AF605832

Art through a Lifetime

The Mary Griggs Burke Collection

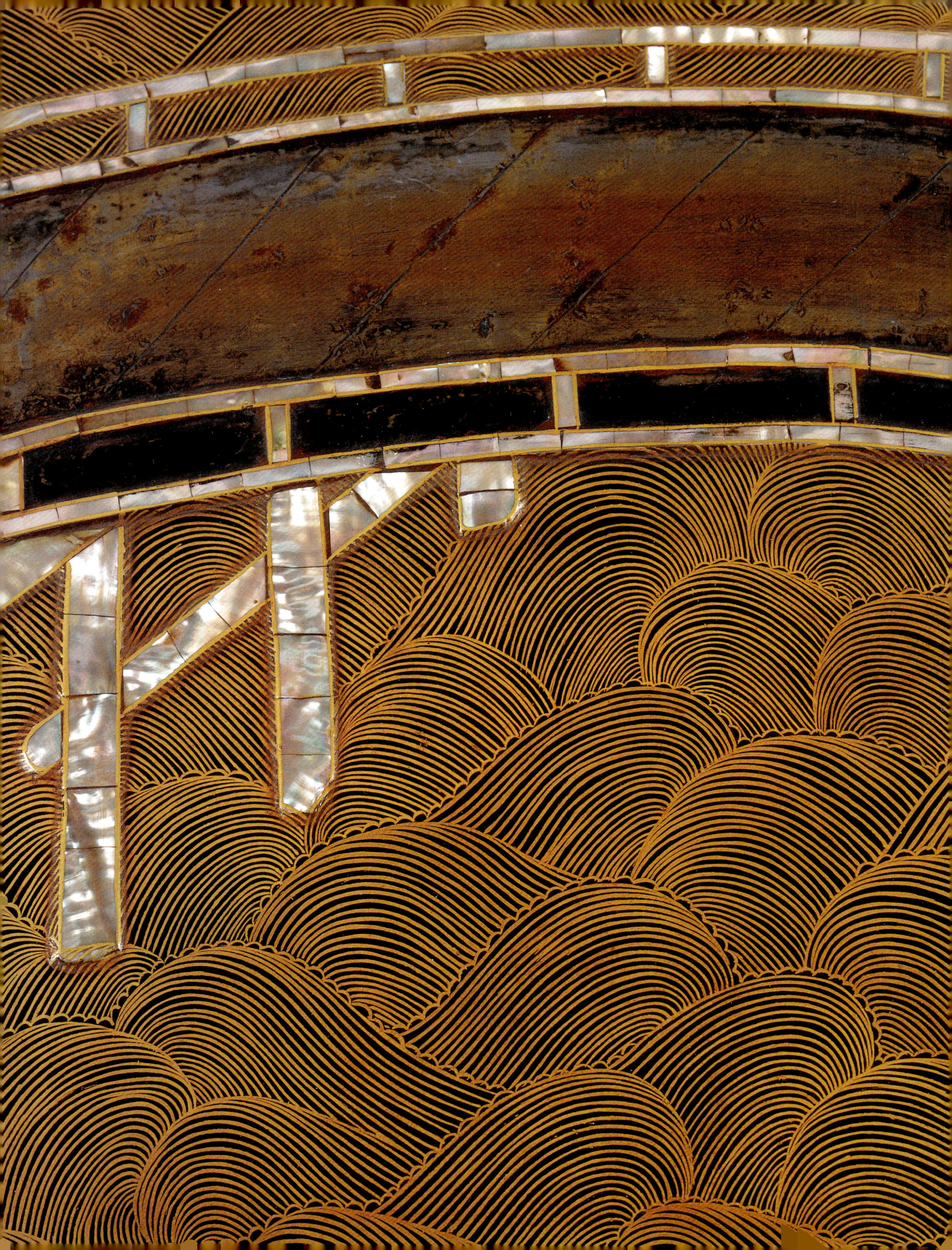

Art through a Lifetime

THE MARY GRIGGS BURKE COLLECTION

Volume 2: Japanese Objects, Korean Art, Chinese Art

Miyeko Murase, Soyoung Lee, David Ake Sensabaugh
Il Kim, Shi-yee Liu, Gratia Williams Nakahashi, Stephanie Wada

MARY AND JACKSON BURKE FOUNDATION
Distributed by University of Washington Press, Seattle

Gratia Williams Nakahashi, Curator
Stephanie Wada, Associate Curator

Mary Gladue, Project Manager
Bruce Campbell, Designer
Amanda Freymann, Production Manager
Aardvark Type, Desktop Publishing
Mary Cason, Bibliography Editor / Proofreader
Il Kim, Special Consultant

Color separations by Professional Graphics, Inc., Rockford, IL
Printed and bound by Conti Tipocolor, Calenzano, Italy

Distributed by:
University of Washington Press
P.O. Box 50096
Seattle, Washington 98145-5096
USA
www.washington.edu/uwpress/

Library of Congress Control Number: 2013949640
ISBN 978-0-295-99268-6

Cover: Six of the Group of Twelve Guardians (*Jūni Shinshō*, 十二神将)
Kamakura period, 14th century
Lacquered, polychromed, and gilded wood with inlaid crystal eyes
Detail from No. 557

Frontispiece: Writing box (*suzuribako*, 硯箱) with bridge and waves
Edo period, 18th century
Black lacquer with gold *maki-e* and mother-of-pearl and metal inlay
Detail from No. 761

Contents

Chronology

Japan

Protoliterate Era	ca. 12,500 B.C.–A.D. 538
Jōmon period, ca. 12,500–ca. 300 B.C.	
Yayoi period, ca. 300 B.C.–ca. A.D. 300	
Kofun period, ca. A.D. 300–538	
Asuka Period	538–710
Nara Period	710–794
Heian Period	794–1185
Early Heian period, 794–ca. 900	
Late Heian period, ca. 900–1185	
Kamakura Period	1185–1333
Nanbokuchō Period	1333–1392
Muromachi Period	1392–1573
Momoyama Period	1573–1615
Edo Period	1615–1868
Meiji Era	1868–1912
Taishō Era	1912–1926
Shōwa Era	1926–1989
Heisei Era	1989–

Korea

Neolithic Period	ca. 7000–ca. 10th century B.C.
Bronze Age	ca. 10th century B.C.–ca. 3rd century A.D.
Iron Age	ca. A.D. 300
Three Kingdoms Period	57 B.C.–676 A.D.

Silla Kingdom, 57 B.C.–A.D. 676
Baekje Kingdom, 18 B.C.–A.D. 660
Goguryeo Kingdom, 37 B.C.–A.D. 668
Gaya Federation, 42–562

Unified Silla Dynasty	676–935
Balhae, 698–926	
Goryeo Dynasty	918–1392
Joseon Dynasty	1392–1910
Japanese Colonial Period	1910–1945
American and Soviet Occupation	1945–1948
Republic of Korea (ROK; South Korea)	1948–
Democratic People's Republic of Korea (DPRK; North Korea)	1948–

China

Song Dynasty	960–1279

Northern Song, 960–1127
Southern Song, 1127–1279

Yuan Dynasty	1279–1368
Ming Dynasty	1368–1644
Qing Dynasty	1644–1911
Republican Period	1912–1949
People's Republic	1949–

Japanese Objects

Sculpture

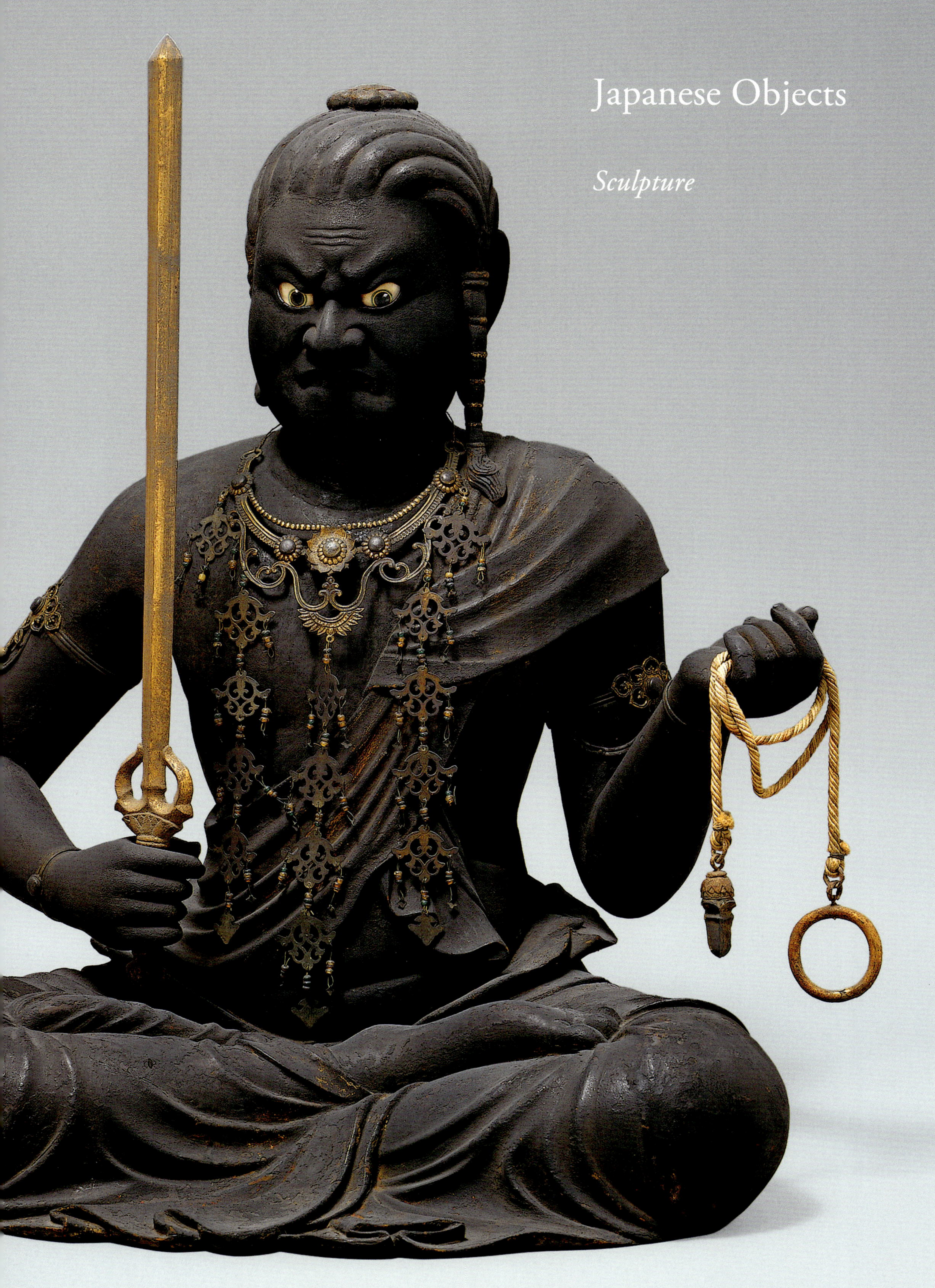

Buddhist

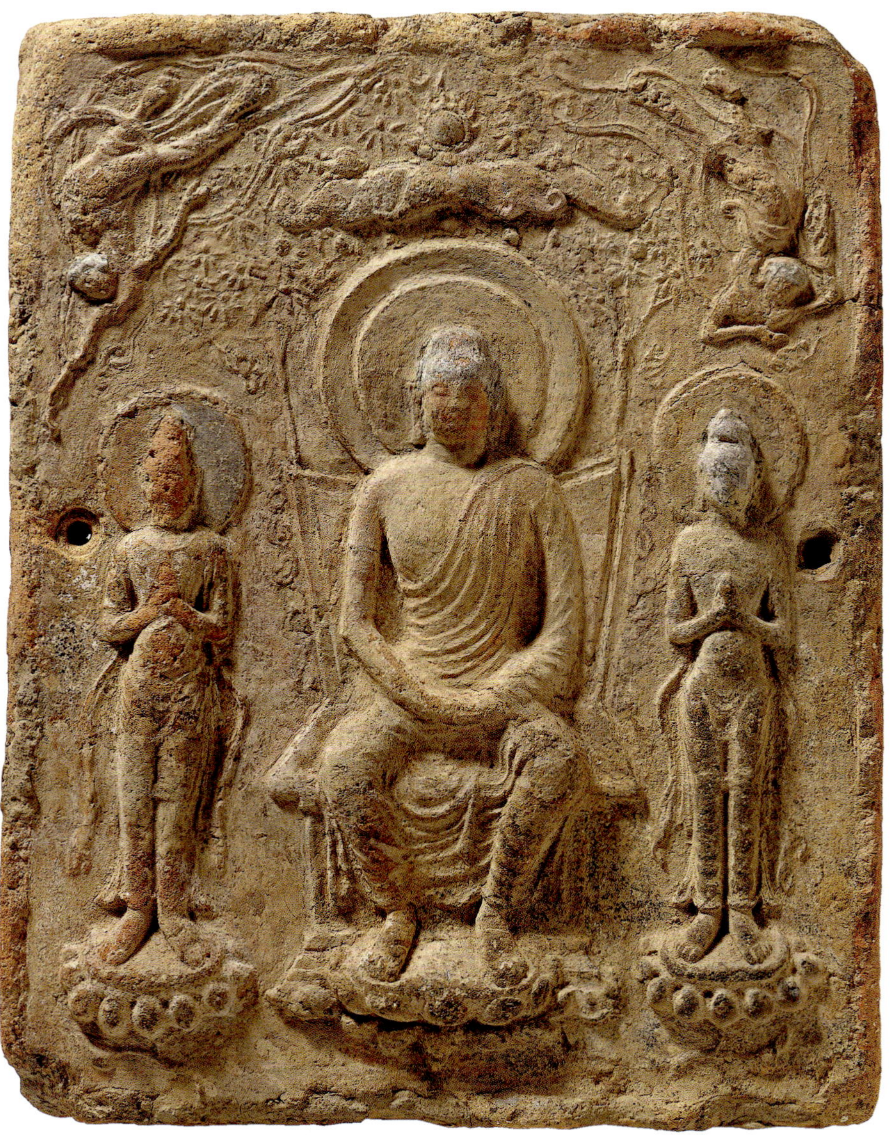

546. Relief tile (*senbutsu*, 塼仏) with Buddha Triad

Asuka period, second half of 7th century
Earthenware with traces of polychrome
24.5 x 19.6 x 3.7 cm (9 5/8 x 7 3/4 x 1 1/2 in.)

Ex coll.: Tachibanadera, Asuka

Literature: Kim 1991, no. 38; Murase 1993, no. 1; Murase 2000, no. 5; Tsuji Nobuo et al. 2005, no. 5; Shirai 2011a, p. 206, fig. 8; Shirai 2011b, p. 55, fig. 8; p. 69, fig. 13; p. 70, figs. 14, 15.

547. Amida Nyorai (阿弥陀如来)

Late Heian period, early 12th century
Polychromed Japanese cypress (*hinoki*)
H. of statue 49.3 cm (19 3/8 in.); h. of pedestal 31.2 cm (12 1/4 in.)

Literature: Kuno Takeshi 1963, pp. 77–79; Rosenfield 1967, no. 27; Olson 1968, pp. 8–9; Murase 1975, no. 3; Mayuyama Junkichi 1976, no. 339; Shimizu Zenzō 1979, no. 110, fig. 113, p. 96; Kurata Bunsaku 1980, no. 12; Kaufman 1985, fig. 1; Avitabile 1990, no. 1; Murase 2000, no. 13; Tsuji Nobuo et al. 2005, no. 11.

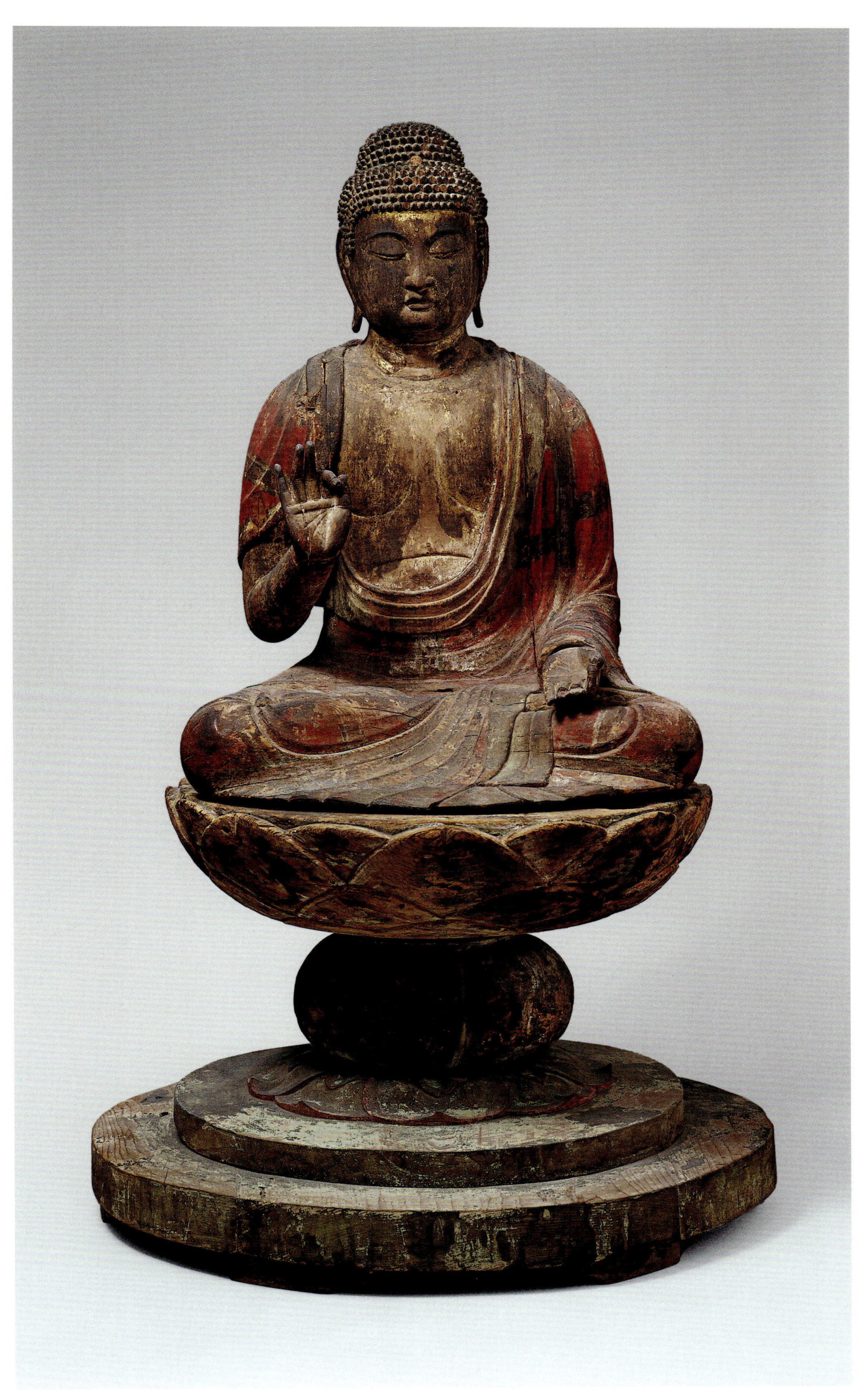

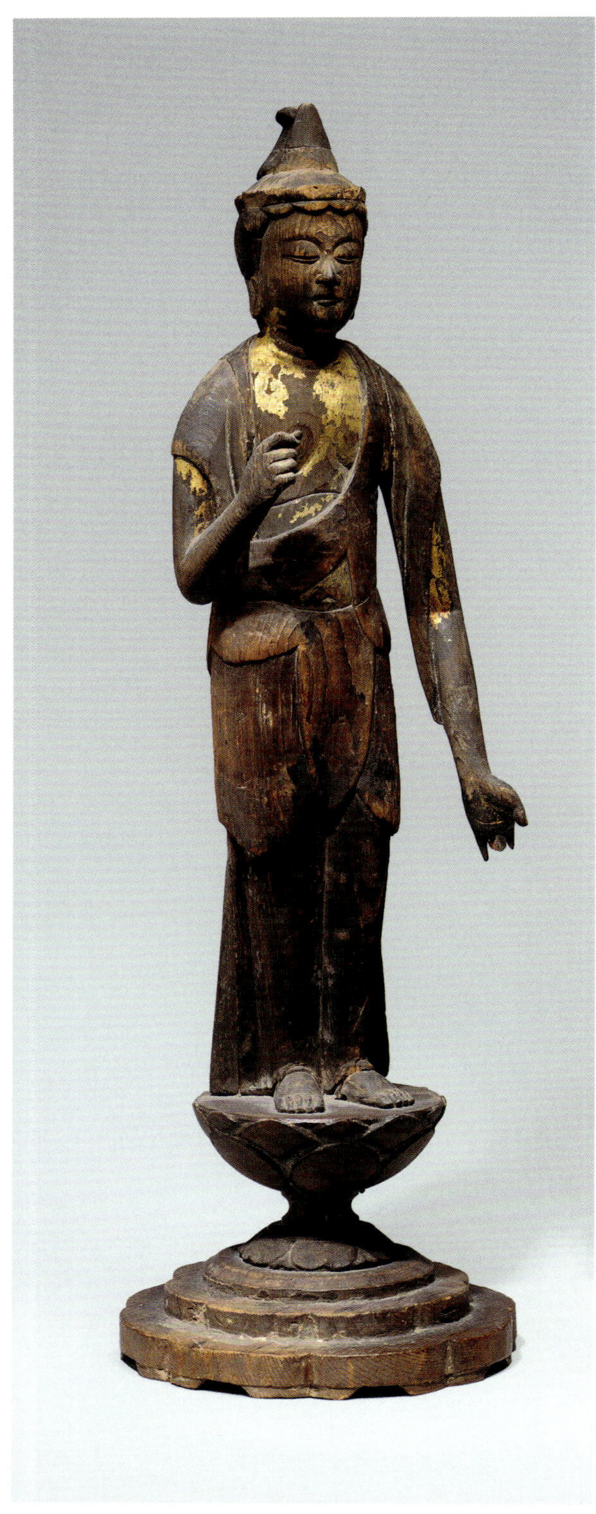

548. Kannon Bosatsu (観音菩薩)

Late Heian period, 12th century (?)
Lacquered and gilded Japanese cypress (*hinoki*)
H. (including pedestal) 46.5 cm (18 1/4 in.)

Literature: Shimizu Zenzō 1979, p. 96, no. 111; Linda 1988, p. 17, no. 4; Morse and Morse 1995, no. 38, p. 100.

Kaikei
(快慶; fl. ca. 1183–1223)

549. Jizō Bosatsu (地蔵菩薩)

Kamakura period, ca. 1202
Lacquered, polychromed, and gilded Japanese cypress (*hinoki*) with *kirikane* and inlaid crystal eyes
H. of statue 51.2 cm (20 1/8 in.); h. of pedestal 4.8 cm (1 7/8 in.)
Text

Literature: Shimizu Zenzō 1979, no. 112, fig. 114, p. 96; Kaufman 1985, figs. 7, 8; Tokyo National Museum 1985a, no. 82; Avitabile 1990, no. 2; Kaneko Hiroaki et al. 1991, pl. 61; Mizuno Keizaburō et al. 1992, fig. 12; Murase 2000, no. 21; Mizuno Keizaburō 2003–10, vol. 2 (2004), pt. 1, *Zuhan*, no. 45, figs. 45-1–45-14, pp. 87–91; pt. 2, *Kaisetsu*, no. 45, pp. 114–17; Tsuji Nobuo et al. 2005, no. 15.

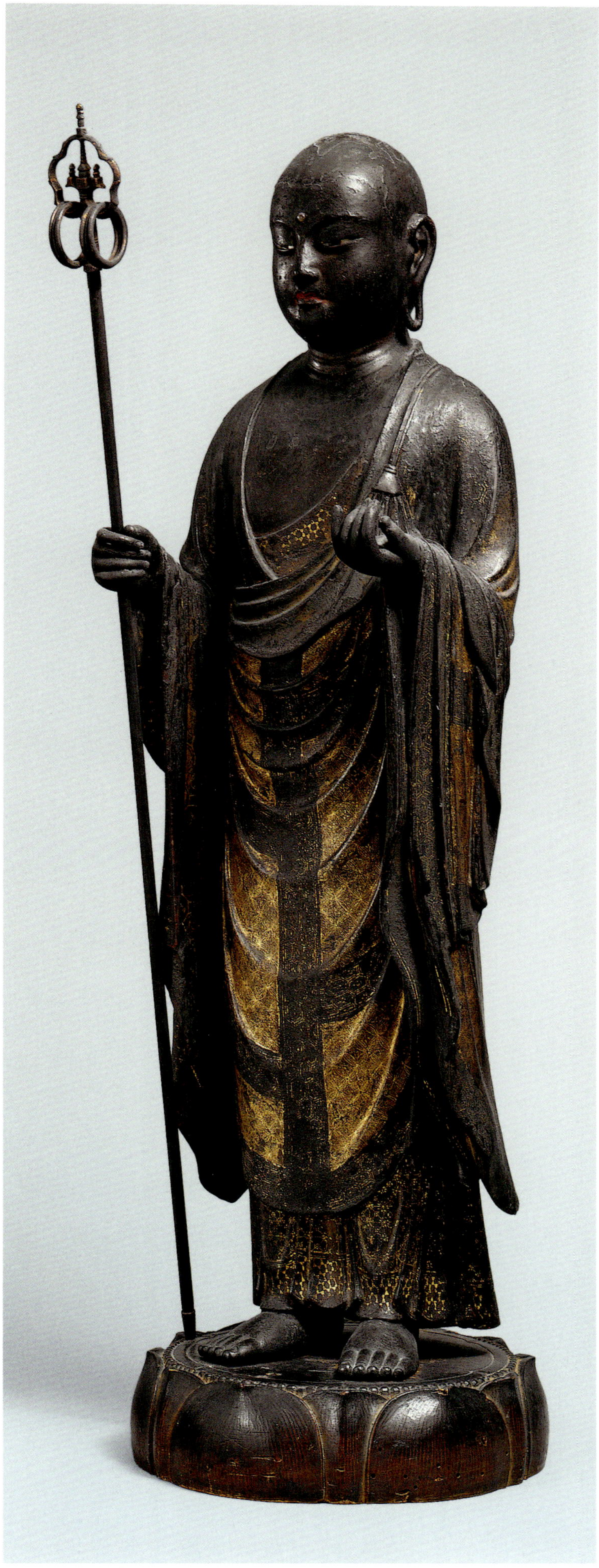

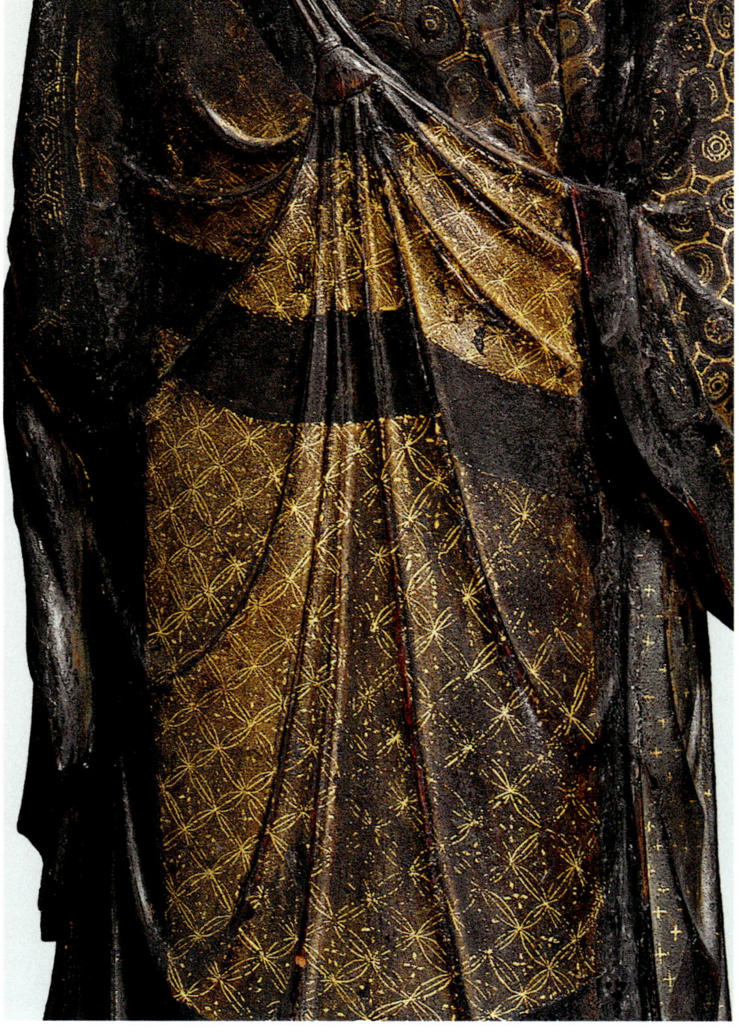

549, detail

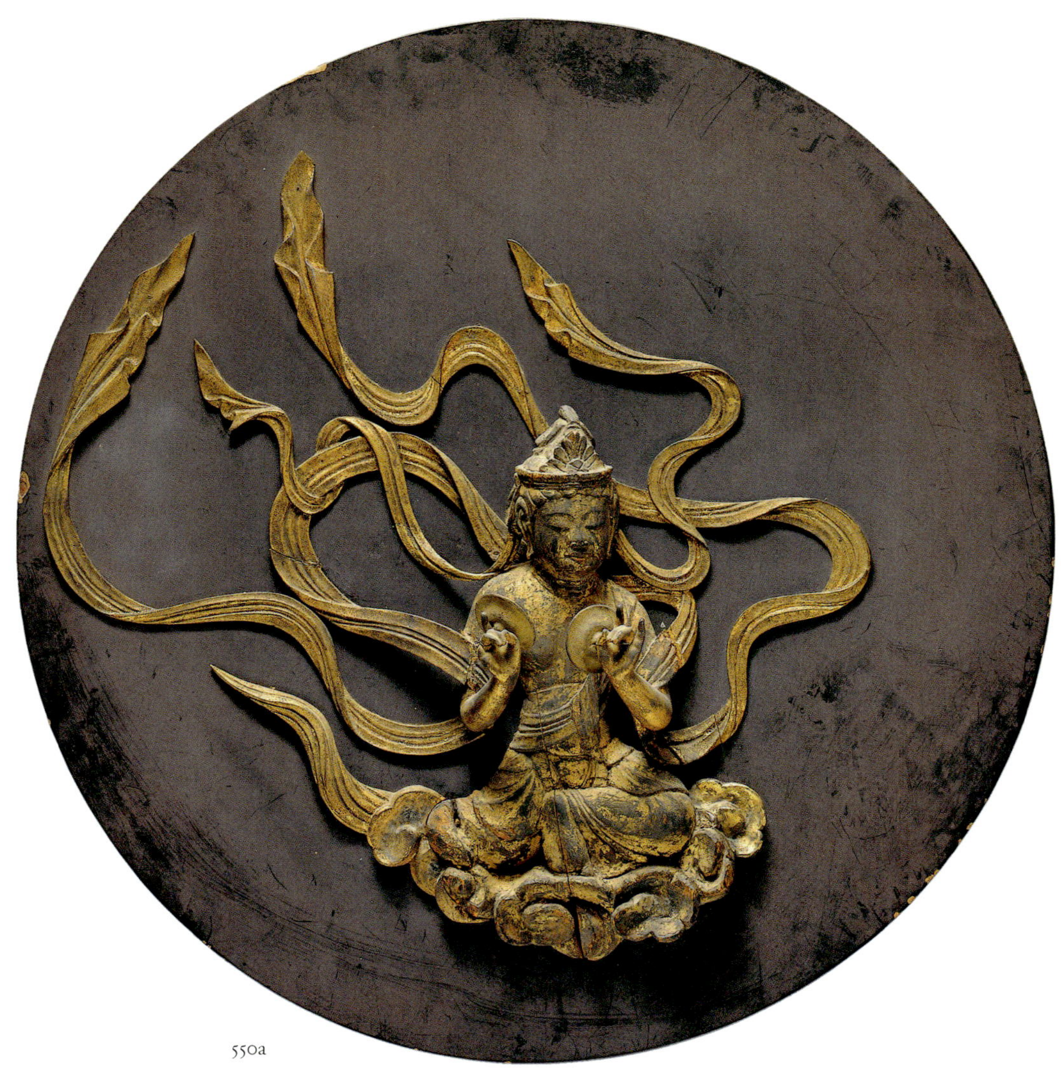

550a

550a, b. Two *hiten* (飛天)

Late Heian period, late 11th–early 12th century
Japanese cypress (*hinoki*) with lacquer and gold
(a) h. 28 cm (11 in.); (b) h. 27.5 cm (10 7/8 in.)

Ex coll.: Koizumi Sakutarō, Japan; Mohr, Germany

Literature: Koizumi Sakutarō 1926, pls. 29, 30; Murase 1993, no. 3; Burke 1996b, p. 45; Murase 2000, no. 14; Tsuji Nobuo et al. 2005, nos. 9, 10.

551. Jizō Bosatsu (地蔵菩薩)

Kamakura period (?)
Wood with traces of polychrome
H. 34.3 cm (13 1/2 in.)

552. Jizō Bosatsu (地蔵菩薩) stone stele in memory of a young girl of the Ohno family

Edo period, 1727
Stone
43 x 25.5 cm (16 7/8 x 10 in.)
Text

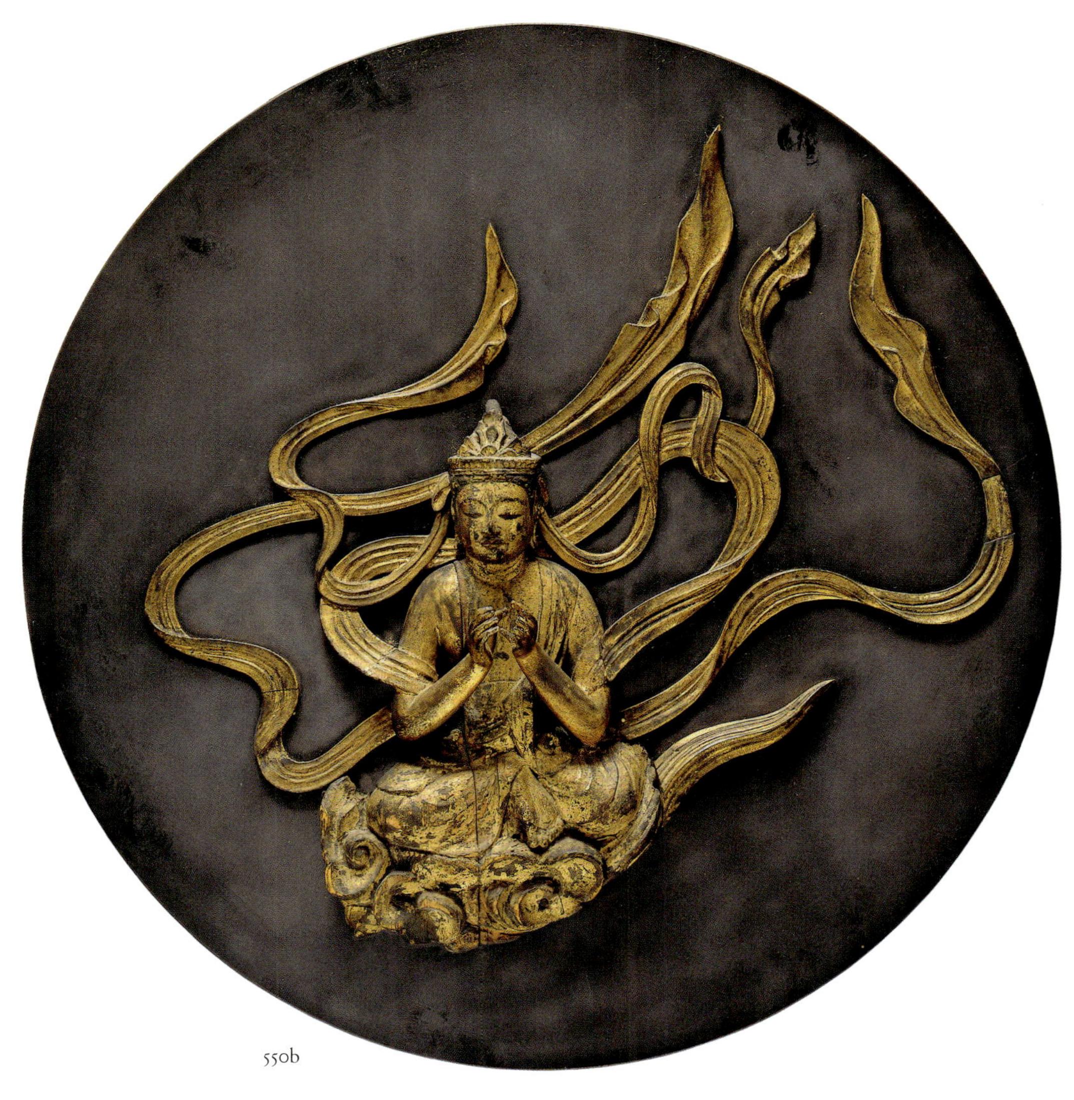

550b

551

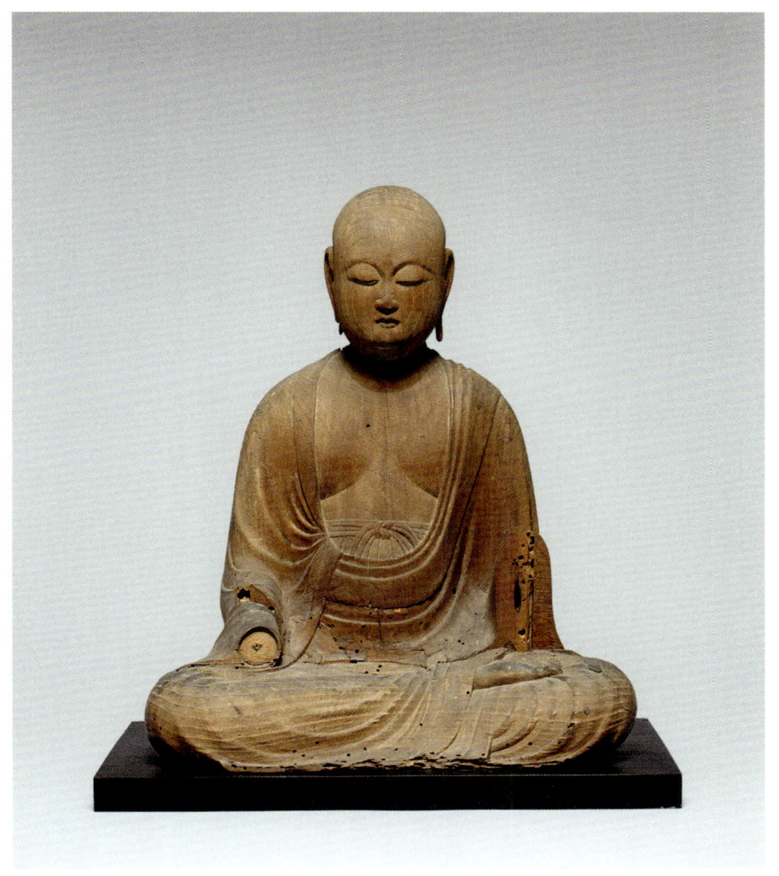

552

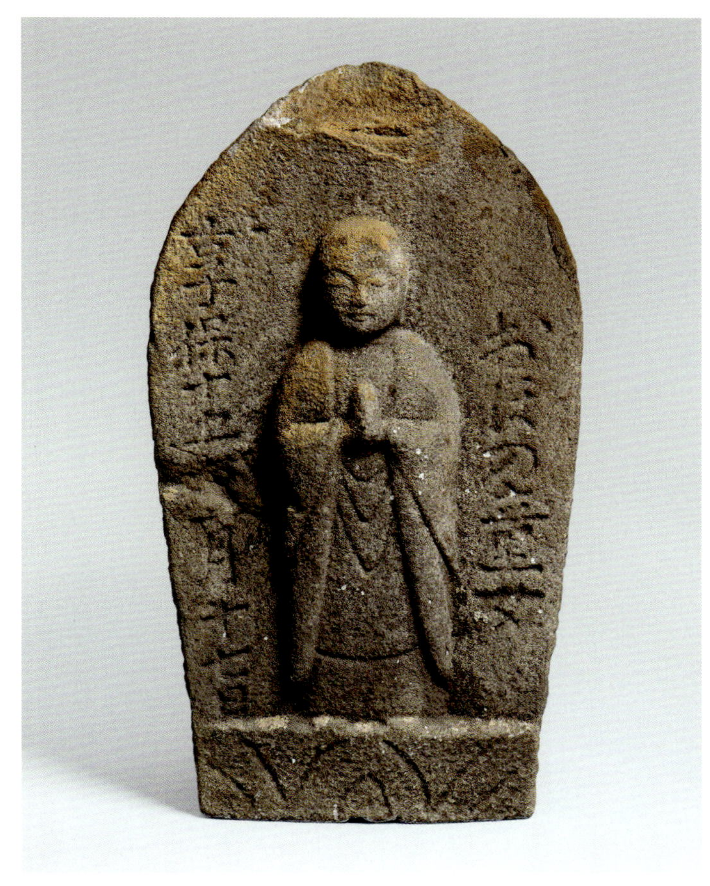

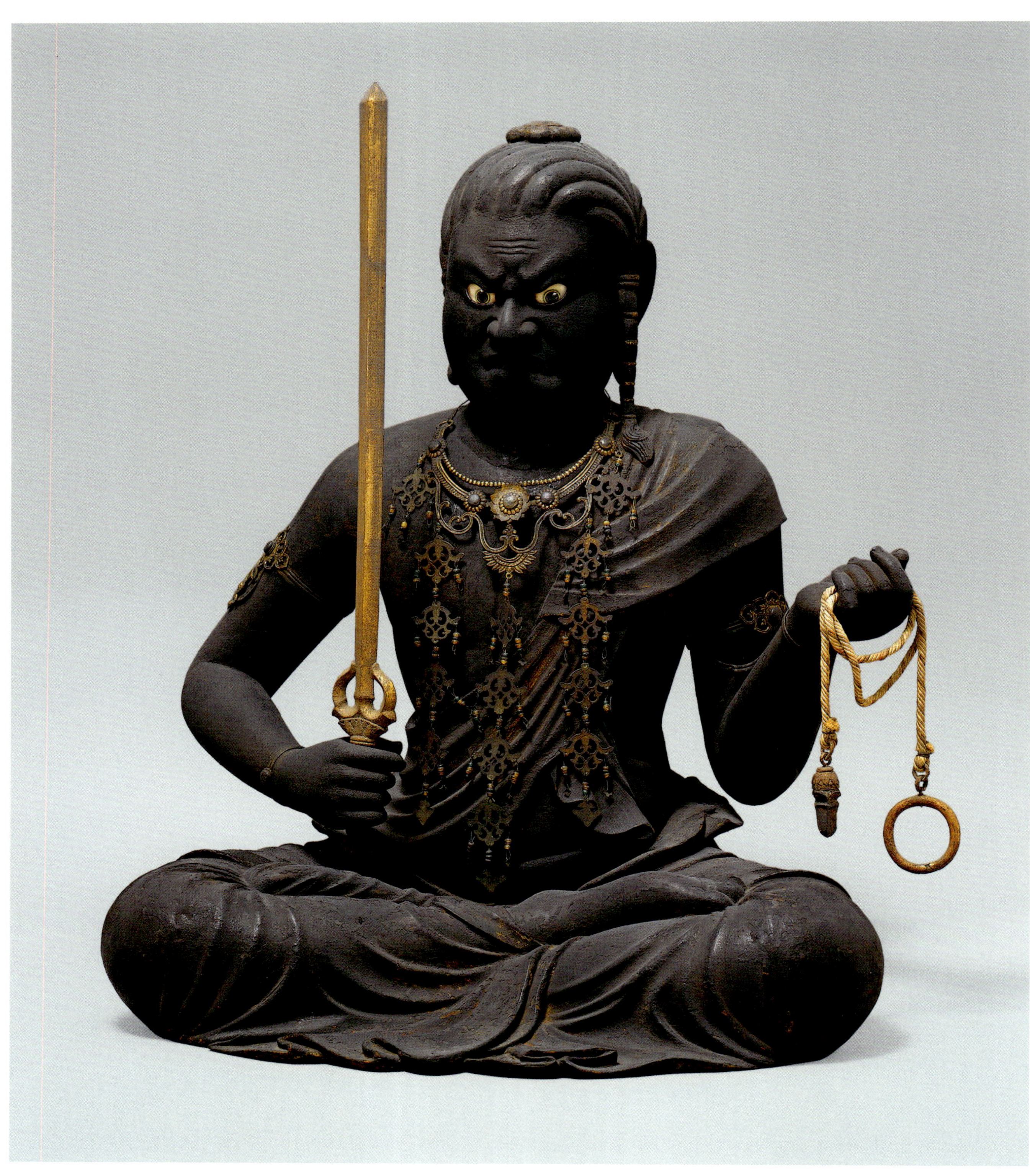

Kaikei
(快慶; fl. ca. 1183–1223)

553. Fudō Myōō (不動明王)

Kamakura period, early 13th century
Lacquered, polychromed, and gilded Japanese cypress (*hinoki*) with *kirikane* and inlaid crystal eyes
H. 51.5 cm (20 1/4 in.)

Ex coll.: Shōrenin, Kyoto

Literature: Dallas Museum of Fine Arts 1969, no. 18; Murase 1975, no. 7; Shimizu Zenzō 1979, no. 113, fig. 115, p. 96; Kurata Bunsaku 1980, no. 70; Kaufman 1985, fig. 5; Tokyo National Museum 1985a, no. 80; Avitabile 1990, no. 3; Mizuno Keizaburō et al. 1992, fig. 30; Morse and Morse 1995, Morse and Morse 1996, fig. 12; no. 36; Murase 2000, no. 22; Tsuji Nobuo et al. 2005, no. 14.

554. Bishamonten (毘沙門天)

Heian period, 11th century
Wood with polychrome
H. including the base 116 cm (45 5/8 in.)

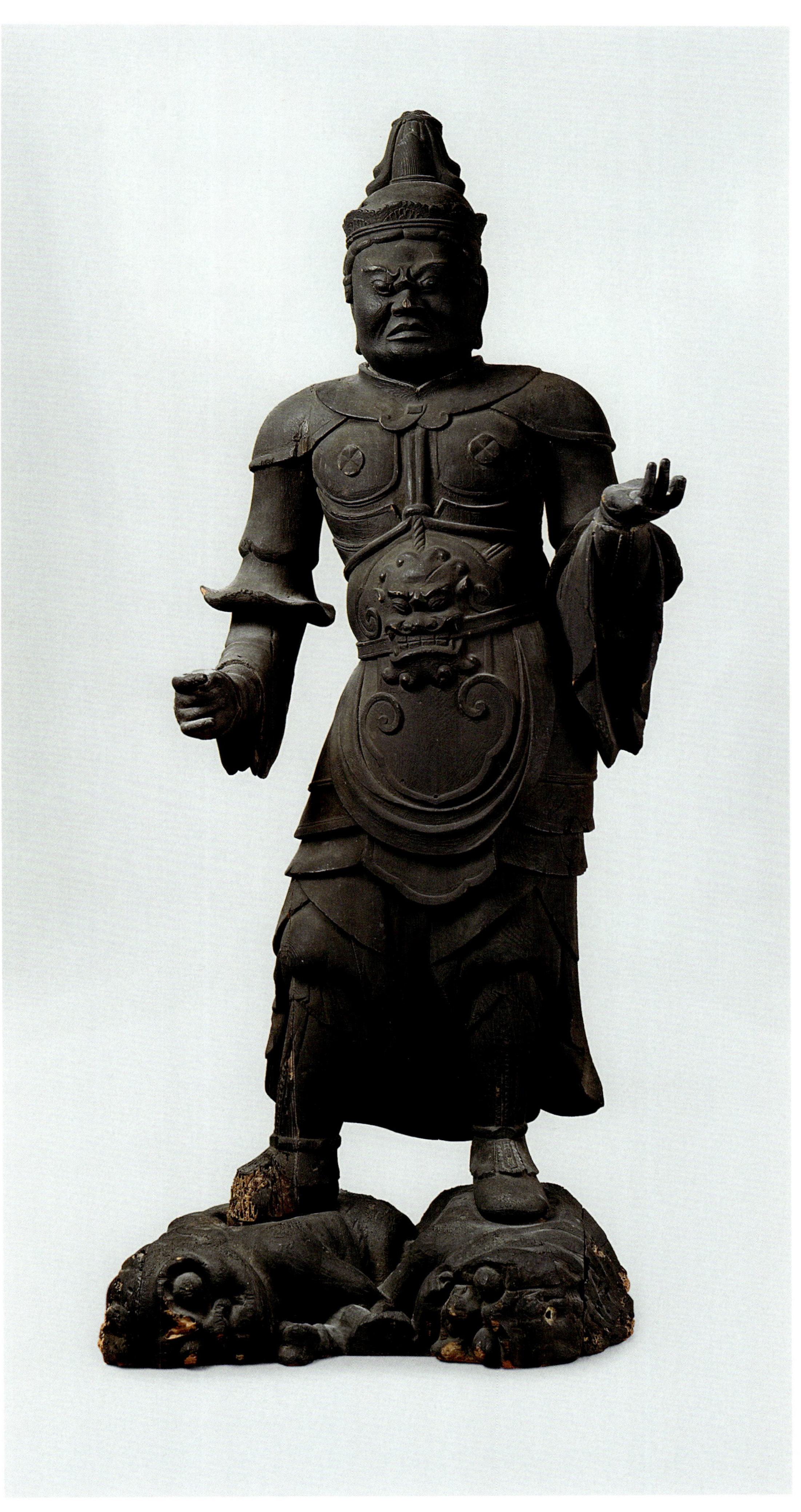

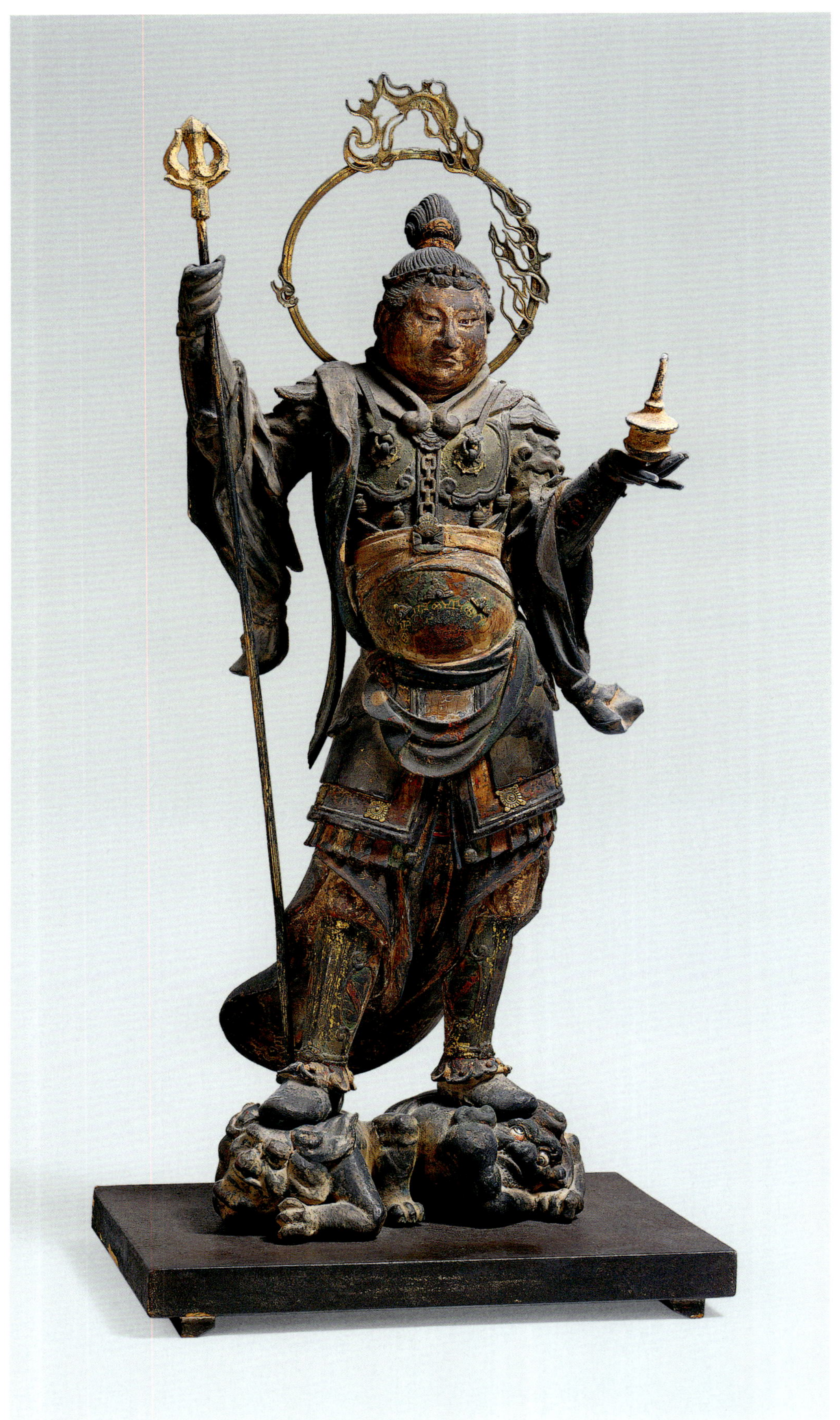

circle of Higo Busshi Jōkei
(肥後仏師定慶; fl. first half of 13th century)

555. Bishamonten (毘沙門天)

Kamakura period
Polychromed and gilded Japanese cypress (*hinoki*) with *kirikane*, inlaid crystal eyes, and gilt metal ornaments
H. 42 cm (16½ in.)

Literature: Murase 1975, no. 8; Shimizu Zenzō 1979, no. 116, fig. 118, p. 97; Tokyo National Museum 1985a, no. 81; Avitabile 1990, no. 4a; Murase 2000, no. 23; Tsuji Nobuo et al. 2005, no. 16.

556. Tobatsu Bishamonten (兜跋毘沙門天)

Late Heian period, late 10th–early 11th century
Polychromed *keyaki* (*Zelkova serrata*)
H. 125 cm (49¼ in.)

Ex coll.: Rishō Gokokuji, Wakayama; Haramoto Torao, Tokyo; Howard C. Hollis, New York

Literature: Ikawa Kazuko 1963, figs. 12–14; Mayuyama Junkichi 1966, no. 18; Rosenfield 1967, no. 3; Murase 1975, no. 2; Mayuyama Junkichi 1976, no. 330; Shimizu Zenzō 1979, no. 117, fig. 119, p. 97; Kurata Bunsaku 1980, no. 57; Murase 2000, no. 9.

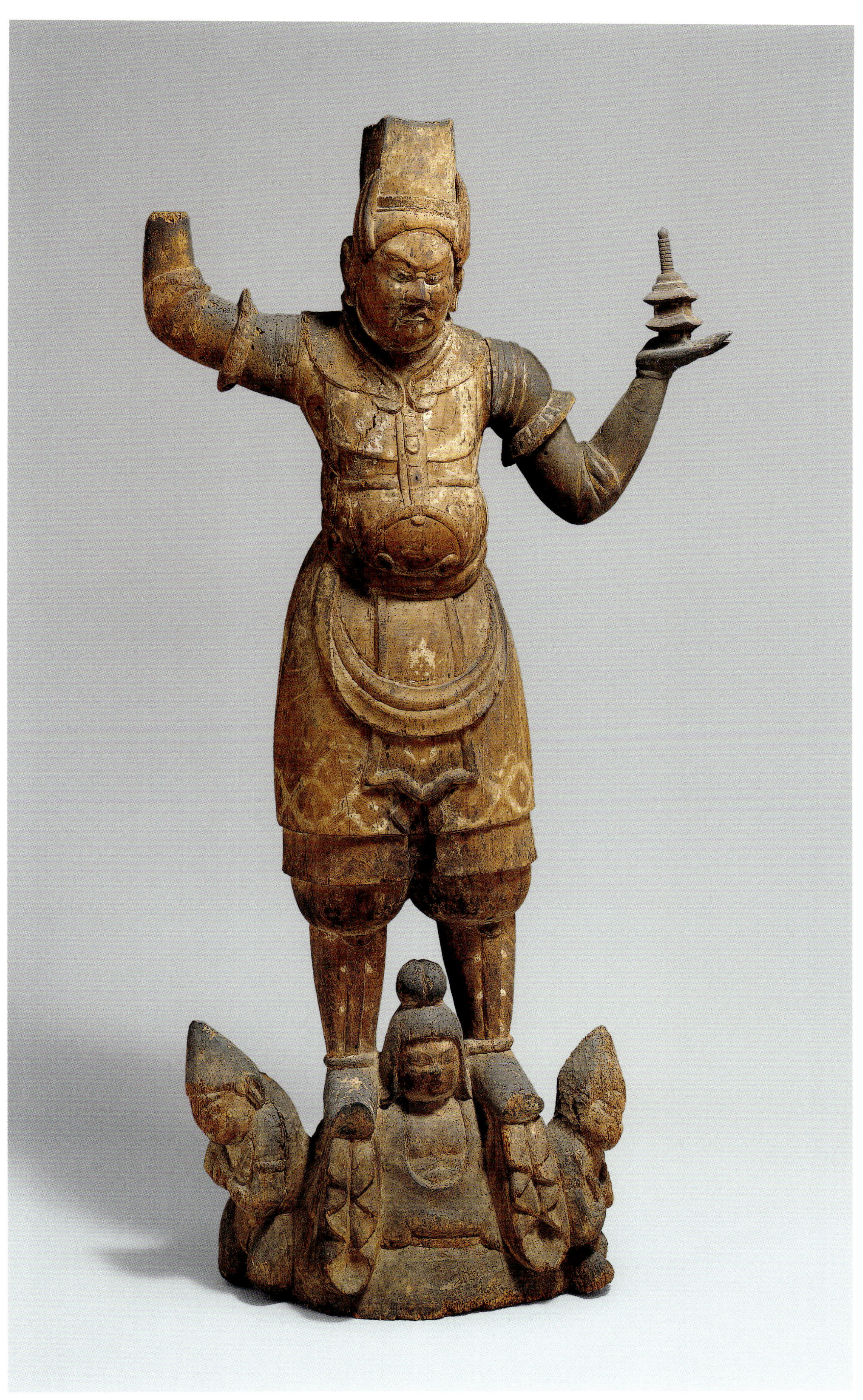

557. Six of the Group of Twelve Guardians (*Jūni Shinshō*, 十二神将)

Kamakura period, 14th century
Lacquered, polychromed, and gilded wood with inlaid crystal eyes
H. 42–46.3 cm (16½–18¼ in.)
The six are tentatively identified as 2. Ox (丑); 4. Rabbit (卯); 6. Snake (巳); 7. Horse (午); 11. Dog (戌); 12. Boar (亥)

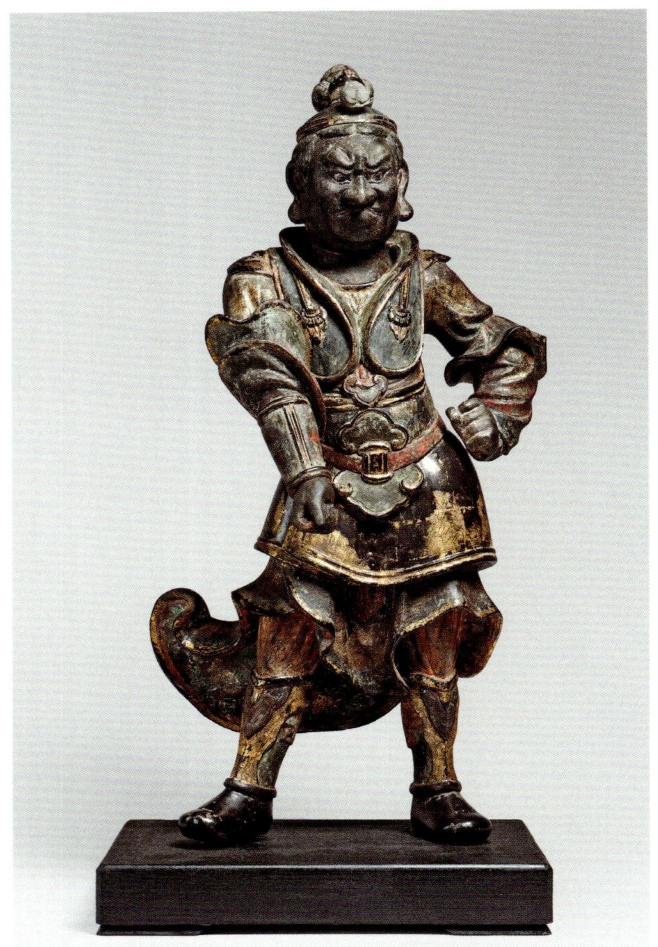

6. Snake

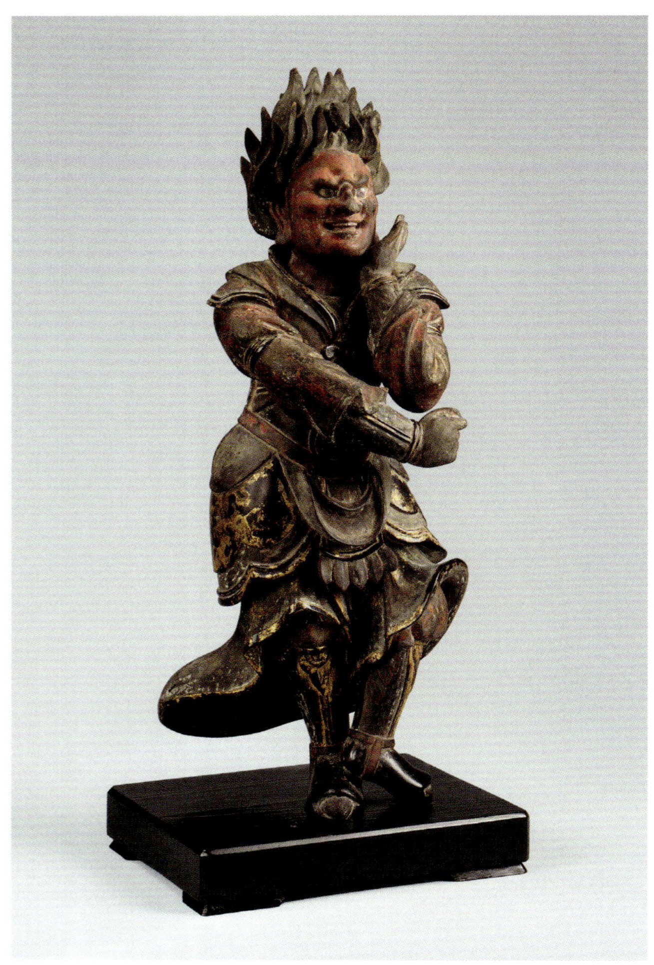

12. Boar

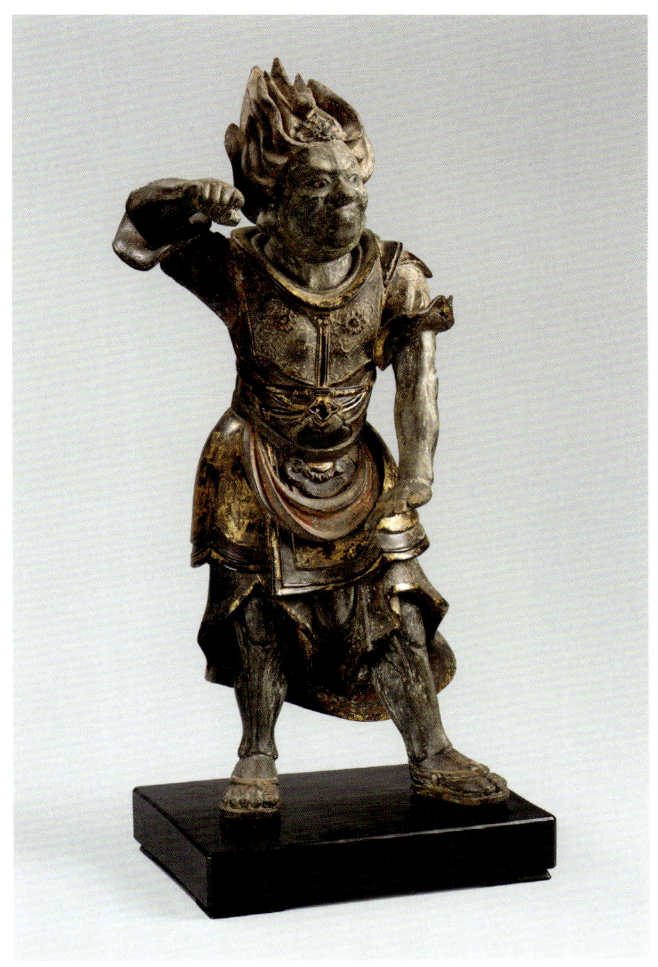

4. Rabbit

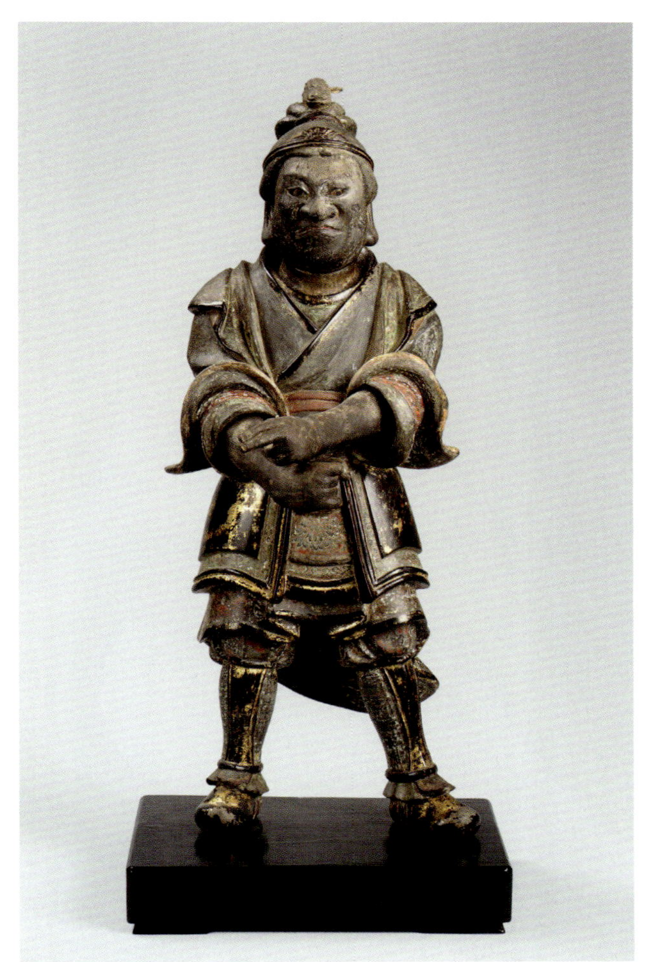

2. Ox

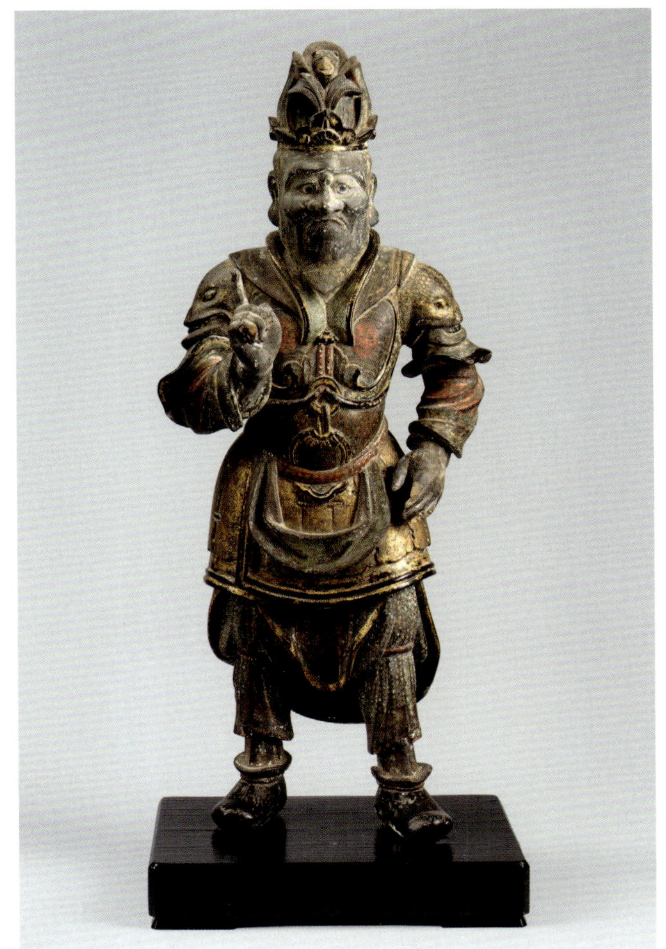

11. Dog

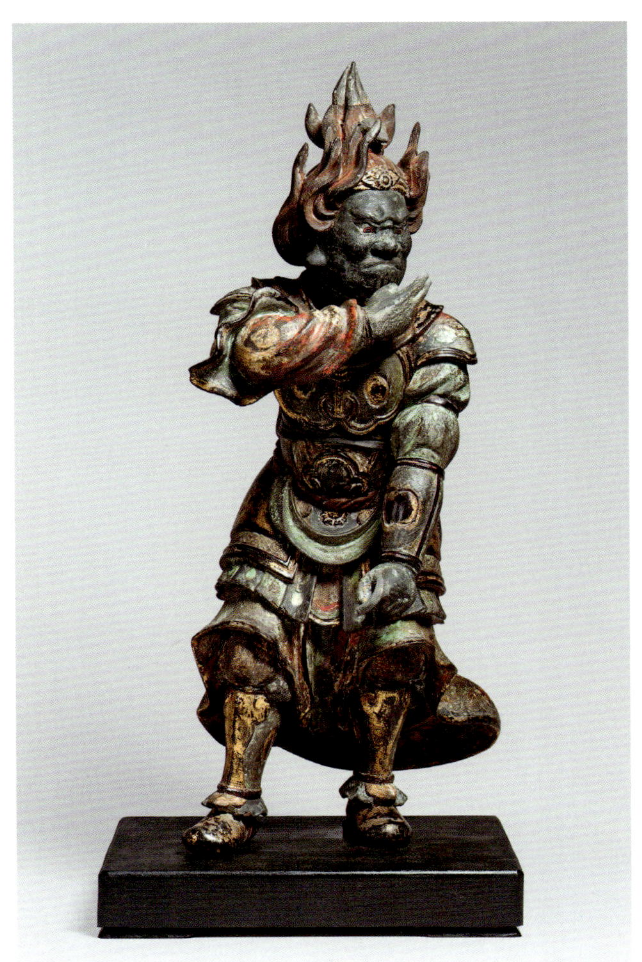

7. Horse

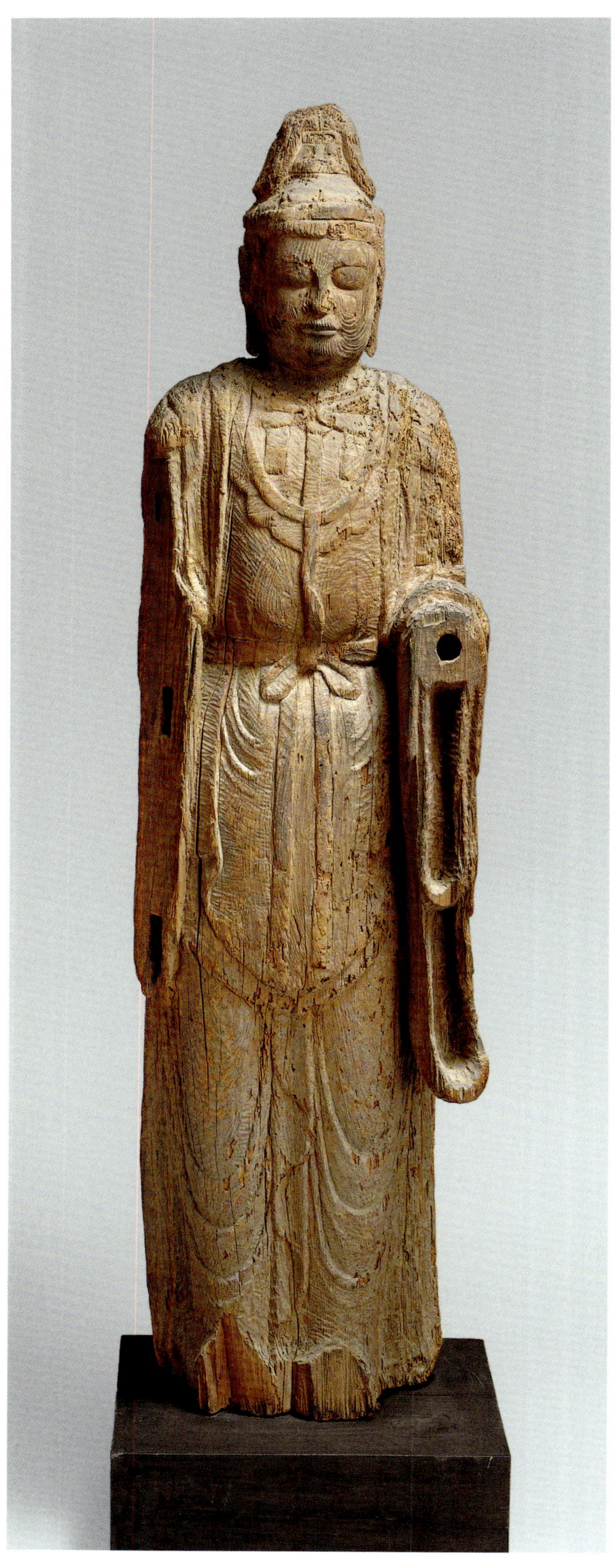

558. Guardian

Heian period, late 10th century
Japanese cypress (*hinoki*)
H. 175.5 cm (69 1/8 in.)

Literature: Murase 1975, no. 1; Shimizu Zenzō 1979, no. 114, fig. 116, p. 97; Sekine Shun'ichi 1997, fig. 88; Murase 2000, no. 8; Tsuji Nobuo et al. 2005, no. 6.

559. Guardian

Kamakura period (?)
Polychromed Japanese cypress (*hinoki*)
H. 39.2 cm (15 3/8 in.)

Literature: Murase 1975, no. 5; Shimizu Zenzō 1979, no. 118, fig. 120, p. 98.

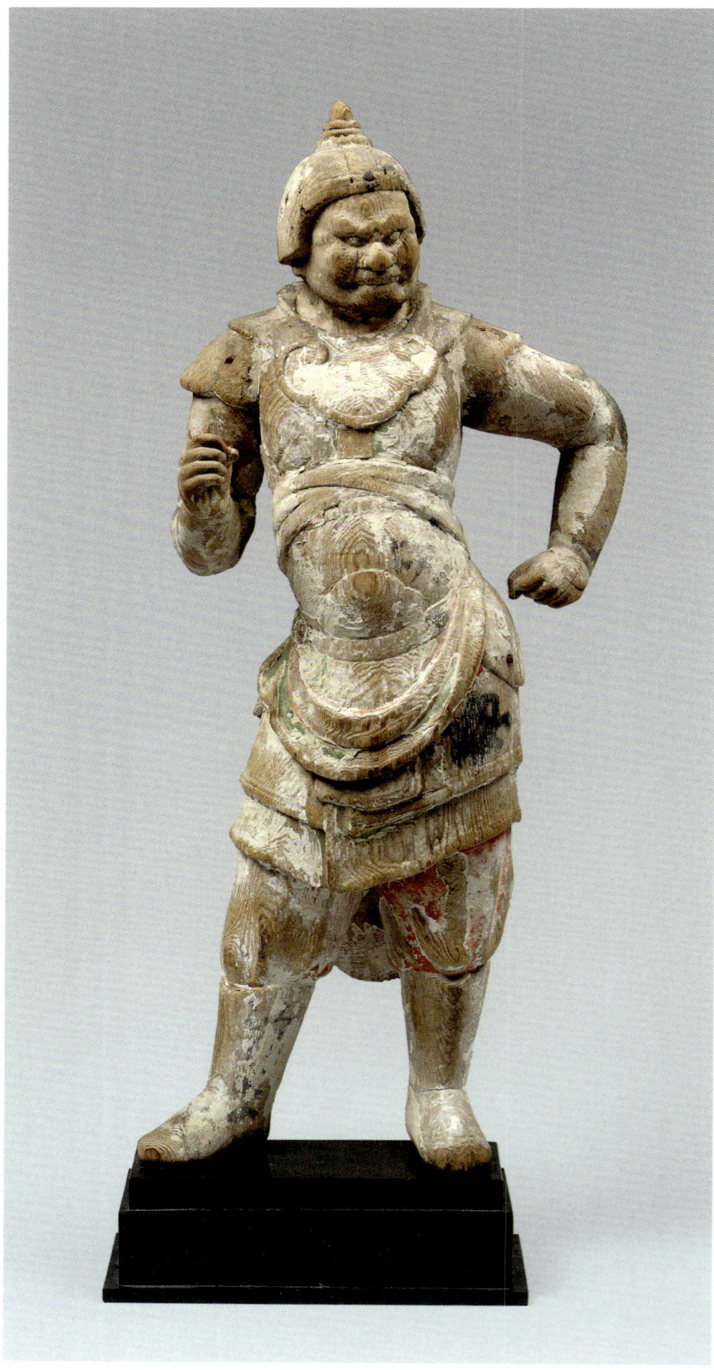

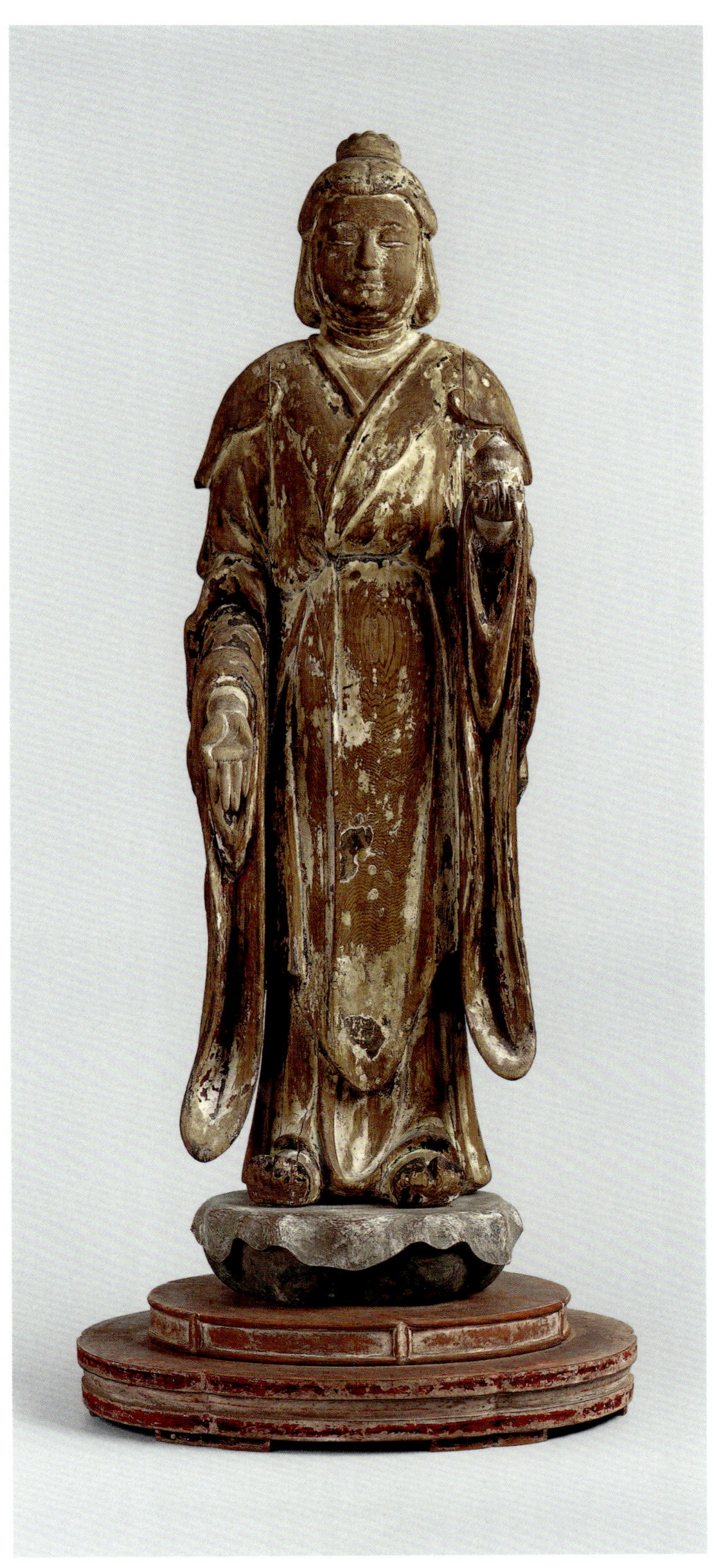

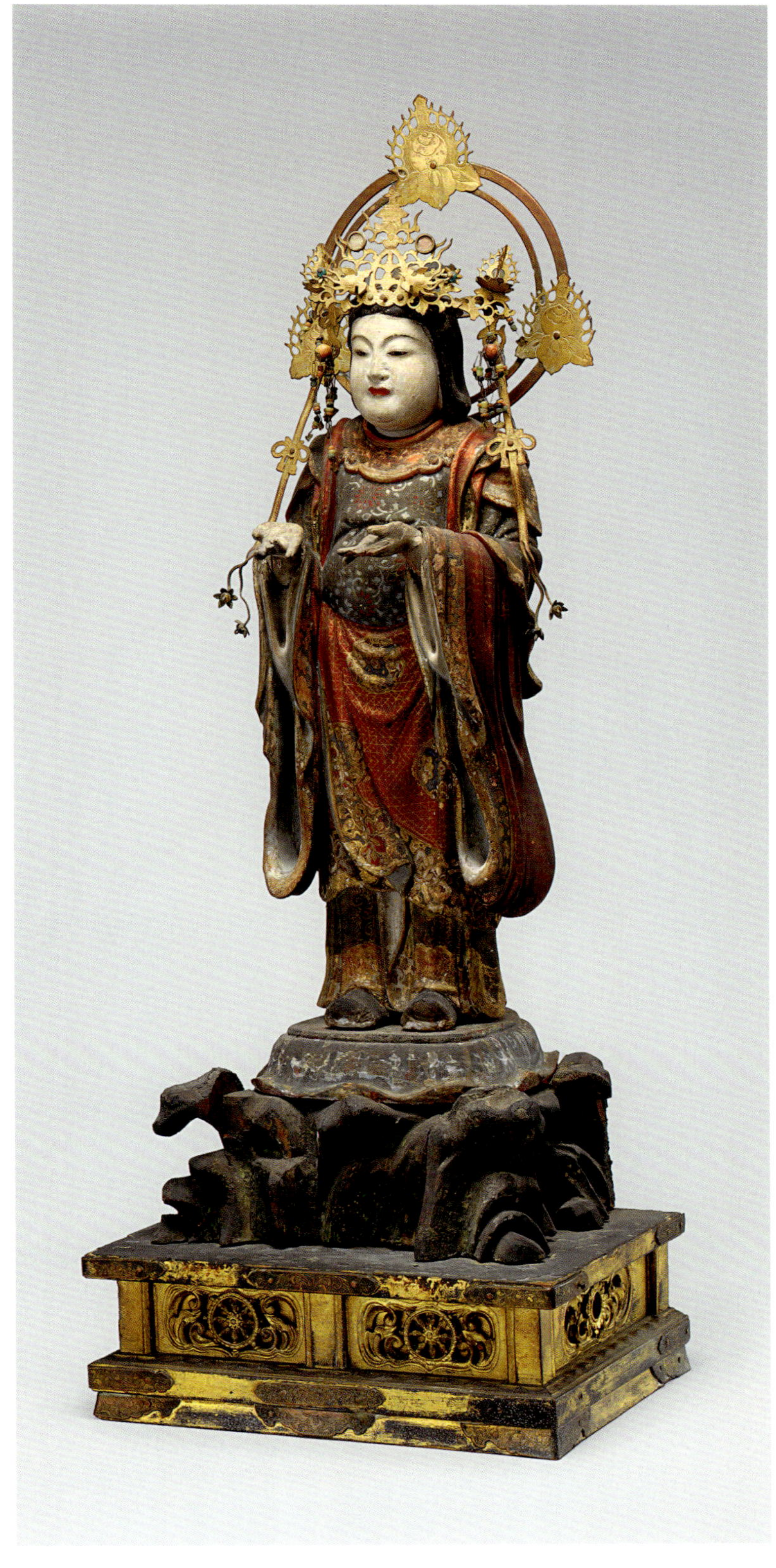

560. Kichijōten (吉祥天)

Kamakura period (?)
Lacquered and polychromed Japanese cypress (*hinoki*)
H. 65.3 cm (25 3/4 in.)

Literature: Murase 1975, no. 6; Shimizu Zenzō 1979, no. 115, fig. 117, p. 97; Japan Society Gallery 1989, no. 3.

561. Zenmyō (善妙)

Edo period, 18th century
Lacquered, polychromed, and gilded Japanese cypress (*hinoki*) with inlaid crystal eyes and gilt metal ornaments
H. 33.2 cm (13 1/8 in.)

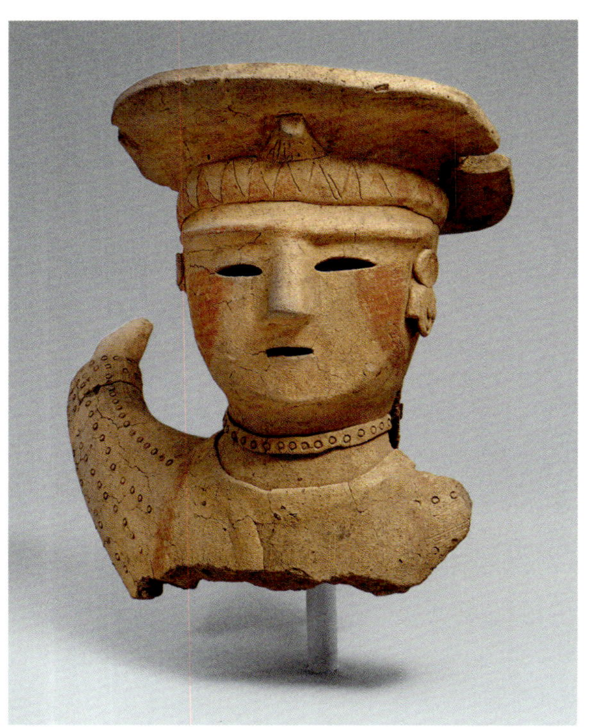

562. Haniwa of a Priestess (埴輪 巫女)

Kofun period, 6th century
Earthenware with traces of polychrome
H. 31.5 cm (12³/₈ in.)

Literature: Murase 1993, no. 57; Murase 2000, no. 3; Tsuji Nobuo et al. 2005, no. 2.

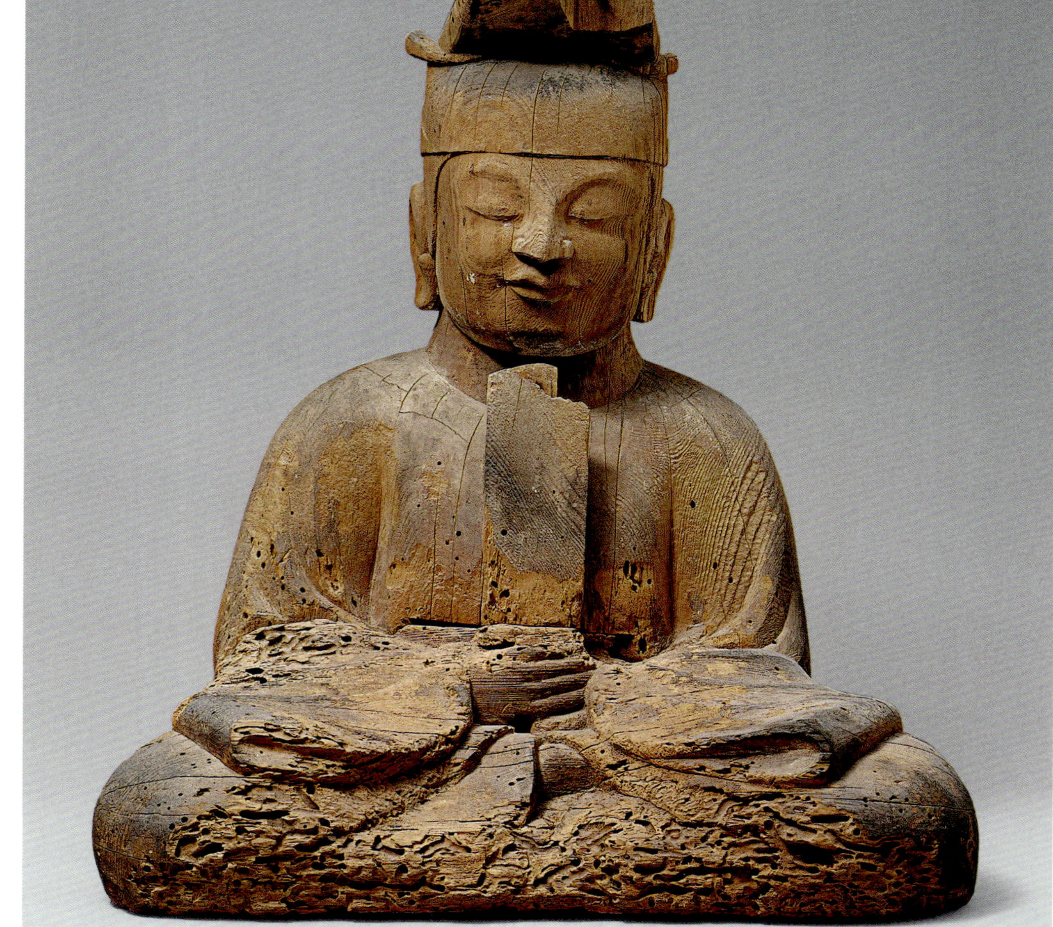

563a

563a, b. Shinto God and Goddess (男神、女神)

Late Heian period, 10th century
Japanese cypress (*hinoki*) with traces of polychrome
H. of each 52.5 cm (20⁵/₈ in.)

Literature: Murata Seiko 1983, pp. 21–31; Kanda 1985, pls. 42–43; Murase 2000, no. 12; Tsuji Nobuo et al. 2005, no. 7.

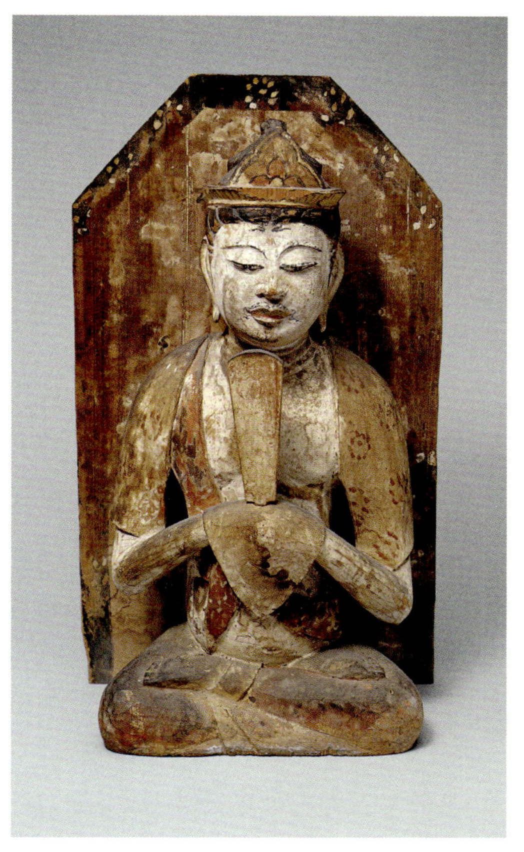
a

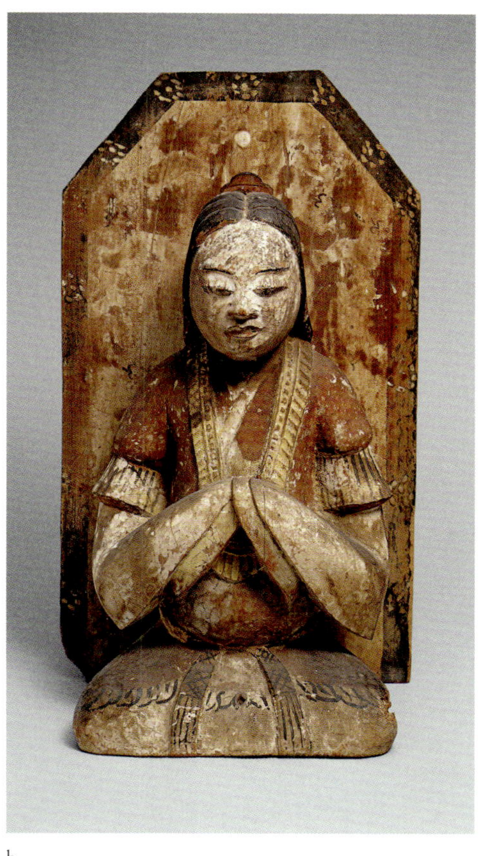
b

564a, b. Shinto God and Goddess (男神、女神)

Late Heian to early Kamakura period, 12th–13th century
Polychromed wood
H. of god 39.1 cm (15 3/8 in.); h. of goddess 39.8 cm (15 5/8 in.)

Literature: Tsuji Nobuo et al. 2005, no. 8.

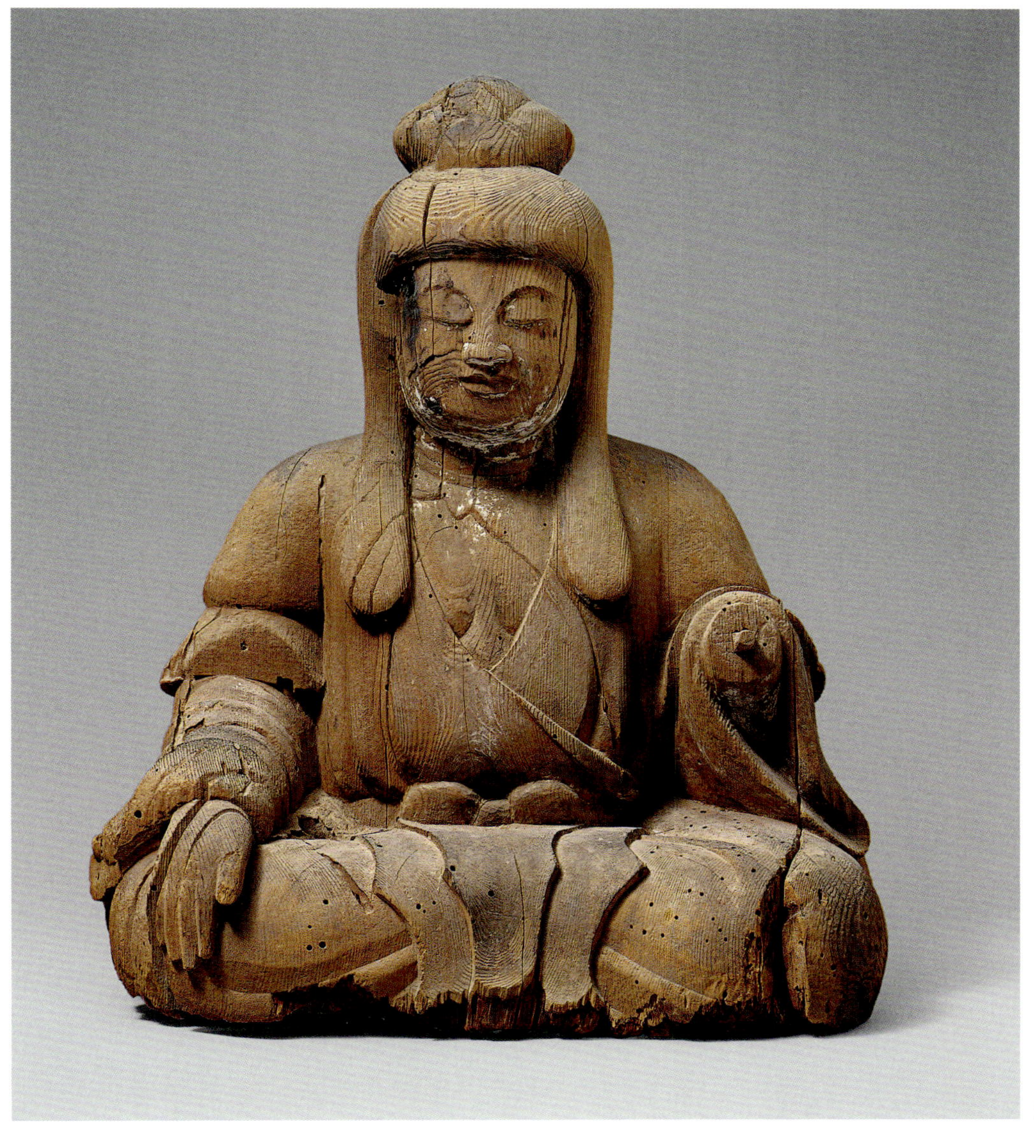
563b

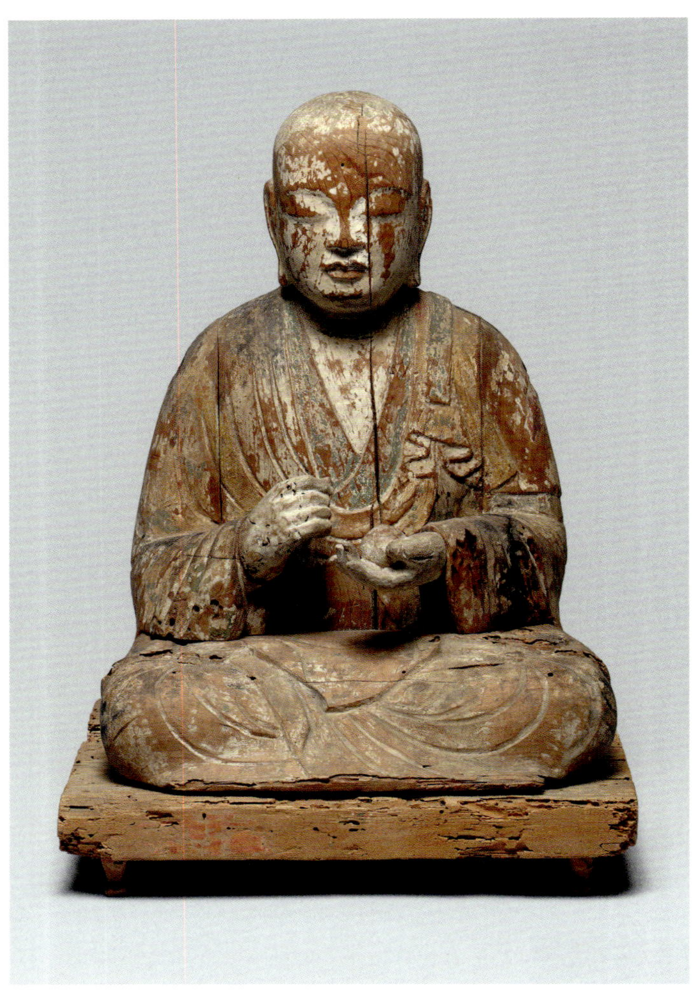

565. Hachiman in the Guise of a Buddhist Monk (Sōgyō Hachiman, 僧形八幡)

Late Heian period, 12th century (?)
Polychromed Japanese cypress (*hinoki*)
H. 34.3 cm (13½ in.)

Literature: Murase 1975, no. 4; Shimizu Zenzō 1979, p. 98, no. 119, fig. 121; Kanda 1985, no. 33; Burke 1993, p. 9, no. 29.

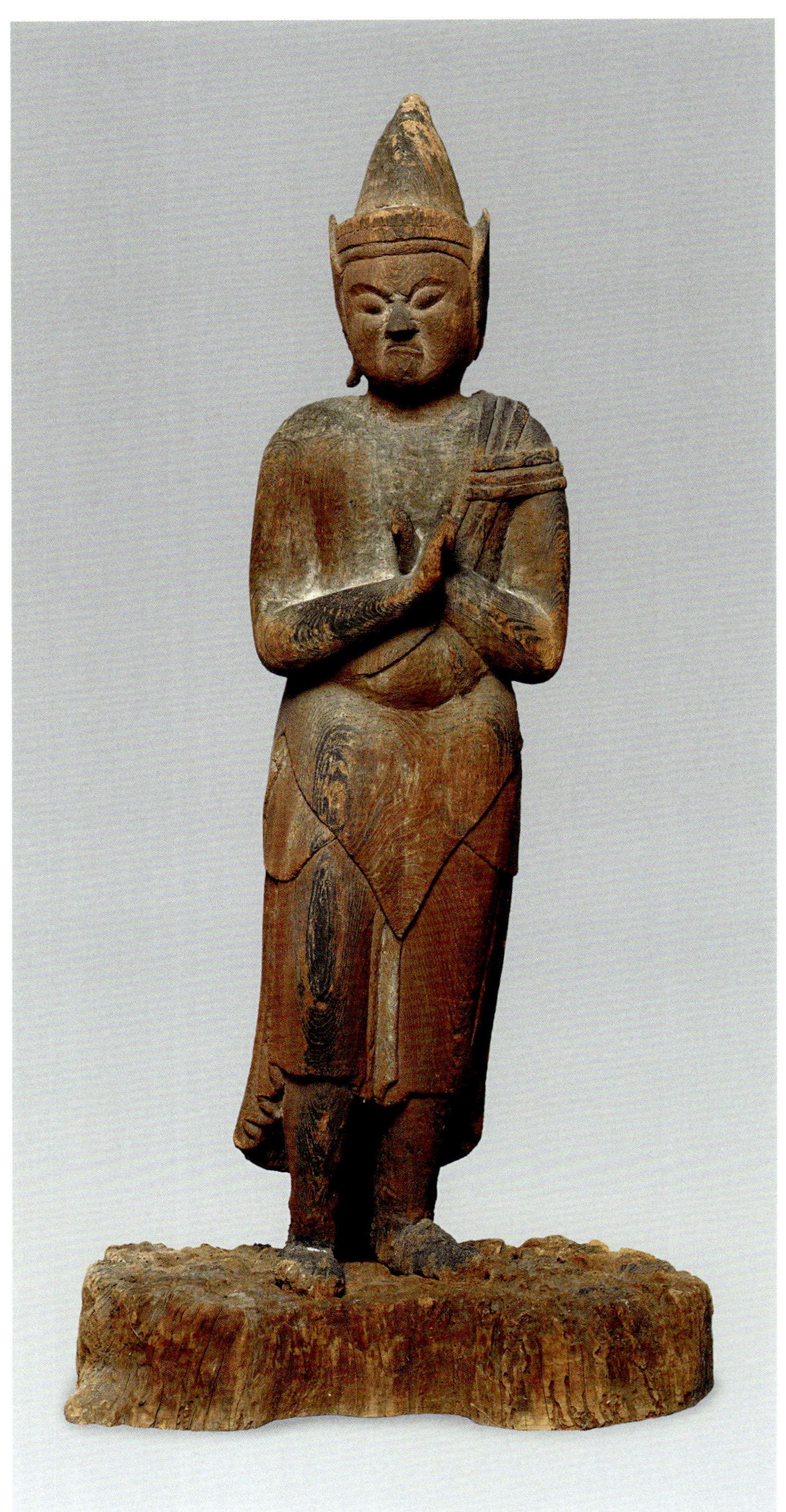

566. Zaō Gongen (蔵王権現)

Heian period
Wood
H. including base 129 cm (50¾ in.)

Ex coll.: Koizumi Sakutarō

Literature: Koizumi Sakutarō 1926, pl. no. 26.

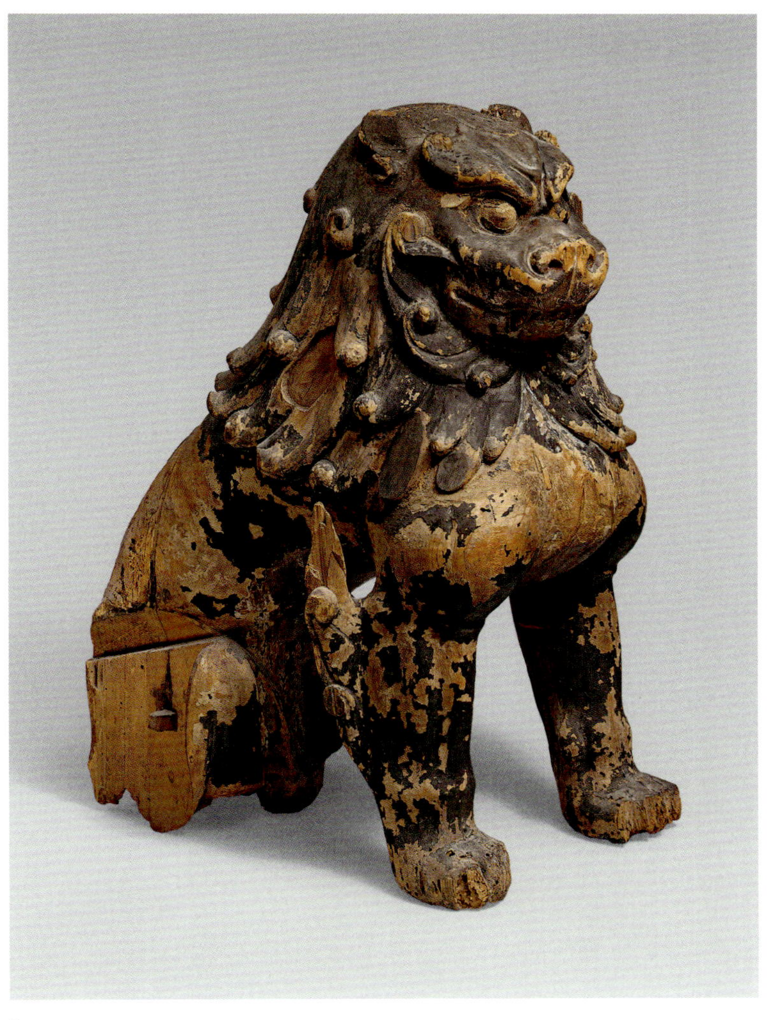

a

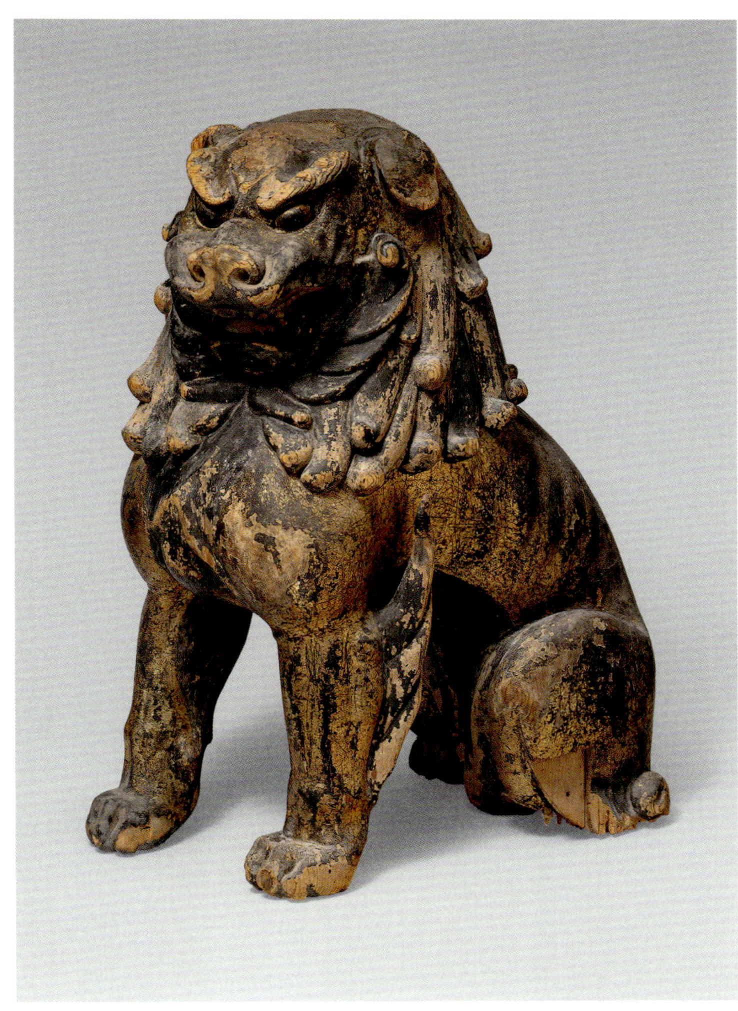

b

567a, b. Pair of Guardian Lion Dogs (*komainu*, 狛犬)

Kamakura period, mid-13th century
Lacquered, polychromed, and gilded Japanese cypress (*hinoki*)
(a) h. 42.4 cm (16 3/4 in.); (b) h. 45.8 cm (18 in.)

LITERATURE: Avitabile 1990, no. 6; Murase 1993, no. 4; Murase 2000, no. 36.

Miscellaneous

568. Daruma (達磨)

Kamakura period, 14th century (?)
Lacquered and gilded wood with inlaid crystal eyes
Overall h. 54 cm (21¼ in.)

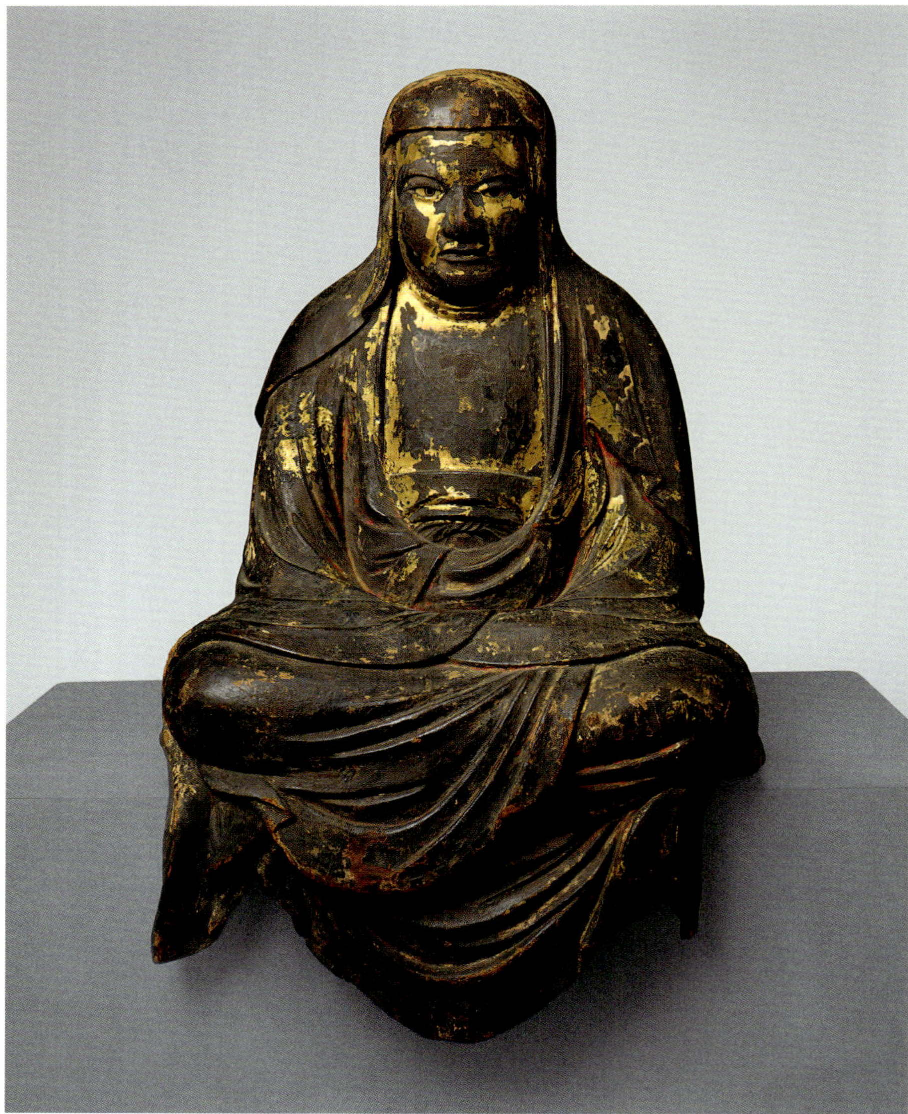

569. Demon mask

Kamakura period (?)
Polychromed wood
H. 33 cm (13 in.)

570. Mask of a man

Muromachi period, 16th century
Polychromed wood
H. 21.5 cm (8½ in.)

Gift from Harry C. Nail, 1967

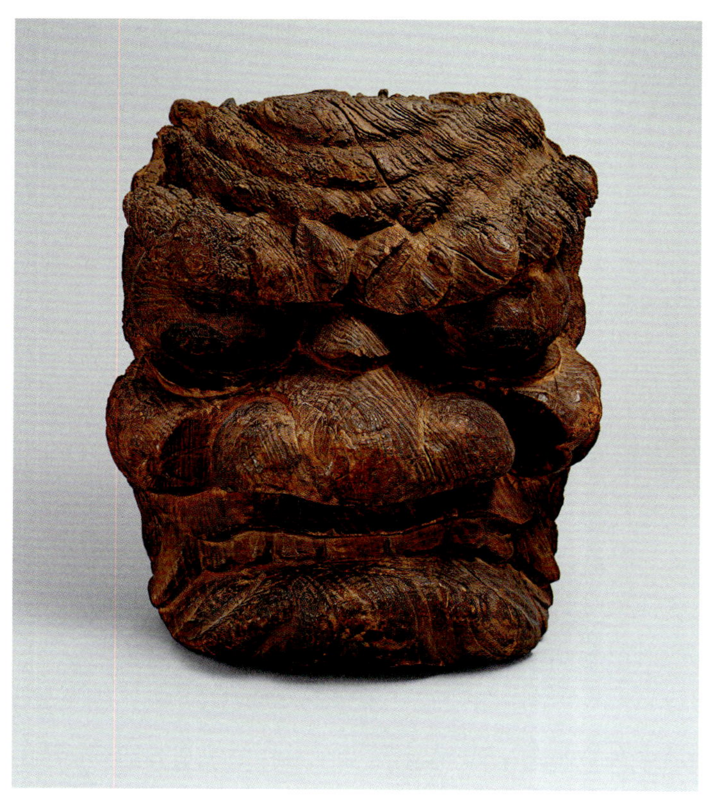

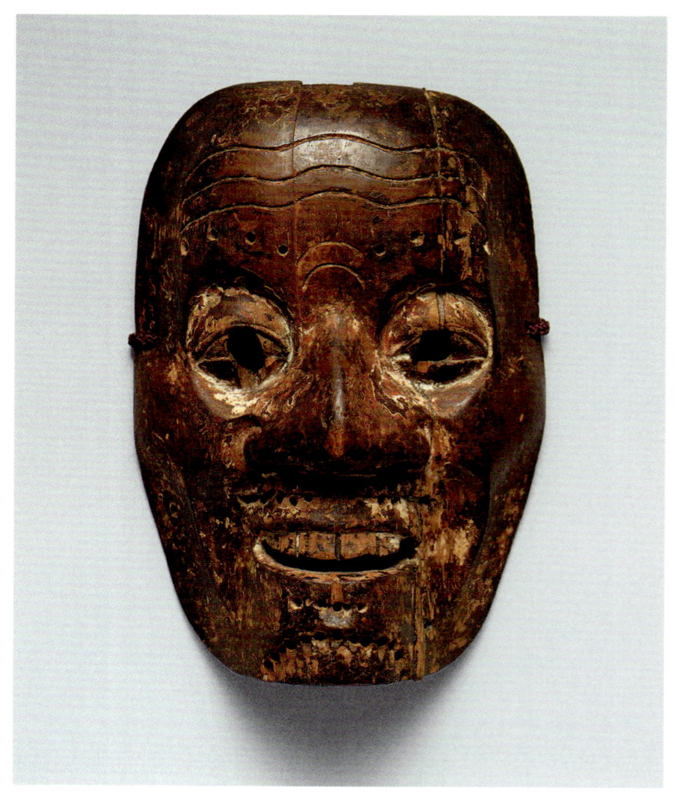

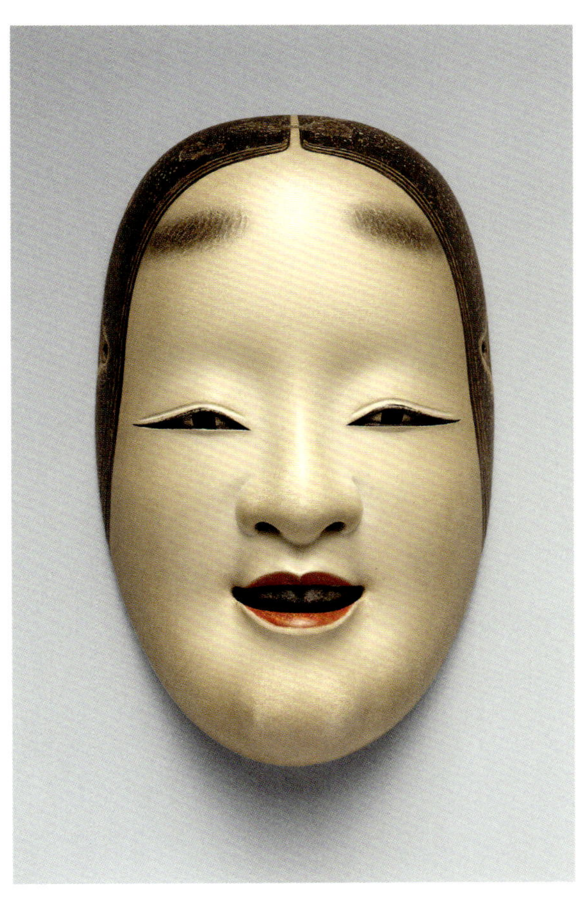

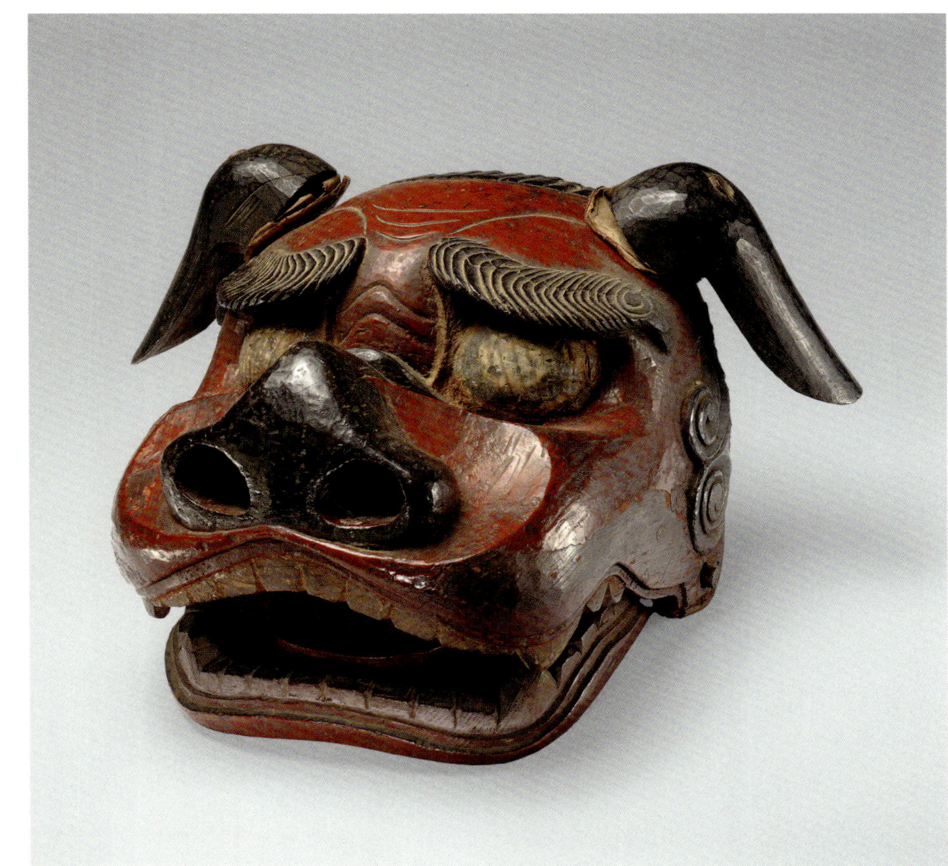

571. Noh mask of a woman

Edo period (?)
Polychromed wood
H. 21.2 cm ($8^3/_8$ in.)

572. Head for Lion Dance

Edo period (?)
Lacquered and polychromed wood
H. 23.1 cm ($9^1/_8$ in.)

573. Lion dancers

Edo period
Lacquered and polychromed wood
H. 17.1 cm ($6^3/_4$ in.)

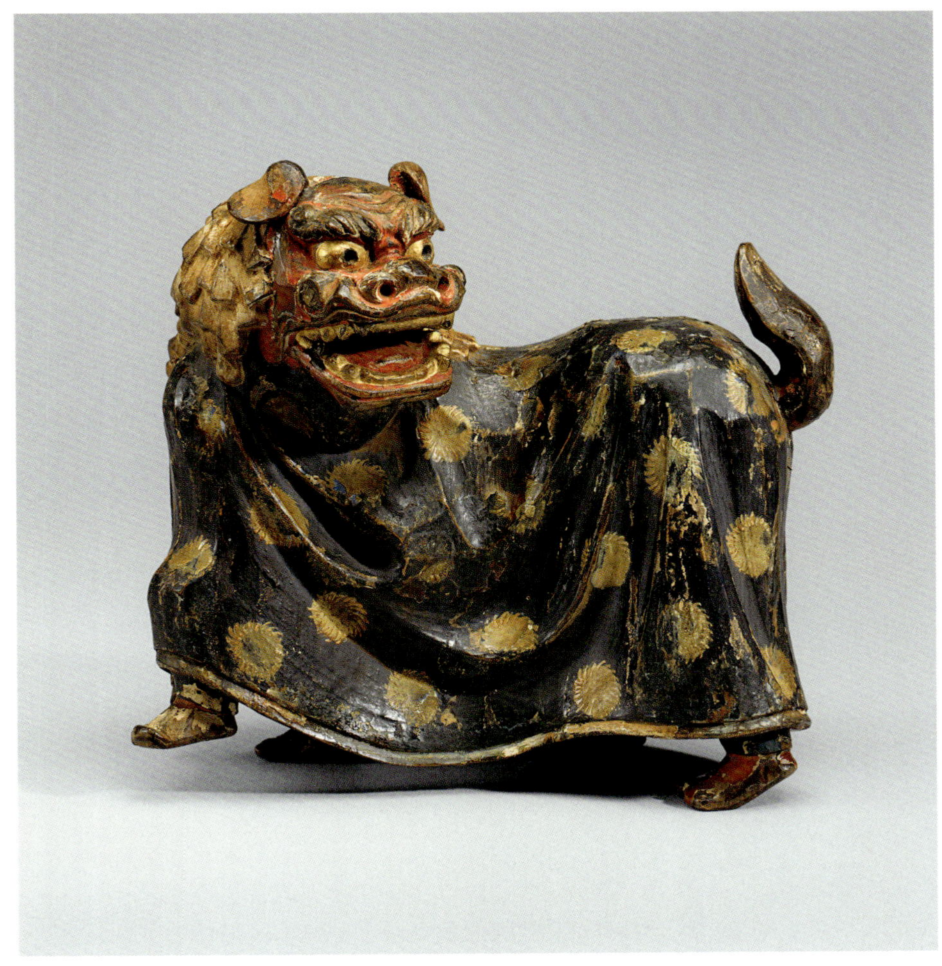

Japanese Sculpture Details

† *denotes illustrated items*

---

† 549. Jizō Bosatsu

Text

[right] seed syllables for *Fugen Bosatsu*, *Kongōkai Dainichi Nyorai*, *Jizō Bosatsu*, and [on lotus pedestal] *Amida Nyorai*
[middle] seed syllables for *Amida Nyorai*, *Fugen Bosatsu*, and *Jizō Bosatsu*
[left] *En Amida Butsu*, seed syllable for *Amida Nyorai*, seed syllable for *Muryōju Nyorai*, *Amida Butsu*, *Monk Shinkai*, *Ryō Amida Butsu*, and seed syllable for *Amida Nyorai*

---

551. Jizō Bosatsu stone stele in memory of a young girl of the Ohno family

Text

A young girl of the Ohno family. On the seventeenth day of the [?] month in 1727.

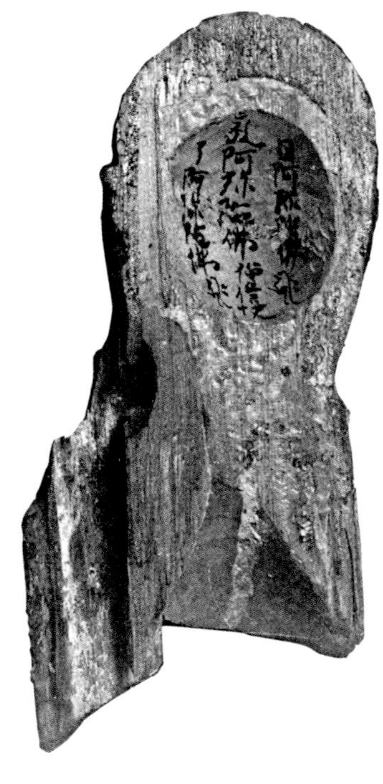

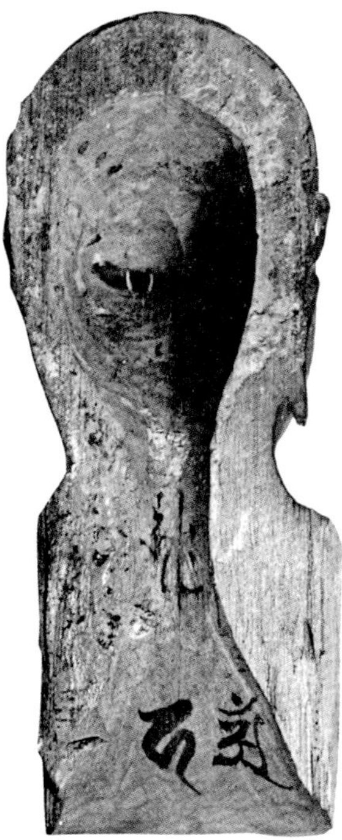

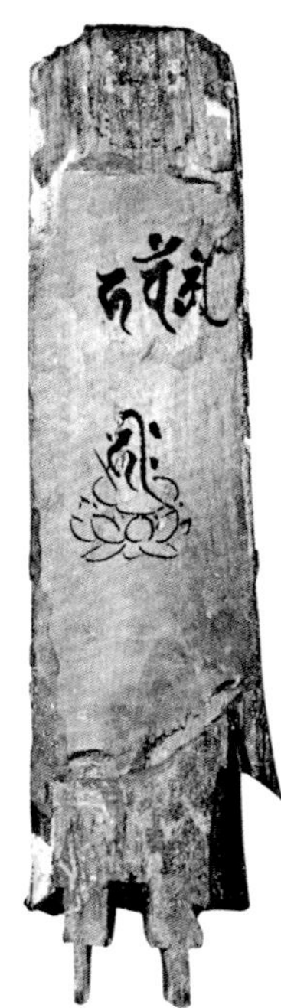

549

Japanese Objects

Ceramics

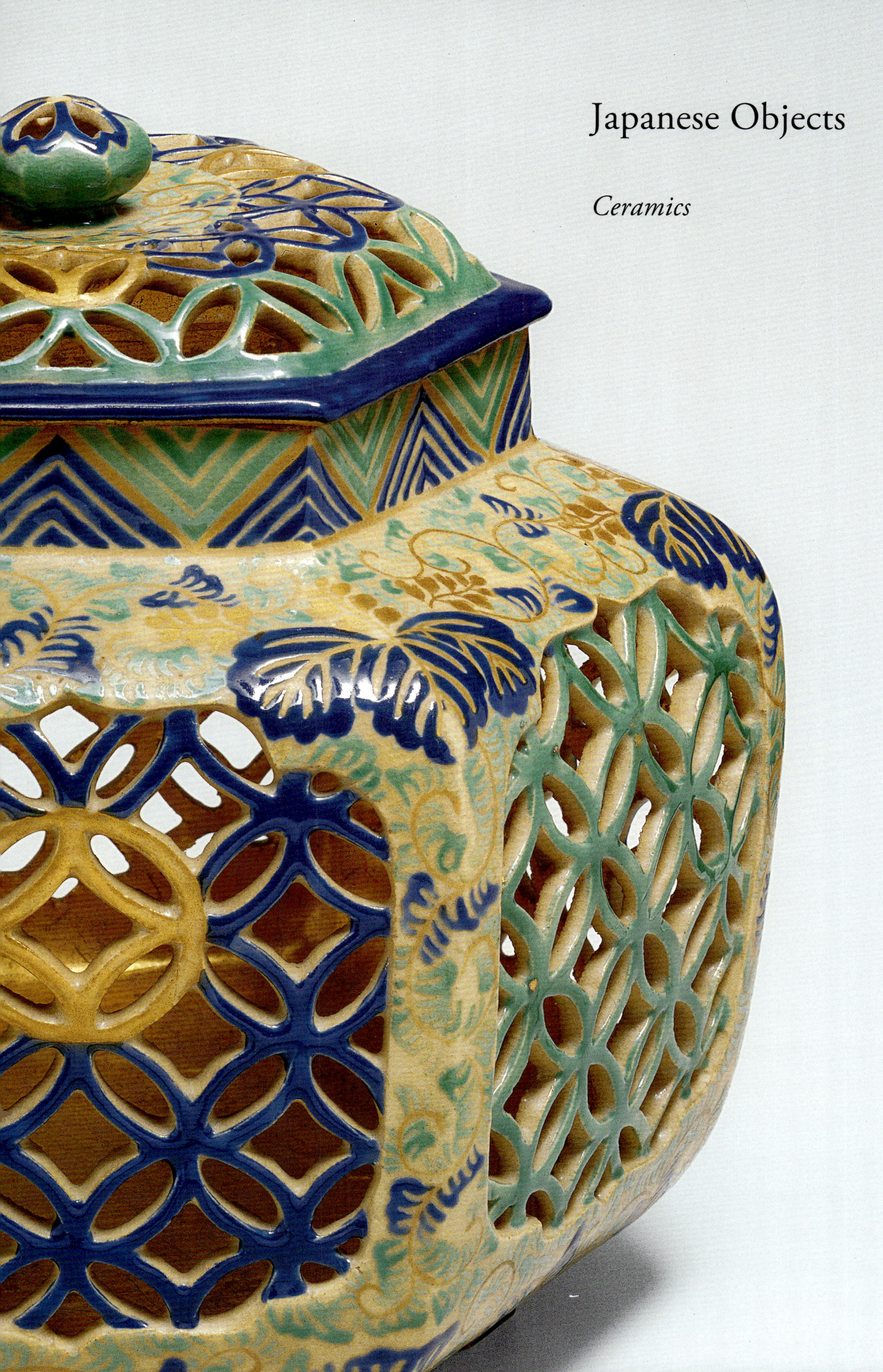

Jōmon–Kamakura Period

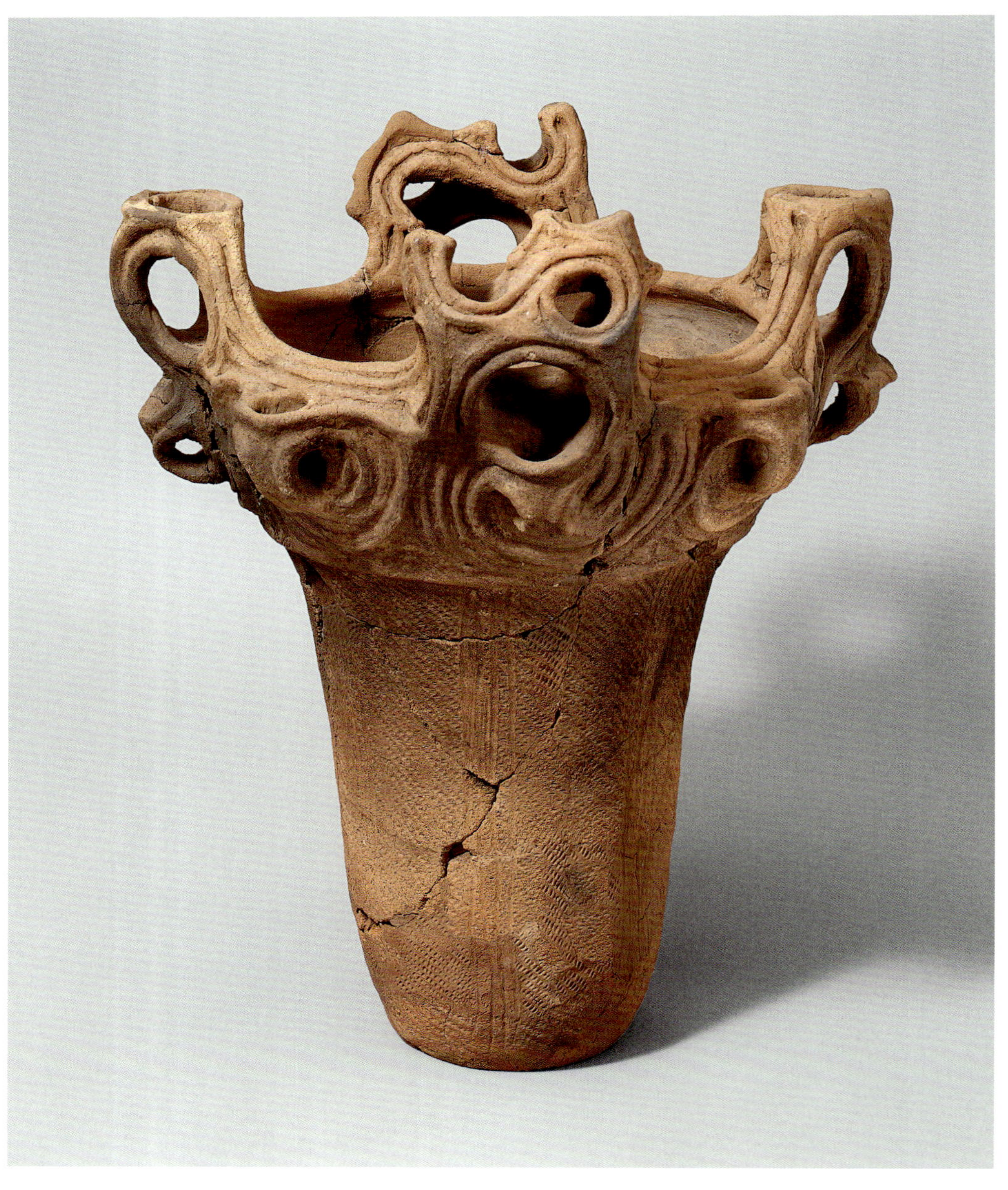

574. Bowl with four projections

Jōmon period, 2500–1500 B.C.
Earthenware
H. 53.1 cm (20⅞ in.)

LITERATURE: Murase 1993, no. 55; Murase 2000, no. 1; Tsuji Nobuo et al. 2005, no. 1.

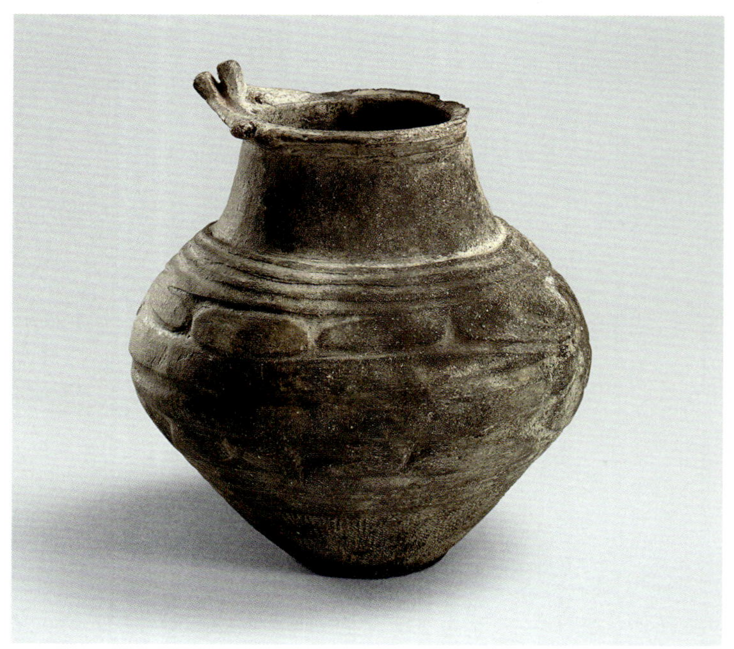

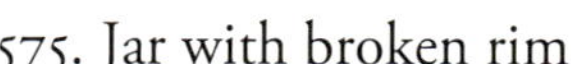

575. Jar with broken rim

Earthenware
Jōmon period, 1000–400 B.C.
H. 13.9 cm (5½ in.)

LITERATURE: Pekarik 1978, no. 4.

576. Jar

Yayoi period, 3rd century A.D.
Earthenware
H. 40.5 cm (16 in.)

LITERATURE: Murase 1993, no. 56; Murase 2000, no. 2; Tsuji Nobuo et al. 2005, no. 3.

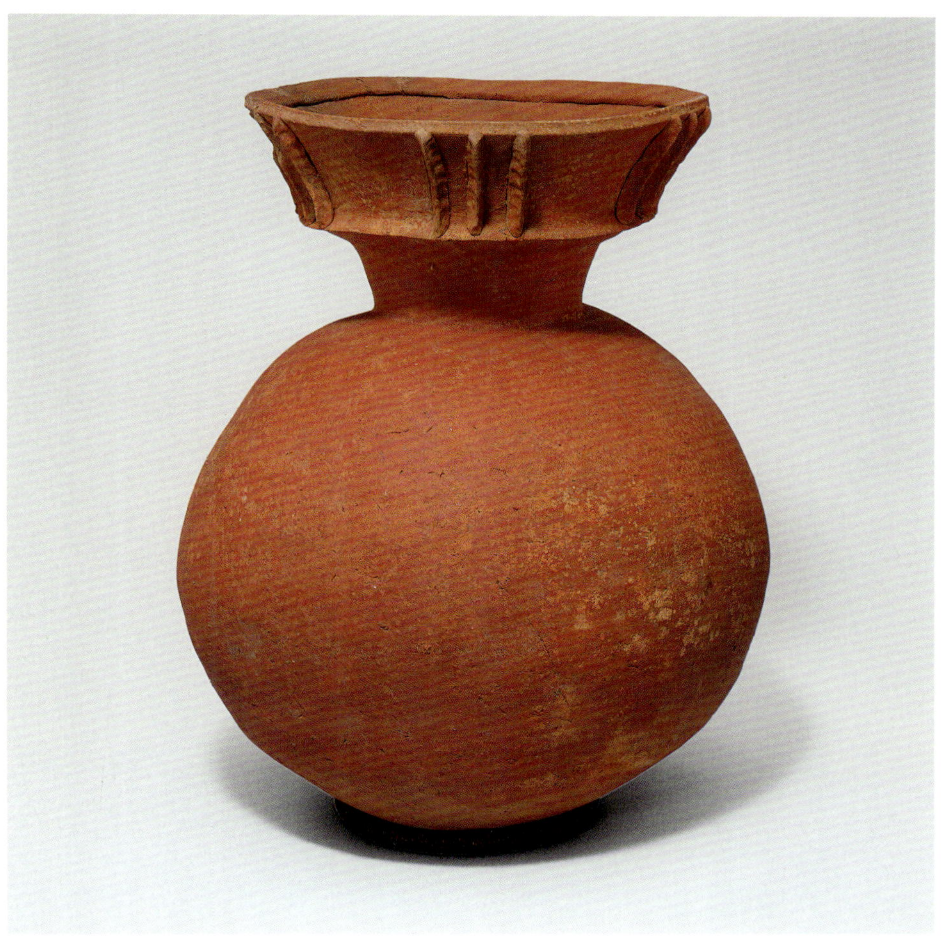

577. Recumbent vessel (*yokobe*, 横瓶)

Kofun period, late 6th century
Sueki (須恵器) stoneware
H. 37 cm (14 5/8 in.)

LITERATURE: Murase 1993, no. 58; Murase 2000, no. 4; Tsuji Nobuo et al. 2005, no. 4.

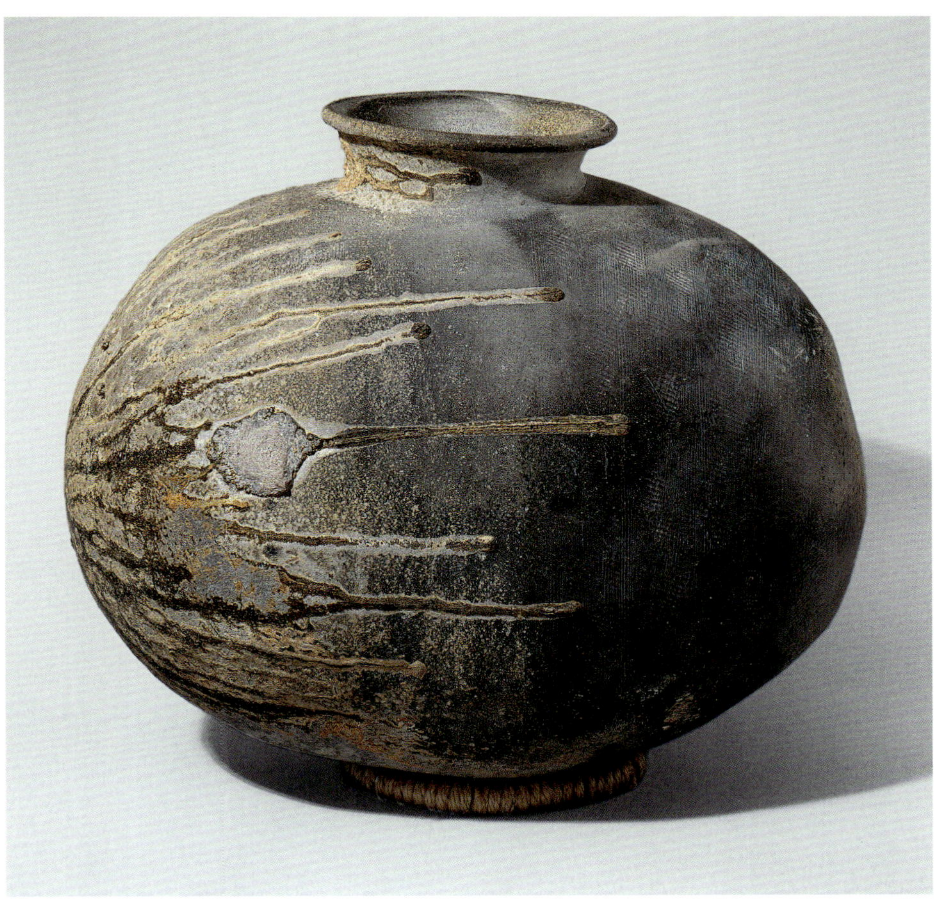

578. Recumbent vessel (*yokobe*, 横瓶) with long neck

Kofun period, 7th century
Sueki (須恵器) stoneware
H. 24.7 cm (9 3/4 in.)

Literature: Murase 1975, no. 96; Pekarik 1978, no. 11.

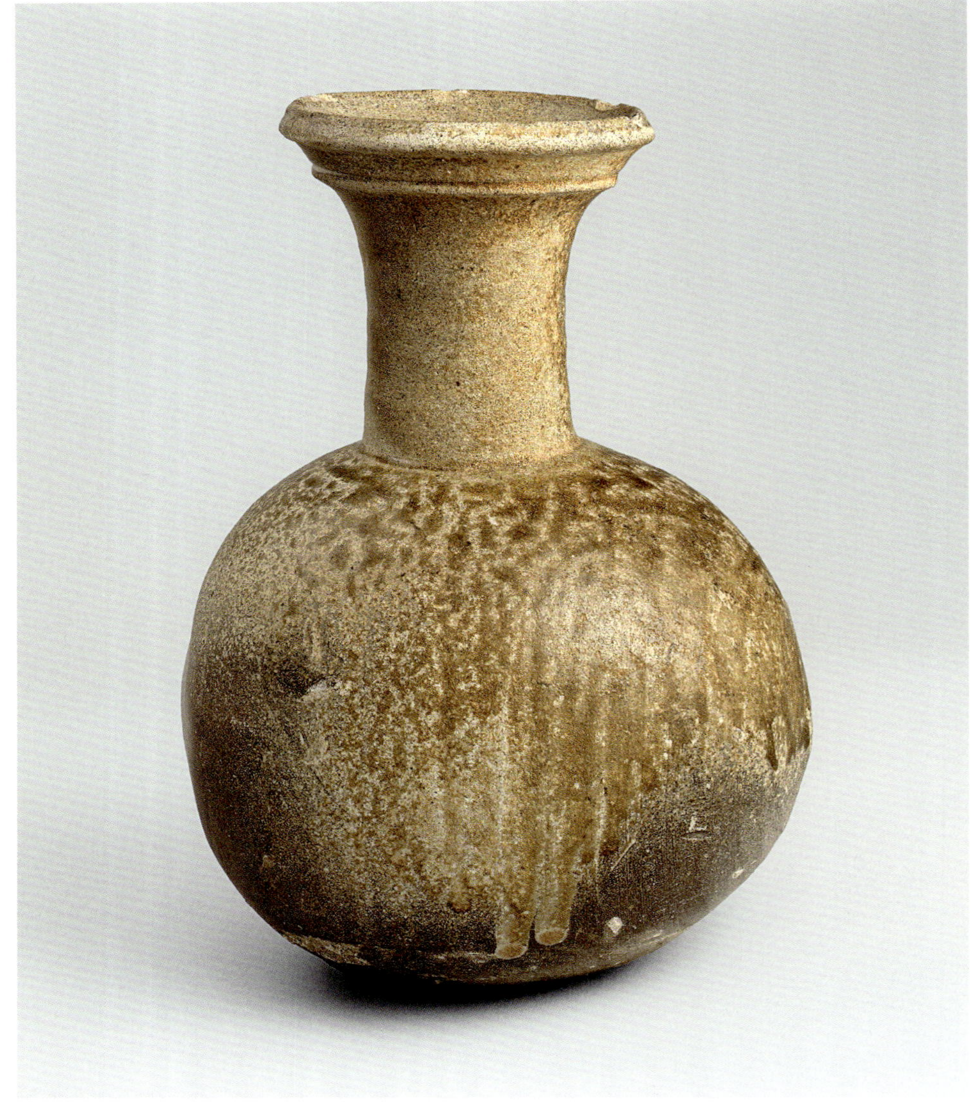

579. Jar with flared mouth

Kofun period, ca. 400
Sueki (須恵器) stoneware
H. 11.6 cm (4 5/8 in.)

580. Jar

Kofun period, 250–600
Sueki (須恵器) stoneware
H. 16.5 cm (6 1/2 in.)

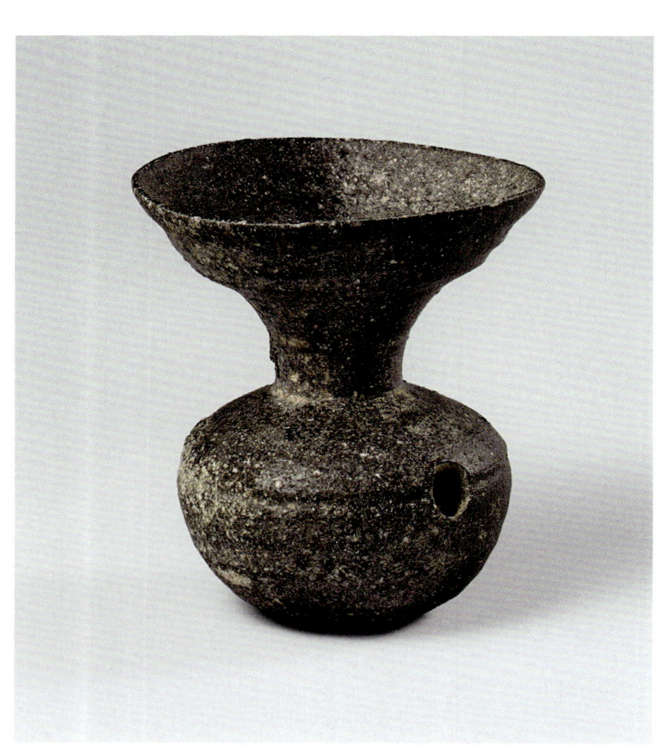

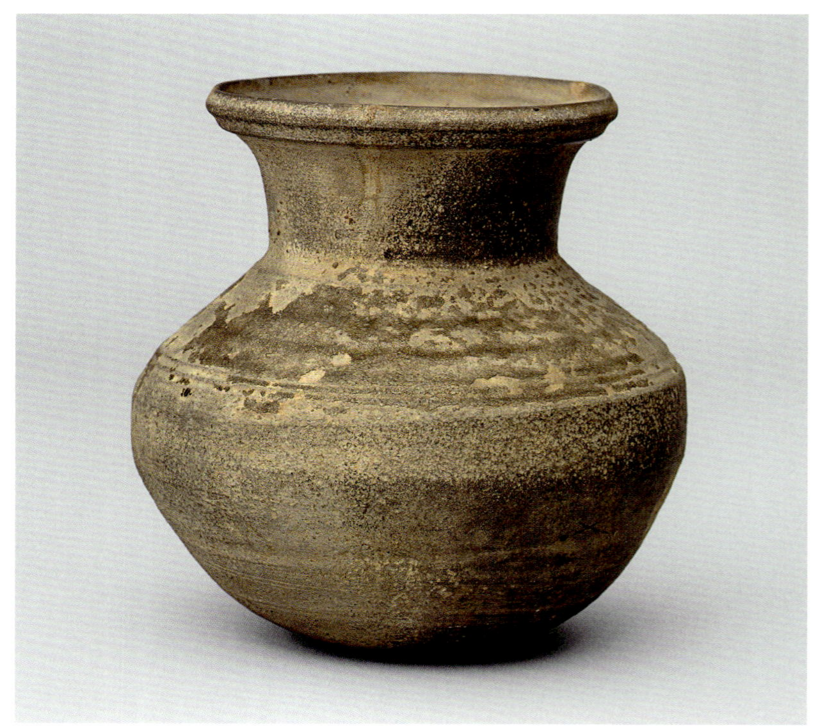

581. Jar

Heian period, 9th–10th century
Hajiki (土師器) earthenware, with dark firing marks
H. 32.5 cm (12 3/4 in.)

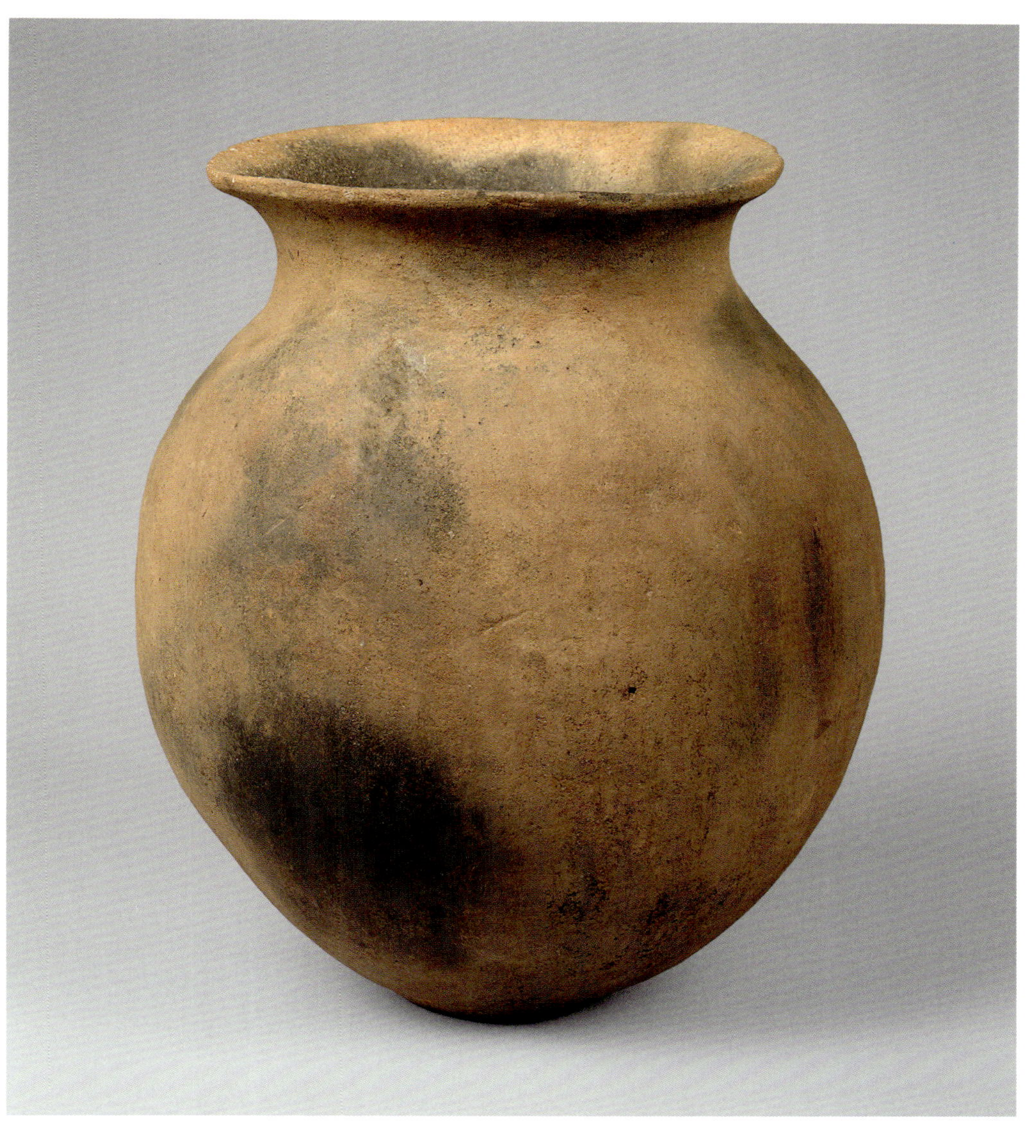

582. Bowl

Heian period, 12th century
Sanage (猿投) ware; stoneware
Diam. 15.5 cm (6 1/8 in.)

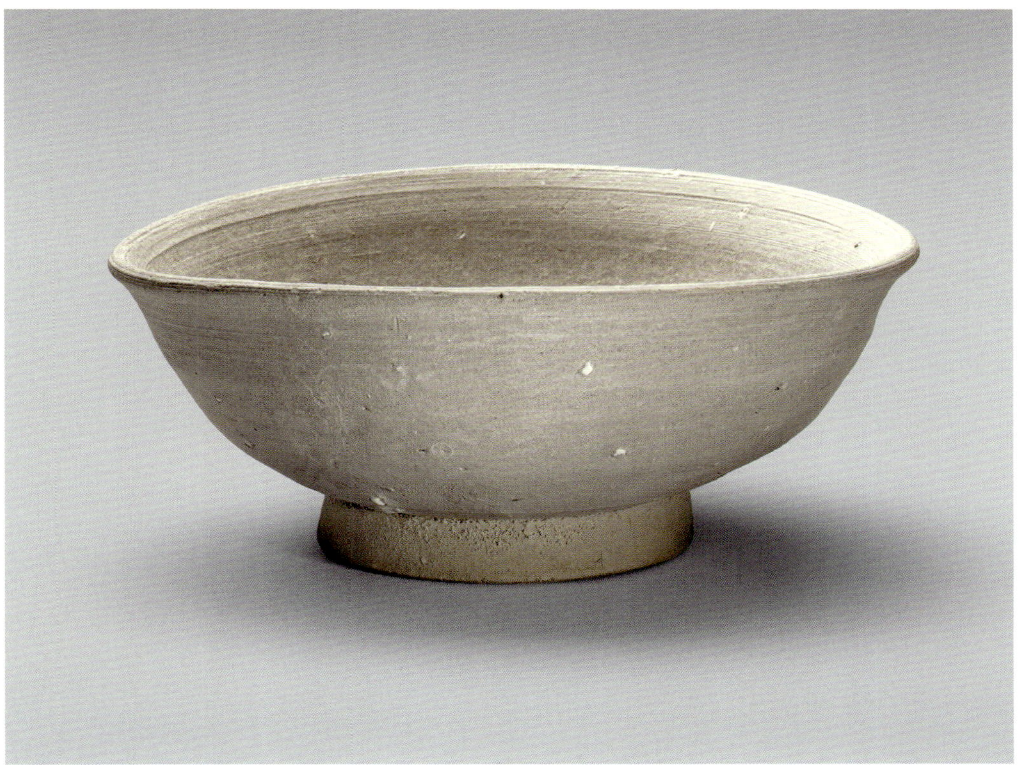

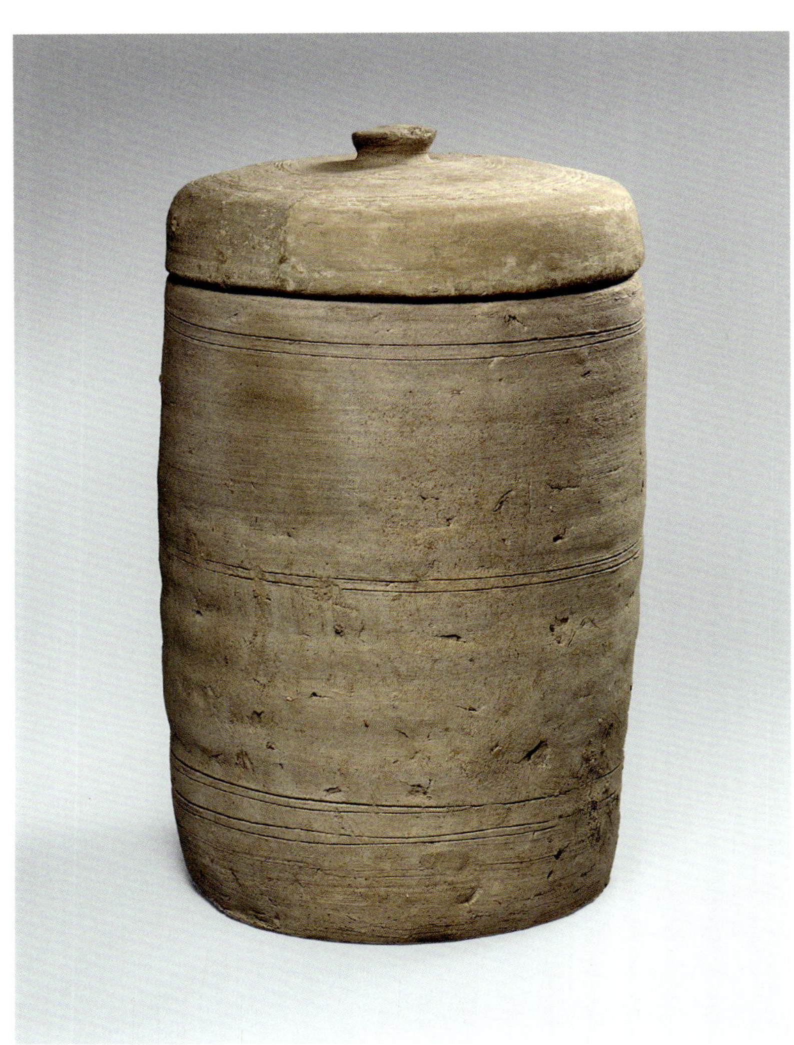

583. Sutra container

Heian period, 12th century
Sanage (猿投) ware; stoneware
H. 34.3 cm (13 1/2 in.), diam. 20.3 cm (8 in.)

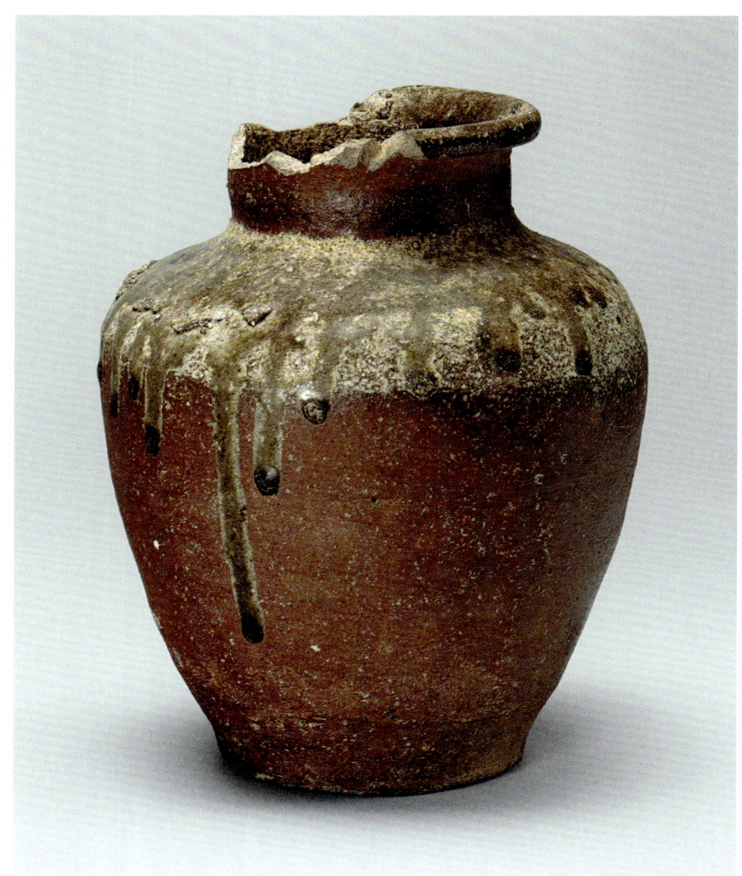

584. Jar with broken rim

Kamakura period, 13th century
Tokoname (常滑) ware; stoneware with natural ash glaze
H. 22.2 cm (8 3/4 in.)

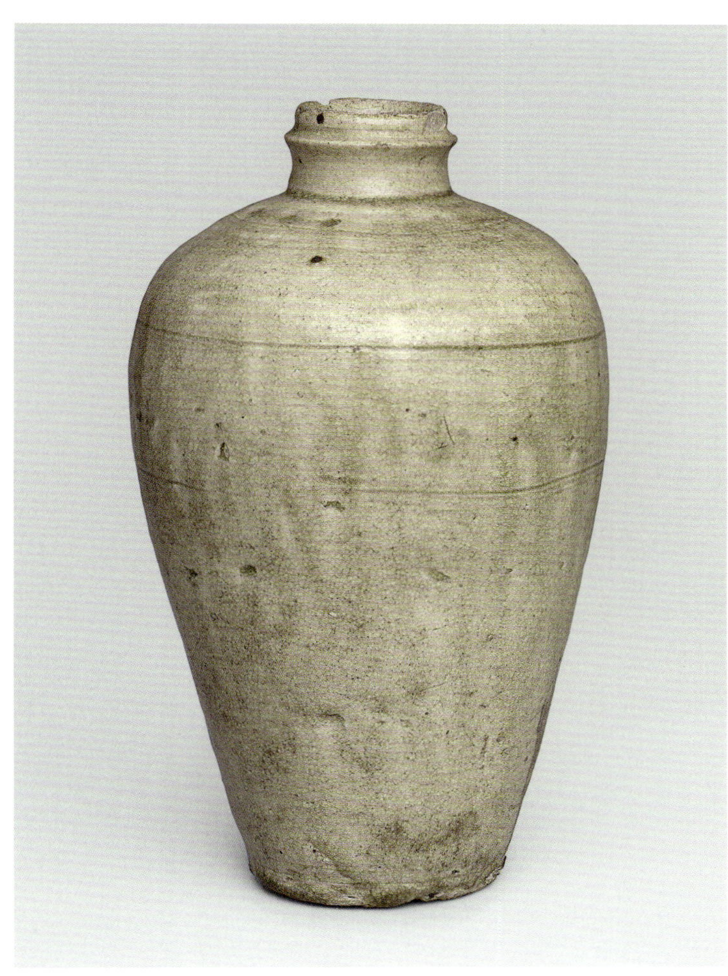

585. *Meiping* (梅瓶) jar

Kamakura period, 13th century
Seto (瀬戸) ware, *Ko Seto* (古瀬戸) type;
stoneware with light-green ash glaze
H. 27.9 cm (11 in.)

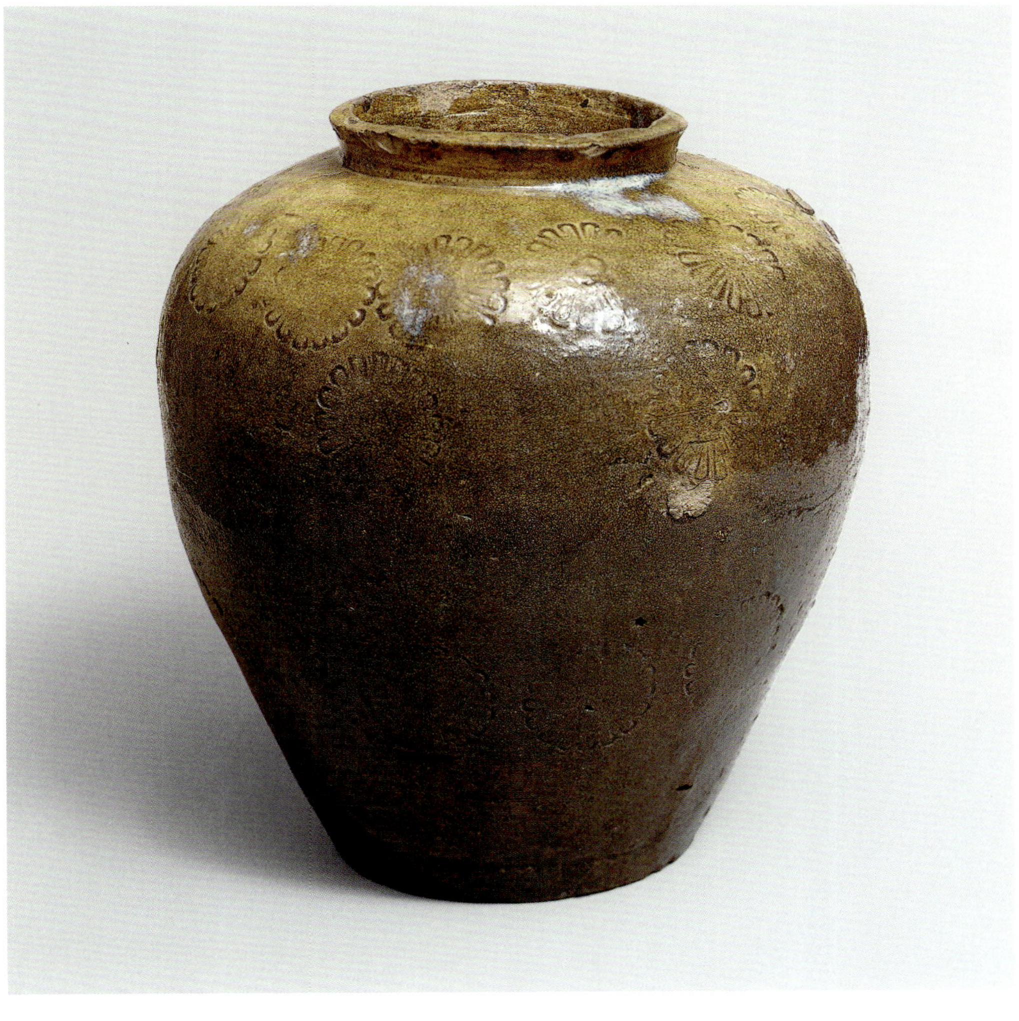

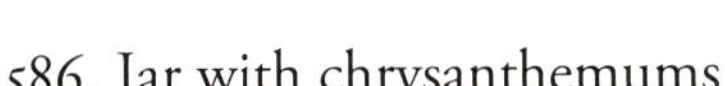

586. Jar with chrysanthemums

Kamakura period, late 13th–early 14th century
Seto (瀬戸) ware, *Ko Seto* (古瀬戸) type;
stoneware with glaze and stamped decoration
H. 24.8 cm (9 3/4 in.)

LITERATURE: Murase 1975, add. no. 115; Pekarik 1978, no. 15; Tokyo National Museum 1985a, no. 86; Avitabile 1990, no. 128; Murase 2000, no. 47; Tsuji Nobuo et al. 2005, no. 17.

587. Tea caddy (*chaire*, 茶入れ)

Edo period, 18th–19th century
Banko (万古) ware; stoneware with brown glaze
H. 5.7 cm (2¼ in.)

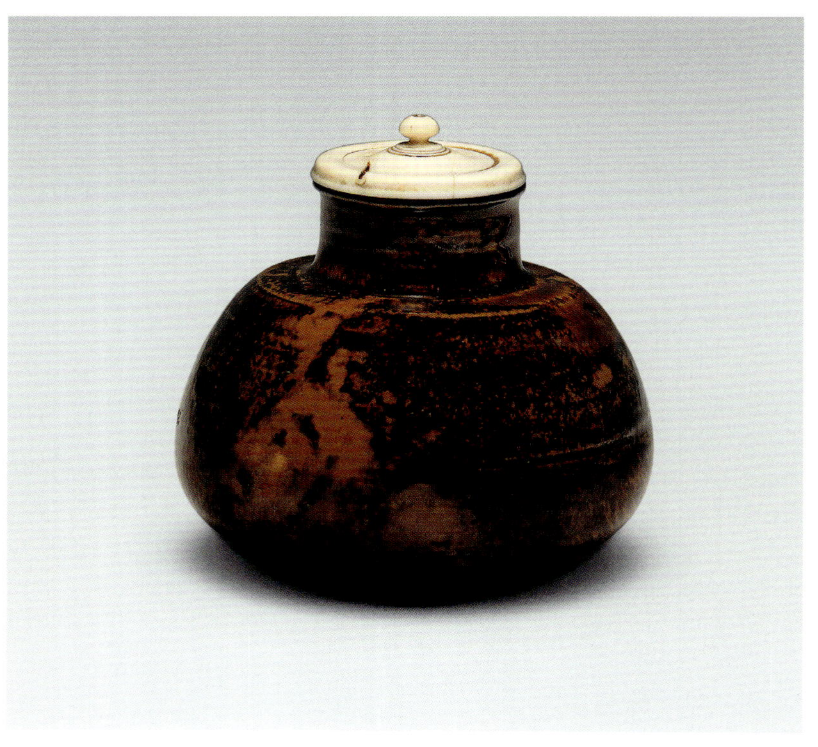

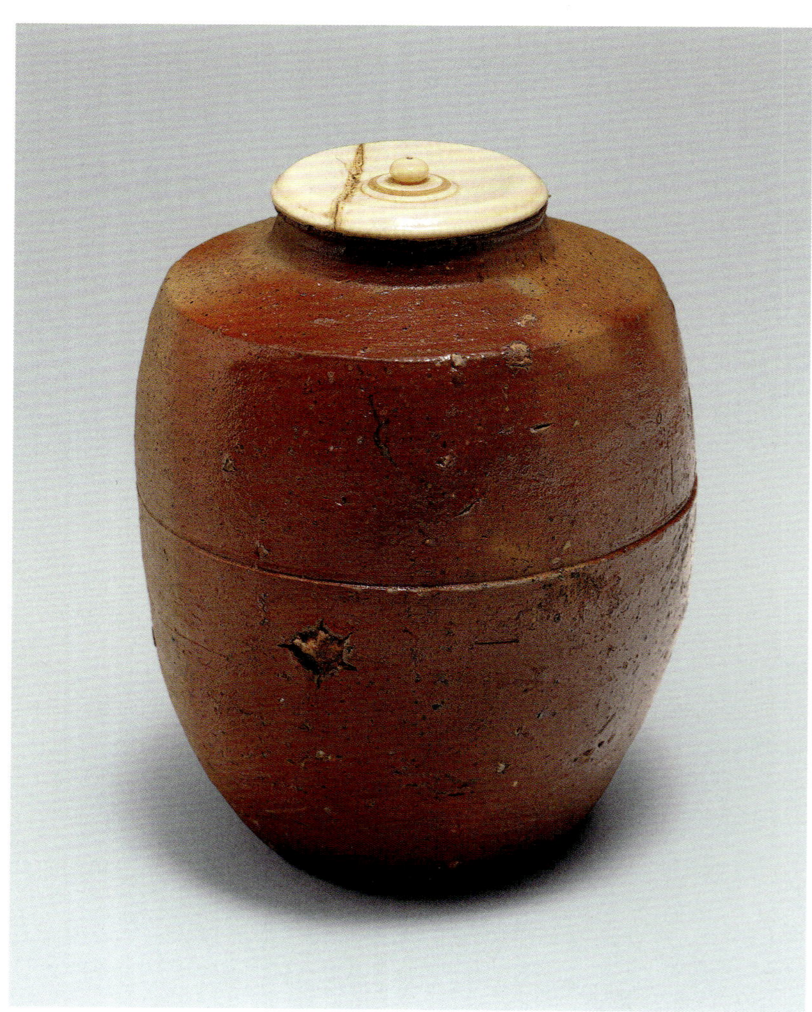

588. Tea caddy (*chaire*, 茶入れ)

Momoyama period, 16th century
Bizen (備前) ware; stoneware with natural ash glaze
H. 7.5 cm (3 in.)

Literature: Tokyo National Museum 1985a, no. 95; Avitabile 1990, no. 139; Murase 2000, no. 102.

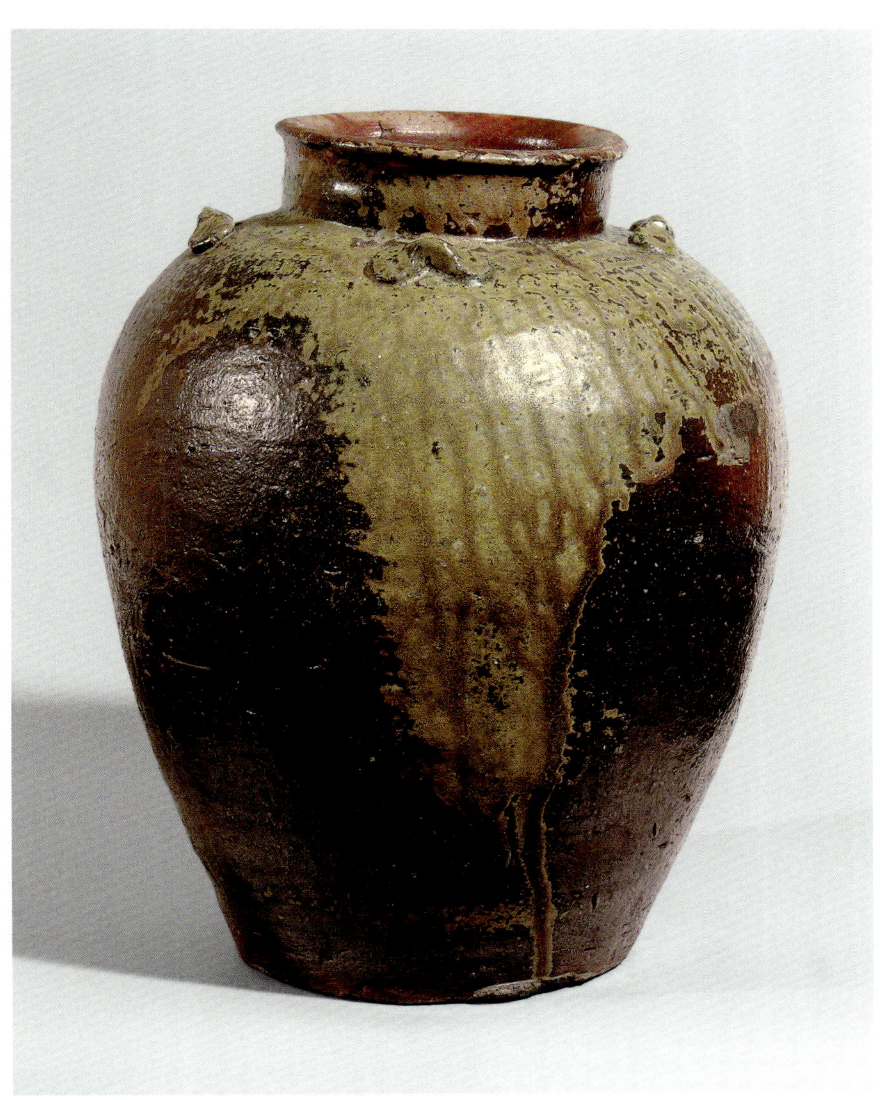

589. Tea-leaf storage jar

Momoyama period, 16th century
Bizen (備前) ware; stoneware with natural ash glaze and straw fire marks around mouth
H. 30.7 cm (12 1/8 in.)
Mark

LITERATURE: Tokyo National Museum 1985a, no. 89; Avitabile 1990, no. 137.

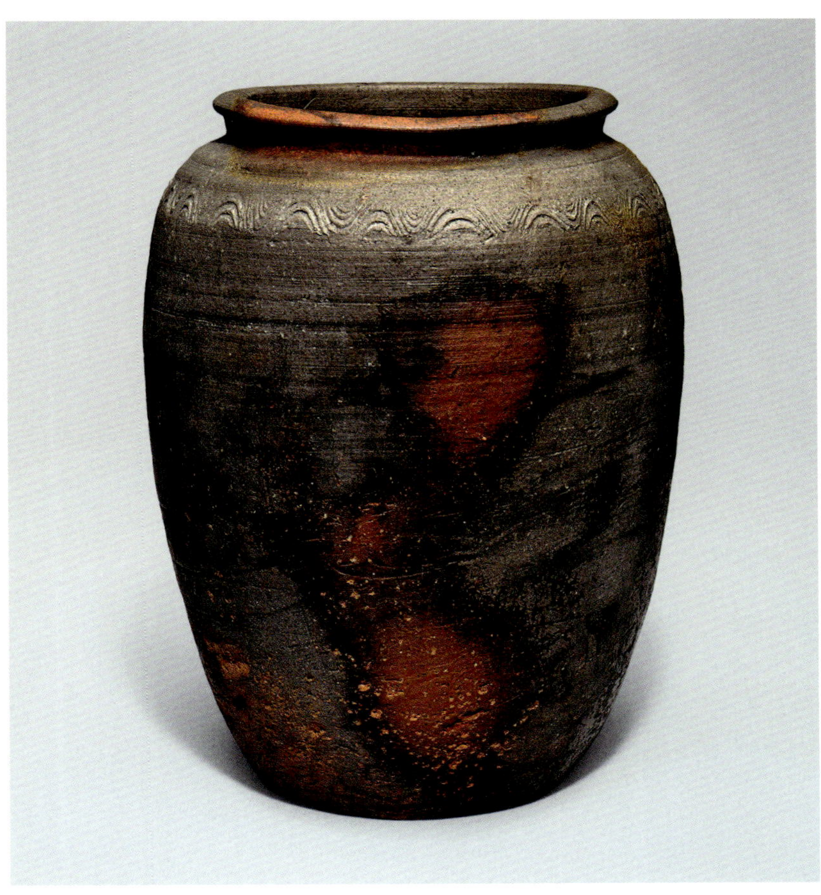

590. Jar with wave pattern

Momoyama period, 16th century
Bizen (備前) ware; stoneware with incising and fire marks
H. 25.7 cm (10 1/8 in.)

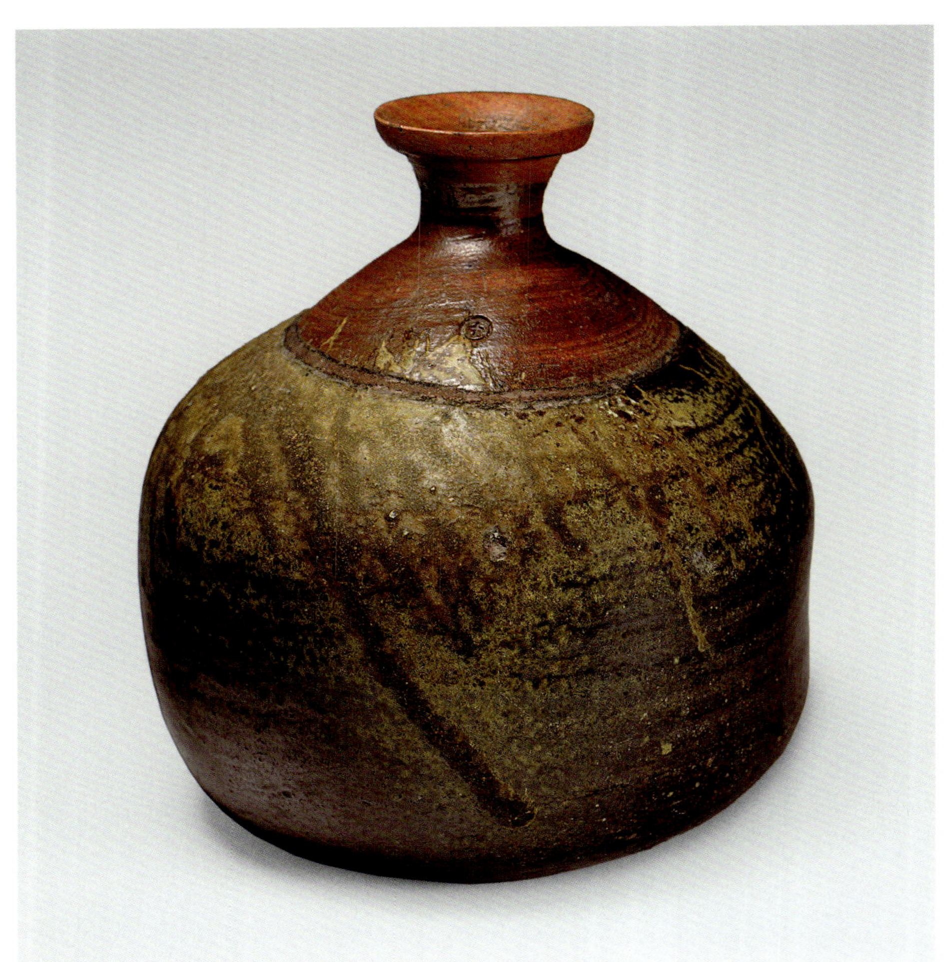

591. Sake bottle

Momoyama period, 16th century
Bizen (備前) ware; stoneware with natural ash glaze
H. 21.9 cm (8⅝ in.)
Mark

Literature: Tokyo National Museum 1985a, no. 91; Avitabile 1990, no. 138.

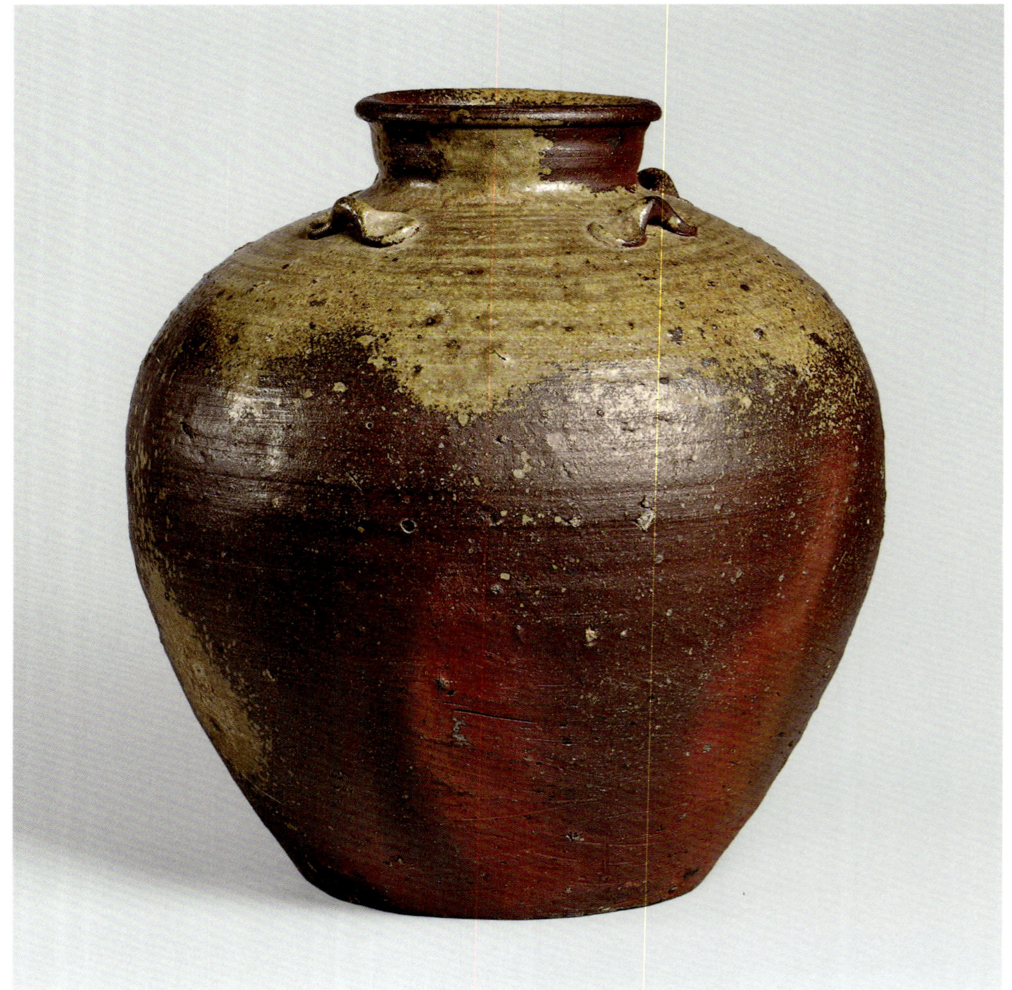

592. Jar with four loops on shoulder

Momoyama period, 16th century
Bizen (備前) ware; stoneware with natural ash glaze and fire marks
H. 32 cm (12⅝ in.)
Mark

593. Platter

Momoyama period, early 17th century
Bizen (備前) ware; stoneware with natural ash glaze
Diam. 30.5 cm (12 in.)

Literature: Cort 1985, fig. 4; Tokyo National Museum 1985a, no. 90; Avitabile 1990, no. 140; Murase 2000, no. 103; Murase 2003, no. 106; Tsuji Nobuo et al. 2005, no. 53.

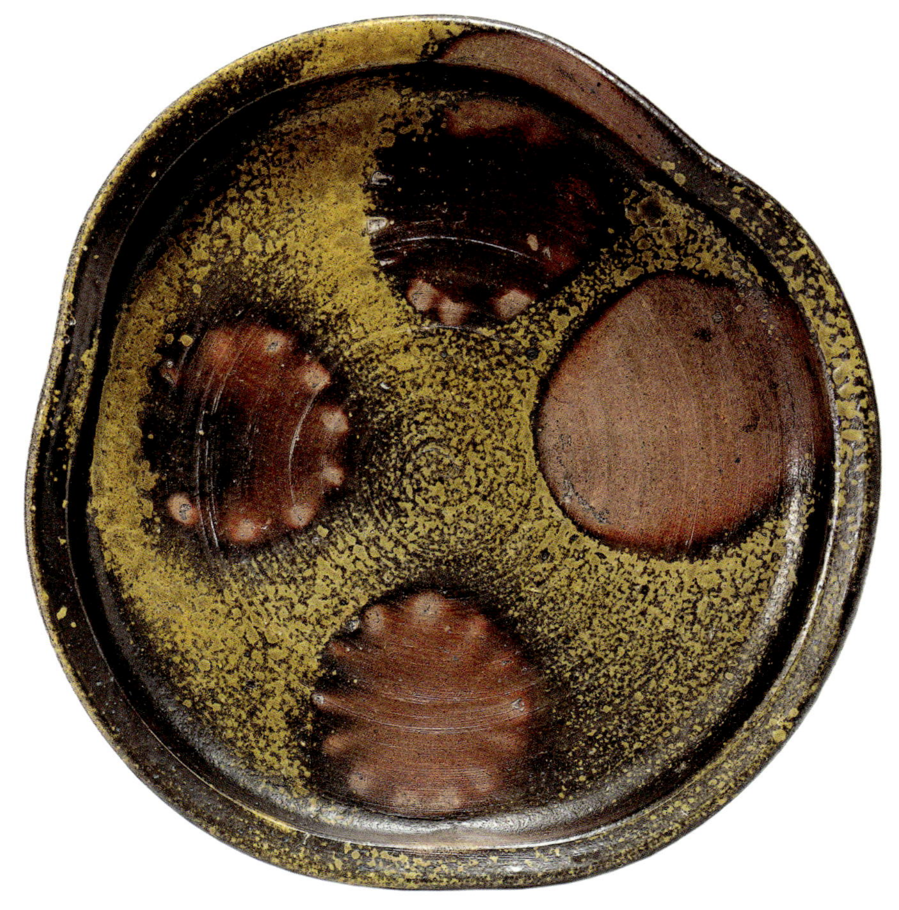

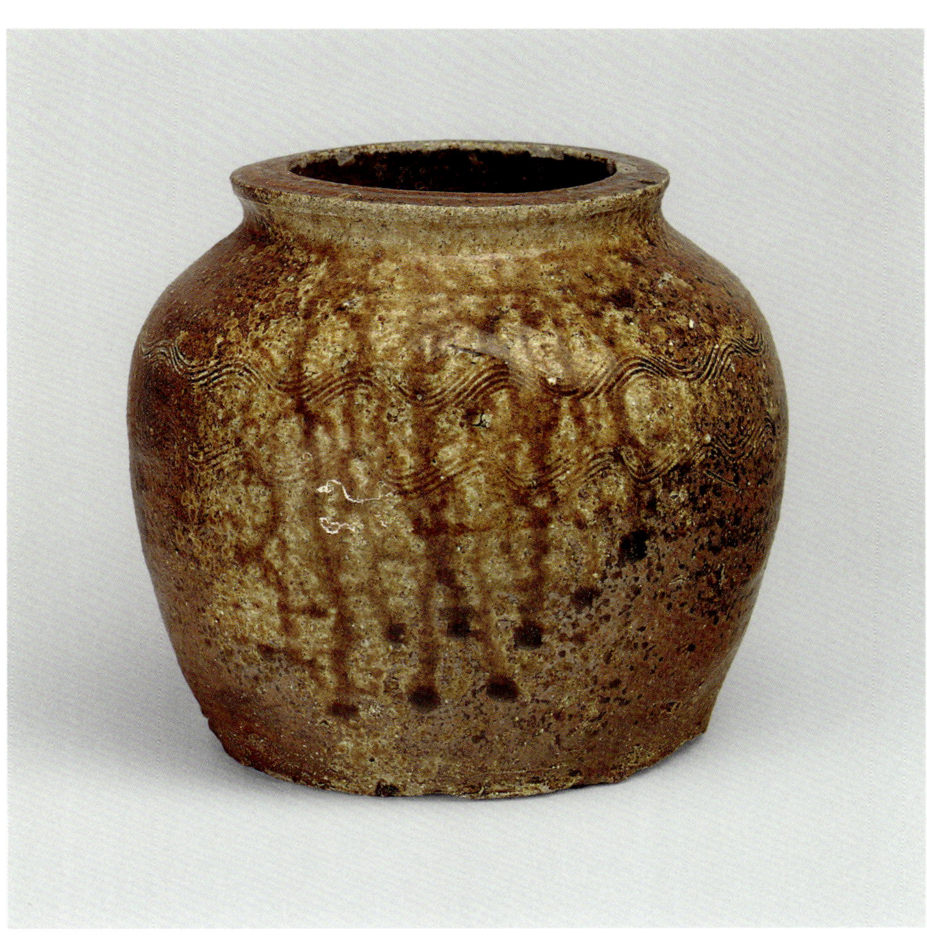

594. Oil jar

Edo period, 18th century
Echizen (越前) ware; stoneware with natural ash glaze
H. 16.3 cm (6 3/8 in.)

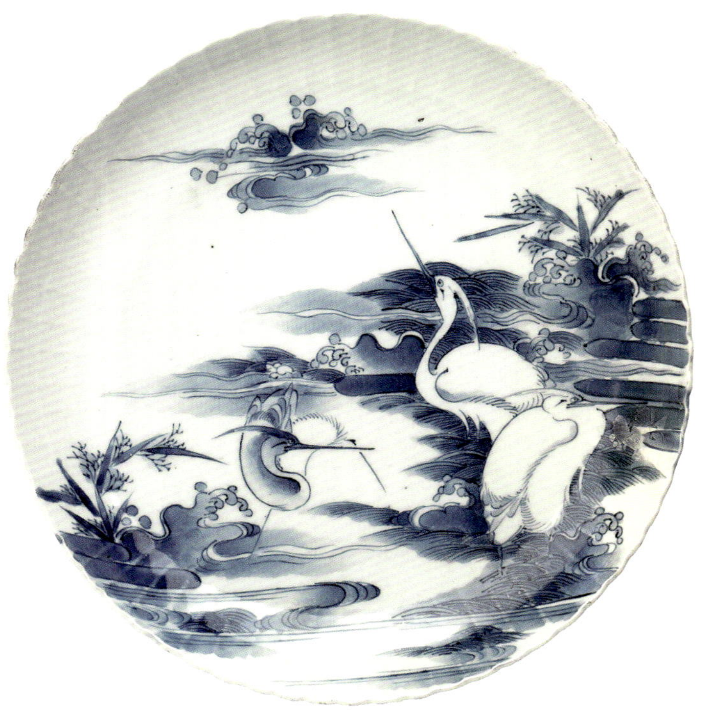

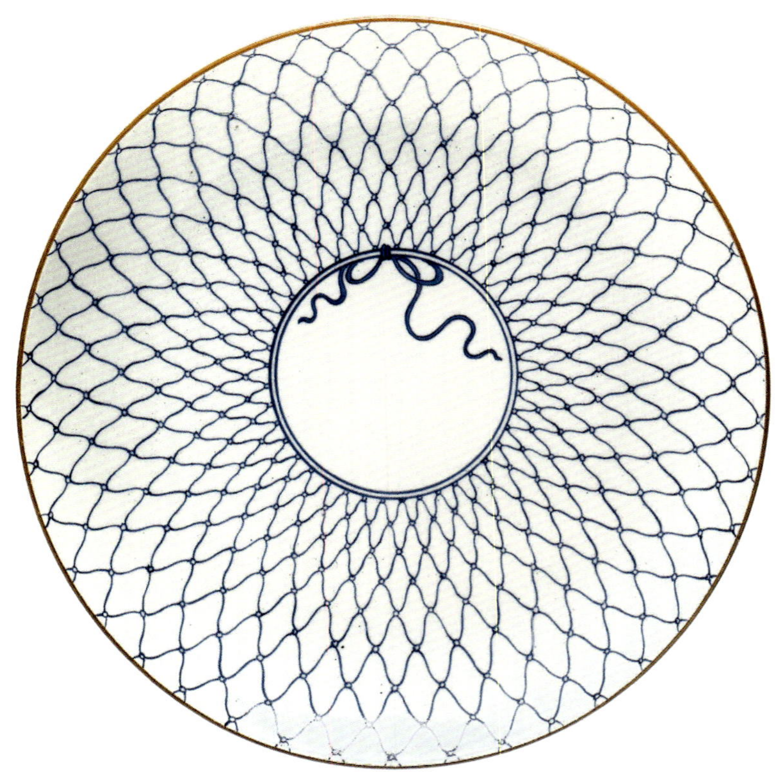

596. Dish with fishnet design

Edo period, 17th–18th century
Hizen (肥前) ware, *Ai Kakiemon* (藍柿右衛門) style; porcelain with underglaze cobalt blue
Diam. 21 cm (8¼ in.)

LITERATURE: Rousmaniere 2002, no. 123.

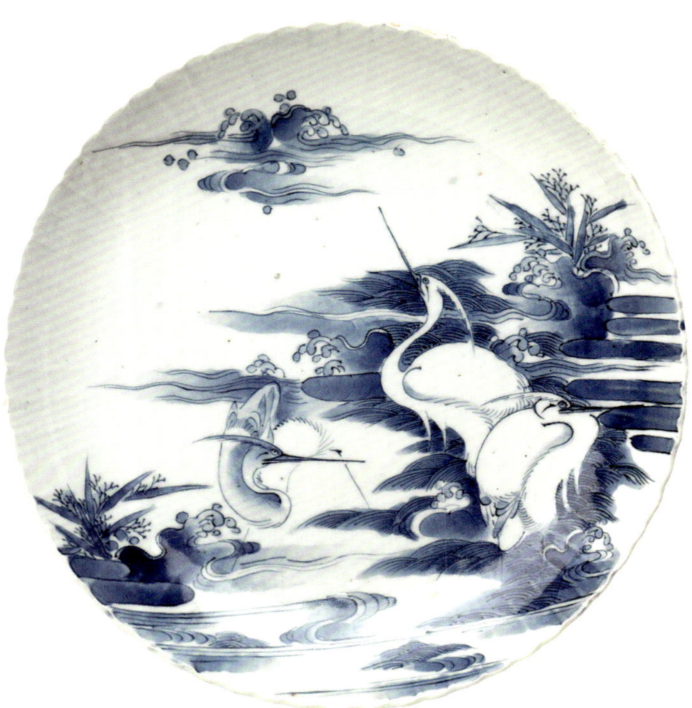

595. Pair of dishes with herons

Edo period, 18th century
Hizen (肥前) ware, *Ai Kakiemon* (藍柿右衛門) style; porcelain with underglaze cobalt blue
Diam. 21.6 cm (8½ in.)

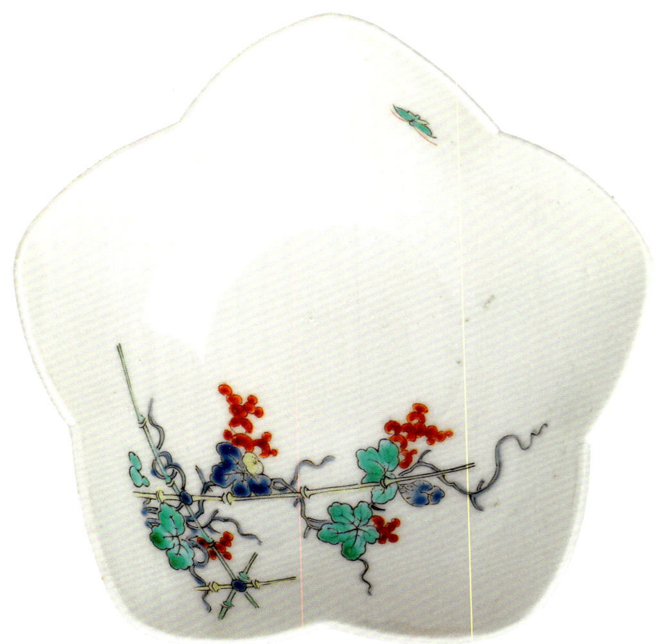

597. Dish with grapevine

Edo period, 17th century
Hizen (肥前) ware, *Kakiemon* (柿右衛門) style; porcelain with overglaze enamels
Diam. 12.7 cm (5 in.)

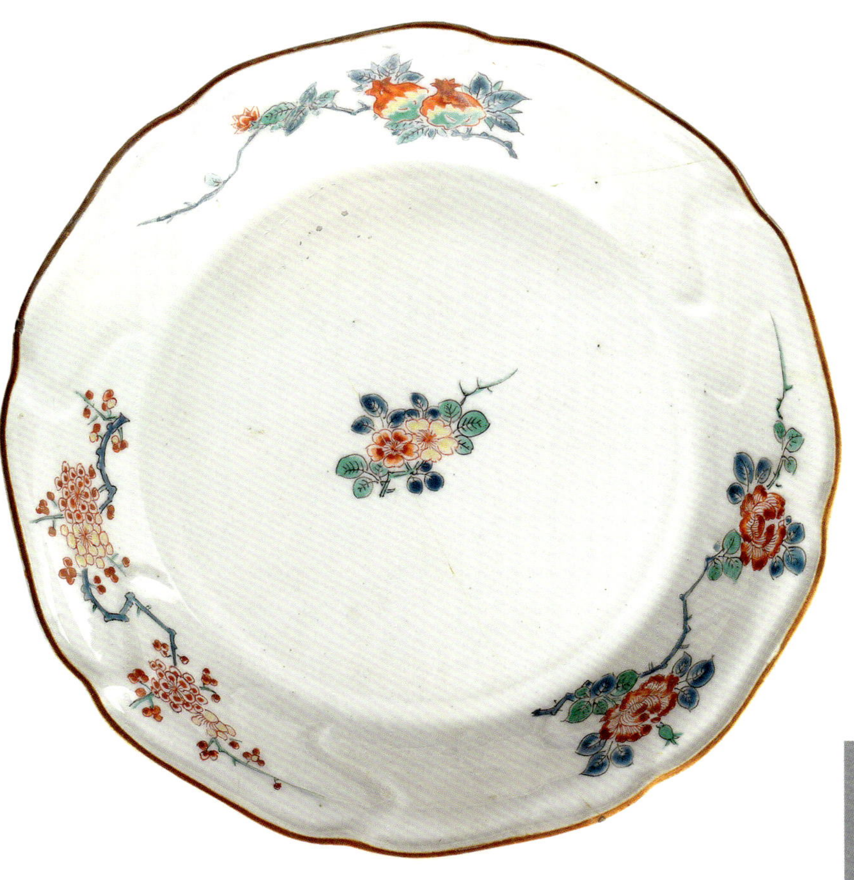

598. Dish with plum, peony, and pomegranate

Edo period, 18th century
Hizen (肥前) ware, *Kakiemon* (柿右衛門) style; porcelain with overglaze enamels
H. 3.8 cm (1½ in.), diam. 18.7 cm (7⅜ in.)

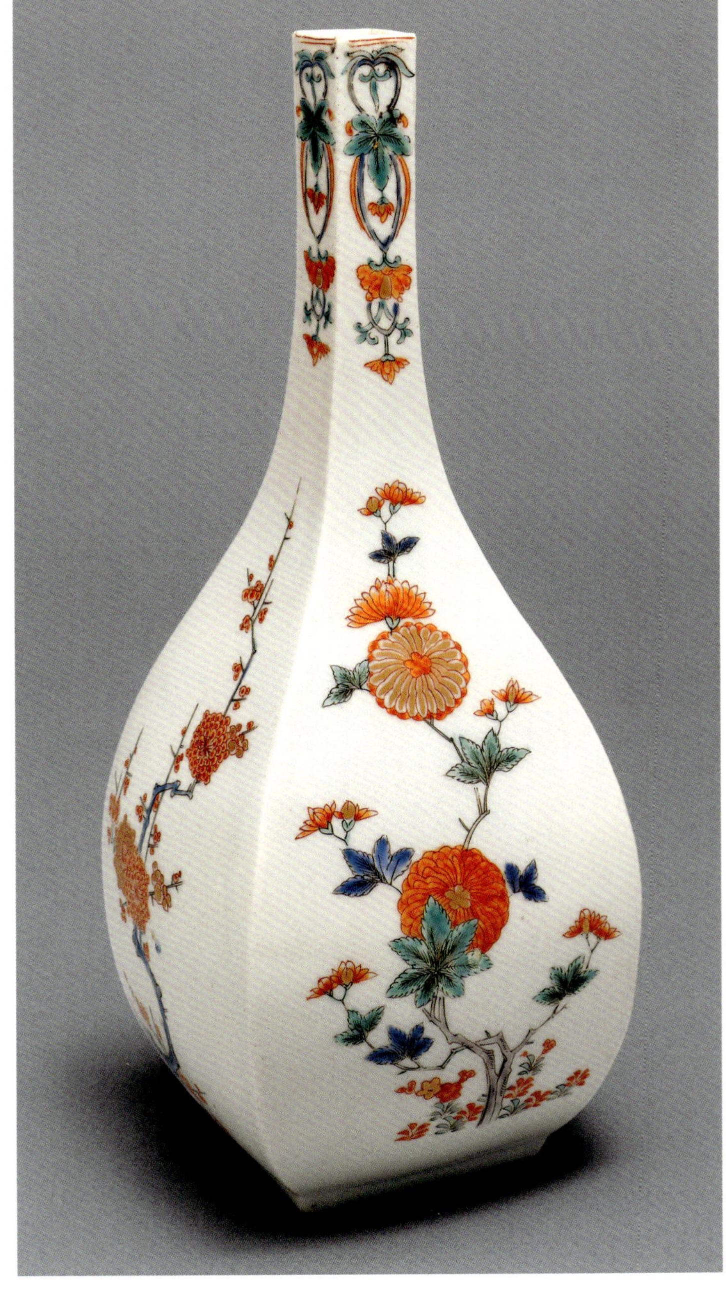

599. Bottle with chrysanthemums and plums

Edo period, late 17th century
Hizen (肥前) ware, *Kakiemon* (柿右衛門) style; porcelain with overglaze enamels
H. 22.8 cm (9 in.)

Ex coll.: Augustus II, king of Poland and elector of Saxony

Literature: Tsuji Nobuo et al. 2005, no. 58.

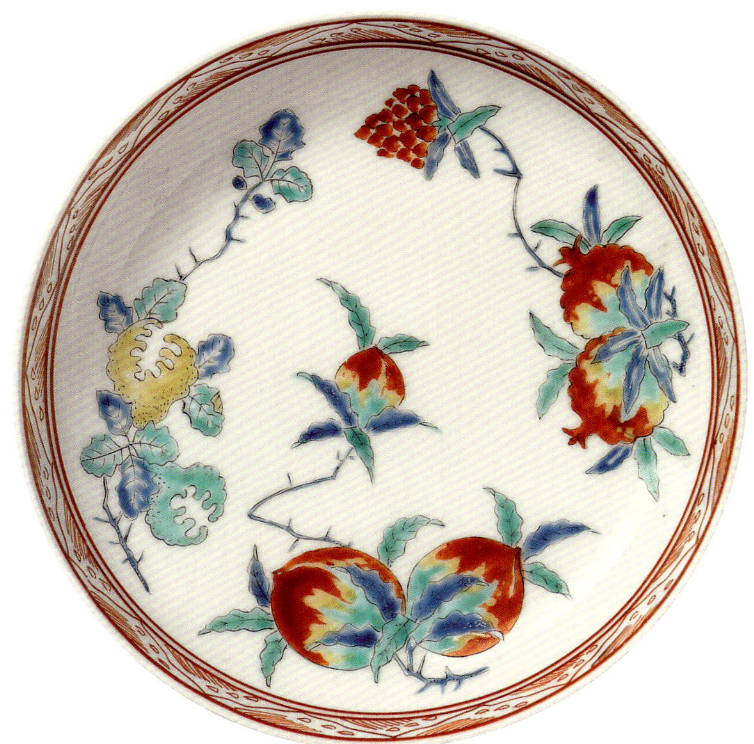

600. Dish with pomegranates, peaches, and finger citron

Edo period, 18th–19th century
Hizen (肥前) ware, *Kakiemon* (柿右衛門) style;
porcelain with overglaze enamels
Diam. 13.9 cm (5½ in.)

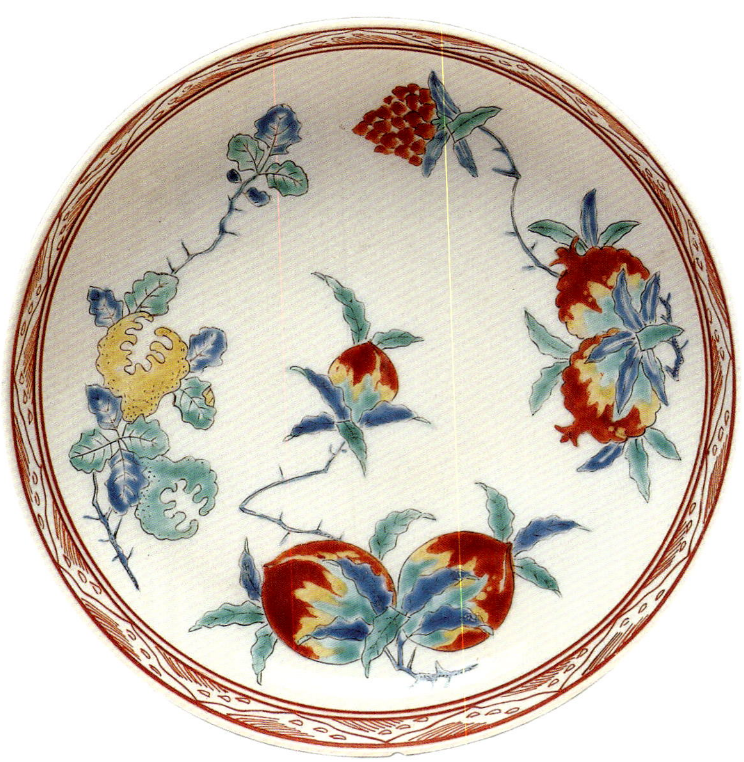

601. Dish with pomegranates, peaches, and finger citron

Edo period, 18th–19th century
Hizen (肥前) ware, *Kakiemon* (柿右衛門) style;
porcelain with overglaze enamels
Diam. 13.9 cm (5½ in.)

LITERATURE: Burke 1993, no. 43.

602. Incense burner (*hiire*, 火入れ) with three birds

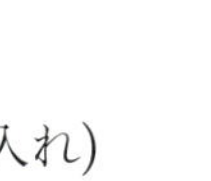

Momoyama period, 16th century
Hizen (肥前) ware, *Karatsu* (唐津) type;
stoneware with underglaze iron oxide
H. 10.2 cm (4 in.)

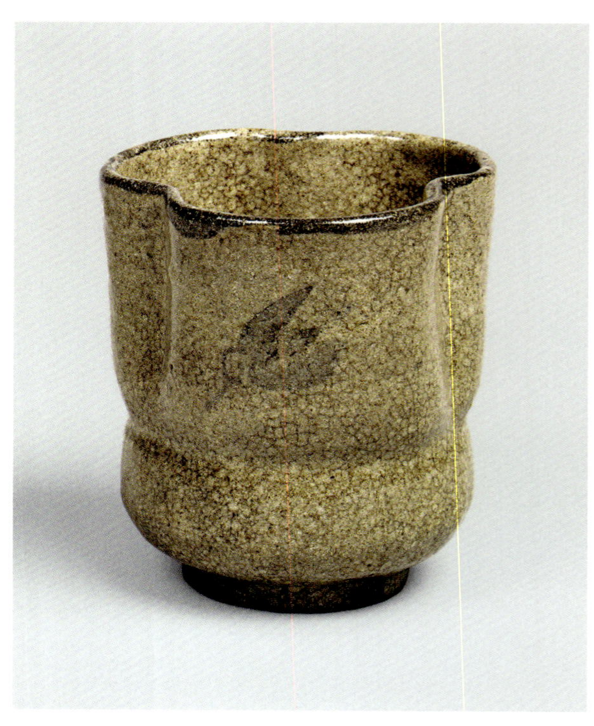

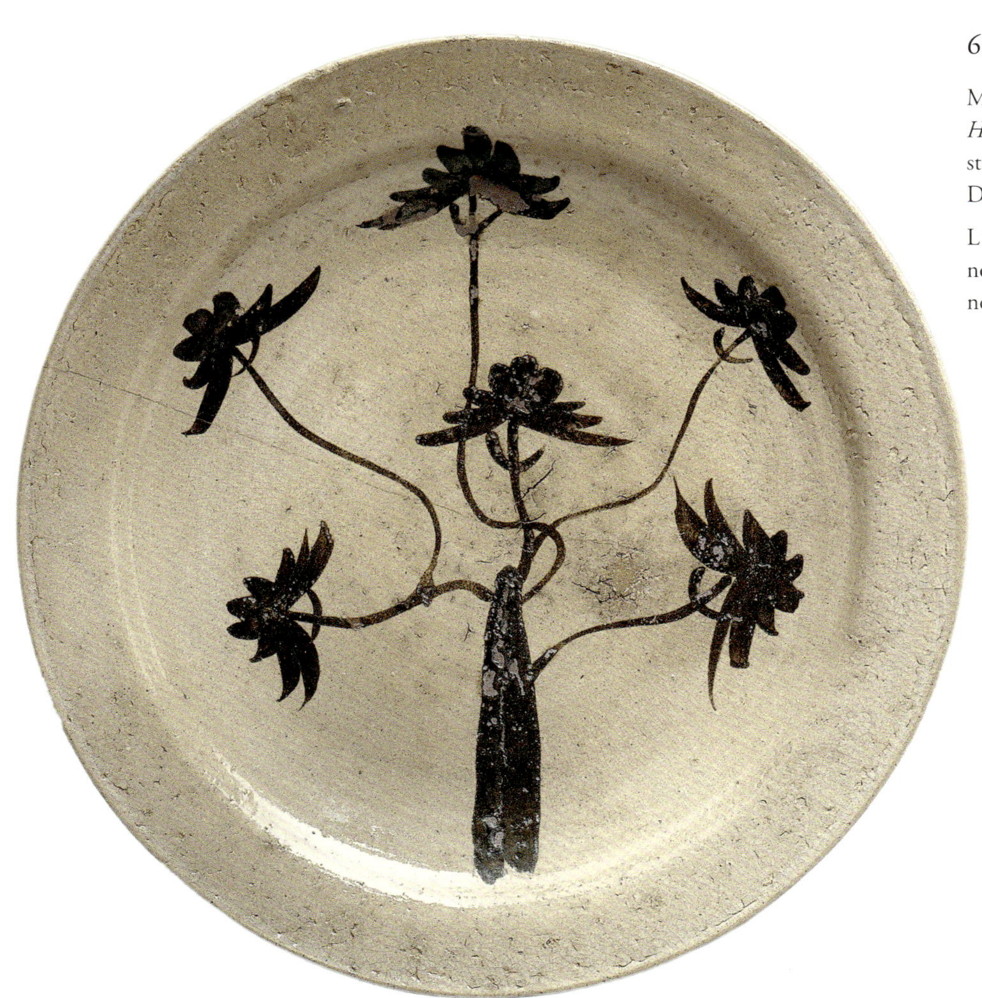

603. Platter with pine tree

Momoyama period, early 17th century
Hizen (肥前) ware, *Karatsu* (唐津) type;
stoneware with underglaze iron oxide
Diam. 32 cm (12 5/8 in.)

LITERATURE: Tokyo National Museum 1985a, no. 101; Avitabile 1990, no. 142; Murase 2000, no. 105.

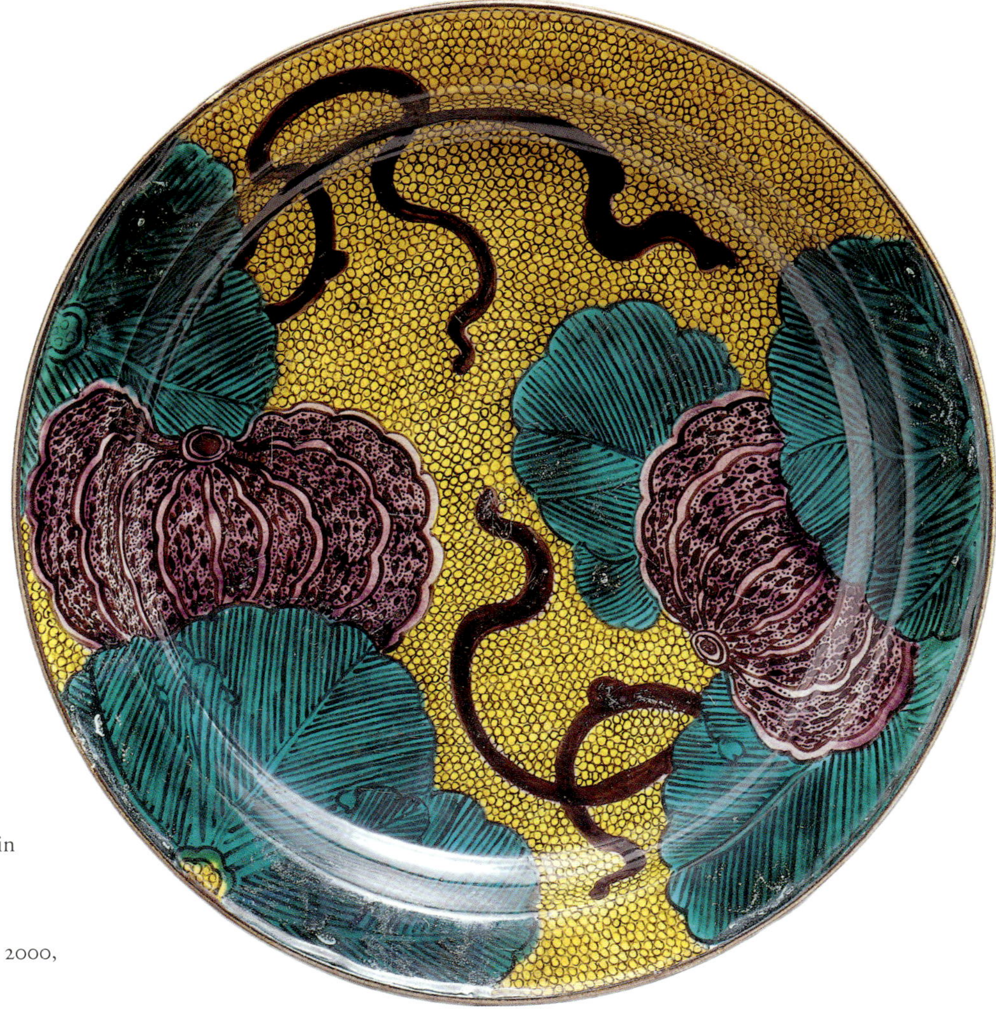

604. Plate with pumpkins

Edo period, ca. 1660s
Hizen (肥前) ware, *Kutani* (九谷) type,
Aode Kokutani (青手古九谷) style; porcelain
with overglaze enamels
Diam. 37.8 cm (14 7/8 in.)

LITERATURE: Murase 1993, no. 59; Murase 2000, no. 128; Tsuji Nobuo et al. 2005, no. 57.

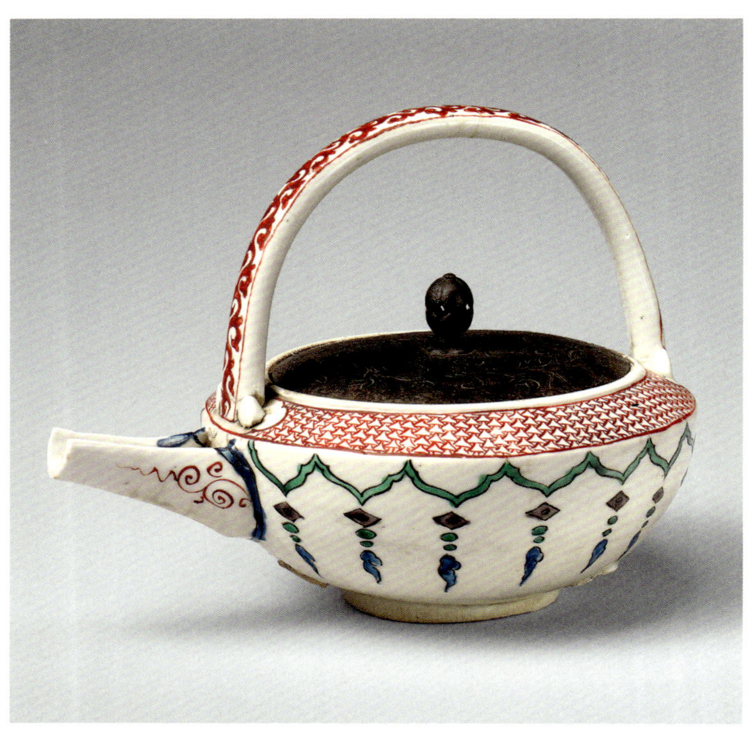

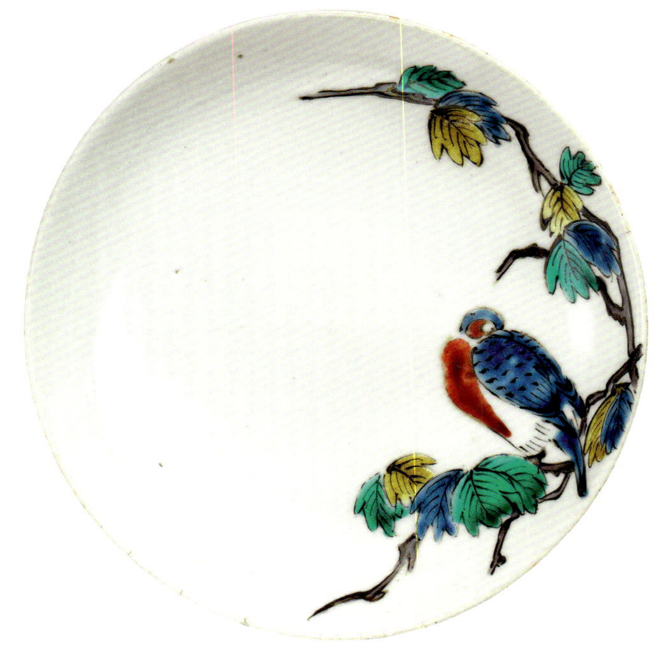

605. Sake ewer with abstract design

Edo period, 18th century
Hizen (肥前) ware, *Kutani* (九谷) type, *Ko Kutani* (古九谷) style; porcelain with overglaze enamels; metal (lid)
H. 14.8 cm (5 7/8 in.)

Literature: Murase 1980b, no. 51.

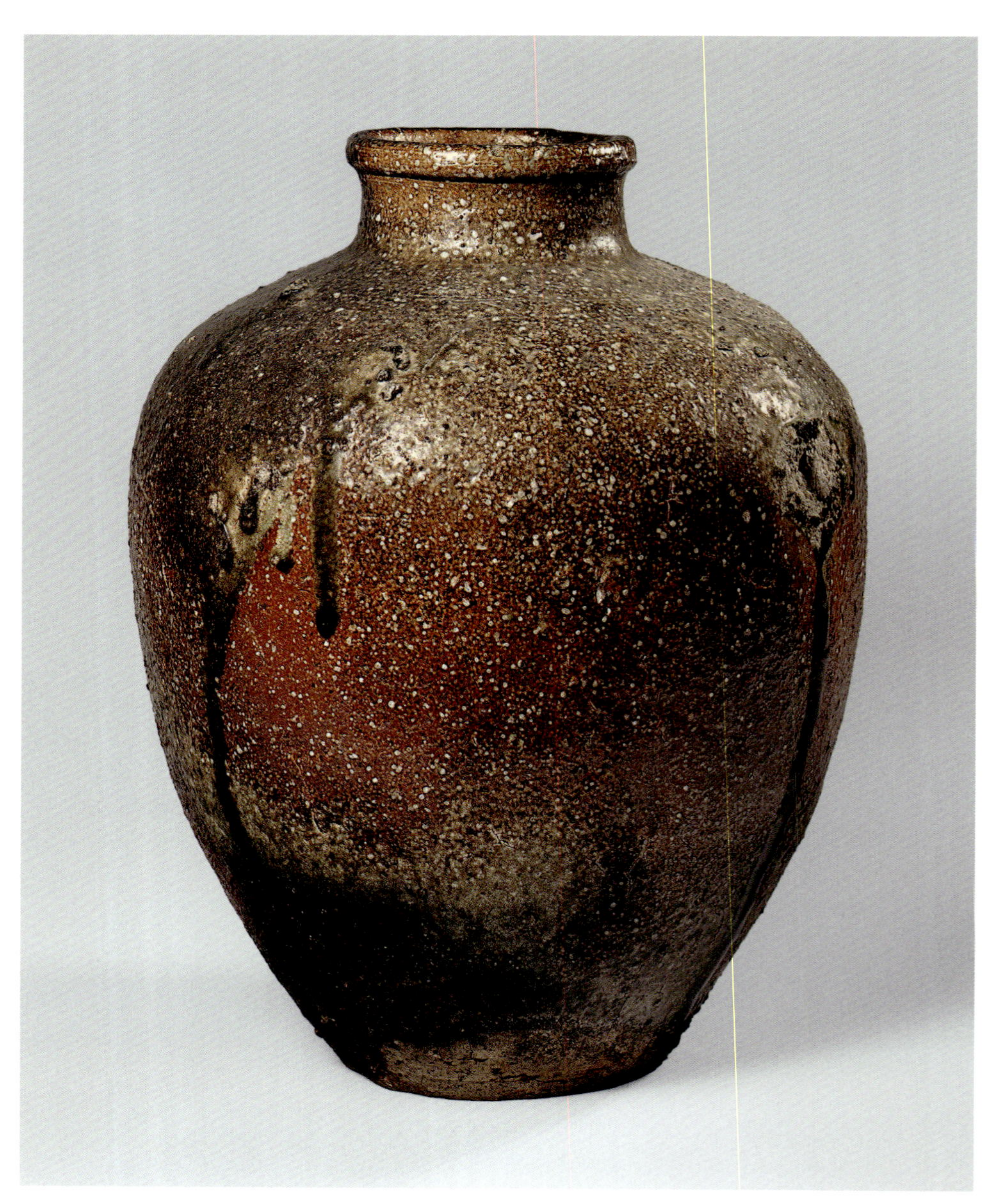

606. Plate with bird on branch

Edo period, 17th century
Hizen (肥前) ware, *Kutani* (九谷) type, *Ko Kutani* (古九谷) style; porcelain with overglaze enamels
Diam. 14.6 cm (5 3/4 in.)

607. Storage jar

Momoyama period, 16th–17th century
Iga (伊賀) ware; stoneware with natural ash glaze
H. 37.5 cm (14 3/4 in.), diam. 29.2 cm (11 1/2 in.)

Literature: Pekarik 1978, no. 18.

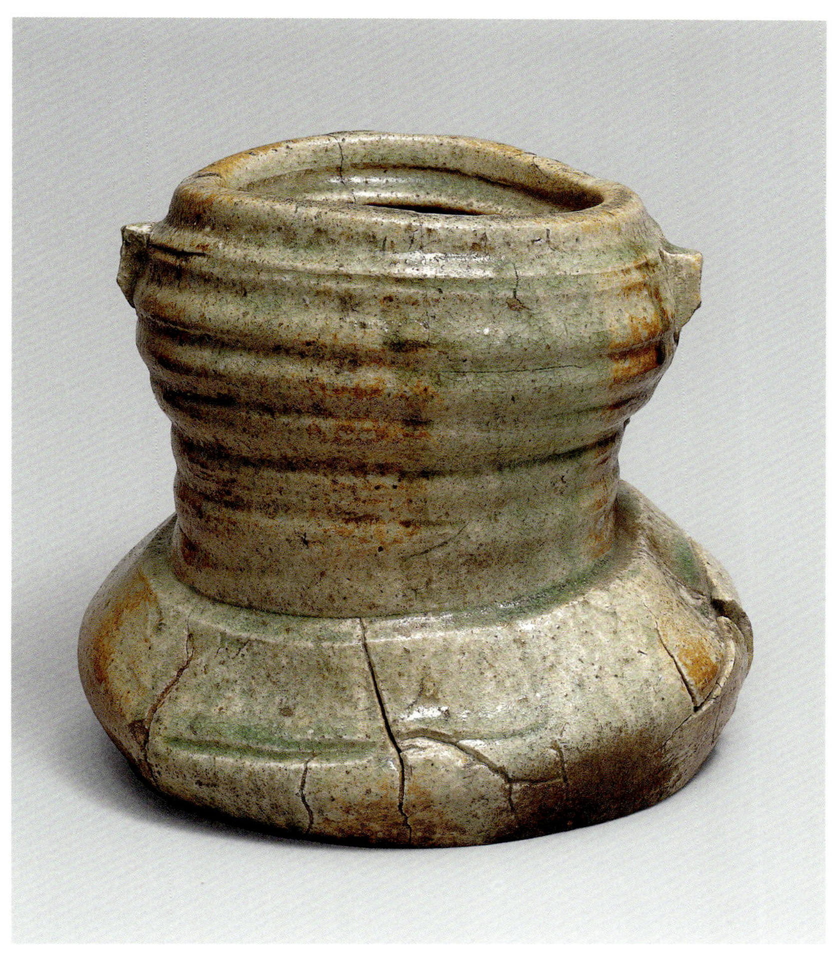

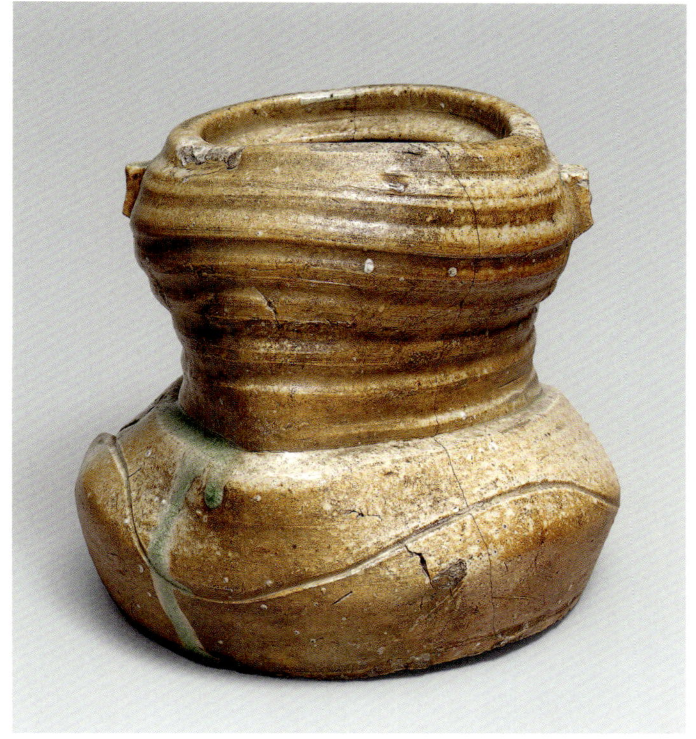

608, reverse

608. "Burst Bag" freshwater jar (*mizusashi*, 水指)

Momoyama period, 16th–17th century
Iga (伊賀) ware; stoneware with natural ash glaze
H. 20.6 cm (8 1/8 in.)

Ex coll.: Count Matsu'ura

Literature: Rhodes 1970, fig. 10; Hayashiya Seizō 1972a, pp. 93–94; Hayashiya Seizō 1972b, pl. 352; Murase 1975, no. 97; Pekarik 1978, no. 25; Hayashiya Seizō 1981, no. 15; Tokyo National Museum 1985a, no. 94; Avitabile 1990, no. 136; Murase 2000, no. 97; Murase 2003, no. 10; Tsuji Nobuo et al. 2005, no. 49.

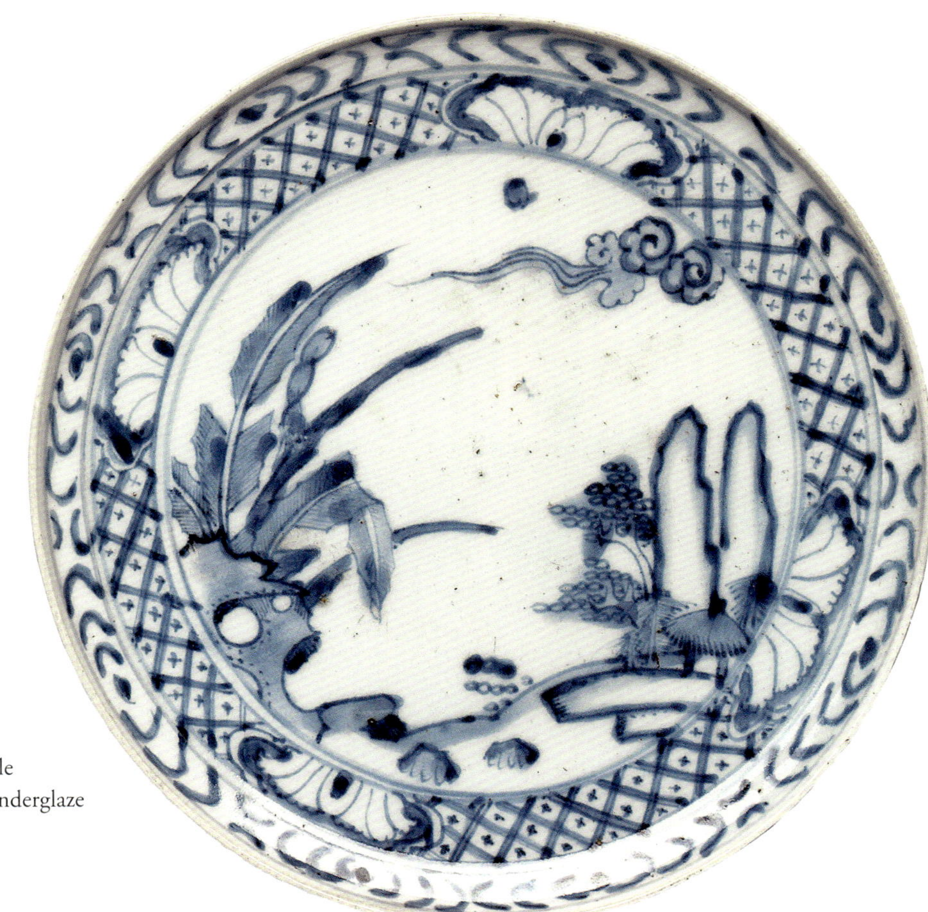

609. Dish with landscape

Edo period, early 17th century
Imari (伊万里) ware; *Shoki Imari* style (初期伊万里); porcelain with pale underglaze cobalt blue
Diam. 19 cm (7 1/2 in.)
Text

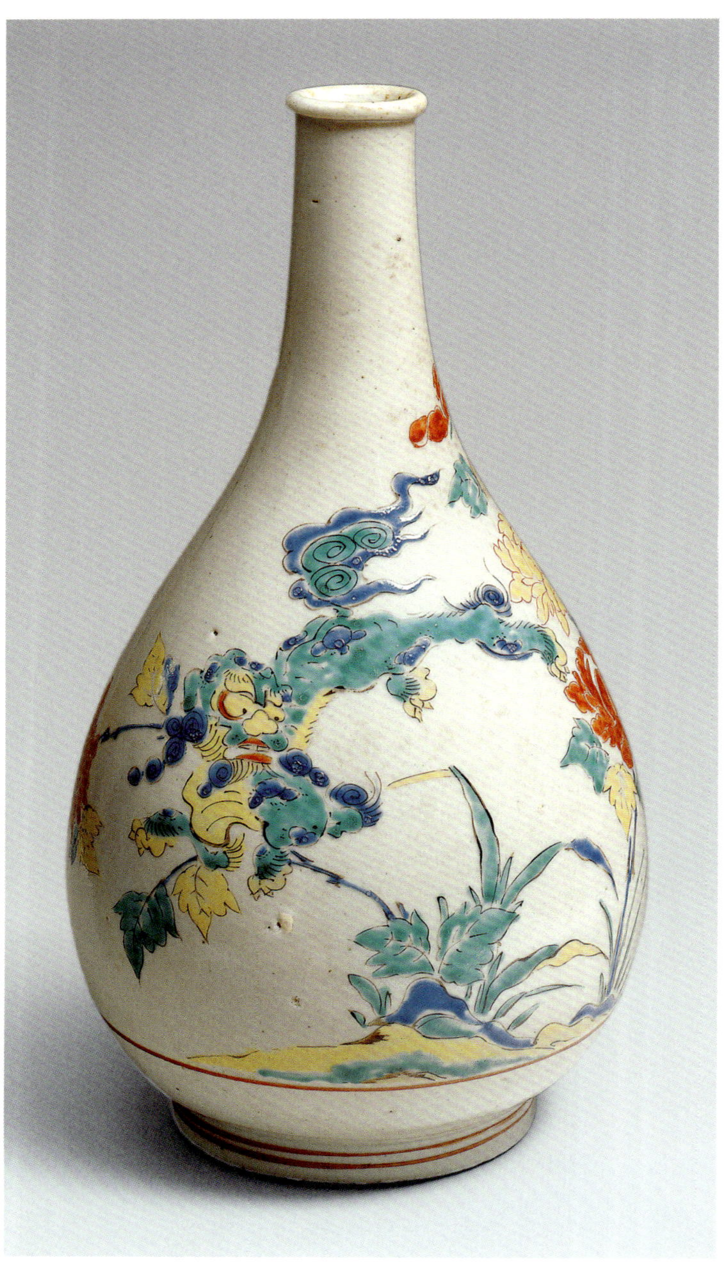

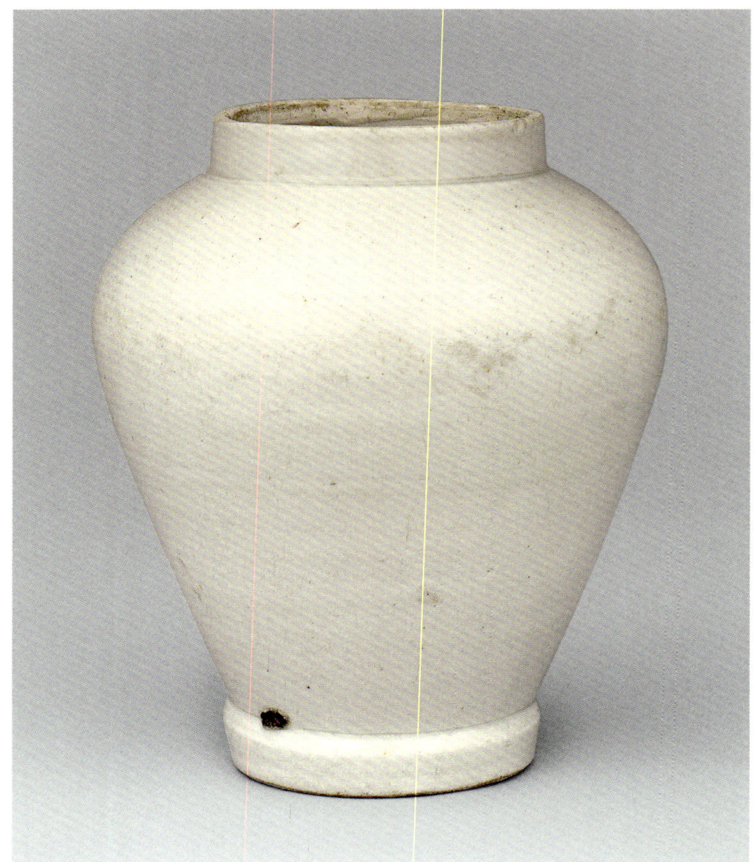

611

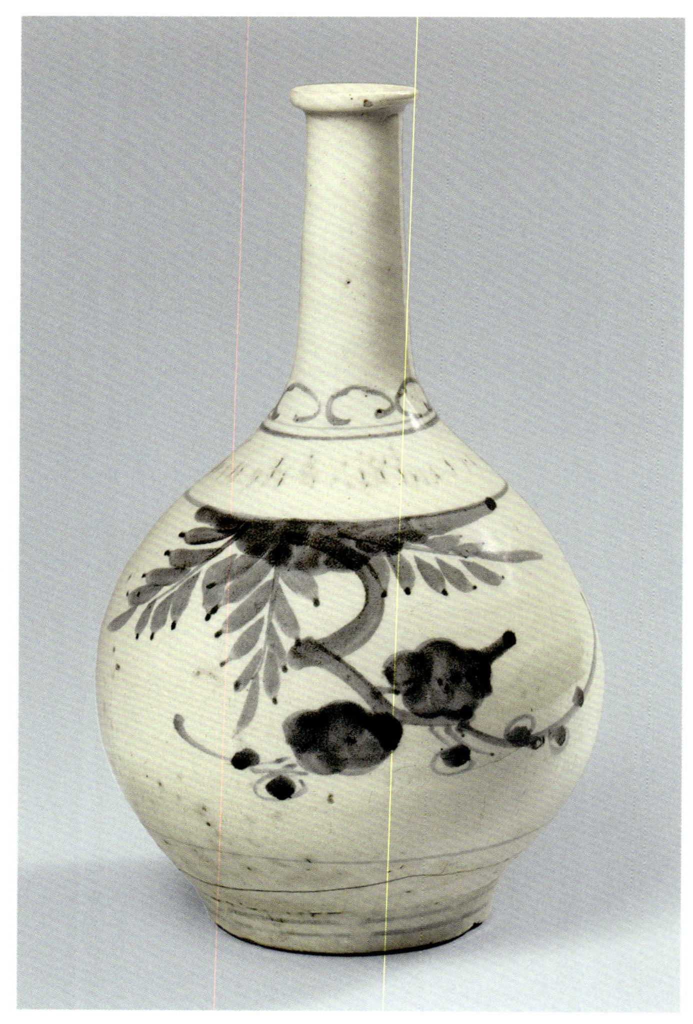

610. Bottle with peonies and Chinese lion

Edo period, ca. 1660s
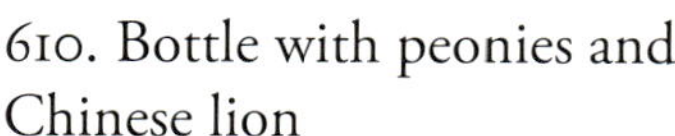
Imari (伊万里) ware, *Ko Imari* (古伊万里) style; porcelain with overglaze enamels
H. 28.3 cm (11⅛ in.)

Literature: Murase 1993, no. 60; Murase 2000, no. 129.

611. Vase

Edo period, 17th century
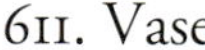
Imari (伊万里) ware; porcelain with light-green glaze
H. 16.5 cm (6½ in.)

612. Sake bottle with tree branches

Edo period, 17th century
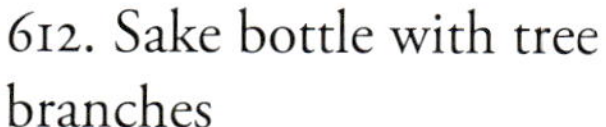
Imari (伊万里) ware; porcelain with underglaze cobalt blue
H. 26.7 cm (10½ in.)

613. Dish with flowers

Edo period, 17th century
Imari (伊万里) ware; porcelain with overglaze enamels
Diam. 17.2 cm (6 3/4 in.)

Gift from The Crane Gallery, Inc., 1989

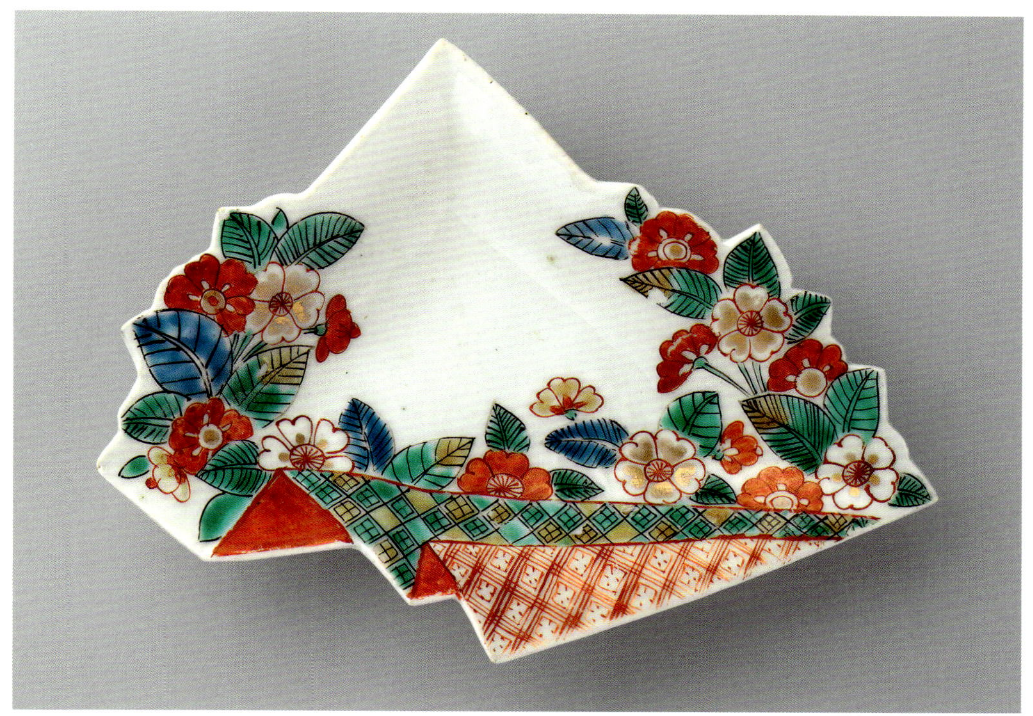

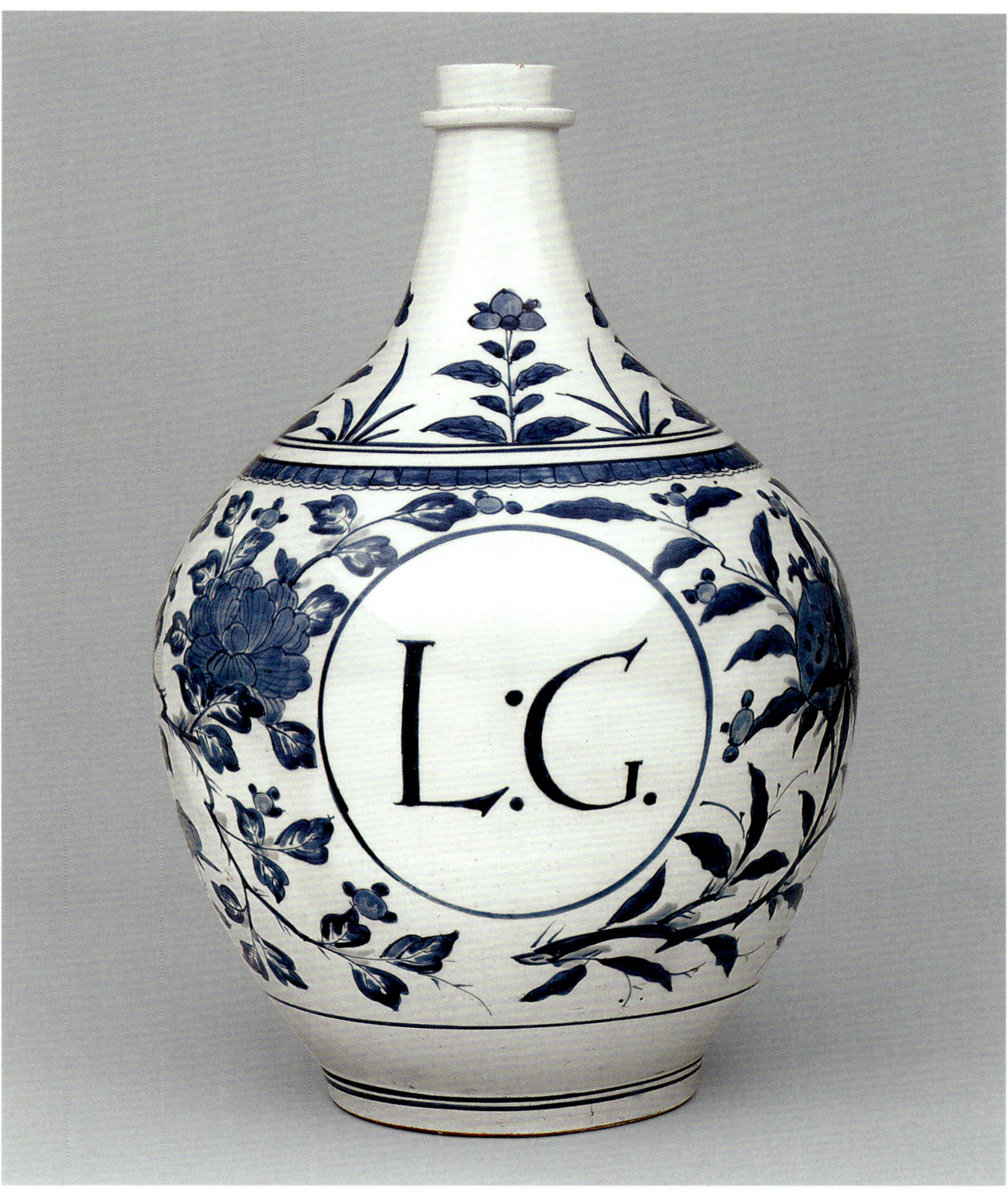

614. Bottle with the initials L.G.

Edo period, 1660–80
Imari (伊万里) ware; porcelain with underglaze cobalt blue; missing original lid
H. 49 cm (19 1/4 in.)

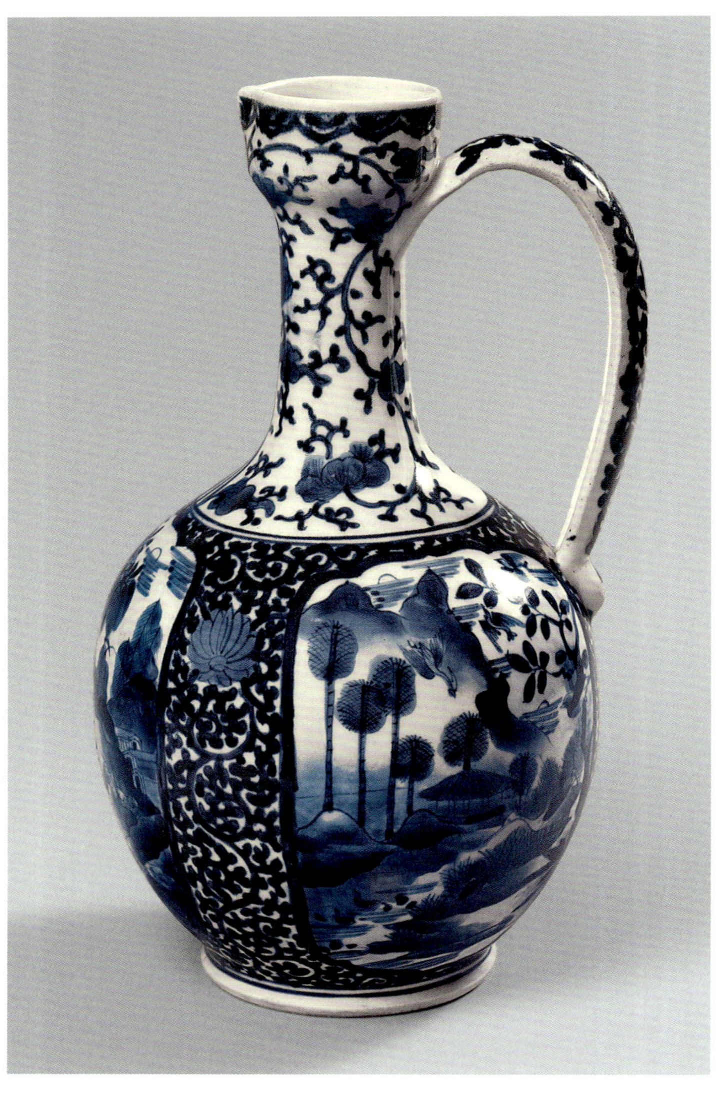

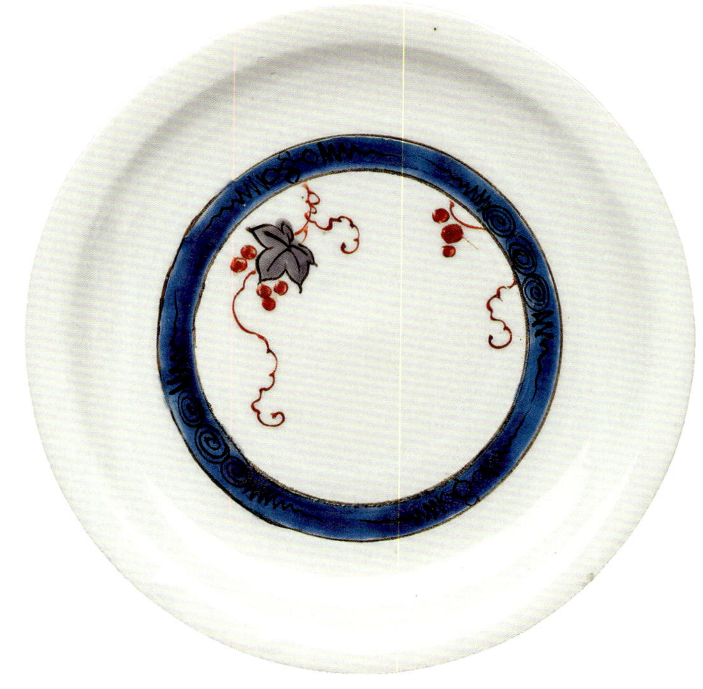

616. Plate with grapevine

Edo period, 17th century
Imari (伊万里) ware; porcelain with underglaze cobalt blue
Diam. 14.6 cm (5 3/4 in.)

615. Ewer with landscapes and flowers

Edo period, 1660–80
Imari (伊万里) ware; porcelain with underglaze cobalt blue
H. 28.2 cm (11 1/8 in.), diam. 16.6 cm (6 1/2 in.)

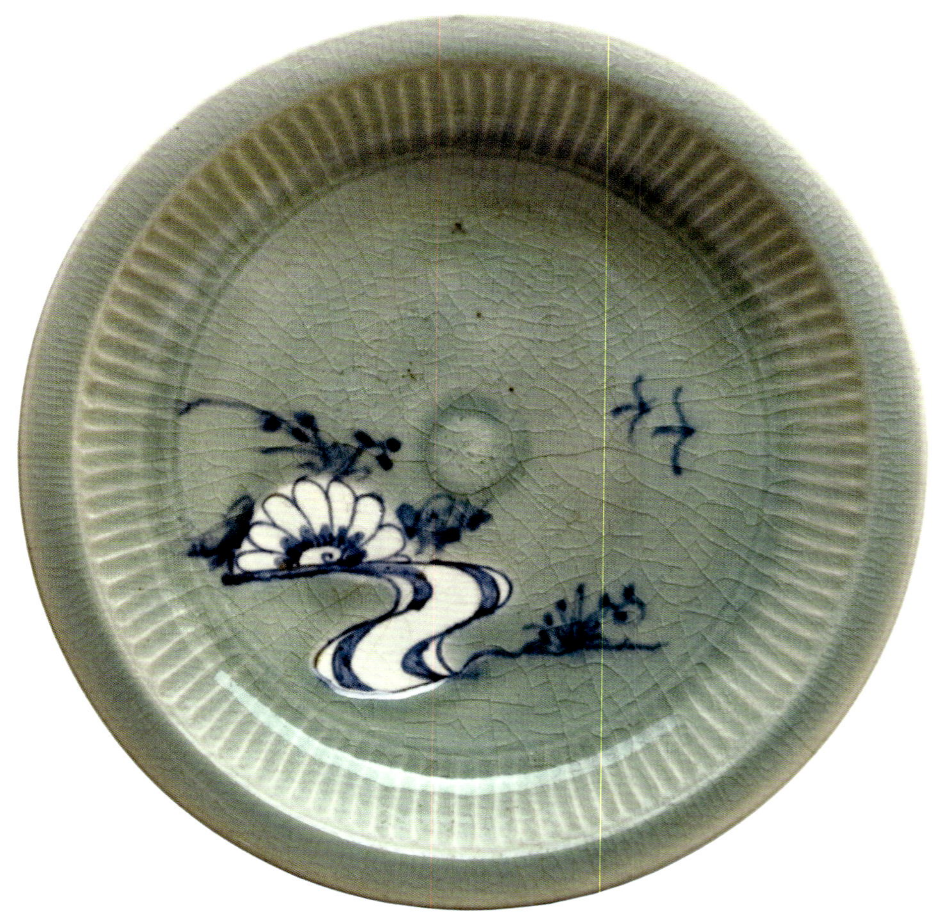

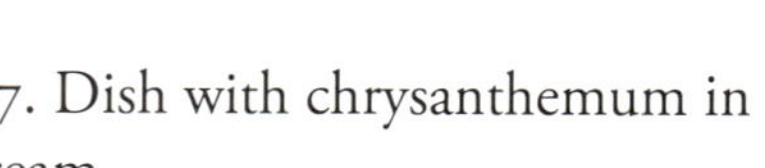

617. Dish with chrysanthemum in stream

Edo period, second half of 17th century
Imari (伊万里) ware; porcelain with celadon glaze and underglaze cobalt blue
Diam. 30.4 cm (12 in.)

Literature: Murase 1993, no. 61.

618. Apothecary bottle with mynah birds and peonies

Edo period, 1660–80
Imari (伊万里) ware; porcelain with underglaze cobalt blue
H. 51 cm (20$^{1}/_{8}$ in.)

LITERATURE: Murase 1993, no. 62.

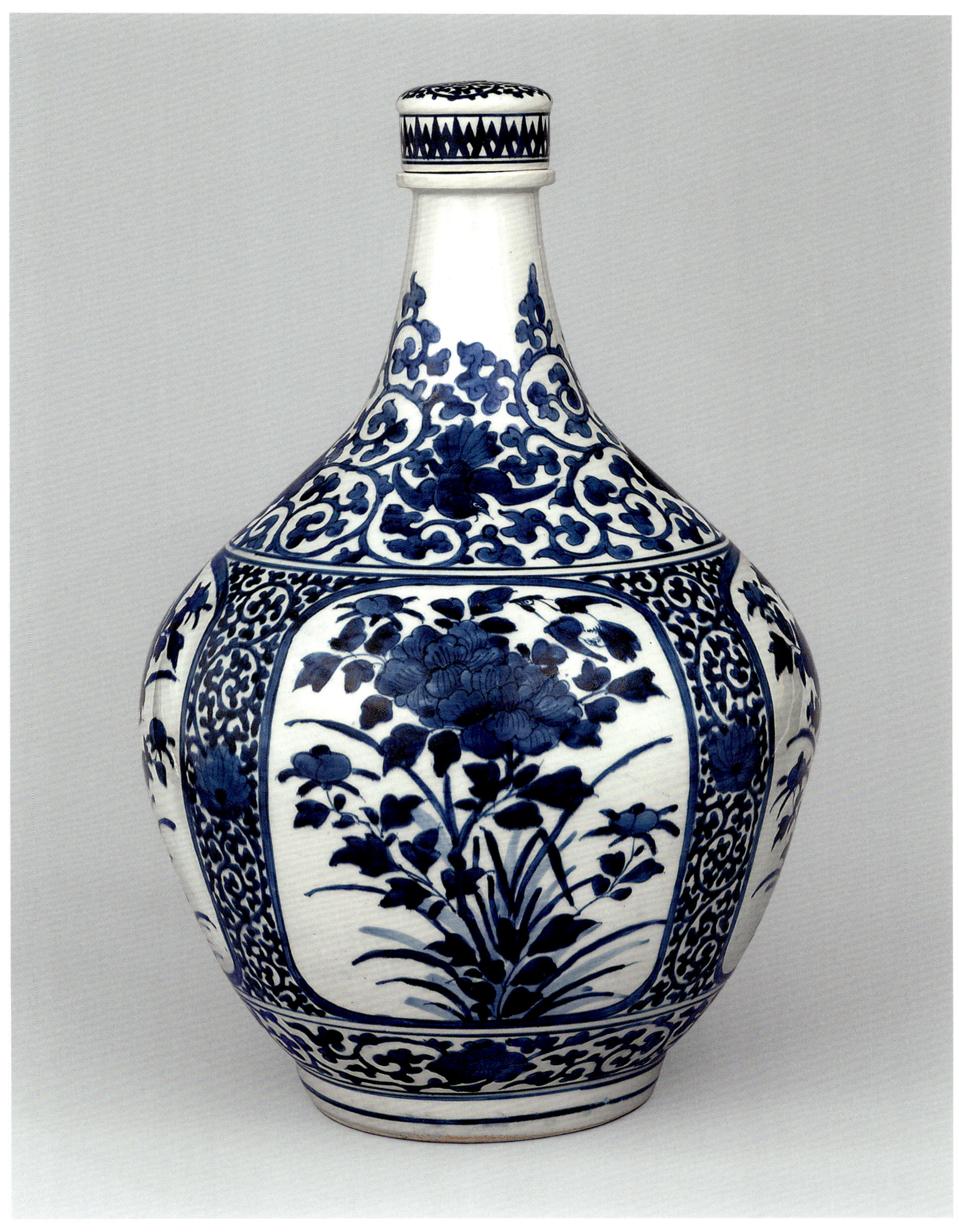

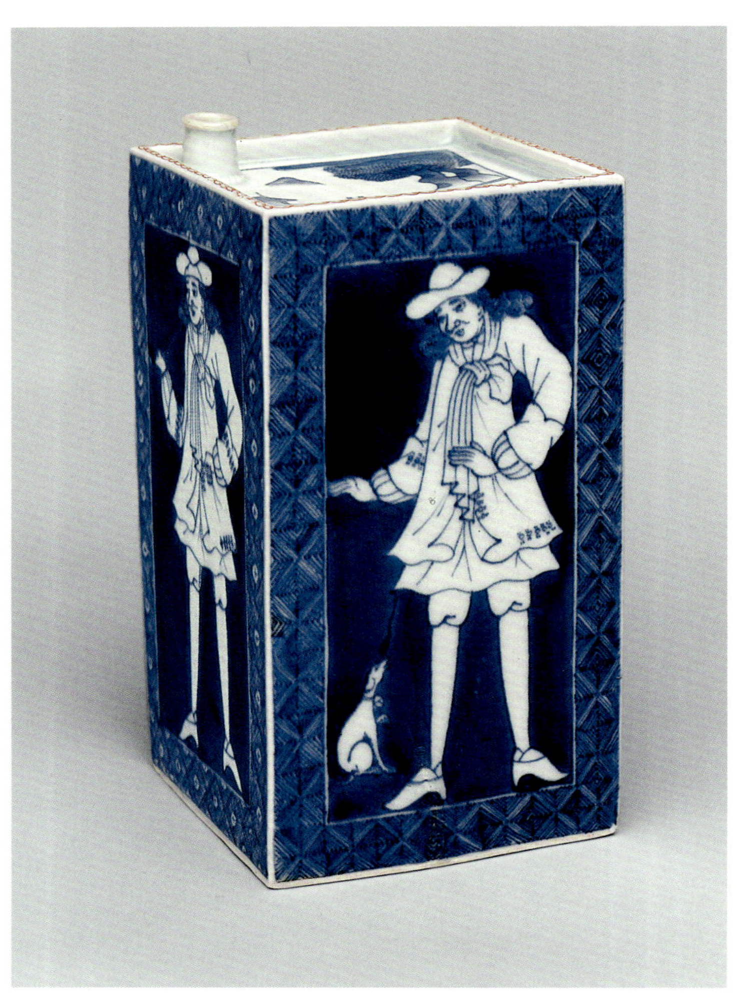

619. Sake bottle with Dutchmen

Edo period, 18th century
Imari (伊万里) ware; porcelain with underglaze cobalt blue
H. 20.7 cm (8 1/8 in.), diam. 11.2 cm (4 3/8 in.)

Literature: Burke 1993, no. 42.

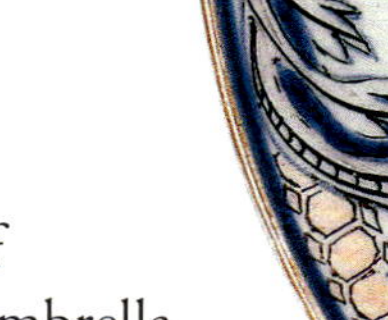

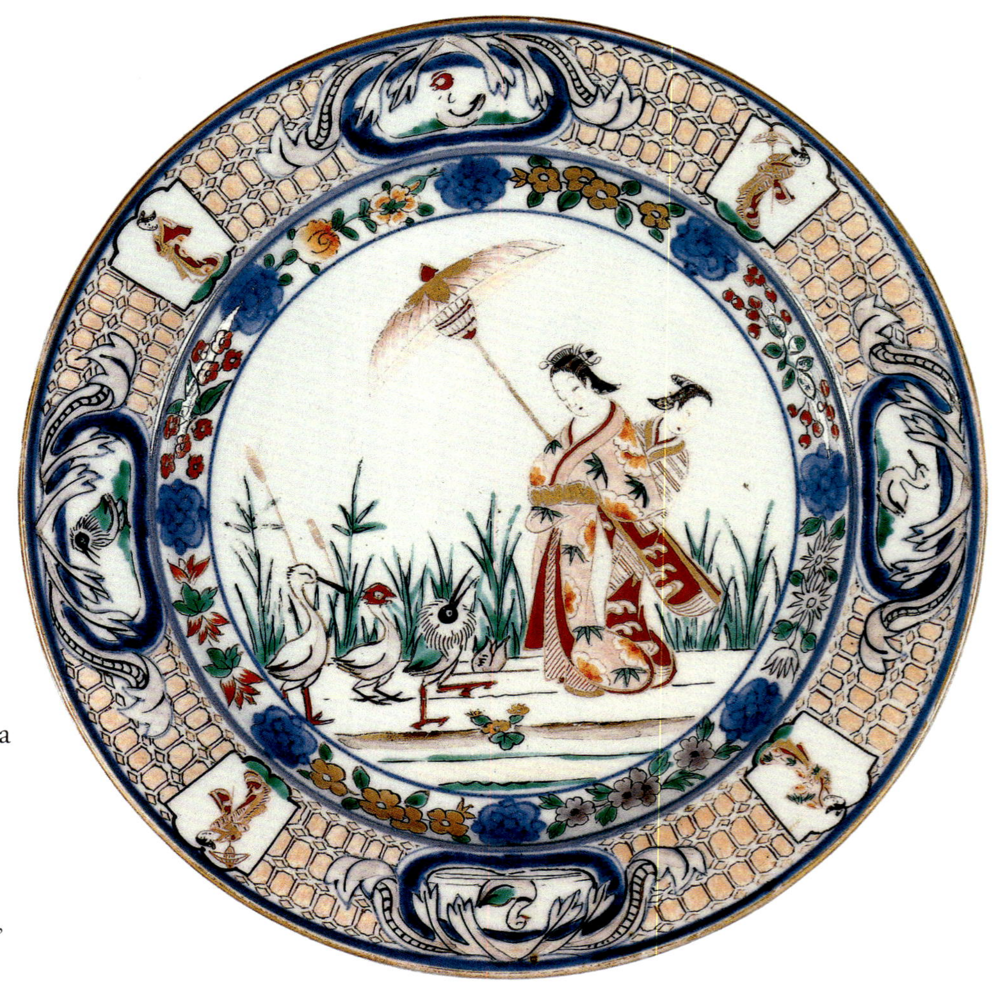

620. Plate with Pronk design of courtesan and attendant with umbrella

Edo period, 18th century
Imari (伊万里) ware; porcelain with underglaze cobalt blue, overglaze enamels, and gold
Diam. 23.5 cm (9 1/4 in.)

Literature: Meech 1993, no. 123; Murase 1993, no. 63.

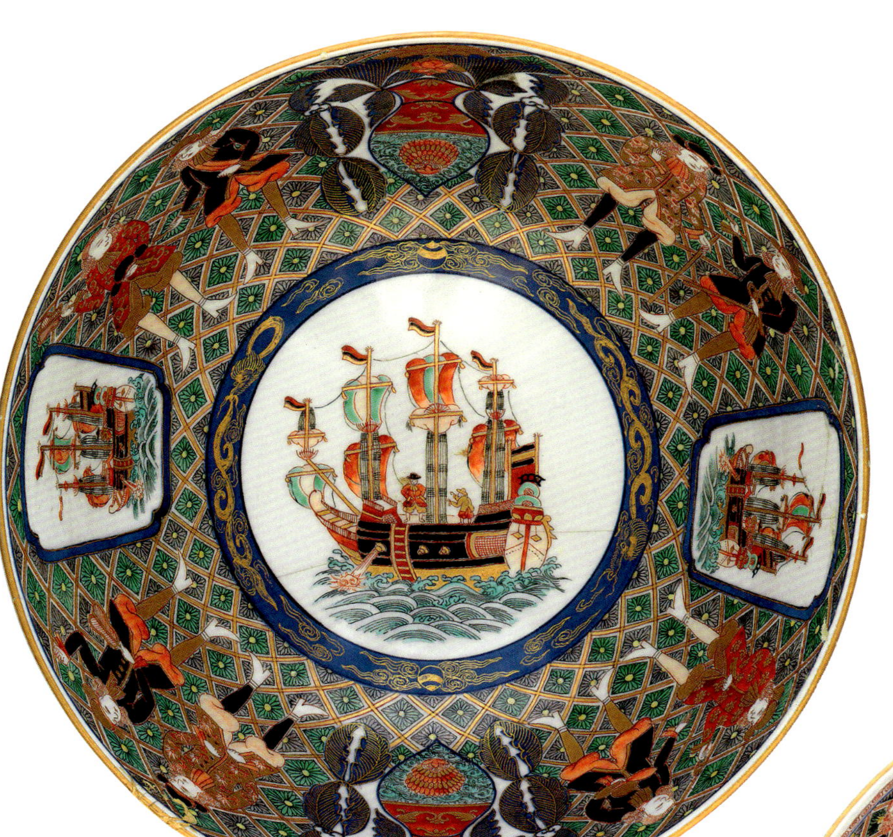

621. Bowl with Europeans and ships

Edo period, 18th century
Imari (伊万里) ware; porcelain with underglaze cobalt blue, overglaze enamels, and gold
H. 15.8 cm ($6\frac{1}{4}$ in.), diam. 33.5 cm ($13\frac{1}{4}$ in.)
Text

622. Bowl with Europeans and ships

Edo period, 18th century
Imari (伊万里) ware; porcelain with underglaze cobalt blue, overglaze enamels, and gold
H. 14.2 cm ($5\frac{5}{8}$ in.), diam. 30 cm ($11\frac{3}{4}$ in.)
Text

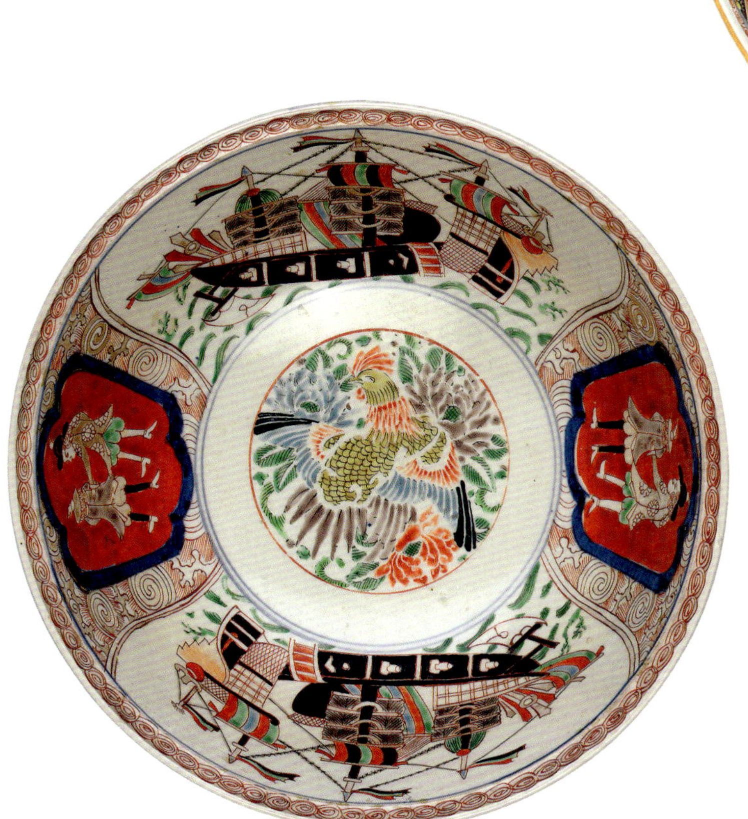

623. Bowl with Europeans and ships

Edo period, 18th century
Imari (伊万里) ware; porcelain with underglaze cobalt blue, overglaze enamels, and gold
H. 8.8 cm ($3\frac{1}{2}$ in.), diam. 25.1 cm ($9\frac{7}{8}$ in.)
Mark

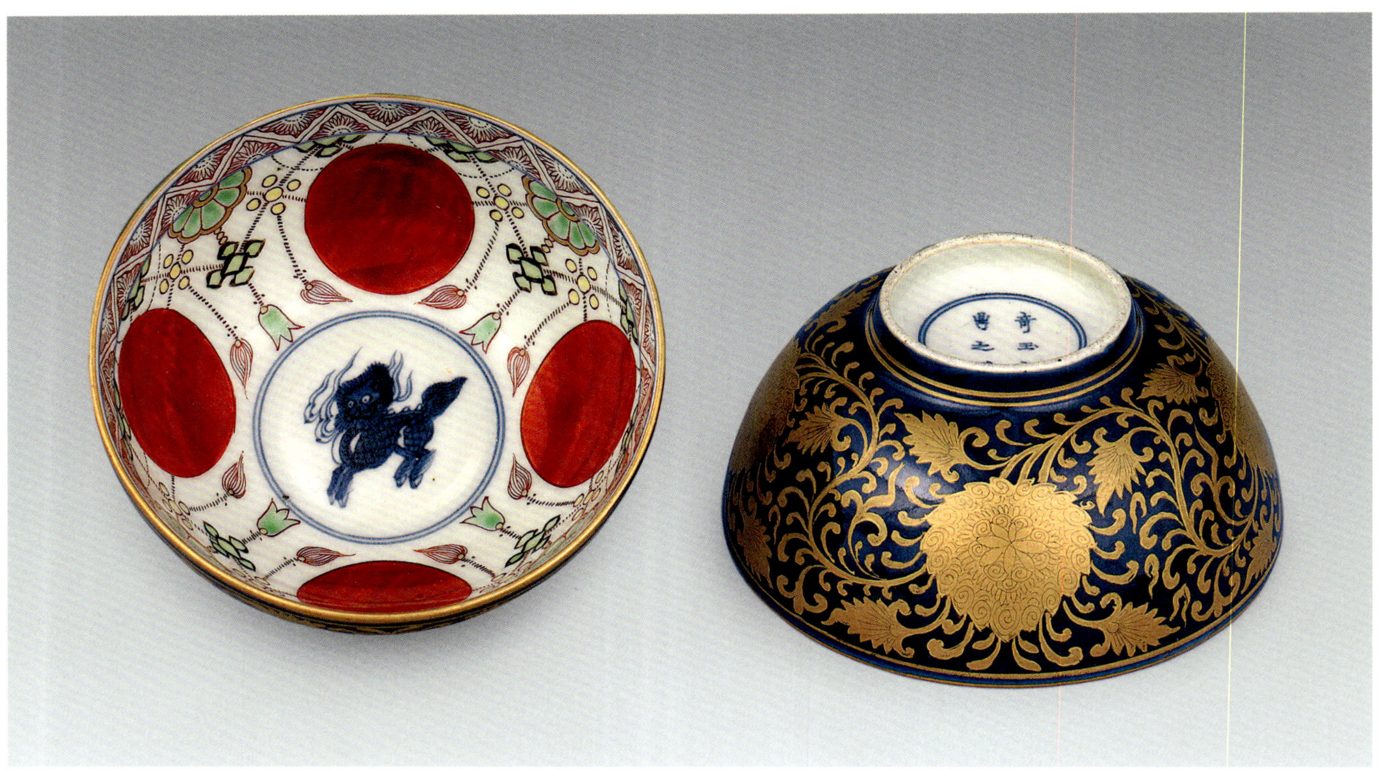

624. Pair of bowls

Edo period, 18th century
Imari (伊万里) ware; porcelain with underglaze cobalt blue, overglaze enamels, and gold
Diam. of each 13 cm (5$^{1}/_{8}$ in.)
Text

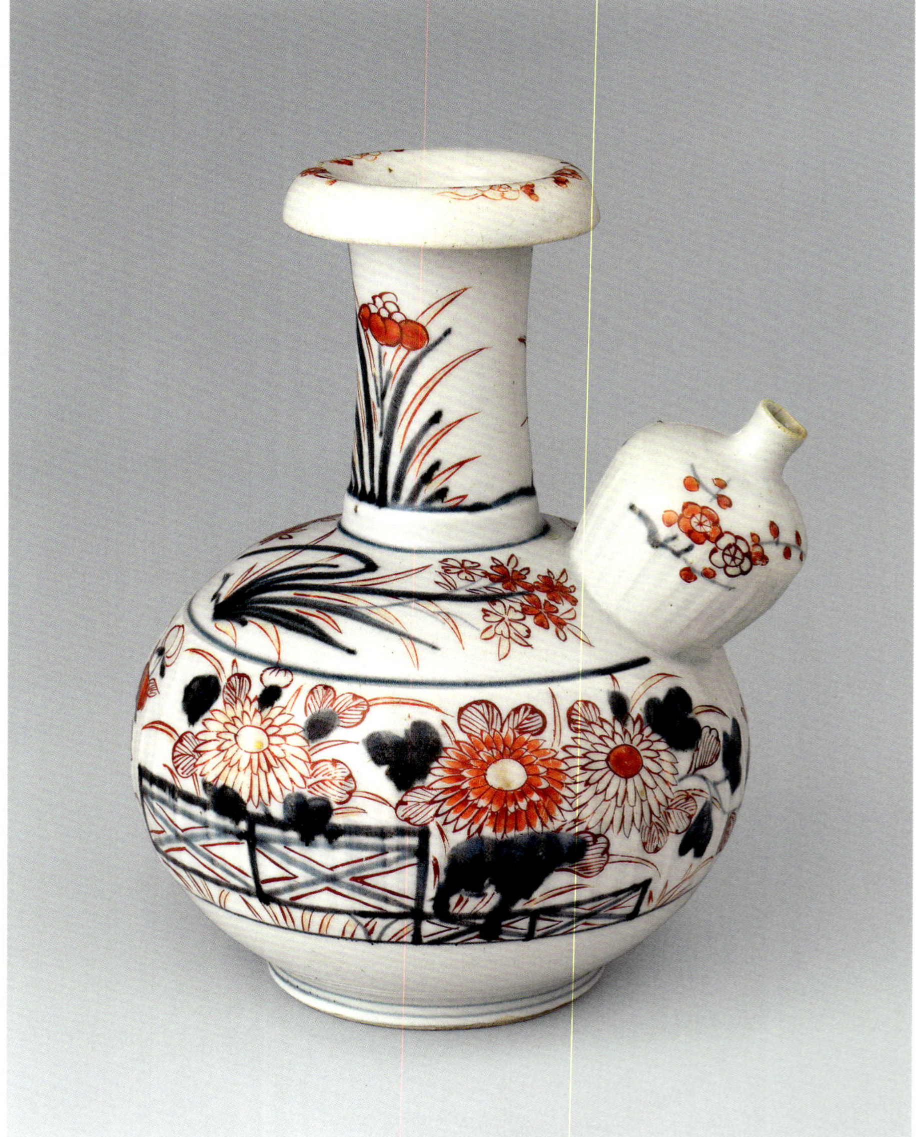

625. Wine pitcher with peonies, chrysanthemums, and other floral motifs

Edo period, 18th–19th century
Imari (伊万里) ware; porcelain with underglaze cobalt blue, overglaze enamels, and traces of gold
H. 20.3 cm (8 in.)

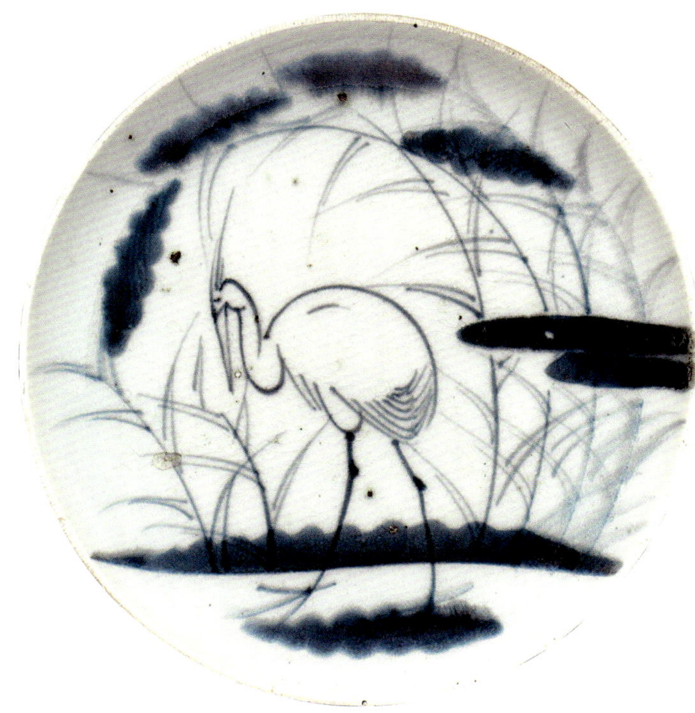

626. Plate with heron and grasses

Edo period, 18th century
Imari (伊万里) ware; porcelain with underglaze cobalt blue
Diam. 20.1 cm (7⅞ in.)

Gift from Matsuo Sumio, 1977

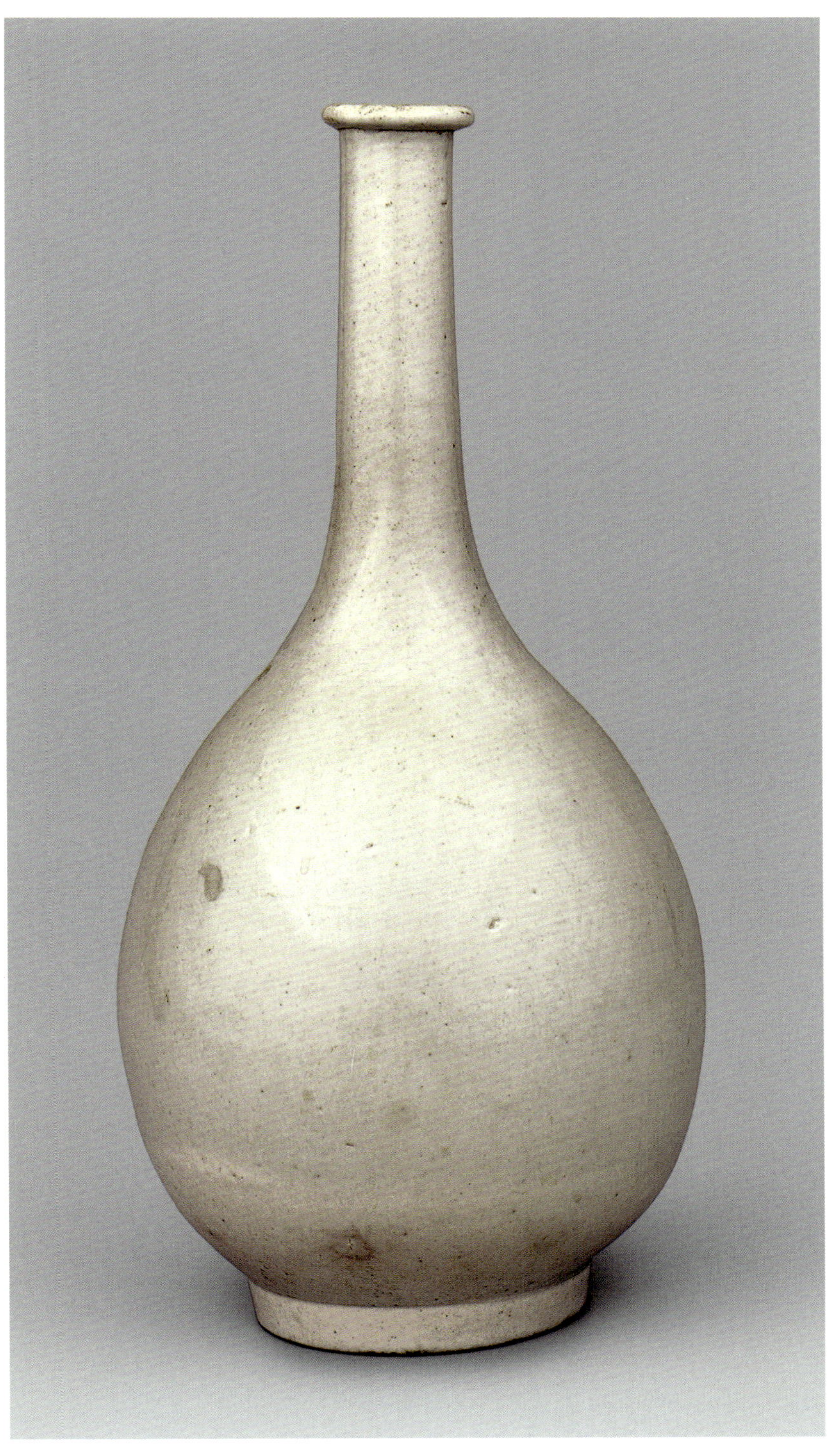

627. Bottle

Edo period, 18th century
Imari (伊万里) ware; porcelaneous stoneware with glaze
H. 40.6 cm (16 in.)

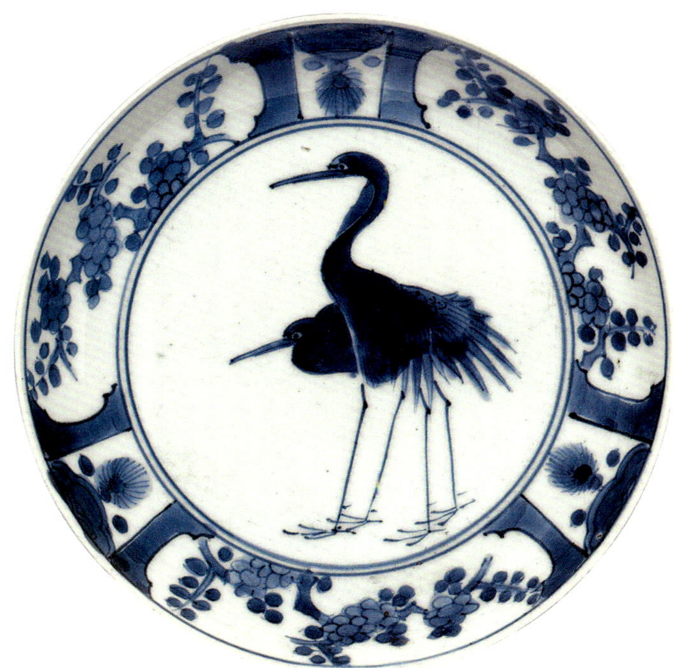

628. Plate with cranes

Edo period, 18th–19th century
Imari (伊万里) ware; porcelain with underglaze cobalt blue

Diam. 18.2 cm (7 1/8 in.)

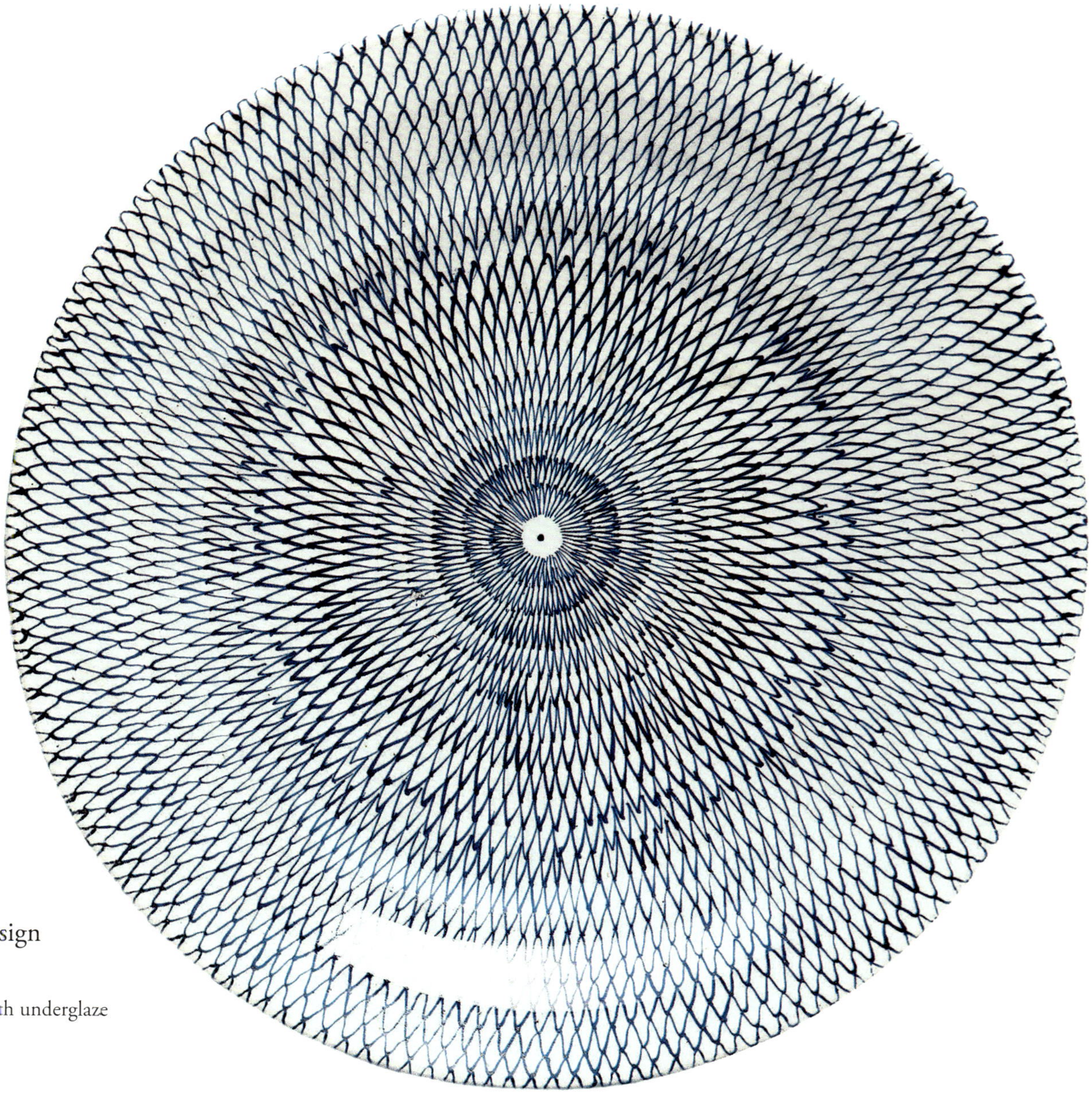

629. Platter with fishnet design

Edo period, 18th–19th century
Imari (伊万里) ware; porcelain with underglaze cobalt blue
Diam. 46.5 cm (18 1/4 in.)

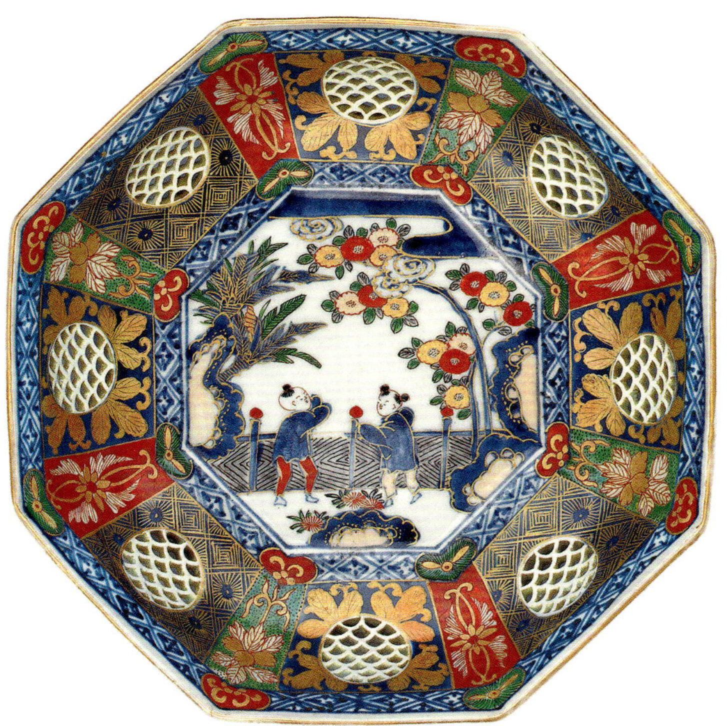

630. Dish with two Chinese boys in a garden

Edo period, 19th century
Imari (伊万里) ware; porcelain with underglaze cobalt blue, overglaze enamels, and gold
Diam. 24.2 cm (9½ in.)
Text

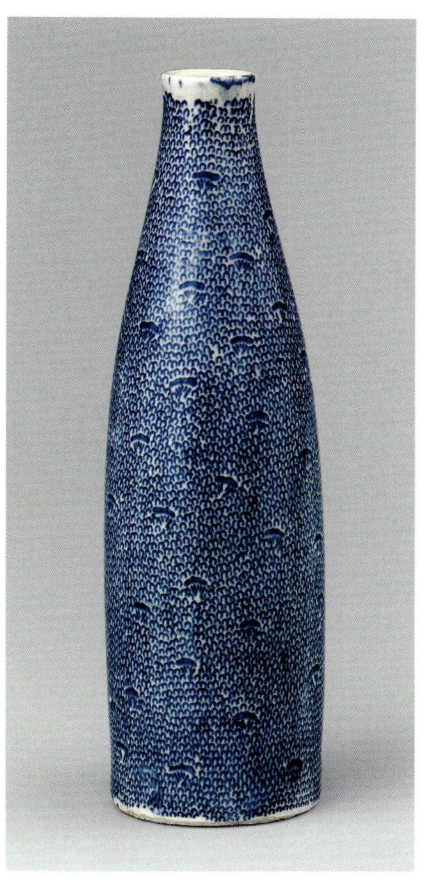

631. Sake bottle

Edo period, 19th century
Imari (伊万里) ware; porcelain with underglaze cobalt blue
H. 20.7 cm (8⅛ in.)

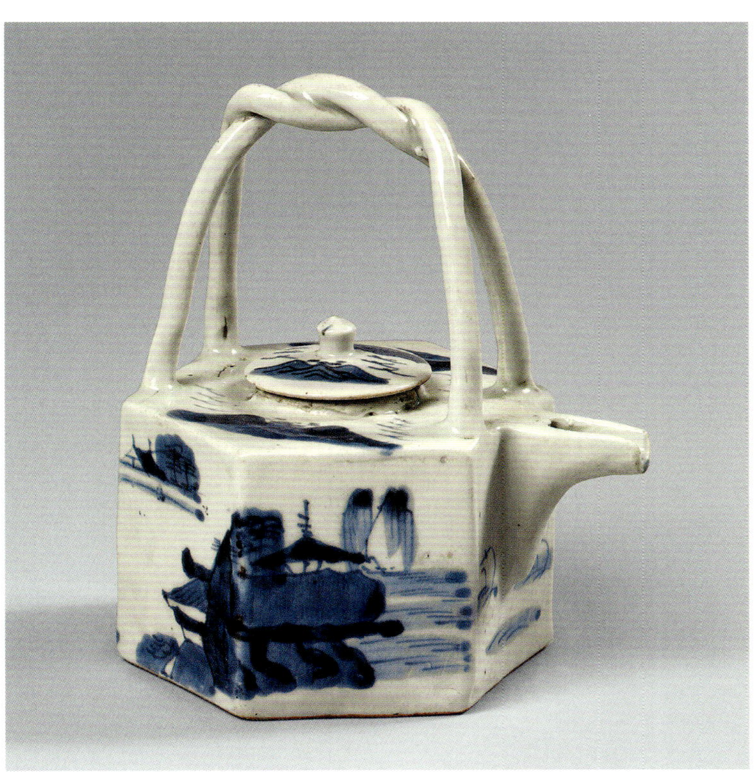

632. Ewer with landscape

Edo period, 19th century
Imari (伊万里) ware; porcelain with underglaze cobalt blue
H. 14.3 cm (5⅝ in.), diam. 10.2 cm (4 in.)

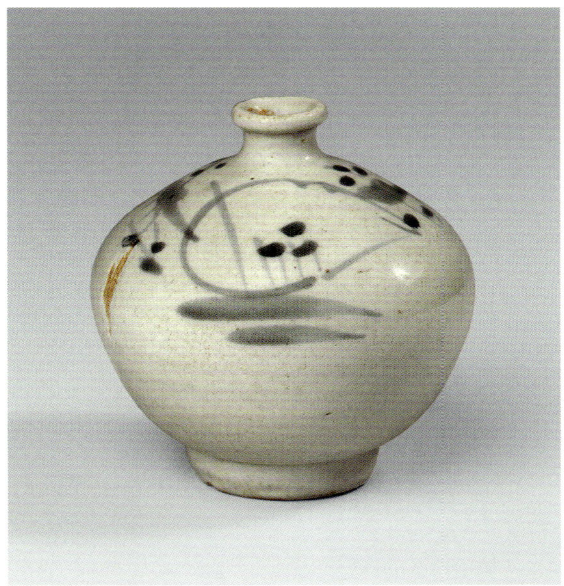

633. Bottle

Edo period, 19th century
Imari (伊万里) ware; porcelain with underglaze cobalt blue
H. 9.8 cm (3⅞ in.)

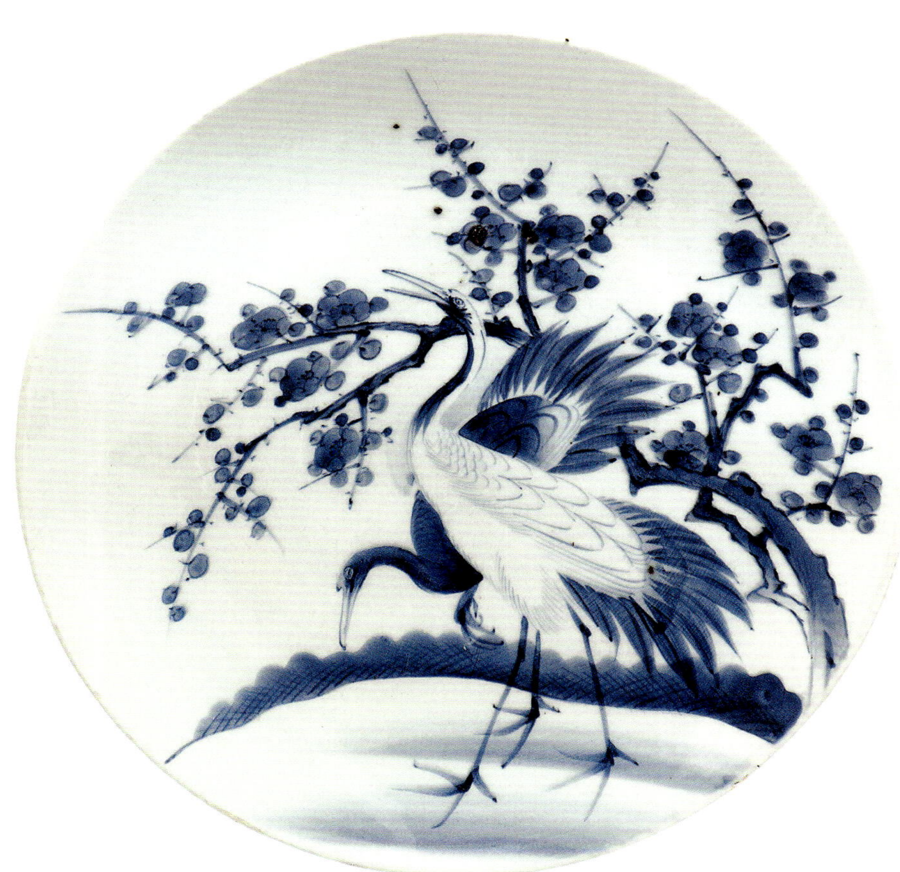

634. Platter with plum tree and cranes

Edo period, 19th century
Imari (伊万里) ware; porcelain with underglaze cobalt blue
Diam. 36.6 cm (14 3/8 in.)

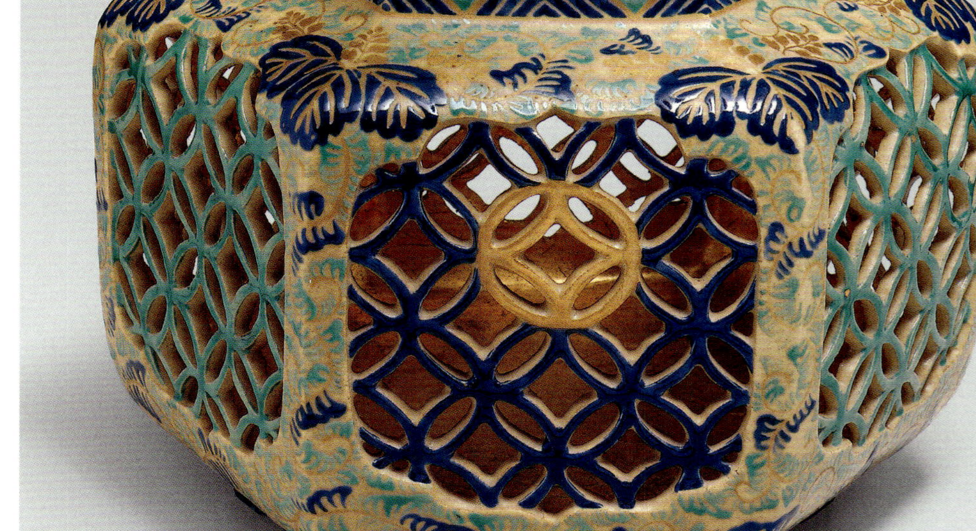

635. Lidded brazier with paulownia and geometric design

Edo period, late 17th century
Kyoto (*Kyōyaki* 京焼) ware, *Ko Kiyomizu* (古清水) type; stoneware with overglaze enamels and gold
H. including lid 21.1 cm (8 1/4 in.)

Literature: Hayashiya Seizō 1975, no. 49; Murase 2000, no. 130.

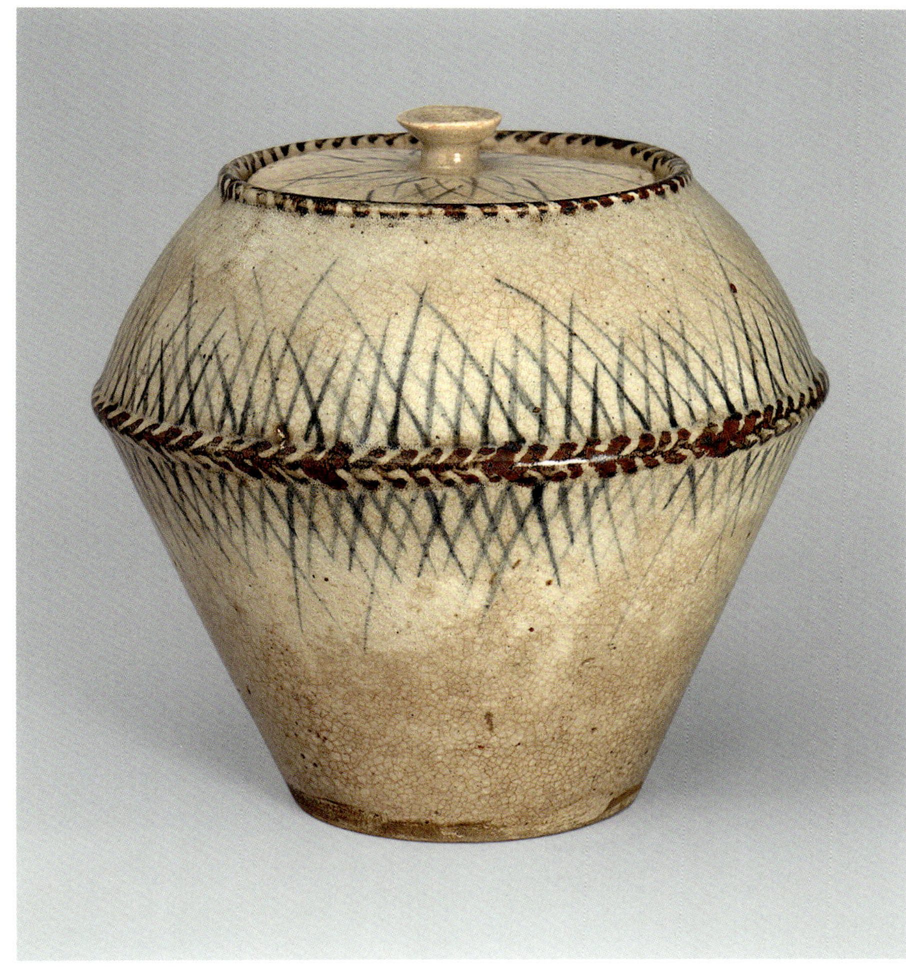

636

636. Freshwater jar (*mizusashi*, 水指)

Edo period, 17th–18th century
Kyoto (*Kyōyaki* 京焼) ware, *Ko Kiyomizu* (古清水) type; stoneware with iron oxide and underglaze cobalt blue
H. with lid 18.3 cm (7¼ in.), diam. 19.2 cm (7½ in.)

Ex coll.: Dr. Hiroshi Iwasaki

637. Sake bottle with paulownia

Edo period, 17th–18th century
Kyoto (*Kyōyaki* 京焼) ware; porcelain with underglaze iron oxide
H. 15.4 cm (6⅛ in.), diam. 12.8 cm (5 in.)

Nonomura Ninsei
(野々村仁清; fl. ca. 1646–ca. 1694)

638. Tea caddy (*chaire*, 茶入れ)

Edo period, after 1657
Kyoto (*Kyōyaki* 京焼) ware; glazed stoneware
H. including lid 11.5 cm (4½ in.)
Seal

Literature: Tokyo National Museum 1985a, no. 102; Avitabile 1990, no. 144; Murase 2000, no. 131.

637

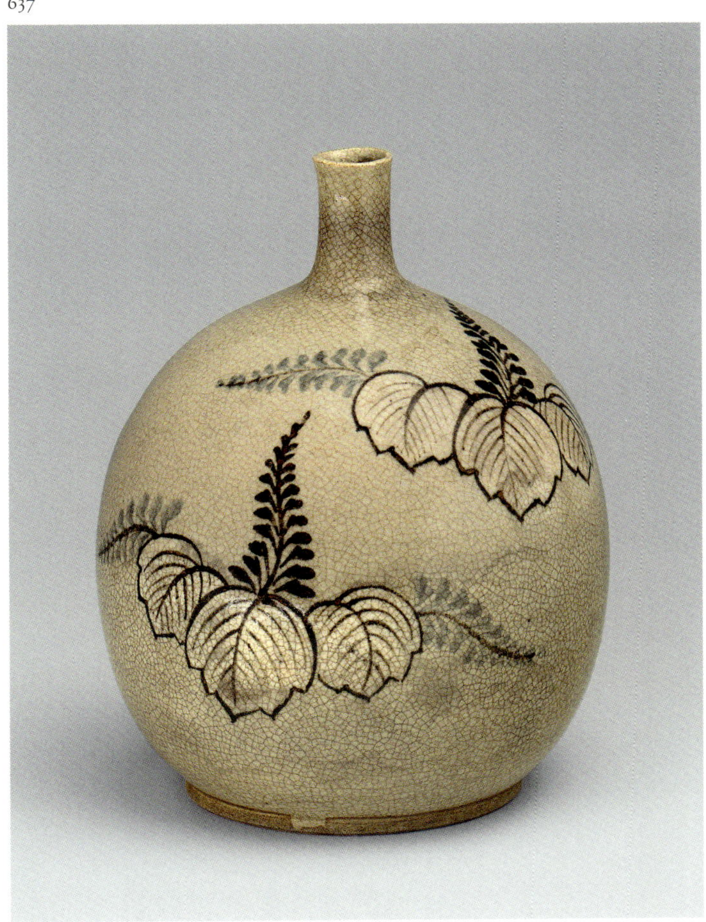

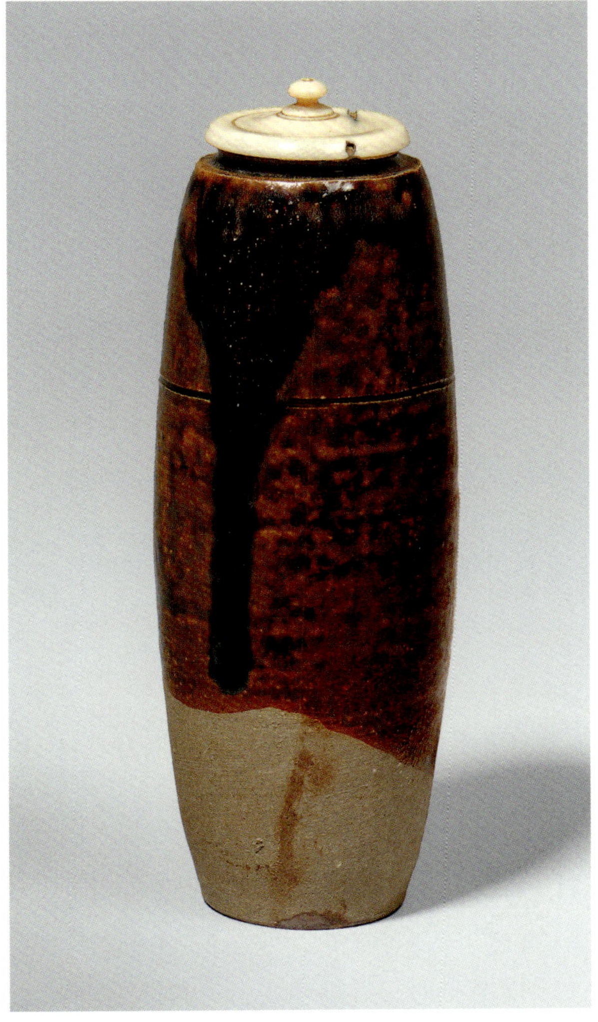

638

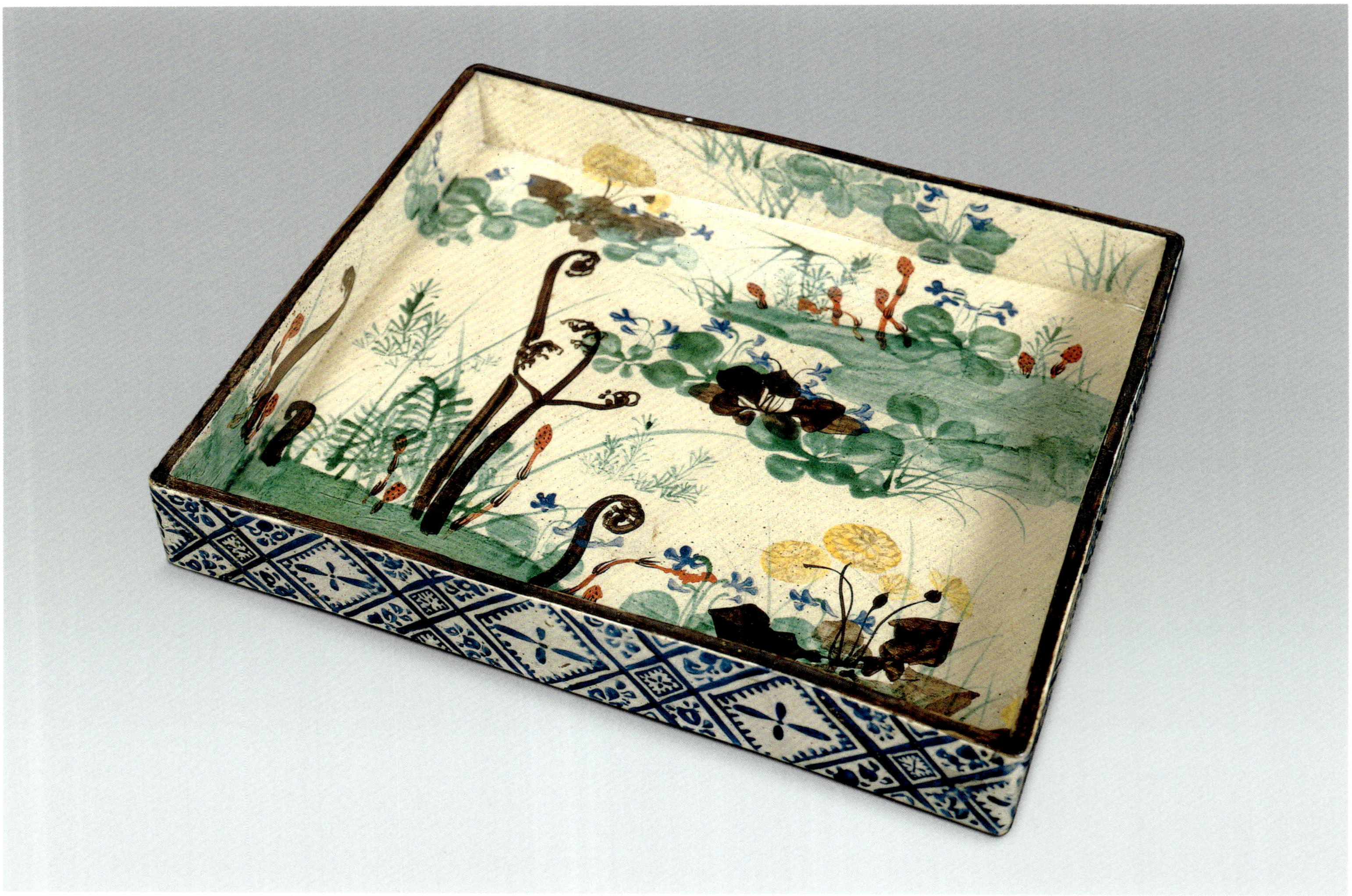

639

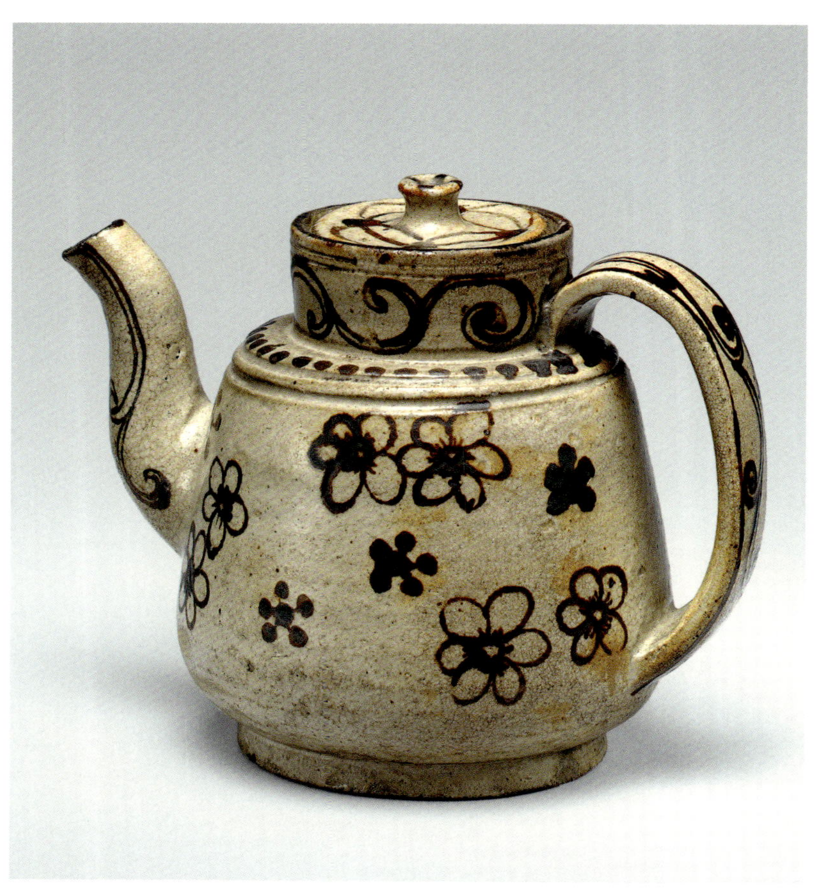

640

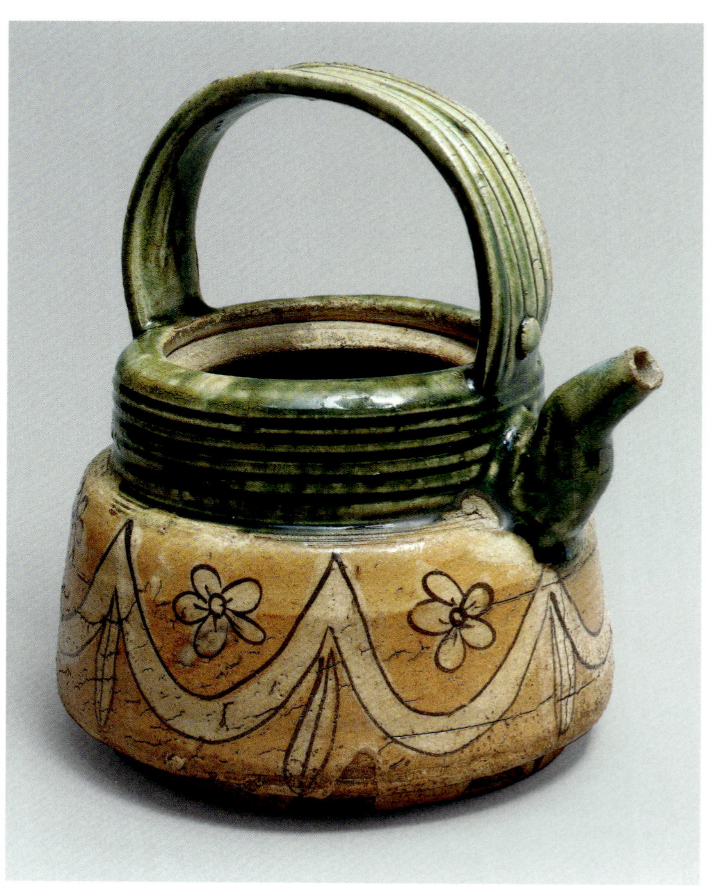

641

Ogata Kenzan
(尾形乾山; 1663–1743)

639. Platter with spring flowers

Edo period, 18th century
Kyoto (*Kyōyaki* 京焼) ware; stoneware with underglaze enamels and cobalt blue
31.6 x 36.7 cm (12½ x 14½ in.)
Signature, seal

Literature: Carpenter 2012, no. 82.

640. Ewer with willow and cherry blossoms

Edo period, early 17th century
Mino (美濃) ware, *Oribe* (織部) type; stoneware with iron oxide
H. 16.5 cm (6½ in.)

641. Ewer with blossoms and outdoor curtain

Momoyama or Edo period, early 17th century
Mino (美濃) ware, *Narumi-Oribe* (鳴海織部) type; stoneware with underglaze iron oxide; original lid missing
H. including handle 21 cm (8¼ in.)

Literature: Murase 1975, no. 99; Tokyo National Museum 1985a, no. 100; Avitabile 1990, no. 143; Murase 2000, no. 104; Murase 2003, no. 92; Tsuji Nobuo et al. 2005, no. 54.

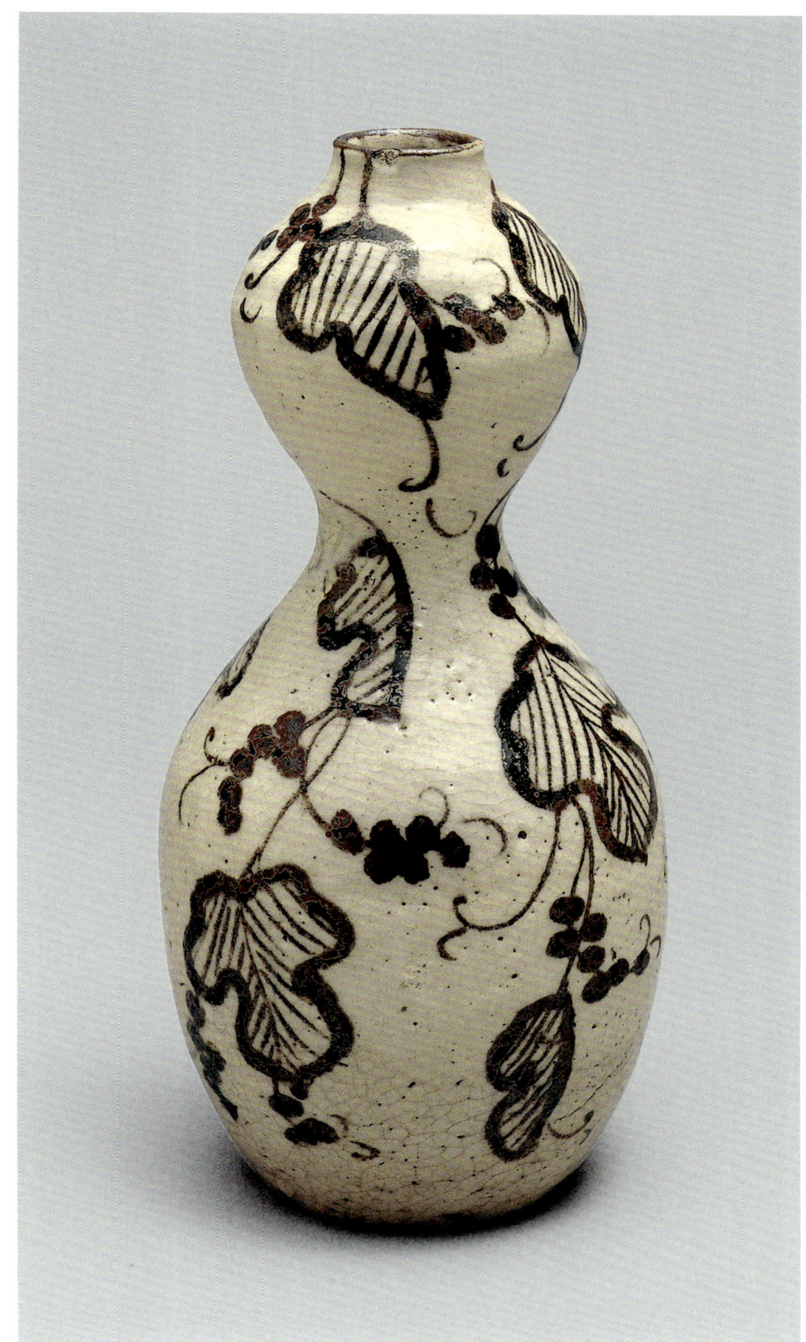

642

642. Sake flask with grapevines

Momoyama period, early 17th century
Mino (美濃) ware, *Oribe* (織部) type; stoneware with underglaze iron oxide
H. 21.9 cm (8⅝ in.)

Literature: Itō Yoshiaki 2000, no. 69; Tsuji Nobuo et al. 2005, no. 55.

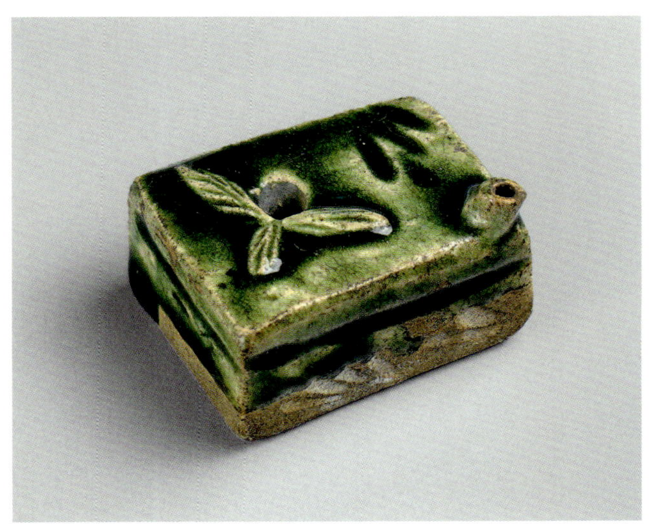

643

643. Water dropper (*suiteki*, 水滴)

Edo period, 19th century
Mino (美濃) ware, *Oribe* (織部) type; glazed stoneware
2 x 4.6 x 3.5 cm (¾ x 1¾ x 1⅜ in.)

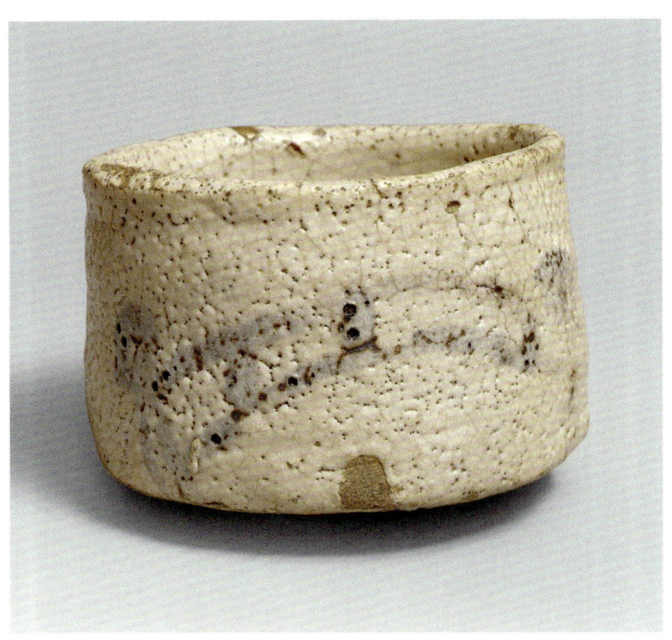

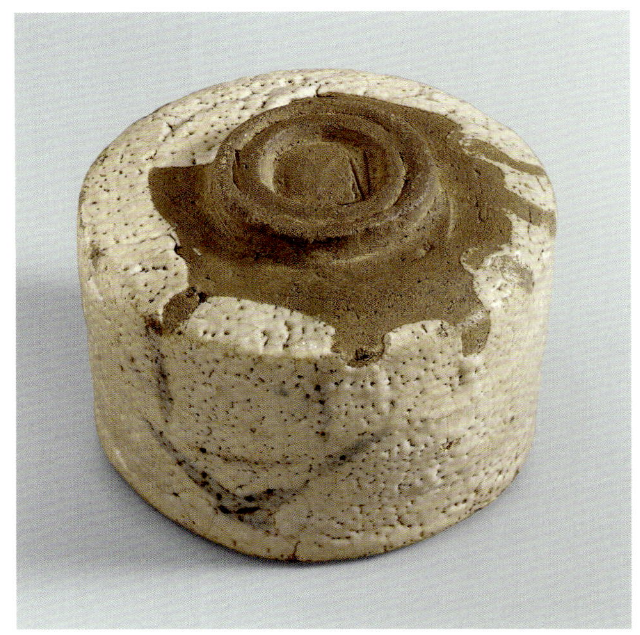

644. "Bridge of the Gods" tea bowl

Momoyama period, late 16th century
Mino (美濃) ware, *Shino* (志野) type;
stoneware with underglaze iron oxide
H. 10.5 cm (4 1/8 in.), diam. 14 cm (5 1/2 in.)

Literature: Murase 1975, no. 98; Pekarik 1978, no. 80; Hayashiya Seizō 1981, no. 22; Tokyo National Museum 1985a, no. 98; Avitabile 1990, no. 131; Murase 2000, no. 100.

645. Plate with grapevines, trellis, and geometric design

Momoyama period, 16th century
Mino (美濃) ware, *Nezumi Shino* (鼠志野)
type; stoneware with underglaze iron oxide
7.3 x 28.5 x 27 cm (2 7/8 x 11 1/4 x 10 5/8 in.)

Ex coll.: Okabe Kan

Literature: Arakawa Toyozō 1959, pl. 49; *Encyclopedia of World Art* 1960, pl. 171; Tokyo National Museum 1971, no. 52; Arakawa Toyozō 1972, pl. 87; Minamoto Toyomune et al. 1973, no. 32; Hayashiya Seizō 1974, no. 42; Murase 1975, add. no. 112; Tokyo National Museum 1985a, no. 99; Avitabile 1990, no. 132; Hayashiya Seizō and Enjōji Jirō 1990, no. 41; Murase 2000, no. 101; Murase 2003, no. 28; Tsuji Nobuo et al. 2005, no. 51.

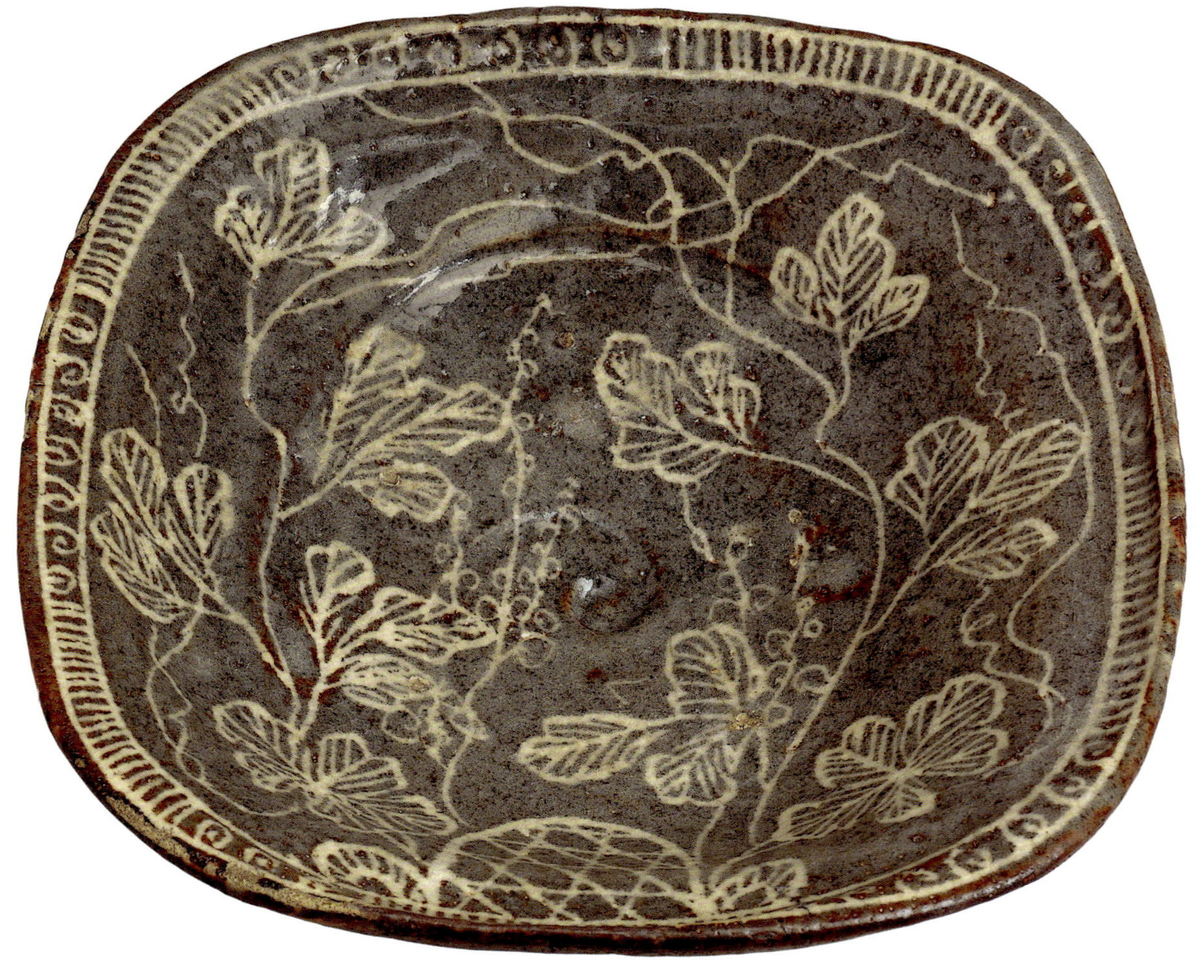

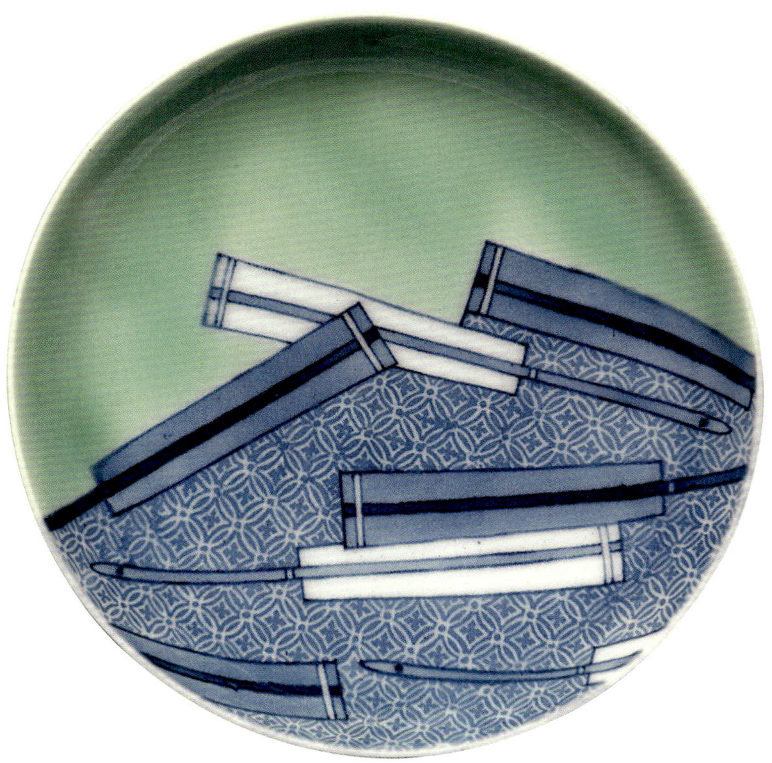

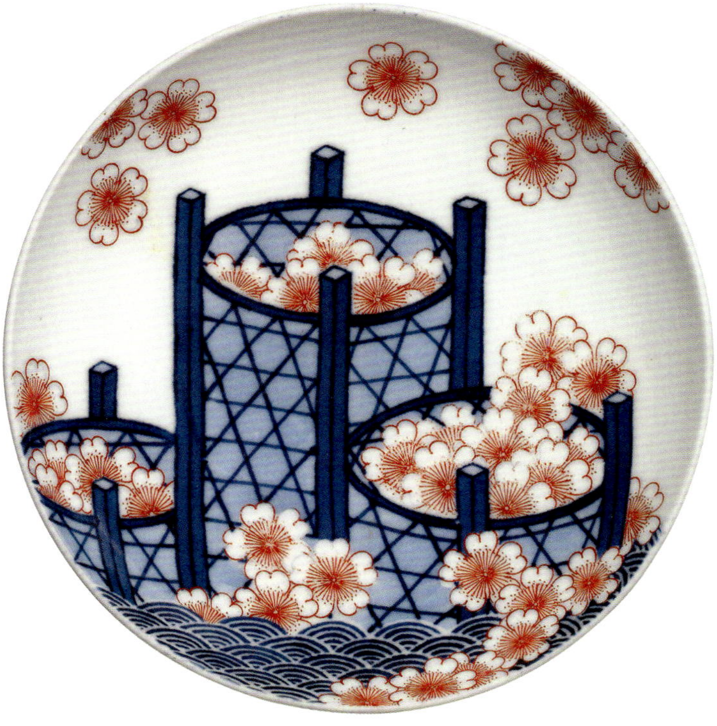

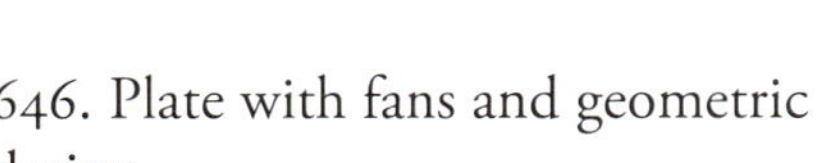

646. Plate with fans and geometric design

Edo period, 1680–90
Nabeshima (鍋島) ware; porcelain with underglaze cobalt blue and celadon glaze
H. 4.9 cm (2 in.), diam. 15.2 cm (6 in.)

LITERATURE: Pekarik 1978, no. 37; Burke 1993, no. 46.

647. Plate with baskets and cherry blossoms

Edo period, late 17th–early 18th century
Nabeshima (鍋島) ware; porcelain with underglaze cobalt blue and overglaze enamels
Diam. 15 cm (5 7/8 in.)

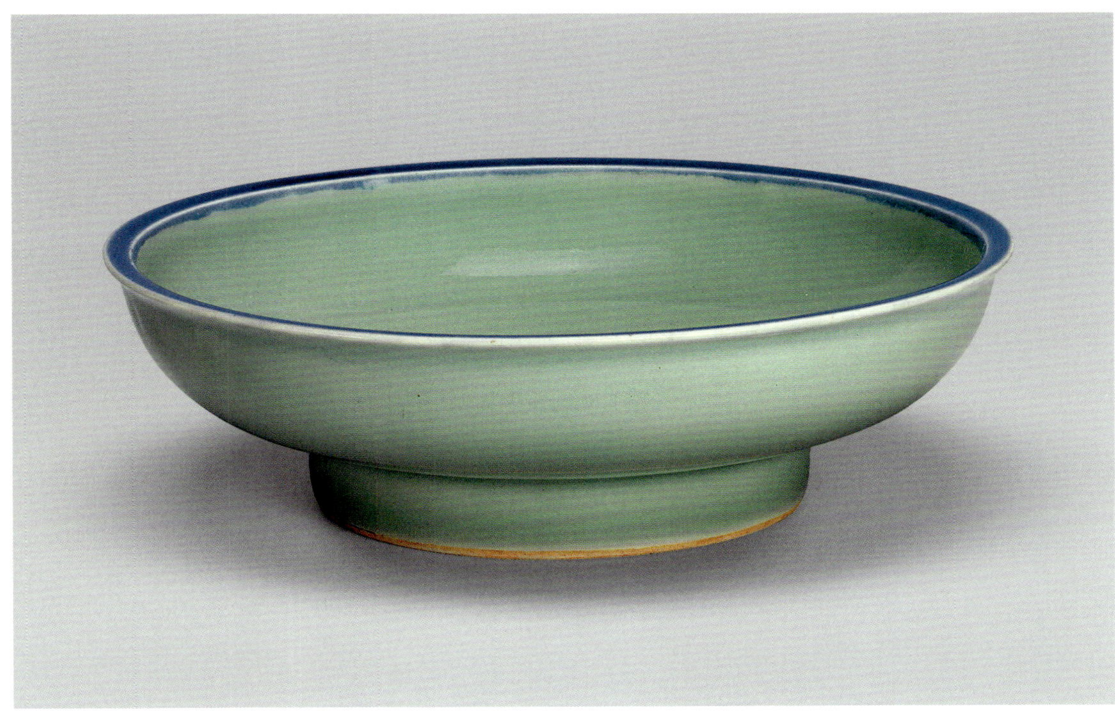

648. Plate

Edo period, ca. 1700
Nabeshima (鍋島) ware; porcelain with underglaze cobalt blue and celadon glaze
Diam. 20.1 cm (7 7/8 in.)

LITERATURE: Pekarik 1978, no. 42.

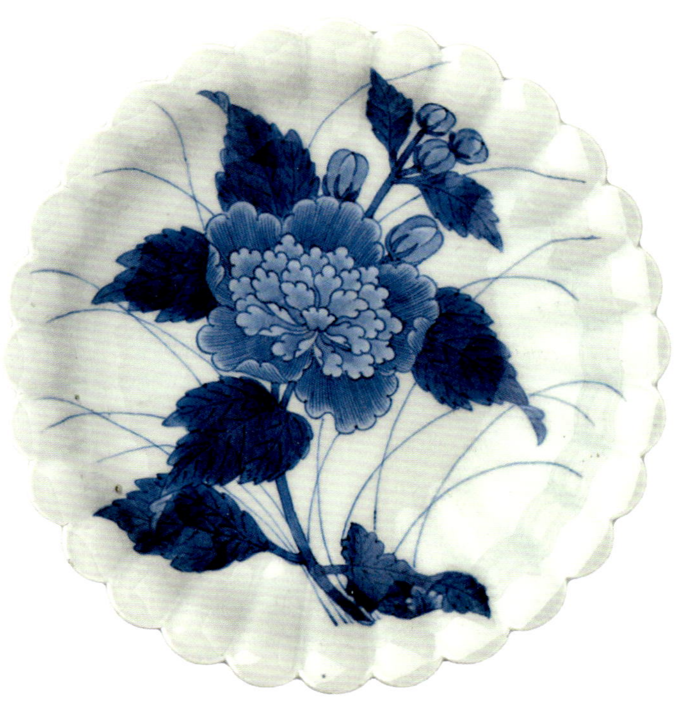

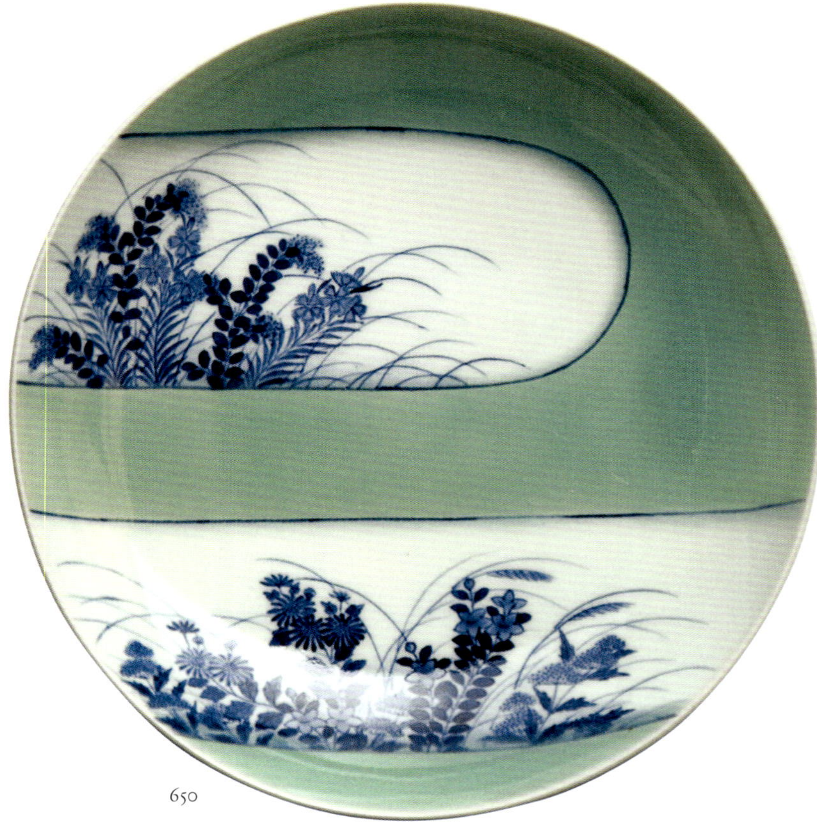

650

649. Plate with peonies

Edo period, ca. 1720
Nabeshima (鍋島) ware; porcelain with underglaze cobalt blue
Diam. 14.5 cm (5 3/4 in.)

650. Plate with autumn grasses

Edo period
Nabeshima (鍋島) ware; porcelain with underglaze cobalt blue and celadon glaze
Diam. 20.2 cm (8 in.)

Literature: Pekarik 1978, no. 36; Tokyo National Museum 1985a, no. 103; Avitabile 1990, no. 145.

Raku Ryōnyū
(樂了入; 1756–1834)

651. Pair of tea bowls with incised cranes and turtles

Edo period, 18th–19th century
Raku (樂) ware; earthenware
H. of each 8.1 cm (3 1/8 in.), diam. of red bowl 12.2 cm (4 3/4 in.), diam. of black bowl 11 cm (4 3/8 in.)
Seals

Literature: Burke 1993, no. 32.

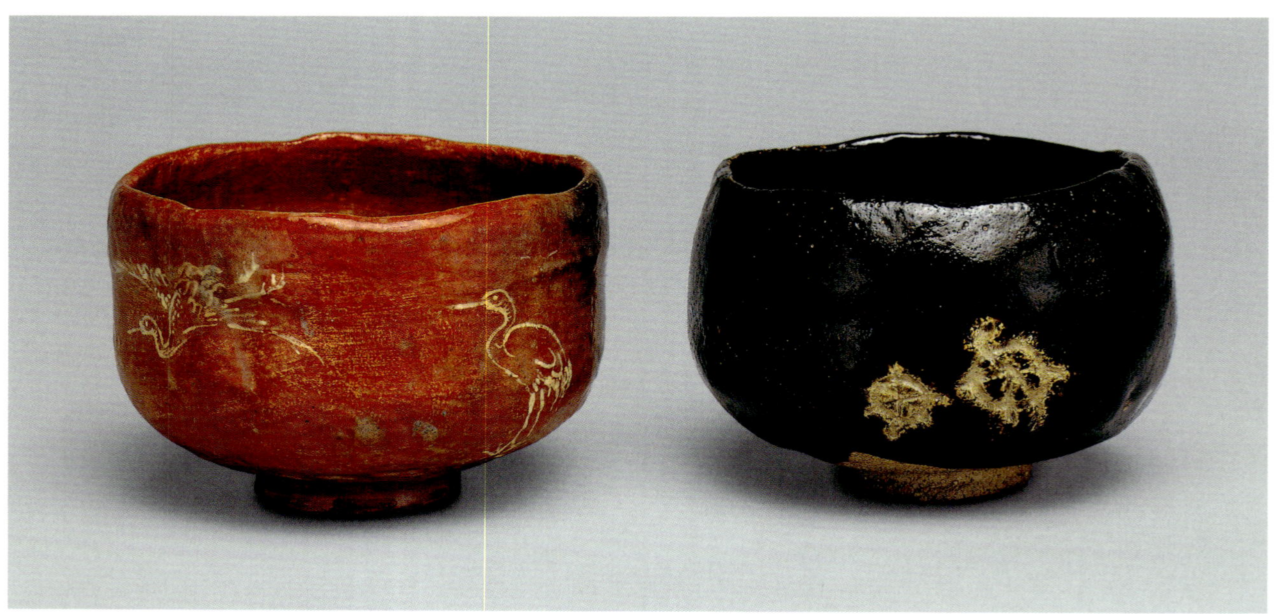

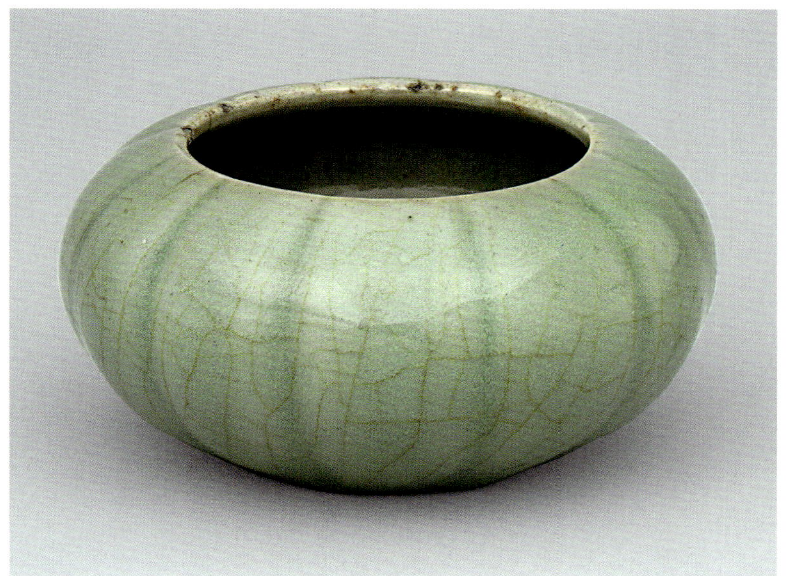

652. Brush washer

Edo period, 19th century
Sanda (三田) ware; stoneware with celadon glaze
H. 5.3 cm (2 1/8 in.), diam. 10.5 cm (4 1/8 in.)

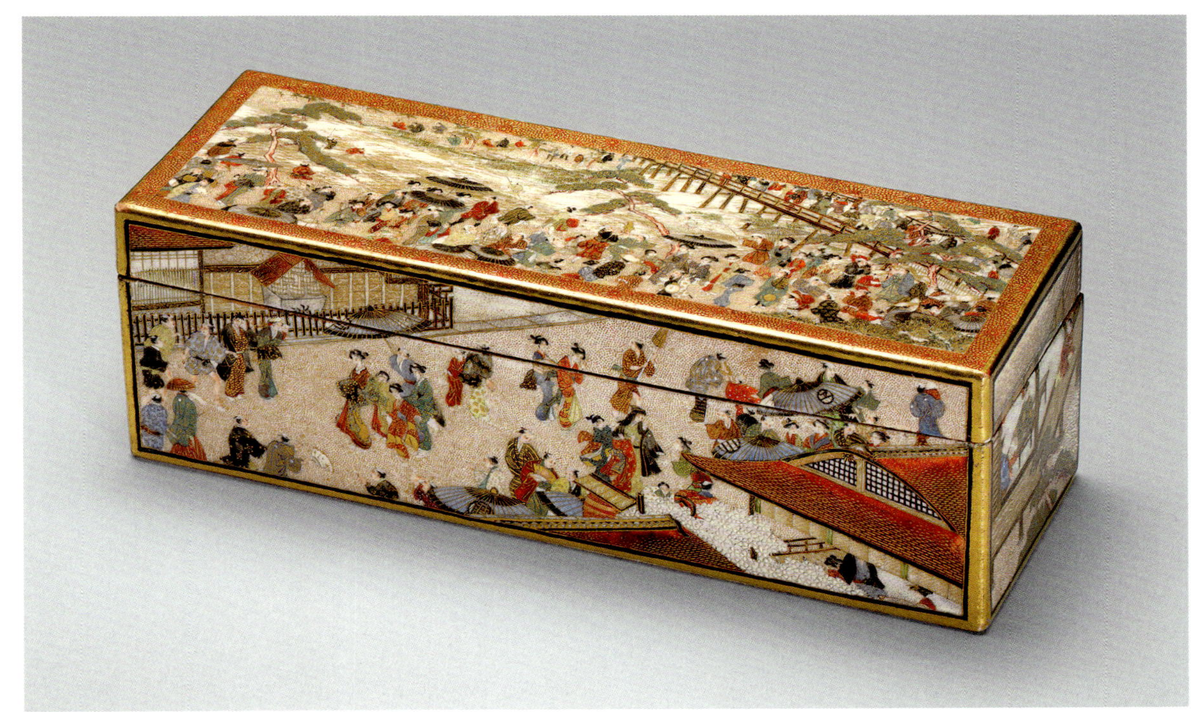

653. Box with scenes of Kyoto

Meiji era, 19th century
Satsuma (薩摩) ware; porcelain with overglaze enamels and gold
6.2 x 18.9 x 6.3 cm (2 3/8 x 7 1/2 x 2 1/2 in.)
Seal

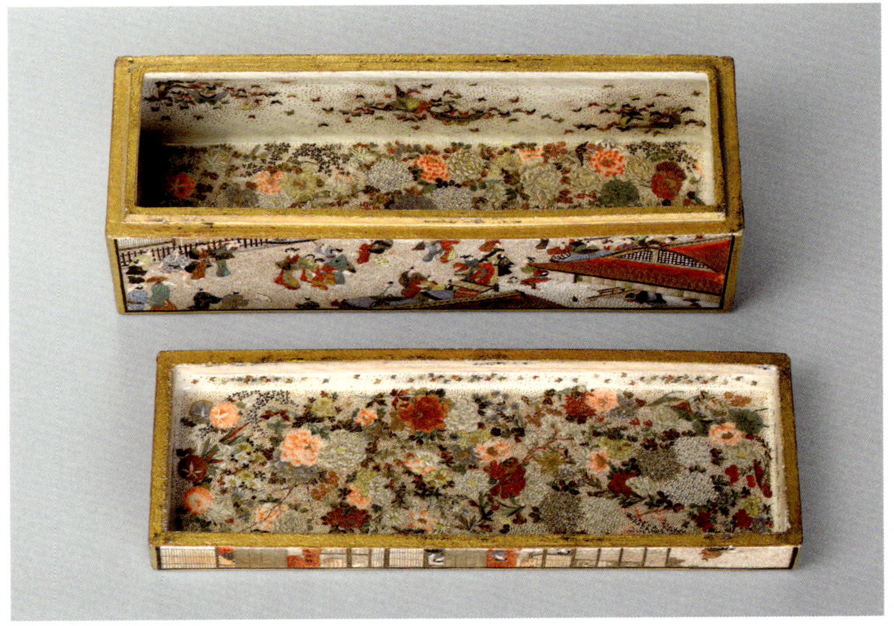

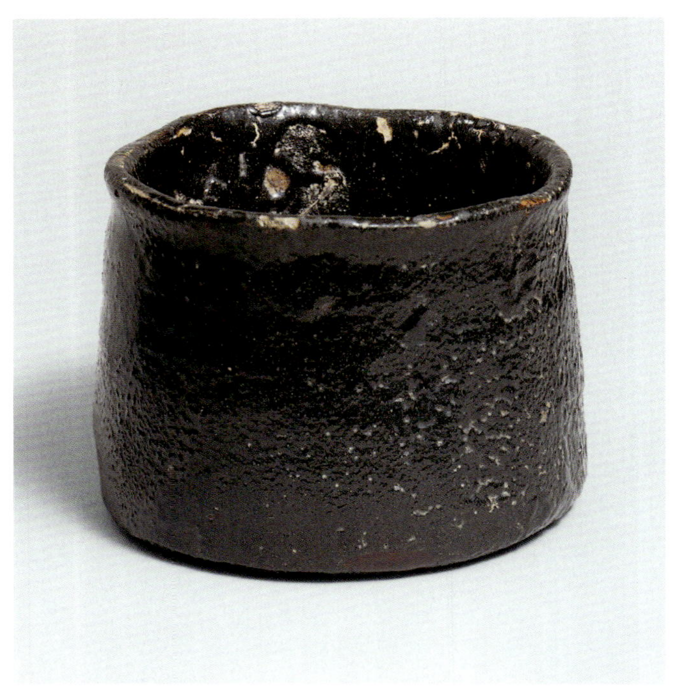

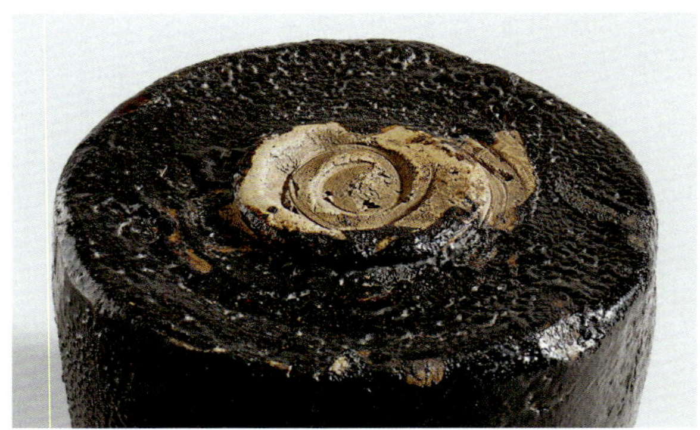

654. "Iron Mallet" tea bowl

Momoyama period, 1580–90
Mino (美濃) ware, *Seto Guro* (瀬戸黒) type; stoneware with black glaze
H. 9 cm (3½ in.), diam. 12 cm (4¾ in.)

LITERATURE: Cort 1985, fig. 3; Tokyo National Museum 1985a, no. 97; Avitabile 1990, no. 129; Murase 2000, no. 98; Murase 2003, no. 20; Tsuji Nobuo et al. 2005, no. 50.

655. Tea caddy (*chaire*, 茶入れ)

Momoyama period, late 16th century
Seto (瀬戸) ware; stoneware with iron-rich glaze
H. including lid 10 cm (4 in.)

LITERATURE: Tokyo National Museum 1985a, no. 96; Avitabile 1990, no. 130; Murase 2000, no. 99.

656. Tea caddy (*chaire*, 茶入れ)

Momoyama period, 16th–17th century
Seto (瀬戸) ware; glazed stoneware
H. including lid 8 cm (3⅛ in.)

LITERATURE: Pekarik 1978, no. 81.

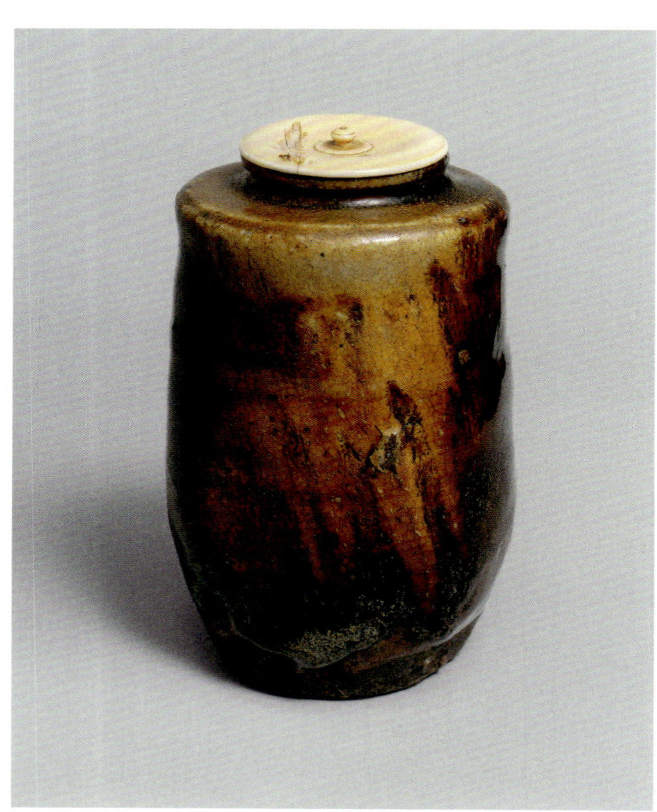

655

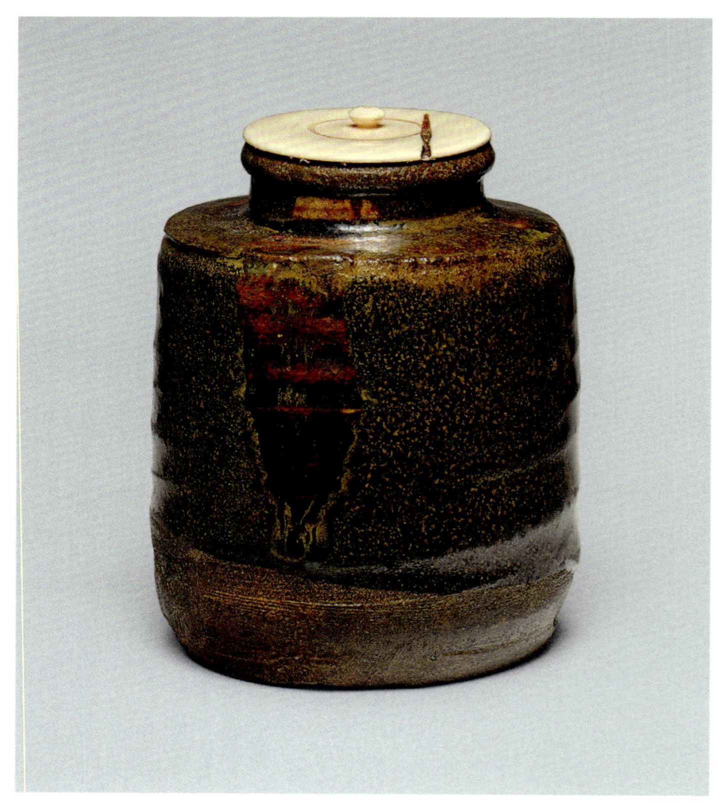

656

657. Plate with willow

Edo period, 18th century
Seto (瀬戸) ware; stoneware with underglaze iron oxide and cobalt blue
Diam. 26.4 cm (10 3/8 in.)

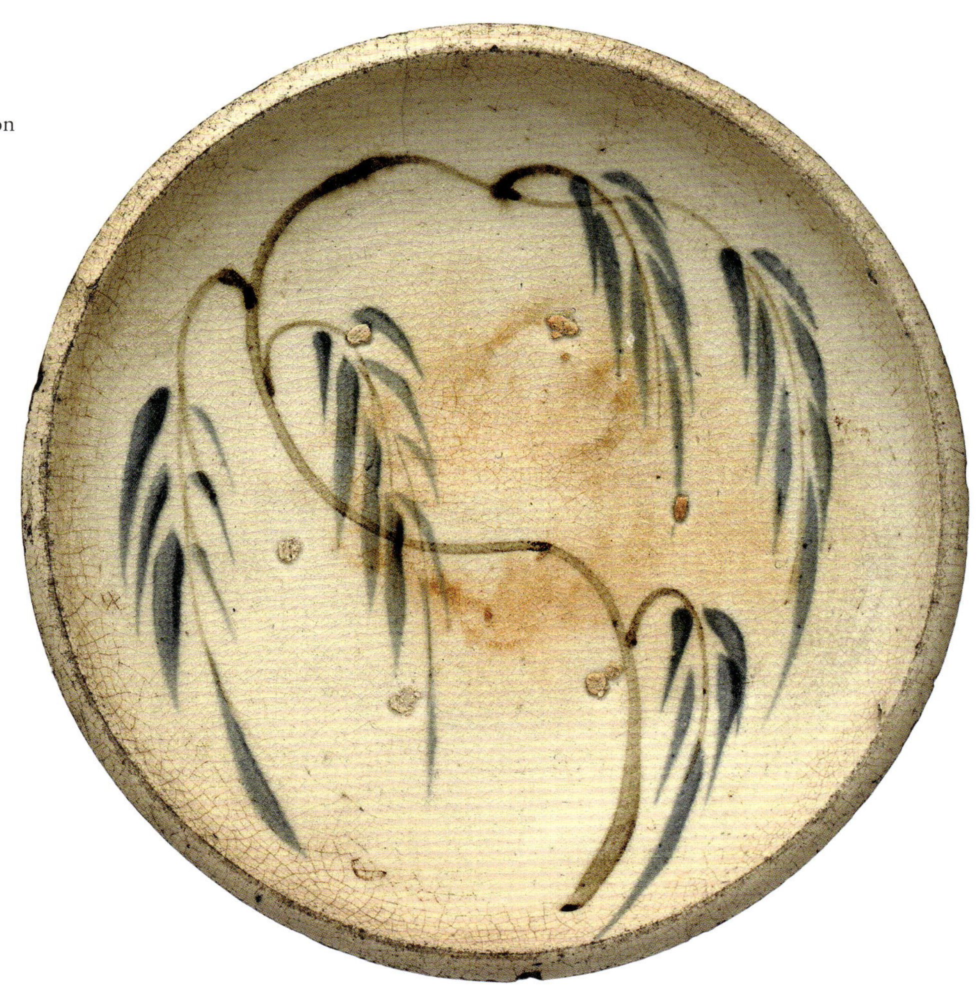

658. Plate with "horse eye" design

Edo period, 18th century
Seto (瀬戸) ware; stoneware with underglaze iron oxide
Diam. 26.5 cm (10 3/8 in.)

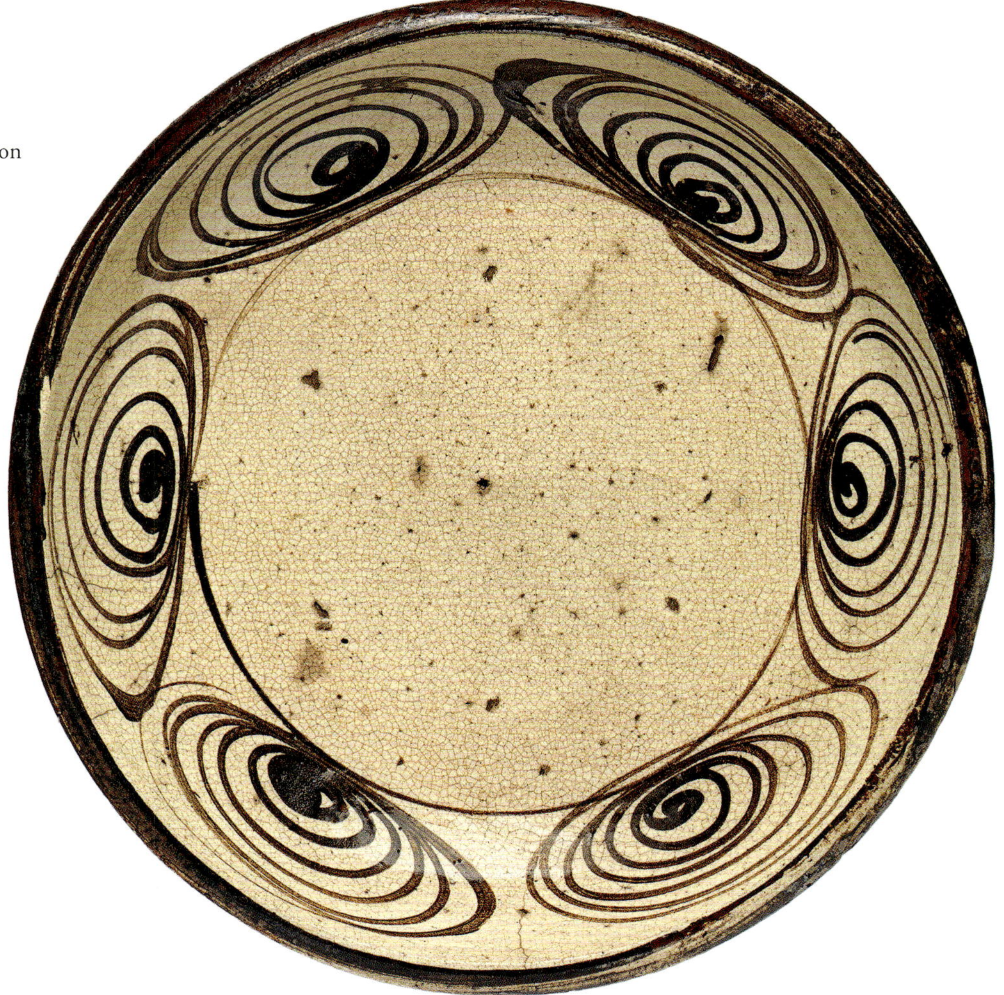

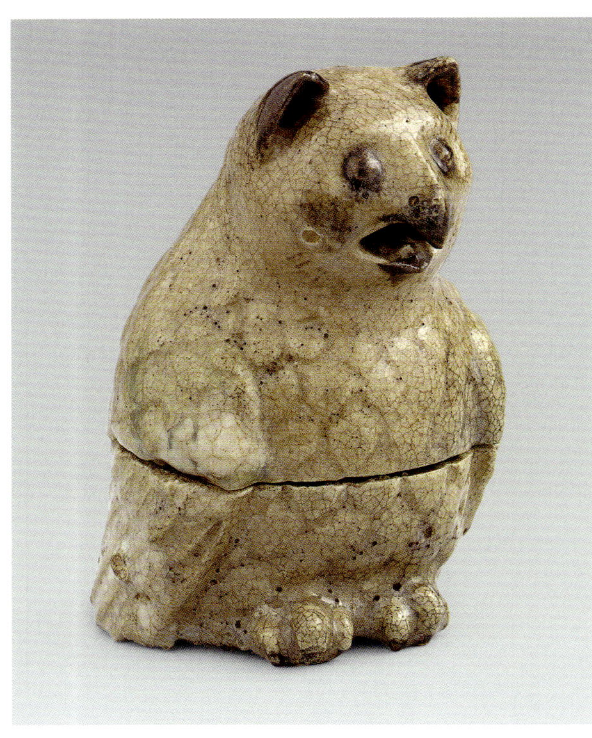

659. Owl-shaped incense burner (*kōro*, 香炉)

Edo period, 18th century
Seto (瀬戸) ware; stoneware with crackled glaze
H. 12.3 cm (4 7/8 in.)

Gift from Setsu Iwao, ca. 1970

660. Storage jar

Muromachi period, 15th century
Shigaraki (信楽) ware; stoneware with natural ash glaze
H. 45.5 cm (17 7/8 in.)

Literature: Pekarik 1978, no. 16; Tokyo National Museum 1985a, no. 87; Avitabile 1990, no. 133; Tsuji Nobuo et al. 2005, no. 18.

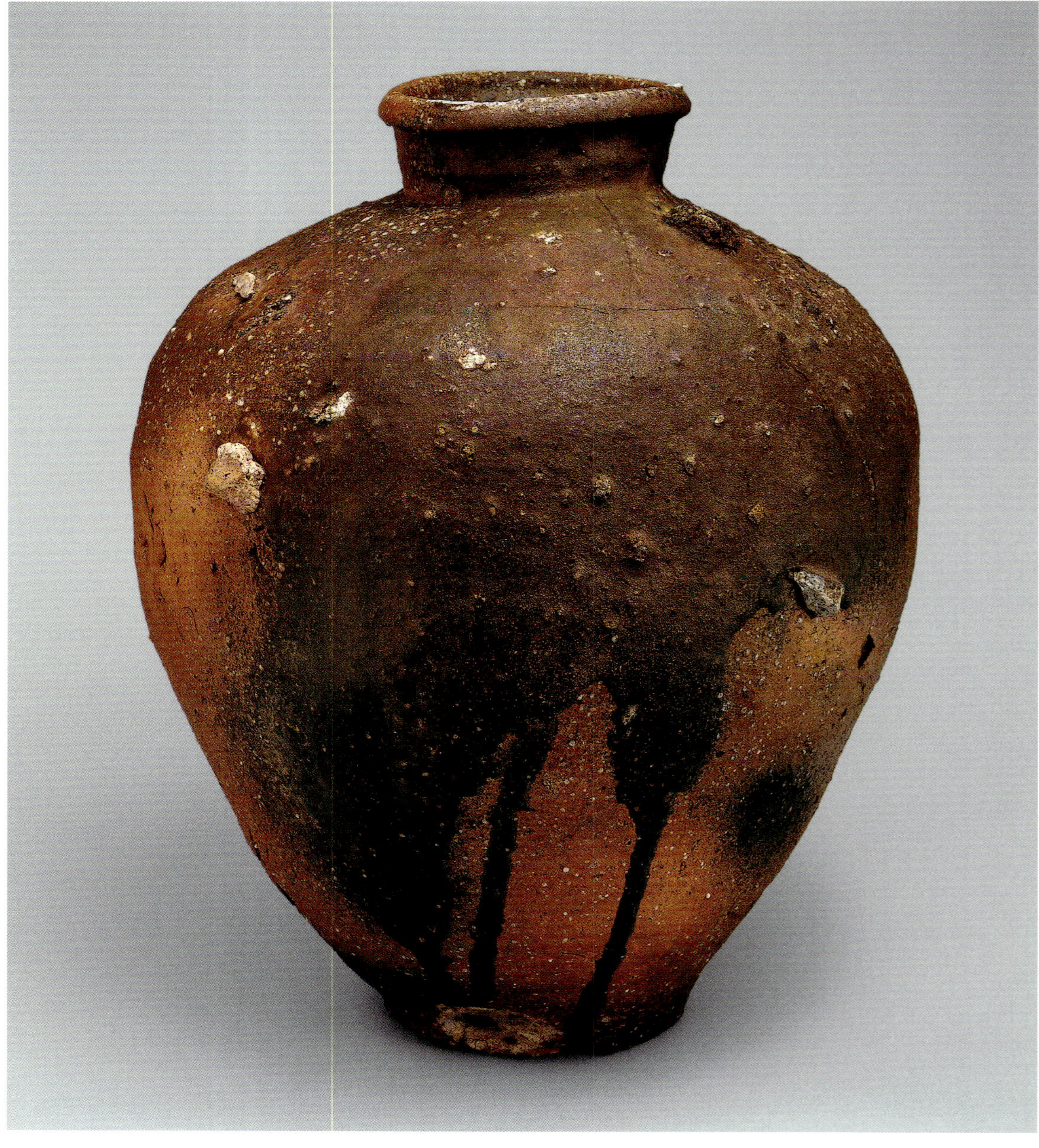

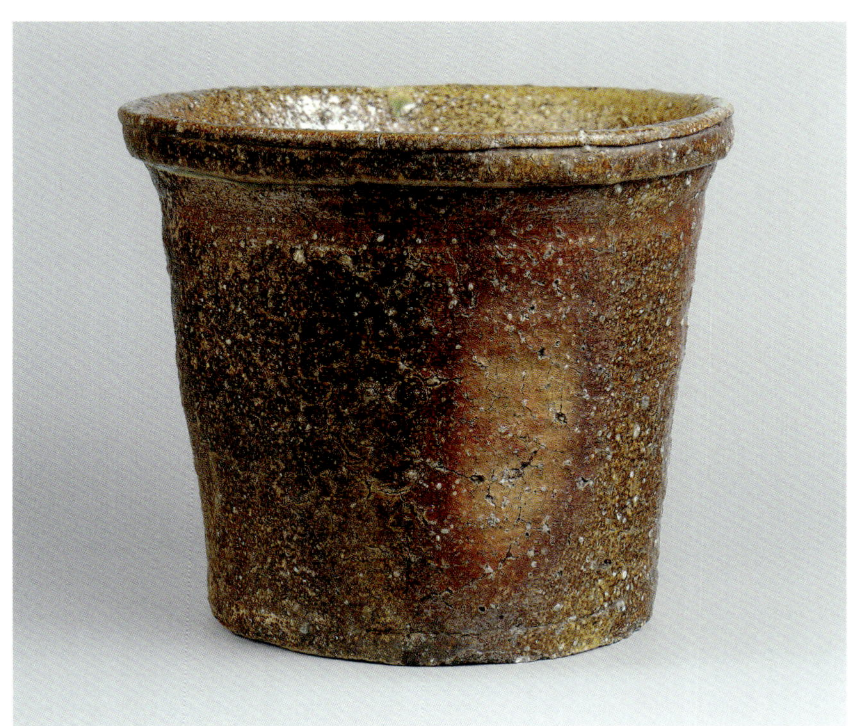

661. Pail-shaped freshwater jar
(*onioke mizusashi*, 鬼桶水指)

Muromachi period, 16th century
Shigaraki (信楽) ware; stoneware with natural ash glaze
H. 23.5 cm (9 1/4 in.)

LITERATURE: Tokyo National Museum 1985a, no. 93; Avitabile 1990, no. 135.

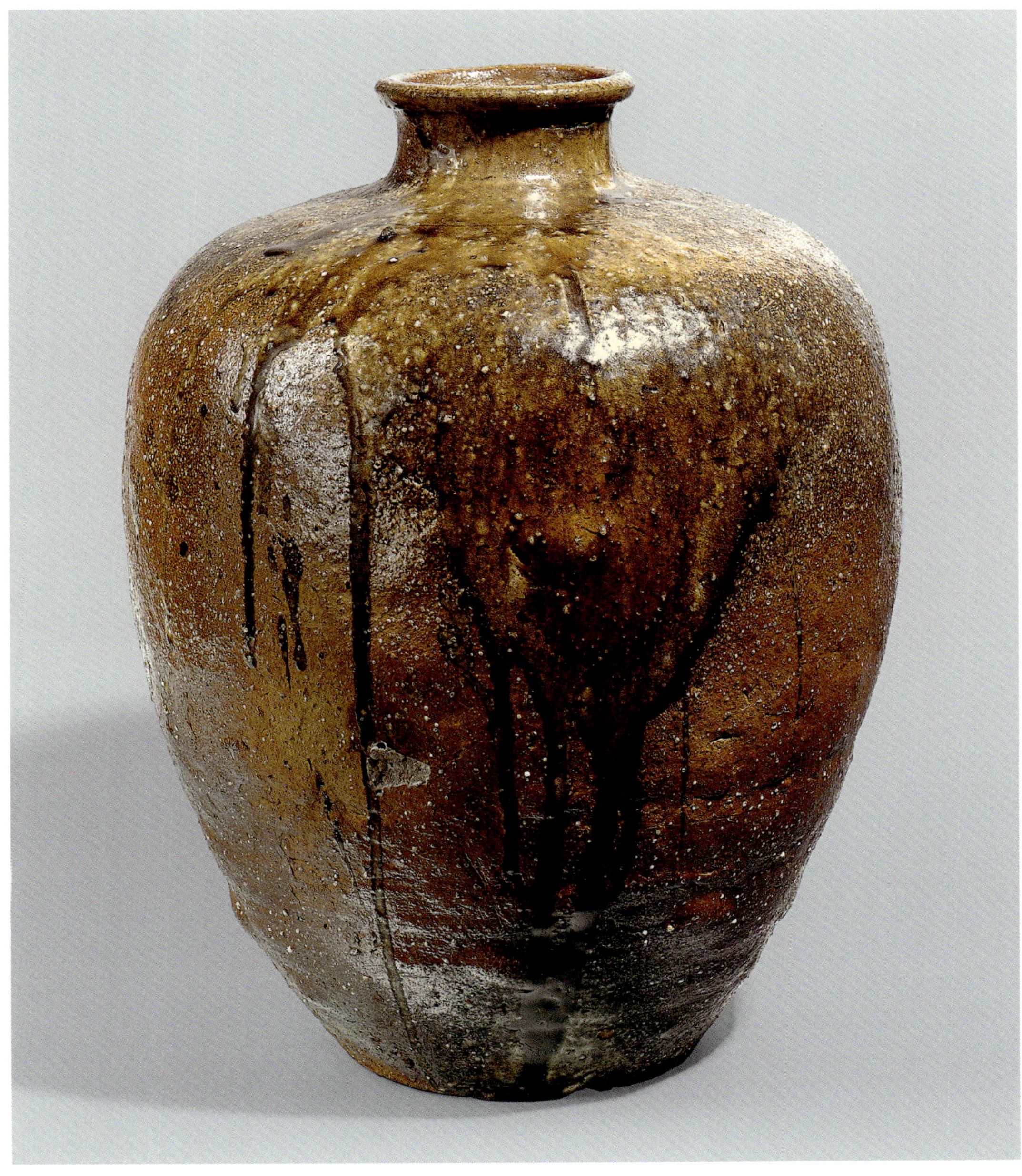

662. Storage jar

Momoyama period, 16th century
Shigaraki (信楽) ware; stoneware with natural ash glaze
H. 46 cm (18 1/8 in.)

LITERATURE: Tokyo National Museum 1985a, no. 92; Avitabile 1990, no. 134.

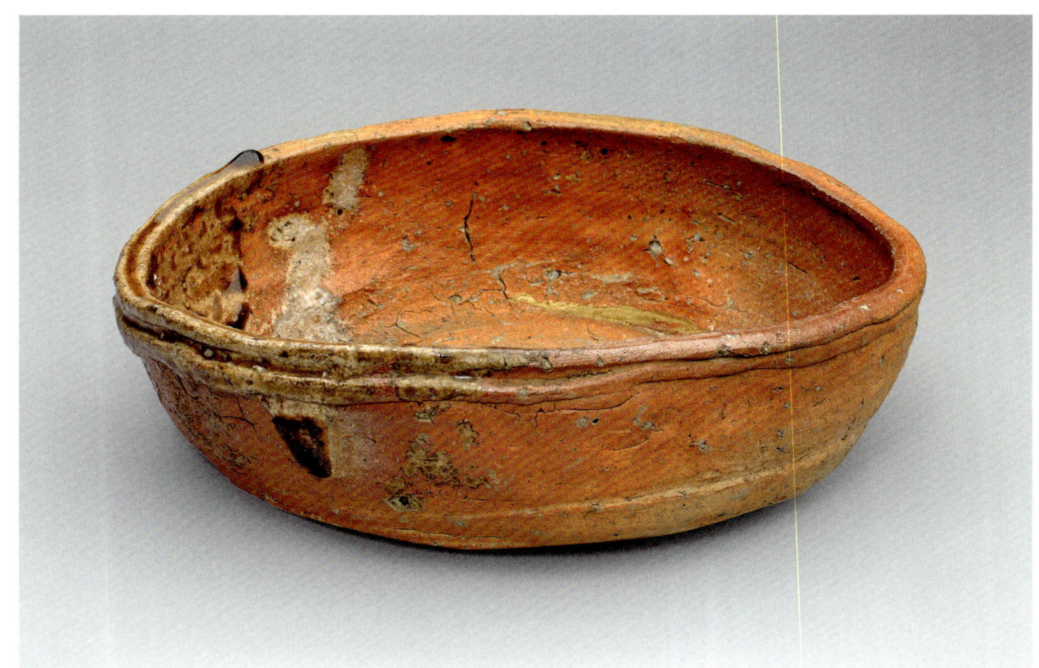

663. Bowl

Momoyama–early Edo period, 16th–17th century
Shigaraki (信楽) ware; stoneware with natural ash glaze
Diam. 23.2 cm (9⅛ in.)

664. Jar

Edo period, 17th century
Kyoto (*Kyōyaki* 京焼) ware, *Shigaraki* (信楽) type; stoneware with natural ash glaze and gold lacquer repairs
H. 26 cm (10¼ in.)

Literature: Pekarik 1978, no. 57; Cort 1979, fig. 117.

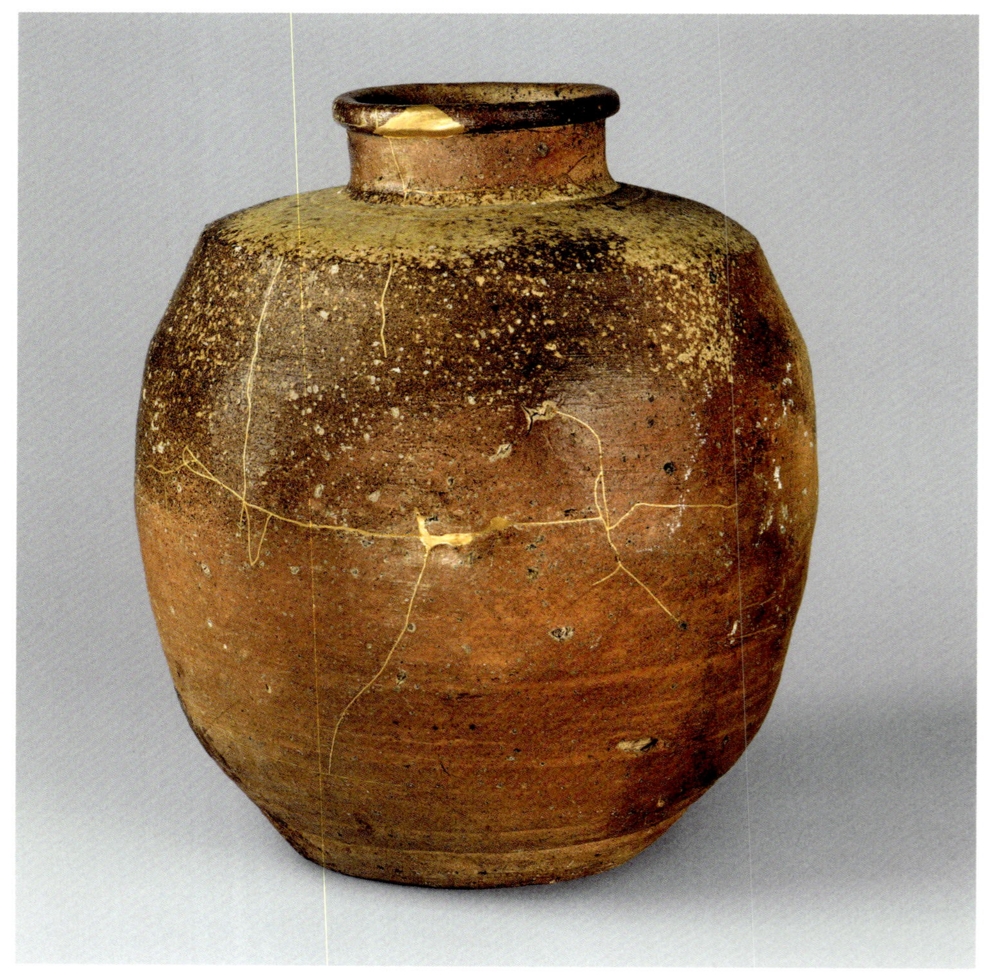

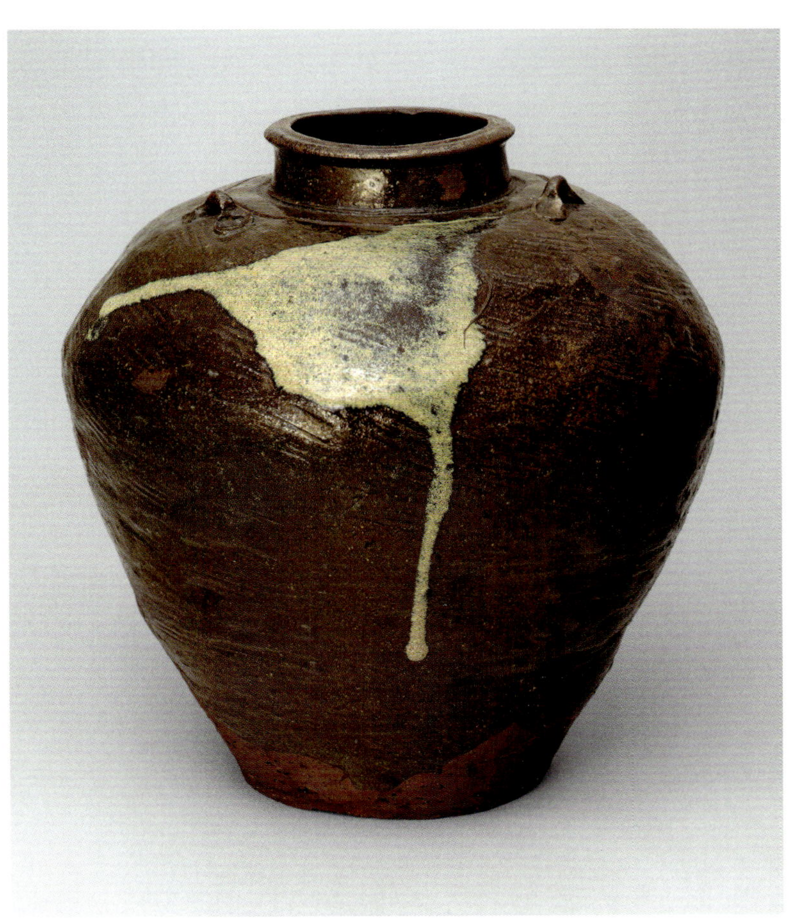

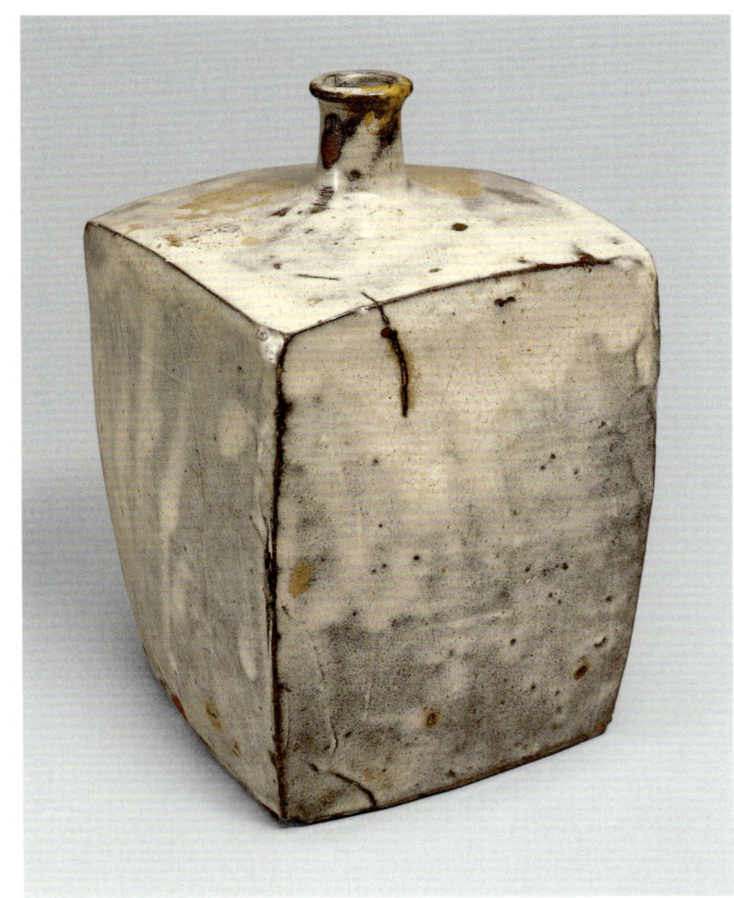

665. Storage jar

Edo period, 17th century
Shōdai (小代) ware; stoneware with white slip
H. 29.8 cm (11 3/4 in.)

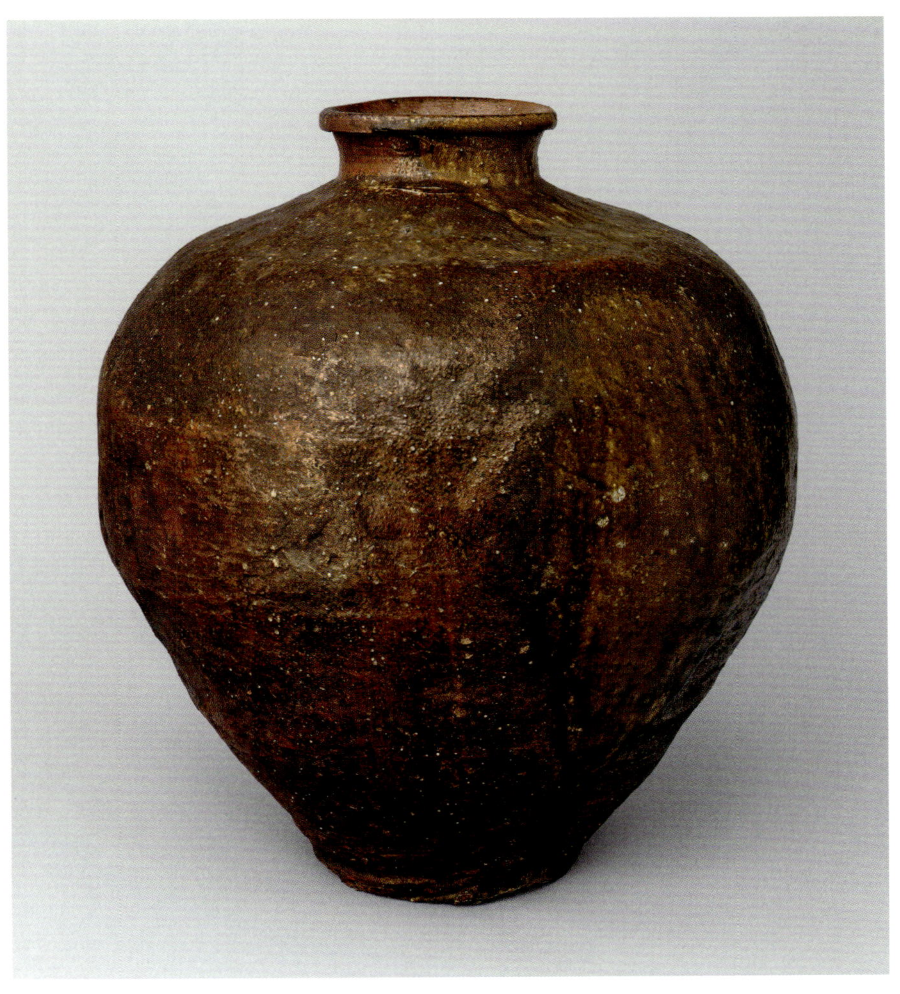

666. Sake bottle

Edo period, 17th century
Shōdai (小代) ware; stoneware with white glaze
H. 26 cm (10 1/4 in.)

Ex coll.: Shirasu Masako

Literature: Shirasu Masako 1997, no pl. number; Tsuji Nobuo et al. 2005, no. 56.

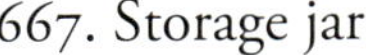

667. Storage jar

Muromachi period, 15th century
Tanba (丹波) ware; stoneware with natural ash glaze
H. 46.8 cm (18 3/8 in.)

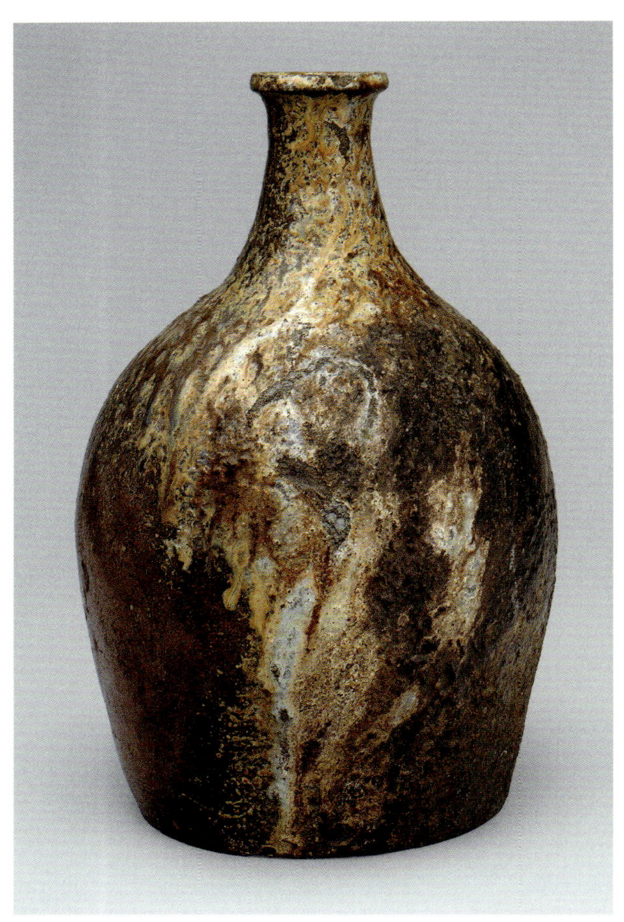

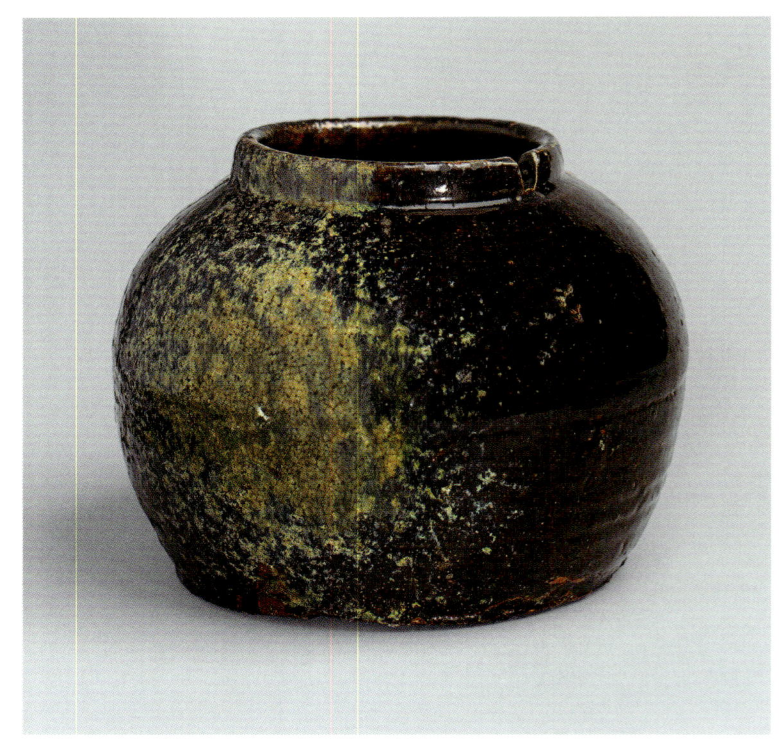

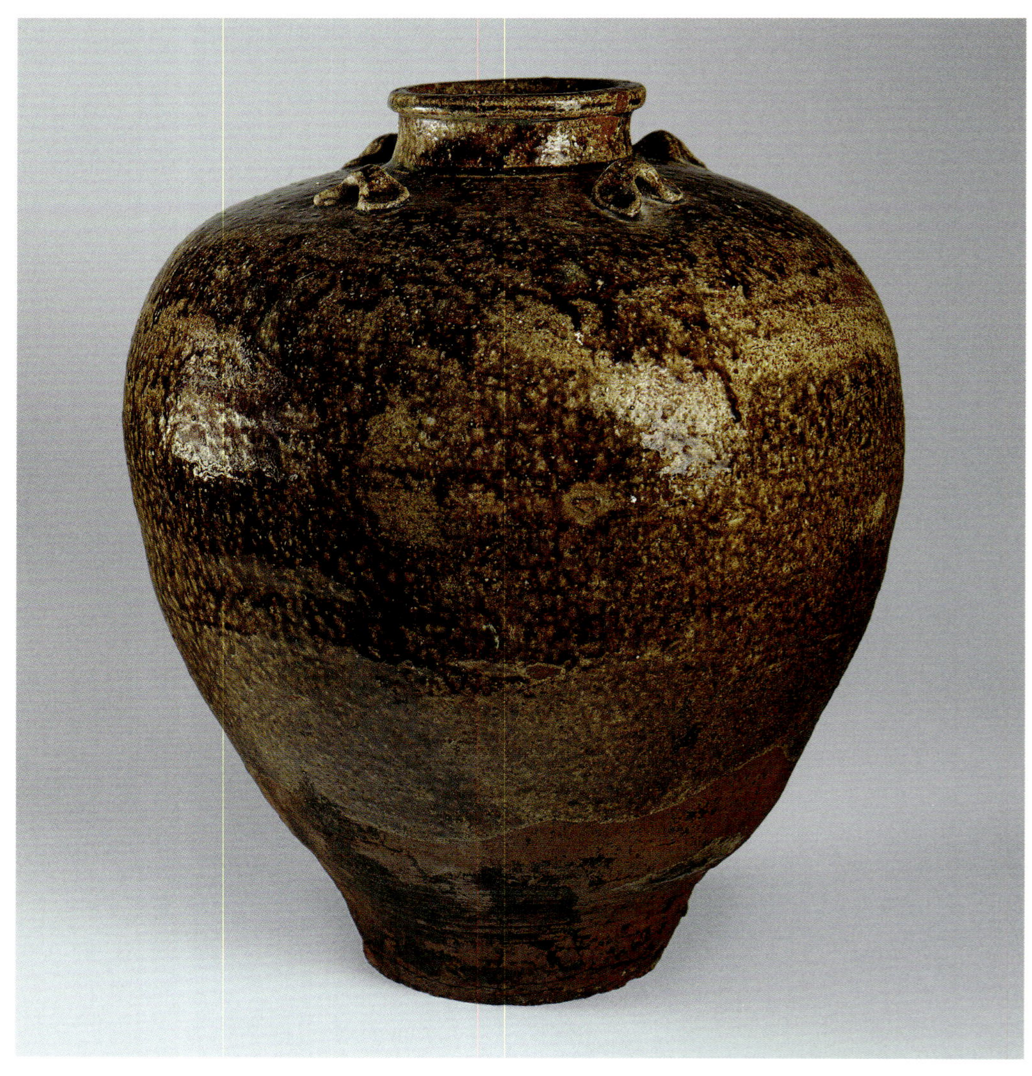

668. Sake bottle

Edo period, 17th–18th century
Tanba (丹波) ware; stoneware with natural ash glaze
H. 34.3 cm (13½ in.)

669. Oil jar

Edo period, 18th century
Tanba (丹波) ware; glazed stoneware
H. 15.3 cm (6 in.), diam. 19.7 cm (7¾ in.)

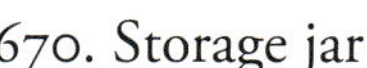

670. Storage jar

Edo period, 18th century
Tanba (丹波) ware; glazed stoneware
H. 40.2 cm (15⅞ in.), diam. 33.5 cm (13¼ in.)

671. Storage jar

Muromachi period, 16th century
Tokoname (常滑) ware; stoneware with natural ash glaze
H. 54.7 cm ($21^{1}/_{2}$ in.)

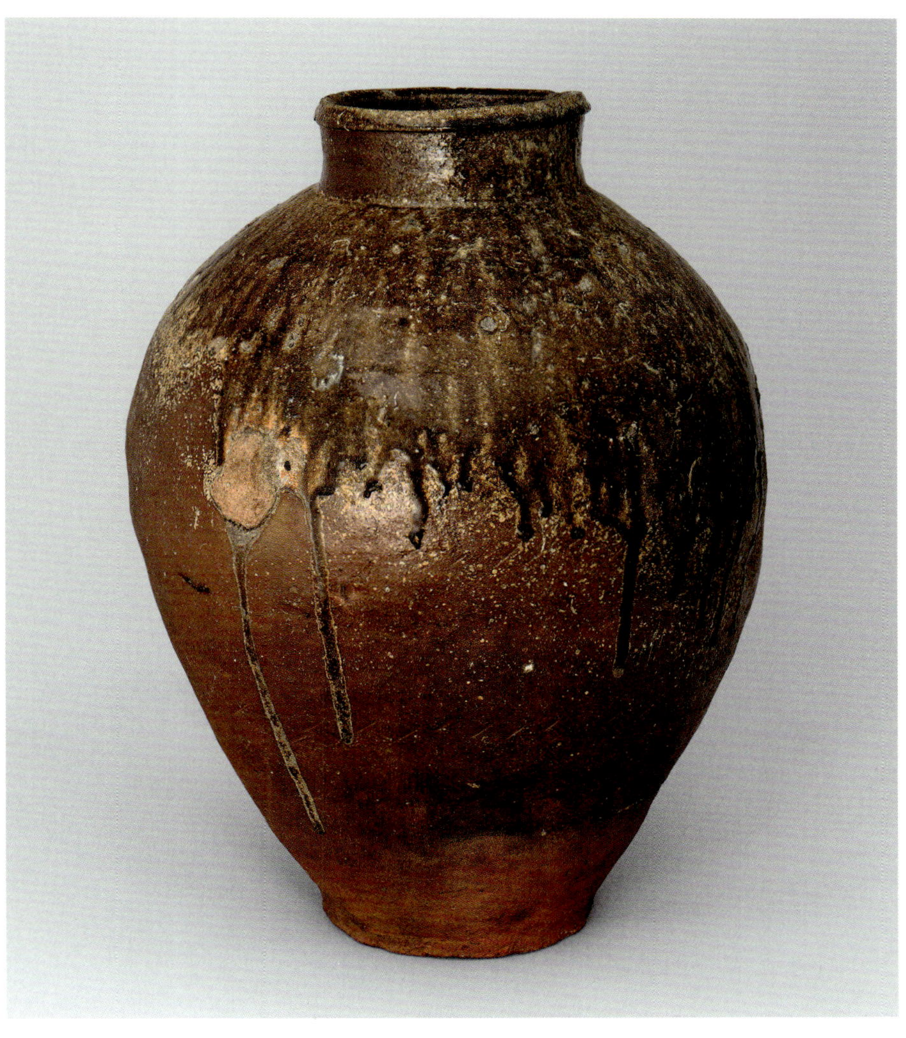

672. Storage jar

Momoyama–Edo period, early 17th century
Tokoname (常滑) ware; stoneware with natural ash glaze
H. 52.4 cm ($20^{5}/_{8}$ in.)

LITERATURE: Tokyo National Museum 1985a, no. 88; Avitabile 1990, no. 141.

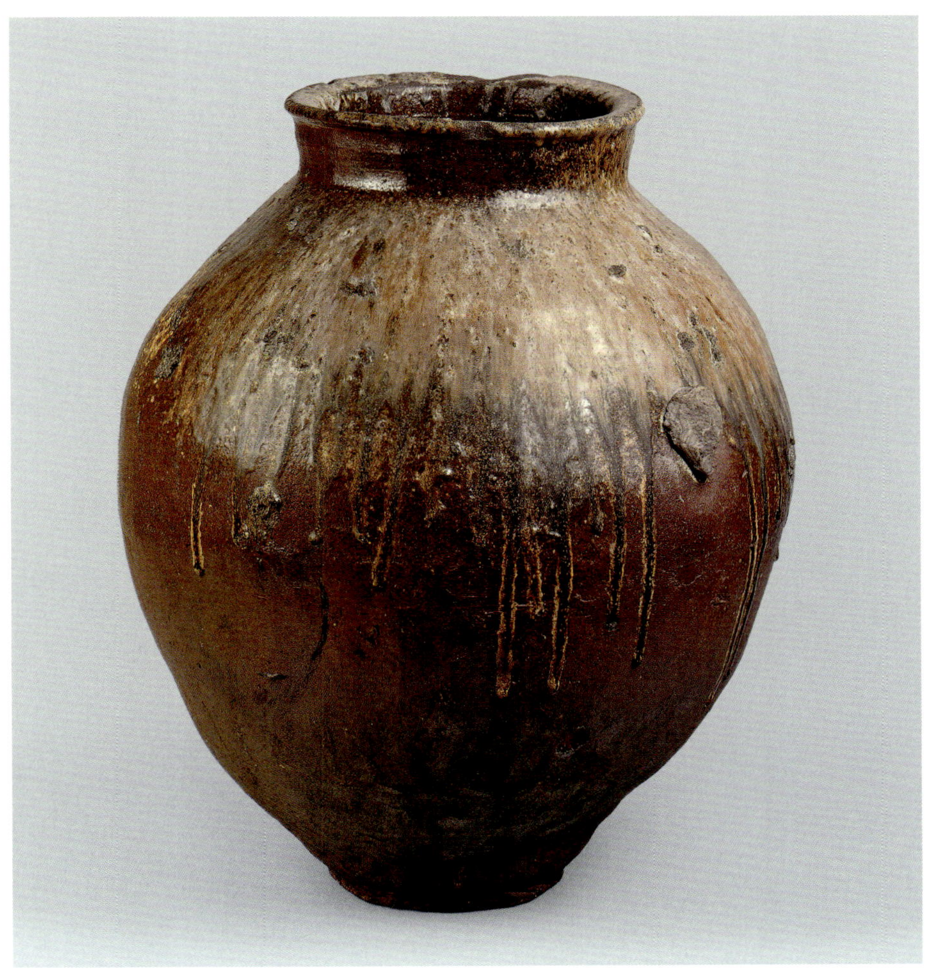

673. Four serving bowls (*mukōzuke*, 向付)

Edo period, first half of 18th century
Utsutsugawa (現川) ware; glazed stoneware
Diam. of each 4.5 cm (1¾ in.)

LITERATURE: Pekarik 1978, no. 52.

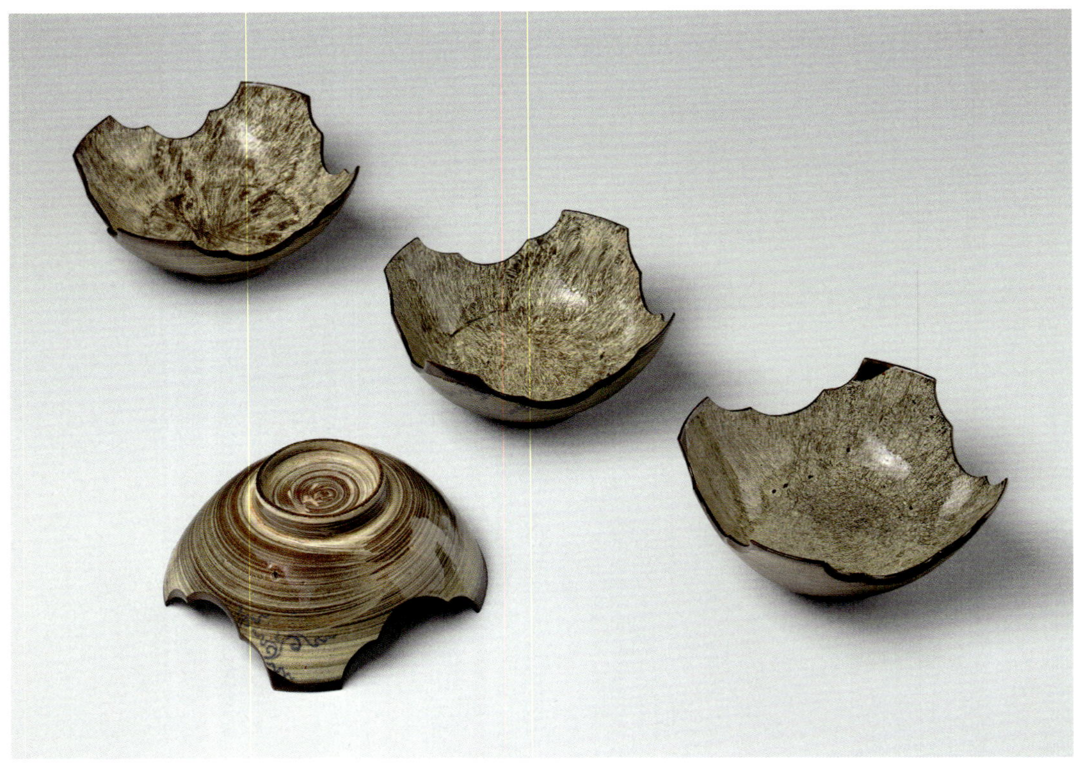

674. Five dishes with wave design

Edo period, first half of 18th century
Utsutsugawa (現川) ware; glazed stoneware
Diam. of each 11.5 cm (4½ in.)

LITERATURE: Pekarik 1978, no. 53.

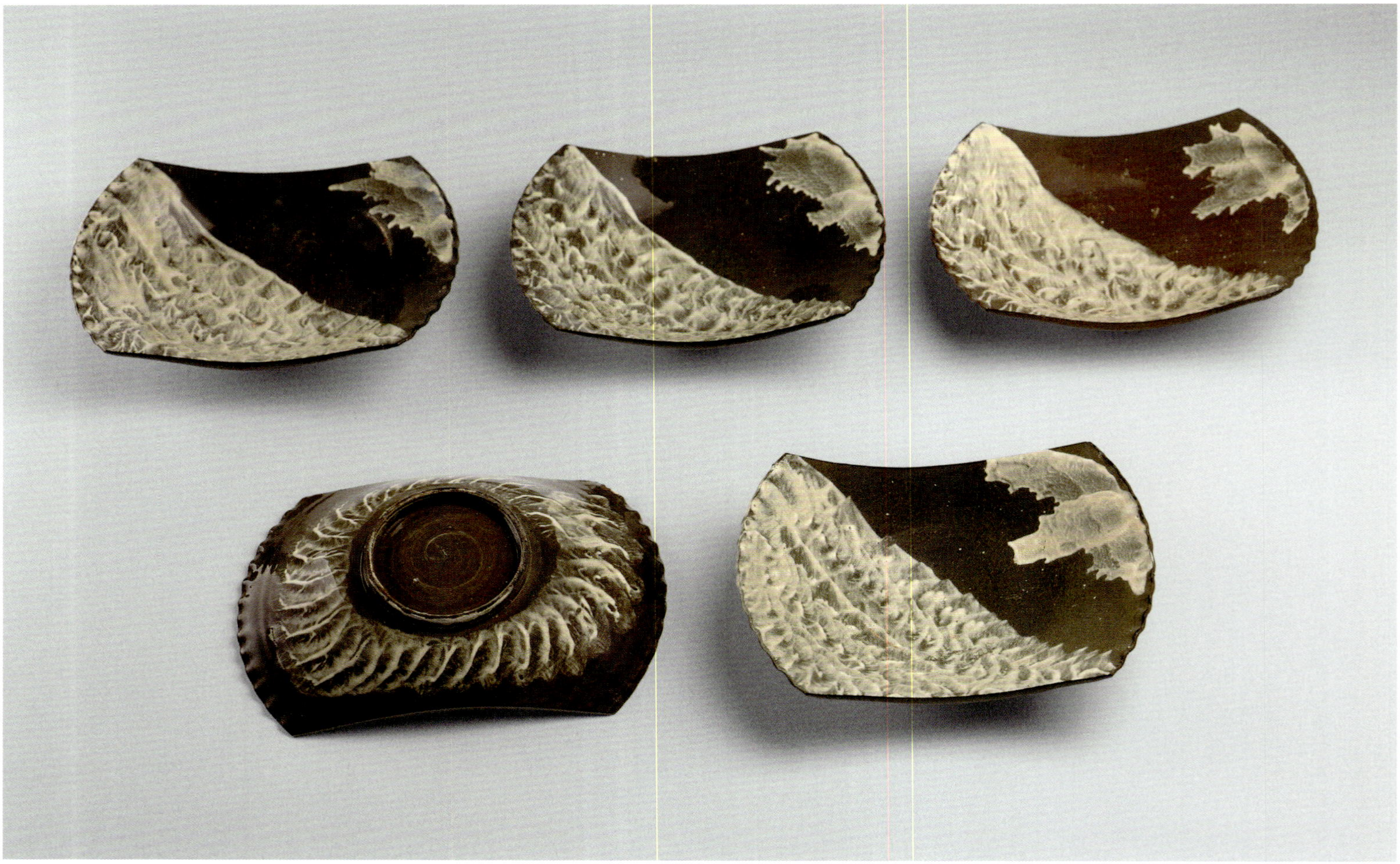

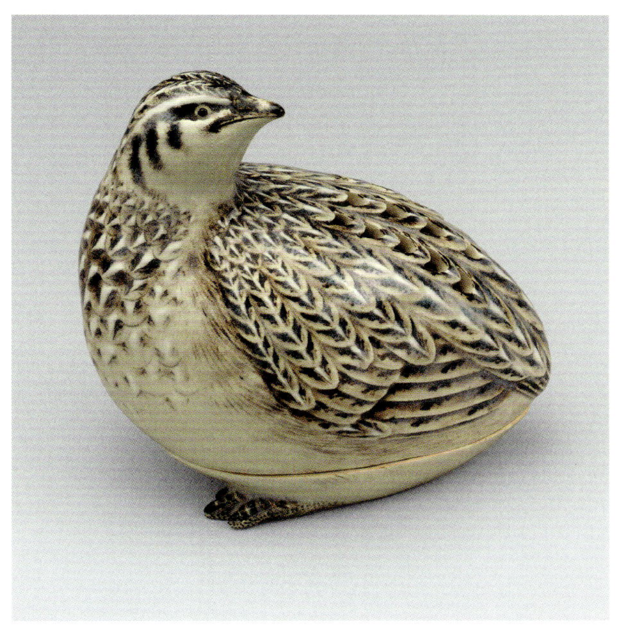

675

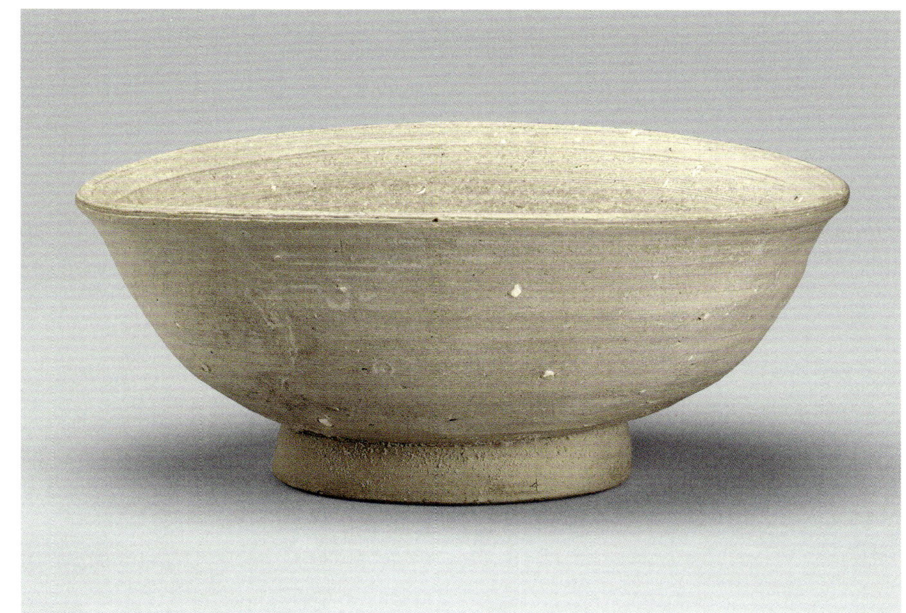

676

Miyagawa Kōzan
(宮川 [also known as Makuzu, 真葛] 香山; 1842–1916)

675. Quail-shaped incense burner

Meiji–Taishō era, 19th–20th century
Porcelain with glaze
H. 11.5 cm (4½ in.)

Arakawa Toyozō
(荒川豊蔵; 1894–1985)

676. Bowl

Shōwa era, 20th century
Shino (志野) type; glazed stoneware
Diam. 17.8 cm (7 in.)

Gift from N. V. Hammer, 1979

677

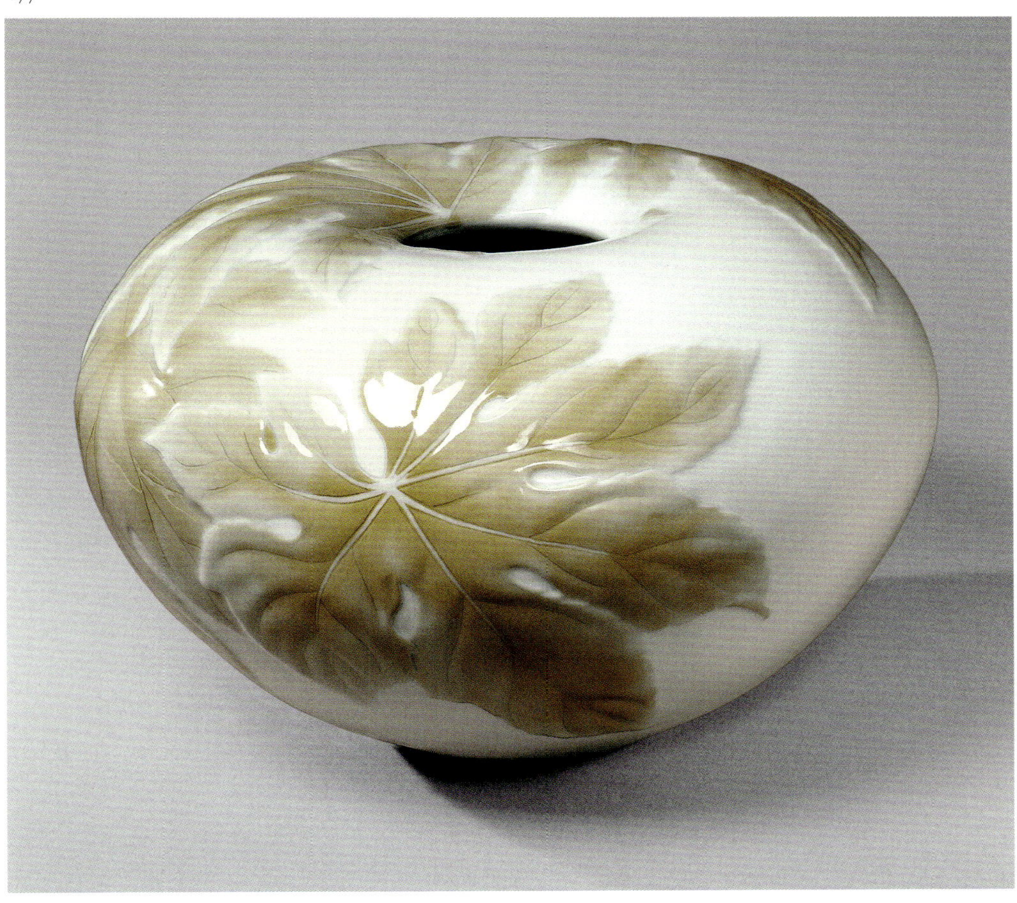

Akashi Ryūtarō
(明石竜太郎; b. 1971)

677. Vase with Japanese aralia design

Heisei era, 20th–21st century
White porcelain with low relief
H. 21.6 cm (8½ in.), diam. 33 cm (13 in.)
Signature

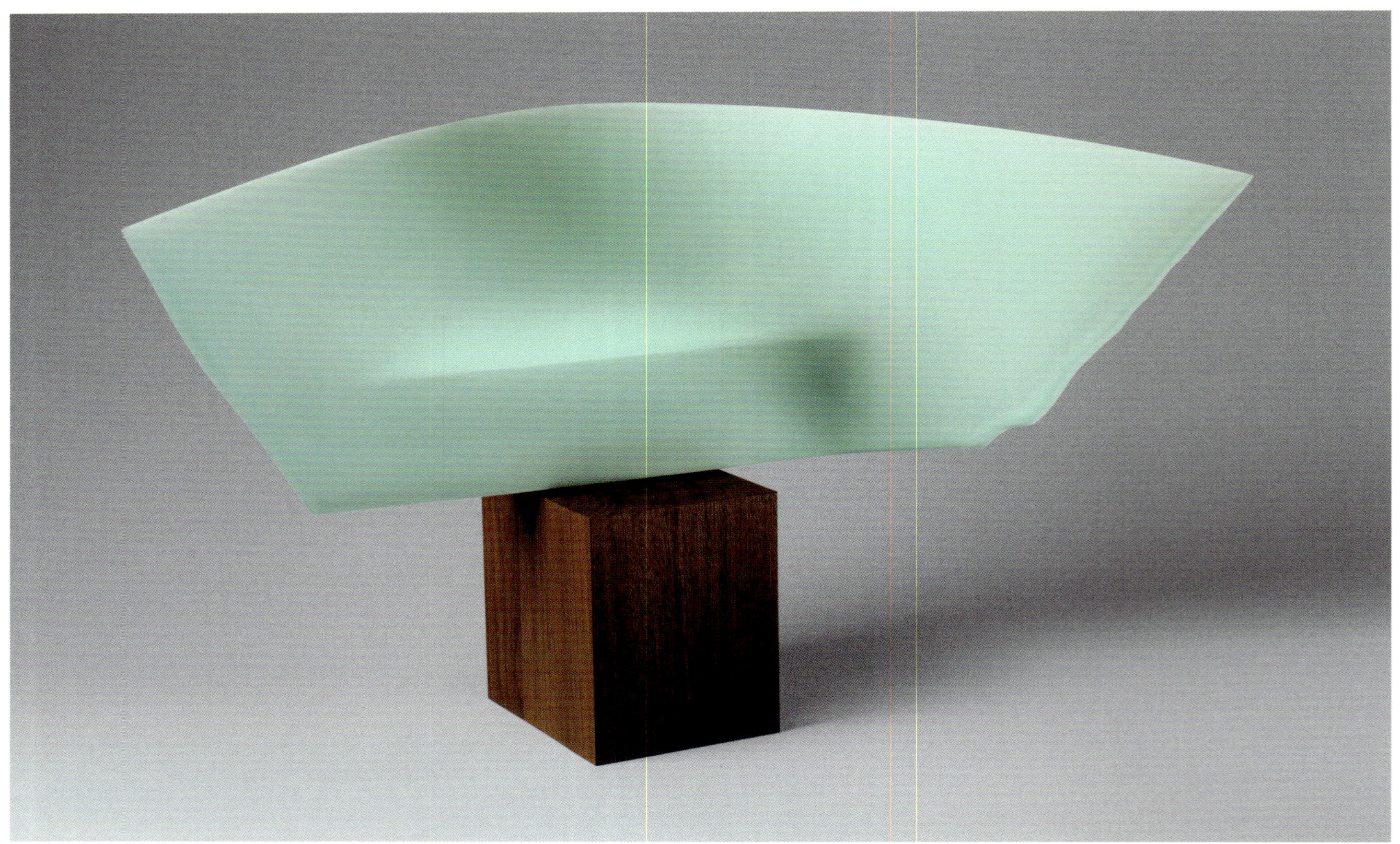

Fukami Sueharu
(深見陶治; b. 1947)

678. *Sky, Soaring*

Shōwa–Heisei era, 20th century
Porcelain with pale bluish-green glaze
L. 59.4 cm ($23\frac{3}{8}$ in.)

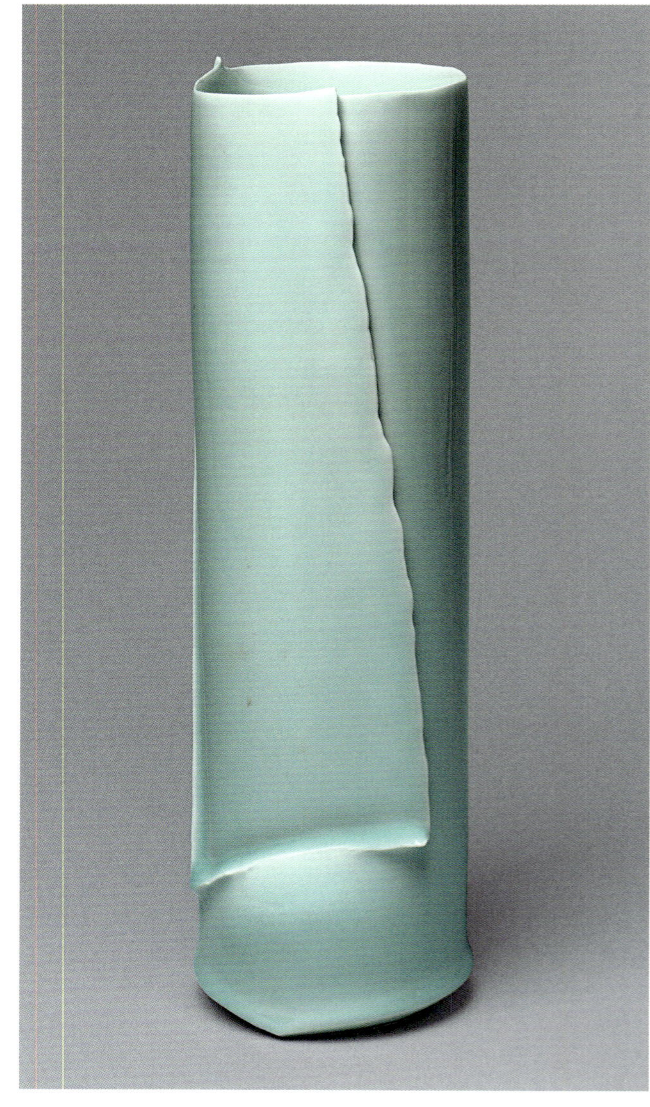

Fukami Sueharu
(深見陶治; b. 1947)

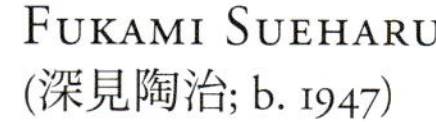

679. Vase

Shōwa–Heisei era, 20th century
Porcelain with pale bluish-green glaze
H. 34.1 cm ($13\frac{3}{8}$ in.)

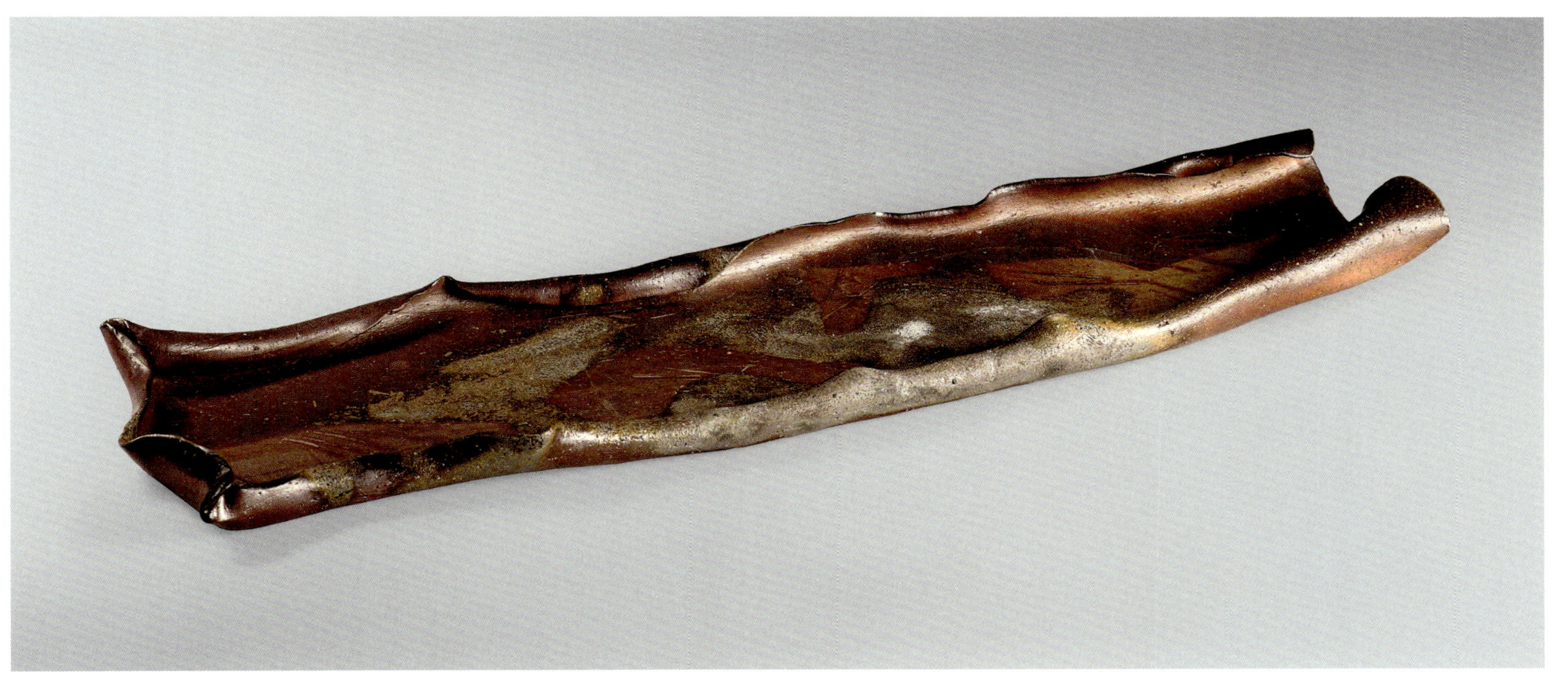

Fukushima Kazuo
(福島一夫; b. 1950)

680. Platter

Shōwa–Heisei era, 20th century
Bizen (備前) ware; stoneware with natural ash glaze
6.4 x 72.4 x 20.3 cm ($2^1/_2$ x $28^1/_2$ x 8 in.)

Furukawa Toshiko
(古川俊子; b. 1939)

681. Box with pampas grass

Shōwa–Heisei era, 20th century
Stoneware with overglaze enamels
4.2 x 19.7 x 19.1 cm ($1^5/_8$ x $7^3/_4$ x $7^1/_2$ in.)

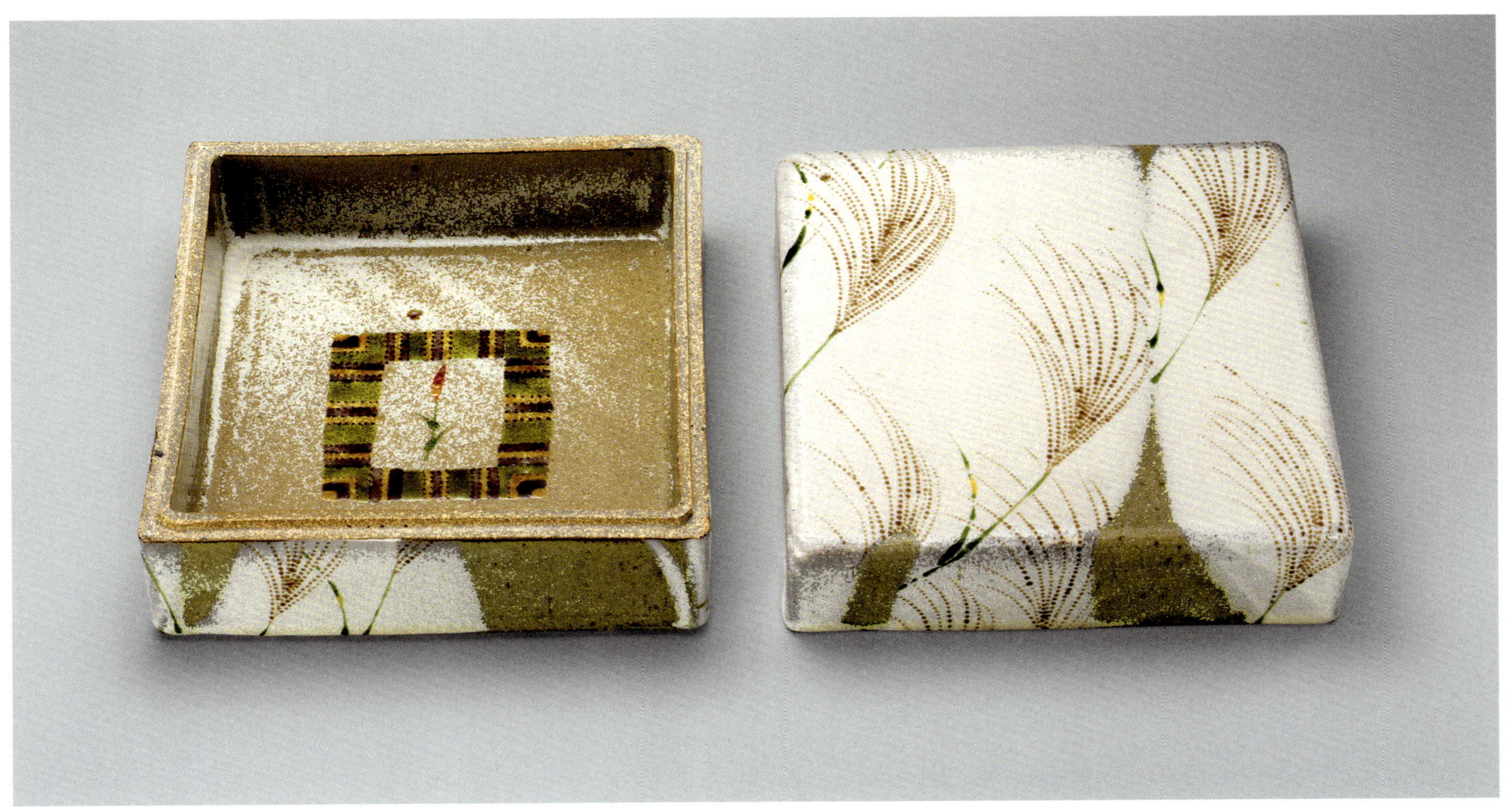

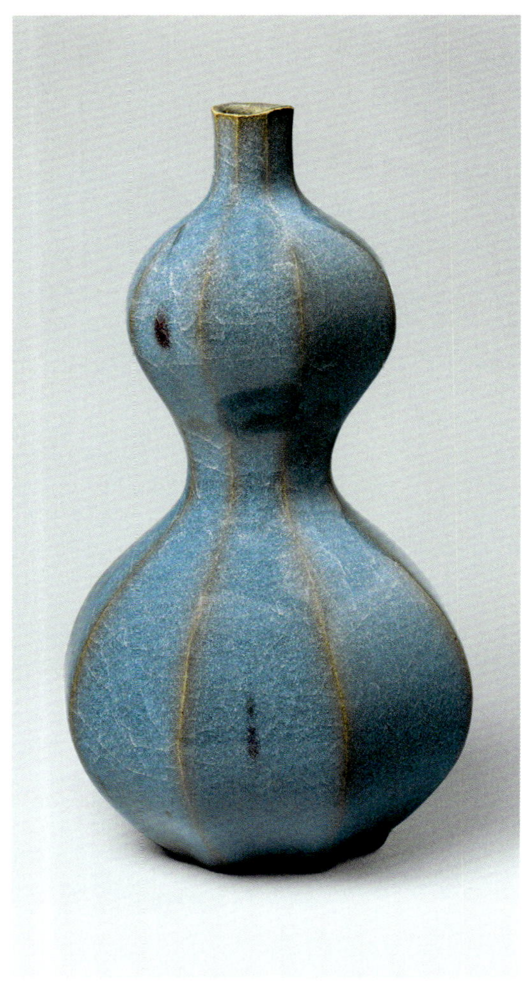

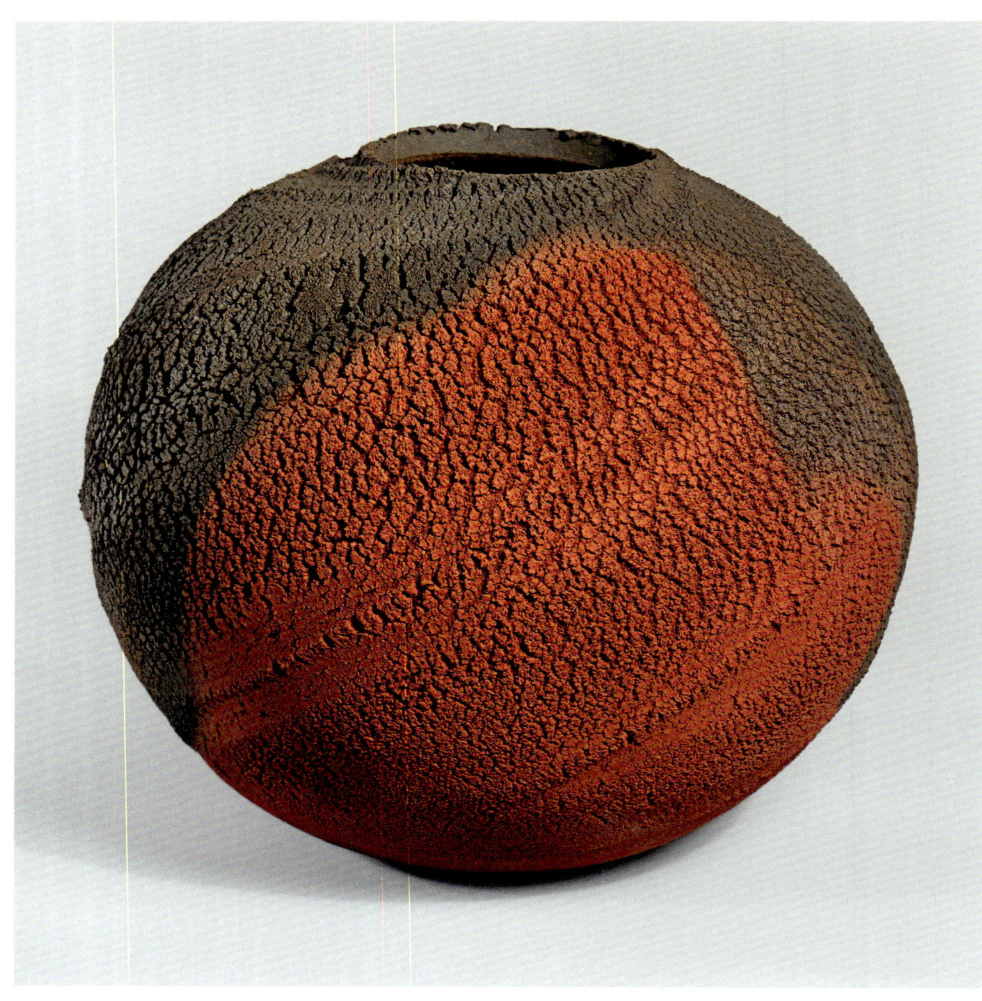

Hara Kiyoshi
(原清; b. 1936)

682. Double gourd–shaped vase

Shōwa era, 20th century
Glazed stoneware
H. 27.4 cm (10 3/4 in.)

Itō Sekisui
(伊藤赤水; b. 1941)

683. Vase

Shōwa era, 1984
Stoneware
H. 26.1 cm (10 1/4 in.)

Literature: Baekeland and Moes 1993, no. 81.

Imai Hyōe
(今井兵衛; b. 1951)

684. Bowl

Heisei era, 20th–21st century
Stoneware
H. 23 cm (9 in.), diam. 45.8 cm (18 in.)

Gift from the artist to the Mary and Jackson Burke Foundation, 2011

Kojima Kenji
(小島憲二; b. 1953)

685. Platter

Shōwa–Heisei era, 20th–21st century
Stoneware with green ash glaze
8.9 cm x 45.7 x 38.7 cm (3 1/2 x 18 x 15 1/4 in.)

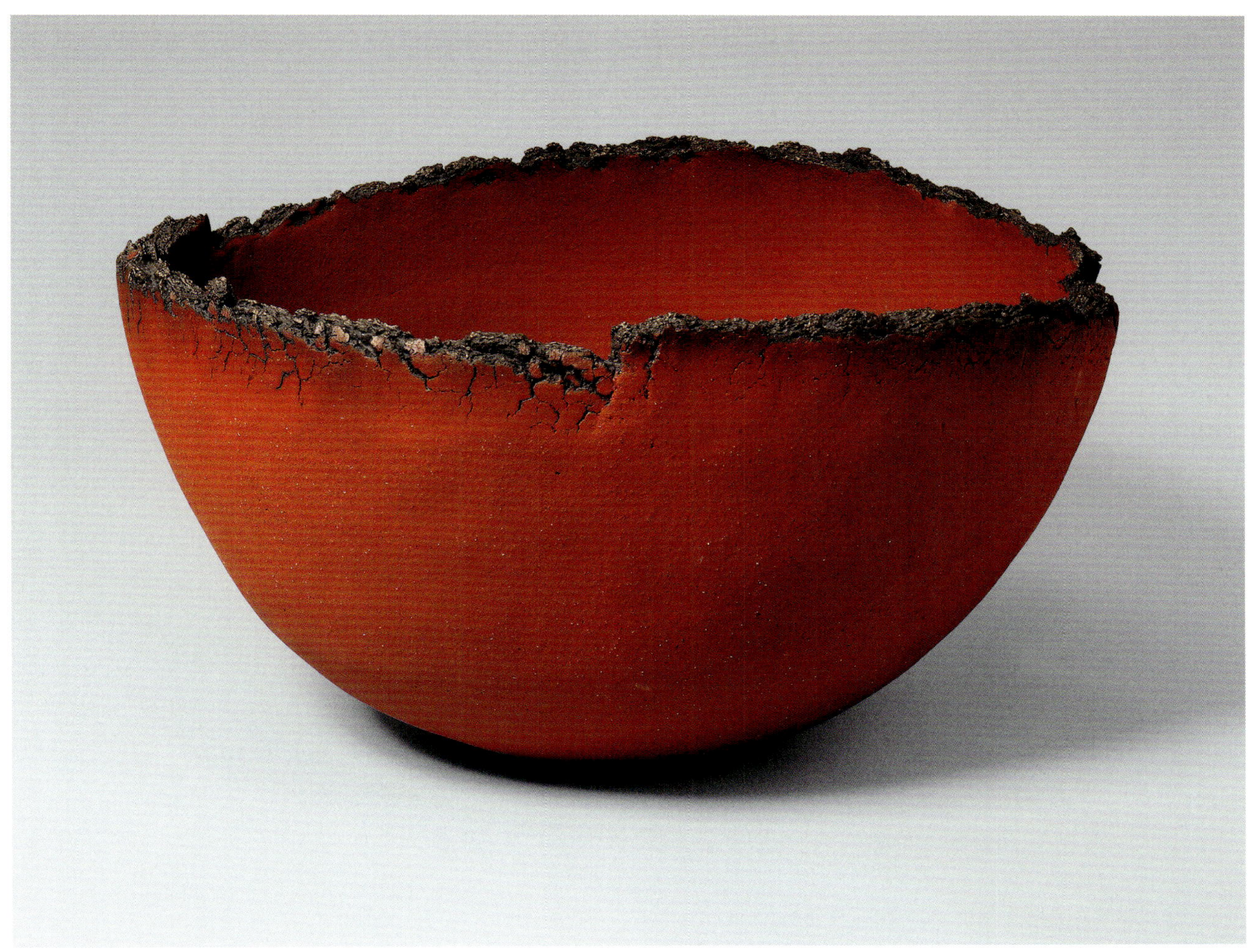

684

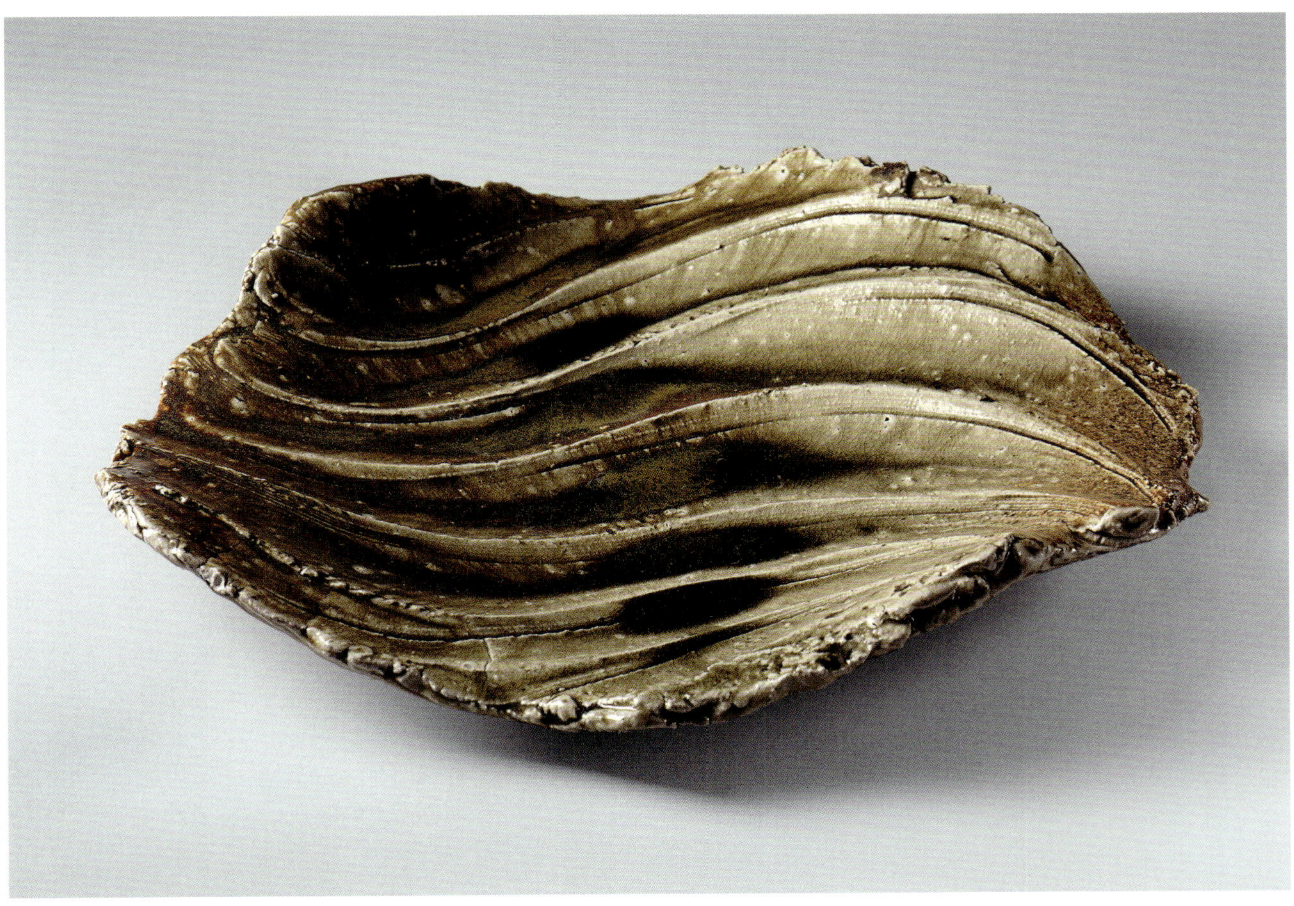

685

Kajitani Ban
(梶谷胖; b. 1941)

686. Vase

Shōwa era, 1980
Marbleized stoneware
H. 27.6 cm (10⅞ in.), diam. 23.3 cm (9⅛ in.)
Signature

Literature: Baekeland and Moes 1993, no. 85.

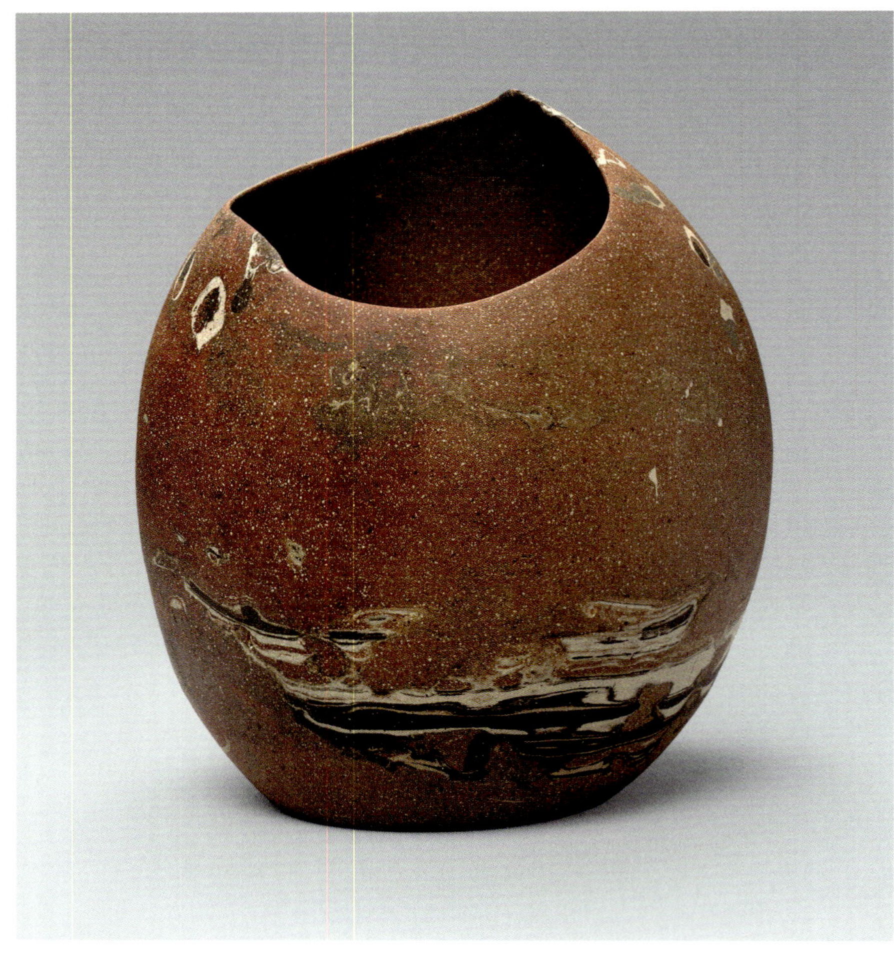

Kawasaki Tadao
(川崎忠夫; b. 1938)

687. Vase with leaves

Shōwa–Heisei era, 20th–21st century
Porcelain with overglaze enamels
H. 17.6 cm (6⅞ in.)

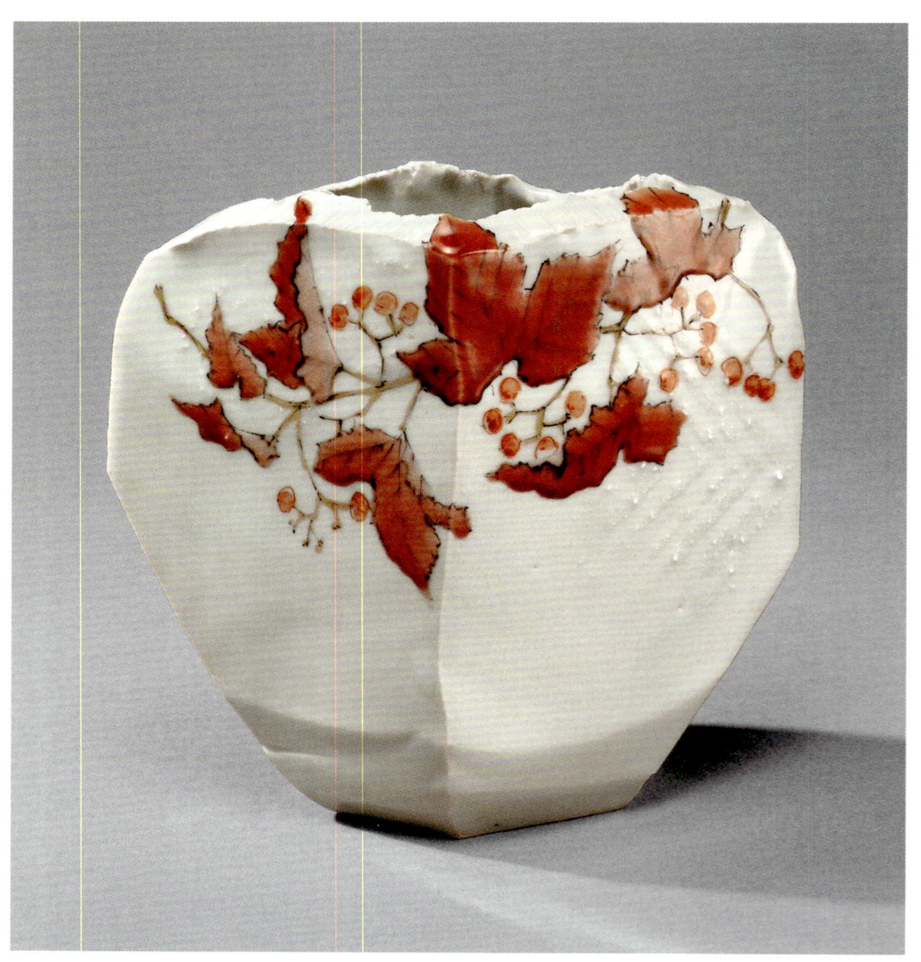

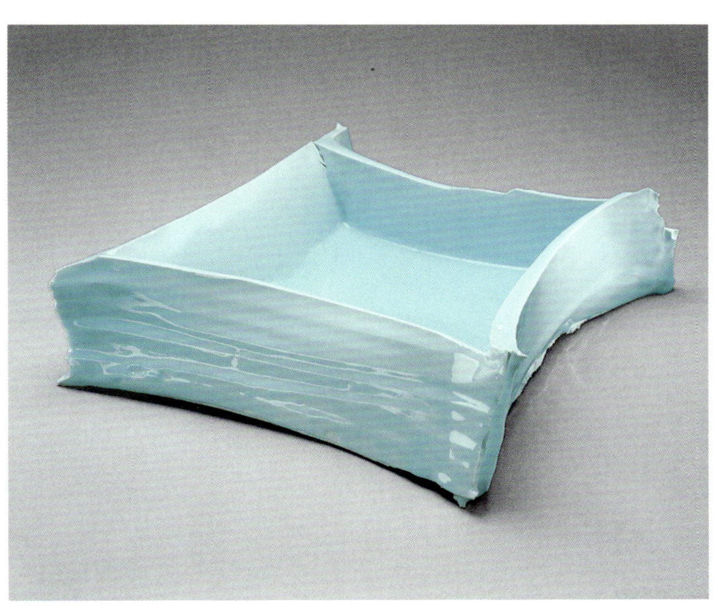

688

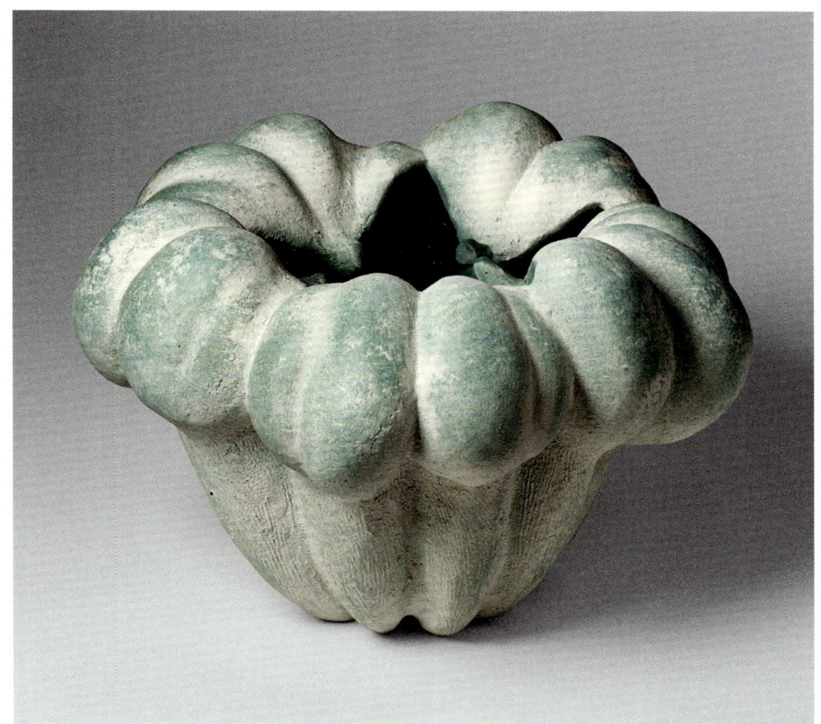

689

Katō Tsubusa
(加藤委; b. 1962)

688. Dish

Heisei era, 2002
Porcelain with glaze
11.4 x 40.6 x 39.4 cm (4 1/2 x 16 x 15 1/2 in.)

Katsumata Chieko
(勝間田千恵子; b. 1950)

689. Biomorphic vessel

Heisei era, 2005
Stoneware with turquoise and white glaze
H. 22.5 cm (8 7/8 in.)

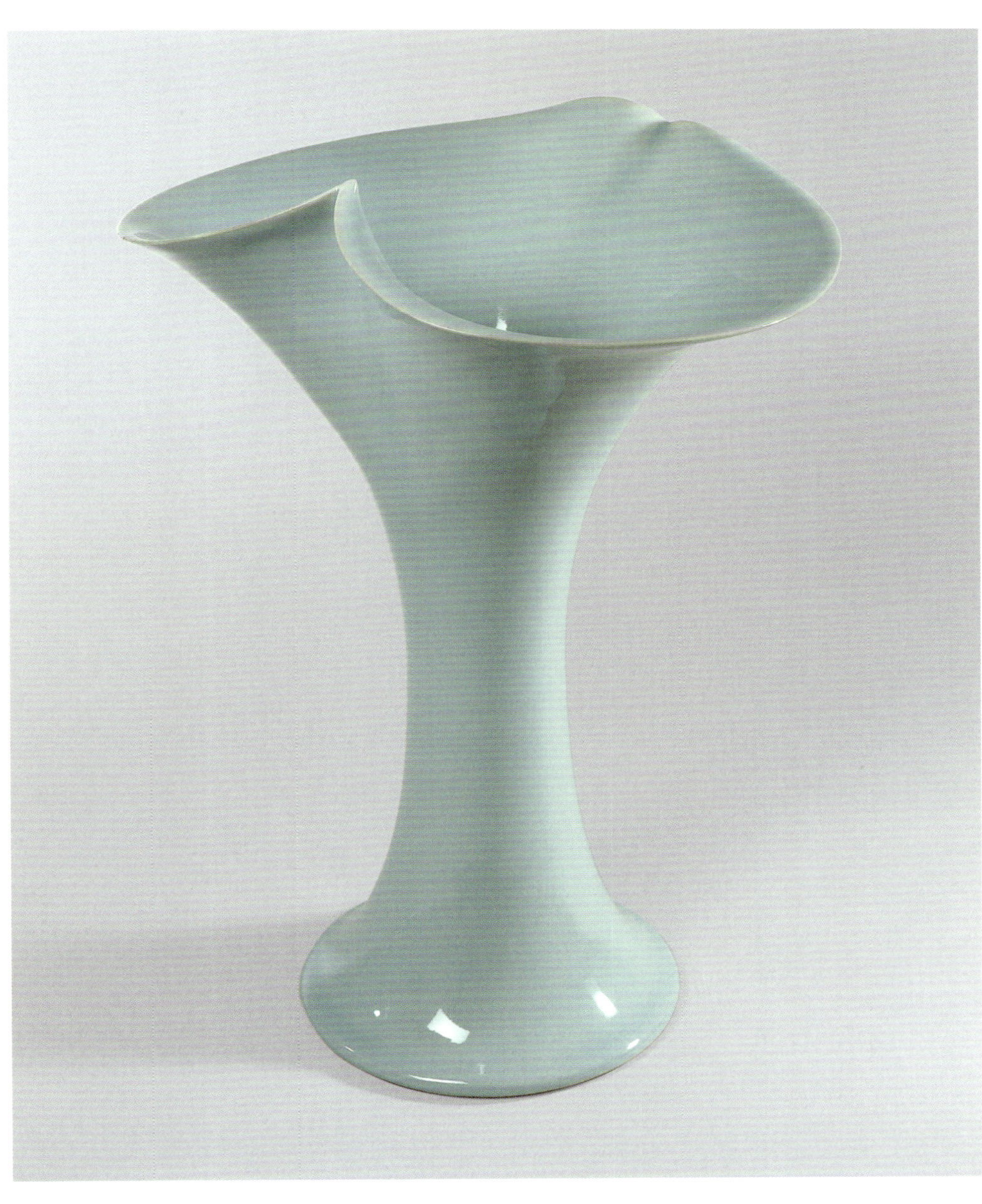

Kawase Shinobu
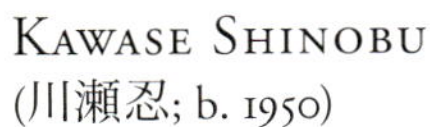
(川瀬忍; b. 1950)

690. Vase with lotus-shaped mouth

Heisei era, ca. 1996
Porcelaneous stoneware with bluish-green glaze
H. 28.4 cm (11 1/8 in.)

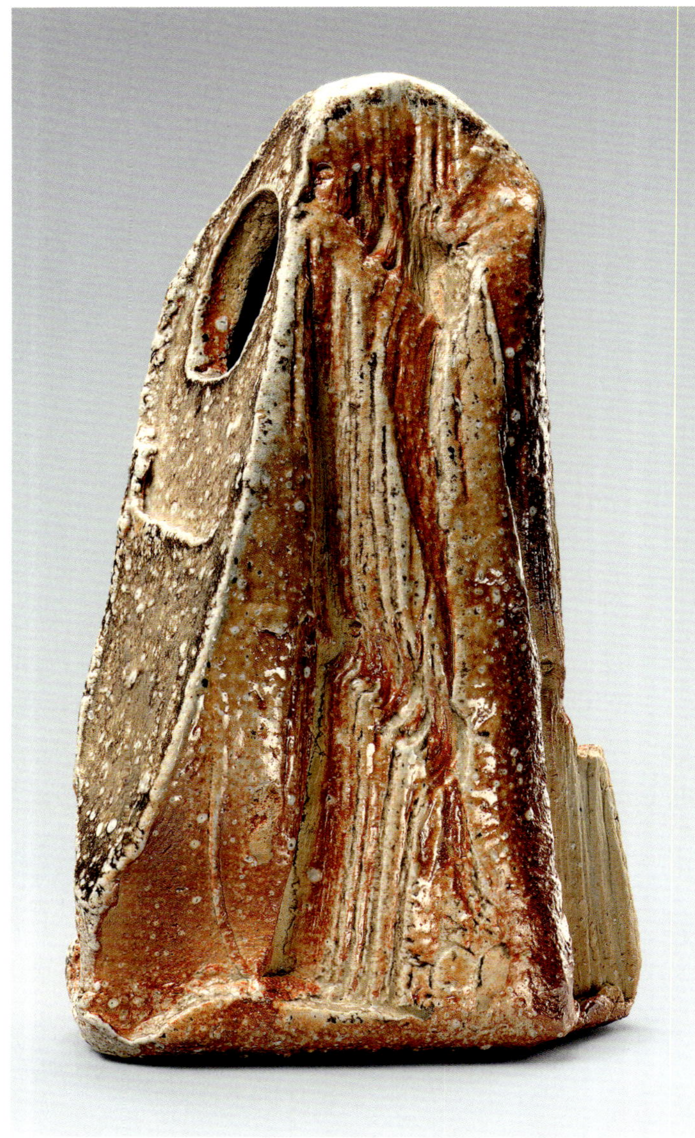

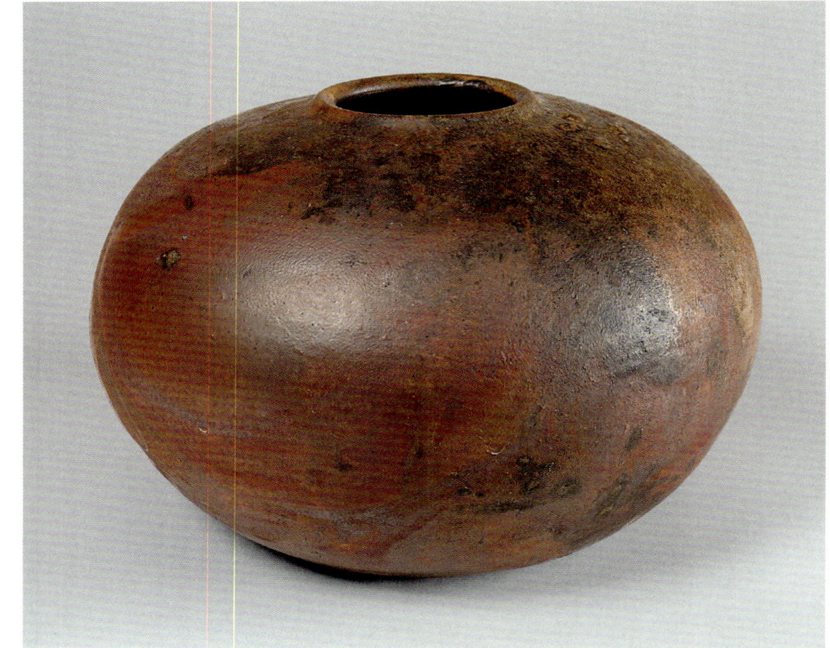

692

Kishimoto Kenji
(岸本謙仁; b. 1934)

691. Flower container

Shōwa era, 20th century
Iga (伊賀) type; stoneware with ash glaze
H. 33.5 cm (13¼ in.)

691

Kiyomizu Hisao
(清水久夫, also known as Honoho Tankyū, 炎探久; b. 1932)

692. Vase

Shōwa era, 1988
Tanba (丹波) ware; stoneware with natural ash glaze
H. 19.7 cm (7¾ in.), diam. 30.5 cm (12 in.)

Literature: Baekeland and Moes 1993, no. 12.

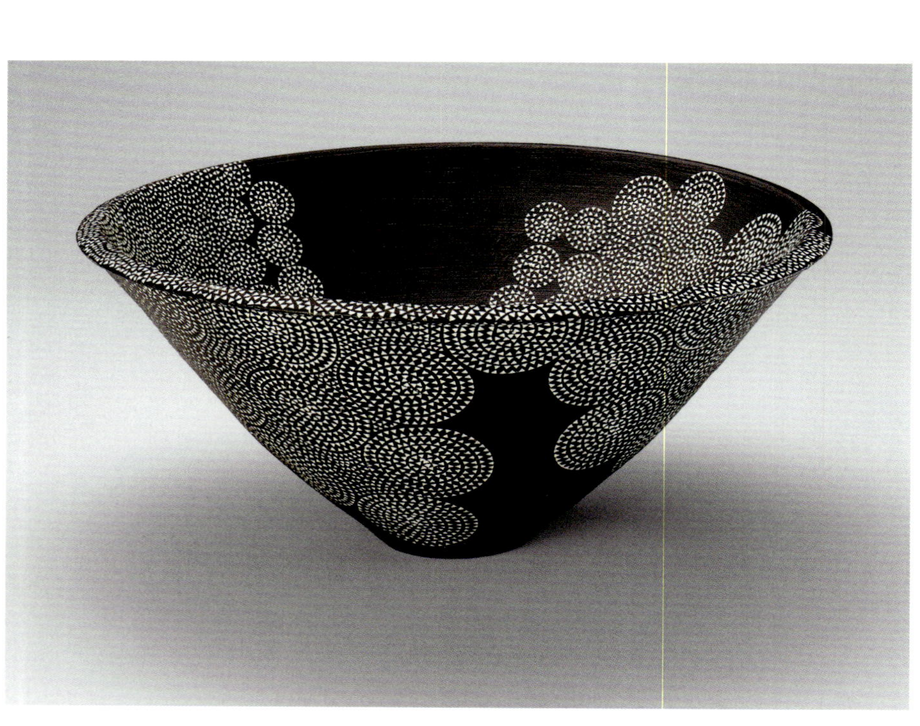

Kitamura Junko
(北村純子; b. 1956)

693. Bowl with abstract design

Heisei era, 1990
Stoneware with black glaze and punching with white slip inlay
H. 11.9 cm (4¾ in.), diam. 26.9 cm (10⅝ in.)

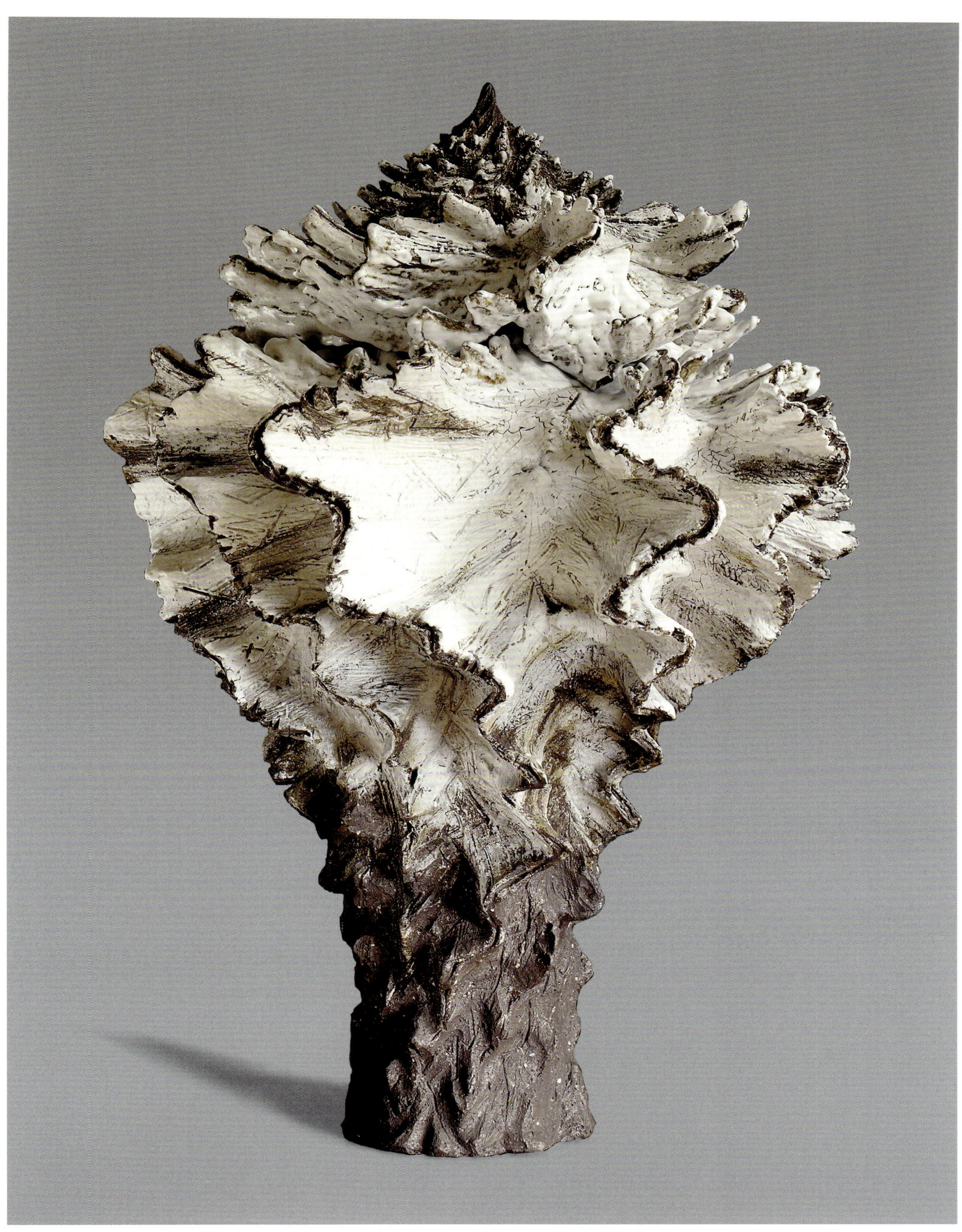

Koike Shōko
(小池頌子; b. 1943)

694. *Shell Vessel*

Heisei era, 1997
Stoneware with white glaze
H. 60 cm (23 5/8 in.)

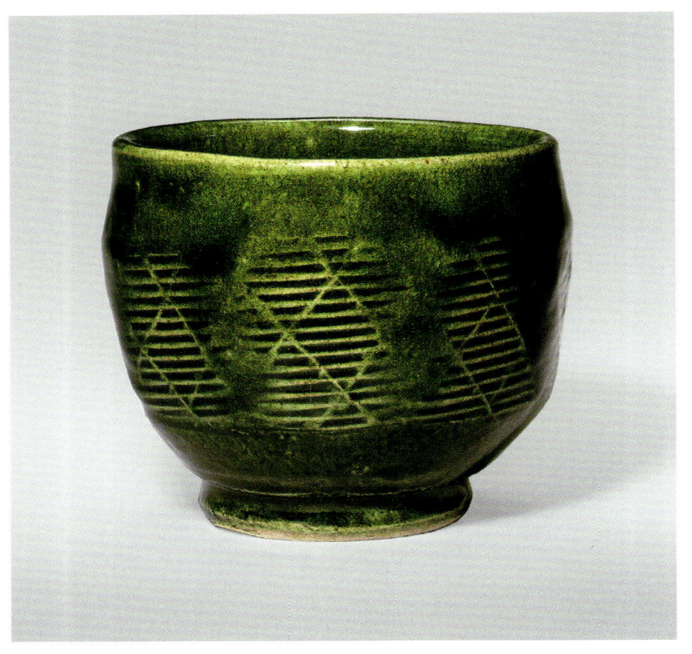

Maeda Yasuaki
(前田泰昭; b. 1937)

695. Tea bowl with diamond design

Shōwa era, 20th century
Stoneware with green glaze
H. 9.4 cm (3 3/4 in.)

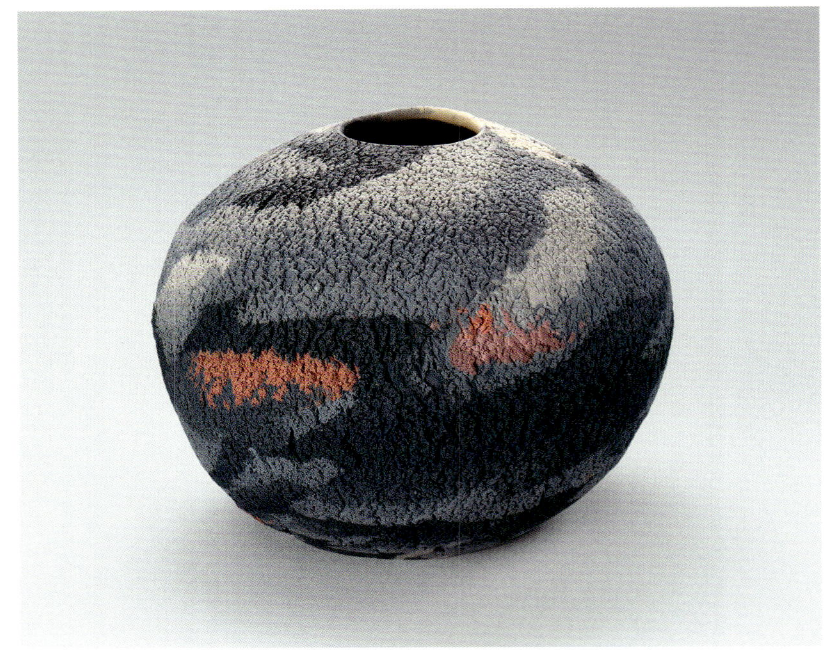

Matsui Kōsei
(松井康成; 1927–2003)

696. Vase

Shōwa era, 1980s
Marbleized stoneware
H. 10.9 cm (4 1/4 in.)
Signature

Matsuda Yuriko
(松田百合子; b. 1943)

697. *Itonamu* (Conduct)

Heisei era, 1990s
Porcelain with overglaze enamels and gold
Left foot: 9 x 25 cm (3 1/2 x 9 7/8 in.)
Right foot: 9 x 20 cm (3 1/2 x 7 7/8 in.)

Gift from Eleanor Briggs, 2004

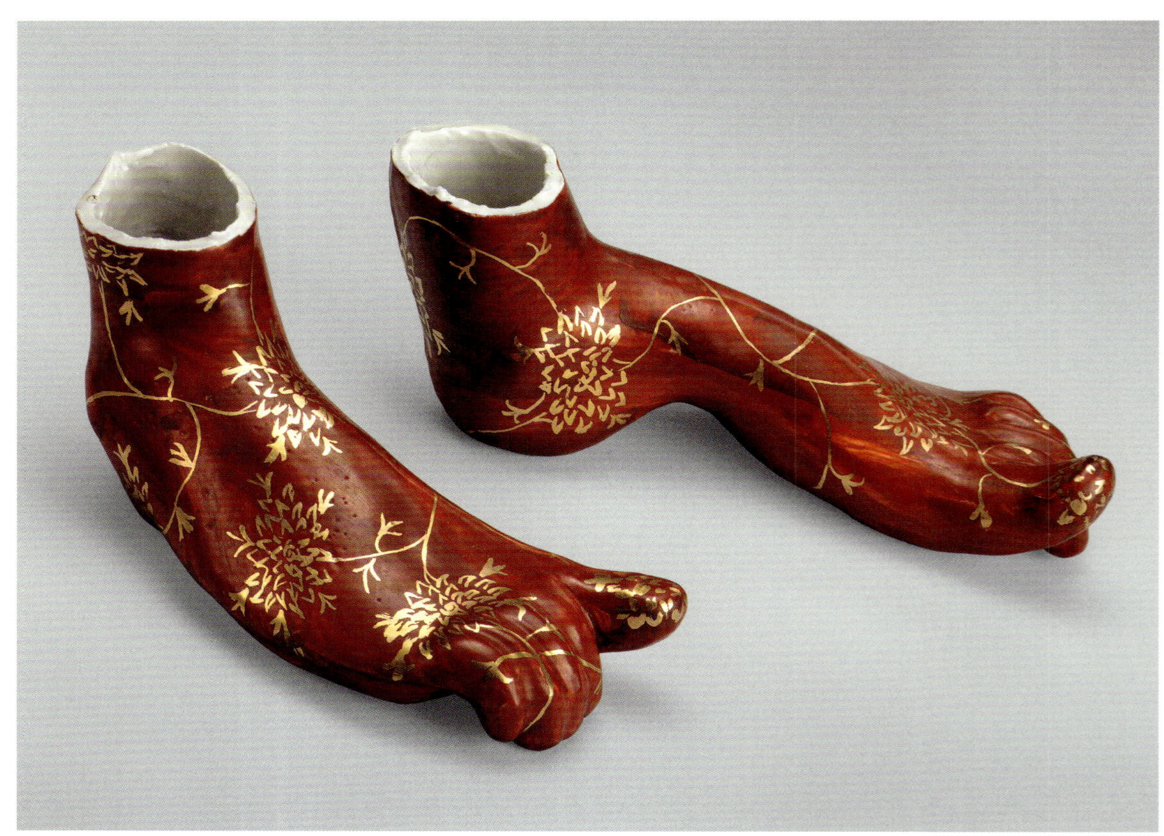

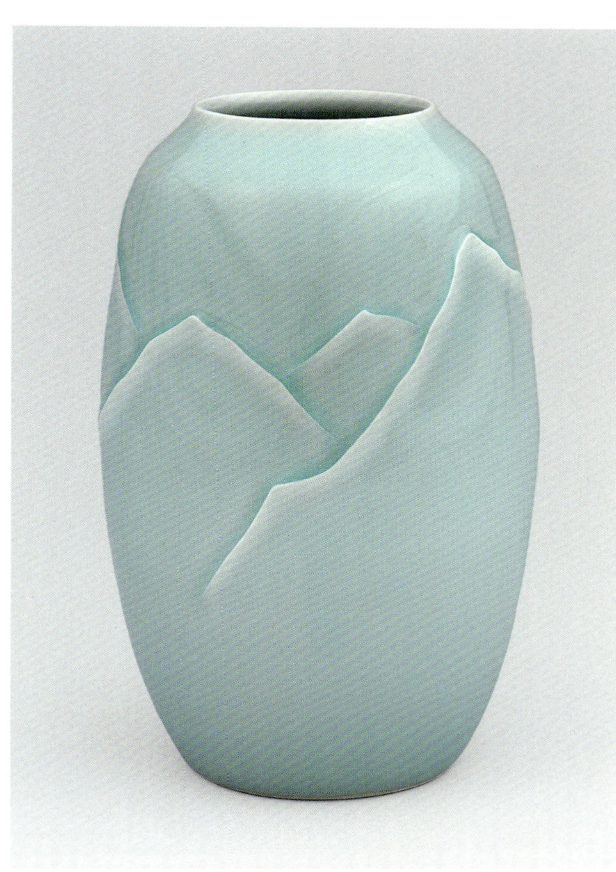

Matsumoto Isami
(松本為佐視; b. 1931)

698. Vase with mountains

Shōwa–Heisei era, 20th century
Porcelain with low relief and pale bluish-green glaze
H. 21.7 cm (8½ in.)
Seal

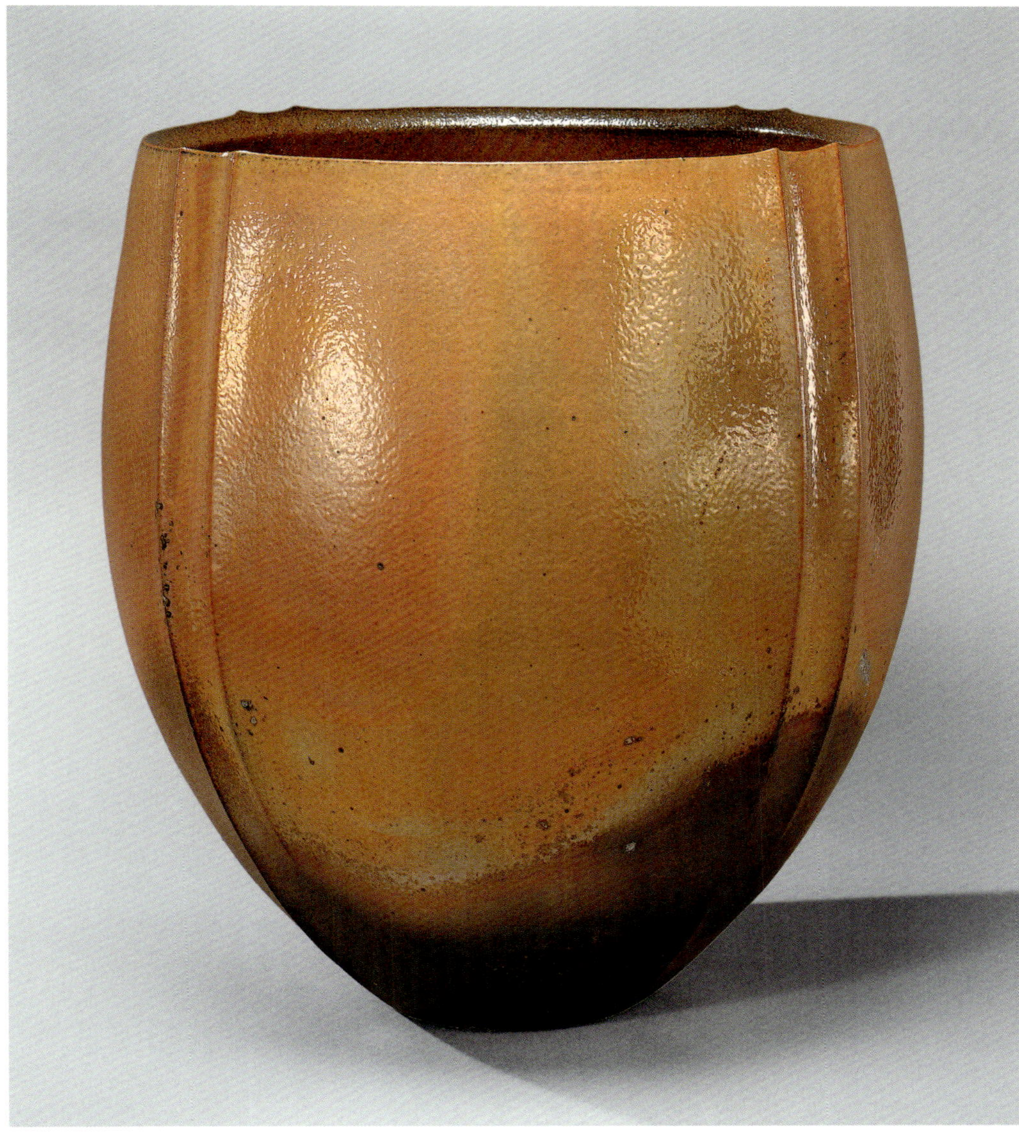

Matsuo Jun
(松尾潤; b. 1961)

699. Vessel

Heisei era, 21st century
Stoneware with luster glaze
H. 36.7 cm (14½ in.)
Seal

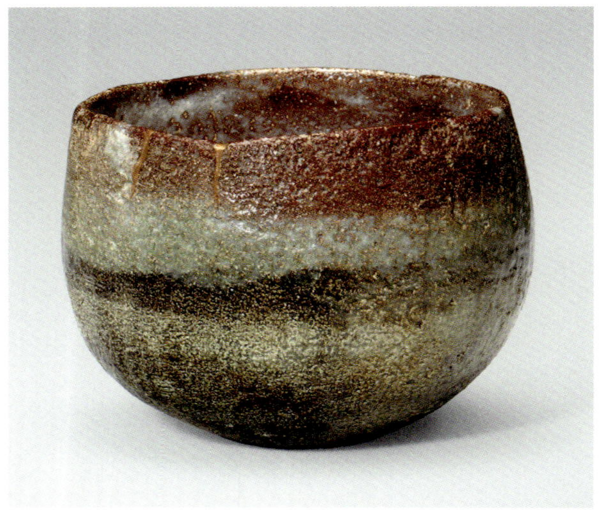

700

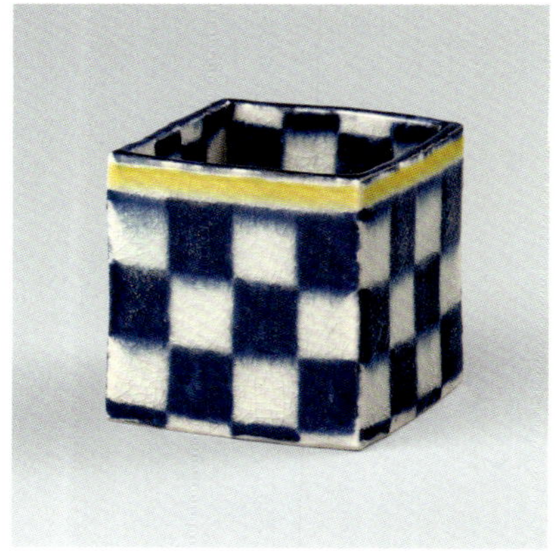

701

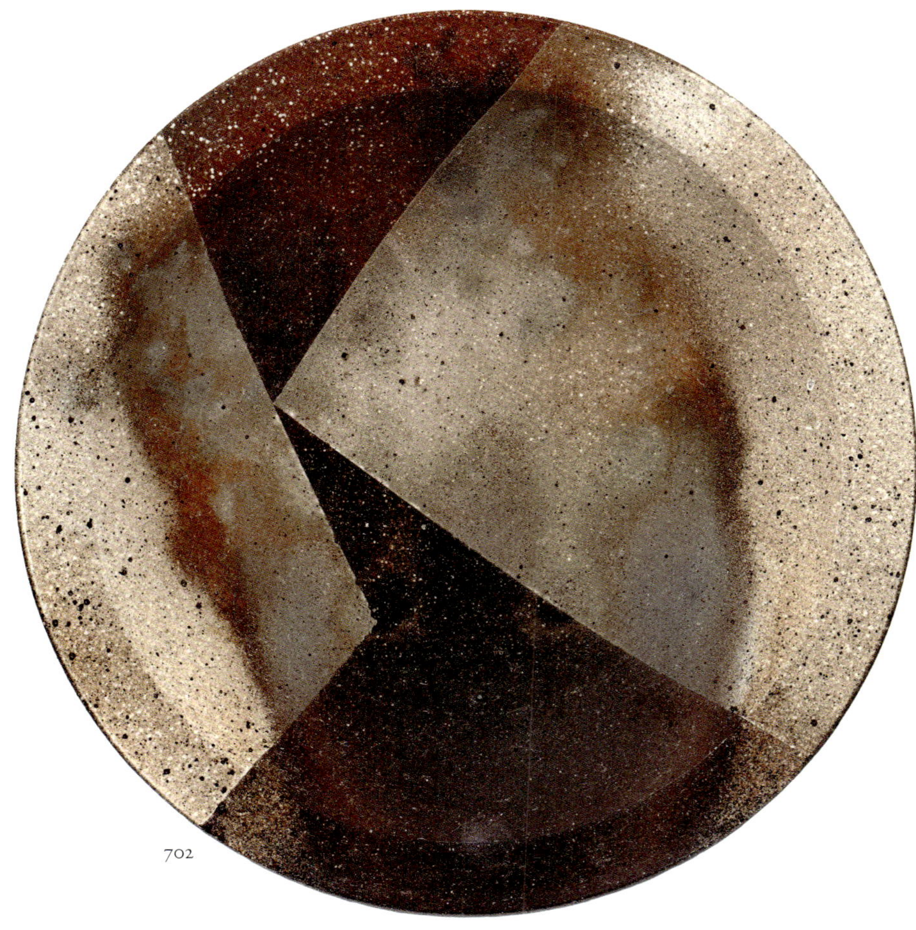

702

MURASE JIHEI
(村瀬治兵衛; 1898–1972)

700. Tea bowl

1964
Raku (楽) type; earthenware with clay of various colors
H. 11.5 cm (4 1/2 in.)
Mark

MURATA MAKOTO
(村田真人; b. 1956)

701. Sake cup with checkerboard design in the style of Ogata Kenzan (尾形乾山; 1663–1743)

Heisei era, 21st century
Porcelain with underglaze cobalt
Diam. at widest point 4.6 cm (1 3/4 in.)
Text, seal

Gift from the Miho Museum, 2005

NOMURA HIROYUKI
(野村博行; b. 1956)

702. Dish with geometric design

Shōwa–Heisei era, 20th century
Stoneware
Diam. 29.4 cm (11 5/8 in.)
Signature

OGATA KAMIO
(尾形香三夫; b. 1949)

703. Beehive-shaped vase

Shōwa–Heisei era, 20th century
Marbleized stoneware
H. 12.5 cm (4 7/8 in.)

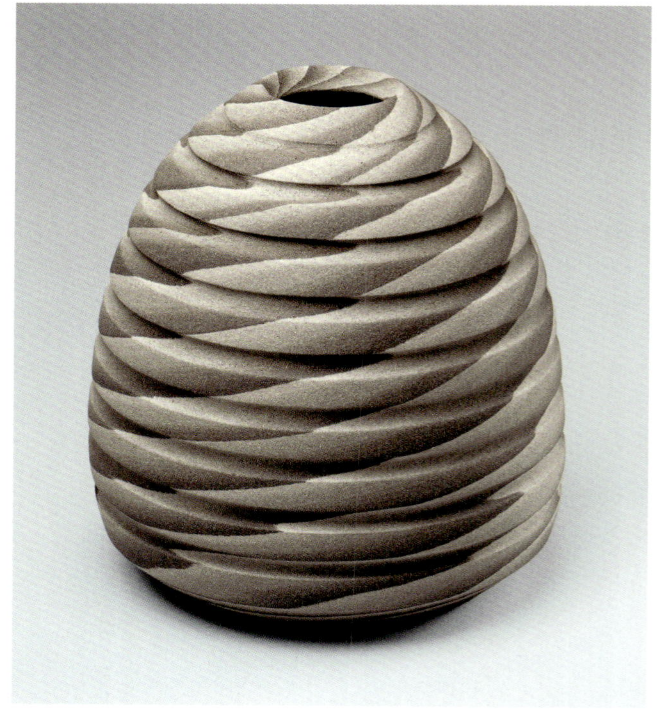

703

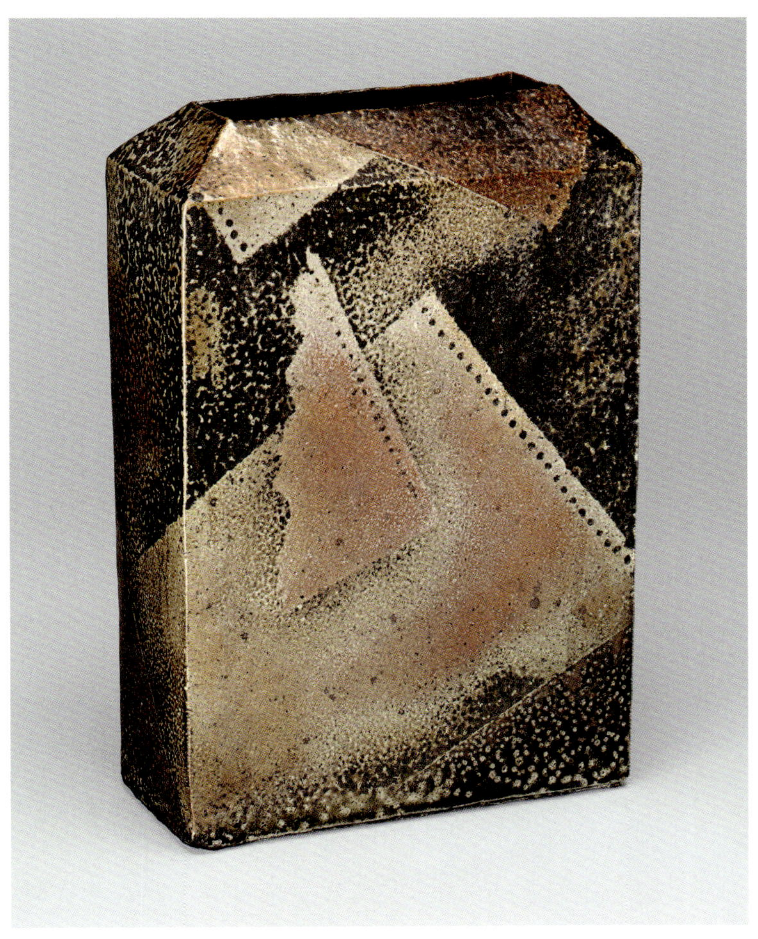

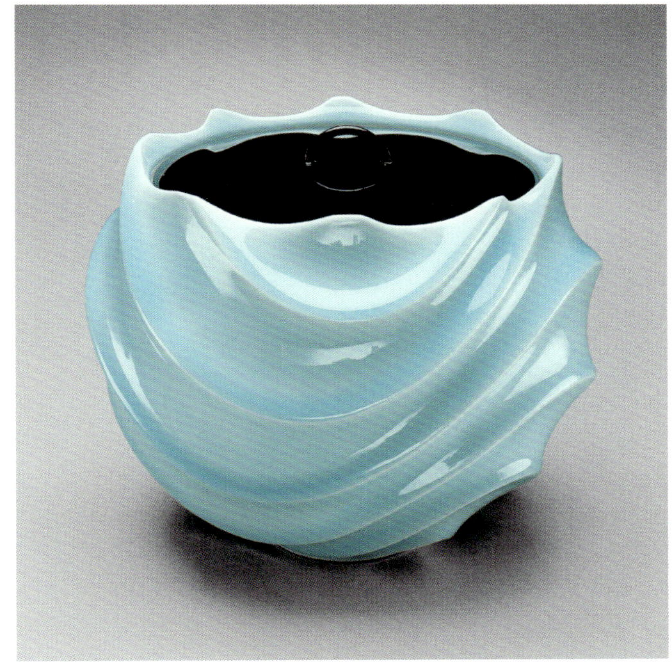

Okada Kenzō
(岡田謙三; b. 1948)

704. Vase

Shōwa–Heisei era, 20th century
Stoneware with salt glaze
H. 29.5 cm (11⅝ in.)

Ōno Kōtaro
(大野耕太郎; b. 1953)

705. Freshwater jar (*mizusashi*, 水差) with lid

Heisei era, 2003
Porcelain with celadon glaze; lacquer (lid)
H. 15.9 cm (6¼ in.)

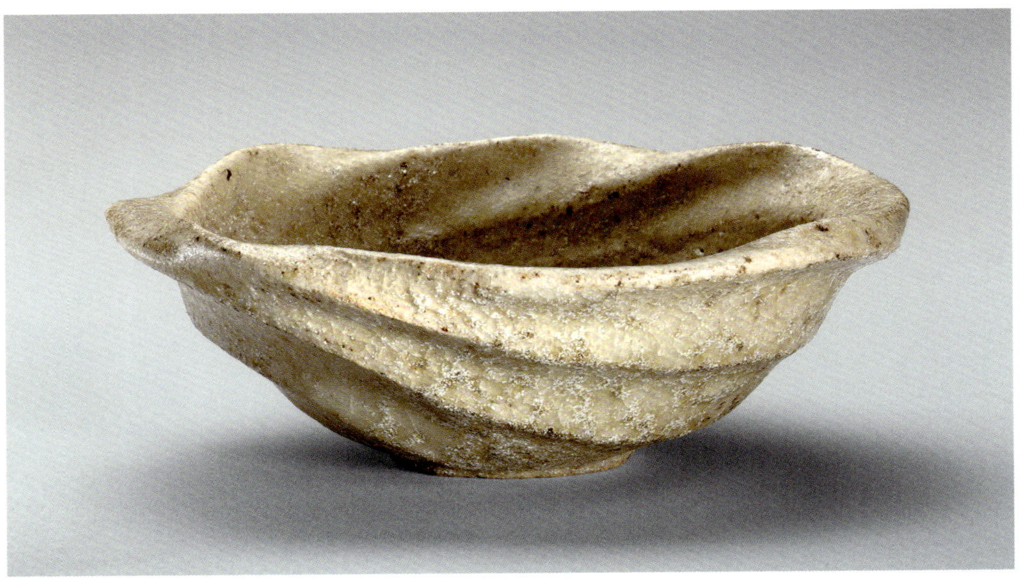

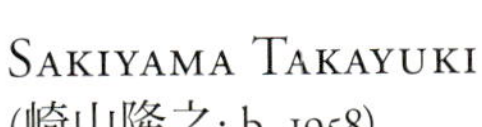

Sakiyama Takayuki
(崎山隆之; b. 1958)

706. *Listening to Waves*

Shōwa–Heisei era, 20th–21st century
Sand-glazed stoneware
5.4 x 14.9 x 12.5 cm (2⅛ x 5⅞ x 4⅞ in.)

Gift from the artist, 2004

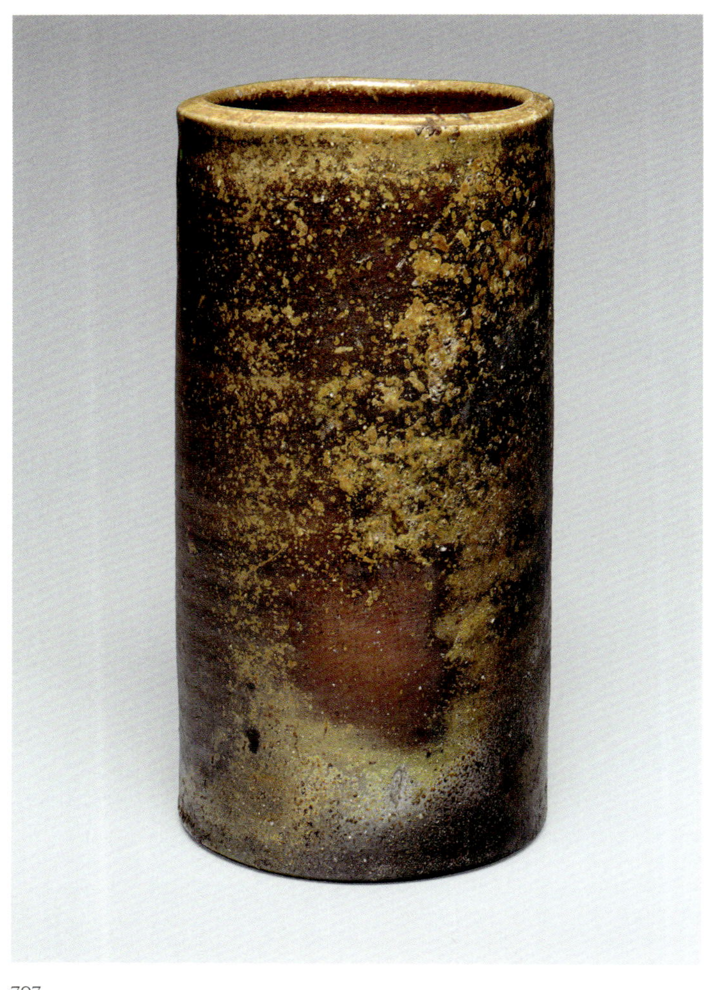

707

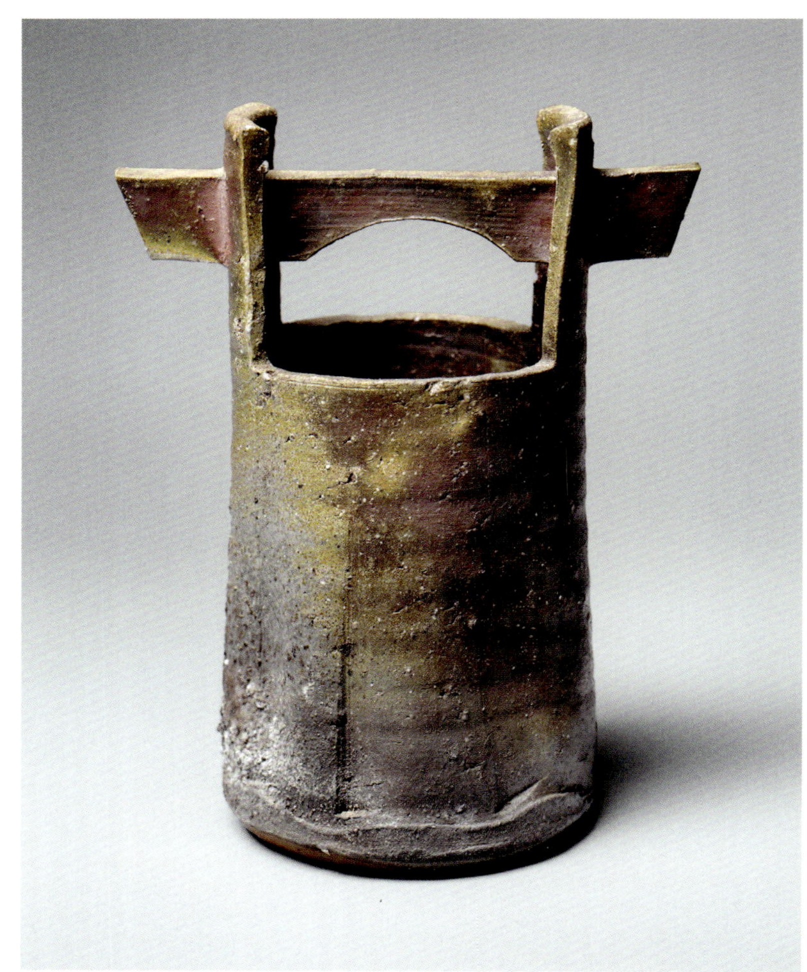

708

Shibaoka Masashi
(柴岡正志; b. 1946)

707. Vase

Shōwa era, late 1970s
Bizen (備前) ware; stoneware with natural ash glaze
H. 26.8 cm (10 1/2 in.)

Suzuki Kōichi
(鈴木黄弌; b. 1942)

708. Bucket-shaped vase with handle

Shōwa era, ca. 1983
Bizen (備前) ware; stoneware with natural ash glaze
H. 26.4 cm (10 3/8 in.)
Signature

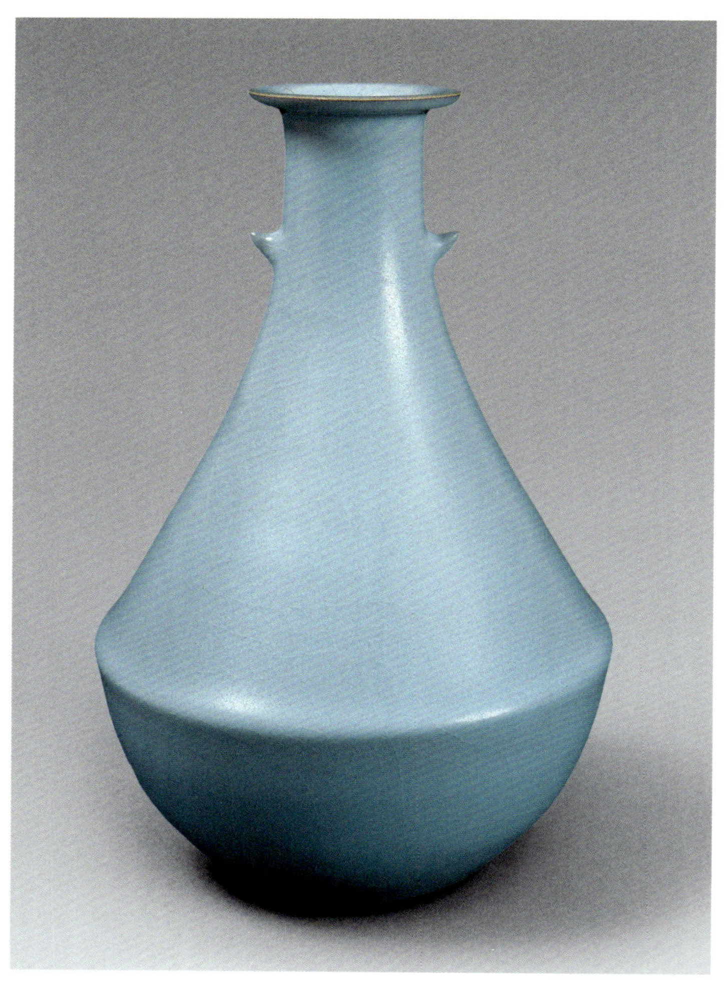

Suzuki Sansei
(鈴木三成; b. 1936)

709. Vase

Shōwa era, 1987
Celadon porcelain
H. 30.1 cm (11 7/8 in.)

Literature: Baekeland and Moes 1993, no. 54.

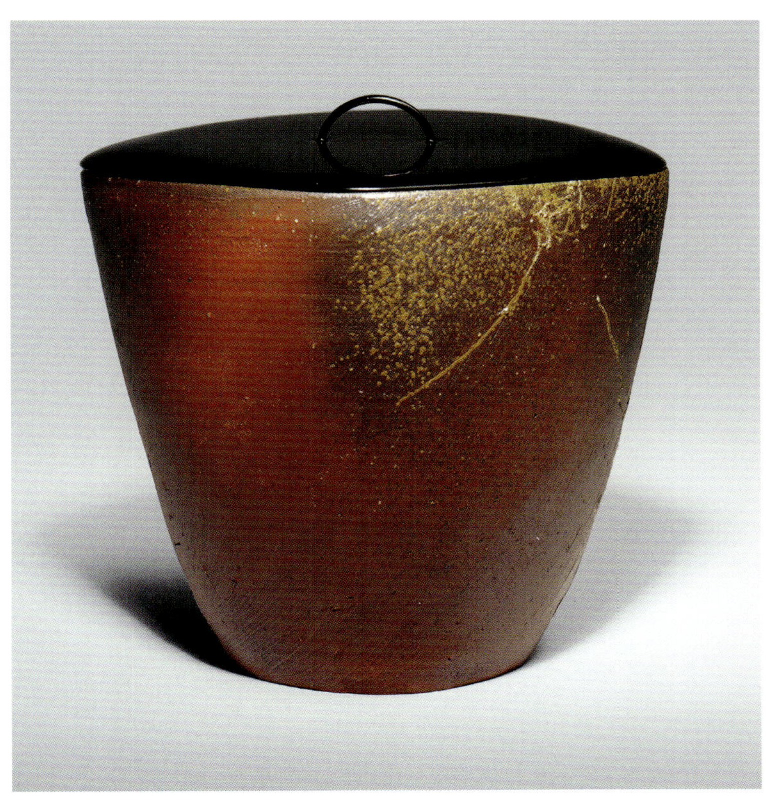

Takahara Shōji
(高原昌治; 1941–2000)

710. Freshwater jar (*mizusashi*, 水差) with lid

Shōwa era, 20th century
Bizen (備前) ware, stoneware with natural ash glaze; lacquer (lid)
H. 16.6 cm (6 1/2 in.)

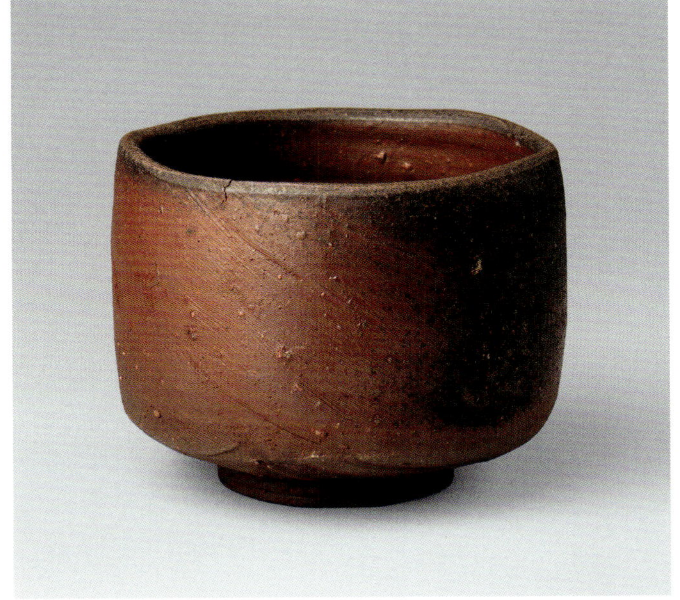

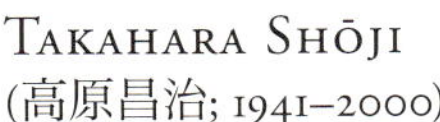

Takahara Shōji
(高原昌治; 1941–2000)

711. Tea bowl

Shōwa era, 20th century
Bizen (備前) ware; stoneware with natural ash glaze
Diam. 11 cm (4 3/8 in.)

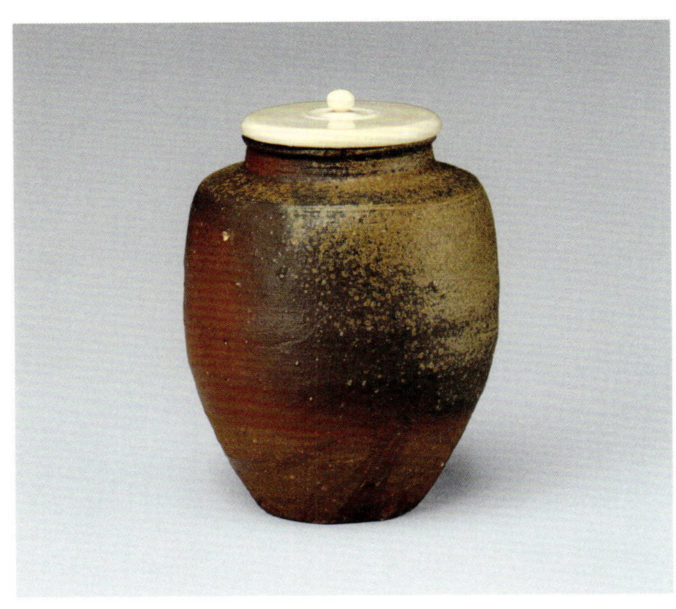

Takahara Shōji
(高原昌治; 1941–2000)

712. Tea caddy (*chaire*, 茶入れ)

Shōwa era, 20th century
Bizen (備前) ware; stoneware with natural ash glaze
H. 9.5 cm (3 3/4 in.)

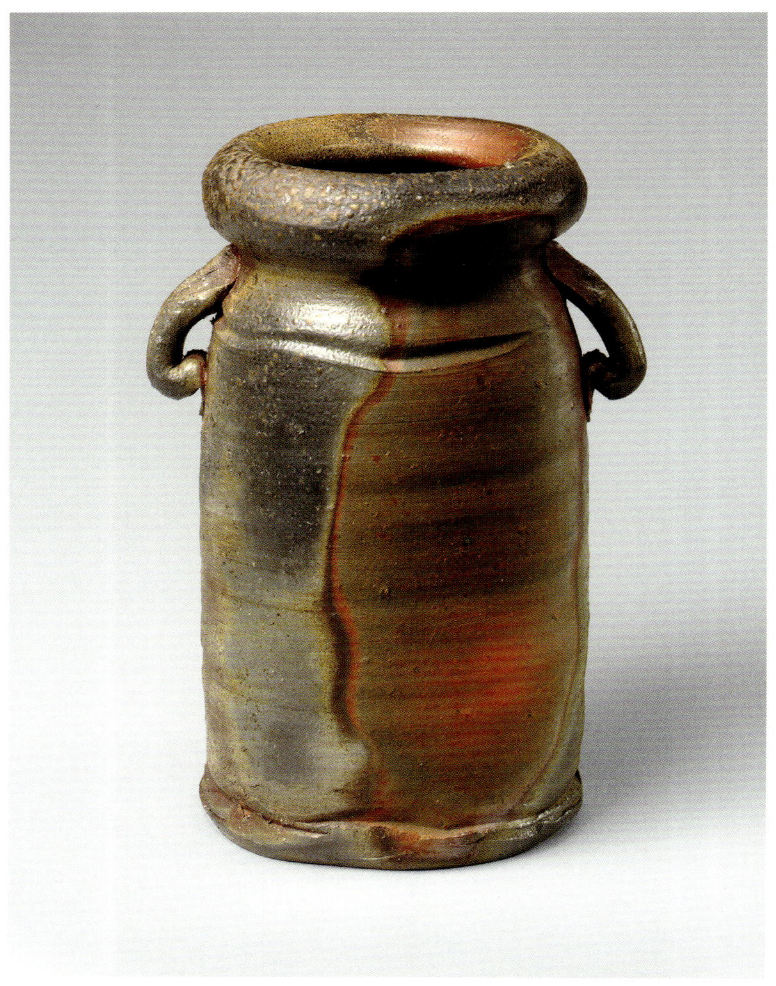

713

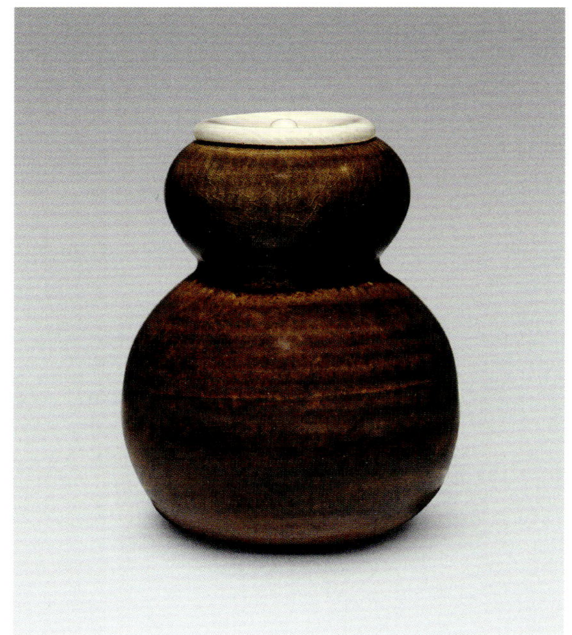

714

Takahara Shōji
(高原昌治; 1941–2000)

713. Vase

Shōwa era, 1986–87
Bizen (備前) ware; stoneware with natural ash glaze
H. 23.5 cm (9 1/4 in.)

Takatori Seizan
(高取静山; 1910–1983)

714. Tea caddy (*chaire*, 茶入れ)

Shōwa era, 1977
Takatori (高取) ware; glazed stoneware
H. 8.9 cm (3 1/2 in.)

Literature: Pekarik 1978, no. 89.

Takahashi Shunsai
(高橋春斎; b. 1927)

715. Bowl

Shōwa era, 20th century
Shigaraki (信楽) ware; stoneware
Diam. 29.5 cm (11 5/8 in.)

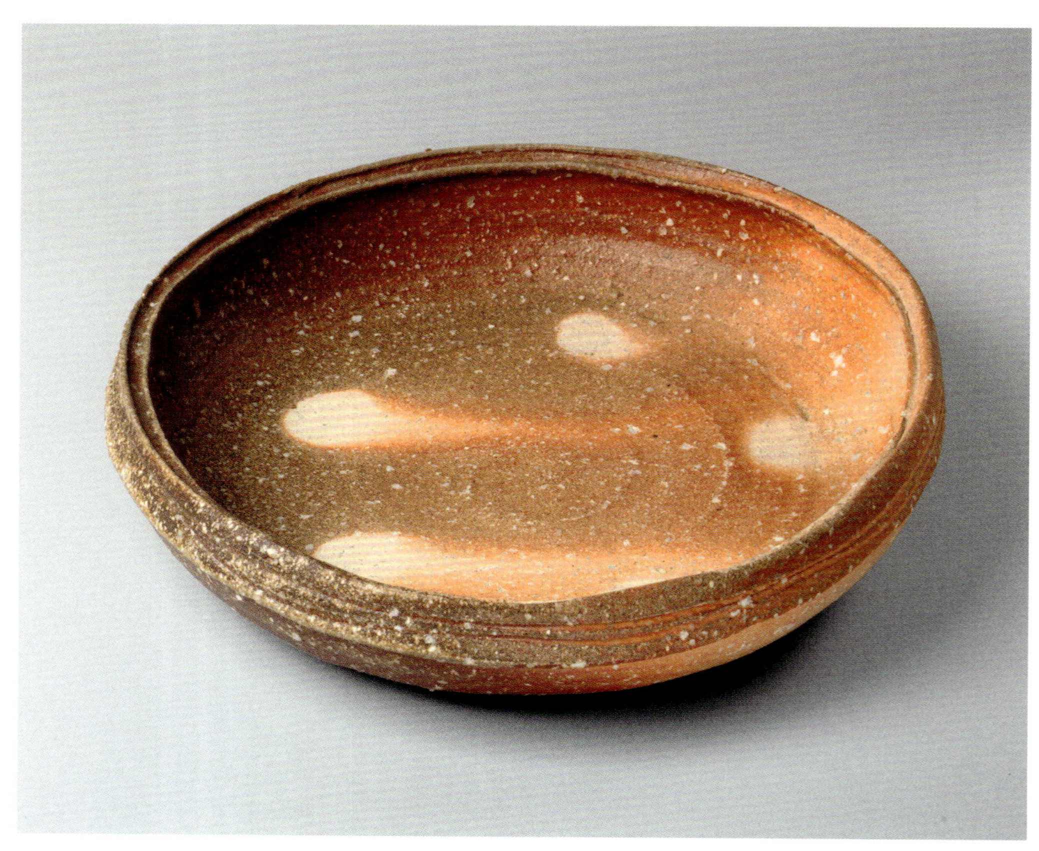

715

Takeda Toshio
(武田敏男; b. 1932)

716. Jar with *murasaki* plant

Shōwa era, 1982
Stoneware with iron and silver oxide
H. 26.7 cm (10 1/2 in.)
Seal

Literature: Baekeland and Moes 1993, no. 5.

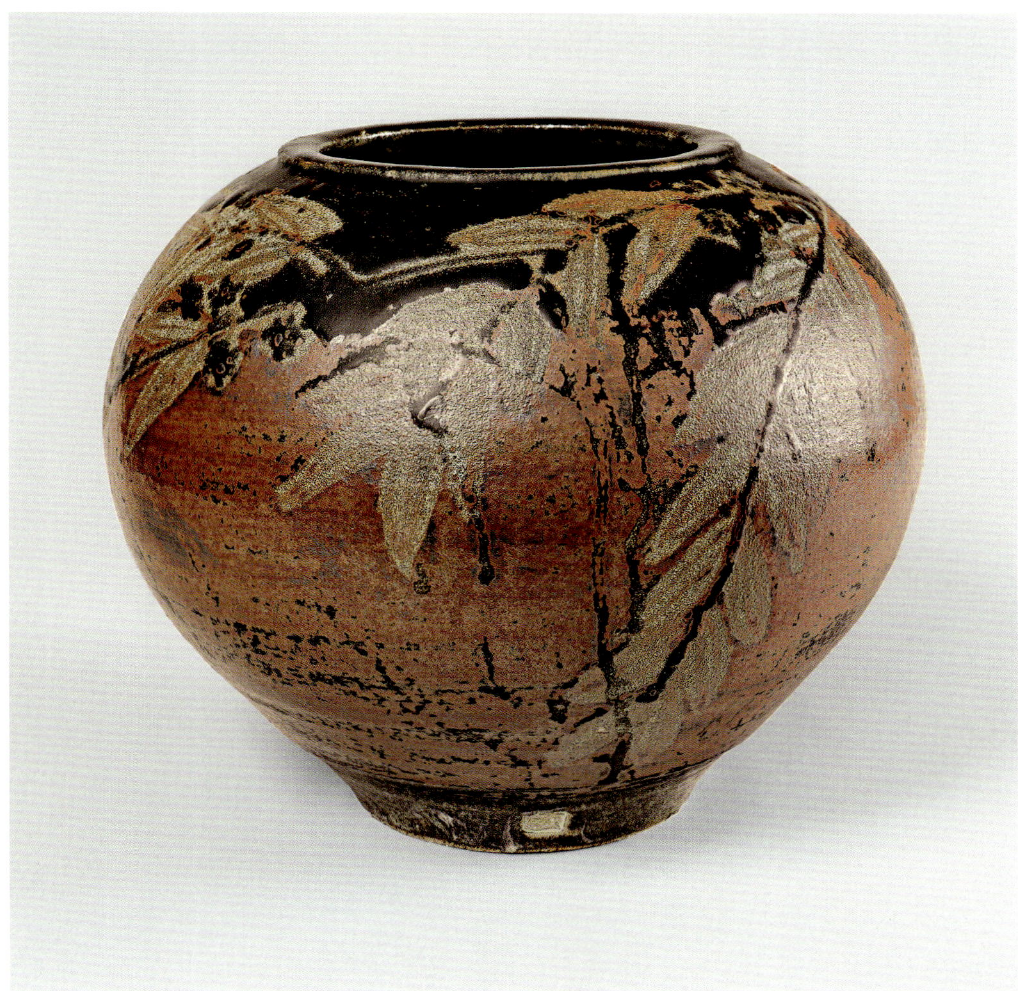

716

Takeda Yōko
(武田洋子; fl. 20th century)

717. *Moonlight*

Shōwa–Heisei era, 20th century
Stoneware
H. 10.5 cm (4 1/8 in.)

Gift from Miyeko Murase, 1999

Takenaka Kō
(竹中浩; b. 1941)

718. Vase

Shōwa–Heisei era, 20th–21st century
Porcelain with white glaze
H. 20 cm (7 7/8 in.)

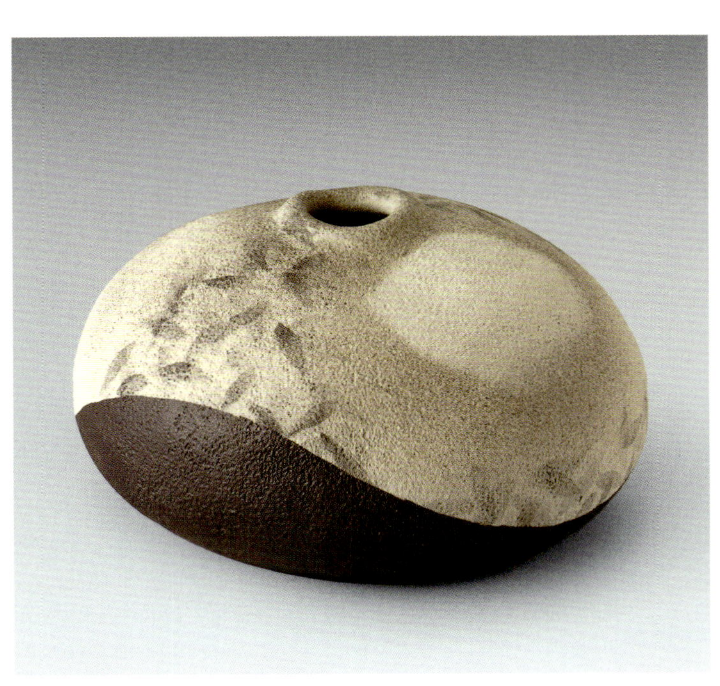

717

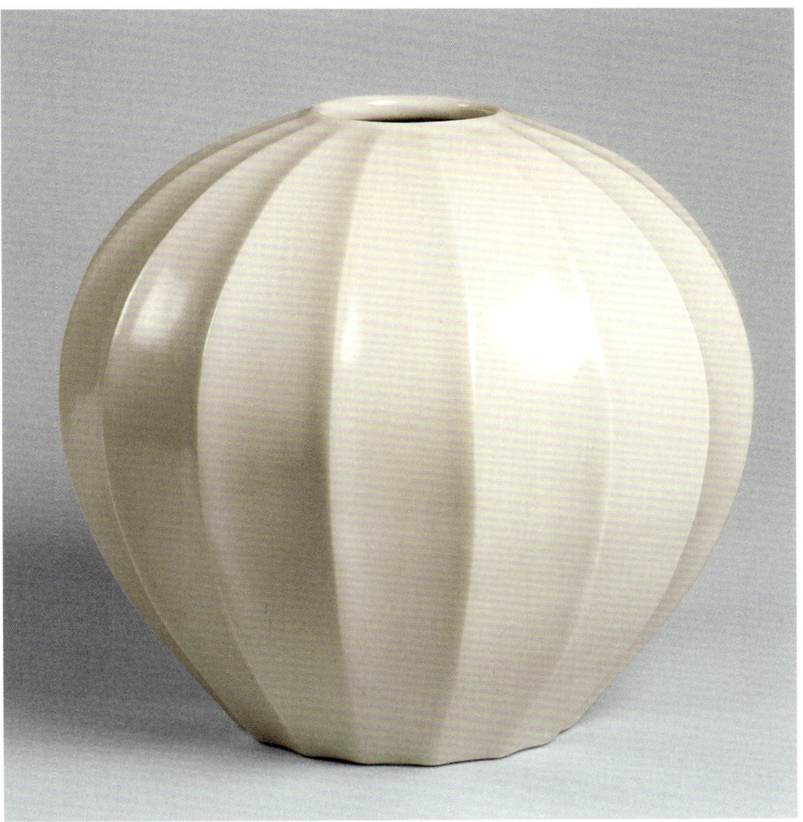

718

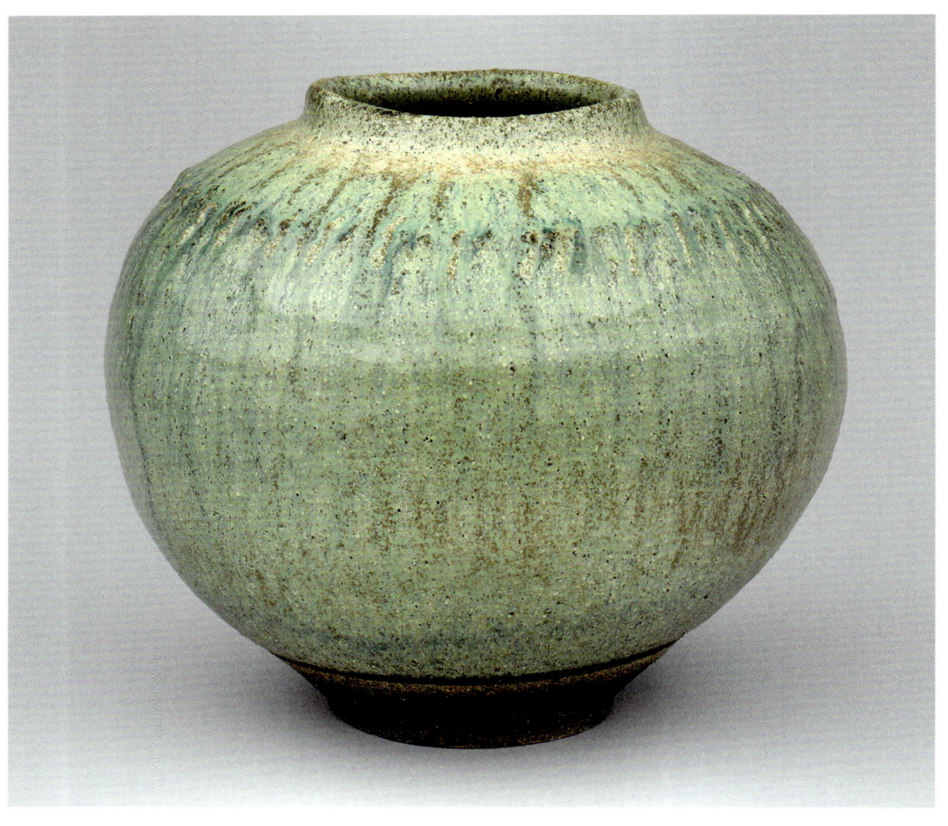

719

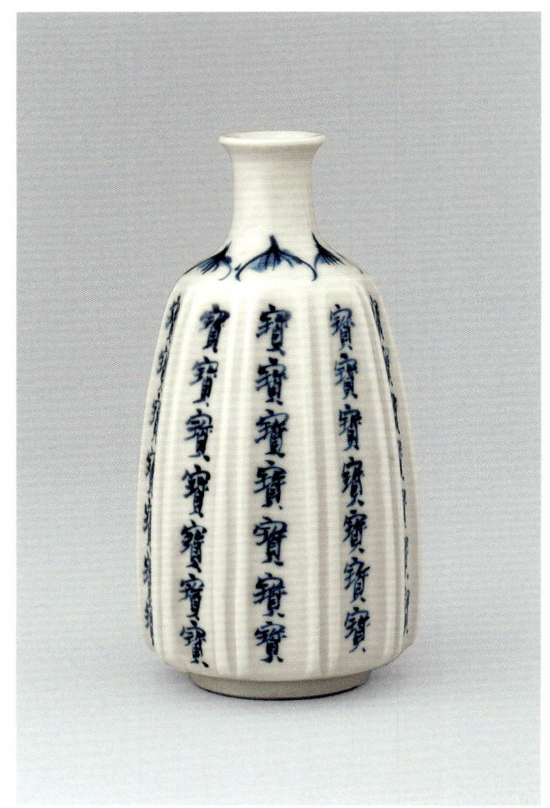

720

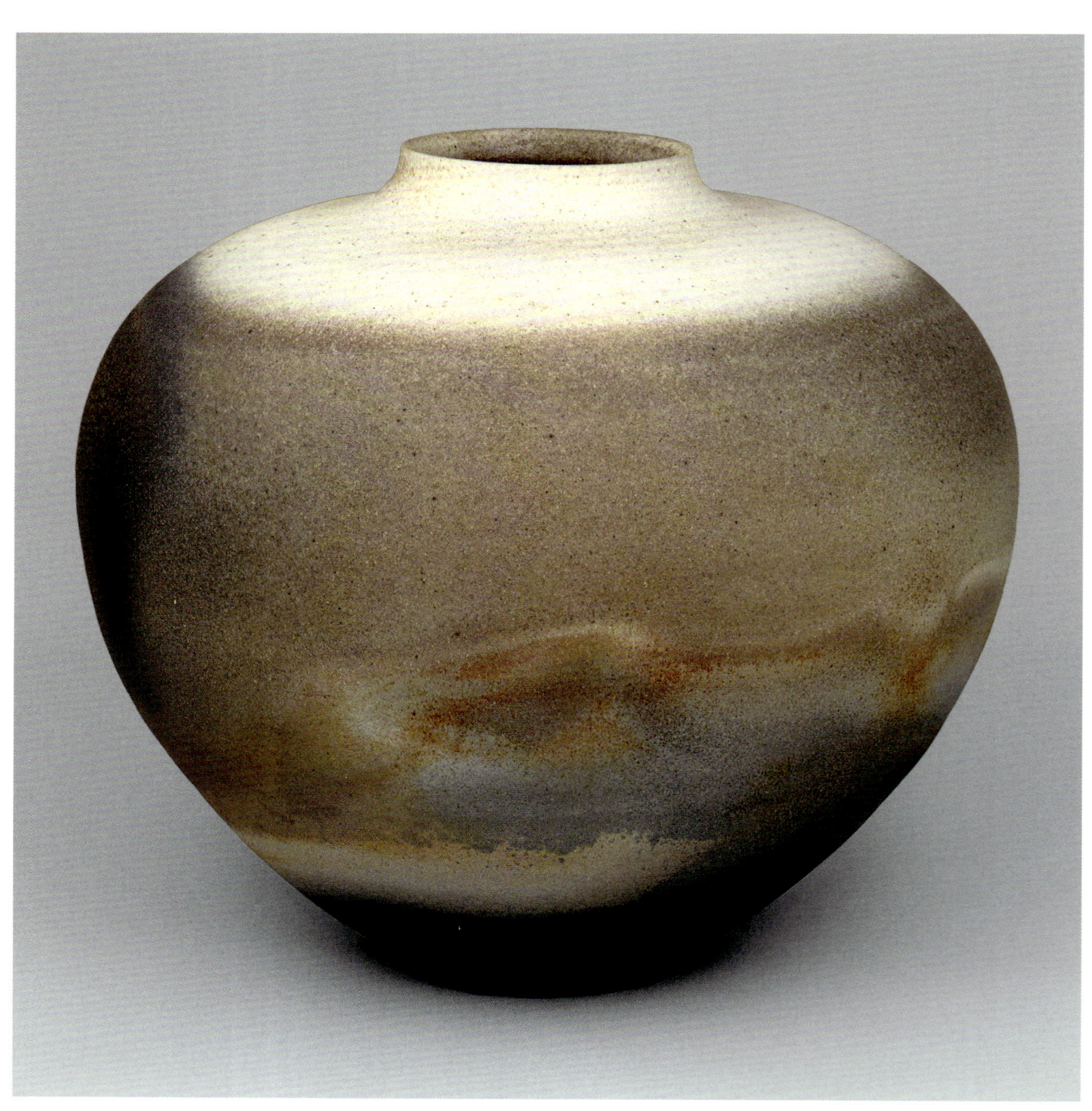

Takeuchi Kimiaki
(竹内公明; b. 1948)

719. Jar

Shōwa–Heisei era, 20th century
Stoneware with bluish green glaze
H. 24.2 cm (9½ in.)

Tatebayashi Gen'emon
(館林源右衛門; 1927–1989)

720. Sake bottle with the Chinese character for "treasure" (*takara*, 寶)

Shōwa era, 1977
Porcelain with underglaze cobalt
H. 16.3 cm (6⅜ in.)

Literature: Pekarik 1978, no. 98.

Takeuchi Kimiaki
(竹内公明; b. 1948)

721. Jar

Shōwa–Heisei era, 20th century
Stoneware
H. 38.1 cm (15 in.)
Signature

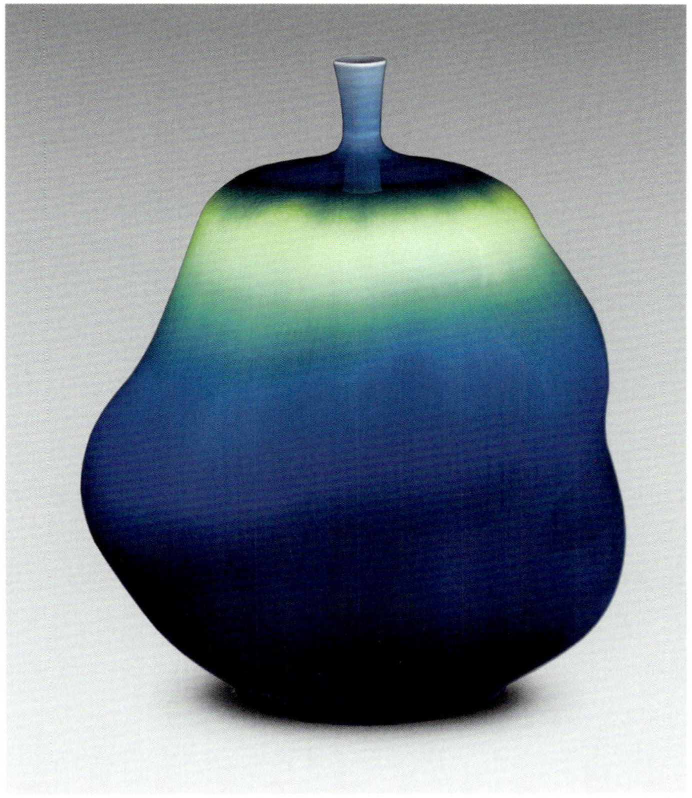

722

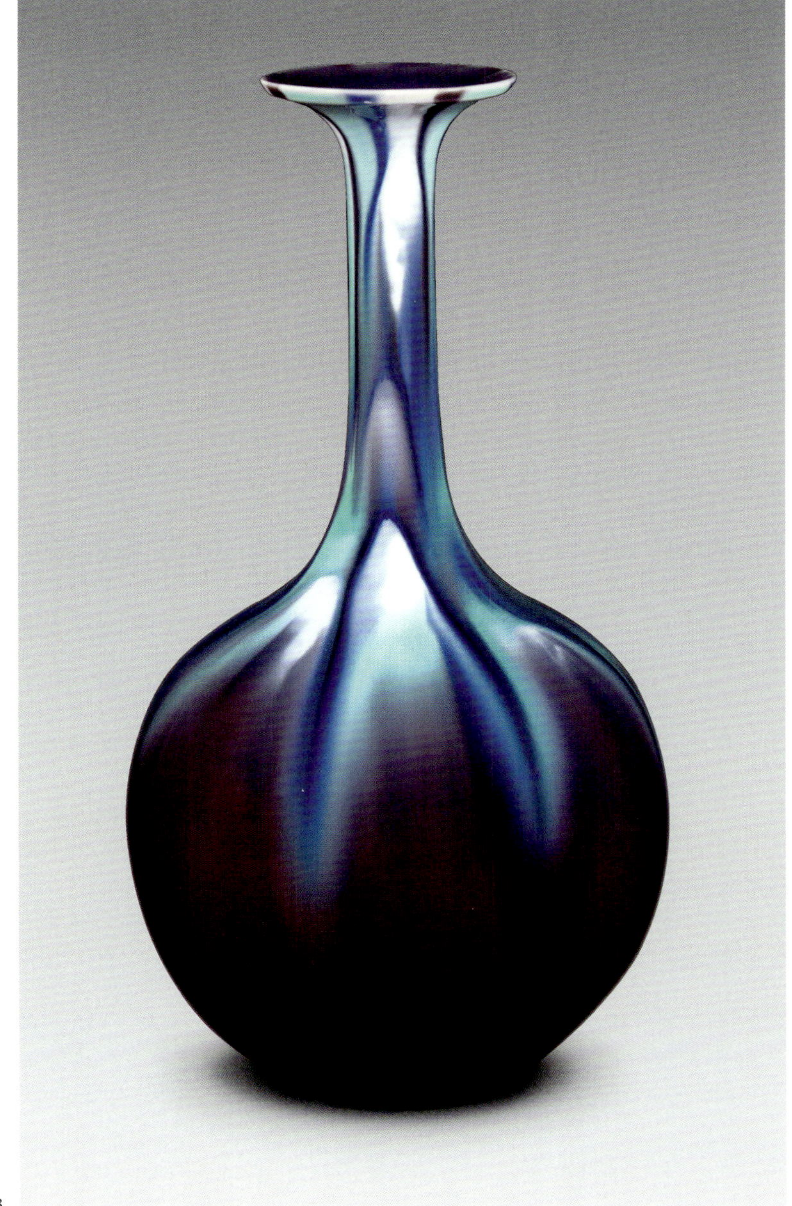

723

Tokuda Yasokichi III
(徳田八十吉; 1933–2009)

722. Bottle

Shōwa–Heisei era, 20th century
Kutani (九谷) type; porcelain with overglaze enamels
H. 19.7 cm (7 3/4 in.)

Gift from Shinichi Doi, 1990

Tokuda Yasokichi III
(徳田八十吉; 1933–2009)

723. Vase

Shōwa–Heisei era, 20th century
Kutani (九谷) type; porcelain with overglaze enamels
H. 26 cm (10 1/4 in.)

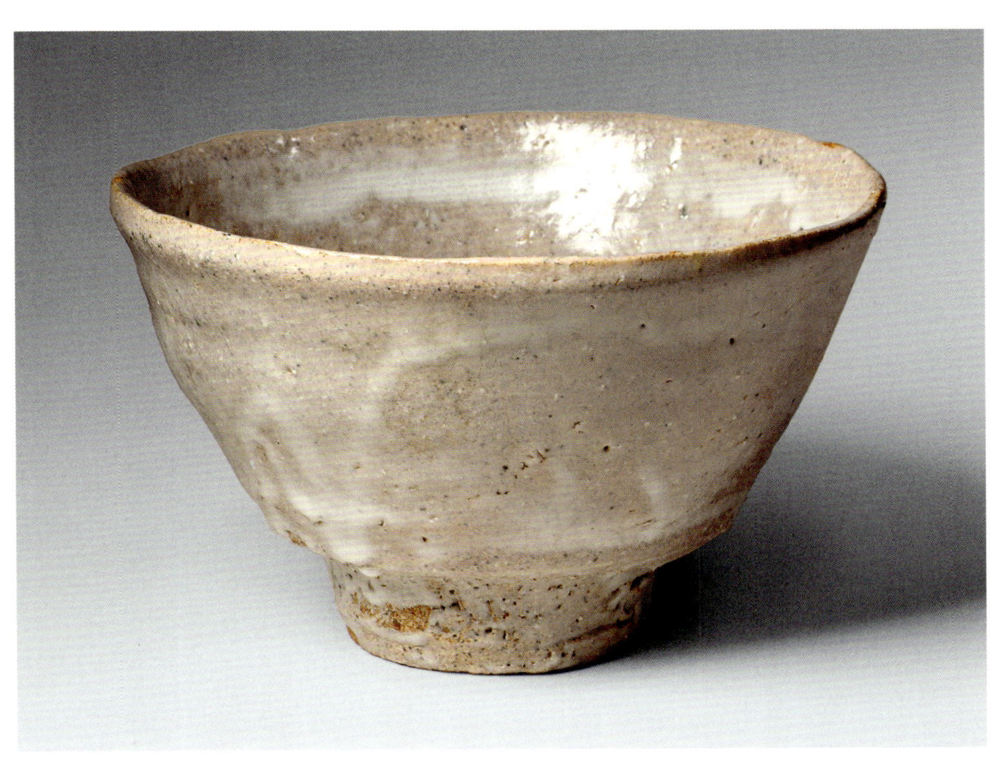

Tsujimura Shirō
(辻村史朗; b. 1947)

724. Tea bowl

Heisei era, 20th century
Ido (井戸) type; glazed stoneware
H. 9.5 cm (3 3/4 in.), diam. 15.9 cm (6 1/4 in.)

Gift from the artist, 2003

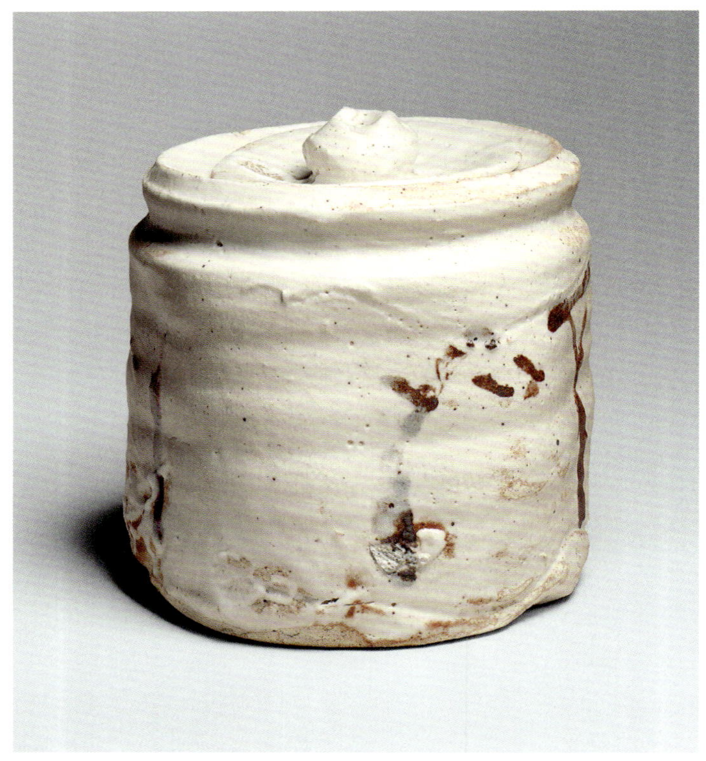

725

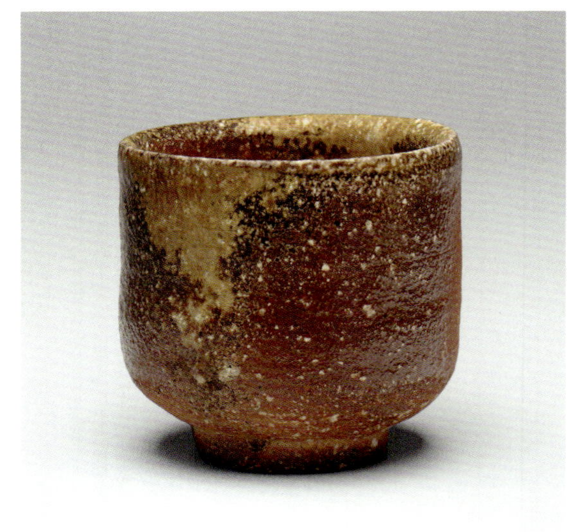

726

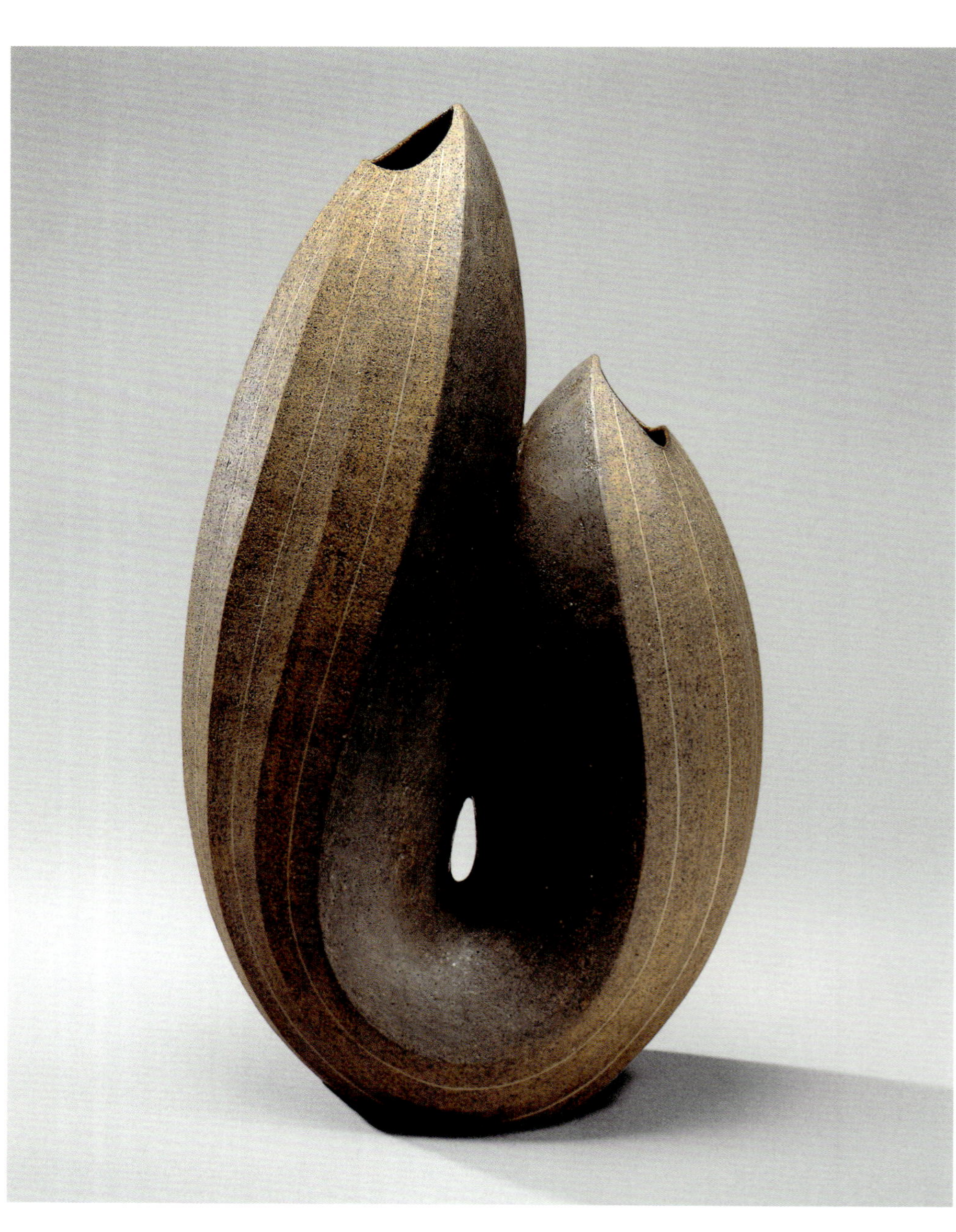

Tsujimura Shirō
(辻村史朗; b. 1947)

725. Freshwater jar (*mizusashi*, 水差)

Heisei era, 21st century
Shino (志野) type; stoneware with white feldspathic glaze and underglaze iron oxide
H. 19.7 cm (7 3/4 in.)

Gift from Eleanor Briggs, 2003

Ueda Naokata
(上田直方; b. 1927)

726. Cylindrical tea bowl (*tsutsu chawan*, 筒茶碗)

Shōwa era, 1985
Shigaraki (信楽) ware; stoneware
H. 8.5 cm (3 3/8 in.)

Usui Kazunari
(臼井和成; b. 1954)

727. Vase

Heisei era, 20th–21st century
Stoneware
H. 44.5 cm (17 1/2 in.)
Mark

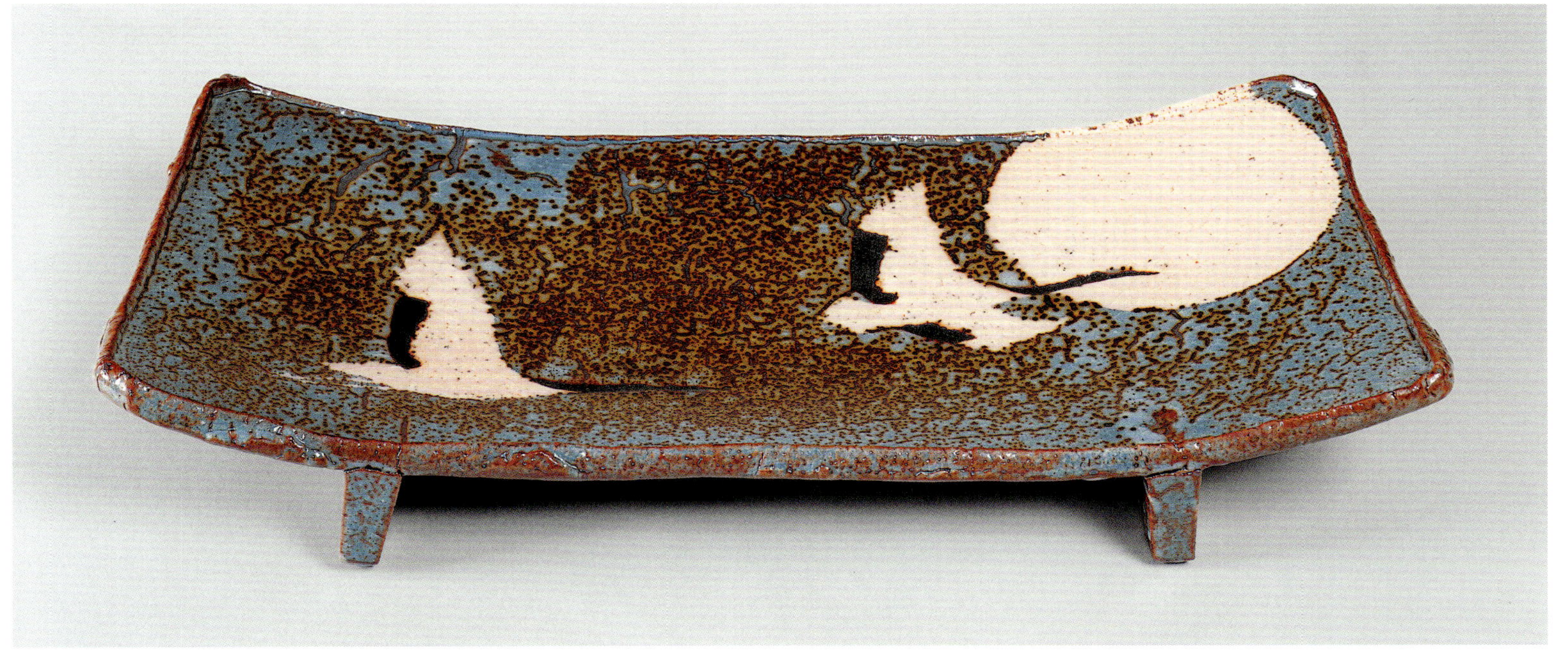

728

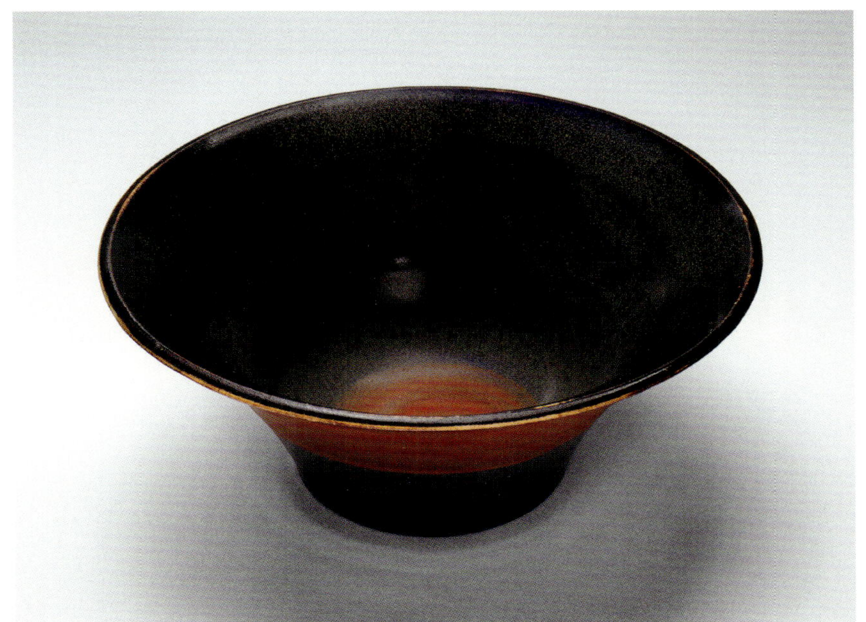

729

Wakao Toshisada
(若尾利貞; b. 1933)

728. Chopping board (*manaita*, まな板) with cranes and sun

Shōwa era, 1985
Mino ware (美濃), *Nezumi Shino* (鼠志野) type; glazed stoneware
L. 57.8 cm (22 3/4 in.)

Literature: Baekeland and Moes 1993, no. 22; Carpenter 2012, no. 59.

Watanabe Asako
(渡辺朝子; b. 1930)

729. *Tenmoku* (天目) bowl

Shōwa–Heisei era, 20th century
Stoneware with red and black glaze
H. 10.9 cm (4 1/4 in.), diam. of mouth 25.7 cm (10 1/8 in.)
Seal

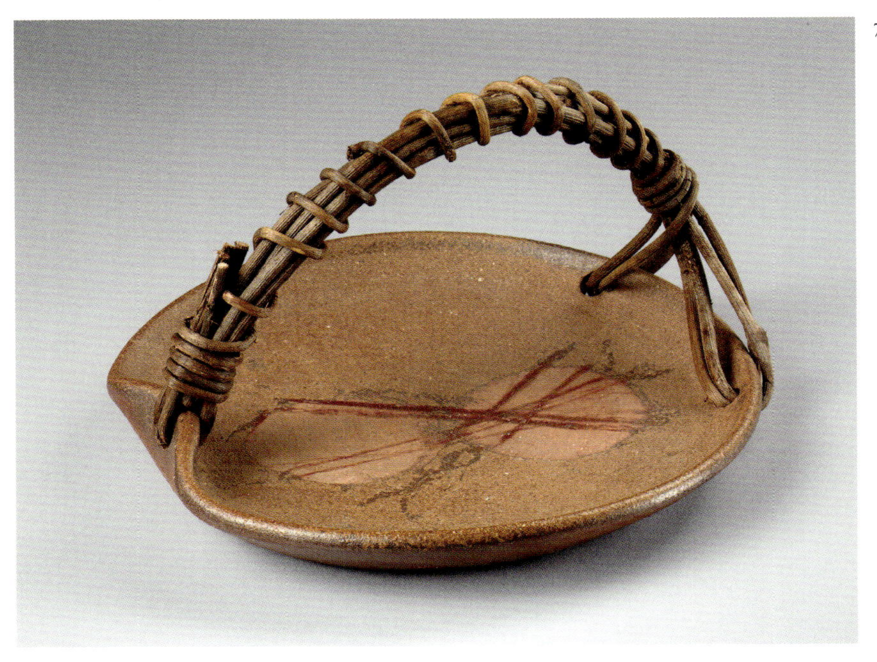

730

Yamauchi Atsuyoshi
(山内厚可; b. 1945)

730. Plate with handle

Shōwa era, 20th century
Bizen (備前) ware; stoneware; bine stems (handle)
Diam. 23.5 cm (9 1/4 in.)

Gift from Miyeko Murase, 1985

Richard Bresnahan
(b. 1953)

731. Dish

1989
Stoneware with navy-bean straw ash glaze over iron oxide
Diam. 18.6 cm (7 3/8 in.)
Signature

Gift from the artist, 1992

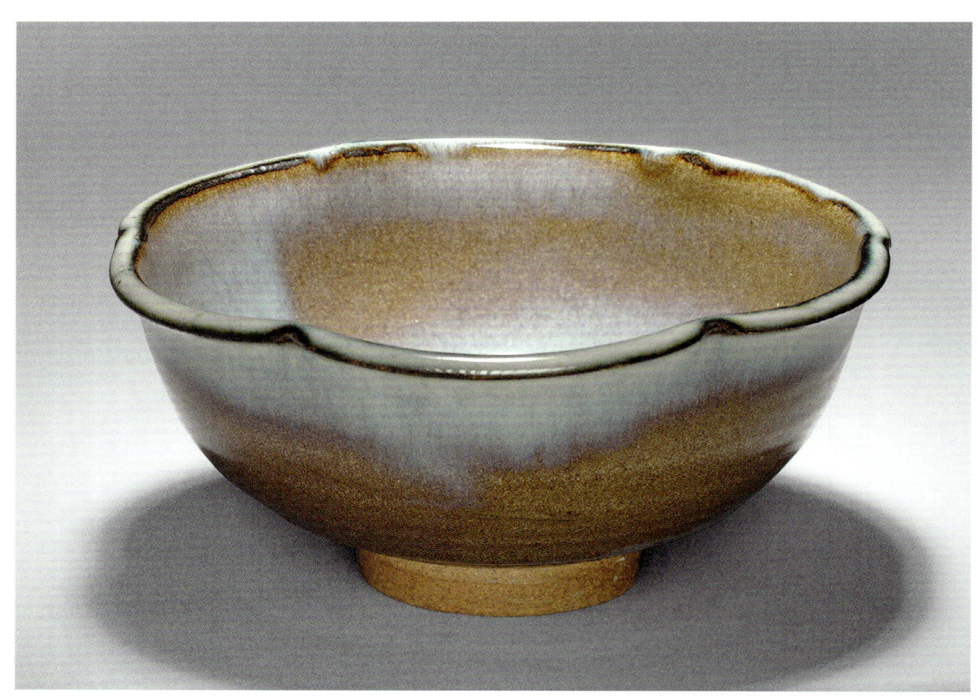

Richard Bresnahan
(b. 1953)

732. Bowl with birds

20th century
Stoneware with navy-bean straw ash glaze over iron oxide
Diam. 35.1 cm (13 7/8 in.)

Gift from the artist, 1997

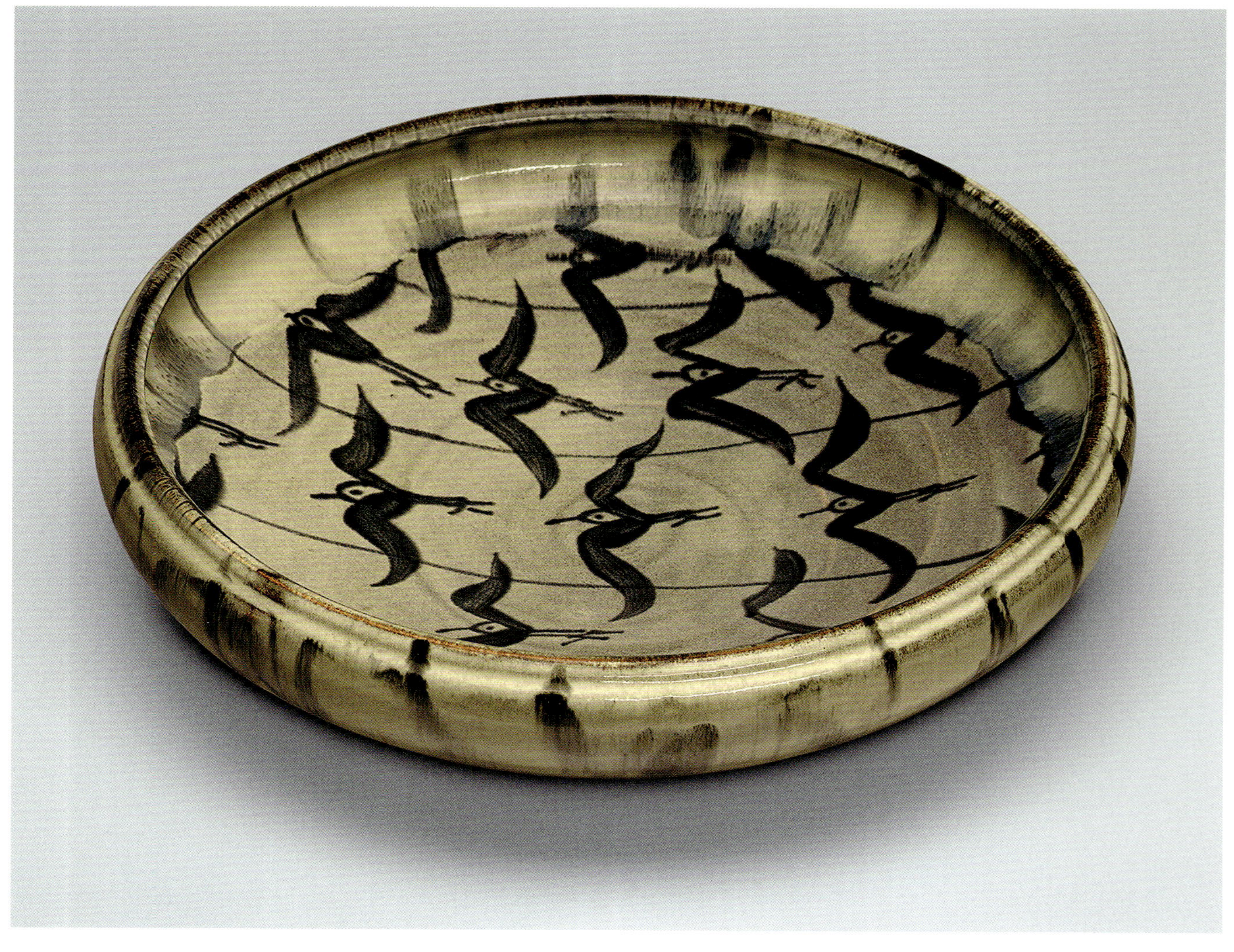

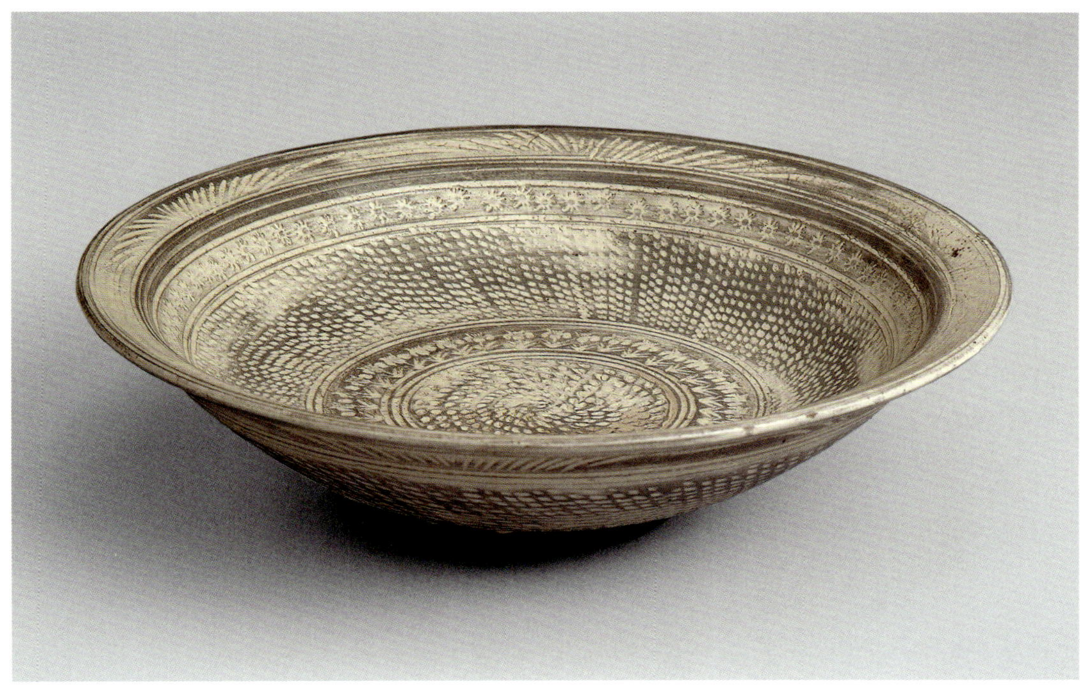

Richard Bresnahan
(b. 1953)

733. Plate

1978
Mishima (三島) type; stoneware with inlaid porcelain and pine ash glaze
H. 22.8 cm (9 in.)
Signature

Ikuta Susumu
(b. 1934)

734. Bowl with butterflies, pine boughs, and flowers

1992
Stoneware with underglaze cobalt blue and gray
Diam. 38.4 cm ($15\frac{1}{8}$ in.)
Signature

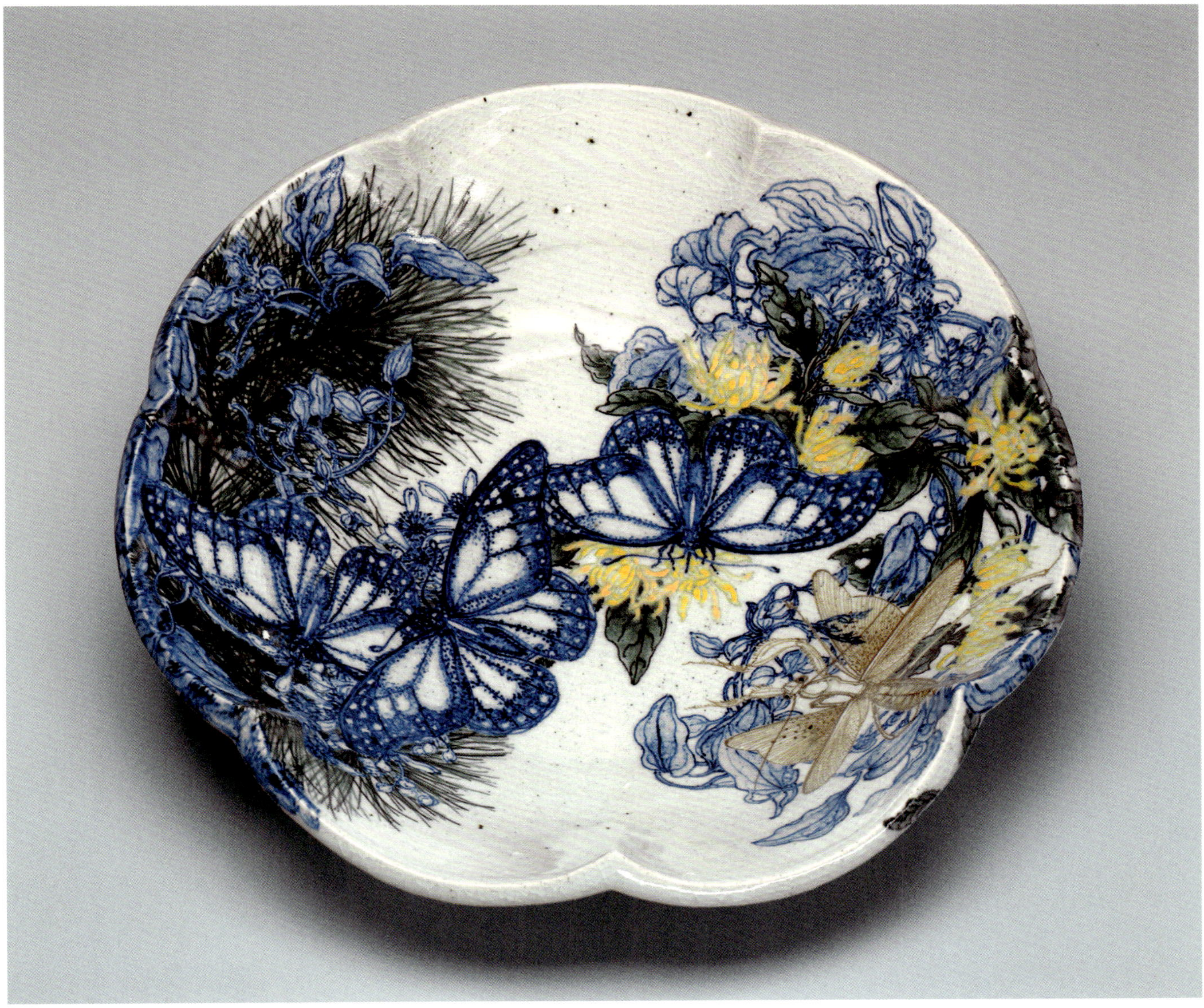

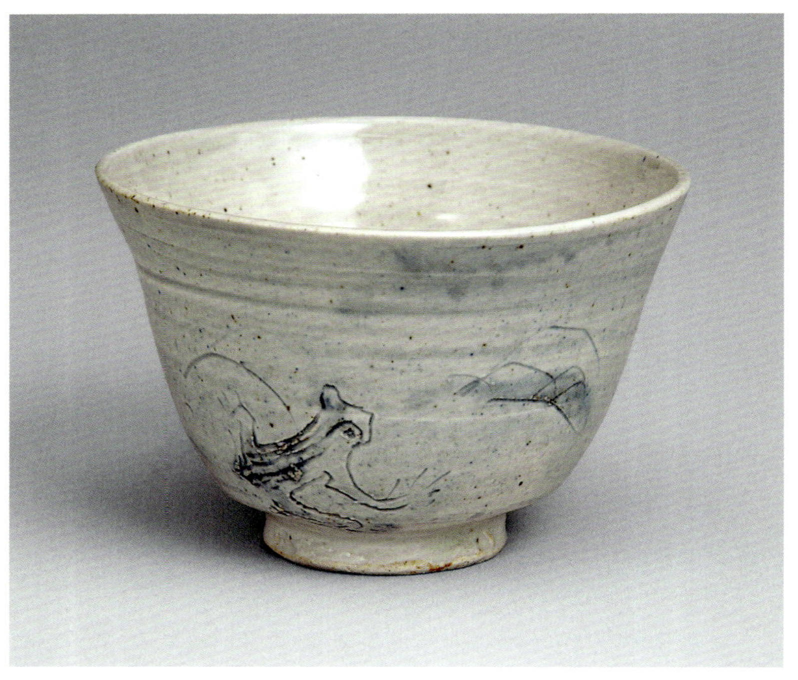

735

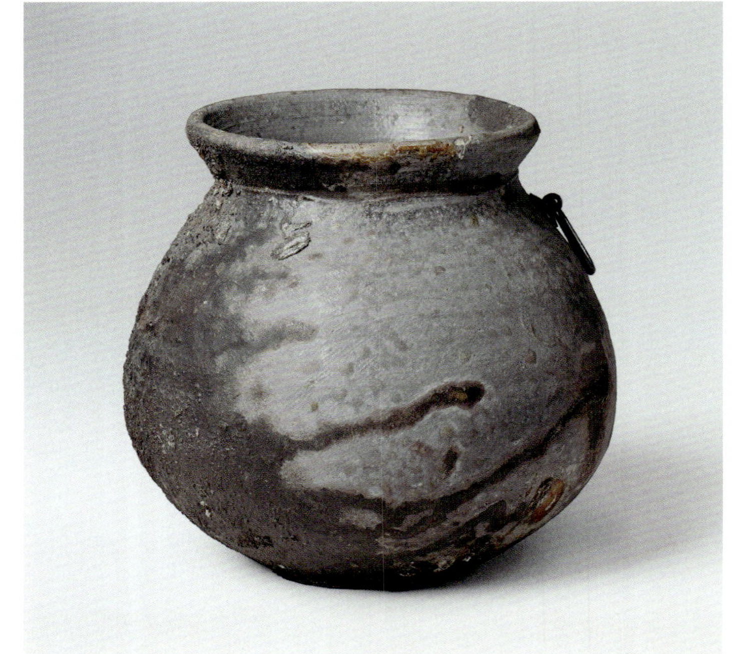

736

Bernard Leach
(1887–1979)

735. Tea bowl with frog

20th century
Stoneware with underglaze cobalt blue
Diam. 12.9 cm (5 1/8 in.)
Mark, seal

Jeff Shapiro
(b. 1949)

736. Hanging vase

1983
Bizen (備) type; unglazed stoneware
H. 12.3 cm (4 7/8 in.)
Mark

Gift from Miyeko Murase, 1981

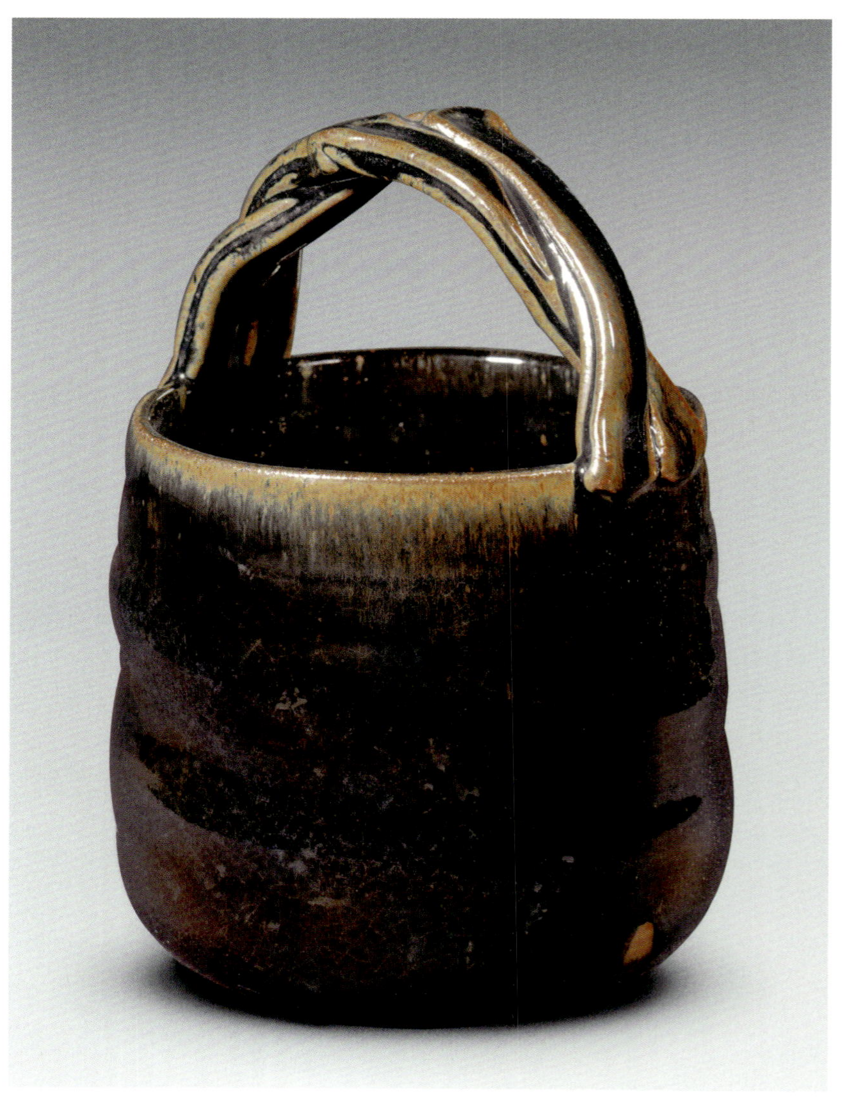

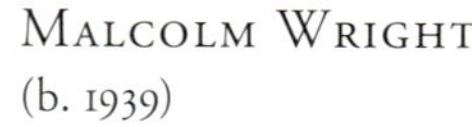

Malcolm Wright
(b. 1939)

737. Basket-shaped vase

20th century
Glazed stoneware
H. 26.1 cm (10 1/4 in.)

Gift from Julia Meech, 1987

Japanese Ceramics Details

† *denotes illustrated items*

† 589. Tea-leaf storage jar

Mark

[on base] potter's mark

† 591. Sake bottle

Mark

[on shoulder] kiln mark

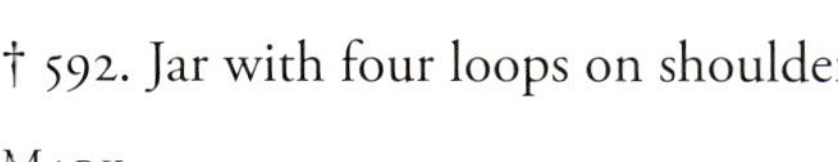

† 592. Jar with four loops on shoulder

Mark

[on base] potter's mark

† 609. Dish with landscape

Text

[on underside] *Fuku*

† 621. Bowl with Europeans and ships

Text

[on underside] *Kotobuki*

† 622. Bowl with Europeans and ships

Text

[on underside] *Kotobuki*

† 623. Bowl with Europeans and ships

Mark

[on underside] floral motif

† 624. Pair of bowls

Text

[on underside] *Rarest among precious jewels and august treasures*

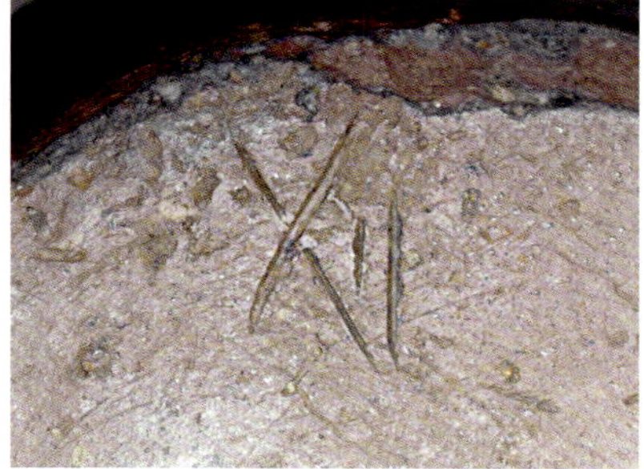

589

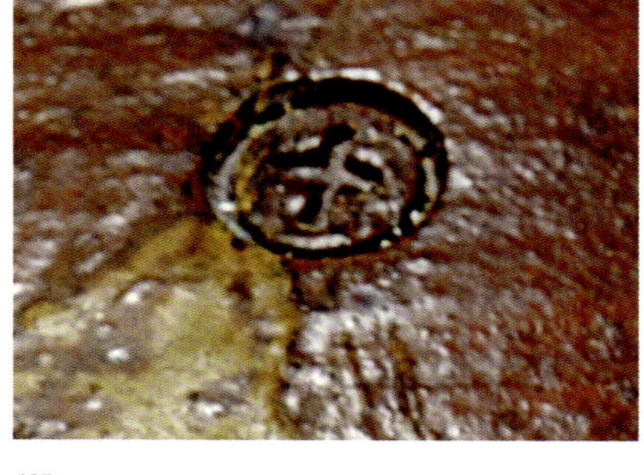

591

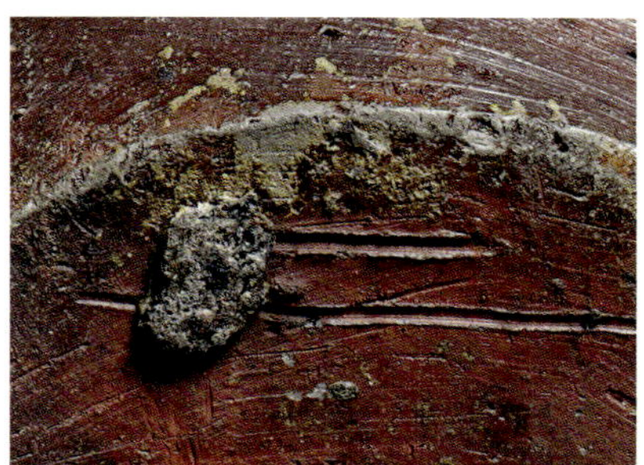

592

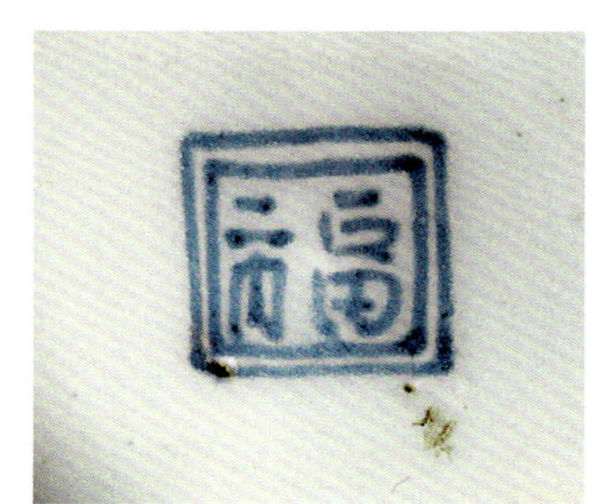

609

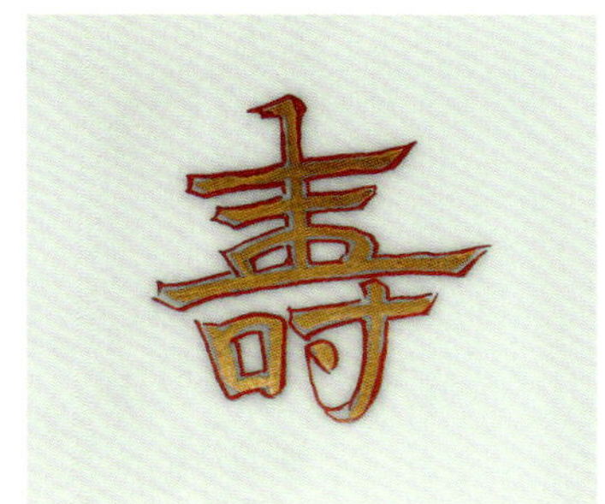

621

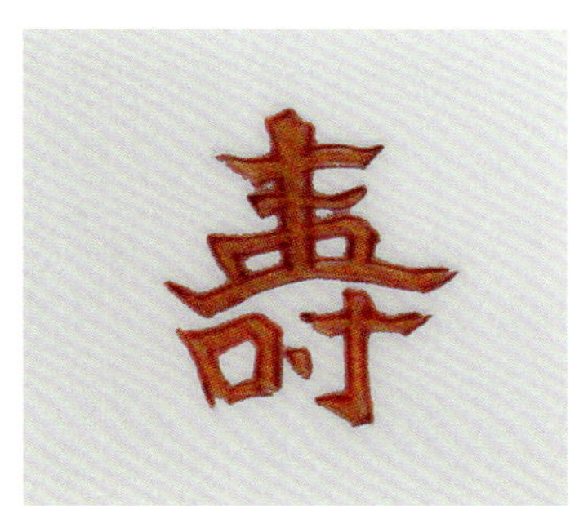

622

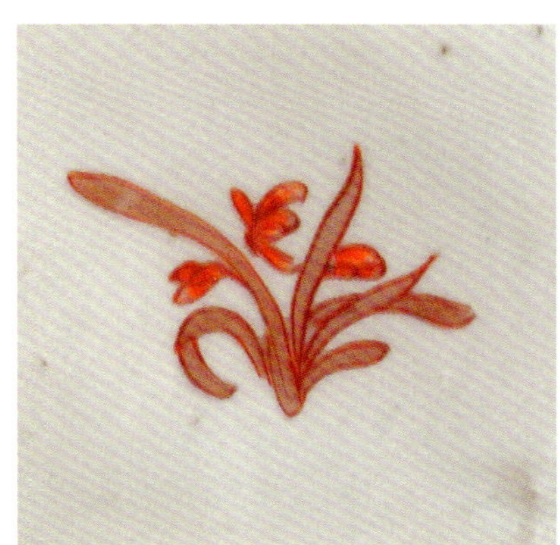

623

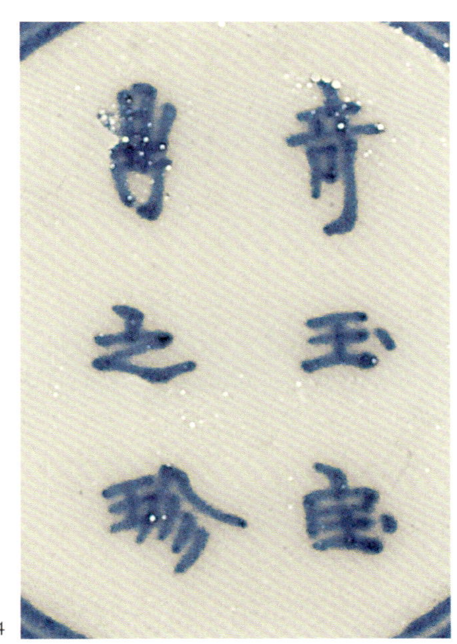

624

† 630. Dish with two Chinese boys in a garden

Text

[on underside] *Wealth and longevity*

† 638. Tea caddy

Seal

[on underside] *Ninsei*

† 639. Platter with spring flowers

Signature

[on underside] *Kenzan Tōin*

Seal

[on underside] *Shōko*

† 651. Pair of tea bowls with incised cranes and turtles

Seals

[on underside of each] *Raku*

† 653. Box with scenes of Kyoto

Seal

[on underside] *Seikōzan*

677. Vase with Japanese aralia design

Signature

[on underside] *Ryū*

686. Vase

Signature

[on underside] *Kajitani '80*

† 696. Vase

Signature

[on underside] *Kō*

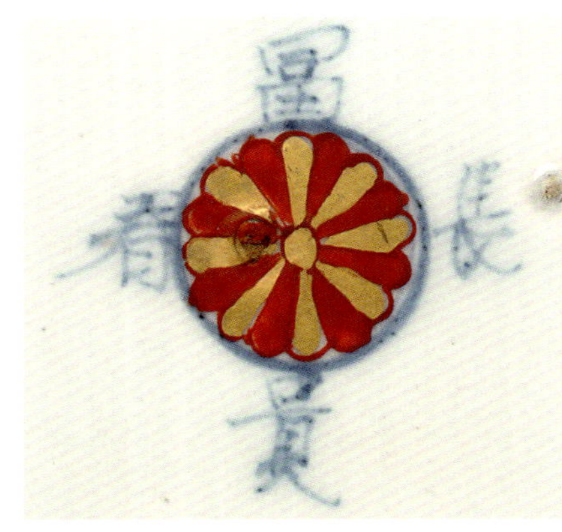

630

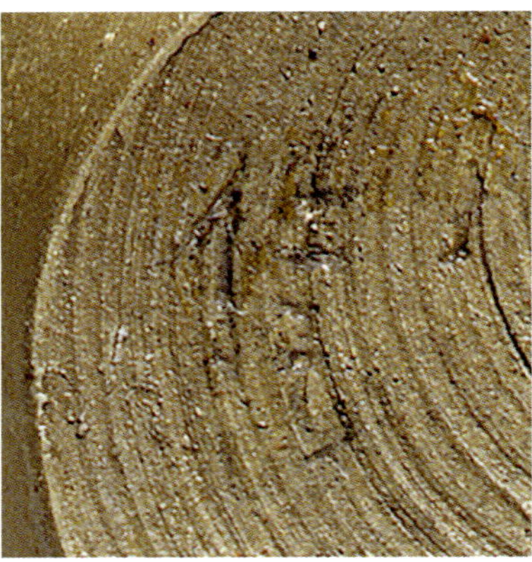

638

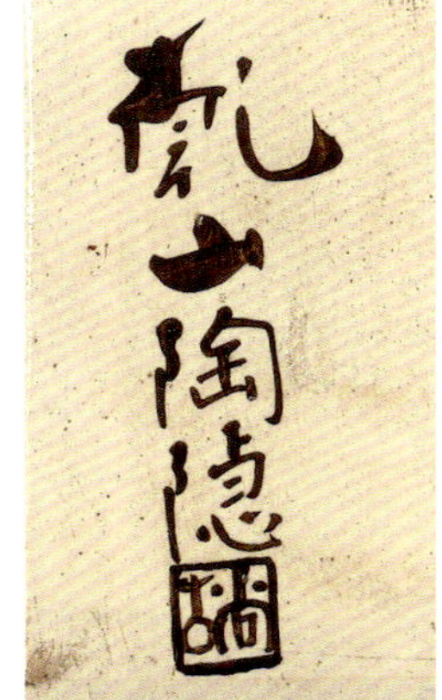

639

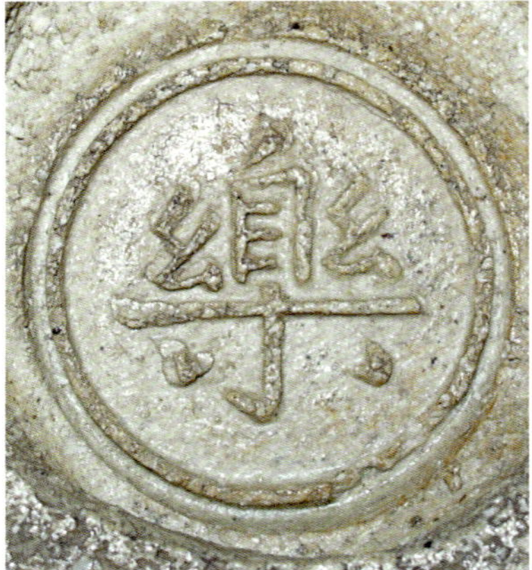

651

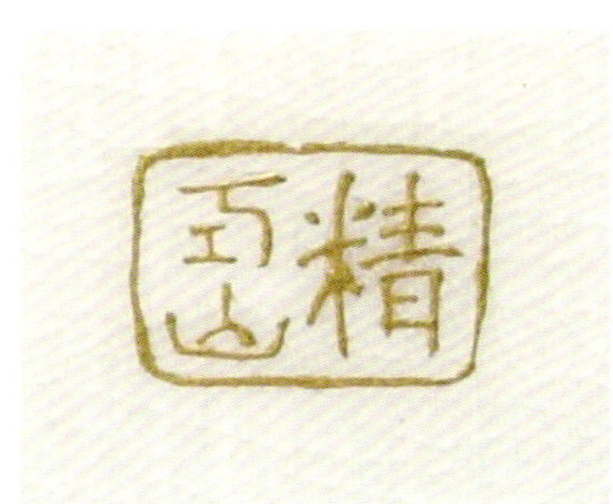

653

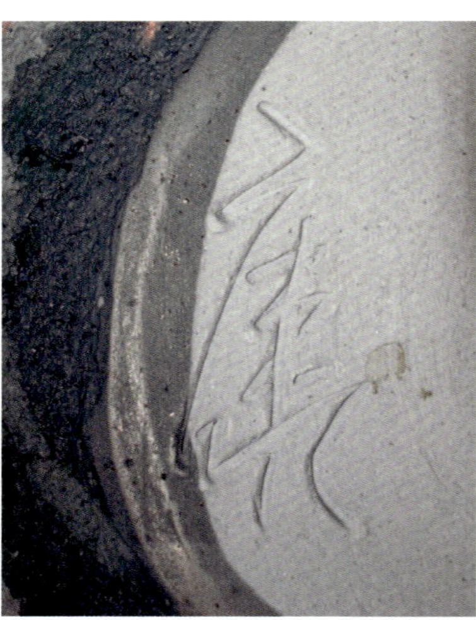

696

698. Vase with mountains

Seal

[on underside] *I[sami]*

† 699. Vessel

Seal

[on underside] *Jun*

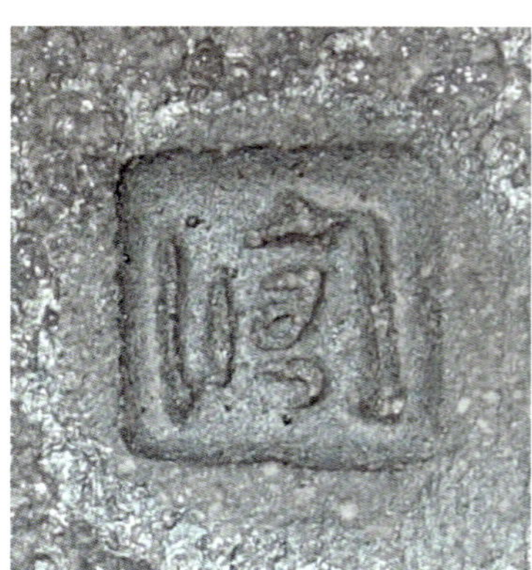

699

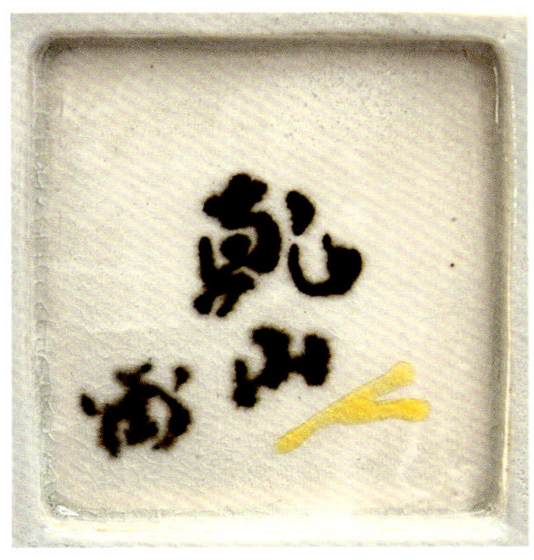

701

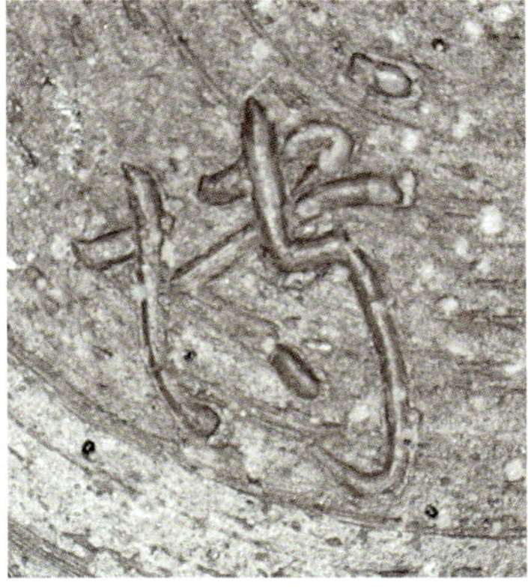

702

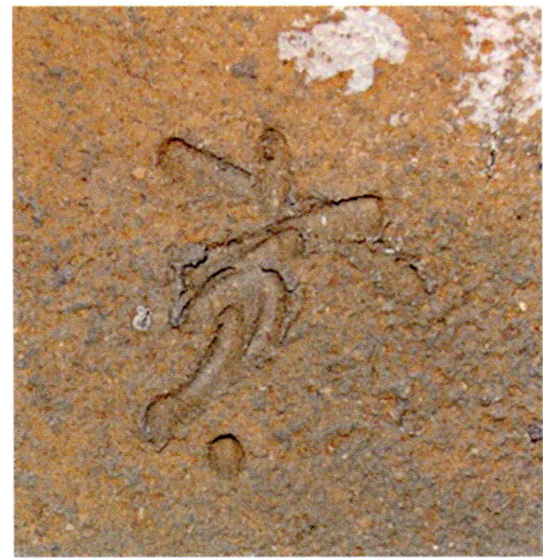

708

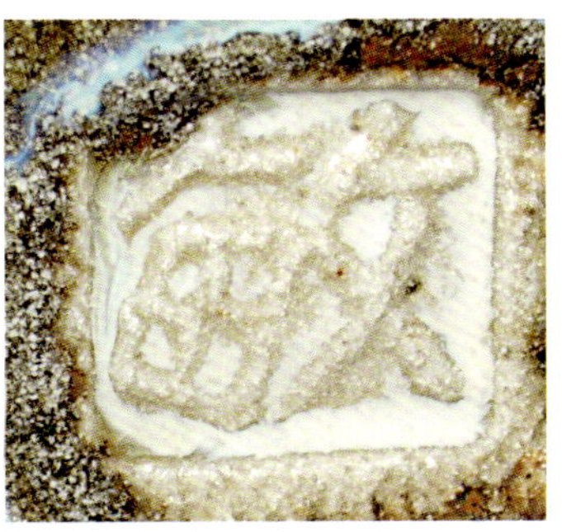

716

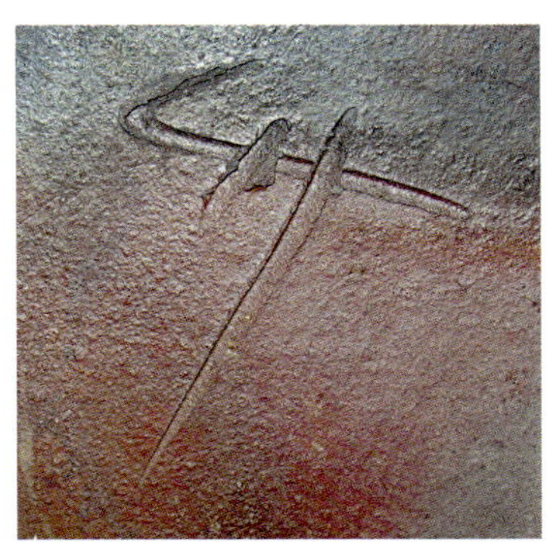

721

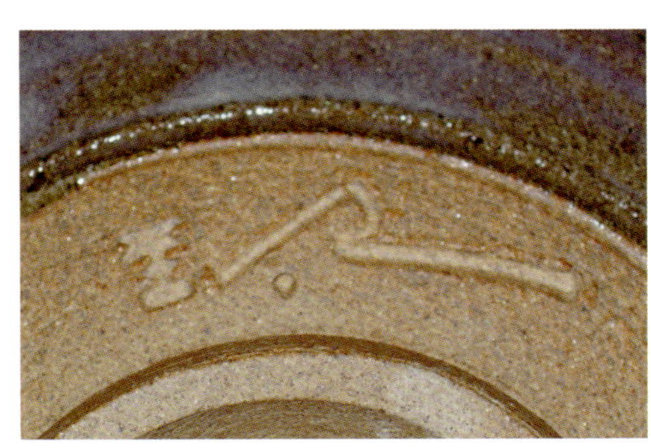

731

700. Tea bowl

Mark

[on underside] Potter's mark

† 701 Sake cup with checkerboard design in the style of Kenzan

Text

[on underside] *Kenzan*; *Ji*

Seal

[on underside] in the shape of pine needles

† 702. Dish with geometric design

Signature

[on underside] *Hiro[shi]*

† 708. Bucket-shaped vase with handle

Signature

[on underside] *Kō*

† 716. Jar with *murasaki* plant

Seal

[on underside of foot] *Toshi*

† 721. Jar

Signature

[on underside] *Take*

727. Vase

Mark

[on underside] Potter's mark

729. *Tenmoku* bowl

Seal

[on underside] *Asa*

† 731. Dish

Signature

[on underside] *RB*

† 733. Plate

Signature

[on underside] *RB*

† 734. Bowl with butterflies, pine boughs, and flowers

Signature

[on underside] *'92, Susumu*

† 735. Tea bowl with frog

Mark

[on underside] Potter's mark

Seal

[on underside] *BL*

† 736. Hanging vase

Mark

[on shoulder] Potter's mark

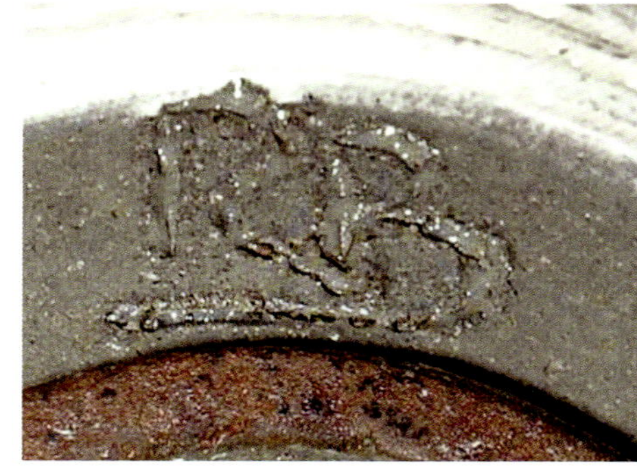

733

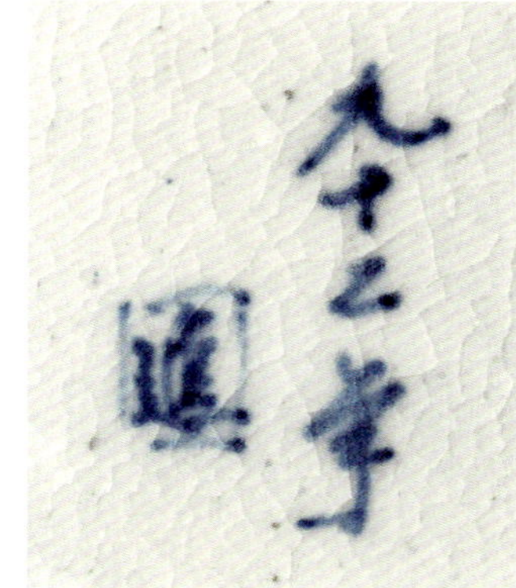

734

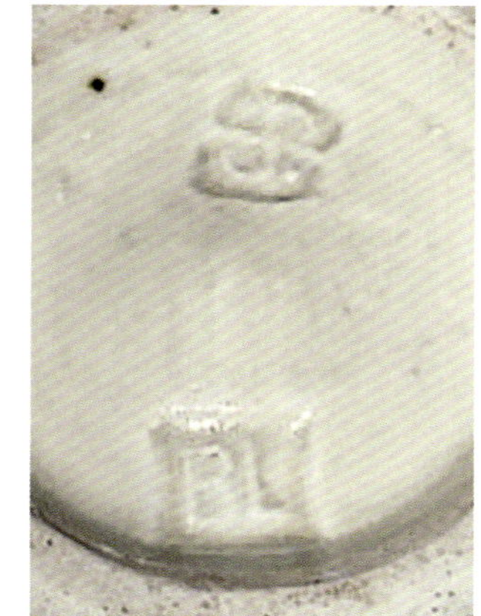

735

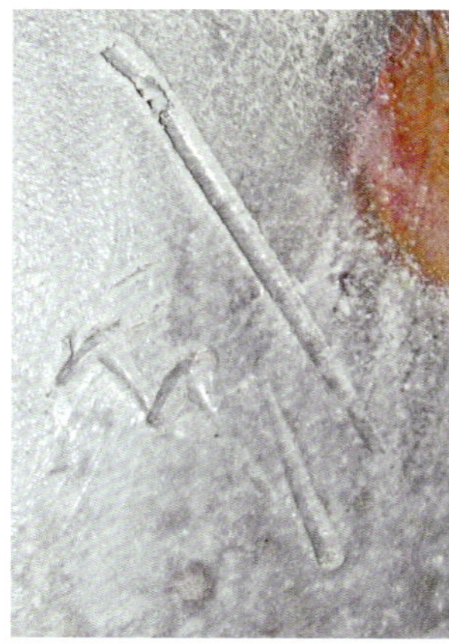

736

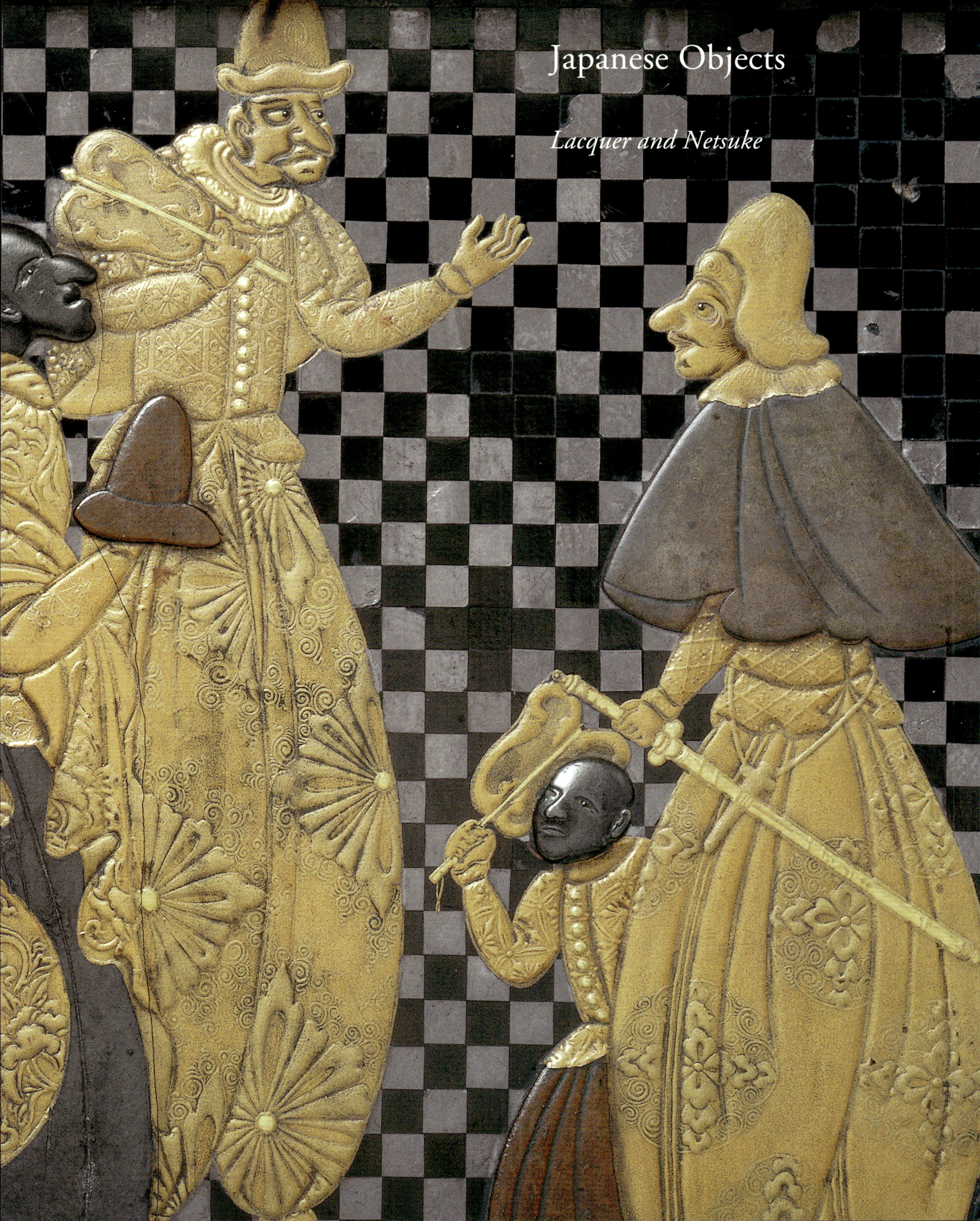

Japanese Objects

Lacquer and Netsuke

MAKI-E (蒔絵, Sprinkled Picture)

738. Incense box (*kōgō*, 香合) with pines and plovers

Kamakura period, early 14th century
Black lacquer with gold *maki-e* on gold pearskin ground (*nashiji*, 梨地)
3.5 x 6.9 x 9.4 cm (1 3/8 x 2 3/4 x 3 3/4 in.)

Literature: Lee 1961, no. 40; Murase 1975, no. 102; Tokyo National Museum 1985a, no. 104; Avitabile 1990, no. 106; Murase 2000, no. 45.

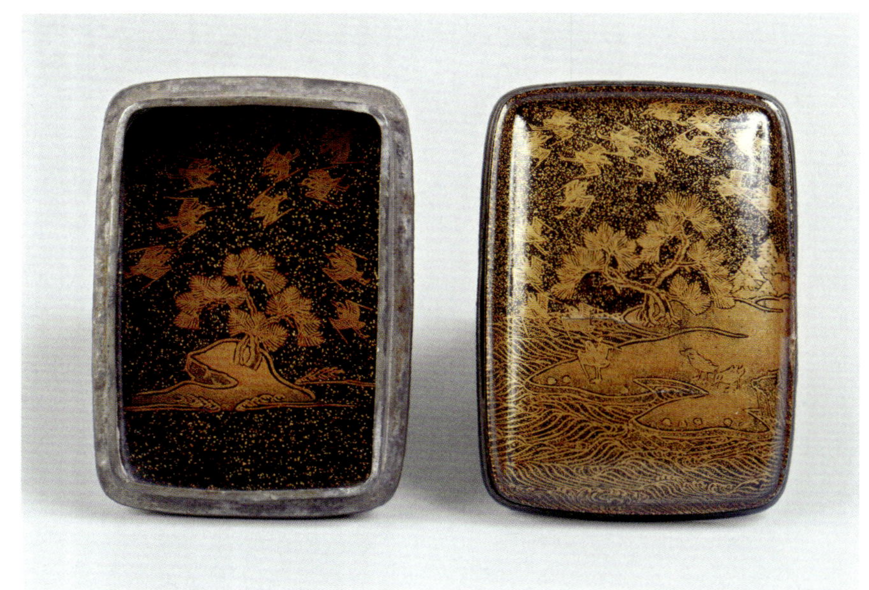

739. Incense box (*kōgō*, 香合) with autumn grasses

Muromachi period, 15th century
Black lacquer with gold *maki-e* on gold pearskin ground (*nashiji*, 梨地)
3.3 x 6.4 x 8.4 cm (1 1/4 x 2 1/2 x 3 1/4 in.)

Literature: Murase 1975, no. 102; Tokyo National Museum 1985a, no. 106; Avitabile 1990, no. 107; Murase 2000, no. 46.

Gift from Muraguchi Shirō, 1970

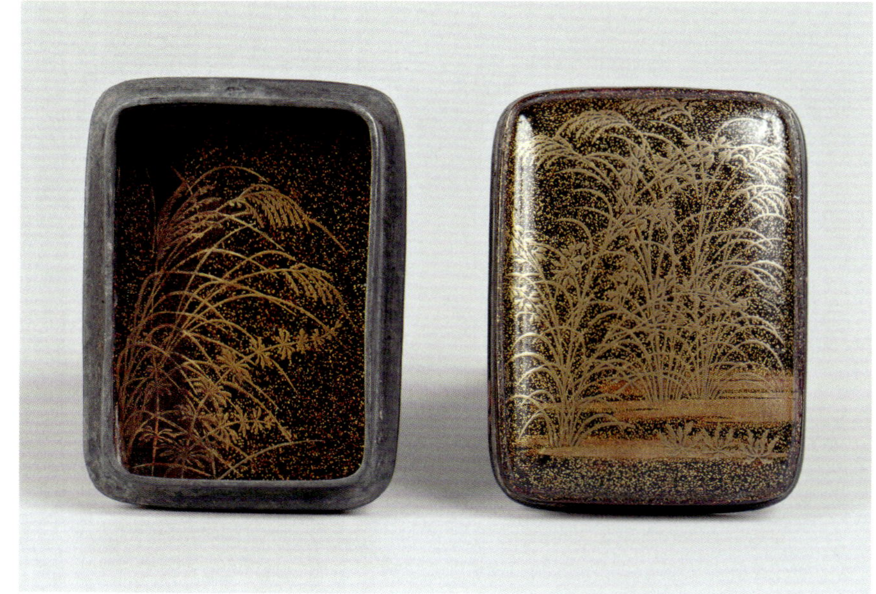

740. Incense box (*kōgō*, 香合) with peacock

Muromachi period, 16th century
Black lacquer with gold *maki-e* and mother-of-pearl inlay
3 x 6.2 x 8.3 cm (1 1/8 x 2 1/2 x 3 1/4 in.)

Literature: Lee 1961, no. 40; Murase 1975, no. 102.

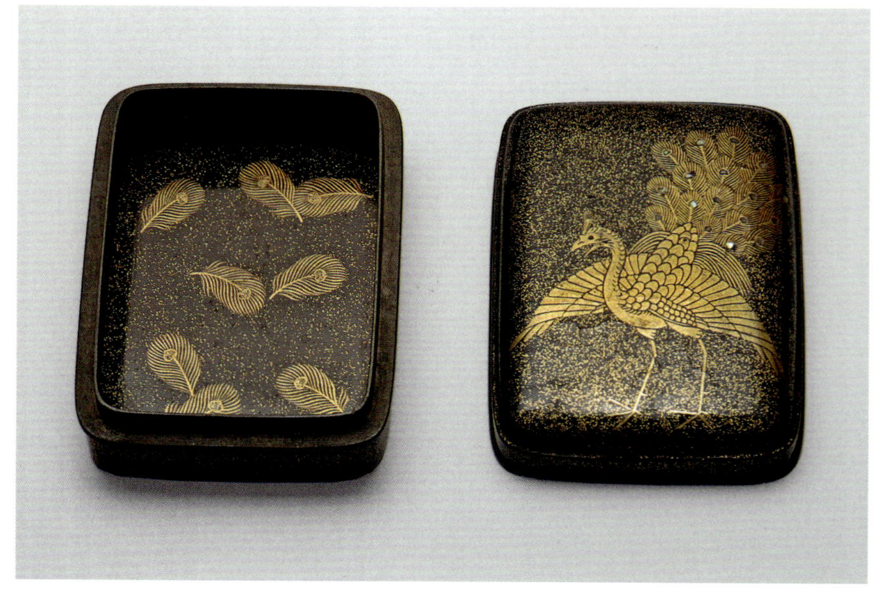

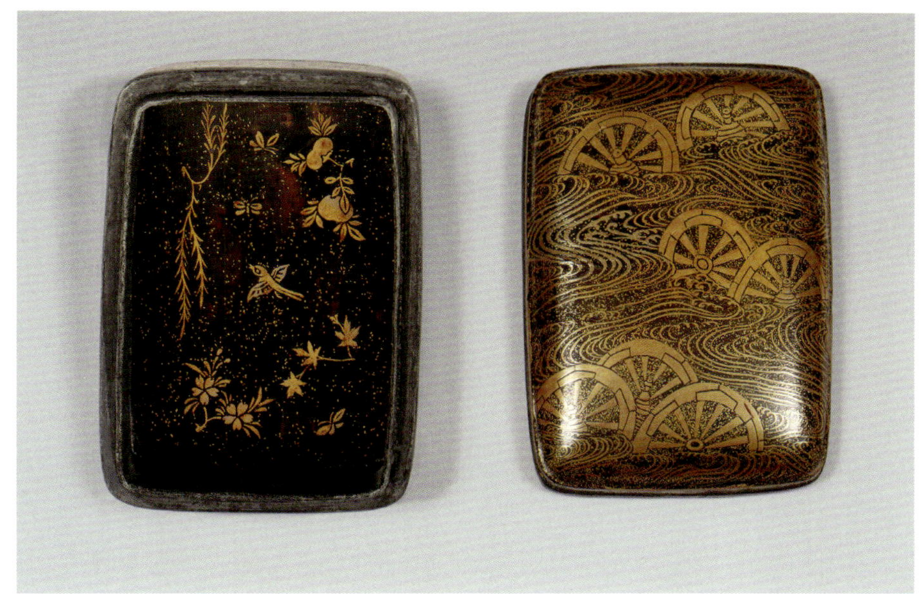

741. Incense box (*kōgō*, 香合) with cart wheels partially submerged in water

Muromachi period, 15th century
Black lacquer with gold *maki-e*
2.9 x 6.2 x 8.3 cm (1 1/8 x 2 1/2 x 3 1/4 in.)

LITERATURE: Murase 1993, no. 64.

742. Box with herdboy on an ox

Muromachi period, 16th century
Black lacquer with gold *maki-e*
4 x 12.2 x 17.2 cm (1 5/8 x 4 3/4 x 6 3/4 in.)

LITERATURE: Wada 2002, p. 25, fig. 5.

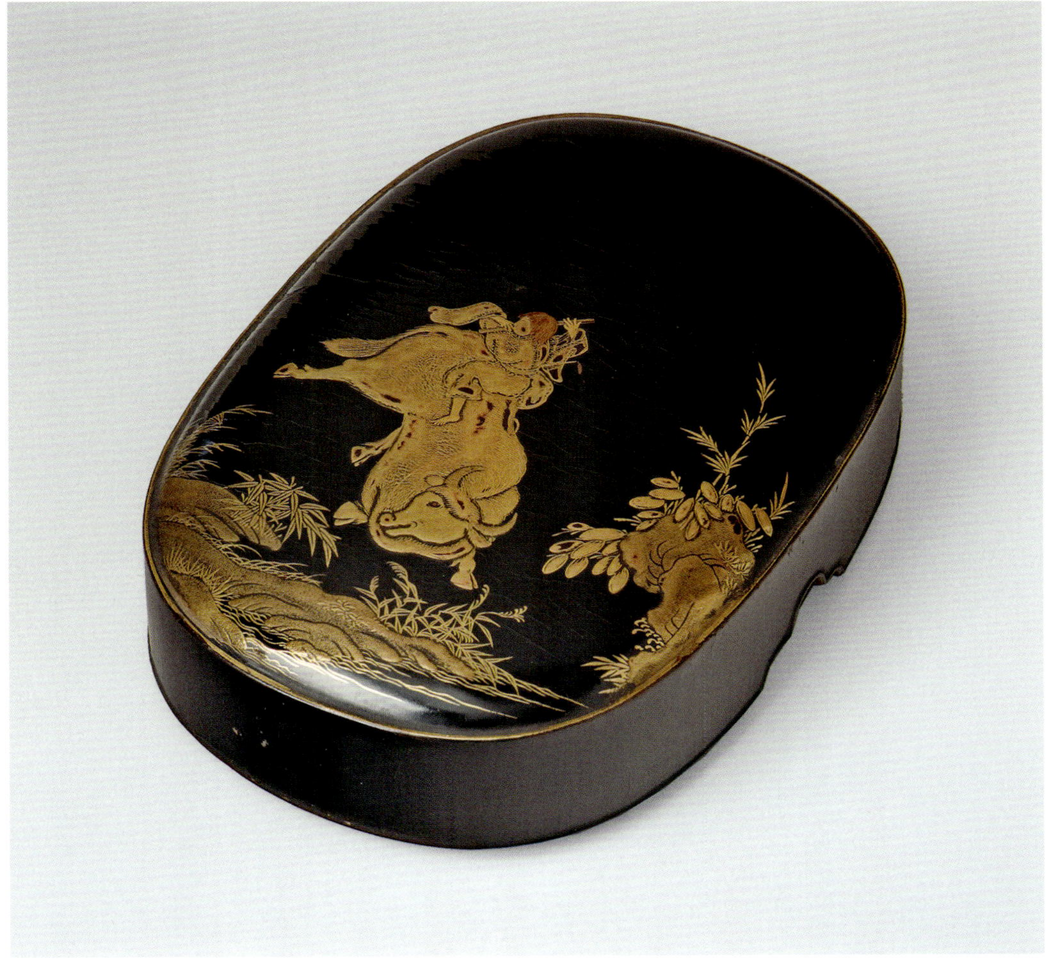

743. *Nanban* (南蛮) cabinet with geometric patterns and deer, birds, fish, plants, and cart wheels partially submerged in water

Momoyama period, early 17th century
Black lacquer with gold and silver *maki-e* and mother-of-pearl inlay
31.4 x 43.4 x 30.5 cm (12 3/8 x 17 1/8 x 12 in.)

LITERATURE: Tokyo National Museum 1985a, no. 111; Murase 2000, no. 95.

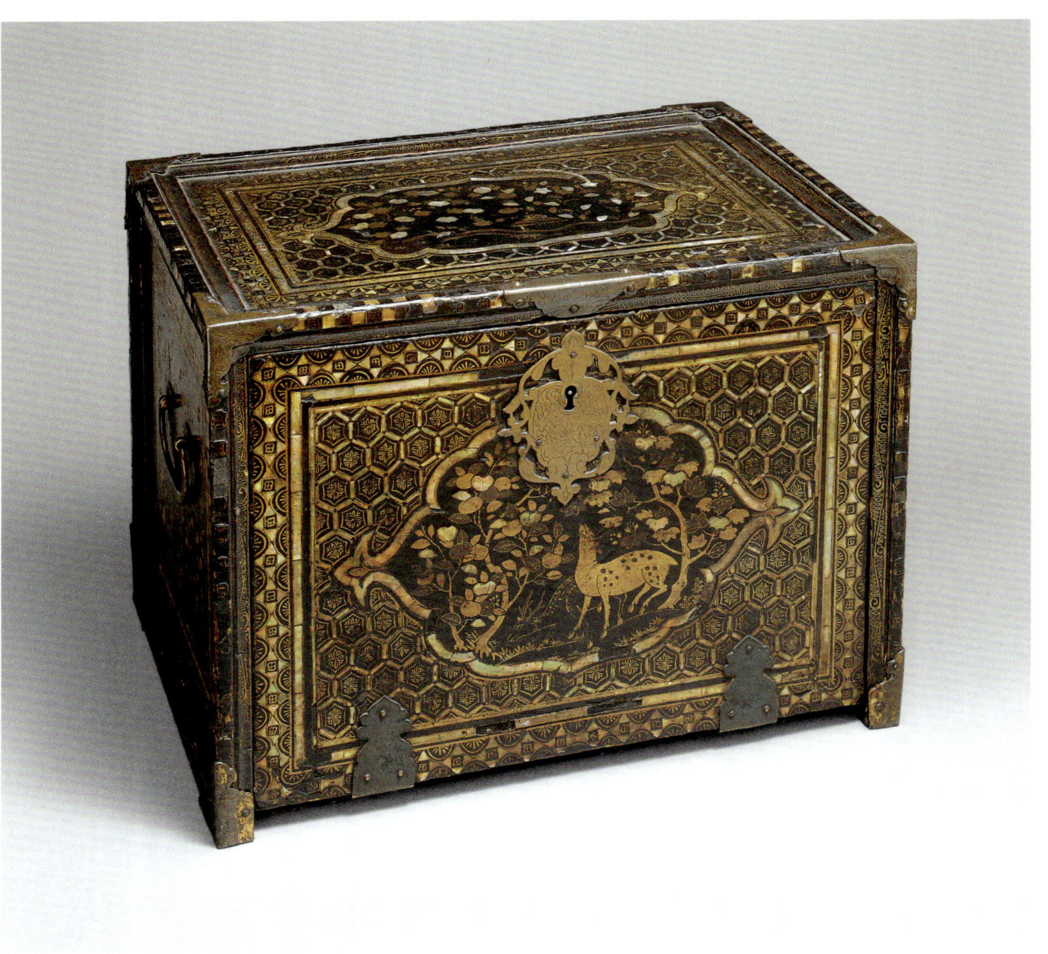

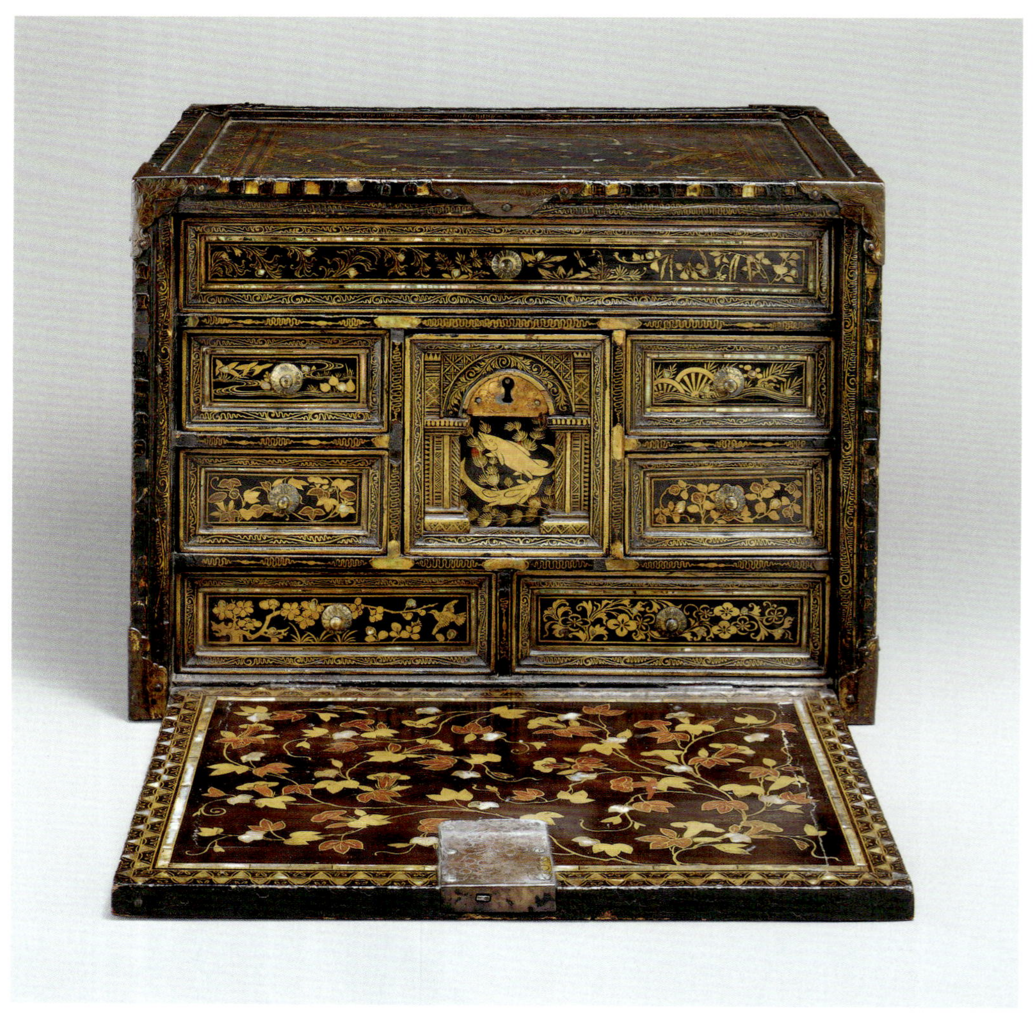

744. Stacked food boxes (*jūbako*, 重箱) with stripes

Momoyama period, early 17th century
Black lacquer with gold *maki-e* and mother-of-pearl and lead inlay
22 x 23.5 x 21.3 cm ($8^{5}/_{8}$ x $9^{1}/_{4}$ x $8^{3}/_{8}$ in.)

LITERATURE: Tokyo National Museum 1985a, no. 112; Avitabile 1990, no. 116; Murase 2000, no. 96.

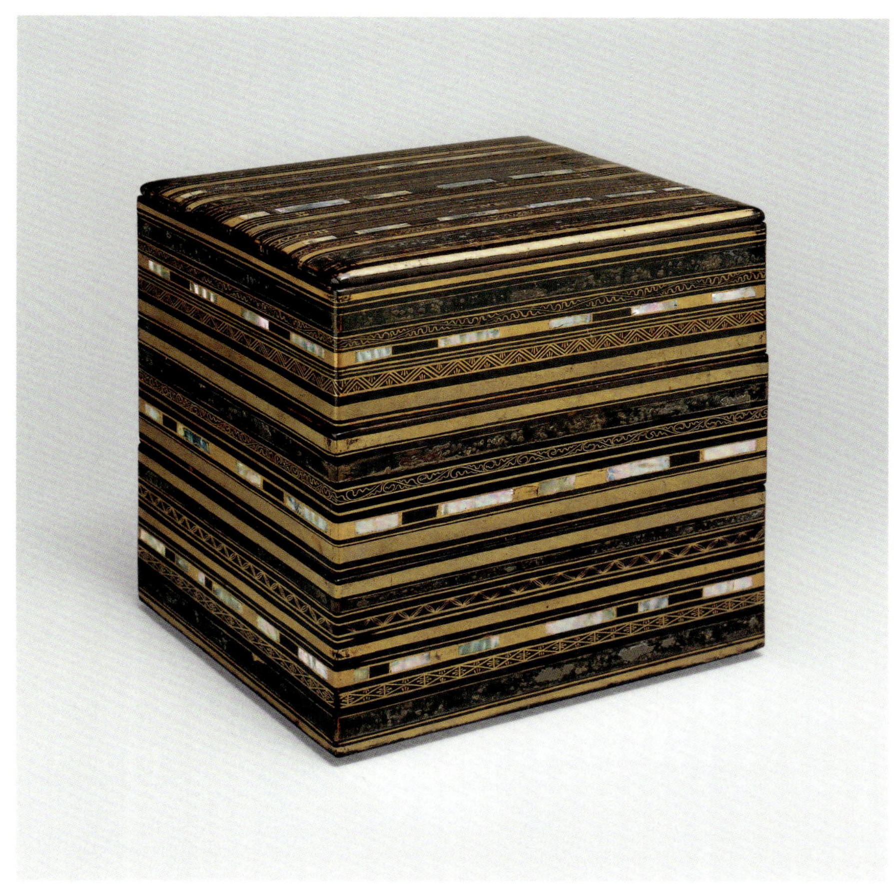

745. Ewer for hot water (*yutō*, 湯桶) with wisteria

Momoyama period, late 16th–early 17th century
Black lacquer with traces of red lacquer and silver and gold *maki-e*
H. with handle 24.9 cm ($9^{3}/_{4}$ in.)

LITERATURE: Wheelwright 1989, fig. 61; Avitabile 1990, no. 117; Murase 1993, no. 72; Murase 2000, no. 123.

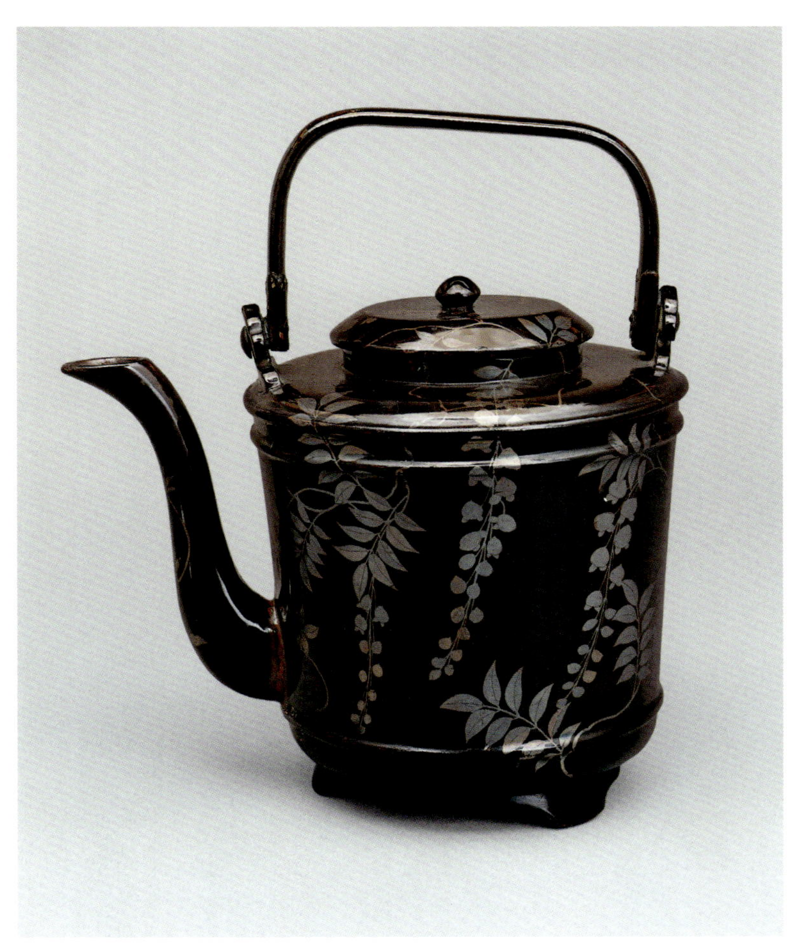

746. Sutra box with lotus flowers and two seed syllables (*shuji*, 種字) for White-Robed Kannon (白衣観音) and Juntei Kannon (准胝観音)

Momoyama period, early 17th century
Black lacquer with gold *maki-e*
L. 32.2 cm (12⅝ in.)

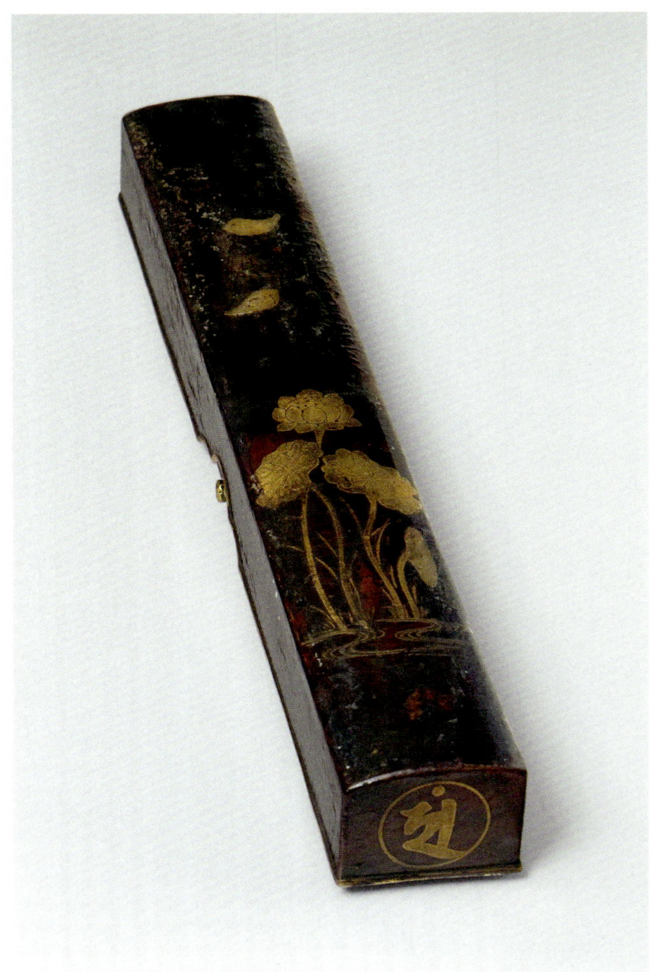

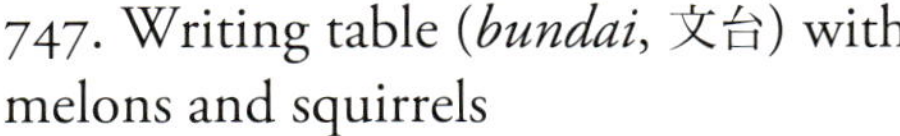

747. Writing table (*bundai*, 文台) with melons and squirrels

Momoyama–Edo period, early 17th century
Black lacquer with gold *maki-e* and pictorial pearlskin ground (*e-nashiji*, 絵梨地)
10 x 58.4 x 34.6 cm (4 x 23 x 13⅝ in.)

LITERATURE: Doi Kumiko 1987, no. 10; Avitabile 1990, no. 113; Murase 1993, no. 70.

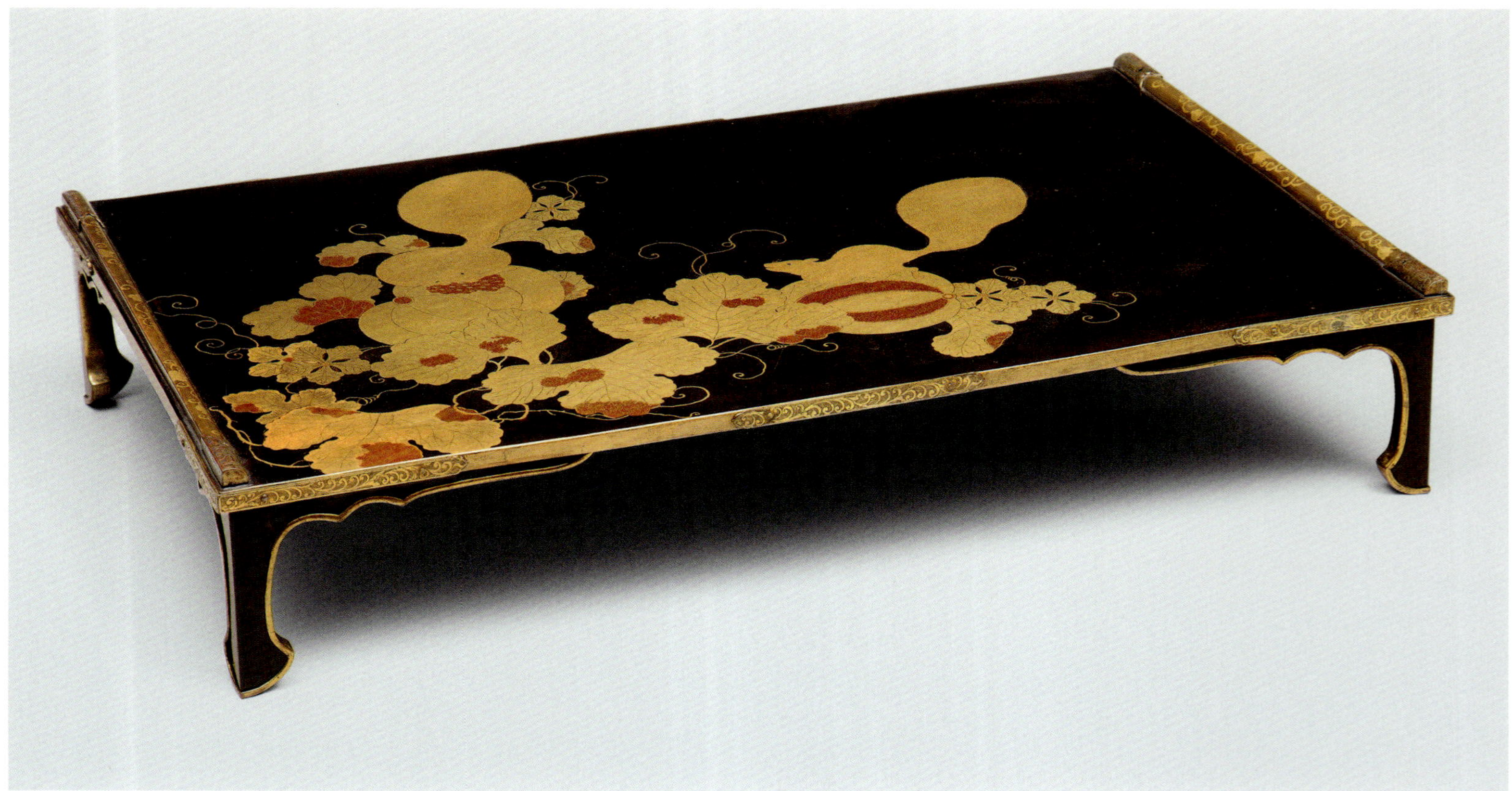

748. Writing box (*suzuribako*, 硯箱) with *Nanban* (南蛮) figures

Edo period, ca. 1633
Black lacquer with gold and silver *maki-e*, polychrome lacquer, and gold and silver foil inlay
4.2 x 20.9 x 22.2 cm (1 5/8 x 8 1/4 x 8 3/4 in.)

Ex coll.: Manno Collection

Literature: Manno Art Museum, 1988, no. 69; Murase 2003, no. 139.

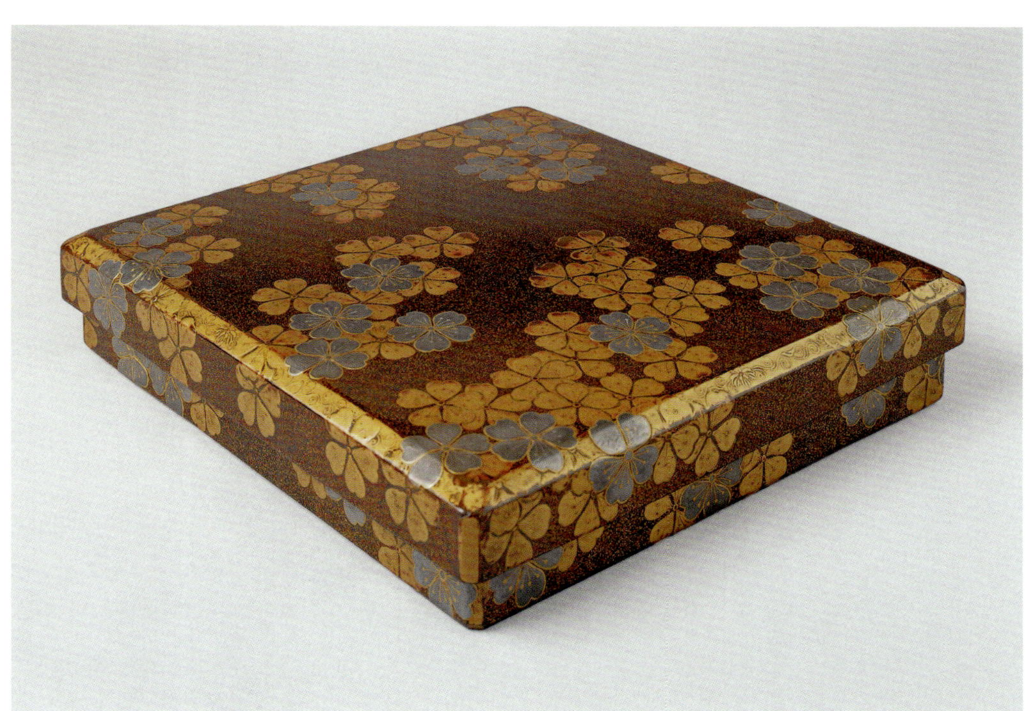

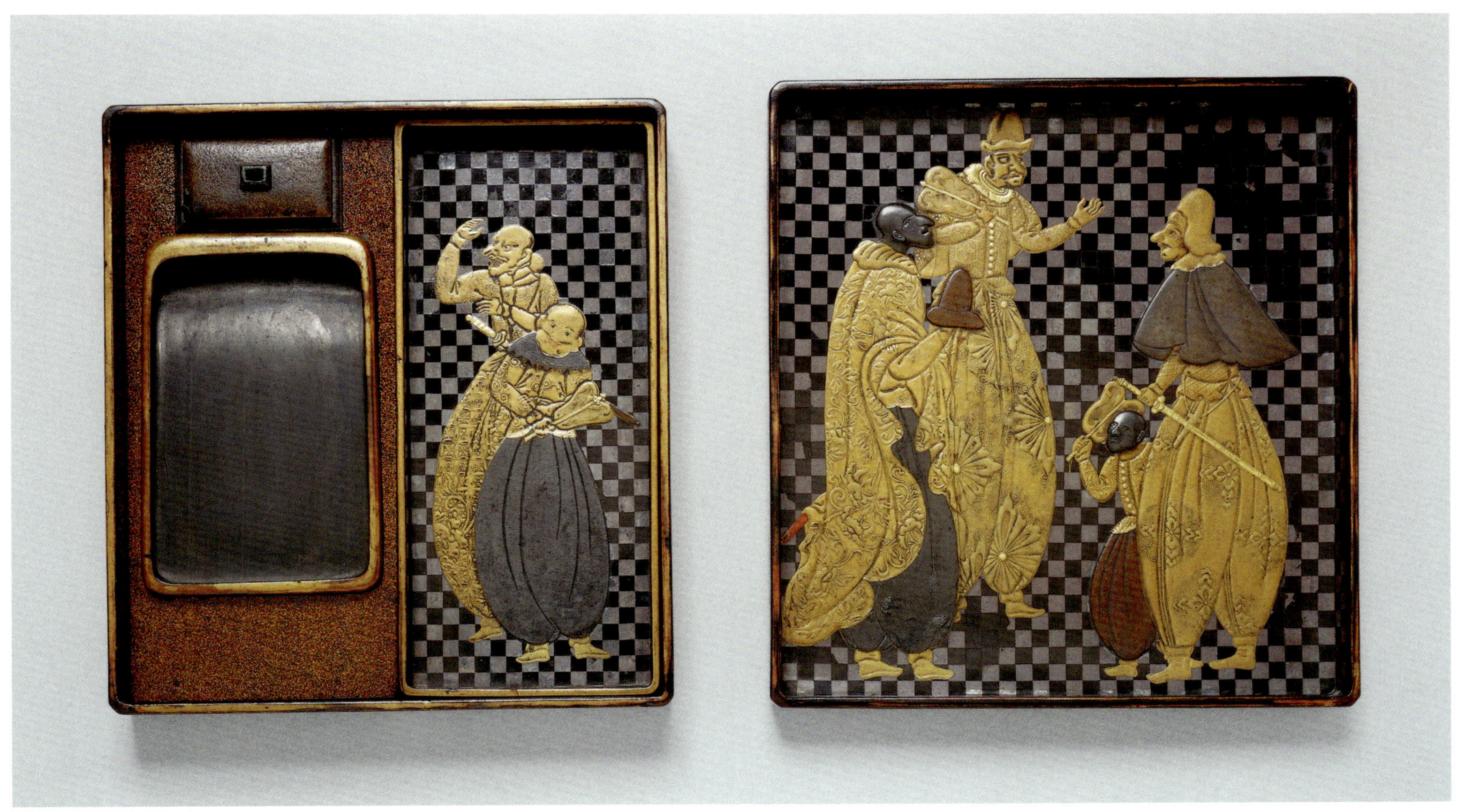

749. Lobed incense burner with metal cover

Edo period, 17th century
Black lacquer with gold *maki-e* on pearskin ground (*nashiji*, 梨地)
Diam. 10 cm (4 in.)

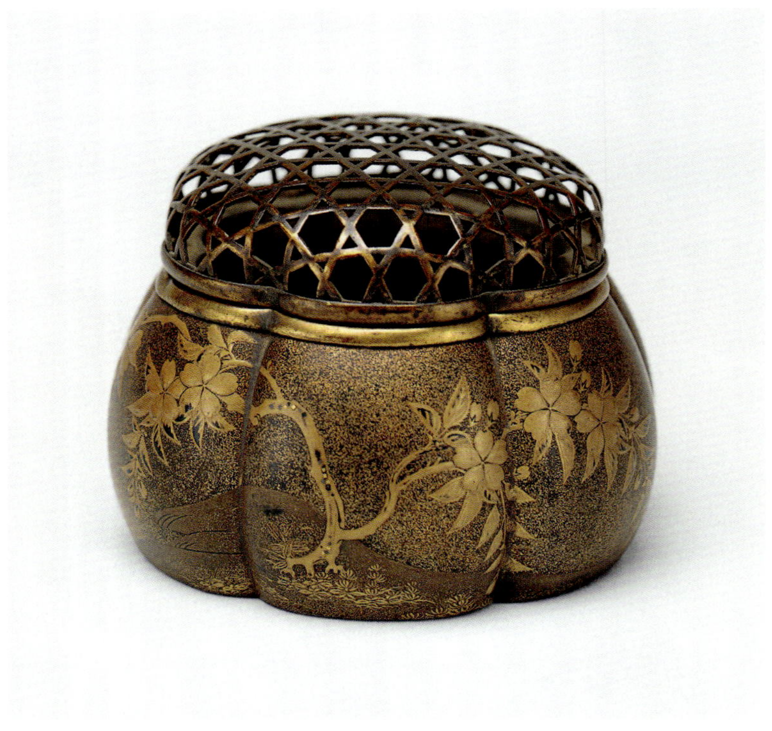

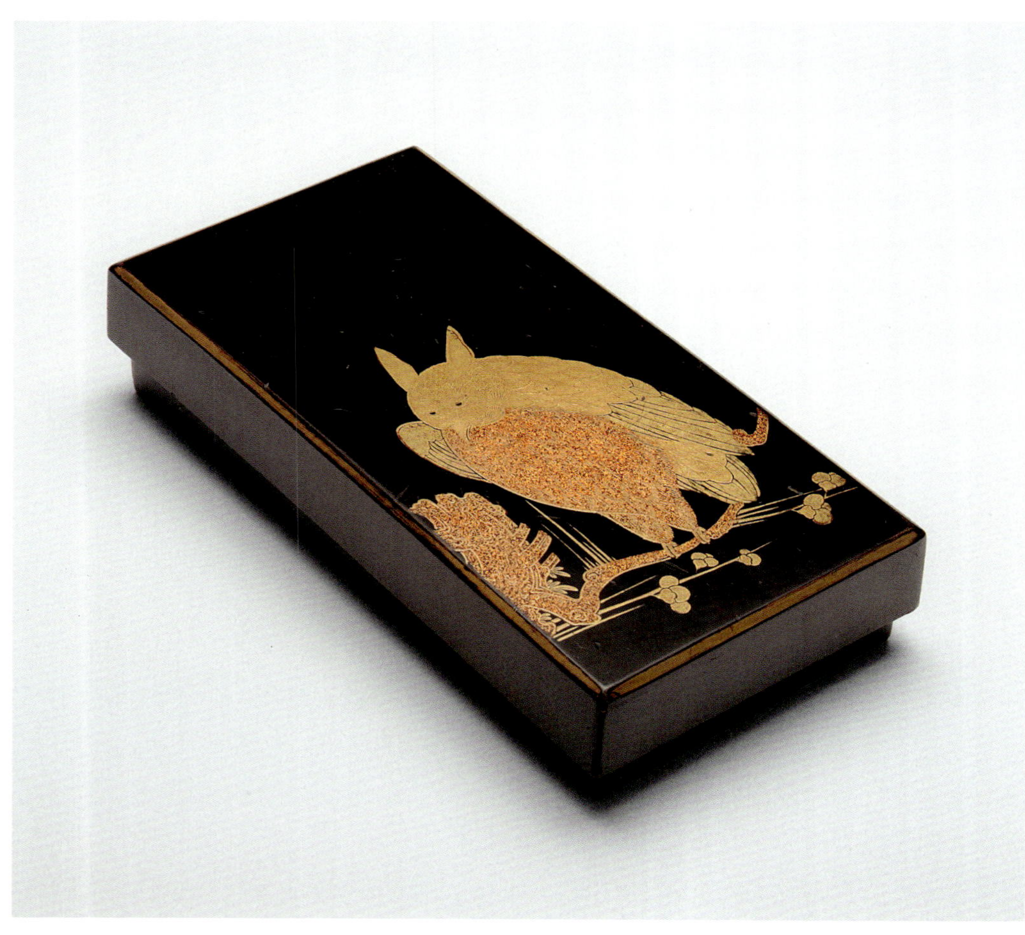

750. Writing box (*suzuribako*, 硯箱) with owl

Edo period, 17th century
Black lacquer with gold *maki-e* and pictorial pearskin ground (*e-nashiji*, 絵梨地)
3.6 x 9.8 x 19.6 cm (1³/₈ x 3⁷/₈ x 7³/₄ in.)

LITERATURE: Tokyo National Museum 1985a, no. 119; Avitabile 1990, no. 122.

Gift from Setsu Iwao

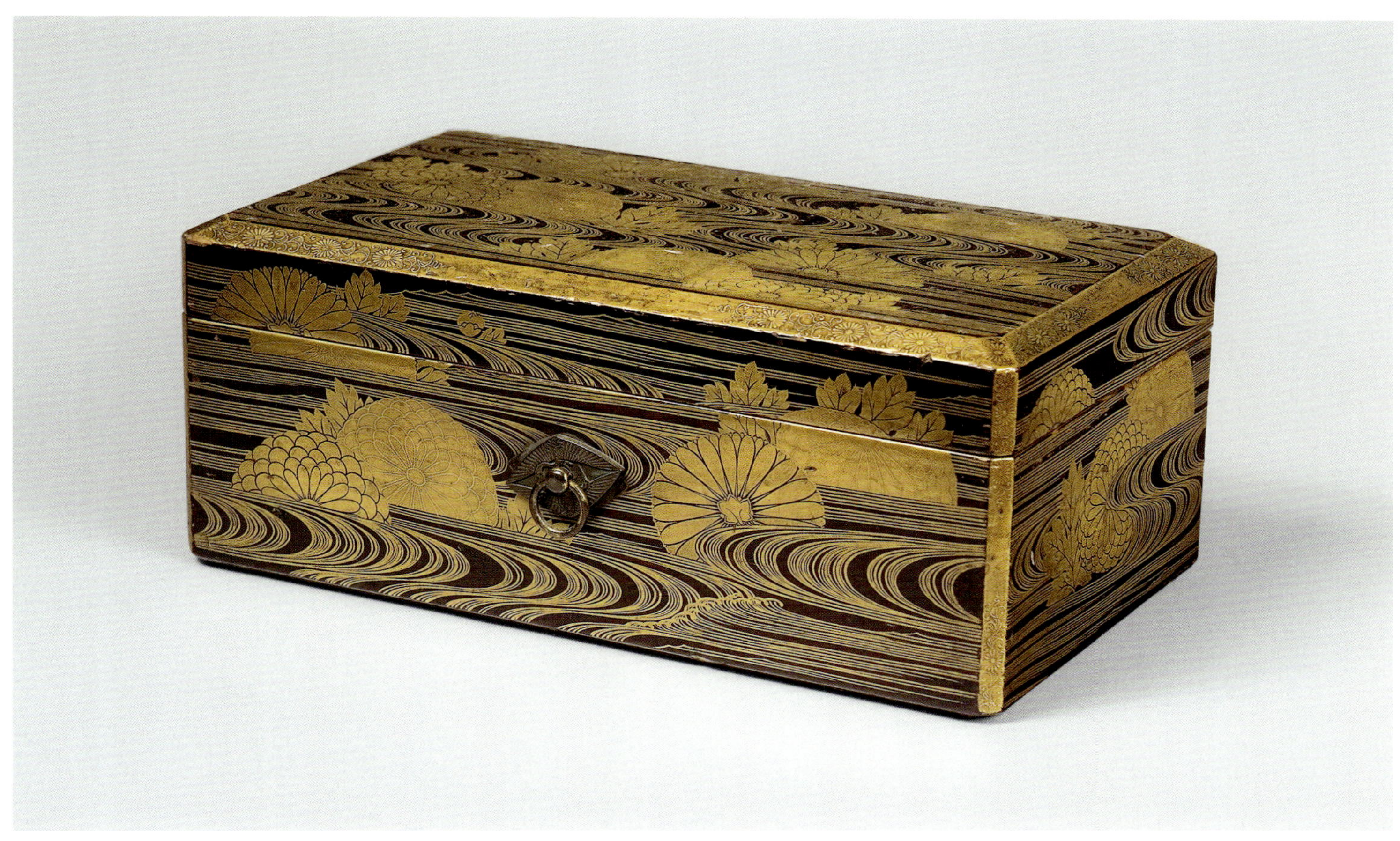

751. Box with chrysanthemums and flowing water

Edo period, 17th century
Black lacquer with gold *maki-e*
12 x 30.5 x 17.5 cm (4 3/4 x 12 x 6 7/8 in.)

Literature: Tokyo National Museum 1985a, no. 116; Avitabile 1990, no. 120.

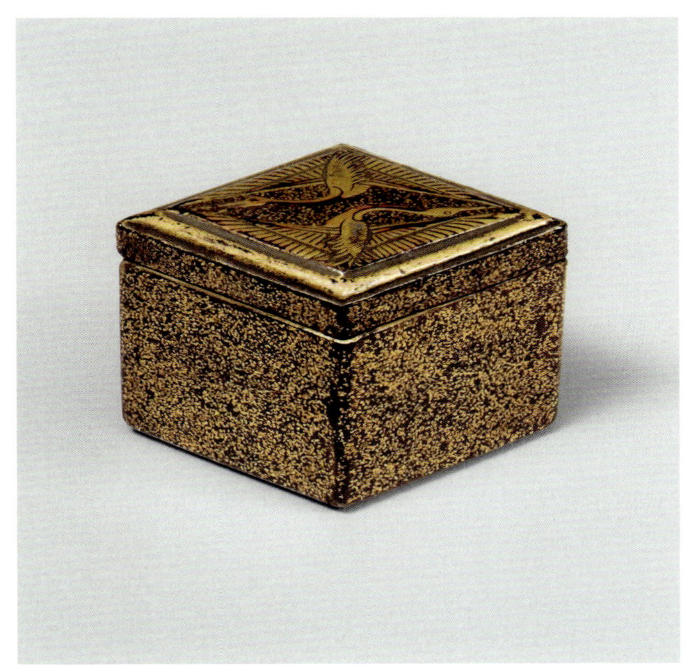

752. Incense box (*kōgō*, 香合) with paired cranes

Edo period, 17th century
Black lacquer with gold *maki-e*
H. 2.8 cm (1 1/8 in.)

Gift from Hosomi Minoru, 1980

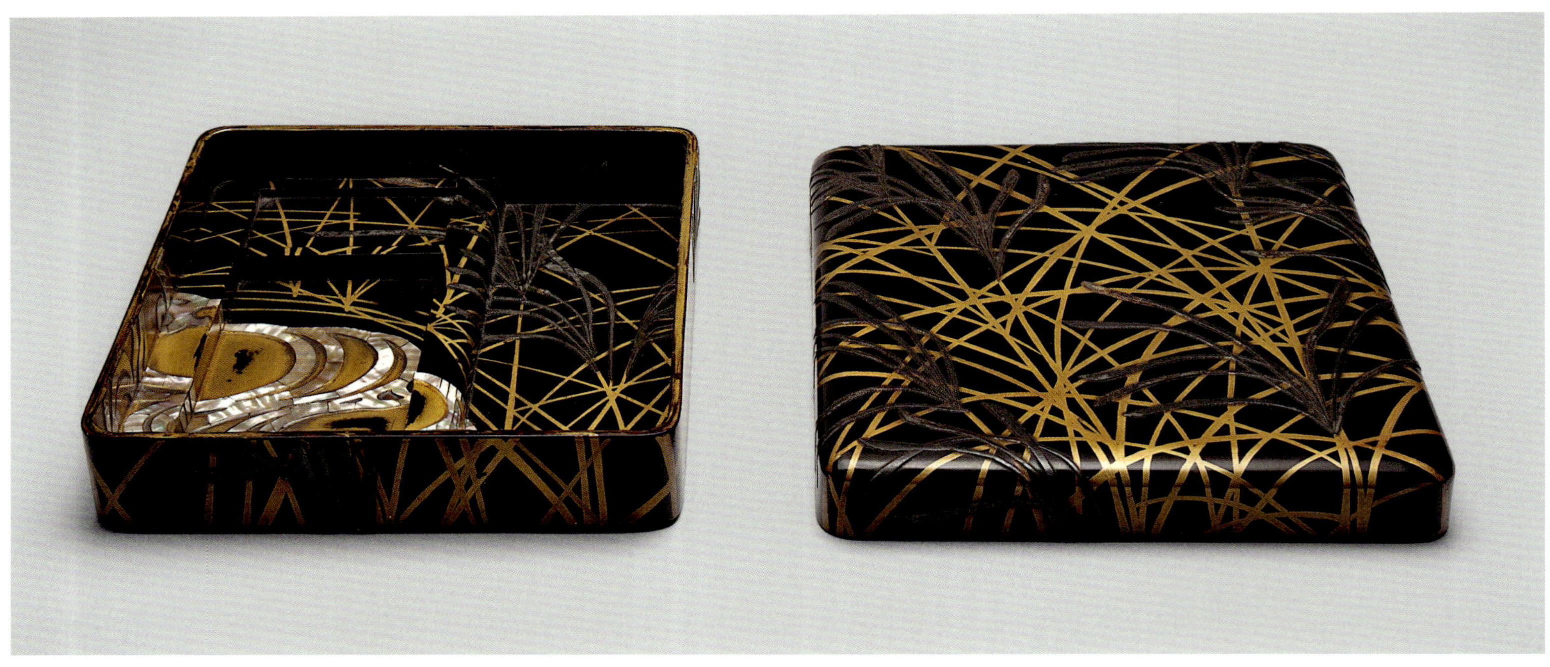

753. Writing box (*suzuribako*, 硯箱) with reeds and water

Edo period, late 17th century
Black lacquer with gold *maki-e* and mother-of-pearl and lead inlay
4.4 x 20.4 x 24.1 cm (1¾ x 8⅛ x 9 in.)

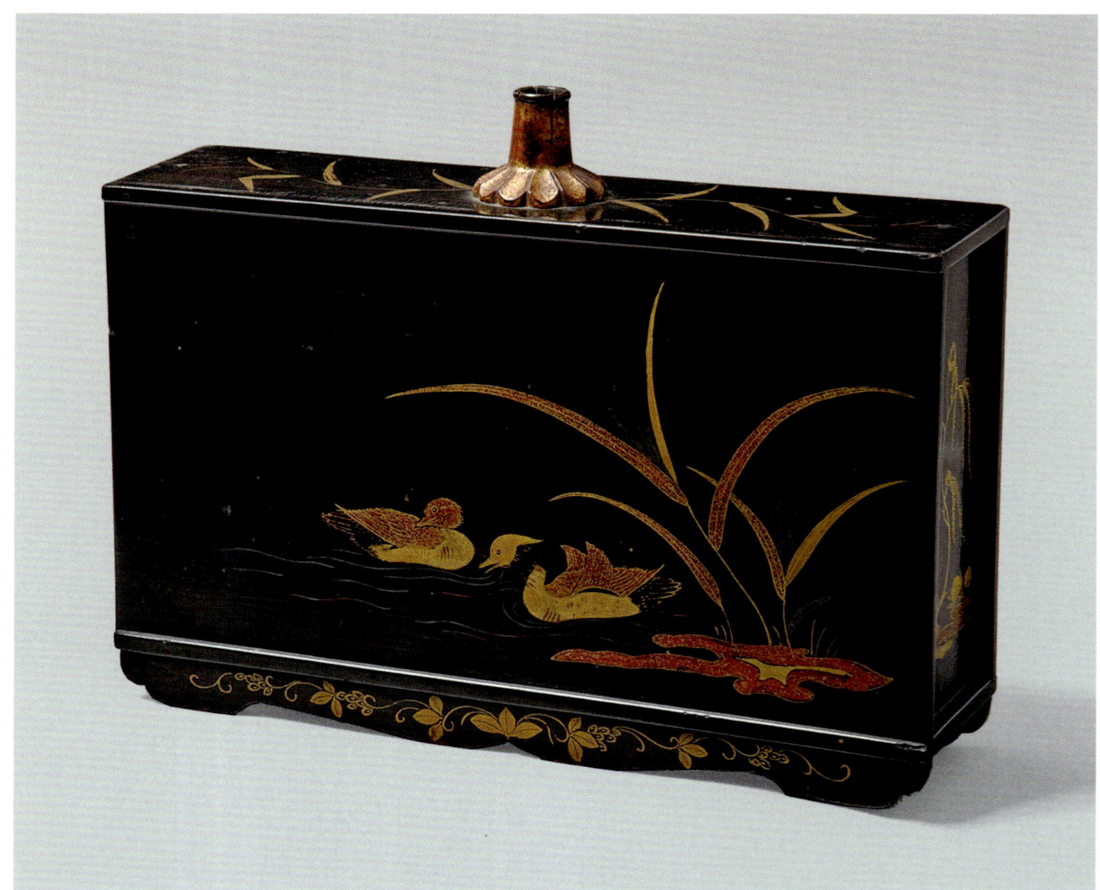

754. Sake container with ducks

Edo period, 17th–18th century
Black lacquer with gold and silver *maki-e* and pictorial pearskin ground (*e-nashiji*, 絵梨地)
22.3 x 30.2 x 8 cm (8¾ x 11⅞ x 3⅛ in.)

LITERATURE: Tokyo National Museum 1985a, no. 117; Avitabile 1990, no. 119.

755. Writing box (*suzuribako*, 硯箱) with poem from *Kokin wakashū* (古今和歌集)

Edo period, 18th century
Black lacquer with gold *maki-e* and lead inlay on pearskin ground (*nashiji*, 梨地)
2.5 x 14.2 x 15.7 cm (1 x $5^{5}/_{8}$ x $6^{1}/_{8}$ in.)
Text

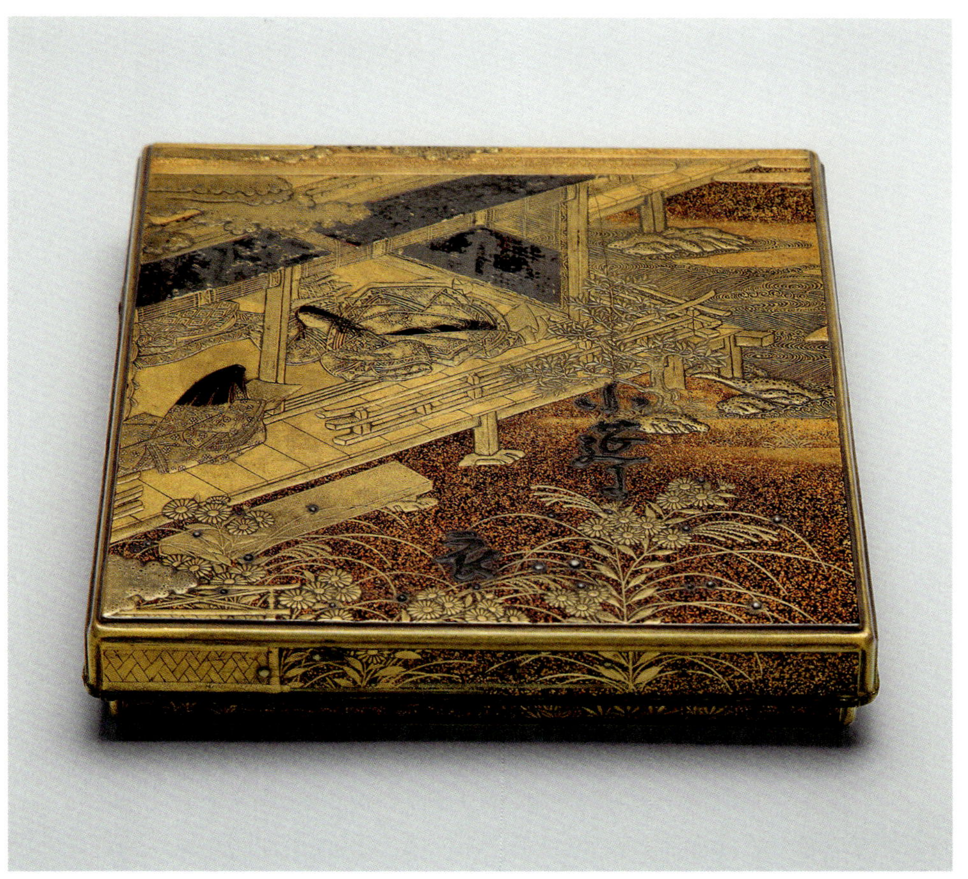

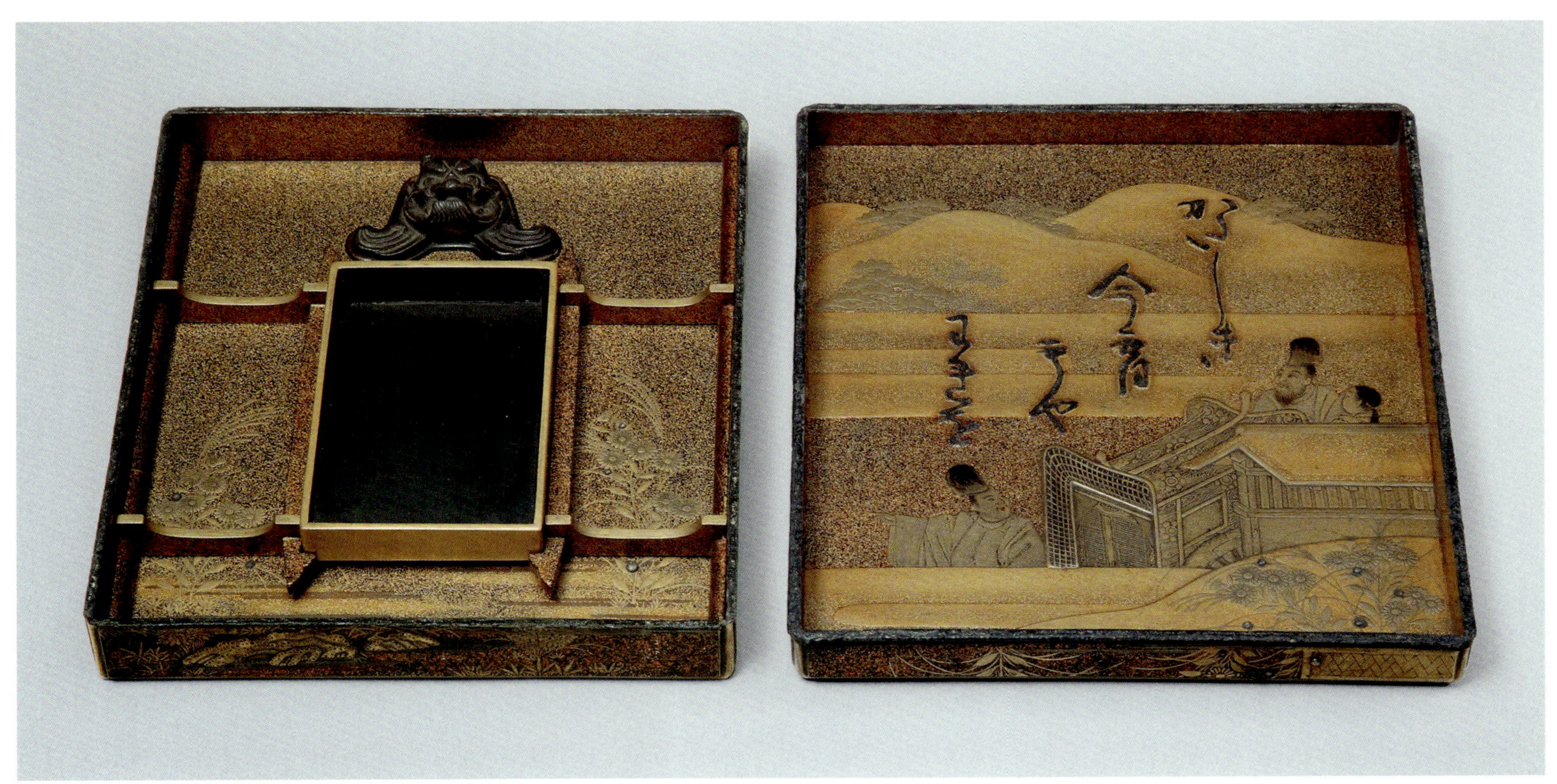

756. Storage box containing handwritten 41-volume *Taiheiki* (太平記)

Edo period, 18th century
Black lacquer with gold *maki-e*
24 x 39.5 x 27.4 cm (9 1/2 x 15 1/2 x 10 3/4 in.)

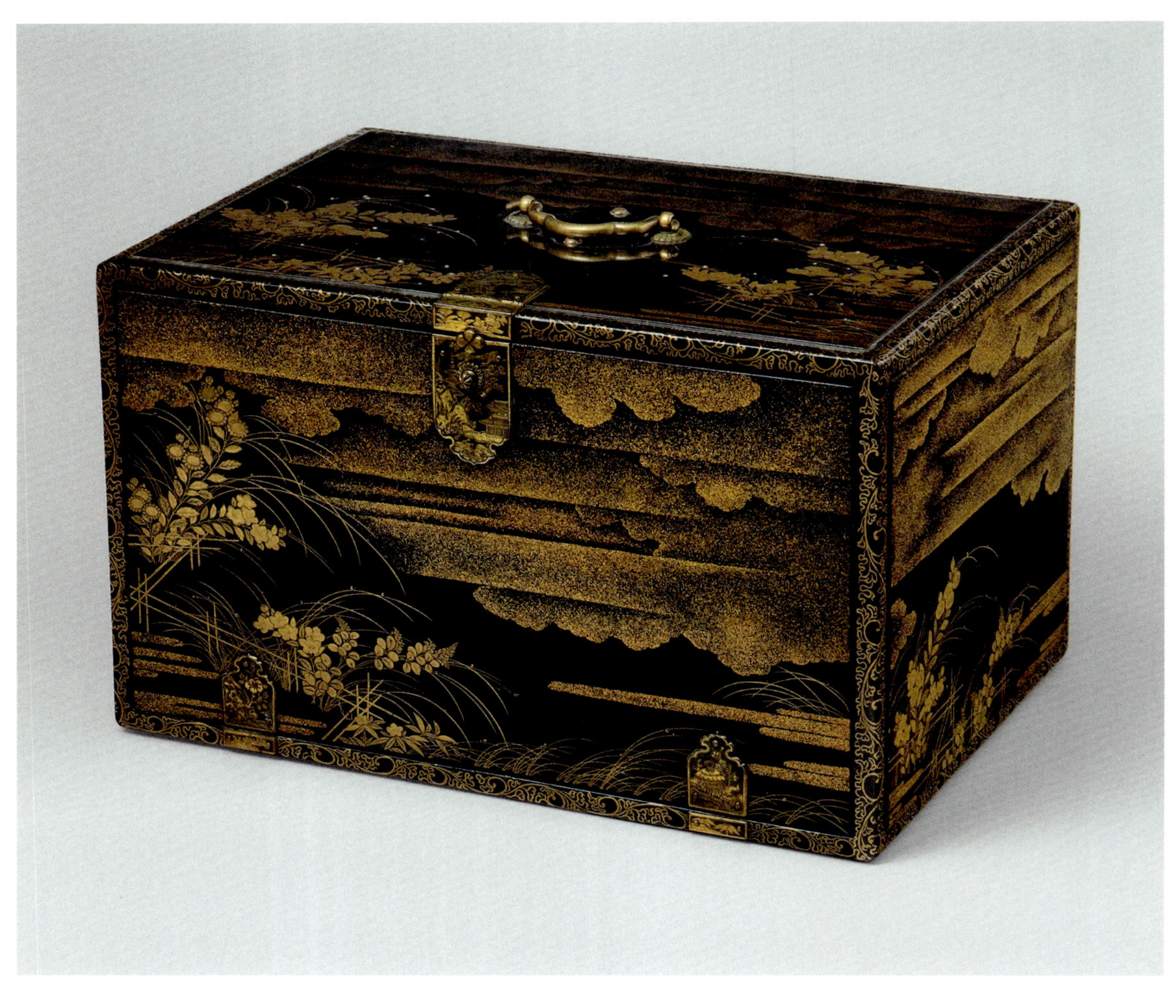

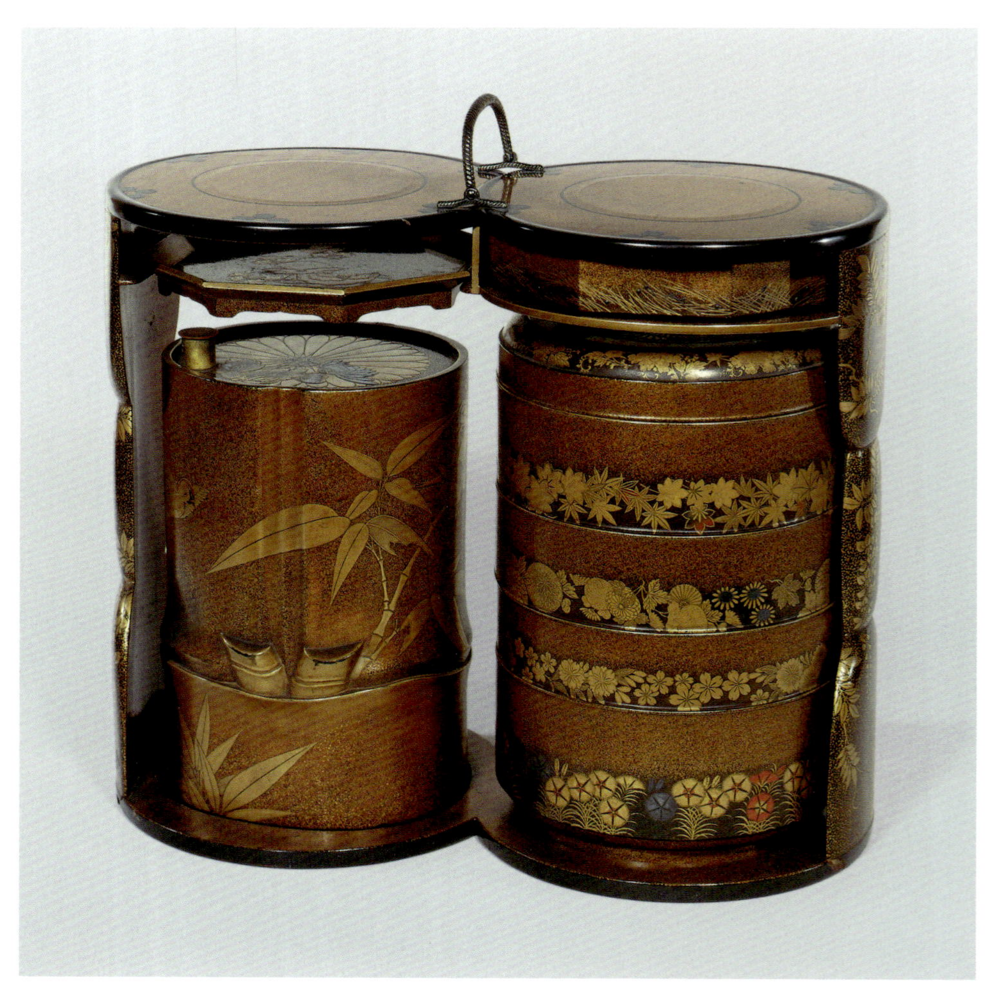

757. Picnic set with plants from the four seasons

Edo period, 18th century
Black lacquer with gold and silver *maki-e* and polychrome lacquer on pearskin ground (*nashiji*, 梨地)
Overall 24.3 x 29.4 x 15.2 cm (9 5/8 x 11 5/8 x 6 in.)

LITERATURE: Tokyo National Museum 1985a, no. 118; Avitabile 1990, no. 121.

758. Portable chest (*sagetansu*, 提箪笥) with wisteria

Edo period, 17th–18th century
Black lacquer with gold *maki-e* and mother-of-pearl and lead inlay
19 x 18.5 x 27.9 cm (7½ x 7¼ x 11 in.)

LITERATURE: Tokyo National Museum 1985a, no. 121; Avitabile 1990, no. 124.

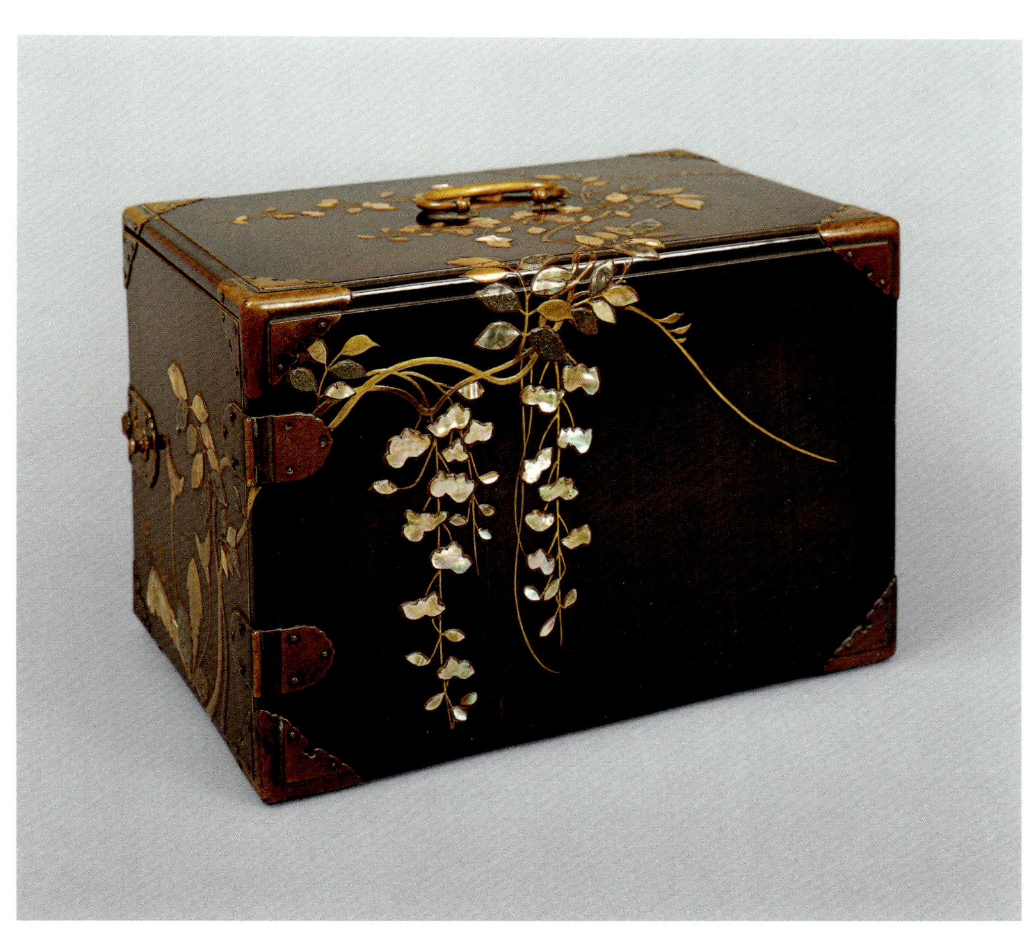

759. Accessories box (*tebako*, 手箱) with scenes from *Genji monogatari* (源氏物語)

Edo period, 17th–18th century
Black lacquer with gold *maki-e*, silver flakes, sheet metal, and pictorial pearskin ground (*e-nashiji*, 絵梨地)
Box 19.1 x 19.9 x 25.2 cm (7½ x 7⅞ x 9⅞ in.)

LITERATURE: Murase 1993, no. 69.

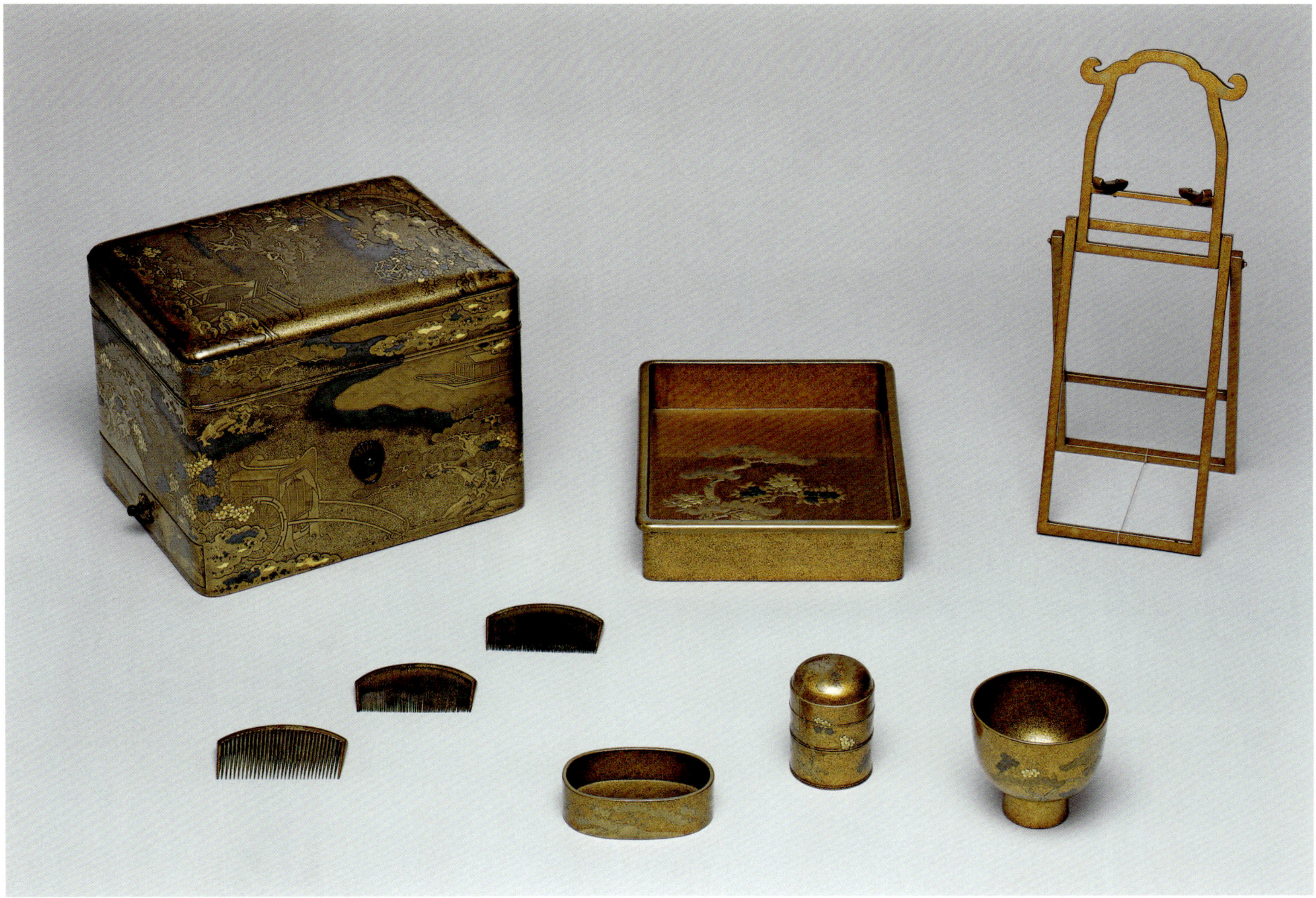

760. Writing box (*suzuribako*, 硯箱) with a poem from *Shin kokin wakashū* (新古今和歌集)

Edo period, 18th century
Black lacquer with gold *maki-e* and lead inlay on pearskin ground (*nashiji*, 梨地)
5.5 x 23 x 24 cm (2 1/8 x 9 x 9 1/2 in.)
Text

LITERATURE: Tokyo National Museum 1985a, no. 120; Avitabile 1990, no. 123; Murase 2000, no. 125.

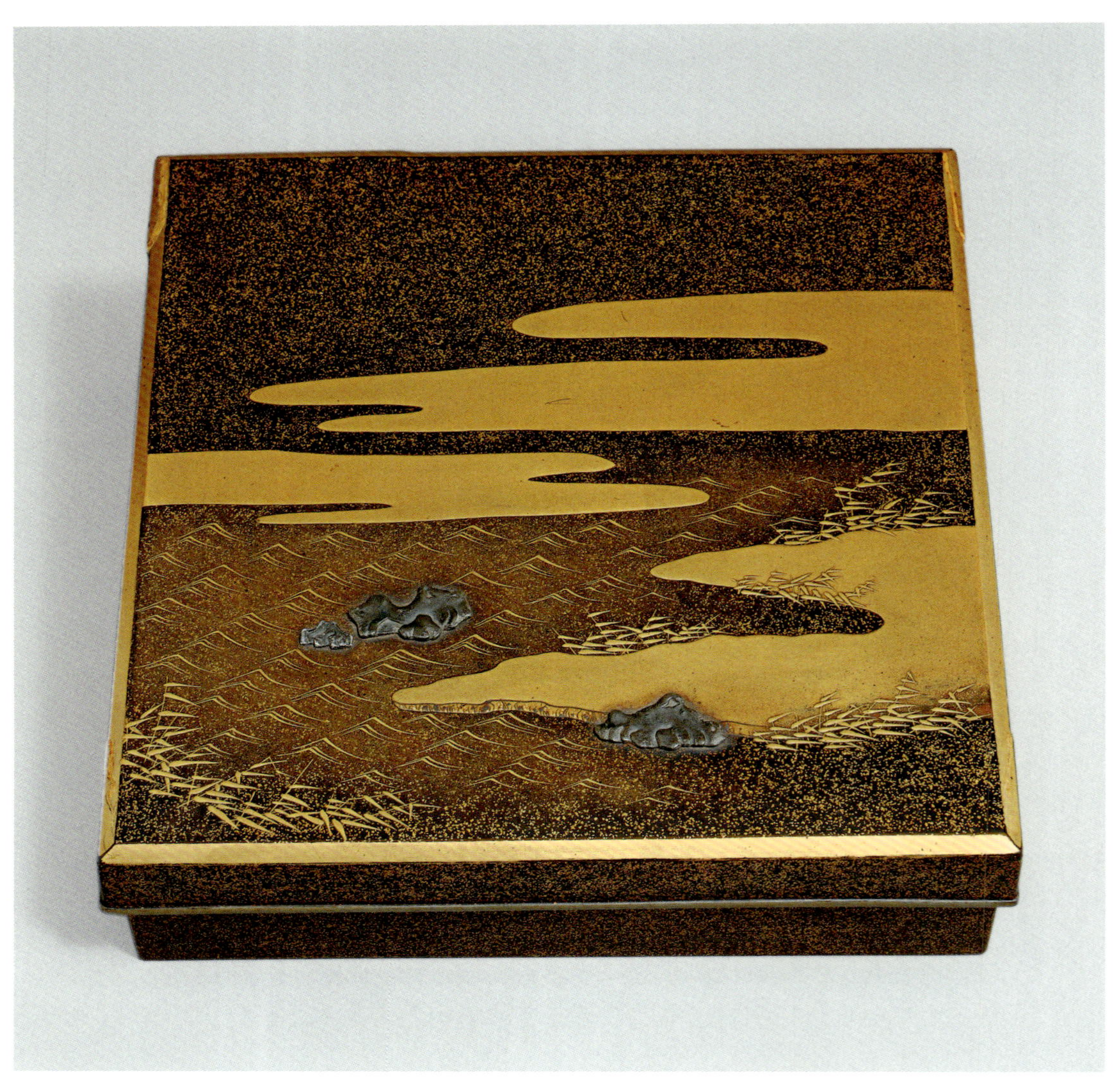

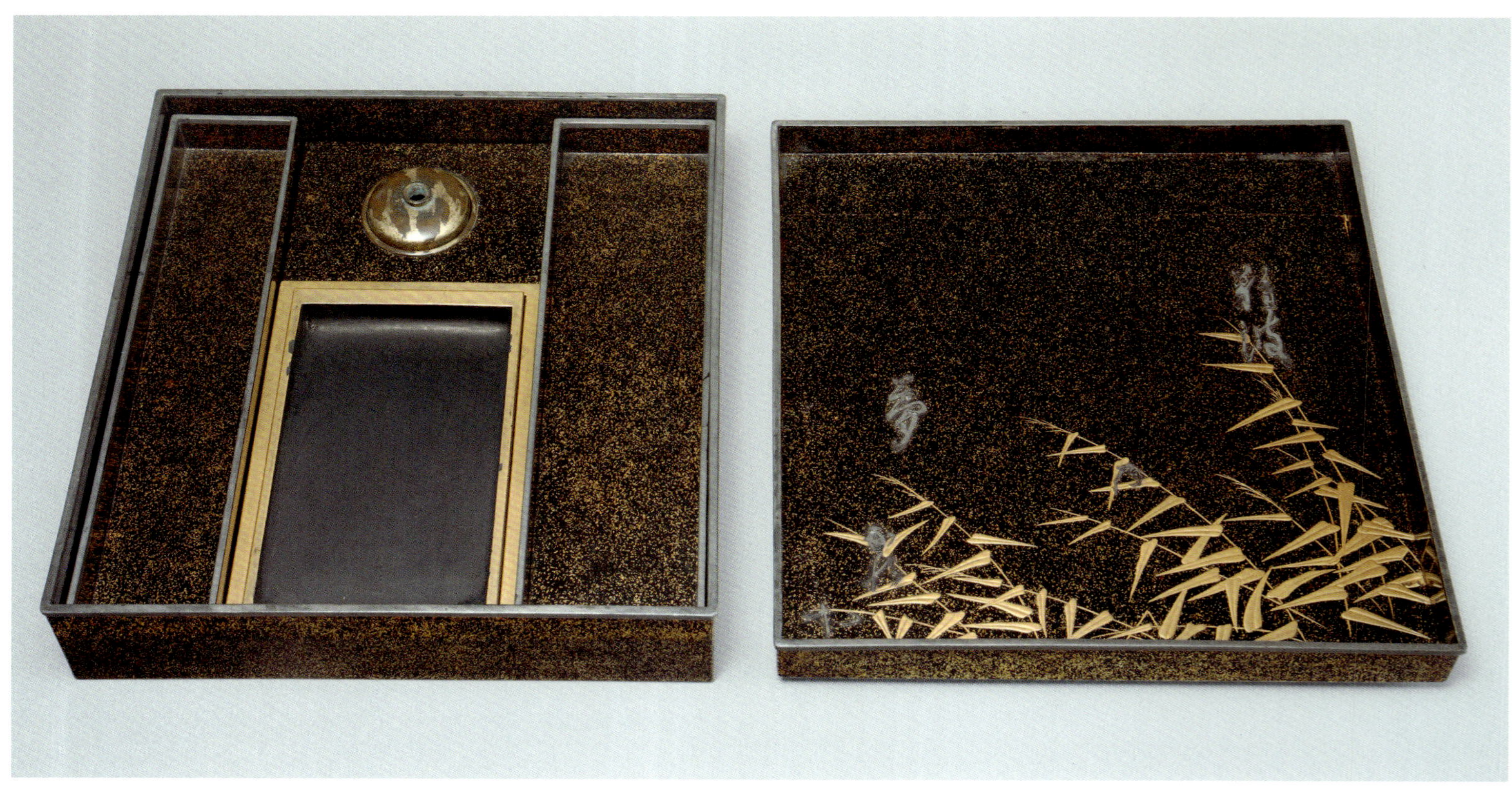

761. Writing box (*suzuribako*, 硯箱) with bridge and waves

Edo period, 18th century
Black lacquer with gold *maki-e* and mother-of-pearl and metal inlay
4.3 x 21 x 22.5 cm ($1^{3}/_{4}$ x $8^{1}/_{4}$ x $8^{7}/_{8}$ in.)

LITERATURE: Burke 1993, no. 50.

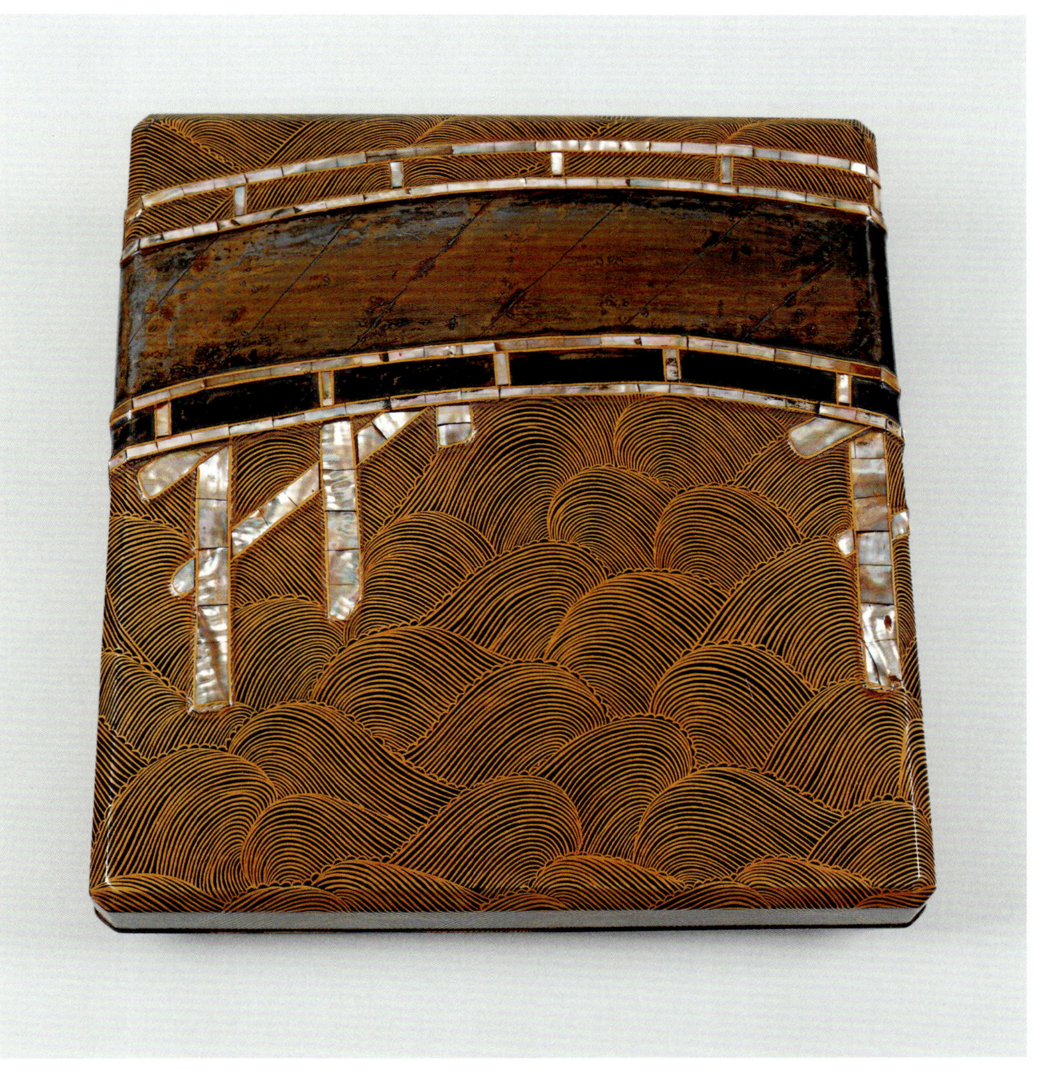

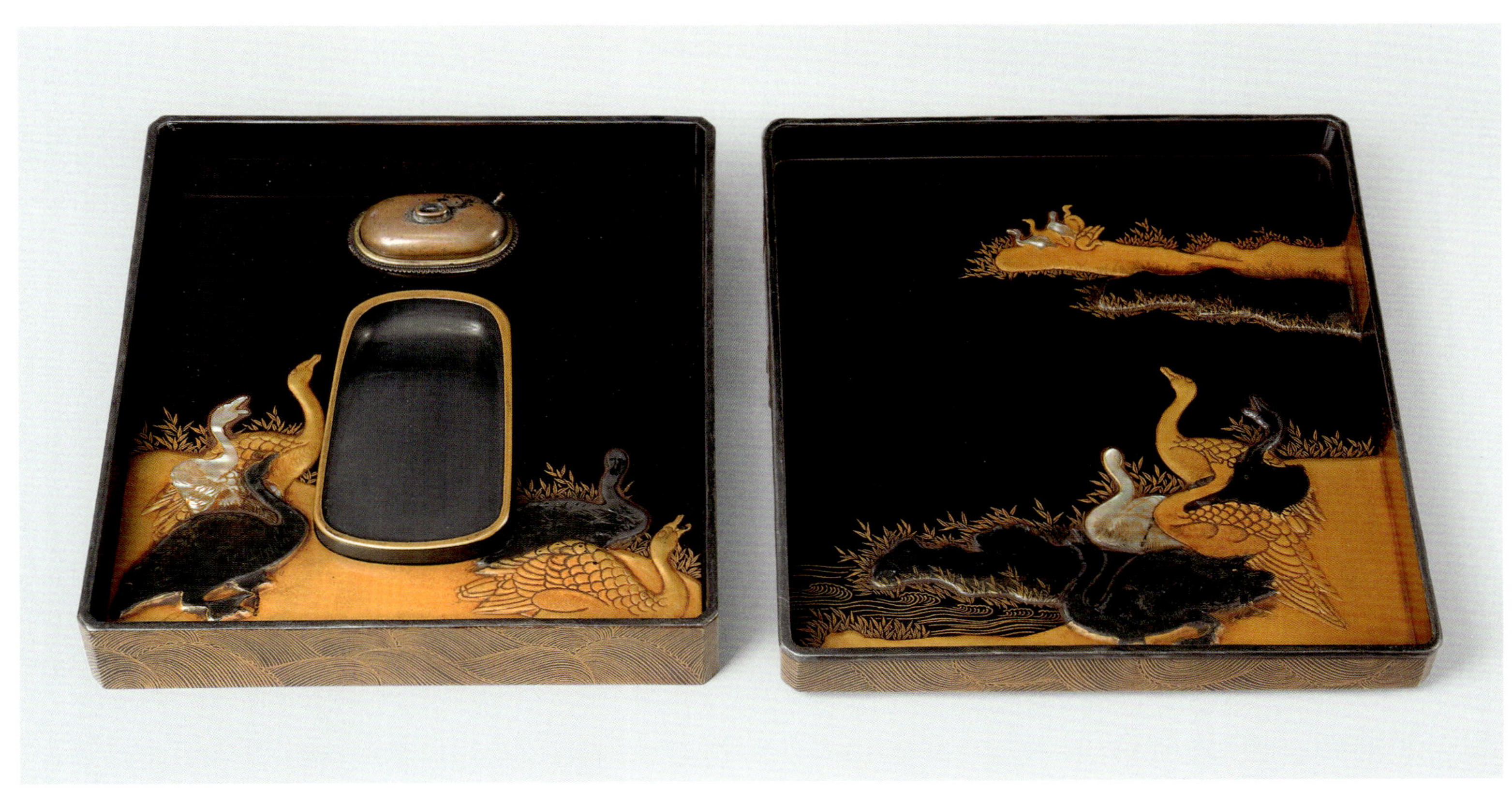

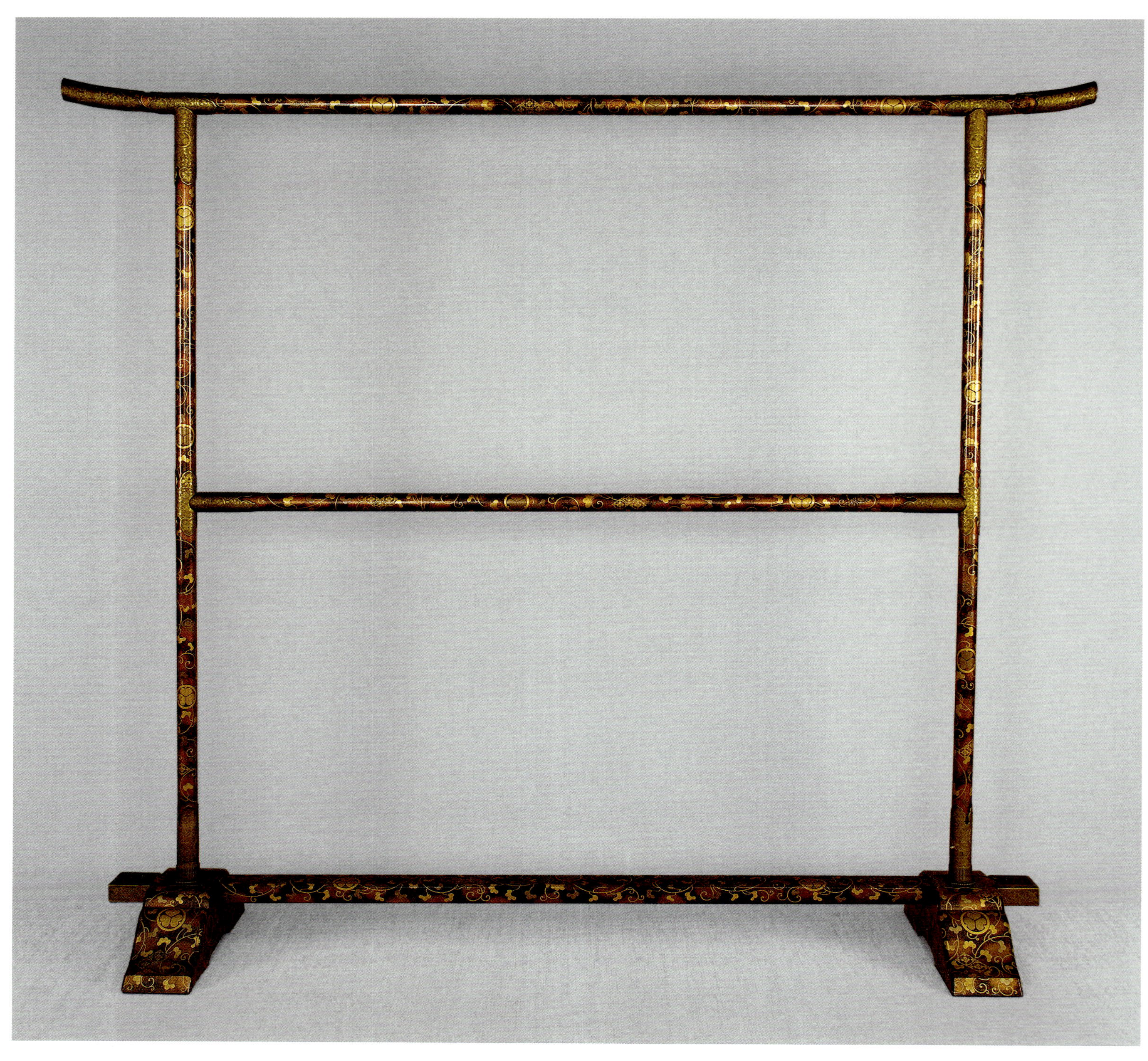

762. Kimono stand (*ikō*, 衣桁) with scrolling foliage and hollyhock crests

Edo period, 18th century
Black lacquer with gold *maki-e* and pictorial pearskin ground (*e-nashiji*, 絵梨地)
Overall 164 x 187 x 42.4 cm (64 5/8 x 73 5/8 x 16 3/4 in.)

LITERATURE: Murase 1980b, no. 47.

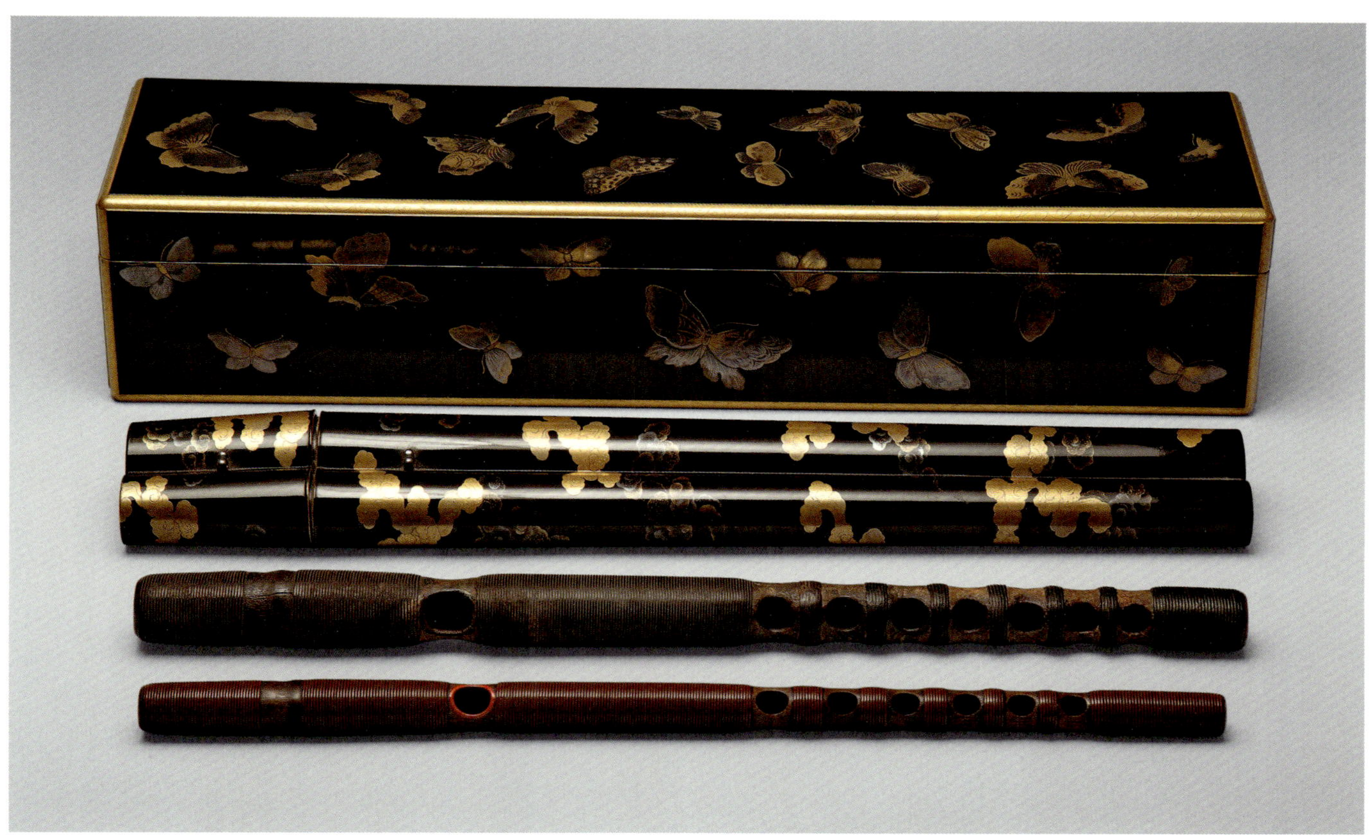

763. Box and case for Noh flutes named "Winter Wind" (*Kogarashi*, 木枯し)

Edo period, 18th century
Black lacquer with gold and silver *maki-e*
Outer box 9 x 12.1 x 46 cm (3½ x 4¾ x 18⅛ in.)
Flute case: L. 42 cm (16½ in.)
Flutes: L. 39.7 cm (15⅝ in.) and 37.3 cm (14⅝ in.)

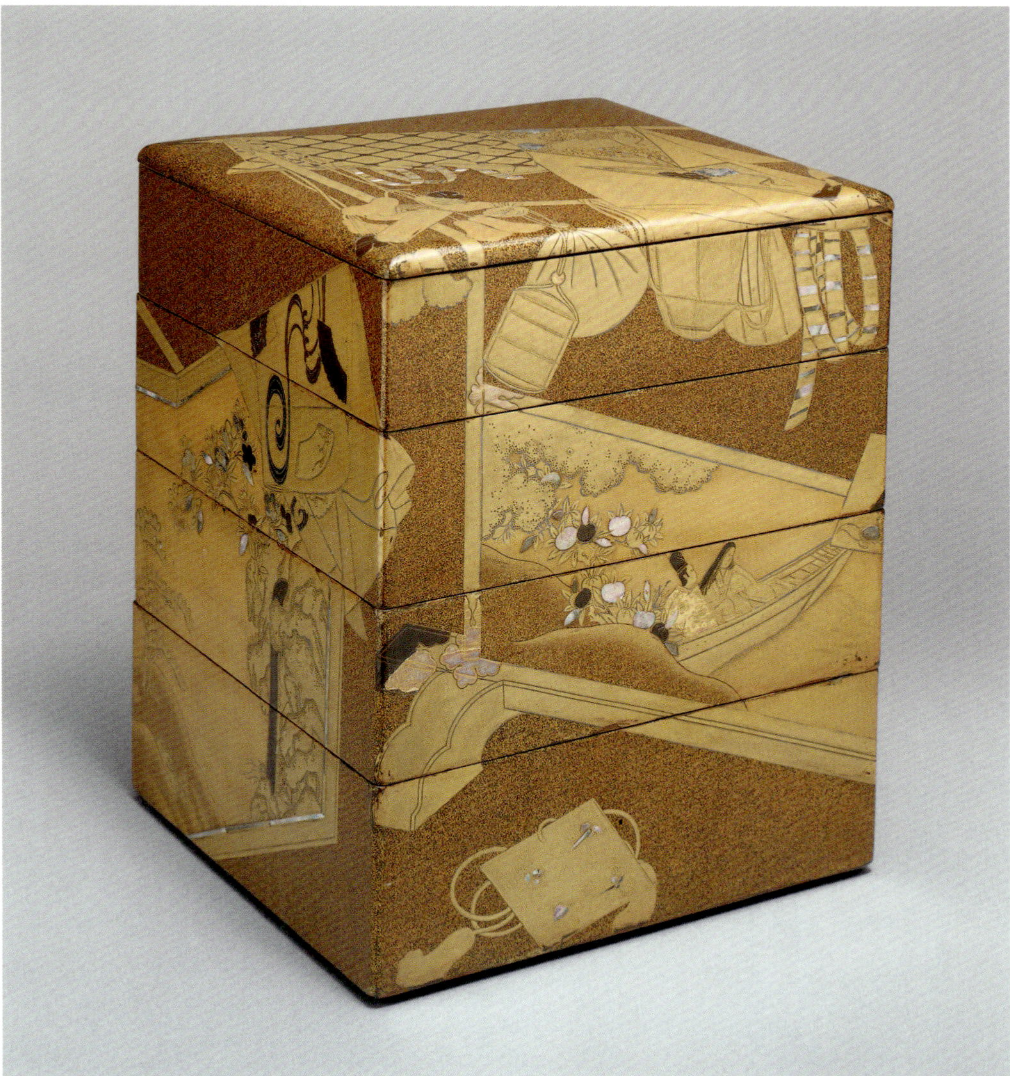

764. Stacked food boxes (*jūbako*, 重箱) with "Whose Sleeves?" (*Tagasode*, 誰袖)

Edo period, 18th century
Black lacquer with gold *maki-e* and mother-of-pearl and lead inlay on pearskin ground (*nashiji*, 梨地)
27.3 x 22.7 x 21 cm (10¾ x 9 x 8¼ in.)

LITERATURE: Murase 2000, no. 126.

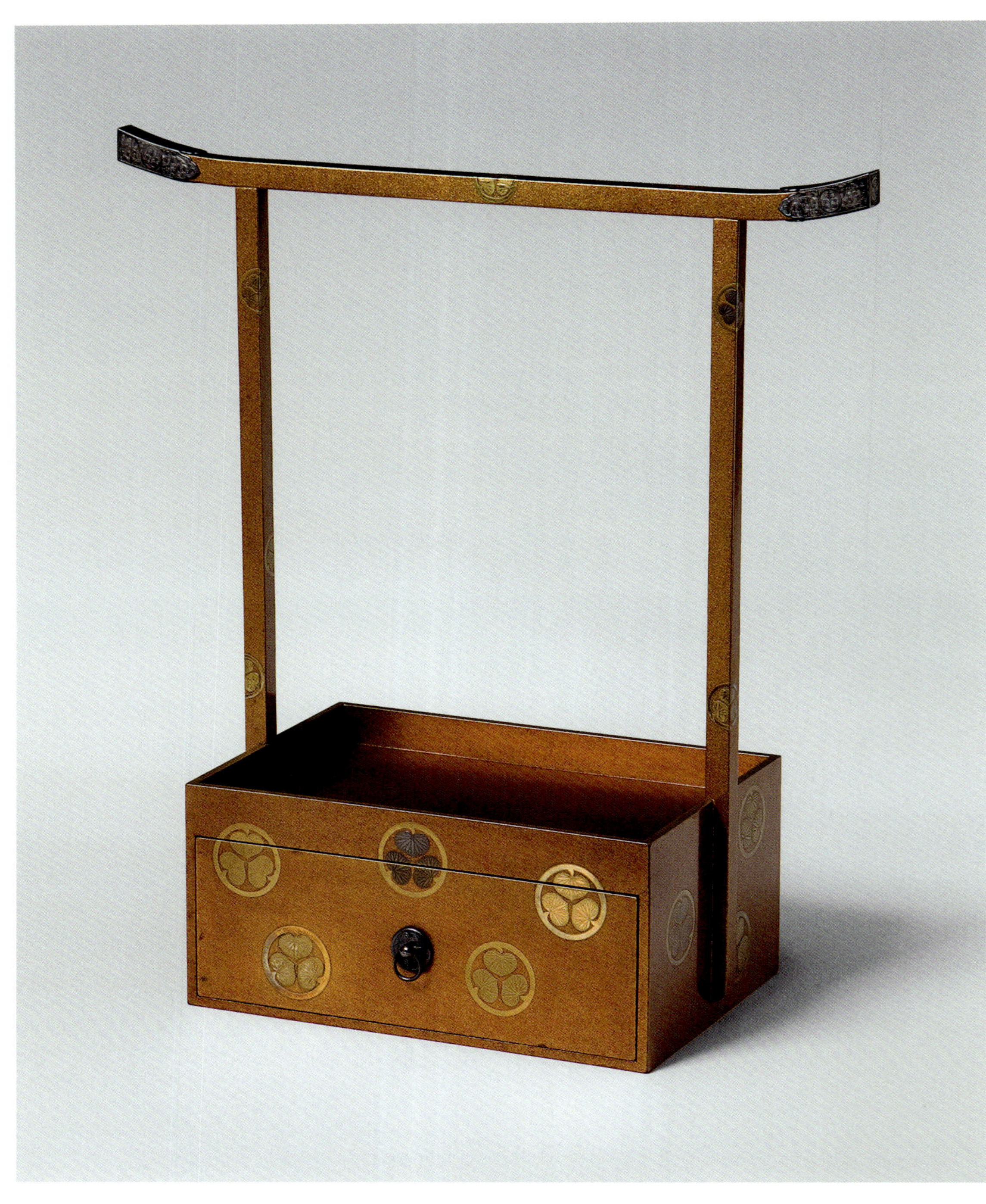

765. Towel stand (*tenugui kake*, 手拭掛) and cosmetic case with hollyhock crests

Edo period, 18th century
Gold and silver *maki-e* on pearskin ground (*nashiji*, 梨地)
45 x 41.5 x 18 cm (17 3/4 x 16 3/8 x 7 1/8 in.)

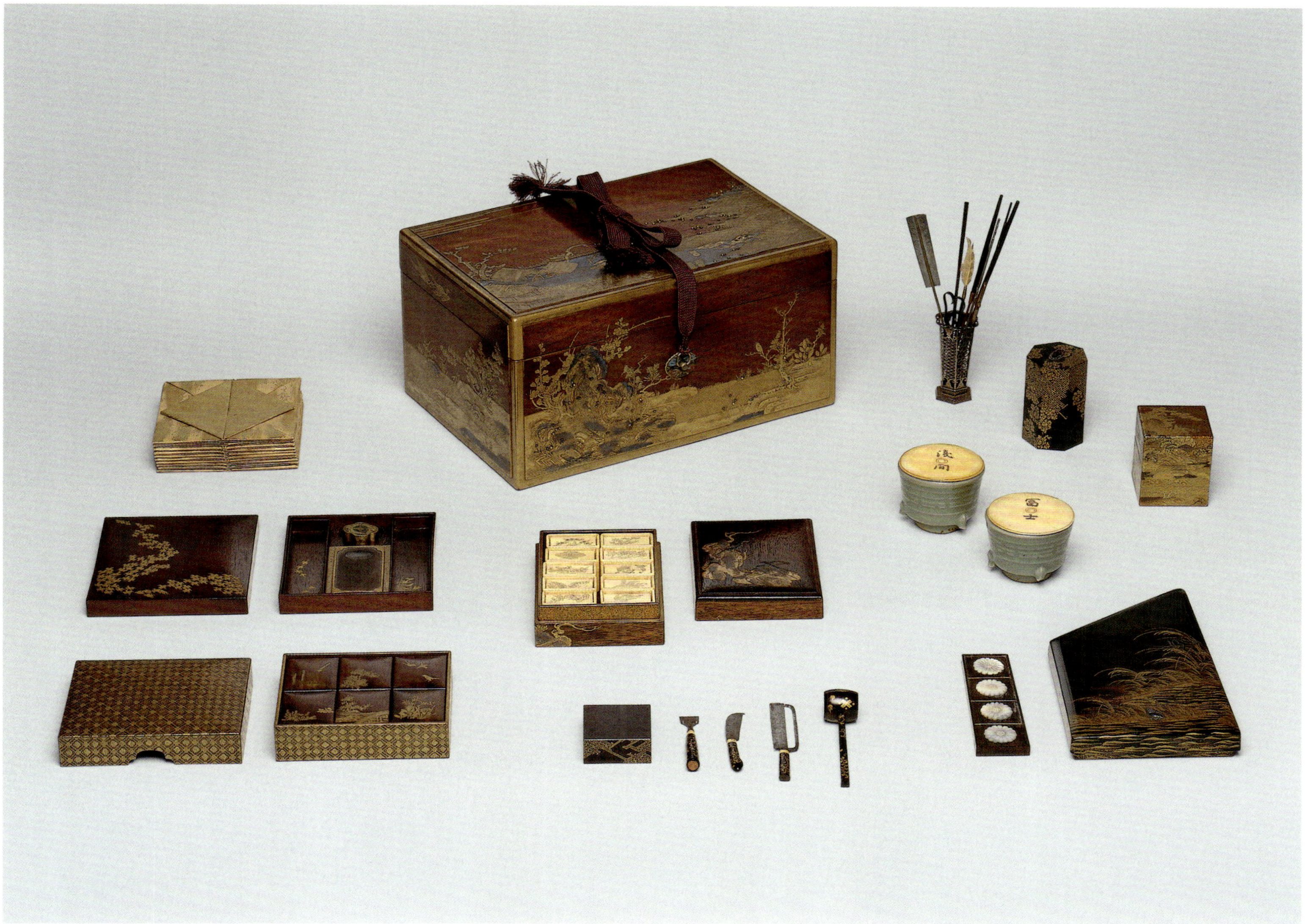

766. Box and assorted implements for the incense game

Edo period, 18th century
Gold *maki-e* and various materials
Outer box 15 x 30 x 20 cm (5 7/8 x 11 7/8 x 7 7/8 in.)

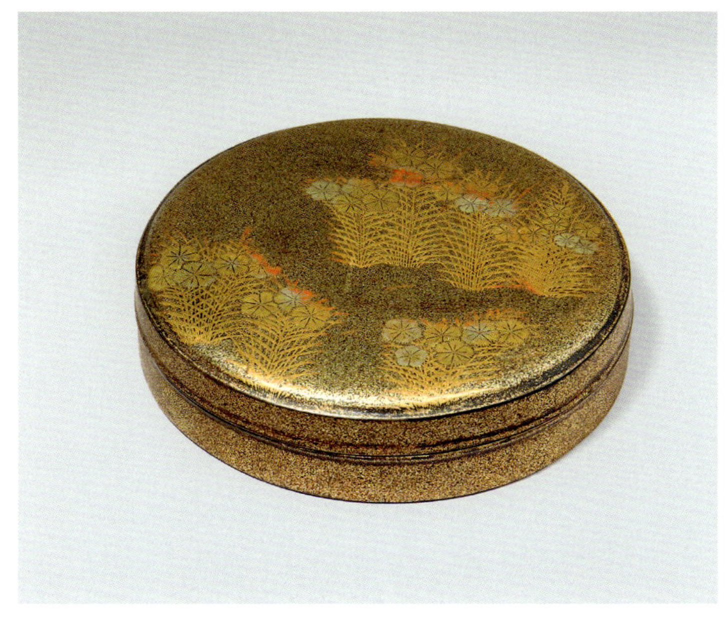

767. Mirror case with design of pinks

Edo period, 19th century
Black and red lacquer with gold *maki-e* on pearskin ground (*nashiji*, 梨地)
Diam. 11 cm (4 3/8 in.)

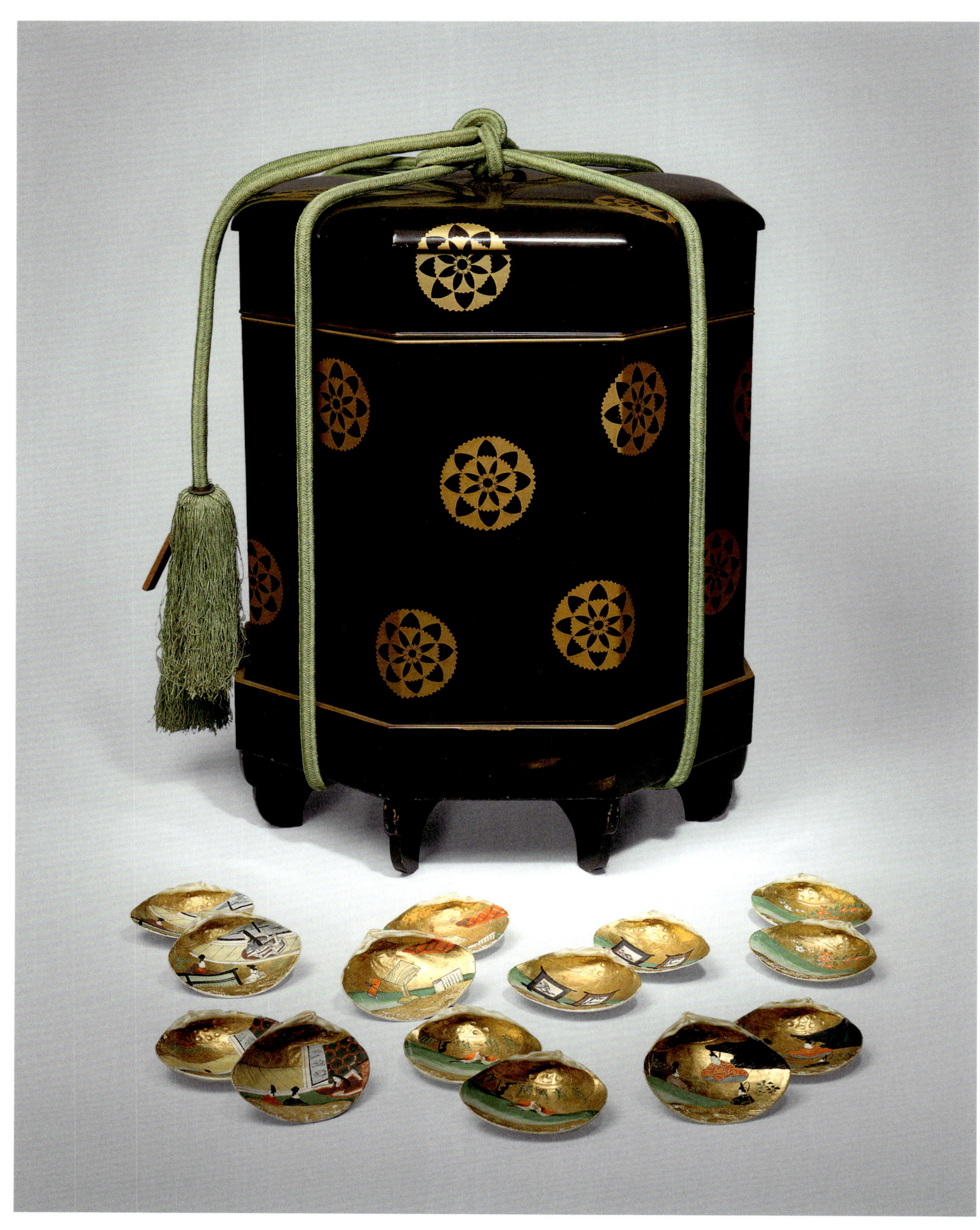

768. Boxed set for shell-matching game (貝合せ)

Edo period, 19th century
Container in black lacquer with gold *maki-e*; shells with polychrome and gold
Container: H. 44 cm (17 3/8 in.), diam. 35.7 cm (14 in.); diam. of shells 7.9–8.3 cm (3 1/8–3 1/4 in.)

Sano Chōkan
(佐野長寛; 1791–1863)

769. Pumpkin-shaped box

Edo period, 1857
Black lacquer with gold *maki-e*
Diam. 16.5 cm (6½ in.)
Signature

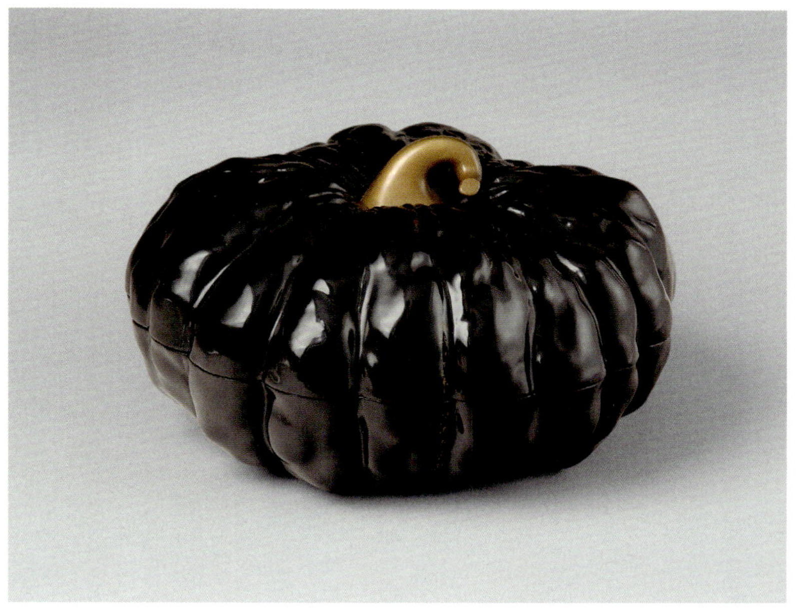

770. Storage box for monk's robe (*kesabako*, 袈裟箱)

Edo–Meiji period, 19th century
Black lacquer with gold *maki-e* and lead inlay
15 x 33.1 x 39.5 cm (5⅞ x 13 x 15½ in.)

Literature: Avitabile 1990, no. 127; Murase 1993, no. 71.

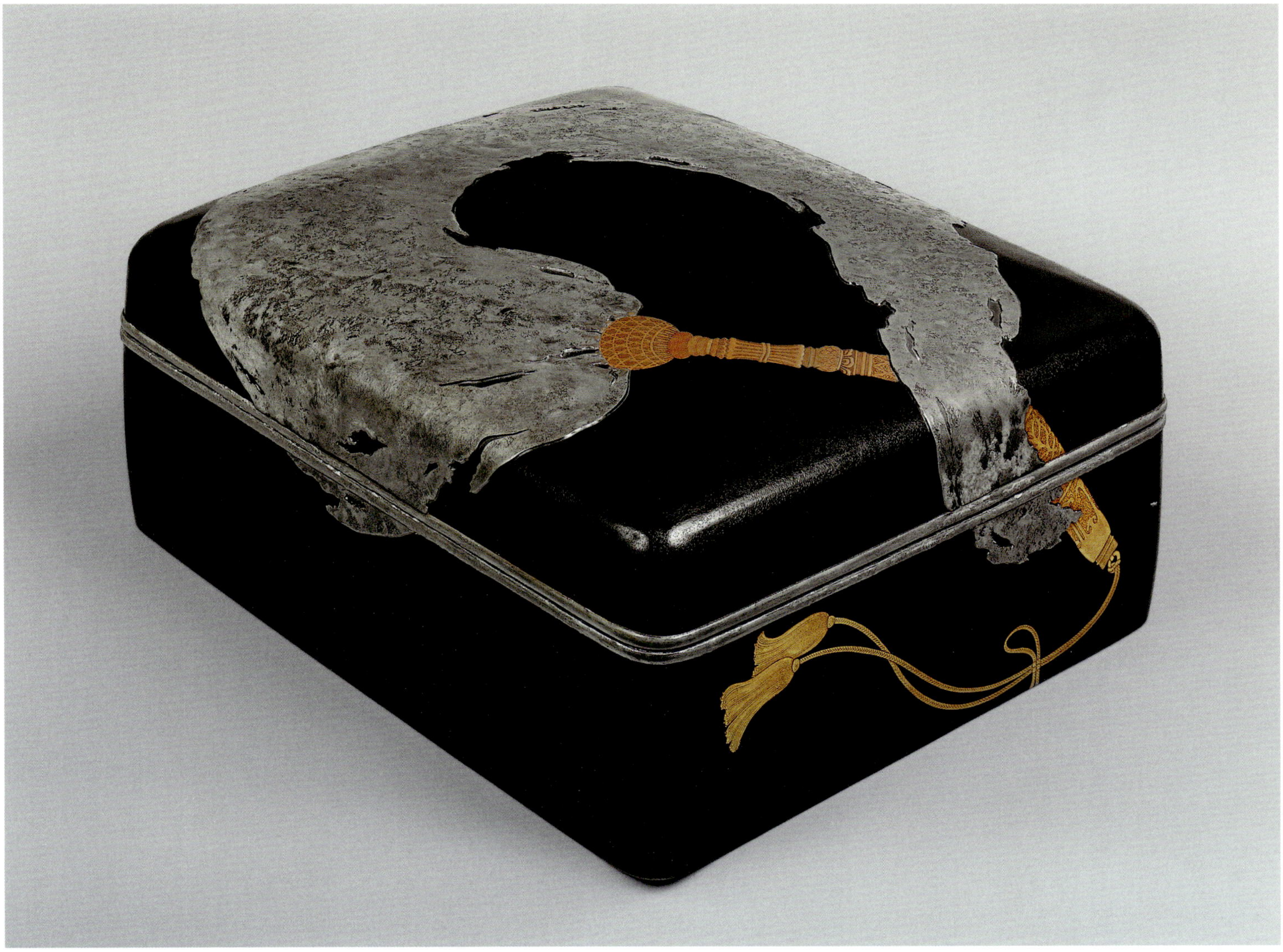

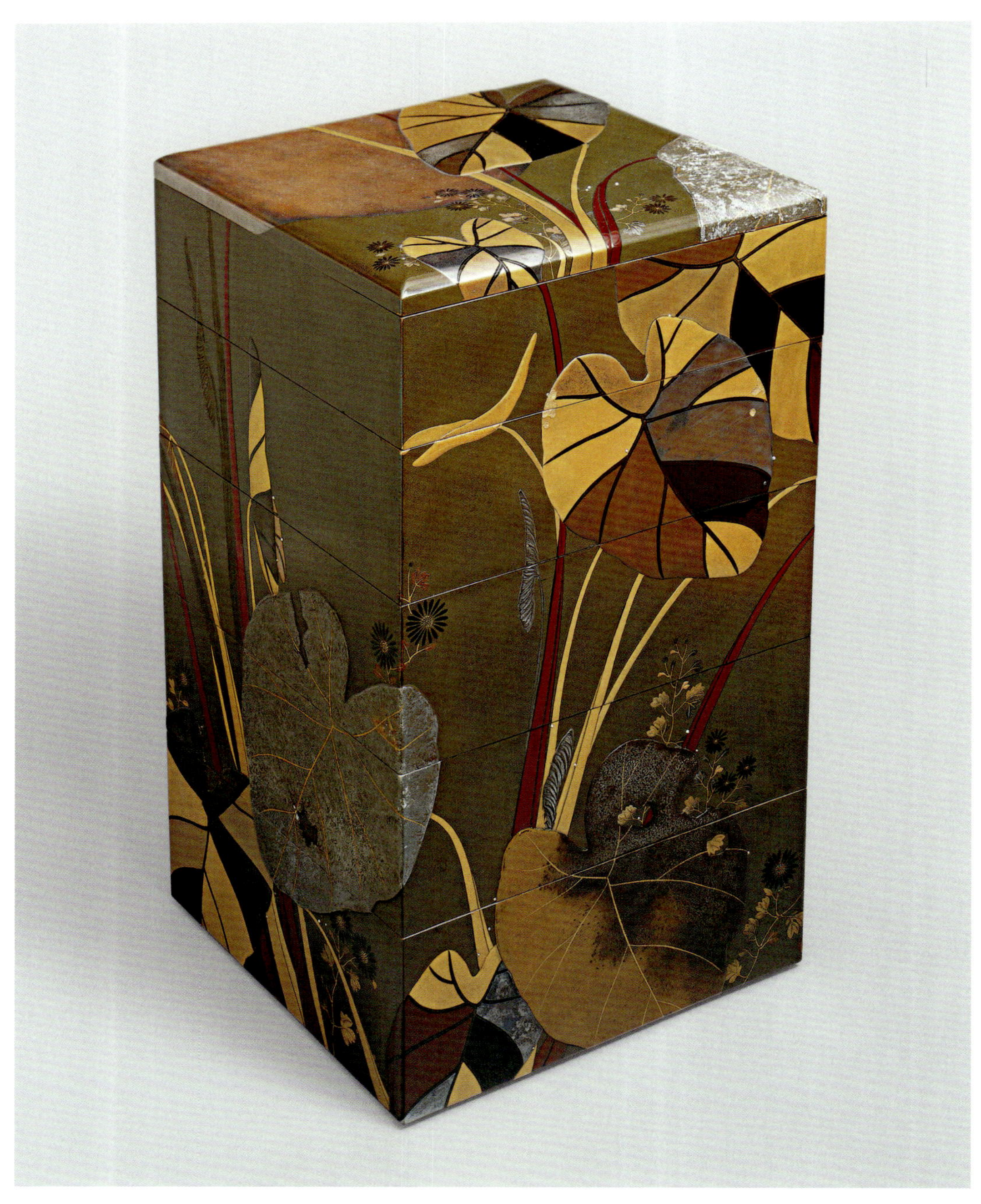

Shibata Zeshin
(柴田是真; 1807–1891)

771. Stacked food boxes (*jūbako*, 重箱) with taro plants and chrysanthemums

Late Edo–early Meiji period, 19th century
Polychrome lacquer with gold and silver *maki-e* and lead inlay
42 x 24.3 x 22.8 cm (16½ x 9⅝ x 9 in.)
Signatures

Literature: Gōke Tadaomi 1981, vol. 1, no. 8; Avitabile 1990, no. 126; Murase 1993, no. 73; Murase 2000, no. 127.

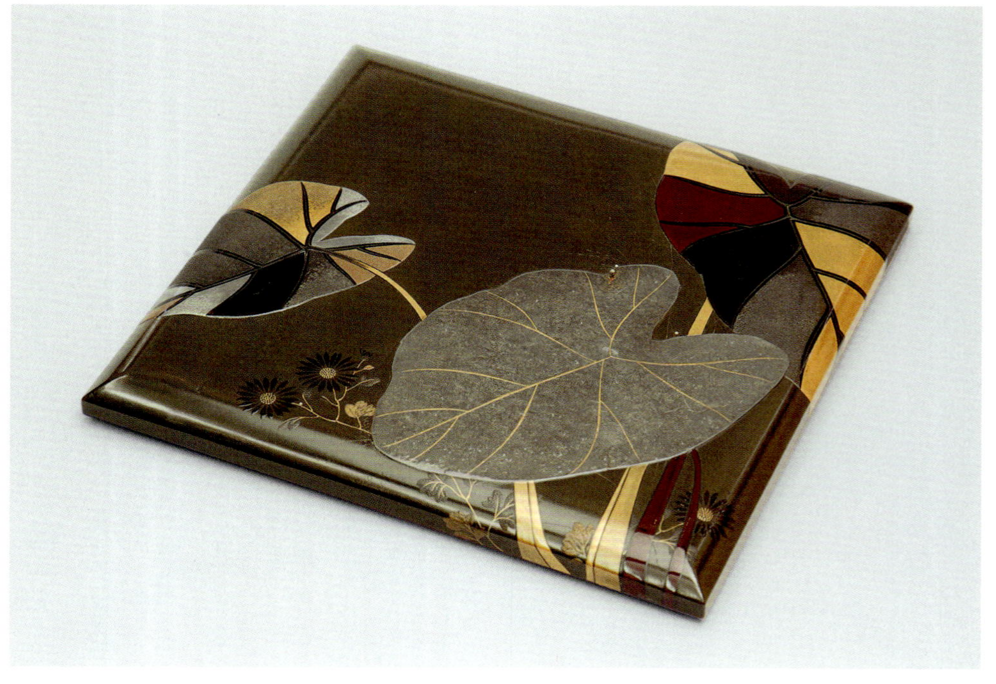

Shibata Zeshin
(柴田是真; 1807–1891)

772a–l. Zodiac calendar in the shape of a hanging scroll

Edo period, 1846
Gold and silver *maki-e* and shell inlay on lacquered wood; 6 plaques decorated on both sides
Container: 25.7 x 7.8 x 4.3 cm (10 1/8 x 3 1/8 x 1 3/4 in.); each plaque approx. 19.9 x 6.3 cm (7 7/8 x 2 1/2 in.)
Signatures, seal

Ex coll.: Itō Shige'emon

Literature: Gōke Tadaomi 1981, vol. 1, nos. 103–15; Burke 1993, no. 53.

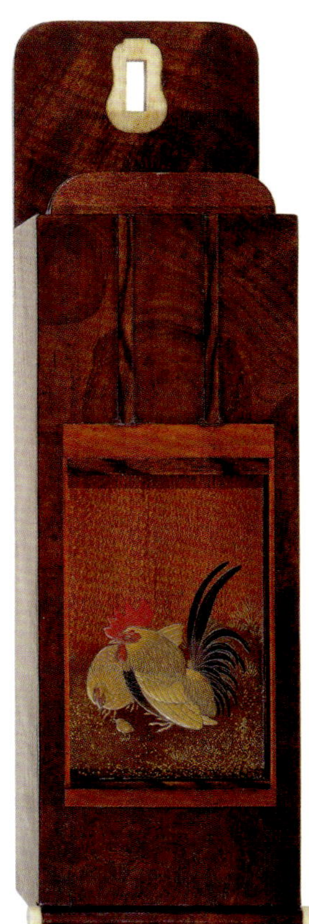

c. Tiger

b. Ox

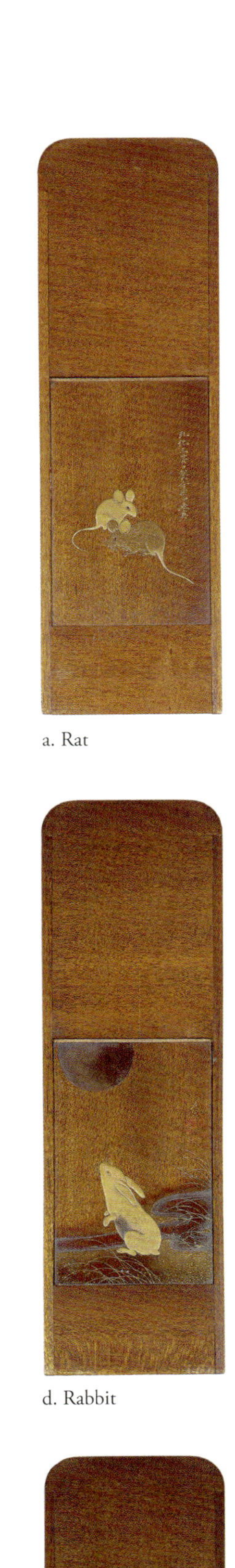

a. Rat

f. Snake

e. Dragon

d. Rabbit

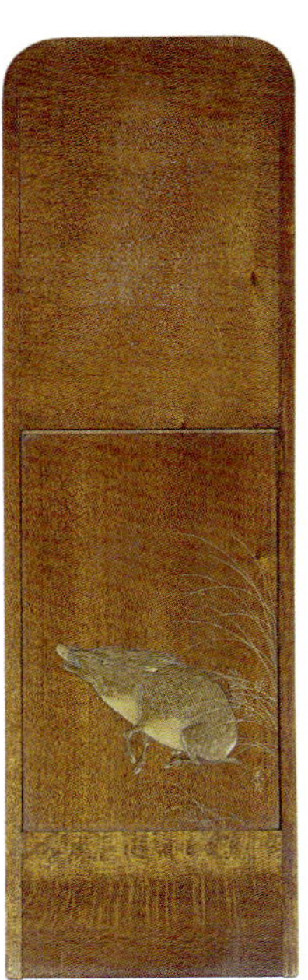

l. Boar

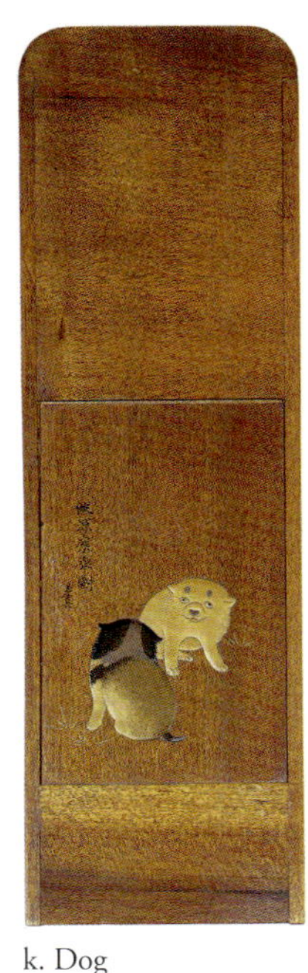

k. Dog

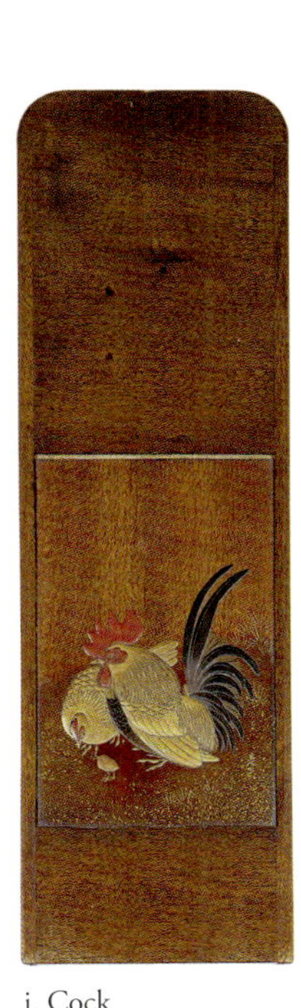

j. Cock

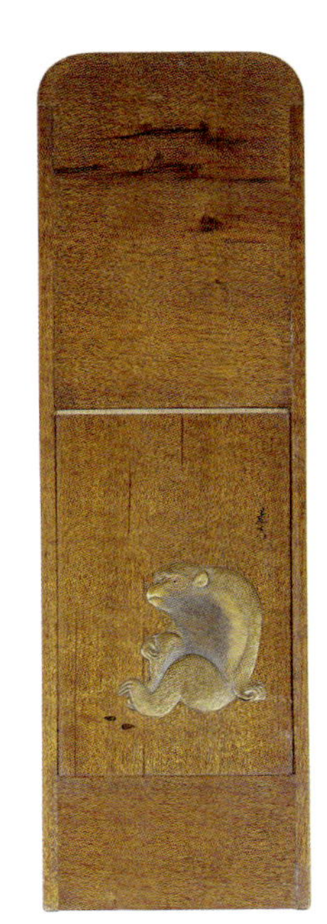

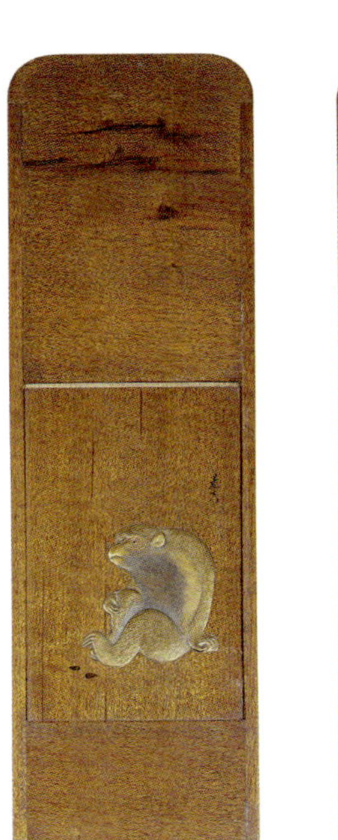

i. Monkey

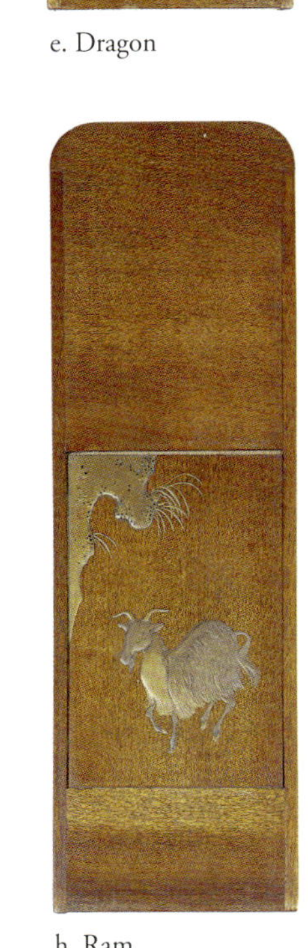

h. Ram

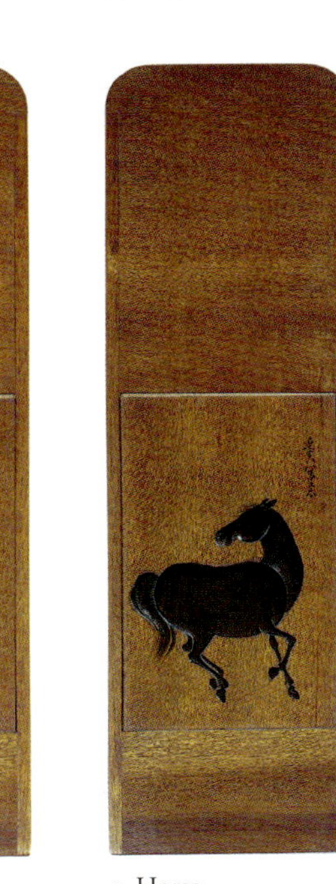

g. Horse

773. Comb and pin with cranes

Meiji period, 19th century
Tortoiseshell with gold *maki-e* and enamels
L. of comb 10.2 cm (4 in.); l. of pin 16 cm (6¼ in.)
Signature

Gift from Uehara Kesami, 1979

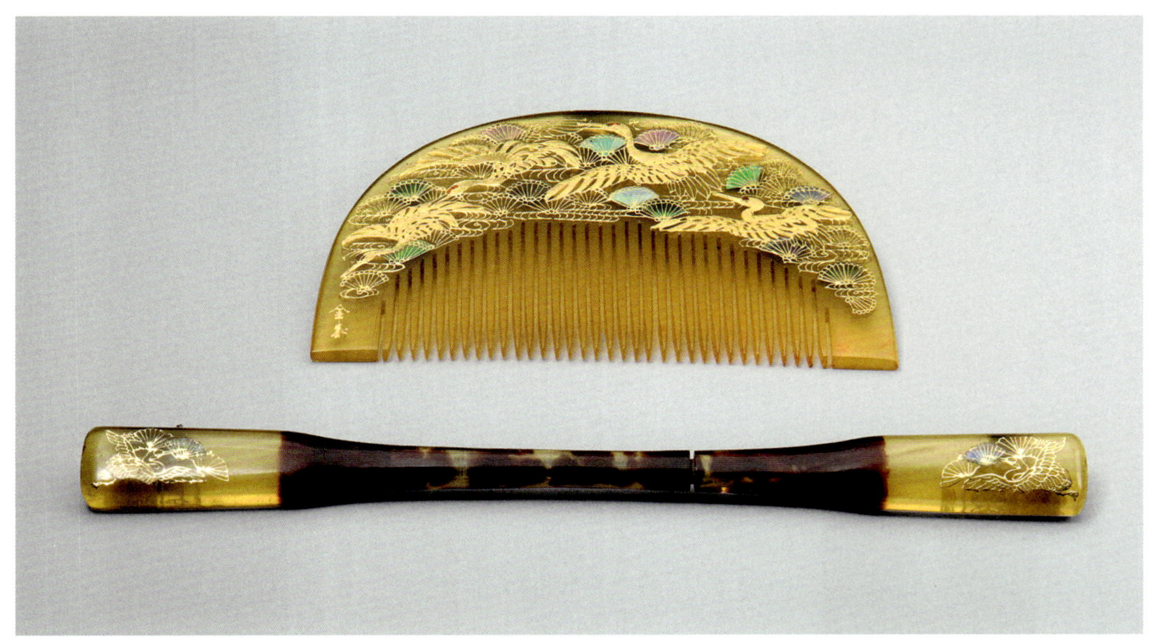

Minota Nagahisa
(箕田長久; fl. early 19th century)

774. Shelf stand with scenes from *Eight Views of Ōmi* (*Ōmi hakkei,* 近江八景)

Meiji period, early 19th century
Black lacquer with gold *maki-e* and tortoiseshell
89.5 x 93.5 x 39 cm
(35¼ x 36⅞ x 15⅜ in.)
Signature, seal

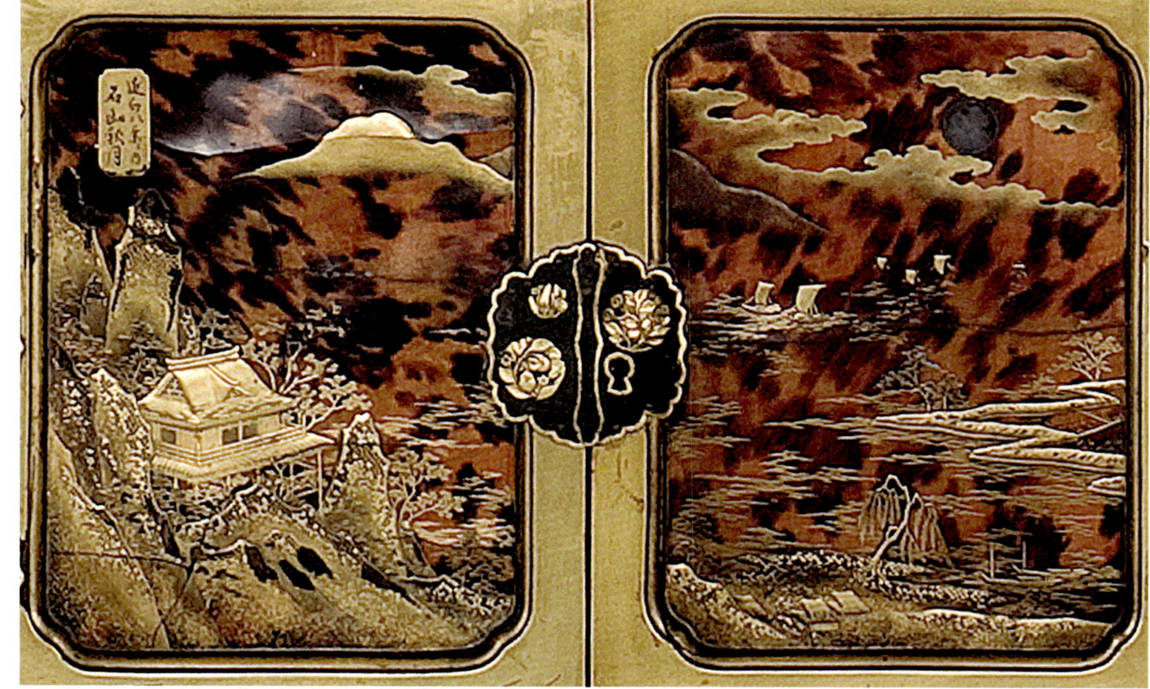

774, door detail

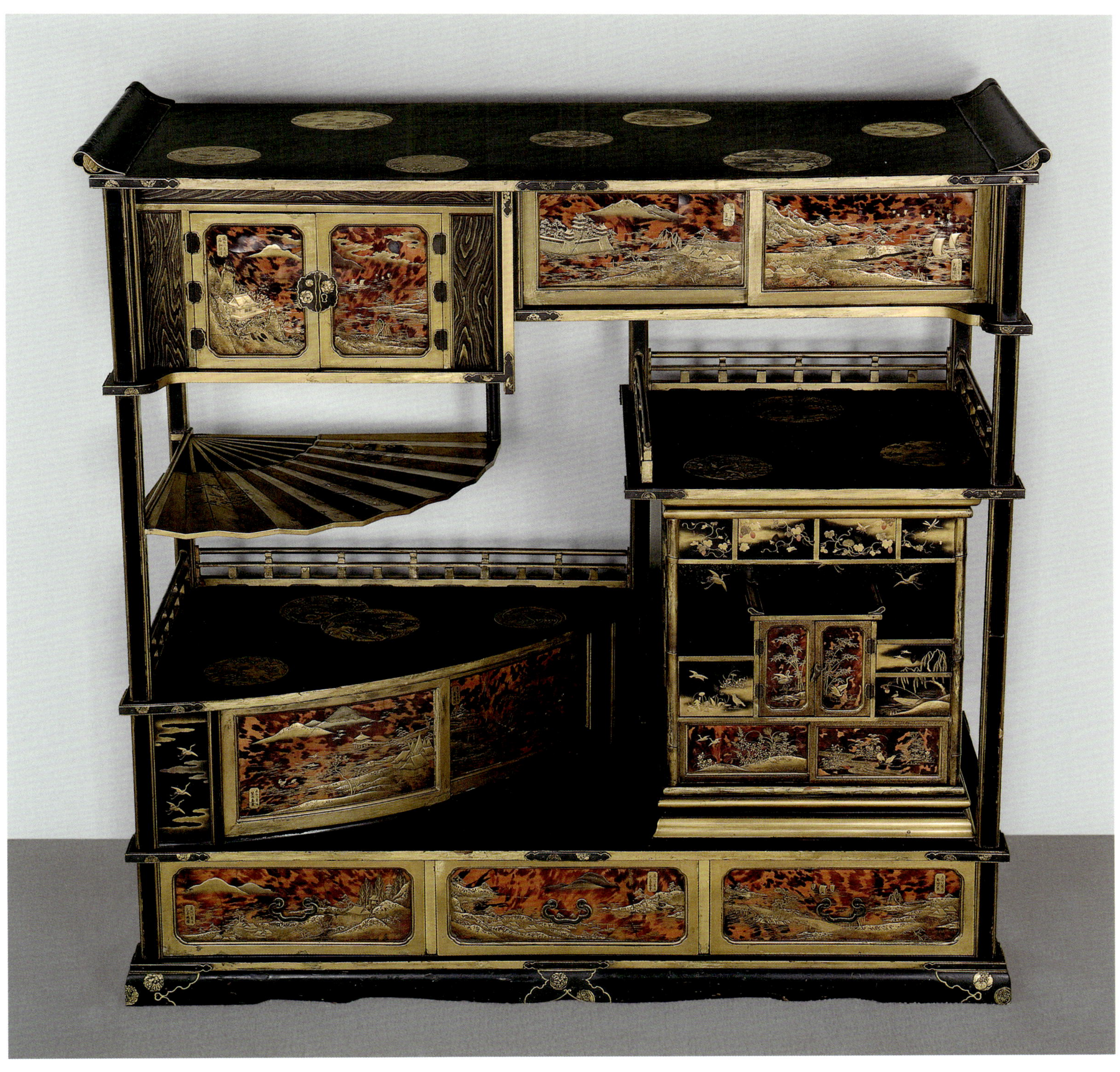

774

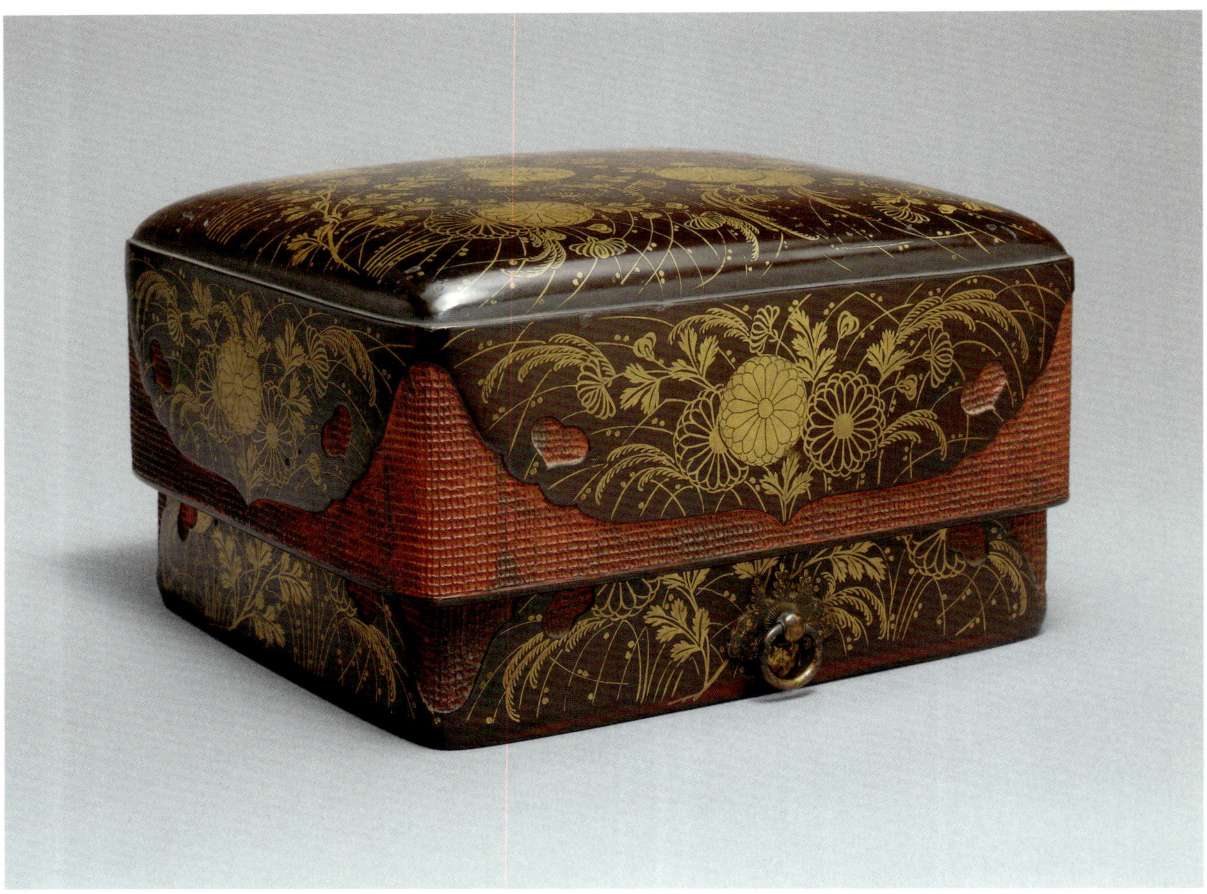

775. Accessories box with red corners (*sumiaka tebako*, 角赤手箱) with chrysanthemums and autumn grasses

Momoyama period, 16th century
Black lacquer with gold *maki-e*; red lacquer over coarse cloth
19 x 32.5 cm x 28 cm (7½ x 12¾ x 11 in.)

LITERATURE: Kyoto Furitsu Sōgō Shiryōkan 1967, pl. 34; Yoshimura Motoo 1976, pl. 2; Murase 1993, no. 65; Murase 2000, no. 88; Tsuji Nobuo et al. 2005, no. 61.

776. Large hand-drum core (*ōtsuzumidō*, 大鼓胴) with grapevines and squirrels

Momoyama period, late 16th century
Black lacquer with gold *maki-e* and pictorial pearskin ground (*e-nashiji*, 絵梨地)
H. 28 cm (11 in.)
Signatures

LITERATURE: Minamoto Toyomune et al. 1973, no. 57; Murase 1975, no. 103; Pekarik 1985b, fig. 2; Tokyo National Museum 1985a, no. 107; Avitabile 1990, no. 110; Murase 2000, no. 89.

777. Large hand-drum core (*ōtsuzumidō*, 大鼓胴) with tigers and pines

Momoyama period, late 16th century
Black lacquer with gold *maki-e* and pictorial pearskin ground (*e-nashiji*, 絵梨地)
H. 27.8 x (11 in.)

LITERATURE: Murase 1993, no. 66; Murase 2000, no. 90; McKelway 2012, no. 24.

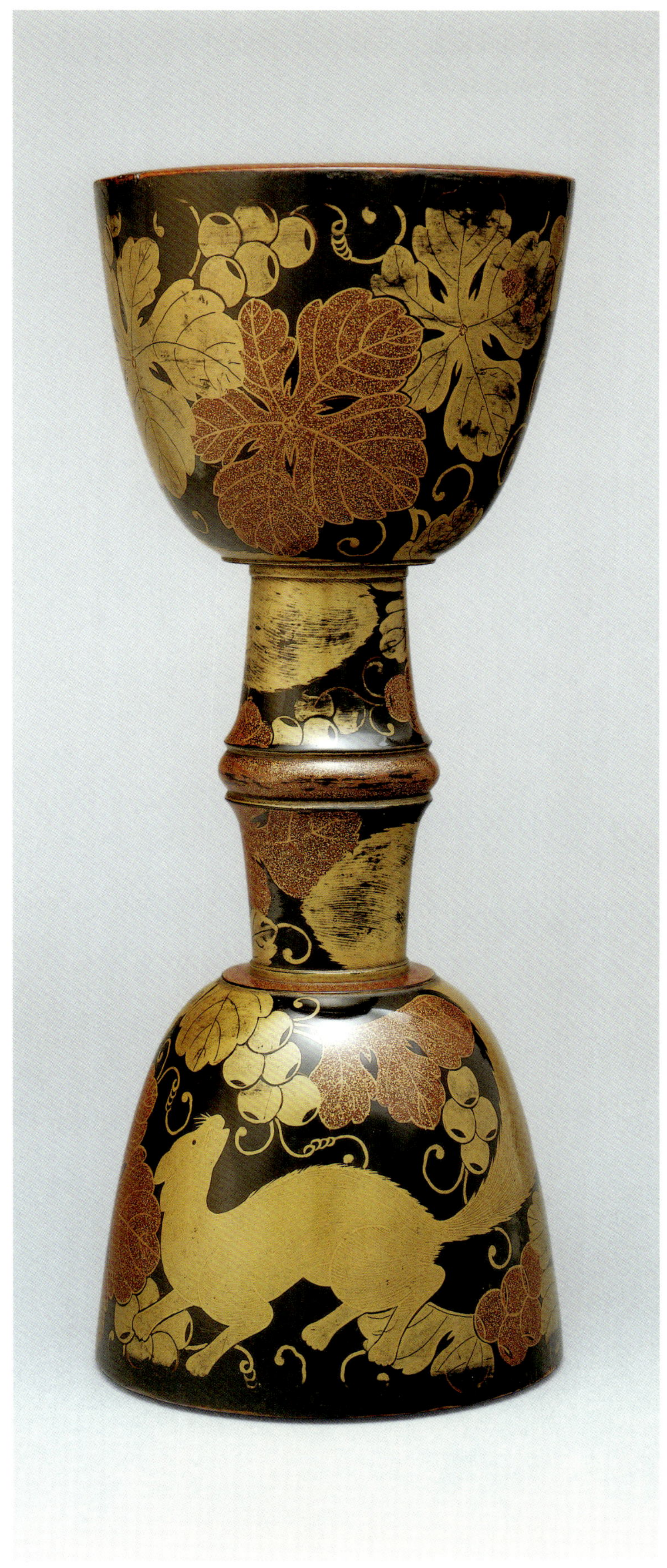
776

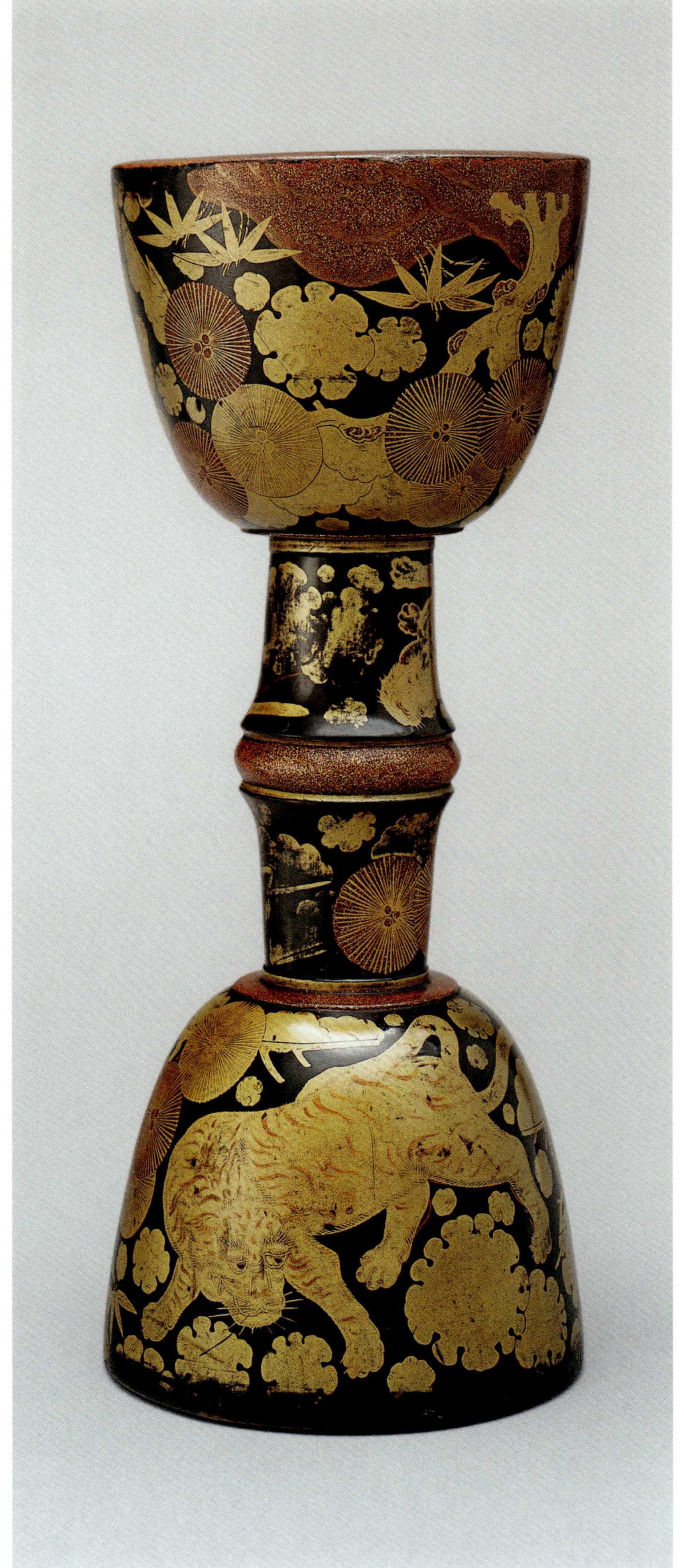
777

778. Table with autumn flowers

Momoyama period, 16th century
Black lacquer with gold *maki-e* and pictorial pearskin ground (*e-nashiji*, 絵梨地)
45.8 x 25.6 x 24 cm (18 x 10⅛ x 9½ in.)
Seal

LITERATURE: Murase 1993, no. 67; Murase 2000, no. 92; Murase 2003, no. 142; Tsuji Nobuo et al. 2005, no. 59.

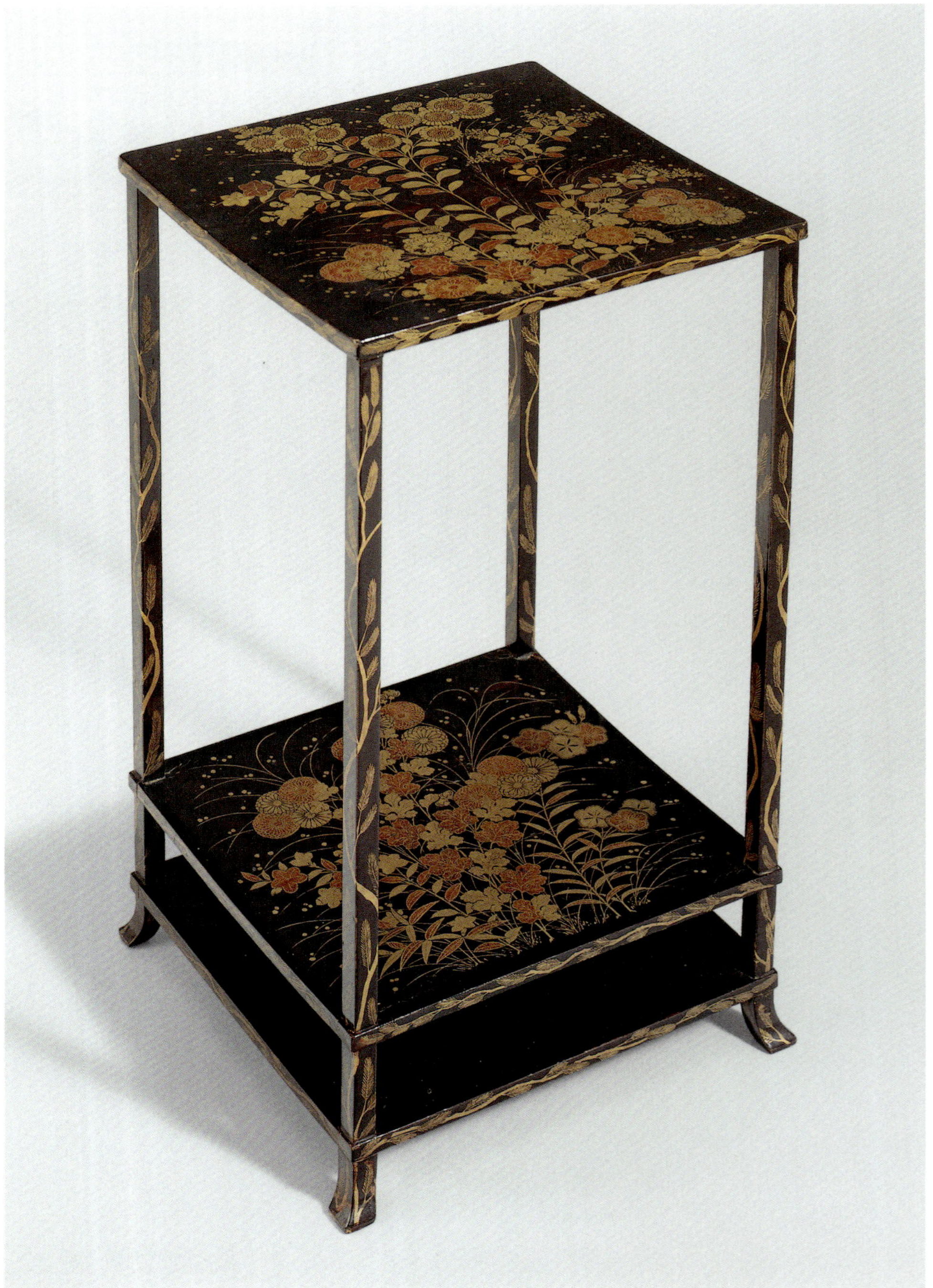

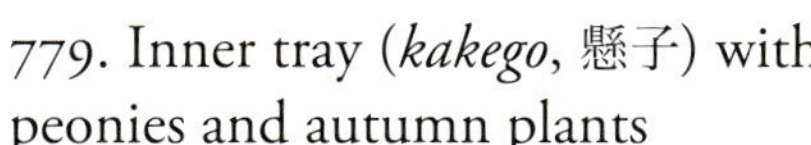

779. Inner tray (*kakego*, 懸子) with peonies and autumn plants

Momoyama period, early 17th century
Black lacquer with gold *maki-e,* pearskin ground (*nashiji*, 梨地), and pictorial pearskin ground (*e-nashiji*, 絵梨地)
9 x 38 x 29.3 cm (3½ x 15 x 11½ in.)

LITERATURE: Tokyo National Museum 1985a, no. 109; Avitabile 1990, no. 114.

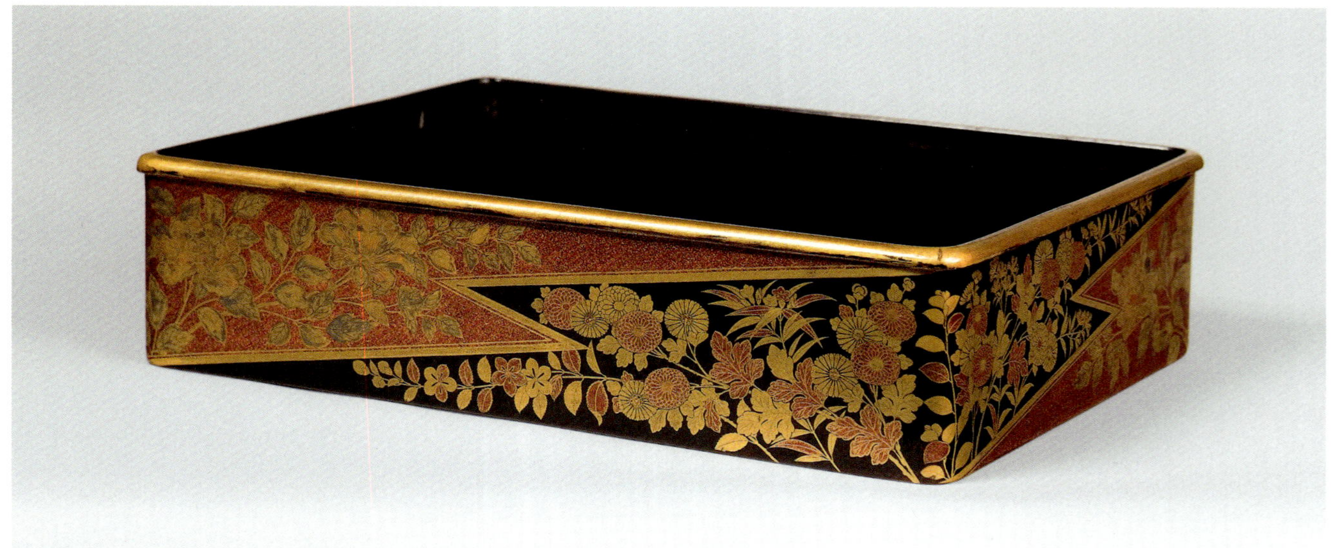

779

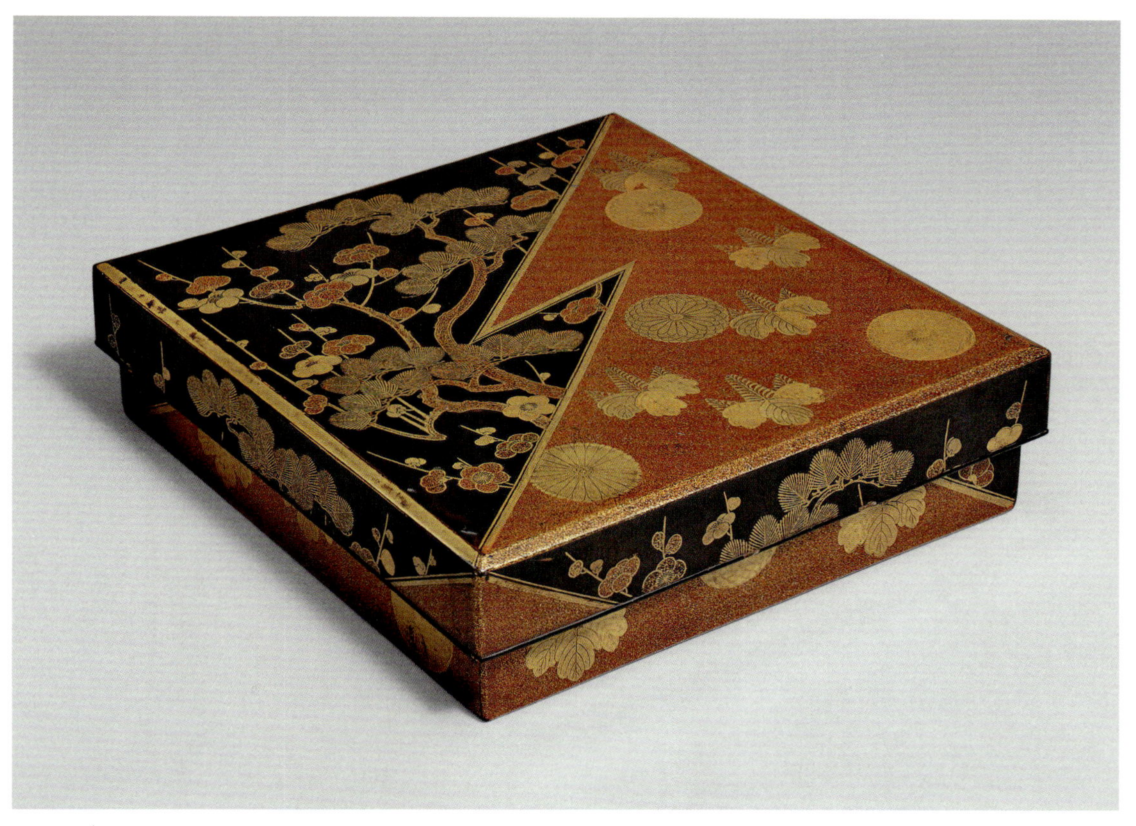

780. Writing box (*suzuribako*, 硯箱) with pines, plum, chrysanthemums, and paulownia

Momoyama period, 16th century
Black lacquer with gold *maki-e*, pearskin ground (*nashiji*, 梨地), and pictorial pearskin ground (*e-nashiji*, 絵梨地)
6.2 x 23.2 x 24.6 cm ($2^{1}/_{2}$ x $9^{1}/_{8}$ x $9^{3}/_{4}$ in.)

LITERATURE: Pekarik 1985b, figs. 4, 5; Tokyo National Museum 1985a, no. 110; Avitabile 1990, no. 112; Murase 2000, no. 91; Murase 2003, no. 143

781. Sutra box with lotus

Momoyama period, early 17th century
Black lacquer with gold *maki-e* and pictorial pearskin ground (*e-nashiji*, 絵梨地)
15 x 20.4 x 36.5 cm ($5^{7}/_{8}$ x 8 x $14^{3}/_{8}$ in.)

LITERATURE: Tokyo National Museum 1985a, no. 108; Pal and Meech-Pekarik 1988, pl. 87; Avitabile 1990, no. 111; Murase 2000, no. 93; Tsuji Nobuo et al. 2005, no. 60.

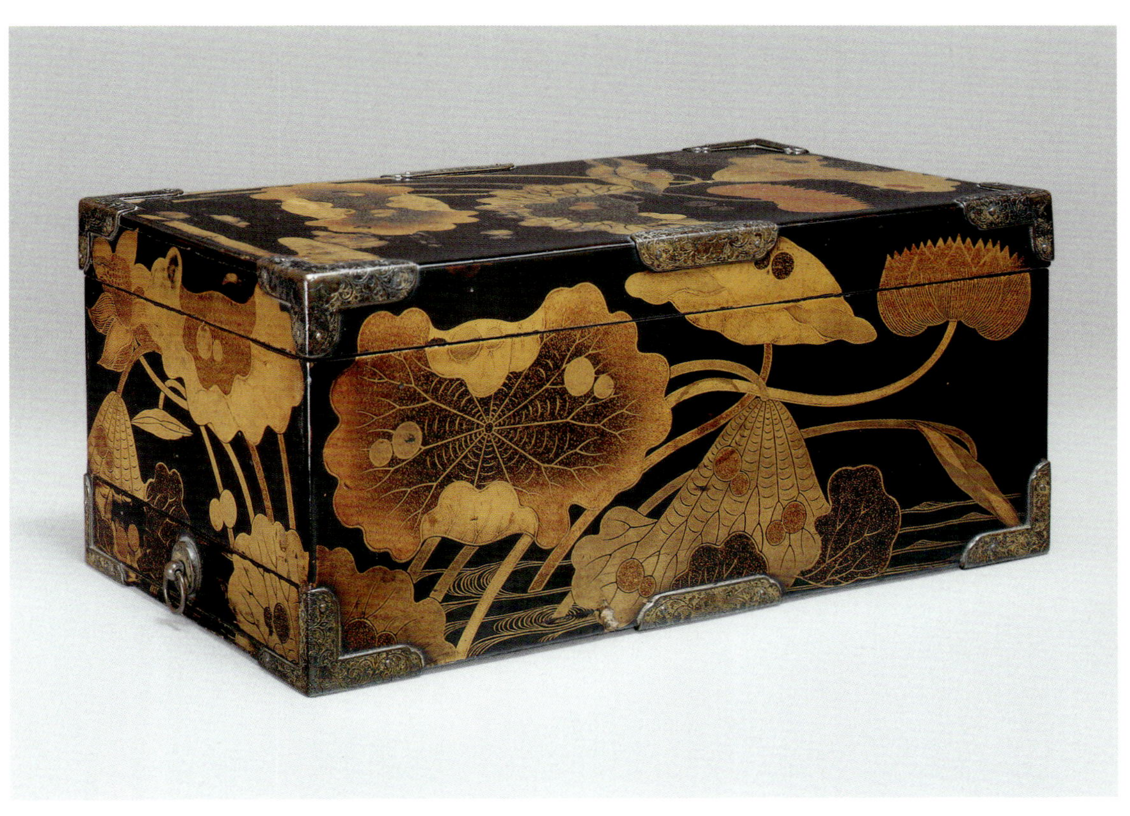

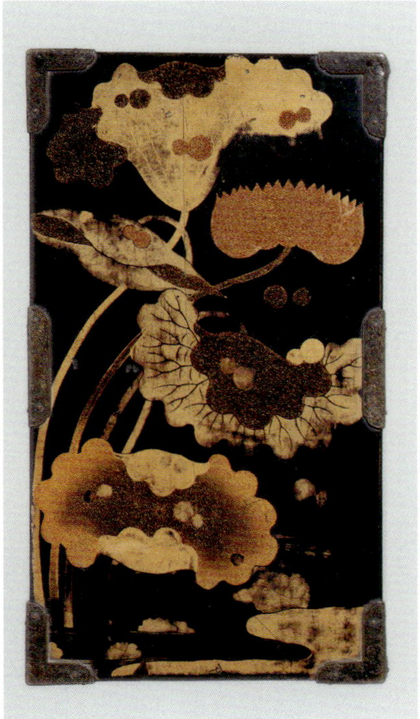

781, top

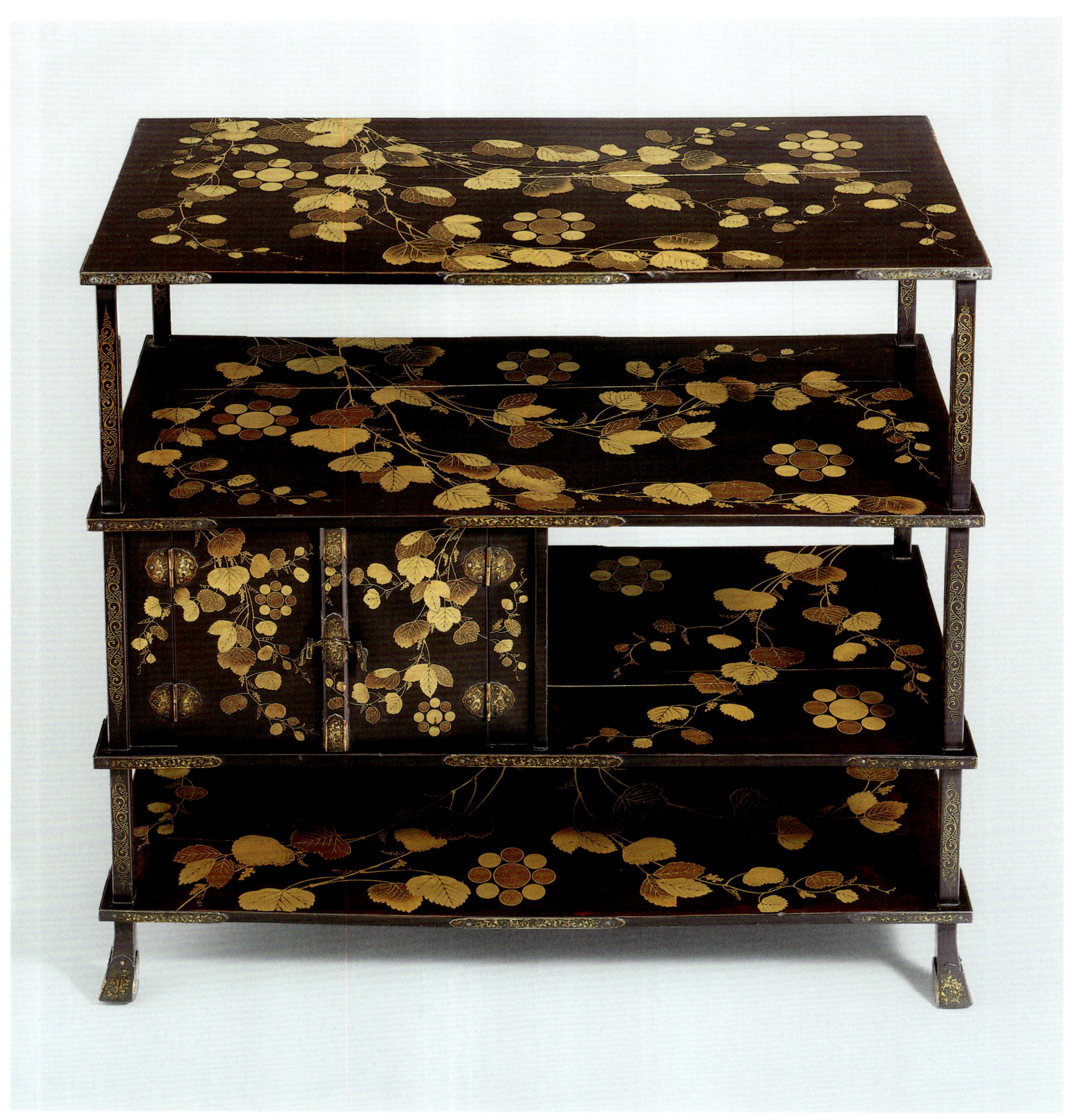

782. Shelf for cosmetic boxes (*kurodana*, 黒棚) with grapevines

Edo period, early 17th century
Black lacquer with gold *maki-e* and pictorial pearskin ground (*e-nashiji*, 絵梨地)
68 x 76.3 x 36 cm (26 3/4 x 30 x 14 1/8 in.)

LITERATURE: Murase 1975, no. 103; Tokyo National Museum 1985a, no. 115; Murase 2000, no. 94.

783. Scroll box with paulownia and grasses

Momoyama–Edo period, 17th century
Black lacquer with gold *maki-e* and pictorial pearskin ground (*e-nashiji*, 絵梨地)
L. 36.4 cm (14 3/8 in.)

LITERATURE: Tokyo National Museum 1985a, no. 113; Avitabile 1990, no. 115.

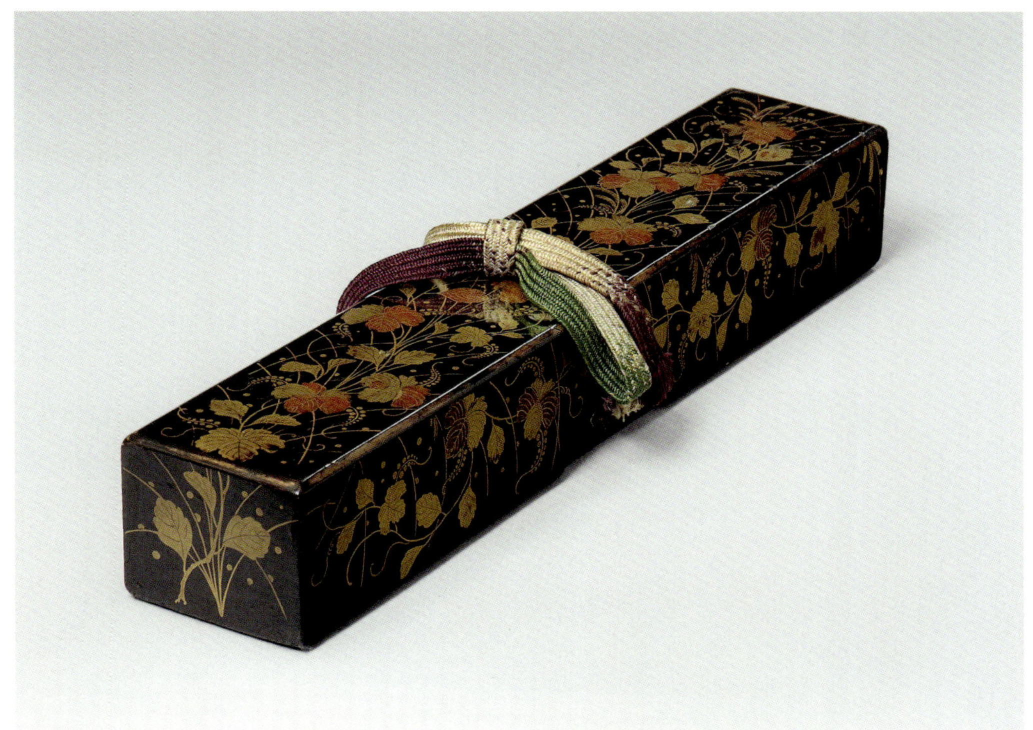

783

784. Cabinet with grapevine

Edo period, 17th century
Black lacquer with gold *maki-e* and pictorial pearskin ground (*e-nashiji*, 絵梨地)
30 x 16 x 19 cm (11 7/8 x 6 1/4 x 7 1/2 in.)

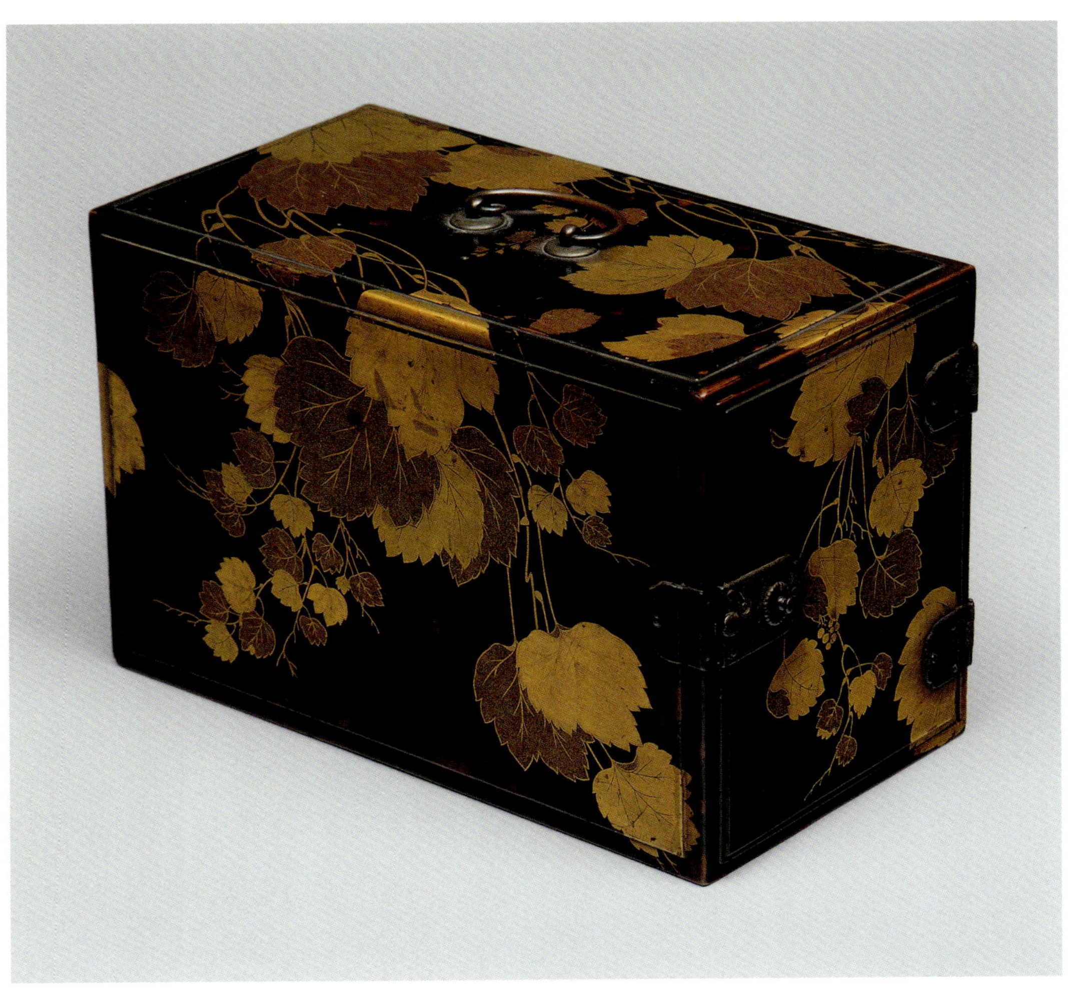

784

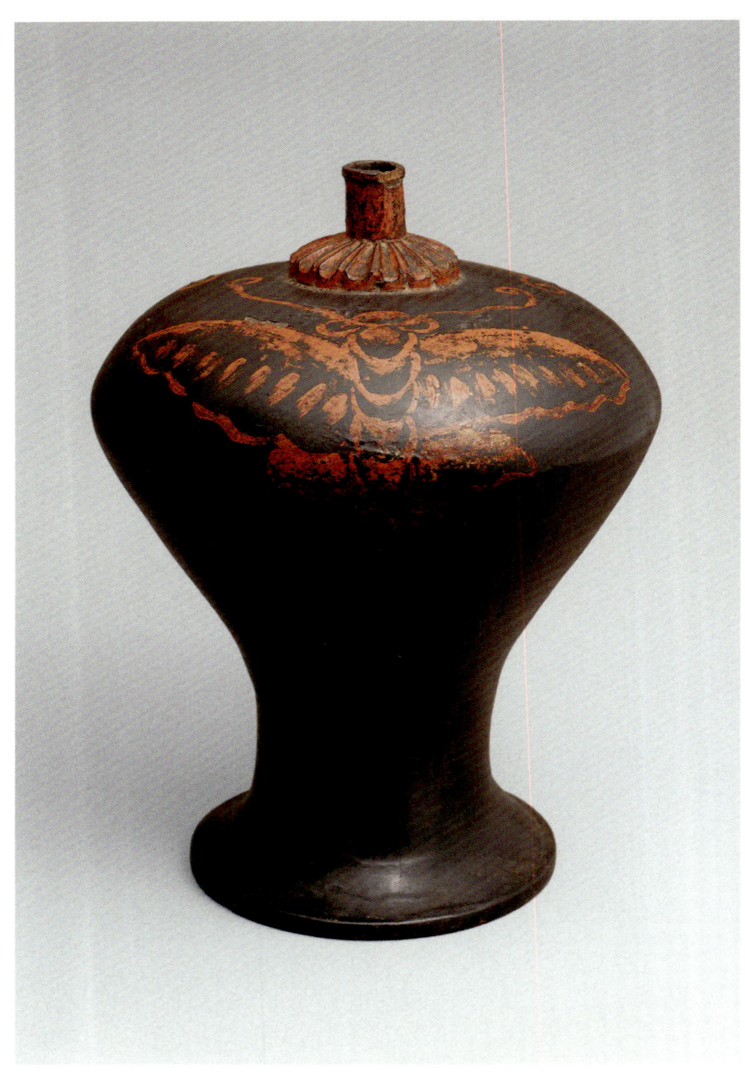

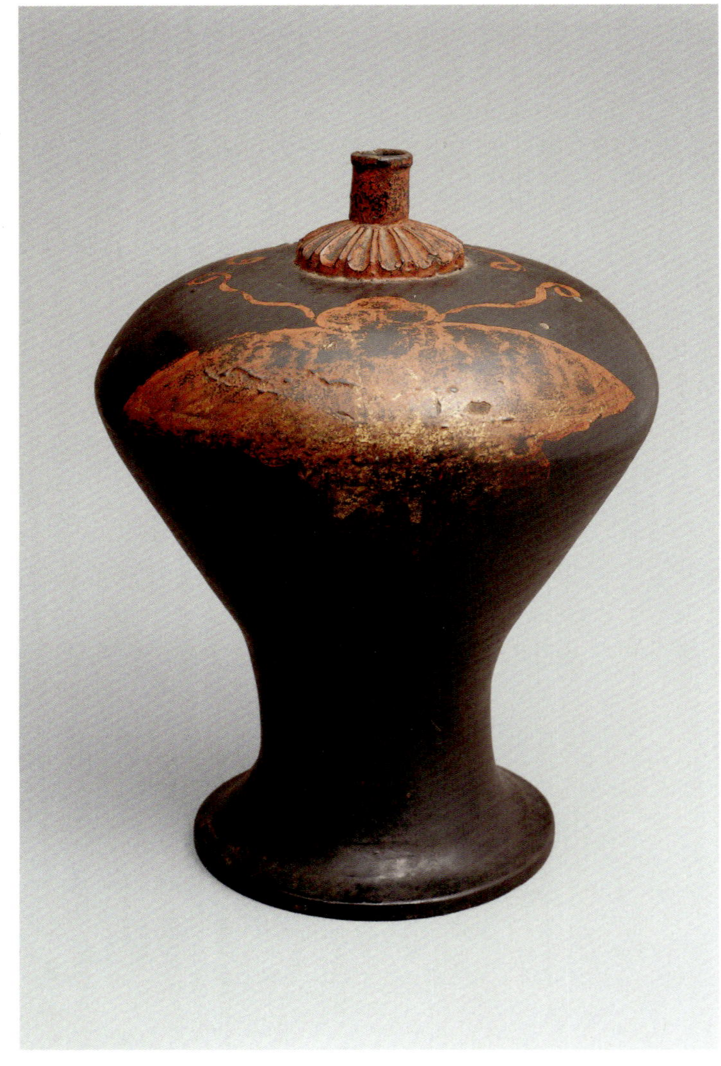

785. Sake vessel (*heishi*, 瓶子) with design of butterflies

Muromachi period, late 14th–15th century
Black and red lacquer with gold leaf
H. 31.5 cm (12 3/8 in.)

LITERATURE: Murase 1993, no. 74; Murase 2000, no. 72; Tsuji Nobuo et al. 2005, no. 19.

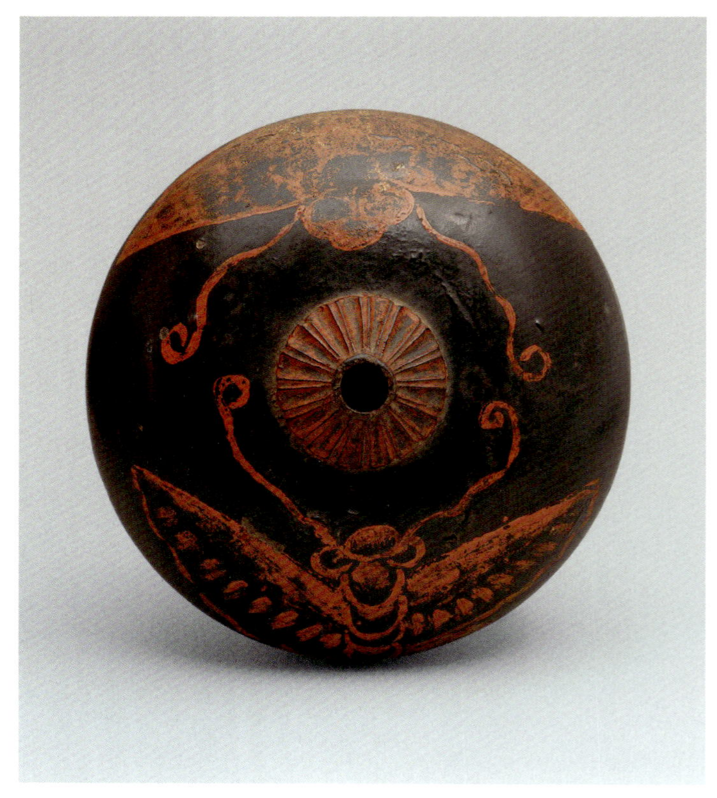

786. Sake vessel (*heishi*, 瓶子)

Muromachi period, 15th century
Red and black lacquer
H. 38.5 cm (15 1/8 in.)

Literature: Murase 1975, no. 101; Tokyo National Museum 1985a, no. 105; Avitabile 1990, no. 108; Murase 2000, no. 73.

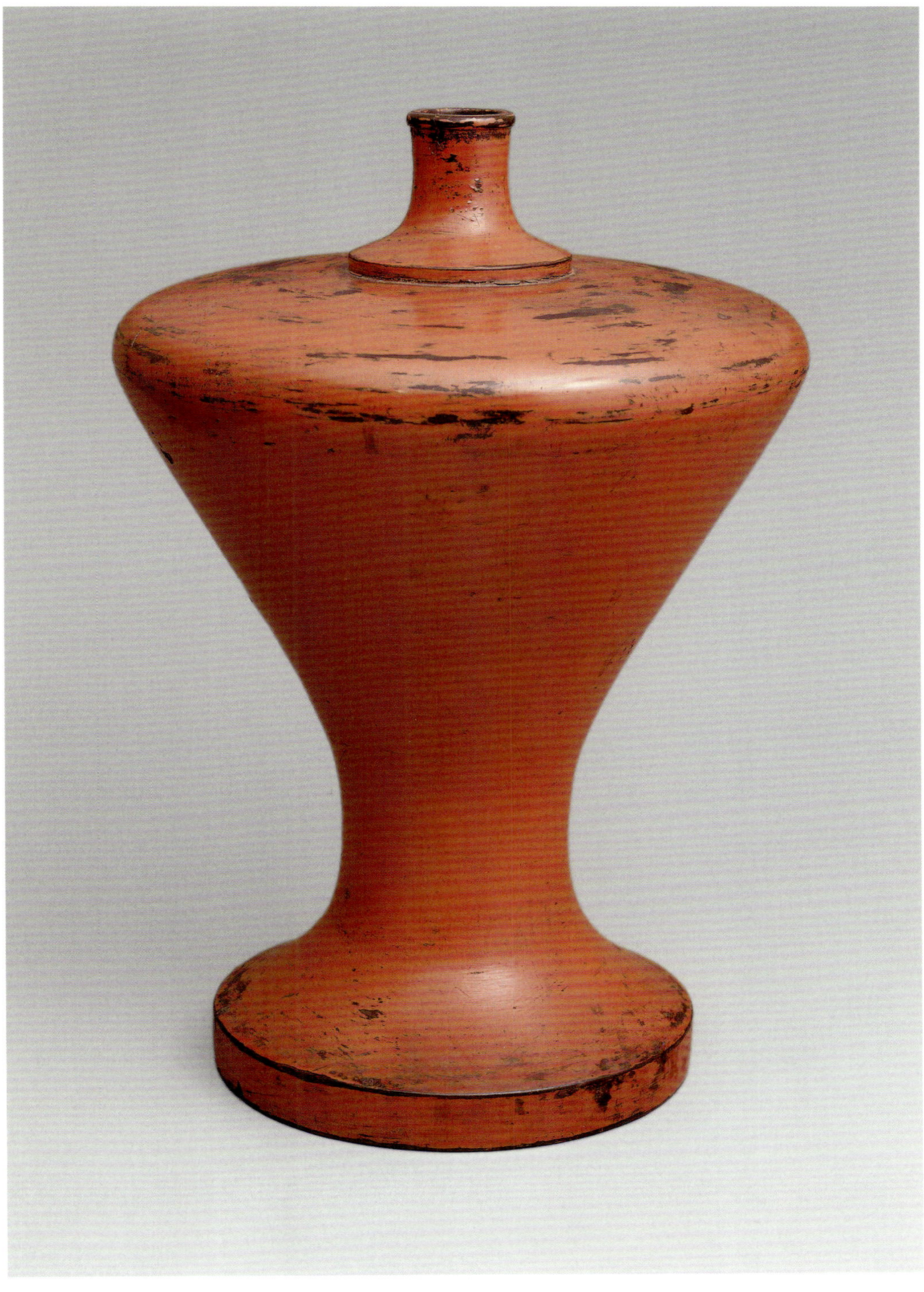

787. Wash basin (*tarai*, 盥)

Muromachi period, 1353 or 1413
Red and black lacquer with exposed *keyaki* (*Zelkova serrata*) wood
H. 16 cm (6¼ in.), diam. 32.8 cm (12⅞ in.)
Text

Literature: Kawada Sadamu 1985, fig. 39; Avitabile 1990, no. 109; Murase 1993, no. 75; Murase 2000, no. 74.

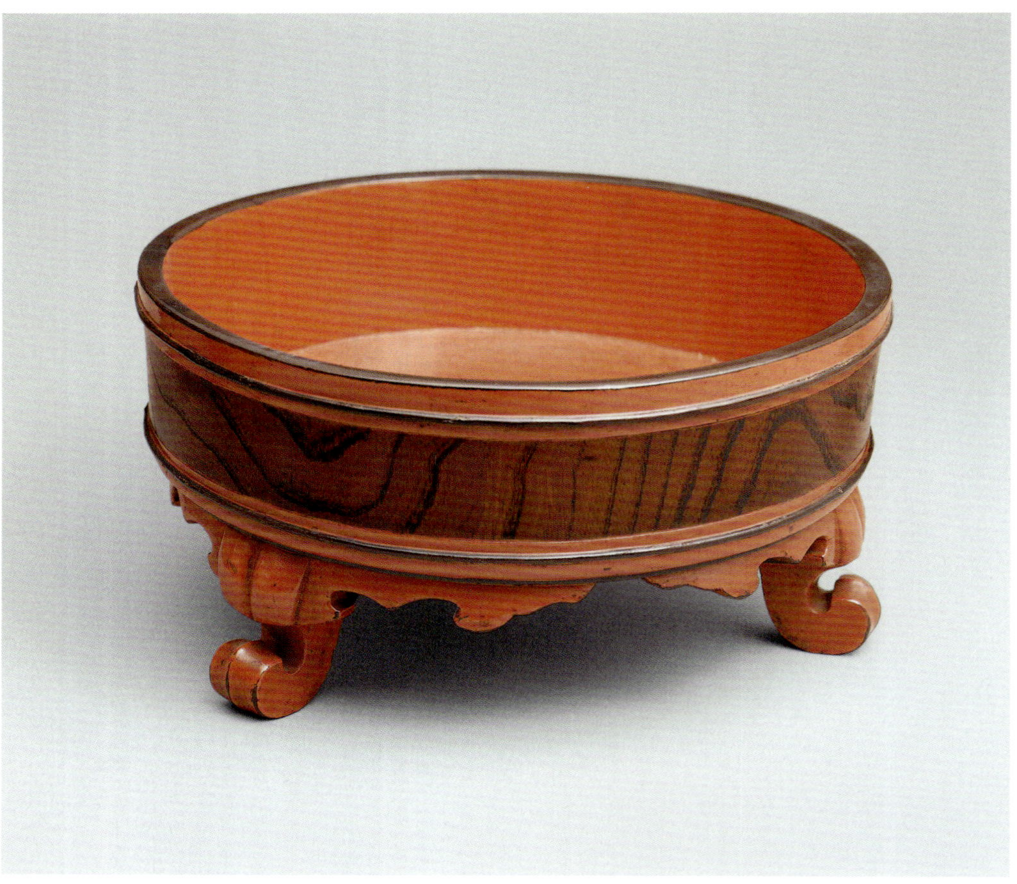

788. Stem table (*takatsuki*, 高坏)

Muromachi period, 1482
Red and black lacquer with gold leaf
27.4 x 29.7 x 29 cm (10¾ x 11¾ x 11⅜ in.)
Text

Ex coll.: Shinra Zenshindō, at Onjōji, Shiga Prefecture

Literature: Kawada Sadamu 1985, no. 27; Ishikawa Wajima Urushi Art Museum 1998, fig. 8; Tsuji Nobuo et al. 2005, no. 20.

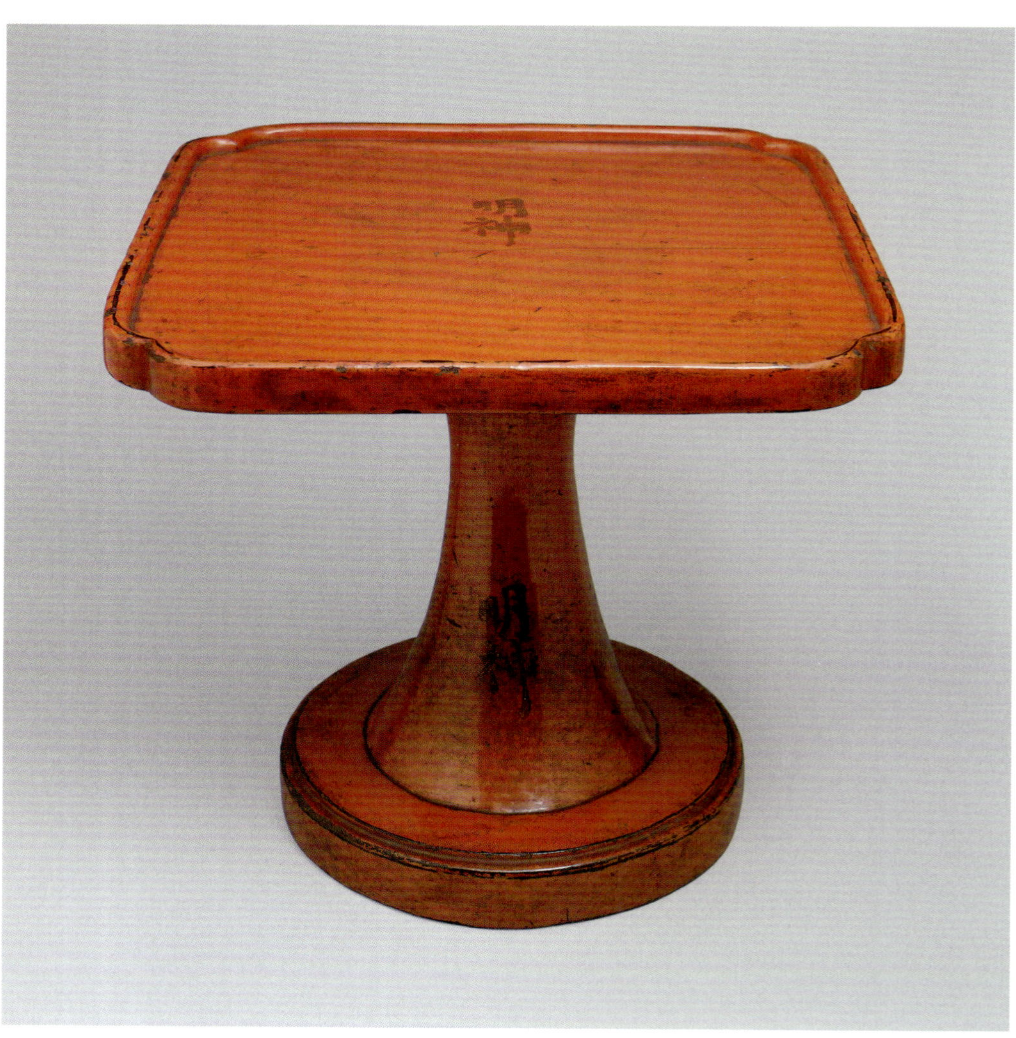

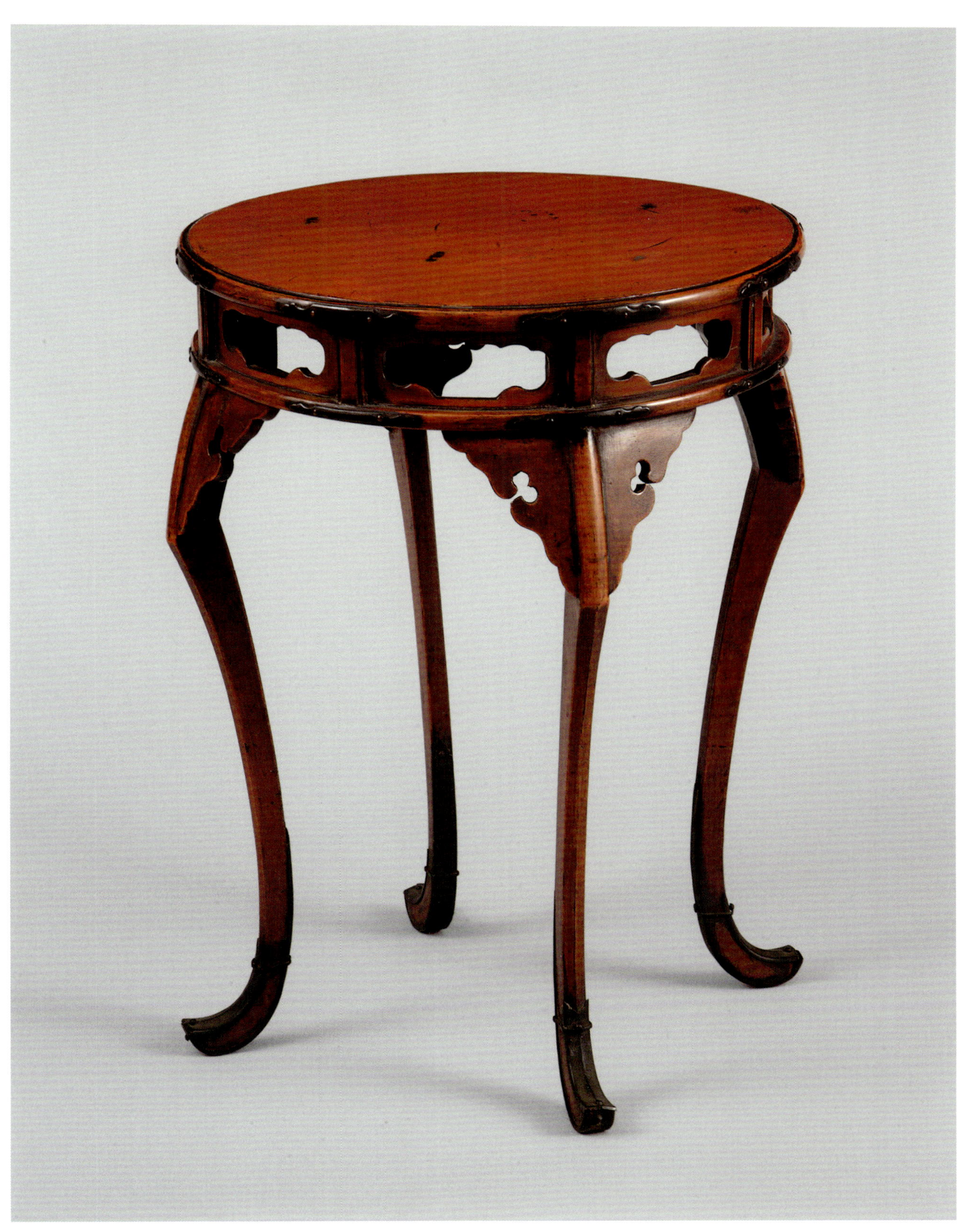

789. Table

Muromachi period, 16th century
Black and red lacquer
H. 39 cm (15 3/8 in.), diam. 28.7 cm (11 1/4 in.)

LITERATURE: Murase 1975, no. 101.

790. Hot-water ewer (*yutō*, 湯桶)

Muromachi period, 16th century
Black and red lacquer
H. 36 cm (14 1/8 in.)
Text

LITERATURE: Hosomi Ryō 1961, p. 1; Murase 1975, no. 101.

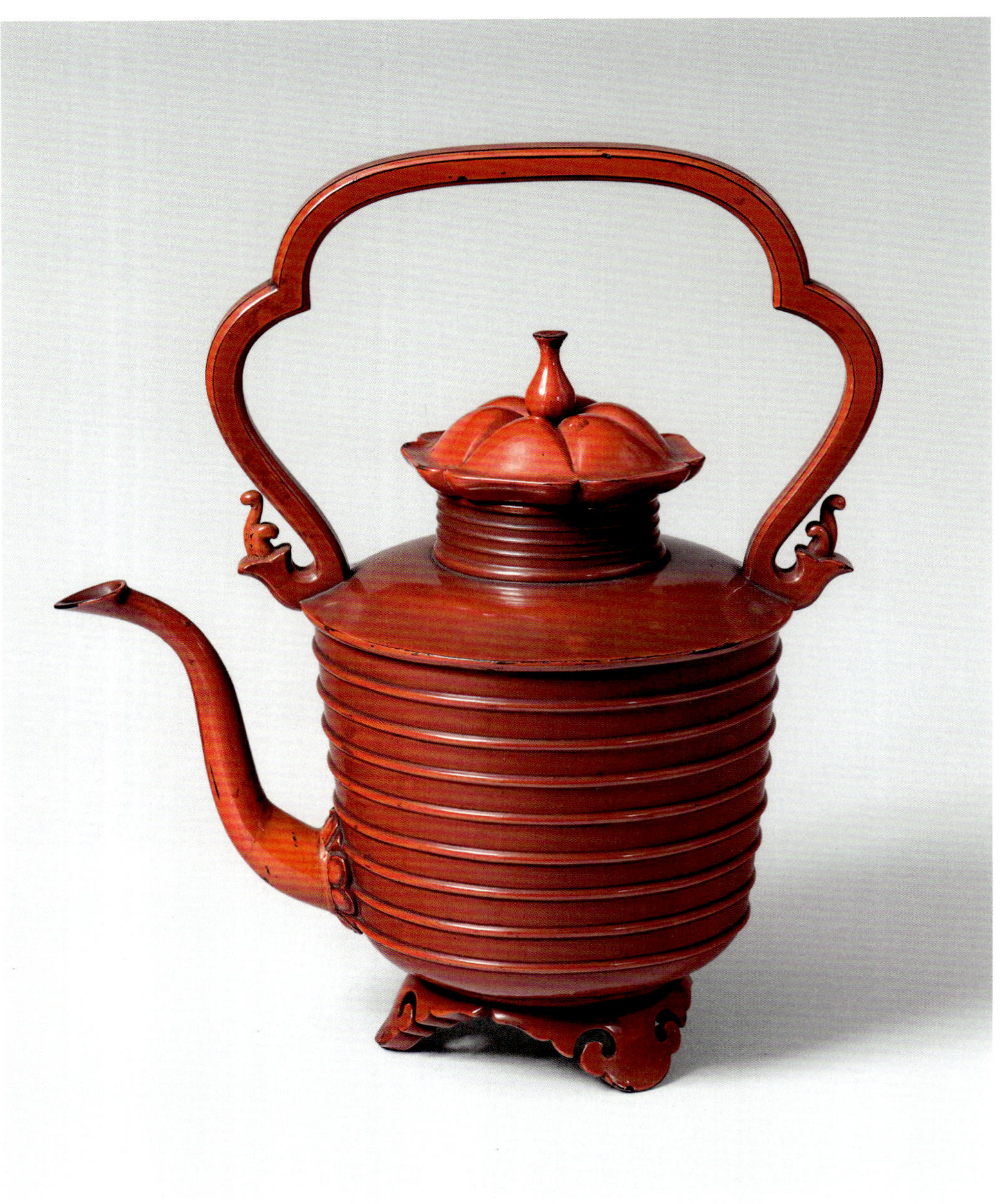

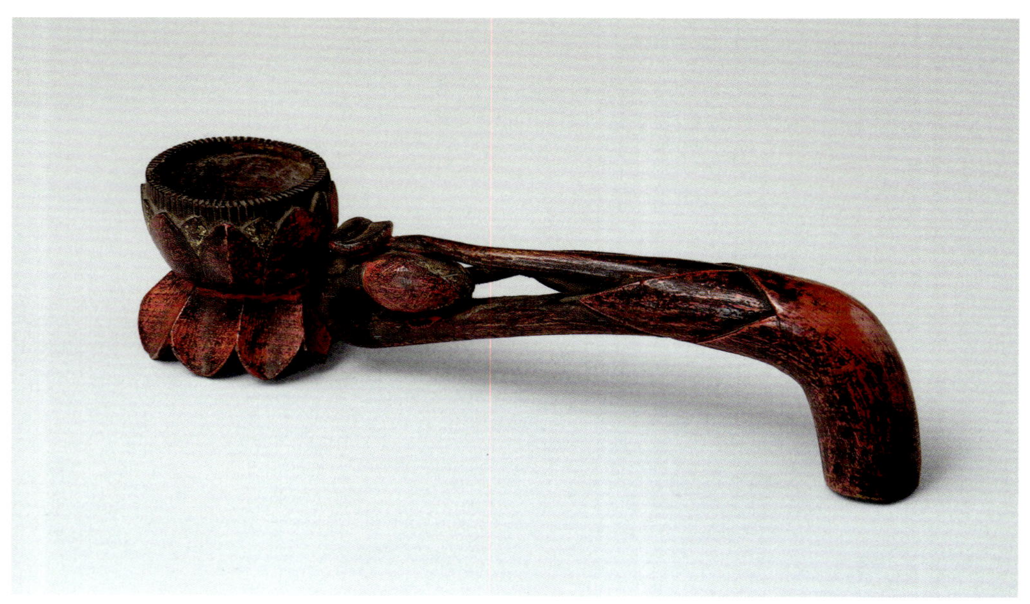

791. Incense holder (*egōro*, 柄香炉)

Momoyama–Edo period, 17th century
Black and red lacquer with gold leaf
6.4 x 27.6 cm (2 1/2 x 10 7/8 in.)

Gift from N. V. Hammer

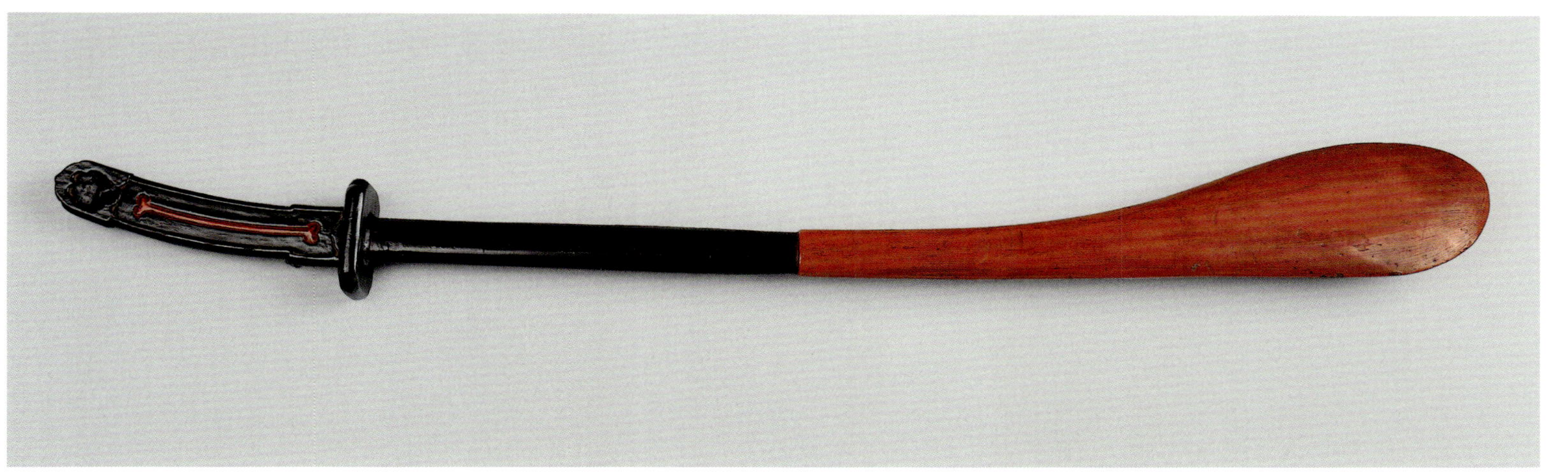

792. Ceremonial sword

Edo period, 17th century
Black and red lacquer
L. 82.8 cm (32 5/8 in.)

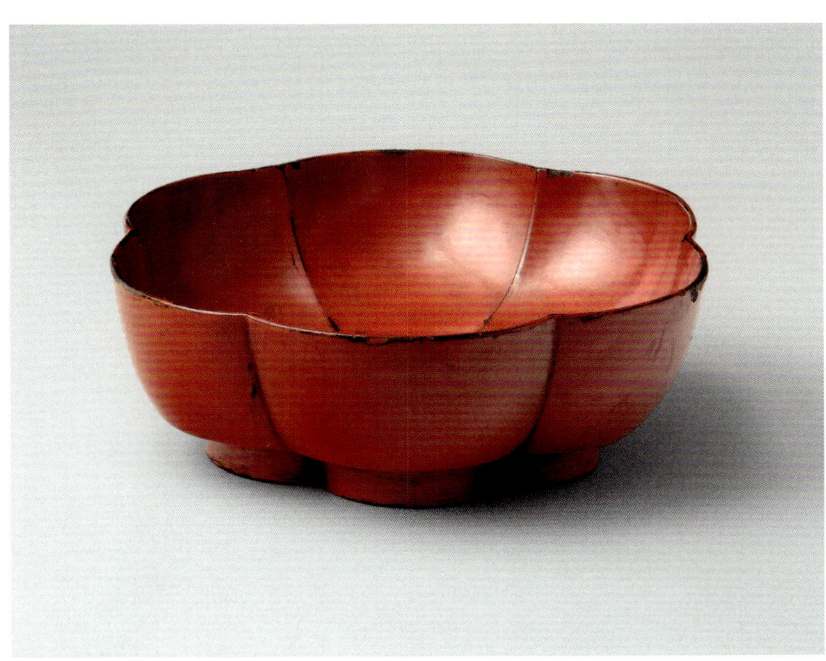

793. Lobed dish

Edo period, 17th century
Black and red lacquer
H. 7.3 cm (2 7/8 in.), diam. 21 cm (8 1/4 in.)

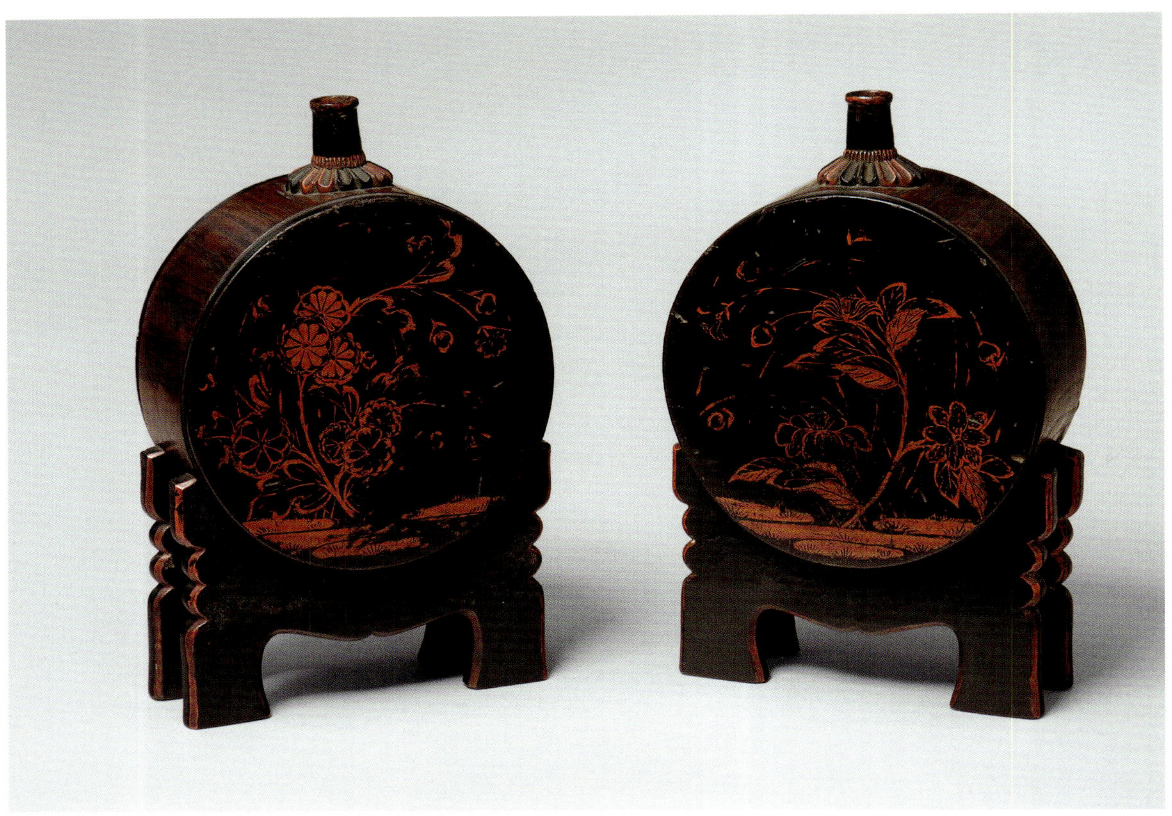

794. Pair of sake containers with grasses and flowers

Momoyama–Edo period, early 17th century
Black lacquer with red lacquer decoration
Each container 27.8 x 17.7 x 8.5 cm (11 x 7 x 3 3/8 in.)

LITERATURE: Tokyo National Museum 1985a, no. 114; Avitabile 1990, no. 118.

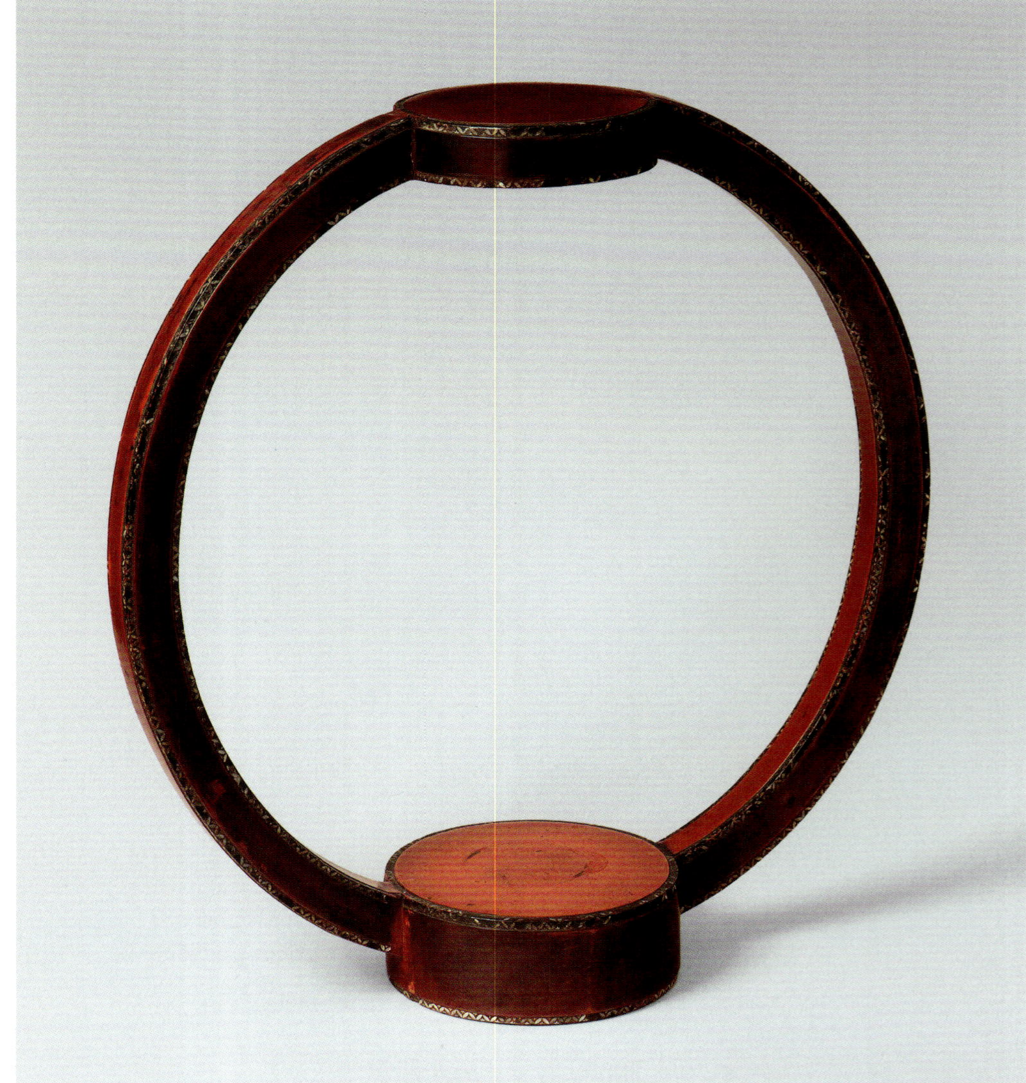

795. Round flower stand

Edo period, 17th century
Black and red lacquer and mother-of-pearl inlay
63.5 x 61.3 cm (25 x 24 1/8 in.)

796. Altar table

Muromachi–Momoyama period,
15th–16th century
Black lacquer
27.5 x 58 x 32.7 cm (10⅞ x 22⅞ x 12⅞ in.)

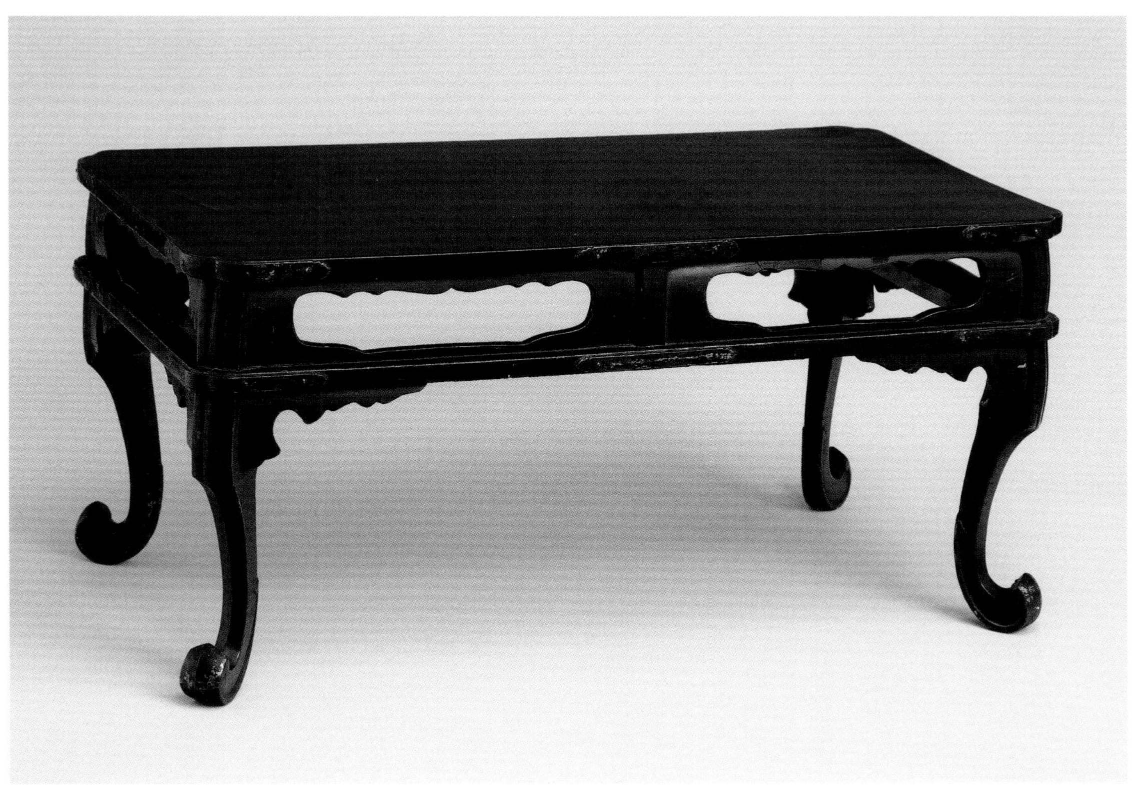

797. Altar table

Momoyama–Edo period, 16th–17th century
Black lacquer
27 x 61 x 32.4 cm (10⅝ x 24 x 12¾ in.)

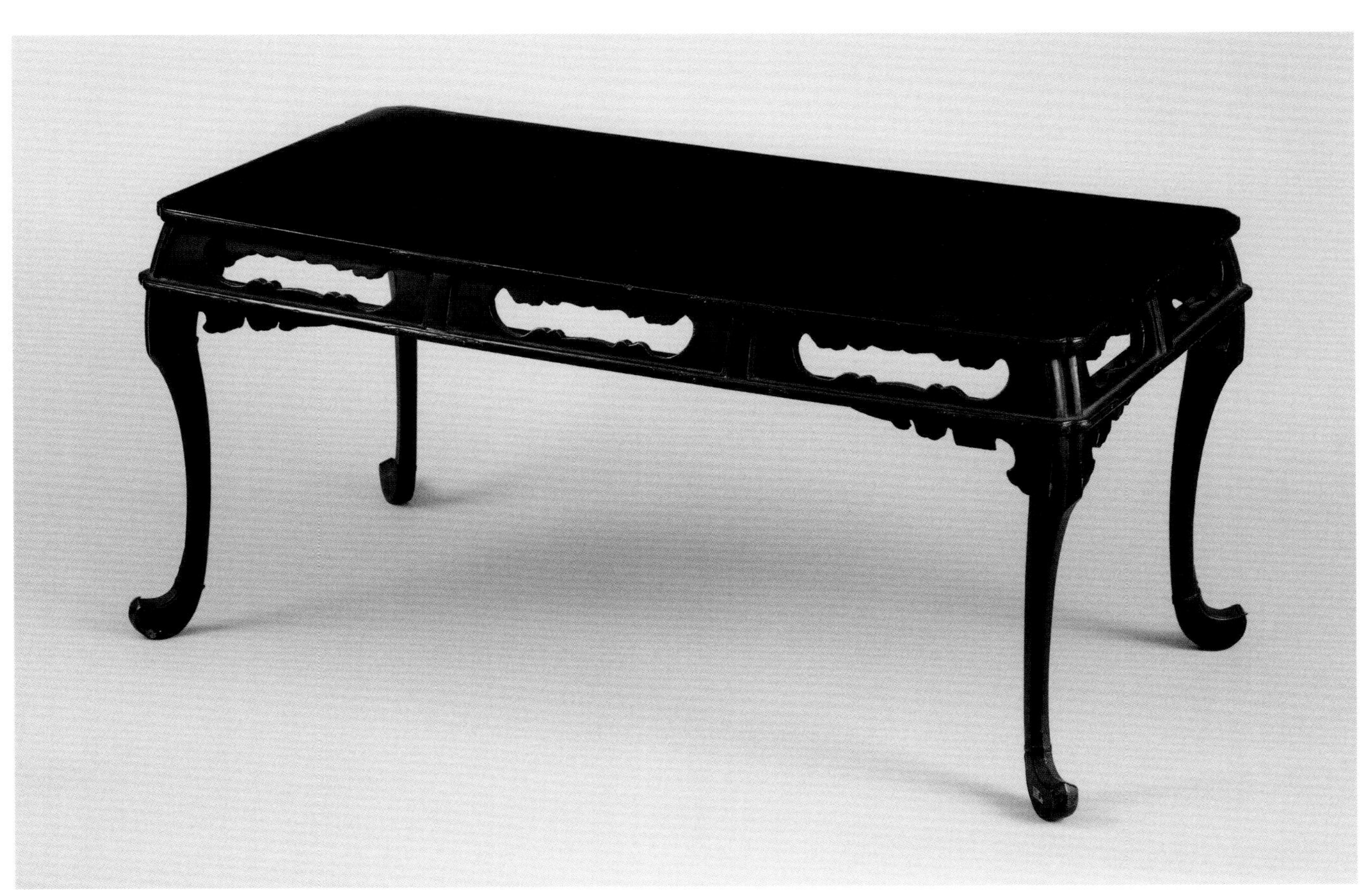

798. Box with sword beans

Edo period, 17th century
Black lacquer with polychrome lacquer
24.5 x 39.5 x 27.7 cm ($9^5/_8$ x $15^1/_2$ x $10^7/_8$ in.)

LITERATURE: Tokyo National Museum 1985a, no. 122; Avitabile 1990, no. 125.

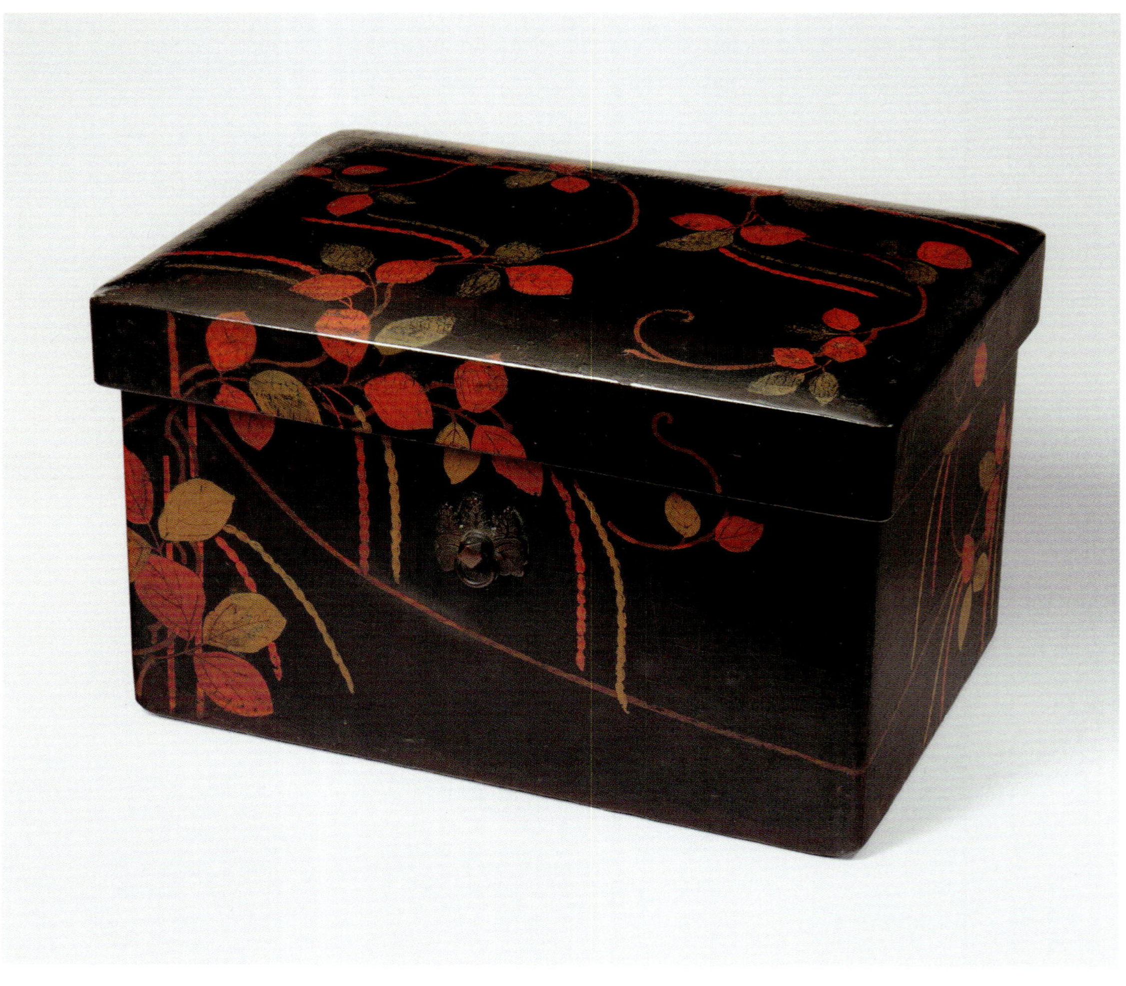

799. Altar table

Edo period, 17th–18th century
Black and red lacquer
20.5 x 54.7 x 32.2 cm ($8^1/_8$ x $21^1/_2$ x $12^5/_8$ in.)

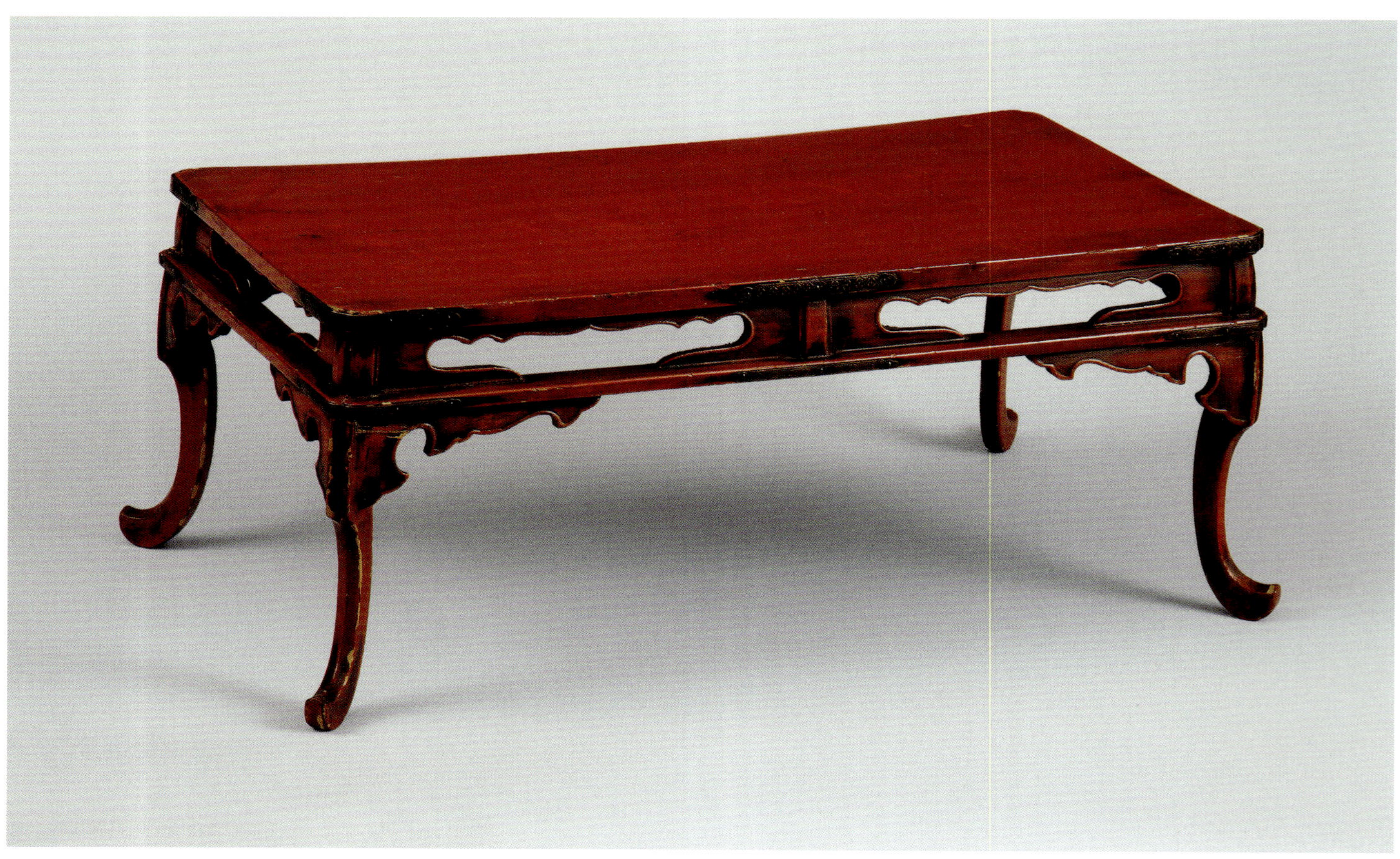

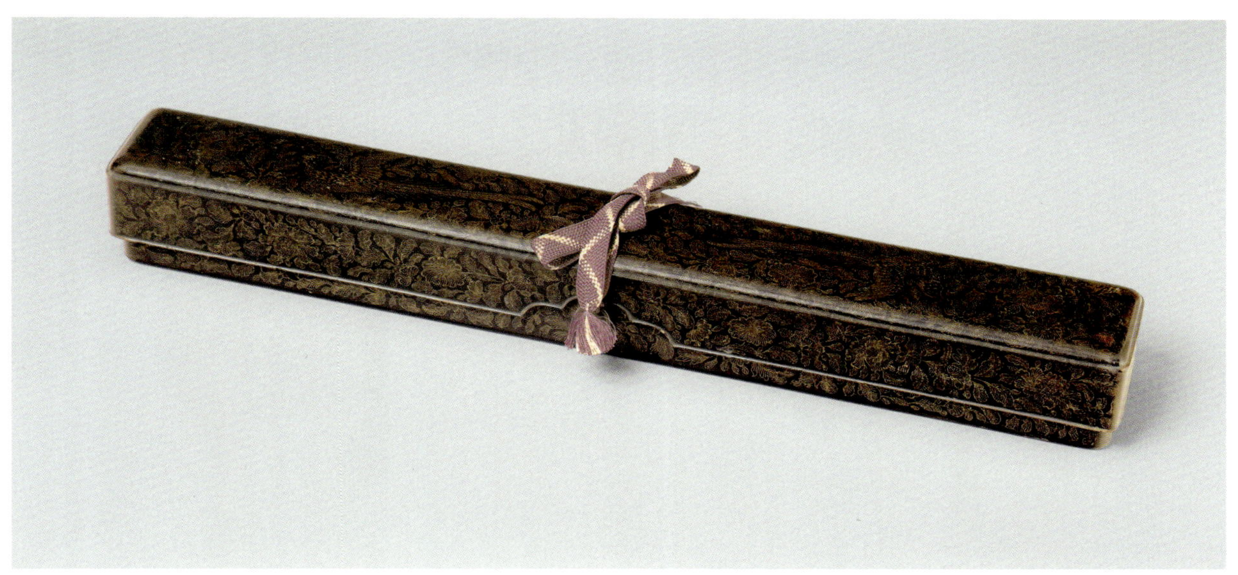

800. Sutra box with phoenixes, from the Ryūkyū Islands

Edo period, 18th century
Black lacquer with gold inlay
L. 41.1 cm (16 1/8 in.)

Gift from Muraguchi Shirō, 1981

Nakamura Sōtetsu
(中村宗哲; fl. 18th century)

801. Zither (*kin*, 琴) named "Flowing Water" (*Ryūsui*, 流水)

Edo period, 1794
Wood with black lacquer and mother-of-pearl inlay
L. (excluding tassels) 82.5 cm (32 1/2 in.)
Text, signature, seals

Literature: Murase 1980b, no. 45.

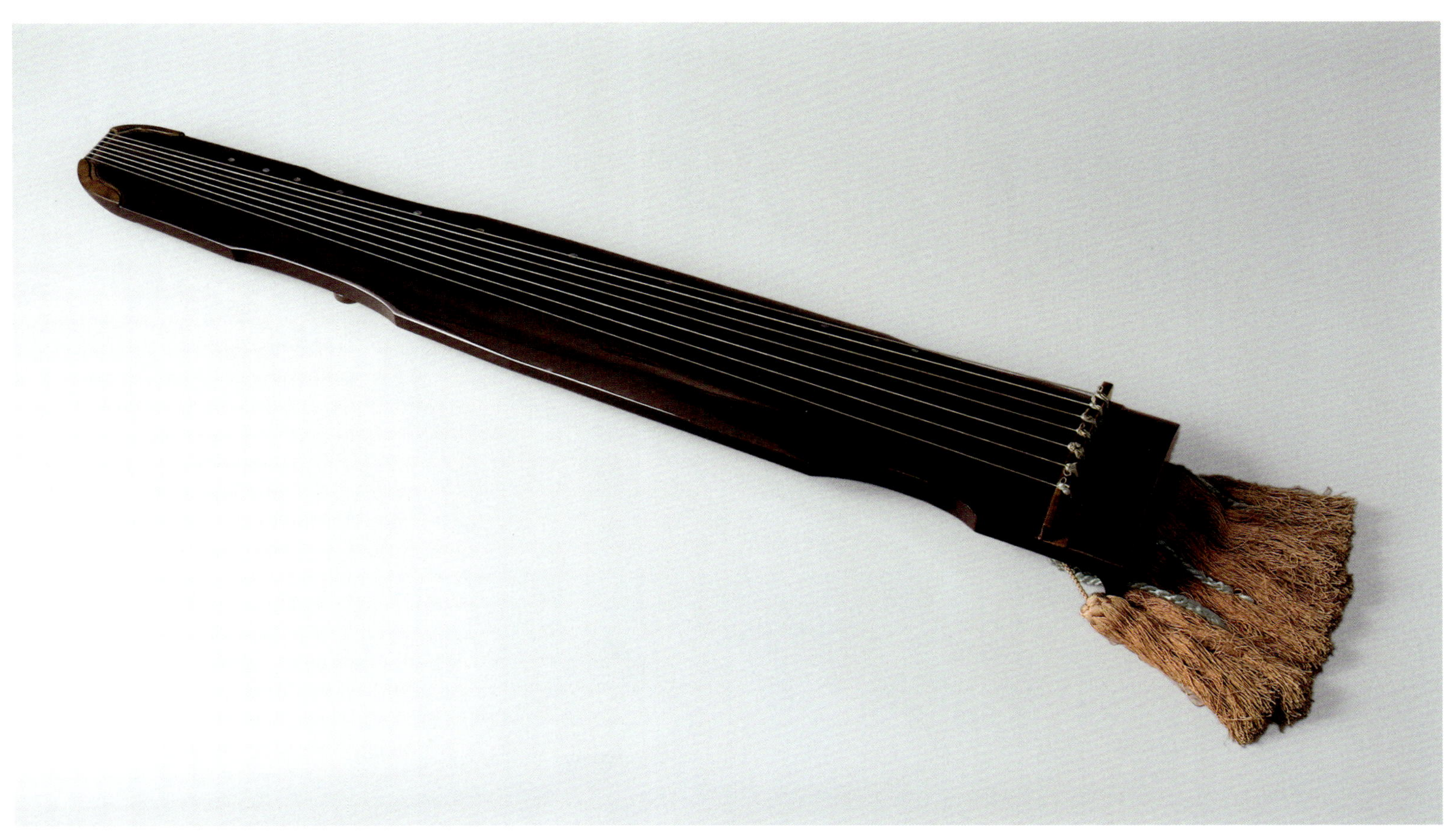

802. Altar table

Edo period, 18th–19th century
Black and red lacquer
28 x 49 x 31 cm (11 x 19¼ x 12¼ in.)

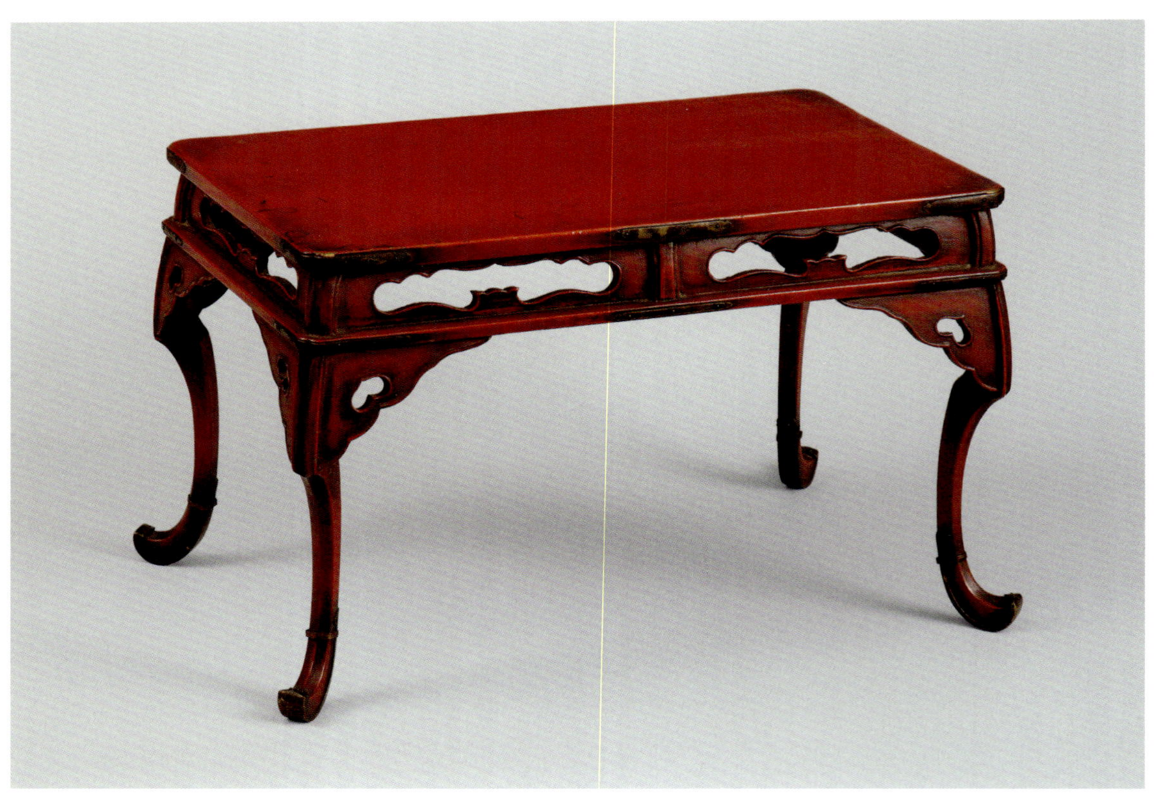

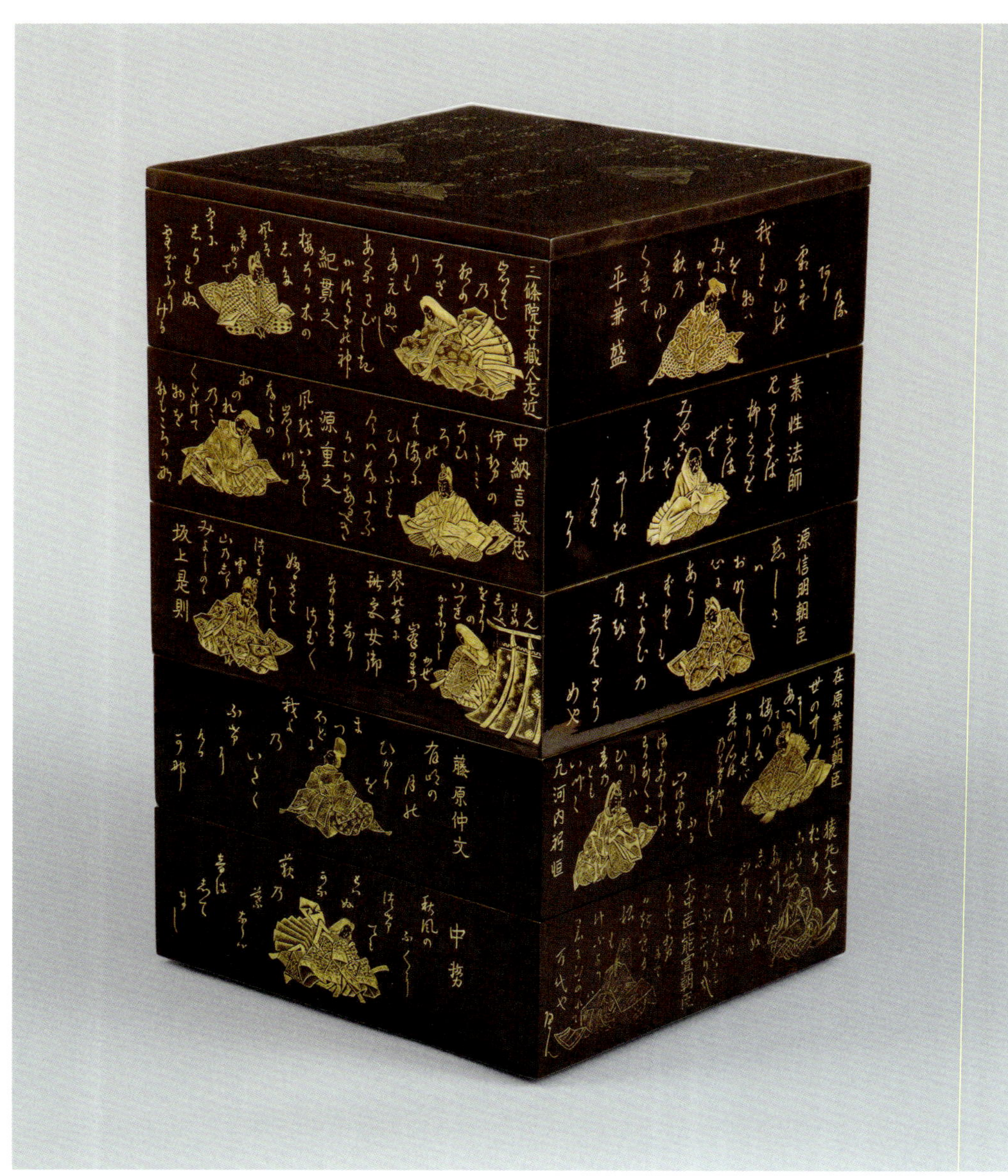

803. Stacked food boxes (*jūbako*, 重箱) with the Thirty-Six Immortal Poets (三十六歌仙)

Edo period, 19th century
Black lacquer, incised and decorated with gold
Overall 41.6 x 25.9 x 24.3 cm (16⅜ x 10¼ x 9⅝ in.)

LITERATURE: Burke 1993, no. 52.

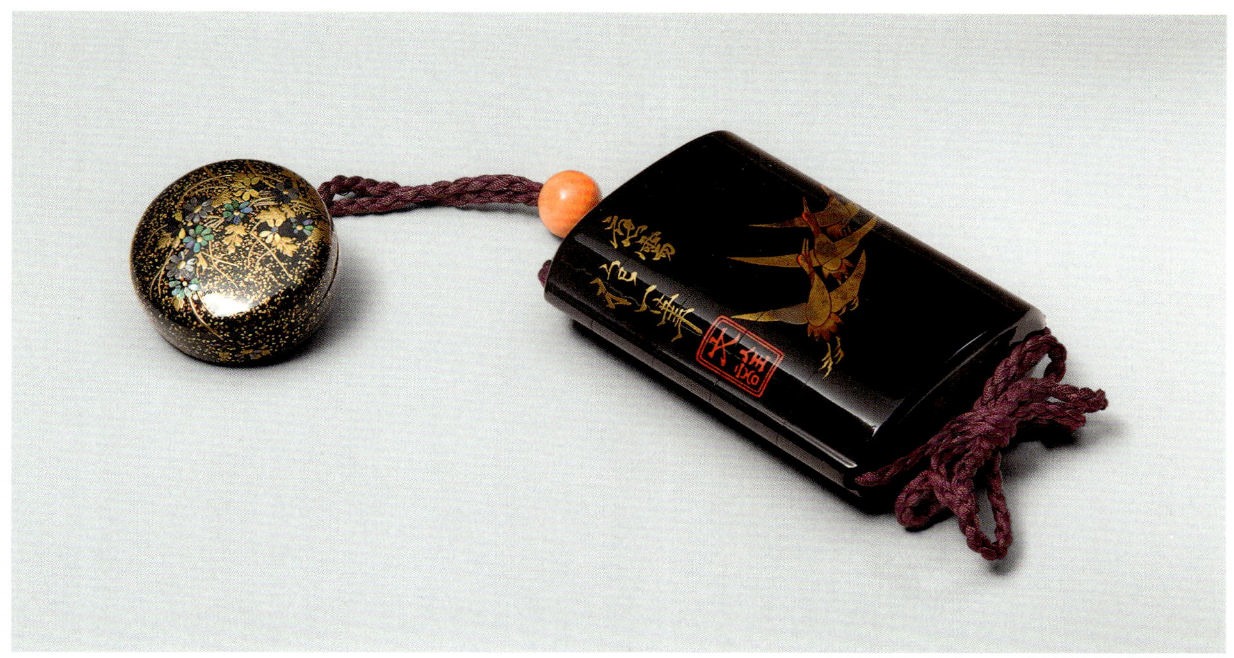

Hara Yōyūsai
(原羊遊斎; 1772–1845)
Design by Sakai Hōitsu
(酒井 抱一, 1761–1828)

804. Medicine case (*inrō*, 印籠) with cranes and waves

Edo period, ca. 1815–45
Black lacquer with gold and silver *maki-e* and shell inlay; silk cord
Case 6.8 x 5.2 cm (2 5/8 x 2 in.); netsuke diam. 3.5 cm (1 3/8 in.)
Signatures, seal

Literature: McKelway 2012, no. 24.

Gift from Mr. and Mrs. Minoru Hosomi, 1987

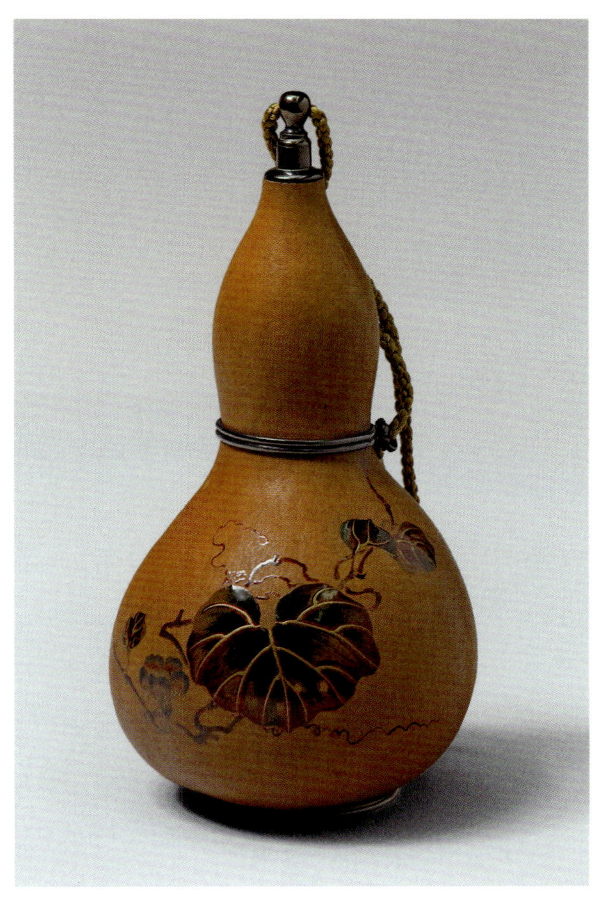

Hara Yōyūsai
(原羊遊斎; 1772–1845)
Design by Sakai Hōitsu
(酒井 抱一, 1761–1828)

805. Painted gourd with vine leaves

Edo period, 19th century
Gourd with lacquer and gold
H. 18.1 cm (7 1/8 in.), diam. 9 cm (3 1/2 in.)
Signatures, seals

Literature: McKelway 2012, no. 25.

Suzuki Mutsumi
(鈴木睦美; 1941–2009)

Suzuki Misako
(鈴木美佐子; b. 1945)

806. Tea caddy (*natsume*, 棗) with clouds

Shōwa era, 20th century
Red lacquer with gold and silver *maki-e*
H. 7.5 cm (3 in.), diam. 7.3 cm (2 7/8 in.)

Literature: Burke 1993, no. 55.

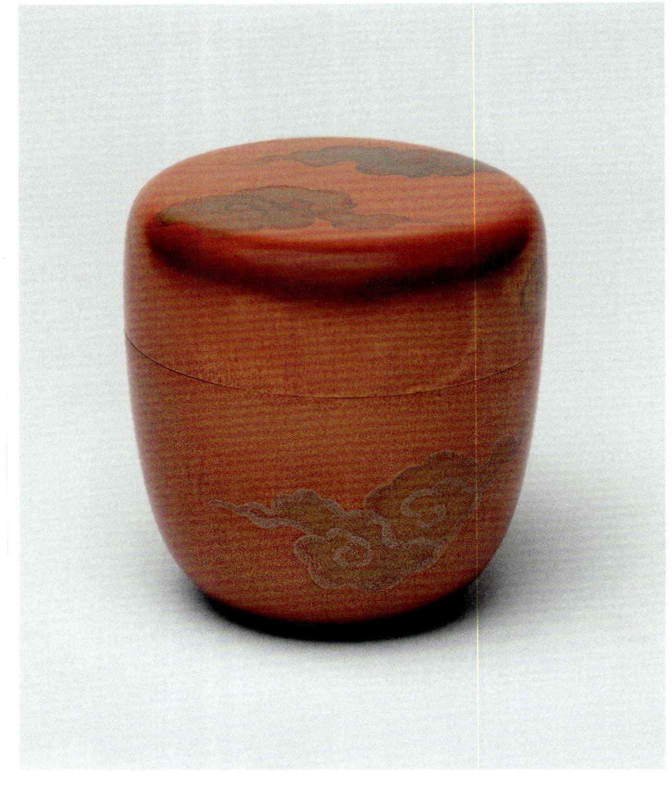

Suzuki Mutsumi
(鈴木睦美; 1941–2009)

Suzuki Misako
(鈴木美佐子; b. 1945)

807. Tea caddy (*natsume*, 棗) with autumn fire

Shōwa era, 20th century
Black and red lacquer with gold *maki-e*
H. 7.5 cm (3 in.), diam. 7.3 cm (2 7/8 in.)

Literature: Burke 1993, no. 54.

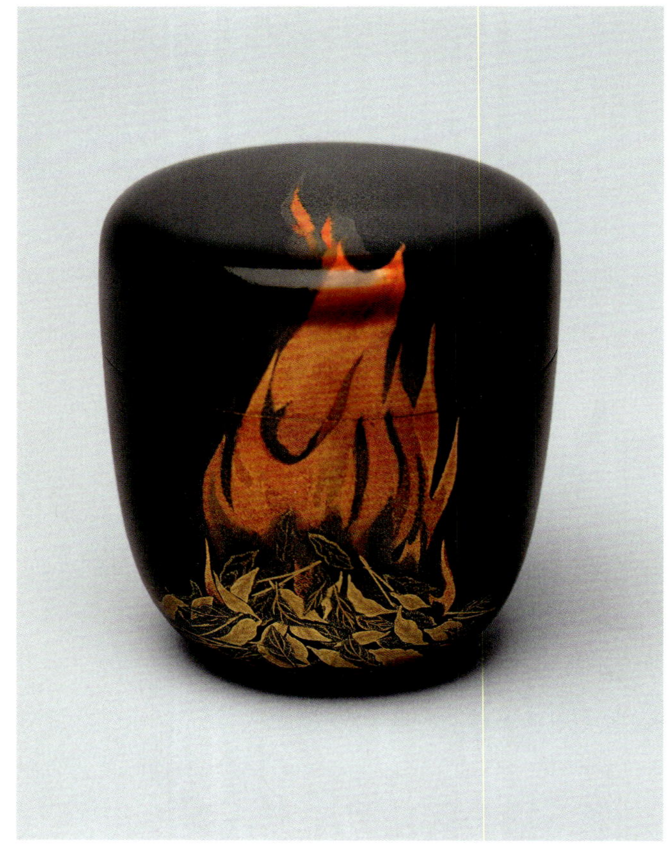

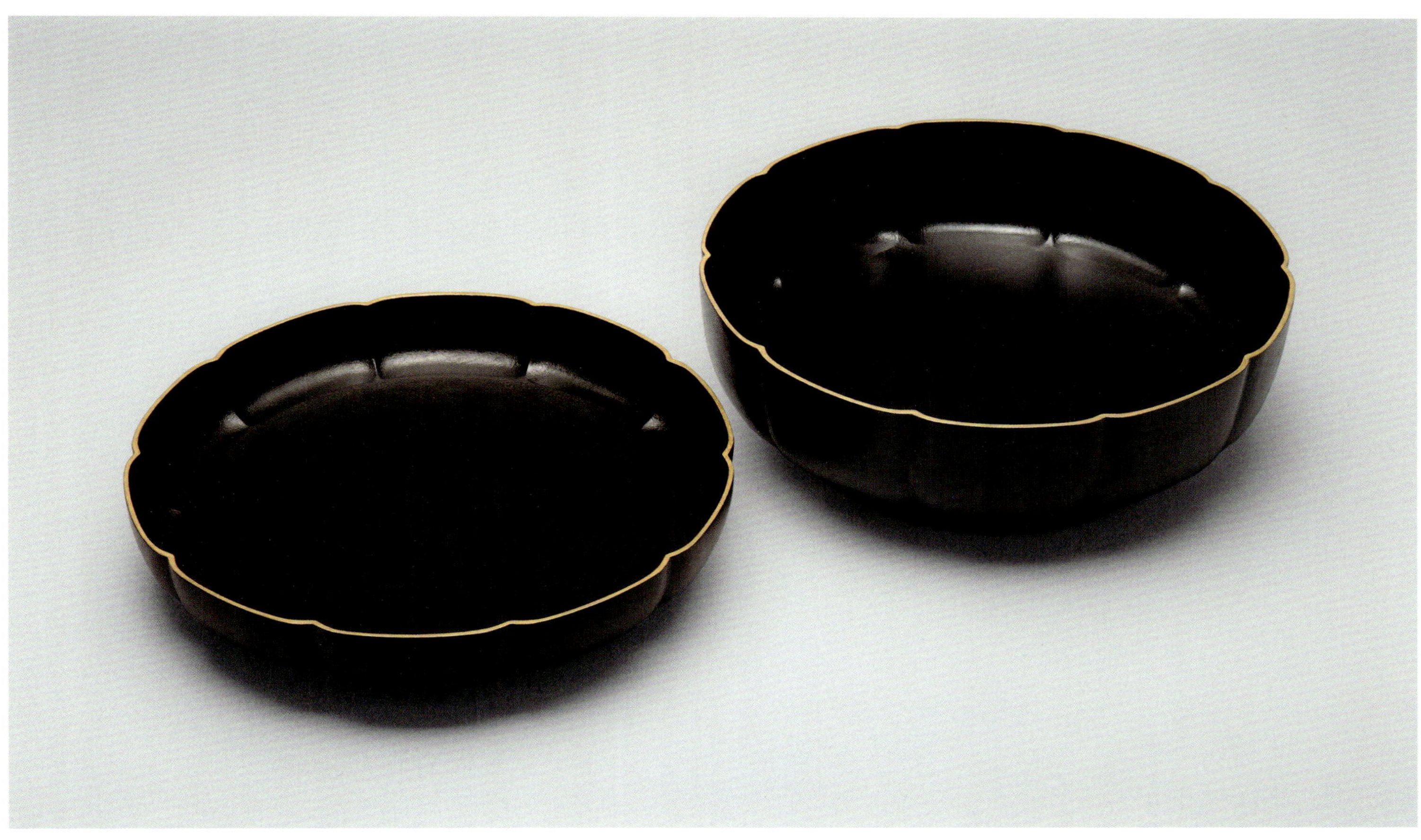

Suzuki Mutsumi
(鈴木睦美; 1941–2009)

808. Two trays for tea sweets

Shōwa era, 20th century
Black lacquer with gold trimming
(*right*) H. 7.9 cm (3 1/8 in.), diam. 23.4 cm (9 1/4 in.);
(*left*) H. 4.9 cm (1 7/8 in.), diam. 22.9 cm (9 in.)

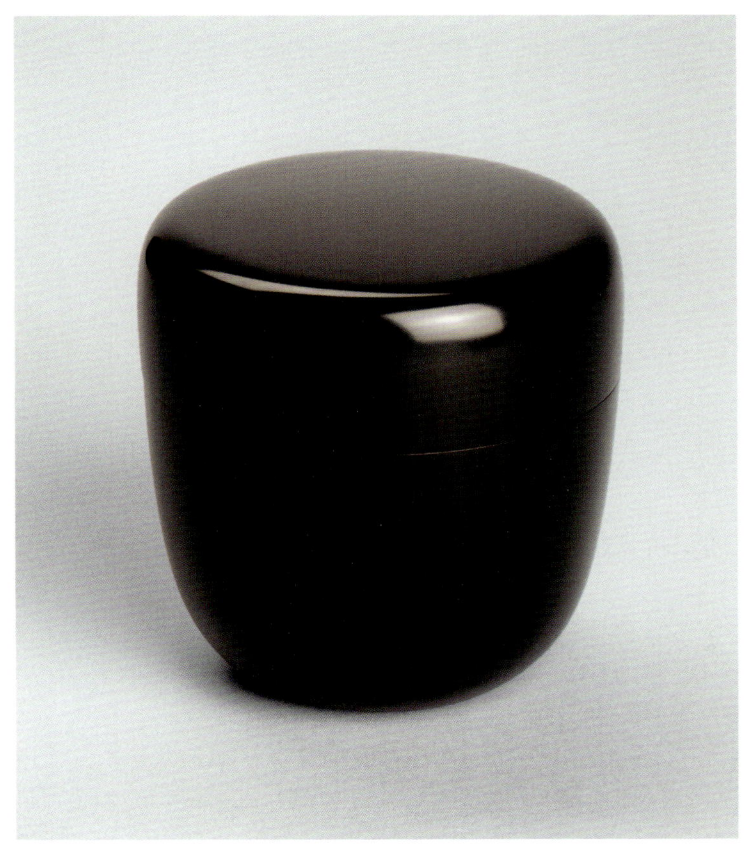

Suzuki Mutsumi
(鈴木睦美; 1941–2009)
Suzuki Misako
(鈴木美佐子; b. 1945)

809. Tea caddy (*natsume*, 棗)

Shōwa era, 20th century
Black lacquer
H. 7.5 cm (3 in.), diam. 7.3 cm (2 7/8 in.)

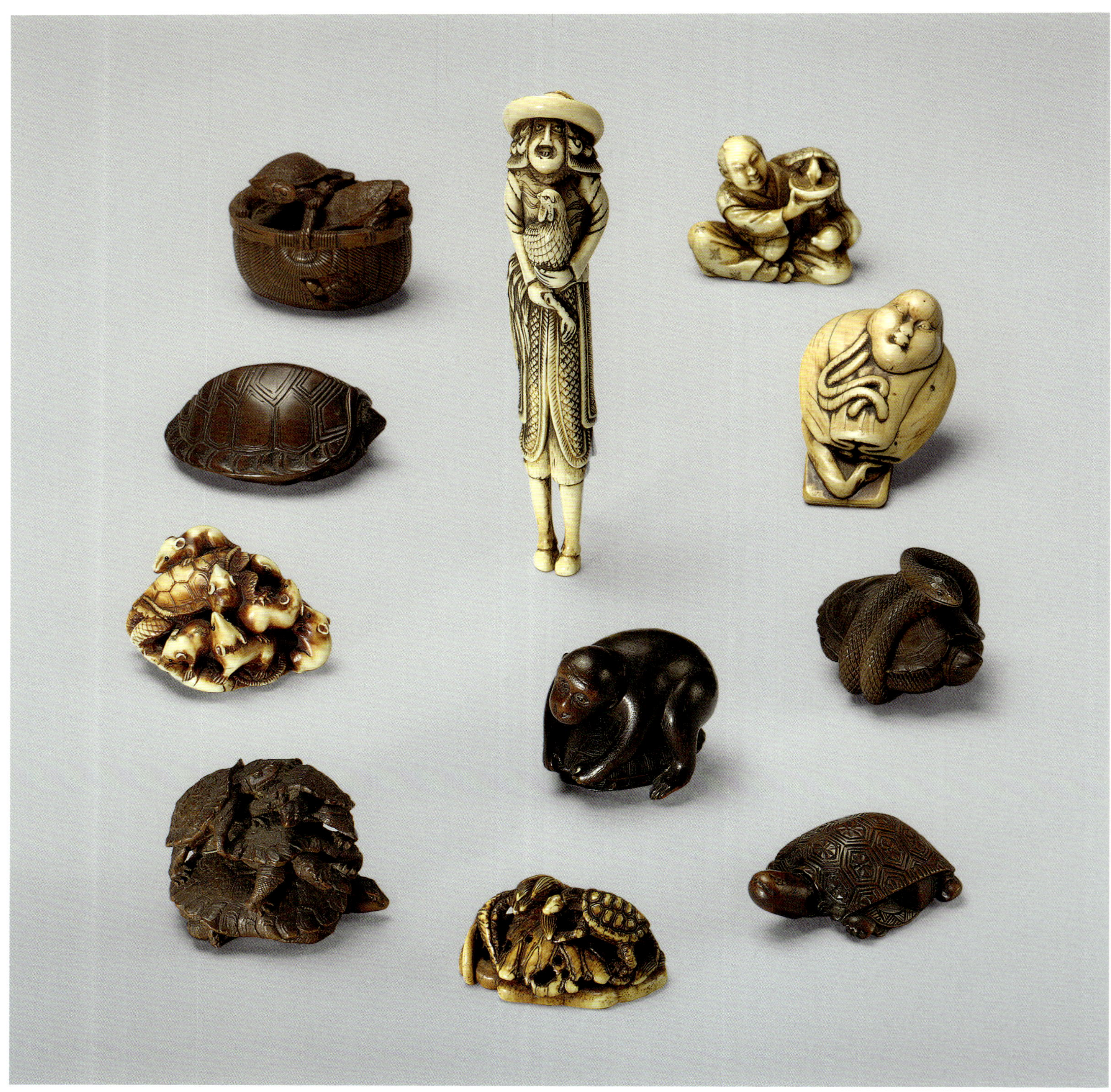

810. Eleven netsuke: Dutchman and others

Edo period, late 18th–19th century
Various materials
Varying sizes

Japanese Lacquer Details

† *denotes illustrated items*

755. Writing box (*suzuribako*) with poem from *Kokin wakashū*

Text

[poem 689]
[top of lid] *Upon the mat,* [inside box] *spreading but one side [of your robe,] / tonight again, [bridge maiden of Uji,] do you wait for me?*

760. Writing box (*suzuribako*) with a poem from *Shin kokin wakashū*

Text

[from poem 625]
Naniwa; *dream*

† 769. Pumpkin-shaped box

Signature

Made by Master of Lacquer Chōkan in 1857

† 771. Stacked food boxes (*jūbako*) with taro plants and chrysanthemums

Signatures

[inside each lid] *Zeshin*

772a–l. Zodiac calendar in the shape of a hanging scroll

Signatures

(a) *Made on a certain day in 1846 by Ta Zeshin upon request*; (b) *Zeshin*; (c) *Drawn by Zeshin*; (d) *Zeshin*; (e) *Tanyū, copied by Zeshin*; (f) *Zeshin*; (g) *Zeshin depicted the spirit*; (h) *Tairyūkyo*; (i) *Zeshin*; (j) *Zeshin*; (k) *Copy of Minamoto Ōkyo's painting, Zeshin*; (l) *Zeshin*

Seals

(a) *Zeshin*; (c) *Shin*; (d) *Zeshin*; (h) illegible; (k) *Zeshin*; (l) *Koma*

† 773. Comb and pin with cranes

Signature

[on pin] *Kinju*

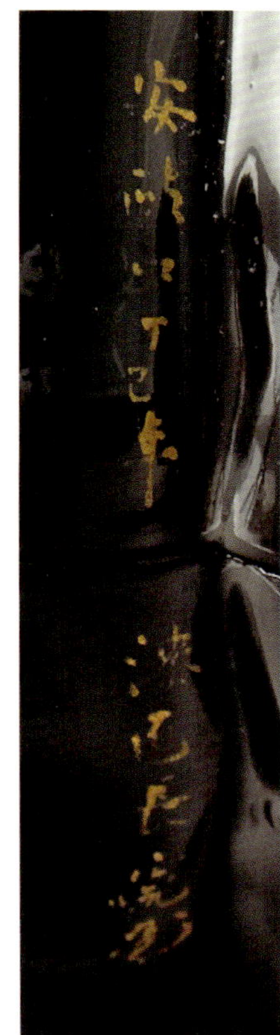

769

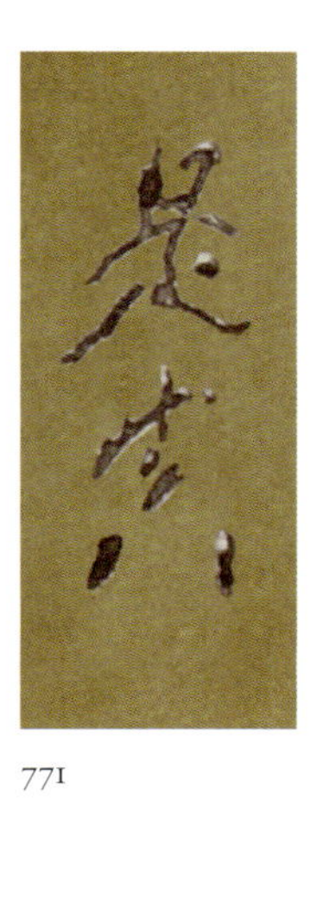

771

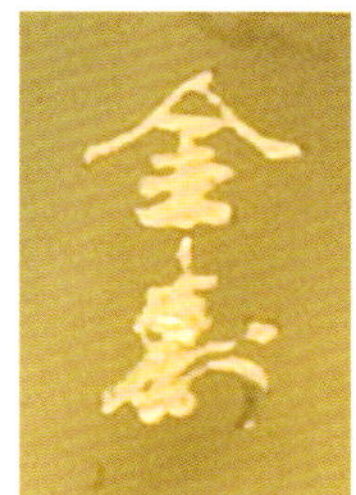

773

† 774. Shelf stand with scenes from *Eight Views of Ōmi* (*Ōmi hakkei*)

Signature

[inside large, hinged door] *Minota Nagahisa*

Seal

[inside large, hinged door] *kaō*

† 776. Large hand-drum core (*ōtsuzumidō*) with grapevines and squirrels

Signatures

Itoku; *Yazaemon*

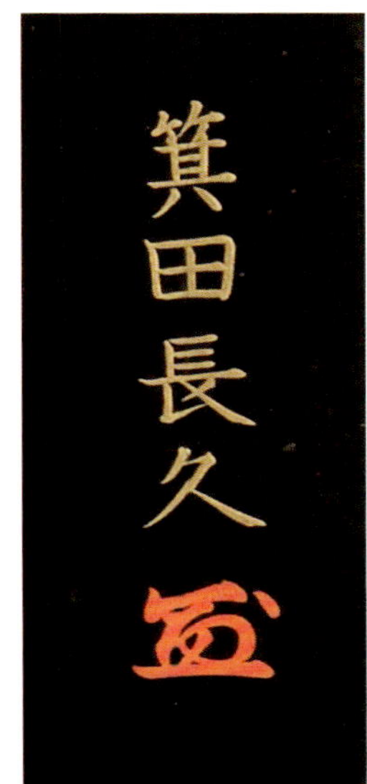

774

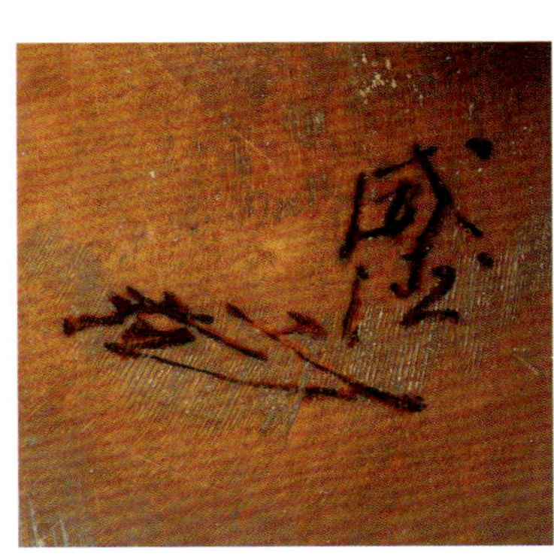

776

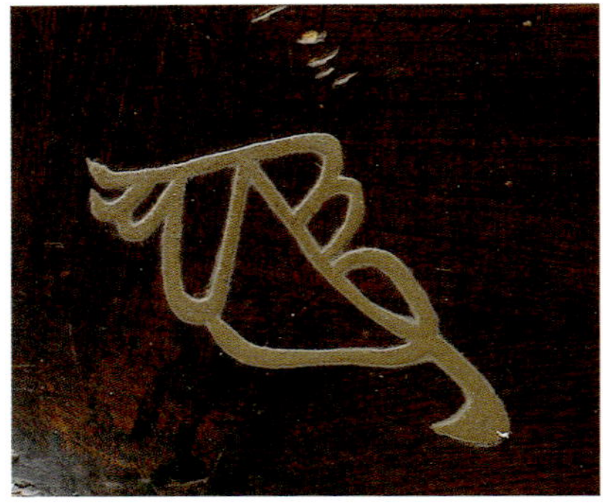

778

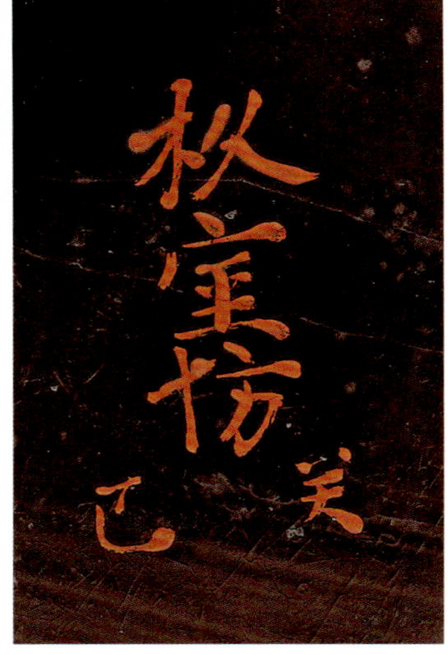

787

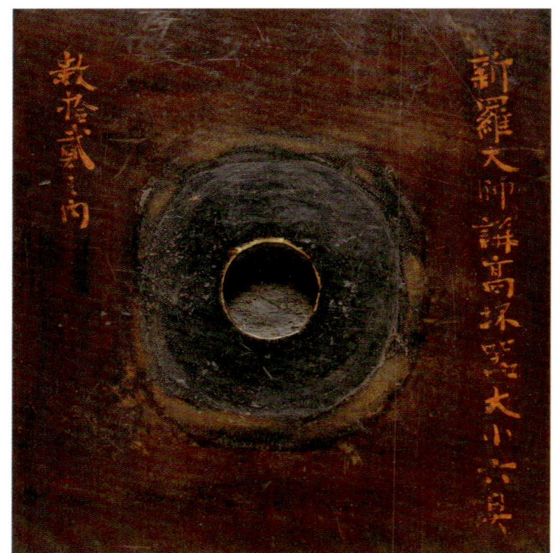

788, underside of tabletop

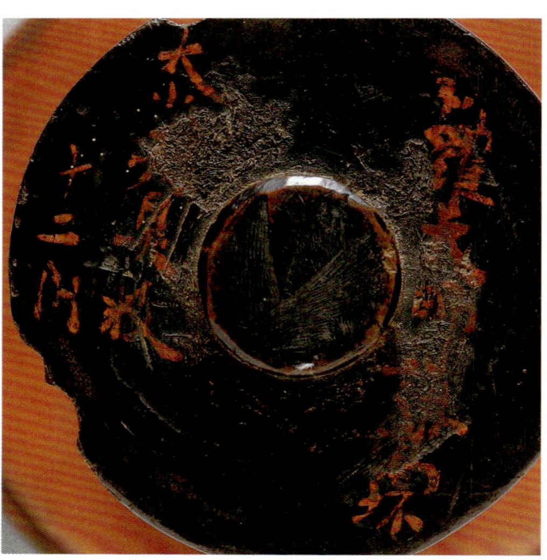

788, top of stem

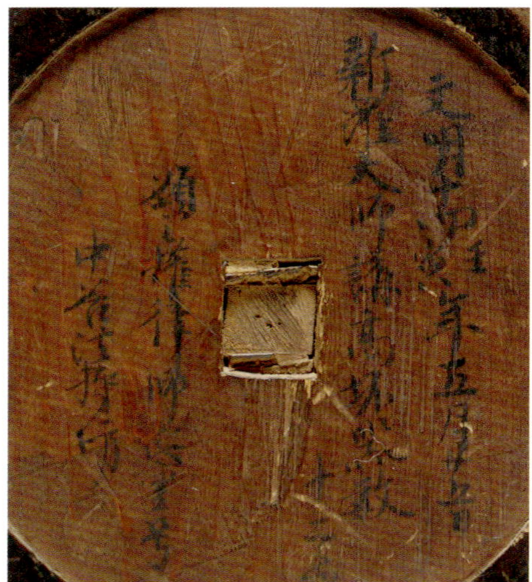

788, bottom of stem

† 778. Table with autumn flowers

SEAL

kaō

† 787. Wash basin (*tarai*)

TEXT

Sanshitsubō; cyclical date of 1353 or 1413

† 788. Stem table (*takatsuki*)

TEXT

[top of table] *Myōjin*; [underside of tabletop] *Society of Shinra Daishi, one of stem tables, six large and six small, total twelve*; [stem] *Myōjin*; [top of stem] *Society of Shinra Daishi, one of stem tables, six large and six small, total twelve*; [bottom of stem] *Fifth month twenty-fifth day of 1482; Society of Shinra Daishi, one of twelve stem tables; petitioner Gon Risshi Ryōjū go Nakatani Hōjibō*

† 790. Hot-water ewer (*yutō*)

TEXT

[under lid and on base] *Enmyō*

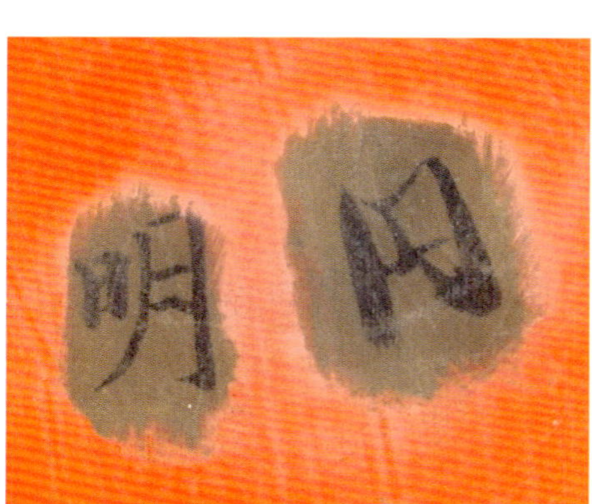

790, under lid

† 801. Zither (*kin*) named "Flowing Water" (*Ryūsui*)

Text

Ryūsui

Signature

Lacquerer Sōtetsu, early winter, 1794

Seals

Yuimin; *Shishō* (?); *kaō*

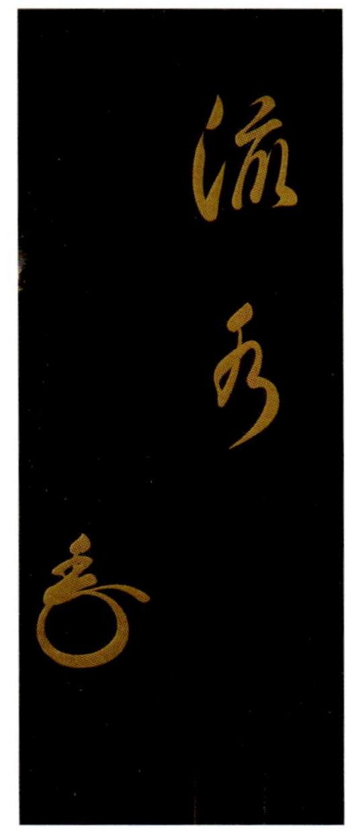

801

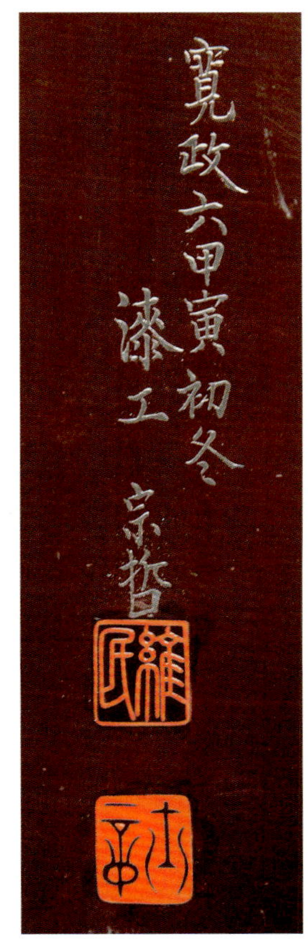

801

† 804. Medicine case (*inrō*) with cranes and waves

Signatures

[on base] *Yōyūsai*; [on body] *Brushed to special order by Hōitsu*; [on netsuke] *Shin'yōsai Tōju*

Seals

[on base] *kaō*; [on body] *Monsen*

† 805. Painted gourd with vine leaves

Signatures

Brushed by Hōitsu; *Yōyūsai*

Seals

Monsen; *kaō*

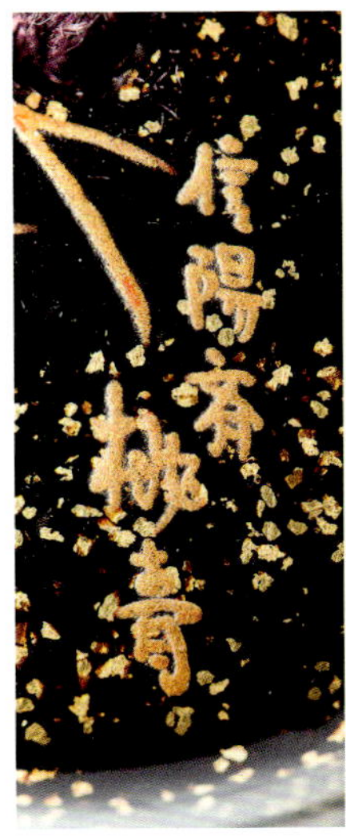

804

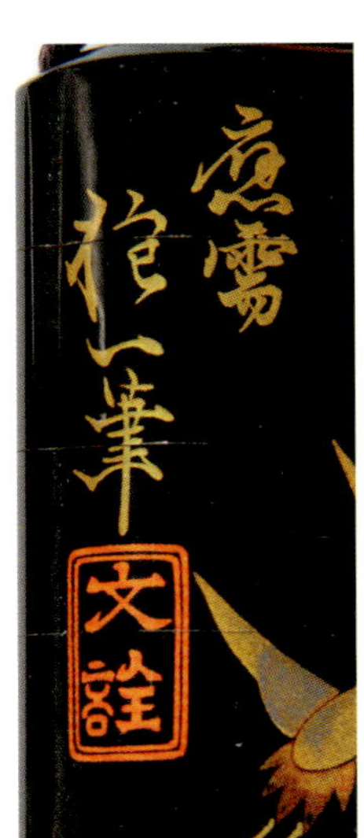

804

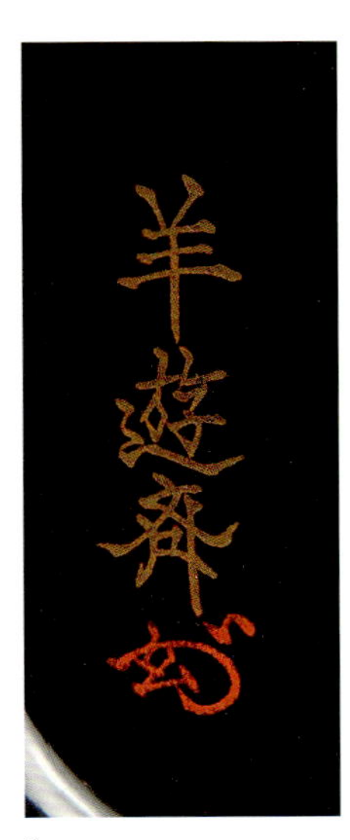

804

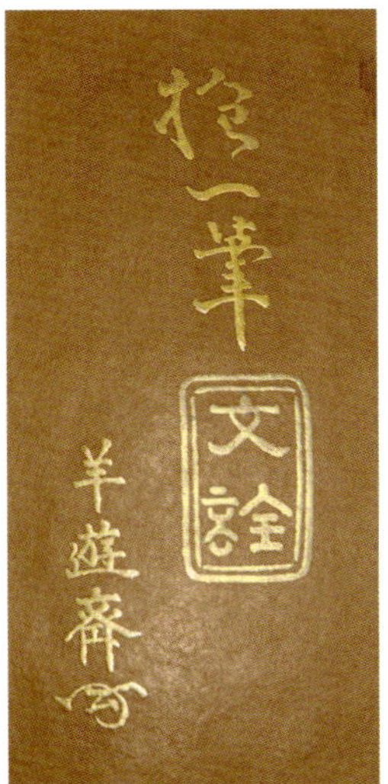

805

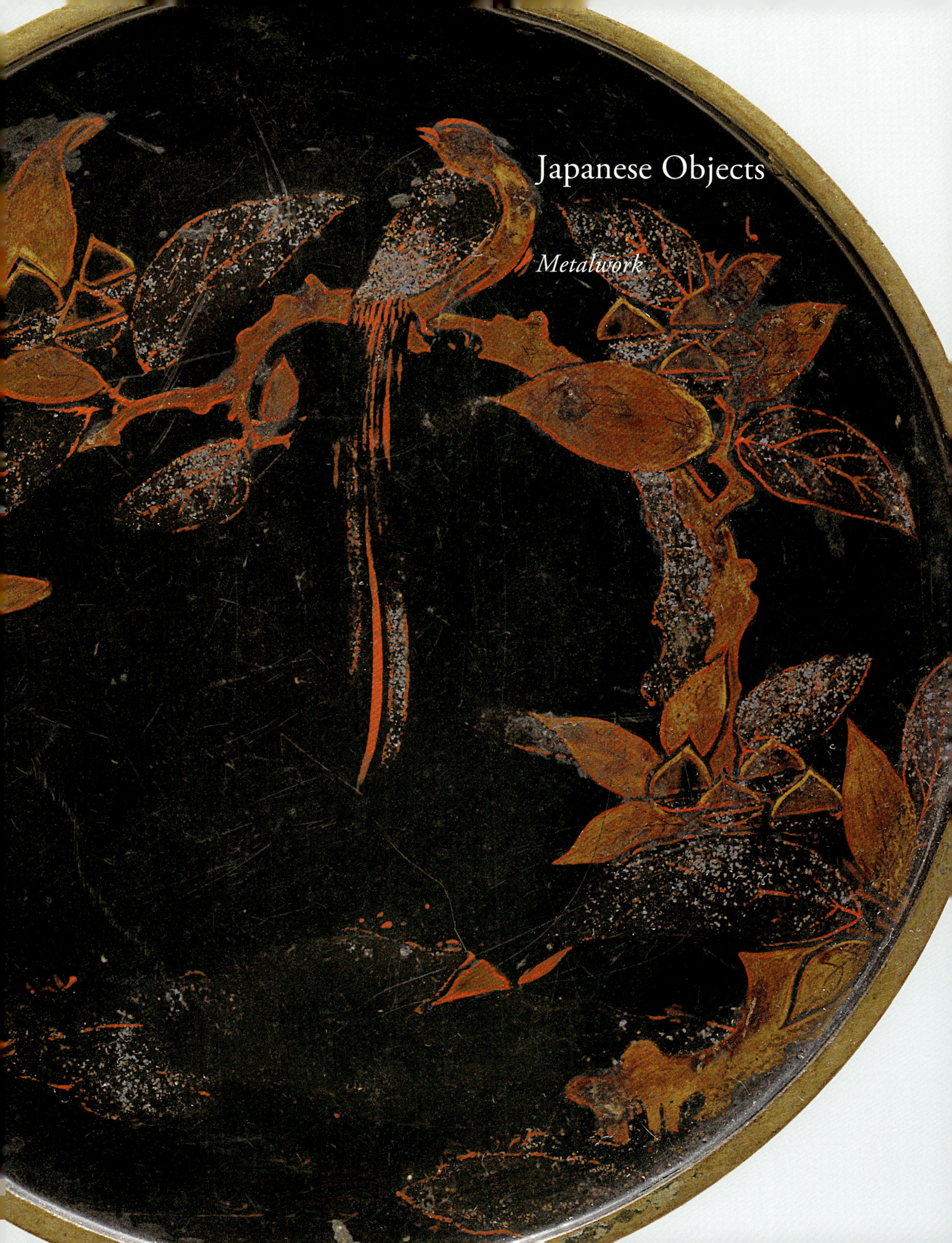

Japanese Objects

Metalwork

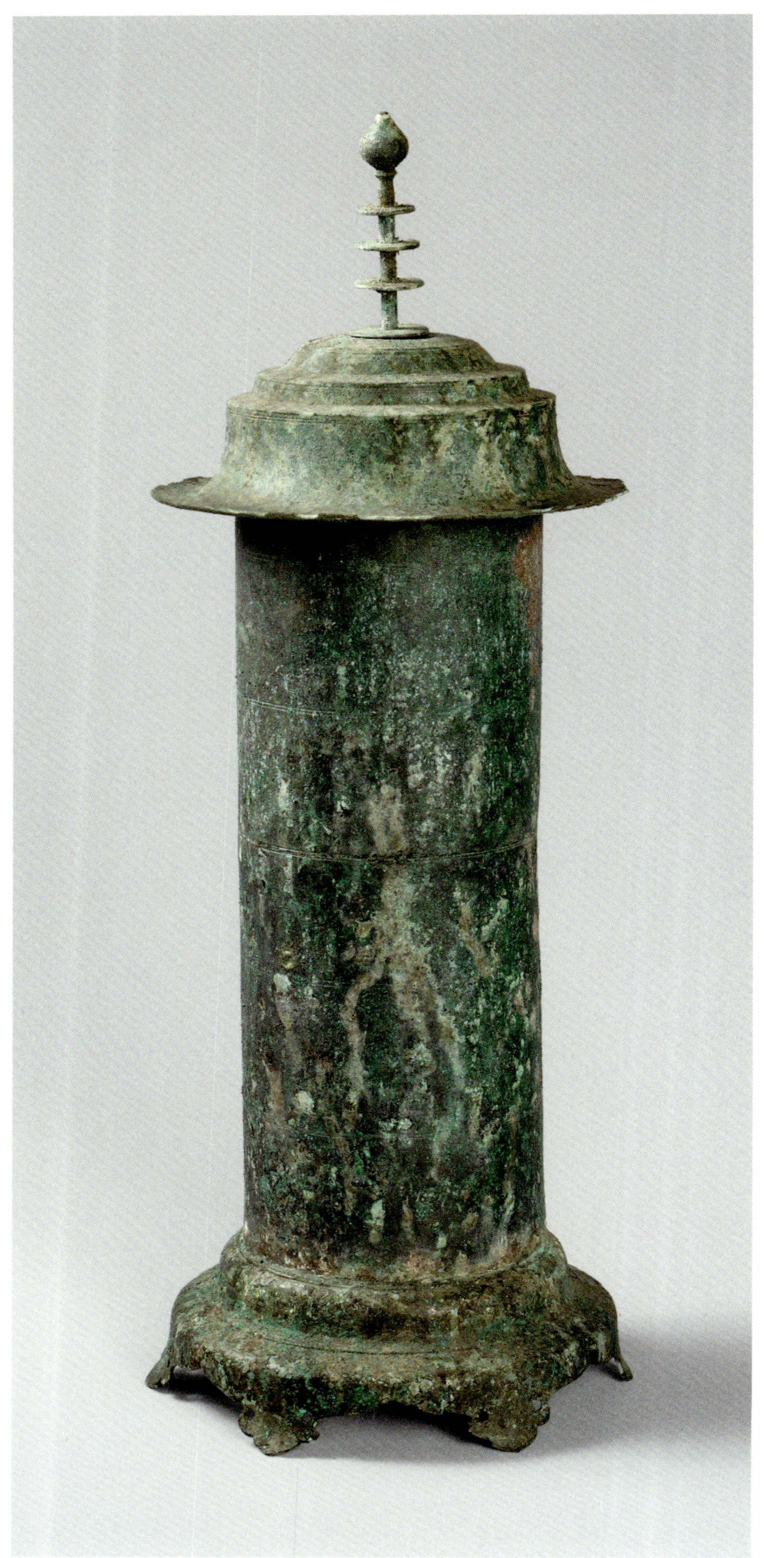

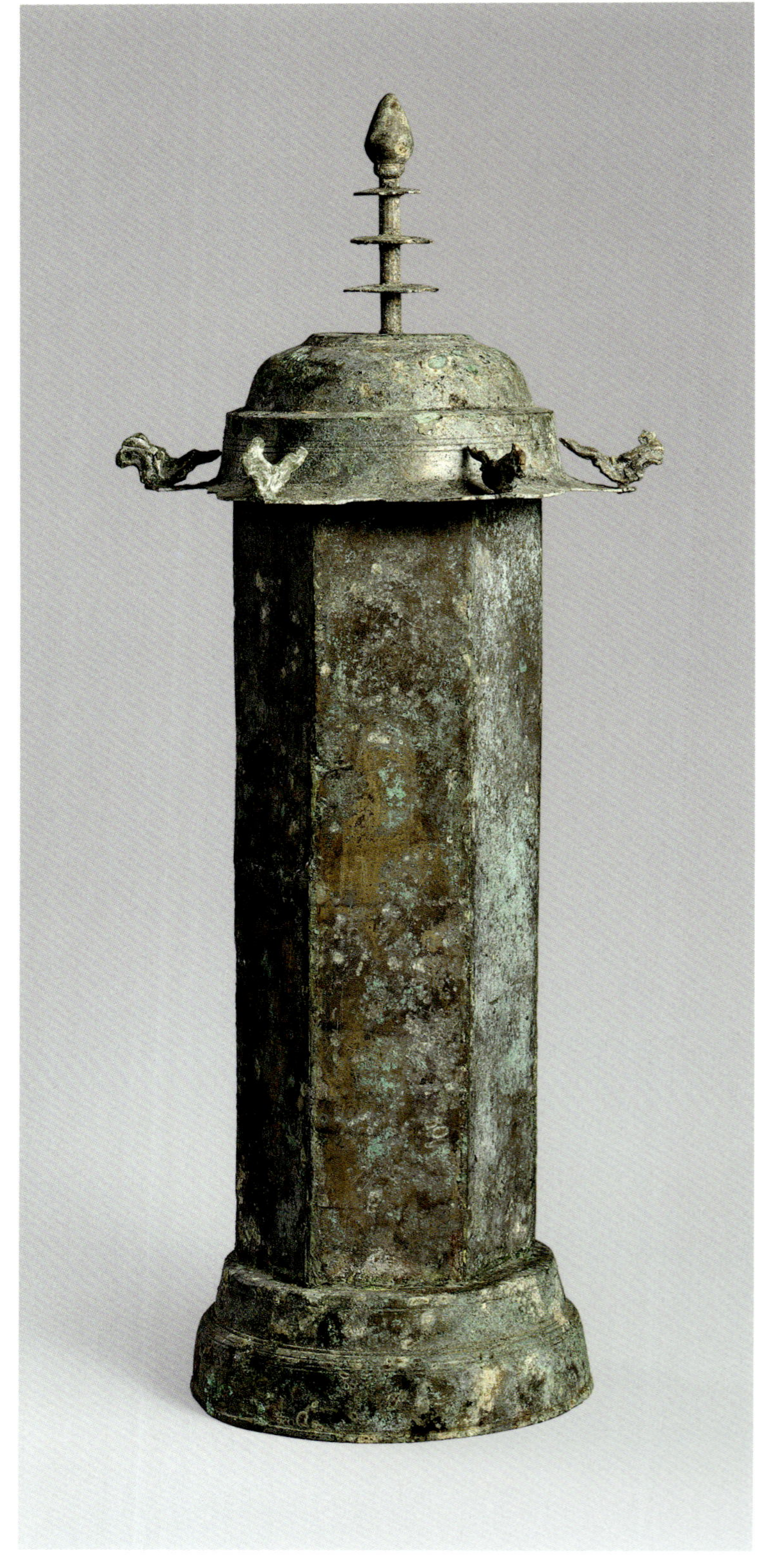

811. Sutra container (*kyōzutsu*, 経筒)

Heian period, 12th century
Bronze
H. with lid 44.5 cm (18½ in.)

Literature: Murase 1975, no.9; Pal and Meech-Pekarik 1988, fig. 113.

812. Hexagonal sutra container (*kyōzutsu*, 経筒)

Heian period, 1127
Bronze
H. with lid 41.5 cm (16⅜ in.)
Text

Literature: Murase 1975, no. 9.

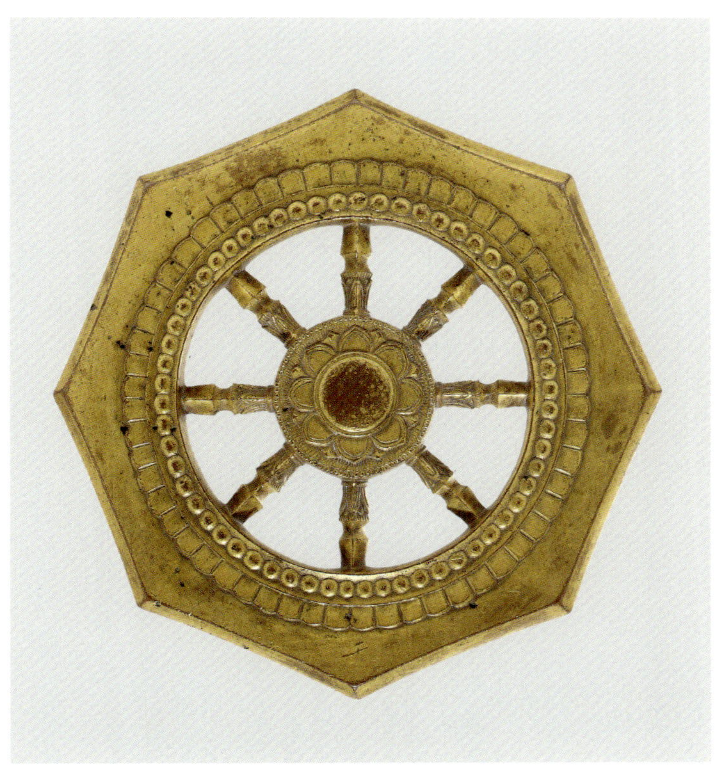

813. Chakra wheel (*rinpō*, 輪宝)

Kamakura period, late 13th century
Gilt bronze
Diam. 12.5 cm (4 7/8 in.)

Literature: Tokyo National Museum 1985a, no. 84; Avitabile 1990, no. 16; Murase 2000, no. 28.

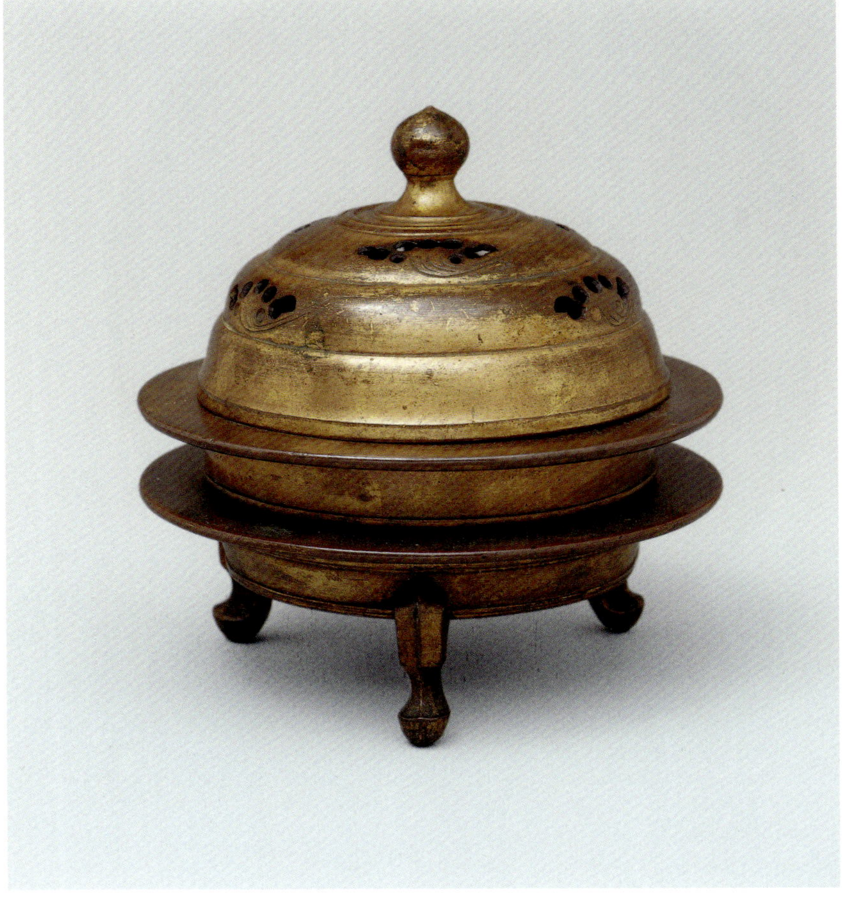

814. Incense burner (*kasha*, 火舎)

Kamakura period, 13th century
Gilt bronze
H. 9.5 cm (3 3/4 in.)

Literature: Tokyo National Museum 1985a, no. 85; Avitabile 1990, no. 18; Murase 2000, no. 29.

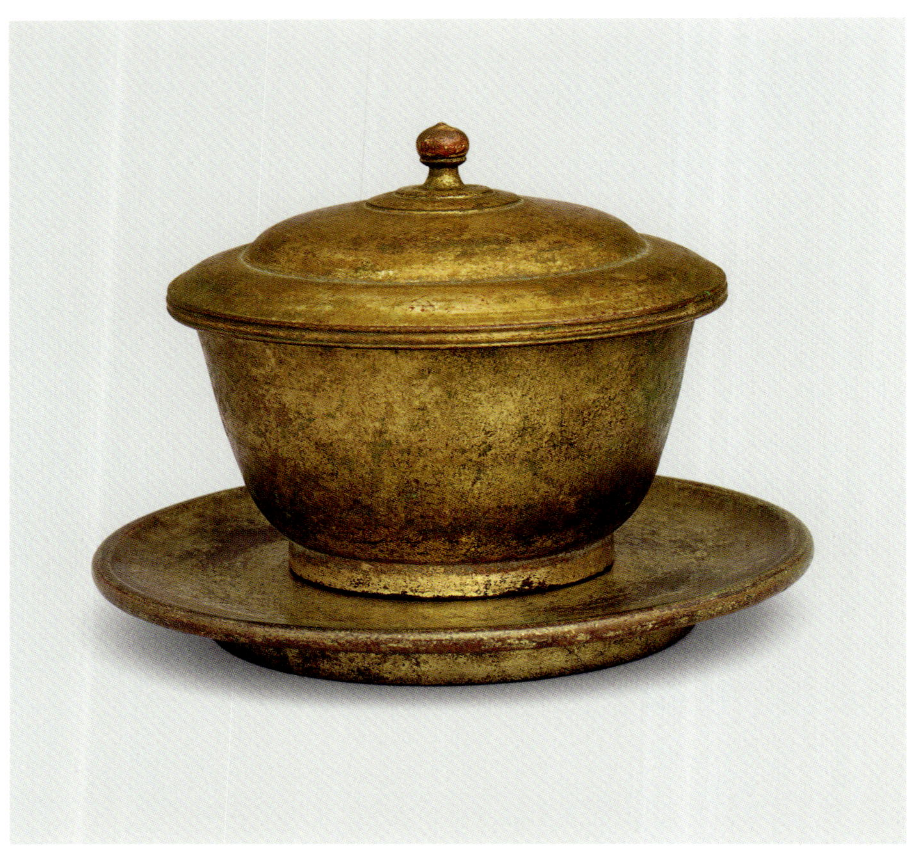

815. Incense container (*zukōki,* 塗香器)

Kamakura period, 14th century
Gilt bronze
H. including lid and saucer 11.2 cm (4 3/8 in.)

817. Five-pronged *vajra* (*sube gokosho,* 都五鈷杵)

Nanbokuchō period, late 14th century
Gilt bronze
L. 14 cm (5 1/2 in.)

Literature: Tokyo National Museum 1985a, no. 83; Avitabile 1990, no. 17; Ishida Mosaku and Okazaki Jōji 1993, no. 275; A. N. Morse and S. C. Morse 1995, no. 8; Murase 2000, no. 30.

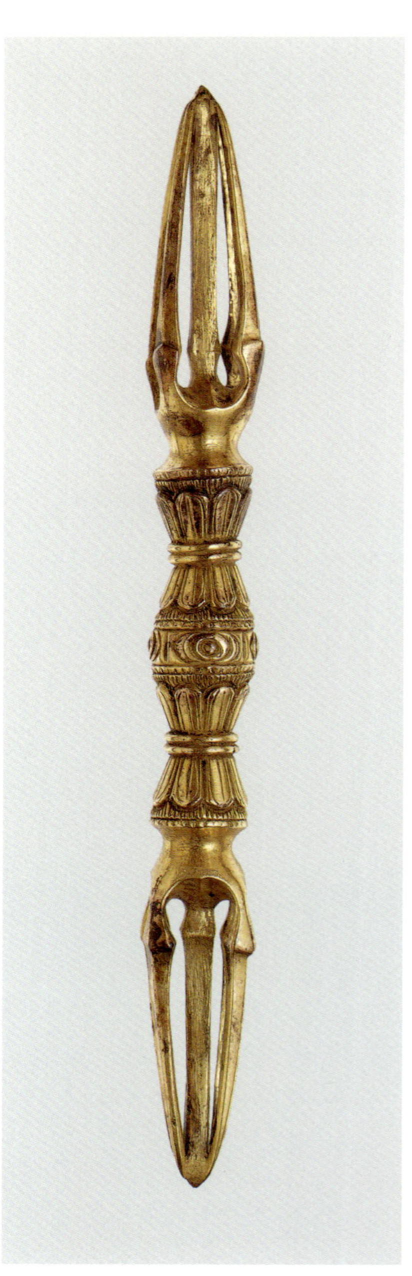

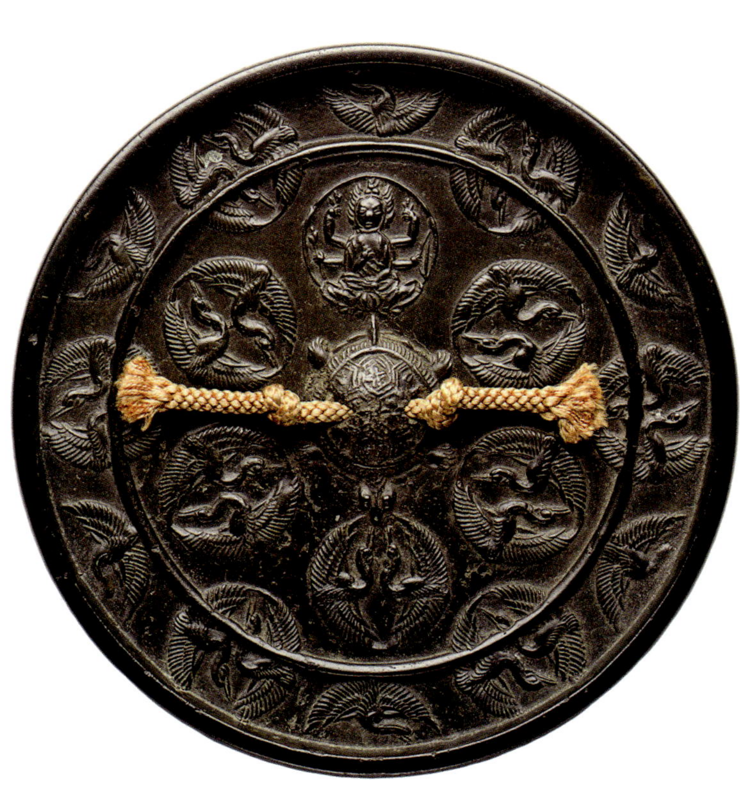

816. Mirror with Aizen Myōō (愛染明王), turtle, and cranes

Kamakura to Nanbokuchō period, 14th century
Gilt bronze
Diam. 11.4 cm (4 1/2 in.)

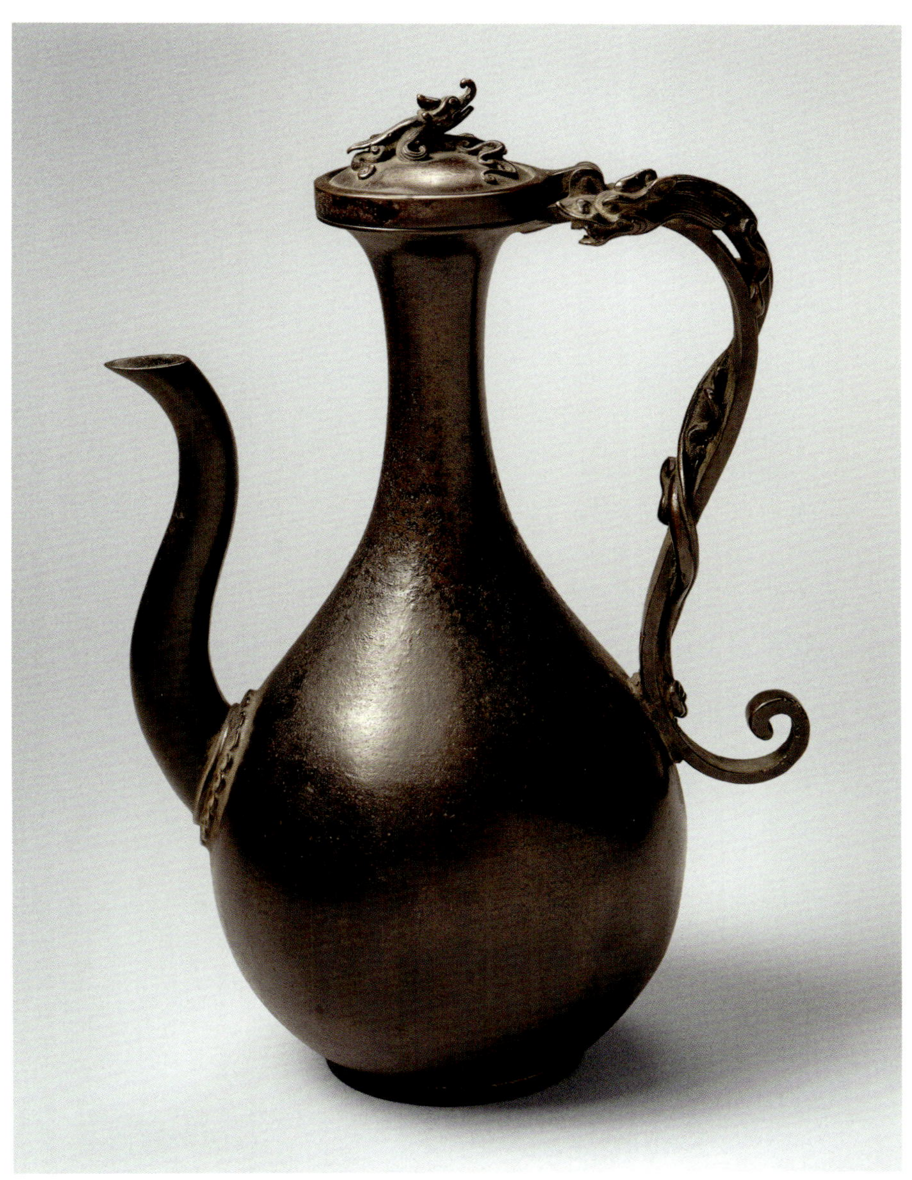

Rihei
(利兵衛; fl. 15th–16th century)

818. Ewer

Muromachi period, 15th–16th century
Bronze
H. 26.5 cm ($10\frac{3}{8}$ in.)
Signature

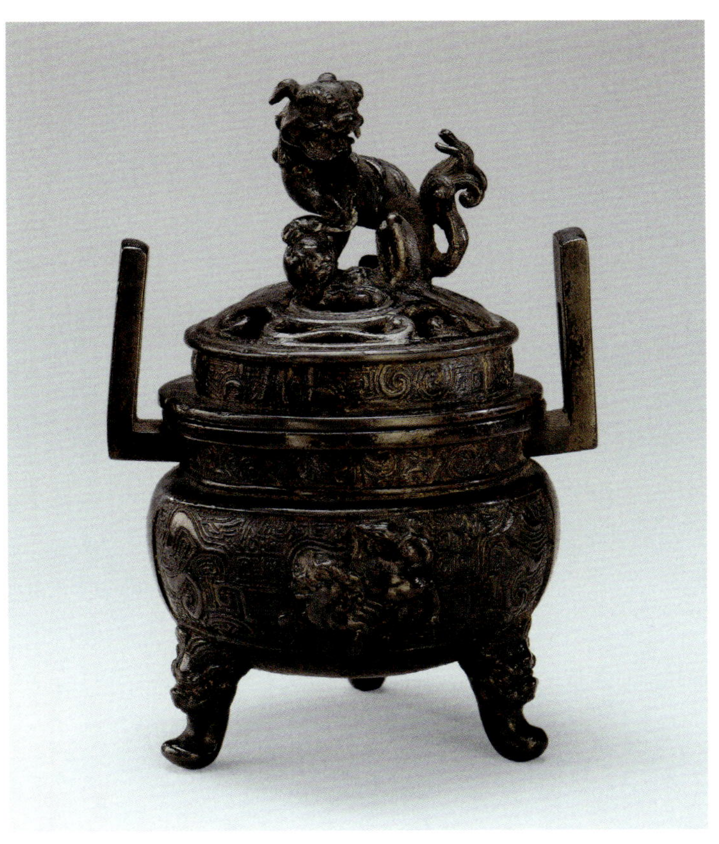

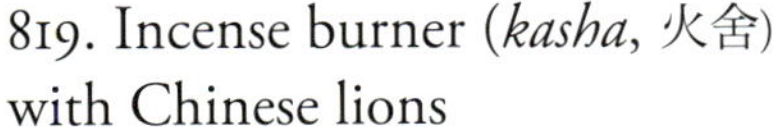

819. Incense burner (*kasha*, 火舎) with Chinese lions

Momoyama period, 16th century
Bronze
H. 14.5 cm ($5\frac{3}{4}$ in.), diam. 10 cm (4 in.)

Literature: Rousmaniere 2002, no. 15; Ohki 2009, pl. 8.

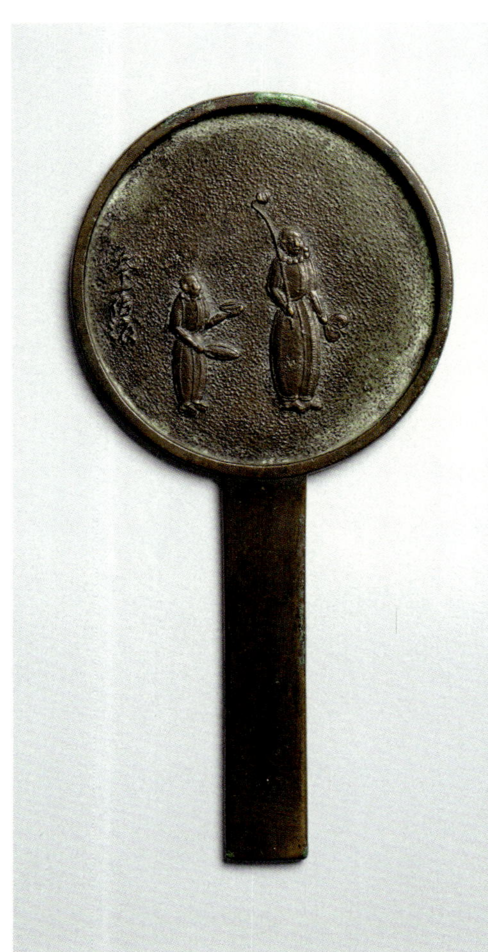

820. Mirror with *Nanban* (南蛮) figures

Edo period, 17th century
Bronze
Diam. 9.7 cm (3⅞ in.); length of handle 9.8 cm (3⅞ in.)
Text

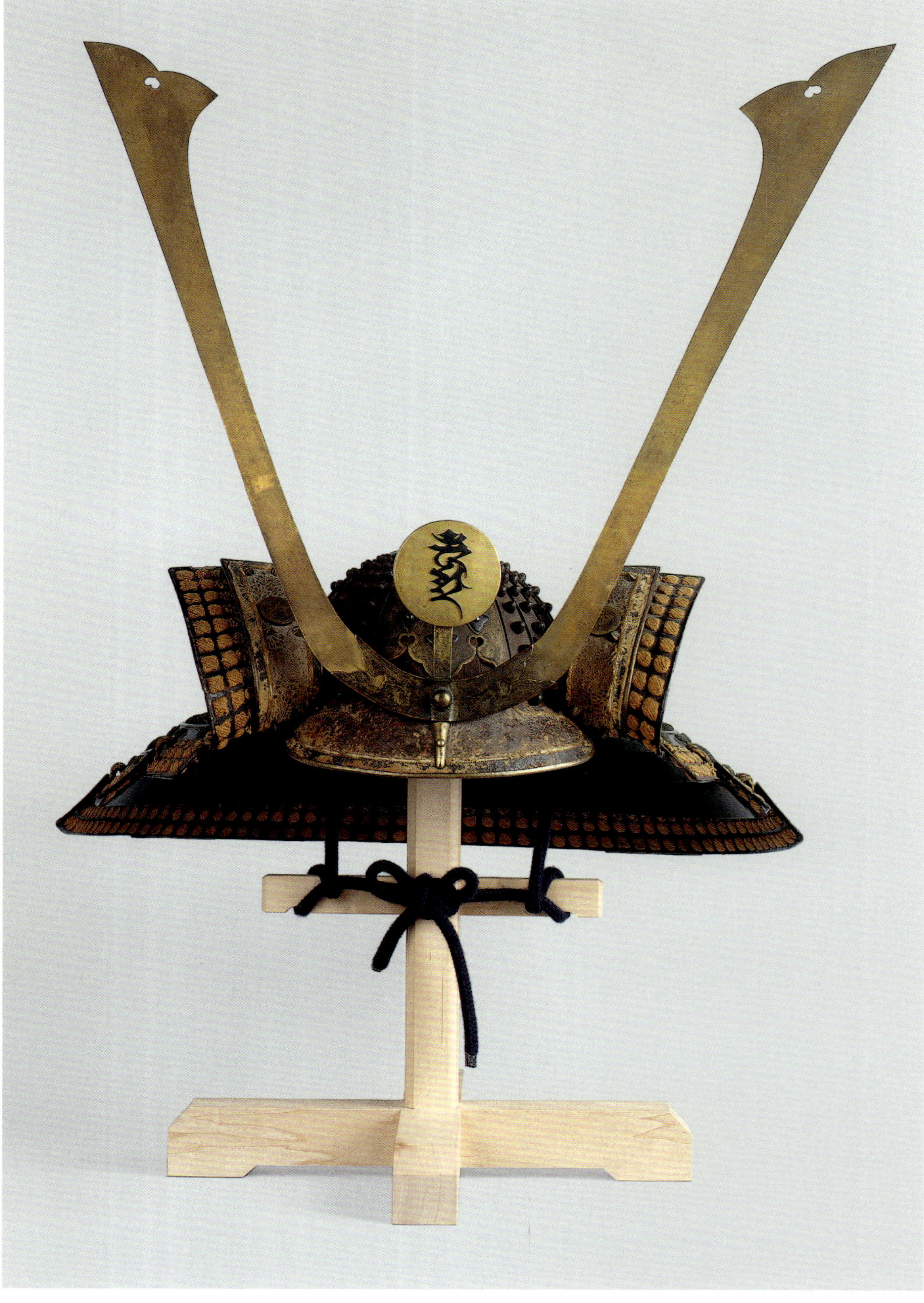

821. Helmet (*hoshi kabuto*, 星兜) with ornament bearing seed syllable for Fudō Myōō

Edo period, 17th century
Iron, gilt copper, deerskin, silk, and lacquer
H. 20 cm (7⅞ in.)

LITERATURE: Avitabile 1990, no. 105.

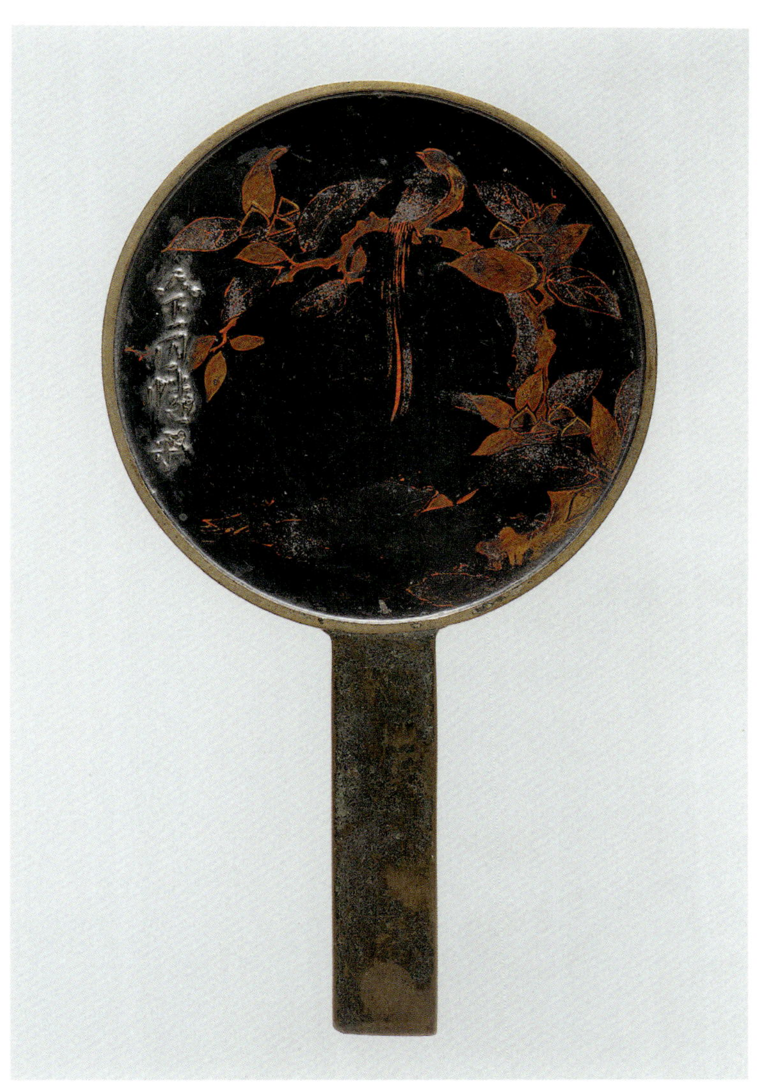

822. Mirror with handle

Edo period, 1661–72
Bronze with black and red lacquer and silver *maki-e*
Diam. 13.6 cm (5 3/8 in.); l. of handle, 9.9 cm (3 7/8 in.)
Signature

Literature: Murase 1993, no. 68; Murase 2000, no. 124.

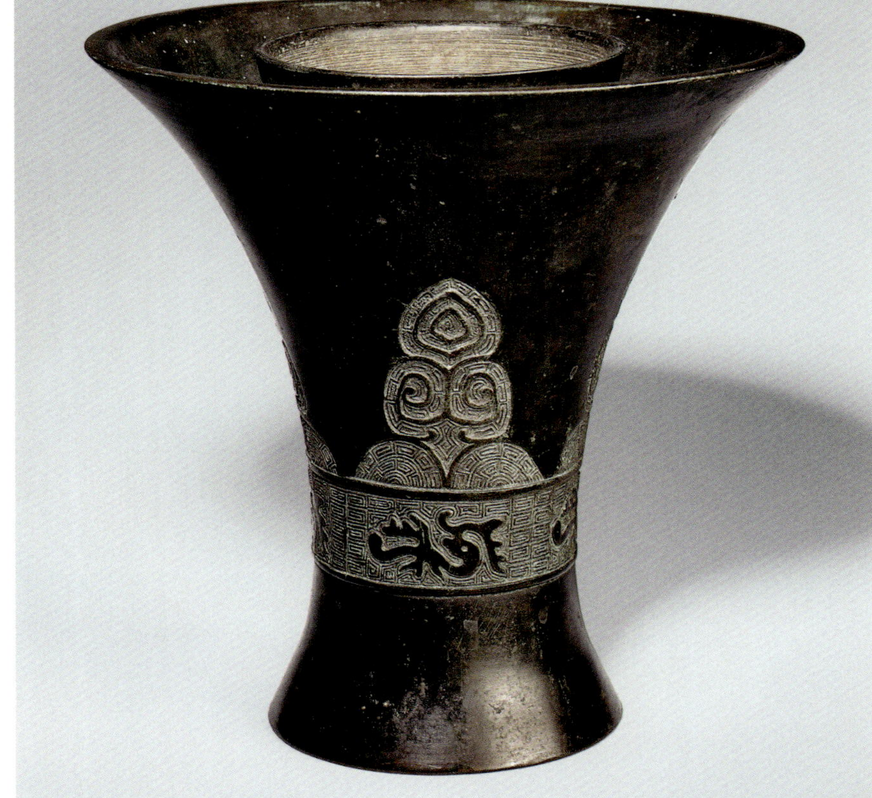

823. Flaring flower vase

Edo period, 18th century
Bronze
H. 21 cm (8 1/4 in.), diam. of mouth 21.9 cm (8 5/8 in.)
Text

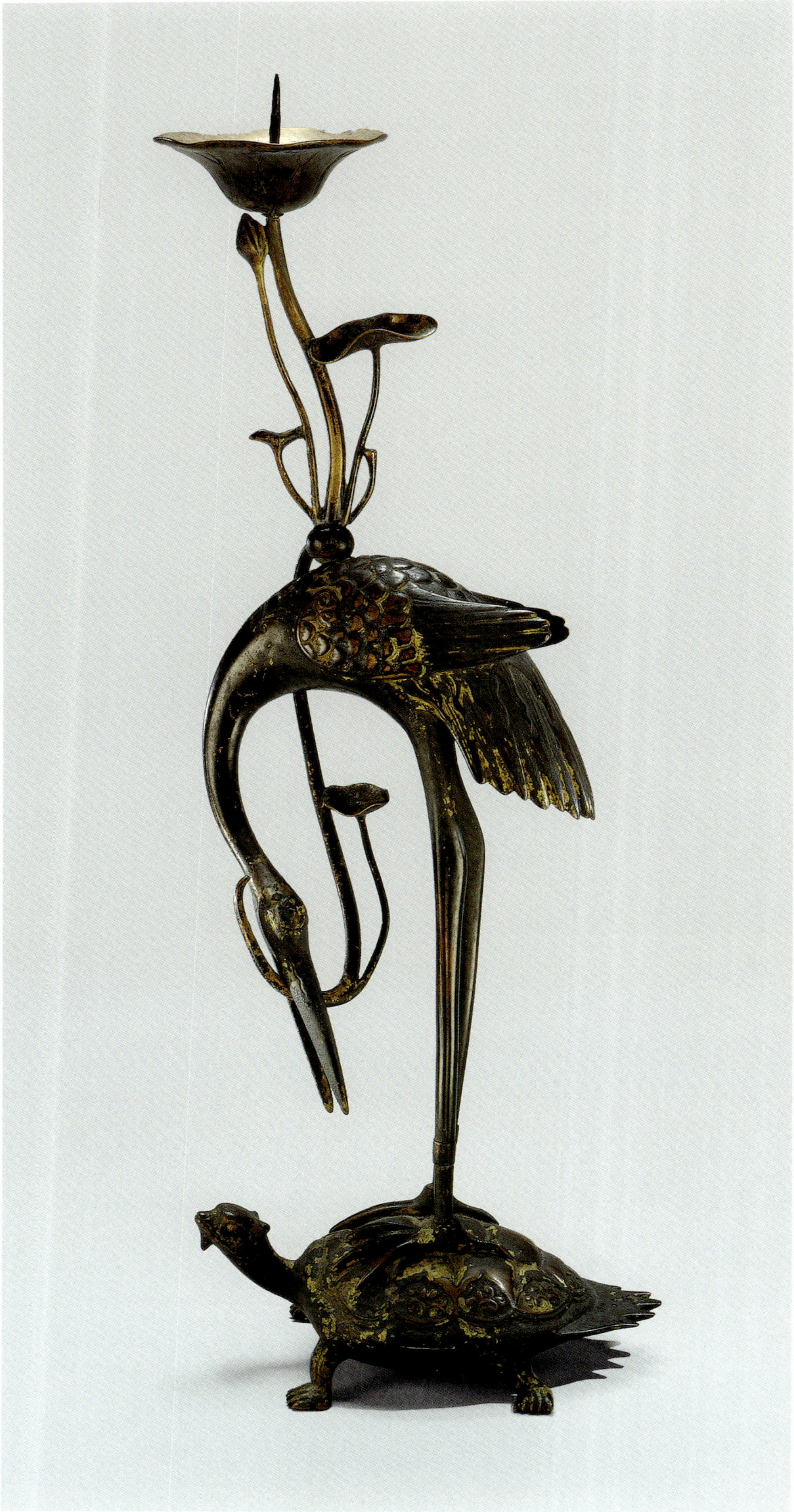

824. Candlestand in the shape of a crane on a long-tailed tortoise (*minogame*, 蓑亀)

Edo period, 18th century
Gilt bronze
H. 40 cm (15¾ in.)

Literature: Rousmaniere 2002, no. 16; Ohki 2009, pl. 7.

825. Ritual bell with handle in the shape of the *vajra* (*gokorei*, 五鈷鈴)

Edo period, 18th century
Bronze
H. 17.2 cm (6¾ in.)
Text

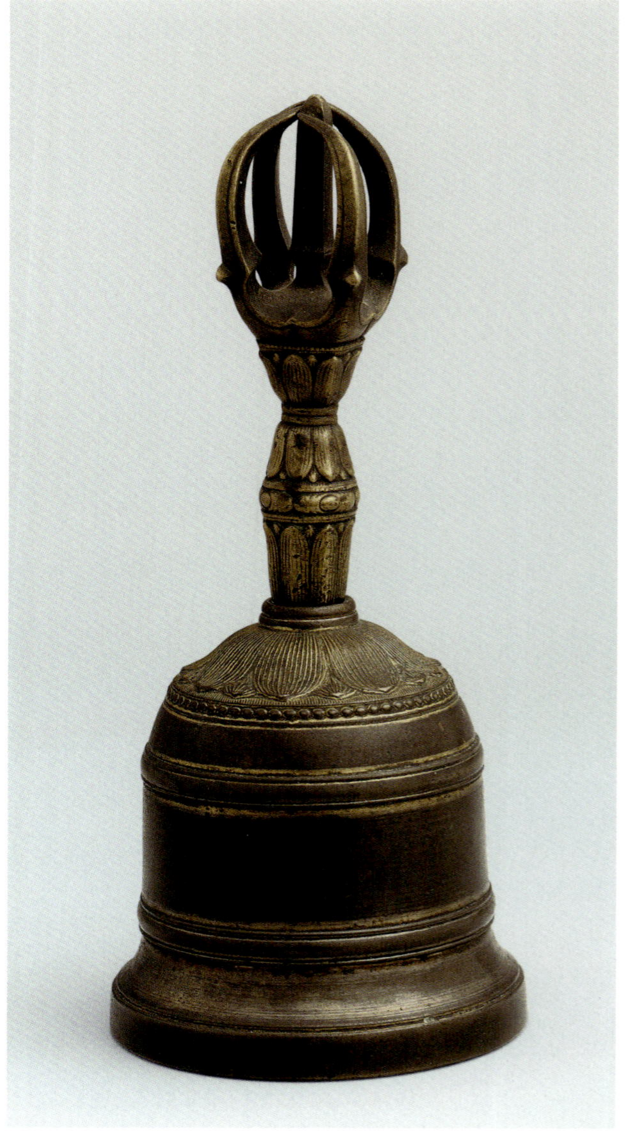

826. Vase with lotus and crab

Edo period, 18th century
Bronze
H. 26.5 cm (10 3/8 in.)

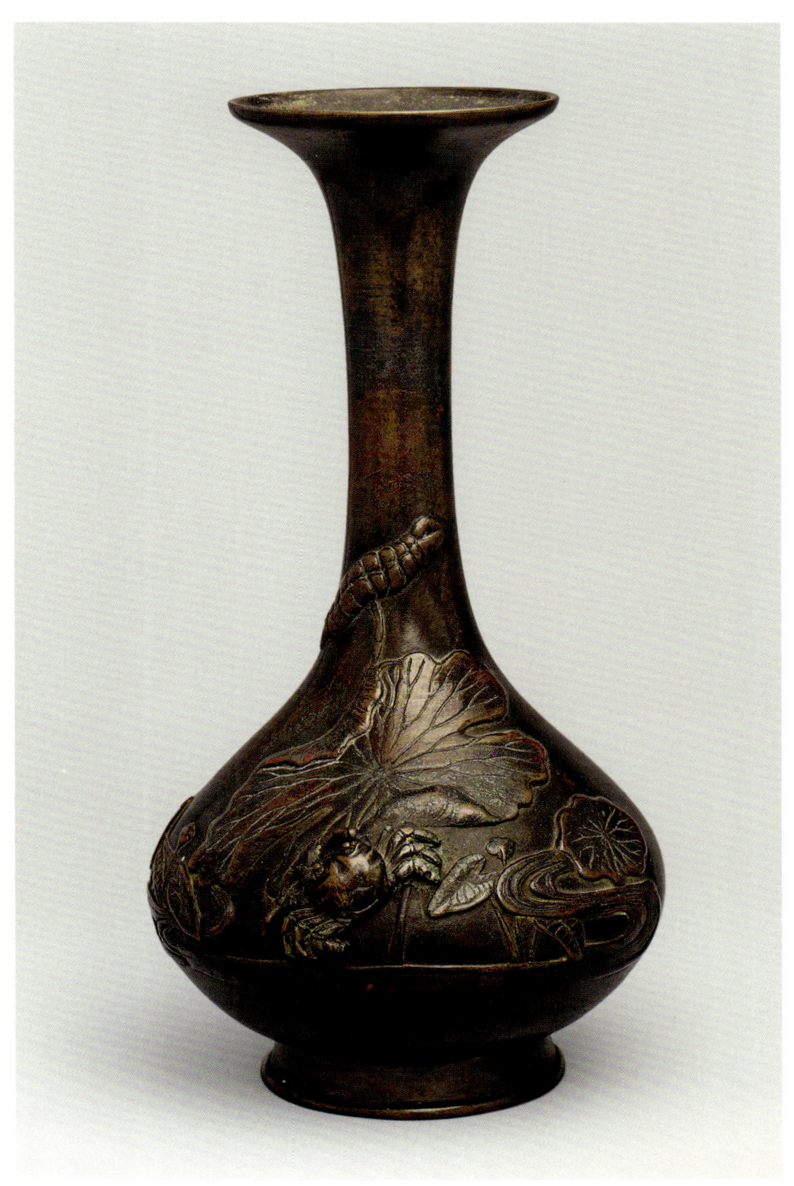

827. Incense burner in the shape of a Chinese boy on a water buffalo

Edo period, 18th century
Bronze
H. 13 cm (5 1/8 in.)

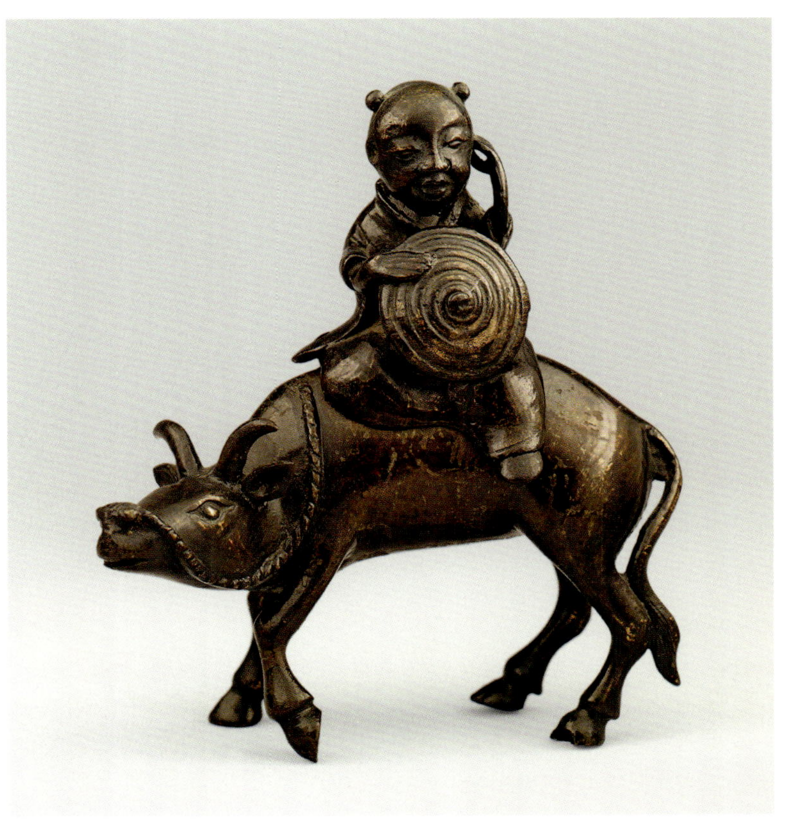

828. Vase with Rinnasei (Ch. Lin Hejing, 林和靖) and crane

Edo period, 18th–19th century
Bronze
H. 22.2 cm (8 3/4 in.), diam. of mouth 14 cm (5 1/2 in.)

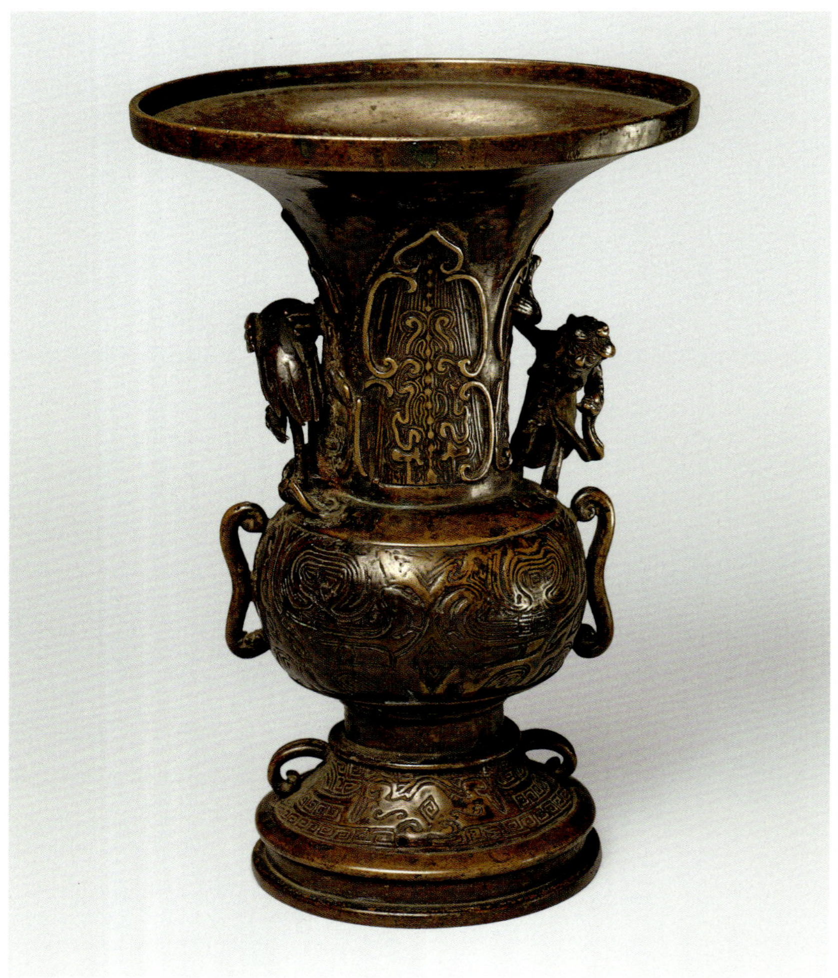

829. Hanging lantern (*tsuridōrō*, 釣燈籠)

Edo period, 1811
Copper
H. 24.5 cm
Text

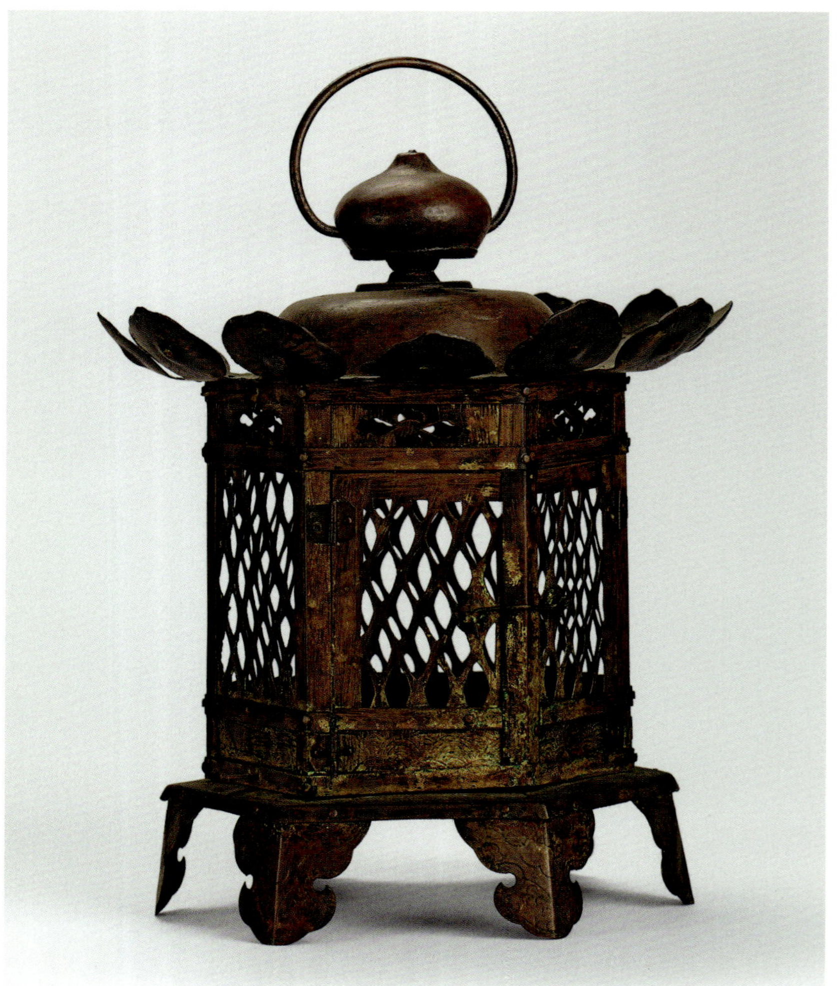

830. Incense burner in the shape of an eggplant with an insect

Edo period, 19th century
Bronze
H. including lid 8.5 cm (3 3/8 in.)

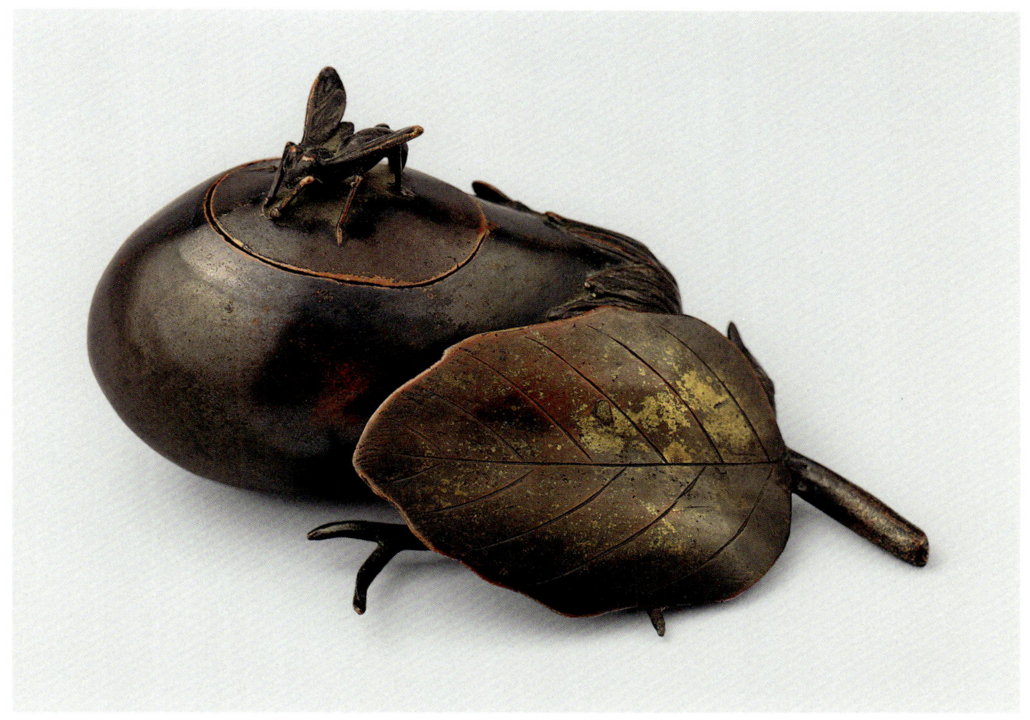

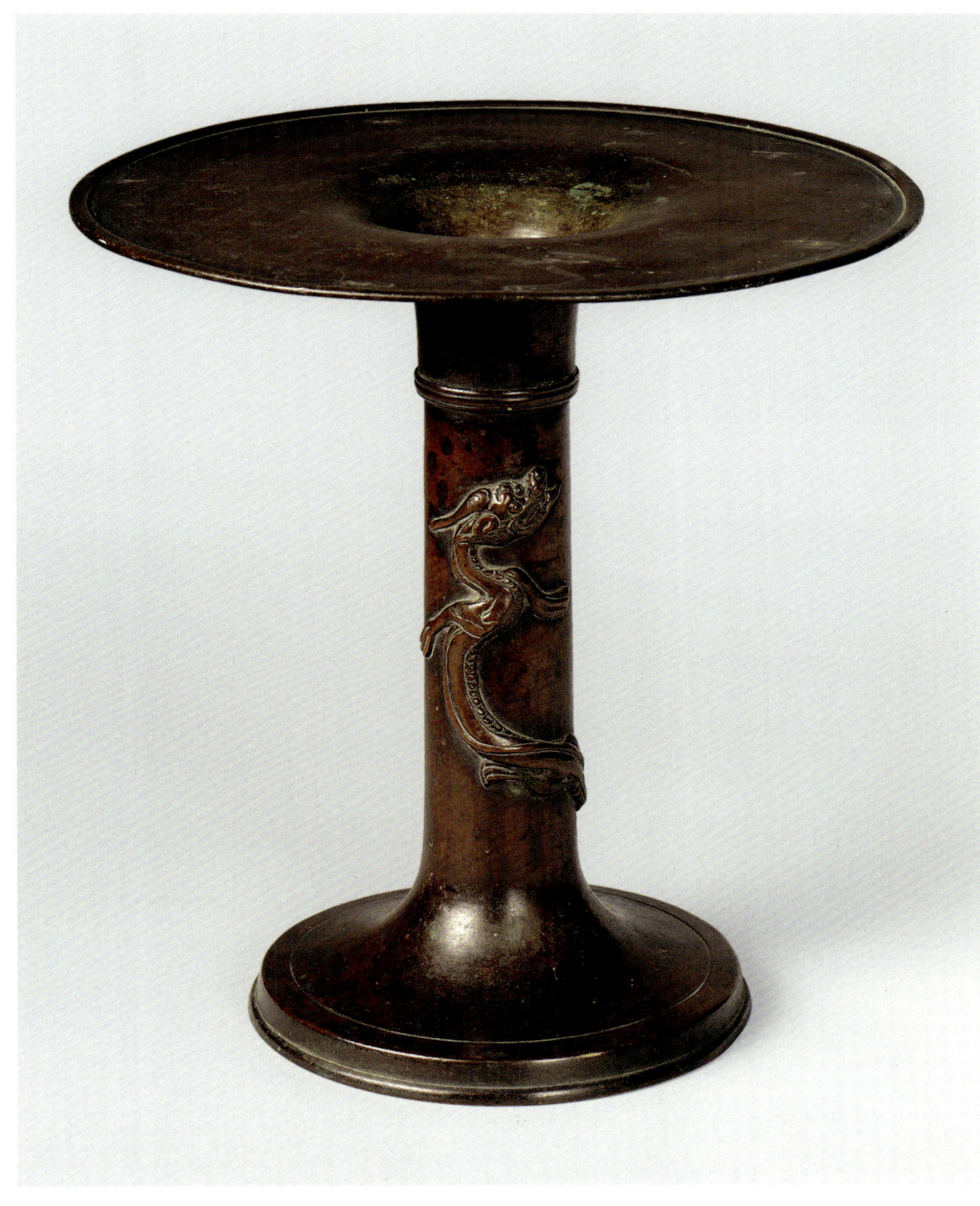

831. Flower vase with dragon

Edo period, 19th century
Bronze
H. 24 cm (9 3/8 in.), diam. of rim 23.3 cm (9 1/8 in.)

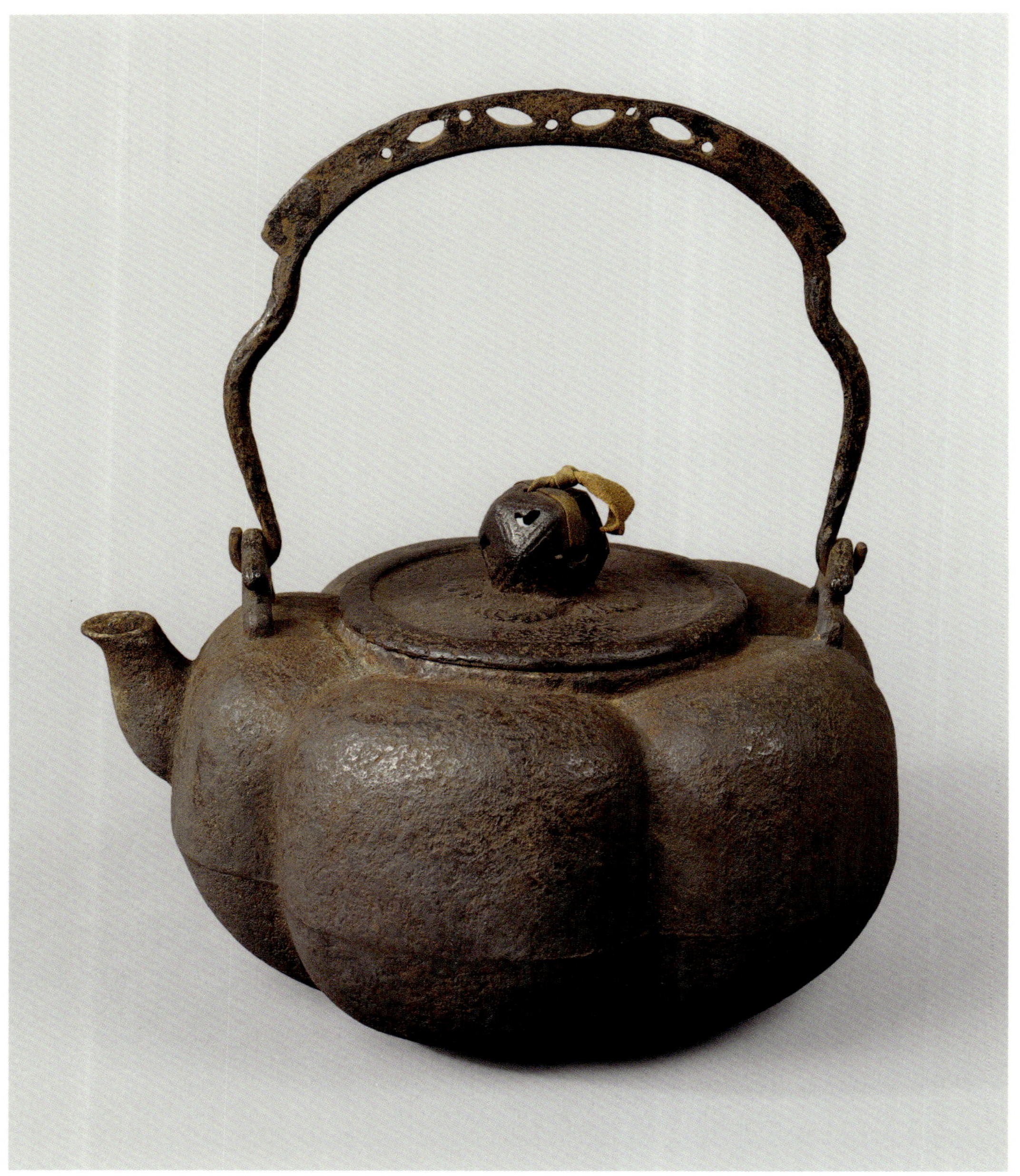

832. Five-lobed kettle

Edo period, 19th century
Iron
H. including handle 23.5 cm ($9^{1}/_{4}$ in.)

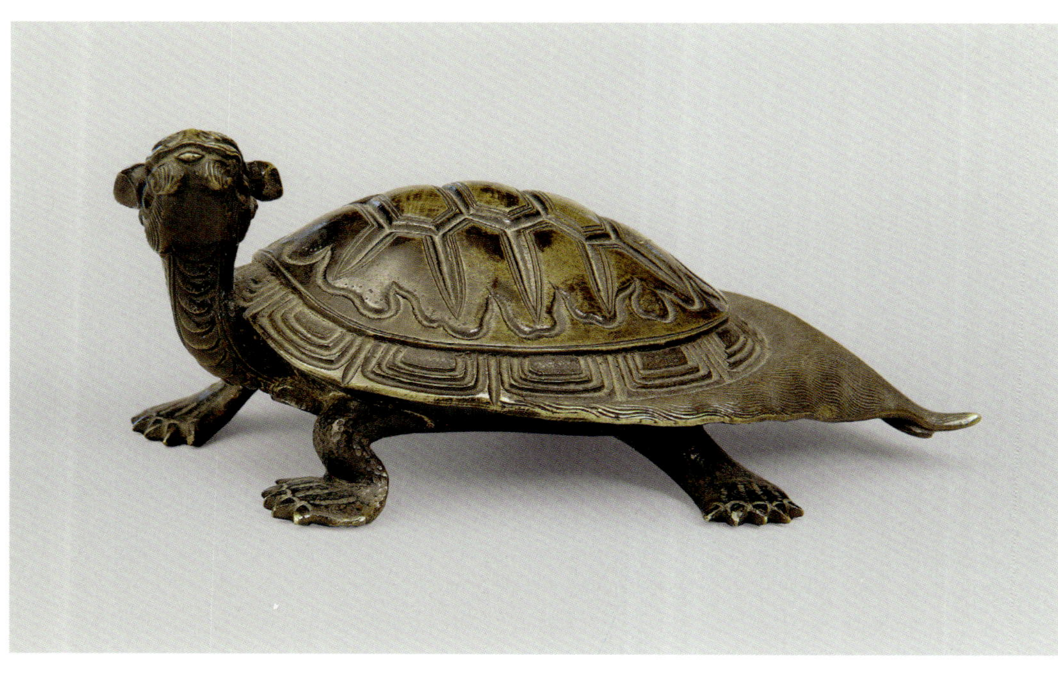

833. Long-tailed tortoise (*minogame*, 蓑亀)

Meiji era, 19th–20th century
Bronze
H. 6 cm ($2^{3}/_{8}$ in.), l. 12 cm ($4^{3}/_{4}$ in.)

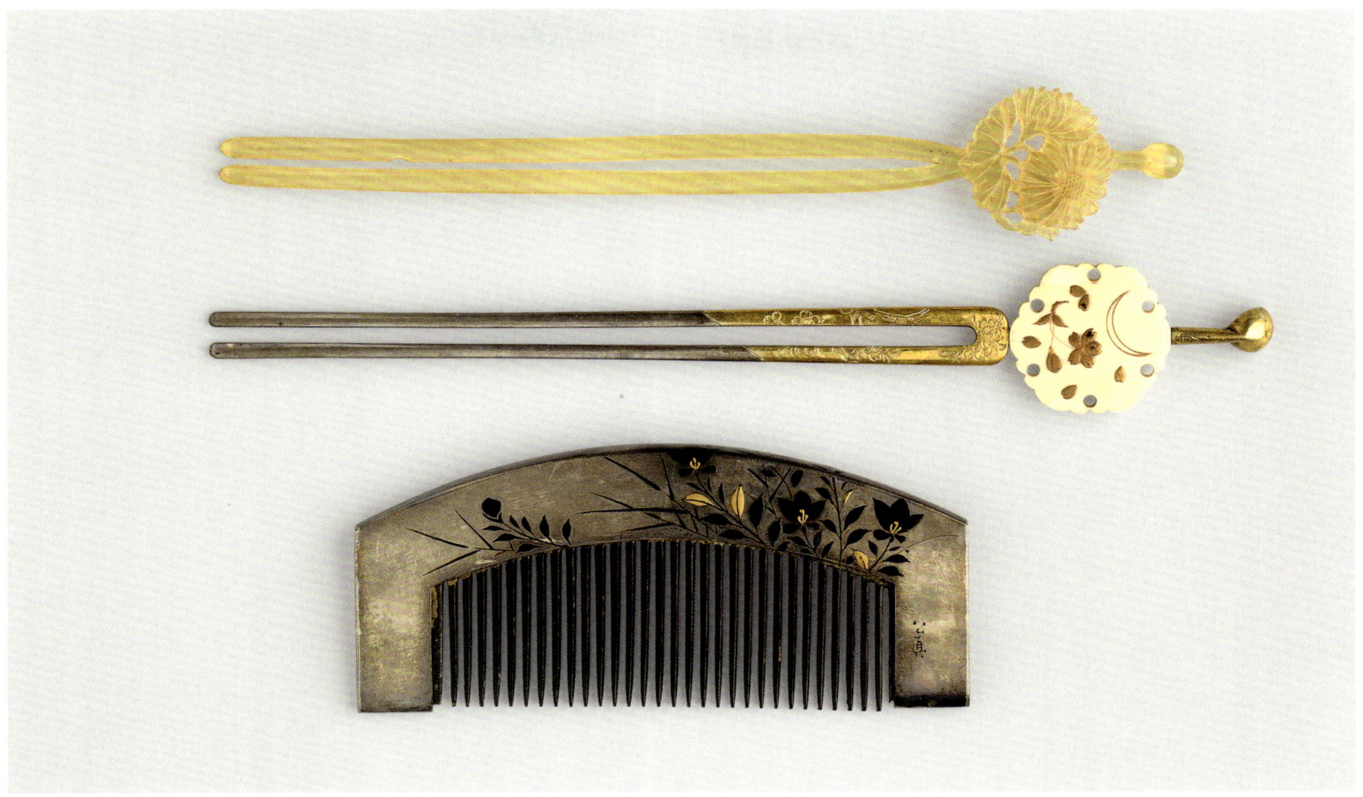

834. Hair pins and comb

Meiji or Taishō era, 19th–20th century
Tortoiseshell (hair pin); metal (comb, hair pin)
L. of hairpins 14.2 cm (5 5/8 in.), 15.7 cm (6 1/8 in.); l. of comb 9 cm (3 1/2 in.)
Signature

Gift from Hosomi Minoru, 1975

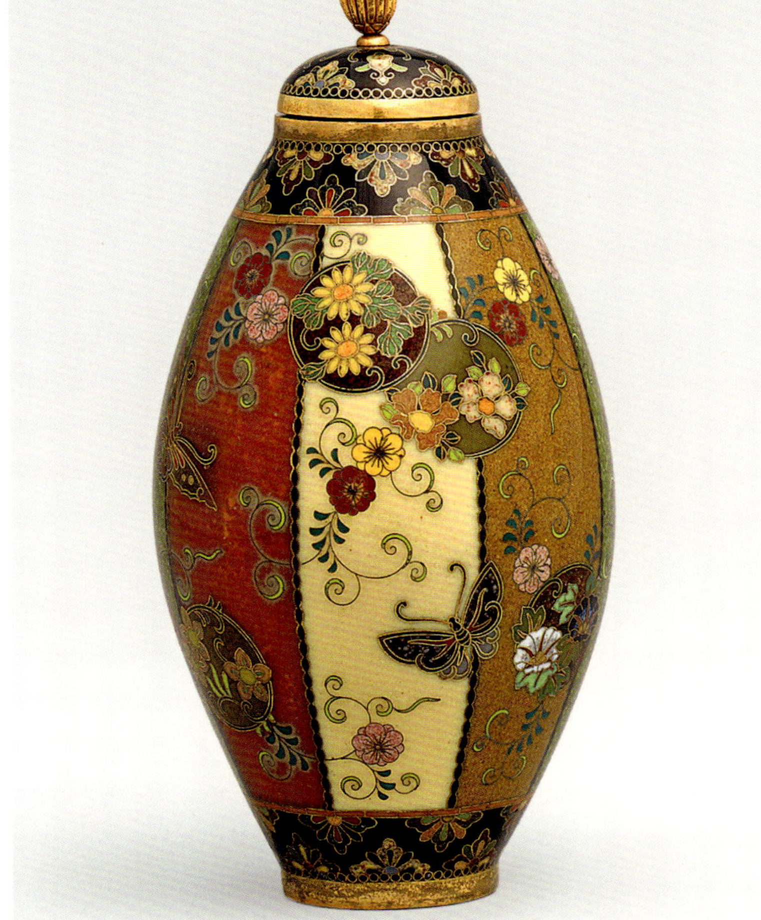

Namikawa Yasuyuki
(並河靖之; 1845–1927)

835. Covered bottle

Meiji or Taishō era, 19th–20th century
Cloisonné
H. including lid 10.7 cm (4 1/4 in.)
Signature

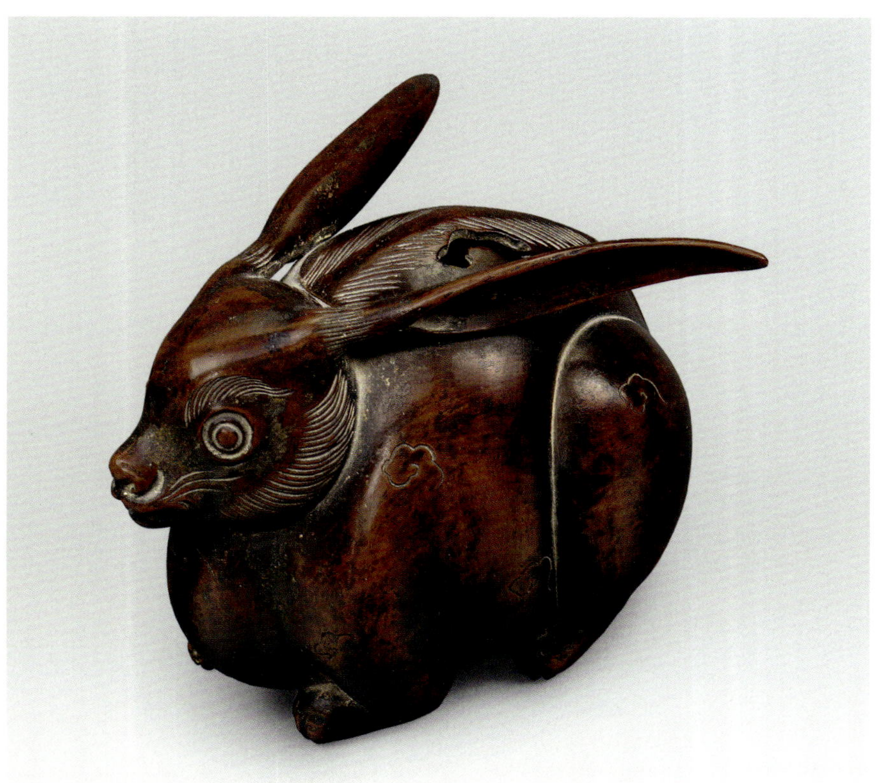

Seimin
(整眠; fl. 18th–19th century)

836. Incense burner in the shape of a rabbit

Edo period
Bronze
H. 9.2 cm (3 5/8 in.), l. 12 cm (4 3/4 in.)
Signature

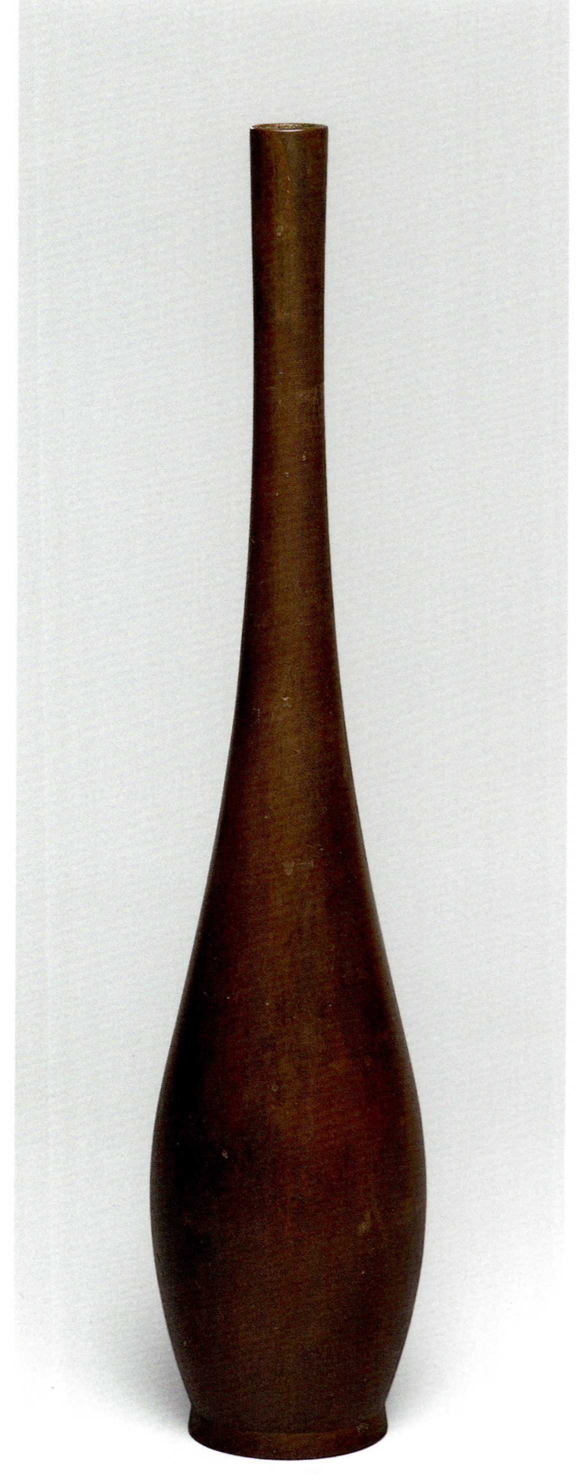

Zōroku IV
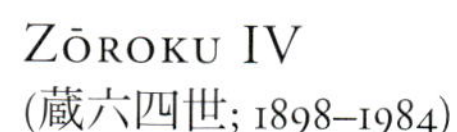
(蔵六四世; 1898–1984)

837. Long-necked flower vase

Shōwa era, 20th century
Bronze
H. 28.7 cm (11 1/4 in.)
Signature

Japanese Metalwork Details

† *denotes illustrated items*

812. Hexagonal sutra container (*kyōzutsu*)

Signature

Monk [illegible] *mei*; *Monk seiyo*; *1127*

† 818. Ewer

Signature

Rihei

† 820. Mirror with *Nanban* figures

Signature

Number one under the Heaven, Sado

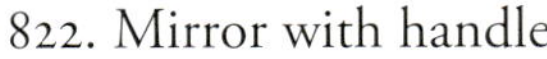

822. Mirror with handle

Signature

Number one under the Heaven, Inbe no Kami

† 823. Flaring flower vase

Text

Manner favored by Sōju

† 825. Ritual bell with handle in the shape of the *vajra* (*gokorei*)

Text

In the generation of the Priest Kōshō

† 829. Hanging lantern (*tsuridōrō*)

Text

For the Thirty Guardian Deities of Myōhōji at Risshōzan in Ogura, dedicated by Adachi Hikobei of Iwamoto in the first month of 1811

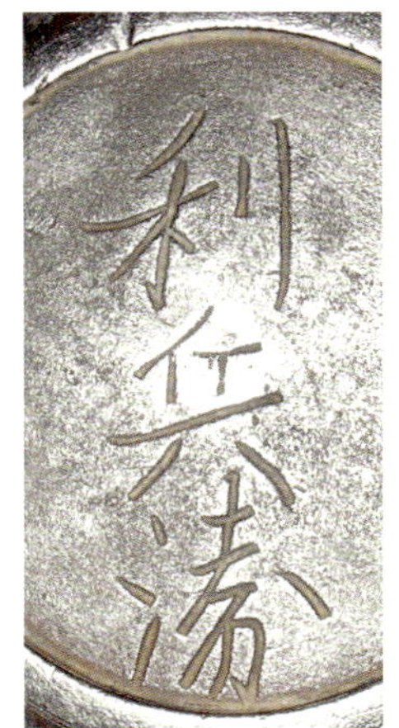

818

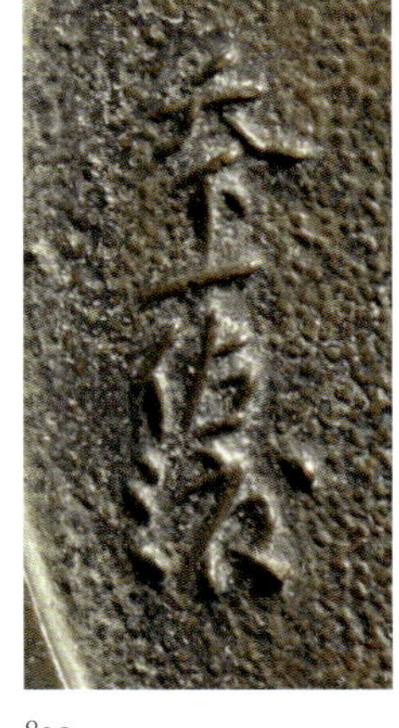

820

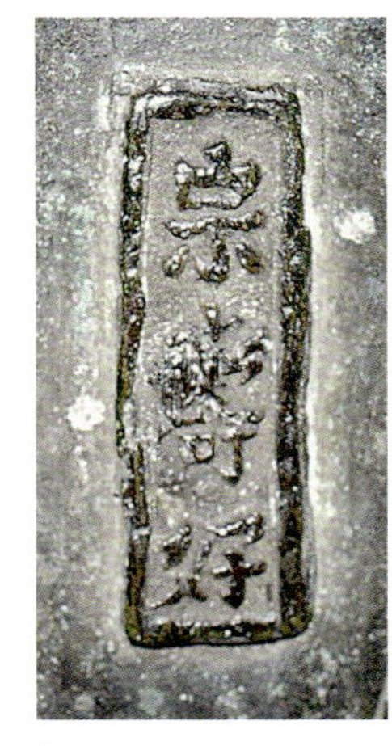

823

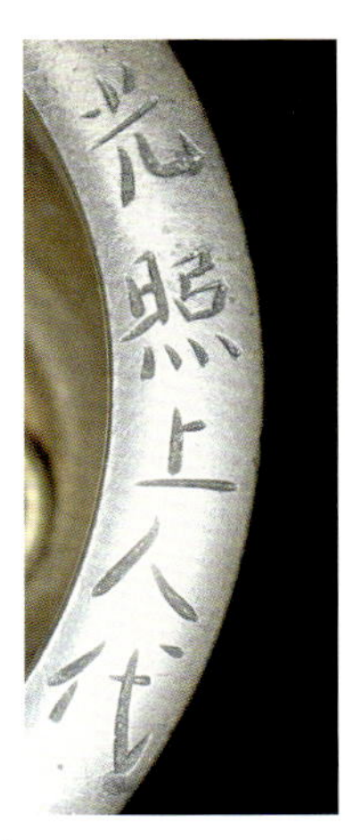

825

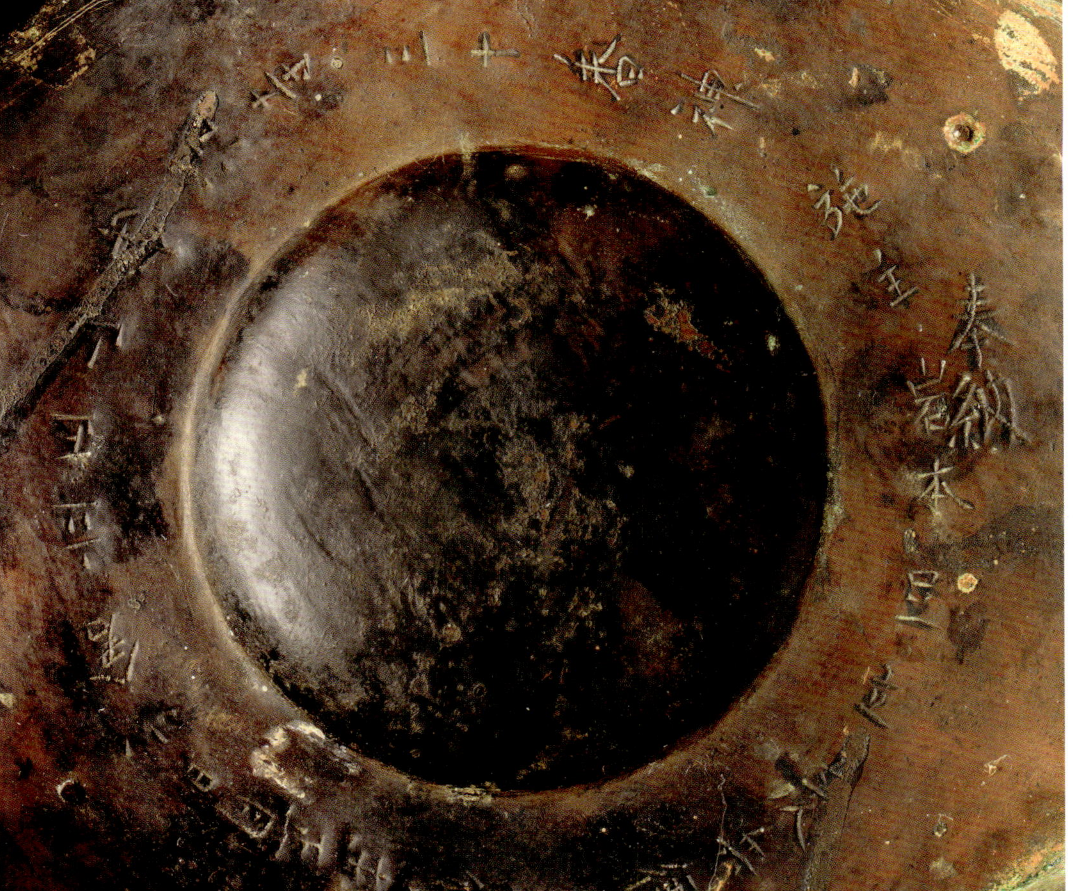

829

† 834. Hair pins and comb

Text

[on comb] *Kōshin*

† 835. Covered bottle

Signature

[on underside] *Kyoto Namikawa*

† 836. Incense burner in the shape of a rabbit

Signature

Made by Seimin

† 837. Long-necked flower vase

Signature

Zōroku

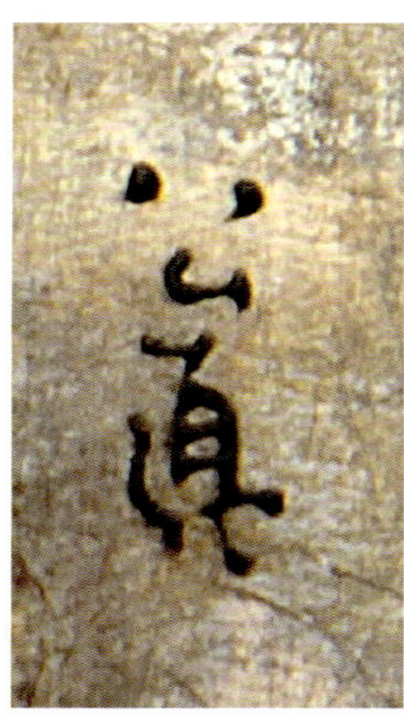

834

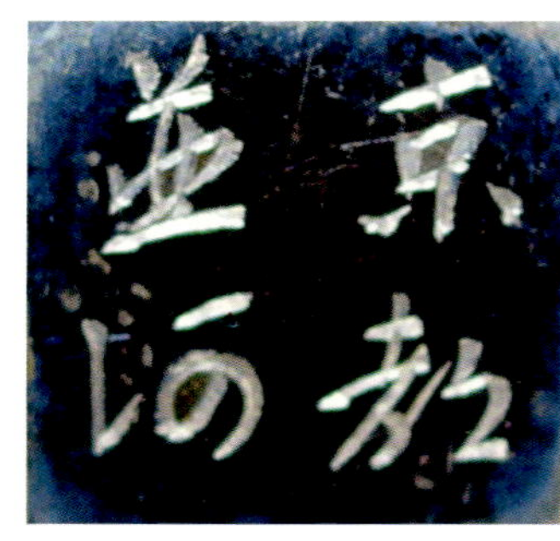

835

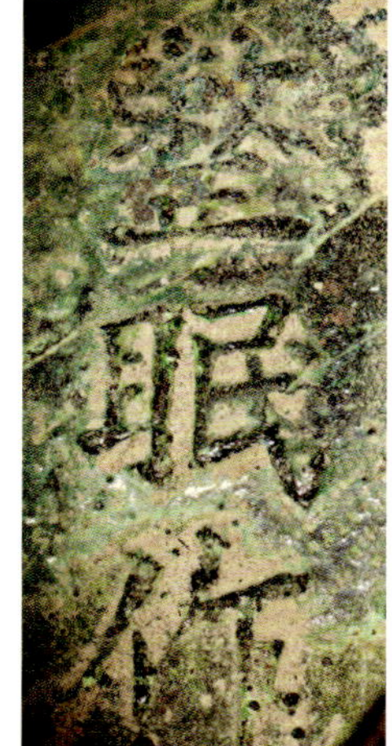

836

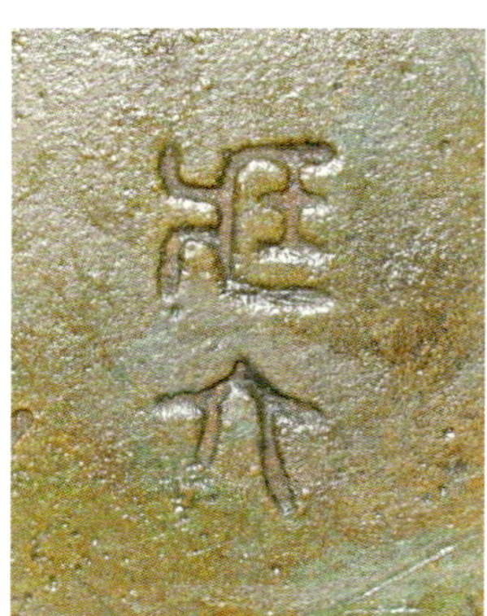

837

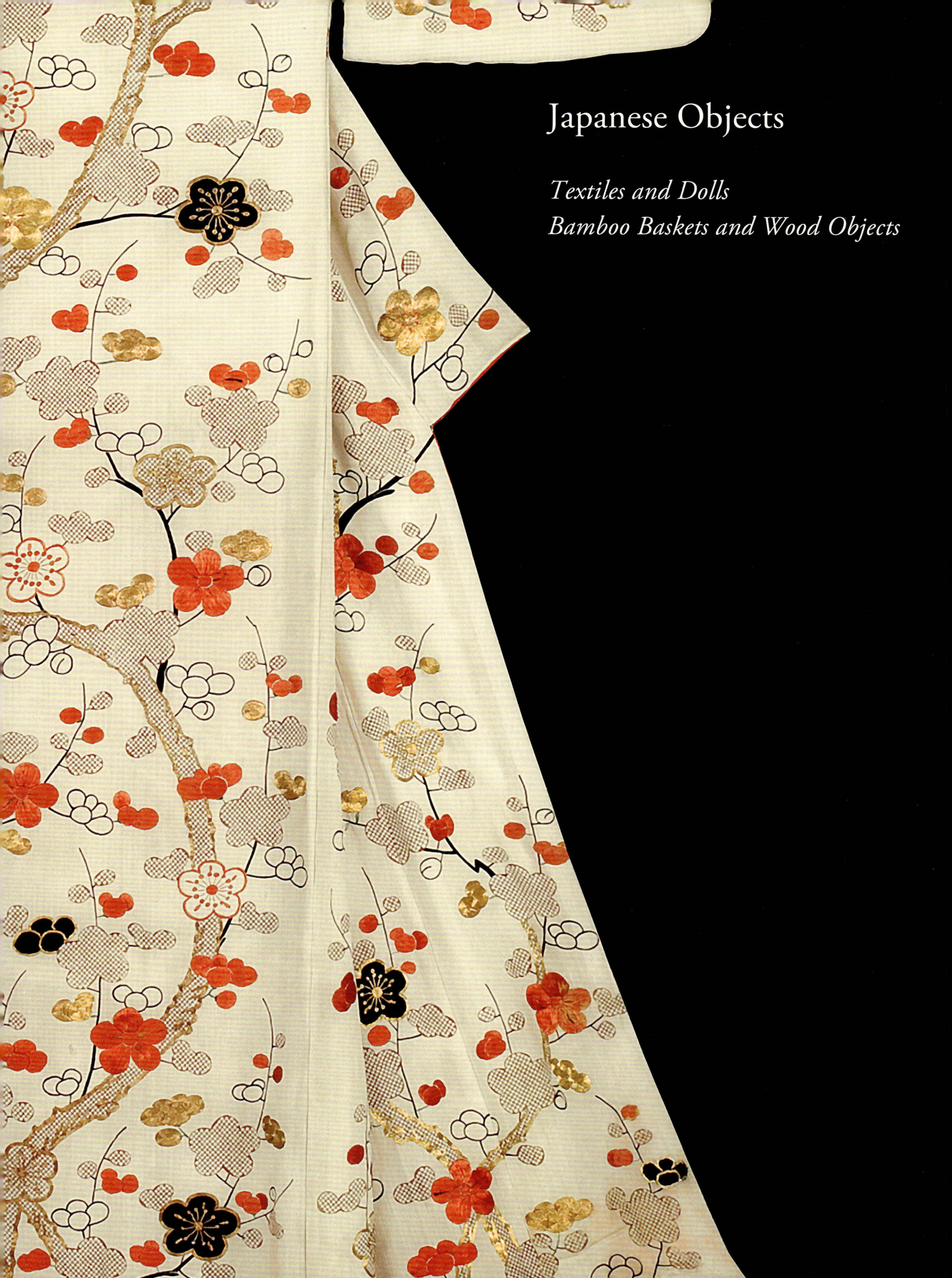

Japanese Objects

Textiles and Dolls
Bamboo Baskets and Wood Objects

838. Sutra Cover

Late Heian period, before 1149
Silk brocade, bamboo, brass, and mica
31.4 x 44 cm (12 3/8 x 17 3/8 in.)

Ex coll.: Jingoji, Kyoto

Literature: Murase 1975, no. 111; Pal and Meech-Pekarik 1988, pl. 83; Murase 2000, no. 17.

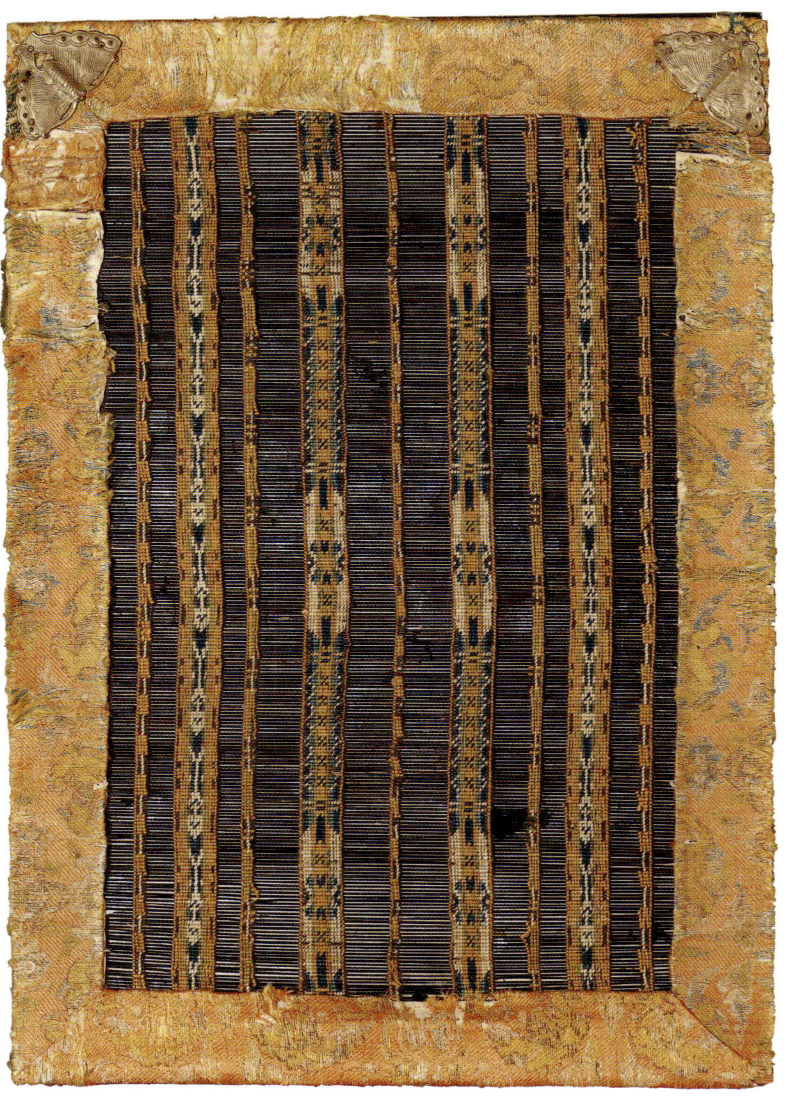

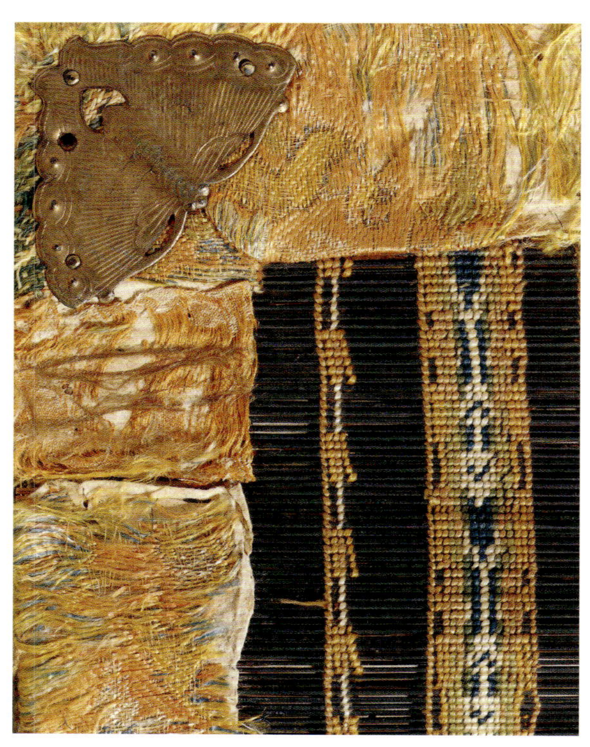

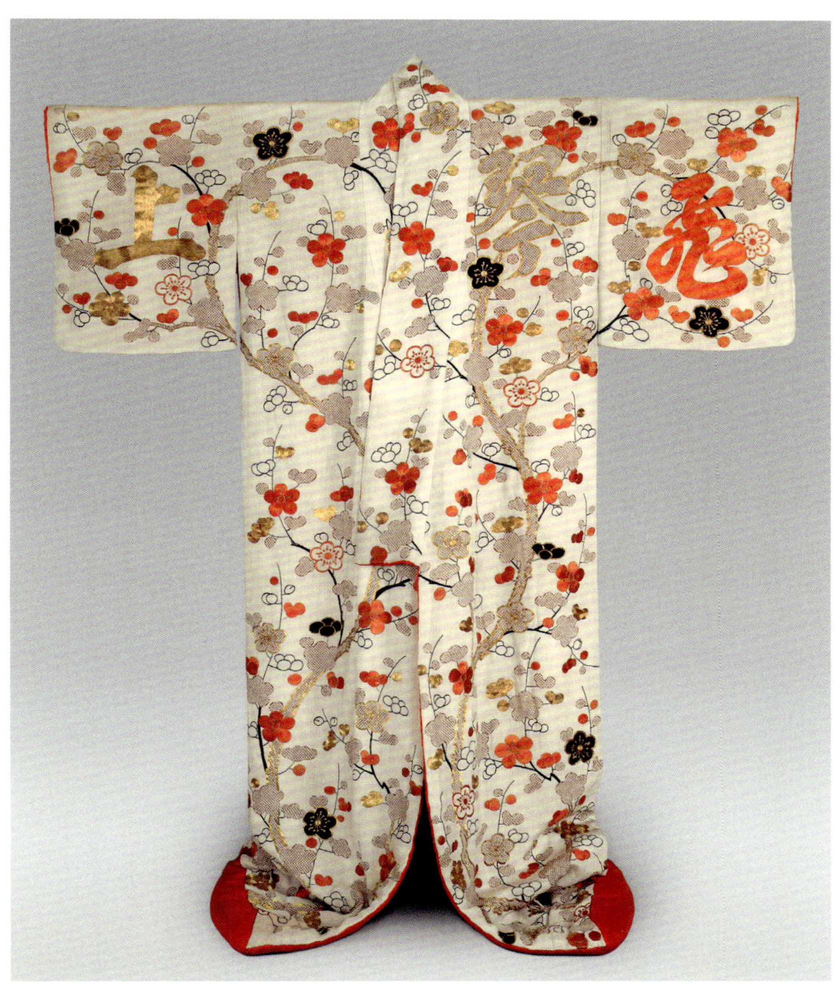

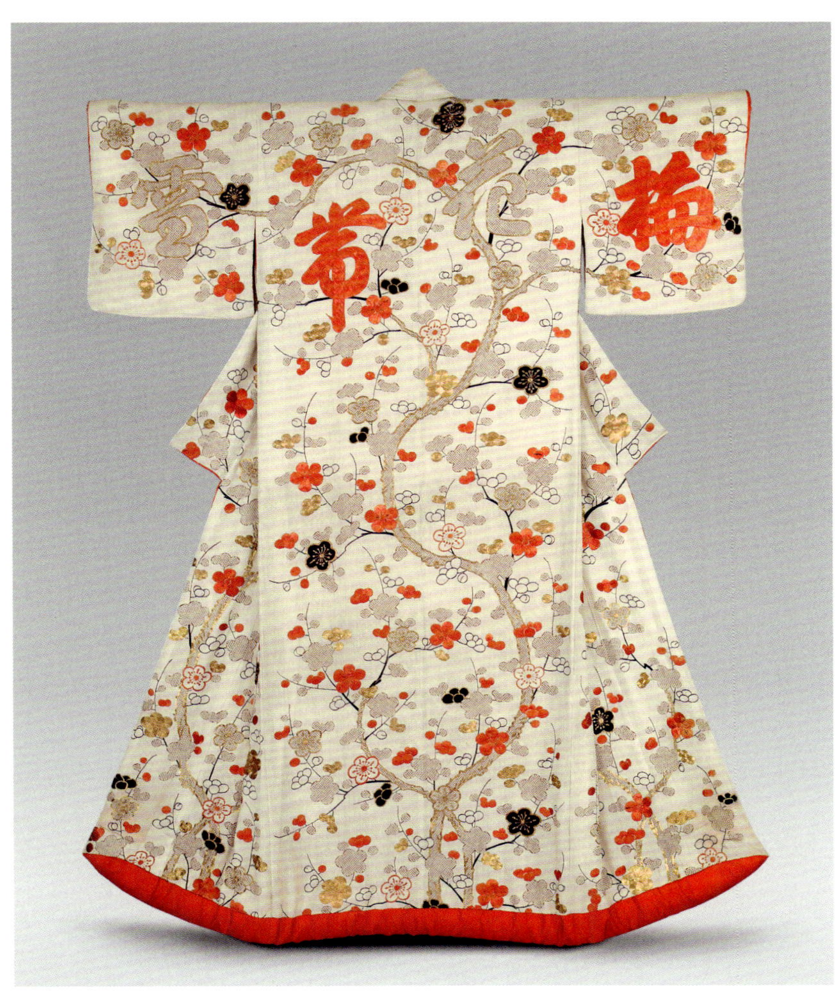

839. Kosode with plum trees and Chinese poem by Zhang Xiaobiao (章孝標, fl. ca. 830)

Edo period, second half of 17th century
Silk, embroidery, and tie-dyeing
L. 167.6 cm (66 in.)
Text

Literature: Murase 1980b, no. 46.

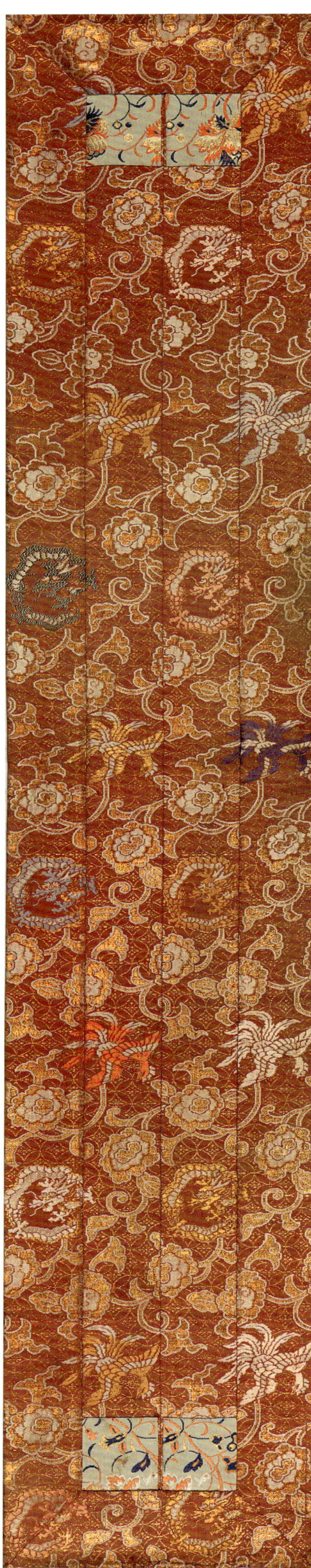

840. Buddhist priest's stole (*ōhi*, 横被)

Edo period, 19th century
Brocaded silk with phoenix, dragon, and flower
151.1 x 31.8 cm (59 1/2 x 12 1/2 in.)

841. Gilded leather (*Kinkarakawa*, 金唐革) tobacco pouch with *Nanban* (南蛮) figures

Edo period, late 18th–early 19th century
Polychrome-lacquered and gilded leather with metal
9.4 x 15.2 cm (3 3/4 x 6 in.)
Signature

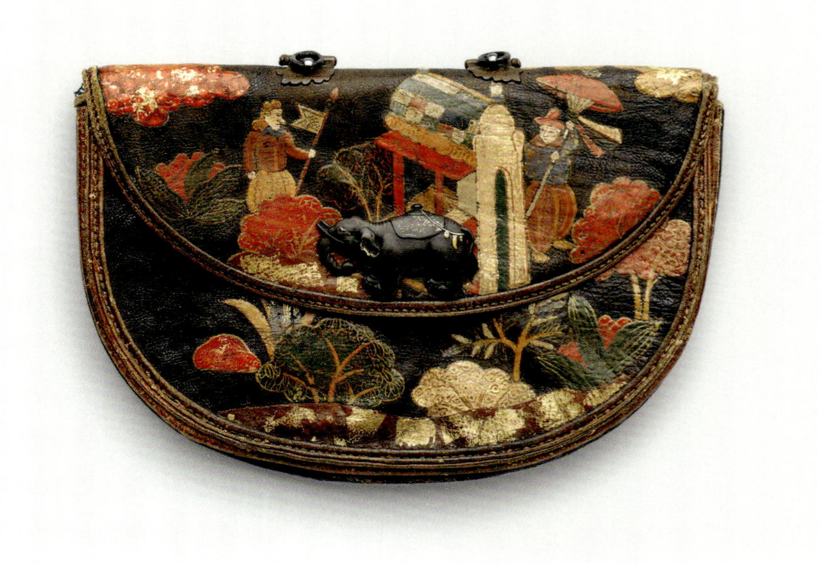

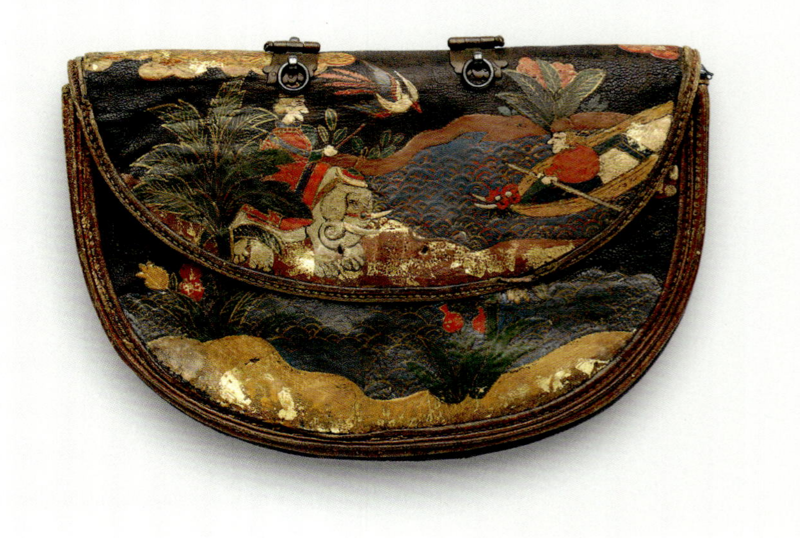

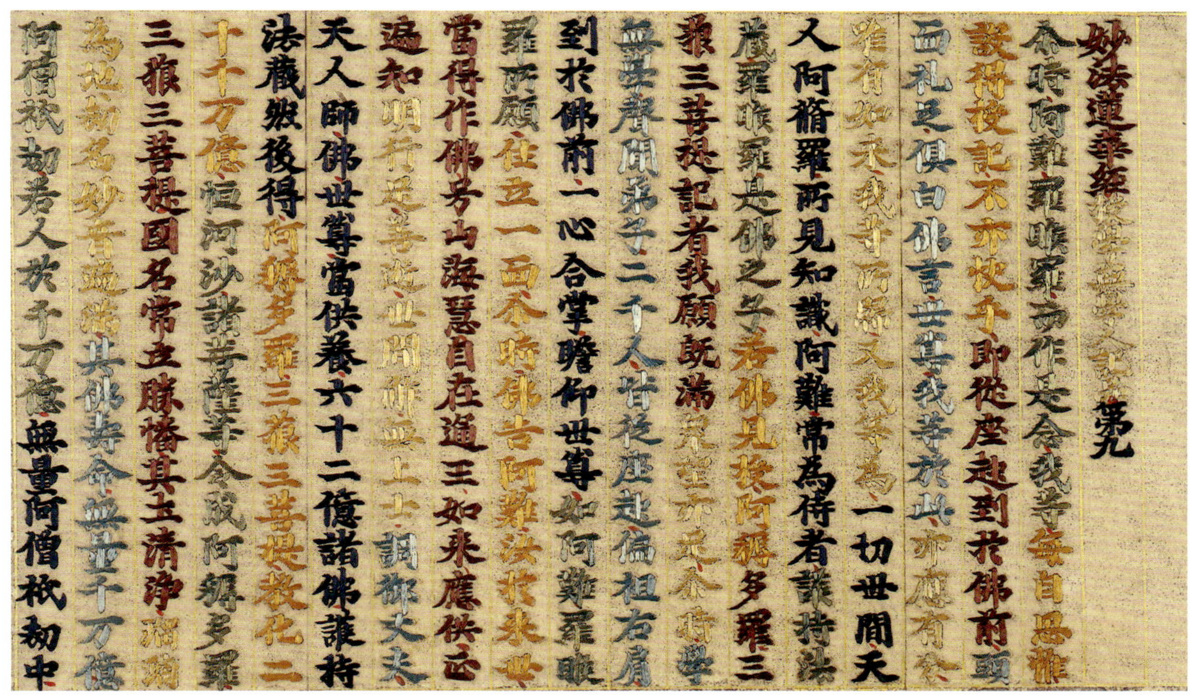

842. Lotus Sutra, Chapter 9
(法華経　第九巻)

Kamakura period, early 14th century
Handscroll fragment, mounted as hanging scroll; silk embroidered on paper
H. 27.6 cm (10⅞ in.), w. 43.7 cm (17¼ in.)

Literature: Kaufman 1985, p. 98, fig. 12; Pal and Meech-Pekarik 1988, p. 311, pl. 96; Katonah Museum of Art 1996, p. 111, no. 49

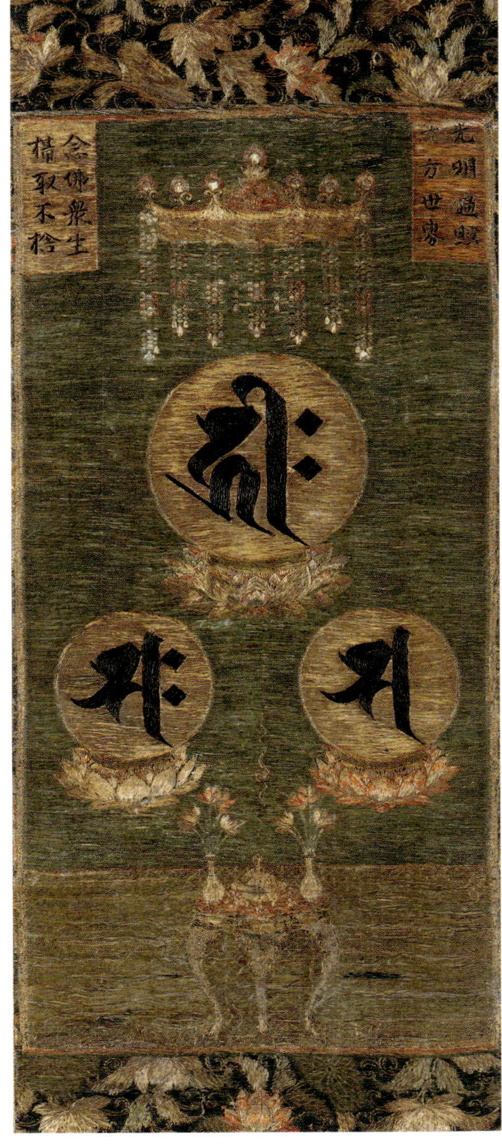

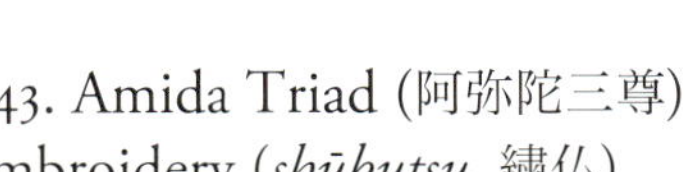

843. Amida Triad (阿弥陀三尊) embroidery (*shūbutsu*, 繡仏)

Kamakura period, 14th century
Hanging scroll; embroidered silk
59 x 25.2 cm (23¼ x 9⅞ in.)
Text

Literature: London Gallery Ltd. 2000, no. 110.

Japanese Textiles Details

† *denotes illustrated items*

---

839. Kosode with plum trees and Chinese poem by Zhang Xiaobiao

Text

[from "A Feast at the Clear Field in Early Spring" by Zhang Xiaobiao]

Plum blossoms amidst the snow flutter over the zither.

---

† 841. Gilded leather (*Kinkarakawa*) tobacco pouch with *Nanban* figures

Signature (?)

[on the metalwork] *Kuzui* [or *Kanazui*]

841

---

† 843. Amida Triad embroidery

Text

[center] seed syllables for (top) *Amida Nyorai*, (right) *Kannon Bosatsu*, and (left) *Seishi Bosatsu*
[above right] *The light of Amida illuminates the entire world.*
[above left] *All who praise Amida will be saved.*

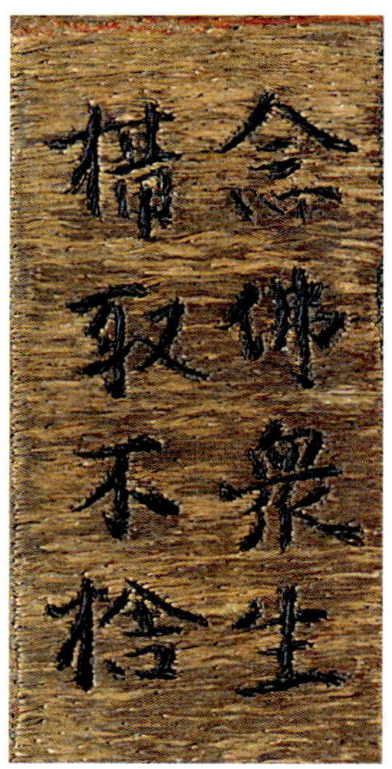

843, left

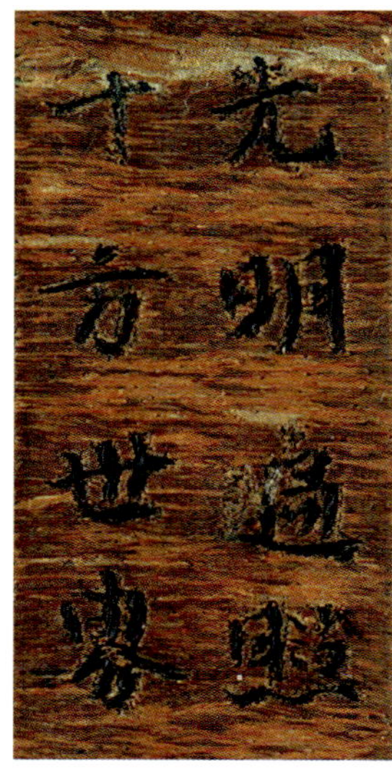

843, right

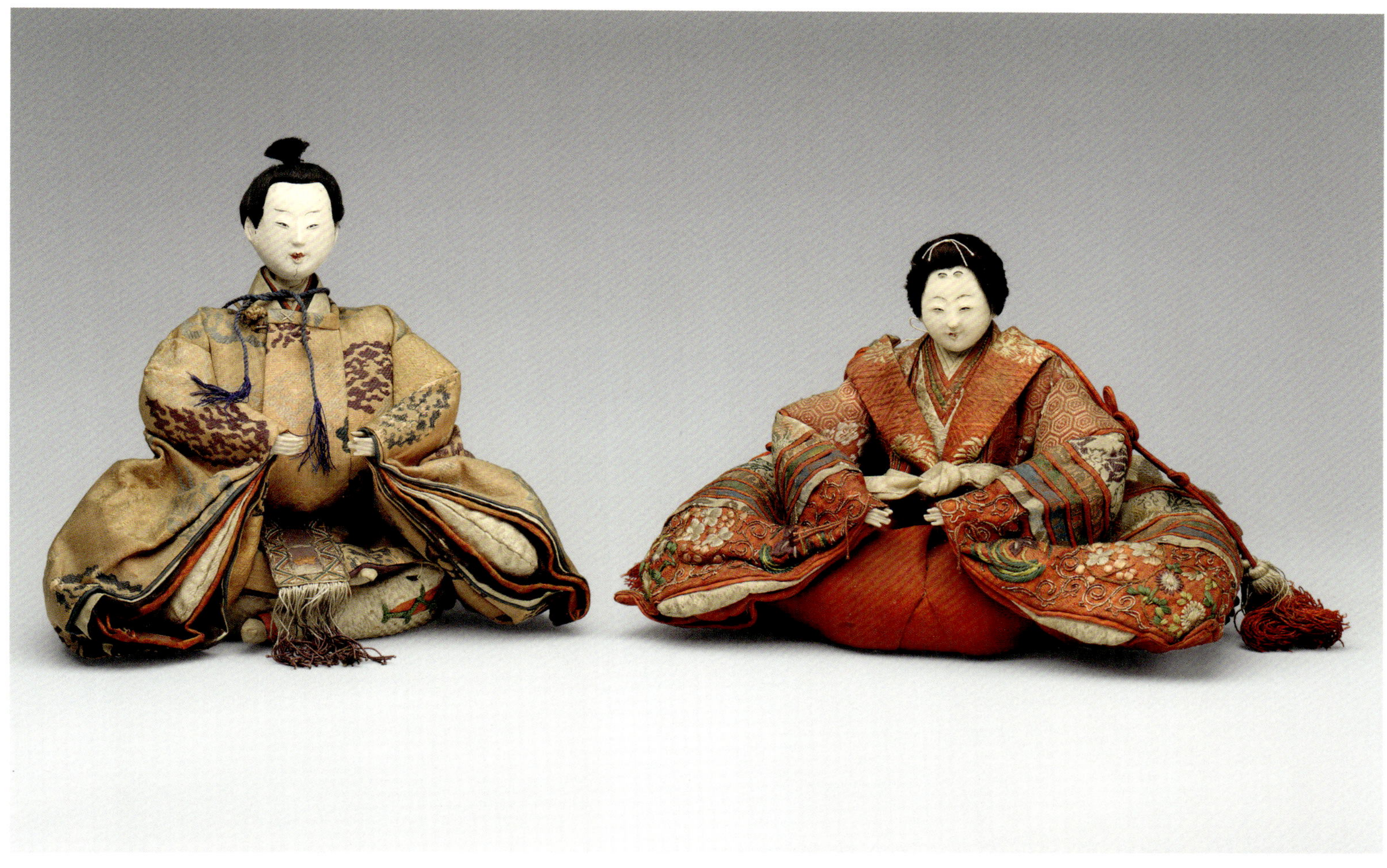

844. Dolls for the *Hina Matsuri* (雛祭)

Edo period, 18th–19th century
Wood, fabric, and powdered seashells (*gofun*, 胡粉)
H. of male (without cap) 21.7 cm (8½ in.); h. of female 17.8 cm (7 in.)

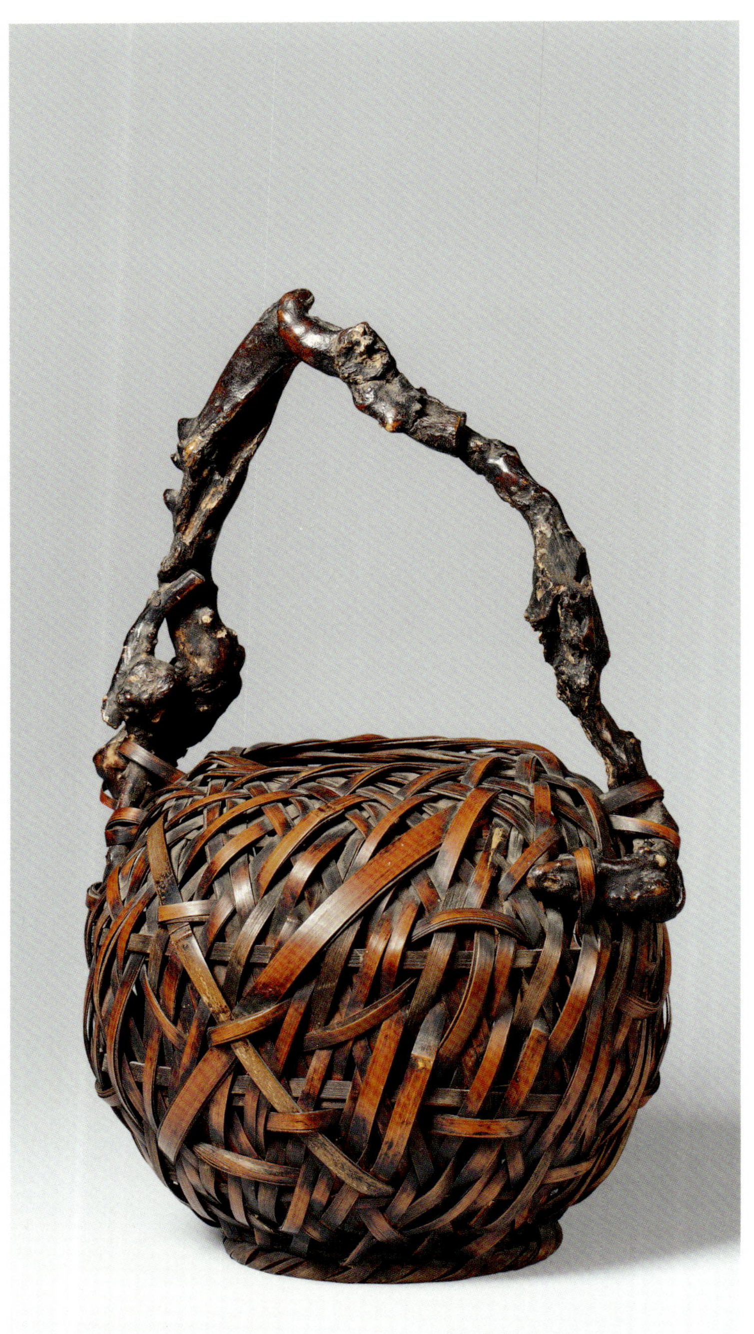

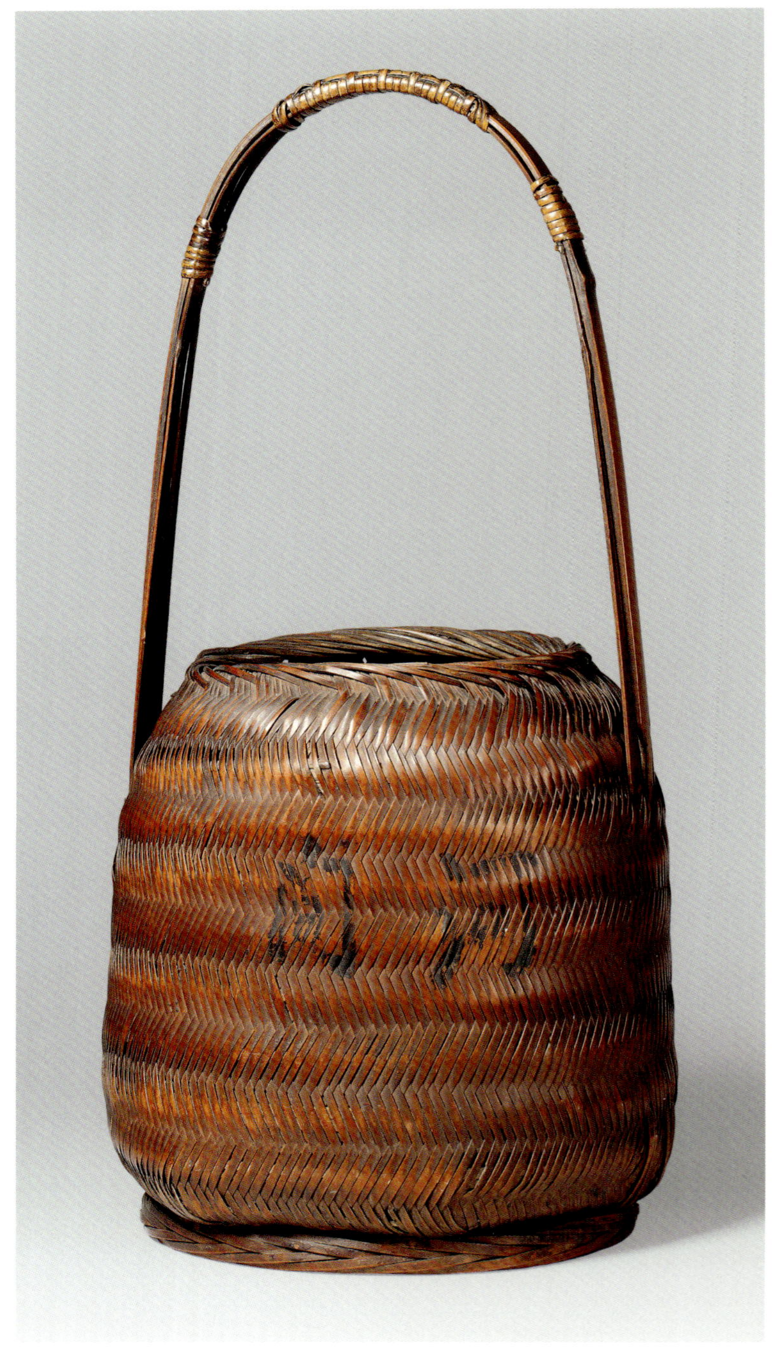

845. Basket with wood handle

Meiji–Shōwa period, 19th–20th century
H. 37.9 cm (14 7/8 in.)

846. Basket with handle

Meiji–Shōwa period, 19th–20th century
H. 51.4 cm (20 1/4 in.)
Text

847. Basket with ring handles

Meiji–Shōwa period, 19th–20th century
H. 23.6 cm (9 1/4 in.)

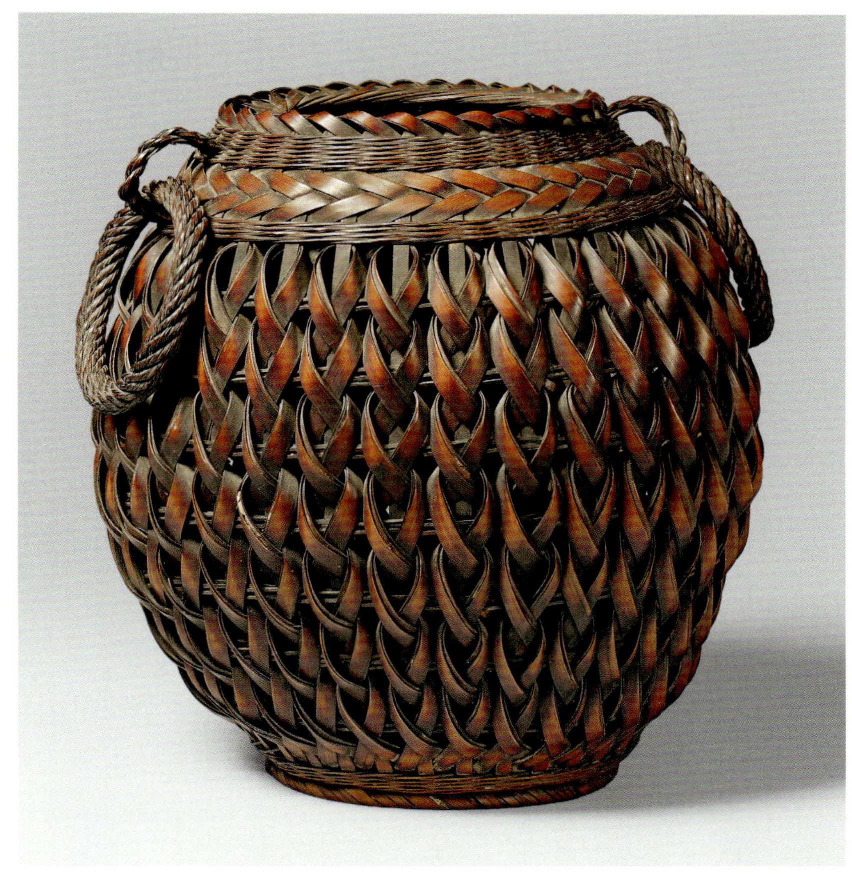

848. Boat-shaped flower container

Meiji–Shōwa period, 19th–20th century
H. 33 cm (13 in.)

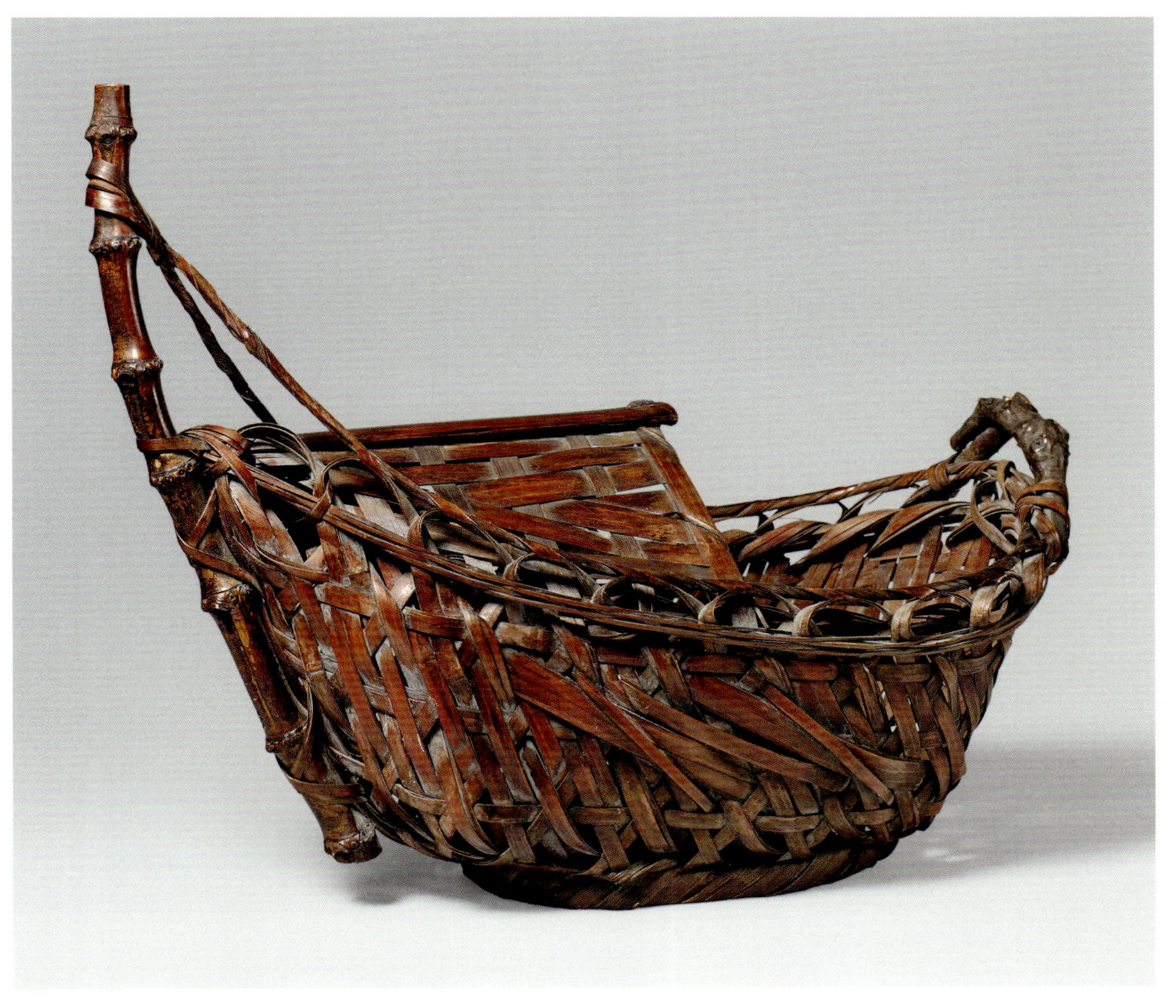

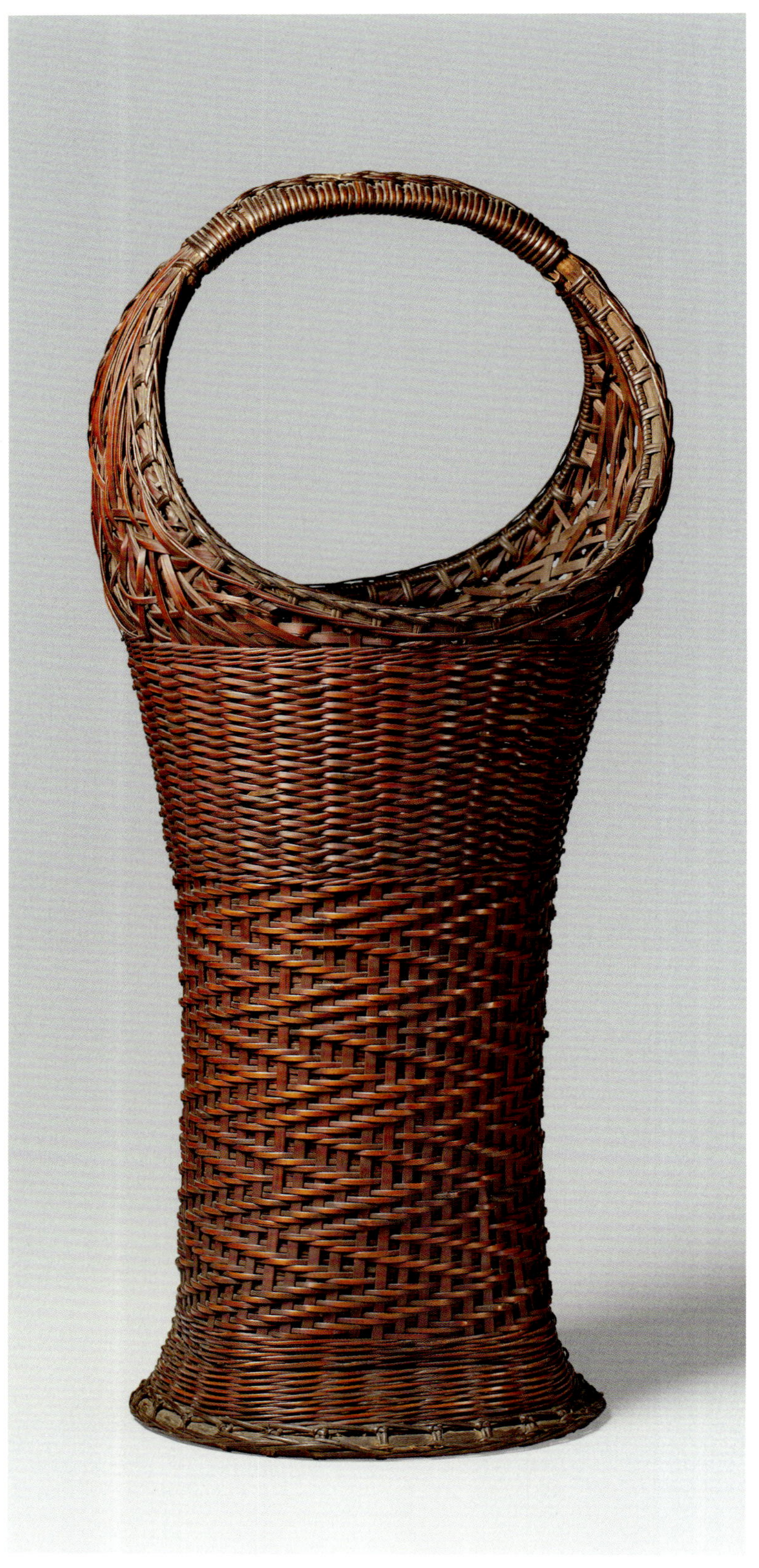

Seichikusai
(誠竹斎; fl. 19th–20th century)

849. Basket with handle

Meiji–Shōwa period
H. 45.1 cm (17 3/4 in.)
Signature

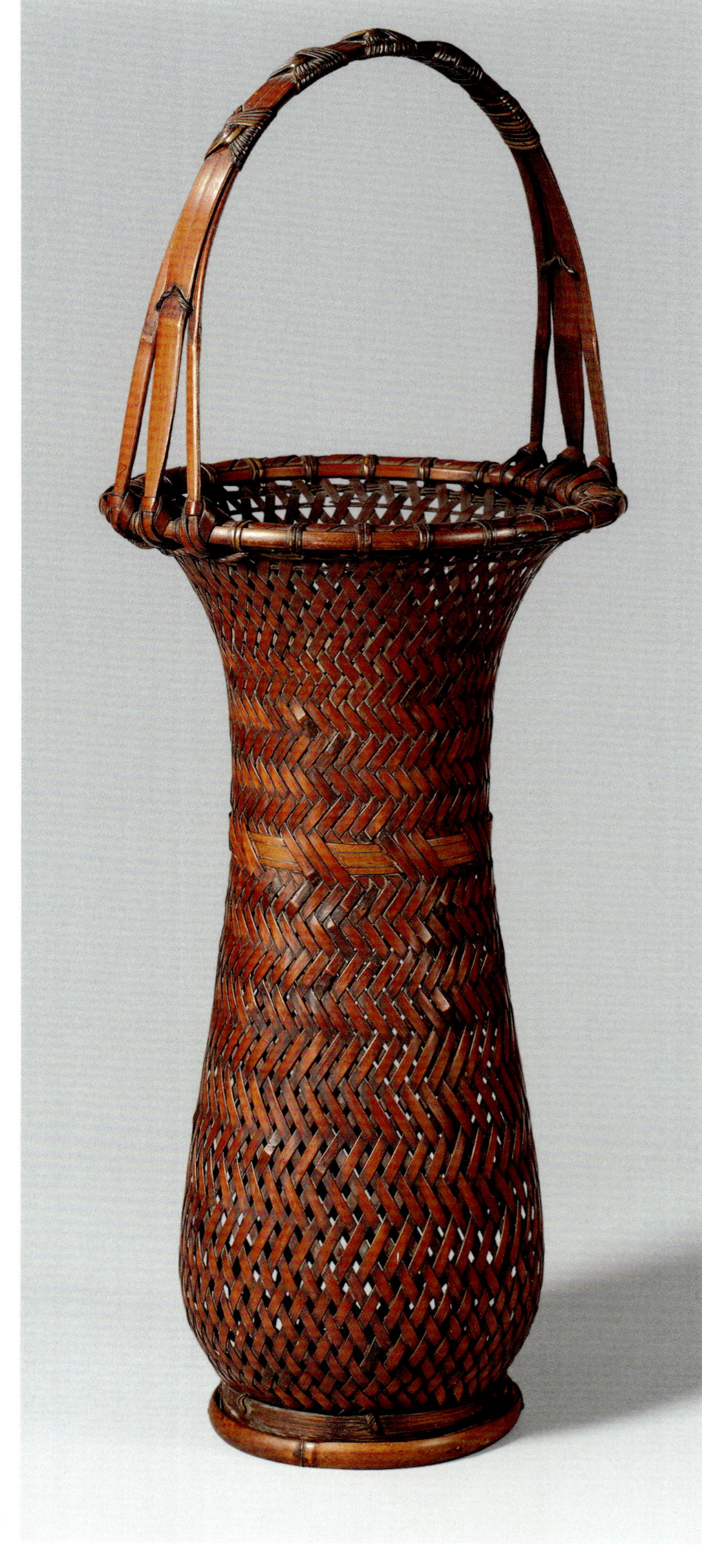

Seigetsu
(清月; fl. 19th–20th century)

850. Basket with handle

Meiji–Shōwa period
H. 57.8 cm (22 3/4 in.)
Signature

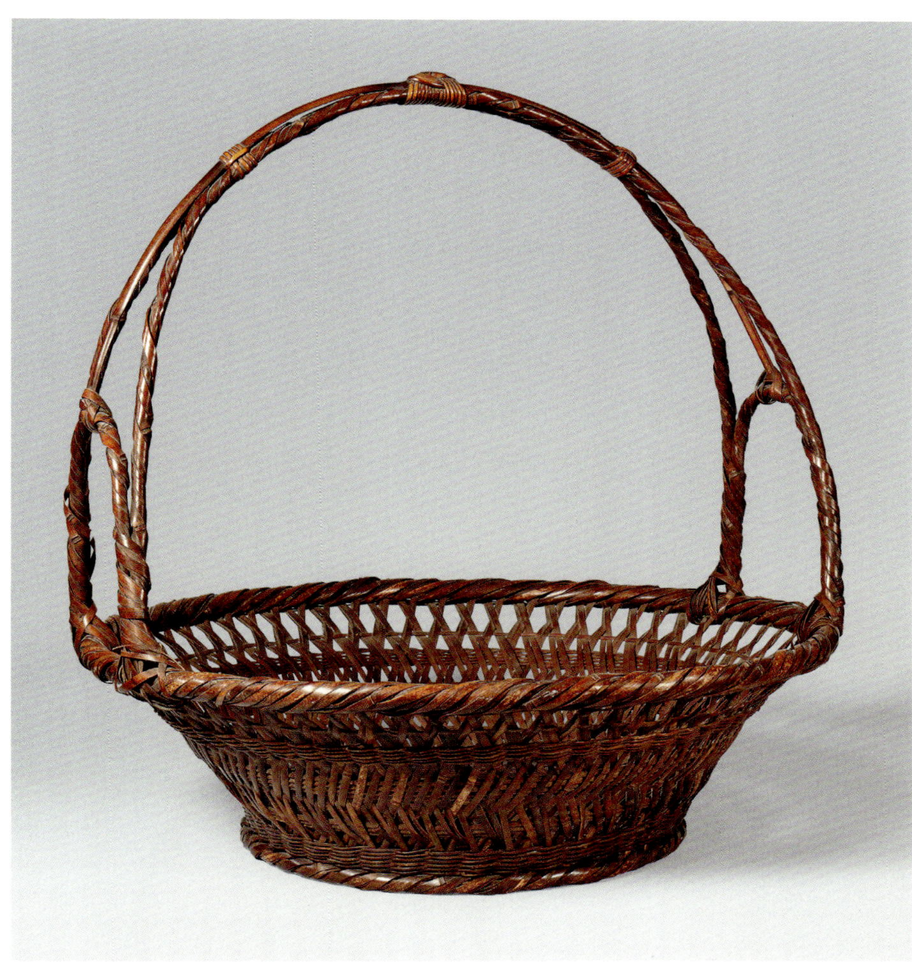

Chikushinsai
(竹心斎; fl. 19th–20th century)

851. Flower container with handle

Meiji–Shōwa period
H. 56.5 cm (22 1/4 in.)
Signature

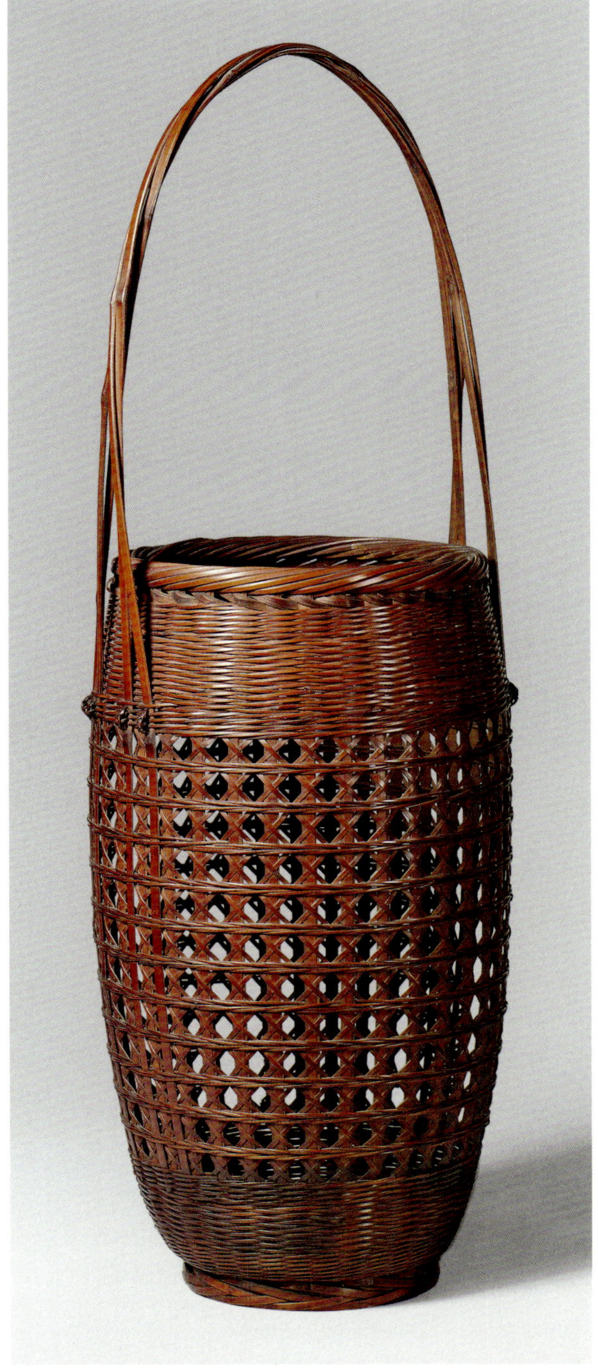

Kōkōsai
(坑々斎; fl. 19th–20th century)

852. Basket with handle

Meiji–Shōwa period
H. 52.8 cm (20 3/4 in.)
Signature

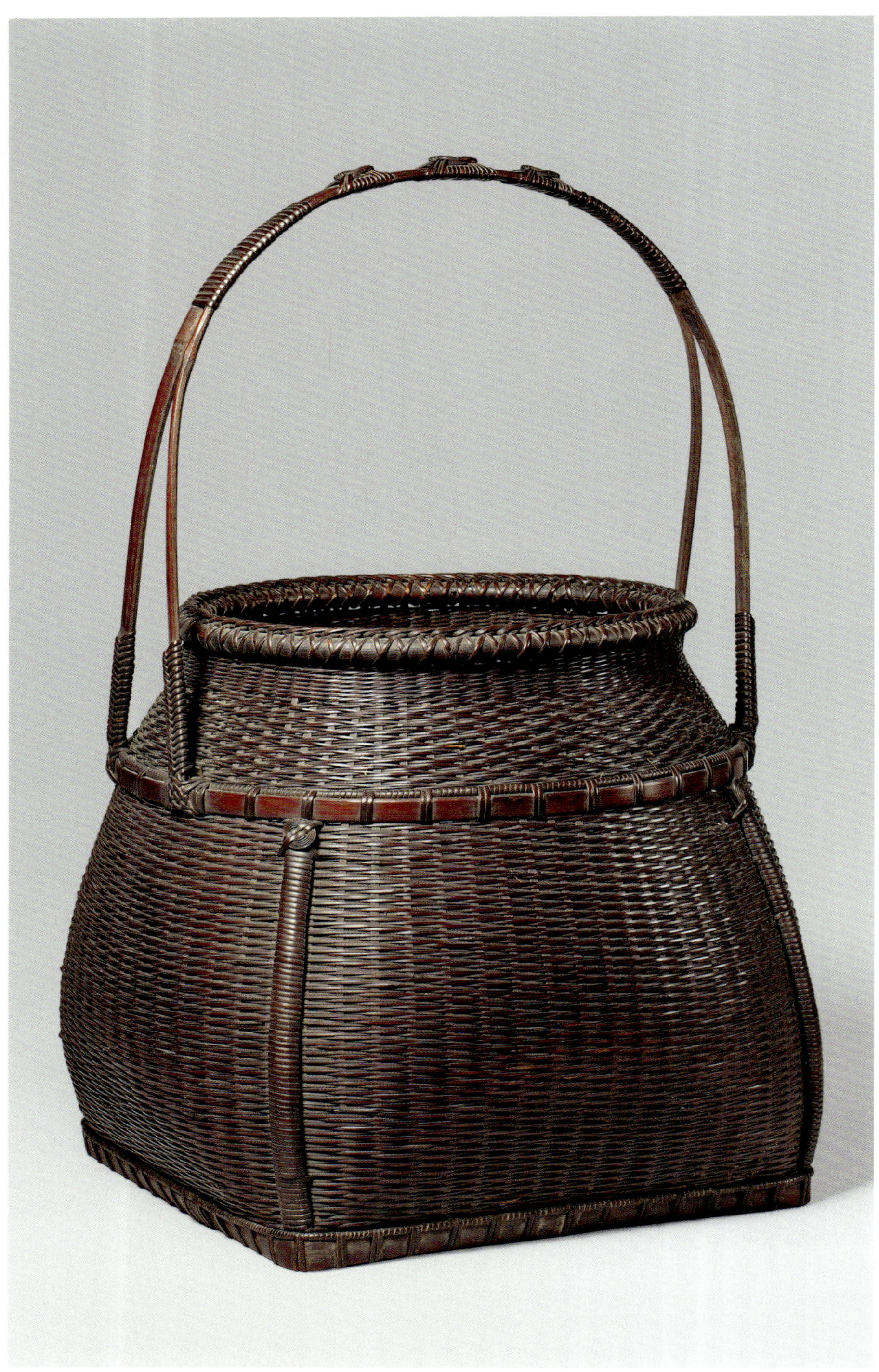

Chikukōen
(竹工園; fl. 19th–20th century)

853. Basket with handle

Meiji–Shōwa period
H. 46.8 cm (18 3/8 in.)
Signature

Chikuami
(竹阿彌; fl. 19th–20th century)

854. Basket with handle

Meiji–Shōwa period
H. 50.1 cm (19 3/4 in.)
Signature

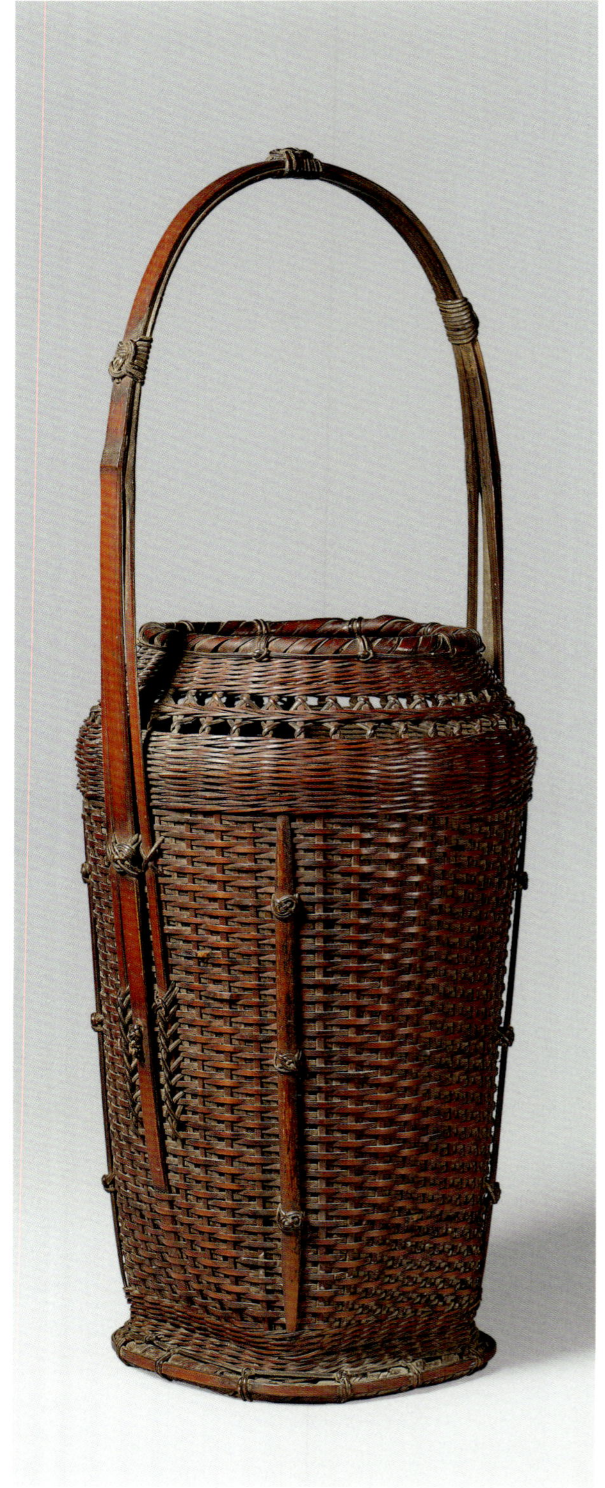

Gyokukōsai
(玉晃斎; fl. 19th–20th century)

855. Basket with handle

Meiji–Shōwa period
H. 51.9 cm (20 3/8 in.)
Signature

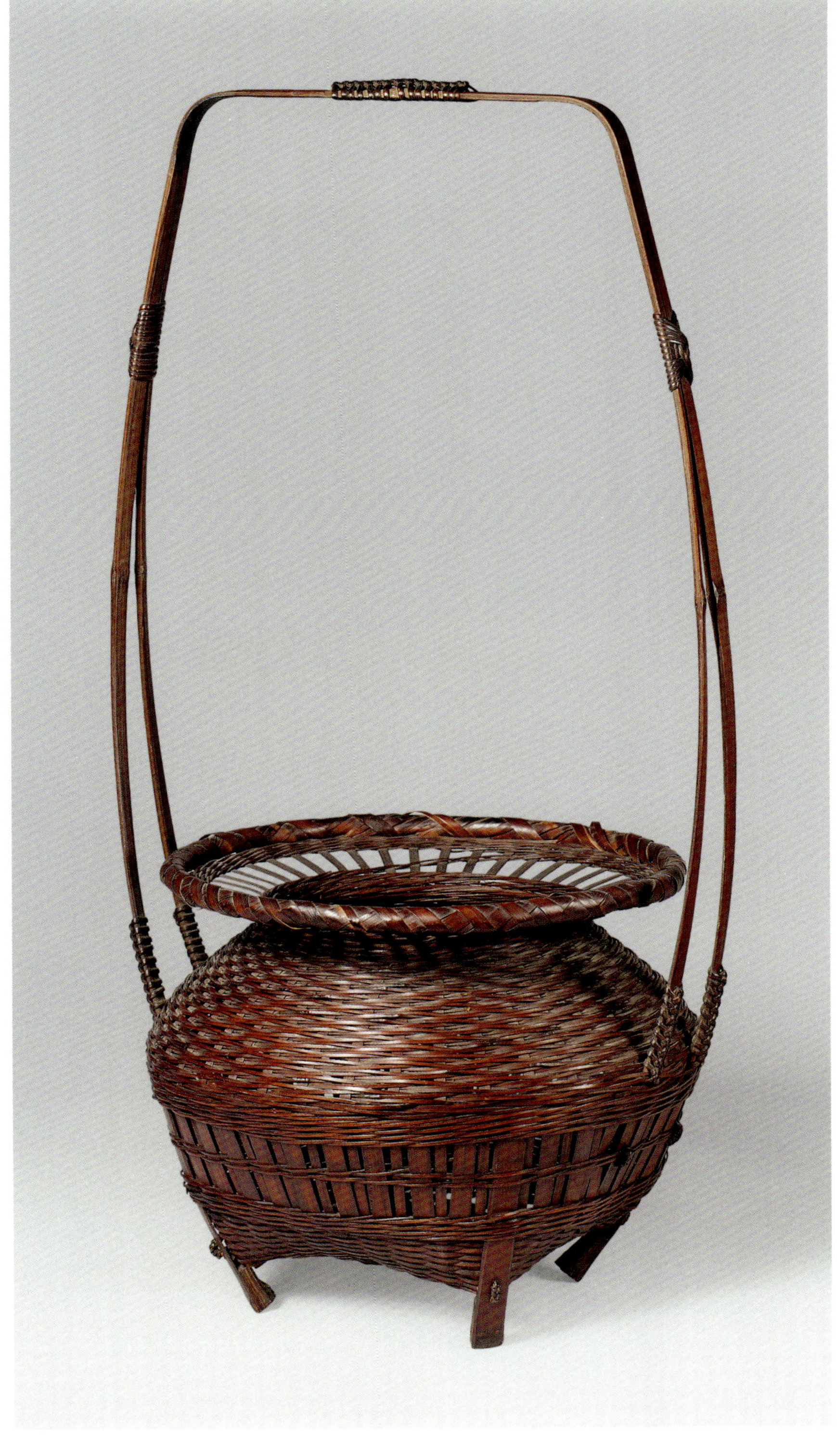

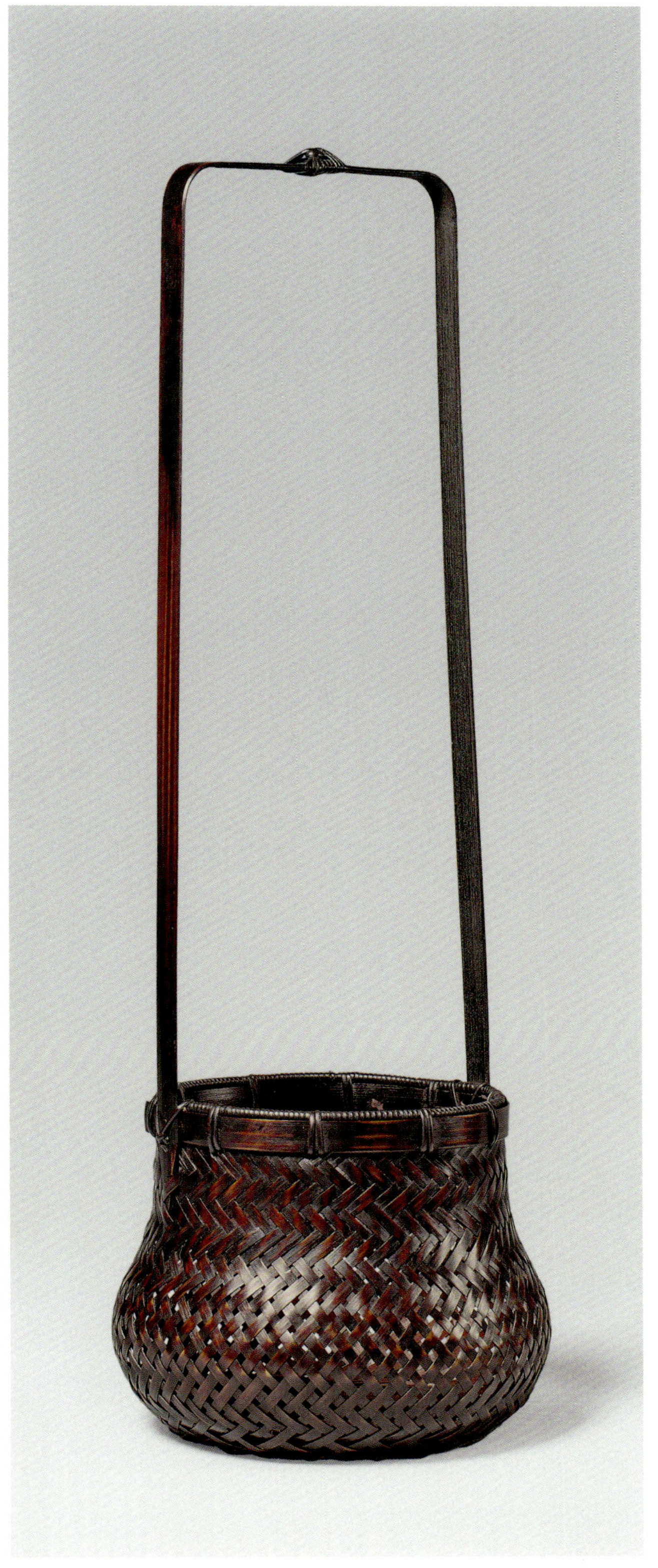

Chikuyūsai
(竹遊斎; fl. 20th century)

856. Basket with handle

Shōwa period
H. 43.8 cm (17 1/4 in.)

Bamboo Baskets Details

† *denotes illustrated items*

---

846. Basket with handle

Text

Kawama

---

† 849. Basket with handle

Signature

Seichikusai

---

† 850. Basket with handle

Signature

Made by Seigetsu

---

† 851. Flower container with handle

Signature

Chikushinsai

---

† 852. Basket with handle

Signature

Made by Kōkōsai

---

† 853. Basket with handle

Signature

Chikukōen

---

† 854. Basket with handle

Signature

Made by Chikuami

---

† 855. Basket with handle

Signature

Gyokukōsai

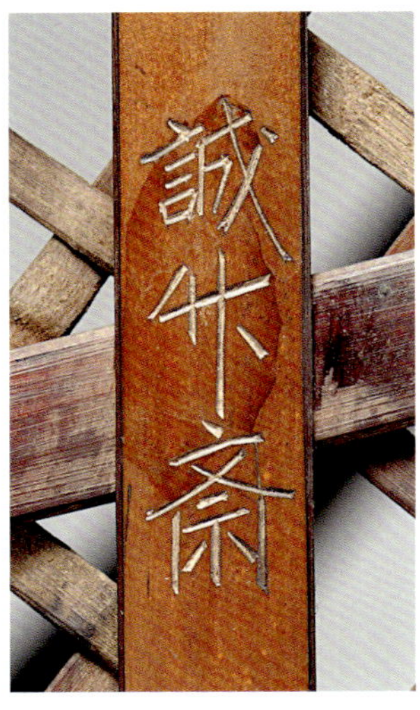

849

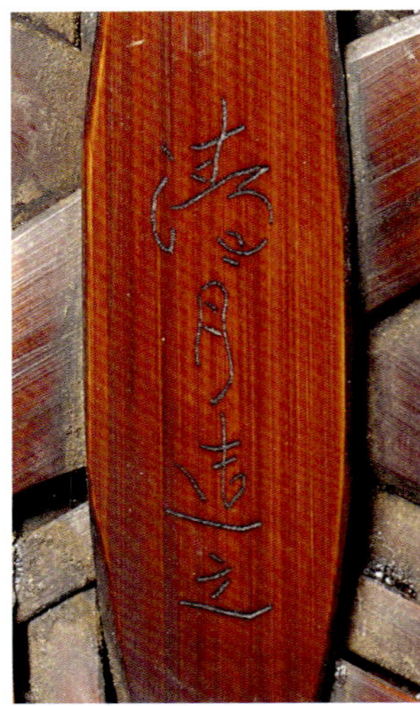

850

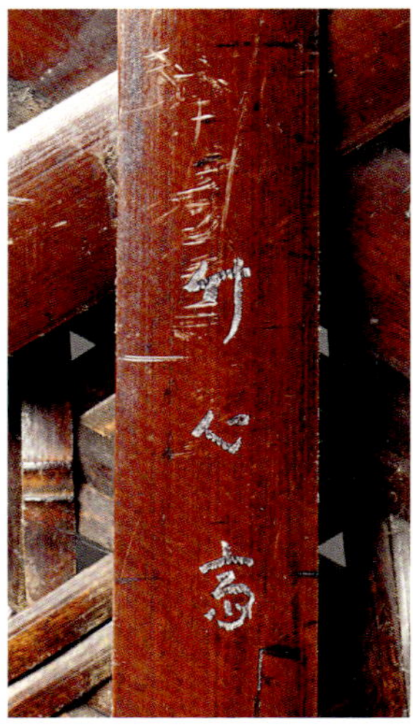

851

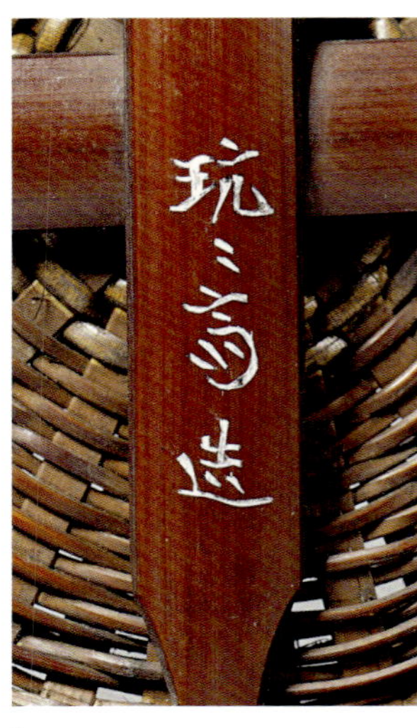

852

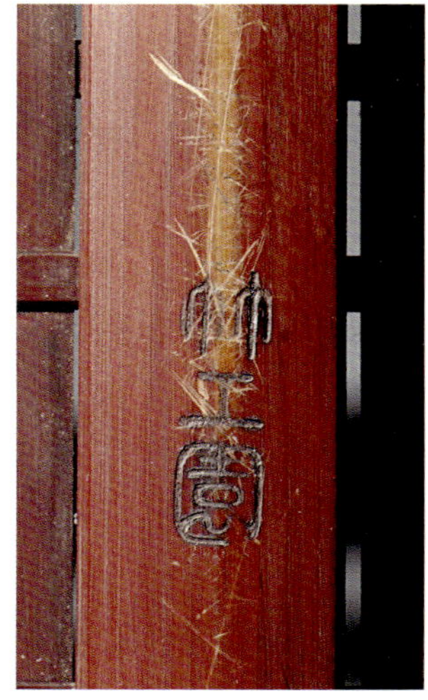

853

854

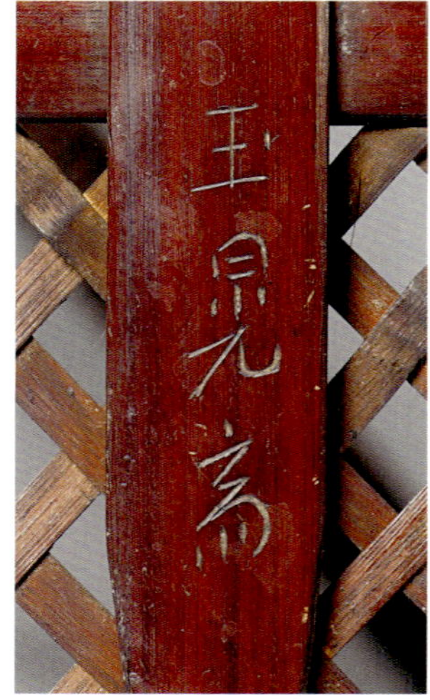

855

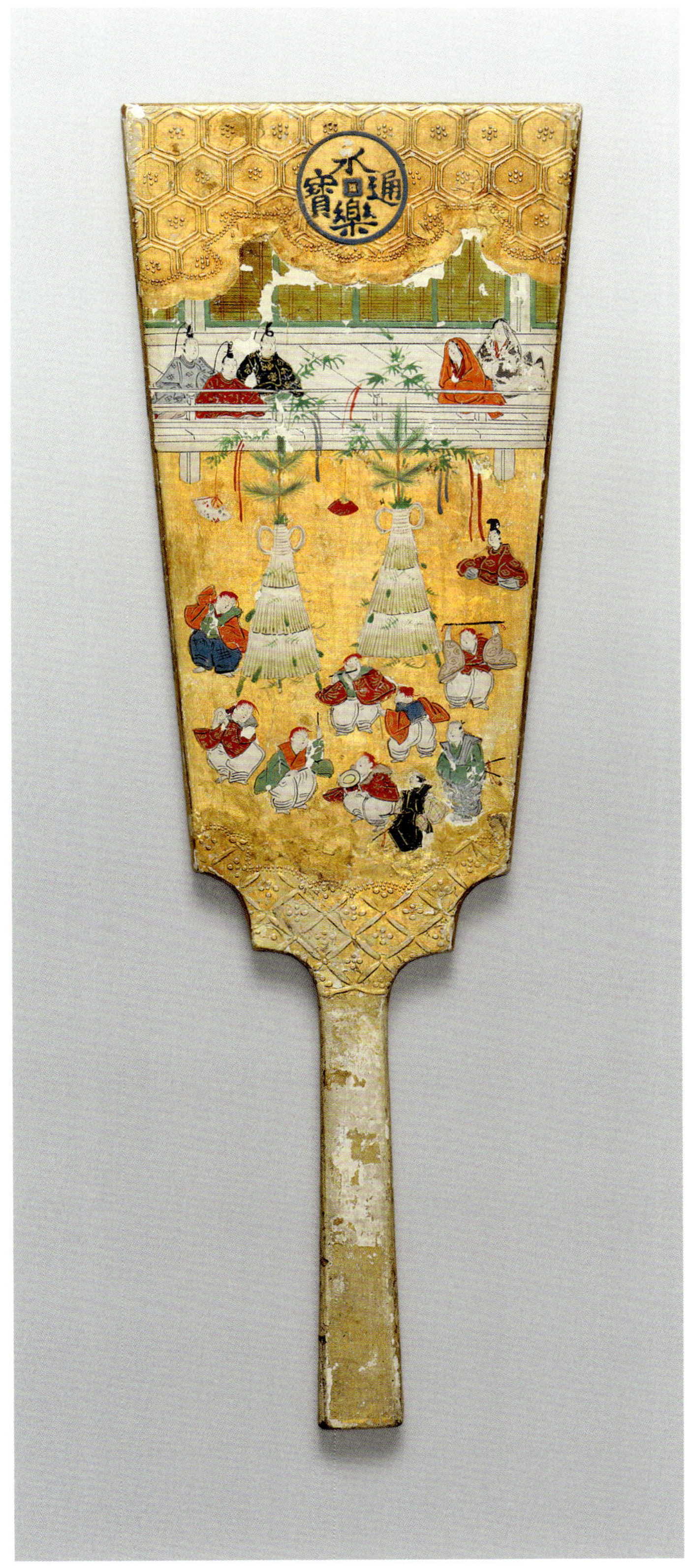

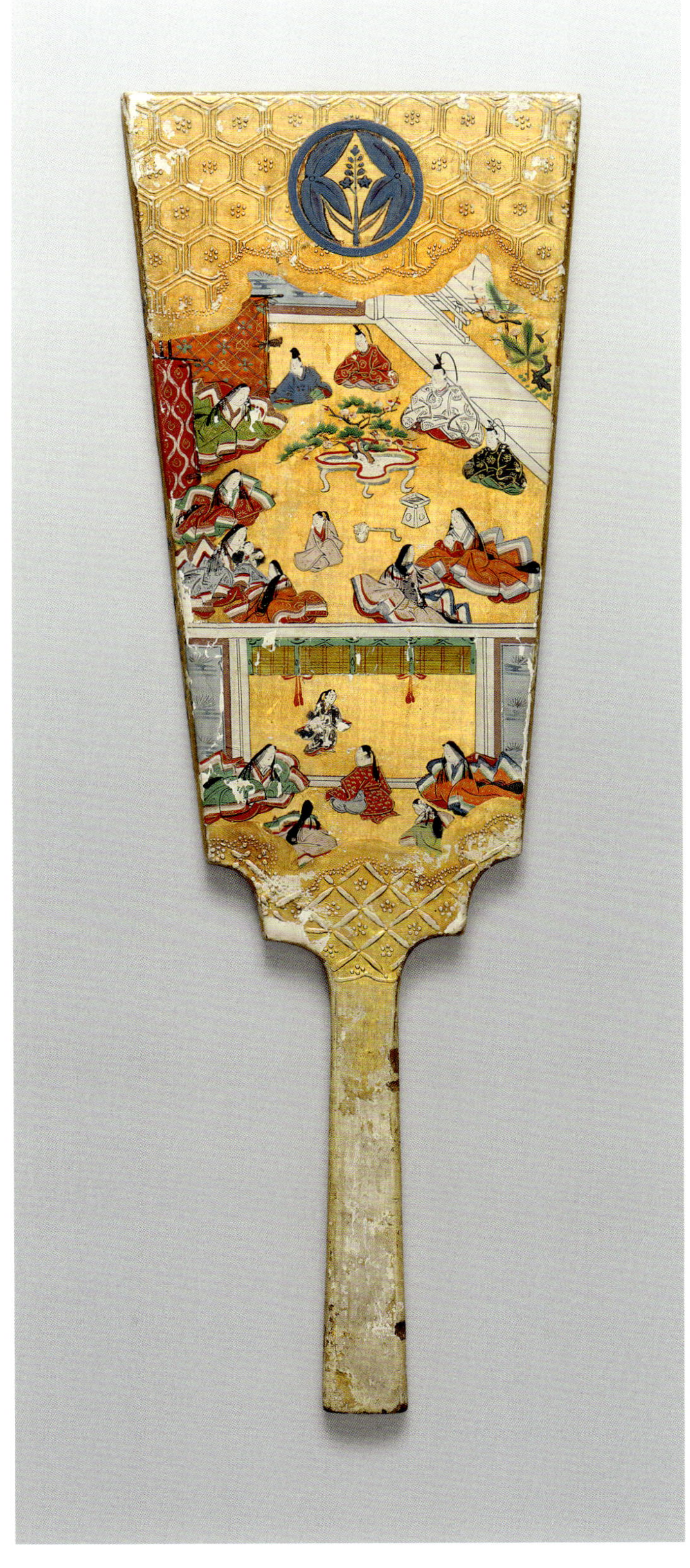

857. Painted battledore (*hagoita*, 羽子板)

Scenes of New Year's Festivities (right) and *Sagichō* (左義長) (left)
Edo period, 18th century
Ink, color, and gold on wood
L. 48 cm (18⅞ in.)
Seals

Gift from N. V. Hammer

858. Stand with cabinet

Edo period, 19th century
Wood, metal, and bamboo
47.6 x 29.7 x 24.5 cm (18 3/4 x 11 3/4 x 9 5/8 in.)

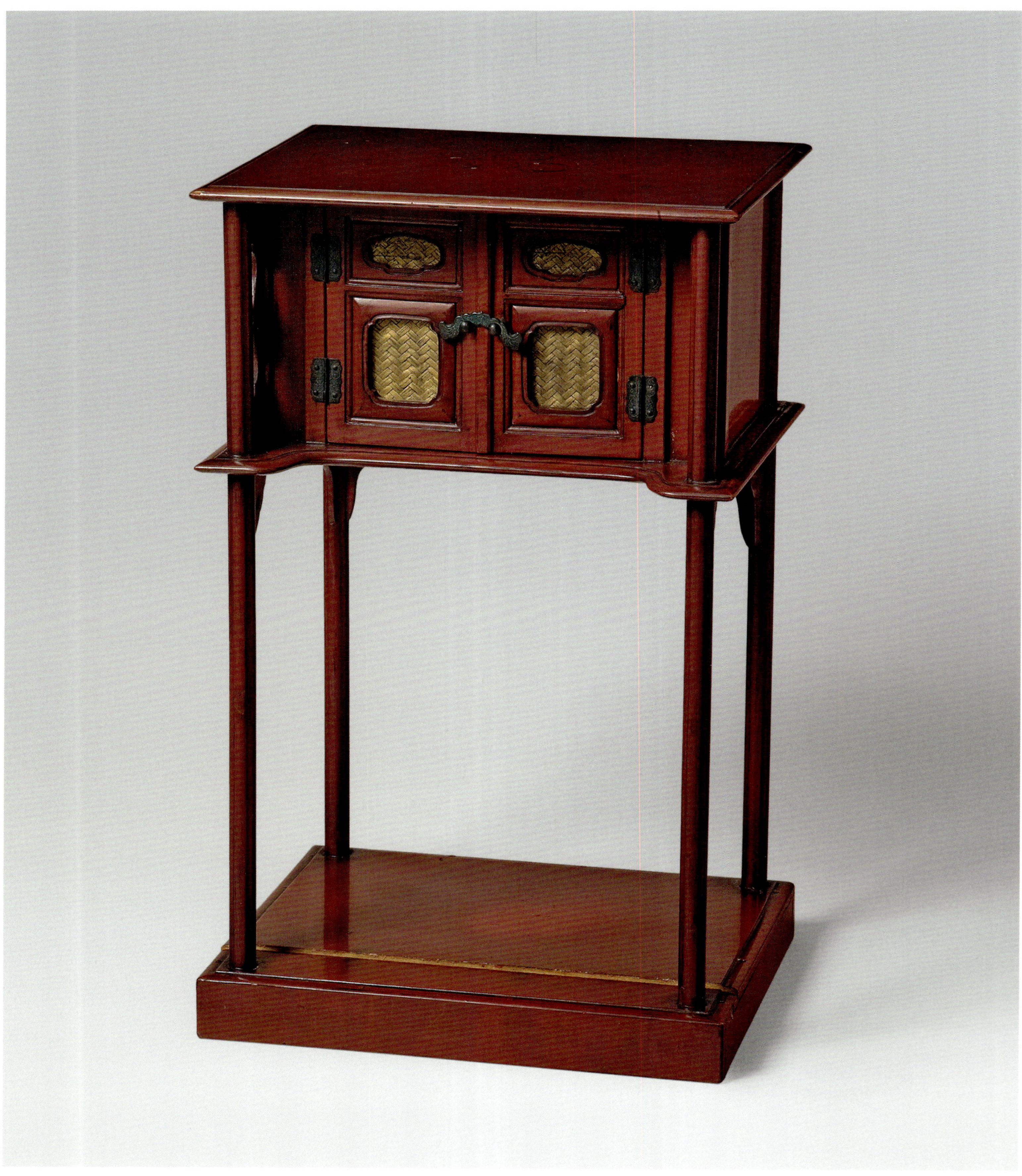

Wood Objects Details

† *denotes illustrated items*

---

† 857. Painted battledore

Seals

[on New Year's Festivities] a family crest; [on *Sagichō*] *Eiraku tsūhō* (Ch. Yongle-era coin design)

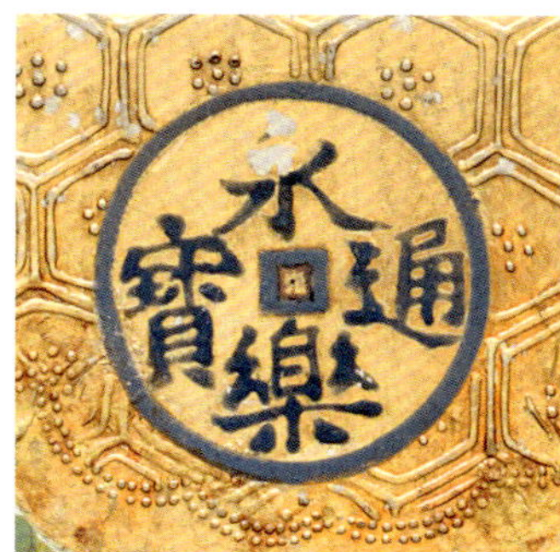

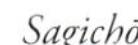

Sagichō

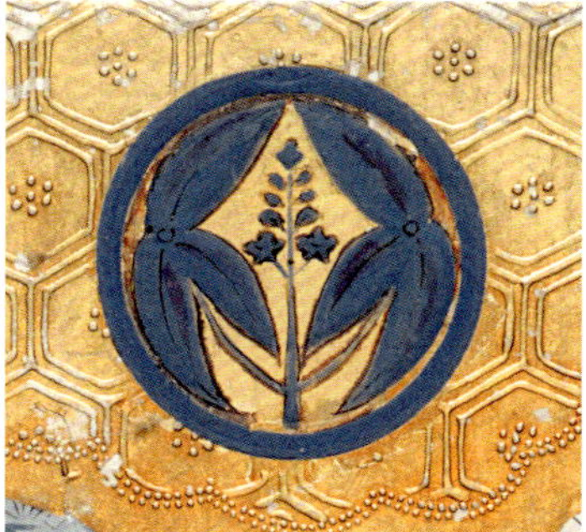

New Year's Festivities

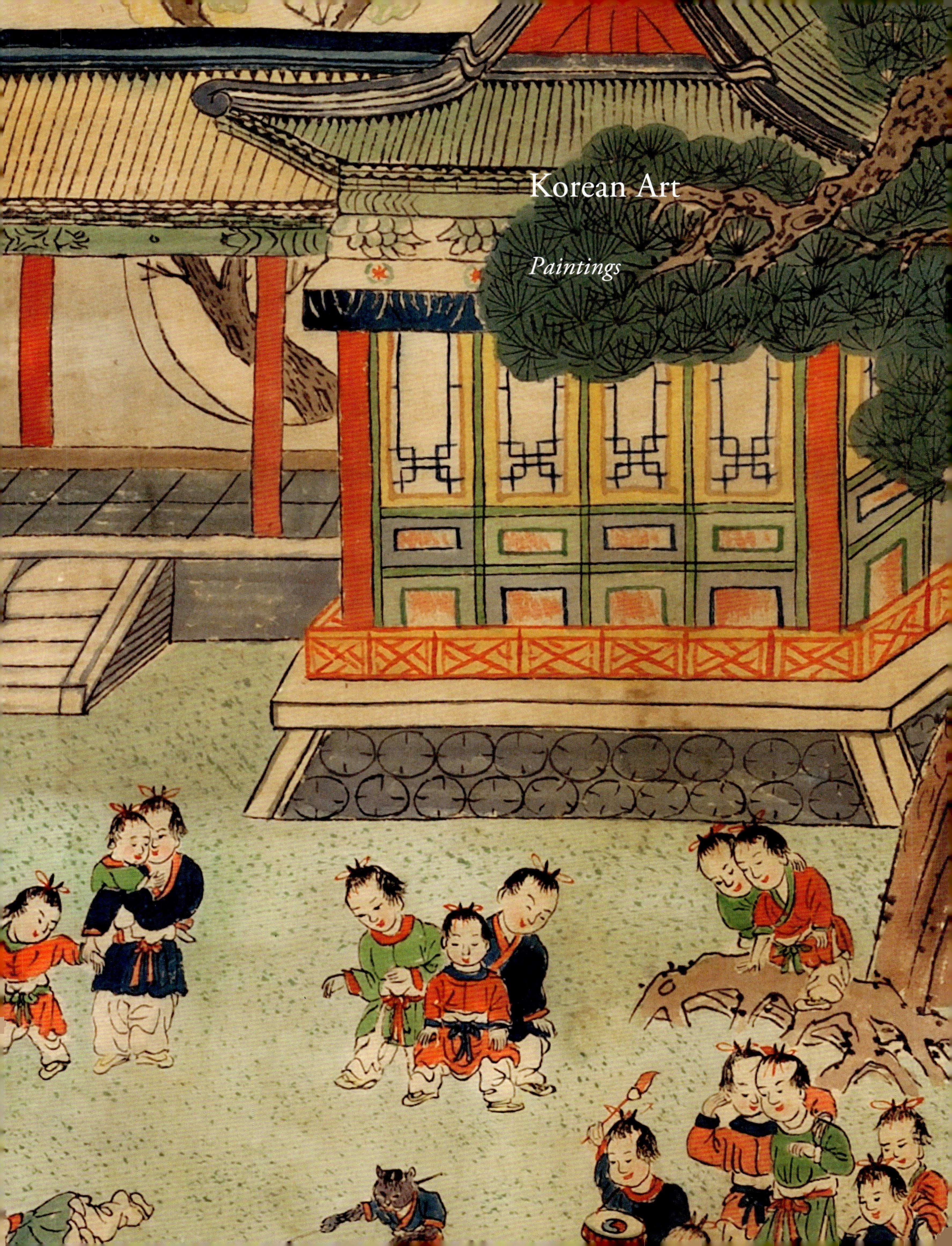

Korean Art

Paintings

859. Shakyamuni (Seokka, 釋迦) Triad

Joseon dynasty, 1565
Hanging scroll; ink, color, and gold on silk
69.3 x 33 cm (27¼ x 13 in.)
Text

LITERATURE: Hongnam Kim 1990, pp. 46–58, no. 12; Hongnam Kim 1991; Chung et al. 1998, pp. 176–77, pl. 80; Poster et al. 1999, pp. 56–57, no. 4; Lee 2009, p. 33, no. 12.

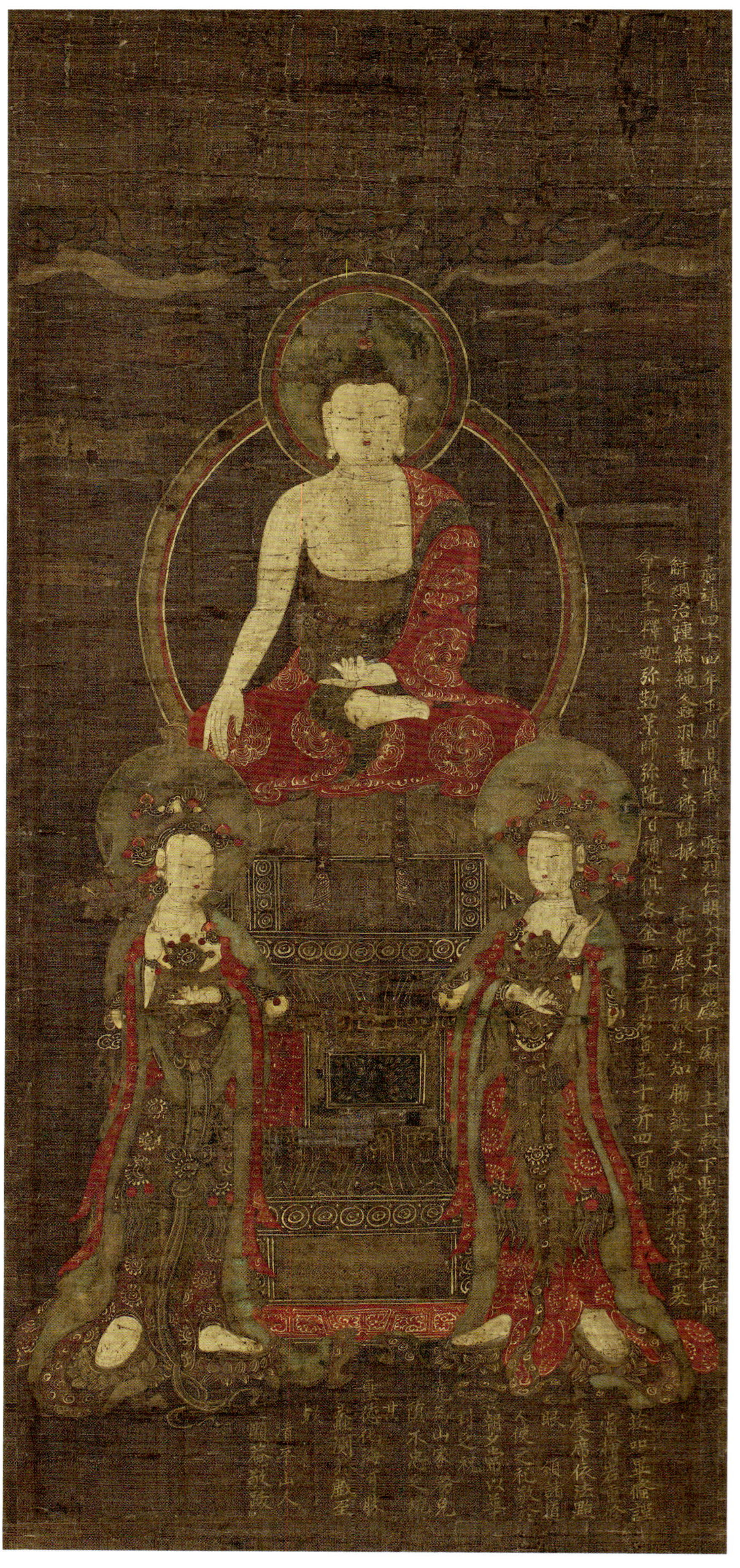

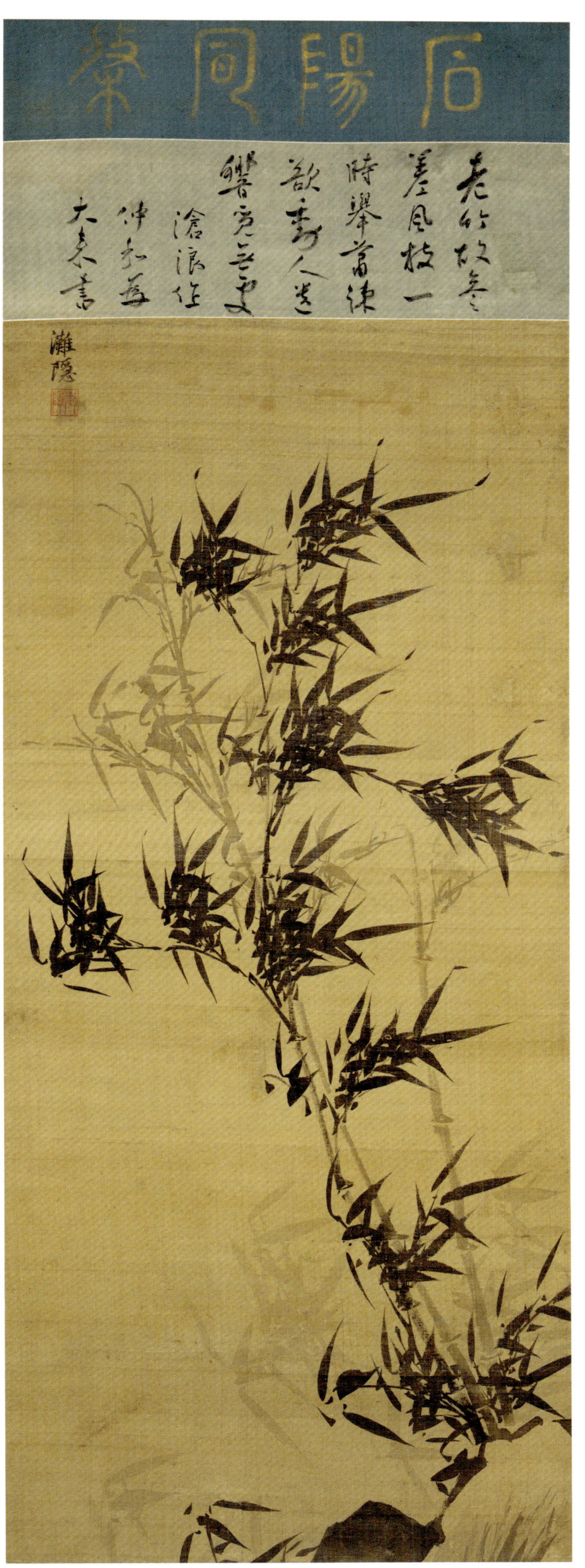

Yi Jeong
(李霆; 1541–1622)

860. *Bamboo in the Wind*

Joseon dynasty, early 17th century
Hanging scroll; ink on silk with gold on colophon
143.6 x 53.1 cm (56½ x 20⅞ in.)
Text, signature, seals

Literature: Korean National Museum [1973], p. 213, no. 505; Choi Sun-u 1973–75, vol. 12, p. 34, no. 23; Rousset 1977, p. 149, no. 121; Yi Song-Mi 1998, p. 61; Lee 2009, pp. 29, 100.

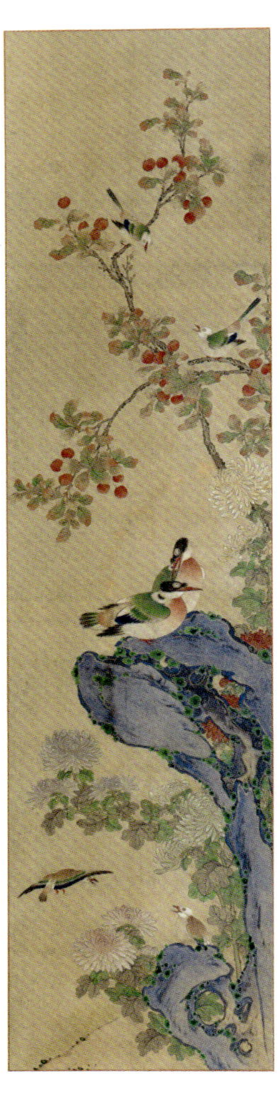
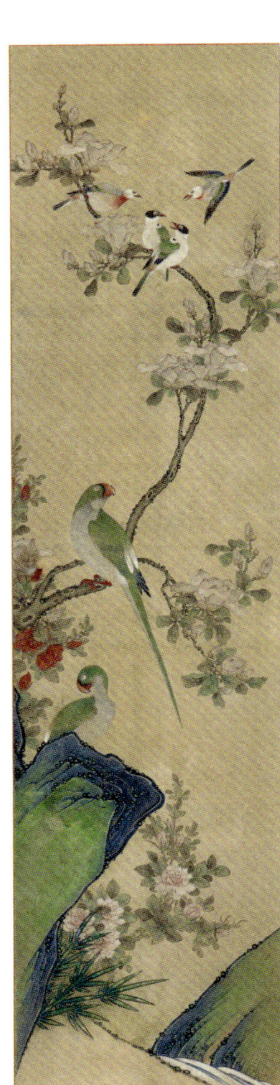
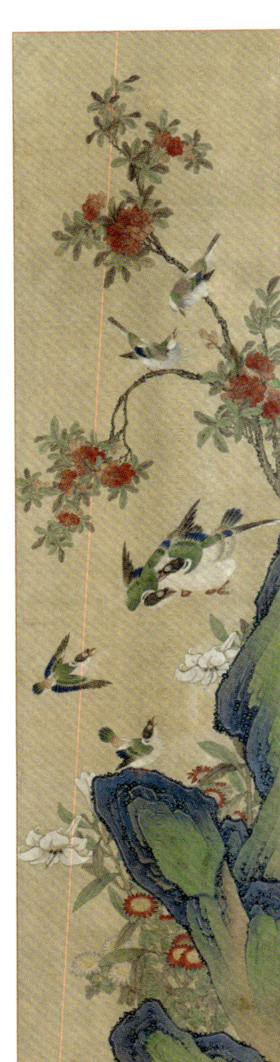
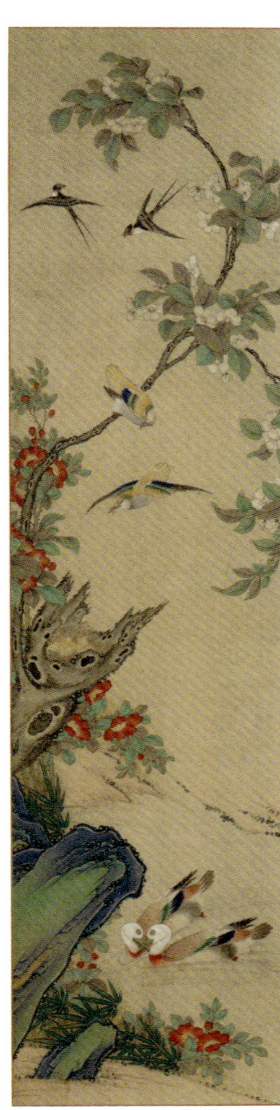
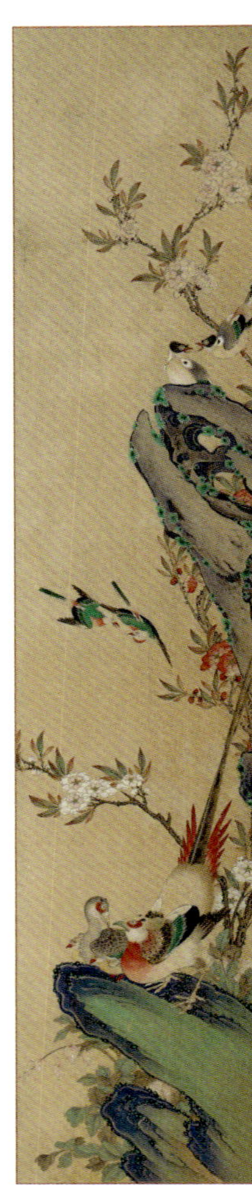

861. Birds and Flowers

Joseon dynasty, first half of 19th century
Eight-panel screen; ink and color on silk
Each panel 150 x 38.4 cm (59 x $15^{1}/_{8}$ in.)

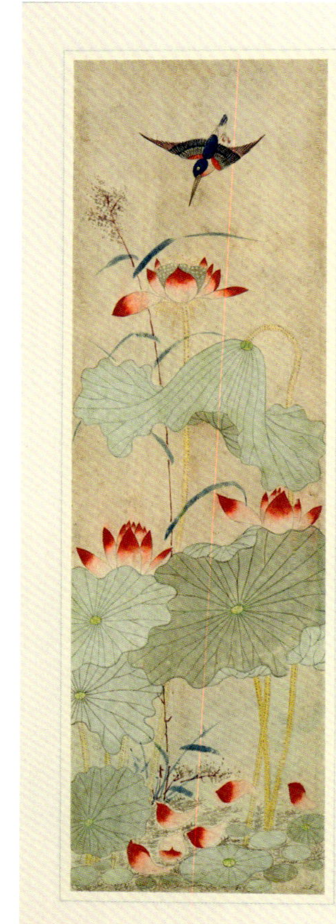
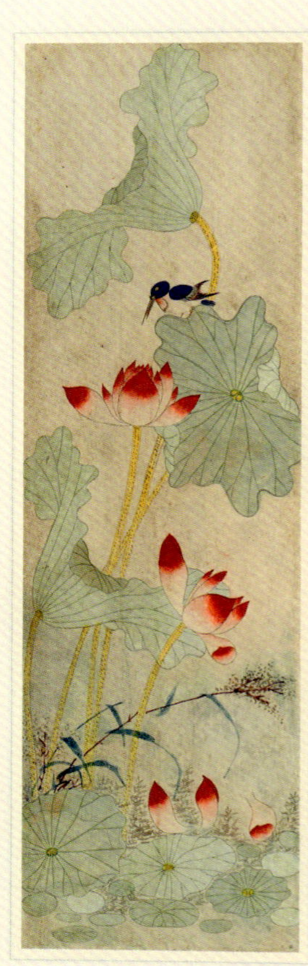
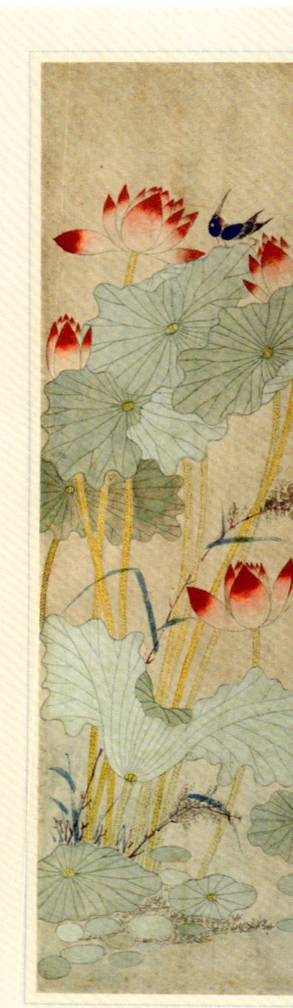

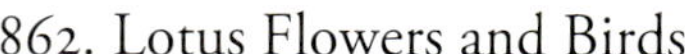

862. Lotus Flowers and Birds

Joseon dynasty, late 19th century
Eight-panel screen; ink and color on paper
Each panel 84 x 29.2 cm ($33^{1}/_{8}$ x $11^{1}/_{2}$ in.)

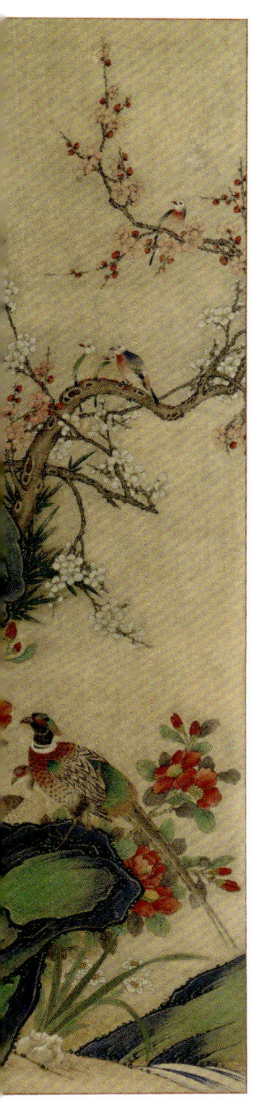
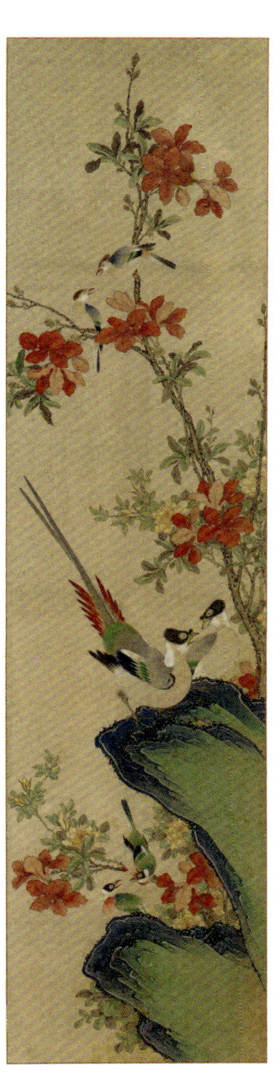
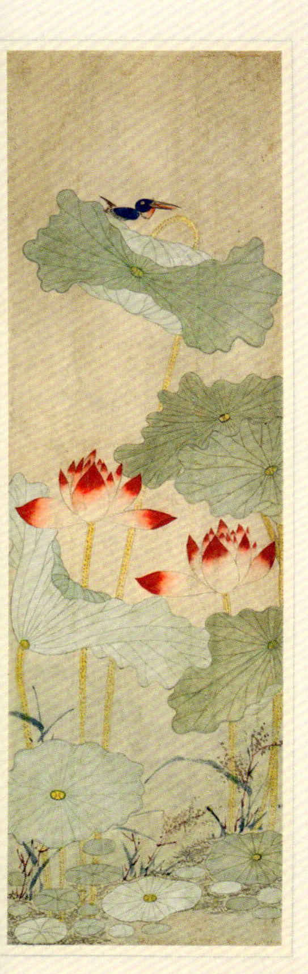
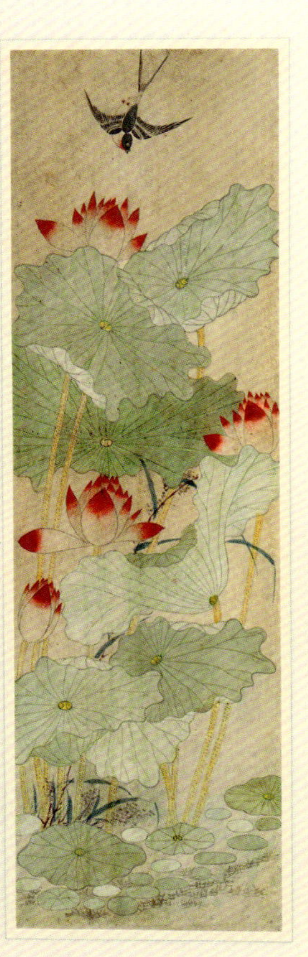
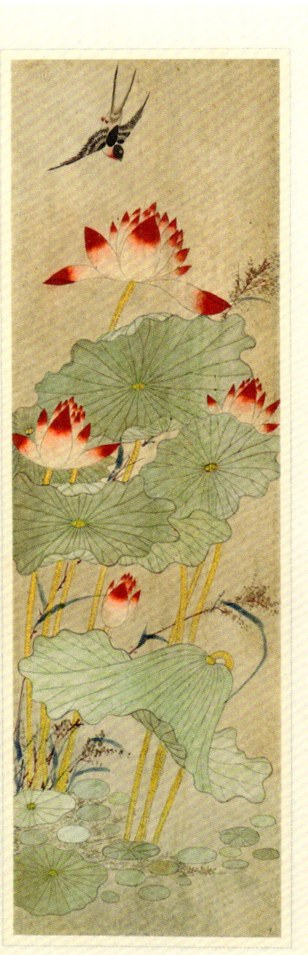
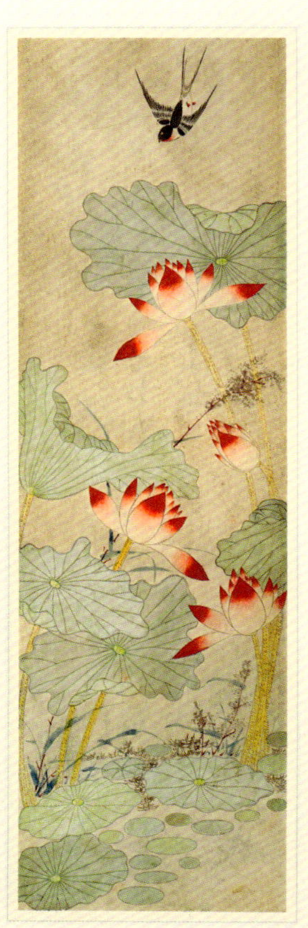
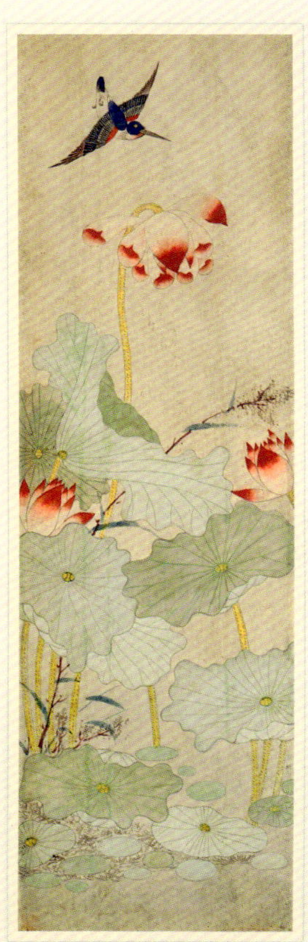

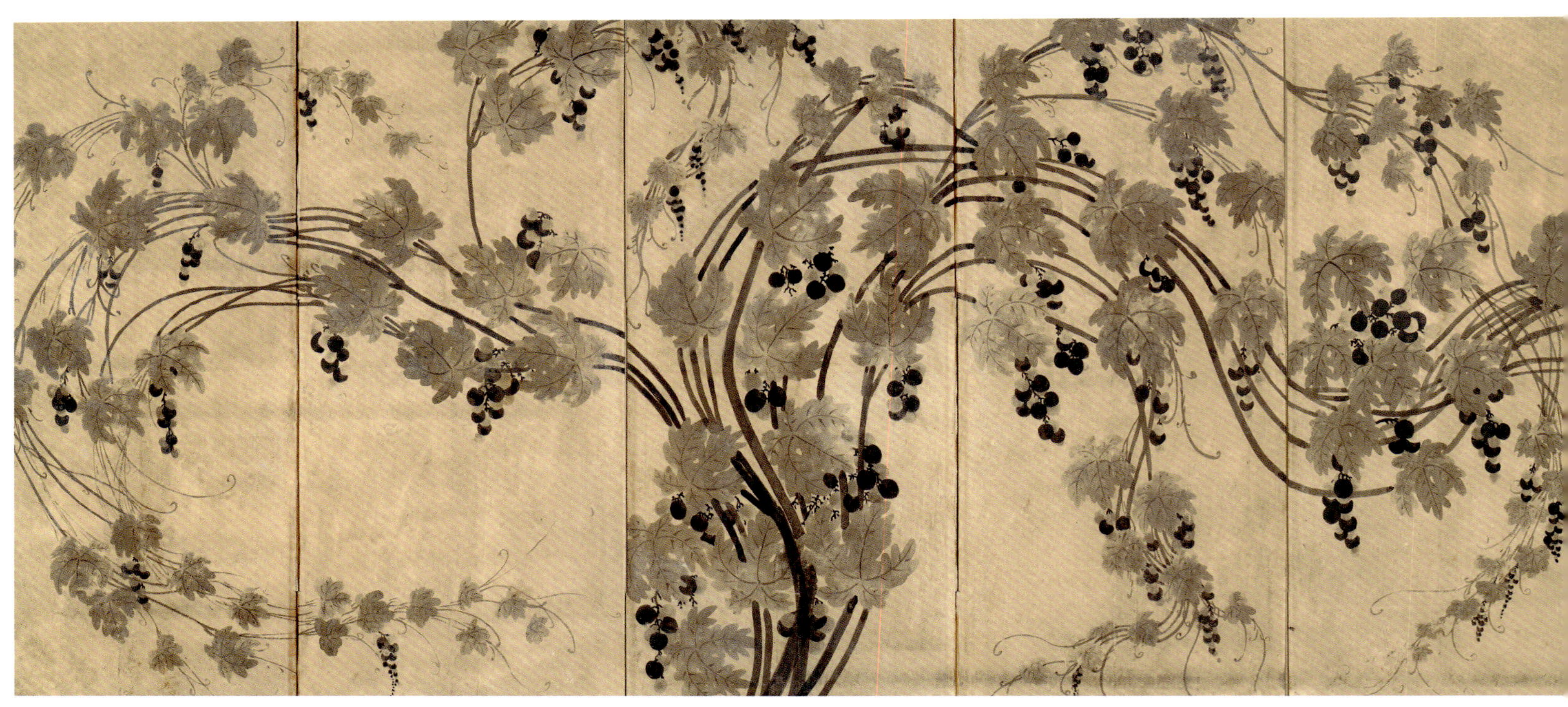

863. Grapevines

Joseon dynasty, late 19th century
Eight-panel screen; ink on paper
80.8 x 305.7 cm (31 3/4 in. x 10 ft. 3/8 in.)

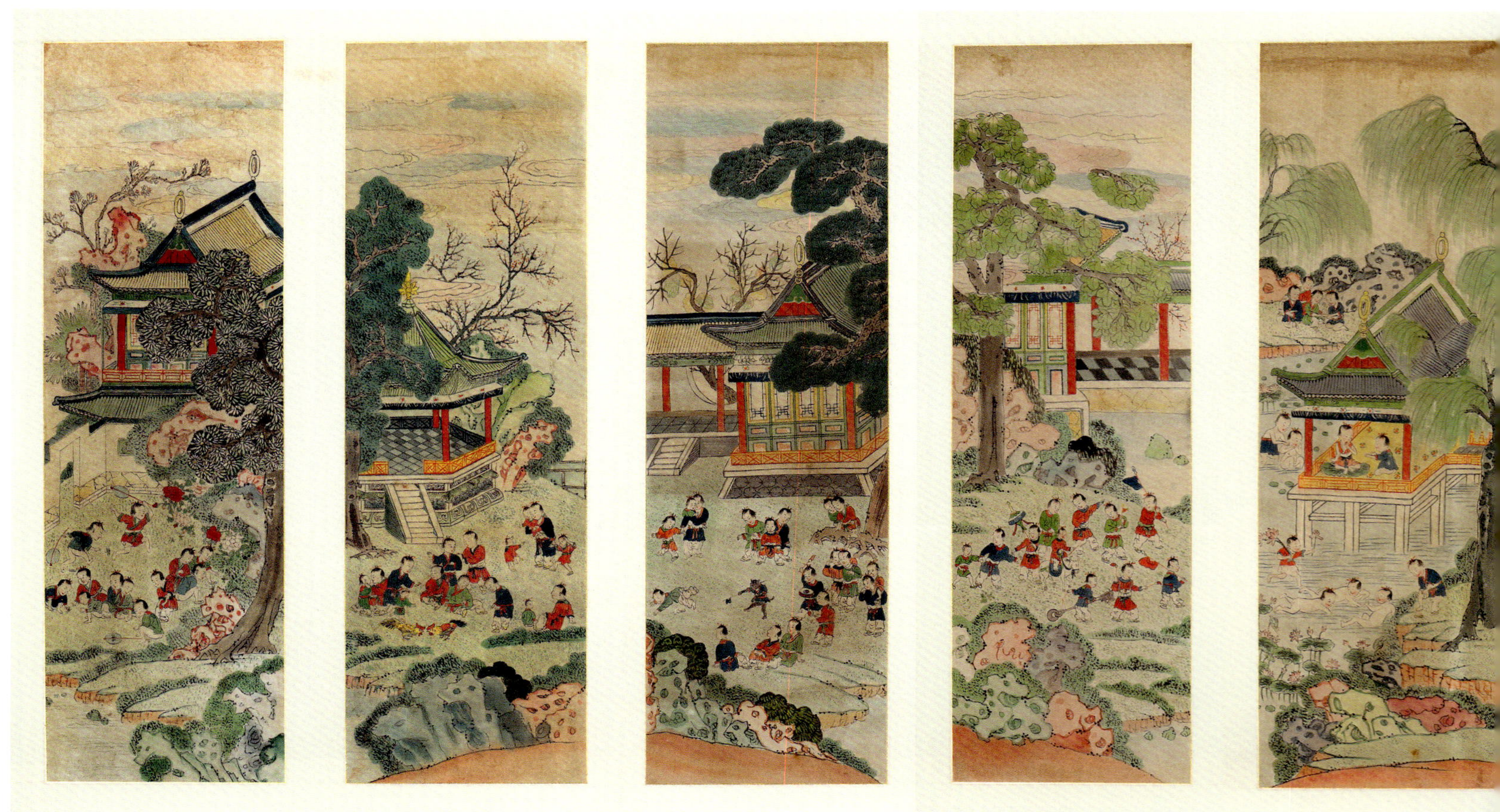

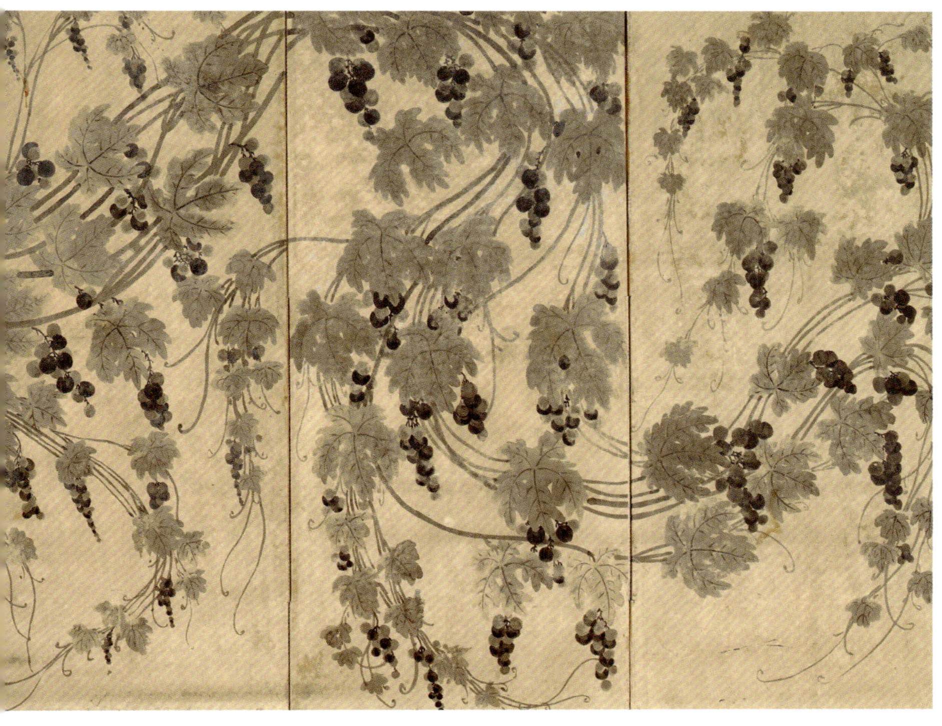

864. One Hundred Children at Play

Joseon dynasty, late 19th century
Ten-panel screen; ink and color on paper
Each panel 90.4 x 29.8 cm (35 5/8 x 11 3/4 in.)

Gift from R. Namkoong, 1978

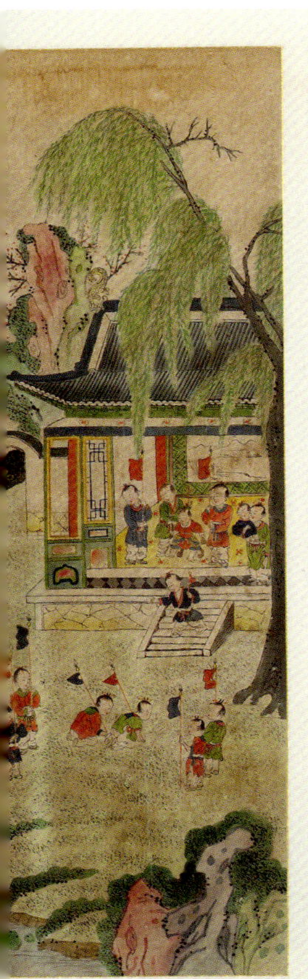
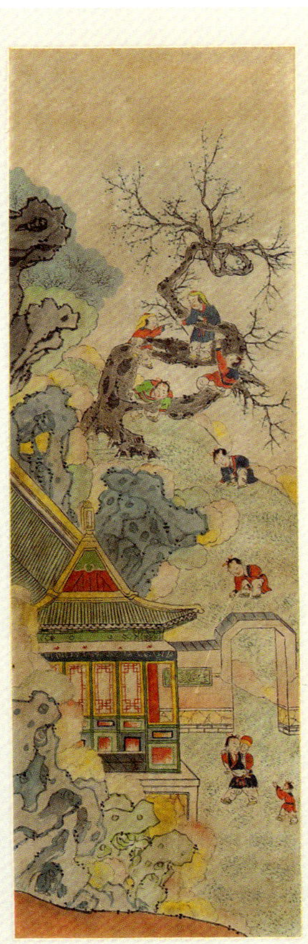
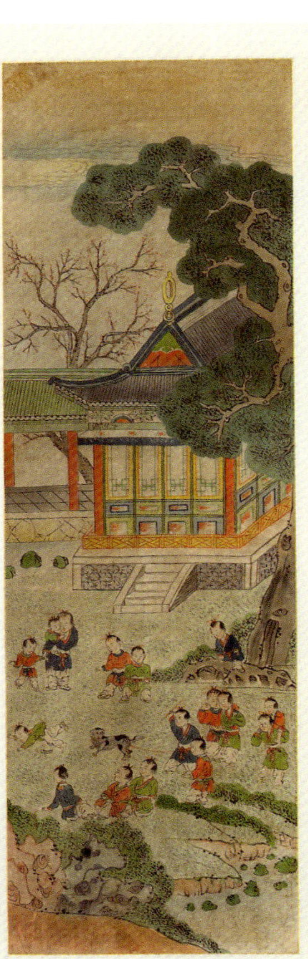
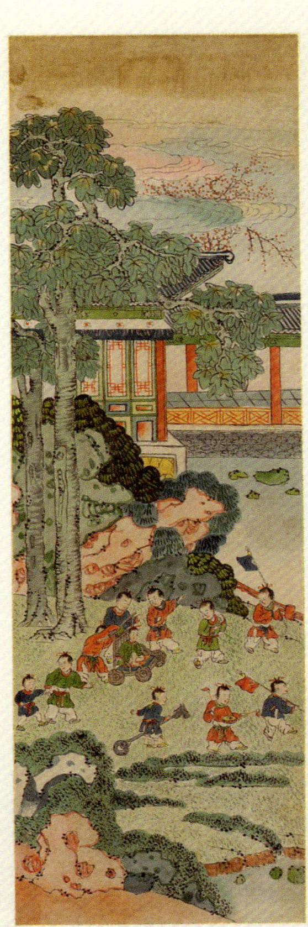
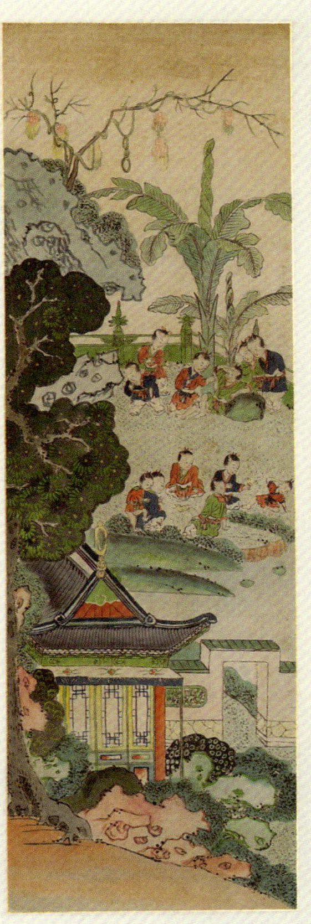

865. Lotus, Turtle, and Fish in Rondel

Joseon dynasty, late 19th century
Framed painting; ink and color on paper
37.5 x 37.6 cm (14 3/4 x 14 3/4 in.)

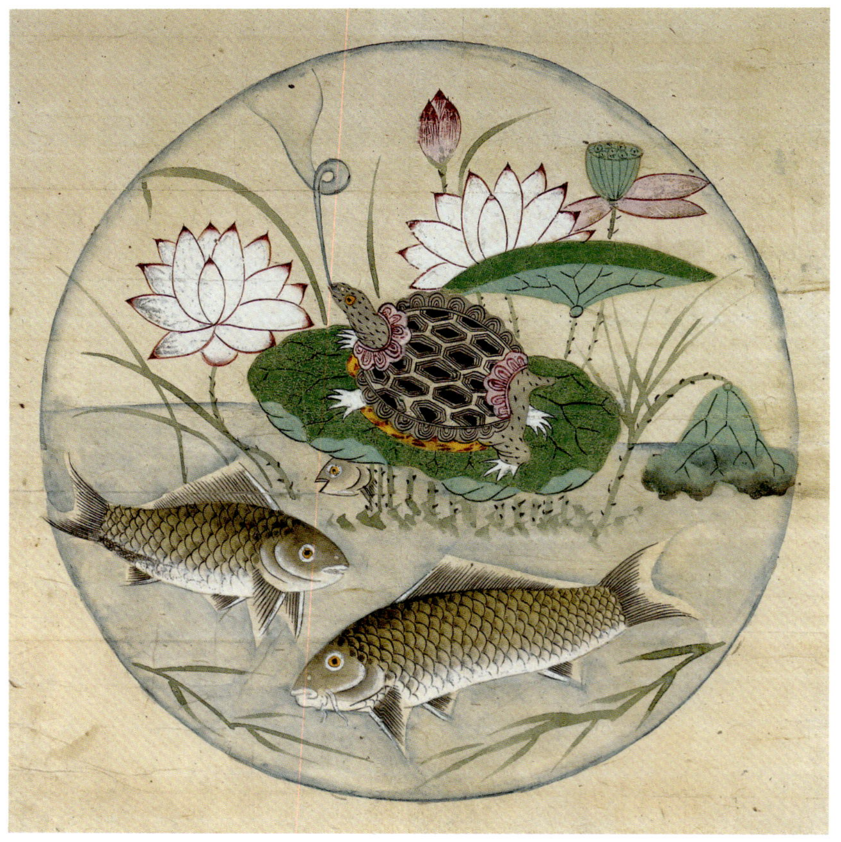

866. Dog Treeing a Cat

Joseon dynasty, 19th century
Framed painting; ink on paper
52.9 x 40.1 cm (20 7/8 x 15 3/4 in.)

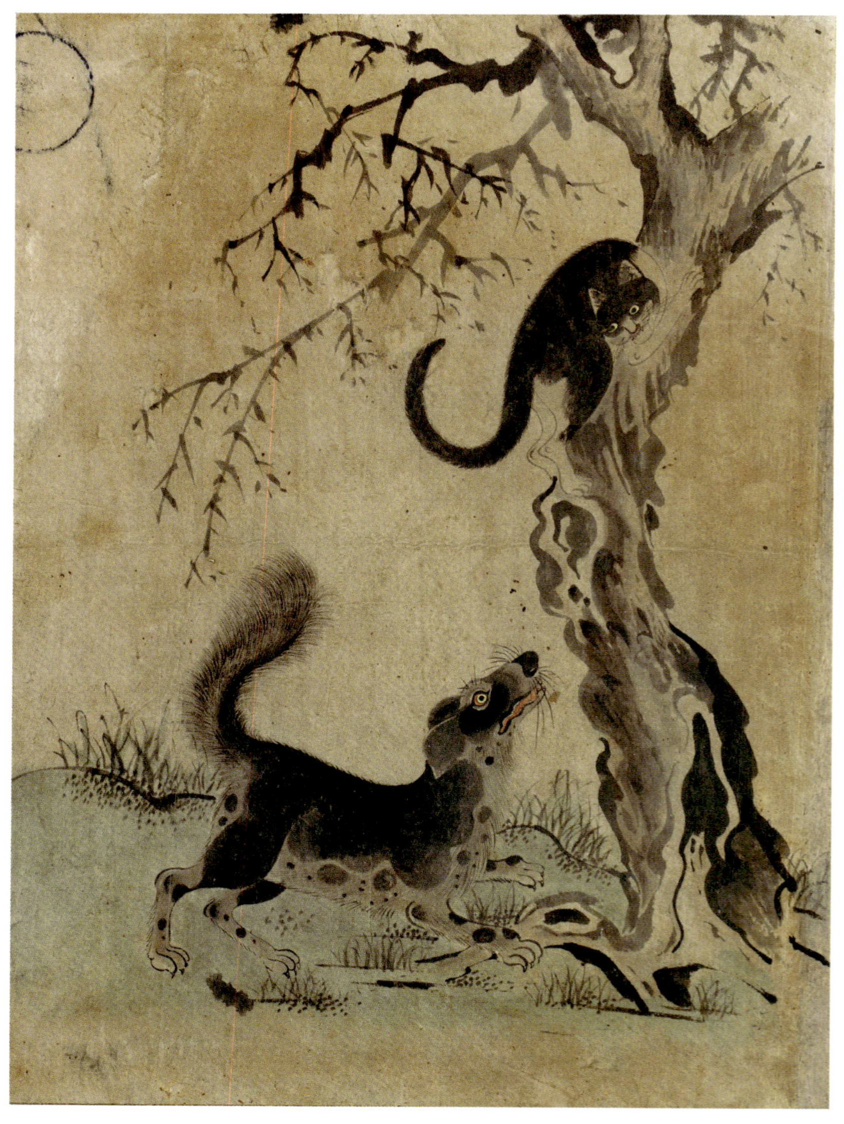

Kim Gyujin
(金圭鎭; 1868–1933)

867. Orchids in Hanging Basket

Early 20th century
Hanging scroll; ink on paper
138 x 42 cm ($54\frac{3}{8}$ x $16\frac{1}{2}$ in.)
Text, signature, seals

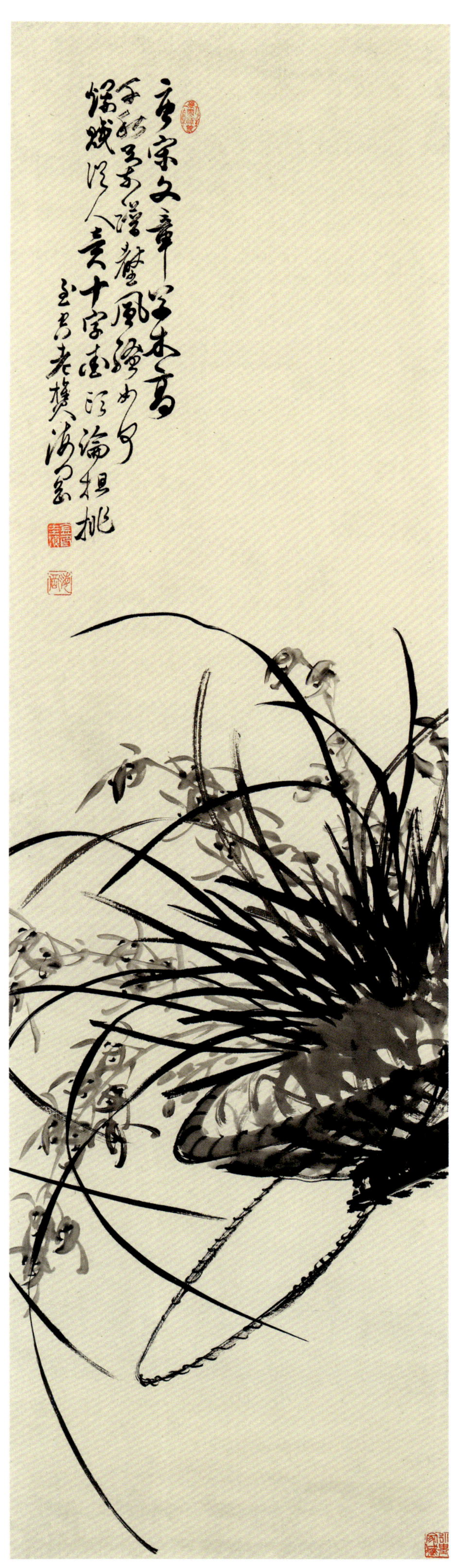

Korean Paintings Details

No illustrated items

859. Shakyamuni (Seokka) Triad

Text

One day in the First Moon in the forty-fourth year of the Jiajing reign [1565], *Our Majesty, Great Queen Dowager Seongryeol Inmyeong Daewang Daebi, wishes that His Noble Majesty the King will enjoy a life of ten thousand years. How boundless is the King's benevolence! It surpasses [that of Emperor Wu, who] "let loose all trapped animals." How great is the King's [wise] rule! It aspires to the [ancient sages' art of governing by the] recording method of "knotted cords." Blessed will he be with countless children. How noble is Her Majesty's birth! She understood [everything] from the time of her birth. How divine is Her Majesty the Queen's birth! Heaven endowed her with brightness. [Thus the Great Queen Dowager] released a fund from the royal treasury to order* yanggong [skilled artists] *to paint Seokka [Shakyamuni], Mireuk [Maitreya], Mita [Amitabha], [all with attendant] bodhisattvas, fifty of each in gold and fifty in color, totaling four hundred in number. They were all splendidly assembled for the ceremony celebrating the restoration of the Hoeam-sa, accompanied by the "eye-dotting" rite. All were ordered to worship them day and night and to offer incense to aid all the people of the kingdom to avoid falling into the trap of being disloyal subjects. Her Majesty's virtue is like the unfathomable ocean. It is truly immeasurable. How admirable! Respectfully inscribed by Cheongpyeong sanin Naam.*

嘉靖四十四年正月日惟我聖烈仁明大王大妃殿下爲主上殿下聖躬萬歲仁踰鮮網治踵結繩螽羽蟄蟄燐趾振振王妃殿下頂娠生和脇誕天縱恭捐帑寶爰命良工釋迦彌勒藥師彌陀百補処俱各金画五十彩画五十幷四百幀莊嚴畢備謹當檜岩重修慶席依法點眼領諸道人使之禮敬於朝夕常以華封之祝堯爲山家務免墮不忠之坑其聖德化海可勝螽測於戲至歟清平山人懶庵敬跋

860. *Bamboo in the Wind*

Text

[at top] *Lord Seogyang's Stylistic Principle* 石陽風條 [Seogyang is the artist's royal title]

[Poem]

Old Bamboo, long and short, all mixed. / The leaves lift simultaneously as the breeze comes. / Calm and restrained is their posture, so impressive as to move people. / Their remaining echo is found nowhere else. // Composed by Changrang, written [transcribed] by Junghwa for Daerae

老竹故參差
風枝一時擧
蕭疎欲動人
遺響覓無處
滄浪作仲和爲大來書

Signature

[on painting] *Taneun* 灘隱 [artist's pen name]

Seal

[at top] *Myeonggok* 明谷
[on painting] *Taneun* 灘隱

867. Orchids in Hanging Basket

Text

Many volumes from Tang to Song dynasties have exalted the plants. / Still, ancient paintings and writings on orchids even surpass Shijing and Lisao. / Having handed over my brilliant verse (i.e., painting of orchid) / why not venture out into the streets and critique its quality (see how it compares to ancient works on orchids).

唐宋文章草木高
千秋蘭譜壓風騷如何
爛賦從人賣十字街頭論担挑

Signature

Jigong nocho Haegang 至空老樵海岡

Seals

[right of inscription] *Life's first* [i.e., highest, number one] *joy* [i.e., that parents and siblings are alive and well]; *clear writing* 人生一樂 筆墨淸良
[below end of inscription, upper seal] *Kim Gyujin in* 金圭鎭印
[below end of inscription, lower seal] *Haegang* 海岡 [artist's pen name]
[bottom right of scroll] *Collection of the Yeonggi family* 永基家藏 [Kim Yeonggi (1911–2003) was the artist's son]

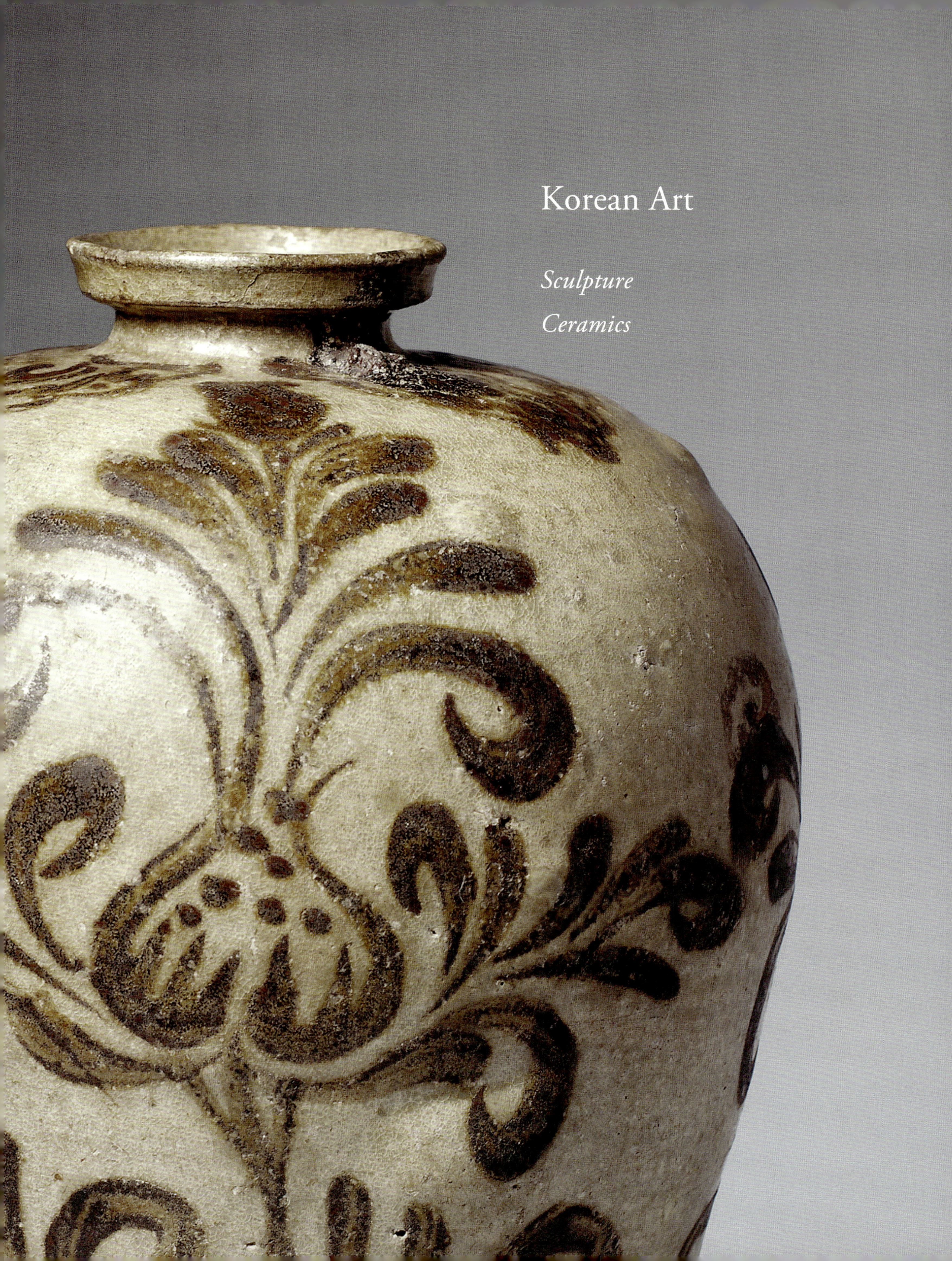

Korean Art

Sculpture

Ceramics

KOREAN SCULPTURE

868. Seated Bodhisattva (left attendant of a triad)

Joseon dynasty, mid-17th century
Gilded wood
H. 51.4 cm (20 1/4 in.)

LITERATURE: Lee 2004.

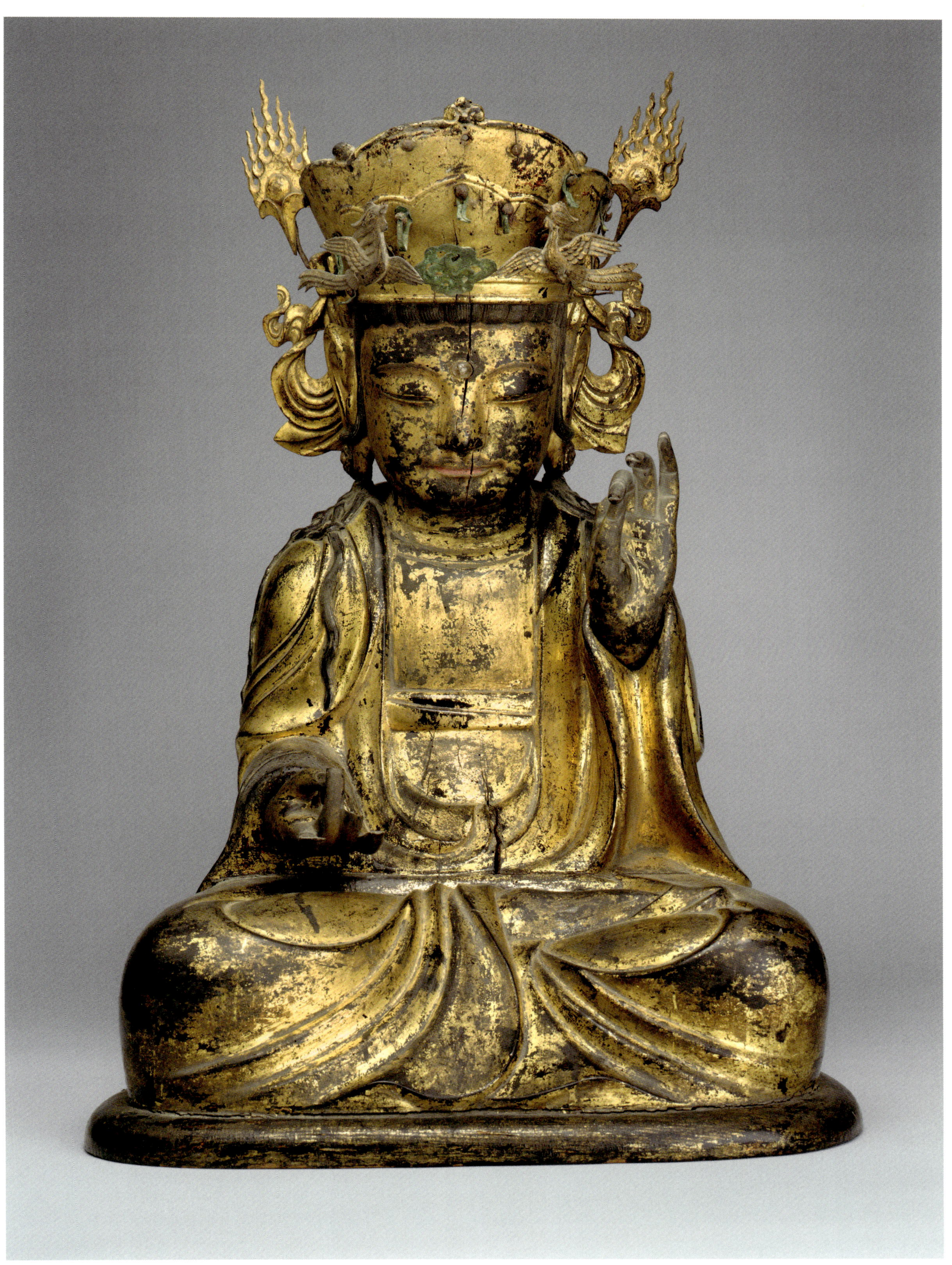

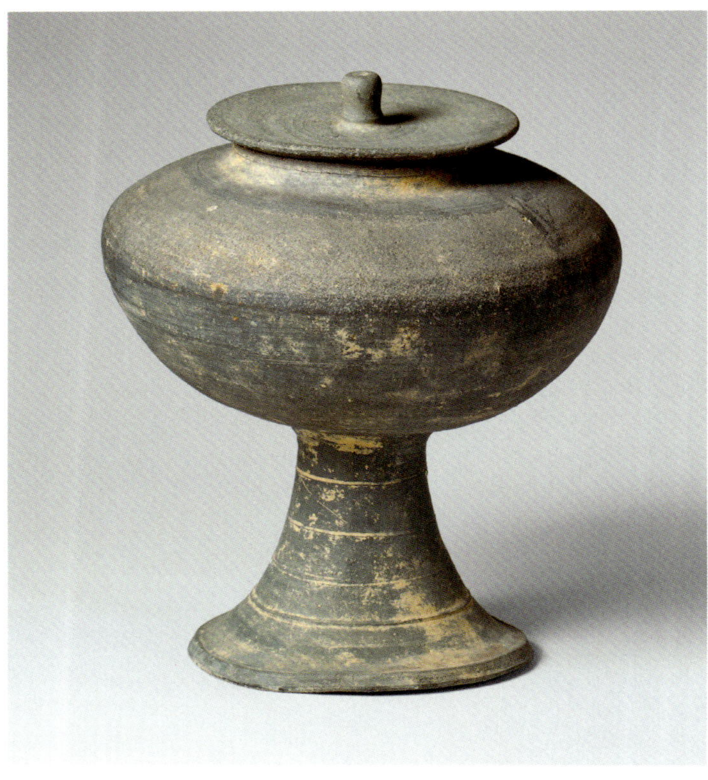

869

869. Lidded bowl with tall base

Three Kingdoms period, Gaya federation (42–562), first half of 6th century
Stoneware; lid is not original
H. 21.5 cm (8½ in.), diam. 9 cm (3½ in.)

870. Cup with handle

Three Kingdoms period, Silla kingdom, 5th century
Stoneware
H. 10.5 cm (4⅛ in.), diam. 10 cm (3⅞ in.)

871. Long-necked jar

Three Kingdoms period, Silla kingdom, first half of 5th century
Stoneware with incidental ash glaze
H. 19 cm (7½ in.), diam. 14 cm (5½ in.)

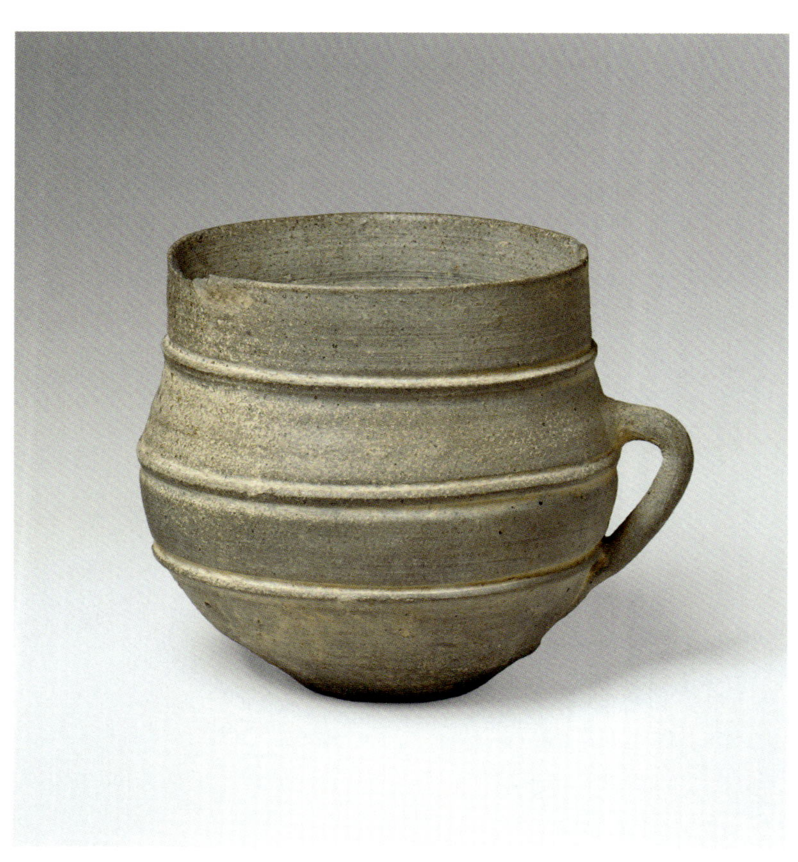

870

871

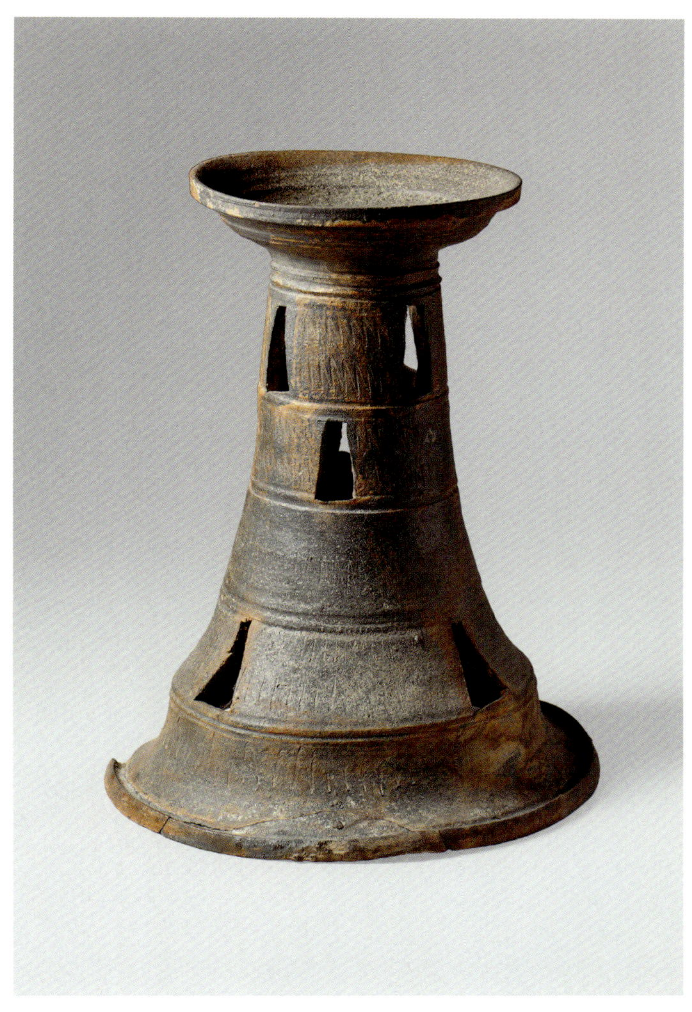

872

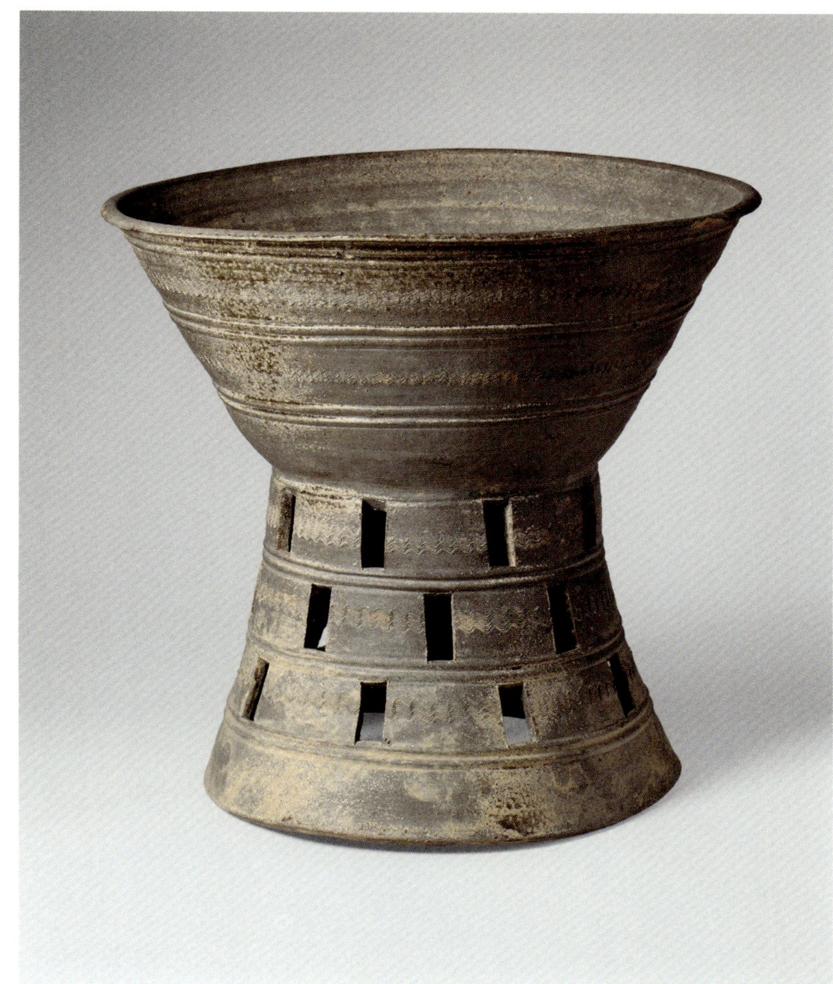

873

872. Shallow stand with tall, perforated base

Three Kingdoms period, 5th century
Stoneware with incised design
H. 34 cm (13 3/8 in.), diam. 17.6 cm (6 7/8 in.)

873. Stand with tall, perforated base

Three Kingdoms period, Silla kingdom, first half of 5th century
Stoneware with incised design of wavy lines
H. 34 cm (13 3/8 in.), diam. 36.7 cm (14 1/2 in.)

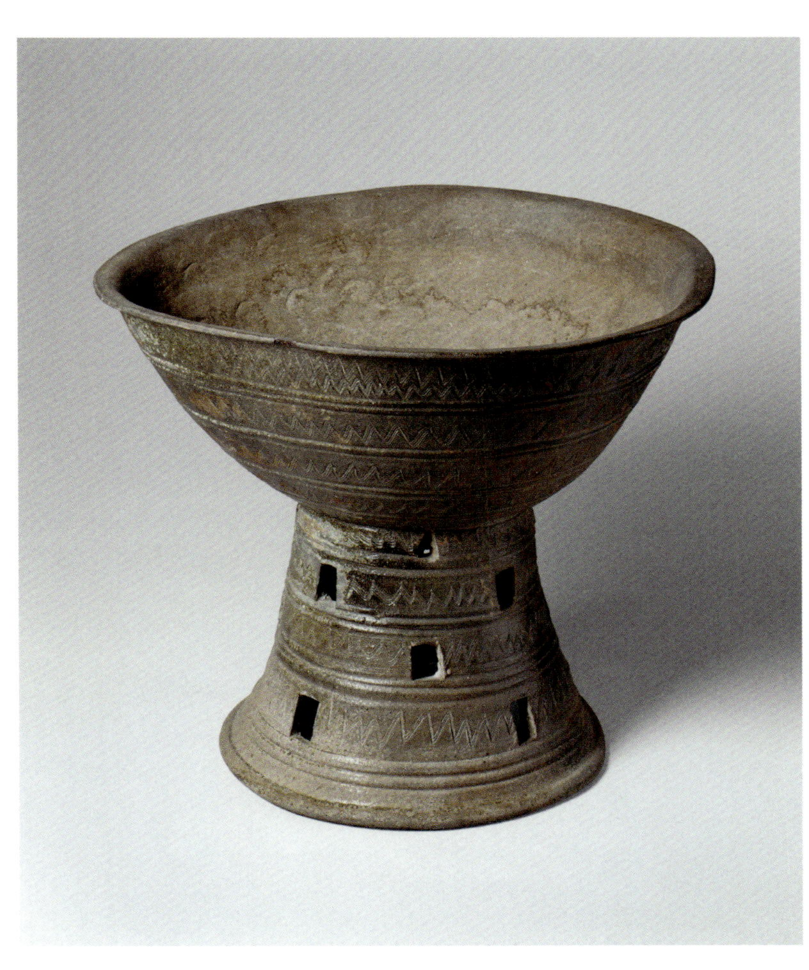

874. Stand with tall, perforated base

Three Kingdoms period, Silla kingdom, second half of 5th century; from Daegu
Stoneware with incised design and incidental ash glaze
H. 27 cm (10 5/8 in.), diam. 32.3 cm (12 3/4 in.)

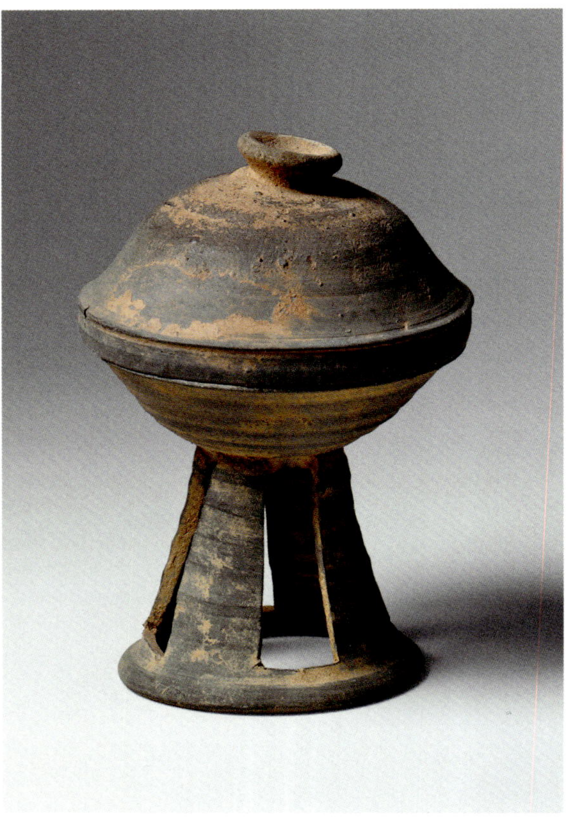

875

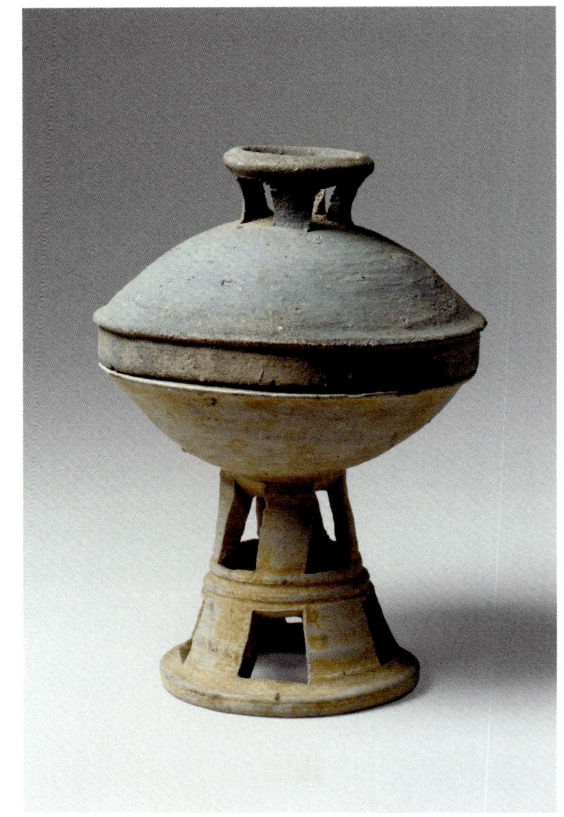

876

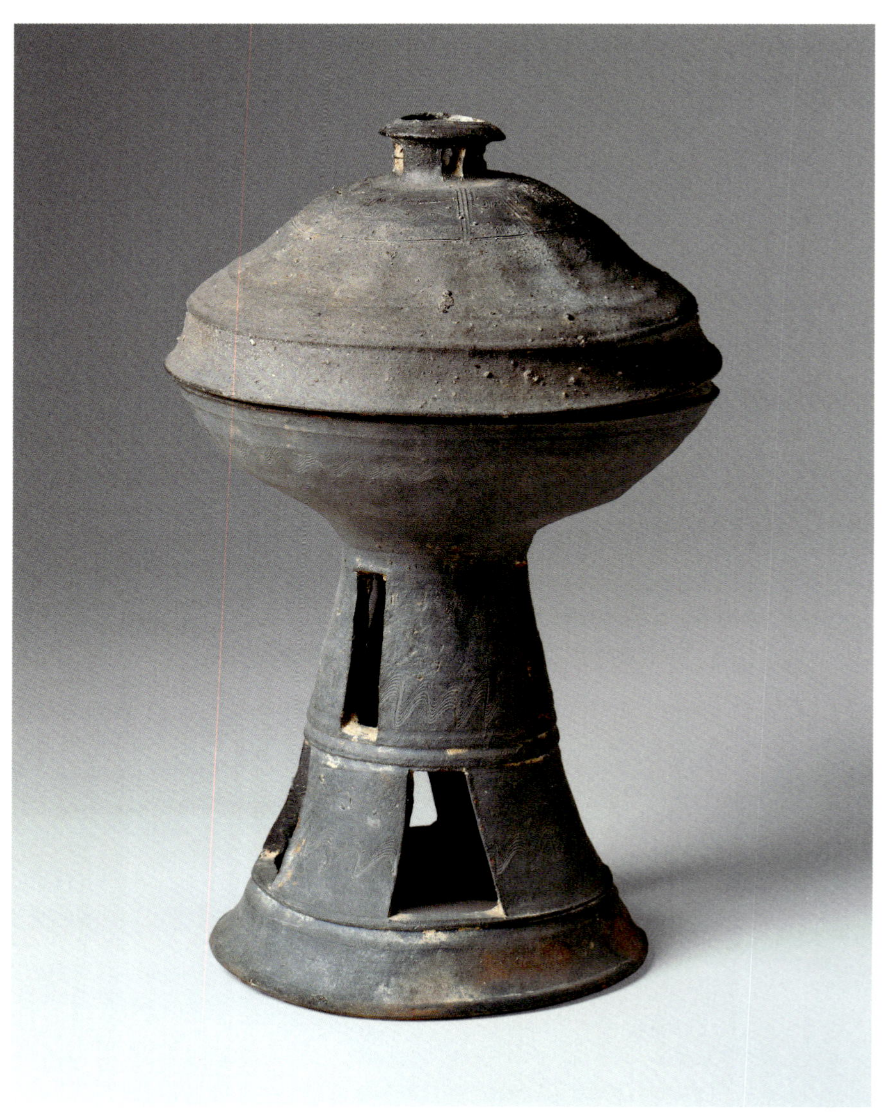

875. Lidded dish with tall, perforated base

Three Kingdoms period, Silla kingdom, second half of 5th century; from Gyeongju
Stoneware
H. 17.5 cm (6⅞ in.), diam. 11 cm (4⅜ in.)

876. Lidded dish with tall, perforated base

Three Kingdoms period, Silla kingdom, second half of 5th century; from Gyeongju
Stoneware
H. 17 cm (6¾ in.), diam. 10.6 cm (4⅛ in.)

877. Lidded dish with tall, perforated base

Three Kingdoms period, Silla kingdom, second half of 5th century; from Seongju
Stoneware with incised design of wavy lines
H. 25.5 cm (10 in.), diam. 14.2 cm (5⅝ in.)

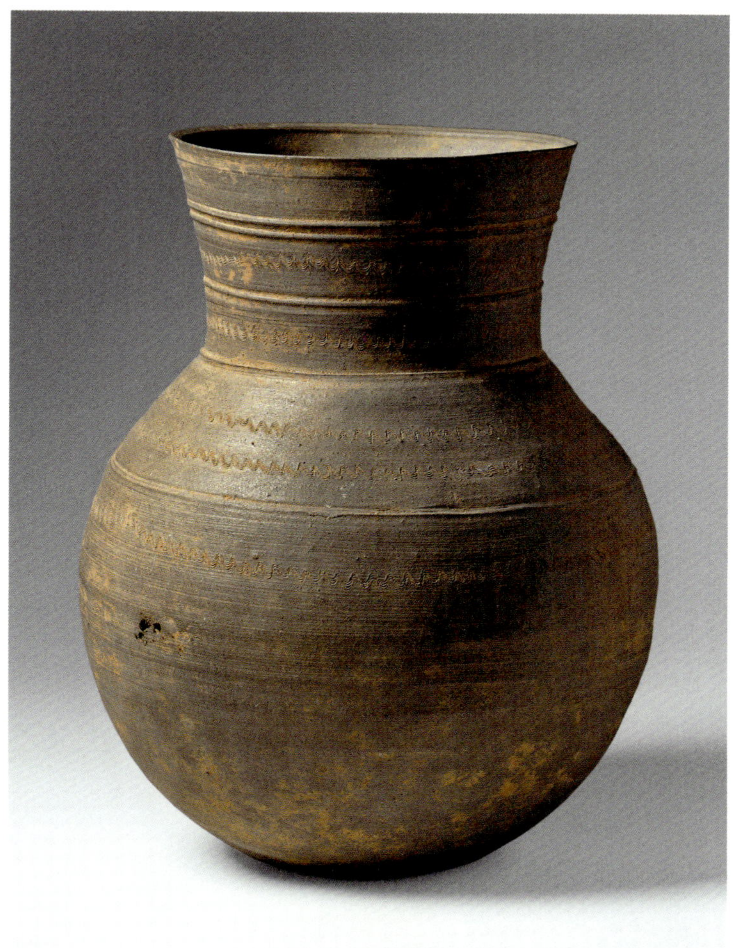

878

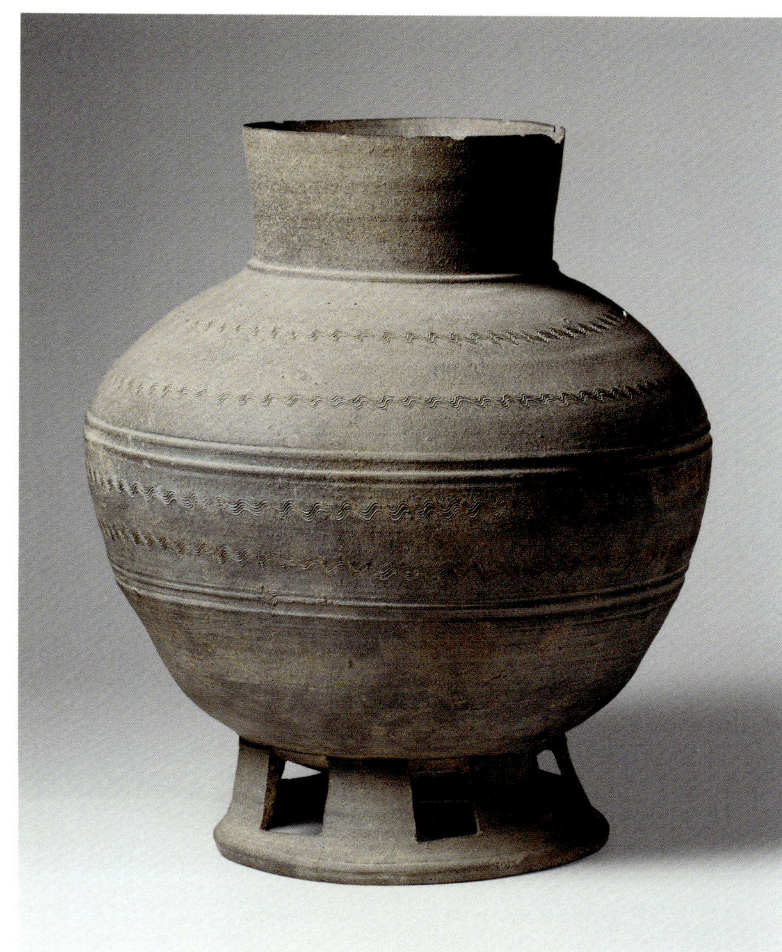

879

878. Long-necked jar

Three Kingdoms period, Silla kingdom, second half of 5th century
Stoneware with incised design of wavy lines
H. 32.6 cm (12 7/8 in.), diam. 18.2 cm (7 1/8 in.)

879. Long-necked jar with perforated base

Three Kingdoms period, Silla kingdom, second half of 5th century; from Gyeongju
Stoneware with incised design of wavy lines
H. 31.7 cm (12 1/2 in.), diam. 14.2 cm (5 5/8 in.)

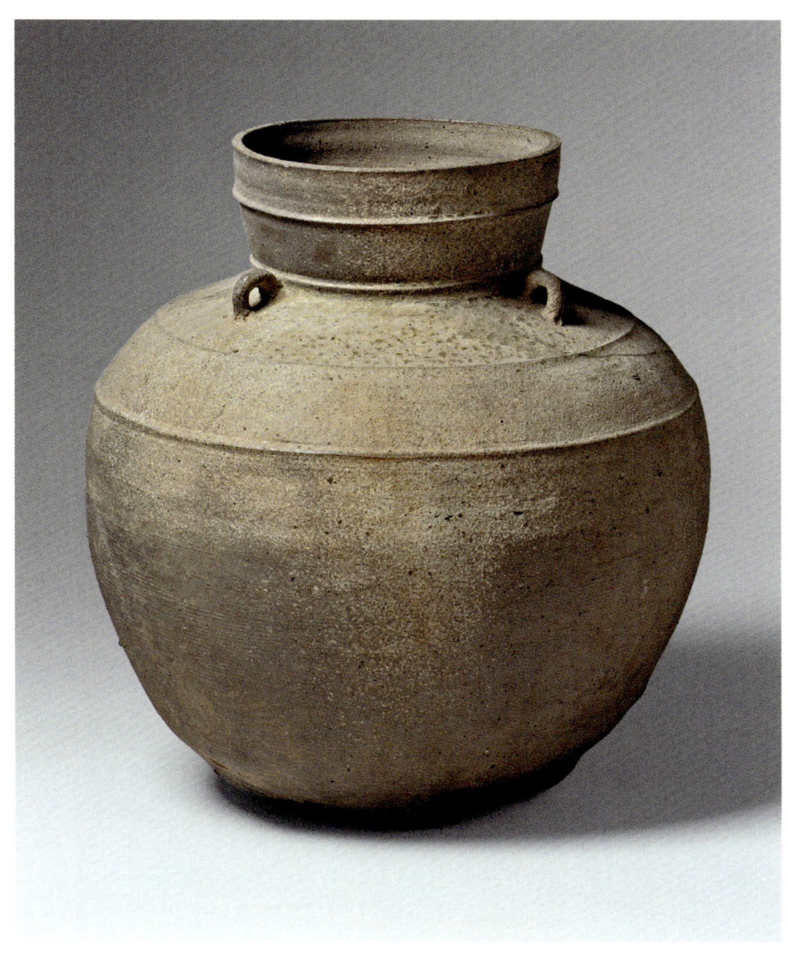

880. Long-necked jar with three loop-handles

Three Kingdoms period, Silla kingdom, second half of 5th century
Stoneware with incidental ash glaze
H. 30 cm (11 3/4 in.), diam. 15 cm (5 7/8 in.)

881. Jar

Three Kingdoms period, Silla kingdom, late 5th–early 6th century
Stoneware with incidental ash glaze
H. 18.1 cm (7 1/8 in.), diam. 12 cm (4 3/4 in.)

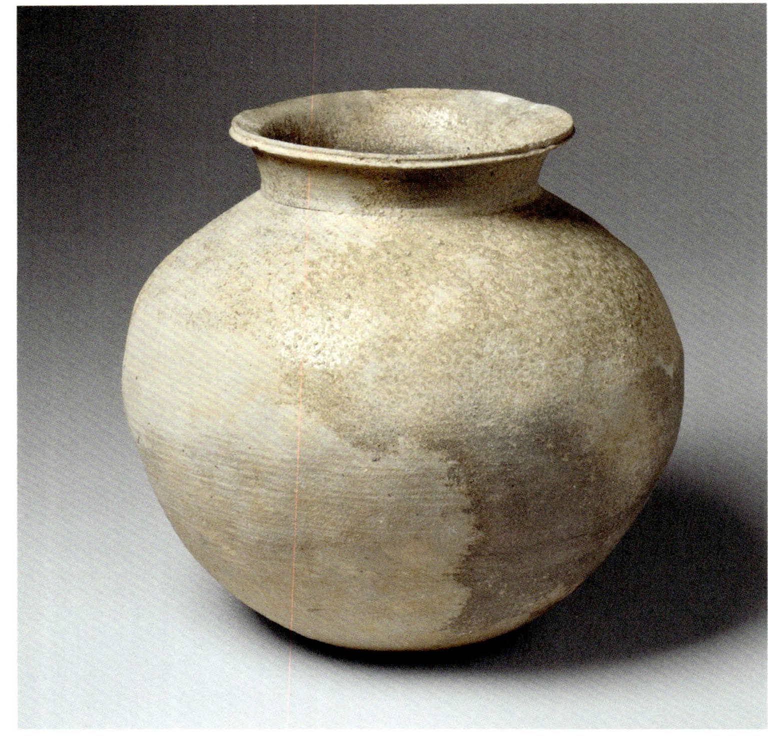

882. Small lidded jar with handle

Three Kingdoms period, Silla kingdom, second half of 5th century
Earthenware
H. 11.5 cm (4 1/2 in.), diam. 7.5 cm (3 in.)

Gift from Keum Ja Kang, 1986

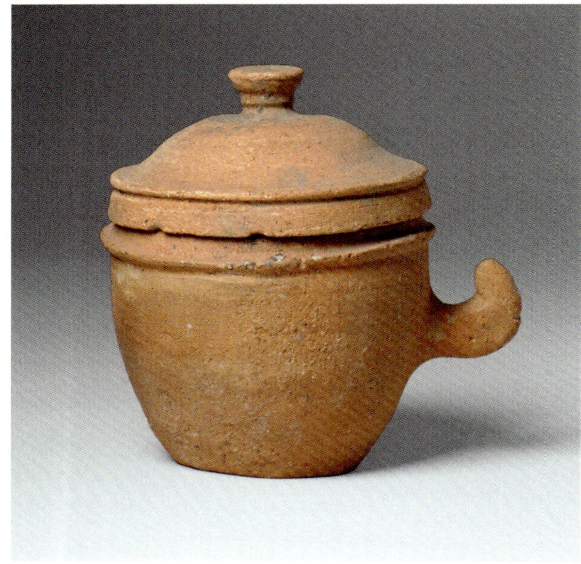

883. Jar with four knobs

Three Kingdoms period, Silla kingdom, late 5th–early 6th century; from Daegu-Uiseong region
Stoneware with incised design
H. 19.7 cm (7 3/4 in.), diam. 11 cm (4 3/8 in.)

884. Jar with three knobs

Three Kingdoms period, Silla kingdom, late 5th–early 6th century; from Daegu-Uiseong region
Stoneware with incised design
H. 19.5 cm (7 5/8 in.), diam. 11.4 cm (4 1/2 in.)

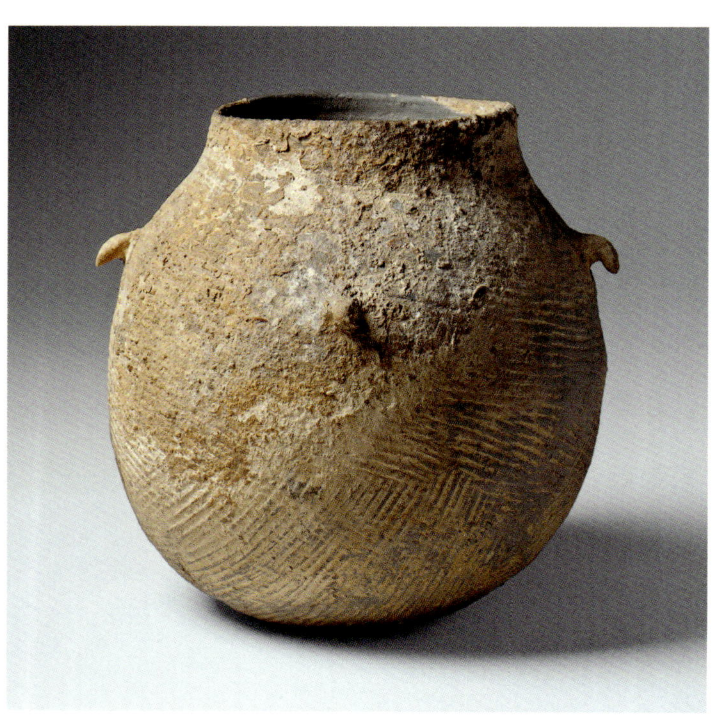

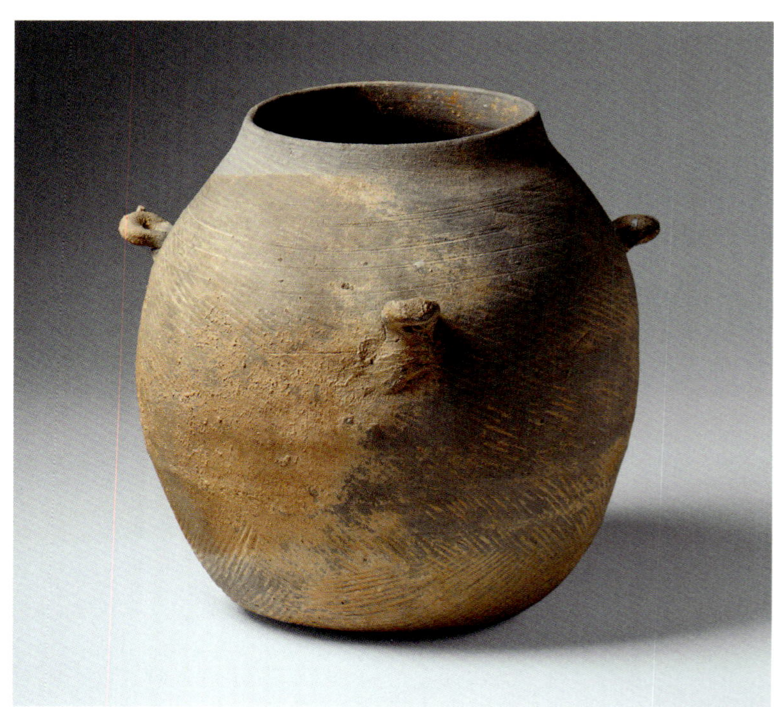

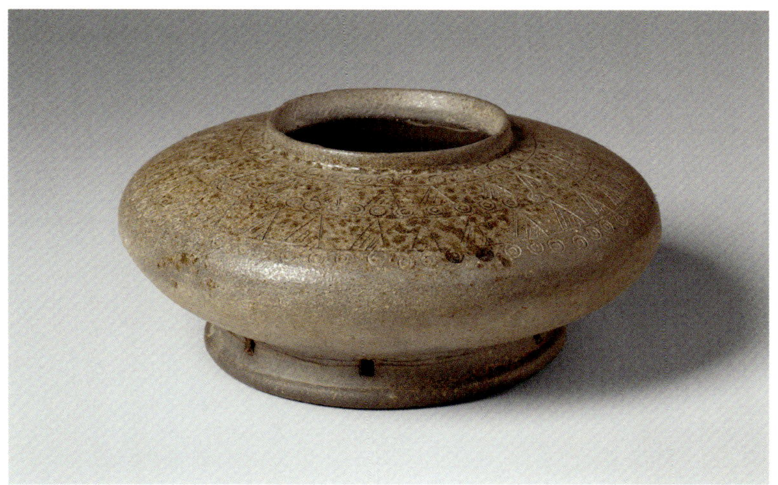

885. Small jar with perforated base

Unified Silla period, late 6th–early 7th century
Stoneware with stamped and incised design and incidental ash glaze
H. 9 cm (3 1/2 in.), diam. 9.2 cm (3 5/8 in.)

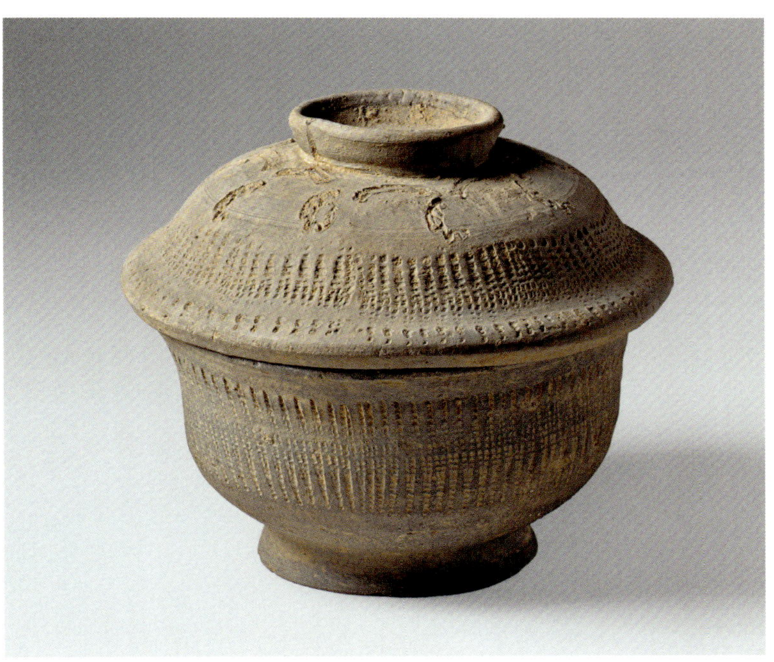

886. Covered bowl with abstract and geometric pattern

Unified Silla period, 7th–8th century
Stoneware with stamped and incised design
H. 14 cm (5 1/2 in.), diam. 16.5 cm (6 1/2 in.)

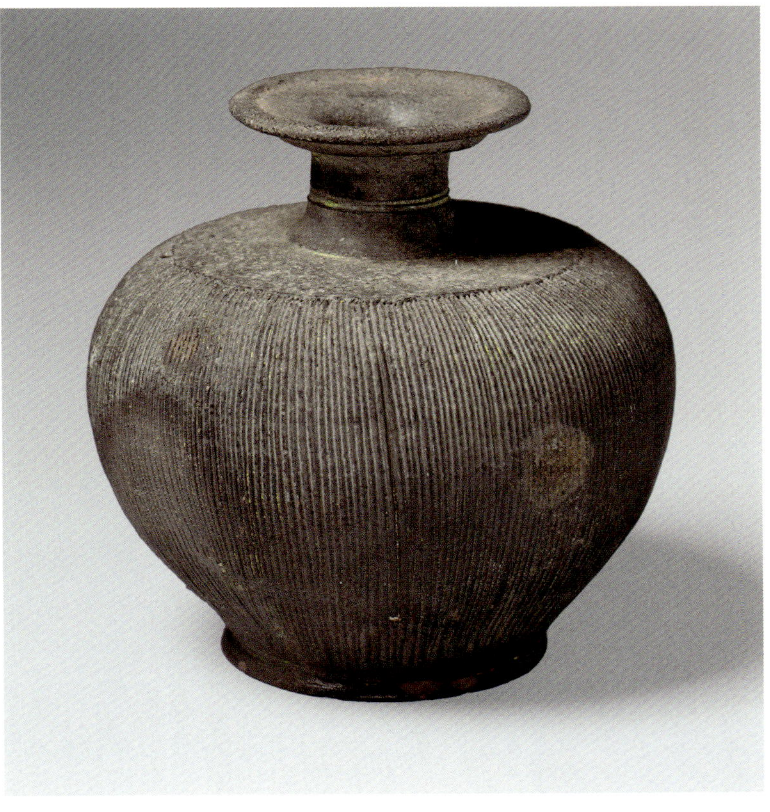

887. Bottle with flared mouth and combed pattern

Unified Silla period, 9th century
Stoneware with incidental ash glaze
H. 12 cm (4 3/4 in.)

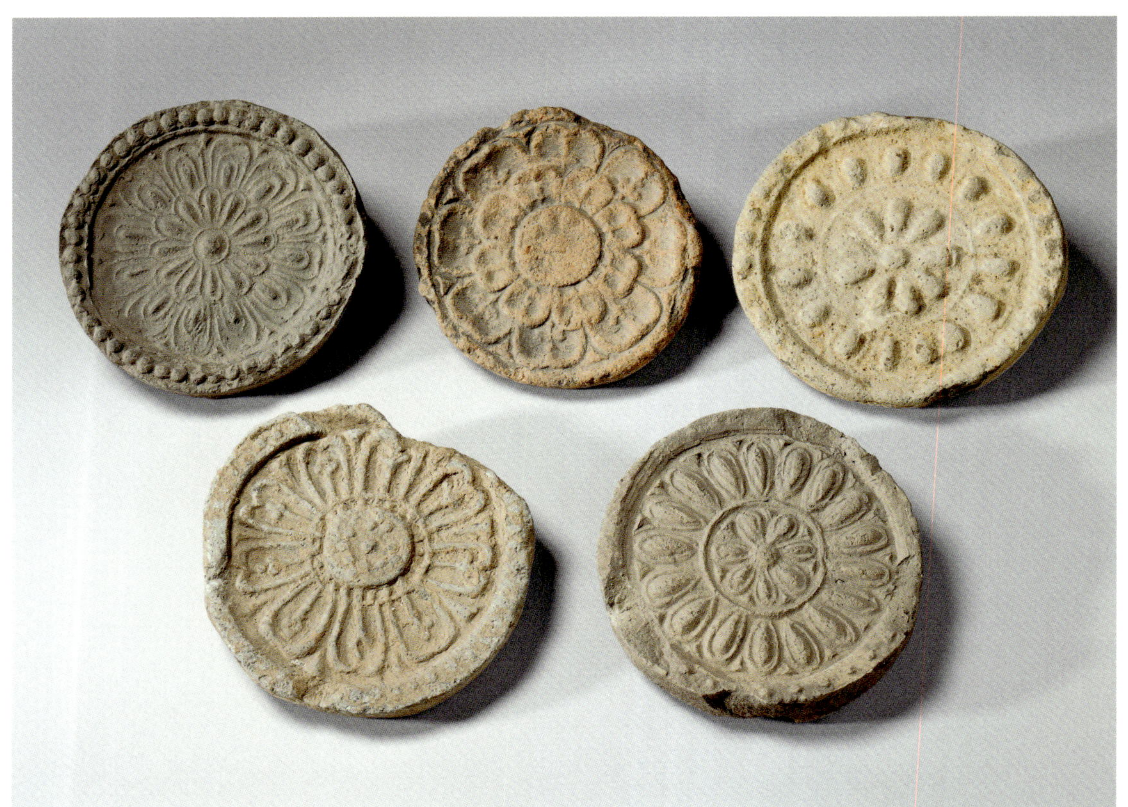

888

888. Five roof-end tiles with lotus

Unified Silla period
Stoneware
Various diameters: 14.7 cm ($5^{3}/_{4}$ in.); 15.5 cm ($6^{1}/_{8}$ in.); 13.5 cm ($5^{3}/_{8}$ in.); 14 cm ($5^{1}/_{2}$ in.); 14.2 cm ($5^{5}/_{8}$ in.)

889. Bottle with leaves

Goryeo dynasty, 11th century
Stoneware with iron-brown design under celadon glaze
H. 25 cm ($9^{7}/_{8}$ in.)

890. Bottle with leaves

Goryeo dynasty, 11th century
Stoneware with iron-brown design under celadon glaze
H. 27 cm ($10^{5}/_{8}$ in.)

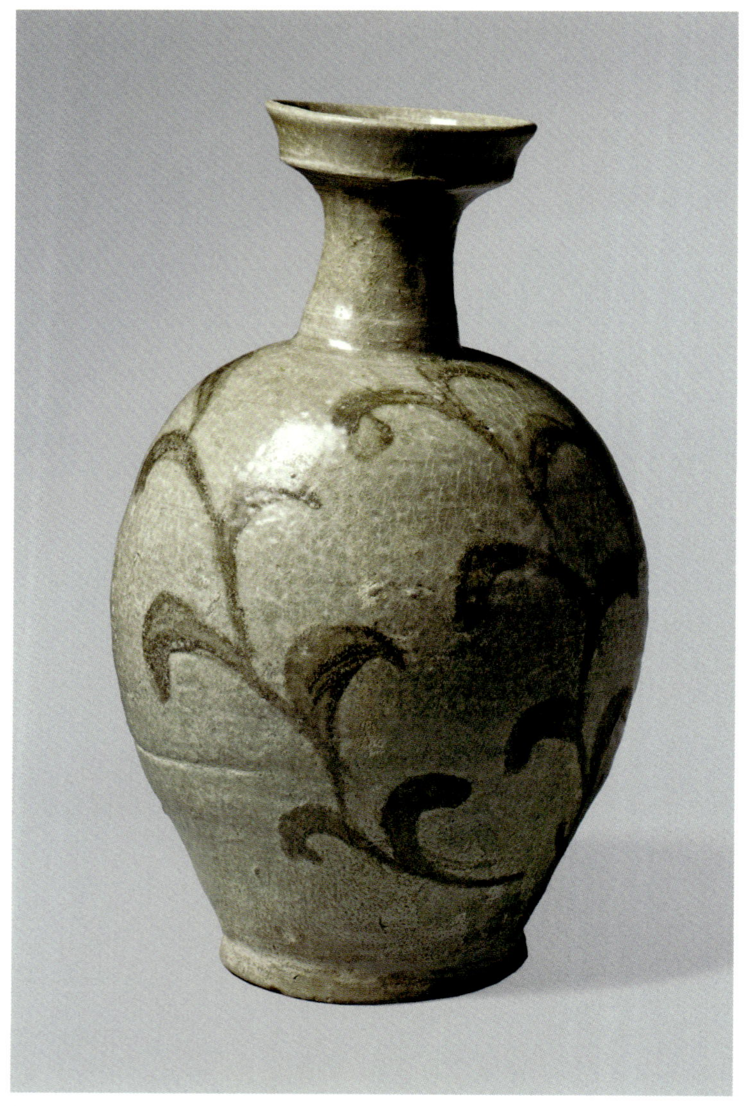

889

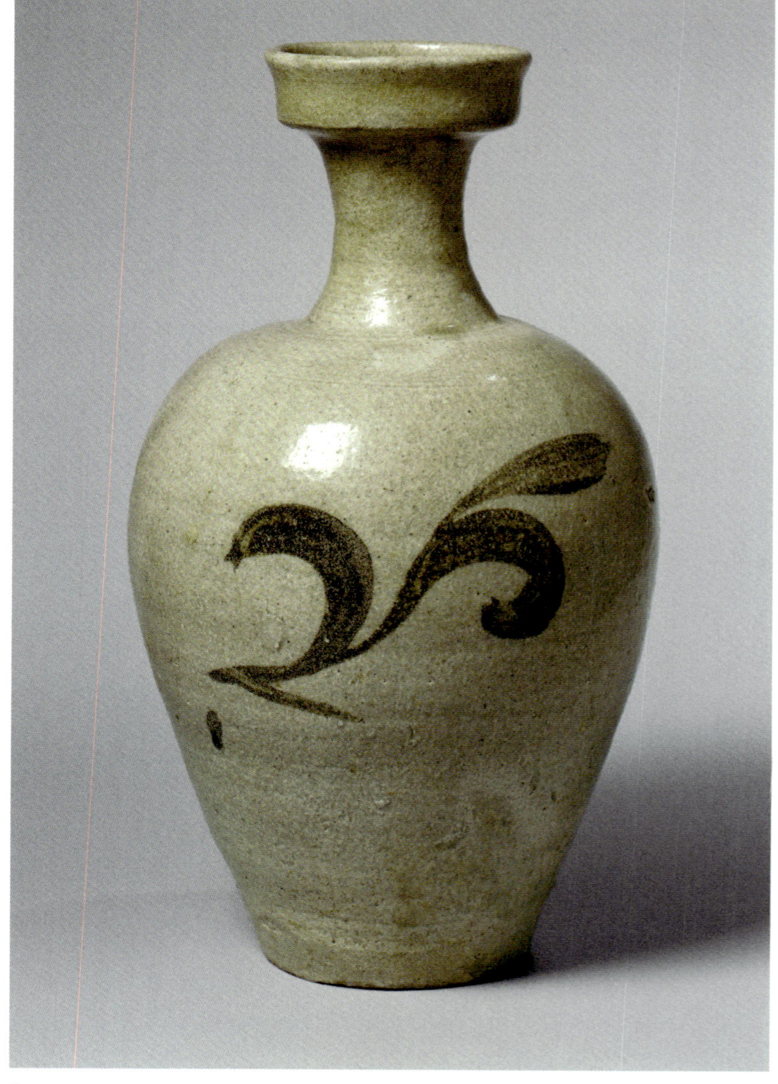

890

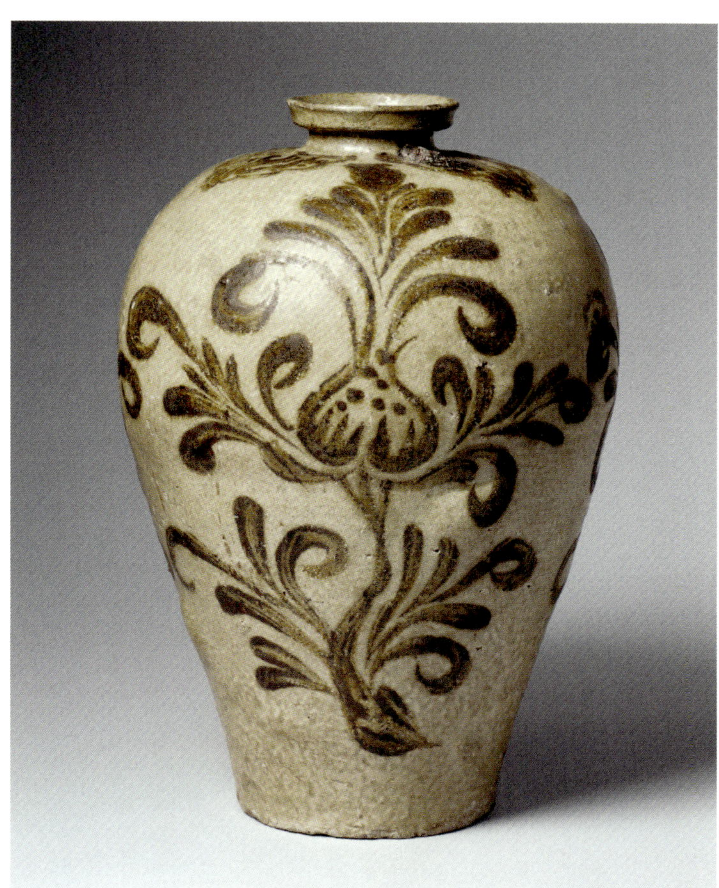

891. Maebyeong (梅瓶) with peonies

Goryeo dynasty, 11th–12th century
Stoneware with iron-brown design under celadon glaze
H. 24 cm (9½ in.)

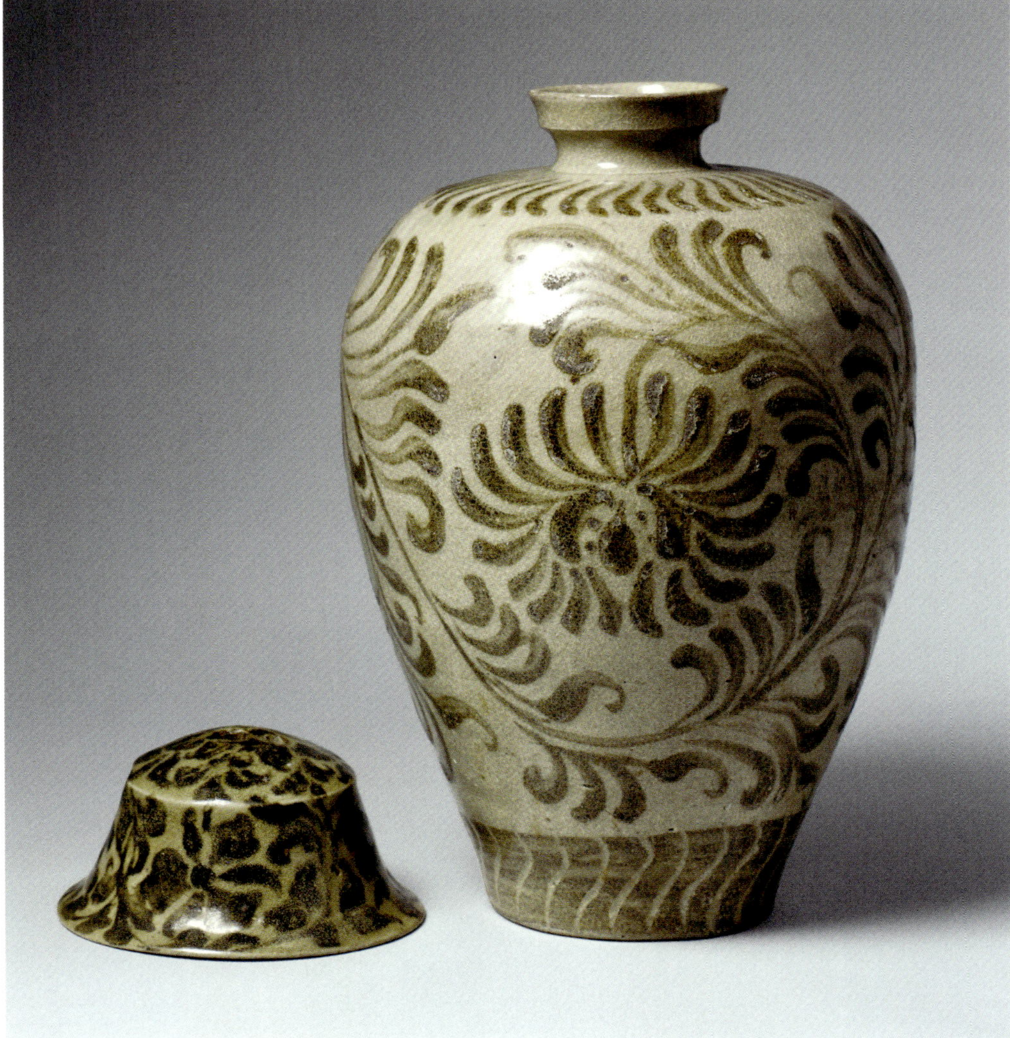

892. Maebyeong(梅瓶) with chrysanthemums

Goryeo dynasty, 11th–12th century
Stoneware with iron-brown design under celadon glaze; lid is of the period but not original
H. excluding lid 24 cm (9½ in.)

893. Bowl with lotus petals

Goryeo dynasty, first half of 12th century
Stoneware with carved design under celadon glaze
H. 5 cm (2 in.), diam. 15.9 cm ($6^1/_4$ in.)

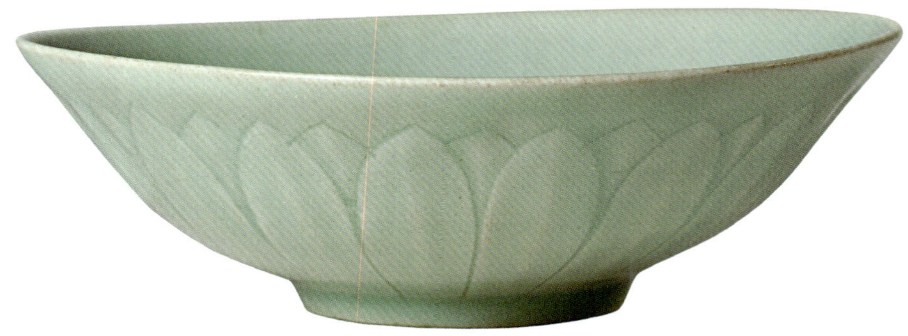

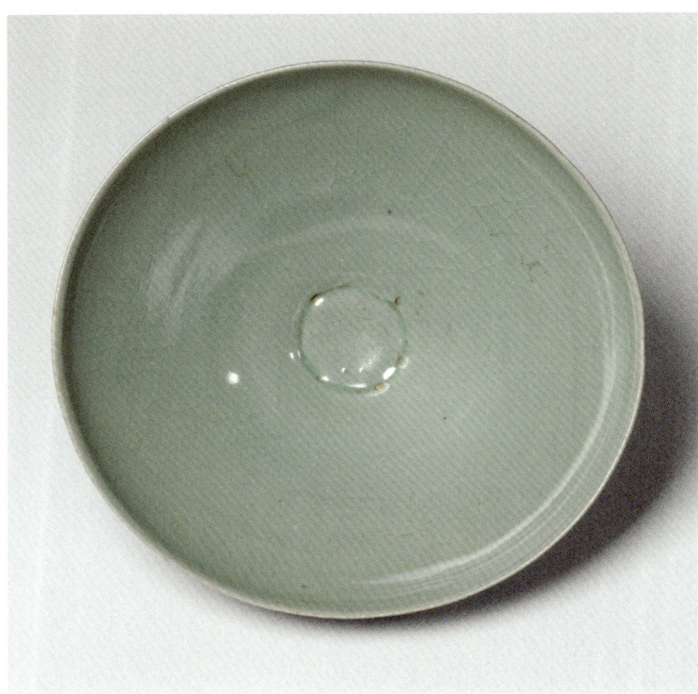

894, detail

894. Bowl with flying parrot

Goryeo dynasty, first half of 12th century
Stoneware with incised design under celadon glaze
H. 7.5 cm (3 in.), diam. 18 cm ($7^1/_8$ in.)

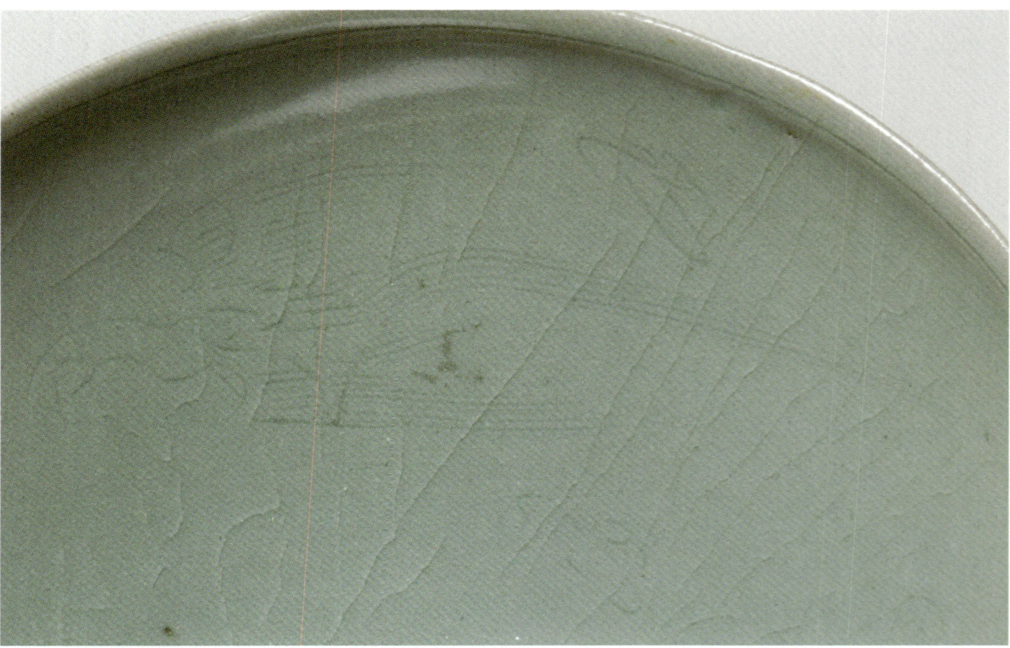

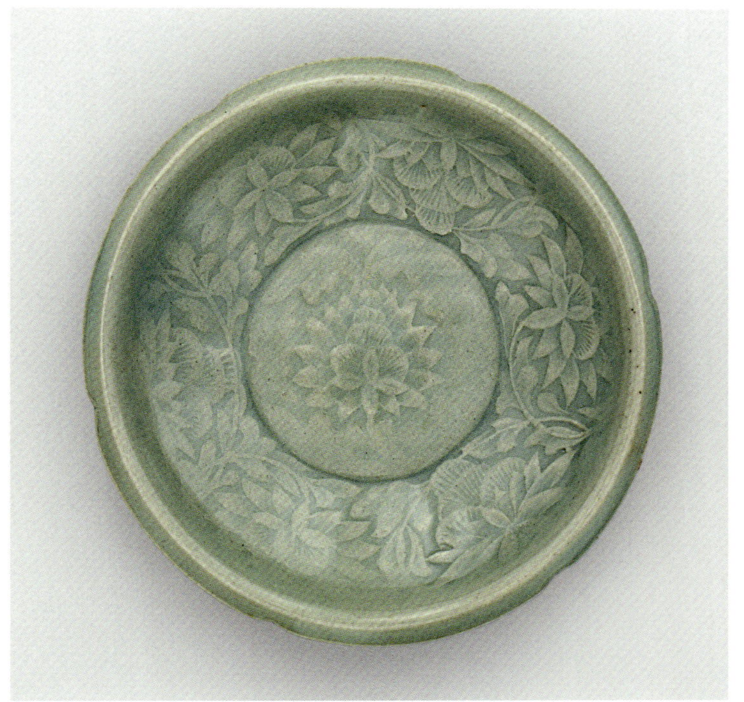

895. Small dish with foliate rim and peony

Goryeo dynasty, first half of 12th century
Stoneware with mold-impressed design under celadon glaze
H. 2.4 cm (1 in.), diam. 9.9 cm (3 7/8 in.)

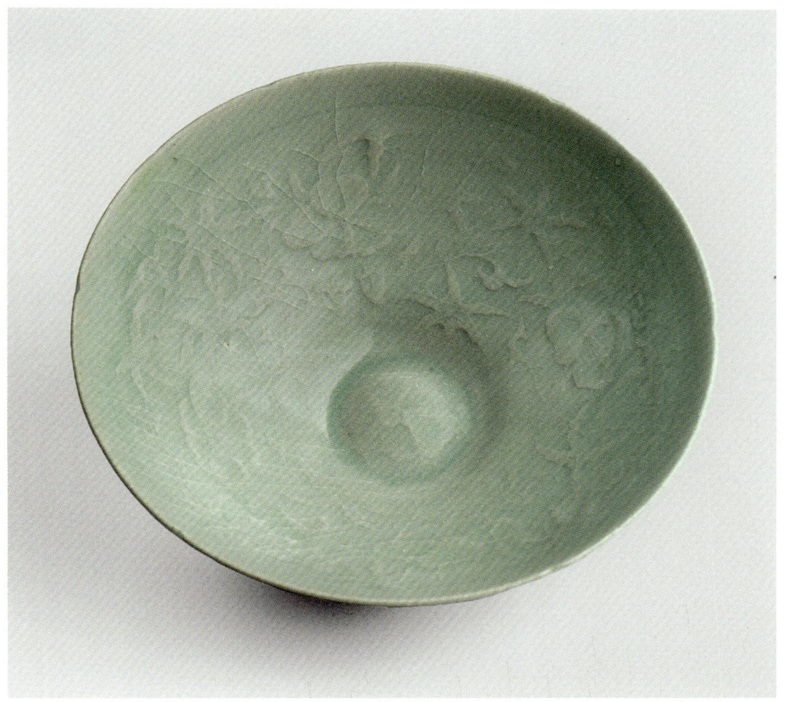

896. Bowl with floral design

Goryeo dynasty, first half of 12th century
Bowl with mold-impressed design under celadon glaze
H. 7 cm (2 3/4 in.), diam. 18.6 cm (7 3/8 in.)

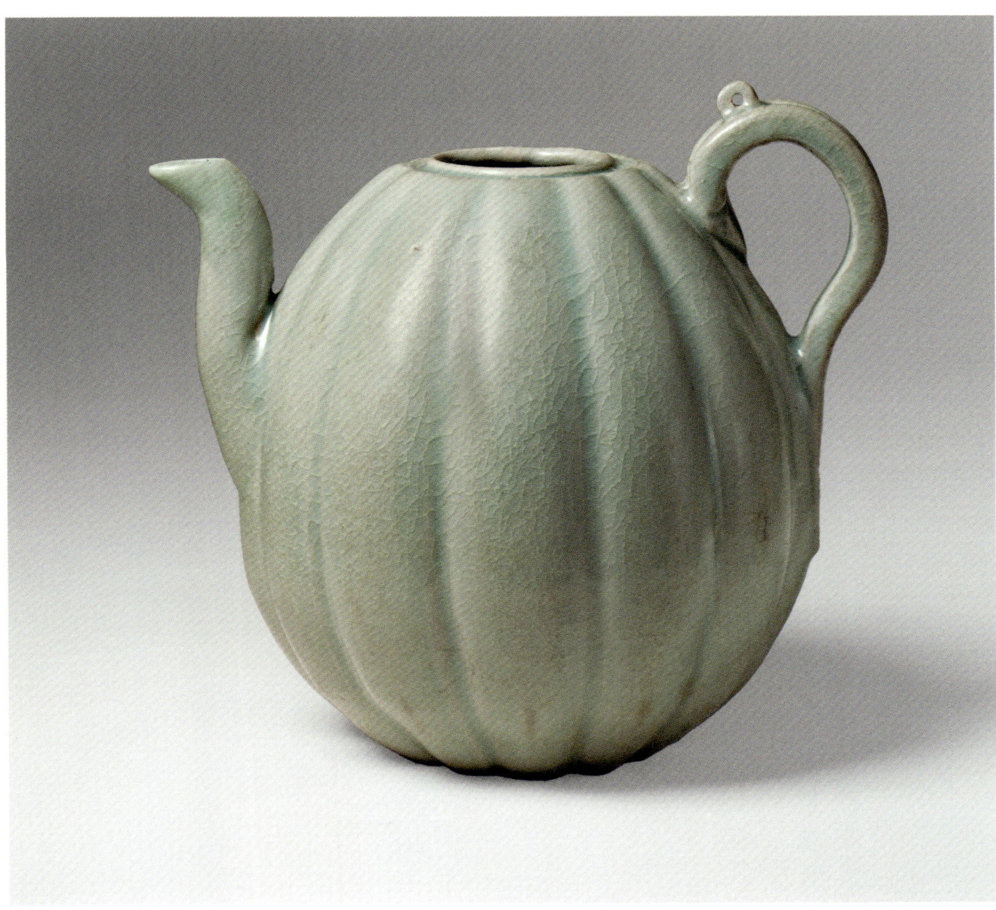

897. Ewer in the shape of a melon

Goryeo dynasty, first half of 12th century
Stoneware with celadon glaze; lid missing
H. (to highest point on handle) 18.8 cm (7 3/8 in.)

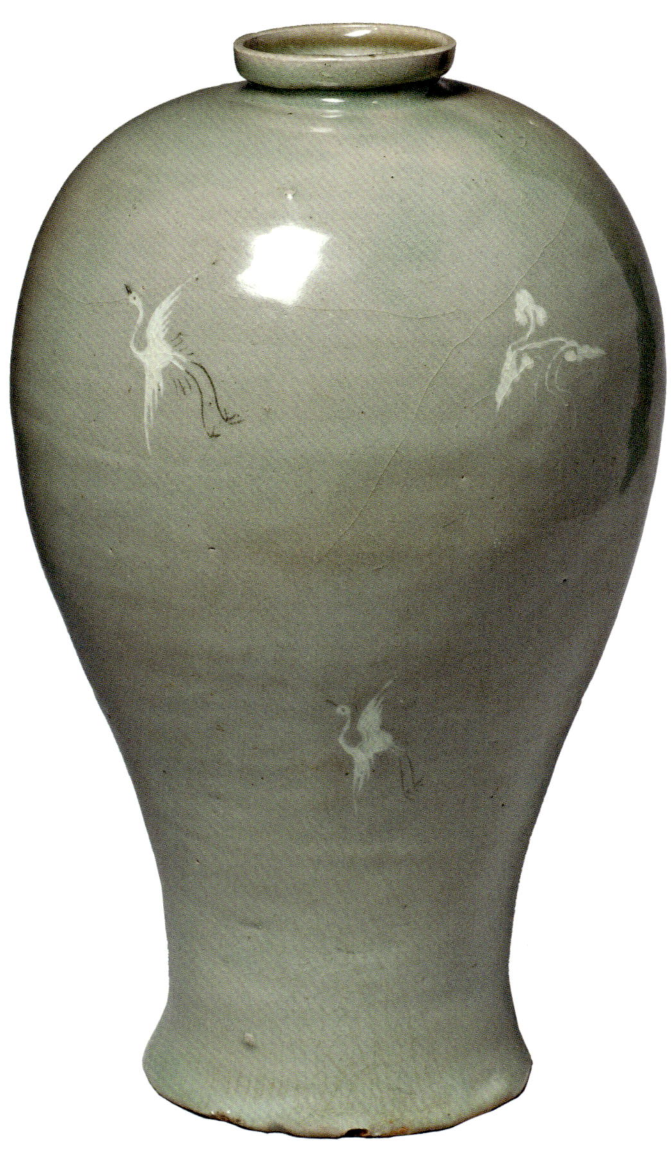

898. Maebyeong (梅瓶) with flying cranes and clouds

Goryeo dynasty, 12th century
Stoneware with inlaid design under celadon glaze
H. 31.6 cm (12½ in.)

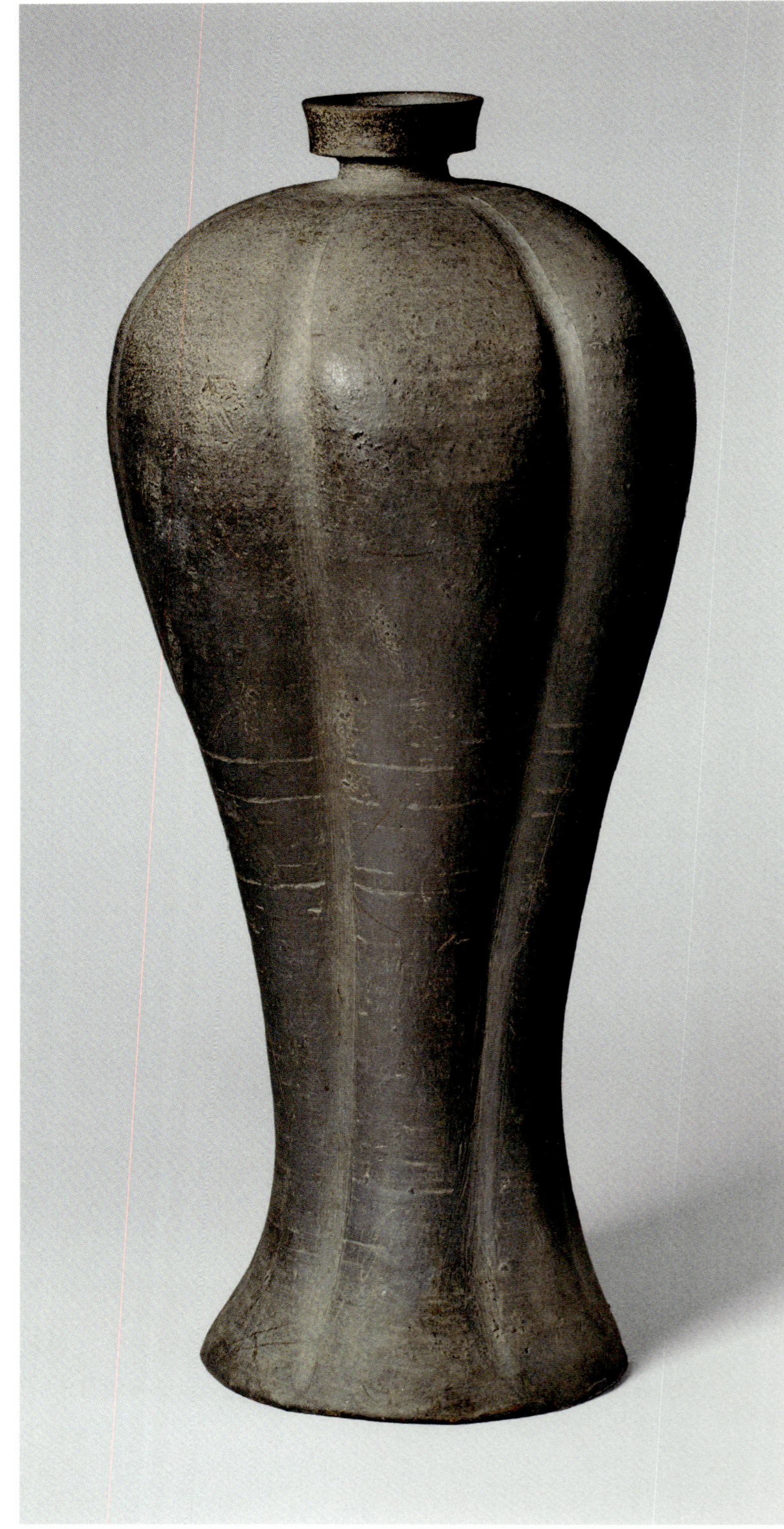

899. Maebyeong (梅瓶)

Goryeo dynasty, 13th century
Stoneware with incidental ash glaze
H. 45.7 cm (18 in.)

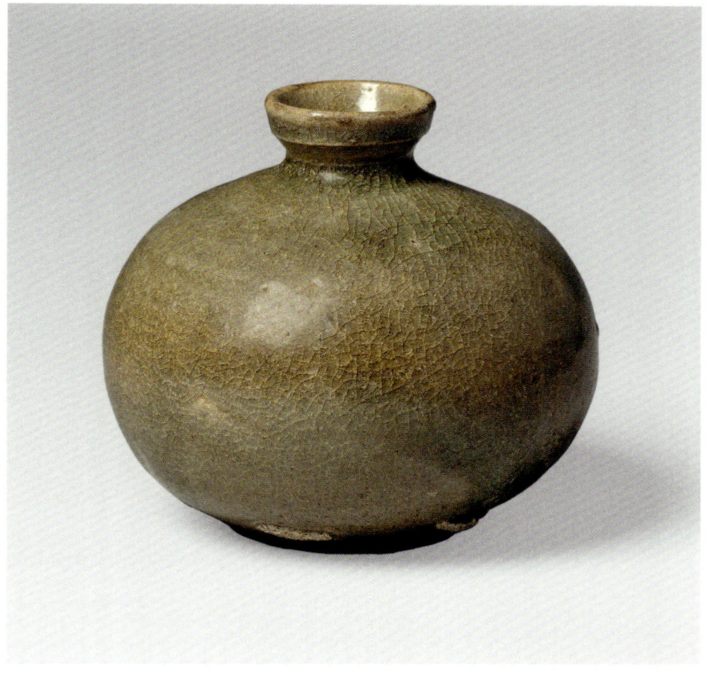

900

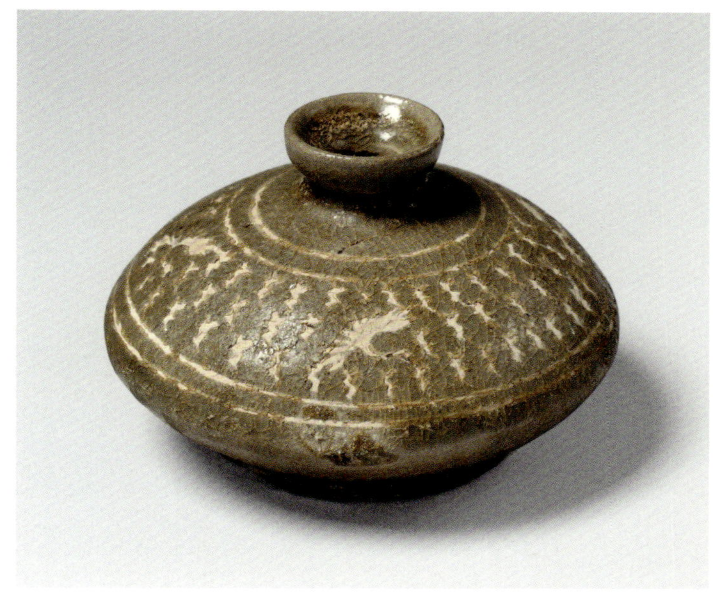

901

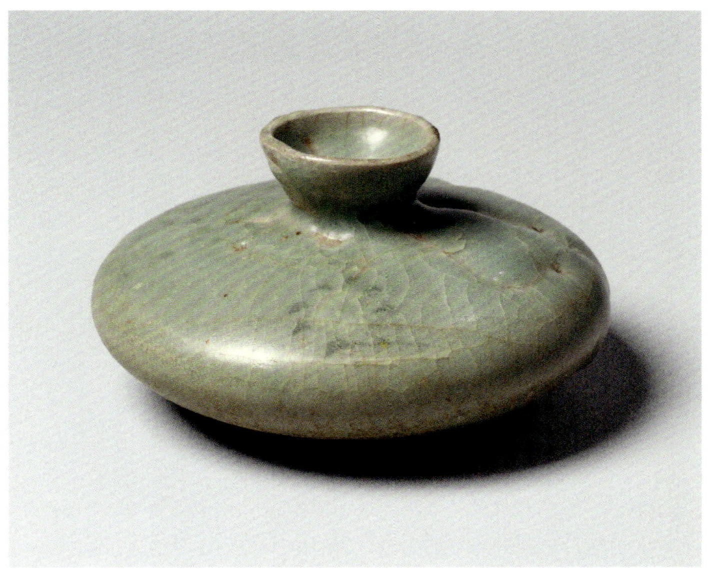

902

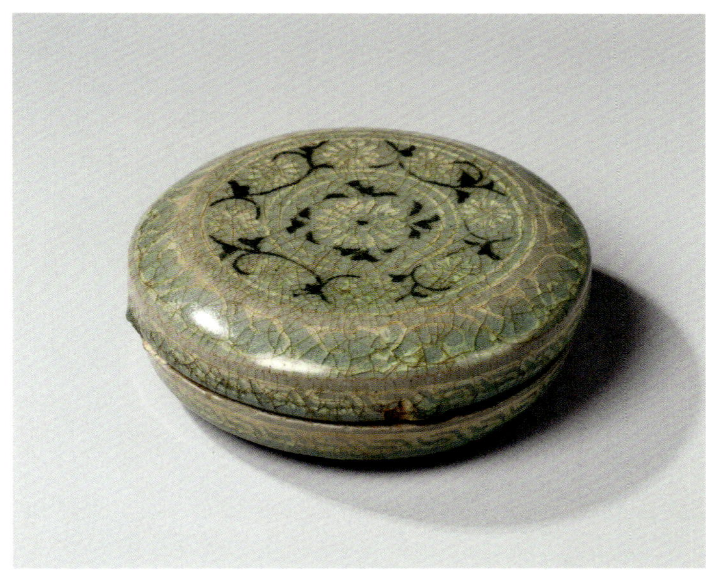

903

900. Oil bottle

Goryeo dynasty, 11th–12th century
Stoneware with celadon glaze
H. 9 cm (3 1/2 in.)

902. Oil bottle with chrysanthemums

Goryeo dynasty, 13th century
Stoneware with inlaid design under celadon glaze
H. 5 cm (2 in.)

901. Oil bottle with flying cranes and clouds

Goryeo dynasty, first half of 14th century
Stoneware with inlaid design under celadon glaze
H. 5.3 cm (2 1/8 in.), diam. 7.5 cm (3 in.)

903. Covered incense or cosmetic box with chrysanthemums

Goryeo dynasty, 13th century
Stoneware with inlaid design under celadon glaze
H. 3.2 cm (1 1/4 in.), diam. 7.2 cm (2 7/8 in.)

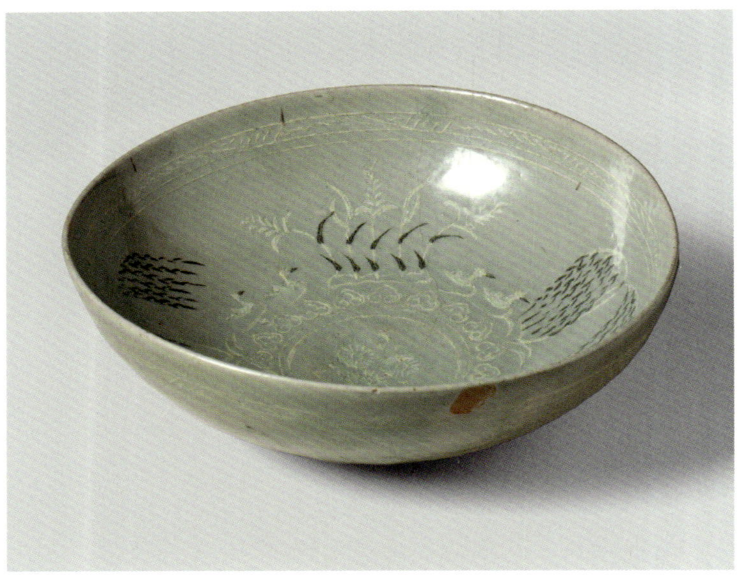

904

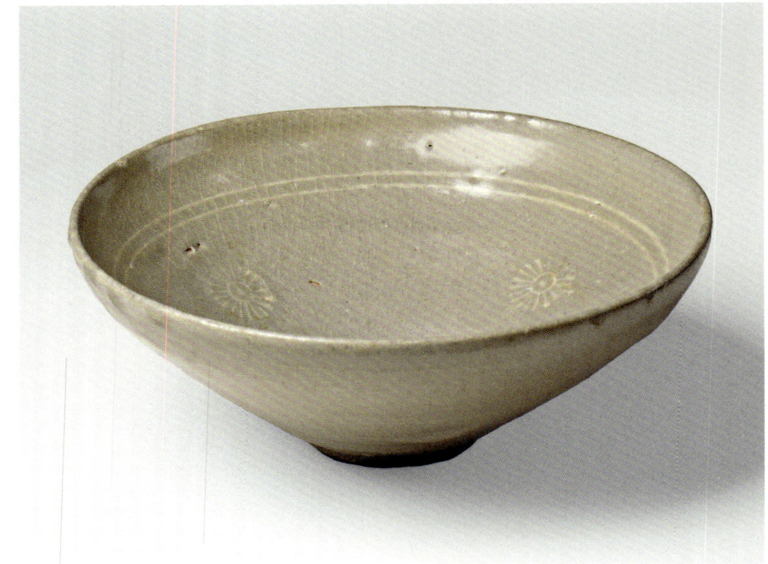

905

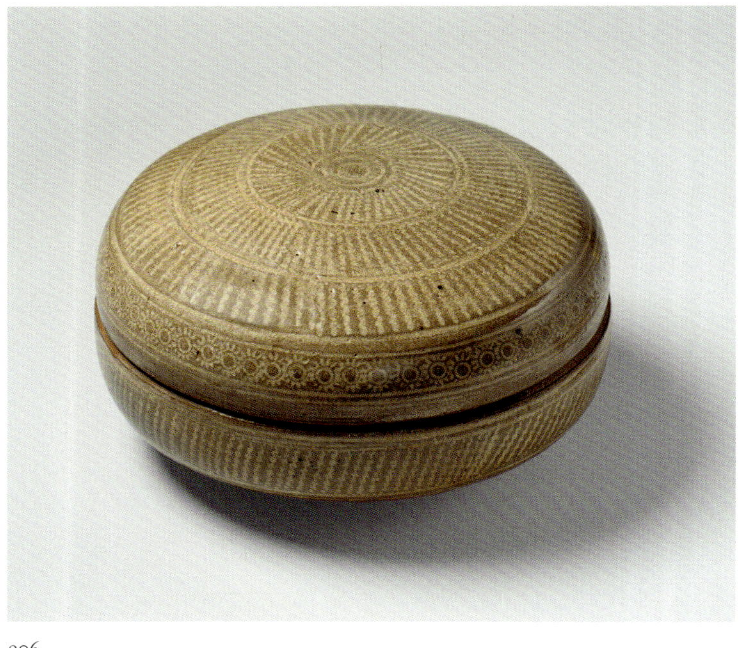

906

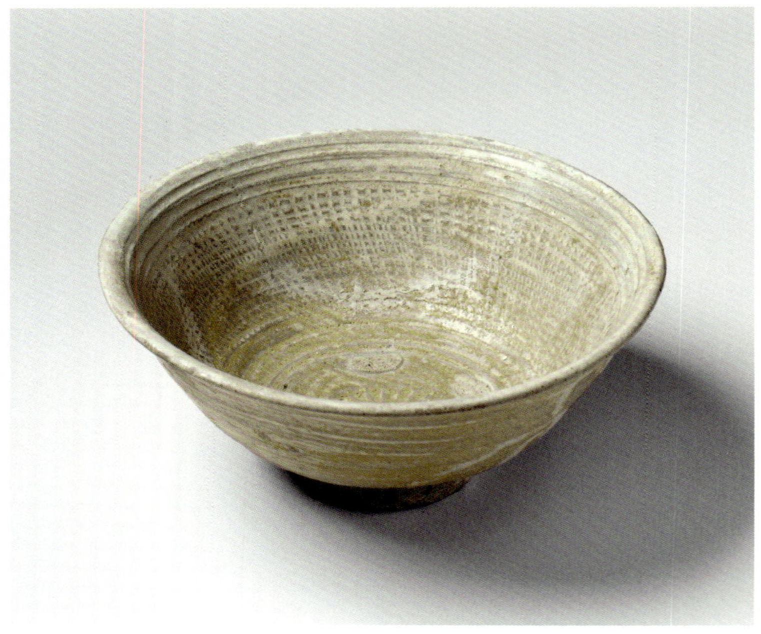

907

904. Bowl with waterfowl, willows, and reeds

Goryeo dynasty (918–1392), late 13th–14th century
Stoneware with inlaid design under celadon glaze
H. 7.3 cm (2 7/8 in.), diam. 20 cm (7 7/8 in.)

905. Bowl with chrysanthemums

Goryeo dynasty, late 14th century
Stoneware with stamped and inlaid design under celadon glaze
H. 7.5 cm (3 in.), diam. 19.5 cm (7 5/8 in.)

Gift from Jean Archbold, 1987

906. Covered box with wavy lines and chrysanthemums

Joseon dynasty (1392–1910), second half of 15th century
Buncheong ware with stamped design
H. 9 cm (3 1/2 in.), diam. 14.5 cm (5 3/4 in.)

907. Bowl with rows of square dots and chrysanthemums

Joseon dynasty, mid-15th century
Buncheong ware with stamped and brushed-slip design
H. 5.7 cm (2 1/4 in.), diam. 13.4 cm (5 1/4 in.)

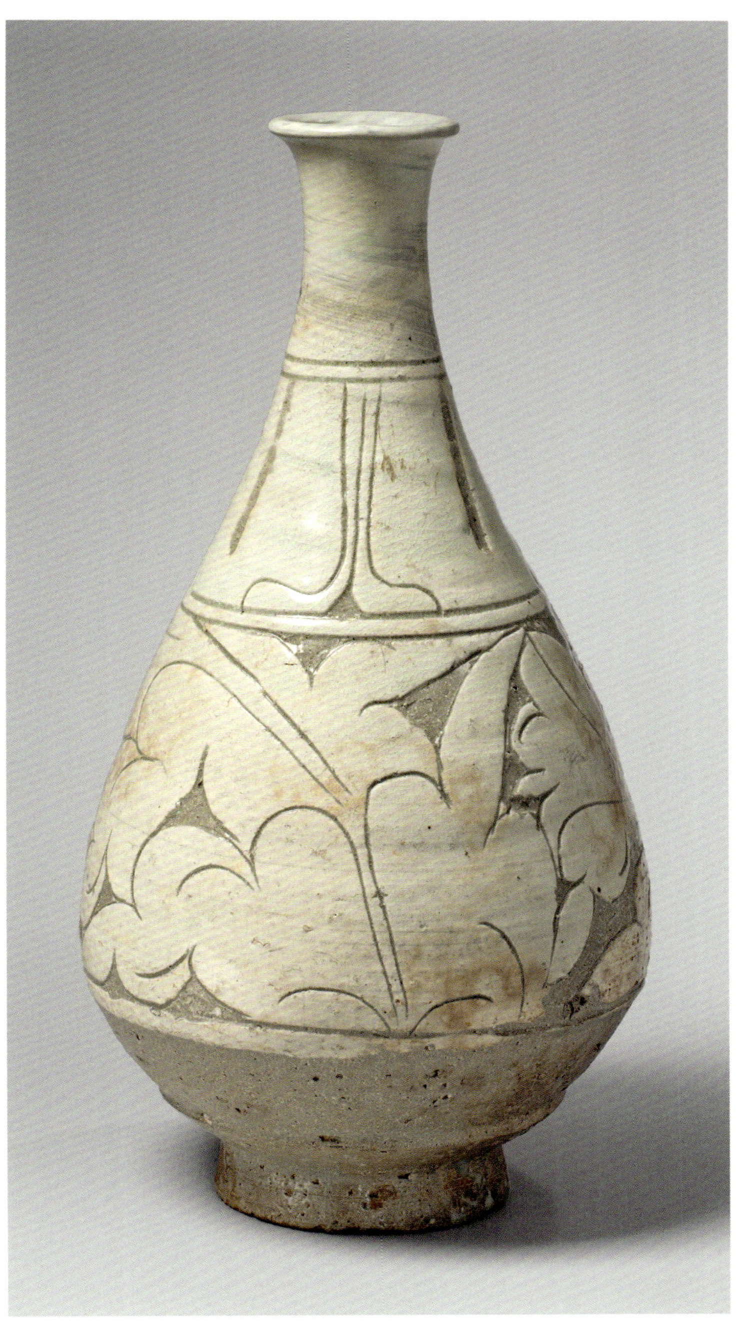

908. Bottle with peony leaves

Joseon dynasty, second half of 15th century
Buncheong ware with sgraffito design
H. 32 cm (12 5/8 in.)

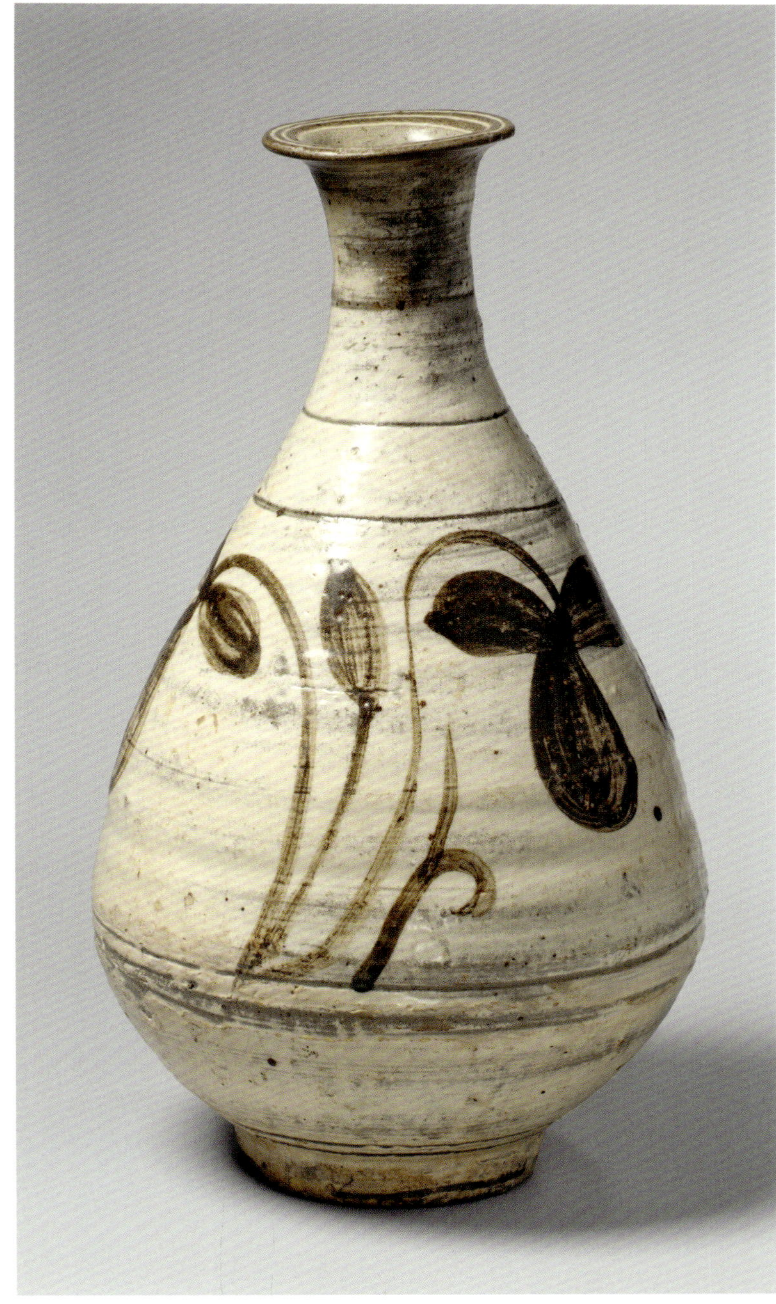

909. Bottle with floral design

Joseon dynasty, late 15th century
Buncheong ware with iron-brown design;
Gyeryongsan Hakbong-ri kilns
H. 28.5 cm (11 1/4 in.)

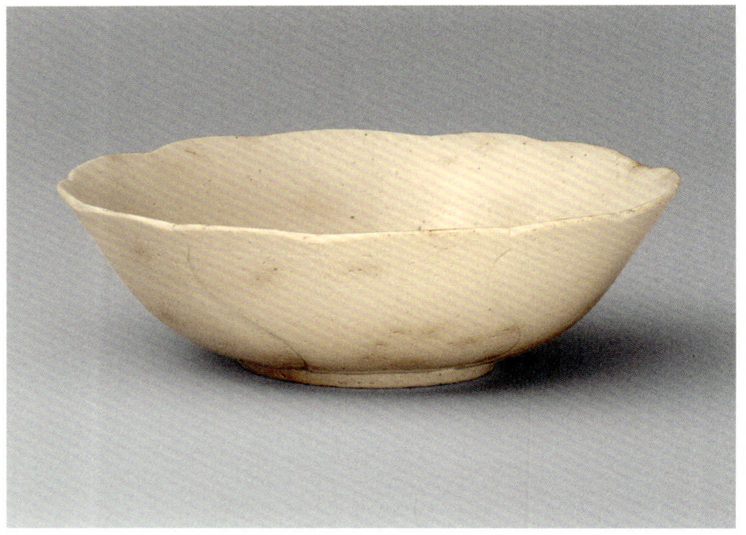

910

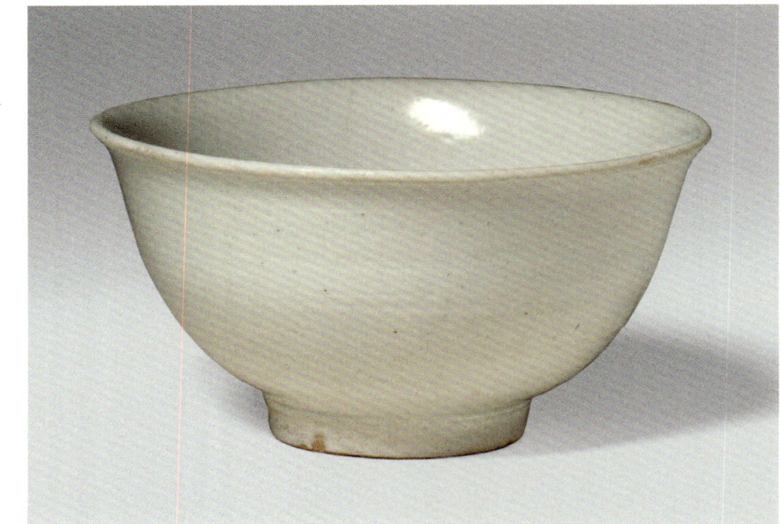

911

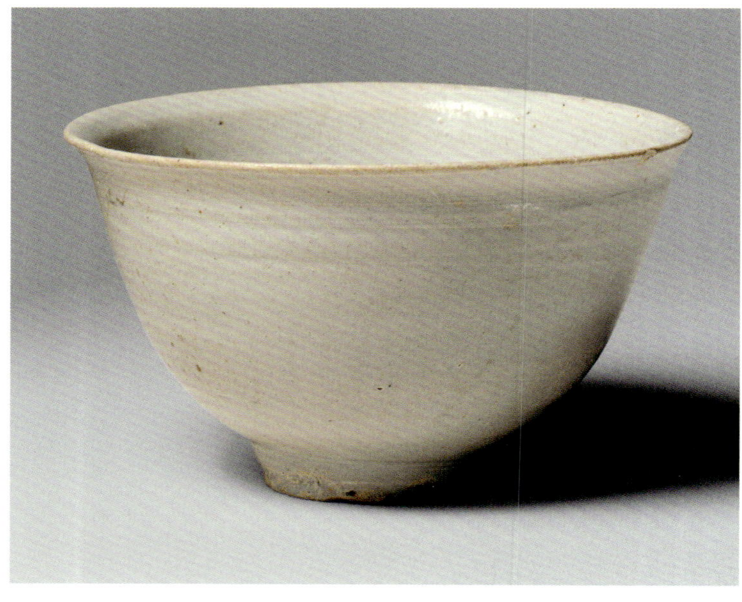

912

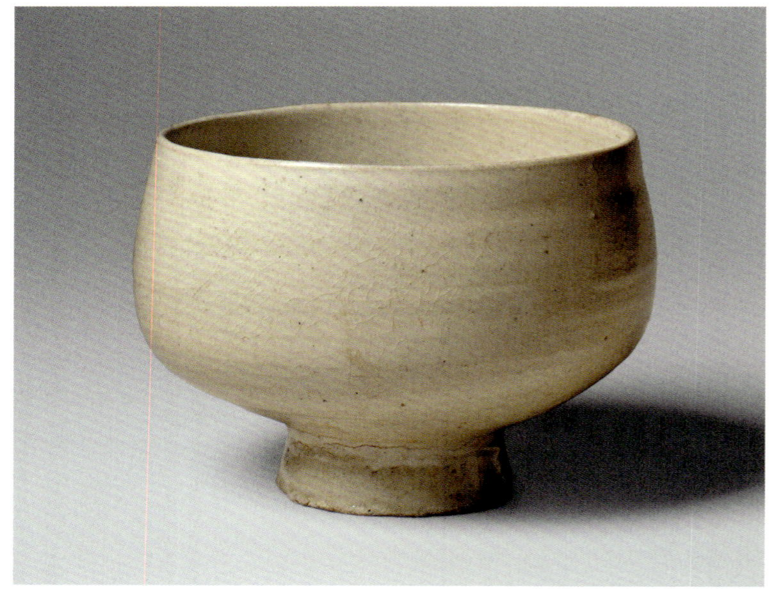

913

910. Flower-shaped dish

Joseon dynasty, 15th–16th century
Porcelain
H. 4.5 cm (1 3/4 in.), diam. 14.1 cm (5 1/2 in.)

911. Bowl

Joseon dynasty, 16th century
Porcelain
H. 6.8 cm (2 5/8 in.), diam. 13.1 cm (5 1/8 in.)

912. Bowl

Joseon dynasty, 16th century
Porcelain
H. 9.7 cm (3 7/8 in.), diam. 16.5 cm (6 1/2 in.)

913. Bowl

Joseon dynasty, 17th century
Porcelain
H. 10.7 cm (4 1/4 in.), diam. 13.7 cm (5 3/8 in.)

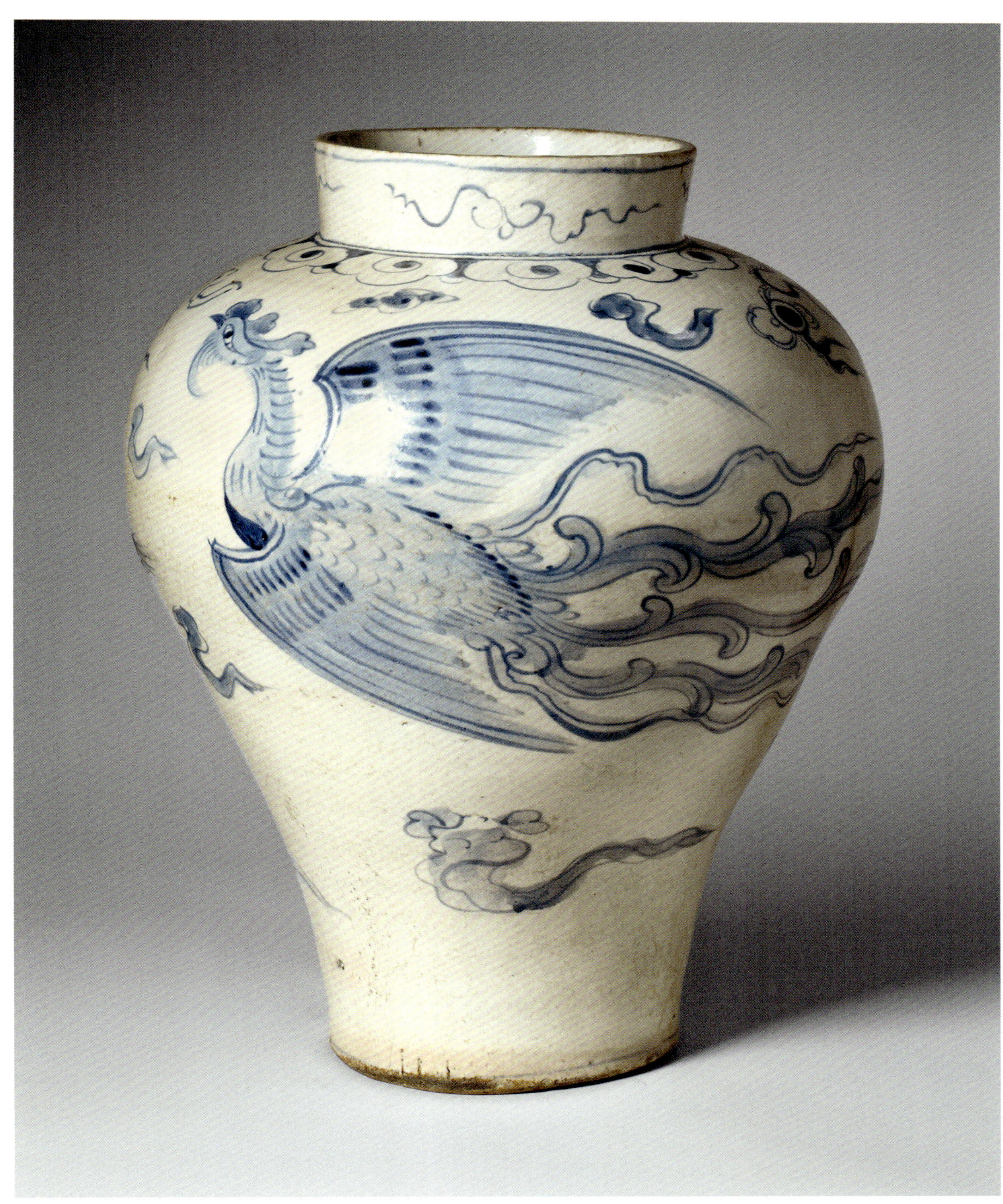

914. Jar with phoenix among clouds

Joseon dynasty, late 18th–early 19th century
Porcelain with cobalt-blue design under clear glaze
H. 39.6 cm (15 5/8 in.), diam. 16.5 cm (6 1/2 in.)

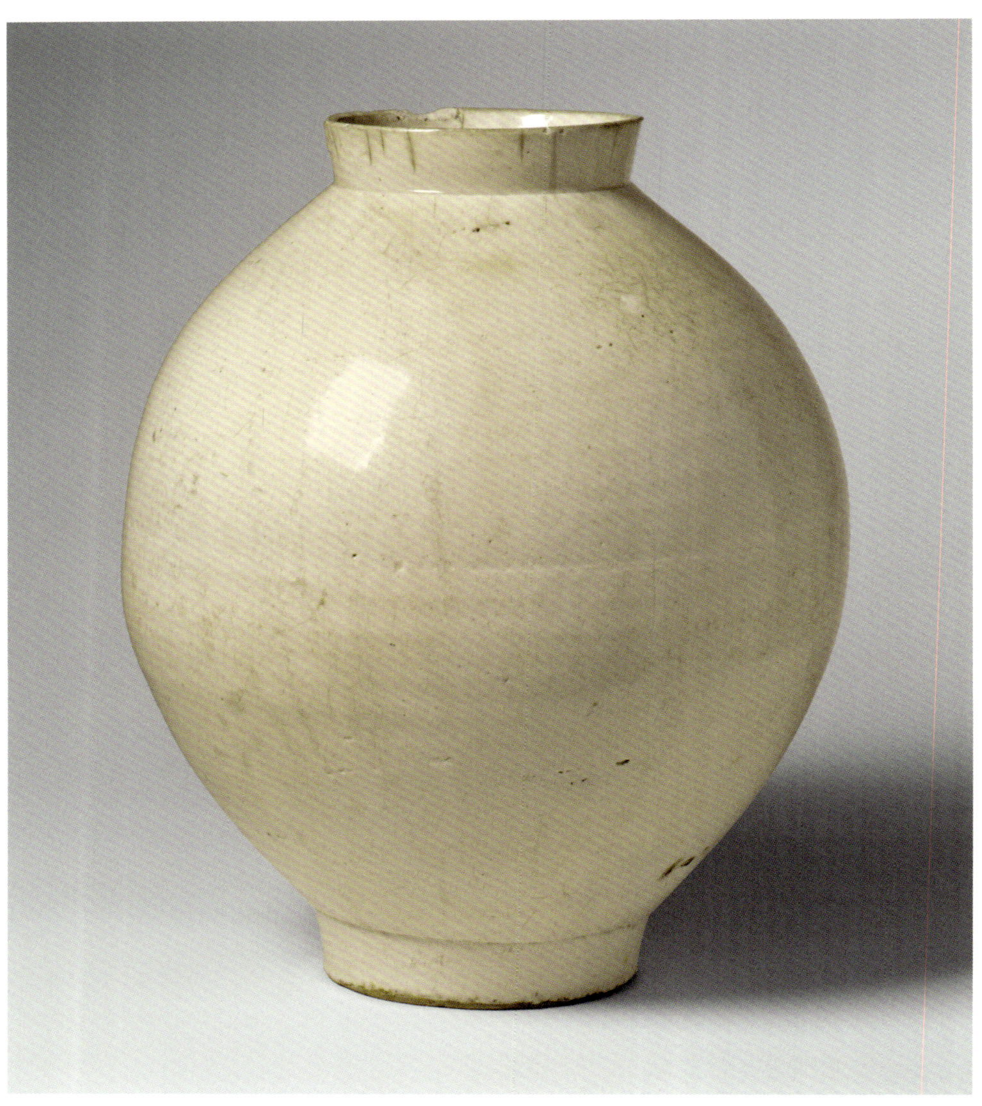

915. Moon Jar

Joseon dynasty, late 18th century
Porcelain
H. 35.4 cm (13 7/8 in.), diam. 13 cm (5 1/8 in.)

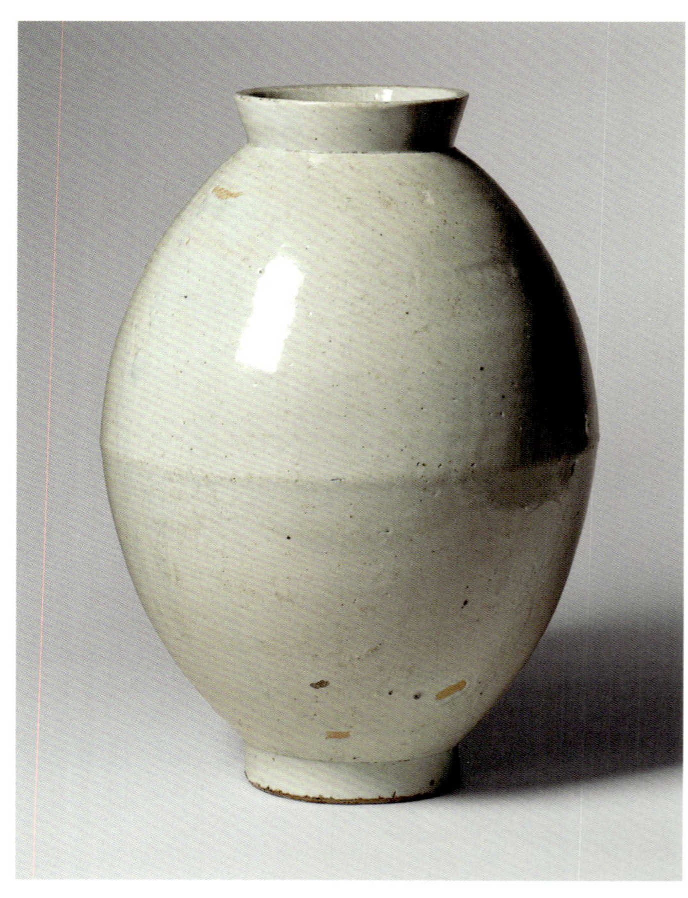

916. Jar

Joseon dynasty, 19th century
Porcelain
H. 33.4 cm (13 1/8 in.), diam. 11.5 cm (4 1/2 in.)

917. Bowl with auspicious treasures and Chinese character for longevity (壽)

Joseon dynasty, first half of 19th century
Porcelain with cobalt-blue designs under clear glaze
H. 8.6 cm (3 3/8 in.), diam. 15.8 cm (6 1/4 in.)

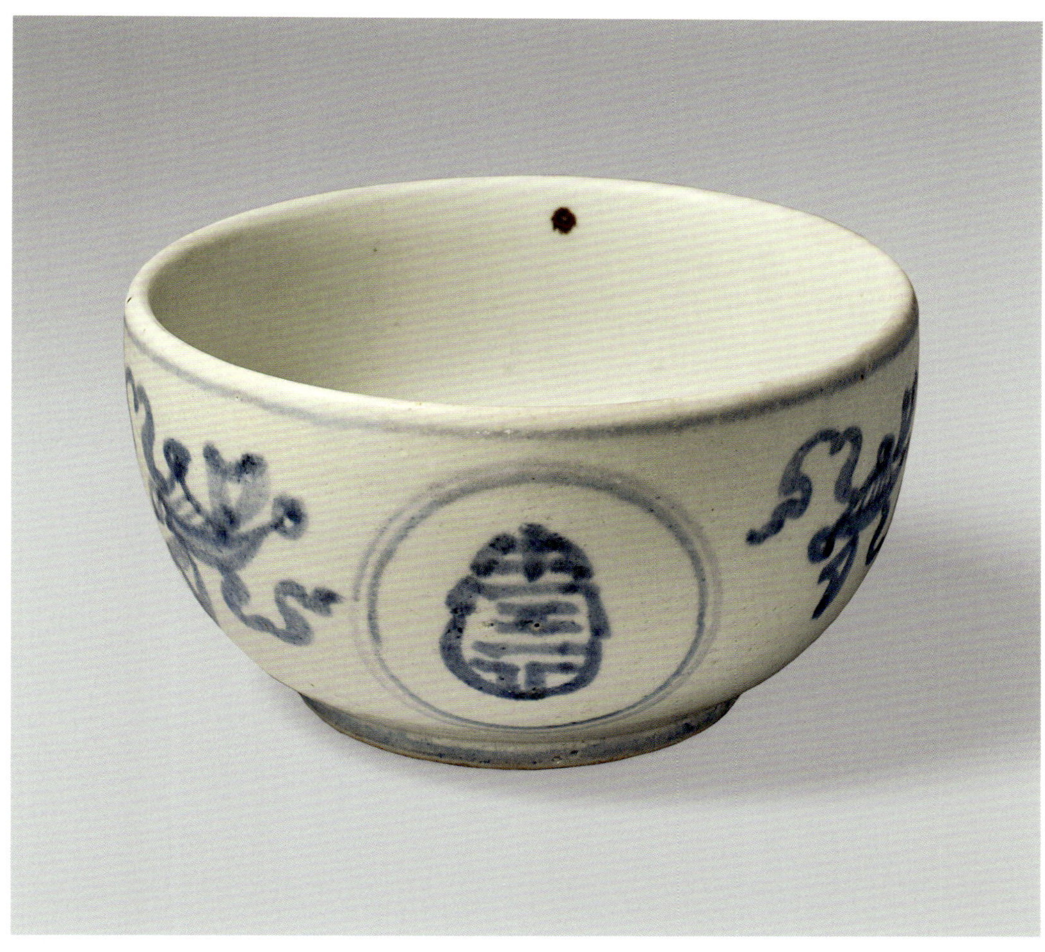

918. Bowl with Chinese character for longevity (壽)

Joseon dynasty, 19th century
Porcelain with cobalt-blue design under clear glaze
H. 6.5 cm (2 1/2 in.), diam. 15.5 cm (6 1/8 in.)

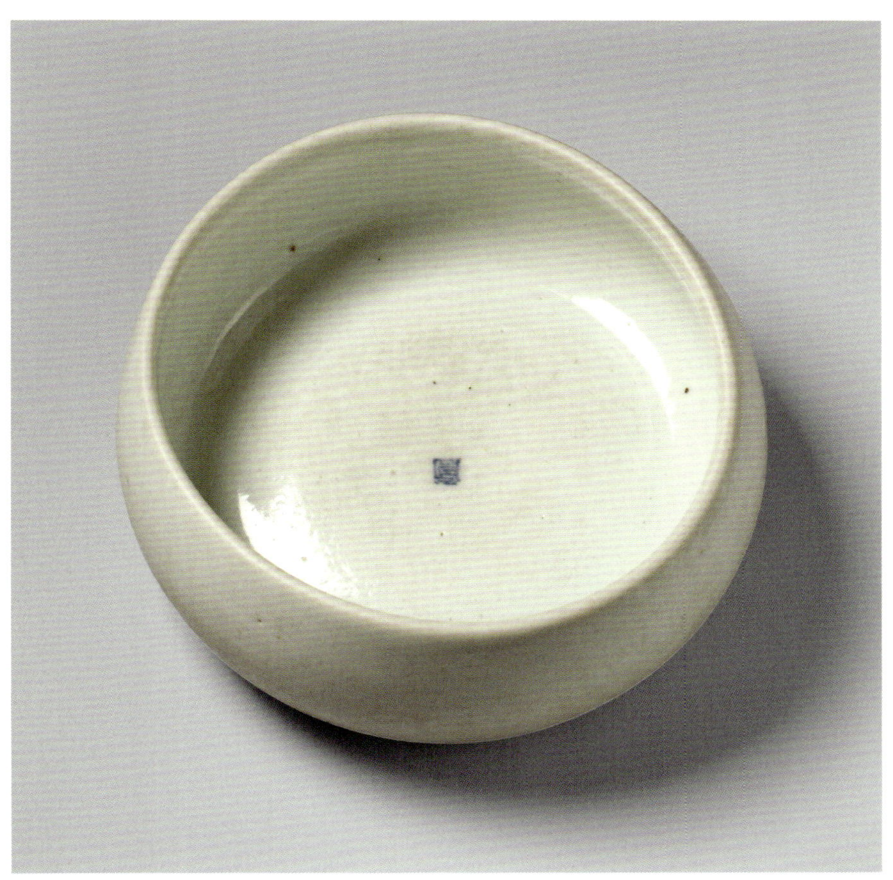

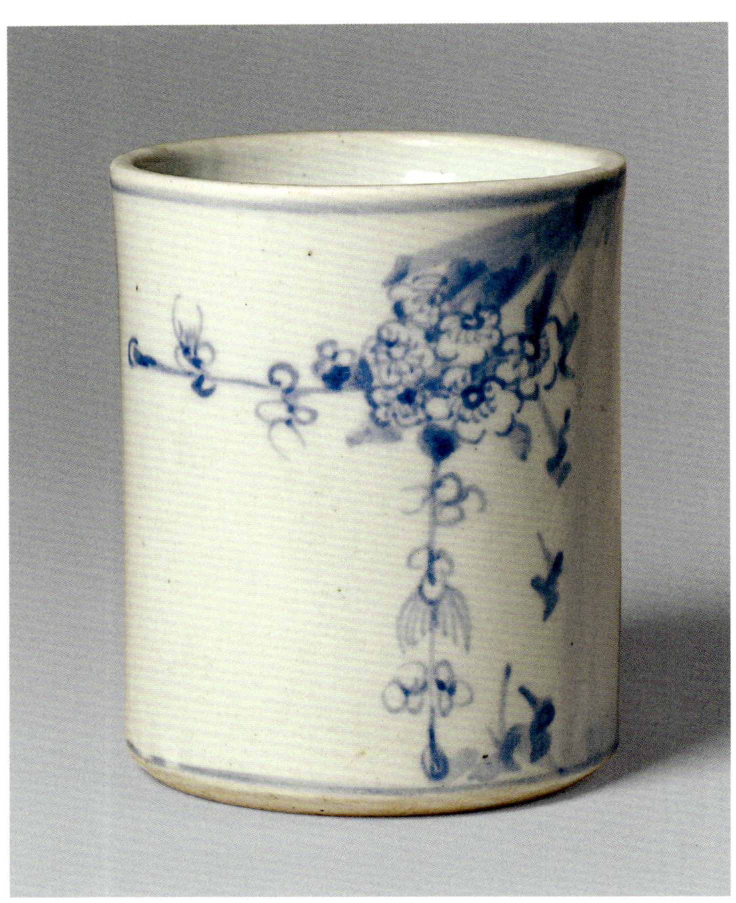

919. Brush holder with bamboo and plum blossoms
Joseon dynasty, 19th century
Porcelain with cobalt-blue design under clear glaze
H. 12.7 cm (5 in.), diam. 10.5 cm (4 1/8 in.)

920. Bottle with bamboo and plum blossoms

Joseon dynasty, 19th century
Porcelain with cobalt-blue design under clear glaze
H. 17.5 cm (6 7/8 in.)

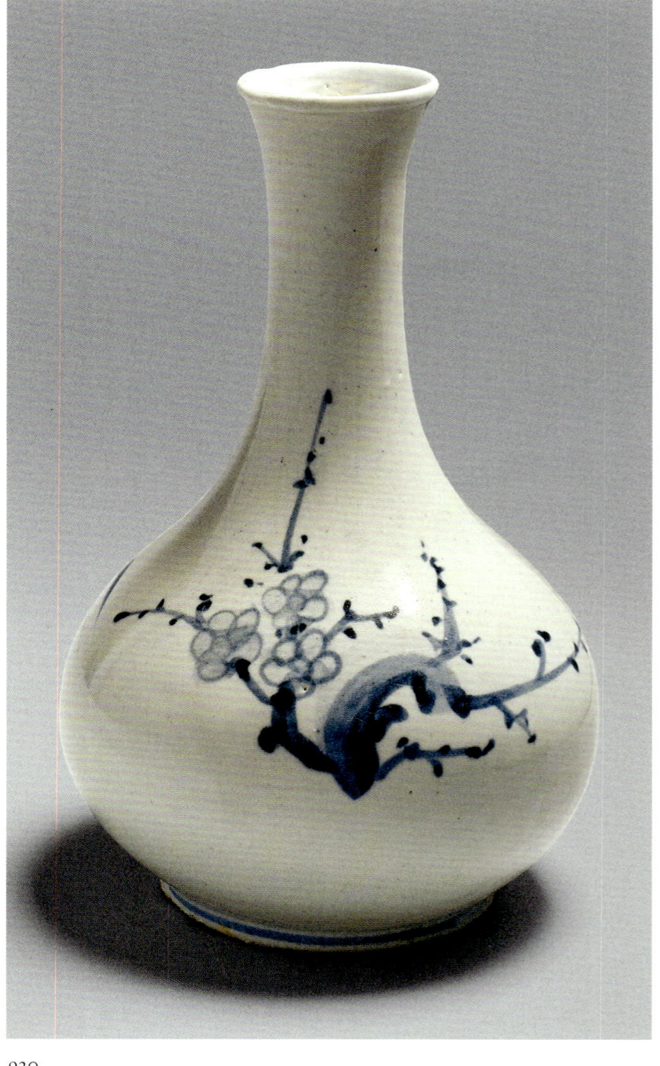

920

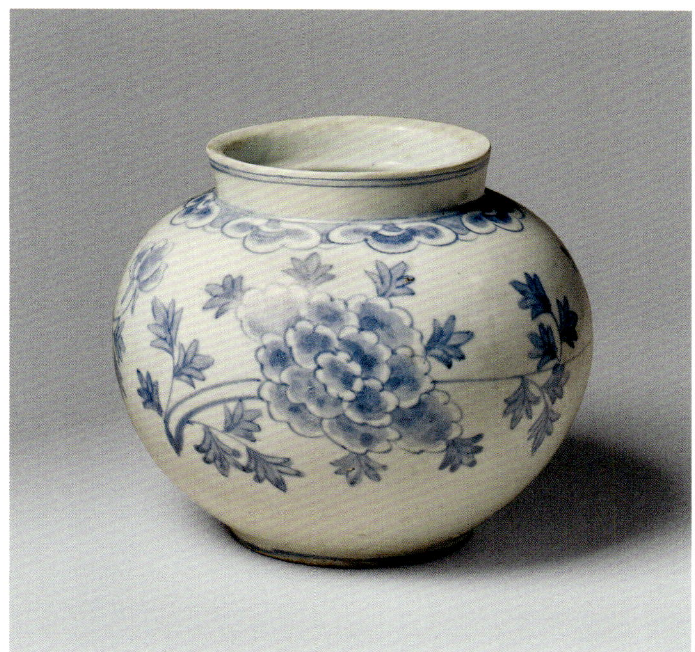

921

921. Jar with peonies

Joseon dynasty, 19th century
Porcelain with cobalt-blue design under clear glaze
H. 14.4 cm (5 5/8 in.), diam. 10 cm (3 7/8 in.)

922. Bottle

Joseon dynasty, 19th century
Porcelain
H. 23.5 cm (9 1/4 in.)

923. Bottle with floral scroll

Joseon dynasty, second half of 19th century
Porcelain with cobalt-blue design under clear glaze
H. 14.2 cm (5 5/8 in.)

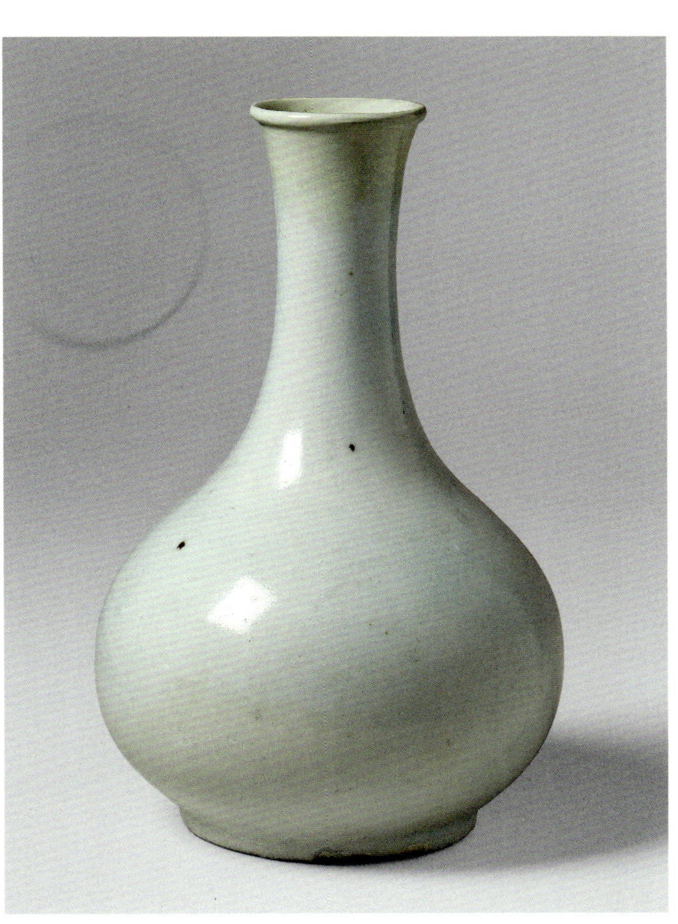

922

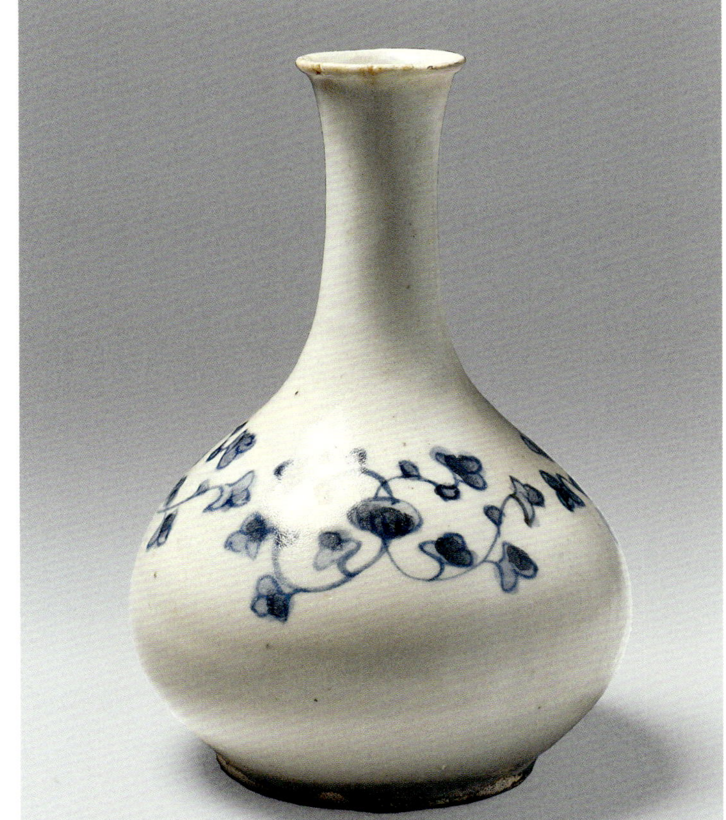

923

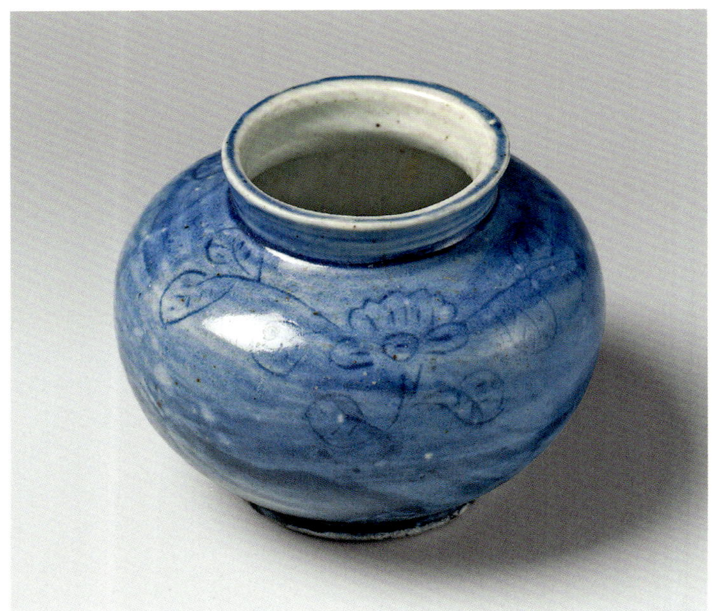

924. Small jar with floral pattern

Joseon dynasty, 19th century
Porcelain painted with cobalt blue under clear glaze
H. 8.3 cm ($3^1/_4$ in.), diam. 6.2 cm ($2^1/_2$ in.)

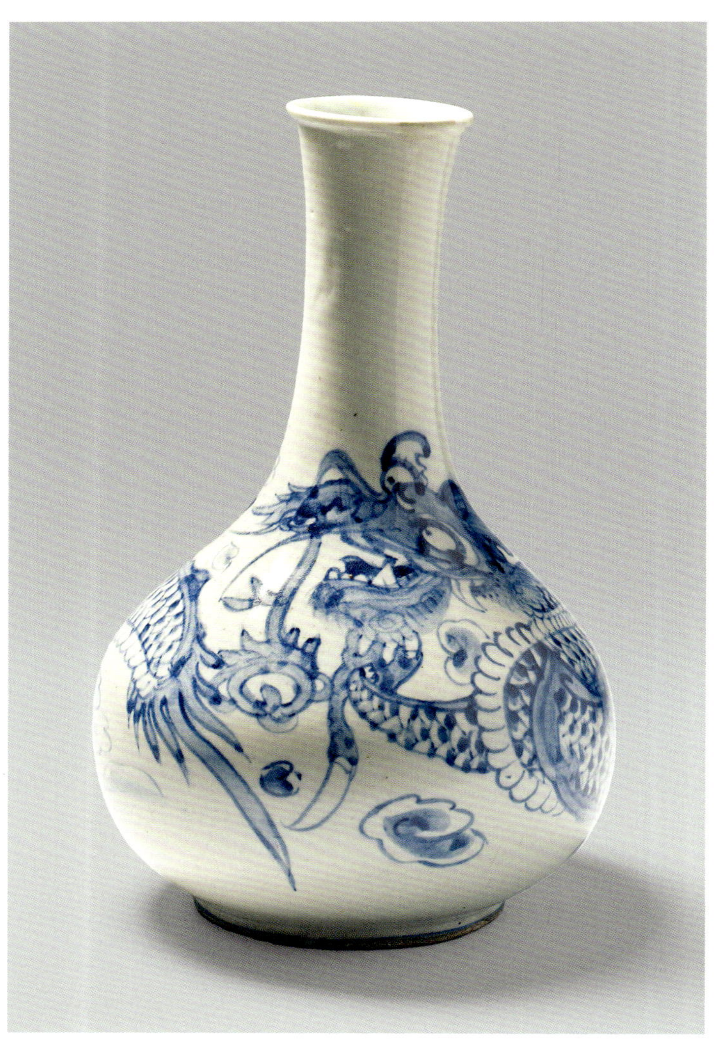

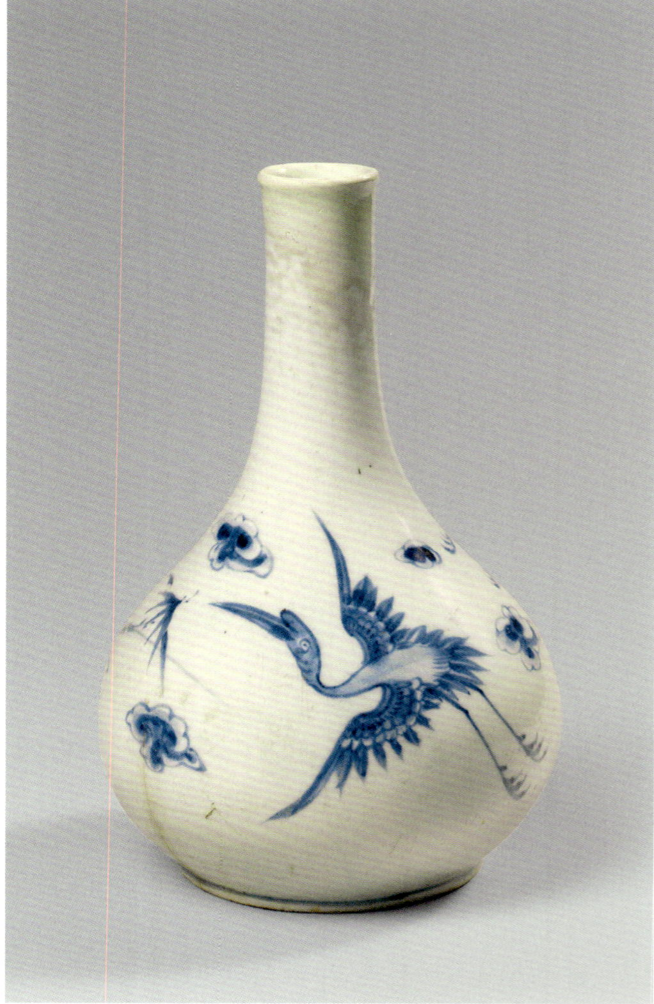

925. Bottle with dragons

Joseon dynasty, 19th century
Porcelain with cobalt-blue design under clear glaze
H. 27.2 cm ($10^3/_4$ in.)

926. Bottle with flying cranes and clouds

Joseon dynasty, 19th century
Porcelain with cobalt-blue design under clear glaze
H. 20.2 cm

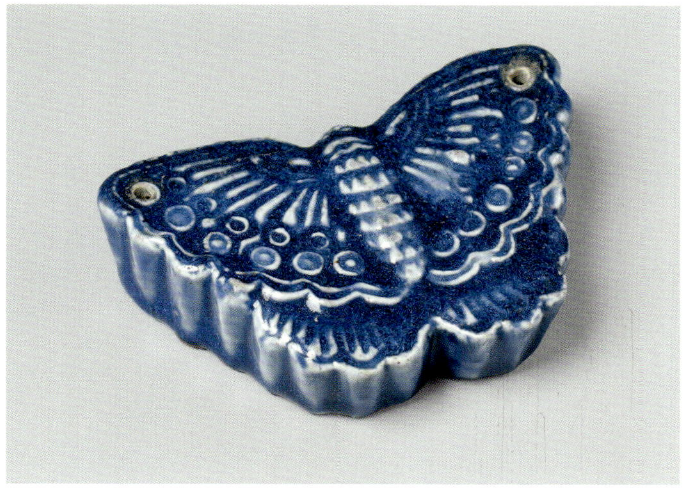

927

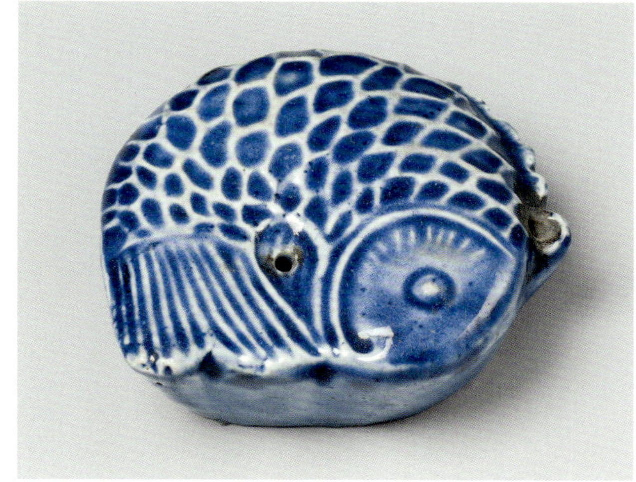

928

927. Water dropper in the shape of a butterfly

Joseon dynasty, late 19th century
Porcelain painted with cobalt blue under clear glaze
H. 2.8 cm (1 1/8 in.)

928. Water dropper in the shape of a fish

Joseon dynasty, late 19th century
Porcelain painted with cobalt blue under clear glaze
H. 3.5 cm (1 3/8 in.)

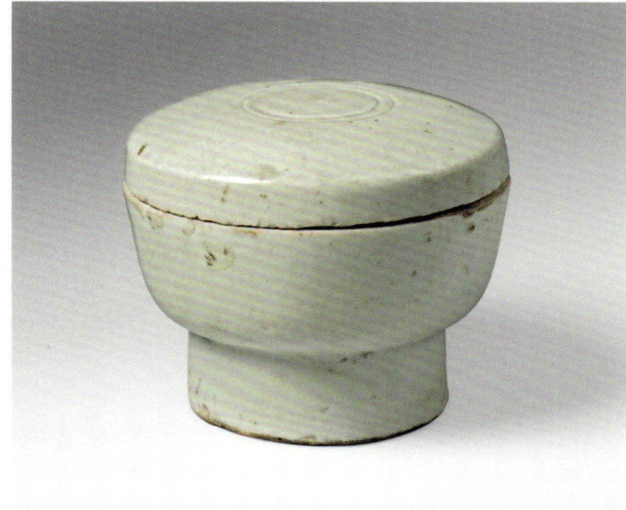

929

929. Covered bowl with tall foot

Joseon dynasty, late 19th century
Porcelain with incised design under clear glaze
H. 8.2 cm (3 1/4 in.), diam. 8.5 cm (3 3/8 in.)

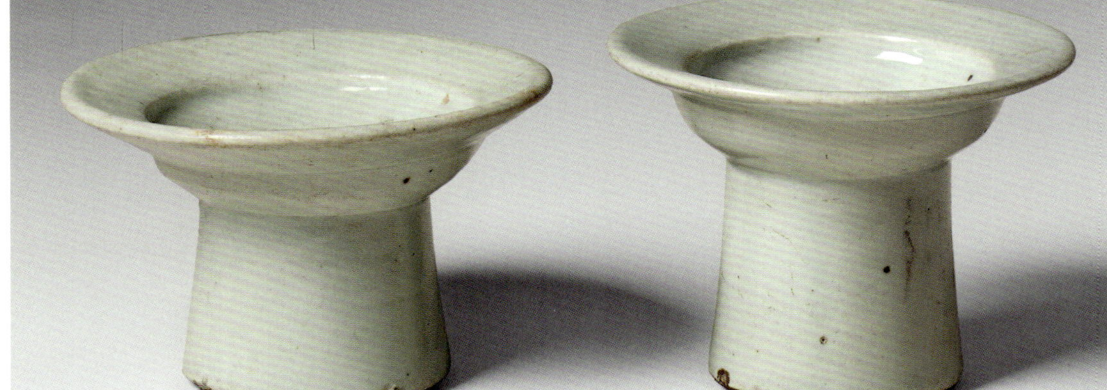

930. Two stands

Joseon dynasty, late 19th century
Porcelain
Left: h. 7.5 cm (3 in.), diam. 12 cm (4 3/4 in.)
Right: h. 8.5 cm (3 3/8 in.), diam. 11.5 cm (4 1/2 in.)

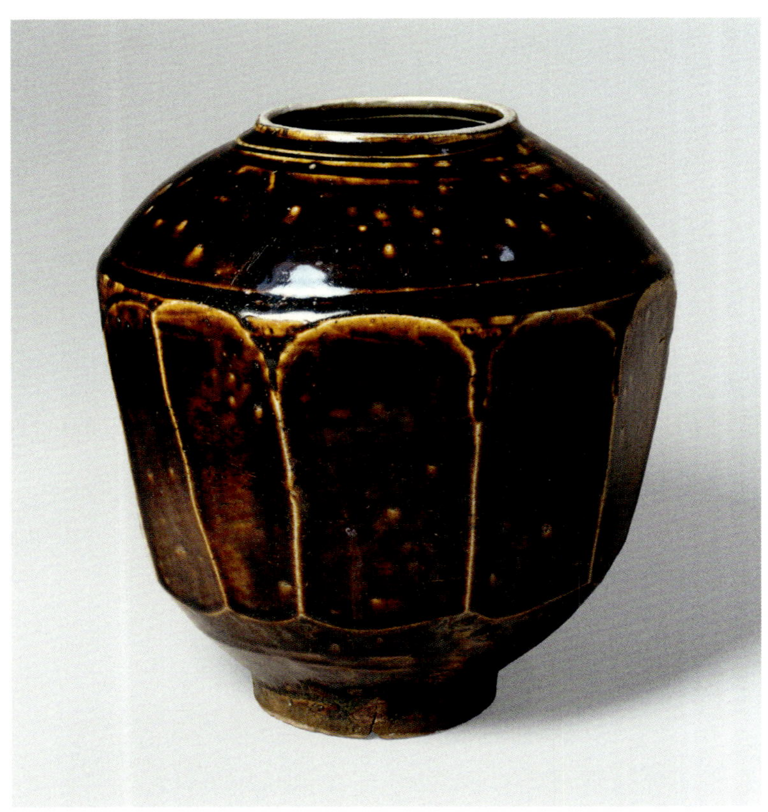

931

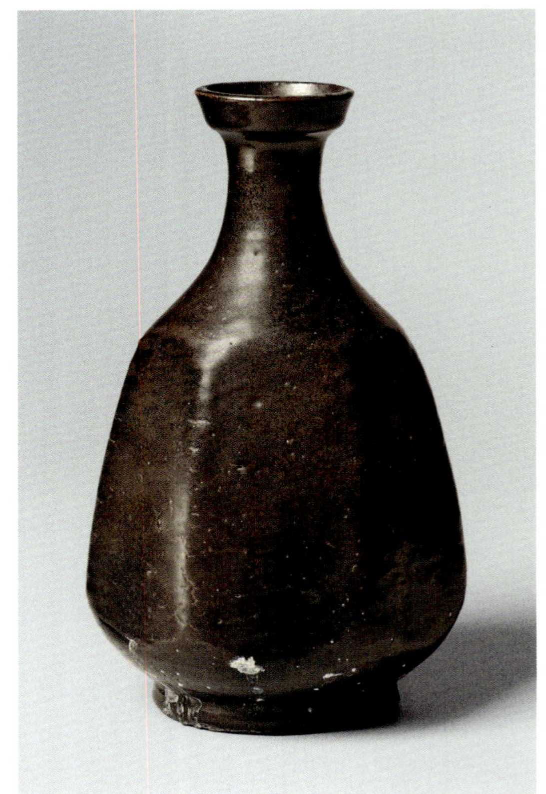

932

931. Faceted jar

Joseon dynasty, late 19th–early 20th century
Stoneware with iron-brown glaze
H. 22 cm ($8\frac{5}{8}$ in.), diam. 9.4 cm ($3\frac{3}{4}$ in.)

Gift from Julia Meech, 1977

932. Faceted bottle

Joseon dynasty, late 19th–early 20th century
Stoneware with iron-brown glaze
H. 19.8 cm ($7\frac{3}{4}$ in.)

933. Bottle with flared mouth

Joseon dynasty, late 19th–early 20th century
Stoneware with iron-brown glaze
H. 31.5 cm ($12\frac{3}{8}$ in.), diam. 11 cm ($4\frac{3}{8}$ in.)

934. Jar with floral sprays

Early 20th century
Porcelain with cobalt-blue and iron-brown design under clear glaze
H. 38 cm (15 in.), diam. 21.5 cm (8½ in.)

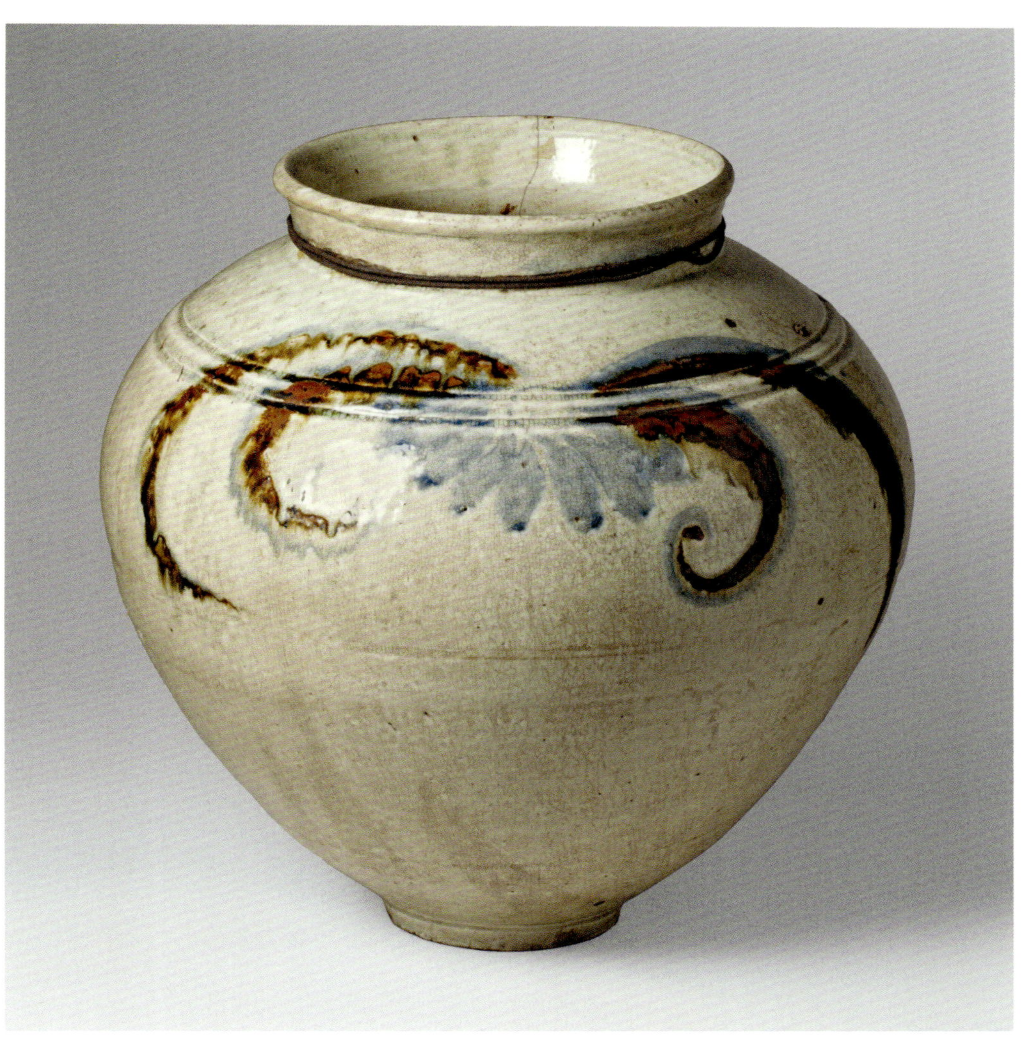

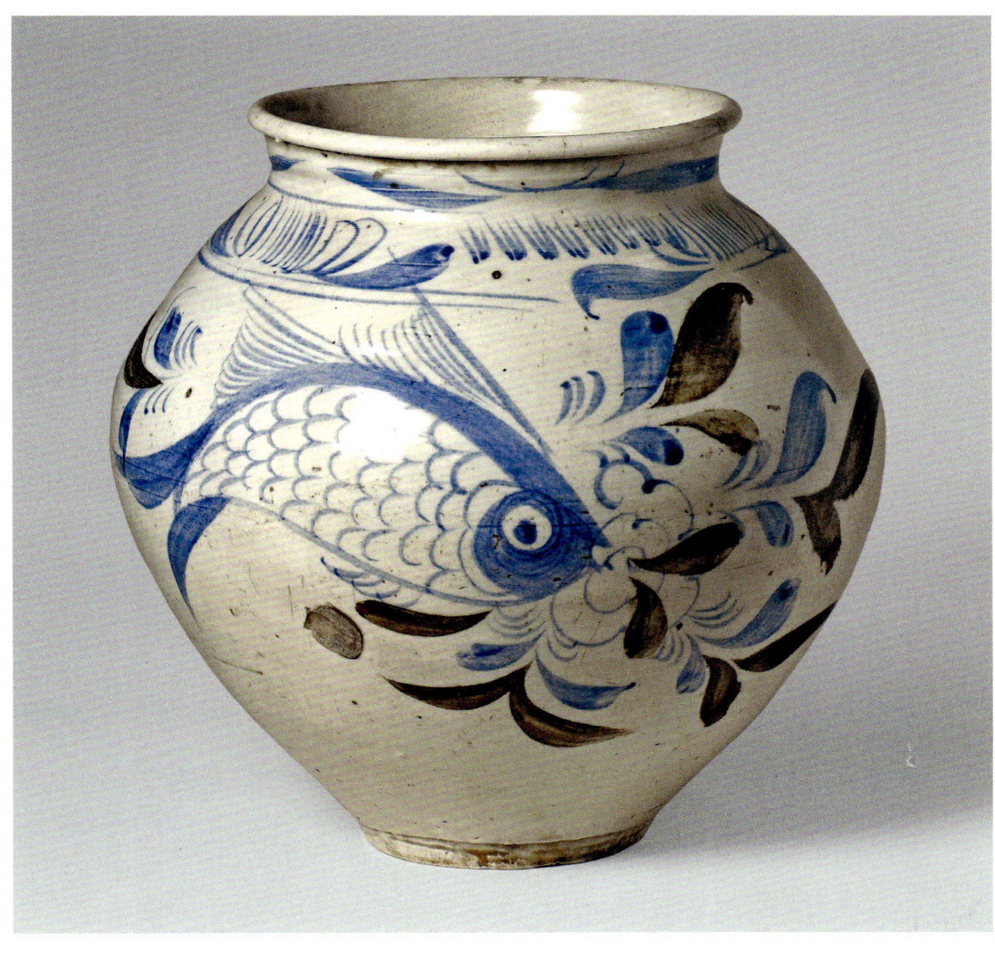

935. Jar with fish and plants

Early 20th century
Porcelain with cobalt-blue and iron-brown design under clear glaze
H. 30 cm (11¾ in.), diam. 19.8 cm (7¾ in.)

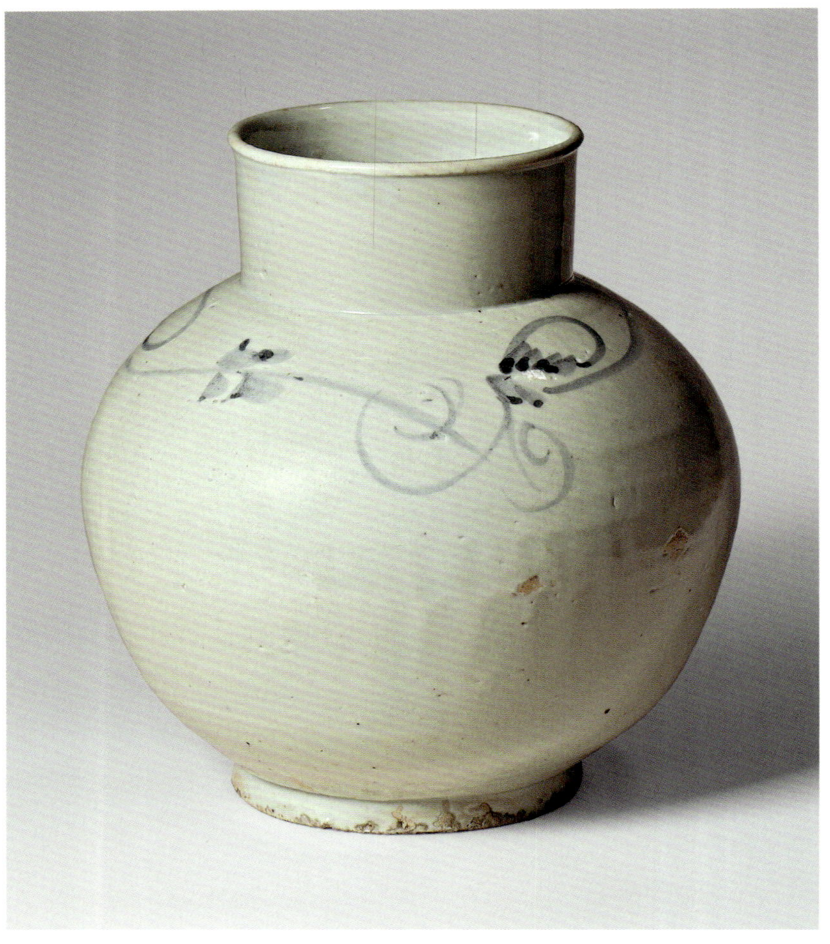

936

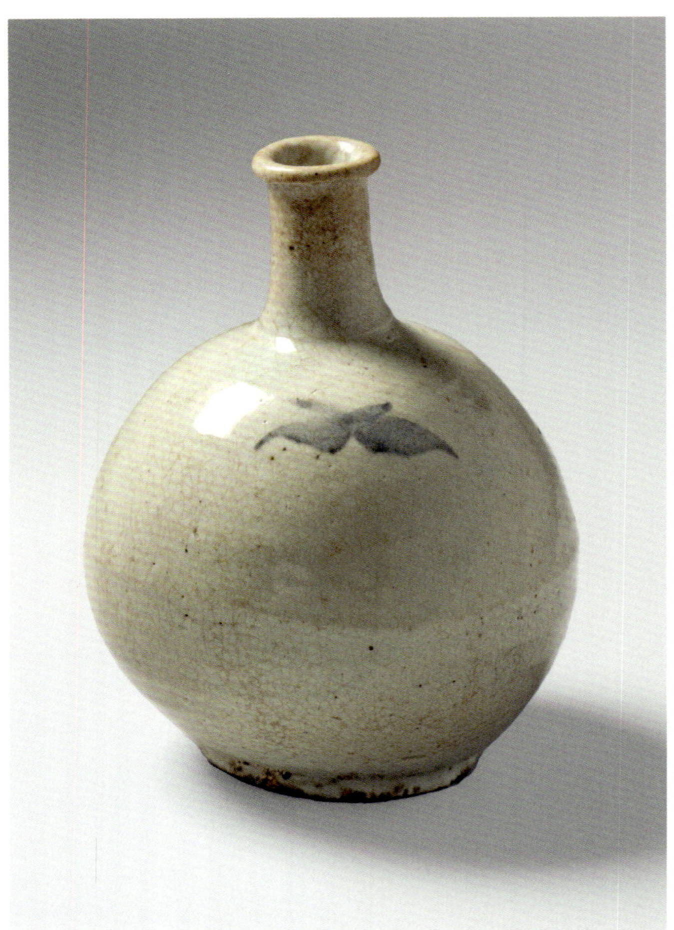

937

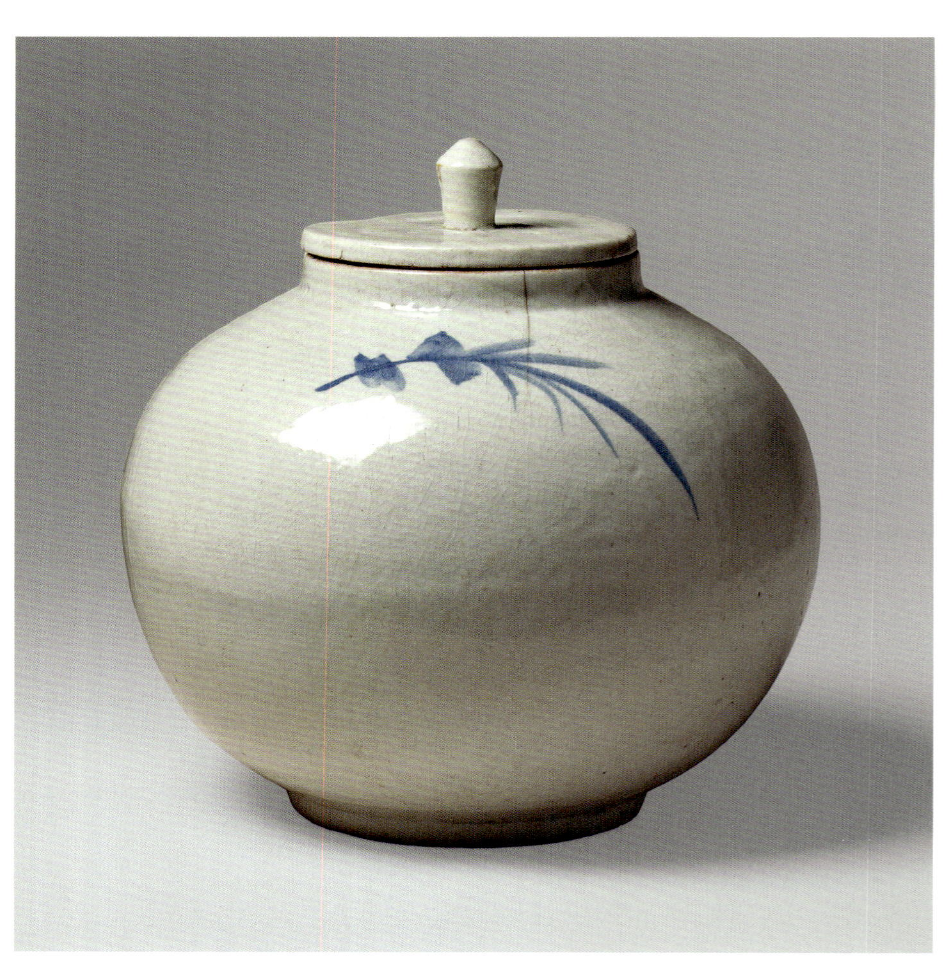

936. Long-necked jar with scrolling plant

Early 20th century
Porcelain with cobalt-blue design under clear glaze
H. 23.2 cm (9 1/8 in.), diam. 12.3 cm (4 7/8 in.)

937. Small bottle with butterfly

Early 20th century
Porcelain with cobalt-blue design under clear glaze
H. 14 cm (5 1/2 in.)

938. Lidded jar with sprig

Early 20th century
Porcelain with cobalt-blue design under clear glaze
H. with lid 22.7 cm (8 7/8 in.), diam. 11.3 cm (4 1/2 in.)

939. Vase with chrysanthemums and bamboo

Early 20th century
Porcelain with cobalt-blue and copper-red design under clear glaze
H. 25.2 cm (9 7/8 in.), diam. 11.6 cm (4 5/8 in.)

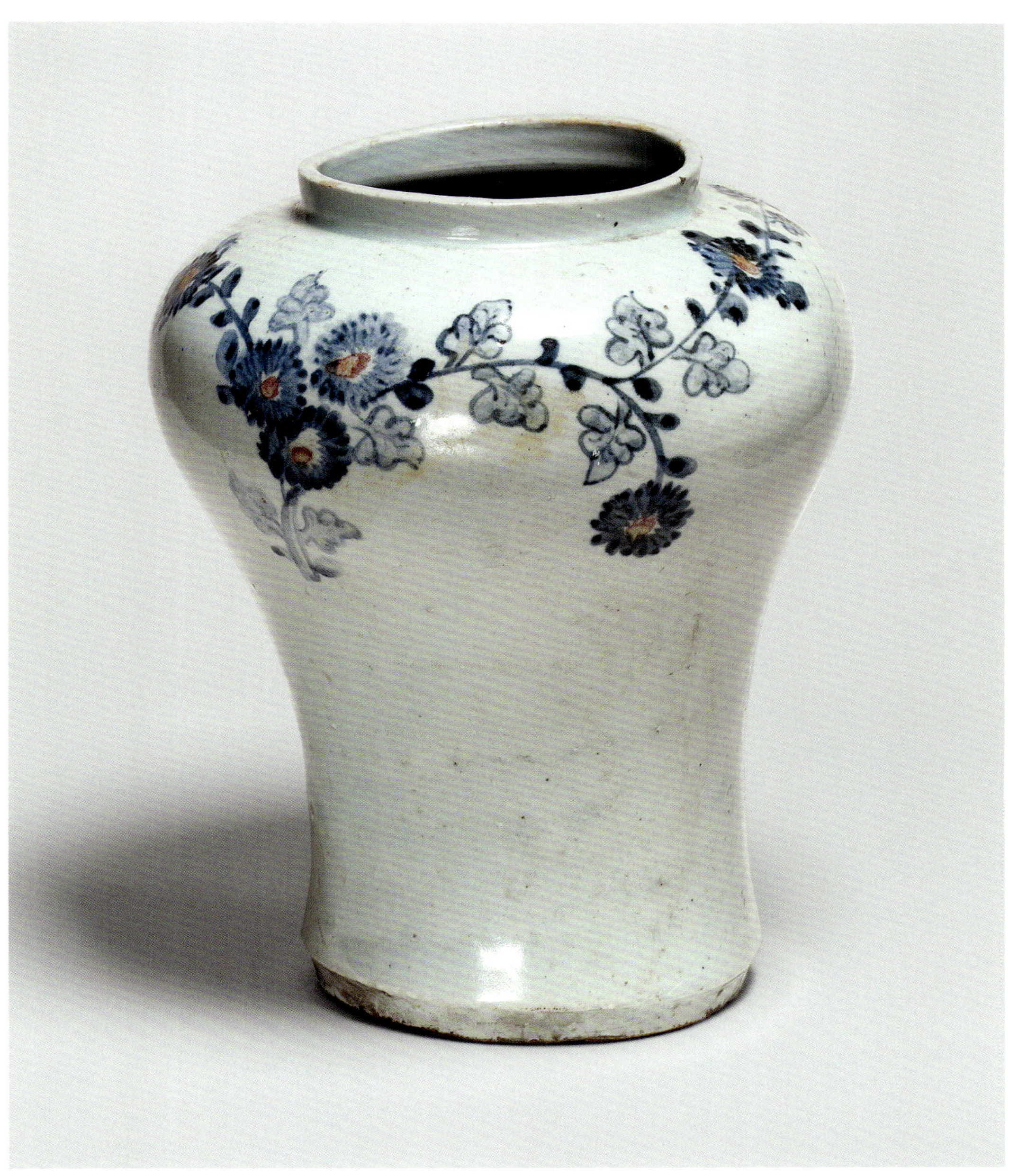

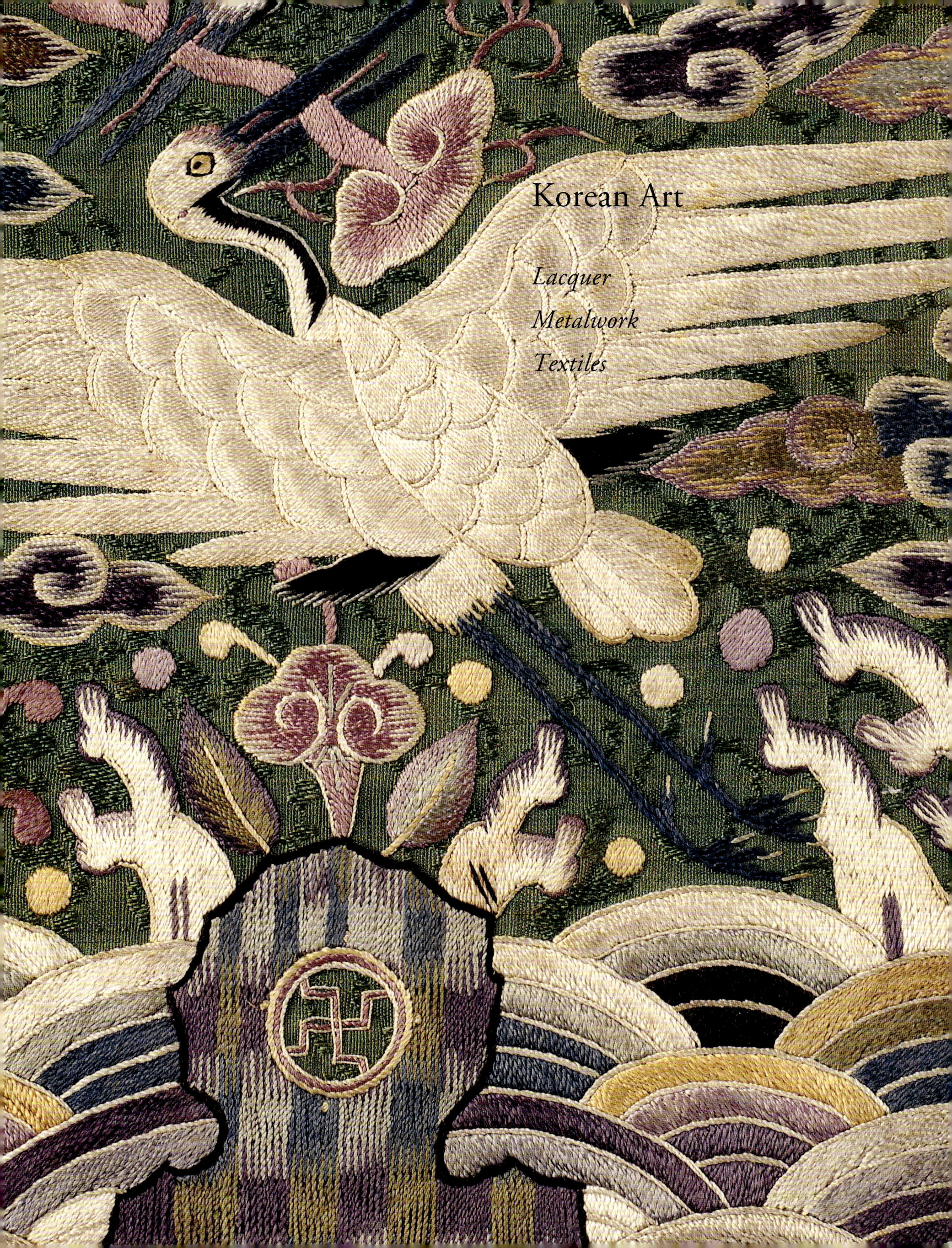

Korean Art

Lacquer

Metalwork

Textiles

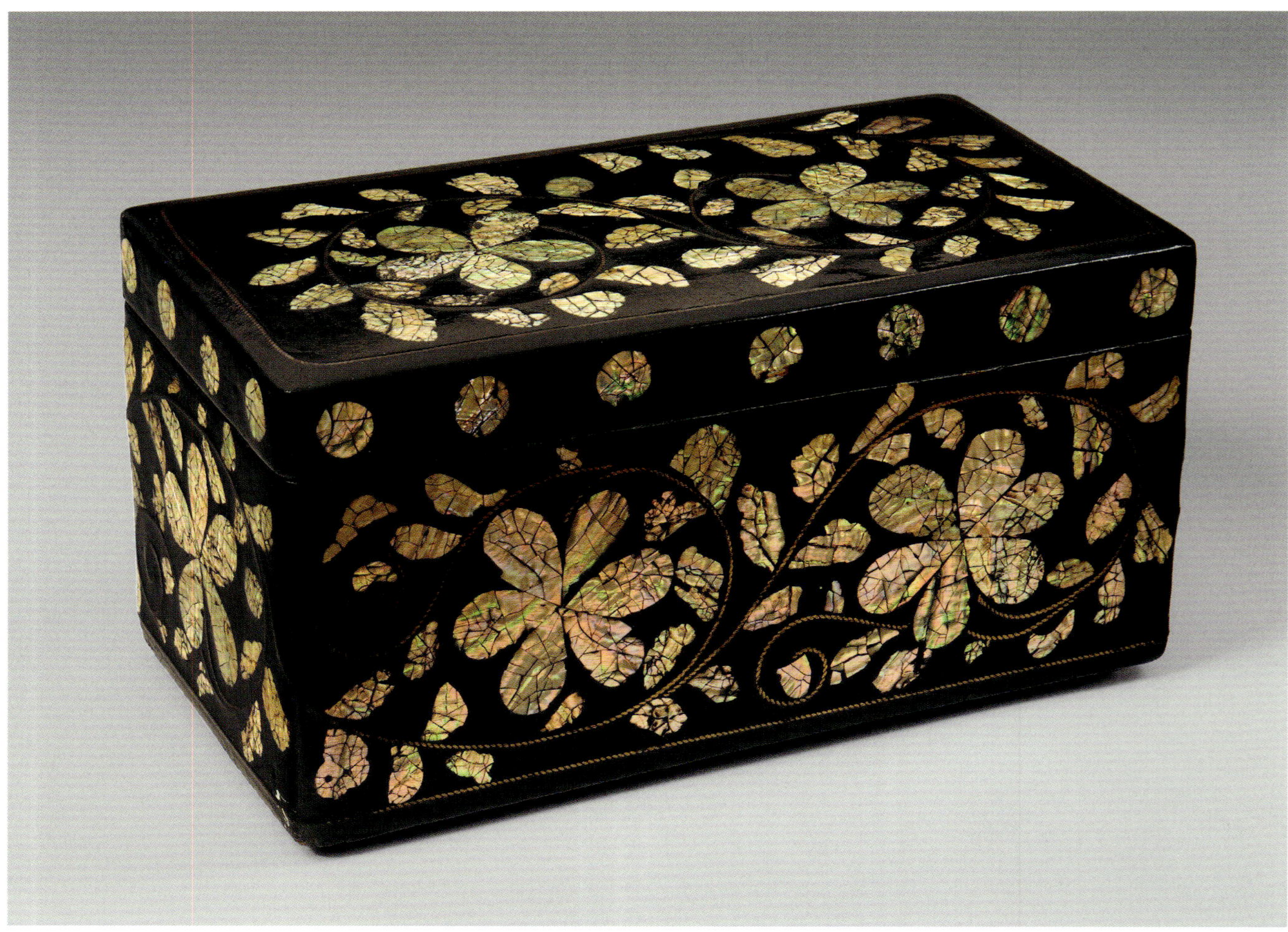

940. Box with floral scrolls

Late Joseon dynasty
Lacquered wood with mother-of-pearl inlay and brass wire
18 x 35.4 x 18.6 cm ($7^{1}/_{8}$ x $13^{7}/_{8}$ x $7^{3}/_{8}$ in.)

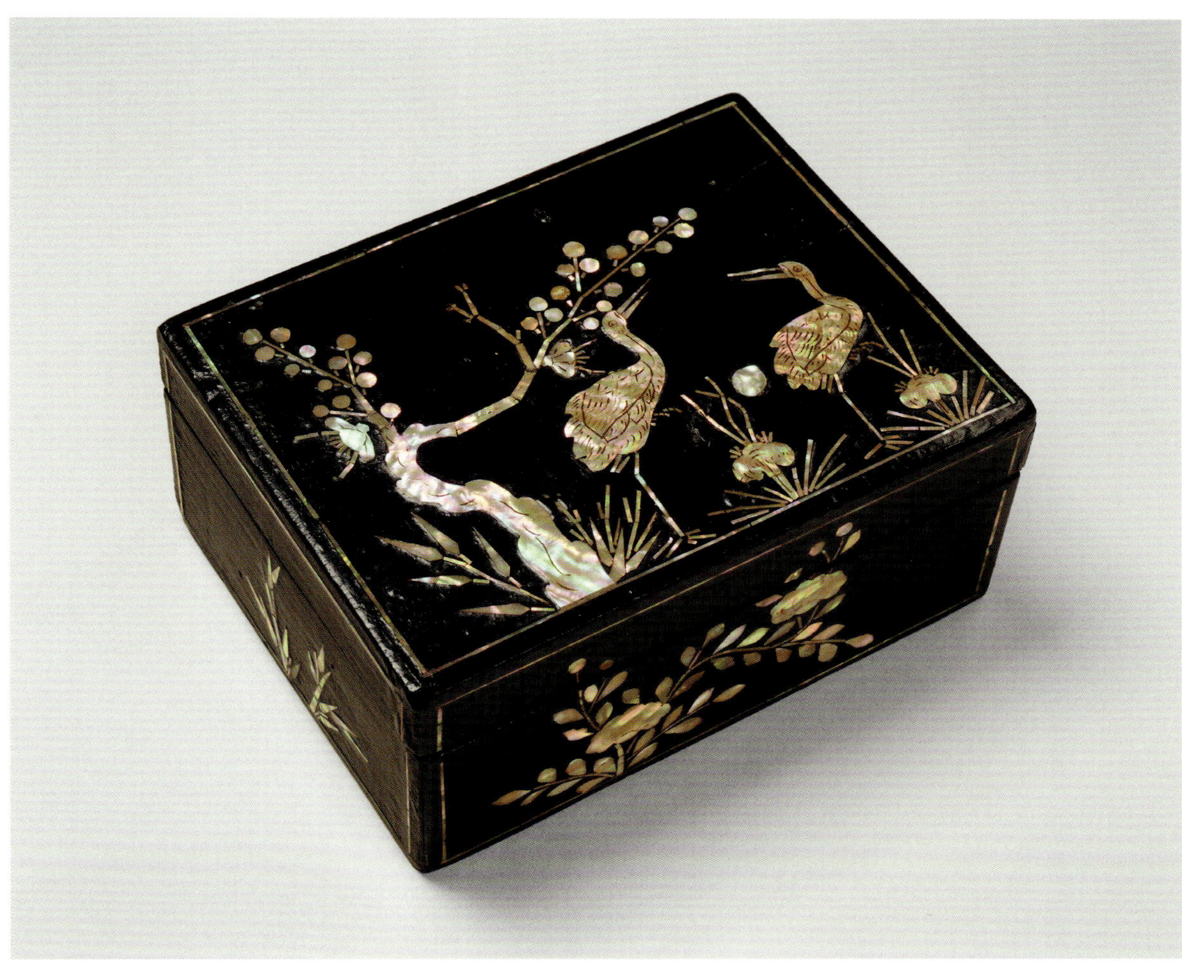

941. Box with cranes and plum tree

Late Joseon dynasty
Lacquered wood with mother-of-pearl inlay
6 x 13.7 x 10.3 cm ($2^3/_8$ x $5^3/_8$ x 4 in.)

Gift from Keum Ja Kang, 1997

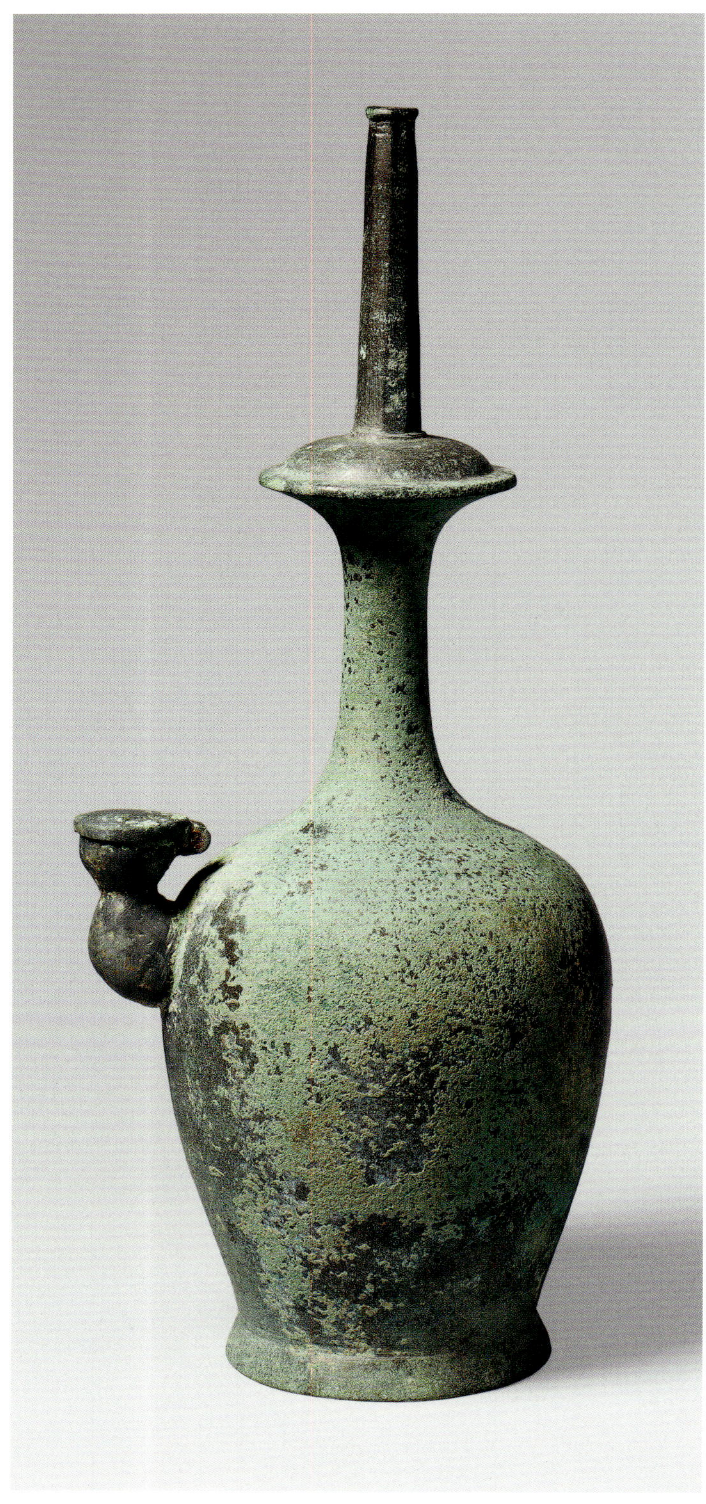

942

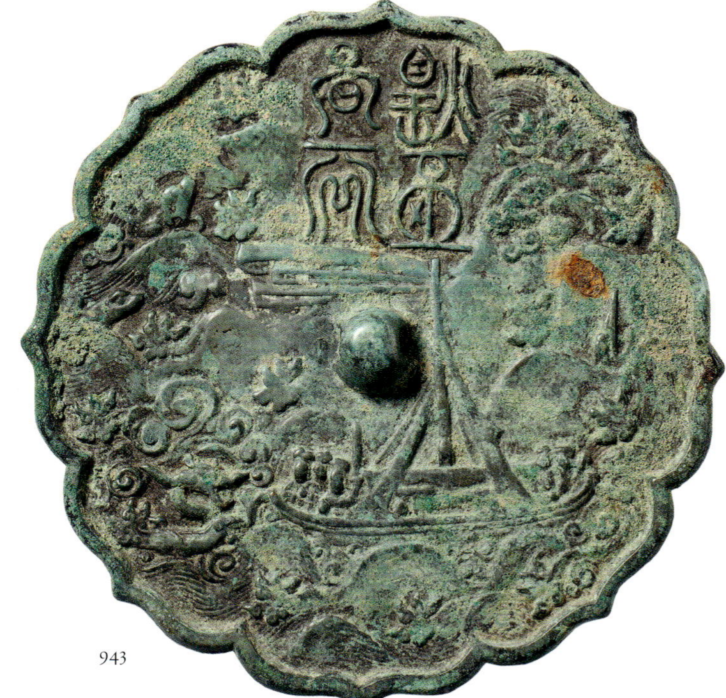

943

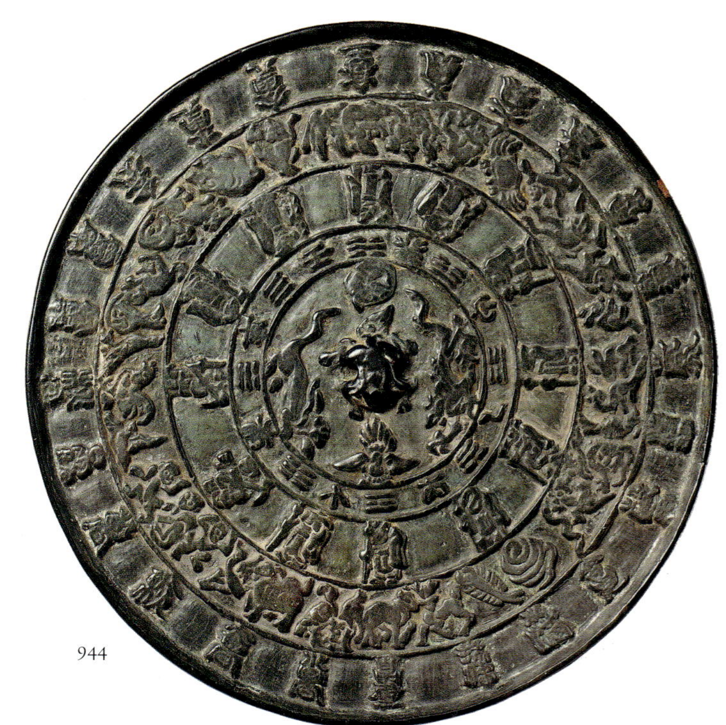

944

942. Water vessel (*kundika*)

Goryeo dynasty
Bronze
H. 35.7 cm (14 in.)

943. Mirror showing a ship at sea and inscription

Goryeo dynasty
Bronze with relief design
Diam. 16.7 cm (6 5/8 in.)
Text (煌丕昌天 *Brightly shining, prosperous sky*)

944. Mirror

Goryeo dynasty [possibly Chinese, Song (960–1279) or Yuan (1271–1368) dynasty]
Bronze with four directional guardian animals and twelve zodiac signs in relief
Diam. 17.7 cm (7 in.)

945. Bottle

Joseon dynasty, 15th–16th century
Bronze
H. 29.2 cm (11 1/2 in.)

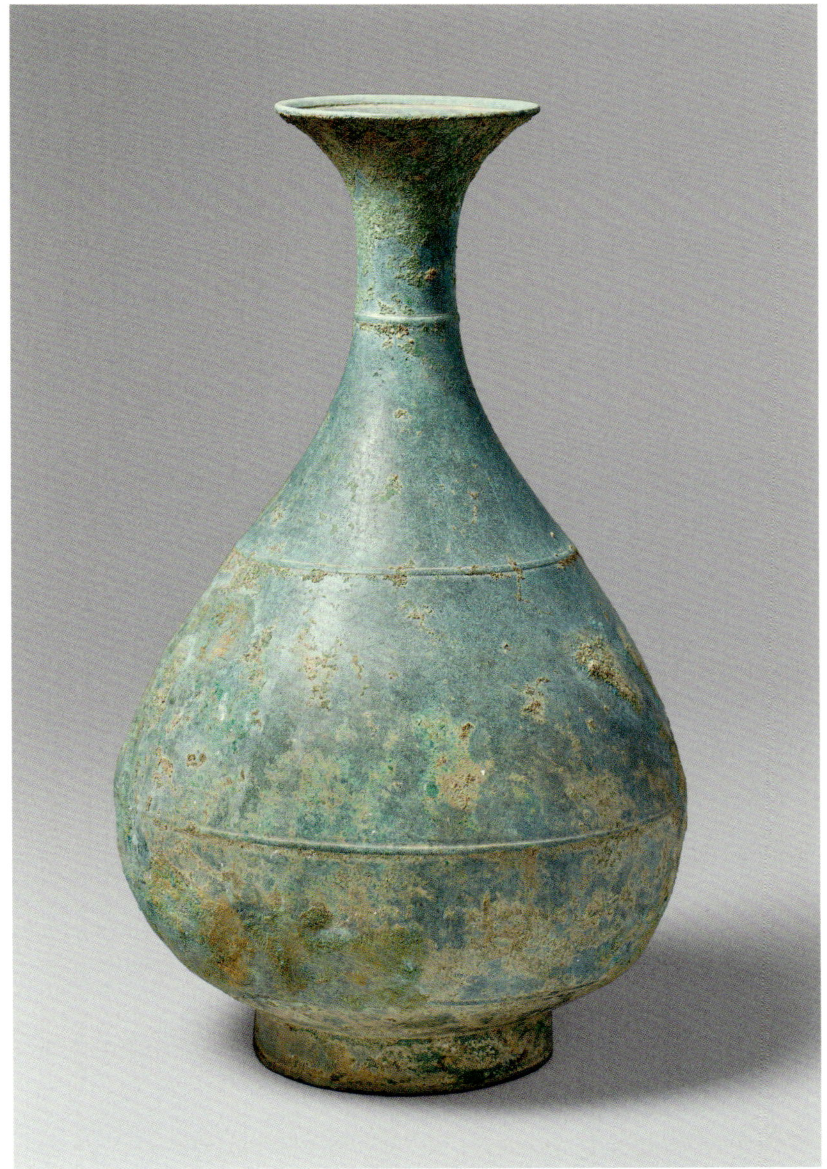

945

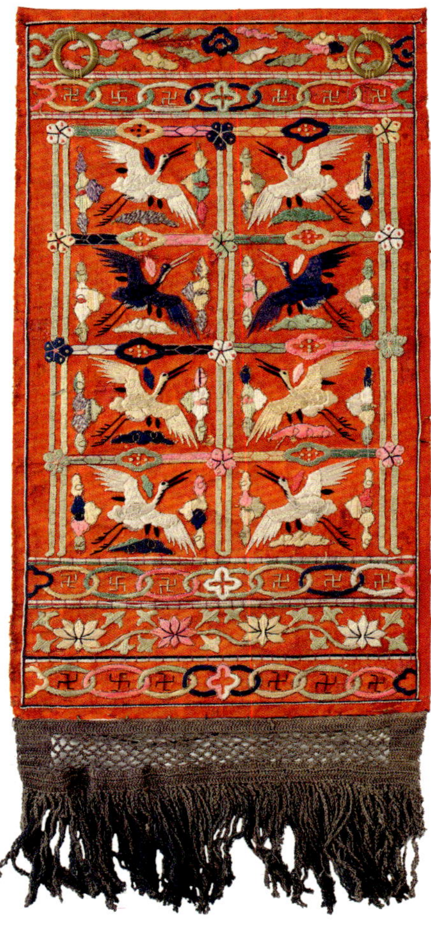

946. Decorative hanging panel for back of official robe (*husu*, 後綬) with cranes

Joseon dynasty, 19th century
Silk thread embroidery on silk
H. excluding fringe 43.8 cm (17 1/4 in.), w. 25.8 cm (10 1/8 in.)

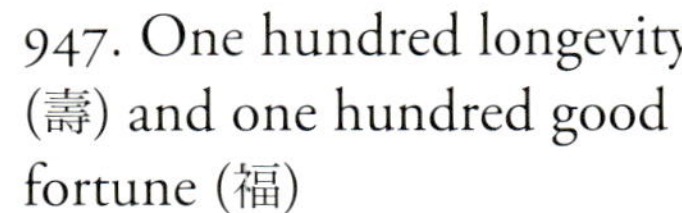

947. One hundred longevity (壽) and one hundred good fortune (福)

Joseon dynasty, 18th–19th century
Six framed panels; gold thread embroidery on silk
Each panel 86.7 x 32.1–32.3 cm (34 1/8 x 12 5/8–12 3/4 in.)

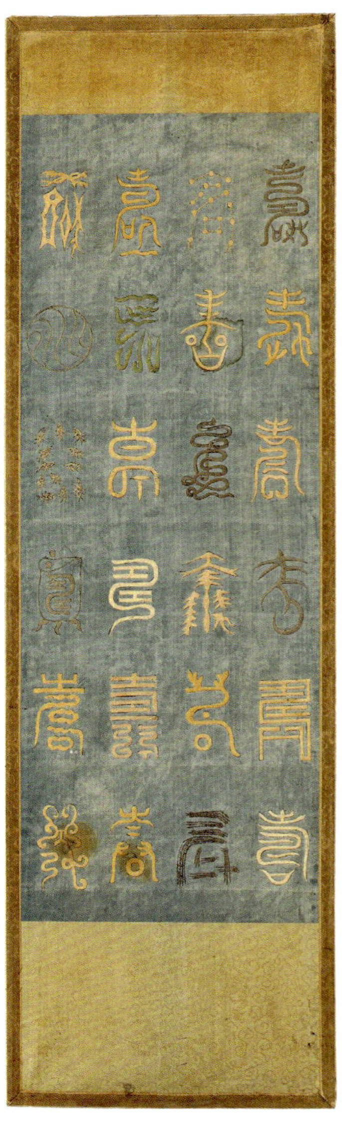

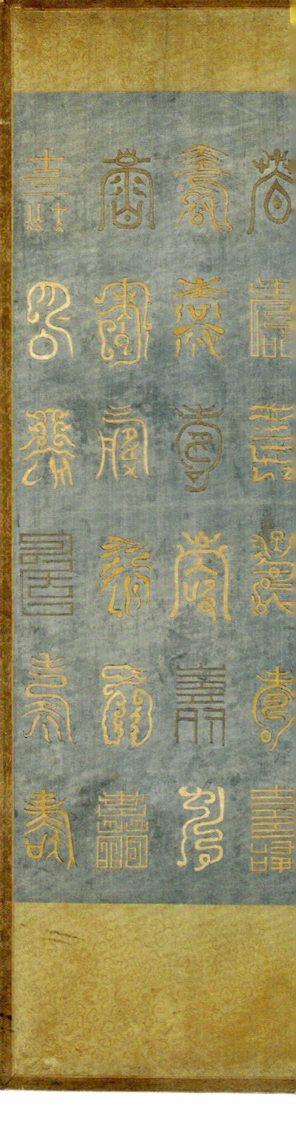

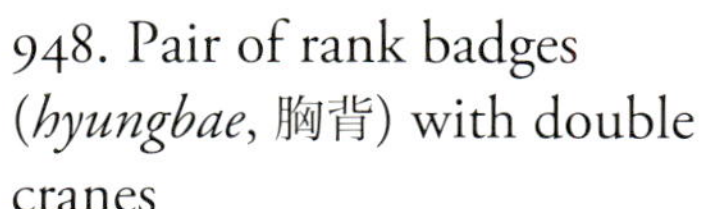

948. Pair of rank badges (*hyungbae*, 胸背) with double cranes

Joseon dynasty, 19th century
Silk thread embroidery on silk
Left: 23.3 x 19.5 cm (9 1/8 x 7 5/8 in.)
Right: 23.2 x 19.5 cm (9 1/8 x 7 5/8 in.)

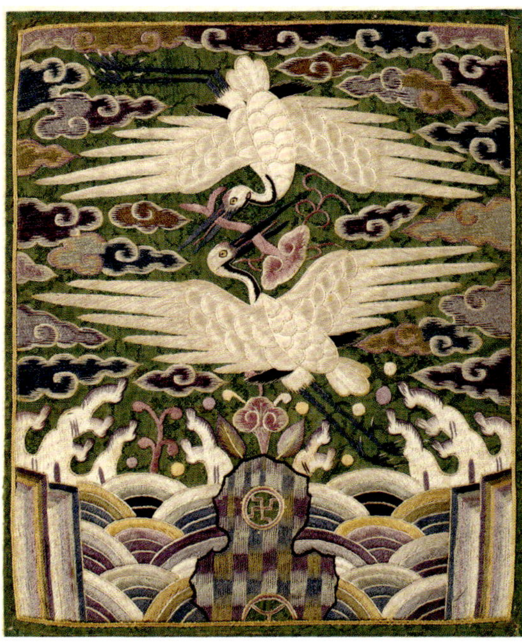

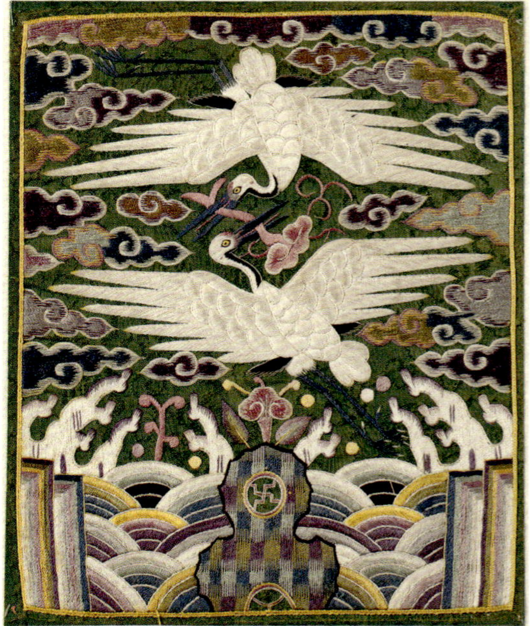

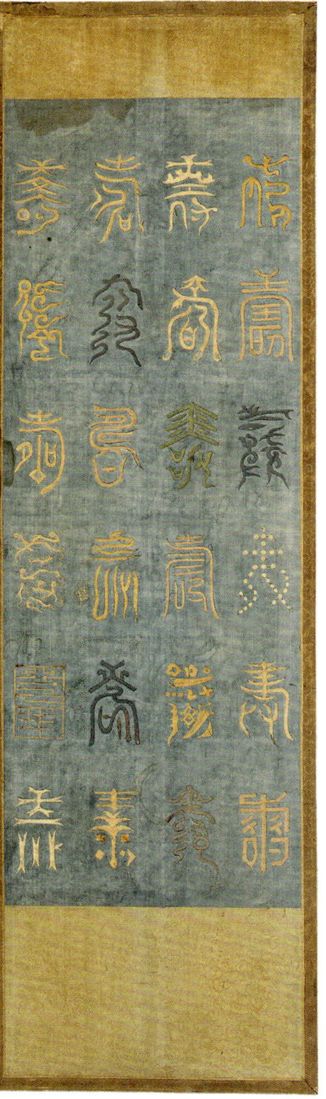
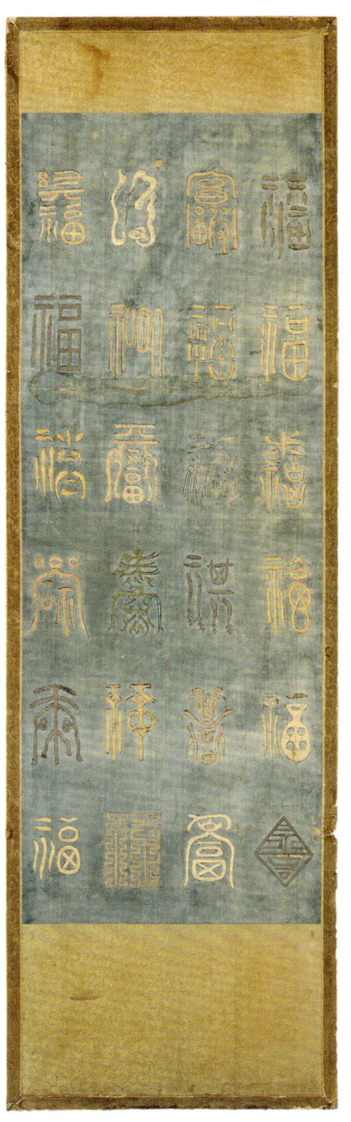
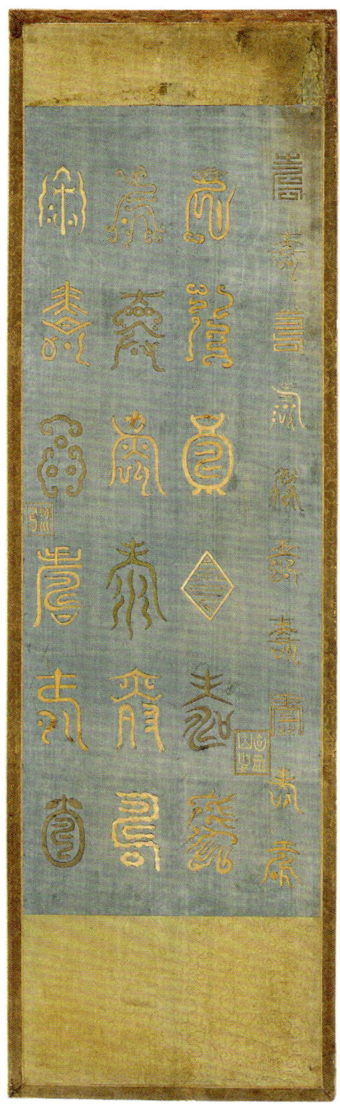
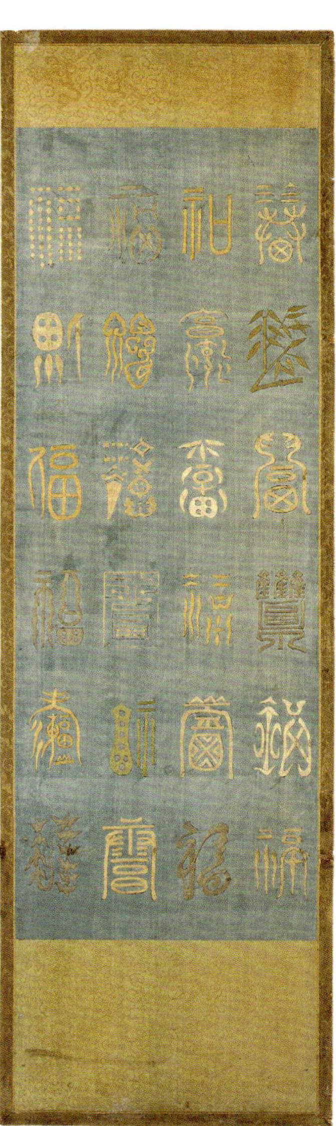
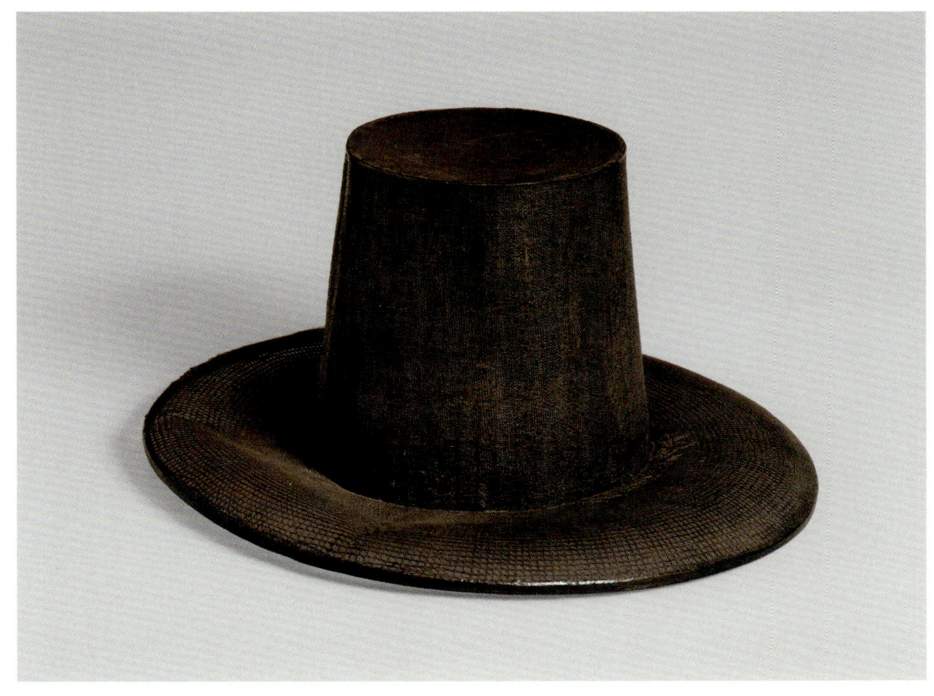

949. Hat

Joseon dynasty, late 19th–early 20th century
Horsetail hair and silk
H. 15 cm (5⅞ in.)

Gift from Julia Meech

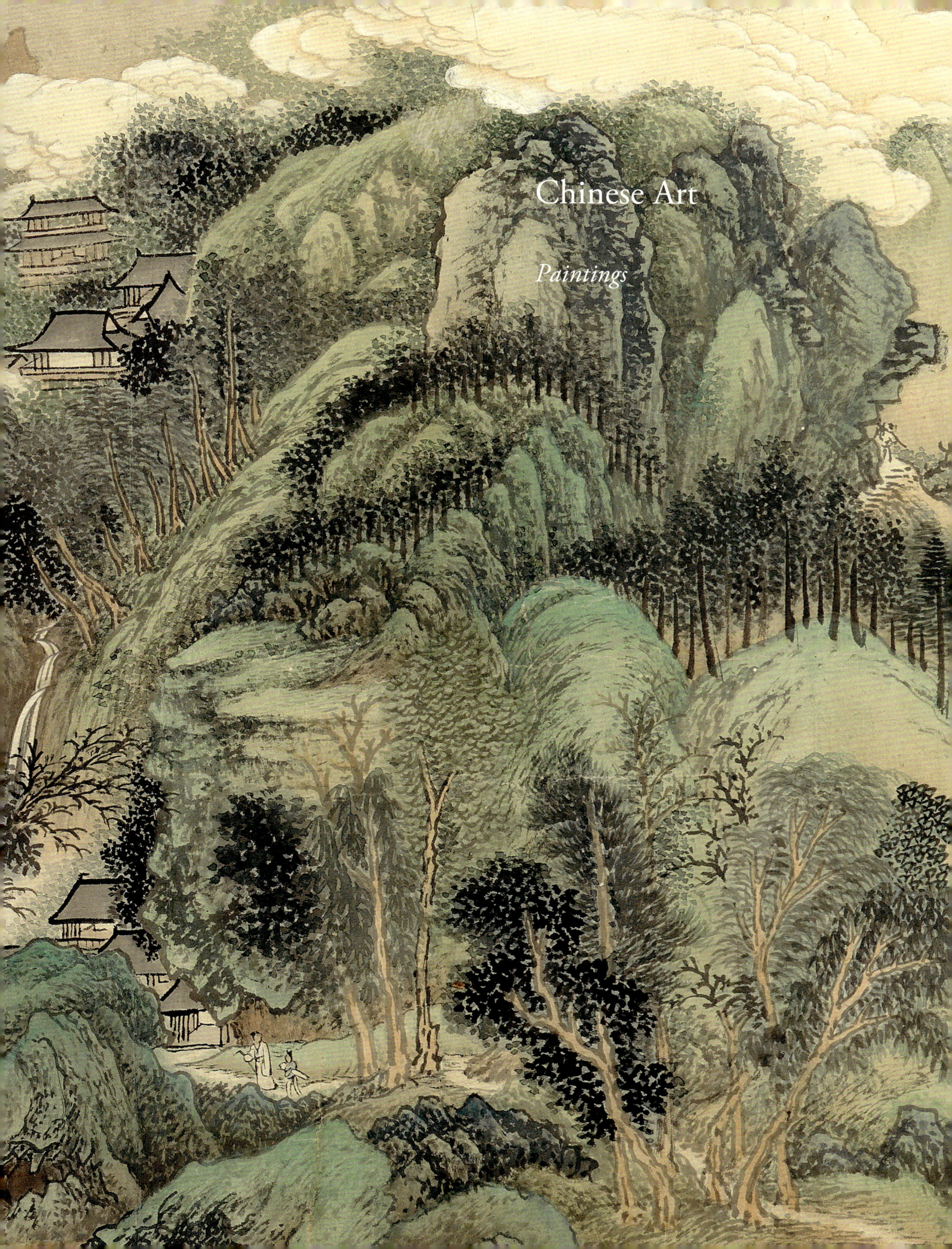

Chinese Art

Paintings

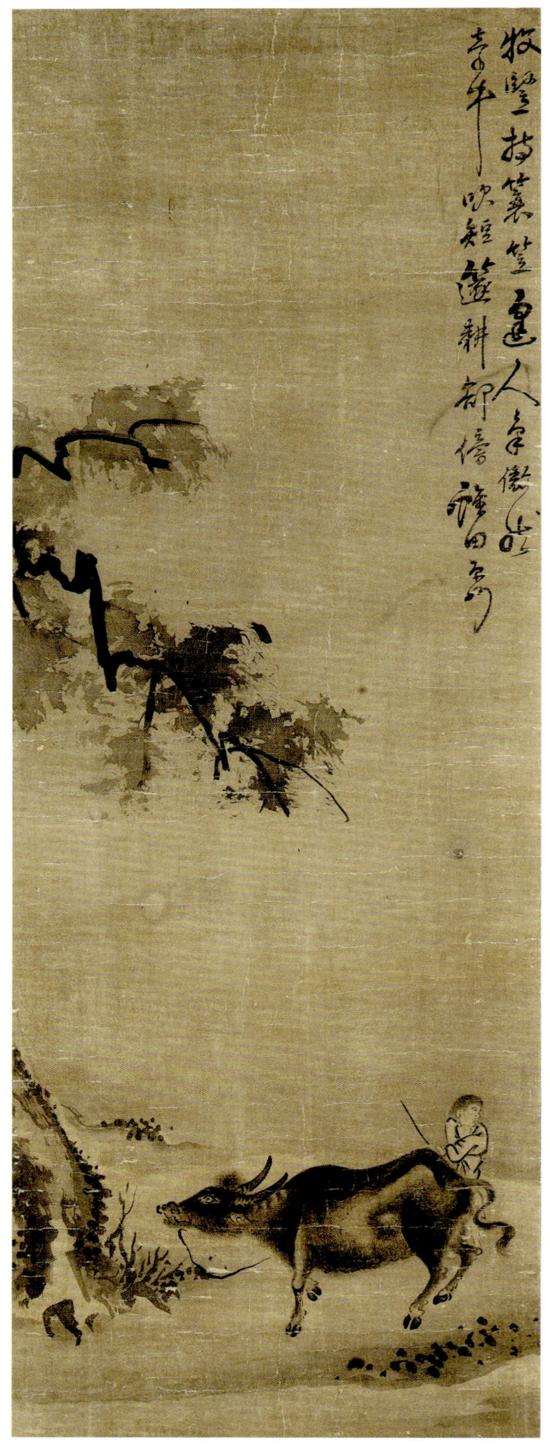

ATTRIBUTED TO YINTUOLUO
(因陀羅; full name Fanyin Tuoluo [梵因陀羅];
fl. late 13th–first half of 14th century)

950. Shide (拾得圖軸)

Yuan dynasty, late 13th century
Hanging scroll; ink on paper
87.5 x 31.2 cm (34½ x 12¼ in.)
Text, signature, seals

EX COLL.: Masaki Naohiko, Tokyo, 1938

LITERATURE: Harada Kinjirō 1938, p. 117.

ANONYMOUS

951. Ox and Herdsman (牧童圖)

Yuan dynasty, late 13th century
Hanging scroll, ink on silk
99.4 x 37.6 cm (39⅛ x 14¾ in.)
Text, signature

EX COLL.: Moriya Kōzō, Kyoto, 1922

LITERATURE: Toda Teisuke et al. 1973, pp. 145, 176, no. 105.

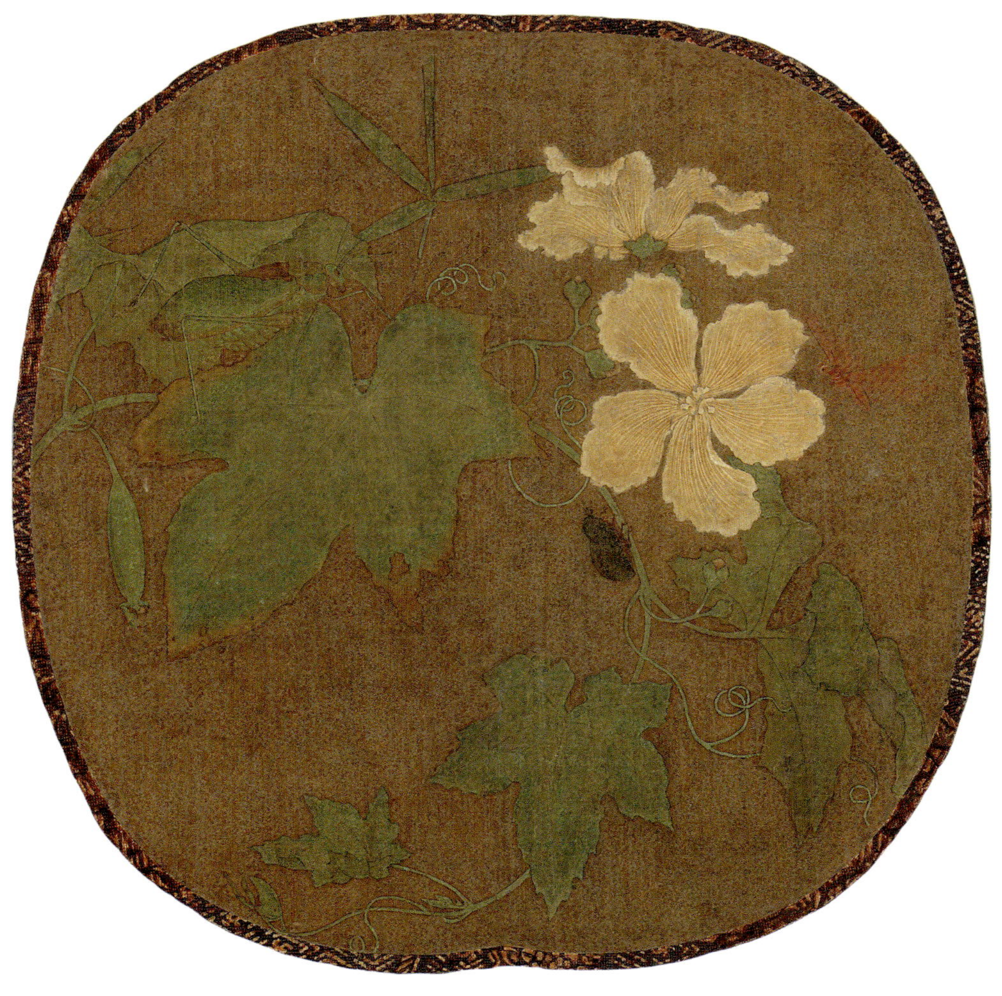

TRADITIONAL ATTRIBUTION TO ZHAO CHANG
(趙昌; ca. 960–after 1016)

952. Melon Flowers and Insects

Yuan dynasty, late 13th–14th century
Fan mounted as a hanging scroll; ink and color on silk
H. 22.4 x 23.2 cm (8 7/8 x 9 1/8 in.)

EX COLL.: Moriya Kōzō, Kyoto, 1922

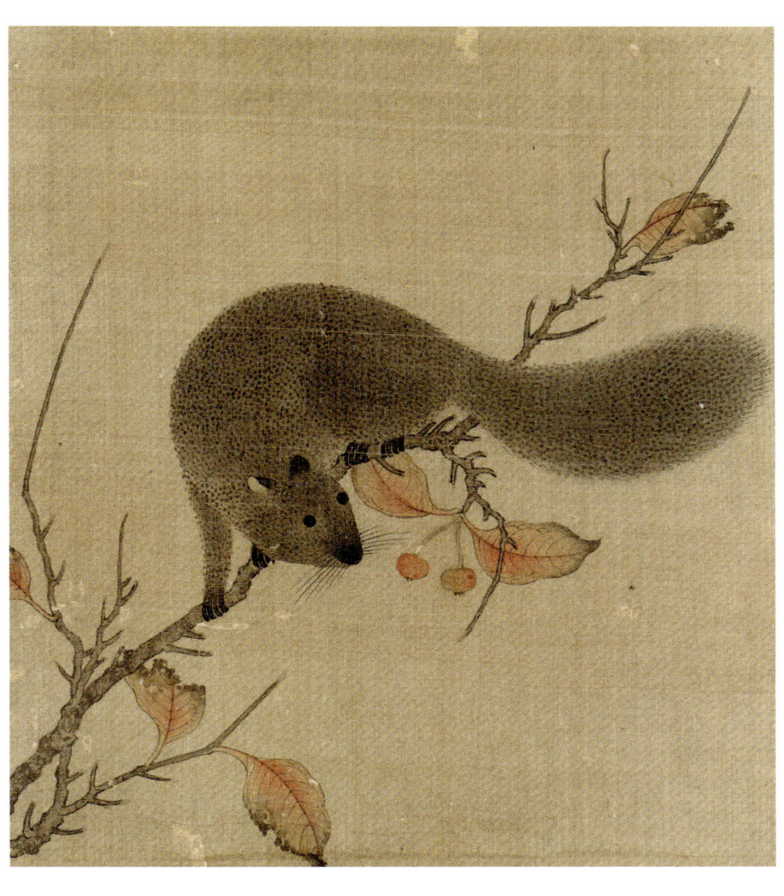

ANONYMOUS
Attributed to Tao Cheng (陶成; fl. mid-15th century) by Kano Eishin (Yasunobu) (狩野永真 [安信]; 1613–1685)

953. Squirrel on a Branch

Ming dynasty, 15th century
Album leaf mounted as a hanging scroll; ink and color on silk
23.5 x 21.5 cm (9 1/4 x 8 1/2 in.)

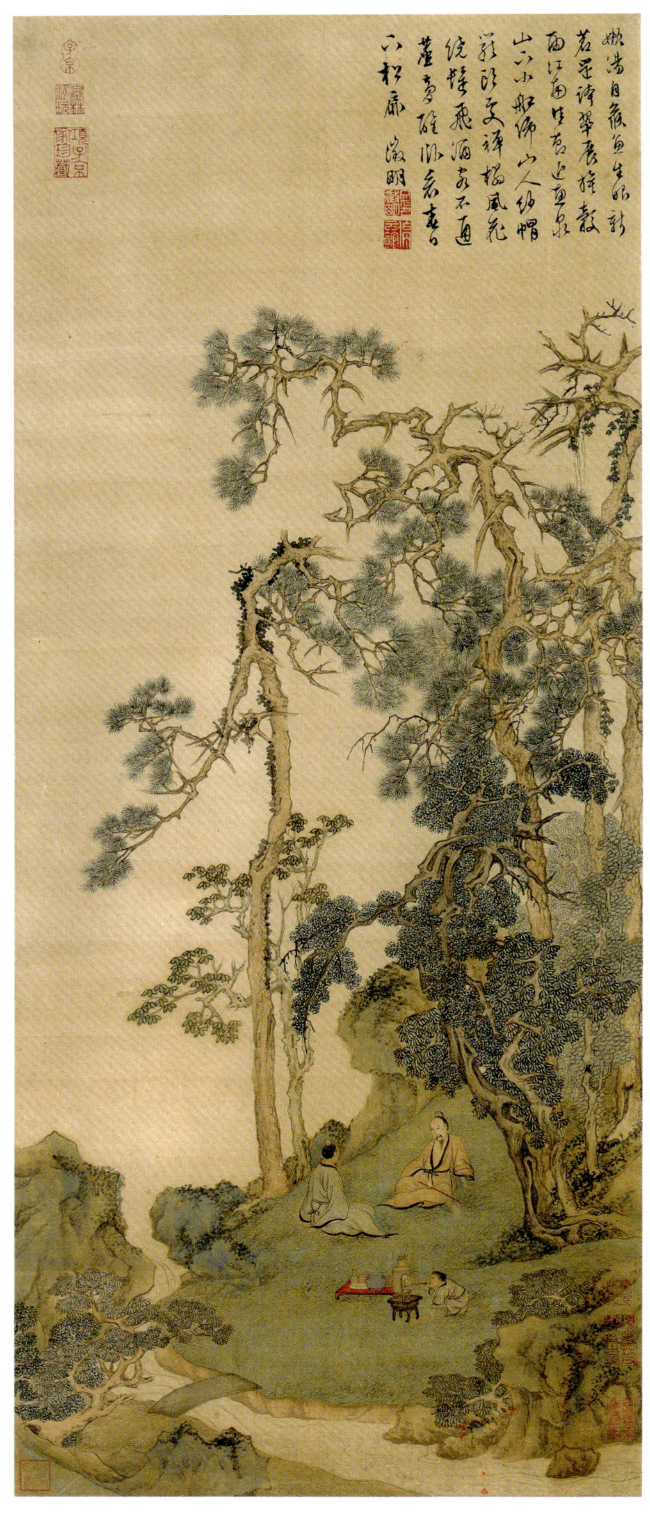

Wen Zhengming
(文徵明; 1470–1559)

954. Brewing Tea on a Spring Evening
(煎茶圖軸)

Ming dynasty, ca. 1540
Framed, formerly a hanging scroll; ink and color on silk
91.5 x 46.5 cm (36 x 18¼ in.)
Text, signature, seals

Literature: Mi Chou Gallery 1962; Clapp 1975, fig. 17, p. XIV; Edwards 1976, no. XXVII, pp. 114–15.

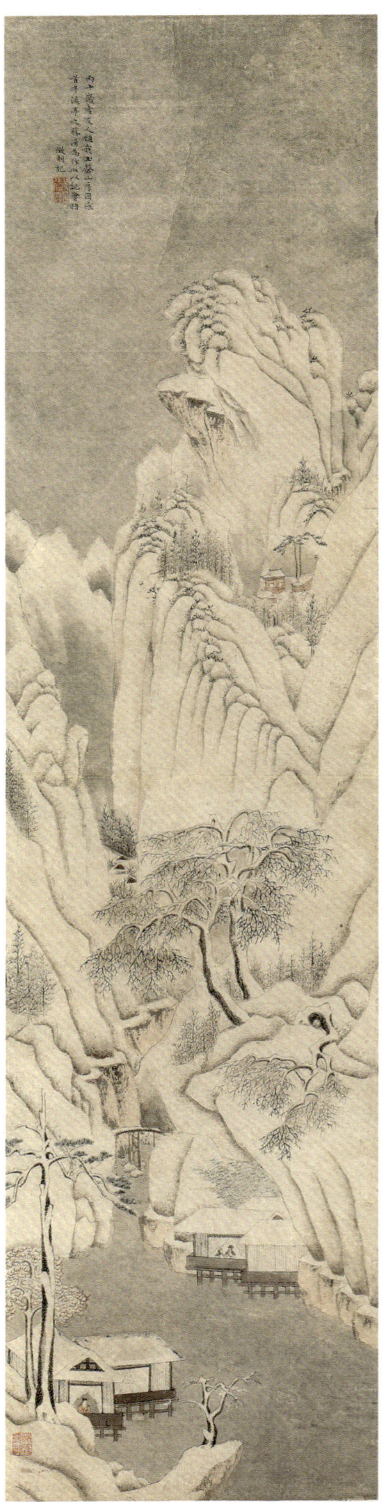

attributed to Wen Zhengming
(傳文徵明; 1470–1559)

955. Deep Snow over Streams and Mountains (溪山深雪圖軸)

Attributed inscription dated to 1546
Qing dynasty, late 18th–early 19th century
Framed, formerly hanging scroll; ink and light color on paper
101.3 x 25.8 cm (39⅞ x 10⅛ in.)
Text, signature, seals

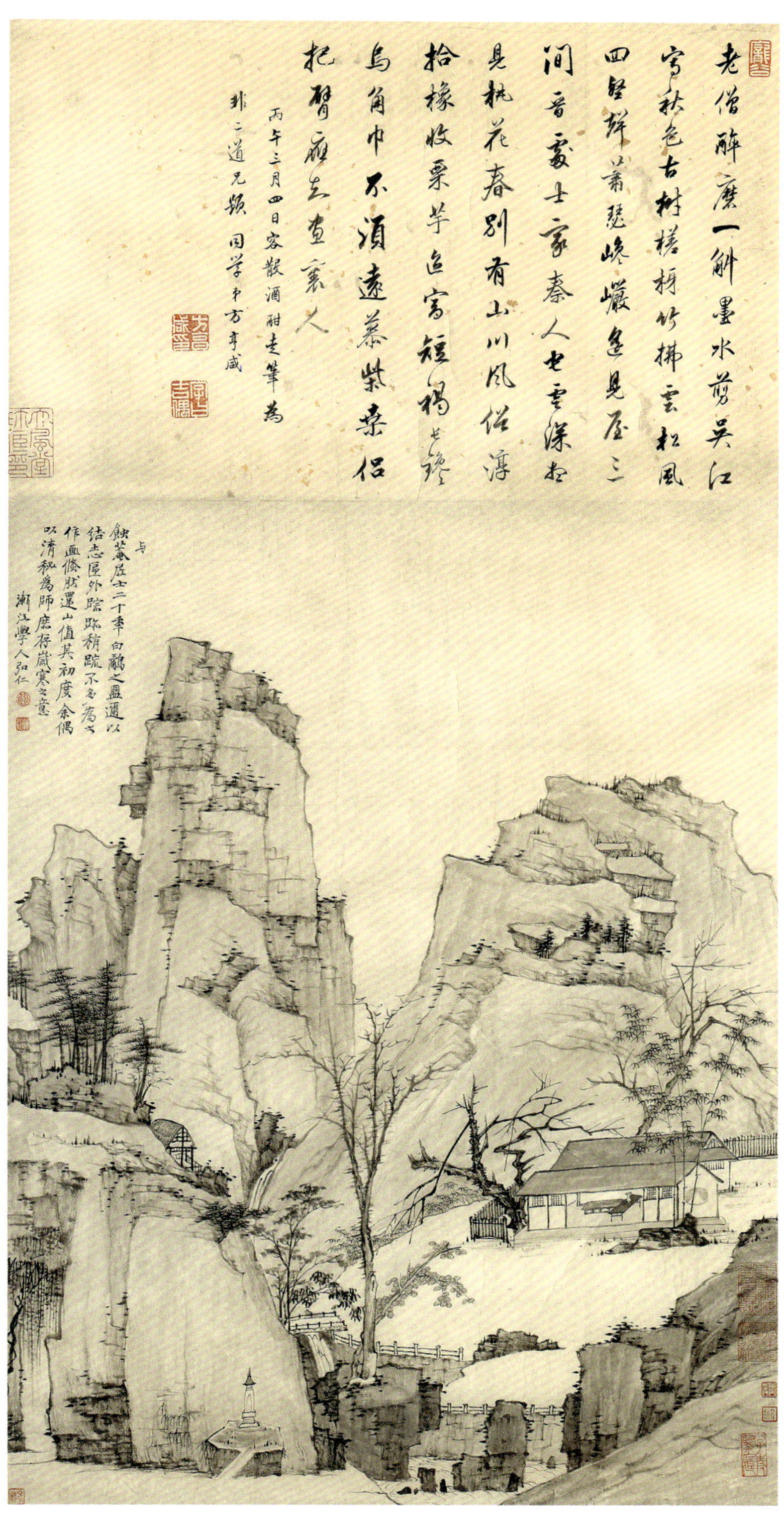

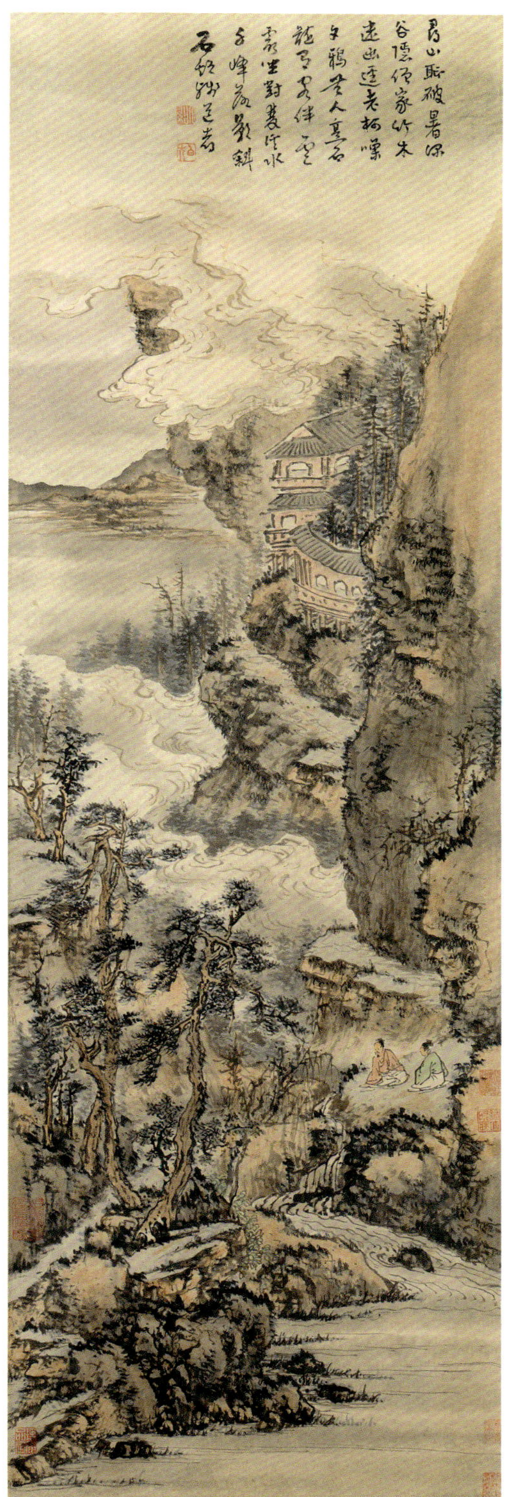

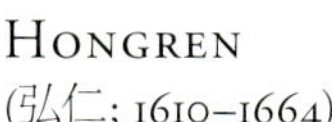

HONGREN
(弘仁; 1610–1664)

956. Landscape for Shian
(為蝕菴寫山水圖軸)

Qing dynasty, ca. 1657–58
Framed, formerly a hanging scroll; ink on paper
Painting 60.2 x 46.8 cm (23 x 18 3/8 in.)
Painting with *shitang* 88.6 x 46.8 cm (34 7/8 x 18 3/8 in.)
Text, signature, seals

LITERATURE: Zhang Wanli and Hu Renmu 1969, pl. 12; Cahill 1981, no. 26; Kuo 1990, p. 214, pl. 172.

KUNCAN
(髡殘; 1612–ca. 1674)

957. A Deep Valley Conceals a Monk's Home (深谷隱僧家圖軸)

Qing dynasty, mid-17th century
Framed, formerly a hanging scroll; ink and color on paper
110.4 x 37.1 cm (43 1/2 x 14 5/8 in.)
Text, signature, seals

LITERATURE: Pang Yuanji [1909], vol. 10, p. 18.

Chen Danzhong
(陳丹衷; *jinshi* 1642)

958. Clouds Rising above Mountains and Streams (山川出雲圖)

Ming–Qing dynasty, 17th century, before 1652
Framed album leaf; ink on paper
24.8 x 32.2 cm (9 3/4 x 12 5/8 in.), excluding frame
Text, signature, seals

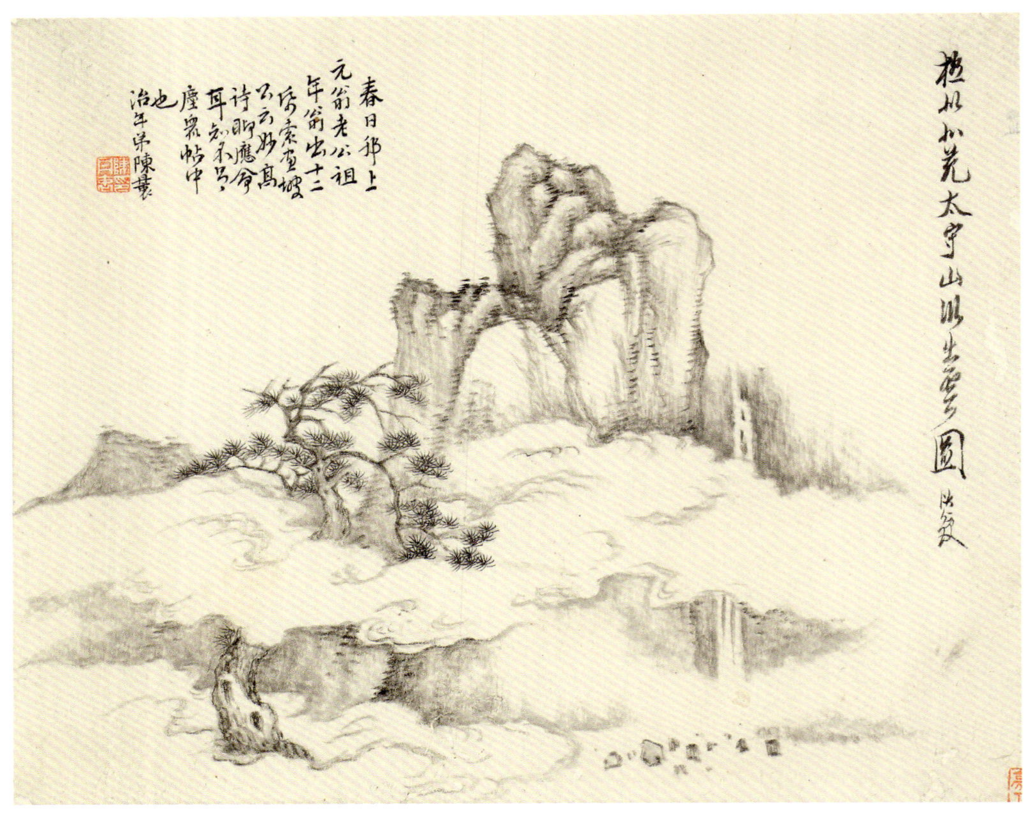

Wang Hui
(王翬; 1632–1717)

959. Landscape

Qing dynasty, 1669
Handscroll; ink and color on paper
38 x 187.5 cm (15 x 73 3/8 in.)
Text, signature, seals

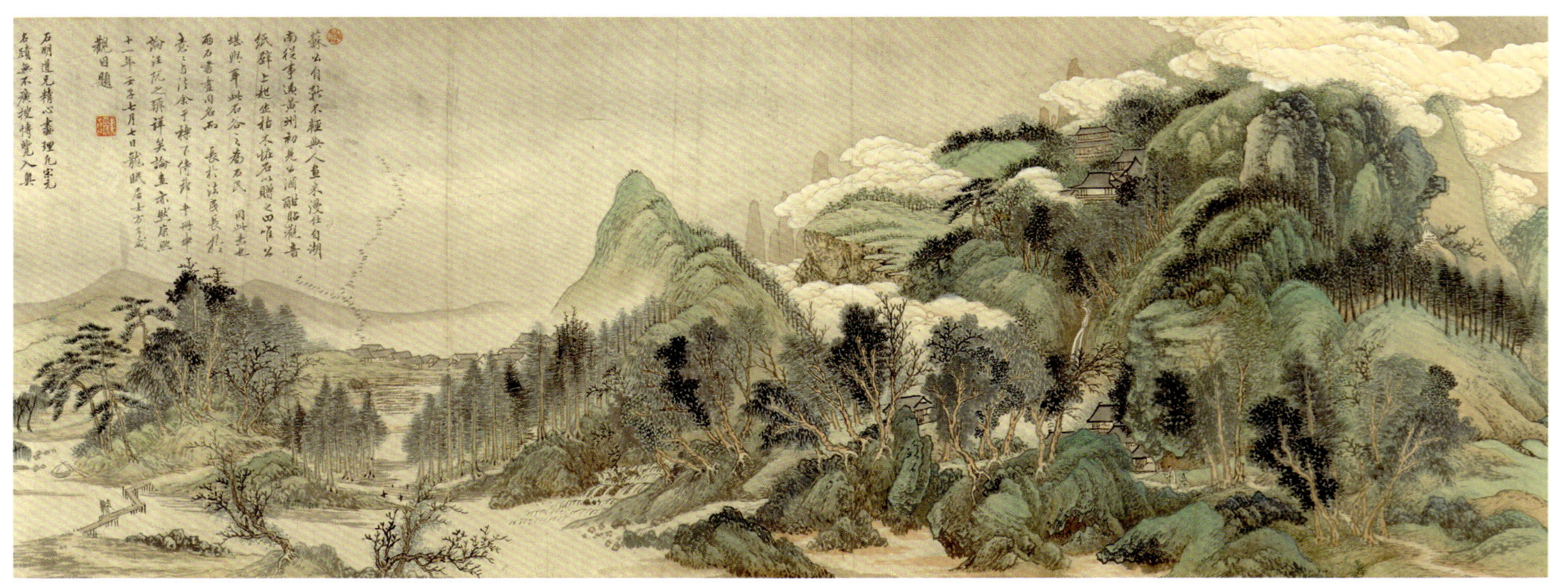

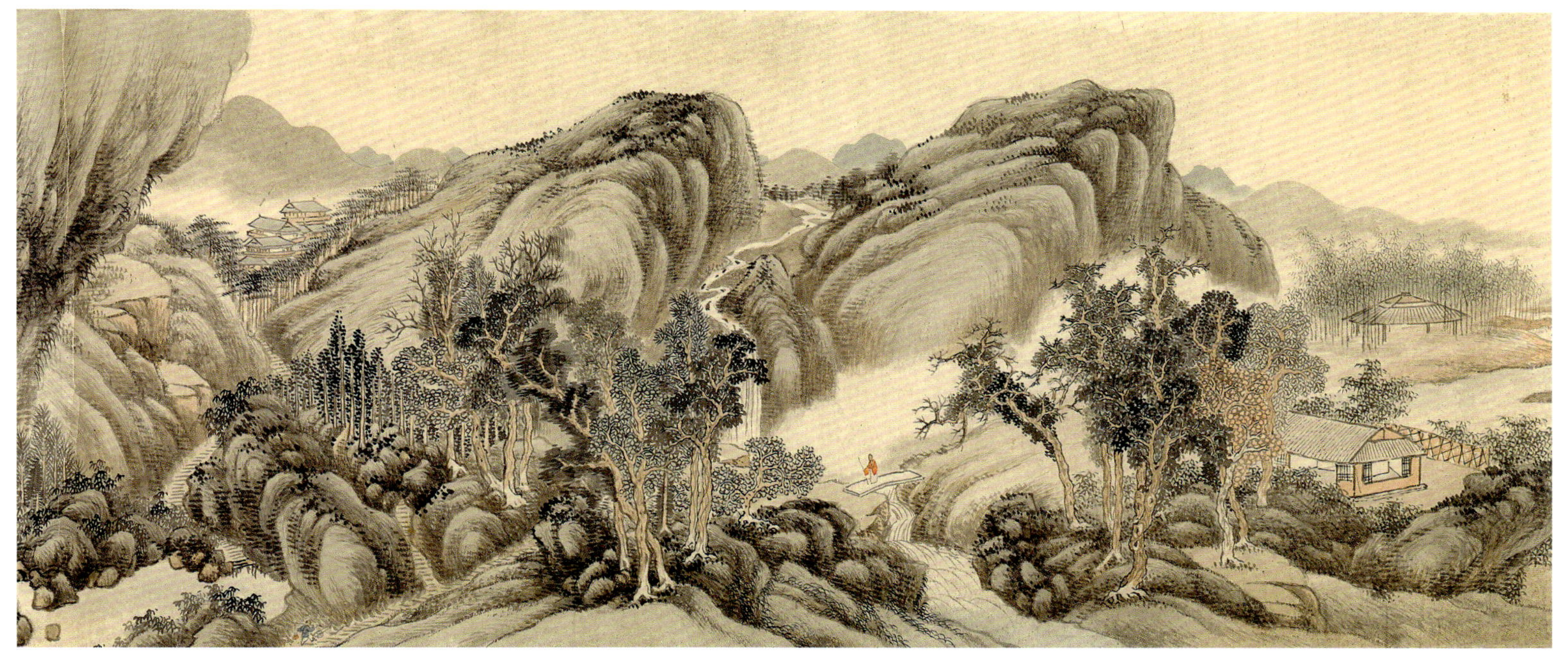

ATTRIBUTED TO HUANG DING
(黃鼎; 1660–1730)

960. Autumn Colors on Streams and Mountains (溪山秋色圖卷)

Qing dynasty, 18th–19th century
Handscroll; ink and color on paper
33.7 x 268.6 cm (13¼ x 105¾ in.)
Text, signature, seals

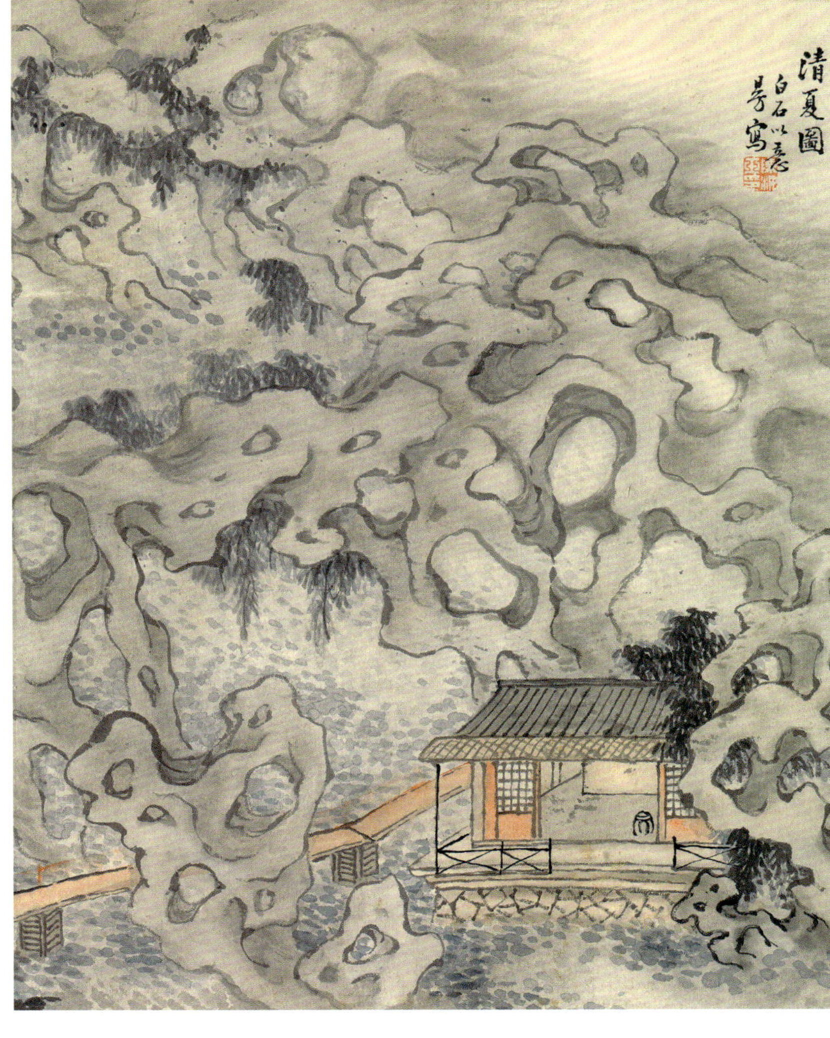

CHEN RUYU
(陳汝玉; fl. 18th–19th century)

961. Clear Summer (清夏圖)

Qing dynasty, 18th–19th century
Framed album leaf; ink and color on paper
41 x 33.7 cm (16⅛ x 13¼ in.), excluding frame
Text, signature, seal

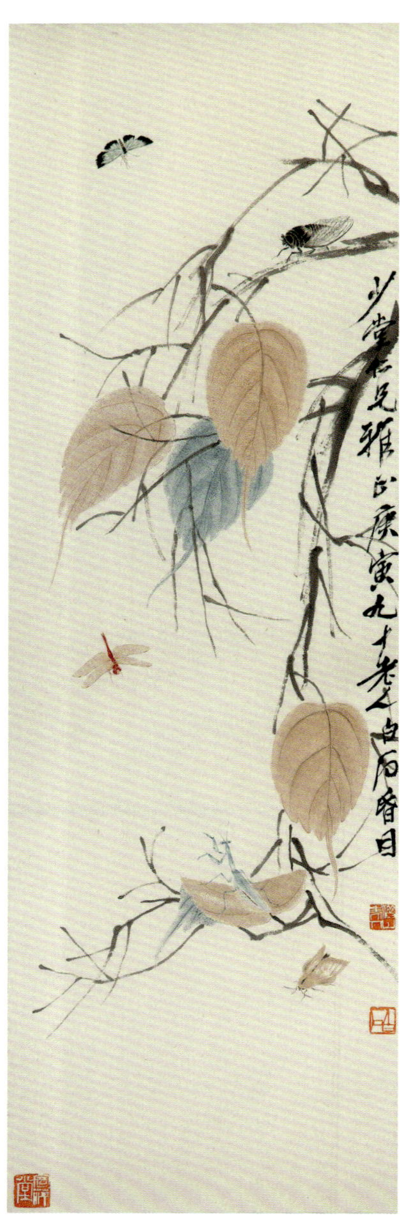

Qi Baishi
(齊白石; 1863–1957)

962. Autumn Insects (秋蟲)

1950
Framed, formerly hanging scroll; ink and color on paper
102.3 x 34.2 cm (40¼ x 13½ in.), excluding frame
Text, signature, seals

Qi Baishi
(齊白石; 1863–1957)

963. Lotus (蓮花)

1950
Framed, formerly hanging scroll; ink and color on paper
68.6 x 34.3 cm (27 x 13½ in.)
Signature, seal

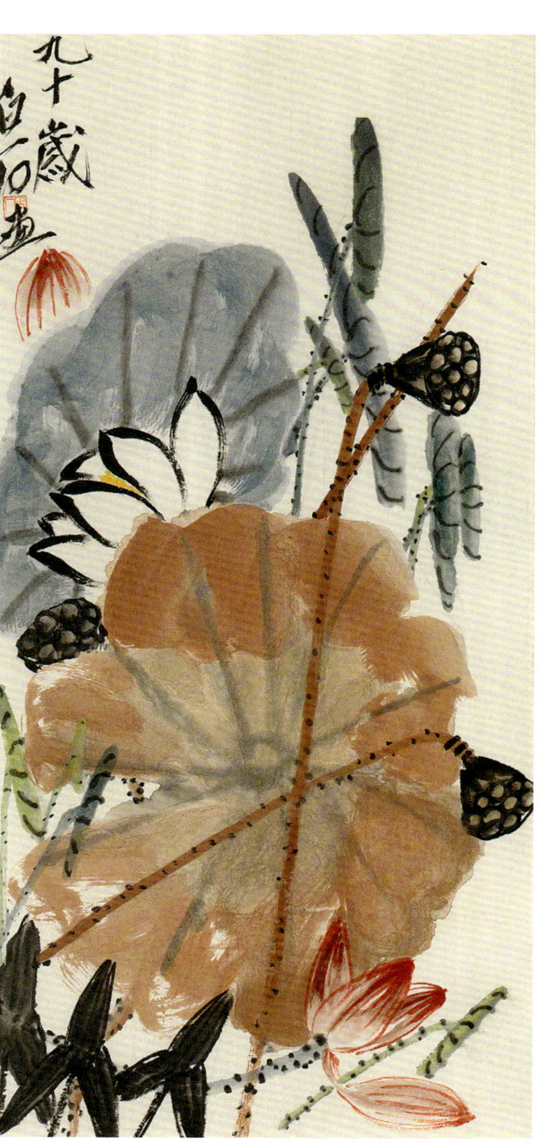

Qi Baishi
(齊白石; 1863–1957)

964. Basket of Litchi (荔枝筐)

1950
Framed, formerly hanging scroll; ink and color on paper
67.9 x 31.8 cm (26¾ x 12½ in.)
Signature, seal

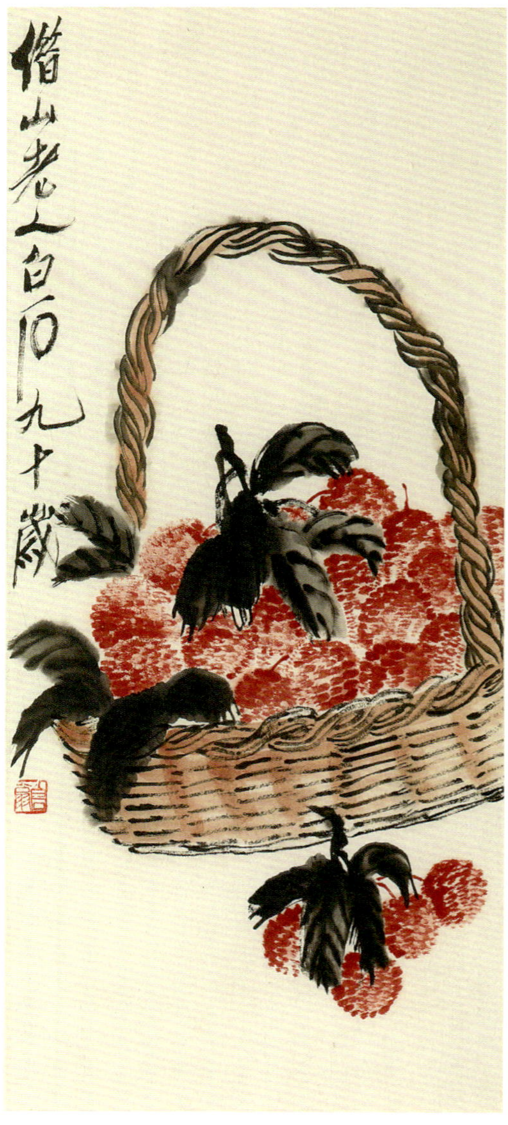

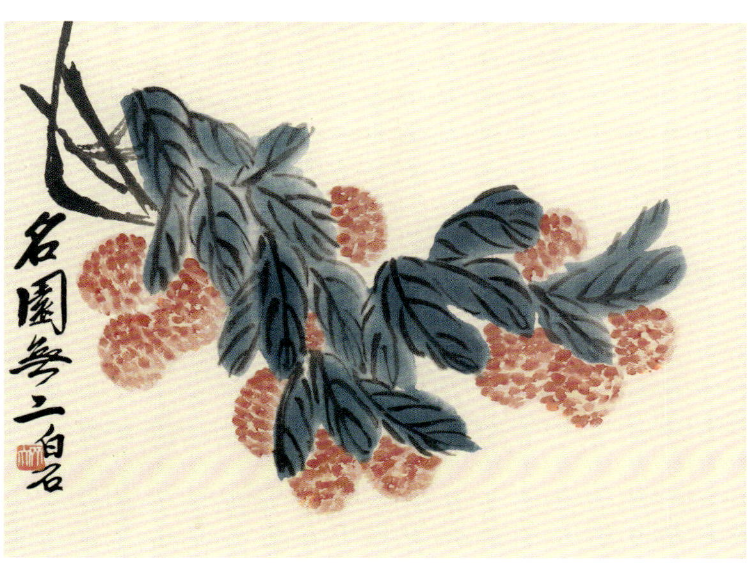

Qi Baishi
(齊白石; 1863–1957)

965. (*a*) Peony (牡丹); (*b*) Branch of Litchi (荔枝)

1950s
Framed album leaves; ink and color on paper
(*a*) 22.3 x 30.5 cm (8¾ x 12 in.); (*b*) 23.1 x 30.6 cm (9⅛ x 12 in.), excluding frames
(*a*) Signature, seal; (*b*) text, signature, seal

Qi Baishi
(齊白石; 1863–1957)

966. Autumn Fragrance (秋香)

1950s
Framed album leaf; ink and color on paper
21.8 x 30.4 cm (8⅝ x 12 in.), excluding frame
Text, signature, seal

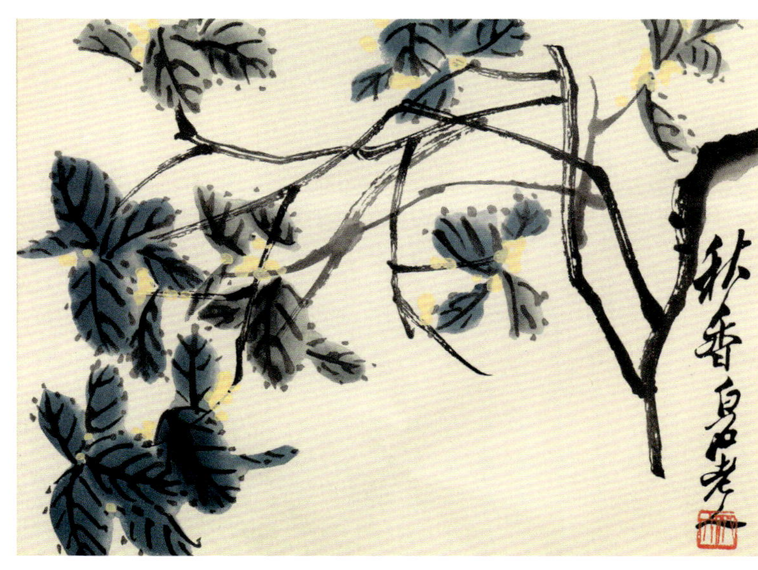

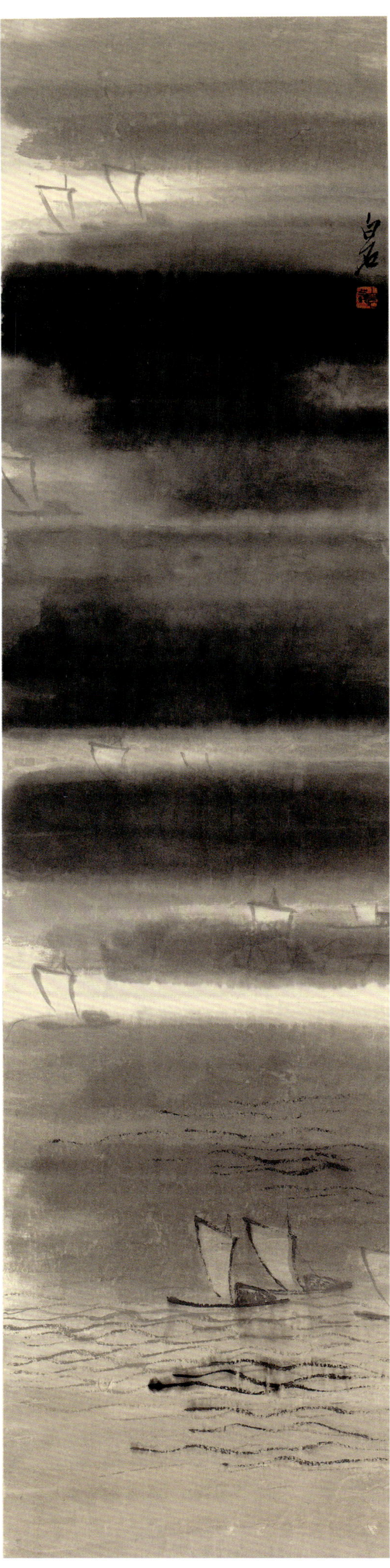

Qi Baishi
(齊白石; 1863–1957)

967. Sails on the Yangzi River
(長江帆船)

Mid-20th century
Hanging scroll; ink on paper
129.8 x 33.1 cm (51 1/8 x 13 in.)
Signature, seal

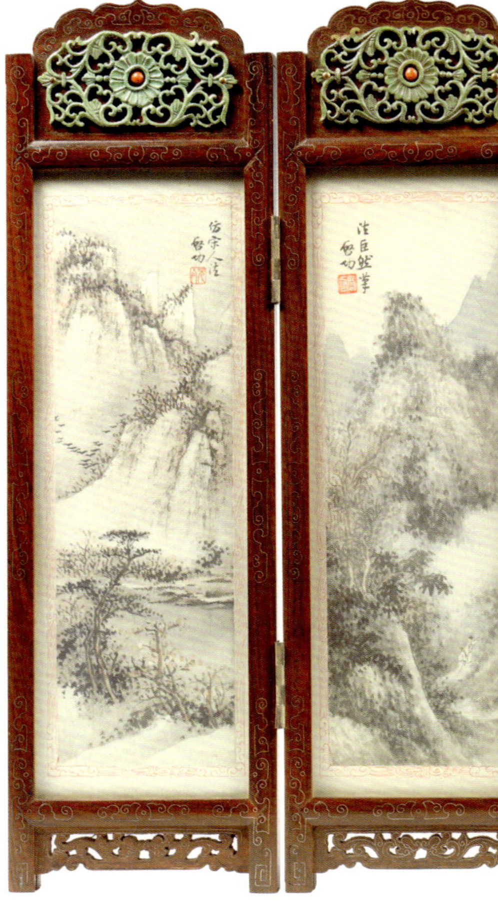

Qi Gong
(啓功; 1912–2005)

968. Landscapes in the Styles of Old Masters

Republic of China (1912–49) or People's Republic of China (1949–present), mid-20th century
Eight-panel table screen; ink and color on paper
23 x 8 cm (9 x 3 1/8 in.)
Text, signatures, seals

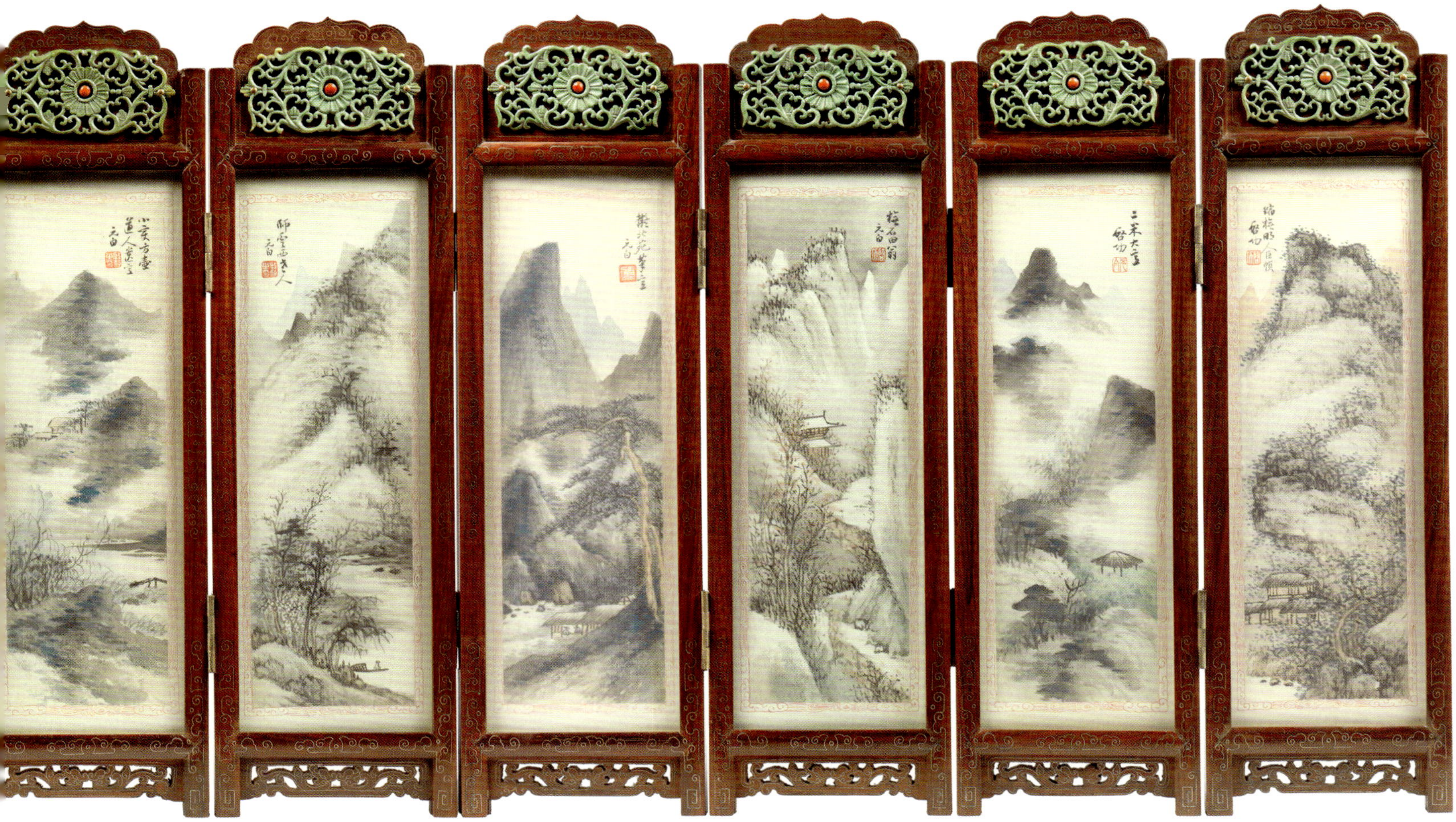

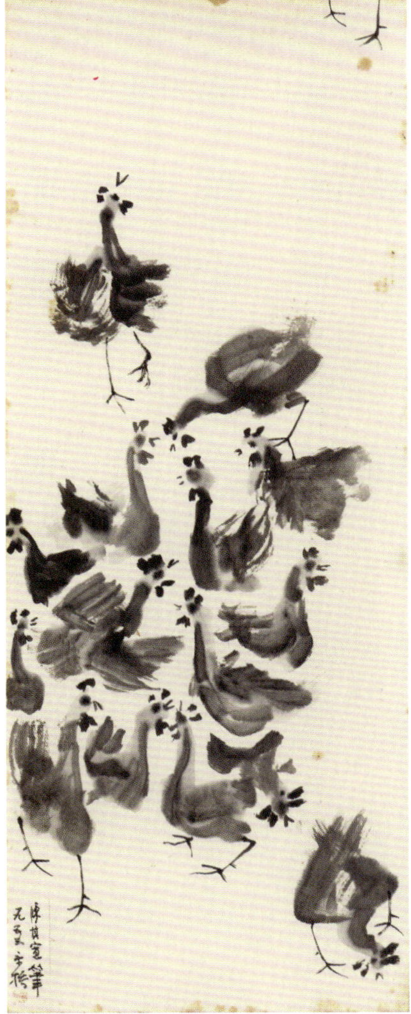

Chen Chi-kwan
(陳其寬, Chen Qikuan; 1921–2007)

969. Untitled (Anxious)

1953
Framed painting; ink on paper
61 x 24.2 cm (24 x 9½ in.)
Signature, seal

Chen Chi-kwan
(陳其寬, Chen Qikuan; 1921–2007)

970. Fishing (漁魚) (Pier)

1953
Framed painting; ink and color on paper
120.7 x 23 cm (47½ x 9 in.)
Signature, seal

Literature: Rahman-Steinert 1996, no. 4.

Chen Chi-kwan
(陳其寬, Chen Qikuan; 1921–2007)

971. Impressions of an American Football Game (美國足球賽印象)

1954
Framed painting; ink on paper
121.5 x 24.4 cm (47⅞ x 9⅝ in.)
Signature, seal

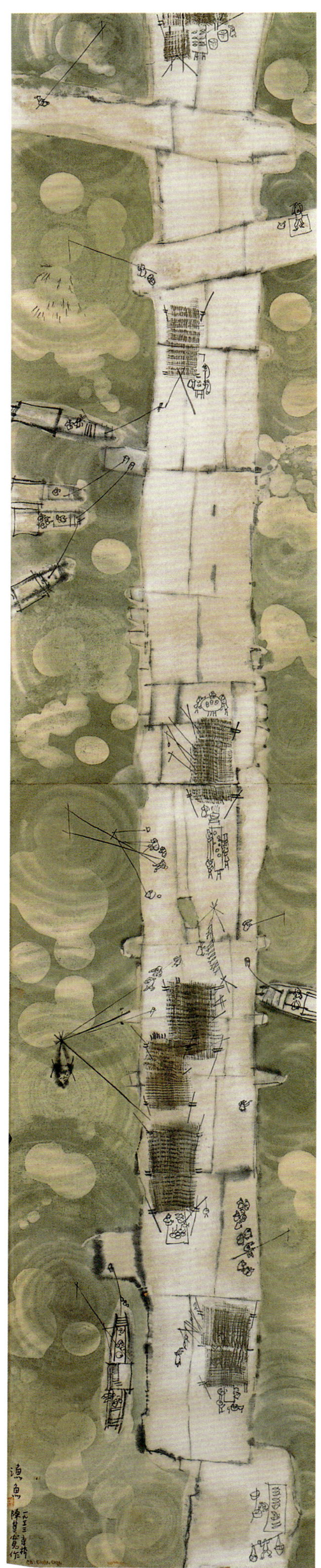

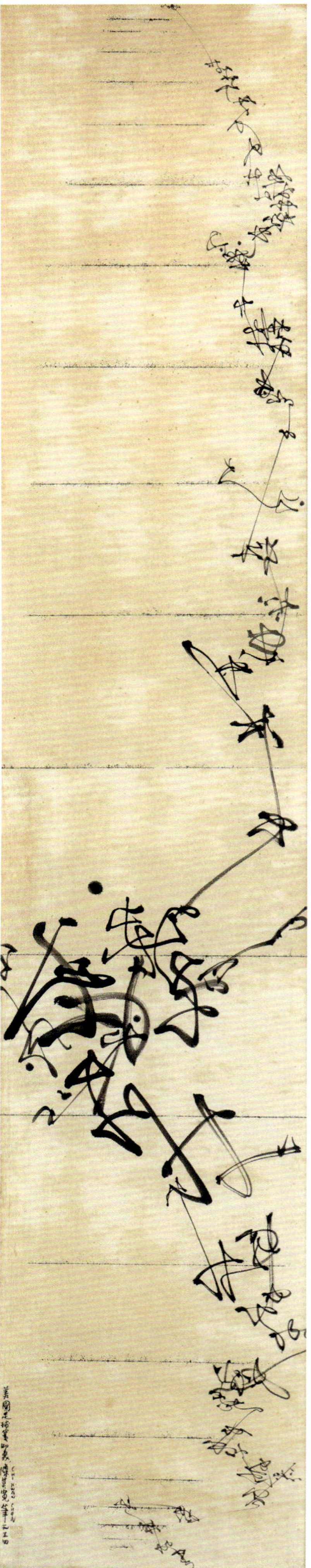

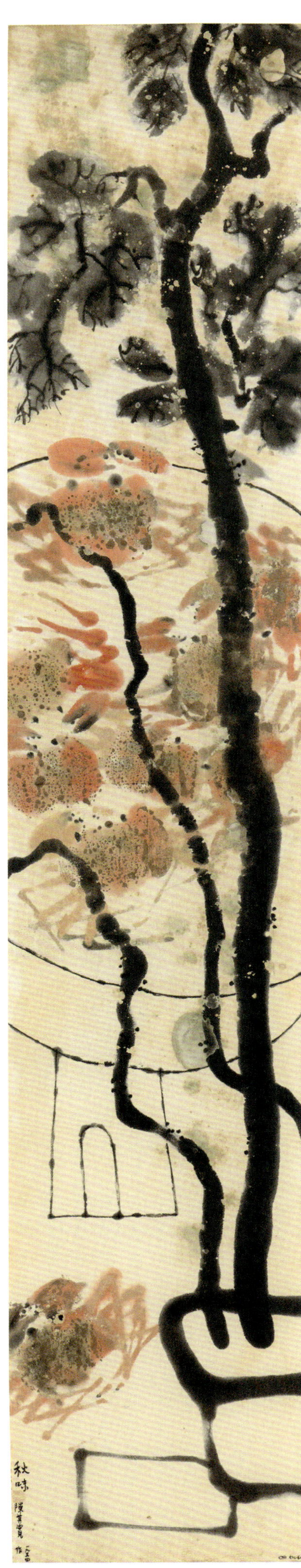

Chen Chi-kwan
(陳其寬, Chen Qikuan; 1921–2007)

972. Autumn Delicacies (秋味)

1954
Framed painting; ink and color on paper
121.6 x 24 cm ($47\frac{7}{8}$ x $9\frac{1}{2}$ in.)
Signature, seal

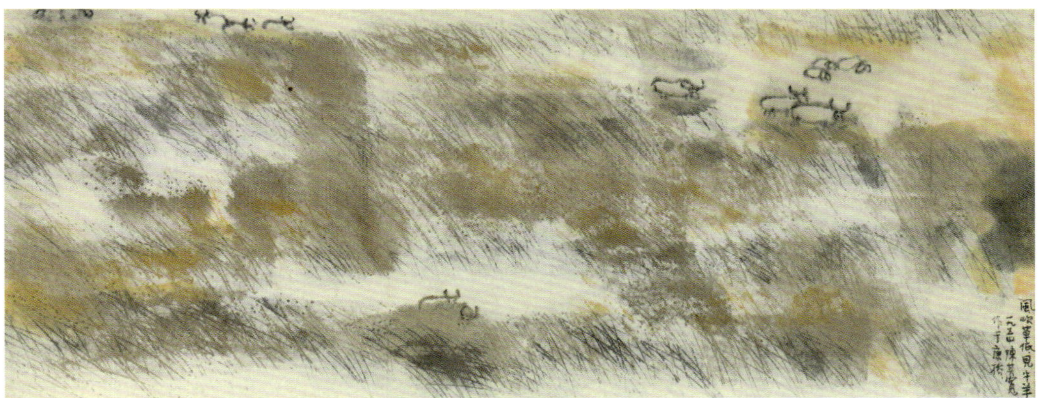

Chen Chi-kwan
(陳其寬, Chen Qikuan; 1921–2007)

973. Untitled (Where the Buffalo Roam)

1954
Framed painting; ink and color on paper
23.3 x 61 cm ($9\frac{1}{8}$ x 24 in.)
Text, signature

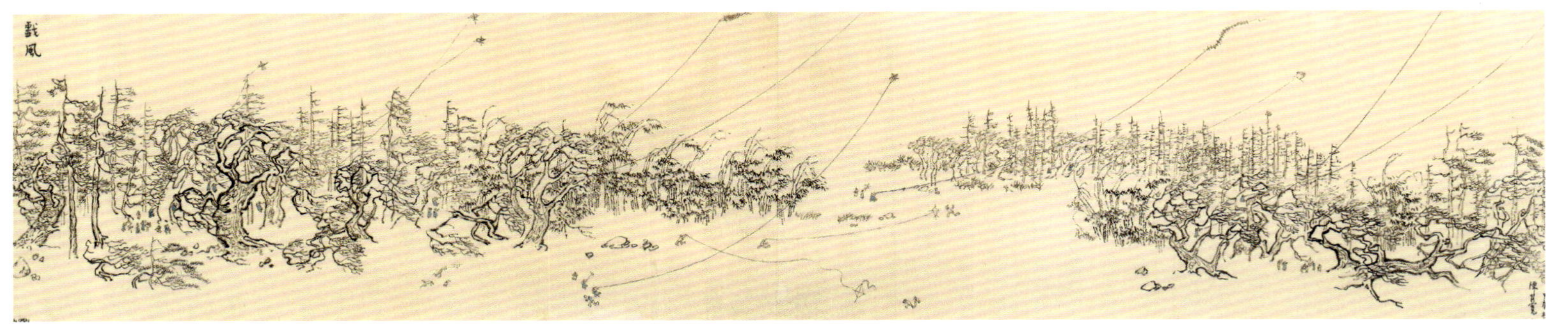

Chen Chi-kwan
(陳其寬, Chen Qikuan; 1921–2007)

974. Playing in the Wind (戲風)

1954
Framed painting; ink on paper
23.3 x 121 cm (9 5/8 x 47 5/8 in.)
Signature, seal

Chen Chi-kwan
(陳其寬, Chen Qikuan; 1921–2007)

975. Untitled (Monkeys)

1955
Framed painting; ink on paper
23.8 x 60.5 cm (9 3/8 x 23 7/8 in.)
Signature

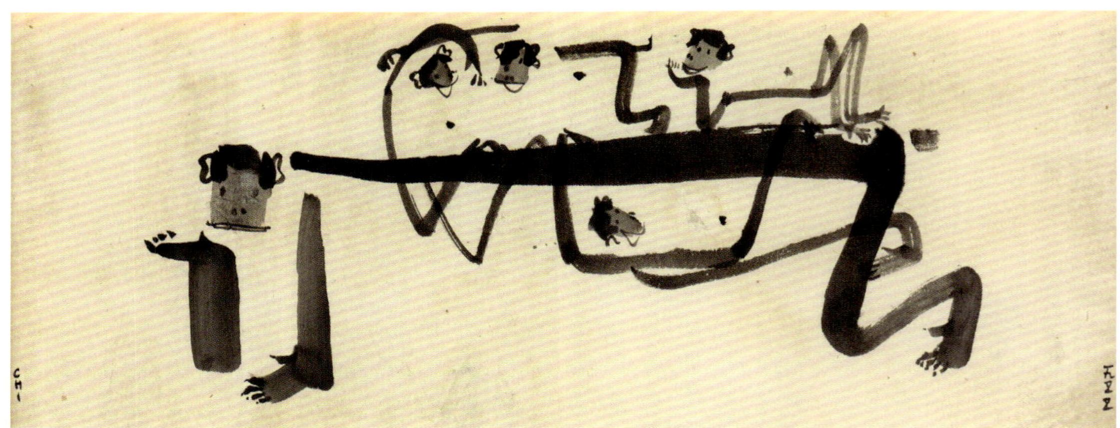

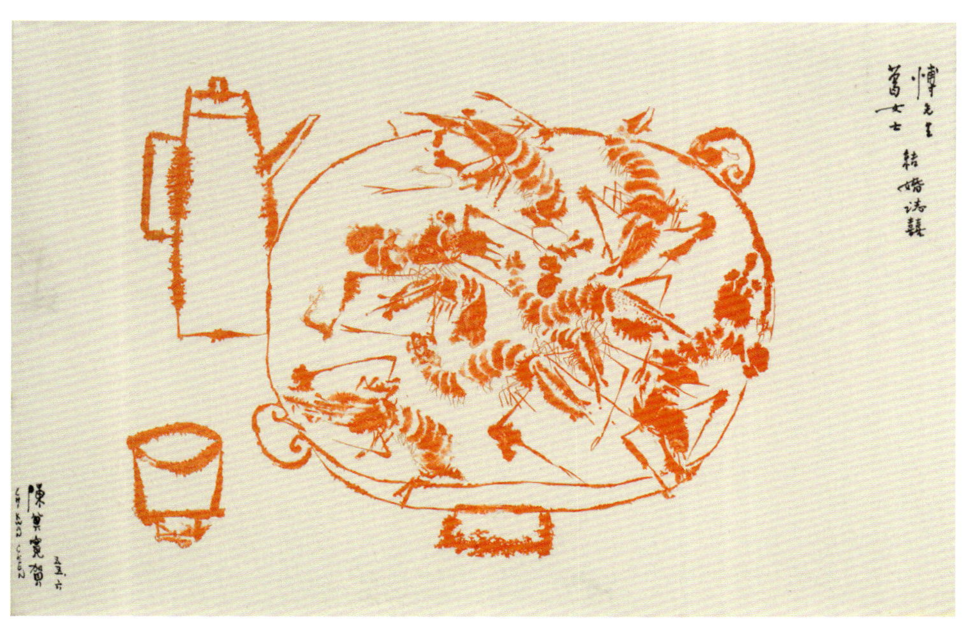

Chen Chi-kwan
(陳其寬, Chen Qikuan; 1921–2007)

976. Untitled (Wedding Gift)

1955
Framed painting; ink and color on paper
30 x 48 cm (11 3/4 x 18 7/8 in.)
Text, signature

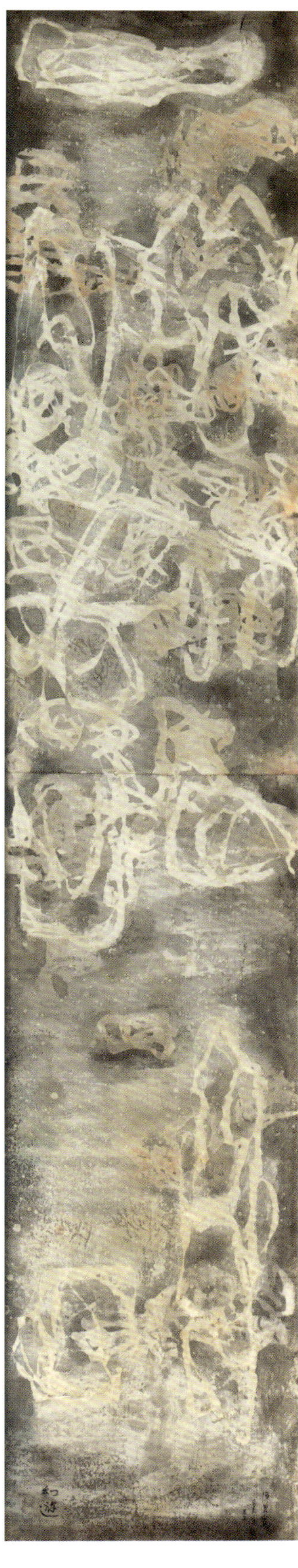

Chen Chi-kwan
(陳其寬, Chen Qikuan; 1921–2007)

977. Imaginary Journey (幻游)

1955
Framed painting; ink and color on paper
121.5 x 24 cm (47⅞ x 9¾ in.)
Signature

Chen Chi-kwan
(陳其寬, Chen Qikuan; 1921–2007)

978. To Have No Contact Until Old and Dead (No. 2) (老死不相往來 [其二]) (Isolated)

1956
Framed painting; ink and color on paper
24.1 x 120 cm (9½ x 47¼ in.)
Signature

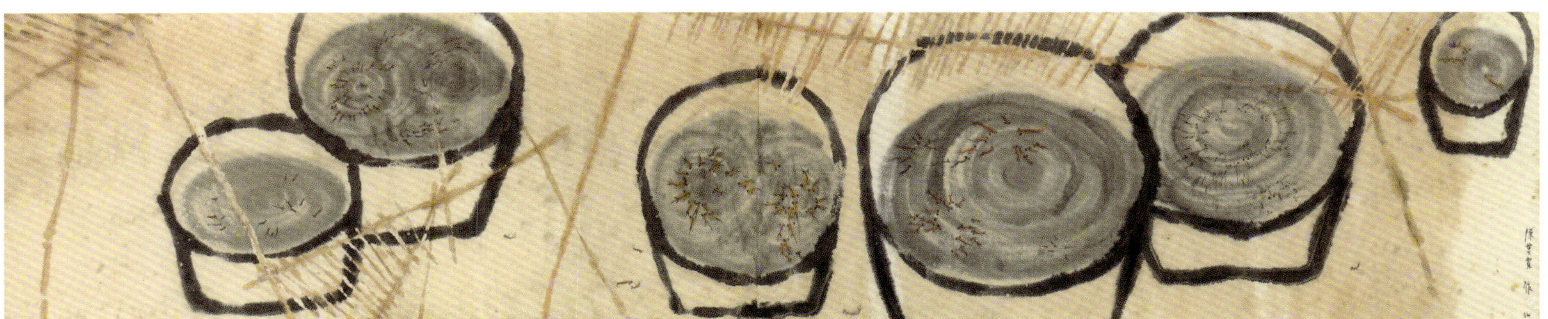

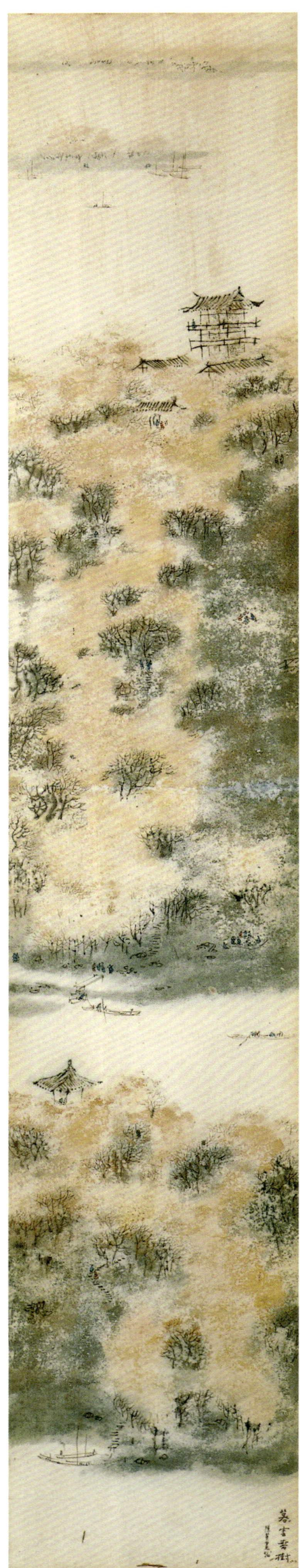

979

980

CHEN CHI-KWAN
(陳其寬, Chen Qikuan; 1921–2007)

979. Evening Clouds, Spring Trees (暮雲春樹)

1956
Framed painting; ink and color on paper
119 x 23.6 cm (46 7/8 x 9 1/4 in.)
Signature

LITERATURE: Rahman-Steinert 1996, no. 7.

CHEN CHI-KWAN
(陳其寬, Chen Qikuan; 1921–2007)

980. Boats Passing by the Window (窗上行舟)

1957
Framed painting; ink and color on paper
120 x 23.7 cm (47 1/4 x 9 3/8 in.)
Signature

LITERATURE: Rahman-Steinert 1996, no. 10.

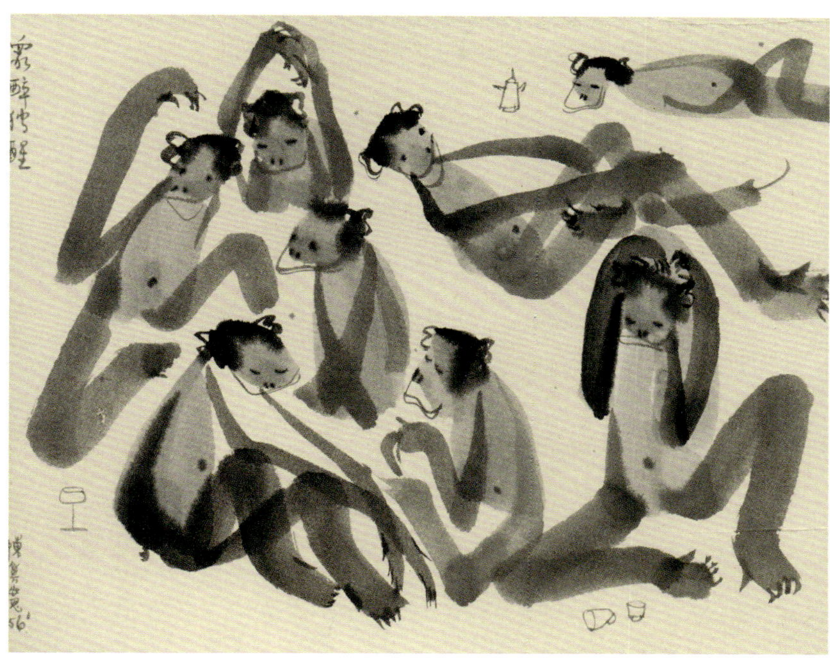

Chen Chi-kwan
(陳其寬, Chen Qikuan; 1921–2007)

981. "All Men Are Drunk and I Alone Am Sober" (眾醉獨醒)

1956
Framed painting; ink on paper
23.2 x 30.8 cm ($9^1/_8$ x $12^1/_8$ in.)
Signature

Chen Chi-kwan
(陳其寬, Chen Qikuan; 1921–2007)

982. Untitled (Vermillion)

1957
Framed painting and collage; ink and color on paper and patterned paper
24.8 x 121 cm ($9^3/_4$ x $47^5/_8$ in.)
Signature

Literature: Rahman-Steinert 1996, no. 13.

Chen Chi-kwan
(陳其寬, Chen Qikuan; 1921–2007)

983. Dream Journey (臥遊)

1957
Framed painting; ink and color on paper
22.6 x 118.6 cm ($8^7/_8$ x $46^3/_4$ in.)
Signature

Literature: Rahman-Steinert 1996, no. 12.

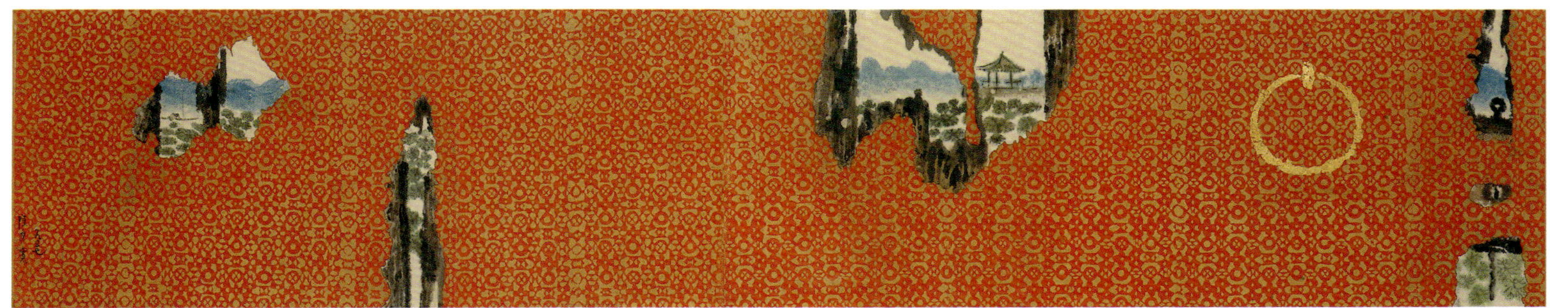

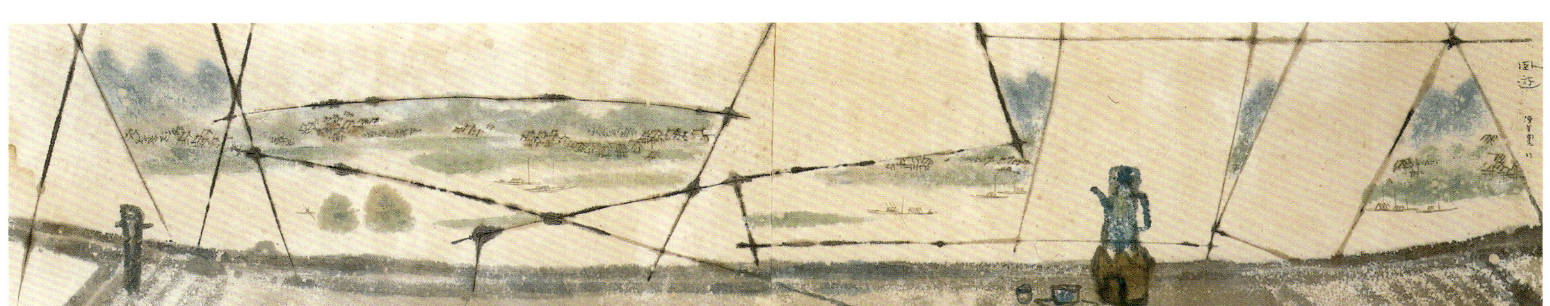

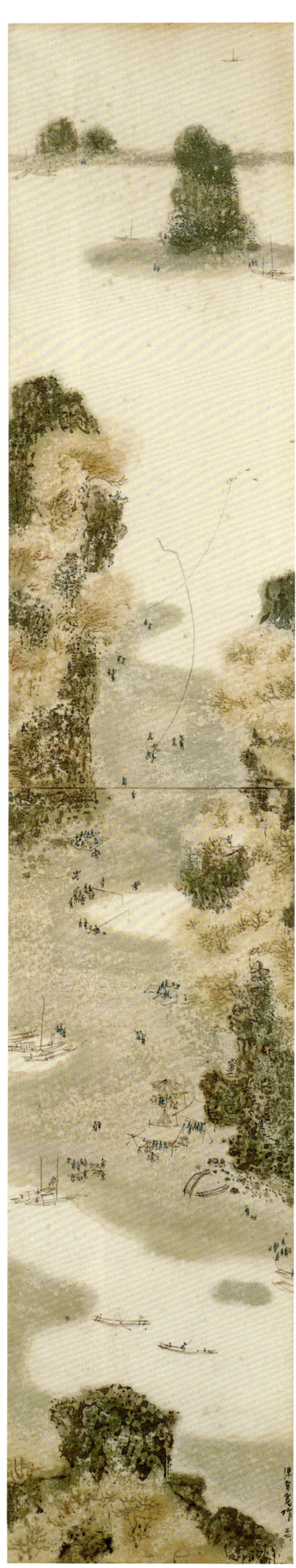

Chen Chi-kwan
(陳其寬, Chen Qikuan; 1921–2007)

984. Untitled (Picnic)

1957
Framed painting; ink and color on paper
118.6 x 22.7 cm (46¾ x 9 in.)
Signature

Literature: Rahman-Steinert 1996, no. 8.

Chen Chi-kwan
(陳其寬, Chen Qikuan; 1921–2007)

985. Monkey Show (猴戲)

1957(?)
Framed painting; ink and color on paper
22 x 31.8 cm (8⅝ x 12½ in.)
Seal

Literature: Rahman-Steinert 1996, no. 11.

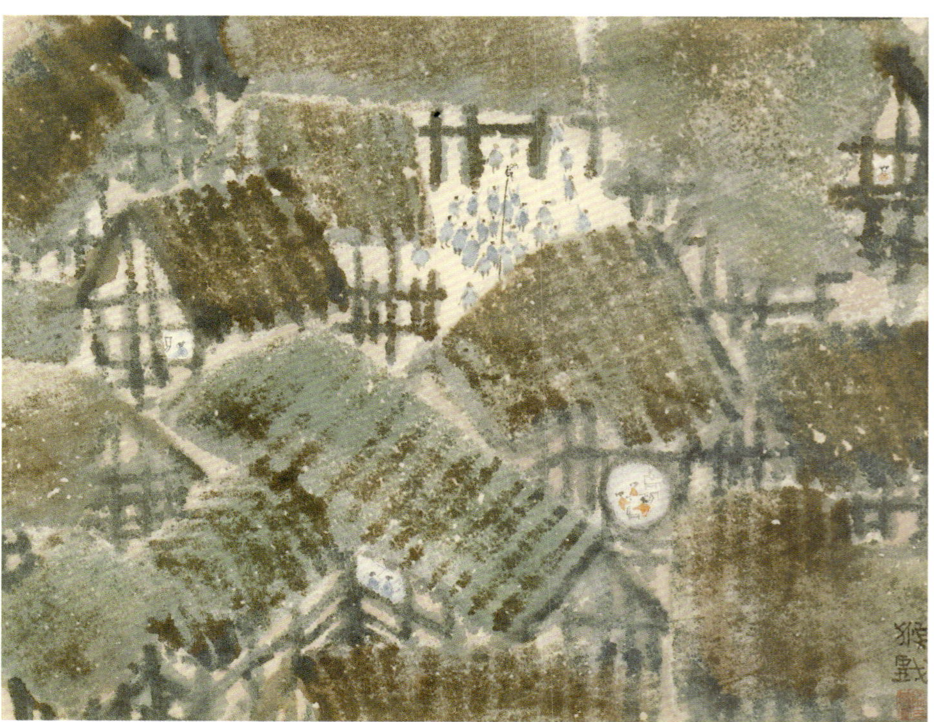

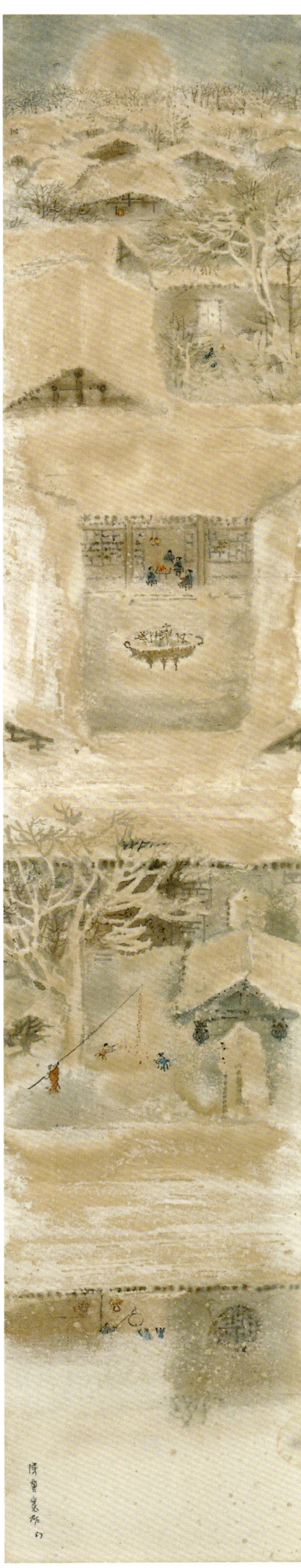

Chen Chi-kwan
(陳其寬, Chen Qikuan; 1921–2007)

986. Untitled (New Year's Eve)

1957
Framed painting; ink and color on paper
119.5 x 23.6 cm (47 x 9¼ in.)
Signature

Literature: Rahman-Steinert 1996, no. 9.

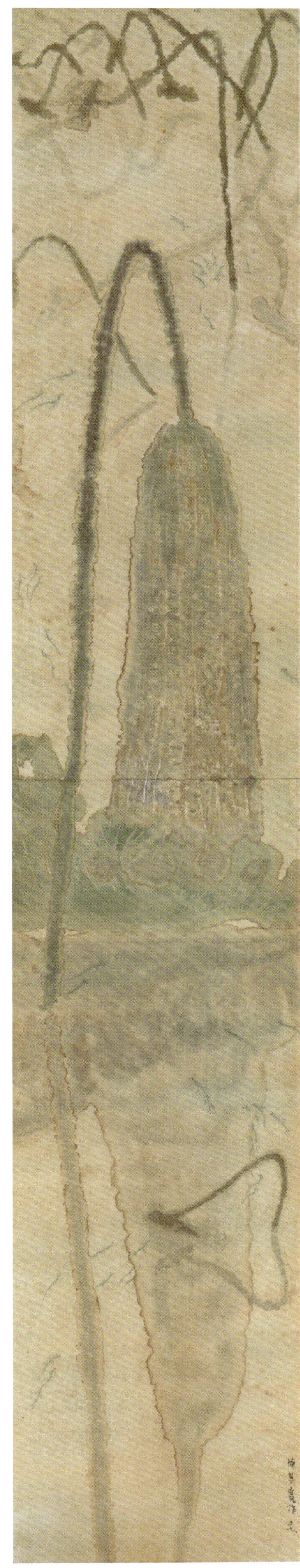

Chen Chi-kwan
(陳其寬, Chen Qikuan; 1921–2007)

987. Untitled (Lotus Reflected)

1957
Framed painting; ink and color on paper
120.2 x 23.1 cm (47⅜ x 9⅛ in.)
Signature

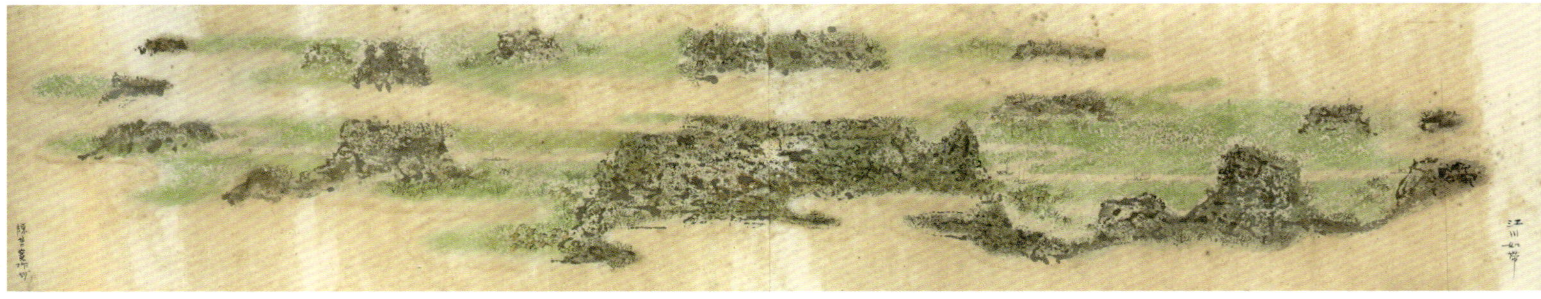

988

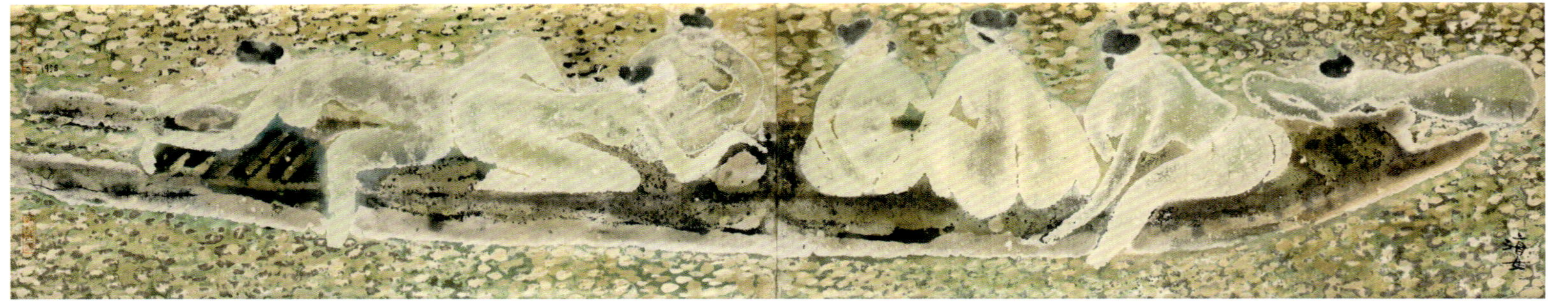

989

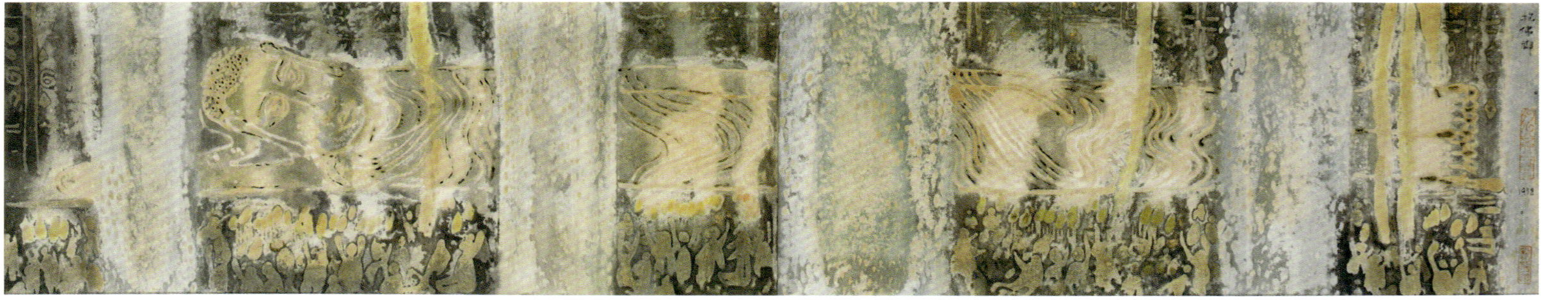

990

Chen Chi-kwan
(陳其寬, Chen Qikuan; 1921–2007)

988. Rivers and Streams like Sashes (江川如帶)

1957
Framed painting; ink and color on paper
22.7 x 118.5 cm (8 7/8 x 46 5/8 in.)
Signature

Chen Chi-kwan
(陳其寬, Chen Qikuan; 1921–2007)

989. Fisher Women (海女)

1958
Framed painting; ink and color on paper
23.5 x 120.2 cm (9 1/4 x 47 3/8 in.)
Signature, seals

Chen Chi-kwan
(陳其寬, Chen Qikuan; 1921–2007)

990. Clasping the Feet of Buddha (抱佛腳)

1958
Framed painting; ink and color on paper
22.8 x 120 cm (9 x 47 1/4 in.)
Signature, seals

Chen Chi-kwan
(陳其寬, Chen Qikuan; 1921–2007)

991. Untitled (Blue Mosque)

1959 (?)
Framed painting, ink and color on paper
121 x 23.5 cm (47 5/8 x 9 1/4 in.)
Seal

Chen Chi-kwan
(陳其寬, Chen Qikuan; 1921–2007)

992. Untitled (Frozen Landscape)

1959
Framed painting, ink and color on paper
121 x 23.5 (47 5/8 x 9 1/4 in.)
Signature, seal

Chen Chi-kwan
(陳其寬, Chen Qikuan; 1921–2007)

993. Nüti Mountain (女體山)

1958
Framed painting, ink and color on paper
93.4 x 25.8 cm (36 3/4 x 10 1/8 in.)
Signature, seals

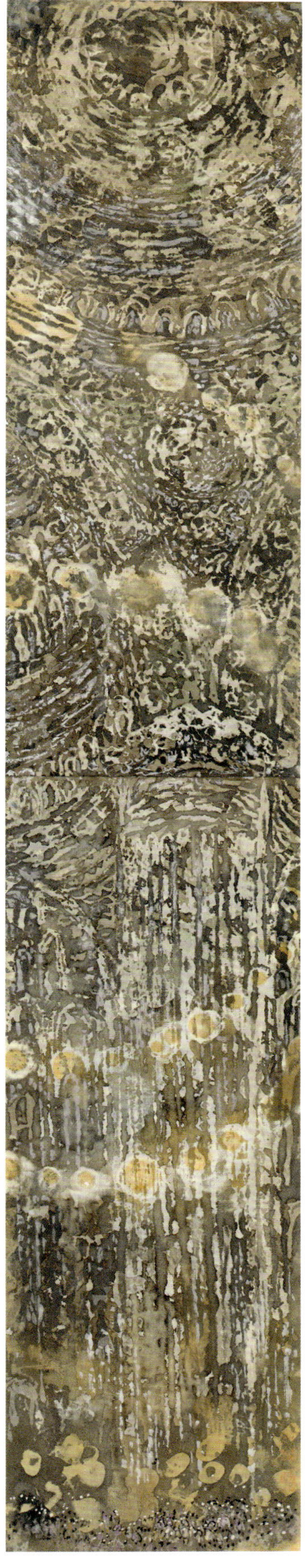

991

992

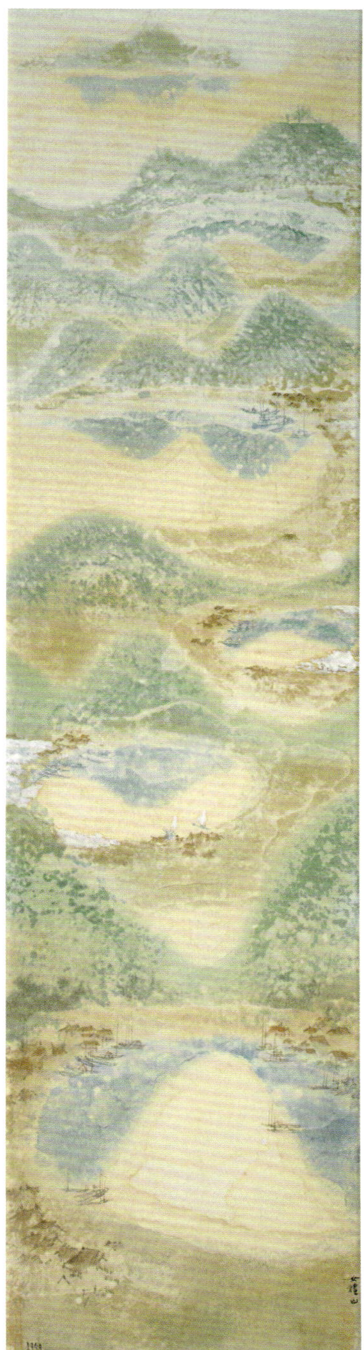

993

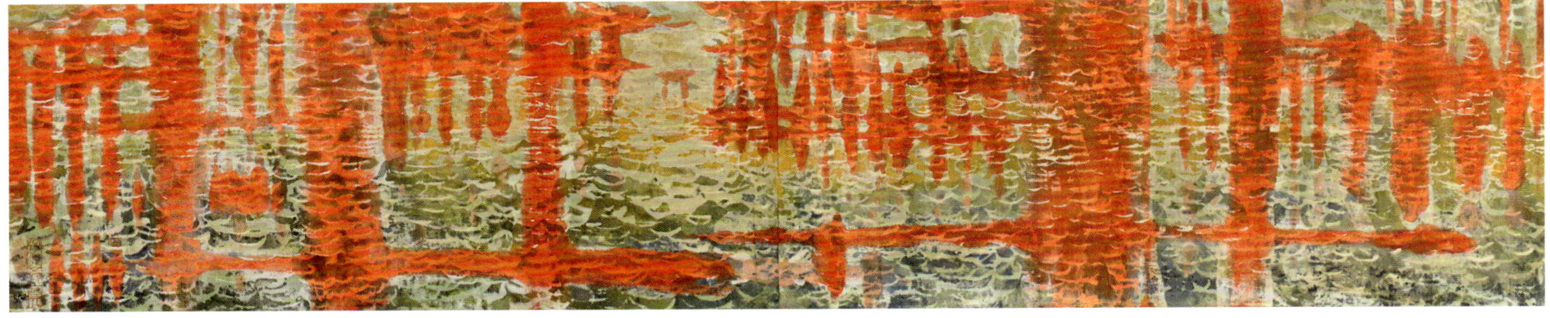
994

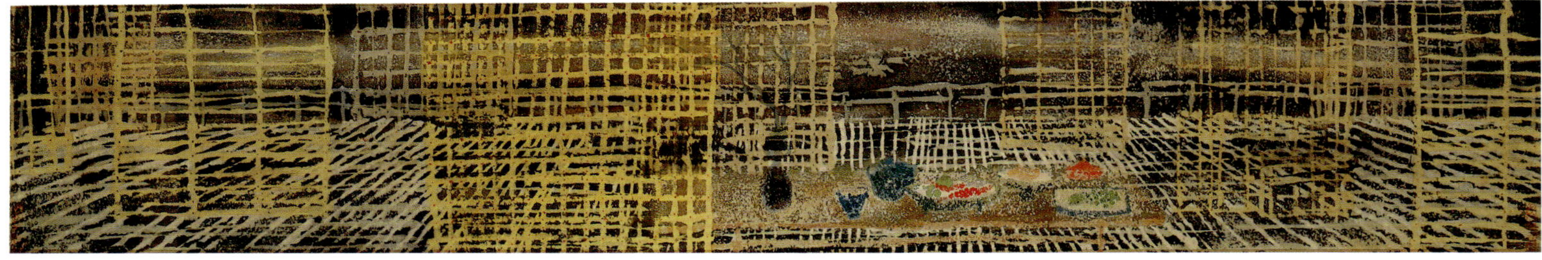
995

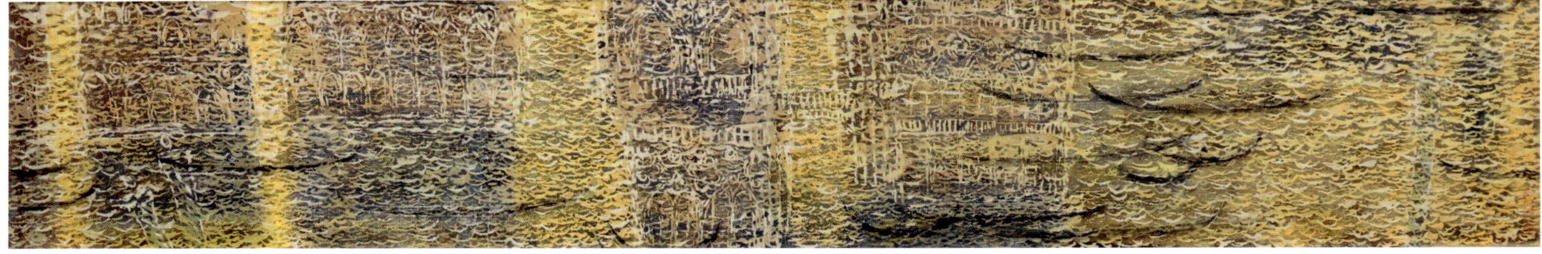
996

CHEN CHI-KWAN
(陳其寬, Chen Qikuan; 1921–2007)

994. Untitled (Itsukushima)

1959
Unframed painting; ink and color on paper
24.3 x 120.5 cm ($9^{5}/_{8}$ x $47^{3}/_{8}$ in.)
Signature, seal

CHEN CHI-KWAN
(陳其寬, Chen Qikuan; 1921–2007)

995. Untitled (Mergence) (交融)

1960
Framed painting; ink and color on paper
30 x 181.7 cm ($11^{3}/_{4}$ x $71^{1}/_{2}$ in.)
Signature, seals

LITERATURE: Rahman-Steinert 1996, no. 14.

CHEN CHI-KWAN
(陳其寬, Chen Qikuan; 1921–2007)

996. Untitled (Fishing Boats / Venice)

1960
Framed painting; ink and color on paper
29.8 x 181 cm ($11^{3}/_{4}$ x $71^{1}/_{4}$ in.)
Signature, seal

LITERATURE: Rahman-Steinert 1996, no. 15 (as *Venice*).

CHEN CHI-KWAN
(陳其寬, Chen Qikuan; 1921–2007)

997. Forest of Flesh (肉林)

1960
Framed painting; color on paper
21.8 x 29.3 cm ($8^{5}/_{8}$ x $11^{1}/_{2}$ in.)
Signature, seal

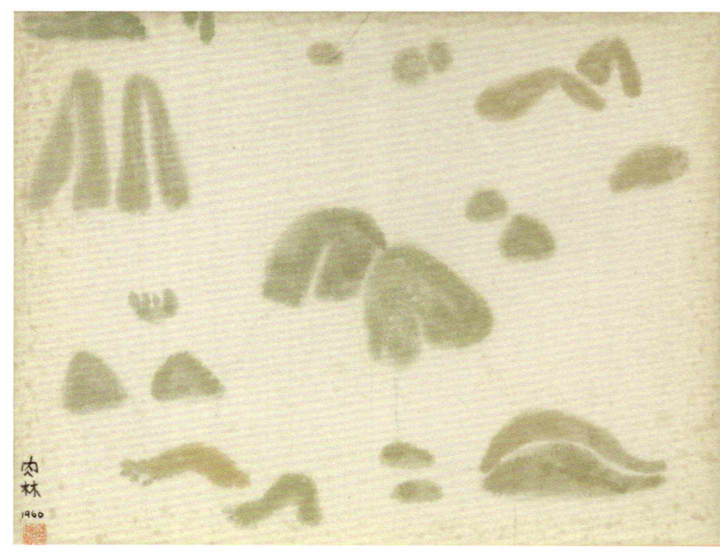

997

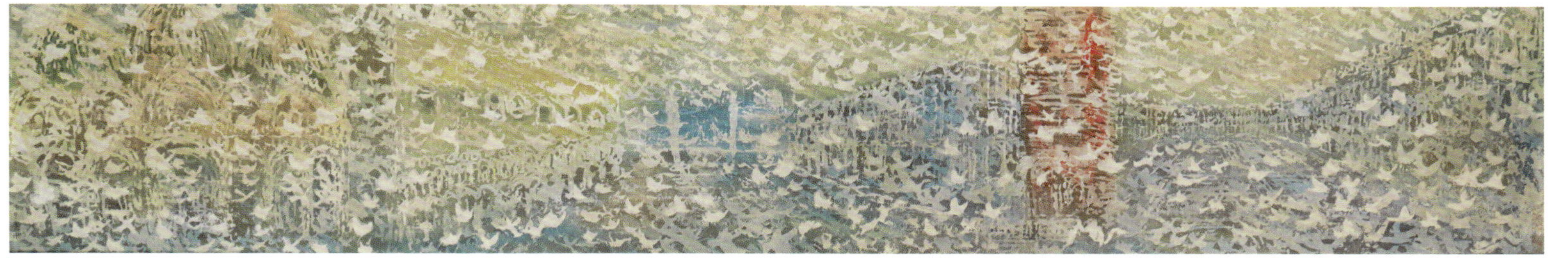

998

Chen Chi-kwan
(陳其寬, Chen Qikuan; 1921–2007)

998. Untitled

1960
Framed painting; ink and color on paper
30 x 181.5 cm (11 3/4 x 71 1/2 in.)
Signature, seal

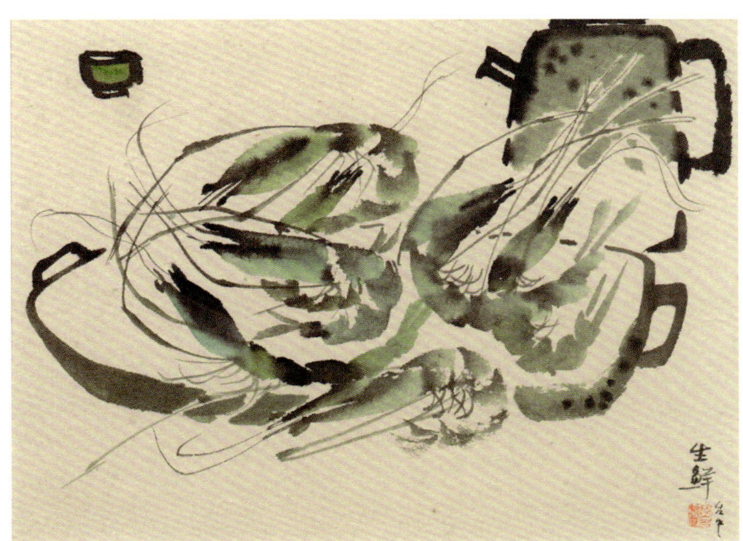

a

Chen Chi-kwan
(陳其寬, Chen Qikuan; 1921–2007)

999. (*a*) Fresh Seafood (生鮮); (*b*) Conciliatory but Not Accommodating (合而不同)

1962 (?)
Framed paintings; ink and color on paper
(*a*) 22 x 30 cm (8 5/8 x 11 3/4 in.); (*b*) 22.5 x 29.8 cm (8 3/4 x 11 3/4 in.)
(*a*) Signature, seal; (*b*) seal

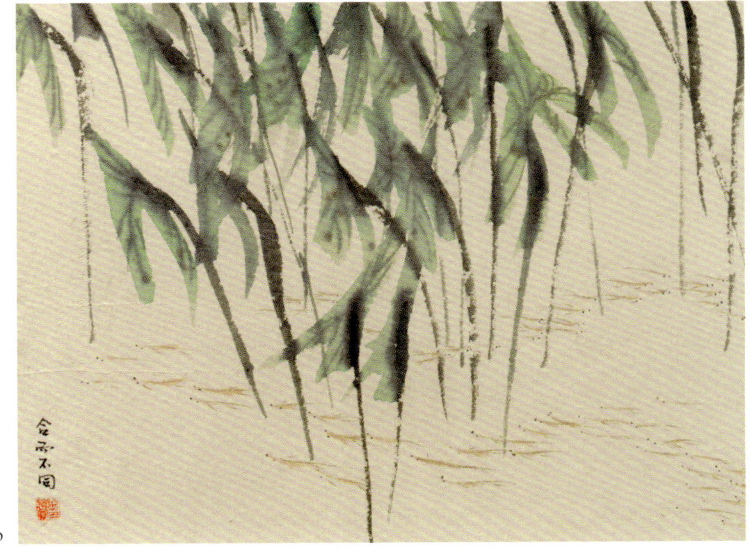

b

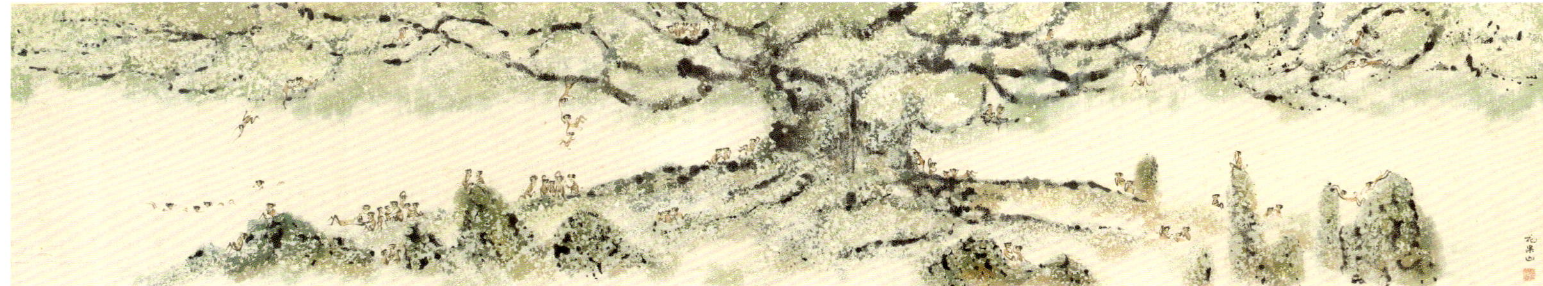

Chen Chi-kwan
(陳其寬, Chen Qikuan; 1921–2007)

1000. Mount Huaguo: Home of the Monkey King (花果山)

1964 (?)
Framed painting; ink and color on paper
22.9 x 119.4 cm (9 x 47 in.)
Seal

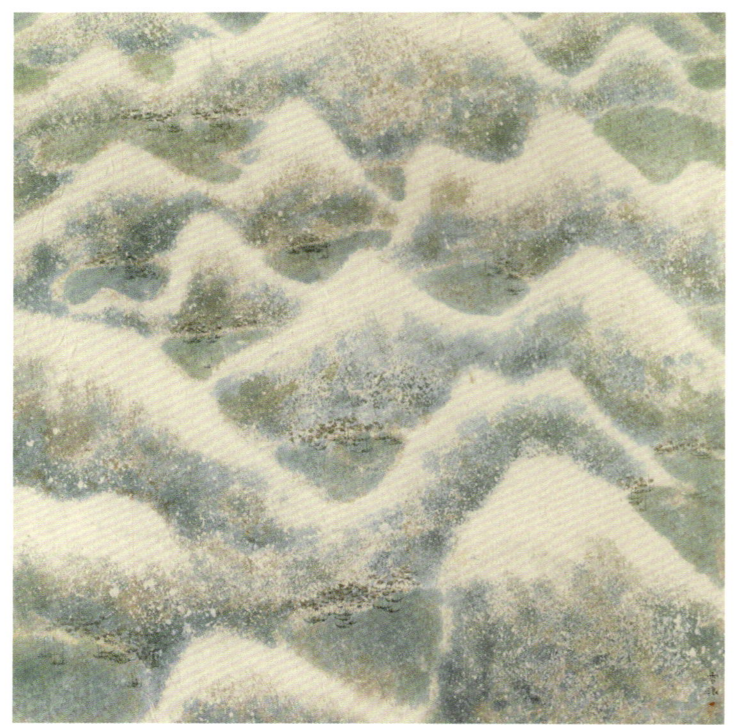

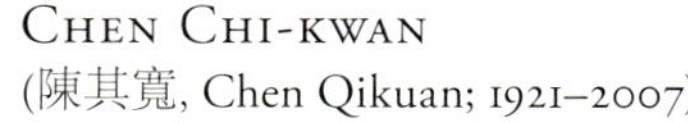

Chen Chi-kwan
(陳其寬, Chen Qikuan; 1921–2007)

1001. Waves of Snow (雪浪)

1964 (?)
Framed painting; ink and color on paper
45.7 x 45.7 cm (18 x 18 in.)
Seal

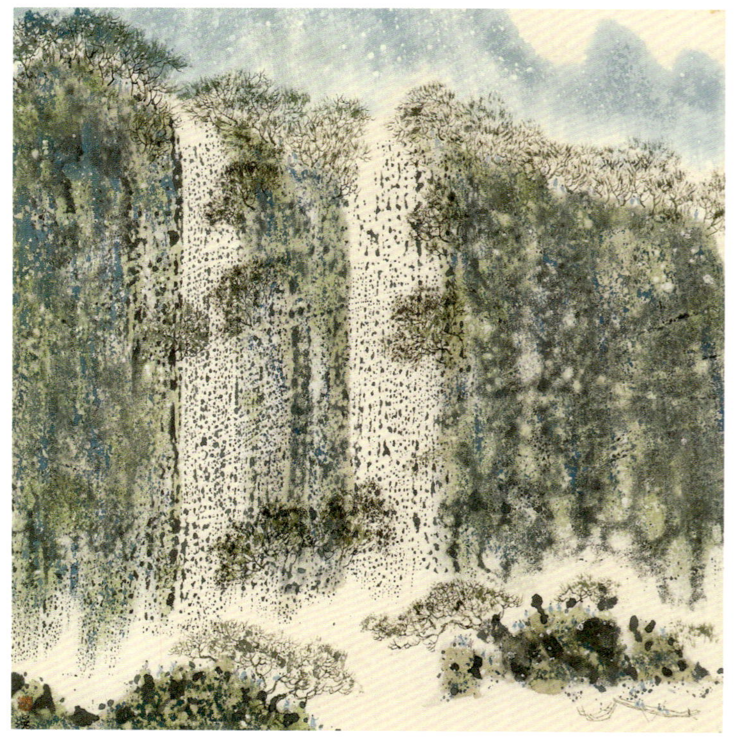

Chen Chi-kwan
(陳其寬, Chen Qikuan; 1921–2007)

1002. Waterfall (瀑)

n.d.
Framed painting; ink and color on paper
45.3 x 45.7 cm ($17\frac{7}{8}$ x 18 in.)
Seal

Literature: Rahman-Steinert 1996, no. 17.

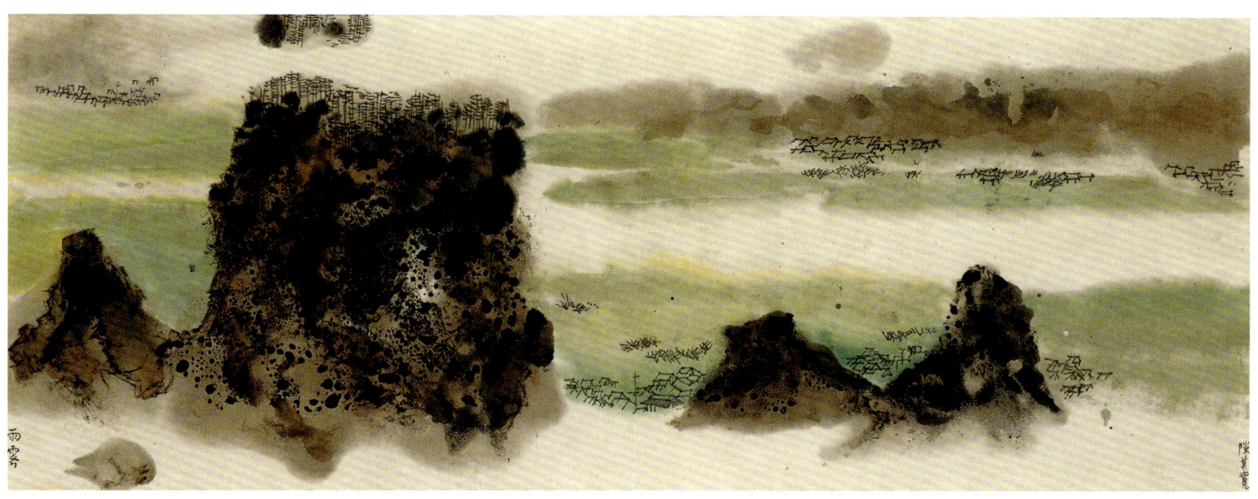

Chen Chi-kwan
(陳其寬, Chen Qikuan; 1921–2007)

1003. Clearing after Rain (雨霽)

n.d.
Framed painting; ink and color on paper
24 x 60.5 cm ($9^{1}/_{2}$ x $23^{7}/_{8}$ in.)
Signature

Literature: Rahman-Steinert 1996, no. 16.

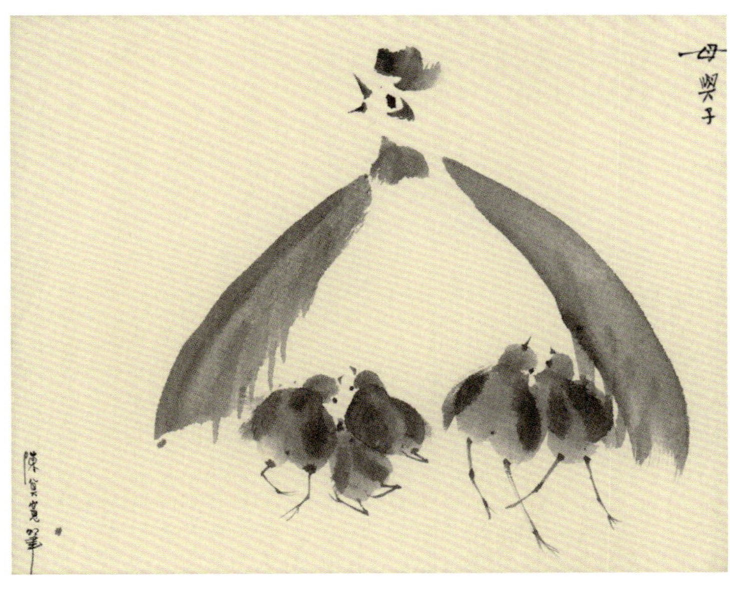

Chen Chi-kwan
(陳其寬, Chen Qikuan; 1921–2007)

1004. Mother Hen and Chicks (母與子)

n.d.
Framed painting; ink on paper
23.3 x 30 cm ($9^{1}/_{8}$ x $11^{3}/_{4}$ in.)
Signature

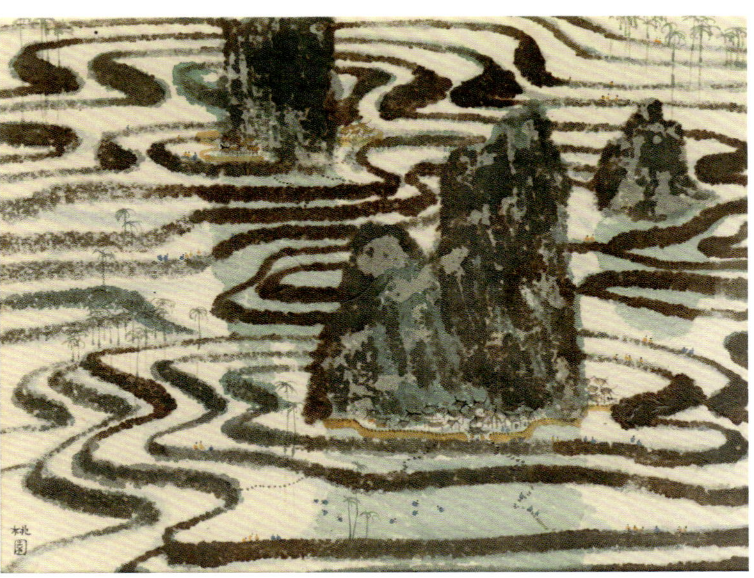

Chen Chi-kwan
(陳其寬, Chen Qikuan; 1921–2007)

1005. Taoyuan (桃園)

n.d.
Framed painting; ink and color on paper
29.8 x 22.2 cm ($11^{3}/_{4}$ x $8^{3}/_{4}$ in.)
Text

Chinese Paintings Details

† *denotes illustrated items*

† 950. Shide

Seal

Perpetual state of *Samadhi* [*Sanmei yongshou*, 三昧永受] (square, *intaglio*)

Text

[attributed to Yuji Zhihui (愚極智慧; ca. 1215–1300)]

Clapping hands he comes, opening wide his smiling mouth. / Reciting verses incompletely and composing poems without rhymes, / he abandons [worldly concerns] and works with a bamboo broom. / In front of Five Peaks, behind Twin Torrents, / in the lion's cave, there is no other animal.

Signature

Yuji of Jingci [Monastery] *eulogizes* (Jingci Yuji *zan* 淨慈愚極贊)

Seals

Yuji [愚極] (square, relief); *Foxin* [佛心] (square, relief)

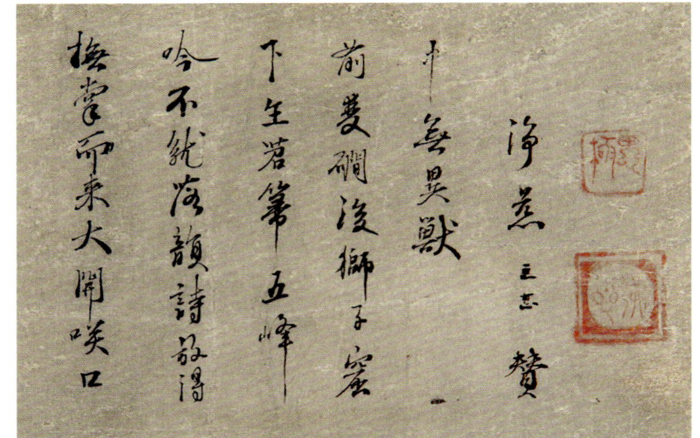

950

950

† 951. Ox and Herdsman

Text

The herd boy wearing a rain cloak and bamboo hat / meets people with a proud air. / Leading his ox, he plays a piccolo; / done with plowing, he rests by the field.

Signature

Yuanmiao [原妙; possibly Gaofeng Yuanmiao, 高峰原妙; 1238–1295]

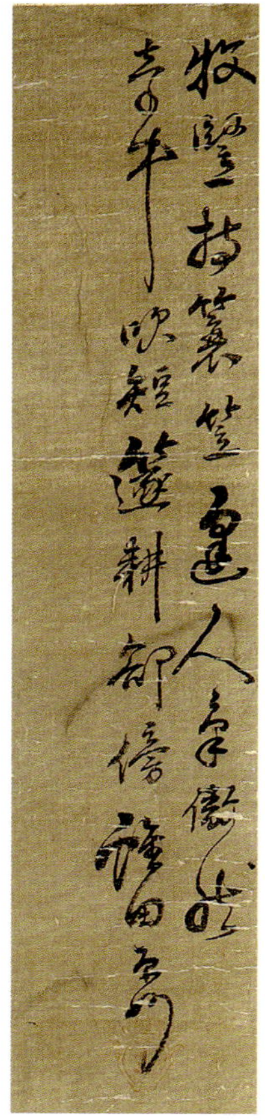

951

† 954. Brewing Tea on a Spring Evening

Text

[by artist] *Fresh water waiting to boil, / the proud new tea swelling like green banners; / Jiangnan's "grain rains"—the festival is near. / Under Mount Hui's springs, a skiff returns, / Gauze cap and mountain man at "the place of the halter." // The meditation mat, wind-borne flowers, the flying, swirling beard; /the blocked-up wine guest wakes from a dream of dust, / reclines, and watches the spring sun sink through the pine door.*

Signature

[of artist] *Zhengming* 徵明

954

Seals

[of artist]
Seal of Wen Zhengming [*Wen Zhengming yin* 文徵明印] (square, intaglio);
Tingyun Lodge [*Tingyun guan* 停雲館] (square, intaglio)

[of collectors]
Xiang Yuanbian 項元汴 (1525–1590): *Zijing* 子京 (gourd-shaped, relief); *Carefully guarded and enjoyed by Molin* [*Molin miwan* 墨林祕玩] (square, relief); *Prized and owned by the family of Xiang Zijing* [*Xiang Zijing jia zhencang* 項子京家珍藏] (rectangular, relief); *Seal of Xiang Yuanbian* [*Xiang Yuanbian yin* 項元汴印] (square, relief); *Seal of the treasure boxes of father Xiang Molin* [*Xiang Molin fu miji zhi yin* 項墨林父祕笈之印] (rectangular, relief)
Wang Jiqian 王季遷 (C. C. Wang, 1907–2003)
Formerly collected at Wang Jiqian's dwelling [*Zengcang Wang Jiqian chu* 曾藏王季遷處] (rectangular, relief)
Unidentified collector: Undeciphered

† 955. Deep Snow over Streams and Mountains

TEXT

[attributed to artist] *During snow in the* bingwu *year* [1546] *a friend visited me at my Jade-chime Mountain House (Yuqing shanfang). Because we reminisced about the beautiful scenery of streams and pavilions in former years I did this to record our meeting.*

SIGNATURE

[attributed to artist] *Recorded by Zhengming* 徵明記

SEALS

[attributed to artist]
Zhengming 徵明 (rectangular, intaglio)

[of collector] *Treasured and carefully guarded by Qiuhe* [*Qiuhe zhenmi* 秋鶴珍秘] (square, relief)

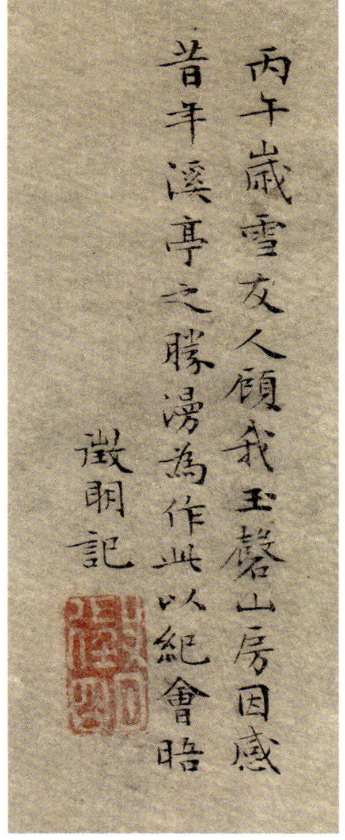

955

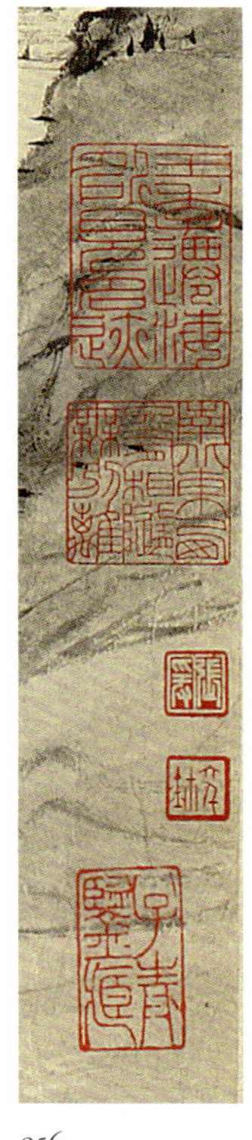
956

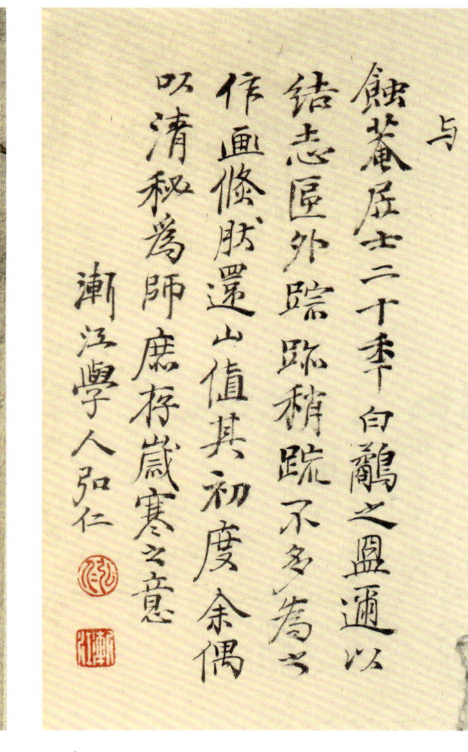
956

† 956. Landscape for Shian

TEXT

[by artist]

I have had a sworn pact with the Buddhist Recluse Shian for twenty years. Recently because he made acquaintances away from the region his traces were few, and I have not often painted for him. Suddenly he has returned to the mountains, [and since] it happened to be his birthday [in this picture] by chance I have taken Qingmi (Ni Zan) as a teacher, perhaps preserving the idea of when the years turned cold.
與蝕菴居士, 二十年白鷴之盟, 邇以結志區外, 踪跡稍疏, 不多為之作畫。倏然還山, 值其初度, 余偶以清秘為師庶存歲寒之意。

SIGNATURE

[of artist] *Jianjiang xueren Hongren* 漸江學人弘仁

SEALS

[of artist] *Hongren* 弘仁 (circular, relief); *Jianjiang* 漸江 (square, intaglio)

[of collectors and connoisseurs]
Zhang Zhiwan 張之萬 (1811–1897):
Judged and owned by Ziqing [*Ziqing jiancang* 子青鑒藏] (rectangular, relief)
Zhang Daqian 張大千 (Chang Dai-chien; 1899–1983):
South, north, east or west to follow [me] only and not to leave [my side] [*Nanbei dongxi zhi you xiangsui wu bieli* 南北東西只有相隨無別離] (square, relief); *Zhang Yuan* 張爰 (square, intaglio); *Seal of Daqian* [*Daqian xi* 大千鉩 (鉥)] (square, relief)
Wang Jiqian 王季遷 (C. C. Wang; 1907–2003):
A famous work seen abroad by Wang Jiqian [*Wang Jiqian haiwai suojian mingji* 王季遷海外所見名跡] (square, relief)
Unidentified collector
Huimifang 卉米舫 (square, relief)
Inscription in *shitang* by Fang Hengxian 方亨咸 (*jinshi* 1647) dated to 1666:
Seal of Fang Hengxian [*Fang Hengxian yin* 方亨咸印] (square, intaglio)
Style name Jiou [*Zi yue Jiou* 字曰吉偶] (square, intaglio)
Pang gong 龐公 (rectangular, intaglio)
Collector's seal in *shitang*
Zhang Daqian 張大千 (Chang Dai-chien; 1899–1983)
Seal of the treasured possessions of the Great Wind Hall [*Dafengtang zhencang yin* 大風堂珍藏印] (rectangular, relief)

† 957. A Deep Valley Conceals a Monk's Home

TEXT

[by artist] *Seeking in the mountains to escape the summer heat, / a deep valley conceals a monk's home. / Bamboo and trees obscure the remote trail; / on old branches, crows squawk at dusk. / Without anyone to boil stone marrow, / yet there is a guest to keep company with the rosy clouds. / We sit facing each other by Shuangxi Stream; / the shadows of a thousand peaks fall obliquely.*

SIGNATURE

[of artist] *Shiqi Can daozhe* 石谿殘道者

SEALS

[of artist]
Shiqi 石谿 (square, intaglio); *Baitu* 白禿 (square, relief)

[of collectors and connoisseurs]

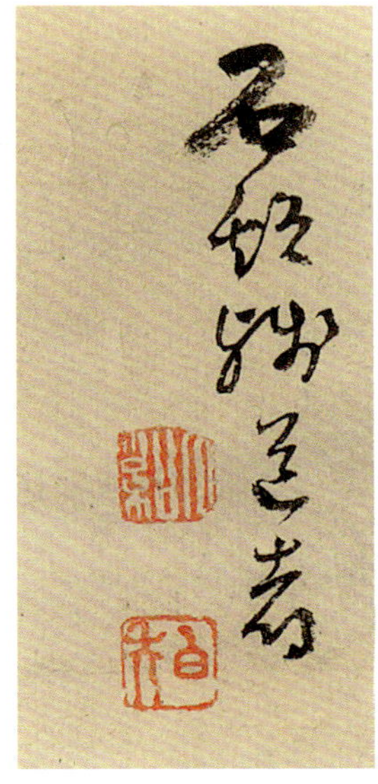
957

He Yuanyu 何瑗玉 (fl. 19th century):
Seal of books, ancient inscriptions, calligraphy, and paintings that have passed the eyes of younger brother He Yuanyu, sobriquet Quhe, of Duanxi [*Duanxi He shuzi Yuanyu hao Quhe guoyan jingji jinshi shuhua yinji* 端谿何叔子瑗玉号蘧盦過眼經籍金石書畫印記] (rectangular, relief)
Lin Qingtang 林慶堂 (19th century?):
Owned by the Zhilanwei Studio of Mr. Lin Qingtang [*Zhilanwei Zhai Lin shi Qingtang cang* 芝蘭味齋林氏慶堂藏] (square, relief)
Pang Yuanji 龐元濟 (1864–1949)
Examined and authenticated by Xuzhai [*Xuzhai shending* 虛齋審定] (square, relief)
Wang Jiqian 王季遷 (C. C. Wang; 1907–2003)
A famous work seen abroad by Wang

Jiqian [*Wang Jiqian haiwai suojian mingji* 王季遷海外所見名跡] (square, relief)
Unidentified collectors:
Evaluated and authenticated by Li'an [*Li'an pinding* 理庵品定] (possibly Zhao Hongxie 趙宏燮 [Qing dynasty]) (square, intaglio)
Owned by Jingtang [*Jingtang suocang* 鏡塘所藏] (possibly Wang Baolin 王寶林 [Qing dynasty]) (square, relief)

---

† 958. Clouds Rising above Mountains and Streams

TEXT

[by artist] *On a spring day, Yuan weng* [Zhou Lianggong] *of Hanshang* [Yangzhou], *the esteemed official, our fathers being of the same year in the examinations, took out twelve sheets of paper requesting paintings. Master Po* [Su Shi] *said: "My poem on Miaogao[tai] was composed fulfilling a request." I know that my paintings are not worthy of even being in a commonplace album.*

SIGNATURE

[of artist] *Your younger subordinate Chen Danzhong* (*zhiniandi Chen Danzhong* 治年第陳丹衷)

SEAL

[of artist] *Seal of Chen Danzhong* [*Chen Danzhong yin* 陳丹衷印] (square, intaglio)

TEXT

[by Chen Hongshou (陳洪綬, 1598–1652)] *This closely resembles Administrator Beiyuan's* [Dong Yuan, d. 967] Clouds Rising above Mountains and Streams (*ji si Beiyuan taishou Shanchuan chuyun tu* 極似北苑太守山川出雲圖)

SIGNATURE

[of inscriber] *Hongshou* 洪綬

SEAL

[of collector] Zhou Lianggong (1612–1672): *Lianggong* 亮工 (rectangular, relief)

---

† 959. Landscape

TEXT

[by artist] *Shiming, my fellow artist, is an expert in the principles of painting. He collects widely and studies broadly the famous works of the Song and Yuan dynasties, understanding their profundities and searching out their subtleties. Moreover he has traveled to almost all of the tall mountains and great rivers to the north and south of the Yangzi River. With true landscapes in his mind each [of his paintings] is planned and expansive with free transformations that cannot be thoroughly fathomed. When faced with such paintings, I want to withdraw. Now that I have returned to Yushan he often visited, stimulating me*

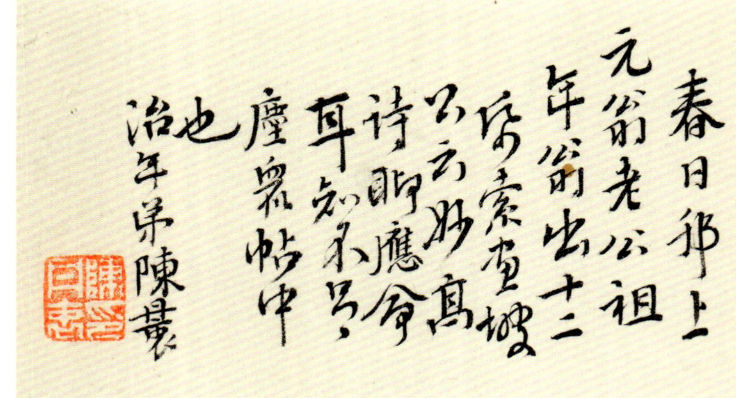

958

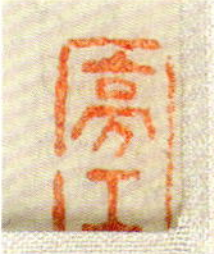

958

958

959

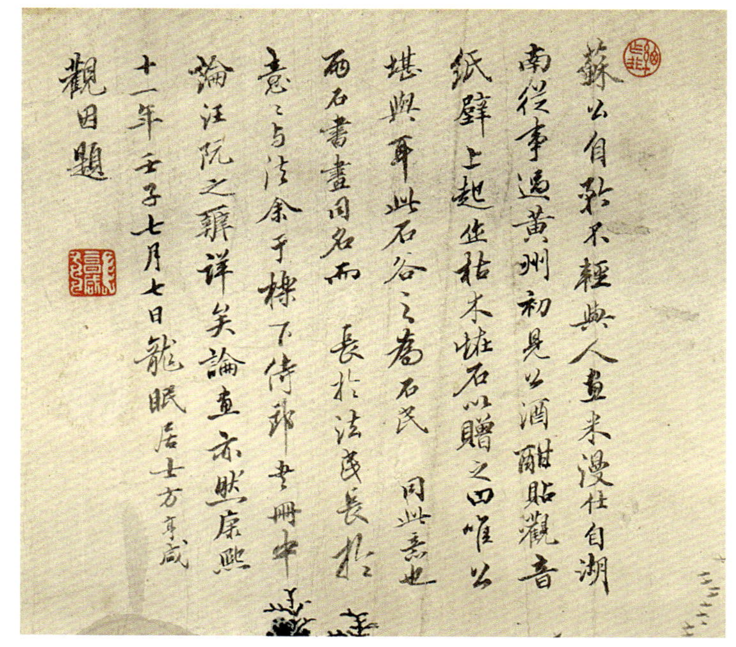

959

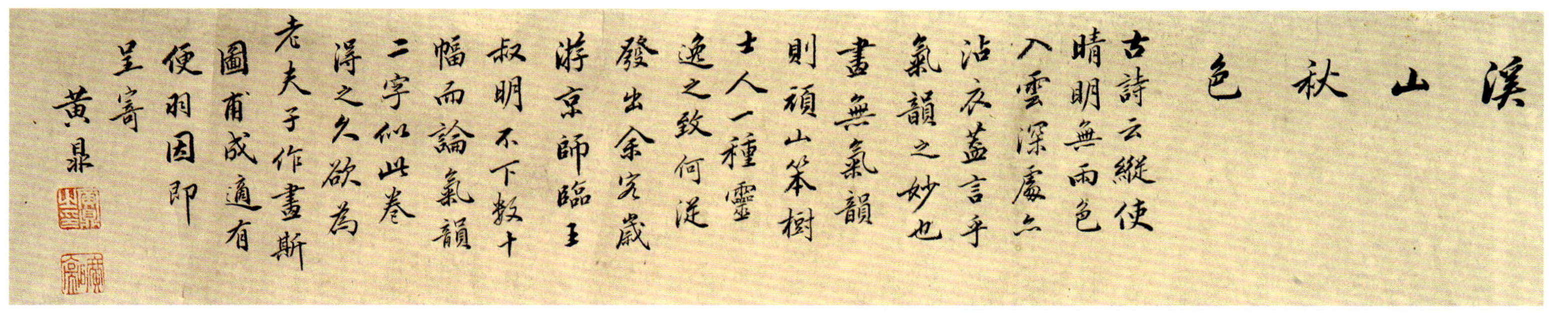

960

with the teachings of the ancients. He does not consider my awkward brushwork as ugly and repeatedly asks for it. I have exerted myself to paint this scroll in response to his request. Ashamed at the shallowness of my learning, even in my dreams I cannot see the least resemblance to Huayuan (Fan Kuan). As a great connoisseur you certainly have something to teach me.

Signature

[of artist] *On the ninth day of the third month of the* jiyou *year* [1669], *the Man of Wumu Mountain, Wang Hui [painted] and inscribed (jiyou sanyue jiuri Wumu shan zhongren Wang Hui bing zhi* 己酉三月九日烏目山中人王翬并識*)*

Seal

[of artist] *Seal of Wang Hui* [*Wang Hui zhi yin* 王翬之印] (square, intaglio)

Text

[by inscriber Fang Hengxian (*jinshi* 1647)] *Master Su [Shi] was boastful, rarely doing paintings for anyone. Mi Manshi [Fu] coming from Hunan on business passed by Huangzhou. Tipsy at their first meeting, he [Mi] rose to put a piece of Guanyin paper on the wall and [Su] painted withered trees and strange rocks to give to him, saying "only you deserve this work." Shigu [Wang Hui] did this for Shimin in the same vein. Both Shi [Shigu and Shimin] enjoy equal reputations in calligraphy and painting: [Shigu] excels in techniques, while [Shi]min excels in conceptions. Concerning conceptions and techniques, I have discussed in detail the distinctions between Wang and Ruan in Vice Minister Lixia's [Zhou Lianggong] calligraphy album. Discussing painting is the same.*

Signature

[of inscriber] *On the seventh day of the seventh month of the eleventh year,* renzi, *of the Kangxi reign* [1672], *the Retired Scholar of Longmian, Fang Hengxian, viewed and therefore inscribed (Kangxi shiyi nian renzi qiyue qiri Longmian jushi Fang Hengxian guan yin ti* 康熙十一年壬子七月七日龍眠居士方亨咸觀因題)

Seals

[of inscriber Fang Hengxian (*jinshi* 1647)] *xizuoxing* 細作行 (circular, relief); *Hengxian* [*Hengxian* 亨咸] (square, intaglio); *Viewed by Fang Shaocun* [*Fang Shaocun zengguan* 方邵村曾觀] (square, relief)

960

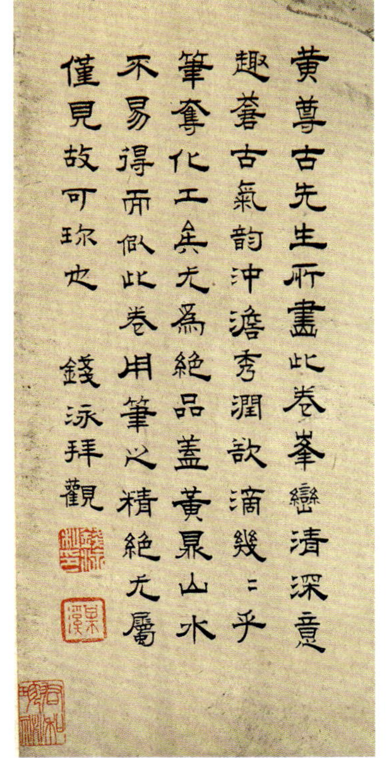

960

† 960. Autumn Colors on Streams and Mountains

Text

[attributed to Huang Ding] *An old poem reads: "Even if it is a clear and bright day without a hint of rain, Entering into a place deep within the clouds will dampen one's clothing." This speaks to the subtleties of spirit resonance. Paintings without spirit resonance are nothing but coarse mountains and awkward trees. How can a scholar painter's exquisite elegance emanate from such works? Last year when I traveled to the capital, I copied no less than several tens of Wang Shuming's [Wang Meng] paintings. As far as his spirit resonance is concerned, it seems as though this handscroll obtains it. I have long wanted to paint a picture for you, venerable master. Right after I completed this painting, there happened to be a messenger, and I am therefore presenting it to you and sending it [along with the messenger].*

Signature

[attributed to artist] *Huang Ding* (黃鼎)

Seals

[attributed to artist] *Seal of Huang Ding* [*Huang Ding zhi yin* 黃鼎之印] (square, intaglio); *Kuangting* [*Kuangting* 曠亭] (square, relief)

Text

[by Qian Yong (錢泳; 1759–1844)]

In this scroll by Master Huang Zungu [Huang Ding], *the peaks and ranges are clear and profound, the conception and flavor are hoary and ancient, and the spirit resonance is tranquil. Its elegance and richness are on the point of dripping [from the surface]. The brushwork almost steals the skills of Nature. It is a particularly rare work. Huang Ding's landscapes are not easy to obtain, moreover as in this scroll his exquisite use of the brush is especially classed as hardly ever seen. Thus it should be treasured.*

Signature

[of Qian Yong] *Qian Yong respectfully viewed* [*Qian Yong baiguan* 錢泳拜觀]

Seals

[of Qian Yong] *Private Seal of Qian Yong* [*Qian Yong siyin* 錢泳私印] (square, intaglio); *Plum Stream*

[*Meixi* 梅溪] (square, relief)
[of unidentified collector] *Prized and carefully guarded by Junhe* [*Junhe zhenmi* 君和珍祕] (rectangular, relief)

---

† 961. Clear Summer

Text

[by artist]

Picture of Clear Summer [*Qingxia tu* 清夏圖]

Signature

[of artist] *Casually painted by Baishi according to his conception* [*Baishi yi yi manxie* 白石以意曼寫]

Seal

Seal of Chen Ruyu [*Chen Ruyu yin* 陳汝玉印] (square, intaglio)

---

962. Autumn Insects

Text

Shaotang, dear friend, please correct my errors, gengyin *year* [1950] [少堂仁兄雅正庚寅]

Signature

The ninety-year-old-man Baishi, with unclear eyesight [*jiushi laoren Baishi hunmu* 九十老人白石昏目]

Seals

[of artist] *The old man who borrows mountains* [*Jieshan laoren* 借山老人] (square, intaglio); *Baishi* [白石] (square, relief); *Jiping Hall* [*Jipingtang* 寄萍堂] (square, relief)

---

963. Lotus

Signature

Painted by the ninety-year-old Baishi [*jiushi sui Baishi hua* 九十歲 / 白石畫]

Seal

[of artist] *Dullard* [literally "wood man," or carpenter] (*muren* 木人) (square, relief)

---

964. Basket of Litchi

Signature

The old man who borrows mountains, Baishi at 90 sui [*Jieshan laoren Baishi jiushi sui* 借山老人白石久十歲]

Seal

[of artist] *Old man Baishi* [*Baishi weng* 白石翁] (square, relief)

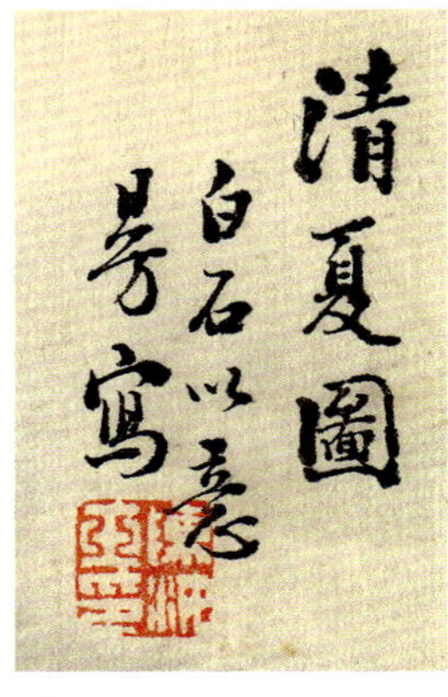

961

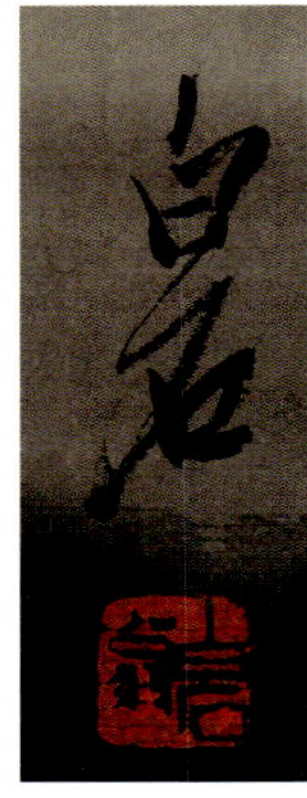

967

---

965. (*a*) Peony; (*b*) Branch of Litchi

Signature

[a] *Baishi* 白石

Seal

[a] [of artist] *The eldest son of the Qi family* [*Qida* 齊大] (square, intaglio)

Text

[b] [by artist]

A famous garden without doubt [*ming yuan wuer* 名園無二]

Signature

[b] *Baishi* 白石

Seal

[b] [of artist] *The eldest son of the Qi family* [*Qida* 齊大] (square, intaglio)

---

966. Autumn Fragrance

Text

Autumn fragrance [*Qiuxiang* 秋香]

Signature

Old man Baishi [*Laoren Baishi* 老人白石]

Seal

The eldest son of the Qi family [*Qida* 齊大] (square, relief)

---

† 967. Sails on the Yangzi River

Signature

Baishi 白石

Seal

[of artist] *Old man Baishi* [*Baishi weng* 白石翁] (square, intaglio)

---

† 968. Landscapes in the Styles of Old Masters

Text

[by artist]
[Panel 1] *Reducing a large work of a Ming painter*
[Panel 2] *General idea of the two Mi*
[Panel 3] *After Shitian weng*
[Panel 4] *Following the brush ideas of Beiyuan*
[Panel 5] *Copying Yunxi Daoren*
[Panel 6] *Small changes on the received ideas of Fanghu Daoren*
[Panel 7] *Modeling the brushwork of Juran*
[Panel 8] *Imitating the methods of a Song painter*

Signatures

[of artist] *Qi Gong* (啓功); *Yuanbai* (元白)

Seals

[of artist] *Qi Gong* [*Qi Gong* 啓功] (square, intaglio); *Seal of Qi Gong* [*Qi Gong zhi yin* 啓功之印] (square, intaglio); *Yuanbai* [*Yuanbai* 元白] (square, relief)

---

969. Untitled (Anxious)

Signature

Brushed by Chen Qikuan, 1953, Cambridge [陳其寬筆 一九五三 康橋]

Seal

Seal of Chen Qikuan [*Chen Qikuan yin* 陳其寬印] (square, relief)

---

† 970. Fishing [*Yuyu* 漁魚] (Pier)

Signature

1953 Painted by Chen Qikuan of Cambridge (一九五三康橋陳其寬作)

Seal

Seal of Chen Qikuan [*Chen Qikuan yin* 陳其寬印] (square, relief)

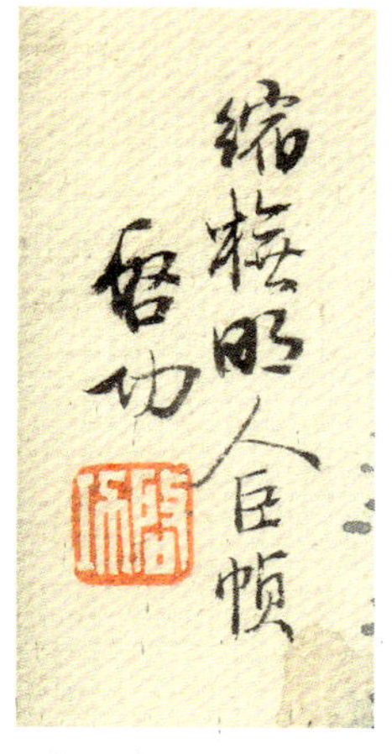

968

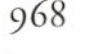

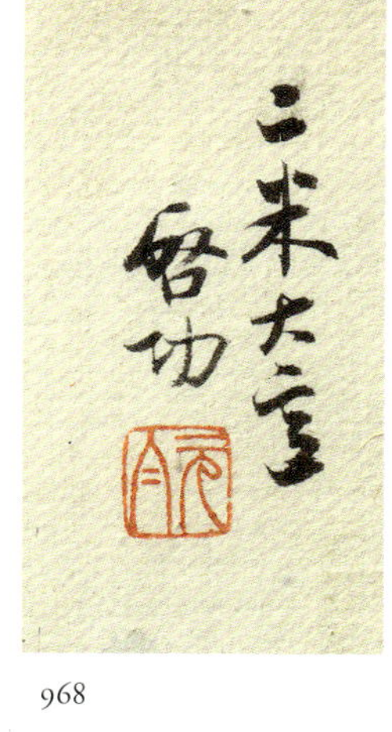

968

968

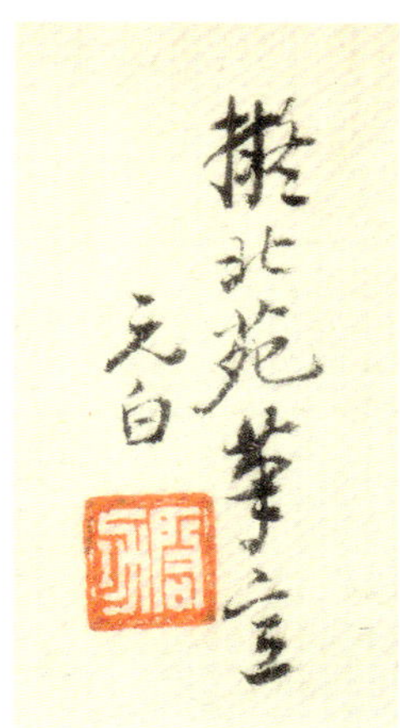

968

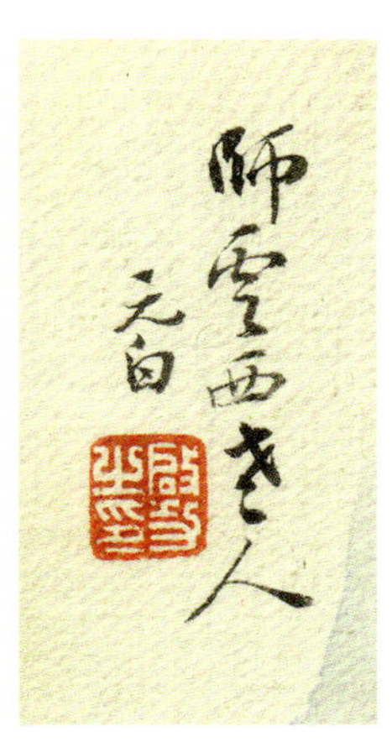

968

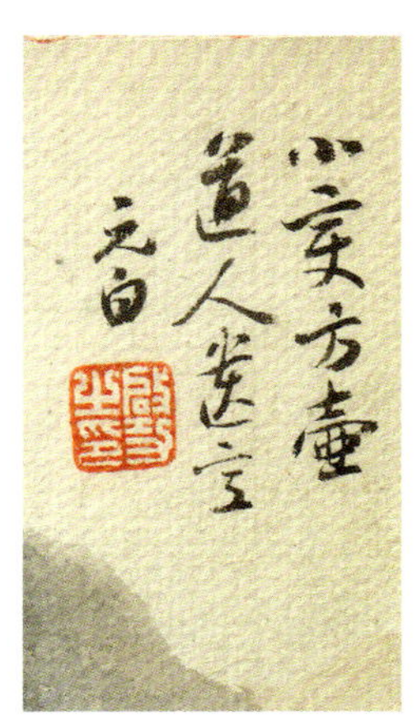

968

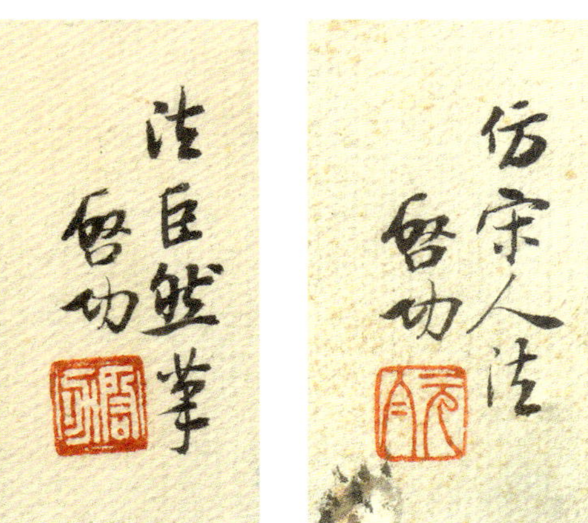

968

968

† 971. Impressions of an American Football Game [美國足球賽印象]

Signature

CHI KWAN CHEN Brushed by Chen Qikuan 1954 [*CHI KWAN CHEN* 陳其寬筆 一九五四]

Seal

Seal of Chen Qikuan [*Chen Qikuan yin* 陳其寬印] (square, relief)

† 972. Autumn Delicacies [*Qiuwei* 秋味]

Signature

Painted by Chen Qikuan in 1954 [陳其寬 一九五四 作]

Seal

Seal of Chen Qikuan [*Chen Qikuan yin* 陳其寬印] (square, relief)

973. Untitled (Where the Buffalo Roam)

Text

When the wind blows the grass bends and one sees the buffalo [風吹草低見牛羊]

Signature

Painted by Chen Qikuan in Cambridge 1954 CHI KWAN CHEN [一九五四 陳其寬 / 作于康橋 / *CHI KWAN CHEN*]

† 974. Playing in the Wind [*Xifeng*, 戲風]

Signature

1954 in Cambridge Painted by Chen Qikuan [CHI] KWAN CHEN [一九五四年 / 于康橋 / 陳其寬作 / *[CHI] KUAN CHEN*]

Seal

Seal of Chen Qikuan [*Chen Qikuan yin,* 陳其寬印] (square, relief)

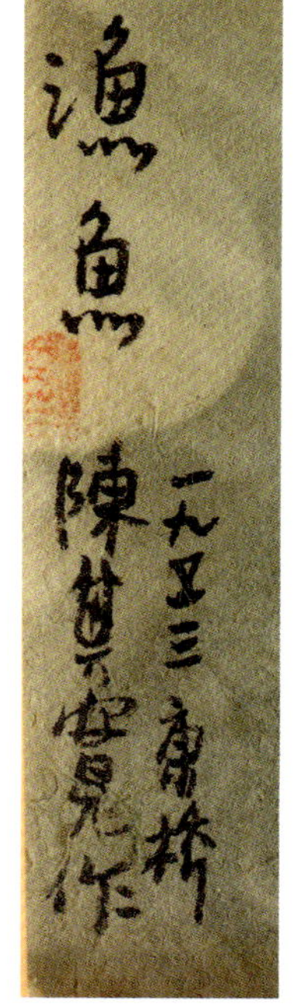

970

971

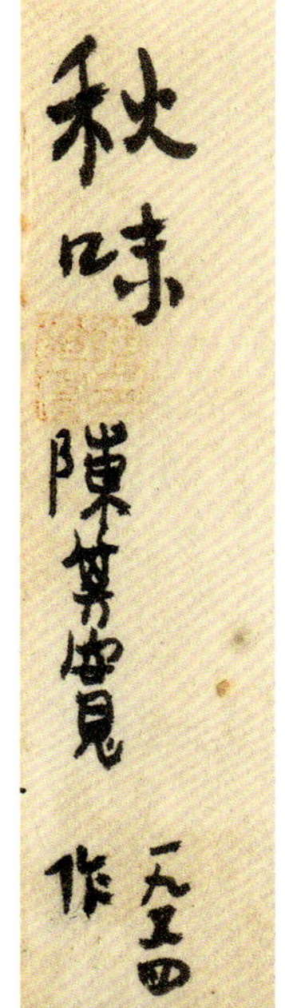

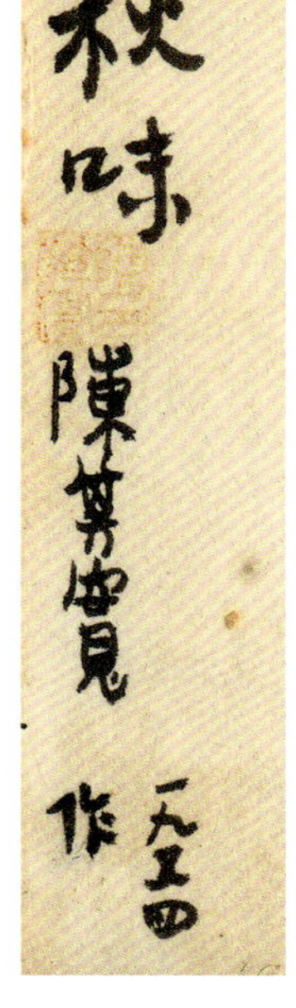

972

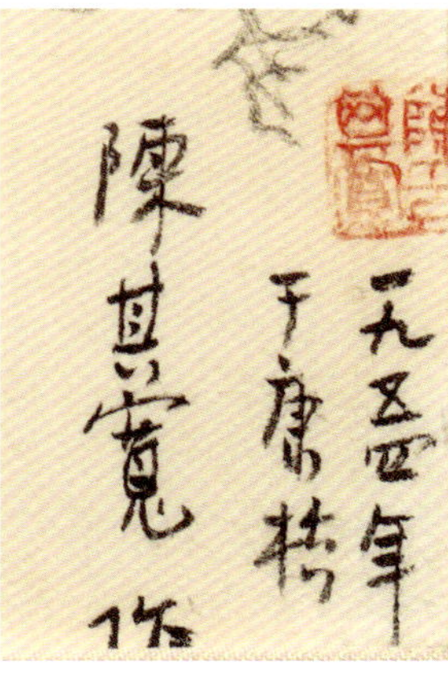

974

974

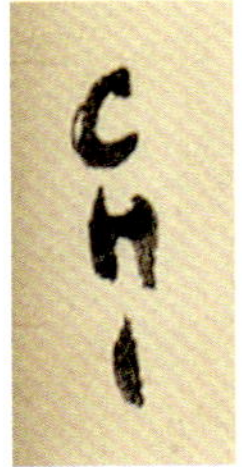

975

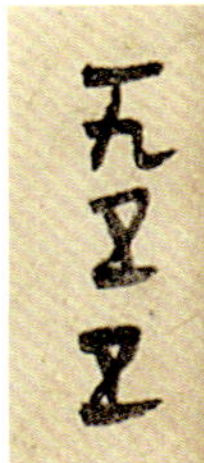

975

† 975. Untitled (Monkeys)

Signature

1955 / Chi [一九五五, *CHI*]

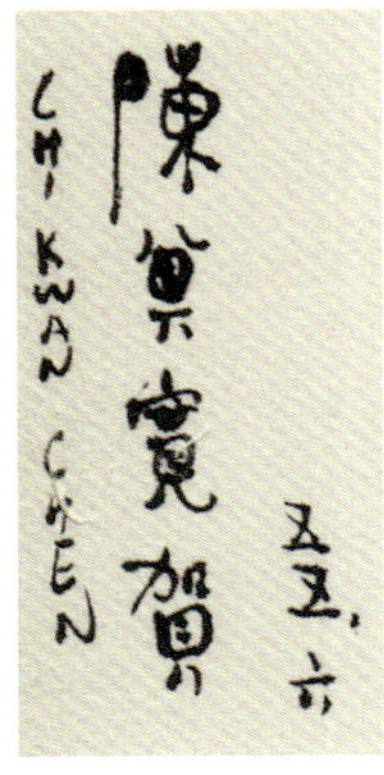

976

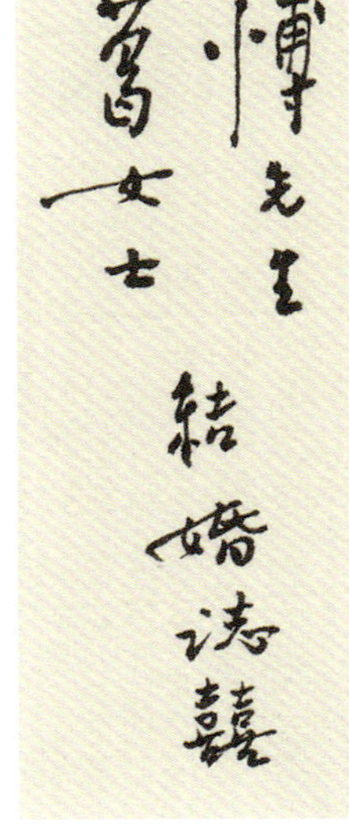

976

† 976. Untitled (Wedding Gift)

Text

Mr. Burke, Miss Griggs: Wishing Happiness for Your Wedding [博先生 / 葛女士 / 結婚誌喜]

Signature

June 1955 Chen Qikuan gives congratulations CHI KWAN CHEN [五五。六 陳其寬賀, *CHI KWAN CHEN*]

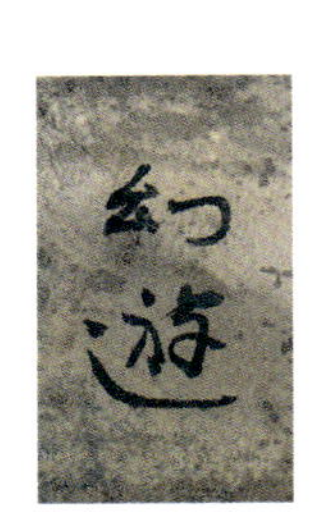

977

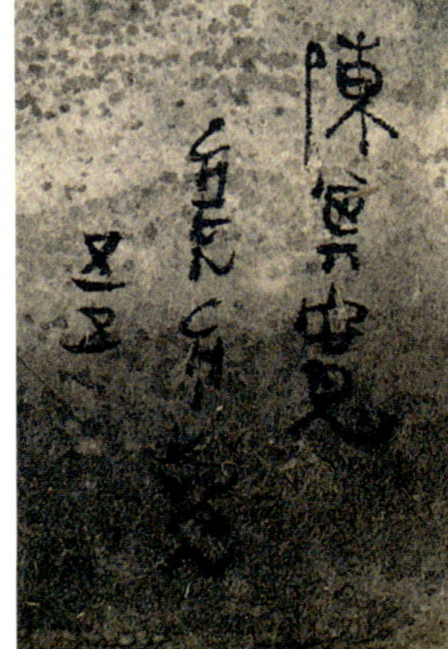

977

† 977. Imaginary Journey [*huanyou*, 幻游]

Signature

Chen Qikuan CHEN CHI KWAN '55 [陳其寬 *CHEN CHI KWAN* 五五]

978

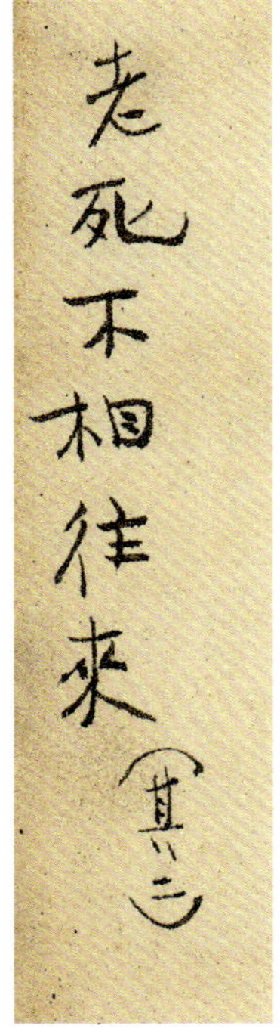

978

† 978. To Have No Contact Until Old and Dead (No. 2) [老死不相往來 (其二)] (Isolated)

Signature

Painted by Chen Qikuan '56 [陳其寬作 *'56*]

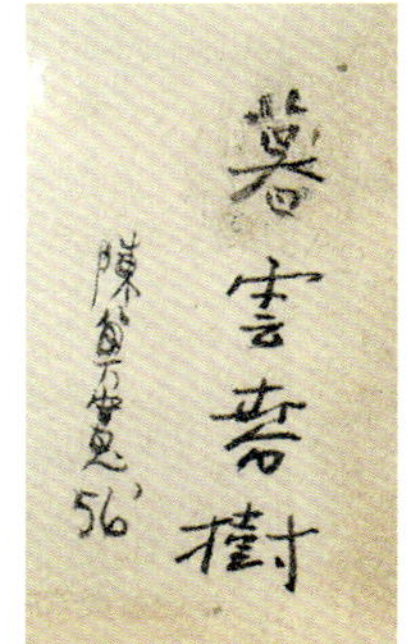

979

† 979. Evening Clouds, Spring Trees [暮雲春樹, *muyun chunshu*; "Thinking of a Friend Far Away" from a poem by Du Fu]

Signature

Chen Qikuan '56 [陳其寬 *56*]

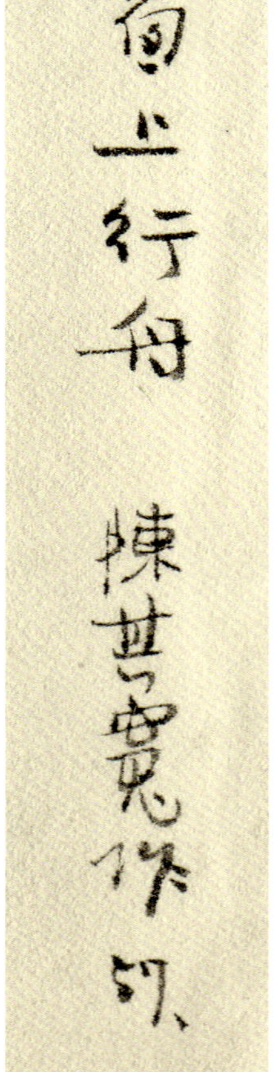

980

† 980. Boats Passing by the Window [*chuangshang xingzhou*, 窗上行舟]

Signature

Painted by Chen Qikuan '57 [陳其寬作 *57 Chen Qikuan zuo 57*]

† 981. "All Men Are Drunk and I Alone Am Sober" [*zhongzui duxing*, 眾醉獨醒]

Signature

Chen Qikuan '56 [陳其寬 56]

† 982. Untitled (Vermillion) [*zhuyan*, 朱顏]

Signature

1957 Chen Qikuan [一九五七 陳其寬]

† 983. Dream Journey [*woyou*, 臥遊]

Signature

Chen Qikuan '57 [陳其寬 57]

† 984. Untitled (Picnic) [*jiaoyou*, 郊遊]

Signature

Painted by Chen Qikuan '57 [陳其寬作 五七]

† 985. Monkey Show [*houxi*, 猴戲]

Seal

Seal of Chen Qikuan [*Chen Qikuan yin* 陳其寬印] (square, relief)

986. Untitled (New Year's Eve)

Signature

Painted by Chen Qikuan '57 [陳其寬作 57]

† 987. Untitled (Lotus Reflected)

Signature

Painted by Chen Qikuan '57 [陳其寬作 五七]

† 988. Rivers and Streams Like Sashes [*jiangchuan ru dai*, 江川如帶]

Signature

Painted by Chen Qikuan '57 [陳其寬作 57]

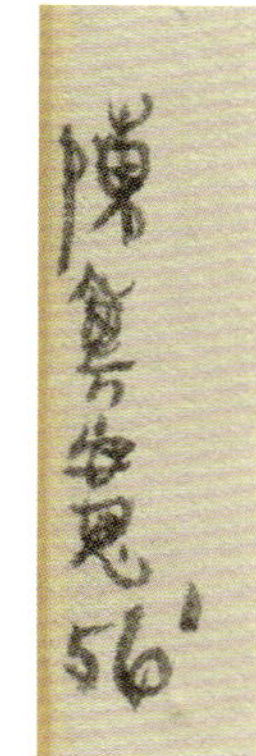

981

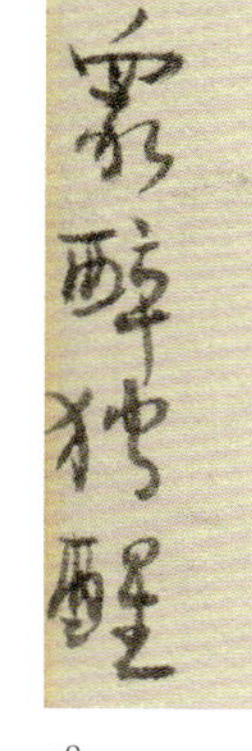

981

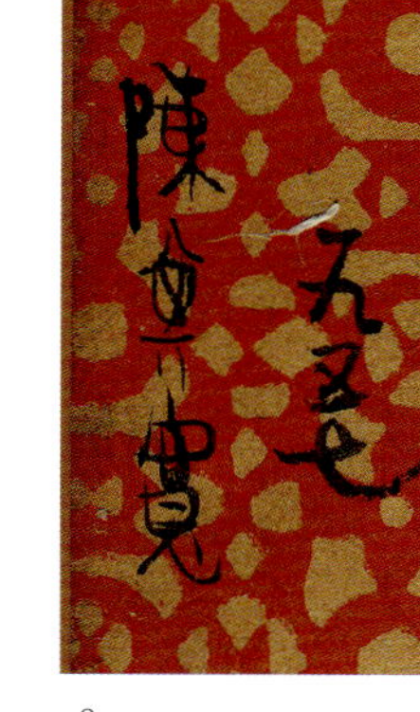

982

983

984

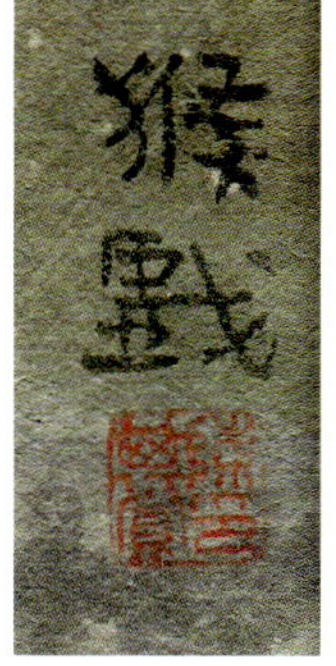

985

987

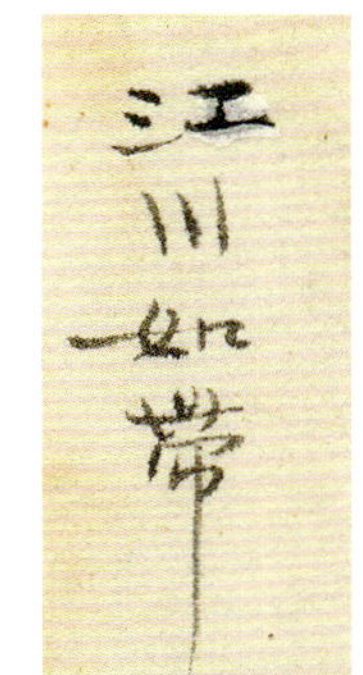

988

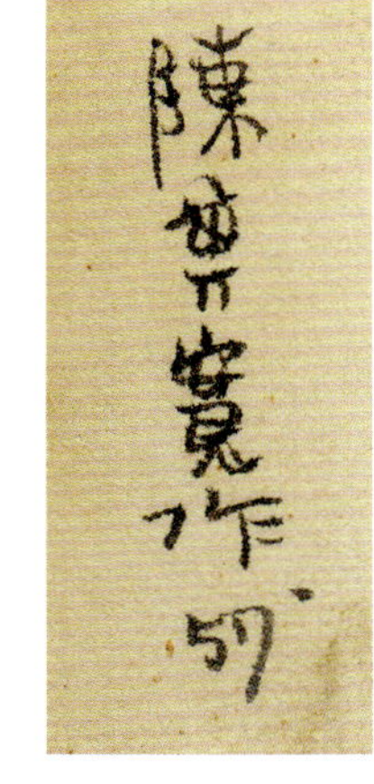

988

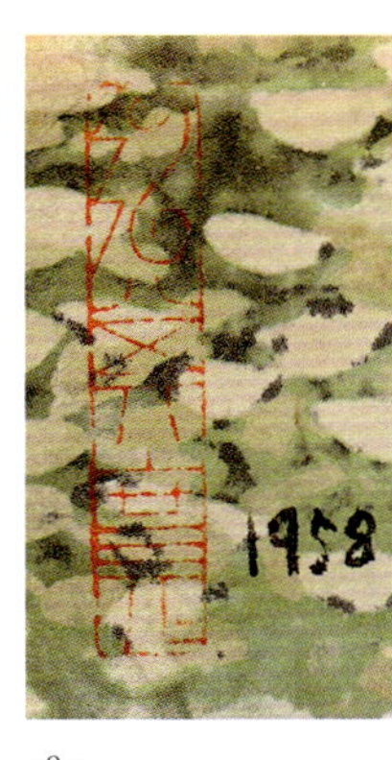

989

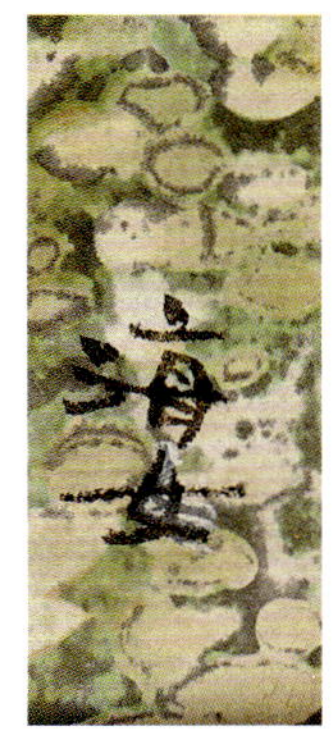

989

† 989. Fisher Women [*hainü*, 海女]

Signature

1958

Seals

Chen Qikuan [*Chen Qikuan* 陳其寬] (rectangular, relief); *To travel this far* (*Dao ci yu you* 到此于遊) (rectangular, relief)

† 990. Clasping the Feet of Buddha (抱佛脚)

Signature

1958

Seals

Chen Qikuan [*Chen Qikuan yin* 陳其寬印] (rectangular, relief); *To travel this far* (*Dao ci yu you* 到此于遊) (rectangular, relief)

† 991. Untitled (Blue Mosque)

Seal

Chen Qikuan [*Chen Qikuan* 陳其寬] (rectangular, relief)

† 992. Untitled (Frozen Landscape)

Signature

59

Seal

Chen Qikuan [*Chen Qikuan* 陳其寬] (rectangular, relief)

† 993. Nüti Mountain [*Nüti shan*]

Signature

1958

Seals

Chen Qikuan; [*Chen Qikuan* 陳其寬] (rectangular, relief); *To travel this far* (*Dao ci yu you* 到此于遊) (rectangular, relief)

† 994. Untitled (Itsukushima)

Signature

59

Seal

Chen Qikuan [*Chen Qikuan* 陳其寬] (rectangular, relief)

† 995. Untitled (Mergence) [*jiao rong* 交融]

Signature

Chen Qikuan 1960 [陳其寬 *1960*]

Seals

[two impressions of same seal] *Chen Qikuan* [*Chen Qikuan* 陳其寬] (rectangular, relief)

990

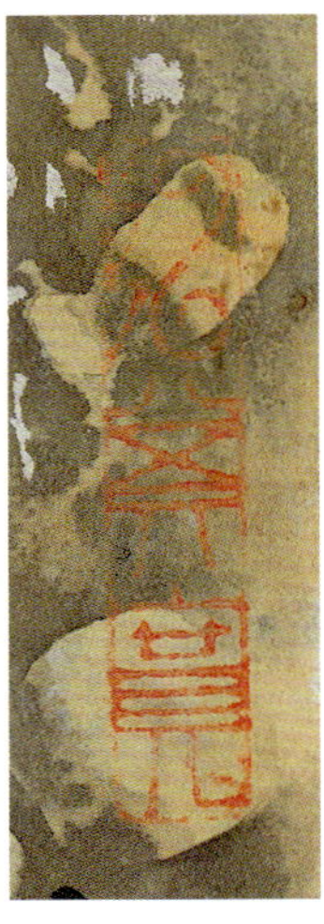

991

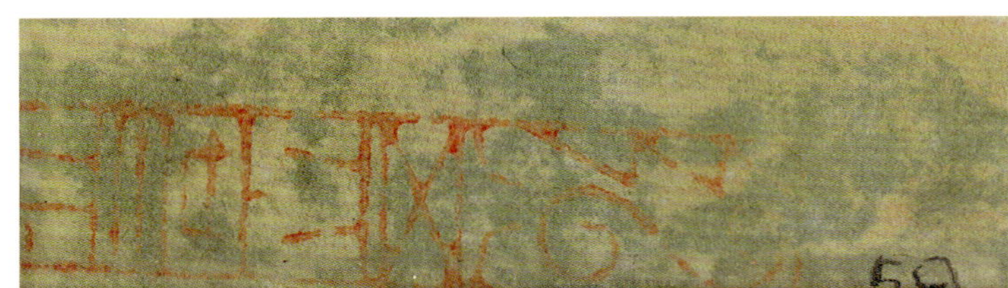

992

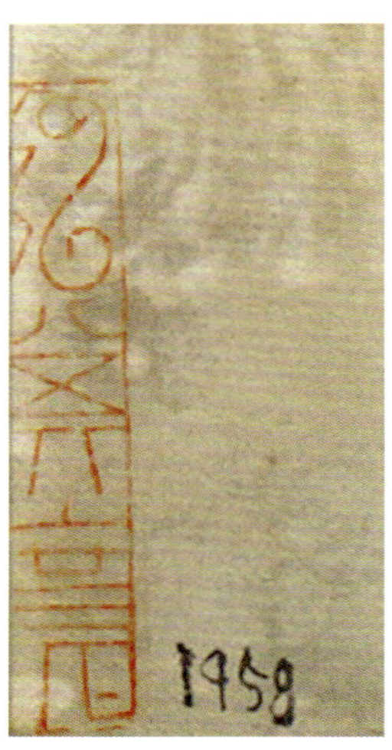

993

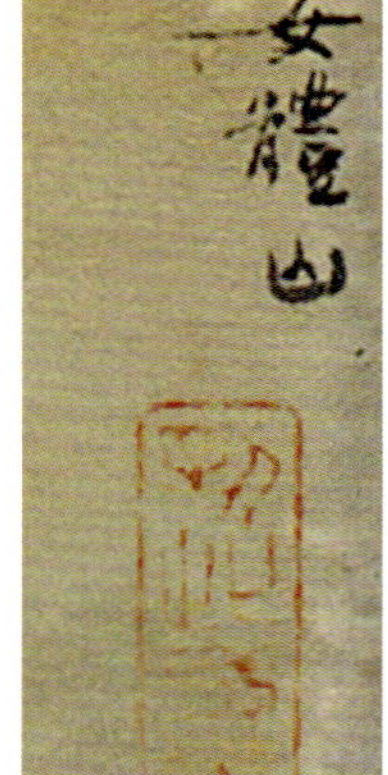

993

994

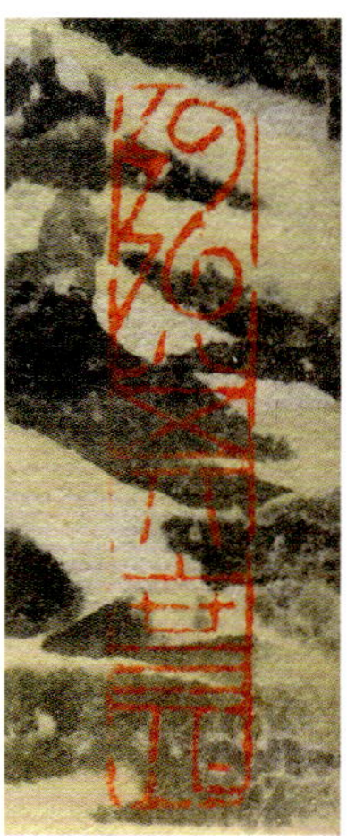

995

995

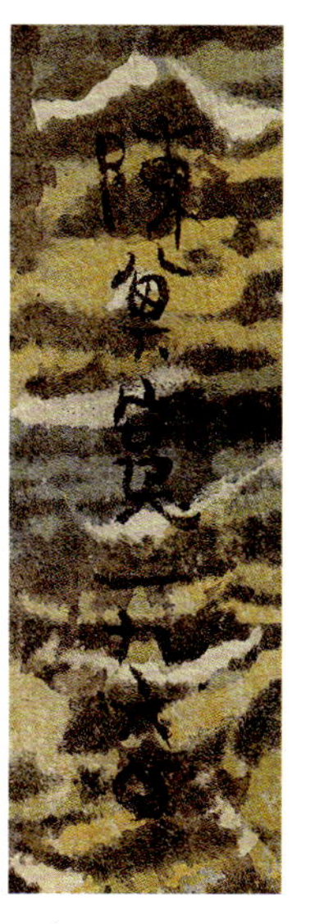

996

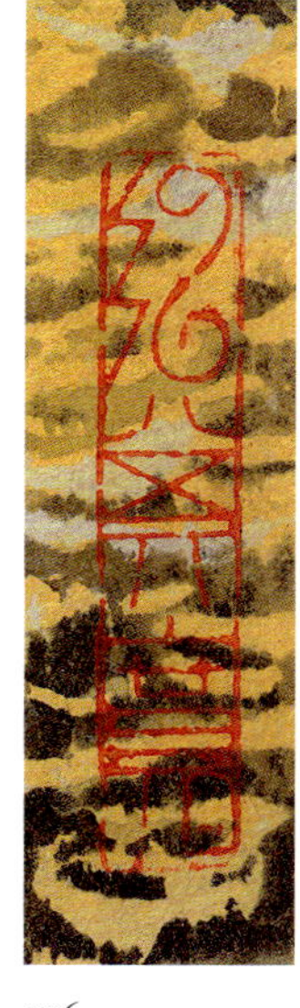

996

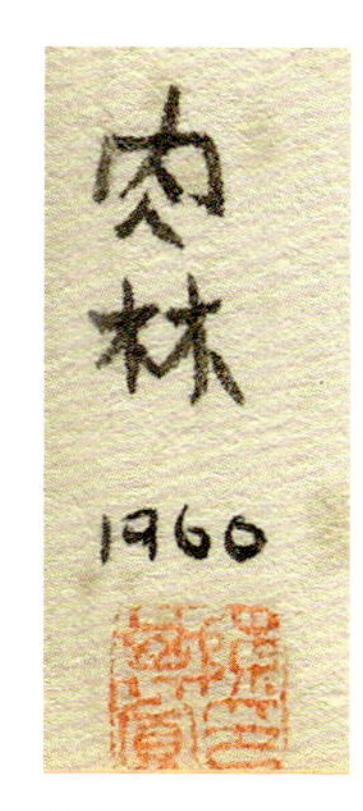

997

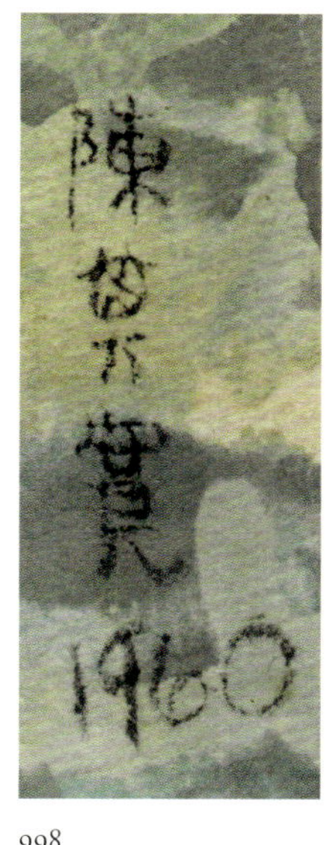

998

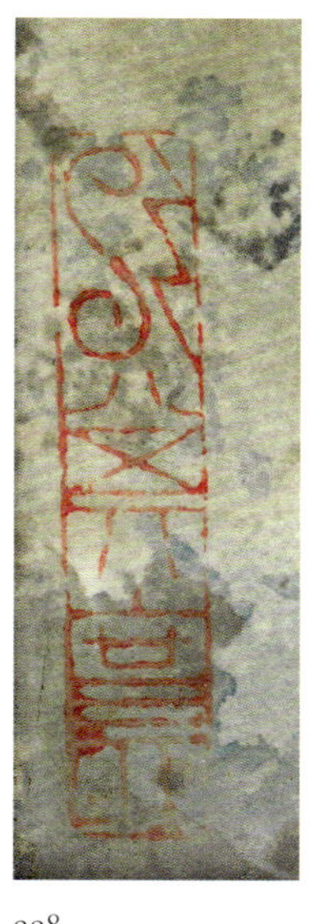

998

† 996. Untitled (Fishing Boats / Venice)

Signature

Chen Qikuan 1960 [陳其寛 一九六0]

Seal

Chen Qikuan [*Chen Qikuan* 陳其寛] (rectangular, relief)

† 997. Forest of Flesh [*Roulin* 肉林 "lavish lifestyle" from 肉林酒池 / 酒池肉林]

Signature

1960

Seal

Seal of Chen Qikuan [*Chen Qikuan yin* 陳其寛印] (square, relief)

† 998. Untitled

Signature

Chen Qikuan 1960 [陳其寛 *1960*]

Seal

Chen Qikuan [*Chen Qikuan* 陳其寛] (rectangular, relief)

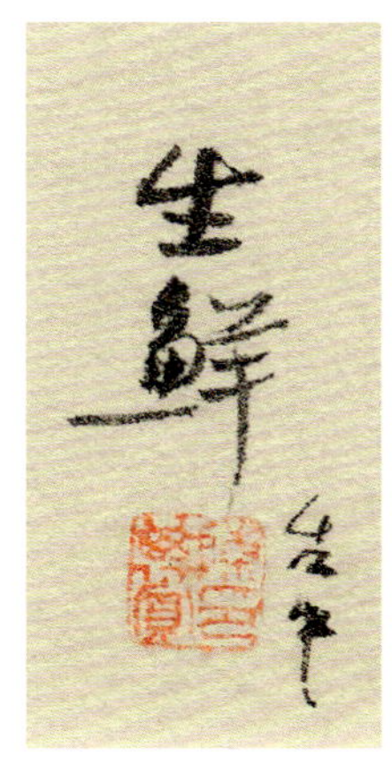

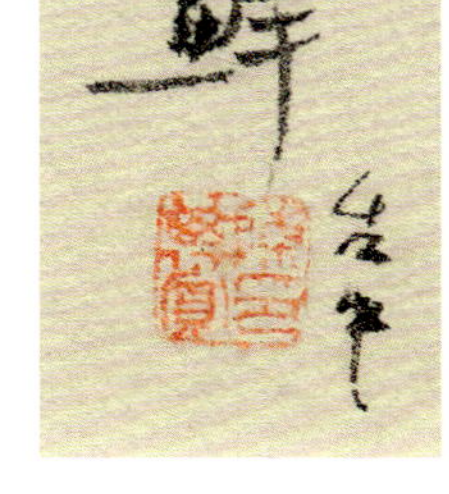

999

999

† 999. (*a*) Fresh Seafood [*shengxian*, 生鮮]; (*b*) Conciliatory but Not Accommodating [*he er butong*, 合而不同]

[a]

Signature

Taizhong 台中 [name of city in Taiwan]

Seal

Seal of Chen Qikuan [*Chen Qikuan yin* 陳其寛印] (square, relief)

[b]

Seal

Seal of Chen Qikuan [*Chen Qikuan yin* 陳其寛印] (square, relief)

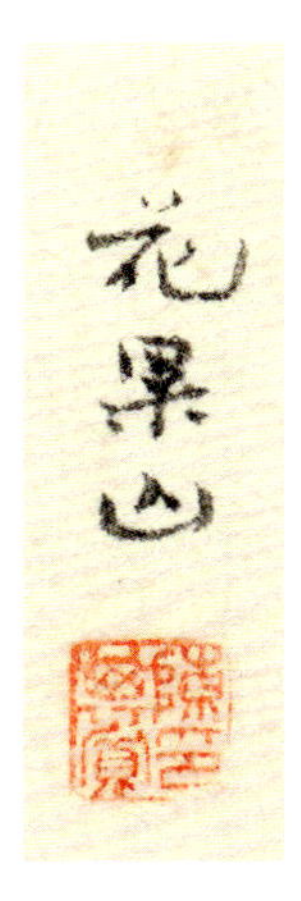

1000

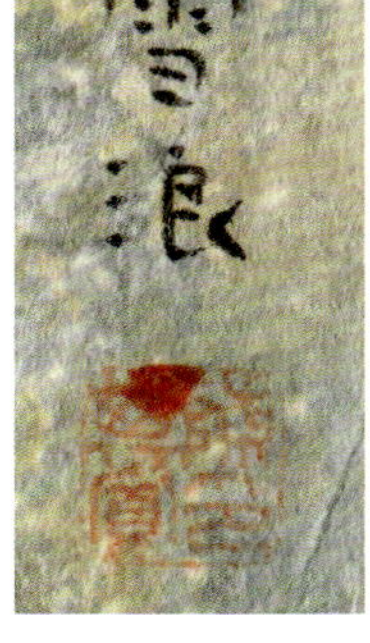

1001

† 1000. Mount Huaguo: Home of the Monkey King [*Huaguo shan*, 花果山]

Seal

Seal of Chen Qikuan [*Chen Qikuan yin* 陳其寛印] (square, relief)

† 1001. Waves of Snow [*xuelang*, 雪浪]

Seal

Seal of Chen Qikuan [*Chen Qikuan yin* 陳其寛印] (square, relief)

† 1002. Waterfall [*bu*, 瀑]

Seal

Seal of Chen Qikuan [*Chen Qikuan yin* 陳其寬印] (square, relief)

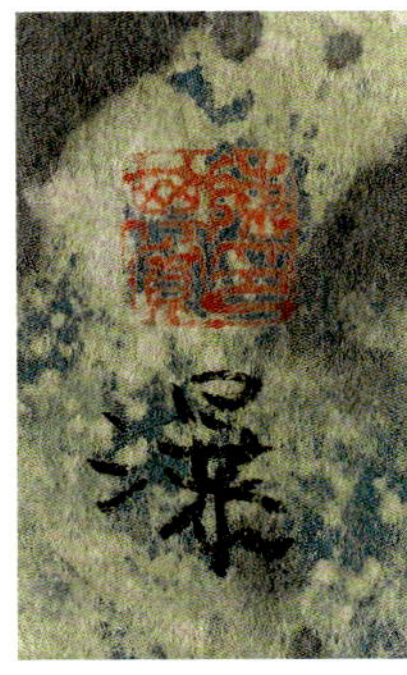

1002

† 1003. Clearing after Rain [*yuji*, 雨霽]

Signature

Painted by Chen Qiquan [陳其寬作]

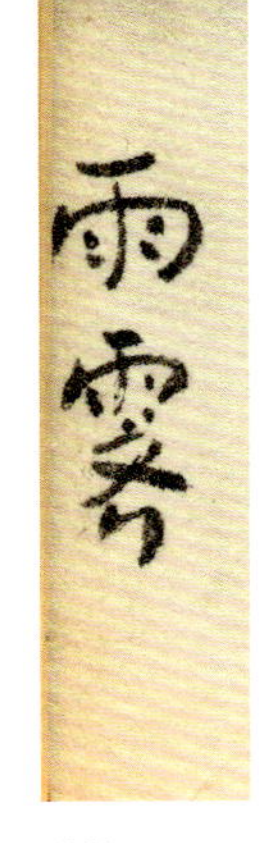

1003

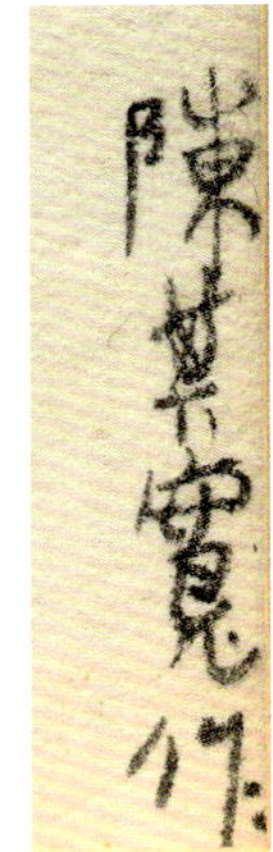

1003

† 1004. Mother Hen and Chicks [*mu yu zi*, 母與子]

Signature

Brushed by Chen Qikuan [*Chen Qikuan bi* 陳其寬筆]

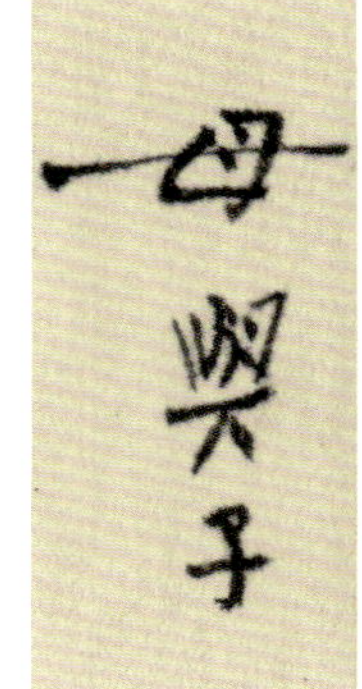

1004

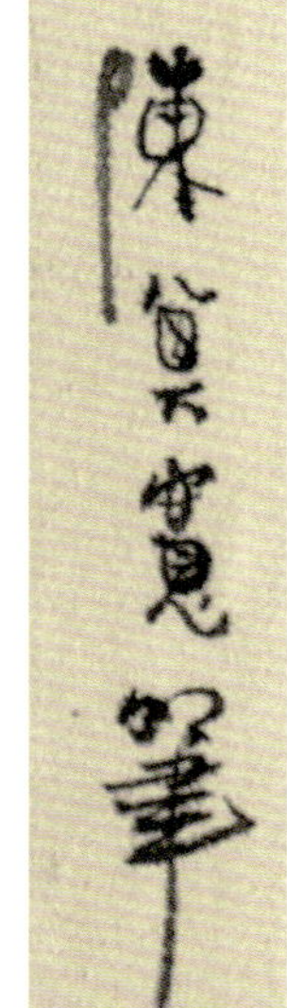

1004

† 1005. Taoyuan [*Taoyuan*, 桃園]

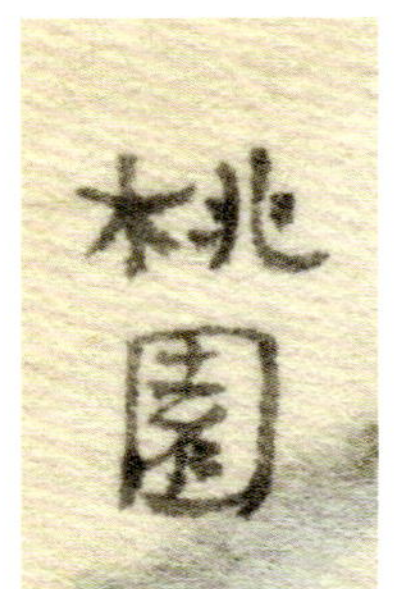

1005

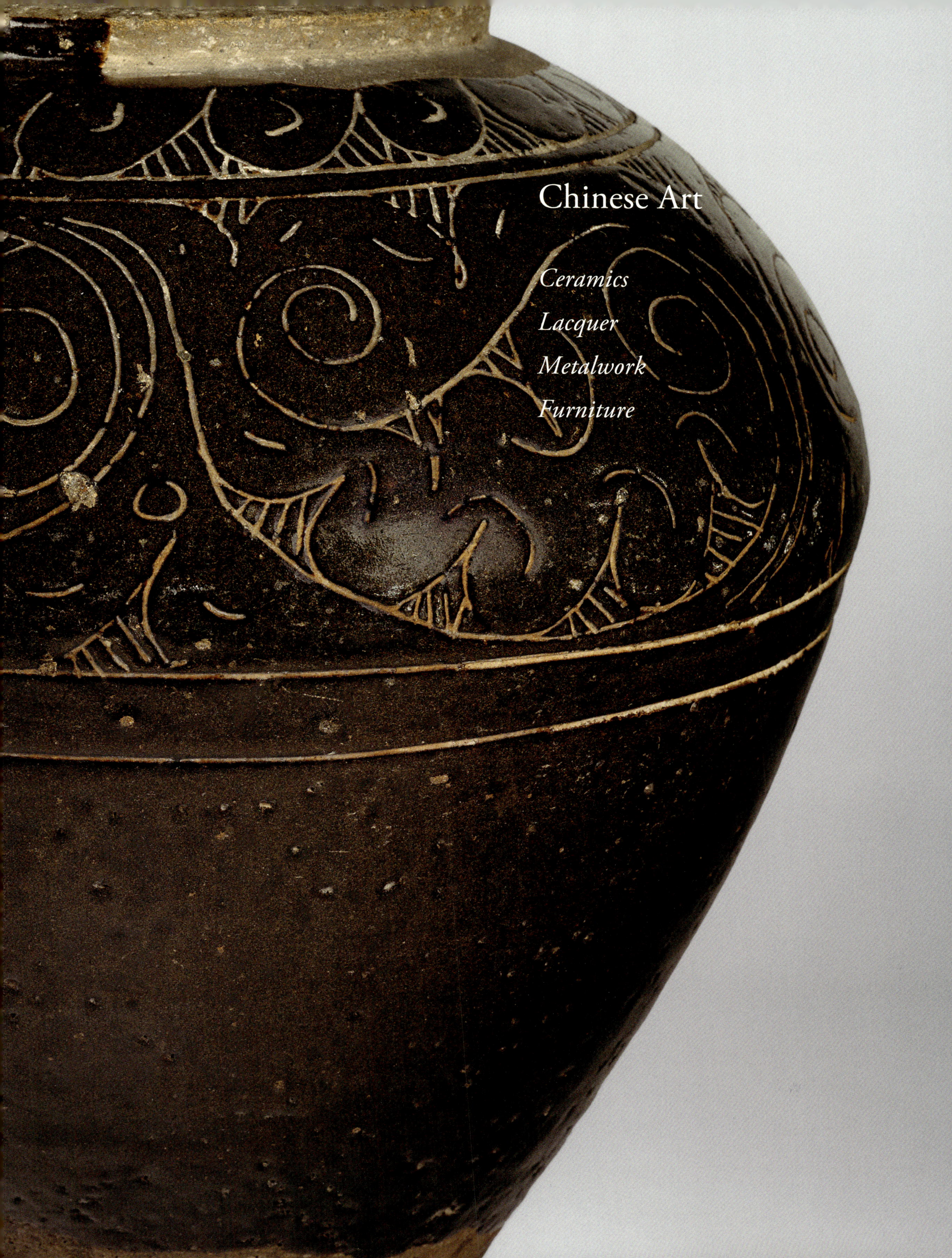

Chinese Art

Ceramics
Lacquer
Metalwork
Furniture

1006. Tea bowl with indented lip

Southern Song dynasty (1127–1279), 13th century
Jian ware (建窯); stoneware with dark brown glaze and hare's-fur markings
H. 60 cm (23 5/8 in.), diam. 12 cm (4 3/4 in.); footring diam. 3.1 cm (1 1/4 in.)

LITERATURE: Rousmaniere 2002, p. 100, no. 10.

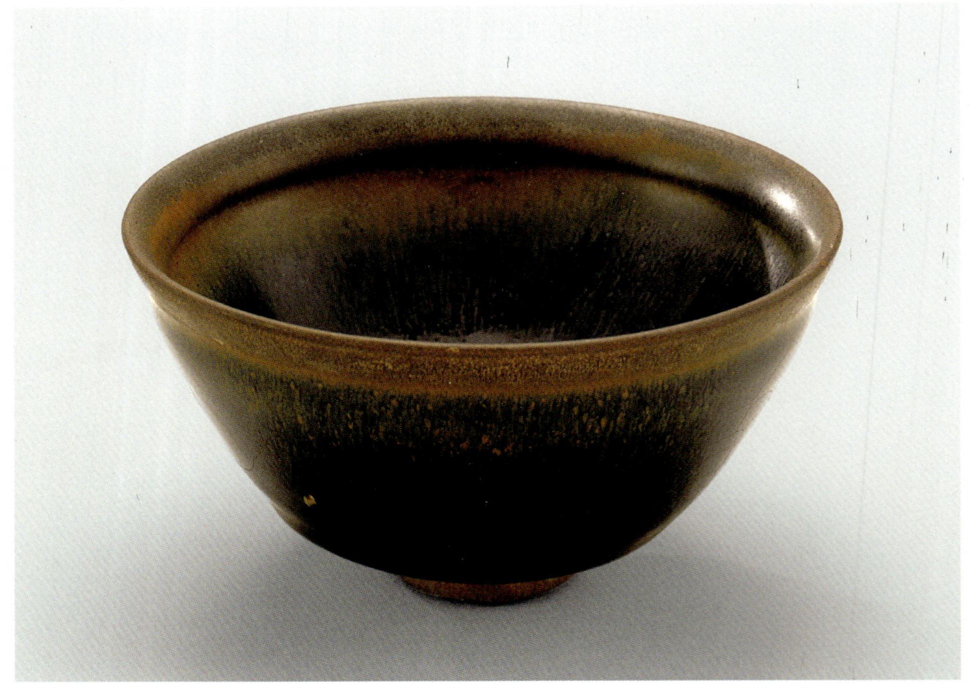

1007. Storage jar

Southern Song–Yuan dynasty, 13th–14th century
South China, possibly Guangdong
Buff stoneware with brown glaze
H. 24.1 cm (9 1/2 in.), diam. 20.3 cm (8 in.)

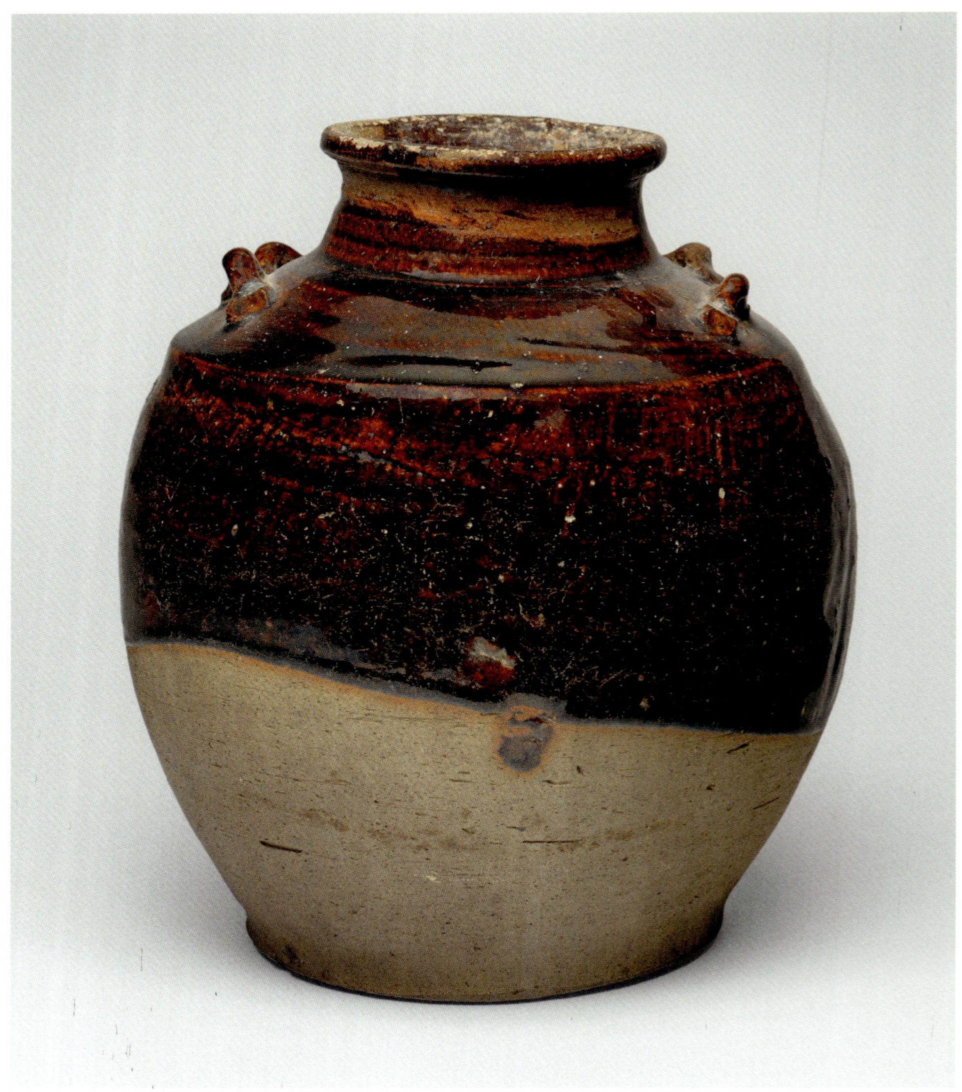

1008. Ovoid jar with incised decoration

Yuan–Ming dynasty, 14th–early 15th century
Cizhou-type ware (磁州窑); buff stoneware with black glaze
H. 33 cm (13 in.)

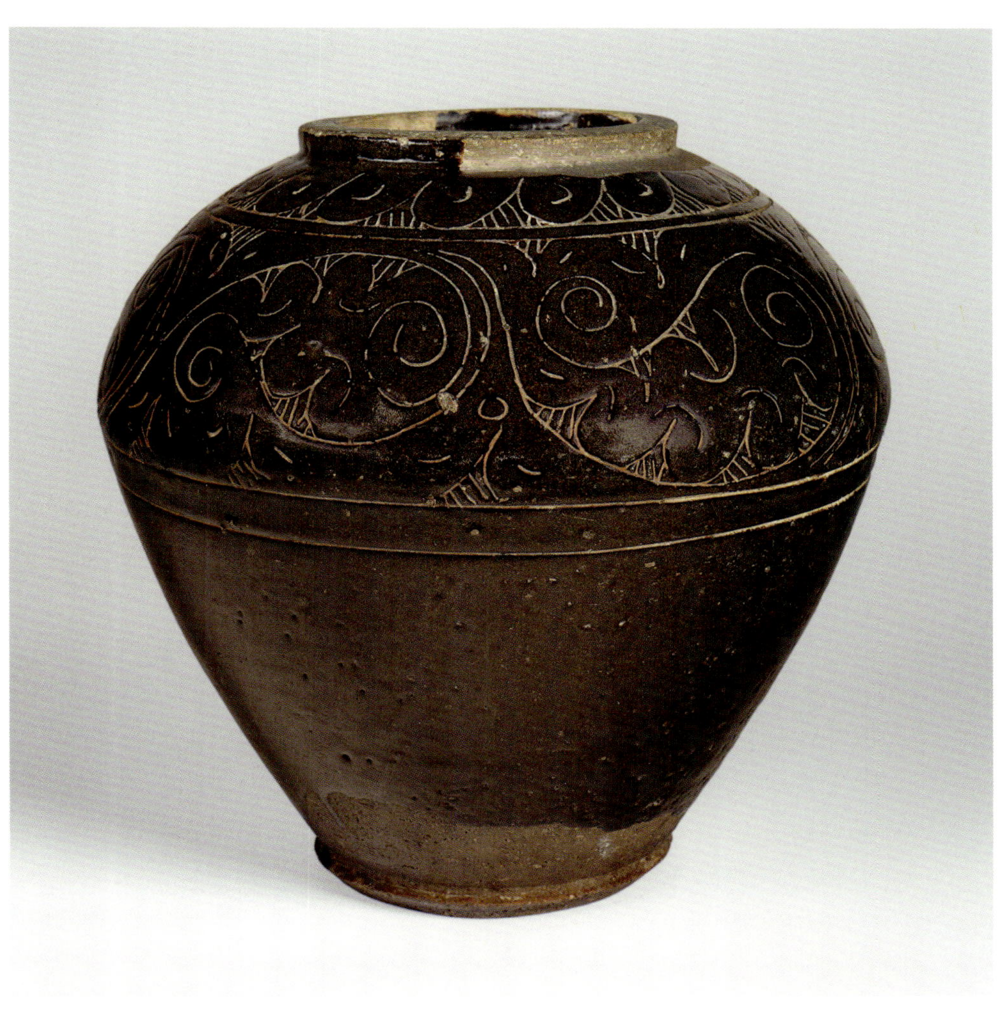

1009. Basin with incised decoration and applied fish

Yuan–Ming dynasty, 14th–early 15th century
Longquan ware (龍泉窑); stoneware with green glaze and applied decoration in unglazed clay
H. 8 cm (3 1/8 in.); diam. 28.6 cm (11 1/4 in.)

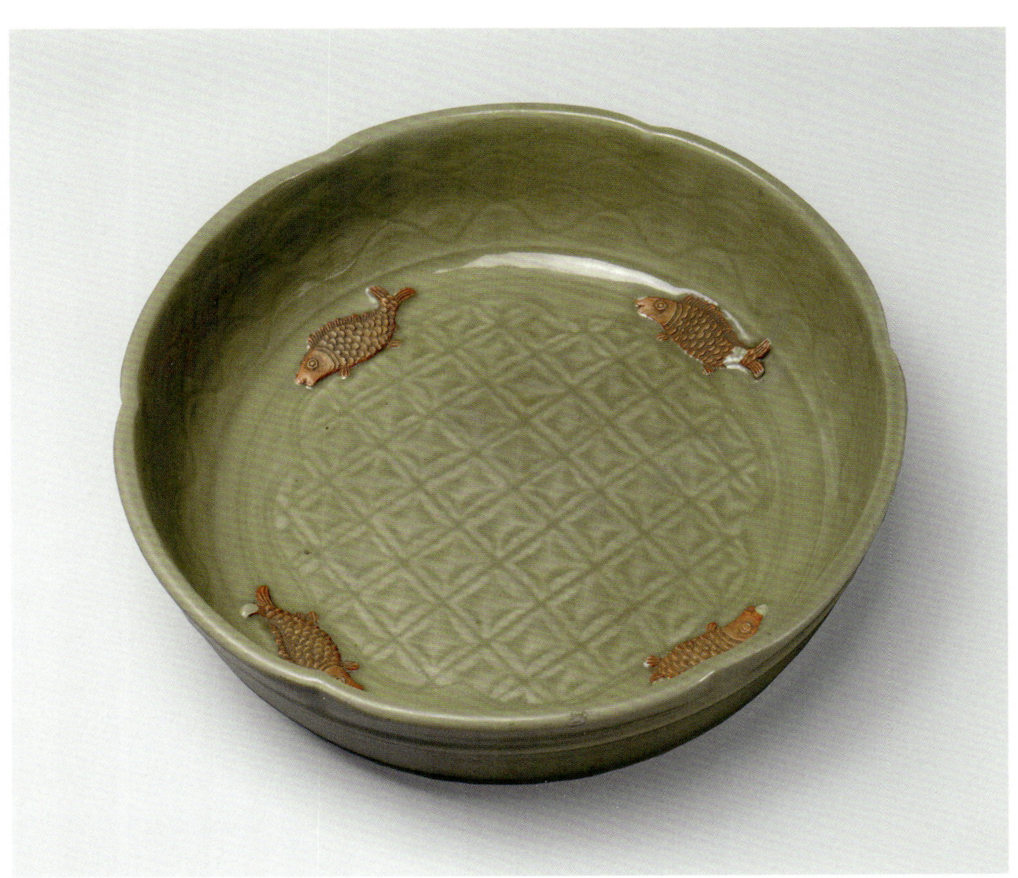

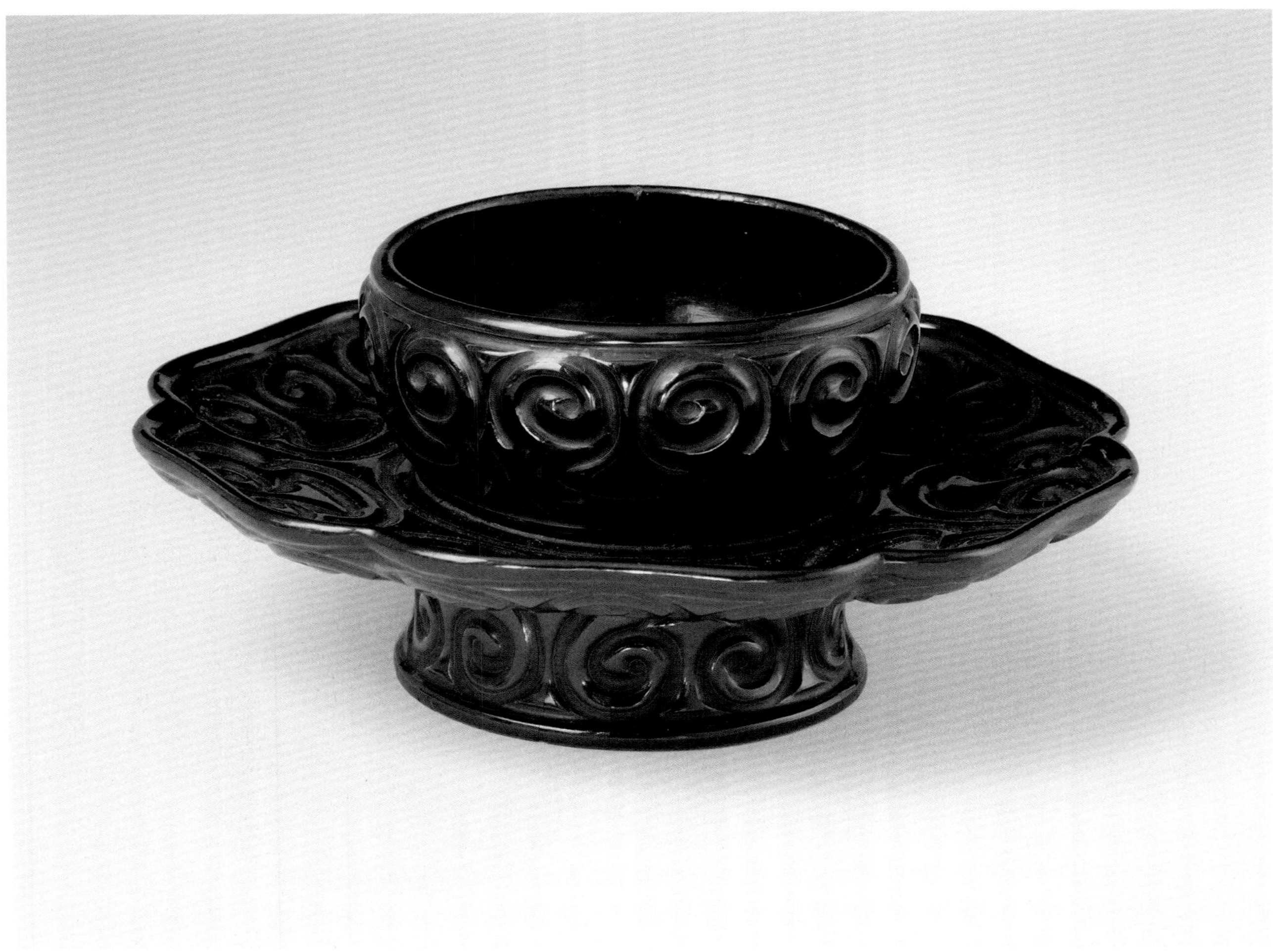

1010. Tea bowl stand (剔犀茶托)

Ming dynasty (1368–1644), 16th century
Carved red and black lacquer on wood
H. 7.1 cm (2 3/4 in.); diam. 15.2 cm (6 in.)

LITERATURE: Rousmaniere 2002, p. 101, no. 11.

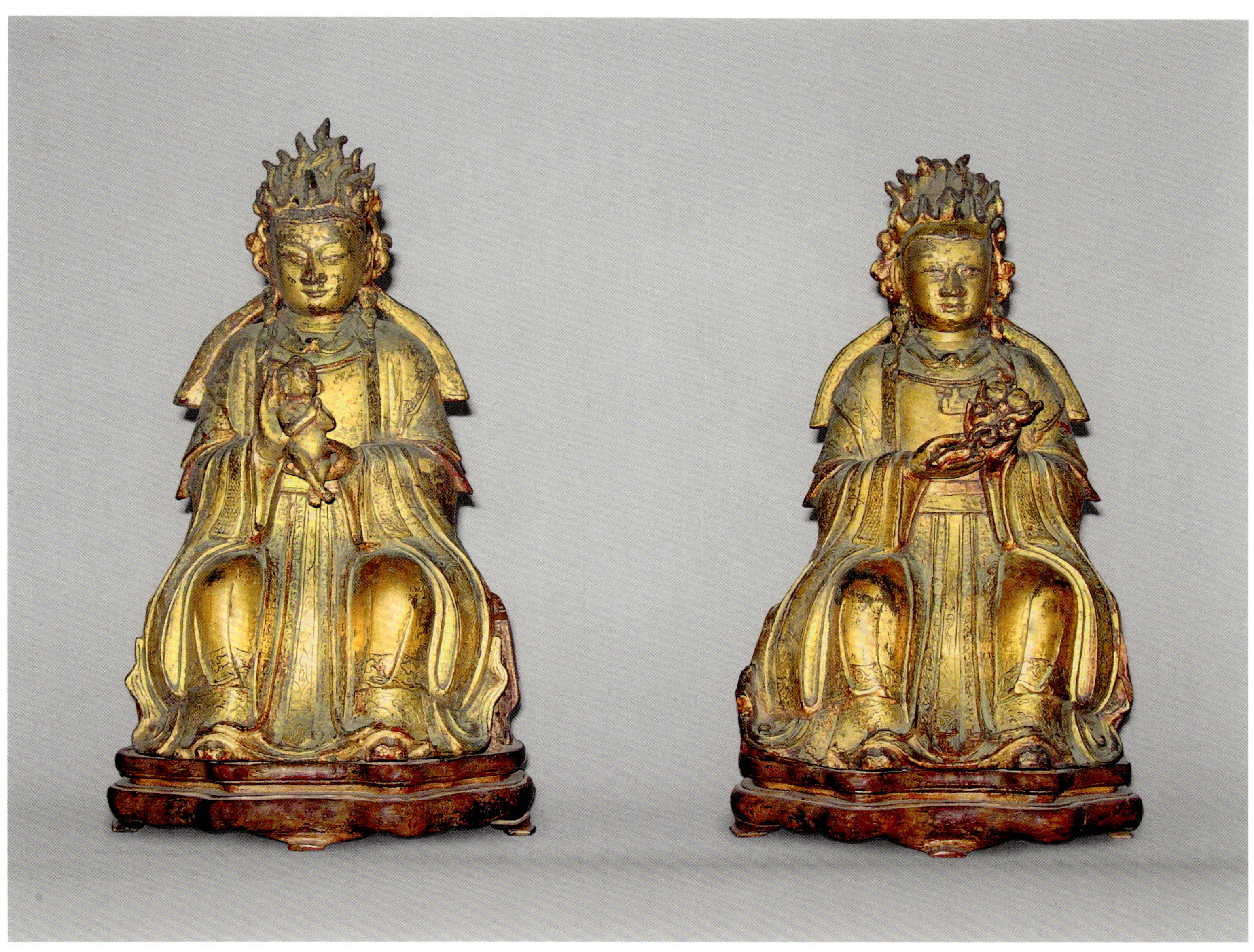

1011. Pair of Daoist Deities:
(*left*) Songzi Niangniang (送子娘娘) and
(*right*) Yanguang Niangniang (眼光娘娘)

Ming dynasty, late 16th–early 17th century
Gilt bronze with blue and red lacquer; wood bases
H. of each 21 cm (8 1/4 in.); (*left*) h. with base 23.6 cm (9 1/4 in.); (*right*) h. with base 23.1 cm (9 1/8 in.)

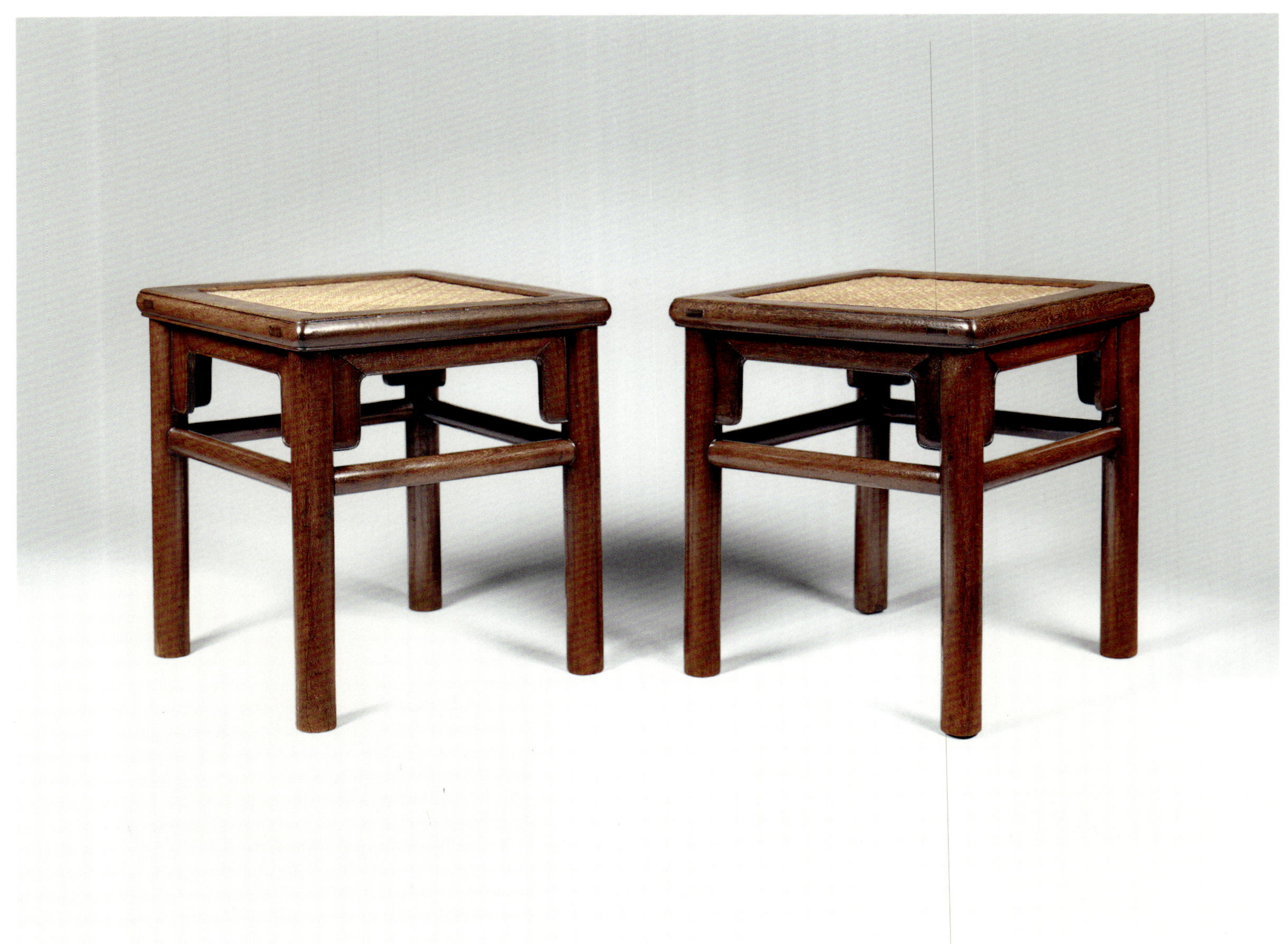

1012. Pair of square stools (方櫈一對)

Late Ming–early Qing dynasty, 17th century
Jichimu wood (鸂鶒木)
Each 45.2 x 41.3 x 41.3 cm (17¼ x 16¼ x 16¼ in.)

Ex coll.: Peter Lai Antiques, Hong Kong;
Mr. and Mrs. Robert Piccus, Hong Kong;
Christie's New York, 1997

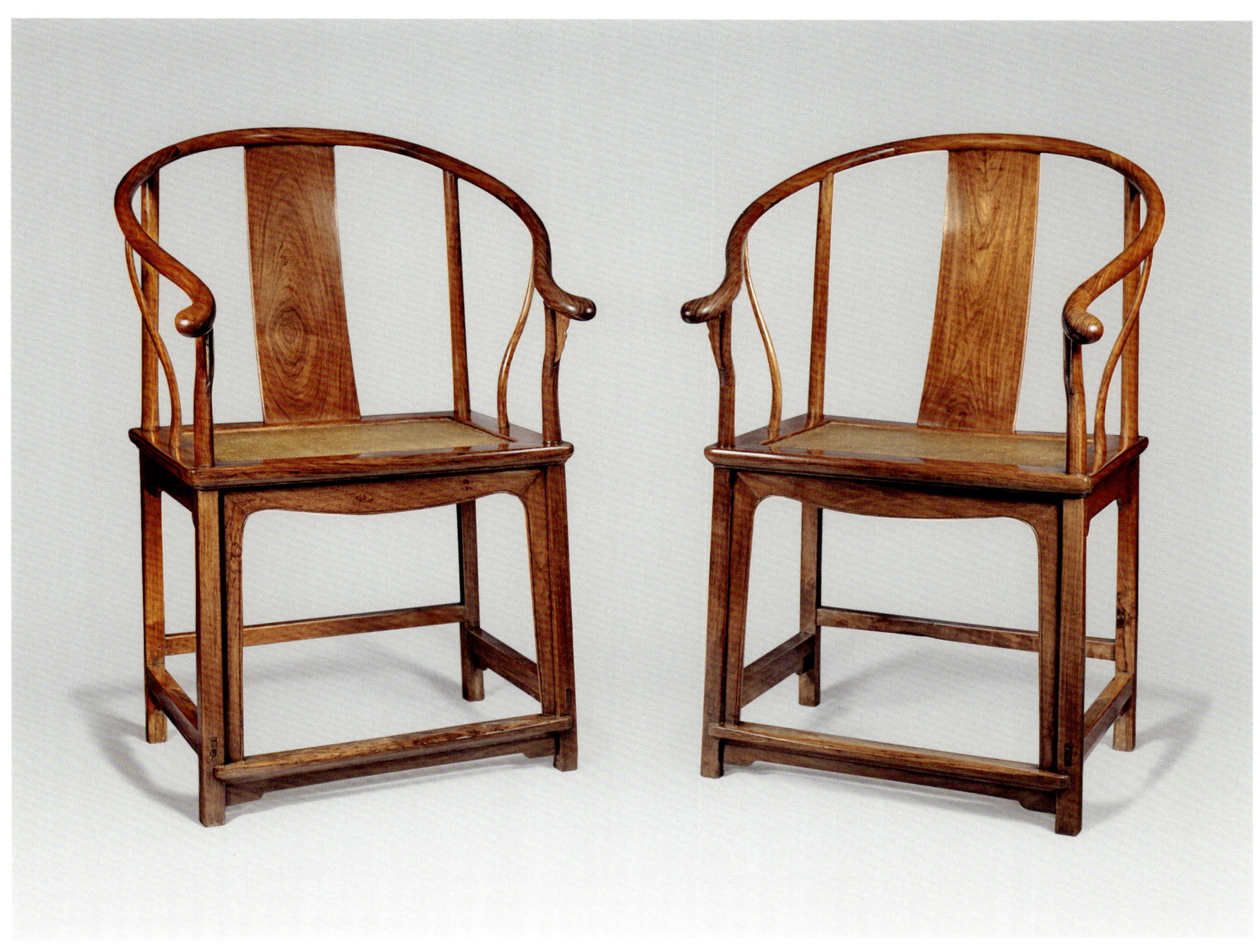

1013. Pair of horseshoe-back armchairs
(圈椅一對)

Late Ming–early Qing dynasty, 17th century
Huanghuali wood (黄花梨)
99 x 66 x 54.6 cm (39 x 26 x 21½ in.)

Ex coll.: Leo Ephrussi, Peking; Robin Curtis; Alice Boney, 1962; Nicholas Grindley, 1997

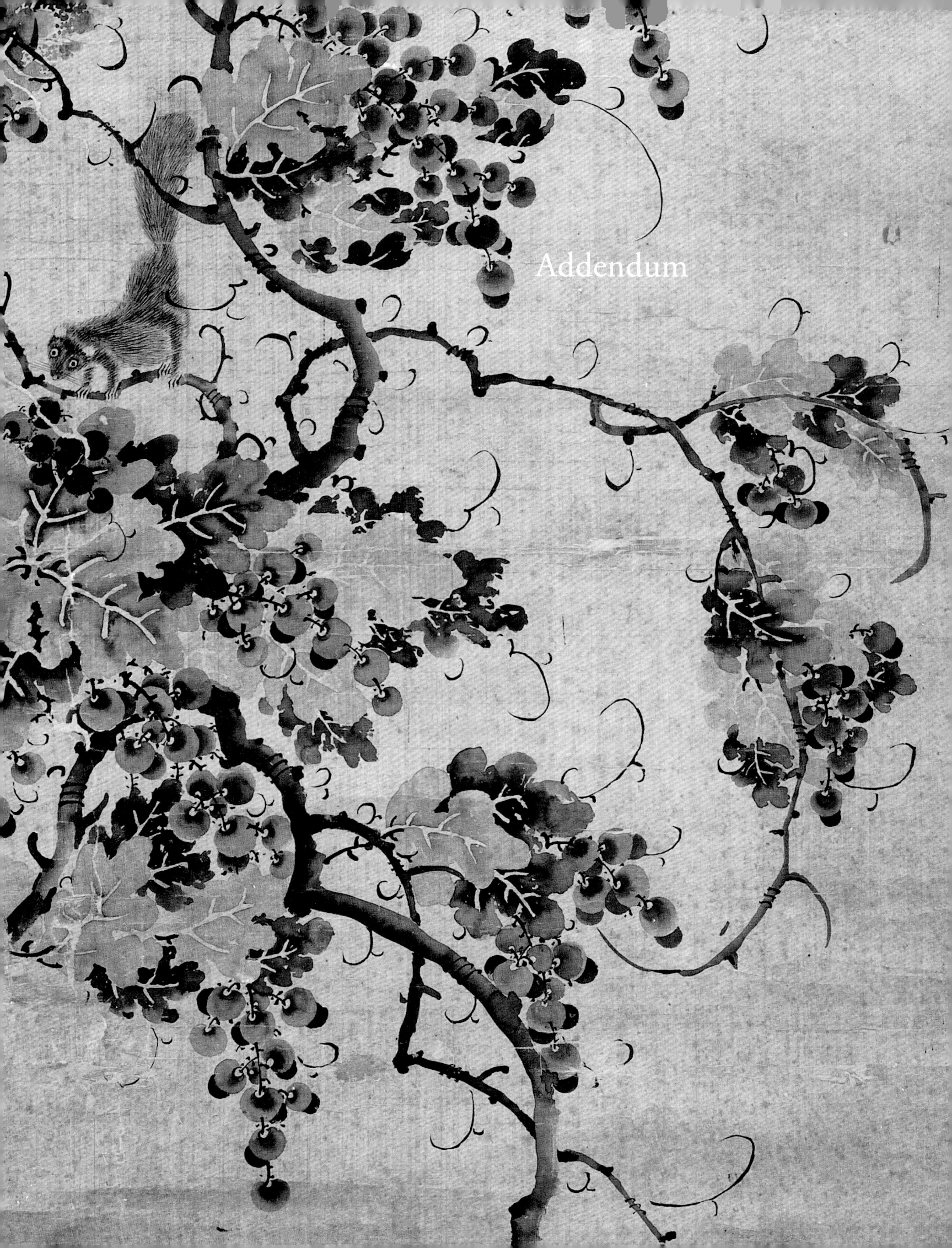

Addendum

1014. Grapevine and Squirrels

Ryūkyū Islands(?), 18th–19th century
Hanging scroll; ink on silk
142 x 57.2 cm ($55^{7}/_{8}$ x $22^{1}/_{2}$ in.)
Seal

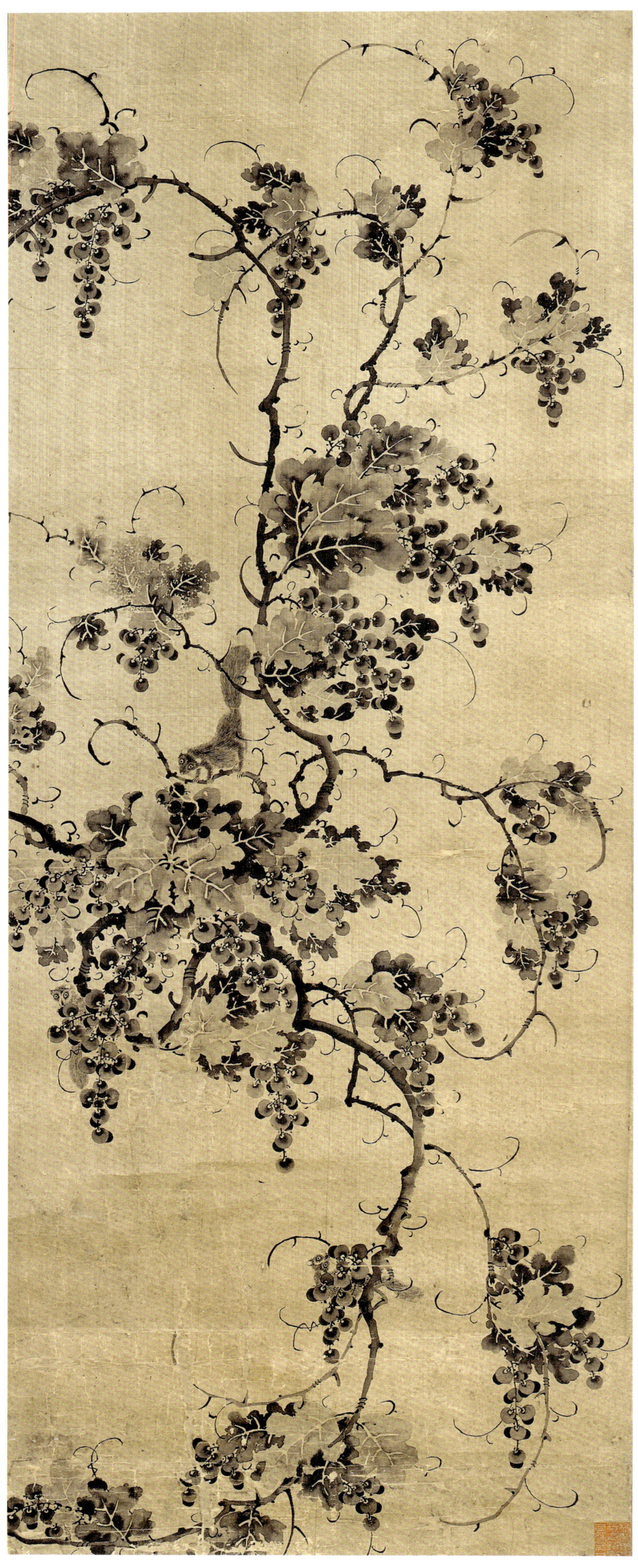

Detail

† *denotes illustrated item*

---

† 1014. Grapevine and Squirrels

Seal

Retaining spring in the plum studio, / Whiling away summer at the lotus pavilion. / I just enjoy myself.

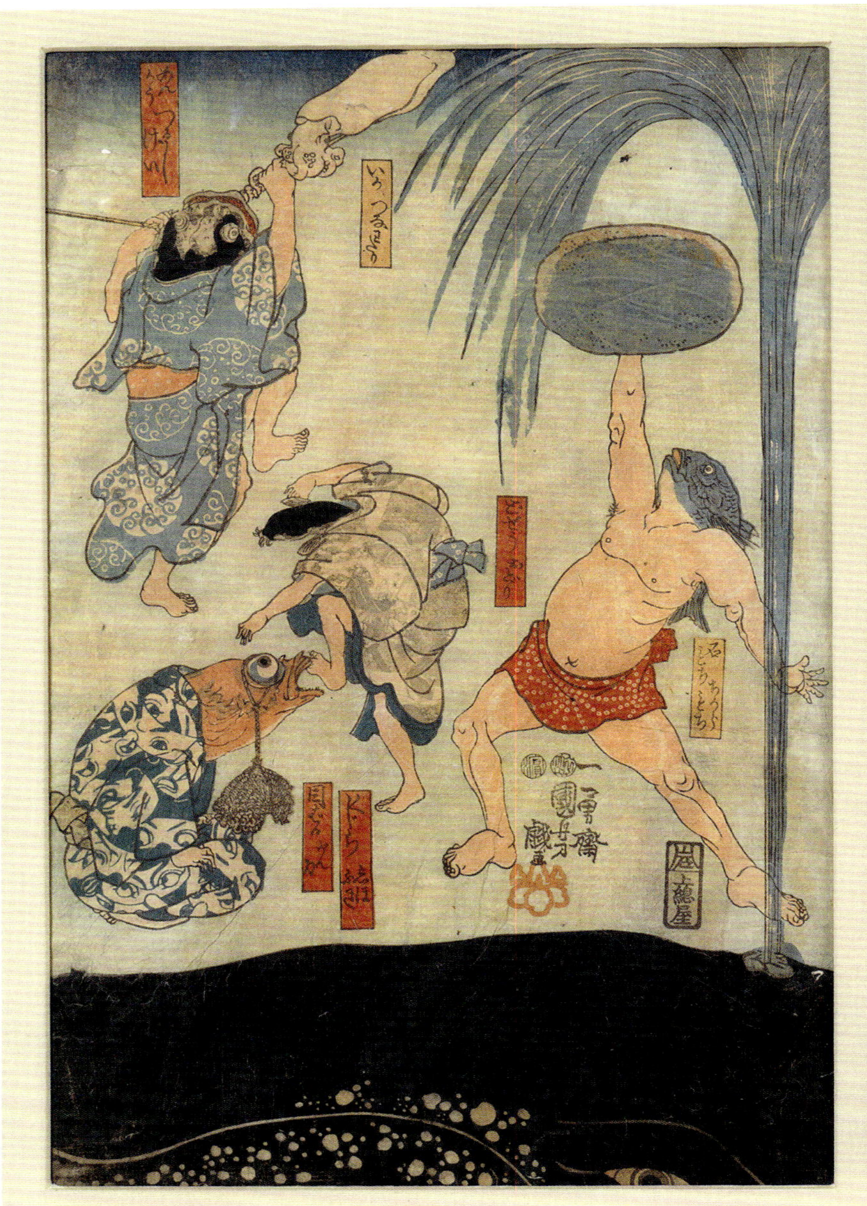

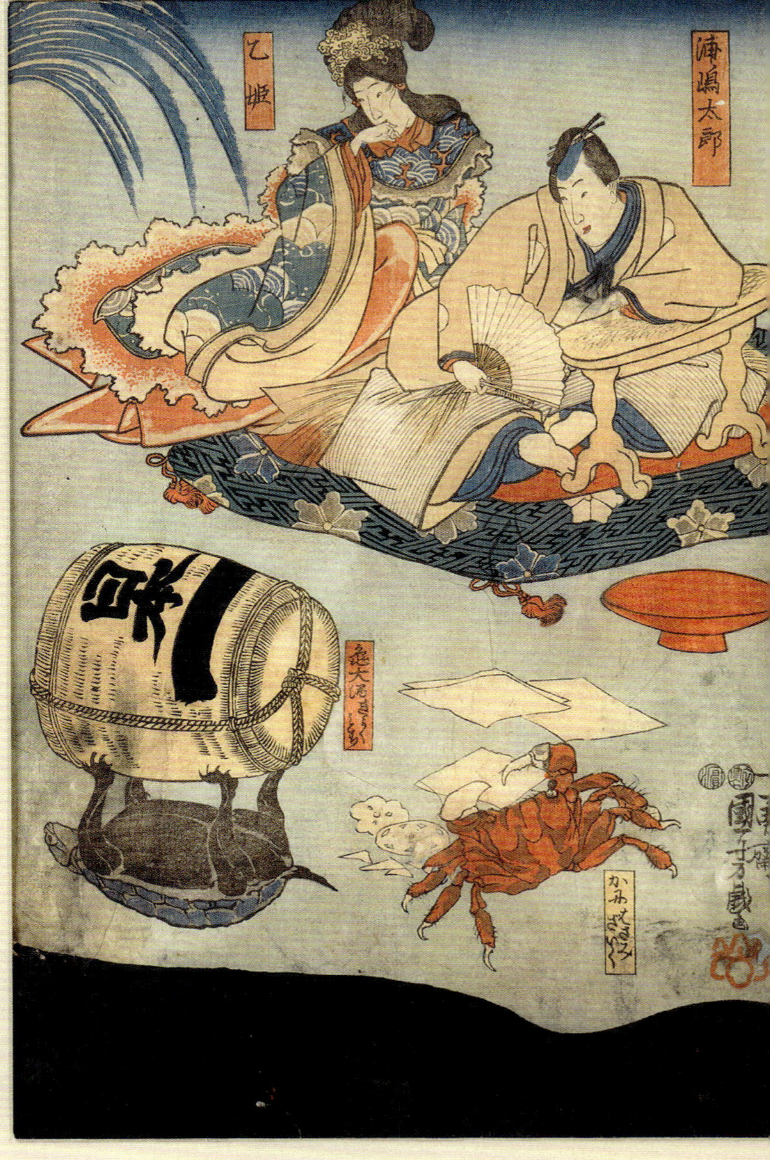

Utagawa Kuniyoshi
(歌川 国芳; 1797–1861)

1015. Sea creatures entertain Urashima Tarō and Oto Hime at the undersea Dragon Palace

Edo period, 1847/48
Ōban tate-e woodblock print triptych; ink and color on paper
Overall 35 x 74 cm (13$\frac{3}{4}$ x 29$\frac{1}{8}$ in.)
Signature, seals

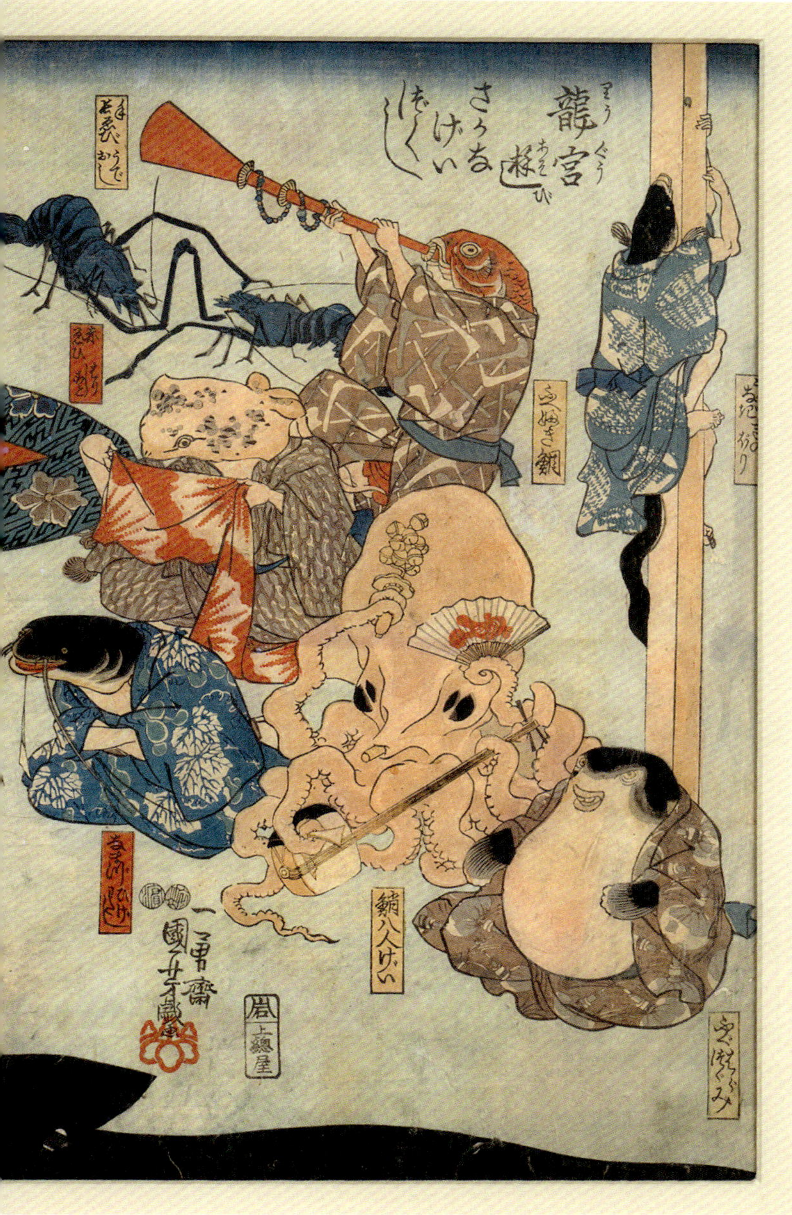

Detail

† *denotes illustrated items*

---

† 1015. Sea creatures entertain Urashima Tarō and Oto Hime at the undersea Dragon Palace

SIGNATURE

Playfully painted by Ichiyūsai Kuniyoshi

SEALS

[publisher's seal] *Kazusaya Iwazō*
[censor's seal, on the right] *Kinugasa Fusajirō*
[censor's seal, on the left] *Hama Yahei*
[artist's seal] red paulownia

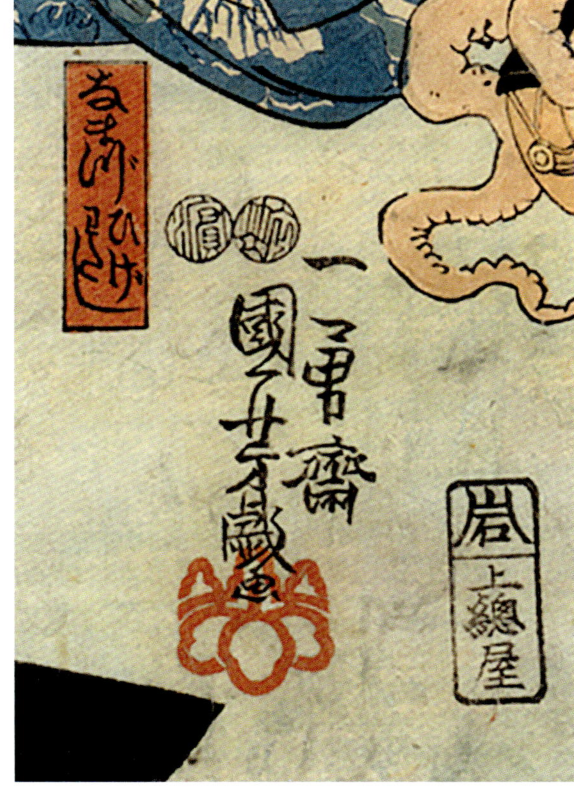

Index of Artists

Artists are listed by family name. The number following artist's name and dates refers to catalogue number.

Record of Ownership

These objects, listed by catalogue number, include only those in the Estate of Mary Griggs Burke and those in the collection of the Mary and Jackson Burke Foundation. If a work is now in the collection of another institution, a credit line appears in the entry itself.

Estate of Mary Griggs Burke

547, 549, 552, 555, 559, 560, 565, 569–573, 575, 578–584, 590, 591, 594–596, 601, 602, 605–608, 611–613, 615, 620–628, 631–634, 637, 638, 641, 643, 646–648, 651–653, 656–660, 662–664, 667–671, 673–676, 678–683, 685, 686, 688–693, 695, 697, 698, 700–702, 704–720, 722–725, 727, 729–737, 739–743, 750, 752–754, 757, 758, 760, 761, 763, 765, 767–769, 773, 774, 776, 780, 782, 783, 786, 789–792, 794, 796, 797, 799–802, 804, 805, 808, 809, 811, 812, 815–818, 822, 823, 825–838, 840, 844–858, 861, 864–866, 869–888, 890, 891, 893, 895, 900–903, 905–908, 910–913, 915–918, 920–924, 926–933, 936, 938, 939, 941–945, 947, 949, 953–1006, 1008, 1009, 1011–1013, 1015

Mary and Jackson Burke Foundation

546, 548, 550, 551, 553, 554, 556–558, 561–564b, 566–568, 574, 576, 577, 585–589, 592, 593, 597–600, 603, 604, 609, 610, 614, 616–619, 629, 630, 635, 636, 639, 640, 642, 644, 645, 649, 650, 654, 655, 661, 665, 666, 672, 677, 684, 687, 694, 696, 699, 703, 721, 726, 728, 738, 744–749, 751, 755, 756, 759, 762, 764, 766, 770–772, 775, 777–779, 781, 784, 785, 787, 788, 793, 795, 798, 803, 806, 807, 810, 813, 814, 819–821, 824, 839, 841–843, 859, 860, 862, 863, 867, 868, 889, 892, 894, 896–899, 904, 909, 914, 919, 925, 934, 935, 937, 940, 946, 948, 950–952, 1007, 1010, 1014

Bibliography

Adachi Keiko

1990 "Nishu no ryūkyō zu byōbu" (Two screen paintings of Bridge and Willows). *Kokka*, no. 1135 (June): 7–22.

Addiss, Stephen

1984 *The World of Kameda Bōsai: The Calligraphy, Poetry, Painting, and Artistic Circle of a Japanese Literatus*. Exh. cat. New Orleans: New Orleans Museum of Art; Lawrence: University Press of Kansas.

1987 *Tall Mountains and Flowing Waters: The Arts of Uragami Gyokudō*. Honolulu: University of Hawai'i Press.

1999 *The Resonance of the Qin in East Asian Art*. Exh. cat. New York: China Institute Gallery.

Addiss, Stephen, and Kwan S. Wong

1978 *Ōbaku: Zen Painting and Calligraphy*. Exh. cat., Helen Foresman Spencer Museum of Art, Lawrence, and New Orleans Museum of Art. Lawrence, Kan.: Helen Foresman Spencer Museum of Art.

The Age of Navigation and Japan

1978 *The Age of Navigation and Japan*. Tokyo: Shōgakukan.

Akamatsu Shinshū

1951 "Kami Daigo no Kiyotaki Myōjin zō" (The statue of Kiyotaki Myōjin in the Upper Temple of Daigo). *Bijutsushi* 1, no. 3 (March): 1–26.

Akazawa Eiji

1980 [Editor]. *Muromachi no suibokuga: Sesshū, Sesson, Motonobu* (Ink painting of the Muromachi period: Sesshū, Sesson, and Motonobu). Nihon bijutsu zenshū (Survey of Japanese art), 16. Tokyo: Gakushū Kenkyūsha.

1995 *Nihon chūsei kaiga no shinshiryō to sono kenkyū* (Research on recently discovered Japanese medieval paintings). Tokyo: Chūōkōron Bijutsu.

Akiyama Ken

1998 *Genji no ishō* (Genji design). Shōtō Museum. Tokyo: Shōgakkan.

Akiyama Ken, Akiyama Terukazu, and Tsuchida Naoshige [Akiyama Ken et al.]

1978 *Genji monogatari* (*The Tale of Genji*). Zusetsu Nihon no koten (Illustrated analyses of Japanese classics), 7. Tokyo: Shūeisha.

Akiyama Ken and Taguchi Eiichi

1988 *Gōka "Genji-e" no sekai: Genji monogatari* (Splendor in the world of "Genji" illustrations: *The Tale of Genji*). Tokyo: Gakushū Kenkyūsha.

Akiyama Terukazu

1952 "Heiji monogatari-e Rokuhara kassen no maki ni tsuite" (Fragments of a hitherto unknown scroll of *Heiji monogatari*). *Yamato bunka*, no. 7 (July): 1–11.

1964 *Heian jidai sezokuga no kenkyū* (Secular painting in early medieval Japan). Tokyo: Yoshikawa Kōbunkan.

1976 *Genji-e* (Genji pictures). Nihon no bijutsu (Arts of Japan), 119. Tokyo: Shibundō.

1978 "Genji monogatari emaki Wakamurasaki zu dankan no genkei kakunin" (A new attribution for a painting fragment of the twelfth-century *Tale of Genji* scrolls). *Kokka*, no. 1011: 9–26.

1980a [Editor]. *Emakimono* (Narrative scroll painting). Zaigai Nihon no shihō (Japanese art: Selections from Western collections), 2. Tokyo: Mainichi Shinbunsha.

1980b "Jin'ōji engi emaki no fukugen to kōsatsu: Iwayuru Kōnin Shōnin eden o megutte" (The reconstruction and study of the illustrated history of the Jin'ōji Temple: On the illustrated biography of the monk Kōnin). In Akiyama Terukazu 1980a, pp. 98–113.

Allen, Laura W.

2004 "Japanese Exemplars for a New Age: *Genji* Paintings from the Seventeenth-Century Tosa School." In *Critical Perspectives on Classicism in Japanese Painting, 1600–1700*, edited by Elizabeth Lillehoj, pp. 99–132. Honolulu: University of Hawai'i Press.

Amino Yoshihiko, Ōnishi Hiroshi, and Satake Akihiro [Amino Yoshihiko et al.]

1991 [Editors]. *Ten no hashi, chi no hashi* (The heavenly bridge, the earthly bridge). Ima wa mukashi, mukashi wa ima (Present is past, past is present), 2. Tokyo: Fukuinkan Shoten.

1993 [Editors]. *Chōjū giga* (Frolicking animals and birds). Ima wa mukashi, mukashi wa ima (Present is past, past is present), 3. Tokyo: Fukuinkan Shoten.

Andrews, Allan A.

1973 *The Teachings Essential for Rebirth: A Study of Genshin's Ōjōyōshū*. A Monumenta Nipponica Monograph. Tokyo: Sophia University.

Aoki Jun

1992 "Kū Amida Butsu Myōhen no kenkyū: Tokuni busshi Kaikei tono kankei o megutte" (A study of Kū Amida Butsu Myōhen and his relationship with the Buddhist sculptor Kaikei). *Indogaku Bukkyōgaku kenkyū*, no. 80 (March): 654–56.

Arakawa Hirokazu

1958 "Kinenmei Negoro nuri ni tsuite" (Dated specimens of Negoro lacquerware). [Tokyo] *Museum*, no. 92 (November): 25–30.

1969 *Maki-e* (Japanese lacquer). Nihon no bijutsu (Arts of Japan), 35. Tokyo: Shibundō.

1971 *Nanban shitsugei* (*Nanban* lacquerware). Tokyo: Bijutsu.

Arakawa Masaaki

1992 "Kan'ei Baroque bunka to Ko Kutani ishō" (Baroque culture of the Kan'ei era and designs on Ko Kutani ware). *Kobijutsu rokushō* 6: 50–63.

1996 "Ōzara no jidai: Kinsei shoki ni okeru ōzara juyō" (The era of the large platter: Demand for large platters in the early modern period). *Idemitsu Bijutsukan kenkyū kiyō* 2: 71–103.

Arakawa Toyozō

1959 *Shino*. Tōki zenshū (Survey of ceramics), 4. Tokyo: Heibonsha.

1972 *Shino, Ki Seto, Seto Guro*. Tōji taikei (Compendium of ceramics), 11. Tokyo: Heibonsha.

Ariga Yoshitaka
1983 *Heian kaiga* (Paintings of the Heian period). Nihon no bijutsu (Arts of Japan), 205. Tokyo: Shibundō.

"Art of Asia"
1966–67 "Art of Asia Recently Acquired by American Museums, 1965." *Archives of Asian Art* 20: 84–106.

Asahi Misako
1984 "Ryūkyō suisha zu byōbu no seiritsu" (The formation of pictures of willows and waterwheels). *Bigaku bijutsushi ronshū*, no. 3: 35–78.

Asahi Shinbunsha
1994–95 *Nihonbi no seika: Rinpa* (Rinpa: The essence of Japanese beauty). Tokyo: Asahi Shinbunsha.

Asano Shūgō
1994 "Kaigetsudō Ando Tachi bijin zu" ("Standing Beauty," painted by Kaigetsudō Ando). *Kokka*, no. 1183: 24–28.

Asia Society
1970 *Masterpieces of Asian Art in American Collections, 2: An Offering of Treasures Celebrating the Tenth Anniversary of Asia House Gallery*. Exh. cat. New York: Asia Society.

Avitabile, Gunhild
1990 [Editor]. *Die Kunst des alten Japan: Meisterwerke aus der Mary and Jackson Burke Collection, New York*. Exh. cat. Frankfurt: Schirn Kunsthalle Frankfurt.

Ayers, John, O. R. Impey, and J. V. G. Mallet [Ayers et al.]
1990 *Porcelain for Palaces: The Fashion for Japan in Europe, 1650–1750*. Exh. cat., British Museum. London: Oriental Ceramic Society.

Baekeland, Frederick, and Robert Moes
1993 *Modern Japanese Ceramics in American Collections*. Exh. cat. New York, Japan Society.

Bargen, Doris G.
1997 *A Woman's Weapon: Spirit Possession in "The Tale of Genji."* Honolulu: University of Hawai'i Press.

Barnet, Sylvan, and William Burto
1982 *Zen Ink Paintings*. Great Japanese Art. Tokyo: Kōdansha International.
2011 "The Kasuga Deer Mandala Hunt." *Orientations* 42, no. 1 (January/February): 64–72.

Bayou, Hélène
2004 *Images du monde flottant: Peintures et estampes japonaises, XVIIe–XVIIIe siècles*. Exh. cat., Galeries nationales du Grand Palais. Paris: Réunion des musées nationaux.

Becker, Johanna Lucille
1974 "The Karatsu Ceramics of Japan: Origins, Fabrications, and Types." PhD diss., University of Michigan.

"Bokudō zu"
1984 "Bokudō zu" ("Herdboy"). *Kokka*, no. 58 (July): 187.

"Bokushō hitsu Sansui zu"
1942 "Bokushō hitsu Sansui zu" ("Landscape," by Bokushō). *Kokka*, no. 618 (May).

Bowner, Robert H., and Earl Miner
1961 *Japanese Court Poetry*. Stanford Studies in the Civilization of Eastern Asia. Stanford, Calif.: Stanford University Press.

Brinker, Helmut, and Hiroshi Kanazawa
1996 *Zen: Masters of Meditation in Images and Writings*. Translated by Andreas Leisinger. Artibus Asiae, Supplementum, 40. Zurich: Artibus Asiae.

Brown, Kendall H.
1997 *The Politics of Reclusion: Painting and Power in Momoyama Japan*. Honolulu: University of Hawai'i Press.

Buckland, Rosina
2004 *Golden Fantasies: Japanese Screens from New York Collections*. Exh. cat. New York: Asia Society.

Burke, Mary Griggs
1985 "Twisted Pine Branches: Recollections of a Collector." *Apollo* 121, no. 276 (February): 77–83.
1993 *Japanese Art: Personal Selections from the Mary and Jackson Burke Collection*. Delray Beach, Fla.: The Morikami Museum and Japanese Gardens.
1996a "The Delights of Nature in Japanese Art." *Orientations* 27, no. 2 (February): 54–61.
1996b "Miyeko Murase: Friend, Scholar and Mentor." *Orientations* 27, no. 8 (September): 44–45.

Cahill, James
1972 *Scholar Painters of Japan: The Nanga School*. Exh. cat. New York: Asia Society.
1981 [Editor]. *Shadows of Mt. Huang: Chinese Painting and Printing of the Anhui School*. Exh. cat. Berkeley: University Art Museum, University of California.
1983 *Sakaki Hyakusen and Early Nanga Painting*. Japan Research Monograph, 3. Berkeley: Institute of East Asian Studies, University of California.
1996 *The Lyric Journey: Poetic Painting in China and Japan*. Cambridge, Mass.: Harvard University Press.

Carpenter, John T.
2012 *Designing Nature: The Rinpa Aesthetic in Japanese Art*. Exh. cat. New York: The Metropolitan Museum of Art.

Chapin, Helen B.
1933 "The Ch'an Master Pu-tai." *Journal of the American Oriental Society* 53: 47–52.

Chiba Municipal Museum
1996a *Shugyoku no Nihon bijutsu: Hosomi Collection no zenbō to Boston, Cleveland, Sackler no wadaisaku; Kaikan isshūnen kinen* (Masterpieces of Japanese art: An overview of the Hosomi Collection, with highlights from the Boston, Cleveland, and Sackler collections; first anniversary of the Chiba Museum). Exh. cat. Chiba: Chiba Municipal Museum.
1996b *Shukufuku sareta shiki: Kinsei Nihon kaiga no shosō* (Celebrated four seasons: Various aspects of Japanese paintings from the 16th to the 19th century). Exh. cat. Chiba: Chiba Municipal Museum.

Chibbett, David G.
1977 *The History of Japanese Printing and Book Illustration*. Tokyo: Kōdansha International.

"Chikusai monogatari"
1960 Edward Putzar, translator. "Chikusai monogatari." *Monumenta Nipponica* 16, nos. 1–2 (April–July): 161–95.

Chino Kaori
1980 "Meisho-e no seiritsu to tenkai" (The emergence and development of pictures of famous places). In *Keibutsuga: Meisho keibutsu* (Landscape: Famous sceneries), ed. Takeda Tsuneo. Nihon byōbu-e shūsei (Collection of Japanese screen paintings), 10. Tokyo: Kōdansha.

Chiu, Melissa, and Miwako Tezuka
2009 [Editors]. *Yang Fudong: Seven Intellectuals in Bamboo Forest*. Exh. cat. New York: Asia Society.

Chizawa Teiji
1981 *Sakai Hōitsu*. Nihon no bijutsu (Arts of Japan), 186. Tokyo: Shibundō.

Choi Sun-u
1973–75 *Hanguk misul chonjip* (Collection of Korean art). 15 vols. Seoul: Tonghwa Chulpansa.

Chōkoku
1972 *Chōkoku* (Sculpture). Jūyō bunkazai (Important cultural properties), 1–6. Tokyo: Mainichi Shinbunsha.

Chung et al.
1998 *Arts of Korea*. Edited by Judith G. Smith. Exh. cat. New York: The Metropolitan Museum of Art.

Clapp, Anne de Coursey
1975 *Wen Cheng-ming: The Ming Artist and Antiquity*. Ascona: Artibus Asiae, 1975.

Clark, Kenneth
1970 *Masterpieces of Fifty Centuries*. Exh. cat., The Metropolitan Museum of Art. New York: Dutton.

Conant, Ellen P., Steven D. Owyoung, and J. Thomas Rimer [Conant et al.]
1995 *Nihonga: Transcending the Past; Japanese Style Painting, 1868–1968*. Exh. cat. Saint Louis: Saint Louis Art Museum; [Tokyo]: Japan Foundation.

Cort, Louise Allison
1979 *Shigaraki, Potters' Valley*. Tokyo: Kodansha International.
1985 "Ceramics and the Tea Ceremony." *Apollo* 121, no. 276 (February): 120–23.

Cunningham, Louisa [L. Cunningham]
1984 *The Spirit of Place: Japanese Paintings and Prints of the Sixteenth through Nineteenth Centuries*. Exh. cat. New Haven: Yale University Art Gallery.

Cunningham, Michael R., Suzuki Norio, Miyajima Shin'ichi, and Saitō Takamasa [M. Cunningham et al.]
1991 *The Triumph of Japanese Style: Sixteenth-Century Art in Japan*. Exh. cat. Cleveland: Cleveland Museum of Art.

Dallas Museum of Fine Arts
1969 *Masterpieces of Japanese Art*. Exh. cat. Dallas: Dallas Museum of Fine Arts.

Doi Kumiko
1987 *Urushi kōgei no bi* (The beauty of lacquer arts and crafts). Osaka: Osaka City Museum.

Doi Tsugiyoshi
1970 *Kinsei Nihon kaiga no kenkyū* (Study of the painting of the early modern era in Japan). Tokyo: Bijutsu.
1978 *Kano Eitoku, Mitsunobu*. Nihon bijutsu kaiga zenshū (Survey of Japanese painting), 9. Tokyo: Shūeisha.

Donohashi Akiho
1977 "Tōdaiji Shaka Sanzon Jūroku Rakan ni tsuite" (On the Tōdaiji Shaka Triad with Sixteen Rakan). *Bukkyō geijutsu/Ars Buddhica*, no. 112 (April): 58–80.

Earle, Joe
1996 [Editor]. *Treasures of Imperial Japan: Masterpieces by Shibata Zeshin/Meiji no takara: Shibata Zeshin meihinshū*. The Nasser D. Khalili Collection of Japanese Art. London: Kibō Foundation.

Ebine Toshio
1994 *Suibokuga: Mokuan kara Minchō e* (Ink paintings: From Mokuan to Minchō). Nihon no bijutsu (Arts of Japan), 333. Tokyo: Shibundō.

Ebine Toshio and Kōno Motoaki
1993 *Buson, Taiga no jidai* (The era of Buson and Taiga). Nihon suiboku meihin zufu (Survey of masterpieces of Japanese ink painting), 5. Tokyo: Mainichi Shinbun.

Edwards, Richard
1976 [Editor]. *The Art of Wen Cheng-ming (1470–1559)*. Exh. cat., Museum of Art, University of Michigan, and Asia House Gallery, New York. Ann Arbor: University of Michigan.

Edwards, Walter
1997 "Japan's New Past." *Archaeology* 50, no. 2 (March/April): 32–42.

Egami Yasushi
1972 "Sanjūrokunin shū ryōshi sōshoku ni okeru taihō teki hibikiai" (Counterpoint intensity in the decorative patterns on the *ryōshi* of the Anthology of the Thirty-Six Poets). *Kokka*, no. 946 (June): 11–18.

1992 *Senmenga: Kodai hen* (Fan painting: Ancient periods). Nihon no bijutsu (Arts of Japan), 319. Tokyo: Shibundō.

Emura Tomoko
2011 *Tosa Mitsuyoshi to kinsei yamato-e no keifu* (Tosa Mitsuyoshi and the history of Yamato-e in the early modern era). Nihon no bijutsu (Arts of Japan), 543.

Encyclopedia of World Art
1960 *Encyclopedia of World Art*. Vol. 3. New York: McGraw-Hill.

Etō Shun
1969a "Sansui zu: Sesson hitsu" ("Landscape," by Sesson). *Kobijutsu*, no. 25 (March): 67–70.
1969b "Rogan zu: Renmon rōsen bokuga" (Geese and reeds: Ink paintings executed on paper embossed with lotus patterns). *Kobijutsu*, no. 28 (December): 83–84.
1979 *Sōami, Shōkei*. Nihon bijutsu kaiga zenshū (Survey of Japanese painting), 6. Tokyo: Shūeisha.
1982 [Editor]. *Sesson Shūkei zen gashū* (The complete works of Sesson Shūkei). Tokyo: Kōdansha.

Fischer, Felice
2000 With Edwin A. Cranston et al. *The Arts of Hon'ami Kōetsu: Japanese Renaissance Master*. Exh. cat. Philadelphia Museum of Art.
2007 With Kyoko Kinoshita. *Ike Taiga and Tokuyama Gyokuran: Japanese Masters of the Brush*. Exh. cat. Philadelphia: Philadelphia Museum of Art.

Fister, Pat
1988 With Fumiko Yamamoto. *Japanese Women Artists, 1600–1900*. Exh. cat. Lawrence: Spencer Museum of Art, University of Kansas.

Fong, Wen C.
1958 *The Lohans and a Bridge to Heaven*. Freer Gallery of Art Occasional Papers, vol. 3, no. 1. Washington, D.C.

Fontein, Jan
1967 *The Pilgrimage of Sudhana: A Study of Gandavyuha Illustrations in China, Japan and Java*. The Hague: Mouton.

Fontein, Jan, and Money L. Hickman
1970 *Zen Painting and Calligraphy*. Exh. cat. Boston: Museum of Fine Arts.

Ford, Barbara Brennan
1980 "A Study of the Painting of Sesson Shūkei." PhD diss., Columbia University.
1985 "Muromachi Ink Painting." *Apollo* 121, no. 276 (February): 114–19.
1997 "Tragic Heroines of the *Heike monogatari* and Their Representation in Japanese Screen Painting." *Orientations* 28, no. 2 (February): 40–47.

French, Calvin L.
1974 *The Poet-Painters: Buson and His Followers*. Exh. cat. Ann Arbor: University of Michigan Museum of Art.

Fujii Masaharu and Abe Zenryō
1977 *Manpukuji*. Koji junrei Kyoto (Pilgrimage to the old temples in Kyoto), 9. Kyoto: Tankōsha.

Fujioka Ryōichi
1968 *Cha dōgu* (Tea ceremony utensils). Nihon no bijutsu (Arts of Japan), 22. Tokyo: Shibundō.
1970 *Shino to Oribe* (Shino and Oribe). Nihon no bijutsu (Arts of Japan), 51. Tokyo: Shibundō.

Fujisawa Yoshisuke
1982 "Ko Seto chūki yōshiki no seiritsu katei" (The formation of the middle-period style of Ko Seto ware). *Tōyō tōji* 8: 29–56.

Fukui Rikichirō
1935 "Sesson shōki" (Brief notes on Sesson). *Bunka* 2 (November): 131–34.
1944 "Shinshutsu no Heiji monogatari emaki zanketsu" (Newly discovered fragments of the *Heiji monogatari emaki*). *Bunka* 11, nos. 8–9 (September).
1999 *Fukui Rikichirō bijutsushi ronshū 2* (Collected essays on art history by Fukui Rikichirō, 2). Tokyo: Chūōkōron Bijutsu.

Fukushima Prefectural Museum
1992 *Sadanobu to Bunchō: Matsudaira Sadanobu to shūhen no gajin tachi* (Sadanobu and Bunchō: Matsudaira Sadanobu and painters in his circle). Exh. cat. Aizu Wakamatsu: Fukushima Prefectural Museum.
1994 *Gyokudō to Shunkin, Shūkin: Uragami Gyokudō fushi no geijutsu* (Gyokudō, and Shunkin and Shūkin: The arts of Uragami Gyokudō and his sons). Exh. cat. Aizu Wakamatsu: Fukushima Prefectural Museum.

Fukushima Tsunenori
1993a *Muromachi jidai no Sesshū ryū* (The followers of Sesshū in the Muromachi period). Exh. cat. Yamaguchi: Yamaguchi Prefectural Museum of Art.
1993b "Unkei Eii: Tenbun nenkan ni okeru Suō no Sesshū-ha" (Unkei Eii: The Sesshū school in Suō during the Tenbun era). *Bijutsushi* 42, no. 1 (February): 72–92.

Furuta Ryō and Nakamura Reiko
2004 *Rinpa*. Exh. cat., National Museum of Modern Art. Tokyo: Tōkyō Shinbun, 2004.

Furuta Shōkin
1988 "Geirin okudan 9—Ryūkyō zu: Sono Ujibashi zu o megutte sono igi o tou" (An artistic assumption, 9: On Uji bridge, the river, and its banks). *Idemitsu Bijutsukan kanpō* 61: 18–23.

Galerie Janette Ostier
1980 *Les jardins d'or du Prince Genji: Peintures japonaises du XVIIe siècle*. Paris: Galerie Janette Ostier.

Gitter, Kurt A., and Pat Fister
1985 *Japanese Fan Paintings from Western Collections*. Exh. cat. New Orleans: New Orleans Museum of Art.

Goepper, Roger
1993 *Aizen-Myōō: The Esoteric King of Lust; An Iconological Study*. Artibus Asiae, Supplementum, 39. Zurich: Artibus Asiae and Museum Rietberg Zurich.

Gōke Tadaomi
1974 *Shibata Zeshin*. Nihon no bijutsu (Arts of Japan), 93. Tokyo: Shibundō.
1981 *Shibata Zeshin meihinshū: Bakumatsu kaikaki no shikkō kaiga* (Masterpieces by Shibata Zeshin: Painting and lacquer-ware from the late Edo and early Meiji periods). 2 vols. Tokyo: Gakushū Kenkyūsha.

The Gotoh Museum
1964 *Daitōkyū Kinenbunko sōritsu jūgo shūnen tokubetsu ten* (Special exhibition commemorating the fifteenth anniversary of the Daitōkyū Memorial Library). Exh. cat. Tokyo: The Gotoh Museum.
1987 *Teika-yō* (Teika: The stylistic legacy of a master calligrapher). Gotō Bijutsukan tenrankai zuroku (The Gotoh Museum exhibition catalogue), 107. Tokyo: The Gotoh Museum.
1996 *Mokkei: Shōkei no suibokuga* (Ink mists: Zen paintings by Muqi). Exh. cat. Gotō Bijutsukan tenrankai zuroku (The Gotoh Museum exhibition catalogue), 118. Tokyo: The Gotoh Museum.

Gotō Shigeo
1997 [Editor]. *Nihon no bi: Momoyama ten, 1997* (The beauty of Japan: Exhibition of Momoyama-period arts, 1997). Exh. cat. Tokyo: NHK Puromōshon.

Graham, Patricia Jane
1983 "Yamamoto Baiitsu: His Life, Literati Pursuits, and Related Paintings." 2 vols. PhD diss., University of Kansas.
1986 "Yamamoto Baiitsu no Chūgokuga kenkyū" (Yamamoto Baiitsu's approach to the study of Chinese painting). *Kobijutsu*, no. 80 (October): 62–75.
1998 *Tea of the Sages: The Art of Sencha*. Honolulu: University of Hawai'i Press.
2007 *Faith and Power in Japanese Buddhist Art, 1600–2005*. Honolulu: University of Hawai'i Press.

Guoan
1969 *The Ox and His Herdsman: A Chinese Zen Text*. Translated by M. H. Trevor. Tokyo: Hokuseidō.

Guth, Christine
1992 *Asobi: Play in the Arts of Japan*. Exh. cat., Katonah Museum of Art, San Antonio Museum of Art, and Los Angeles County Museum of Art. Katonah, N.Y.: Katonah Museum of Art.
1996 *Art of Edo Japan: The Artist and the City, 1615–1868*. Perspectives. New York: Harry N. Abrams.
2004 *Longfellow's Tattoos: Tourism, Collecting, and Japan*. Seattle: University of Washington Press.

Gyōtoku Shin'ichirō
1993 "Yōgō to shizen to: Yōmei Bunko zō Kasuga shika mandara zu" (Sacred manifestation and nature: The *Kasuga shika mandara* in the Yōmei Bunko). *Kokka*, no. 1173: 3–17.
1994 "Suijakuga no kenkyū: Miya mandara o chūshin ni" (A study of Shinto syncretic paintings: Primarily shrine mandalas). *Kajima Bijutsu Zaidan nenpō* 11: 240–57.
1996 "Kasuga Miya mandara zu no fūkei hyōgen: Busshō to shinsei no katachi" (Landscape in the Kasuga Shrine Mandala, symbol of Buddha-dhatu and

Shinto). [Tokyo] *Museum*, no. 541 (April): 13–42.

Haga Kōshirō
1979 [Editor]. *Takuan*. Bunjin shofū (Types of literati), 5. Kyoto: Tankōsha.
1981 *Chūsei zenrin no gakumon oyobi bungaku ni kansuru kenkyū* (Studies of scholarly and literary works by medieval Zen monks). 1956. Haga Kōshirō rekishi ronshū (Historical studies by Haga Kōshirō), 3. Kyoto: Shibunkaku.

Haga Kōshirō and Nishiyama Matsunosuke
1962 [Editors]. *Cha no bunka shi* (Cultural history of tea). Zusetsu sadō taikei (Illustrated compendium of the tea ceremony), 2. Tokyo: Kadokawa Shoten.

Haga Tōru and Hayakawa Monta
1994 *Buson*. Suibokuga no kyoshō (Great masters of ink painting), 12. Tokyo: Kōdansha.

Haino Akio
1980 "Shitsugeihin ni miru bungaku ishō" (Lacquer designs derived from literature). In *Kōgei ni miru koten bungaku ishō* (The world of Japanese classical literature in craft design). Exh. cat. Kyoto National Museum.
1985 *Shikkō* (Lacquerware: Early modern period). Nihon no bijutsu (Arts of Japan), 231. Tokyo: Shibundō.

Hamada Giichirō
1963 *Ōta Nanpo*. Jinbutsu sōsho (Biographical series), 102. Edited by Nihon Rekishi Gakkai. Tokyo: Yoshikawa Kōbunkan.

Hamada Takashi
1980 *Mandara* (Mandalas). Nihon no bijutsu (Arts of Japan), 173. Tokyo: Shibundō.

Hamada Takashi et al.
1989 *Hiten* (Apsaras). Asuka Shiryōkan Catalogue, 22. Nara: Asuka Shiryōkan.

Hanshin Department Store
1971 *Sekai no gasei Sesshū ten* (Sesshū, the world's great master). Exh. cat. Osaka: Hanshin Department Store.

Harada Kinjirō
1938 *Nihon genzai Shina meiga mokuroku* (Catalogue of Chinese masterpiece paintings in Japan). Tokyo: Ōtsuka Kōgeisha.

Harunari Hideji
1990 *Yayoi jidai no hajimari* (The beginning of the Yayoi period). Kōkogaku sensho (Selected studies in archaeology), 11. Tokyo: Tōkyō Daigaku.

Hasegawa Nobuyoshi
1979 "Sanjūrokkasen no seiritsu" (Emergence of the Thirty-Six Immortal Poets). In Mori Tōru 1979.

Hashimoto Ayako
1969 "Maruyama Ōkyo no sakufū ni tsuite: Ōkyo kenkyū josetsu" (On the style of Maruyama Ōkyo: An introduction to the study of Ōkyo). *Bigaku*, no. 78 (Fall): 10–39.

Hashimoto Fumio
1970 [Editor]. *Kunaichō Shoryōbu zō Goshobon Sanjūrokuninshū* (Deluxe version of the *Sanjūrokuninshū* in the collection of the Imperial Library). Tokyo: Rinsen Shoten.

Hashimoto Shinji
1997 "Muromachi jidai no itsuden gajin, 1: 'Rikō' in no sakuhin ni tsuite" (Lesser-known painters of the Muromachi period, 1: On the paintings bearing "Rikō" seals). *Tochigi Kenritsu Hakubutsukan kiyō* 14 (March): 108–16.

Hasumi Shigeyasu
1935 "Nara Hōgen Kantei." *Nihon bijutsu kyōkai hōkoku*, n.s., no. 38 (October): 1–7.

Hayakawa Monta and Yamamoto Kenkichi
1984 *Buson gafu* (Paintings by Yosa Buson). Tokyo: Mainichi Shinbunsha.

Hayashi Masahiko
2007 [Editor]. *Kumano: Sono shinkō to bungaku, bijutsu, shizen* (Kumano: Beliefs and literature, art and nature). Tokyo: Shibundō.

Hayashi Susumu
1980 "Sesson hitsu Chikurin Shichiken zu byōbu (Hatakeyama Kinenkan zō) ni tsuite" (Screen Painting of "The Seven Sages of the Bamboo Grove," by Sesson, in the collection of the Hatakeyama Memorial Museum). In *Jinbutsuga: Kanga kei jinbutsu* (Figure paintings: Figures in Chinese-inspired paintings). Nihon byōbu-e shūsei (Survey of Japanese screen paintings), 4. Reprint, 1982.
1984 "Sesson Shūkei no kenkyū" (Study of Sesson Shūkei). *Kajima bijutsu zaidan nenpō* 2: 68–73.

Hayashiya Seizō
1967 *Chawan* (Tea bowls). Nihon no bijutsu (Arts of Japan), 14. Tokyo: Shibundō.
1972a [Editor]. *Bizen, Tanba, Iga, Shigaraki*. Nihon no tōji (Japanese ceramics), 2. Tokyo: Chūōkōronsha.
1972b "Iga mimitsuki mizusashi" (Iga-ware water jar with handles). *Kobijutsu*, no. 37 (June): 101–2.
1974 [Editor]. *Shino*. Nihon no tōji (Japanese ceramics), 2. Deluxe color ed. Tokyo: Chūōkōronsha.
1975 [Editor]. *Kyōyaki*. Nihon no tōji (Japanese ceramics), 13. Tokyo: Chūōkōronsha.
1977 [Editor]. *Iga*. Nihon tōji zenshū (Survey of Japanese ceramics), 13. Tokyo: Chūōkōronsha.
1981 [Editor]. *Tōji* (Ceramics). Zaigai Nihon no shihō (Japanese art: Selections from Western collections), 9. Tokyo: Mainichi Shinbunsha.
1985 "Kyōyaki no nagare" (Currents of *kyōyaki*). In *Kyōyaki no sekai: Ninsei kara Hōzen made* (The world of *kyōyaki*: From Ninsei to Hōzen). Exh. cat. Matsue, Shimane Prefecture: Tabe Museum.

Hayashiya Seizō and Enjōji Jirō
1990 [Editors]. *Nihon no meitō hyakusen ten* (One hundred masterpieces of Japanese ceramics). Exh. cat., Takashimaya Department Store. Tokyo: Nihon Keizai Shinbunsha.

Hayashiya Tatsusaburō et al.
1964 *Kōetsu*. Tokyo: Daiichi Hōki Shuppansha.

Hayashiya Tatsusaburō, Yamane Yūzō, and Takeda Tsuneo [Hayashiya Tatsusaburō et al.]
1984 *Kuge buke. Kinsei fūzoku zufu* (Courtiers and warriors: Fashion trends in the early modern era). 11. Tokyo: Shōgakukan.

Hayashi Yoshikazu
1963 *Shunshō*. Enpon kenkyū (Studies of erotic books), 4. Tokyo: Yūkō Shobō.

"Heian *jinbutsushi*"
1936 "An'ei yonen-ban Heian jinbutsushi" (Heian *jinbutsushi*: An address book of artists and scholars in Kyoto, published in the fourth year of An'ei, 1775). *Bijutsu kenkyū*, no. 54 (June): 257–64.
1943 "Tenmei ninen-ban Heian jinbutsushi" (Heian *jinbutsushi*: An address book of artists and scholars in Kyoto, published in the second year of the Tenmei era, 1782). *Bijutsu kenkyū*, no. 132: 227–34.

Hickman, Money L., and Satō Yasuhiro
1989 *The Paintings of Jakuchū*. Exh. cat. New York: Asia Society Galleries.

Hillier, Jack Ronald
1974 *The Uninhibited Brush: Japanese Art in the Shijō Style*. London: Hugh M. Moss.

Hirata Hisashi
1912 [Editor.] *Taishikai zuroku* (Catalogue of the Taishikai tea ceremony). Tokyo: Hirata Hisashi.

Hirata Yutaka
1985 "Takuma ha ni okeru dentō sei" (The traditionalism of the Takuma School). *Kokka*, no. 1085 (July): 11–26.

Hiroshima Prefectural Museum of Art, Kyoto Cultural Museum, and Tōhoku Historical Museum [Hiroshima Prefectural Museum of Art et al.]
2005 *Nihon Sankei ten: Matsushima, Amano hashidate, Itsukushima* (The three great views of Japan—Matsushima, Amanohashidate, Itsukushima). Exh. cat., Hiroshima Prefectural Museum of Art, Kyoto Cultural Museum, and Tōhoku Historical Museum. Hiroshima: Hiroshima Prefectural Museum of Art.

Hitomi Shōka
1940 "Ike Taiga hyōden" (The life of Ike Taiga). *Nanga kanshō* 9 (September): 2–5.

Hōgen monogatari
1971 William R. Wilson, translator. *Hōgen monogatari: Tale of the Disorder in Hōgen*. Monumenta Nipponica Monographs. Tokyo: Sophia University.

Hon'ami gyōjōki to Kōetsu
1965 Masaki Tokuzō, editor. *Hon'ami gyōjōki to Kōetsu* (Annals of the Hon'ami family and Kōetsu). Tokyo: Chūōkōron Bijutsu.

Honma Art Museum
1961 *Dai nikai Nihon nanga ten* (Second exhibition of Japanese Nanga). Exh. cat. Sakata, Yamagata Prefecture: Honma Art Museum.
1968 *Sesson no geijutsu* (The art of Sesson). Exh. cat. Sakata, Yamagata Prefecture: Honma Art Museum.
1969 *Sakai Hōitsu meisaku ten* (Exhibition of Sakai Hōitsu's masterpieces). Exh. cat. Sakata, Yamagata Prefecture: Honma Art Museum.

Horibe Seiji
1943 *Chūko Nihon bungaku no kenkyū: Shiryō to jisshō* (Study of medieval Japanese literature: Supporting documents). Kyoto: Kyōiku Tosho.

Horikawa Takashi
1989 "Shōshō hakkei shi ni tsuite" (On the poems of the Eight Views of the Xiao and Xiang Rivers). *Chūsei bungaku*, no. 34: 101–10.

Hōryūji Shōwa Shizaichō Henshū Iinkai
1991 [Editor]. *Hyakumantō, Daranikyō*. Hōryūji no shihō: Shōwa shizaichō (Treasures of Hōryūji: Shōwa-era record of the temple's holdings), 5. Tokyo: Shōgakukan.

Hoshino Rei
1977 "Ike Gyokuran hitsu Bokubai zu, Sansui zu" ("Landscape" and "Plum Tree," by Ikeno Gyokuran). *Kokka*, no. 998: 36–38.

Hoshiyama Shin'ya
1976 "Gyokuen Bonpō ni tsuite" (On Gyokuen Bonpō). *Geijutsugaku kenkyū* 2: 33–57.

Hosomi Ryō
1961 "Negoro ni tsuite I" (On Negoro ware, 1). *Nihon bijutsu kōgei* 284 (May): 1.

Hosono Masanobu
1979 *Kindai kaiga no reimei: Bunchō, Kazan to yōfūga* (The dawn of modern painting: Bunchō, Kazan, and Western-style painting). Nihon bijutsu zenshū (Survey of Japanese art), 25. Tokyo: Gakushū Kenkyūsha.
1988 *Edo no Kano ha* (The Kano School during the Edo period). Nihon no bijutsu (Arts of Japan), 262. Tokyo: Shibundō.

"Hyakusen"
1939 "Sakaki Hyakusen tokushū gō" (Special issue on Hyakusen). *Nanga kanshō* 8, no. 4 (April).

Ibaraki Prefectural Museum of History
1992 *Sesson: Hitachi kara no tabidachi* (Sesson: A journey begun in Hitachi Province). Exh. cat. [Ibaraki Prefecture]: Ibaraki Prefectural Museum of History.

Idemitsu Museum of Arts
1991 *Selected Masterpieces from the Idemitsu Collection*. Tokyo: Idemitsu Museum of Arts.
1991–96 *Kanzō meihinsen daini shū* (Masterpieces from the collection, second volume). 3 vols. Tokyo: Idemitsu Museum of Arts.

Iizuka Beiu
1932a [Editor]. *Kano ha* (Kano School). 3 vols. Nihonga taisei (Survey of Japanese painting), 5–7. Tokyo: Tōhō Shoin.
1932b [Editor]. *Nanshū ha* (Southern School). 4 vols. Nihonga taisei (Survey of Japanese painting), 9–11. Tokyo: Tōhō Shoin.
1932c [Editor]. *Shoka* (Miscellaneous painters). Nihonga taisei, 15. Tokyo: Tōhō Shoin.

Ikawa Kazuko
1963 "Chiten ni sasaerareta Bishamonten chōzō: Tobatsu Bishamonten zō ni tsuite no ichi kōsatsu" (Statues of Bishamonten supported by Chiten: Research on the Tobatsu Bishamonten). *Bijutsu kenkyū*, no. 229 (July): 53–73.

Ikeda Toshiko
1996 "Shōshō hakkei zu no chōsa hōkoku" (Study of paintings of the Eight Views of the Xiao and Xiang Rivers). *Kajima bijutsu zaidan nenpō* 13: 521–35.

Inamoto Mariko
2008 "Genji monogatari emaki. Sakaki no maki no shōkei sentaku ni kansuru ichikōsatsu" (*Tale of Genji* handscrolls: Thoughts on the selection of settings for illustrations of the "Sakaki" chapter). *Kinko sōsho: Shigaku bijutsushi ronbunshū* no. 34 (March).
2011 "Maboroshi no Genji monogatari emaki Baaku-bon ni tsuite" (The lost picture scrolls of *The Tale of Genjii* owned by the Mary and Jackson Burke Foundation). *Rikkyō Daigaku Nihongaku kenkyūjo nenpō*, no. 8 (March): 15–21.

Inazuka Takeshi
1919 "Goshun ni tsuite" (On Goshun). *Kokka*, no. 348 (May): 417–21 (pt. 1); no. 349 (June): 451–56 (pt. 2).
1920 "Goshun tetsubun" (On the life of Goshun). *Kokka*, no. 358 (March): 392–96 (pt. 1).

Inokuma Kanekatsu
1979 *Haniwa*. Nihon no genshi bijutsu (Prehistoric arts of Japan), 6. Tokyo: Kōdansha.

Inoue Ken'ichirō
1977 "Chūsei no shiki keibutsu: Waka shiryō ni yoru shiron" (Depiction of the four seasons in the medieval period: *Waka* as historical documents). In Takeda Tsuneo 1977b.

Inoue Tadashi
1958 "Jōgon'in Amida Nyorai zō ni tsuite" (On a Buddhist image of Amitabha in the Jōgon'in Temple). *Kokka*, no. 791 (February): 39–51.
1963 "Jōruriji kutai Amida Nyorai zō no zōryū nendai ni tsuite" (On the date of the production of the nine images of Amitabha in the Jōruriji Temple). *Kokka*, no. 861 (December): 7–20.

Inryōken nichiroku
1978–79 *Inryōken nichiroku* (Chronicles at Inryōken). Edited by Takeuchi Rizō. 5 vols. 1953. Reprint, Zōho zoku shiryō taisei (Second compendium of historical material: Enlarged supplement), 21–25. Kyoto: Rinsen Shoten.
1989 *Inryōken nichiroku sakuin* (Index to the chronicles at Inryōken). Edited by Kageki Hideo. Kyoto: Rinsen Shoten.

Institute of Japanese Culture
2013 *Sōtatsu Ise monogatari zu shikishi* (Scenes from the Tale of Ise on *shikishi*, by Sōtatsu). Institute of Japanese Culture, Hagoromo University of International Studies. Kyoto: Shibunkaku.

Ishida Mosaku
1976 *Shōtoku Taishi sonzō shūsei* (Collection of noble images of Shōtoku Taishi). 2 vols. Tokyo: Kōdansha.

Ishida Mosaku and Okazaki Jōji
1993 *Mikkyō hōgu* (Furnishings for esoteric Buddhist rituals). Exh. cat. Kyoto: Rinsen Shoten.

Ishida Mosaku et al.
1955 *Tōshōdaiji*. Tokyo: Kadokawa Shoten.

Ishikawa-ken Kyōiku Iinkai
1971–72 *Daiichiji, Niji Kutani koyō chōsa gaihō* (Reports on the first and second excavations of the old kilns at Kutani). Ishikawa: Ishikawa-ken Kyōiku Iinkai.

Ishikawa Prefectural Art Museum and MOA Museum of Art
1992 *Nonomura Ninsei ten: Edo jidai—Kyōyaki iroe no taiseisha* (Exhibition of Nonomura Ninsei, who perfected polychrome glazing techniques during the Edo period). Exh. cat. Kanazawa: Ishikawa Prefectural Art Museum; Atami: MOA Museum of Art.

Ishikawa Tomohiko
2007 "Kumano shinkō to bijutsu" (Kumano cult and art). In Hayashi Masahiko 2007.

Ishikawa Wajima Urushi Art Museum
1998 *Negoro: Sono katachi to iro* (Negoro: Form and color). Exh. cat. [Wajima]: Ishikawa Wajima Urushi Art Museum.

Itō Shirō
1989 *Komainu* (Lion dogs). Nihon no bijutsu (Arts of Japan), 279. Tokyo: Shibundō.

Itō Toshiko
1970 "Den Kōetsu hitsu Utaibon to Kanze Kokusetsu (A book of *utai* ascribed to Kōetsu and Kokusetsu Kanze). *Kokka*, no. 922: 5–22.
1974 "Den Sōtatsu hitsu Ise monogatari zu shikishi no kotobagaki ni tsuite" (Study of the texts of the *Ise monogatari shikishi* attributed to Sōtatsu). *Yamato bunka*, no. 59 (March): 28–55.
1978 "Kōetsu no sho" (The calligraphy of Kōetsu). In *Kōetsu sho Sōtatsu kingindei-e* (Kōetsu's calligraphy on gold and silver paintings by Sōtatsu). Vol. 1, 95–103. Tokyo: Asahi Shinbunsha, 1978.
1984 [Editor]. *Ise monogatari-e* (Illustrated tales of Ise). Book 5. Tokyo: Kadokawa Shoten.

Itō Yoshiaki
2000 *Momoyama tōgei no hana ten: Kiseto, Setoguro, Shino, Oribe* (Exhibition of the masterpieces of Momoyama ceramics: Kiseto, Setoguro, Shino, Oribe). Nagoya: NHK Nagoya Hōsōkyoku.

Iwama Kaoru
1986 "Kinsei shoki Tosa ha no kenkyū: Kyoto Shiritsu Geijutsu Daigaku shozō Tosa ha shiryō o chūshin ni" (Study of the Tosa School in the early modern period: Materials of the Tosa School primarily in the collection of the Kyoto Municipal University of the Arts). *Kajima bijutsu zaidan nenpō* 4: 164–69.

Izzard, Sebastian
1983 *Hiroshige: An Exhibition of Selected Prints and Illustrated Books*. Exh. cat., Pratt Graphics Center. New York: Ukiyo-e Society of America.

Japan Society Gallery
1989 *The Collector's Eye: Japanese Art Lent by Friends of the Japan Society Gallery*. Exh. cat. New York: Japan Society.

Jenkins, Donald
1971 *Ukiyo-e Prints and Paintings: The Primitive Period, 1680–1745*. Exh. cat. Chicago: Art Institute of Chicago.
1993 [Editor]. *The Floating World Revisited*. Exh. cat. Portland, Ore.: Portland Art Museum.

Jishi sōsho
1915 *Jishi sōsho 3* (Historical records of temples, 3). In Dai Nihon Bukkyō zenshū (The collected works of Japanese Buddhism), 119. Tokyo: Bussho Kankōkai.

Jörg, C. J. A.
1980 *Pronk porselein: Porselein naar ontwerpen van Cornelis Pronk / Pronk Porcelain: Porcelain after Designs by Cornelis Pronk*. Exh. cat. Groningen: Groninger Museum.

Kachōga no sekai
1981–83 *Kachōga no sekai* (The world of bird-and-flower painting). 11 vols. Tokyo: Gakushū Kenkyūsha.

Kageyama Haruki
1973 *The Arts of Shinto*. Translated by Christine Guth. Arts of Japan, 4. New York: Weatherhill; Tokyo: Shibundō.
1975 "Kasuga shika mandara: Kodai shinkō no hyōkei to shite" (The Shika Kasuga mandala). *Kokka*, no. 981: 7–14.

Kageyama Haruki and Christine Guth Kanda
1976 *Shinto Arts: Nature, Gods, and Man in Japan*. Exh. cat. New York: Japan Society.

Kageyama Sumio
1984 "Unkoku Tōgan den" (The life of Unkoku Tōgan). In Yamaguchi Prefectural Museum of Art 1984, pp. 162–67.

Kaigai shozai Nihon bijutsuhin
1992 *Kaigai shozai Nihon bijutsuhin chōsa hōkoku / Catalogue of Japanese Art in Foreign Collections*. Vol. 2, *Painting and Sculpture of the Mary and Jackson Burke Collection and the Mary and Jackson Burke Foundation, New York*. Tokyo: Kobunkazai Kagaku Kenkyūkai.

Kajitani Ryōji
1987 "Jūroku Rakan zō ni tsuite" (Paintings of the Sixteen Rakan). *Bukkyō geijutsu / Ars Buddhica*, no. 172 (May): 117–33.

"Kakei hitsu Hōgyū zu"
1904 "Kakei hitsu Hōgyū zu" ("A Winter Scene," by Hsia Kuei). *Kokka*, no. 165 (February): 182.

Kameda Tsutomu
1969 *E-Ingakyō* (Illustrated sutra of cause and effect). Nihon emakimono zenshū (Survey of Japanese handscroll paintings), 16. Tokyo: Kadokawa Shoten.
1980 *Sesson*. Nihon bijutsu kaiga zenshū (Survey of Japanese painting), 8. Tokyo: Shūeisha.

Kamei Masamichi
1995 *Jinbutsu, dōbutsu haniwa* (Human and animal *haniwa*). Nihon no bijutsu (Arts of Japan), 346. Tokyo: Shibundō.

Kamens, Edward
1988 *The Three Jewels: A Study and Translation of Minamoto Tamenori's Sanbōe.* Michigan Monograph Series in Japanese Studies, 2. Ann Arbor: Center for Japanese Studies, University of Michigan, 1988.

Kanagawa Prefectural Museum of Cultural History
1972 *Kamakura no suibokuga: Gasō Shōkei no shūhen; Tokubetsuten* (Special exhibition: Ink painting of the Kamakura period: The monk-painter Shōkei and his milieu). Exh. cat. Yokohama: Kanagawa Prefectural Museum of Cultural History.
1989 *Go-Hōjō shi to tōgoku bunka* (The Go-Hōjō family and Eastern regional culture). Exh. cat. Yokohama: Kanagawa Prefectural Museum of Cultural History.

Kanazawa Hiroshi
1977 *Kaō, Minchō.* Nihon bijutsu kaiga zenshū (Survey of Japanese paintings), 1. Tokyo: Shūeisha.
1983 *Muromachi kaiga* (Paintings of the Muromachi period). Nihon no bijutsu (Arts of Japan), 207. Tokyo: Shibundō.
1994 *Suibokuga: Josetsu, Shūbun, Sōtan* (Ink painting: Josetsu, Shūbun, and Sōtan). *Nihon no bijutsu* (Arts of Japan), 334. Tokyo: Shibundō.

Kanazawa Hiroshi and Kawai Masatomo
1982 *Suiboku no hana to tori: Muromachi no kachō* (Ink paintings of birds and flowers: Birds and flowers of the Muromachi period). Kachōga no sekai (The world of bird-and-flower painting), 2. Tokyo: Gakushū Kenkyūsha.

Kanda, Christine Guth
1985 *Shinzō: Hachiman Imagery and Its Development.* Harvard East Asian Monographs, 119. Cambridge, Mass.: Council on East Asian Studies, Harvard University.

Kaneko Hiroaki
1992 *Monju Bosatsu zō* (Images of Monju Bosatsu). Nihon no bijutsu (Arts of Japan), 314. Tokyo: Shibundō.

Kaneko Hiroaki, Ōta Hirotarō, Yamane Yūzō, and Yonezawa Yoshiho [Kaneko Hiroaki et al.]
1991 *Unkei, Kaikei.* Shōgakukan Gallery: Shinpen meihō Nihon no bijutsu (Shōgakukan Gallery: Masterpieces of Japanese art; New edition), 13. Tokyo: Shōgakukan.

Kaneko Nobuhisa
2010 *Tabisuru Edo Kaiga: Rinpa kara dōbanga made* (Edo paintings of journeys: From Rinpa to engravings). Tokyo: Pie Bukkusu.

Kano Hiroyuki
1984 "Kinsei itanha gajin no shisōteki kenkyū" (Philosophical aspects of the eccentrics of the Edo period). *Kajima bijutsu zaidan nenpō* 2: 116–20.
1987 *Soga Shōhaku.* Nihon no bijutsu (Arts of Japan), 258. Tokyo: Shibundō.
1993 *Jakuchū.* Kyoto: Shikōsha.

Kano Hiroyuki, Okudaira Shunroku, and Yasumura Toshinobu [Kano Hiroyuki et al.]
1993 *Kōrin to kamigata rinpa* (Kōrin and Rinpa of the Kansai region). Rinpa bijutsukan (Rinpa Museum), 2. Tokyo: Shūeisha.

"Kantei hitsu Sansui zu"
1898 "Kantei hitsu Sansui zu" ("Landscape," by Kantei). *Kokka*, no. 105 (June): 167–69.

Kanzaki Kazuko
1991 "Seto chaire no kisoteki kenkyū: Setogama shutsudo no chaire" (Tea caddies from Seto: Tea caddies excavated from Seto kiln sites). *Aichi-ken Tōji Shiryōkan kenkyū kiyō* 10: 36–44.

Kasanoin, Jikun, and Amy Vladeck Heinrich
1998 *Seasons of Sacred Celebration: Flowers and Poetry from an Imperial Convent.* New York: Institute for Medieval Japanese Studies and Weatherhill, 1998.

Katagiri Yayoi
1996 "Baaku Korekushon no Hakubyō Genji monogatari emaki nishu / Two *Hakubyō Genji Monogatari Emaki* in the Burke Collection." *Nihon Bunka Kenkyū*, no. 8 (March): 69–86.

Katō Hajime
1961 *Oribe.* Tōki zenshū (Survey of ceramics), 5. Tokyo: Heibonsha.

Katsura Matasaburō
1968 *Igayaki tsūshi* (History of Iga ware). Tokyo: Kawade Shobō.

Kaufman, Laura
1985 "Practice and Piety: Buddhist Art in Use." *Apollo* 121, no. 276 (February): 91–99.

Kawada Sadamu
1985 *Negoro.* Kyoto: Shikōsha.

Kawahara Masahiko
1977 *Karatsu.* Nihon no bijutsu (Arts of Japan), 136. Tokyo: Shibundō.

Kawai Masatomo
1966 "Yūshō hitsu Shōshō Hakkei zu" (Hsiao-Hsiang scenery by Kaihō Yūshō). *Bijutsushi* 16, no. 3 (December): 96–104.
1978 *Yūshō, Tōgan.* Nihon bijutsu kaiga zenshū (Survey of Japanese painting), 11. Tokyo: Shūeisha.
1986 [Editor]. *Suibokuga meisaku ten: Drucker Collection* (Sansō Collection: Japanese paintings collected by Prof. and Mrs. P. F. Drucker). Exh. cat., Osaka Municipal Museum of Art. Tokyo: Nihon Keizai Shinbunsha.
1988 "Oguri Sōtan kara Kano Masanobu e" (From Oguri Sōtan to Kano Masanobu). In *International Symposium of the Conservation and Restoration of Cultural Property: Periods of Transition in East Asian Art*, pp. 167–80. Tokyo: Tokyo National Research Institute of Cultural Properties.
1992 *Muromachi jidai suibokuga no keifu: Kaō, Sesshū, Motonobu* (Ink monochrome painting of the Muromachi period: Kaō, Sesshū, Motonobu). Exh. cat. Tokyo: Nezu Institute of Fine Arts.

Kawamoto Keiko
1991 *Yūshō, Sanraku.* Shōgakukan Gallery: Shinpen meihō Nihon no bijutsu (Shōgakukan Gallery: Masterpieces of Japanese art; New edition), 21. Tokyo: Shōgakukan.

Kawamura Tomoyuki
1981 "Kasuga mandara no seiritsu to girei" (Emergence of the Kasuga Mandala and

its ritual background). *Bijutsushi* 30, no. 2 (March): 86–100.

"Keison hitsu Rokuso"
1927 "Keison hitsu Rokuso oyobi Kachō zu kai" ("Priest Yenō as a Faggot-Seller and the Birds," by Keison). *Kokka*, no. 436 (March): 73–74.

Kihara Toshie
1995 "Kano Tan'yū no suibokuga ni okeru futatsu no vision" (Two visions in the ink paintings of Kano Tan'yū). *Bijutsushi* 44, no. 1 (March): 95–115.
1998 *Yūbi no tankyū: Kano Tan'yū ron* (The search for profound delicacy: The art of Kano Tan'yū). 2 vols. Osaka: Osaka Daigaku Shuppankai.

Kikuyama Toneo
1936 "Iga no koyō angya" (Pilgrimage to the old kilns in Iga). *Chawan* 69 (November): 10–15.

Kim, Hongnam
1990 "A Korean Buddhist Triad in the Burke Collection." *Orientations* 21, no. 12 (December): 46–58.
1991 *The Story of a Painting: A Korean Buddhist Treasure from the Mary and Jackson Burke Foundation*. Exh. cat. New York: Asia Society Galleries.

Kimbrough, R. Keller
2001 "Voices from the Feminine Margin: Izumi Shikibu and the Nuns of Kumano and Seiganji." *Women and Performance: A Journal of Feminist Theory* 12, no. 23: 59–78.
2008 *Preachers, Poets, Women, and the Way: Izumi Shikibu and the Buddhist Literature of Medieval Japan*. Michigan Monograph Series in Japanese Studies, 62. Ann Arbor: Center for Japanese Studies, University of Michigan.

Kinoshita Masao
1979 Editor. *Zenshū no bijutsu: Bokuseki to zenshū kaiga* (Arts of Zen Buddhism: Calligraphy and paintings of Zen). Nihon bijutsu zenshū (Survey of Japanese art), 14. Tokyo: Gakushū Kenkyūsha.
1980 *Sanjūrokunin kashū* (Anthologies of poems by the Thirty-Six Immortal Poets). Nihon no bijutsu (Arts of Japan), 168. Tokyo: Shibundō.

Kinoshita Masashi
1982 *Yayoi jidai* (Yayoi period). Nihon no bijutsu (Arts of Japan), 192. Tokyo: Shibundō.

Kinoshita Mitsuun
1975 "Jin'ōji engi" (History of Jin'ōji). *Osaka bunka shi*, no. 1 (May): 154–62.

Kirihata Ken
1983 "Heian, Kamakura, Muromachi no senshoku" (Textiles of the Heian, Kamakura, and Muromachi periods). *Senshoku no bi*, no. 23 (Summer): 9–80.

Kita Haruchiyo
1985 "New York Burke Collection Nihon bijutsu meihin ten" (A selection of Japanese art from the Mary and Jackson Burke Collection). *Kobijutsu*, no. 75 (July): 79–85.

Kiyomi Mutsurō
1936 "Ryū Rikyō" (Yanagisawa Kien). *Nanga kanshō* 5 (February 1936): 26.

Kobayashi Kenji
2010 "Baaku Korekushon zō 'Hachikazuki monogatari'—honkoku to kaidai" / "*Hachikazuki monogatari* of the Mary and Jackson Burke Collection—Republication and Bibliography." *Kokubungaku kenkyū shiryōkan kiyō / The Bulletin of the National Institute of Japanese Literature* 36 (March): 131–52.

Kobayashi Tadashi
1968 "Hanabusa Itchō den: Sono hairu o chūshin to shite" (The life of Itchō Hanabusa). *Kokka*, no. 920 (November): 5–20.
1972a "Ban'nenki Jakuchū no sakuhin: Suiboku ryakuga o chūshin to shite" (The work of Itō Jakuchū in his last years, and the paintings in *suiboku*). *Kokka*, no. 944 (March): 11–19.
1972b *Tosa Mitsunori e-tekagami* (Book of paintings by Tosa Mitsunori). 2 vols. Kyoto: Fuji Art.
1988 *Hanabusa Itchō*. Nihon no bijutsu (Arts of Japan), 260. Tokyo: Shibundō.
1990 [Editor]. *Rinpa*. Vol. 2, *Kachō* (Seasonal flowering plants and birds). Kyoto: Shikōsha, 1990.
1991 [Editor]. *Rinpa*. Vol. 3, *Fūgetsu, chōjū* (Landscapes, animals, and birds). Kyoto: Shikōsha.
1993 *Senmenga*: *Kinsei hen* (Fan painting: Early modern period). Nihon no bijutsu (Arts of Japan), 321. Tokyo: Shibundō.
1994 [Editor]. *Azabu Bijutsu Kōgeikan* (Azabu Museum of Arts and Crafts). Nikuhitsu ukiyo-e taikan (Compendium of Ukiyo-e paintings), 6. Tokyo: Kōdansha, 1994.
2000 *Saikō: Kindai Nihon no bijutsu—Mittsu no kagami ni terashite, bijutsu no Meiji Ishin* (A reconsideration: Japanese art of modern times—Reflections in three mirrors; arts of the Meiji Restoration). Exh. cat. Tokyo: National Museum of Modern Art, Tokyo.

Kobayashi Tadashi and Kano Hiroyuki
1992 [Editors]. *Kano ha to fūzokuga: Edo no kaiga* 1 (The Kano School and genre painting: Painting of the Edo period, 1). Nihon bijutsu zenshū (Survey of Japanese art), 17. Tokyo: Kōdansha.

Kobayashi Tadashi and Kitamura Tetsurō
1982 *Edo no bijinga: Kan'ei, Kanbun-ki no nikuhitsuga* (Paintings of beautiful women of the Edo period: Kan'ei and Kanbun eras). Tokyo: Gakushū Kenkyūsha.

Kobayashi Tadashi, Murashige Yasushi, and Haino Akio [Kobayashi Tadashi et al.]
1990 *Sōtatsu to Kōrin: Edo no kaiga 2, kōgei 1* (Sōtatsu and Kōrin: Painting in the Edo period, 2; Decorative art, 1). Nihon bijutsu zenshū (Survey of Japanese art), 18. Tokyo: Kōdansha.

Kobayashi Tadashi and Sakakibara Satoru
1978 *Morikage, Itchō*. Nihon bijutsu kaiga zenshū (Survey of Japanese painting), 16. Tokyo: Shūeisha.

Kobayashi Tadashi, Tsuji Nobuo, and Yamakawa Takeshi [Koboyashi Tadashi et al.]
1973 *Jakuchū, Shōhaku, Rosetsu*. Suiboku bijutsu taikei (Art of ink painting), 14. Tokyo: Kōdansha.

Kobayashi Tatsuo and Sahara Makoto
1979 *Jōmon doki* (Jōmon earthenware). 2 vols. Nihon no genshi bijutsu (Early arts of Japan), 1–2. Tokyo: Kōdanshha.

Kobayashi Yukio
1990 *Haniwa*. Nihon tōji taikei (Survey of Japanese ceramics), 3. Tokyo: Heibonsha.

Kobe Municipal Museum
1986 *Momoyama jidai no sairei to yūraku: Tokubetsuten* (Festivals and recreations of the Momoyama Period: Special exhibition). Exh. cat. Kobe: Kobe Municipal Museum.

"Kōdaiji"
1995 "Kōdaiji maki-e tokushū" (Special issue: Kōdaiji). *Kokka*, no. 1192.

Koizumi Sakutarō
1926 *Kain Shōja shinkan* (True mirrors of Kain Shōja). Tokyo: Ōtsuka Kōgeisha.

Kojima Naoko
2008 "Genji monogatari emaki / Handscrolls of 'The Tale of Genji'; The Feast of Light and Shadow." *Iichiko: A Journal for Transdisciplinary Studies of Pratiques*, no. 100 (Autumn): 76–79.

Kojima Naoko, Komine Kazuaki, and Watanabe Kenji [Kojima Naoko et al.]
2008 [Editors]. *Genji monogatari to Edo bunka: Kashikasareru gazoku* (*Genji monogatari* and Edo-period culture: Visualizing "Ga" and "Zoku"). Tokyo: Shinwasha.

"Ko Kano hitsu Hakuga dankin zu kai"
1937 "Ko Kano hitsu Hakuga dankin zu kai" ("Po-ya Playing the Koto," attributed to Motonobu). *Kokka*, no. 556 (March): 74–78.

Kokinshū
1984 Laurel Rasplica Rodd, with Mary Catherine Henkenius, translators. *Kokinshū: A Collection of Poems Ancient and Modern*. Princeton Library of Asian Translations. Princeton: Princeton University Press.
1996 Laurel Rasplica Rodd, with Mary Catherine Henkenius, translators. *Kokinshū: A Collection of Poems Ancient and Modern*. Boston: Cheng and Tsui.

Komatsu Shigemi
1963 "Kōetsu to Kōetsu-ryū no sho" (The development of the calligraphy of Kōetsu and his school). *Yamato bunka*, no. 45: 10–29.
1977a [Editor]. *Shigisan engi* (History of Shigisan). Nihon emaki taisei (Survey of Japanese handscroll paintings), 4. Tokyo: Chūōkōronsha.
1977b [Editor]. *Heiji monogatari ekotoba* (Illustrated Tale of the Heiji). Nihon emaki taisei (Survey of Japanese handscroll paintings), 13. Tokyo: Chūōkōronsha.
1981 [Editor]. *Kan'ei sanpitsu* (Three great calligraphers of the Kan'ei era). Nihon no sho (Japanese calligraphy), 10. Tokyo: Chūōkōronsha.
1983 [Editor]. *Zen Kunen kassen ekotoba: Heiji monogatari emaki; Yūki kassen ekotoba* (Scroll of the Former Nine Years' War: Illustrated Tale of the Heiji; Scroll of the Battle of Yūki). Zoku Nihon emaki taisei (Survey of Japanese handscroll paintings: Supplement), 17. Tokyo: Chūōkōronsha.
1984a [Editor]. *San'nō reigenki; Jizō Bosatsu reigenki* (Record of miracles performed at the San'nō Shrine; Record of miracles performed by Jizō Bosatsu). Zoku Nihon emaki taisei (Survey of Japanese handscroll paintings: Supplement), 12. Tokyo: Chūōkōronsha.
1984b [Editor]. *Tsuchigumo zōshi; Tengu zōshi; Ōeyama ekotoba* (The story of Tsuchigumo; The story of Tengu; The illustrated story of Ōeyama). Zoku Nihon emaki taisei (Survey of Japanese handscroll paintings: Supplement), 19. Tokyo: Chūōkōronsha.
1985a [Editor]. *Boki ekotoba* (Illustrated biography of the monk Kakunyo). Zoku Nihon emaki taisei (Survey of Japanese handscroll paintings: Supplement), 4. Tokyo: Chūōkōronsha.
1985b [Editor]. *Kohitsu meihin shō* (Selected masterpieces of old calligraphy). 3 vols. Nihon meiseki sōkan (Collection of famous calligraphies of Japan), 95–97. Tokyo: Nigensha.
1994–95 [Editor]. *Heike monogatari emaki* (Illustrated Tale of the Heike). 12 vols. Tokyo: Chūōkōronsha.

Komatsu Taishū
1985 *Shikkō* (Lacquerware: Prehistoric and ancient periods). Nihon no bijutsu (Arts of Japan), 229. Tokyo: Shibundō.

Kōno Motoaki
1971 "Tani Bunchō hitsu Bakufu zu" ("A Water-Fall," by Bunchō Tani). *Kokka*, no. 930 (February): 32–38.
1978 "Hōitsu no yūnenki sakuhin" (Dated works by Hōitsu). In Yamane Yūzō 1979.
1982a [Editor]. *Bakumatsu no hyakka-fū: Edo makki no kachō* (One hundred flowers from the late Edo period). Kachōga no sekai (The world of bird-and-flower painting), 8. Tokyo: Gakushū Kenkyūsha.
1982b *Kano Tan'yū*. Nihon no bijutsu (Arts of Japan), 194. Tokyo: Shibundō.
1983 "Suzuki Kiitsu no gagyō" (Works of Suzuki Kiitsu). *Kokka*, no. 1067 (October): 9–25.
1993 [Editor]. *Kano ha to Rinpa* (The Kano School and Rinpa). Nihon suiboku meihin zufu (Survey of masterpieces of Japanese ink painting), 4. Tokyo: Mainichi Shinbunsha.
1995 "Rosetsu shiron" (A preliminary study on Rosetsu). *Bijutsushi ronsō* (Collection of essays on art history), no. 11: 107–50.
2002 "Sankyo shūkōzu" (Scholar in a mountain hut). *Kokka*, no. 1286: 29–31.

Korean National Museum
[1973] *2000 Years of Korean Art*. Exh. cat.

Koshinaka Tetsuya, Tokuyama Hikaru, and Kimura Shigekazu [Koshinaka Tetsuya et al.]
1981 [Editors]. *Nagasaki ha no kachōga: Shen Nanpin to sono shūhen* (Bird-and-flower painting of the Nagasaki School: Shen Nanpin and his followers). 2 vols. Kyoto: Fuji Art.

Kumagai Nobuo
1933 "Gyokuen Bonpō den" (Bonpō: An artist and priest of the Ashikaga period; A biographical study). *Bijutsu kenkyū*, no. 15 (March): 95–113.

Kuno Takeshi
1963 "Shui kontai no Amida Nyorai zō" (A statue of Golden Amitabha in a red robe). *Kobijutsu*, no. 1 (January): 81–83.
1972 "Heian shoki ni okeru Nyorai zō no tenkai 2" (The stylistic development of Buddha statues in the early Heian period 2). *Bijutsu kenkyū*, no. 283 (September): 93–115.
1976 *Oshidashi butsu to senbutsu* (Repoussé Buddhist plaques and clay relief tiles). Nihon no bijutsu (Arts of Japan), 118. Tokyo: Shibundō.

Kuo, Jason C.
1990 *The Austere Landscape: The Paintings of Hung-jen*. Taipei: SMC Publishing.

Kuraku Yoshiyuki
1979 *Yayoi doki* (Earthenware of the Yayoi culture). Nihon no genshi bijutsu (Early arts of Japan), 3. Tokyo: Kōdansha.

Kurata Bunsaku
1980 [Editor]. *Chōkoku* (Sculpture). Zaigai Nihon no shihō (Japanese art: Selections from Western collections), 8. Tokyo: Mainichi Shinbunsha.

Kurata Bunsaku and Ogawa Kōzō
1978 *Kaijūsenji, Gansenji, Jōruriji*. Yamato koji taikan (Ancient Yamato temples), 7. Tokyo: Iwanami Shoten.

Kurata Osamu
1967 *Butsugu* (Buddhist ritual implements). Nihon no bijutsu (Arts of Japan), 16. Tokyo: Shibundō.

Kuroda Taizō, Melinda Takeuchi, and Yamane Yūzō [Kuroda Taizō et al.]
1995 *Worlds Seen and Imagined: Japanese Screens from the Idemitsu Museum of Arts*. Exh. cat. New York: Asia Society Galleries.

Kurokawa Harumura
1885–1901 *Zōho Kōko gafu* (Survey of old paintings; supplement). Edited by Kurokawa Mayori. 12 vols. Tokyo: Yūrindō.

Kyoto Furitsu Sōgō Shiryōkan
1967 *Maki-e*. Kyoto: Kyoto Furitsu Sōgō Shiryōkan.

Kyoto Municipal University of the Arts Archives
1993 *Tosa ha kaiga shiryō mokuroku* (Catalogue of documentary materials on Tosa School paintings). Vol. 4, *Hōōdō ita-e; Dōshakuga funpon* (Copies of wood-panel paintings at Hōōdō; Paintings of Buddhist, Daoist, and other religious figures). Kyoto: Kyoto Municipal University of the Arts Archives.

Kyoto National Museum
1933 *Ike Taiga iboku tenrankai mokuroku* (Catalogue of the exhibition of the work of Ike Taiga). Exh. cat. Kyoto: Kyoto National Museum.
1974a *Heike nōkyō* (Sutras donated by the Heike clan). Exh. cat. Kyoto: Kōrinsha.
1974b *Kami gami no bijutsu* (The arts of Japanese gods). Exh. cat. Kyoto: Kyoto National Museum.
1980–81 *Tan'yū shukuzu* (Small sketches by Kano Tan'yū). 2 vols. Kyoto: Kyoto National Museum.
1981 *Gazō Fudō Myōō* (The iconography of Fudō Myōō). Exh. cat. Tokyo: Dōhōsha.
1986 *Byakue Kannon zō* (Images of Byakue Kannon). Exh. cat. Kyoto: Kyoto National Museum.
1990 *Komainu* (Lion dogs). Exh. cat. Kyoto: Kyoto National Museum.
1995 *Maki-e: Shikkoku to ōgon no Nihon bi* (*Maki-e*: The beauty of black-and-gold Japanese lacquer). Exh. cat. Kyoto: Kyoto National Museum.
1996 *Muromachi jidai no Kano ha: Gadan seiha e no michi* (The Kano School in the Muromachi period: On the road to artistic predominance). Exh. cat. Kyoto: Kyoto National Museum.
1997 *Ōgon no toki, yume no jidai: Momoyama kaiga sanka* (The age of gold, the days of dreams: In praise of the paintings in the Momoyama period). Exh. cat. Kyoto: Kyoto National Museum.
2000 *Jakuchū: Tokubetsu tenrankai botsugo 200-nen; Bunkazai hogohō 50-nen kinen jigyō* (Jakuchū: Special exhibition; The 200th anniversary of Jakuchū's death). Exh. cat. Kyoto: Kyoto National Museum.

Kyūsoshin Noboru
1966 *Nishi Honganjibon Sanjūrokuninshū seisei* (The Nishi Honganji Sanjūrokuninshū: Deluxe edition). Tokyo.

Lee, Sherman E. [S. E. Lee]
1961 *Japanese Decorative Style*. Cleveland: Cleveland Museum of Art, 1961.

Lee, Soyoung [S. Lee]
2004 "A Seated Bodhisattva in the Collection of the Mary and Jackson Burke Foundation." *Orientations* 35, no. 7 (October): 90–91.
2009 [Editor]. *Art of the Korean Renaissance, 1400–1600*. Exh. cat. New York: The Metropolitan Museum of Art; New Haven: Yale University Press.

Leidy, Denise Patry, and Robert A. F. Thurman
1997 *Mandala: The Architecture of Enlightenment*. Exh. cat. New York: Asia Society Galleries and Tibet House; Boston: Shambala.

Levine, Gregory P. A., and Yukio Lippit
2007 *Awakenings: Zen Figure Paintings in Medieval Japan*. Exh. cat. New York: Japan Society.

Lillehoj, Elizabeth Ann
1989 "Soga Chokuan to Nichokuan no zaibei sakuhin ni tsuite" (Paintings by Soga Chokuan and Nichokuan in American collections). In Nara Prefectural Museum of Art 1989, pp. 46–53.

Linda, Mary F.
1988 *The Real, the Fake, and the Masterpiece*. Exh. cat. New York: Asia Society Galleries.

Link, Howard A., and Tōru Shinbo
1980 *Exquisite Visions: Rimpa Paintings from Japan*. Exh. cat. Honolulu: Honolulu Academy of Arts.

Little, Stephen
1991 *Visions of the Dharma: Japanese Buddhist Paintings and Prints in the Honolulu Academy of Arts*. Honolulu: Honolulu Academy of Arts.

London Gallery Ltd.
2000 [Editor]. *Buddha's Smile: Masterpieces of Japanese Buddhist Art*. Exh. cat. Tokyo: London Gallery.

Mackenzie, Colin, and Irving Finkel
2004 [Editors]. *Asian Games: The Art of the Contest*. Exh. cat., Asia Society Museum, New York, and Arthur M. Sackler Gallery, Smithsonian Institution, Washington, D.C. New York: Asia Society.

Maeda Taiji
1977 *Tokyo Geijutsu Daigaku shozō meihin ten: Sōritsu kyūjusshū-nen kinen* (Masterpieces from the collection of the Tokyo Geijutsu Daigaku: Commemorating its ninetieth anniversary). Exh. cat., Tokyo National Museum and Tokyo National University of Fine Arts and Music. Tokyo: Tokyo Geijutsu Daigaku.

Manno Art Museum
1988 *Manno korekushon senshū* (Selected masterpieces of the Manno Collection). Osaka: Manno Kinen Bunka Zaidan.

Man'yōshū
1981 Ian Hideo Levy, translator. *The Ten Thousand Leaves: A Translation of the Man'yōshū, Japan's Premier Anthology of Classical Poetry*. Princeton Library of Asian Translations. Princeton: Princeton University Press.

Maruo Shōzaburō
1966 [Editor]. *Nihon chōkokushi kiso shiryō shūsei—Heian jidai: Zōzō meiki hen* (Collection of source materials for the history of Japanese sculpture: Heian-period Buddhist sculpture and inscriptions). 8 vols. Tokyo: Chūōkōron Bijutsu Shuppan.

Maruyama Masatake
1963 [Editor]. *Kanshō bijutsu* (Appreciation of art). Tokyo: Bijutsu Shuppansha.

Mason, Penelope
1977 *Japanese Literati Painters: The Third Generation*. Exh. cat. Brooklyn: The Brooklyn Museum.

Masuda Takashi
1980 *Kōetsu no tegami* (Kōetsu's correspondence). Tokyo: Kawade Shobō Shinsha.

Matsubara Shigeru
1981 "Beni girai to Kansei no kaikaku" (Beni girai and the renovation of the Kansei era). [Tokyo] *Museum*, no. 358 (January): 27–33.
1985 "Beni girai no hassei to sono haikei" (The emergence of *beni girai* and its background). [Tokyo] *Museum*, no. 408 (March): 4–15.
1996 "Sekigaisen no kōyō—kasen-e no shihai sumigaki o yomu" (The benefit of infrared examination: Reading ink inscriptions on verso of poem sheets accompanying pictures of the immortal poets). *Mizuguki*, no. 20: 58–68.

Matsuo Bashō
1966 *Bashō: The Narrow Road to the Deep North; and Other Travel Sketches*. Translated and introduction by Nobuyuki Yuasa. Harmondsworth: Penguin Books.

Matsushima Ken
1985 "Busshi Kaikei no kenkyū" (Study of the Buddhist sculptor Kaikei). *Kajima bijutsu zaidan nenpō* 3: 93–99.

Matsushita Hidemaro
1959 *Kuwayama Gyokushū*. Tokyo: Chūōkōron Bijutsu Shuppan.
1970 *Taiga no sho* (The calligraphy of Taiga). Tokyo: Chūōkōronsha.

Matsushita Takaaki
1960 *Muromachi suibokuga* (Suiboku painting of the Muromachi period). Tokyo: Muromachi Suibokuga Kankōkai.
1967 *Suibokuga* (Ink painting). Nihon no bijutsu (Arts of Japan), 13. Tokyo: Shibundō.
1968 "Hidemori no sūten no sakuhin" (On several paintings by Hidemori). *Bukkyō geijutsu/Ars Buddhica*, no. 69 (December): 135–43.
1975 [Editor]. *Heiji monogatari emaki; Mōko shūrai ekotoba* (Illustrated Tale of the Heiji; Illustrated story of the Mongol invasions). Shinshū Nihon emakimono zenshū (Survey of Japanese handscroll paintings: New edition), 10. Tokyo: Kadokawa Shoten.
1977 [Editor]. *Kawaharadera urayama iseki shutsudohin ni tsuite* (Archaeological finds from the site on the hill behind Kawahara-dera). Josei Kenkyūkai hōkokusho, Bukkyō Bijutsu Kenkyū Ueno Kinen Zaidan (Committee on Research, The Ueno Memorial Foundation for the Study of Buddhist Art), 4. Kyoto: Josei Kenkyūkai hōkokusho, Bukkyō Bijutsu Kenkyū Ueno Kinen Zaidan.
1978 *Josetsu, Shūbun*. Nihon bijutsu kaiga zenshū (Survey of Japanese painting), 2. Tokyo: Shūeisha.

Matsushita Takaaki and Tamamura Takeji
1974 *Josetsu, Shūbun, San Ami*. Suiboku bijutsu taikei (Compendium of ink painting), 6. Tokyo: Kōdansha.

Matsuura Masaaki
1992 *Bishamonten zō* (Images of Bishamonten). Nihon no bijutsu (Arts of Japan), 315. Tokyo: Shibundō.
1998 "Bishamonten hō no shōrai to Rajōmon anchi zō" (The transmission to Japan of the Bishamonten doctrine and the Bishamonten statue enshrined on the Rajōmon Gate). *Bijutsu kenkyū*, no. 370 (March): 285–315.

Mayuyama Junkichi
1966 [Editor]. *Ōbei shūzō Nihon bijutsu zuroku* (Japanese art in the West). Tokyo: Mayuyama Ryūsendō.
1976 *Mayuyama, Seventy Years/Ryūsen shūhō, sōgyō shichijusshūnen kinen*. 2 vols. Tokyo: Mayuyama Ryūsendō.

McCormick, Melissa
2008 "Monochromatic Genji: The Hakubyō Tradition and Female Commentarial Culture." In Shirane 2008a, pp. 101–28.

McKelway, Matthew P.
1997 "The Partisan View: *Rakuchū-rakugai* screens in the Mary and Jackson Burke Collection." *Orientations* 28, no. 2 (February): 48–57.
2002 "Autumn Moon and Lingering Snow: Kano Sansetsu's West Lake Screens." *Artibus Asiae* 62, no. 1: 39–43.
2012 *Silver Wind: The Arts of Sakai Hōitsu (1761–1828)*. Exh. cat. New York: Japan Society Gallery.

McMillan, Peter
2008 *One Hundred Poets, One Poem Each: A Translation of the Ogura Hyakunin Isshu*. New York: Columbia University Press, 2008.

Meech, Julia
1993 [Editor]. *Rain and Snow: The Umbrella in Japanese Art*. Exh. cat. New York: Japan Society.

Meech, Julia, and Jane Oliver
2008 [Editors]. *Designed for Pleasure: The World of Edo Japan in Prints and Paintings, 1680–1860*. Exh. cat. New York: Asia Society and Japanese Art Society of America.

Meech-Pekarik, Julia
1982 "The Artist's View of Ukifune." In *Ukifune: Love in "The Tale of Genji,"* edited by Andrew Pekarik, pp. 173–215. New York: Columbia University Press.
1985 "Death of a Samurai." *Apollo* 121, no. 276 (February): 108–13.
1986 *The World of the Meiji Print: Impressions of a New Civilization*. New York: Weatherhill.

Mi Chou Gallery
1962 *Five Hundred Years of Tradition: Chinese Painting, Fifteenth to Twentieth Century*. Exh. cat. New York: Mi Chou Gallery; St. Paul, Minn.: St. Paul Art Center.

Minamoto Toyomune
1930 "Tobatsu Bishamonten zō no kigen" (The origin of Tobatsu Vaisravana). *Bukkyō bijutsu* 15 (January): 40–55.
1973 *Budō* (Grapes). Nihon no mon'yō (Decorative designs of Japan), 13. Kyoto: Kōrinsha.

Minegishi Yoshiaki
1958 *Uta awase no kenkyū* (Study of poetry competitions). Tokyo: Sanseidō.

Miner, Earl Roy, Hiroko Odagiri, and Robert E. Morrell [Miner et al.]
1985 *The Princeton Companion to Classical Japanese Literature*. Princeton: Princeton University Press.

Mitamura Masako and Geijutsu Shinchō Henshūbu
2008 [Editors]. *Genji monogatari: Tennō ni narenakatta ōji no monogatari* (*The Tale of Genji*: The story of a prince who could not become emperor). Tokyo: Shinchōsha.

Mitani Kazuma
1977 *Edo Yoshiwara zushū* (Pictures of Yoshiwara in Edo). Tokyo: Rippū Shobō.

Mitsumori Masashi

1985 "Senbutsu zatsu sōkan" (Miscellaneous views concerning *senbutsu*). In *Suenaga Sensei beiju kinen kentei ronbunshū* (Studies dedicated to Dr. Masao Suenaga on the occasion of his 88th birthday), edited by Suenaga Sensei Beiju Kinenkai, vol. 2, pp. 1531–51. Nara: Nara Meishinsha.

1986 *Amida Nyorai zō* (Images of Amida Buddha). Nihon no bijutsu (Arts of Japan), 241. Tokyo: Shibundō.

Mitsuoka Tadanari

1966 *Shigaraki, Iga, Bizen, Tanba*. Tōki zenshū (Survey of ceramics), 20. Tokyo: Heibonsha.

Miyajima Shin'ichi

1980 "Shōbyōga ni miru kaiga no hen" (Historical changes in Japanese screen painting). *Bijutsushi* 29, no. 2 (March): 119–26.

1984 *Nagasawa Rosetsu*. Nihon no bijutsu (Arts of Japan), 219. Tokyo: Shibundō.

1986 *Tosa Mitsunobu to Tosa ha no keifu* (Tosa Mitsunobu and the lineage of the Tosa School). Nihon no bijutsu (Arts of Japan), 247. Tokyo: Shibundō.

1993 *Senmenga: Chūsei hen* (Fan painting: Medieval period). Nihon no bijutsu (Arts of Japan), 320. Tokyo: Shibundō.

1994 *Suibokuga: Daitokuji ha to Jasoku* (Ink painting: The Daitokuji School and Jasoku). Nihon no bijutsu (Arts of Japan), 336. Tokyo: Shibundō.

Miyake Hidekazu

2005 "Kinsei meisho zu byōbu no Yoshino to Itsukushima: Sono kumiawase to Toyotomi seiken to no kakawari ni tsuite" (Yoshino and Itsukushima in the early-modern folding screens of celebrated places—The relationship between the thematic combination of these places and the Toyotomi regime). *Gakushūin Daigaku jinbungaku ronshū* (Compilation of papers in the humanities from the faculty of Gakushūin University), 14. Tokyo: Gakushūin Daigaku.

Miyake Hisao

1986 "Kamakura jidai no Jōdo shūkyōdan ni okeru zōzō ni kansuru kenkyū" (Study of sculptural activities in the religious circles of the Jōdo sect during the Kamakura period). *Kajima bijutsu zaidan nenpō* 4: 135–39.

Miyake Kyūnosuke

1955 *Uragami Gyokudō shinsekishū 1* (The authentic works of Uragami Gyokudō, 1). Tokyo: Bijutsu Shuppansha.

Miyama Susumu

1988 [Editor]. *Kamakura Bukkyō* (Buddhism in Kamakura). Zusetsu Nihon no Bukkyō (Illustrated history of Japanese Buddhism), 4. Tokyo: Shinchōsha.

Miya Tsugio, Shinbo Tōru, and Yoshida Yūji [Miya Tsugio et al.]

1995 [Editors]. *Kadokawa emakimono sōran* (Kadokawa comprehensive survey of illustrated handscrolls). Tokyo: Kadokawa Shoten.

Mizoguchi Teijirō, Matsuoka Eikyū, and Tanaka Ichimatsu [Mizoguchi Teijirō et al.]

1942 [Editors]. *Inabadō engi; Ōeyama ekotoba; Kitano honchi* (History of Inabadō; The illustrated story of Ōeyama; The origins of the Kitano Shrine). Zoku Nihon emakimono shūsei (Japanese handscroll paintings: Second series), 1. Tokyo: Yūzankaku.

Mizuno Keizaburō

2003–10 [Editor]. *Nihon chōkokushi kiso shiryō shūsei: Kamakura jidai: zōzō meiki hen* (History of Japanese sculpture: Records of sculpture-making in the Kamakura period). 9 vols. Tokyo: Chūōkōron Bijutsu Shuppan.

Mizuno Keizaburō, Kon'no Toshifumi, and Suzuki Kakichi [Mizuno Keizaburō et al.]

1992 [Editors]. *Mikkyō jiin to butsuzō* (Esoteric Buddhist temples and sculpture). *Heian no kenchiku, chōkoku* (Architecture and sculpture of the Heian period), vol. 1. Nihon bijutsu zenshū (Survey of Japanese art), 5. Tokyo: Kōdansha.

Mizuno Keizaburō, Kudō Yoshiaki, and Miyake Hisao [Mizuno Keizaburō et al.]

1991 [Editors]. *Unkei to Kaikei: Kamakura no kenchiku, chōkoku* (Unkei and Kaikei: Architecture and sculpture of the Kamakura period). Nihon bijutsu zenshū (Survey of Japanese art), 10. Tokyo: Kōdansha.

Mizuo Hiroshi

1965–66 *Sōtatsu-Kōrin ha gashū* (Paintings of the Sōtatsu-Kōrin School). 4 vols. Kyoto: Kōrinsha.

1968 "Getsuya hakubai zu" ("White Plum Blossoms in the Moonlight"). *Kokka*, no. 910 (January): 32–36.

Moes, Robert

1973 *Rosetsu: Exhibition of Paintings by Nagasawa Rosetsu*. Exh. cat. Denver: Denver Art Museum.

1975 *A Flower for Every Season: Japanese Paintings from the C. D. Carter Collection*. New York: The Brooklyn Museum of Art.

"Mokubei"

1967 "Mokubei tokushū" (Special number devoted to the works of Aoki Mokubei). *Yamato bunka*, no. 47 (October).

Mōri Hisashi

1961 *Busshi Kaikei ron* (On the Buddhist sculptor Kaikei). Tokyo: Yoshikawa Kōbunkan.

1969 "Kaikei shūi" (Notes on the sculptor Kaikei). *Bukkyō geijutsu/Ars Buddhica*, no. 71 (July): 22–41.

Mori Senzō

1934 "Maruyama Ōkyo den zakki" (Biographical notes on Maruyama Ōkyo). *Bijutsu kenkyū*, no. 36 (December): 584–93.

Mori Tōru

1958 "Den Fujifusa hitsu no kasen-e ni tsuite" (Portraits of immortal poets, attributed to Fujifusa). *Yamato bunka*, no. 26 (June): 37–47.

1965 "Jidai fudō uta awase-e ni tsuite" (Paintings of poetry competitions of different periods). *Kobijutsu*, no. 8 (March): 25–57.

1978 *Uta awase-e no kenkyū: Kasen-e* (Studies of paintings of poetry competitions: Portraits of the Immortal Poets). Rev. ed. Tokyo: Kadokawa Shoten.

1979 [Editor]. *Sanjūrokkasen-e* (Portraits of the Thirty-Six Immortal Poets). Shinshū Nihon emakimono zenshū (Survey of Japanese handscroll paintings: New edition), 19. Tokyo: Kadokawa Shoten.

Morse, Anne Nishimura, and Samuel Crowell Morse

1995 *Object as Insight: Japanese Buddhist Art and Ritual*. Exh. cat. Katonah, N.Y.: Katonah Museum of Art.

1996 "Object as Insight: Japanese Buddhist Art and Ritual." *Orientations* 27, no. 2 (February): 36–45.

Murai Iwao
1971 *Kofun* (Ancient tumuli). *Nihon no bijutsu* (Arts of Japan), 57. Tokyo: Shibundō.

Murakami Genzō
1975 "Heike monogatari no sekai" (The world of the Tale of the Heike). In *Heike monogatari emaki* (Illustrated Tale of the Heike). Bessatsu Taiyō, 13. Tokyo: Heibonsha.

Muraki Chii
1960 "Kusaba Akira shi" (Mr. Aira Kusaba). *Nihon bijutsu kōgei*, no. 260 (May): 42–48.

Murasaki Shikibu
1976 *The Tale of Genji*. Translated by Edward G. Seidensticker. 2 vols. New York: Alfred A. Knopf.
1982 *Murasaki Shikibu: Her Diary and Poetic Memoirs; A Translation and Study*. Translated by Richard Bowring. Princeton Library of Asian Translations. Princeton: Princeton University Press.

Murase, Miyeko
1967 "Japanese Screen Paintings of the Hōgen and Heiji Insurrections." *Artibus Asiae* 29 (Spring): 193–228.
1971 *Byōbu: Japanese Screens from New York Collections*. Exh. cat. New York: Asia Society.
1975 *Japanese Art: Selections from the Mary and Jackson Burke Collection*. Exh. cat. New York: The Metropolitan Museum of Art.
1977 "A Recent Arrival in the Ranks of the Great Collectors." *Smithsonian* 8, no. 3 (June): 84–91.
1980a "Sumiyoshi monogatari emaki" (Illustrated Tale of Sumiyoshi). In Akiyama Terukazu 1980a, pp. 114–21.
1980b *Urban Beauties and Rural Charms: Japanese Art from the Mary and Jackson Burke Collection*. Exh. cat. Orlando, Fla.: Loch Haven Art Center.
1983a *Emaki: Narrative Scrolls from Japan*. Exh. cat. New York: Asia Society.
1983b *Iconography of "The Tale of Genji": Genji monogatari ekotoba*. New York: Weatherhill.
1985 "Themes from Three Romantic Narratives of the Heian Period." *Apollo* 121, no. 276 (February): 100–107.
1986 *Tales of Japan: Scrolls and Prints from the New York Public Library*. Exh. cat. Oxford: Oxford University Press.
1990 *Masterpieces of Japanese Screen Painting: The American Collections*. New York: George Braziller.
1992 *Il Giappone*. Storia universale dell'arte: La civiltà dell'Oriente. Turin: UTET.
1993 *Jewel Rivers: Japanese Art from the Burke Collection*. Exh. cat. Richmond: Virginia Museum of Fine Art.
1995 "The Evolution of *Meisho-e* and the Case of *Mu Tamagawa*." *Orientations* 26, no. 1 (January): 94–100.
1997 "Youthful Manjusri as the Child God of the Wakamiya at the Kasuga Shrine." *The Metropolitan Museum of Art Bulletin* (Fall): 92.
2000 *Bridge of Dreams: The Mary Griggs Burke Collection of Japanese Art*. Exh. cat. New York: The Metropolitan Museum of Art.
2001 *The Tale of Genji: Legends and Paintings*. New York: George Braziller.
2003 [Editor]. *Turning Point: Oribe and the Arts of Sixteenth-Century Japan*. Exh. cat. New York: The Metropolitan Museum of Art; New Haven: Yale University Press.
2008 "Kaihō Yūsetsu hitsu Genji monogatari emaki" ("Tale of Genji," by Kaihō Yūsetsu. *Kokka*, no. 1358 (December): 39–41.

Murashige Yasushi
1989 [Editor]. *Rinpa*. Vol. 1, *Kachō* (Birds and flowers). Kyoto: Shikōsha.
1991 [Editor]. *Rinpa*. Vol. 4, *Jinbutsu* (Scenes from literature, people). Kyoto: Shikōsha.
1993 [Editor]. *Sōtatsu, Kōrin, Hōitsu: Rinpa*. Edo meisaku gajō zenshū (Survey of masterpieces of painted albums from the Edo period), 6. Tokyo: Shinshindō.

Murashige Yasushi and Kobayashi Tadashi
1992 [Editors]. *Rinpa*. Vol. 5, *Sōgō* (Assorted themes; Supplementary works). Kyoto: Shikōsha, 1992.

Murata Seiko
1983 "Yamato Bunkakan zō Heian jidai mokuchō joshinzō ni tsuite" (On a wooden Shinto goddess of the Heian period, owned by the Museum Yamato Bunkakan). *Yamato bunka*, no. 71 (March): 21–31.

Museum of Fine Arts, Boston
1936 *Illustrated Catalogue of a Special Loan Exhibition of Art Treasures from Japan*. Exh. cat. Boston: Museum of Fine Arts.

Museum of Kyoto
2008 *Genji monogatari sennenkiten* (The millennium of *The Tale of Genji*). Exh. cat. Kyoto: Museum of Kyoto.

Mushanokōji Saneatsu
1942 *Bijutsu o kataru* (Talking about the arts). Tokyo: Bungei Shunjūsha.

Nagahiro Toshio
1949 *Hiten no geijutsu* (*Hiten* in the arts). Tokyo: Asahi Shinbunsha.

Nagasaki Iwao
1993 *Kosode*. Nihon no senshoku, Kyoto Shoin bijutsu sōsho (Kyoto Shoin's art library of Japanese textiles), 4. Kyoto: Kyoto Shoin.

Nagazumi Yasuaki, Takeda Tsuneo, and Uwayokote Masataka [Nagazumi Yasuaki et al.]
1979 [Editors]. *Heike monogatari* (The Tale of the Heike). Zusetsu Nihon no koten (Survey of illustrated Japanese classics), 9. Tokyo: Shūeisha.

Nagoya City Museum
1984 *Tokubetsu ten, Shirarezaru Nanga-ka Hyakusen* (Special exhibition: The unappreciated Nanga artist Hyakusen). Exh. cat. Nagoya: Nagoya City Museum.

Naitō Masato
1989 "Katsukawa Shunshō no nikuhitsu bijinga ni tsuite" (On the paintings of beautiful women by Katsukawa Shunshō). *Bijutsushi* 38, no. 1 (March): 57–81.

Naitō Tōichirō
1932 *Nihon Bukkyō zuzō shi:* 1, *Yakushi Nyorai, Amida Nyorai* (History of Japanese Buddhist images: 1, Yakushi Buddha and Amida Buddha). Tokyo: Tōhō Shoin.

Nakabe Yoshitaka
1989 "Mokuhan kingindei ryōshi sōshoku ni tsuite: Hangi to sono katsuyōhō o chūshin ni" (Concerning the ornamentation of papers imprinted with gold and silver pigments by block printing, with primary attention to the woodblocks and their application in the printing process). *Yamato bunka*, no. 81 (March): 30–42.
1991 "Den Sōtatsu hitsu Ise monogatari zu shikishi kenkyū josetsu" (Introduction to the study of the poem cards of the Tales of Ise attributed to Sōtatsu). In Murashige Yasushi 1991, pp. 241–45.

Nakagawa Chisaku
1974 *Kutaniyaki* (Kutani ware). Nihon no bijutsu (Arts of Japan), 103. Tokyo: Shibundō.

Nakahashi, Gratia Williams

1990 "'The Bodhisattva Jizō Playing a Flute,' by Kano Tan'yū: A New Interpretation." *Orientations* 21, no. 12 (December): 36–45.

2002 "Kano Tan'yū hitsu Fuefuki Jizō-zu" ("The Bodhisattva Jizō Playing a Flute," by Kano Tan'yū). *Kokka (*December), no. 1286: 37–42.

Nakajima Junji

1968 "Sozai keishiki shugi eno tenraku: Sesshū kei kachōzu byōbu kenkyū 2" (Study of flower-and-bird screens by Sesshū and artists of his school, 2: Trend for dominance of formalistic units in compositions). [Tokyo] *Museum*, no. 205 (April): 4–21.

1994 *Suibokuga: Shōkei to Sesson* (Ink painting: Shōkei and Sesson). *Nihon no bijutsu* (Arts of Japan), 337. Tokyo: Shibundō.

Nakajima Ryōichi

1982 "Tani Bunchō no Chūgoku sansuiga kenkyū josetsu" (Introduction to the study of Chinese landscape painting by Bunchō Tani). *Kobijutsu*, no. 61 (January): 47–56.

Nakamachi Keiko

1990 "Sakai Hōitsu ni okeru Kōrin ga no keishō to tenkai" (The preservation and development of Kōrin's art in Hōitsu's oeuvre). *Kajima bijutsu zaidan nenpō* (Kajima Foundation for the Arts annual report) 8: 87–90.

1992a *Sakai Hōitsu*. Shūkan Artists Japan. Tokyo: Shinshūsha.

1992b "Shinshutsu no Sōtatsu ha Ise monogatari-e shikishi ni tsuite" (Recently discovered Sōtatsu School *shikishi* paintings on the Ise monogatari). *Kokka*, no. 1154: 11–28.

1998 "Nihon kinsei Bijutsu ni okeru Bunjinshumi no kenkyū 1" (A study of trends among Japanese literati artists of the early modern era, 1). *Jissen Joshidai bigaku bijutsushigaku* (Study in aesthetics and art history at Jissen Women's University), 13.

2010 [Editor]. *Edo Rinpa no suijin: Sakai Hōitsu* (Sakai Hōitsu: A sophisticate of Edo Rinpa). Nihon no kokoro (Spirit of Japan), 177. Tokyo: Heibonsha.

2012 "Egaita josei tachi—Heian jidai kara Edo jidai o chūshin ni" (Women who painted: Focusing on the Heian to Edo periods). *Kokka* (March), no. 1397: 25–39.

Nakamura Kōji

1993 "Jūroku Rakan zuzōgaku kotohajime" (The origin of the iconography of the Sixteen Arhats). *Bukkyō geijutsu/Ars Buddhica*, no. 206 (January): 15–29.

1996 "Jūroku Rakan zuzōgaku kotohajime: Fukko Rakan zu" (The origin of the iconography of the Sixteen Arhats: A picture of Tiger and Arhat). *Bukkyō geijutsu/Ars Buddhica*, no. 227 (July): 79–97.

Nakamura Tanio

1959a *Sumi-e no bi* (The beauty of ink painting). Tokyo: Meiji Shobō.

1959b "Tagasode zu byōbu" (Tagasode screen paintings). *Kokka*, no. 804 (March): 84–91.

1959c "Tesshū Tokusai no gaji" (Paintings by Tesshū Tokusai). [Tokyo] *Museum*, no. 98 (May): 20–22.

1966 "Gyokuen Bonpō hitsu Bokuran zu sōfuku" (A pair of "Orchids" by Gyokuen Bonpō). *Kobijutsu*, no. 14 (August): 105–8.

1967a "Kenzan hitsu kōbai, tachiaoi zu byōbu" (Kenzan's screens of red plum and hollyhocks). *Kobijutsu*, no. 16 (January 1967): 89–90.

1967b "Nagasawa Rosetsu hitsu Yūku zu fusuma-e" ("Fusuma Sliding Doors with Puppies," by Nagasawa Rosetsu). *Kobijutsu*, no. 18 (July 1967): 91.

1970 "Bokudō zu, Sekkyakushi hitsu" (Sekkyakushi's painting of the Ox and Herdboy). *Nihon bijutsu kōgei*, no. 379 (January): 98–99.

1971 *Sesson to Kantō suibokuga* (Sesson and ink painting of the Kantō region). Nihon no bijutsu (Arts of Japan), 63. Tokyo: Shibundō.

1972 "Tesshū Tokusai hitsu Rogan zu" ("Geese and Reeds," by Tesshū Tokusai). *Kobijutsu*, no. 38 (September): 79–81.

1973 "Tesshū Tokusai hitsu Ranchikuseki zu" ("Orchids, Bamboos, and Stones," by Tesshū Tokusai). *Kobijutsu*, no. 40 (March): 69–71.

1979 [Editor]. *Hōitsu ha kachōga fu*. (Edo: Rinpa and artists surrounding Sakai Hōitsu). 6 vols. Kyoto: Shikōsha.

1985 "Koka ni hisui zu: Senka Sōsetsu hitsu" ("Withered Lotus Leaf and a Kingfisher," by Senka Sōsetsu). *Kobijutsu*, no. 76 (October): 129–33.

Nakano Genzō

1986 *Fudō Myōō zō* (Images of Fudō Myōō). Nihon no bijutsu (Arts of Japan), 238. Tokyo: Shibundō.

Nakano Masaki

1969 *Wakyō* (Japanese mirrors). Nihon no bijutsu (Arts of Japan), 42. Tokyo: Shibundō.

Namiki Seiji

1989 "Kōdaiji Mitamaya zushi maki-e kō: Kōdaiji maki-e shiron 1" (Study of maki-e on the Kōdaiji Mitamaya Shrine: A preliminary study on Kōdaiji maki-e, 1). *Uryū* 12: 1–10.

Nara National Museum

1964a *Suijaku bijutsu* (Shinto syncretic art). Tokyo: Kadokawa Shoten.

1964b *Suijaku mandara* (Shinto syncretic mandalas). Tokyo: Kadokawa Shoten.

1976 *Asuka no senbutsu to sozō: Kawaradera urayama shutsudohin o chūshin to shite* (Senbutsu and clay sculptures from Asuka: Archaeological finds from the hill behind Kawaradera). Exh. cat. Nara: Nara National Museum.

1992 *Tokubetsuten: Mikkyō kōgei—shinpi no katachi* (Special exhibition: Applied art of Japanese esoteric Buddhism—Forms of mystic ritual). Exh. cat. Nara: Nara National Museum.

Nara Prefectural Museum of Art

1989 *Soga Chokuan, Nichokuan no kaiga* (Paintings of Soga Chokuan and Nichokuan). Exh. cat. Nara: Nara Prefectural Museum of Art.

1994 *Jūsan, jūyonseiki Nihon no suibokuga* (Japanese ink painting of the thirteenth and fourteenth centuries). Exh. cat. Nara: Nara Prefectural Museum of Art.

Narazaki Muneshige

1953 "Shinshutsu Tosa Mitsuyoshi hitsu Genji monogatari ejō ni tsuite" (On a newly discovered picture-album of the Genji monogatari). *Kokka*, no. 736 (July): 191–203.

1955 "Uragami Gyokudō hitsu Yakyō Hōkin zu" ("Landscape," by Uragami Gyokudō). *Kokka*, no. 756 (March): 84–89.

1964 "Kyō meisho fūzoku zu byōbu ni tsuite" (On a folding-screen picture of the famous places and the manners and customs of Kyoto). *Kokka*, no. 868 (July): 11–17.

1966 "Unchō hitsu Ryūka bijin zu" ("Beautiful Women under a Willow Tree," by Unchō). *Kokka*, no. 894 (September): 34.

1969 [Editor]. *Zaigai hihō: Ōbei shūzō Nihon kaiga shūsei* (Japanese paintings in Western collections). Vol. 3, *Nikuhitsu ukiyo-e* (Ukiyo-e paintings). Tokyo: Gakushū Kenkyūsha.

1971 "Kan'ō gyoraku zu byōbu" ("Cherry-Blossom Viewing and Pleasurable Fishing"). *Kokka*, no. 933 (May): 20–25.

1974 *Shunshō*. Ukiyo-e taikei (Compendium of ukiyo-e), 3. Tokyo: Shūeisha.

1982 [Editor]. *Shunshō*. Nikuhitsu ukiyo-e (Ukiyo-e paintings), 4. Tokyo: Shūeisha.

1987 *Nikuhitsu ukiyo-e* (Ukiyo-e paintings). Pt. 1, *Kanbun–Hōreki* (From the Kanbun to the Hōreki era). Nihon no bijutsu (Arts of Japan), 248. Tokyo: Shibundō.

Narazaki Muneshige and Yamaguchi Keizaburō

1983 *Kiyonaga, Shigemasa* (Kiyonaga and Shigemasa: Ukiyo-e paintings). Nikuhitsu ukiyo-e (Ukiyo-e paintings), 5. Tokyo: Shūeisha.

Narukami Yoshio

1968 *Ekagami hyakusen* (A selection of 100 masterpieces of mirrors with handles). Tsu, Mie Prefecture: Ekagami Sansō; Kyōto: Unsōdō.

Narusawa Katsutsugu

1985 "Kano Naizen kō" (On Kano Naizen). *Kobe Shiritsu Hakubutsukan kenkyū kiyō* 2 (March): 3–17.

Naruse Fujio

1980 *Fuji no e: Kamakura jidai kara gendai made, kaikan 20-shūnen kinen tokubetsuten/Paintings of Mt. Fuji: Special Exhibition Celebrating the 20th Anniversary of the Museum Yamato Bunkakan*. Exh. cat., Museum Yamato Bunkakan. Nara: Bunkakan.

Nedachi Kensuke

1997 *Aizen Myōō zō* (Images of Aizen Myōō). Nihon no bijutsu (Arts of Japan), 376. Tokyo: Shibundō.

Nezu Institute of Fine Arts

1962 *Shōshō hakkei gashū* (Paintings of the Eight Views of the Xiao and Xiang Rivers). Exh. cat. Tokyo: Nezu Institute of Fine Arts.

1981 *Kobayashi Collection ten: Muromachi suibokuga o chūshin to shite* (Exhibition of the Kobayashi Collection: With emphasis on Muromachi-period ink painting). Exh. cat. Tokyo: Nezu Institute of Fine Arts.

Nezu Institute of Fine Arts and Tokugawa Art Museum

1977 *Chaire* (Tea caddies). Tokyo: Nezu Institute of Fine Arts; Nagoya: Tokugawa Art Museum.

1998 *Kanan no yakimono: Ki Seto, Oribe, Aode Ko Kutani no genryū o motomete* (The ceramics of South China: Sources for Ki Seto, Oribe, and Aode Ko Kutani). Kanshō shirīzu (Appreciation Series), 1. Exh. cat. Tokyo: Nezu Institute of Fine Arts.

Nihon sankei-ten

2005 *Nihon sankei-ten: Matsushima, Amanohashidate, Itsukushima* (Exhibition of Japan's three scenic spots: Matsushima, Amanohashidate, and Itsukushima). Exh. cat. Hiroshima Prefectural Museum of Art, Museum of Kyoto, and Tōhoku History Museum, Miyagi. Hiroshima: Hiroshima Prefectural Museum of Art.

Nishida Hiroko

1976 *Ko Imari*. Nihon tōji zenshū (Survey of Japanese ceramics), 23. Tokyo: Chūōkōronsha.

1990 *Kutani*. Nihon tōji taikei (Survey of Japanese ceramics), 22. Tokyo: Heibonsha.

Nishigōri Ryōsuke

2006 "Kano Tan'yū hitsu Fuefuki: Jizō zō no zuzō" (Iconography of Jizō Playing a Flute). *Kokka* (March), no. 1325: 29–36.

Nishikawa Kyōtarō

1983 *Ichiboku zukuri to yosegi zukuri* (Techniques of one-block and assembly-block carving). Nihon no bijutsu (Arts of Japan), 202. Tokyo: Shibundō.

Ogino Museum of Art

1991 *Ogino bijutsukan meihin sen* (Collected masterworks from the Ogino Museum). Kurashiki, Okayama Prefecture: Ogino Bijutsukan.

Ogisu Jundō

1982 *Takuan oshō nenpu* (Chronology of the monk Takuan). Kinsei zensō den (Biographies of Zen monks of the early modern period), 1. Kyoto: Shibunkaku.

Ōhashi Katsuaki

1980 "Kawaradera no zōbutsu to Hakuhō chōkoku no jōgen ni tsuite" (The production of Buddhist sculpture at Kawaradera and the earliest Buddhist sculpture made in the Hakuhō era). *Bukkyō geijutsu/Ars Buddhica*, no. 128 (January): 11–25.

Ohki, Sadako

2007 "What Makes a Japanese Painting Japanese?" *Yale University Art Gallery Bulletin*: 64–81.

2009 *Tea Culture of Japan*. Exh. cat. New Haven: Yale University Art Gallery.

Okada Gyokuzan

1937 *Konrei dōgu zushū* (Illustrated guide to marriage trousseaux). Vol. 2, *Konrei dōgu sho kikei sunpōsho, ten, chi, jin-kan* (Trousseaux items: Various shapes and sizes, three volumes), edited by Masamune Atsuo. Nihon koten zenshū (Survey of Japanese classics). Tokyo: Nihon Koten Zenshū Kankōkai.

Okada Rihei

1960 "Matsumura-ke ryakkei to Gekkei (Goshun) den" (The history of the Matsumura family and biography of Goshun). *Nihon bijutsu kōgei*, no. 266: 2–8.

1978 *Buson*. Haijin no shoga bijutsu (Calligraphy and painting of the *haikai* poets), 5. Tokyo: Shūeisha.

Okamoto Ryōichi and Wakisaka Atsushi

1984 *Kuge, buke* (Courtiers and warriors). Kinsei fūzoku zufu (Fashion trends in the early modern era), 11. Tokyo: Shōgakukan.

Okamoto Yoshitomo and Takamizawa Tadao

1970 *Nanban byōbu* (*Nanban* screens). 2 vols. Tokyo: Kajima Shuppankai.

Okayama Art Museum

1970 *Uragami Gyokudō to sono jidai* (Uragami Gyokudō and his time). Okayama: Okayama Art Museum.

Okazaki Jōji

1984 "Mikkyō hōgu" (Sacred implements of Japanese esoteric Buddhism). In *Ten, hōgu, soshi* (Devas, implements, and patriarchs). Mikkyō bijitsu taikan (Compendium of Japanese esoteric Buddhist art), 4. Tokyo: Asahi Shinbunsha.

Ōkubo Jun'ichi

2006 *Bijin fūzokuga* (Genre paintings of the beautiful women). Nihon no bijutsu (Arts of Japan), 482 (July). Tokyo: Shibundō.

Okudaira Shunroku
1987 "Yūraku zu ni dai: Kiyomizudera yūrakuzu, Shunjū yūrakuzu" (Two pictures of merrymaking). *Kobijutsu*, no. 81 (January): 105–10.
1989 "Ensaki no bijin: Kanbun bijin zu no ichi shikei o megutte" (Beauty on a veranda: One form of Kanbun bijin; or, Beauties of the Kanbun era). In *Nihon kaigashi no kenkyū* (Studies in the history of Japanese painting), edited by Yamane Yūzō Sensei Koki Kinenkai, pp. 646–90. Tokyo: Yoshikawa Kōbunkan.

Ōkura Shūkokan
2000 *Nenge mishō: Bukkyō bijutsu no miryoku / Buddha's Smile: Masterpieces of Japanese Buddhist Art*. Exh. cat., Ōkura Shūkokan. Tokyo: London Gallery.

"Ōkura Shūkokan zō"
1934 "Ōkura Shūkokan zō no Jūroku Rakan zukai" (The Sixteen Rakan paintings owned by the Ōkura Shūkokan). *Kokka*, no. 527 (October): 281–82.

Olson, Eleanor
1968 *Japanese Sculpture and Painting: From the 9th to the 19th Centuries*. The Museum (Newark), n.s., 20, no. 2 (Spring).

Ōmura Seigai
1919–22 [Editor]. *Bukkyō zuzō shūko* (Collection of Buddhist images). Tokyo: Bukkyō Zuzō Shūko Kankōkai.

Onoe Hachirō
1954–68 *Shodō zenshū* (Compendium of calligraphy). 26 vols. Tokyo: Heibonsha.

Osaka Municipal Museum of Art
1990 *Tokubetsu ten "Kōetsu no sho": Keichō, Gen'na, Kan'ei no meihitsu* (A special exhibition, "The calligraphy of Kōetsu": Great brushes from the Keichō, Gen'na, and Kan'ei eras). Exh. cat. Osaka: Osaka Municipal Museum of Art.

Osaka Municipal Museum of Art, Tokugawa Art Museum, and Nezu Institute of Fine Arts [Osaka Municipal Museum of Art et al.]
1971 *Mino kotō* (Old potteries from Mino). Exh. cat. Osaka: Osaka Municipal Museum of Art; Nagoya: Tokugawa Art Museum; Tokyo: Nezu Institute of Fine Arts.

Ōta Hirotarō, Yamane Yūzō, and Yonezawa Yoshiho [Ōta Hirotarō et al.]
1990 [Editors]. *Katsura Rikyū* (Katsura Imperial Villa). Shōgakukan Gallery: Shinpen meihō Nihon no bijutsu (Shōgakukan Gallery: Masterpieces of Japanese art; New edition), 22. Tokyo: Shōgakukan, 1990.

Ōta Shōko
1993 *"Byōbue o miru: 'Taishokukan byōbu o megutte'"* (Looking at screen painting: Concerning the screens of the Taishokukan story). In *Miru yomu wakaru Nihon no rekishi: Genshi, kodai kara kindai, gendai made* (Viewing, reading, and understanding Japanese history: From ancient times to recent and modern times), vol. 5, *Jibun de yatte miyō* (Let's do it ourselves), edited by Shoseki Daiichi Henshūshitsu, pp. 18–31. Tokyo: Asahi Shinbunsha.

Ōtsu City Museum of History
1997 *Ōmi no kyoshō Kaihō Yūshō* (Kaihō Yūshō: Master artist of Ōmi). Exh. cat. Ōtsu, Shiga Prefecture: Ōtsu City Museum of History.

Ōwaki Kiyoshi
1986 "Senbutsu to oshidashi butsu no dōgenkei shiryō: Natsumehaiji no senbutsu o chūshin to shite" (Senbutsu and oshidashi butsu having common models: Primarily on senbutsu from the temple ruin of Natsume). [Tokyo] *Museum*, no. 418 (January): 4–25.

Ōyama Ninkai
1983 "Tōdaiji zō Konshi ginji Kegongyō zankan (Nigatsudō Yakekyō)" (On the repair of an important cultural property: Remnants of the Kegongyō sutra written in silver on indigo paper and saved from a fire ["Nigatsudō Yakekyō"]). *Gakusō* 5: 143–50.

Ōyama Ninkai and Takasaki Chokudō
1987 *Nihon no shakyō* (Hand-copied sutras of Japan). Kyoto: Kyoto Shoin.

Ozaki Yoshiyuki
1988 "Nishi Honganji no Goshun hitsu Kōsaku zu ni tsuite" ("Farming Scenes" painting by Goshun at the Nishi Honganji). *Kobijutsu*, no. 85: 51–69.
1989 "Kansei ki ikō no Goshun ni tsuite" (Goshun in Kansei and later periods). [Tokyo] *Museum*, no. 455: 24–34.

Pal, Pratapaditya, and Robert L. Brown
1984 *Light of Asia: Buddha Sakyamuni in Asian Art*. Exh. cat. Los Angeles: Los Angeles County Museum of Art.

Pal, Pratapaditya, and Julia Meech-Pekarik
1988 *Buddhist Book Illuminations*. New York: Ravi Kumar.

Pang Yuanji
[1909] *Xuzhai minghua lu*. Shenjiang: Printed by author.

Pearson, Richard J., and Takashi Doi
1992 [Editors]. *Ancient Japan*. Exh. cat. Washington, D.C.: Arthur M. Sackler Gallery; New York: George Braziller.

Pearson, Richard J., et al.
1991 *The Rise of a Great Tradition: Japanese Archaeological Ceramics from the Jōmon through Heian Periods (10,500 BC–AD 1185)*. Exh. cat., IBM Gallery of Science and Art, New York. [Tokyo]: Agency for Cultural Affairs, Government of Japan; New York: Japan Society.

Pekarik, Andrew
1978 *Japanese Ceramics from Prehistoric Times to the Present*. Exh. cat. Southampton, N.Y.: Parrish Art Museum.
1985a "Japanese Calligraphy and Self-Expression." *Apollo* 121, no. 276 (February): 84–90.
1985b "Japanese Lacquer: Some Aesthetic Considerations." *Apollo* 121, no. 276 (February): 124–27.

Pollack, David
1985 *Zen Poems of the Five Mountains*. Studies in Religion/American Academy of Religion, 37. New York: Crossroad; Decatur, Ga.: Scholars Press, 1985.

Poster, Amy G., Richard M. Barnhart, and Christine M. E. Guth [Poster et al.]
1999 *Crosscurrents: Masterpieces of East Asian Art from New York Private Collections*. Exh. cat. New York: Japan Society in association with the Brooklyn Museum of Art, 1999.

Proser, Adriana G.
2010 [Editor]. *Pilgrimage and Buddhist Art*. Exh. cat. New York: Asia Society; New Haven: Yale University Press.

Ragué, Beatrix von
1976 *A History of Japanese Lacquerwork.* Translated by Annie R. de Wasserman. Toronto: University of Toronto Press.

Rahman-Steinert, Uta
1996 *Chen Chi-kwan, geb 1921: Chinesische Malerei*. Exh. cat., Museum für Ostasiatische Kunst, Berlin. Berlin: G & H Verlag.

Rathbun, William J., and Sasaki Jōhei
1980 *Ōkyo and the Maruyama-Shijō School of Japanese Painting.* Exh. cat. Saint Louis: Saint Louis Art Museum.

Rhodes, Daniel
1970 *Tamba Pottery: The Timeless Art of a Japanese Village.* Tokyo: Kōdansha International.

Ronnberg, Ami, and Kathleen Martin
2010 *The Book of Symbols.* The Archive for Research in Archetypal Symbolism. Cologne: Taschen.

Rosenfield, John M.
1967 *Japanese Arts of the Heian Period, 794–1185.* Exh. cat. New York: Asia Society.
1979 [Editor]. *Song of the Brush: Japanese Paintings from the Sansō Collection.* Exh. cat. Seattle: Seattle Art Museum.

Rosenfield, John M., and Elizabeth ten Grotenhuis
1979 *Journey of the Three Jewels: Japanese Buddhist Paintings from Western Collections.* Exh. cat. New York: Asia Society.

Rosenfield, John M., and Fumiko E. Cranston
1999 *Extraordinary Persons: Works by Eccentric, Nonconformist Japanese Artists of the Early Modern Era (1580–1868) in the Collection of Kimiko and John Powers.* 3 vols. Cambridge, Mass.: Harvard University Art Museums.

Rosenfield, John M., and Shimada Shūjirō
1970 *Traditions of Japanese Art: Selections from the Kimiko and John Powers Collection.* Exh. cat. Cambridge, Mass.: Fogg Art Museum, Harvard University.

Rousmaniere, Nicole Coolidge
2002 [Editor]. *Kazari: Decoration and Display in Japan, 15th–19th Centuries.* Exh. cat. New York: Japan Society.

Rousset, Hugette
1977 *Arts de la Corée* (Arts of Korea). Fribourg: Office du livre.

Ruch, Barbara
1979 [Editor]. *Kaigai shozō Nara ehon* (Nara Ehon from outstanding foreign collections). Tokyo: Kōdansha, 1979.
1991 *Mō hitotsu no chūseizō: Bikuni, otogizōshi, raise* (Another perspective on medieval Japan: Itinerant nuns, short prose narratives, and the afterlife). Kyoto: Shibunkaku.
2002 [Editor]. *Engendering Faith: Women and Buddhism in Premodern Japan.* Ann Arbor: Center for Japanese Studies, University of Michigan.

"Ryūkyō hitsu Kachō zu kai"
1929 "Ryūkyō hitsu Kachō zu kai" ("Birds and Flowers," by Ryūkyō). *Kokka*, no. 461 (April): 100–105.

Saga Prefectural Museum of Kyūshū Ceramics
1991 *Hizen no iro-e "sono hajimari to hensen" ten* (Polychrome porcelain in Hizen: Its early type and change of style; Special exhibition). Exh. cat. Arita: Saga Prefectural Museum of Kyūshū Ceramics.

Saigyō
1991 *Saigyō: Poems of a Mountain Home.* Translated by Burton Watson. Translations from the Oriental Classics. New York: Columbia University Press.

Sakai Hōitsu
1815 *Kōrin hyakuzu* (A selection of one hundred paintings by Kōrin). 2 vols. Kyoto: Hosokawa Kaiekidō.

Sakamoto, Gen
1992 "Painting of Jakō Neko and Problems Concerning the 'Uto Gyoshi' Seal." Unpublished ms., Columbia University.
1997 "Kano Gyokuraku: Enigmatic Leader of the Odawara Kano School." *Orientations* 28, no. 2 (February): 32–39.

Sakamoto Mitsuru
1977 [Editor]. *Nanban byōbu* (*Nanban* screen painting). Nihon no bijutsu (Arts of Japan), 135. Tokyo: Shibundō.
1982 *Fūzokuga: Nanban fūzoku* (Genre painting: Genre with *Nanban*). Nihon byōbu-e shūsei (Survey of Japanese screen paintings), 15. 2nd ed. Tokyo: Kōdansha.
2008 *Nanban byōbu shūsei* (Survey of screen paintings of *Nanban*). Tokyo: Chūōkōron Bijutsu.

Sanari Kentarō
1930–31 [Editor]. *Yōkyoku taikan* (Compendium of Nō texts). 7 vols. Tokyo: Meiji Shoin.

Sanjōnishi Sanetaka
1979–80 *Sanetakakō ki* (The diary of Lord Sanetaka). Edited by Takahashi Ryūzō. 3rd ed. 13 vols. in 19. Tokyo: Zoku Gunsho Ruijū Kanseikai.

Sano Midori
2011 *Genji-e shūsei* (Compendium of Genji illustrations). 2 vols. Tokyo: Geika Shoin.

"Sansui zu byōbu"
1910 "Sansui zu byōbu" ("Landscapes," by Tan'yū Kano). *Kokka*, no. 241 (June): 385–86.

Sasaki Jōhei
1996a *Edo ki no Kyō gadan: Tsuruzawa ha o chūshin to shite* (Painters in Kyoto during the Edo period: Primarily of the Tsuruzawa School). Kyoto: Museum of the School of Humanities, Kyoto University.
1996b "Ōkyo-ga tōjō no butai: Tsuruzawa ha" (Background of the emergence of Ōkyo's painting: The Tsuruzawa school of painters). *Nihon bijutsu kōgei*, no. 694 (July): 26–33.

Sasaki Jōhei and Sasaki Masako
1996 *Maruyama Ōkyo kenkyū* (Study of Maruyama Ōkyo). 2 vols. Tokyo: Chūōkōron Bijutsu Shuppan.

Sasaki Kōzō
1977 *Mokubei, Chikuden.* Nihon bijutsu kaiga zenshū (Survey of Japanese painting), 21. Tokyo: Shūeisha.
1983 "Nihon gaka no sakuhin yōshiki no tenkan no keiki ni tsuite: Tanomura Chikuden no baai" (On the motivations of stylistic changes among Japanese painters: The case of Tanomura Chikuden). *Bijutsushi kenkyū* 20: 27–39.

Sasaki Kōzō and Okumura Hideo
1979 [Editors]. *Shinto no bijutsu: Kasuga, Hie, Kumano* (Art of Shinto: Kasuga, Hie, and Kumano). Nihon bijutsu zenshū (Survey of Japanese art), 11. Tokyo: Gakushū Kenkyūsha.

Satō Yasuhiro
1981 "Jakuchū ni okeru mosha no igi" (Significance of copying in Jakuchū paintings). [Tokyo] *Museum*, no. 364 (July): 18–34.

1987 *Itō Jakuchū*. Nihon no bijutsu (Arts of Japan), 256. Tokyo: Shibundō.

1991 *Jakuchū, Shōhaku*. Shōgakukan Gallery: Shinpen meihō Nihon no bijutsu (Shōgakukan Gallery: Masterpieces of Japanese art; new edition), 27. Tokyo: Shōgakukan, 1991.

1992 "Un'u no jōkei: Uragami Gyokudō no eroticism" (A scene of clouds and rain: Eroticism expressed in the paintings of Uragami Gyokudō). [Tokyo] *Museum*, no. 491 (February): 27–38.

Saunders, Ernest Dale

1985 *Mudra: A Study of Symbolic Gestures in Japanese Buddhist Sculpture*. Bollingen Series, 58. New York, 1960. Bollingen Series, 58. Reprint, Princeton: Princeton University Press.

Sawa Ryūken

1962 *Butsuzō zuten* (Encyclopedia of the iconography of Buddhist icons). Tokyo: Yoshikawa Kōbunkan.

Screech, Timon

1995 *Ō-Edo ijin ōrai* (A foreigner in the great city of Edo). Translated by Takayama Hiroshi. Maruzen Books, 36. Tokyo: Maruzen.

Sei Shōnagon

1958 *Makura no sōshi*. In *Makura no sōshi; Murasaki Shikibu nikki* (The Pillow Books; The diary of Murasaki Shikibu), edited by Ikeda Kikan et al. Nihon koten bungaku taikei (Compendium of Japanese classical literature), 19. Tokyo: Iwanami Shoten.

1991 *The Pillow Book of Sei Shōnagon*. Translated by Ivan Morris. New York: Columbia University Press.

Seigle, Cecilia Segawa

1993 *Yoshiwara: The Glittering World of the Japanese Courtesan*. Honolulu: University of Hawai'i Press.

Sekine Shun'ichi

1997 *Bonten, Taishakuten zō* (Images of Bonten and Taishakuten). Nihon no bijutsu (Arts of Japan), 375. Tokyo: Shibundō.

Sen Sōshitsu

1967 *Sadō koten zenshū* (Survey of classic writings on the tea ceremony). Edited by Nagashima Fukutarō. 12 vols. 2nd ed. Kyoto: Tankōsha.

"Sesson hitsu Shichiken suibu zu"

1940 "Sesson hitsu Shichiken suibu zu" ("The Seven Wise Men of the Bamboo Grove in a Drunken Revelry," by Sesson). *Kokka*, no. 591 (February): 40–41.

Shibayama Zenkei

1954 *Jūgyū zu* (Paintings of the Ten Ox-Herding Songs). Zen sōsho (Books on Zen), 3. Tokyo: Kōbundō.

Shibue Jirō

1962 *Kamakura no suibokuga* (Ink paintings of Kamakura). Kamakura Kokuhōkan zuroku (Catalogue of the Treasure House of Kamakura), 9. Kamakura: Kamakura Kokuhōkan.

Shimada Shūjirō

1941 "Sōteki no Shōshō hakkei" (Sung Ti and the Eight Views of the Xiao and Xiang Rivers). *Nanga kanshō* 10, no. 4 (April): 6–13.

1969 [Editor]. *Zaigai hihō: Ōbei shūzō Nihon kaiga shūsei* (Japanese paintings in Western collections). Vol. 1, *Bukkyō kaiga, yamato-e, suibokuga* (Buddhist painting, yamato-e, and ink painting). Vol. 2, *Shōbyōga, Rinpa, bunjinga* (Screen paintings, rinpa, and literati painting). Vol. 3, *Nikuhitsu ukiyoe* (Hand-painted ukiyo-e). Tokyo: Gakushū Kenkyūsha.

1979 [Editor]. *Suibokuga* (Ink painting). Zaigai Nihon no shihō (Japanese art: Selections from Western collections), 3. Tokyo: Mainichi Shinbunsha.

1981 [Editor]. *Tenjin engi emaki; Hachiman engi; Amewakahiko sōshi; Nezumi no sōshi; Bakemono sōshi; Utatane sōshi* (History of the Kitano Tenjin Shrine; History of the Hachiman Shrine; The Story of Amewakahiko; The Story of Mice; The Story of Goblins; The Story of Catnapping). Shinshū Nihon emakimono zenshū, bekkan 2, zaigai hen (Compendium of Japanese handscroll paintings: New edition, supplement 2, overseas collections). Tokyo: Kadokawa Shoten.

Shimada Shūjirō and Iriya Yoshitaka

1987 *Zenrin gasan: Chūsei suibokuga o yomu* (Painting colophon from Japanese Zen milieu). Tokyo: Mainichi Shinbunsha.

Shimao Arata

1989 "Jūgo seiki ni okeru Chūgoku kaiga shumi" (The taste for Chinese painting in the fifteenth century). [Tokyo] *Museum*, no. 463 (October): 22–34.

Shimizu, Yoshiaki

1981 "Seasons and Places in Yamato Landscape and Poetry." *Ars Orientalis* 12: 1–14.

1988 [Editor]. *Japan: The Shaping of Daimyo Culture, 1185–1868*. Exh. cat. Washington, D.C.: National Gallery of Art.

Shimizu, Yoshiaki, and John M. Rosenfield

1984 *Masters of Japanese Calligraphy, 8th–19th Century*. Exh. cat. New York: Asia Society Galleries and Japan House Gallery.

Shimizu, Yoshiaki, and Carolyn Wheelwright

1976 [Editors]. *Japanese Ink Paintings from American Collections: The Muromachi Period; An Exhibition in Honor of Shūjirō Shimada*. Exh. cat. Princeton: The Art Museum, Princeton University.

Shimizu Yoshiko

1960 "Genji monogatari kaiga no ichi hōhō (Techniques for illustrating *The Tale of Genji*). *Kokugo kokubun*, no. 309: 1–14.

Shimizu Zenzō

1979 "Amerika · Kanada ni aru Nihon chōkoku (2)" (Japanese sculptures in America and Canada, 2). *Bukkyō geijutsu/Ars Buddhica*, no. 127 (November).

Shimonaka Kunihiko

1954–68 [Editor]. *Shodō zenshū* (Compendium of calligraphy). 28 vols. Tokyo: Heibonsha.

Shinbo Tōru

1970 *Hakubyō emaki* (Handscroll narrative paintings in the *hakubyō* style). Nihon no bijutsu (Arts of Japan), 48. Tokyo: Shibundō.

1974 "Shinshutsu no Kōanbon Jūgyū zukan: Sorimachi Jūrō shi zō" (Recently discovered paintings depicting Zen enlightenment: The kōan scroll of Jūgyū zu). *Bukkyō geijutsu/Ars Buddhica*, no. 96 (May): 77–79.

1985 *Besson mandara* (Mandalas of individual deities). Tokyo: Mainichi Shinbunsha.

1990 "Hakubyō Kitano Honji-e" (Kitano honji-e with ink drawings). *Bijutsu kenkyū*, no. 347 (March): 1–16.

Shinkai Taketarō and Nakagawa Tadayori

1921 *Rock-Carvings from the Yün-kang Caves*. Tokyo: Bunkyūdō; Peking: Yamamoto Photographic Studio.

Shin Kokinshū

1970 Heihachirō Honda, translator. *The Shin Kokinshū: The Thirteenth-Century*

Anthology Edited by Imperial Edict. Tokyo: Hokuseidō and Eirinsha.

Shinto Taikei Hensankai
1985 *Kasuga*. Shinto taikei: Jinja hen (Compendium on Shinto: Shrines), 13. Tokyo: Shinto Taikei Hensankai.

Shirai, Yoko Hsueh
2011a "The Buddha Triad *Senbutsu* Unearthed in Japan: Replicating and Reinventing the Chinese Prototype in the Seventh Century." *Artibus Asiae* 71, no. 2: 185–219.
2011b "Nihon shutsudo no sanzon senbutsu: sono seisaku no hajimari" (Buddhist triad relief tiles from Japanese archaeological sites: The origins of their production). *Kōkogaku ronkō: Kashihara kōkogaku kenkyūjo kiyō* 34 (March).

Shirasu Masako
1997 *Shirasu Masako no sekai* (The world of Shirasu Masako). Corona Books, 23. Tokyo: Heibonsha.

Shirahata Yoshi
1964 "Saigyō monogatari byōbu" (Screens illustrating the biography of the priest Saigyō). *Kobijutsu*, no. 5 (August): 103–4.
1975 *Rinpa kaiga senshū* (A selection of Rinpa paintings). 3 vols. Kyoto: Kyoto Shoin.
1980a "Heian jidai no kōgei teki mon'yō: Omoni waka tono kanren ni tsuite" (Designs on decorative objects in the Heian period, especially in relation to waka). In Kyoto National Museum 1980–81, vol. 1.
1980b *Kōgei ni miru koten bungaku ishō* (The world of Japanese classical literature in craft design). Exh. cat., Kyoto National Museum. Kyoto: Shikōsha.

Shirane, Haruo
2008a [Editor]. *Envisioning "The Tale of Genji": Media, Gender, and Cultural Production*. New York: Columbia University Press.
2008b "*The Tale of Genji* and the Dynamics of Cultural Production: Canonization and Popularization." In Shirane 2008a, pp. 1–46.

Shiten'nōji no Hōmotsu
1992 *Shiten'nōji no Hōmotsu to Shōtoku Taishi shinkō* (Treasures of the Shiten'nōji Temple and the worship of Prince Shōtoku). Exh. cat., Osaka Municipal Museum of Art and Suntory Museum of Art, Tokyo. Osaka: Executive Committee for the Exhibition "Treasures of the Shiten'nōji Temple and the Worship of Prince Shōtoku."

"Shōhaku hitsu Shakkyō zu"
1899 "Shōhaku hitsu Shakkyō zu" ("Stone Bridge," by Shōhaku). *Kokka*, no. 118 (October): 193.

Shōtō Art Museum of Shibuya Ward
1995 *Kinsei shūkyō bijutsu no sekai: Hen'yō suru shinbutsu tachi* (The world of religious arts in the early modern period: Transformations of Buddhas and Shinto gods). Exh. cat. Tokyo: Shōtō Art Museum of Shibuya Ward.
1996 *Moji-e to e-moji no keifu: Kaikan jūgo-shūnen kinen tokubetsuten* (Special fifteen-year anniversary exhibition: Traditions of writing-pictures and picture-writings). Exh. cat. Tokyo: Shōtō Art Museum of Shibuya Ward.

Singer, Robert T.
1998 [Editor]. *Edo: Art in Japan, 1615–1868*. Exh. cat. Washington, D.C.: National Gallery of Art.

Sin Ki-su and Nakao Hiroshi
1996 *Taikei Chōsen tsūshinshi: Zenrin to yūkō no kiroku / Sekinin henshū Shin Kishū* (Korean missions to Japan: Records of good neighborly relations). 8 vols. Tokyo: Akashi Shoten.

Society of the Four Arts
1963 *Japanese Paintings from the Frank E. Hart Collection*. Exh. cat. Palm Beach, Fla.: Society of the Four Arts.

Soper, Alexander C.
1942 "The Rise of Yamato-e." *Art Bulletin* 24 (December): 351–79.

Stanley-Baker, Richard
1974 "Gakuō's Eight Views of Hsiao and Hsiang." *Oriental Art*, n.s., 20 (Autumn): 284–303.

Stern, Harold P.
1971 *Rimpa: Masterworks of the Japanese Decorative School*. Exh. cat. New York: Japan Society.

Sugahara, Hisao
1967 *Japanese Ink Painting and Calligraphy from the Collection of the Tokiwayama Bunko, Kamakura, Japan*. Translated by Miyeko Murase et al. Exh. cat. Brooklyn: The Brooklyn Museum.

Sugimoto Hidetarō
2007 *Kyoto mugenki* (Kyoto, dreams and fantasies). Tokyo: Shinchōsha.

Sugimoto Hidetarō and Hoshino Suzu
1994 *Gyokudō*. Suibokuga no kyoshō (Great masters of ink painting), 13. Tokyo: Kōdansha.

Sugimoto Sonoko and Kawai Masatomo
1994 *Yūshō*. Suibokuga no kyoshō (Great masters of ink painting), 4. Tokyo: Kōdansha.

Sugimura Eiji
1985 *Kameda Bōsai no sekai* (The world of Kameda Bōsai). Tokyo: Miki Shobō.

"Sumiyoshi Monogatari"
1901 Harold Parlett, translator. "The Sumiyoshi Monogatari." *Transactions of the Asiatic Society of Japan* 29: 35–123.

Suntory Museum of Art
1981 *Itsuō Bijutsukan meihin ten: Buson to Goshun* (Exhibition of masterpieces from the Itsuō Art Museum: Buson and Goshun). Exh. cat. Tokyo: Suntory Museum of Art.
1982 *Sakai Hōitsu to Edo Rinpa ha* (Sakai Hōitsu and Edo Rinpa). Tokyo: Suntory Museum of Art.
1986 *Sanjūrokkasen-e: Satakebon o chūshin ni* (Sanjūrokkasen-e, with emphasis on the Satake version). Exh. cat. Tokyo: Suntory Museum of Art.
1997 *Momoyama Hyakusō: Kinsei byōbu-e no sekai* (One hundred screens of Momoyama: The world of screen painting in the early modern period). Exh. cat. Tokyo: Suntory Museum of Art.

Suzuki Hideo and Kitani Mariko
2006 [Editors]. *Ōchō no miyabi: Genji monogatari no sekai* (Courtly elegance: The world of *The Tale of Genji*). Bessatsu Taiyō, supplement: Nihon no kokoro (Spirit of Japan), 140. Tokyo: Heibonsha.

Suzuki Hiroyuki
1989 "Enjinsai Katō Nobukiyo hitsu Amida sanzon zō" ("Amidtabha Triad," by Katō Nobukiyo). *Bijutsu kenkyū*, no. 343 (February): 37–45.
2007 *Meisho fūzokuzu* (Genre paintings of famous places). Nihon no bijutsu (Arts of Japan), 491. Tokyo: Shibundō.

Suzuki Kei
1964 "Gyokkan Jakufun shiron" (A study of Yü-chien Jo-fen). *Bijutsu kenkyū*, no. 236 (September): 79–92.

Suzuki Keizō
1952 "Heiji monogatari emaki: Rokuhara kassen no maki" (Paintings in the scroll of the Heiji monogatari: "Battle at Rokuhara"). *Kokka*, no. 727 (October): 309–16.

Suzuki Norio
1985 *Shikkō* (Lacquerware: Medieval period). Nihon no bijutsu (Arts of Japan), 230. Tokyo: Shibundō.

Suzuki Susumu
1963 *Chikuden*. Tokyo: Nihon Keizai Shinbunsha.
1970 "Uragami Gyokudō hitsu Zan'u hanson zu" ("Hamlet in Lingering Rain," by Gyokudō Uragami). *Kobijutsu*, no. 30 (June): 143–44.
1972 "Kinsei byōbu-e meisaku ten ni omou koto" (Newly found screens). *Kobijutsu*, no. 36 (March): 47–56.
1973 "Yamamoto Baiitsu hitsu Shiki sansui zu" ("Landscape of Four Seasons," by Yamamoto Baiitsu). *Kobijutsu*, no. 40 (March): 79–82.
1975 *Ike Taiga*. Nihon no bijutsu (Arts of Japan), 114. Tokyo: Shibundō.
1978 *Uragami Gyokudō*. Nihon no bijutsu (Arts of Japan), 148. Tokyo: Shibundō.

Suzuki Susumu and Sasaki Jōhei
1979 *Ike Taiga*. Nihon bijutsu kaiga zenshū (Survey of Japanese painting), 18. Tokyo: Shūeisha.

Swinton, Elizabeth de Sabato, Kazue Edamatsu Campbell, Liza Crihfield Dalby, and Mark Oshima [Swinton et al.]
1995 *The Women of the Pleasure Quarter: Japanese Paintings and Prints of the Floating World*. Exh. cat., Worcester Art Museum; Equitable Gallery, New York; and Kimbell Art Museum, Fort Worth. New York: Hudson Hills Press.

Takasaki Fujihiko
1985 *Rakan zu* (Rakan paintings). Nihon no bijutsu (Arts of Japan), 234. Tokyo: Shibundō.

Takashimaya Department Store
1965 *Byōbu-e meisaku ten* (Exhibition of masterpieces of folding-screen painting). Exh. cat., Takashimaya Department Store. Tokyo: Nihon Keizai Shinbunsha Kikakubu.

Takashina Shūji
2000 *Nimai no e / Two Paintings*. Tokyo: Mainichi Shinbunsha.

Takeda Kōichi
1986 "Sō Shiseki no kōzu" (Composition in the paintings of Sō Shiseki). In Yamakawa Takeshi et al. 1986.

Takeda Tsuneo
1966 *Rakuchū-rakugai zu* (Scenes in and around the capital). Exh. cat., Kyoto National Museum. Tokyo: Kadokawa Shoten.
1967 *Kinsei shoki fūzokuga* (Genre painting of the early modern period). Nihon no bijutsu (Arts of Japan), 20. Tokyo: Shibundō.
1974 *Kano Eitoku*. Nihon no bijutsu (Arts of Japan), 94. Tokyo: Shibundō.
1976 "Tosa Mitsuyoshi to saiga: Kyoto Kokuritsu Hakubutsukan Genji monogatari zujō o megutte" (Tosa Mitsuyoshi and miniature painting: The album of scenes from the *Genji monogatari* in the collection of the Kyoto National Museum). *Kokka*, no. 996 (December): 11–24.
1977a *Kano Eitoku*. Translated and adapted by H. Mack Horton and Catherine Kaputa. Japanese Arts Library, 3. Tokyo: Kōdansha International.
1977b [Editor]. *Keibutsuga: Shiki keibutsu* (Landscape: Scenes of four seasons). Nihon byōbu-e shūsei (Survey of Japanese screen paintings), 9. Tokyo: Kōdansha.
1978a [Editor]. *Fūzokuga: Rakuchū-rakugai* (Genre painting: Scenes in and around the capital). Nihon byōbu-e shūsei, 11. Tokyo: Kōdansha.
1978b *Kano Tan'yū*. Nihon bijutsu kaiga zenshū (Survey of Japanese painting), 15. Tokyo: Shūeisha.
1979 *Chūsei byōbu-e* (Folding-screen paintings of medieval Japan). Exh. cat., Osaka Municipal Museum of Art. Kyoto: Kyoto Shoin.
1980 [Editor]. *Shōheiga* (Screen painting). Zaigai Nihon no shihō (Japanese art: Selections from Western collections), 4. Tokyo: Mainichi Shinbunsha.

Takeda Tsuneo and Matsunaga Goichi
1994 *Tan'yū, Morikage*. Suibokuga no kyoshō (Great masters of ink painting), 5. Tokyo: Kōdansha.

Takeda Tsuneo, Yamane Yūzō, and Yoshizawa Chū [Takeda Tsuneo et al.]
1977 [Editors]. *Fūzokuga: Yūraku, Tagasode* (Genre painting: Pleasures and "Whose Sleeves"). Nihon byōbu-e shūsei (Survey of Japanese screen paintings), 14. Tokyo: Kōdansha.

Takeuchi, Melinda
1992 *Taiga's True Views: The Language of Landscape Painting in Eighteenth-Century Japan*. Stanford, Calif.: Stanford University Press.
1995 "The Golden Link: Place, Poetry, and Paradise in a Medieval Japanese Design." In Kuroda Taizō et al. 1995, pp. 30–55.

Takeuchi Jun'ichi et al.
1989 *Court and Samurai in an Age of Transition: Medieval Paintings and Blades from The Gotoh Museum, Tokyo*. Exh. cat. New York: Japan Society.

Takeuchi Misako
1990 "Ryūkyō suisha zu byōbu: Shinshutsubon no shōkai o kanete" (On willow-bridge and waterwheel screens: Also introducing a newly discovered example). *Kokka*, no. 1138 (September): 20–34 (pt. 1); no. 1139 (October): 7–18 (pt. 2).

Takeuchi Shōji
1972 "Kyū Date-ke bon Hakuga dankin zu to Daisen'in Hōjō Ihatsu-kaku shōhekiga" ("Immortal Playing a Harp," formerly owned by the Date family, and the screen paintings of the main hall of the Daisen'in Temple). *Kobijutsu*, no. 39 (December): 87–88.

Tale of the Heike
1988 Helen Craig McCullough, translator. *The Tale of the Heike*. Stanford, Calif.: Stanford University Press.

Tales of Ise
1968 Helen Craig McCullough, translator. *Tales of Ise: Lyrical Episodes from Tenth-Century Japan*. Stanford, Calif.: Stanford University Press.

Tamagami Takuya
1943 "Byōbu-e to uta to monogatari to" (Screen paintings, poetry, and tales). *Kokugo kokubun*, no. 221 (June): 1–20.

Tamamura Takeji
1983 *Gozan zensō denki shūsei* (Biographies of Zen priests of Gozan temples). Tokyo: Kōdansha.

Tamamushi Satoko

1991 "Muromachi jidai no kingindei-e to Nōami hitsu Shū Hyakku no renga (Gold and silver painting in the Muromachi period and the "Shū Hyakku no renga," by Nōami). *Kokka*, no. 1146: 21–41.

1997 *Sakai Hōitsu*. Shinchō Nihon bijutsu bunko (Shincho Japanese art library), 18. Tokyo: Shinchōsha.

2004 *Toshi no naka no e: Sakai Hōitsu no kaiji to sono efekuto* (Painting born in the urban environment of Edo: The art of Sakai Hōitsu and his followers). Tokyo: Seiunsha.

2008 *Motto shiritai Sakai Hōitsu: Shōgai to sakuhin* (I want to know more about Sakai Hōitsu: His training and oeuvre). Tokyo: Tōkyō Bijutsu.

Tamura Etsuko

1967 "Heiji emaki Rokuhara kassen no maki kotoba-gaki no dankan ni tsuite: Fusete genzon sankan no shoseki ni oyobu" (A textual fragment of the Battle of Rokuhara Scroll of the Heiji War Scroll paintings, with a detailed examination of the calligraphy of the texts of the three existing scrolls). *Bijutsu kenkyū*, no. 252 (May): 13–31.

Tanabe, Willa J.

1988 *Paintings of the Lotus Sutra*. New York: Weatherhill.

Tanabe Saburōsuke

1989 [Editor]. *Shinbutsu shūgō to shugen* (The syncretism of Buddhism and Shinto and Shugen). Zusetsu Nihon no Bukkyō (Illustrated history of Japanese Buddhism), 6. Tokyo: Shinchōsha.

Tanabe Shōzō

1989 *Sue*. Nihon tōji taikei (Survey of Japanese ceramics), 4. Tokyo: Heibonsha.

Tanaka Ichimatsu

1953 "Kontai butsuga-jō to Takuma Tametō" (Buddhist iconographical manuscripts of the twelfth century and the Buddhist painter Tametō). *Yamato bunka*, no. 12 (December): 22–27.

1957 "Ike Taiga hitsu Rantei kyokusui, Gako shajitsu zu byōbu" ("Rantei kyokusui" and "Gako shajitsu," by Taiga Ike). *Kokka*, no. 780 (March): 89–97.

1958 "Sesson hitsu Shiki sansui zu byōbu ni tsuite" (The screen painting "Landscapes of Four Seasons," by Sesson). *Bijutsu kenkyū*, no. 198 (May): 1–10.

1962 [Editor]. *Tokugawa Bijutsukan* (Tokugawa Art Museum). Tokyo: Tōkyō Chūnichi Shinbun Shuppanbu.

1965a "E-Ingakyō dankan gōma zu" (Illustrated Ingakyō sutra). *Kokka*, no. 881 (August): 24.

1965b [Editor]. *Kōrin* (The art of Kōrin). Rev. ed. Tokyo: Nihon Keizai Shinbunsha.

1966 *Nihon kaigashi ronshū* (Collection of essays on the history of Japanese painting). Tokyo: Chūōkōron Bijutsu Shuppan.

1971 "Soga Jasoku to Sōjō o meguru shomondai" (Several problems regarding Soga Jasoku and Sōjō)." *Bukkyō geijutsu/Ars Buddhica*, no. 79 (April): 15–35.

1972 *Japanese Ink Painting: Shūbun to Sesshū*. Translated by Bruce Darling. Heibonsha survey of Japanese art, 12. New York: Weatherhill.

1974 *Kaō, Mokuan, Minchō*. Suiboku bijutsu taikei (Art of ink painting), 5. Tokyo: Kōdansha.

Tanaka Ichimatsu and Nakamura Tanio

1973 *Sesshū, Sesson*. Suiboku bijutsu taikei (Art of ink painting), 7. Tokyo: Kōdansha.

Tanaka Ichimatsu and Yonezawa Yoshiho

1970 *Suibokuga* (Ink painting). Genshoku Nihon no bijutsu (Japanese art in color), 11. Tokyo: Shōgakukan.

1978 *Hakubyōga kara suibokuga e no tenkai* (The development of ink painting from hakubyō). Suiboku bijutsu taikei (Art of ink painting), 1. 1975: Tokyo: Kōdansha.

Tanaka Ichimatsu, Yamanaka Rankei, and Kosugi Hōan [Tanaka Ichimatsu et al.]

1957–59 [Editors]. *Ike Taiga sakuhin gafu* (The works of Ike Taiga). 5 vols. Tokyo: Chūōkōron Bijutsu Shuppan.

1960 [Editors]. *Ike Taiga sakuhinshū* (The works of Ike Taiga). 2 vols. Tokyo: Chūōkōron Bijutsu Shuppan.

Tanaka Kaidō

1942 *Koshakyō sōkan* (Collection of hand-copied sutras). Nara: Ikaruga Koshakyō Shuppanbu.

Tanaka Kisaku

1933 "Sōtatsu zakkō" (Studies on Sōtatsu, a Japanese painter of the seventeenth century). *Bijutsu kenkyū*, no. 20 (August): 362–73.

1936 "Gashi Shūtoku" (Shūtoku, a priest painter of the Ashikaga period). *Bijutsu kenkyū*, no. 54 (June): 236–42.

1941 *Den Sōtatsu hitsu Ise monogatari zu* (Paintings of the Tales of Ise attributed to Sōtatsu). Tokyo: Zōkei Geijutsusha.

Tanaka Migaku

1981 *Kokyō* (Old mirrors). Nihon no bijutsu (Arts of Japan), 178. Tokyo: Shibundō.

Tanaka Shinbi

1932 *Sōtatsu hitsu Ise monogatari* (Paintings of the Tales of Ise by Sōtatsu). Tokyo: Shōkokai.

1960 [Editor]. *Nishihonganjibon Sanjūro-kuninshū* (Anthology of poems by the Thirty-Six Poets, Nishihonganji edition). Tokyo: Nihon Keizai Shinbunsha.

Tanaka Tatsuya

1984 *Nikuhitsu ukiyo-e meihin ten: Saki kaoru Edo no josei bi* (Exhibition of masterpieces of ukiyo-e paintings: The beauty of Edo women, fragrant and blossoming). Exh. cat. Nagoya: Asahi Shinbunsha.

Tanaka Yūko

1998 "Watarenai hashi" (Uncrossable Bridge). *Nihon no bigaku* 28: 36–51.

2000 *Edo hyakumu: Kinsei zuzōgaku no tanoshimi* (Myriad dreams of Edo: An appreciation of early–modern iconographies). Tokyo: Asahi Shinbunsha.

Tanikawa Tetsuzō, Kawabata Yasunari, and Narasaki Shōichi [Tanikawa Tetsuzō et al.]

1990 *Hajiki, Sueki*. Nihon no tōji: Kodai, chūsei hen (Japanese ceramics: Ancient and medieval), 1. Tokyo: Chūōkōronsha.

Tani Shin'ichi

1964 "Rakuchū-rakugai zu byōbu" (Screen paintings of rakuchū-rakugai). *Nihon rekishi*, nos. 191–92 (April–May): 2–4.

ten Grotenhuis, Elizabeth

1999 *Japanese Mandalas: Representations of Sacred Geography*. Honolulu: University of Hawai'i Press.

Teramoto Naohiko

1964 "Genji-e chinjō kō" (Debates on the production of illustrations of *The Tale of Genji*). *Kokugo to kokubungaku* (Japanese language and Japanese literature), no. 486 (September): 26–44 (pt. 1); no. 488 (November): 24–38 (pt. 2).

Tobacco and Salt Museum

1985 *Tabako to Shio no Hakubutsukan* (Tobacco and Salt Museum). Tokyo: Tobacco and Salt Museum.

Toby, Ronald

2008 "Sakoku to iu gaikō" (The politics of national seclusion). Nihon no rekishi (Japanese history), 9. Tokyo: Shōgakukan.

Tochigi Prefectural Museum

1994 *Kanzan Jittoku: Egakareta fūkyō no soshi tachi* (Kanzan and Jittoku: A pair of eccentrics). Exh. cat. Utsunomiya: Tochigi Prefectural Museum.

Tochigi Prefectural Museum and Kanagawa Prefectural Museum of Cultural History

1998 *Kantō suibokuga no nihyakunen: Chūsei ni miru kata to imēji no keifu* (Two hundred years of ink painting in the Kantō region: Lineage of stylistic models and themes in fifteenth- and sixteenth-century Japan). Exh. cat. Utsunomiya: Tochigi Prefectural Museum; Yokohama: Kanagawa Prefectural Museum of Cultural History.

Toda Teisuke

1973 *Mokkei, Gyokkan*. Suiboku Bijutsu taikei (Art of ink painting), 3. Tokyo: Kōdansha.

Tokugawa Art Museum

1966 *Rimpa meihin ten* (Exhibition of the art of the Kōrin School). Exh. cat. Nagoya: Tokugawa Art Museum.

Tokugawa Yoshinobu, Ōishi Shinzaburō, and Saitō Keizō [Tokugawa Yoshinobu et al.]

1983 *The Shogun Age Exhibition from the Tokugawa Art Museum, Japan*. Exh. cat., Los Angeles County Museum of Art; Dallas Museum of Art; Haus der Kunst, Munich; Espace Pierre Cardin, Paris. Tokyo: Shogun Age Exhibition Executive Committee.

Tokyo Metropolitan Teien Art Museum

1986 *Muromachi bijutsu to Sengoku gadan: Ōta Dōkan kinen bijutsu ten* (Art of the Muromachi and Sengoku periods: Ōta Dōkan Memorial Art Exhibition). Exh. cat. Tokyo: Tōkyō-to Bunka Shinkōkai.

Tokyo National Museum

1917 *Nanshū-ga shū* (Southern-style paintings). [Tokyo]: Tokyo Imperial Museum.

1918 *Nansōgashu* (A book of Nanga). [Tokyo]: Tokyo Imperial Museum.

1952 *Sōtatsu-Kōetsu ha zuroku* (The art of the Sōtatsu-Kōetsu School). Exh. cat. Tokyo: Benridō.

1965 *Nihon no bunjingaten mokuroku* (Exhibition catalogue of Japanese literati paintings). Exh. cat. Tokyo: Tokyo National Museum.

1971 *Tōyō no tōji: Tōyō tōji ten kinen zuroku* (Commemorative catalogue of the exhibition of Oriental ceramics). Exh. cat. Tokyo: Tokyo National Museum.

1972 *Rinpa: Sōritsu hyakunen kinen tokubetsu ten* (Special 100-year anniversary exhibition). Exh. cat. Tokyo: Tokyo National Museum.

1978 *Nihon no sho* (Japanese calligraphy). Exh. cat. Tokyo: Tokyo National Museum.

1980 *Cha no bijutsu* (Art of the tea ceremony). Exh. cat. Tokyo: Tokyo National Museum.

1985a *Nihon bijutsu meihin ten: New York Burke Collection / A Selection of Japanese Art from the Mary and Jackson Burke Collection*. Exh. cat. Tokyo: Chunichi Shimbun.

1985b *Nihon no tōji* (Japanese ceramics). Exh. cat. Tokyo: Tokyo National Museum.

1988 *Tokubetsu tenkan: Edo-jō shōhekiga no shita-e; Ōhiroma, matsu no rōka kara ōoku made* (Special exhibition: Preliminary paintings for the screen and mural paintings of Edo Castle; From the great hall and pine corridor to the women's quarters). Exh. cat. Tokyo: Tokyo National Museum.

1989a *Edo-jō shōhekiga no shita-e* (Preliminary paintings for the screen and mural paintings at Edo Castle). 2 vols. Tokyo: Daiichi Hōki.

1989b *Muromachi jidai no byōbu-e* (Screen paintings of the Muromachi period). Exh. cat. Tokyo: Asahi Shinbunsha.

1993 *Yamato-e: Miyabi no keifu* (Yamato-e: Japanese painting in the tradition of courtly elegance). Exh. cat. Tokyo: Tokyo National Museum.

1998 *Tokubetsuten kisshō: Chūgoku bijutsu ni komerareta imi* (Special exhibition, Jixiang: Auspicious motifs in Chinese art). Exh. cat. Tokyo: Tokyo National Museum.

2003 *Kokuhō Daitokujī Jukoīn no fusumae* (National treasure, screen paintings from Daitokujī Jukoīn). Exh. cat. Tokyo: NHK, NHK Puromōshon, and Nihon Keizai Shinbunsha.

Tōshi (Karihan) Nakamura-shi kyūzōhin mokuroku

1915 *Tōshi (Karihan) Nakamura-shi kyūzōhin mokuroku* (Auction catalogue of the former collection of the Nakamura Karihan family). Kyoto: Kyoto Bijutsu Kurabu.

Tottori Prefectural Museum

2006 *Oki Ichiga: Tottori-han goyō eshi* (Oki Ichiga: A retrospective, court painter of the Tottori-clan). Exh. cat. Tottori: Tottori Prefectural Museum.

Trinh, Kahn

2003 *Darstellung realer Orte: Die "wahren Landschaften" des "Malenden Reporters" Tani Bunchō (1763–1840)*. Schweizer Asiatische Studien, 47. Bern: Peter Lang.

Tsuboi Kiyotari

1990 *Yayoi*. Nihon tōji taikei (Survey of Japanese ceramics), 2. Tokyo: Heibonsha.

Tsuji Eiko

1999 *Zaigai Nihon emaki no kenkyū to shiryō* (Japanese illustrated handscrolls abroad: Study and records). Kasama sōsho (Kasama series), 328. Tokyo: Kasama Shoin.

Tsuji Nobuo

1968a "Hanabusa Itchō hitsu Ama yadori zu" ("Ama yadori zu," by Itchō). *Kokka*, no. 920 (November): 35.

1968b "Nanban byōbu" (*Nanban* screens). *Kobijutsu*, no. 21: 101–4.

1970 *Kisō no keifu: Matabei—Kuniyoshi* (Lineage of eccentrics: Matabei—Kuniyoshi). Tokyo: Bijutsu Shuppansha.

1974 *Jakuchū* (The life and works of Itō Jakuchū). Tokyo: Bijutsu Shuppansha.

1976 *Rakuchū-rakugai zu* (Scenes in and around the capital). Nihon no bijutsu (Arts of Japan), 121. Tokyo: Shibundō.

1978 "Suzuki Kiitsu shiron" (Preliminary study of the life and work of Kiitsu). In Yamane Yūzō 1977–80, vol. 5, pp. 57–72.

1980 [Editor]. *Bunjinga, shoha* (Literati painting and other schools). Zaigai Nihon no shihō (Japanese art: Selections from Western collections), 6. Tokyo: Mainichi Shinbunsha.

1994 *Sengoku jidai Kano ha no kenkyū: Kano Motonobu o chūshin to shite* (Study on the early Kano School: Primarily on Motonobu and his family of painters). Tokyo: Yoshikawa Kōbunkan.

Tsuji Nobuo and Itō Shiori
1998 [Editors]. *Soga Shōhaku ten: Edo no kisai* (Soga Shōhaku exhibition: Eccentric artists of the Edo period). Exh. cat., Chiba Municipal Museum and Mie Prefectural Art Museum. Asahi Shimbun.

Tsuji Nobuo et al.
2005 *Nyūyōku Bāku korekushon-ten: Nihon no bi sanzennen no kagayaki / Enduring Legacy of Japanese Art: The Mary Griggs Burke Collection*. Exh. cat., Museum of Fine Arts, Gifu; Hiroshima Prefectural Museum of Art; Tokyo Metropolitan Art Museum; and Miho Museum, Shigaraki, Shiga Prefecture. [Tokyo]: Nihon Keizai Shinbunsha.

Tsuji Nobuo, Kobayashi Tadashi, and Kōno Motoaki [Tsuji Nobuo et al.]
1968 "Hōkokuki: Miyake, Mikura, Niijima santō ni nokoru Hanabusa Itchō no gaseki, Miyagawa Isshō, Kaigetsudō Ando no shiryō nado mo awasete" (Reports: Pictures by Itchō remaining in Miyake-jima, Mikura-jima, and Nii-jima islands). *Kokka*, no. 920 (November): 36–46.

Tsuji Nobuo, Kōno Motoaki, and Yabe Yoshiaki [Tsuji Nobuo et al.]
1991 *Eitoku to shōheiga: Momoyama no kenchiku, kōgei 2* (Eitoku and wall decorations: Paintings and crafts of the Momoyama period, 2). Nihon bijutsu zenshū (Survey of Japanese art), 15. Tokyo: Kōdansha.

Tsuji Nobuo, Money L. Hickman, and Kōno Motoaki [Tsuji Nobuo et al.]
1981 *Jakuchū, Shōhaku*. Nihon bijutsu kaiga zenshū (Survey of Japanese painting), 23. Tokyo: Shūeisha.

Tsukamoto Mizuyo
1989 "Tagasode zu byōbu to ishō" (Tagasode screens and clothing). *Gunma Kenritsu Joshi Daigaku kiyō* 9 (March): 51–64.

Tsuruta Takeyoshi
1979 "Sō Shigan ni tsuite: Raihaku gajin kenkyū" (Paintings with a bird on a pomegranate branch and a bird on a plum branch, by Sung Tzu-yen). *Kokka*, no. 1028: 35–39.
1993 *Sō Shiseki to Nanpin ha* (Sō Shiseki and the Shen Nanpin School). Nihon no bijutsu (Arts of Japan), 326. Tokyo: Shibundō.

Tsuzuki Etsuko
1991 "Mokuhan kansubon ryōshi ni okeru Kamishi Sōji no yakuwari" (The role of Kamishi Sōji in the ornamentation of handscroll papers printed by woodblock). *De arte* 7 (March): 9–28.

Uemura Masurō
1940 *Kōrin*. Tokyo: Takamizawa Mokuhansha.

Ueno Kenji
1976 "Tani Bunchō shukuzu gasatsu" (Study on the album of small drawings by Tani Bunchō). *Tochigi Prefectural Museum Bulletin*, no. 4: 37–78.
1986 "Kantō kanryō Uesugi shi to sono shūhen: Kano ha no shutsuji ni furete" (The Uesugi clan: Governors of the Kantō region and their milieu, especially in connection with the origin of the Kano School). In Tokyo Metropolitan Teien Art Museum 1986.

Uetani Hajime
1959 "Gion Nankai nenpu" (Chronological account of the life of Nankai Gion). *Kokka*, no. 811 (October): 388–92.
1960 "Sakaki Hyakusen nenpu" (Chronological account of the life of Hyakusen Sakaki). *Kokka*, no. 825 (December): 483–90.

Ukiyo-e meisaku senshū
1967 Nihon Ukiyo-e Kyōkai, editor. *Ukiyo-e meisaku senshū: Shoki ukiyo-e* (Selected masterpieces of ukiyo-e: Early ukiyo-e). Vol. 1. Tokyo: Yamada Shoin.

Umezu Jirō
1934 "Maruyama Ōkyo den" (Biography of Maruyama Ōkyo [a Japanese painter, 1733–1795; Reprint from the manuscript written by Hōsui Okamura, 1770–1845, with an introduction by Umezu Jirō]). *Bijutsu kenkyū*, no. 33 (September): 441–42.
1961 "Suzuriwari emaki sonota: Ko-e no mondai" (On the Suzuriwari-zōshi picture-scroll). *Kokka*, no. 828 (March): 97–104.
1970a *Emakimono zanketsu no fu* (Thoughts on fragments of *emakimono*). Tokyo: Kadokawa Shoten.
1970b "Zenzai Dōji emaki" (Illustrated handscroll of Zenzai Dōji). In Umezu Jirō 1970a, pp. 17–23.

Usui Nobuyoshi
1961 "Gyokuen no in" (Seals of Gyokuen Bonpō). *Nihon rekishi*, no. 171 (August): 36–39.

Volk, Alicia
2010 *In Pursuit of Universalism: Yorozu Tetsugorō and Japanese Modern Art*. The Phillips Book Prize Series, 1. Berkeley: University of California Press; Washington, D.C.: Phillips Collection.

Volker, T.
1954 *Porcelain and the Dutch East India Company, as Recorded in the Dagh-Registers of Batavia Castle, Those of Hirado and Deshima, and Other Contemporary Papers, 1602–1682*. Mededelingen van het Rijksmuseum voor Volkenkunde, Leiden, 11. Leiden: E. J. Brill.

Wada, Stephanie
2002 *The Oxherder: A Zen Parable Illustrated*. Translations by Gen P. Sakamoto. New York: George Braziller.

Wakayama-ken Kyōiku Iinkai
1981 *Negoroji bōin ato hakkutsu chōsa gaihō 1 (1978), 2 (1979)* (Brief report on the excavations of temple sites at Negoroji, 1 [1978], 2 [1979]). Wakayama: Wakayama-ken Kyōiku Iinkai.

Wakayama Prefectural Museum
1986 *Gion Nankai: Zuroku* (The work of Gion Nankai). Exh. cat. Wakayama: Wakayama Prefectural Museum.

Watanabe, Masako
2000 "Guanxiu and Exotic Imagery in Rakan Paintings." *Orientations* 31, no. 4 (April): 34–42 (plus cover illus.).
2012 *Storytelling in Japanese Art*. Exh. cat. New York: The Metropolitan Museum of Art.

Watanabe Akiyoshi
1976 *Shōshō hakkei zu* (Paintings of the Eight Views of the Xiao and Xiang Rivers). Nihon no bijutsu (Arts of Japan), 124. Tokyo: Shibundō.

Watanabe Hajime
1985 *Higashiyama suibokuga no kenkyū* (Study of ink painting of the late Muromachi period). Rev. ed. Tokyo: Chūōkōron Bijutsu Shuppan.

Watt, James C. Y., and Barbara Brennan Ford
1991 *East Asian Lacquer: The Florence and Herbert Irving Collection*. Exh. cat. New York: The Metropolitan Museum of Art.

Weber, Charles D.

1968 "Chinese Pictorial Bronze Vessels of the Late Chou Period: Part 4." *Artibus Asiae* 30, nos. 2/3 (Spring): 145–236.

Weston, Victoria

2013 [Editor]. *Portugal, Jesuits, and Japan: Spiritual Beliefs and Earthly Goods.* Boston: McMullen Museum of Art, Boston College.

Wheelwright, Carolyn

1981 "Kano Shōei." 2 vols. PhD diss., Princeton University.

1986 "Taking Shelter from the Rain: A Genroku Period Genre Painting by Hanabusa Itchō in the Mary and Jackson Burke Collection." *Orientations* 17, no. 9 (September): 18–25.

1989 [Editor]. *Word in Flower: The Visualization of Classical Literature in Seventeenth-Century Japan*. Exh. cat. New Haven: Yale University Art Gallery.

Wilson, Richard L., and Ogasawara Saeko

1992 *Ogata Kenzan: Zen sakuhin to sono keifu* (Ogata Kenzan: His life and complete work). 4 vols. Tokyo: Yūzankaku.

Wood, Donald A., and Yuko Ikeda

2003 [Editors]. *Kamisaka Sekka: Rimpa Master—Pioneer of Modern Design.* Exh. cat., The National Museum of Modern Art, Kyoto; Sakura City Museum of Art; Los Angeles County Museum of Art; and Birmingham Museum of Art. Kyoto: The National Museum of Modern Art; Birmingham, Ala.: Birmingham Museum of Art; [Tokyo]: Asahi Shimbun.

Yabe Yoshiaki

1989 *Kakiemon*. Nihon tōji taikei (Survey of Japanese ceramics), 20. Tokyo: Heibonsha.

1990 *Bizen*. Nihon no bijutsu (Arts of Japan), 291. Tokyo: Shibundō, 1990.

Yabumoto Kōzō

1974 "Taiga hitsu Rantei zu hengaku to sōkō" (Plaque with painting of "Poetry Party at Lan-t'ing," by Taiga, and its draft). *Kobijutsu*, no. 44 (April): 52–55.

Yamaguchi Prefectural Museum of Art

1984 *Unkoku Tōgan to Momoyama jidai* (Unkoku Tōgan and the Momoyama era). Exh. cat. Yamaguchi: Yamaguchi Prefectural Museum of Art.

1998 *Zen-dera no eshi tachi* (Painters of Zen temples). Exh. cat. Yamaguchi: Yamaguchi Prefectural Museum of Art.

Yamakawa Takeshi

1963 "Nagasawa Rosetsu to sono Nanki ni okeru sakuhin" (Rosetsu Nagasawa and his works remaining in southern Kishū Province). *Kokka*, no. 860 (November): 5–57.

1977a "Maruyama Ōkyo hitsu Shunjū ayu zu" ("Ayu in Spring and Autumn," by Maruyama Ōkyo). *Kokka*, no. 1002 (July): 21.

1977b *Ōkyo, Goshun*. Nihon bijutsu kaiga zenshū (Survey of Japanese painting), 22. Tokyo: Shūeisha.

1981 "Nagasawa Rosetsu hitsu Taki ni tsuru kame zu byōbu: Dō Sekiheki zu byōbu" ("Landscape with Waterfall, Cranes, and Tortoises" and "Red Cliff," by Rosetsu). *Kokka*, no. 1047 (December): 22.

Yamakawa Takeshi and Nakajima Ryōichi

1986 [Editors]. *Sō Shiseki gashū* (The paintings of Sō Shiseki). Tokyo: Nigensha.

Yamakawa Takeshi et al.

1986 *Sō Shiseki to sono jidai: Chūgoku tōrai no shaseijutsu gahō* (Sō Shiseki and his time: Realism imported from China). Edo bunka shirīzu (Series on Edo culture), 7. Exh. cat. Tokyo: Itabashi Ward Art Museum.

Yamamoto Hideo

1988 "Unkoku Tōgan no sakufū tenkai ni tsuite" (Stylistic development in the art of Unkoku Tōgan). *Bijutsushi* 37, no. 2 (April): 148–65.

1994 "Kano Motonobu oyobi sono shūhen gaka no kenkyū: In'ei ni yoru sakuhin no bunrui to seiri" (A study of Kano Motonobu and his school: The classification of their works based on seals). *Kajima bijutsu zaidan nenpō* 11: 363–71.

2000 "On the Attribution of the Metropolitan Museum of Art's *Birds and Flowers* Screens." *Orientations* 31, no. 4 (April): 43–49.

Yamamoto Yukari

2010 *Kamigata fūzokuga no kenkyū: Nishikawa Sukenobu, Tsukioka Settei o chūshin ni* (A study of genre painting in the Kyoto area: With a focus on Nishikawa Sukenobu and Tsukioka Settei). Tokyo: Geika Shoin.

Yamanaka and Company

1939 *Tōyō kobijutsu tenkan zuroku* (Catalogue of an exhibition of antiques). Sales cat. Tokyo: Tokyo Art Club.

Yamane Yūzō

1962a *Konishi-ke kyūzō Kōrin kankei shiryō to sono kenkyū* (The life and works of Kōrin: The Konishi Collection). Vol. 1, *Shiryō* (Documents). Tokyo: Chūōkōron Bijutsu.

1962b *Sōtatsu*. Tokyo: Nihon Keizai Shinbunsha.

1974 "Den Sōtatsu hitsu Ise monogatari zu shikishi ni tsuite" (Study on the Ise Monogatari Shikishi attributed to Sōtatsu). *Yamato bunka*, no. 59 (March): 1–27.

1975 "Tawaraya Sōtatsu to ihon Ise monogatari-e oyobi Shukongōshin engi-e: Shinshutsu no Ise monogatari zu byōbu o chūshin ni" (Tawaraya Sōtatsu and illustrated scrolls of Ise Monogatari and Shukongōshin Engi). *Kokka*, no. 977 (February): 11–33.

1977–80 [Editor]. *Rinpa kaiga zenshū* (Survey of Rinpa paintings). Vols. 1–2, *Sōtatsu ha I–II*. Vols. 3–4, *Korin ha I–II*. Vol. 5, *Hōitsu ha*. Tokyo: Nihon Keizai Shinbunsha.

1979 [Editor]. *Rinpa* (Sōtatsu-Kōrin School). Zaigai Nihon no shihō (Japanese art: Selections from Western collections), 5. Tokyo: Mainichi Shinbunsha.

1989 [Editor]. *Nihon no bi, Rinpa: Sōtatsu, Kōrin, Hōitsu kara gendai made* (The beauty of Japan, Rinpa: from Sōtatsu, Kōrin, and Hōitsu to modern times). Exh. cat., Fukuoka City Museum. [Fukuoka]: Kyushu Asahi Broadcasting; Kitakyushū: Asahi Shinbunsha.

Yamane Yūzō et al.

1978 *Kōetsu sho Sōtatsu kingindei-e* (Kōetsu's calligraphy on gold and silver paintings by Sōtatsu). Tokyo: Asahi Shimbun-sha.

1979 *Jinbutsuga: Yamato-e kei jinbutsu* (Figure painting: Yamato-e figure paintings). Nihon byōbu-e shūsei (Survey of Japanese screen paintings), 5. Tokyo: Kōdansha.

1994 *Tokubetsu ten, Rinpa: Bi no keishō—Sōtatsu, Kōrin, Hōitsu, Kiitsu* (Special exhibition, Rinpa: Succession of beauty—Sōtatsu, Kōrin, Hōitsu, Kiitsu). Exh. cat. Nagoya: Nagoya City Museum.

Yamaoka Taizō
1978 *Kano Masanobu, Motonobu*. Nihon bijutsu kaiga zenshū (Survey of Japanese painting), 7. Tokyo: Shūeisha.

Yamashita Yūji
1985 "Shikibu Terutada no kenkyū: Kantō suibokuga ni kansuru ichi kōsatsu" (A study of Shikibu Terutada: An observation about suiboku painting in the Kantō District). *Kokka*, no. 1084: 11–31.
1993 "Kakei to Muromachi suibokuga" (Xia Gui and Muromachi ink painting). In *Nihon bijutsushi no suimyaku* (Currents in Japanese art history), edited by Tsuji Nobuo Sensei Kanreki Kinenkai. Tokyo: Perikansha.

Yamashita Yūji and Asano Shūgō
2002 *Sesson ten: Sengoku jidai no sūpā ekisentorriku* (Sesson exhibition: Super eccentric of the Warring States period). Exh. cat., Chiba City Museum of Art. Tokyo: Asano Kenkyūjo.

Yamauchi Naosaburō
1918 [Editor]. *Kōrin zuroku: Korin-gasei nihyakunen-ki kinen* (Catalogue of Kōrin's works: The 200th anniversary of the death of the immortal Kōrin). Exh. cat., Mitsukoshi Department Store, Tokyo. Kyoto: Geishudō.

Yanagisawa Taka
1965 "Shōren'in denrai no hakubyō Kongōkai mandara shoson zuyō" (An ink-drawing scroll representing the Vajradhatu-Mandala images in the Shōren'in Temple). *Bijutsu kenkyū*, no. 241 (July): 58–80 (pt. 1); no. 242 (September): 93–100 (pt. 2).
1980 [Editor]. *Bukkyō kaiga* (Buddhist painting). Zaigai Nihon no shihō (Japanese art: Selections from Western collections), 1. Tokyo: Mainichi Shinbunsha.

Yasuda, Ken
1948 *Poem Card (The "Hyakunin isshu" in English)*. Tokyo: Kamakurabunko.

Yasuhara Makoto
2010 *Baaku Korekushon shozō den Miyagawa Chōshun ga "Usugumo monogatari" shōkai* (Painting attributed to Miyagawa Chōshun in the Burke Collection, "Usugumo monogatari"). Tokyo: Rikkyo University.

Yasumura Toshinobu
1978 "Kano Tan'yū no denki shiryō ni tsuite: Fu Kano Tan'yū nenpu" (On the historical materials on Kano Tan'yū's life, supplemented by Kano Tan'yū chronology). *Bunka* 42, nos. 1–2 (September): 17–36.
1993 *Hōitsu to Edo Rinpa* (Hōitsu and Rinpa in Edo). Rinpa Bijutsukan (Rinpa Museum), 3. Tokyo: Shūeisha.
1998 *Kano Tan'yū*. Shinchō Nihon bijutsu bunko (Shinchōsha series on Japanese art), 7. Tokyo: Shinchōsha.

Yiengpruksawan, Mimi Hall
1987 "One Millionth of a Buddha: The *Hyakumantō Darani* in the Scheide Library." *Princeton University Library Chronicle* 48 (Spring): 225–38.

Yi Song-Mi
1998 "Yi Chong: The Foremost Bamboo Painter of the Choson Dynasty." *Orientations*, vol. 29, no. 8 (August): 61–68.

Yokota Tadashi
1976 "Shoki suiboku gaka no rakkan ni tsuite: Omoni zenrin no gaka o chūshin to shite" (Signatures of early ink painters in Zen circles). *Kobijutsu*, no. 50 (February): 33–40.

Yokoyama Kumiko
1994 "Suzuki Kiitsu kō: Denki oyobi zōkeijō no shomondai" (A study of Suzuki Kiitsu's biography and characteristics of his paintings). *Bijutsushi*, no. 136 (March): 193–216.

Yonezawa Yoshiho
1959 "Sekkyakushi hitsu Bokudō zu" ("A Cowboy"). *Kokka*, no. 802 (January): 17–18.

"Yosa Buson hitsu Kachō zu kai"
1930 "Yosa Buson hitsu Kachō zu kai" ("A Willow, a Peach-Tree, and Birds," by Yosa Buson). *Kokka*, no. 477 (August): 233–34.

Yoshimura Motoo
1971 *Kōdaiji maki-e* (Kōdaiji lacquerware). Exh. cat. Kyoto: Kyoto National Museum.
1976 *Maki-e*. Kyoto: Kyoto Shoin.

Yoshioka Yukio
1985 [Editor]. *Fuji, yanagi, harunatsukusa* (Wisteria, willow, and grasses of spring and summer). Nihon no ishō (Japanese design in art), 9. Kyoto: Kyoto Shoin.

Yoshizawa Chū
1959 "Ike Taiga ni okeru yōshiki tenkan: Nijūdai, sanjūdai no sakuhin o chūshin to shite" (On the development of the pictorial style of Taiga Ikeno). *Kokka*, no. 811 (October): 359–66.
1967 "Kō Fuyō hitsu sansui gajō" (An album of landscape images by Kō Fuyō). *Kokka*, no. 905 (August): 21–26.
1968 "Nukina Kaioku hitsu Eigenji Shūkei zu" (Autumn view of Eigenji). *Kokka*, no. 918 (September): 25–27.
1974 "Nyoi Dōjin shūshū shogajō ni tsuite" (The album of painting and calligraphy by Nyoi Dōjin). *Kokka*, no. 975 (November): 9–14.
1975 *Gyokudō, Mokubei*. Suiboku bijutsu taikei (Art of ink painting), 13. Tokyo: Kōdansha.
1978 *Tanomura Chikuden*. Exh. cat. Idemitsu Bijutsukan, 8. Tokyo: Idemitsu Museum of Arts.
1986 "Onaji zu no aru Ike Taiga hitsu Rantei kyokusui zu byōbu ni tsuite" (The screen of the Lan-ting Gathering, by Ikeno Taiga, and its duplicate). *Kokka*, no. 1096: 33–35.

Young, Martie W., and Robert J. Smith
1966 *Japanese Painters of the Floating World*. Exh. cat., Andrew Dickson White Museum of Art, Cornell University. Ithaca, N.Y.: Office of University Publications, Cornell University.

Zaigai Nara Ehon
1981 Barbara Ruch, editor. *Zaigai Nara Ehon / Nara Ehon Abroad: Illustrated Literature from Medieval and Early Modern Japan*. Proceedings, International Research Conference on Nara Ehon, London, Dublin, and New York, 1978; Tokyo and Kyoto, 1979. Tokyo: Kadokawa Shoten.

Zhang Wanli and Hu Renmu
1969 [Editors]. *Jianjiang huaji* (The selected painting of Chien-chiang [Jianjiang]). Hong Kong: Cafa.

Translation Sources

No. 859: From *The Story of a Painting: A Korean Buddhist Treasure from the Mary and Jackson Burke Foundation.* Transcribed and translated by Hongnam Kim.

No. 860: Translated by Chin-Sung Chang.

No. 867: Translated by Soyoung Lee with the assistance of Soojin Kim.

Photography Credits

Many of the photographers also shot separate images of inscriptions, signatures, or seals if those details were not visible in the overall image or were too small to be readable.

Courtesy of Dr. Frederick Baekeland
727*

Courtesy of Kōichi Yanagi
639*

Christopher Burke
688, 705, 840, 1015, plus details

Sheldan C. Collins
592, 718, 845–856, 859, 860, 862–894, 897–909, 911–925, 927–949, 958, 1014, plus details

Gratia Williams Nakahashi
1011, plus details

Carl Nardiello
619, 620, 749, 806, 807

Bruce Schwarz
547, 549, 550, 552–556, 558, 562–564, 567, 574, 576, 577, 586, 588, 593, 603, 604, 608, 610, 634–636, 638, 641, 645, 650, 654, 672, 684, 735, 738–748, 750–805, 808, 809, 813, 814, 817, 822, 833, 839, 858, 950, 1010, plus details

Bruce White
546, 548, 551, 557, 559–561, 565, 566, 568–573, 575, 578–585, 587, 589–591, 594–602, 605–607, 609, 611–618, 621–633, 637, 640, 642, 643, 644, 646–649, 651–653, 655–671, 673–683, 685–687, 689–704, 706–717, 719–726, 728–734, 736, 737, 810–812, 815, 816, 818–821, 823–832, 834–838, 841–844, 857, 861, 895, 896, 910, 926, 951–957, 959–1009, 1012, 1013, plus details